HUMAN SEXUALITY

HUMAN SEXUALITY

Fifth Edition

William H. Masters
Virginia E. Johnson
Robert C. Kolodny

HarperCollins*CollegePublishers*

Sponsoring Editor: Jill Lectka
Development Editor: Jane Tufts
Text and Cover Design, Art Coordination: York Production Services
Cover Illustration/Photograph: © 1995 Succession H. Matisse, Paris/Artists
    Rights Society (ARS), New York
Photo Research: Joanne DiSimone
Eletronic Production Manager: Christine Pearson
Compositor: York Production Services
Printer and Binder: RR Donnelley & Sons Company
Cover Printer: Coral Graphic Services, Inc.

Human Sexuality, Fifth Edition

Library of Congress Cataloging-in-Publication Data

Masters, William H.
    Human sexuality/William H. Masters, Virginia E. Johnson, Robert C.
Kolodny.—5th ed.
        p. cm.
    Includes bibliographical references and index.
    ISBN 0-673-46785-6
    1. Sex 2. Sex (Psychology) 3. Sex (Biology) I. Johnson, Virginia E.
    II. Kolodny, Robert C. III. Title
        HQ21.M46157 1995
        306.7—dc20   94-36210
                                                                            CIP

95 96 97 9 8 7 6 5 4 3

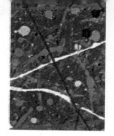

BRIEF CONTENTS

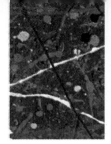

DETAILED CONTENTS

PREFACE

The fifth edition of *Human Sexuality* differs significantly from earlier editions. We have made a number of major changes that we believe make this a more interesting, engaging, topical book. First, we have shifted to the extensive use of color throughout the book, which not only allows us to use photos and illustrations that are more informative, but also gives a warmer (and livelier) look to the book. Second, we have tried to produce a more user-friendly book, which can be seen in the use of more summary tables, more Focus in Brief items, and more Personal Perspective boxes. Third, we have reorganized the fifth edition extensively in ways that we feel make it more logical to follow. Finally, we have added more than 500 new references to this book, providing students with access to the latest research theories and data wherever possible.

Several new chapters have been incorporated into the fifth edition. Notably, completely new material of a practical personal nature has been presented in Chapter 14, "Enhancing Your Sexual Relationships," which we hope will give readers an opportunity to take more than theory from this text. Part of the information presented in this chapter incorporates the sensate focus exercises we devised originally for use in sex therapy but have altered here for use as personal enhancement exercises for couples wishing to improve or refurbish their sexual interaction.

The material on abortion has been revised and expanded into a stand-alone chapter, rather than presenting it as a portion of the chapter discussing birth control, both to provide more detailed coverage of this controversial and important topic and to clarify our firm belief that abortion is NOT a form of birth control. In addition to outlining the legal history of abortion in the United States, this chapter provides the most extensive coverage of any college sexuality textbook on abortion methods, including coverage of RU 486, the so-called "abortion pill," as well as considerable discussion of the psychological side of the abortion process, including its long-range impact.

Two other new chapters in this edition reorganize and expand material from the fourth edition of *Human Sexuality*. Chapter 15, "Sexual Orientation," discusses the broad range of issues concerning the development of sexual orientation, including extensive discussion of new research findings on possible biologic factors that may play a role in predisposing toward homosexuality. This chapter also covers a number of timely topics related to sexual orientation, including the origins and effects of homophobia, cross-cultural aspects of homosexuality, and the nature of bisexuality.

Chapter 16, "Sexual Behavior," combines material previously presented in separate chapters in earlier editions, so that it now covers the full range of sexual behavior, from masturbation, sexual fantasies, and other forms of solitary sex to sexual behavior involving both homosexual, lesbian, and heterosexual couples. The reason behind this reorganization is twofold: to present a more unified view of the spectrum of sexual behavior and to encourage students to see that homosexual and lesbian sexual behavior has much in common with heterosexual forms of sex. Hopefully, this will also help students view homosexual men and women as normal rather than as aberrant in some manner.

One of the other major revisions in this edition is the extensive rewrite of Chapter 11 ("Gender Roles"), which was done in collaboration with Nancy J. Kolodny, M.A., M.S.W., and Linda H. Kolodny, B.A. We believe that this chapter now presents the most up-to-date, dynamic information available on the broad topic of gender roles and is especially useful for its insights into the ways in which male-female differences in socialization and language affect sexual relationships.

Virtually all of the other chapters in this text have been updated with new findings that will help students understand complex aspects of sexuality. Whenever possible, discussion of topical news issues has been included in the text, and we have made an attempt to integrate cross-cultural material throughout, to foster the understanding that views and trends in the United States are not the only ways sexual themes are expressed.

Among the various updated topics in this edition are the following:

Discussion of several new sex research surveys using sophisticated sampling methods has been added to Chapter 2 ("Sex Research: An Overview").

Information on the dangers of silicone breast implants and the FDA's ban on such breast surgery, as well as new findings on the health effects of circumcision, has been added to Chapter 3 ("Sexual Anatomy").

The section on PMS (premenstrual syndrome) has been extensively rewritten and updated in Chapter 4 ("Sexual Physiology").

Updated information has been provided on the length of obstetrical hospitalization following childbirth, and new data on rates of cesarean sections, the safety of ultrasonography, and the success of in vitro fertilization have been added to Chapter 5 ("Human Reproduction").

Chapter 6 ("Birth Control") has been extensively revised, to include new information on virtually all methods of contraception as well as to emphasize the degree of protection (or lack of protection) that each contraceptive method has against HIV infection and other sexually transmitted diseases. Particular attention is devoted to newly approved contraceptive methods, including the Norplant system, the injectable drug Depo-Provera, and the female condom. In addition, a boxed item discussing the delicate issue of how to deal with a partner who doesn't wish to use condoms has been incorporated into this chapter.

Chapter 8 ("Childhood Sexuality") now includes information on prenatal development and sexual differentiation, as well as extensive discussion of the psychology of the development of gender identity and childhood sexuality.

Chapter 9 ("Adolescent Sexuality") now incorporates information on puberty that we had previously provided in a separate chapter, giving better balance to the entire discussion; in addition, we have completely updated the discussion of patterns of sexual behavior in adolescence, drawing on the newest research available to elucidate this area. This chapter also includes a section on gay and lesbian teenagers as part of our effort to include such material in an integrated manner throughout the text.

New findings on patterns of sexual behavior in young adults has been added to Chapter 10 ("Adult Sexuality"), along with updated information on national divorce rates, the menopause, and the safety of hormone replacement therapy in the postmenopausal woman.

Chapter 13 ("Intimacy and Communication Skills") has been expanded considerably to include more information about problems with intimacy and to consider gender differences in communications styles. In addition, a new section on responding to criticism has been added to this chapter as a further means of helping students use material from our text in their personal lives.

Chapter 16 ("Sexual Behavior") now includes a discussion of techniques of lesbian and gay sexual activity as well as a parallel discussion of techniques of heterosexual activity. In a similar vein, this chapter also includes a detailed section on gay and lesbian partners and relationships to parallel our discussion of marital, extramarital, and nonmarital sex for heterosexuals.

An updated and expanded discussion of techniques used to deal with the paraphilias is included in Chapter 17 ("Sexual Variations").

Chapter 18 ("Coercive Sex: The Varieties of Sexual Assault") has had an entirely new topical introduction added, along with updated statistics on rape and sexual harassment. Material on incest has been extensively revised, including more information on the aftermath of incest and a new section on support groups for incest survivors. The discussion of sexual harassment has also been expanded considerably, with more emphasis on the range of harassing behaviors, and the fact that sexual harassment is not really about sex but about power. New material on the cultural under-pinnings of sex victimology has also been added to this chapter.

Chapter 19 ("Sexually Transmitted Diseases and Infections") has been extensively revised, with more than 150 new references added and with updated statistics extensively employed. A new summary table has been developed to help students review this large amount of information in concise format.

Hundreds of new references have also been added to Chapter 20 ("HIV Infection and AIDS"), which has been revised to reflect the growing percentage of cases of heterosexual transmission of HIV in the United States and around the world along with other new trends in the subepidemics of AIDS and HIV infection that are occurring worldwide.

New information about biomedical methods used in treating erectile dysfunction (including the external vacuum pump and self-injections with erection-inducing drugs) has been added to Chapter 21 ("Sexual Dysfunctions and Sex Therapy"), along with a revised discussion of orgasmic problems in women.

Chapter 22 ("Sexual Disorders and Sexual Health") features a completely revised and expanded discussion of breast cancer (including issues of diagnosis and treatment) and cancer of the prostate.

Chapter 23 ("Sex and the Law") now includes a section on legal aspects of sexual harassment, including the Supreme Court's 1993 landmark unanimous decision in which they broadened the definition of sexual harassment in the workplace considerably; as well as new material on legal aspects of rape and child sexual abuse. A new box item examines cross-cultural aspects of sexual offenses.

Chapter 24 ("Religious and Ethical Perspectives on Sexuality") includes expanded discussion of the problem of what to do about frozen human pre-embryos and a new discussion of the ethics of preimplantation genetic diagnosis and the implications of the possibility of human embryo cloning.

We are grateful to a number of individuals whose input provided material assistance to us in the development and production of this edition of *Human Sexuality*. Special mention should be made of the role played by our developmental editor, Jane Tufts, who has worked with us on this project since its inception in the late 1970s and whose personal imprint can be found throughout the book. Her fine judgment and eye for detail are greatly appreciated. Thanks must also be offered to Susan Penney McLaughlin, our editor at HarperCollins College Publishers, and her assistant, Juliana Nocker, for shepherding this project through the various stages from start to finish. We also wish to acknowledge the valuable assistance of Robert Watrous, our copy-editor, Robert Ravas, our permissions editor, and to York Production Services, who developed the design and produced this edition.

We especially wish to acknowledge the role played by a number of college professors who gave us their detailed comments on various drafts of this book. Their names and institutional affiliations are:

Myles Anderson
Walla Walla Community College

Wayne Anderson
University of Missouri

Irvin W. Brandel
The University of Akron

R. Lynn Coward
Virginia Polytechnic Institute

Beverly A. Drinnin
Des Moines Area Community College (IA)

Robin Kowalski
Western Carolina University (NC)

Linda Mealey
College of St. Benedict
St. John's University (MN)

Marilyn Myerson
University of South Florida

Ellen Rosen
College of William and Mary

Peggy Skinner
South Plains College (TX)

Jeffrey Stern
University of Michigan–Dearborn

Deborah McDonald Winters
Boise State University

In all, we have sought to produce a more user-friendly book that is comprehensive, understandable, and topical. We welcome comments from readers and hope that the use of this book will produce some smiles as well as personal insights.

ABOUT THE AUTHORS

William H. Masters, M.D., is internationally acclaimed as one of the pioneer sex researchers and therapists of the twentieth century. Co-author of *Human Sexual Response* (1966), *Human Sexual Inadequacy* (1970), *The Pleasure Bond* (1975), and *Homosexuality in Perspective* (1979), among more than 200 publications, Dr. Masters has been instrumental in establishing the legitimacy of the scientific study of sex. Dr. Masters has been the recipient of more than a dozen awards from professional organizations in recognition of his outstanding career.

Virginia E. Johnson, D.Sc. (Hon.), is world-renowned for her innovative contributions to sex therapy and sex research. As Director of the Masters & Johnson Institute in St. Louis, she oversees clinical, research, and educational operations at this multidisciplinary organization, while continuing to maintain her own special interests in women's studies and the psychology of sexual behavior. Co-author of nine books and hundreds of journal articles, Dr. Johnson has been the recipient of more than a dozen awards from professional organizations during her remarkable career.

Robert C. Kolodny, M.D., is Medical Director of the Behavioral Medicine Institute in New Canaan, Connecticut. He was previously Associate Director and Director of Training at the Masters & Johnson Institute, where he continues to serve as a Consultant. In 1983, he received the National Award from the Society for the Scientific Study of Sex. A member of more than a dozen professional organizations, he currently serves on the Board of Advocates of Planned Parenthood Federation of America. Dr. Kolodny has co-authored a number of previous books with Masters and Johnson, including *Textbook of Sexual Medicine* (1979), *Ethical Issues in Sex Therapy and Research* (Volume 1, 1977; Volume 2, 1980), *On Sex and Human Loving* (1986), *Crisis: Heterosexual Behavior in the Age of AIDS* (1988), and *Heterosexuality* (1994), and has also written two books with his wife on adolescence.

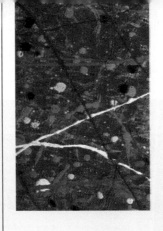

Introduction

1

Perspectives on Sexuality

Every person has sexual feelings, attitudes, and beliefs, but everyone's experience of sexuality is unique because it is processed through an intensely personal perspective. This perspective comes from both private, personal experience and public, social sources. It is impossible to understand human sexuality without recognizing its multidimensional nature.

Sexuality has fascinated people in all walks of life from ancient times until the present. Sexual themes have been common in art and literature. Religions, philosophies, and legal systems—all concerned with shaping human behavior—have typically tried to establish sexual values and sexual taboos. At various times in history, illness, creativity, aggression, emotional disorders, and the rise and fall of cultures have all been "explained" as the result of too much or too little sexual activity or unusual sexual practices or thoughts.

While keeping in mind the private, public, and historical sources of our sexual heritage, we can broaden and deepen our understanding by studying sexuality from biological, psychosocial, behavioral, clinical, and cultural perspectives. In examining sexuality from these varied viewpoints, however, we must be careful not to forget that learning about sexuality, in all its forms, is really learning about people and the complexities of human nature.

WHY STUDY SEXUALITY?

While there are a number of different reasons for studying sexuality, many college students who enroll in sexuality courses do so for personal rather than academic reasons. This is because learning about sexuality—as contrasted to learning about physical chemistry or calculus—can provide people with knowledge that has a high potential for use in their everyday lives. This does not mean that there is no academic value to studying sexuality (since quite the opposite is true), but it does indicate that learning about sexuality has a number of practical applications that other subjects may not provide as easily.

Acquiring accurate information about sexuality can help prevent sexual problems, and it can enable us to educate our children better about sex. Becoming well informed about sex can also help us to deal more effectively with certain types of problems if they occur in our lives (e.g., infertility, sexual dysfunctions, sexually transmitted diseases, sexual harassment). Even more important, studying sexuality can help us become more sensitive and aware in our interpersonal relationships, thus contributing to the growth of intimacy and sexual satisfaction in our lives.

There is a particularly powerful reason to become knowledgeable about sexual matters today. In the age of the HIV epidemic (HIV is the abbreviation for the human immunodeficiency virus that causes AIDS), being knowledgeable can help you make sexual choices that are, quite literally, lifesaving. In addition, since it is now apparent that unless a cure is found, in the decade of the 1990s virtually everyone's life will be touched in some way by the tragedies the HIV/AIDS epidemic engenders, acquiring accurate information about sexuality can increase your tolerance and understanding of the toll this takes on our society and its impact around the world.

Unfortunately, it is also true that these results do not happen automatically. There is no guarantee that careful study of this text will make finding (or keeping) sexual partners any easier, nor that it will lead to sexual bliss. Instead, we believe that learning about sexuality in an objective fashion will enable our readers to examine important sexual issues—some intensely personal, some social, some moral—and emerge with deeper insight into themselves and others. We also believe that sexual knowledge can lead to reasoned, responsible interpersonal sexual behavior and can help people make important personal decisions about sex. In short, learning about sexuality is an invaluable preparation for living.

DIMENSIONS OF SEXUALITY: SOME DEFINITIONS

One would certainly think that there could be no doubt about what is to be understood by the term "sexual." First and foremost, of course, it means the "improper," that which must not be mentioned. *(Freud, 1943, p. 266)*

Sex is not a mere physiological transaction to the primitive South Sea Islander any more than it is to us; it implies love and lovemaking; it becomes the nucleus of such venerable institutions as marriage and the family; it pervades art and it produces its spells and its magic. It dominates in fact almost every aspect of culture. *Sex,* in its widest meaning . . . is rather a sociological and cultural force than a mere bodily relation of two individuals. *(Malinowski, 1929, p. xxiii)*

"Francie, you bloody fucker," I used to say, "you've got the morals of a clam." "But you like me, don't you?" she'd answer. "Men like to fuck, and so do women. It doesn't harm anybody and it doesn't mean you have to love everyone you fuck, does it?" *(Miller, 1961, p. 262)*

What is sexuality? As shown by the preceding quotes, there is no simple answer to this question. Freud saw sex as a powerful psychological and biological force, while Malinowski emphasized its sociological and cultural dimensions. Henry Miller used frank portrayals of sex in his novels to make a philosophical statement about the human condition. In everyday life, the word *sex* is often used to mean male or female (biological gender) or to refer to physical activity involving the genitals ("having sex"). The word **sexuality** generally has a broader meaning since it refers to all aspects of being sexual. Sexuality means a dimension of personality instead of referring to a person's capacity for erotic response alone.

Sexuality is a part of everyone's life, as shown in the following photos.

Unfortunately, our language for talking about sex and sexuality is very limited.[1] We may distinguish between sex acts (such as masturbation, kissing, and sexual intercourse) and sexual behavior (which includes not only specific sex acts but being flirtatious, dressing in certain ways, reading *Playboy*, and dating) without having yet scratched the surface of sexuality. We may describe different types of sex as **procreational** (for having children), **recreational** (for having fun, with no other goal), or **relational** (for sharing with a cared-for person) and find that our categories are still too few. While we cannot fully answer the question "What is sexuality?" in this chapter, we can briefly introduce the dimensions of sexuality that are the subject of this book.

A Case Profile

David and Lynn sat anxiously in the waiting room at the sex therapy clinic. Although feeling embarrassed and unsure, they were determined to seek a solution to the sexual problems that had troubled their relationship for the past three months. Although they had been living together for almost two years and had planned to marry after their graduation from college, the dissatisfactions that now rocked their lives had thrown these future plans into doubt.

Once inside the clinic, they told their story in a straightforward fashion. They had met three years ago, at age 18, during their freshman year at school. Romance blossomed as they discovered many shared interests and easily developed an intimate sexual relationship. Neither David nor Lynn was a virgin when they met, and they felt a strong sexual attraction to each other. Their first shared lovemaking experience was passionate and sensuous. As their relationship matured, their sexual interaction continued to be a major source of pleasure. Living together was a natural outgrowth of these feelings, and it had been fun—until recently.

Trouble first appeared during Christmas vacation when they visited Lynn's parents in Boston. David was upset because he and Lynn were not allowed to share the same bedroom. Lynn was put off by her parents' apparent coolness toward

David. Their only sexual opportunity (on a Sunday morning while Lynn's parents were at church) was hurried and felt mechanical. They were both relieved to return to school in time for a big New Year's Eve party with some friends.

The party lasted until 4:00 a.m. with great quantities of champagne consumed by all. Once back at their apartment, David and Lynn tried to make love but David was unable to get an erection. They laughed it off and fell asleep, happy to be "home."

The next morning David had a terrible hangover. He took some aspirin, ate a quick breakfast, and invited Lynn into their bedroom. She wasn't very enthusiastic, having a slight hangover herself, but didn't object. Once again David was unable to get an erection. Although Lynn was very understanding and supportive, David worried about his sexual performance (or lack of it) all day. He decided he needed some rest and relaxation before trying again, so he went to bed early that evening without any romantic overtures.

David awakened the next day feeling rested and refreshed and immediately turned to embrace Lynn. Despite feeling good he found himself having only a partial erection, and even that disappeared when they tried to have intercourse. From that point on, David was plagued by difficulties getting or keeping an erection, and Lynn—despite initial attempts at helping him—was getting increasingly upset. Whereas their relationship *had* been relaxed and comfortable, now they were becoming short-tempered and abrupt. They talked about splitting up but believed they still loved each other and that they could—with some expert help—overcome this problem.

sexuality a broadly encompassing term used to refer to all aspects of being and feeling sexual.

procreational sex (pro' krē ā' shun ul) sexual intercourse solely for reproduction. Sometimes advocated by some churches and groups as the only acceptable reason for sex.

recreational sex sexual activity primarily for pleasure. Emotional involvement and intimacy are purposefully limited.

relational sex sexual activity in the context of emotional involvement and intimacy in a relationship.

---

[1] Wardell Pomeroy, a leading sexologist, likes to ask an audience for a four-letter word ending in the letter *k* that means "intercourse"—and then pauses knowingly before he says, "talk."

This real-life example, drawn from our files, allows us to introduce the various perspectives on sexuality that we examine in greater detail later in the book. By looking at David's and Lynn's situation, we can see the importance of the different dimensions of sexuality that interact in all of our lives.

The Biological Dimension

David's problem with erections first occurred after he had consumed a lot of champagne. This is not very surprising, since alcohol is a depressant to the nervous system. Because the nervous system normally transmits physical sensations to the brain and activates our sexual reflexes, too much alcohol can block *anyone's* sexual response.

The biological dimension of sexuality is far more inclusive than this, however. Biological factors largely control sexual development from conception until birth and our ability to reproduce after puberty. The biological side of sexuality also affects our sexual desire, our sexual functioning, and (indirectly) our sexual satisfaction. Biological forces are even thought to influence certain sex differences in behavior, such as the tendency of males to act more aggressively than females (Olweus et al., 1980; Reinisch, 1981). And sexual turn-ons, no matter what their source, produce specific biological events: the pulse quickens, the sexual organs respond, and sensations of warmth or tingling spread through our bodies.

The Psychosocial Dimension

David and Lynn reacted to their situation in different ways. David became anxious and goal-oriented and lost his self-confidence, while Lynn, who started out being supportive and understanding, became irritated and aloof. Clearly, the nature of their relationship changed in response to the stress of their sexual problem. David and Lynn even began to doubt whether they were in love and wanted to marry, although while visiting Lynn's parents they were convinced this plan was "right."

These responses illustrate the psychosocial dimension of sexuality, which includes psychological factors (emotions, thoughts, and personalities) in combination with social elements (how people interact). In this case, David's concern about his first sexual "failure" led him into further difficulties even when the original biological "cause"—too much alcohol—was removed from the situation. His anxieties led him into trying too hard to make sex work, with the result being exactly the opposite of what he and Lynn wanted.

The psychosocial side of sexuality is important because it sheds light not only on many sexual problems but also on how we develop as sexual beings. From infancy, a person's **gender identity** (the personal sense of being male or female) is primarily shaped by psychosocial forces. Our early sexual attitudes—which often stay with us into adulthood—are based largely on what parents, peers, and teachers tell us or show us about the meanings and purposes of sex. Our sexuality is also social in that it is regulated by society through laws, taboos, and family and peer group pressures that seek to persuade us to follow certain paths of sexual behavior.

The Behavioral Dimension

Talking with David and Lynn separately, we learned that the pattern of their sexual interaction changed considerably during the three months of their problem. The frequency of attempted lovemaking fell drastically, while in the past it had been four or five times per week. David masturbated several times a week (which he had not done for several years) after finding that he could easily get erections this way. On the other hand, Lynn masturbated only once, since she felt guilty about this activity. She also shied away from initiating sexual activity or even acting romantic with David because she thought this would put extra pressure on him.

These aspects of David's and Lynn's situation reflect the behavioral dimension of sexuality. Sexual behavior is a product of both biological and psychosocial forces, yet studying it in its own right can be enlightening. The behavioral perspective allows us to learn not only *what* people do but to understand more about *how* and *why* they do it. For example, David may have used masturbation to boost his self-confidence by "proving" to himself that he could still get erections. Lynn's withdrawal from initiating physical intimacy may have been well intended, but David may have interpreted it as rejection.

In discussing this topic, we should avoid judging other people's sexual behavior by our own values and experiences. Too often, people have a ten-

"How often is normal?"
Smilby, copyright © Punch (Rothco).

dency to think about sexuality in terms of "normal" versus "abnormal." "Normal" is frequently defined as what we ourselves do and feel comfortable about, while the "abnormal" is what others do that seems different or odd to us. Trying to decide what is normal for others is not only a thankless task but one ordinarily doomed to failure because our objectivity is clouded by our values and experiences.

The Clinical Dimension

David and Lynn entered our sex therapy program and resolved their difficulties within two weeks. Not only did their sexual interaction return to its previously pleasurable state, but both felt that the therapy experience improved their relationship in other ways. As Lynn commented to us: "Overcoming the sexual problem was great, but we've also learned so much about ourselves. Our communication is about a thousand percent better now, and we really feel like we have a solid relationship that can cope with any kind of problem that comes up."

Although sex is a natural function, many types of obstacles can lessen the pleasure or spontaneity of our sexual encounters. Physical problems such as illness, injury, or drugs can alter our sexual response patterns or knock them out completely. Feelings such as anxiety, guilt, embarrassment, or depression and conflicts in our personal relationships can also hamper our sexuality. The clinical perspective of sexuality examines the solutions to these and other problems that prevent people from reaching a state of sexual health and happiness.

Greatly improved results have been obtained in the treatment of a wide variety of sexual difficulties in the last two decades. Two key changes have contributed to this success: a better understanding of the multidimensional nature of sexuality and the development of a new discipline, called sexology, devoted to the study of sex. Doctors, psychologists, nurses, counselors, and other professionals trained in sexology can integrate this knowledge with training in sex counseling or sex therapy to help a high percentage of their patients.

The Cultural Dimension

David's and Lynn's lives, like all of ours, reflect the input of the culture in which they live. For example, Lynn's parents refused to let them sleep in the same bedroom although they knew David and Lynn were living together. As another example, Lynn's sense of guilt toward masturbation stemmed largely from her religious upbringing. And David's anxiety over his sexual difficulties was partly a reaction to the prevailing American notion that men should be instantly erect at the first moment of a sexual encounter.

Our own cultural attitudes toward sexuality are far from universal. In some societies, a man's special obligations to a guest or a friend are discharged by an invitation to have sexual relations with his wife (Voget, 1961). Ford and Beach (1951, p. 49) listed eight cultural groups in which kissing was unknown, pointing out: "When the Thonga first saw Europeans kissing they laughed, expressing this sentiment: 'Look at them—they eat each other's saliva and dirt.'" While these cultural differences may shock or amuse us, they can also help us to understand that our viewpoint is not shared by all people in all places.

gender identity the inner sense a person has of being male or female.

Sexual topics are often controversial and value-laden, but the controversy is often relative to time, place, and circumstance. What is labeled as "moral" or "right" varies from culture to culture, from century to century. Many of the moral issues pertaining to sex relate to certain religious traditions, but religion has no monopoly on morality. People who have no closely held religious creed are just as likely to be moral as those whose values are tied to a religious position. *There is no comprehensive sexual value system that is right for everyone and no single moral code that is indisputably correct and universally applicable.*

In America, messages about sexual behavior that prevailed in the first half of this century have changed considerably in the last 25 years. For example, while there used to be a high cultural premium placed on a woman being a virgin before marriage, today attitudes toward premarital sex have shifted in the opposite direction. Reflecting this change, the age of first sexual intercourse is now lower than it was 20 or 30 years ago, increasing numbers of adolescents are engaging in sexual intercourse, and substantial numbers of couples are living together before marriage. Another example that illustrates how times and attitudes have changed is the current degree of acceptance of masturbation as a harmless, pleasurable act, which is in sharp contrast to earlier views that regarded masturbation as a sign of moral weakness and a cause of physical and mental debility.

Three broad trends have played an important role in the evolution of cultural attitudes toward sex and sexuality in America in the last few decades. The first is a loosening of gender role stereotypes. **Gender role** is the public expression of gender identity—that is, how an individual asserts his or her maleness or femaleness in social settings (Money and Ehrhardt, 1972).[2] Traditionally, women and girls were cast as sexually passive and unresponsive creatures while men were seen as virile sexual aggressors. According to this view, the male was expected to be the sexual initiator and expert, and the female who was aggressive or enjoyed sex too much was frowned upon. This notion has now been replaced for many people by a concept of mutual participation and satisfaction. A second trend is the greater degree of openness about sexuality. All forms of the media from television to cinema to the printed word reflect this change, and, as a result, sex has become less shameful and mysterious. The third trend is the growing acceptance of relational and recreational sex as opposed to reproductive sex. This shift, which has been especially evident in the past 25 years, is due partly to improved contraceptive techniques and concern for overpopulation.

It is a mistake to think that cultural viewpoints are ever frozen in place. Currently, there is some evidence that alarm over increasing rates of sexually transmitted diseases coupled with a growing trend toward political and religious conservatism may cause a shift away from the sexual permissiveness that prevailed in the 1960s and 1970s. In fact, many observers now believe that the so-called sexual revolution is over, with a new era dawning that will emphasize commitment and fidelity in intimate relations instead of experimentation, instant gratification, and sexual variety. But cultural trends are notoriously changeable, so there is no certainty how this new direction will evolve.

HISTORICAL PERSPECTIVES ON SEXUALITY

> A major obstacle to understanding our own sexuality is realizing we are prisoners of past societal attitudes toward sex. *(Bullough, 1976, p. xi)*

To understand the present, it is helpful to begin by examining the past. In certain respects, we are bound by a sexual legacy passed on from generation to generation, but in other ways modern views of sex and sexuality differ drastically from past patterns.

Early Times

Although written history goes back almost 5000 years, only limited information is available describing sexual behavior and attitudes in various societies prior to 1000 B.C. Clearly, a prominent taboo against incest had already been established (Tannahill, 1980), and women were considered as property, with sexual and reproductive value (Bullough, 1976). Men were free to have many sexual partners,

---

[2]Although the term "sex roles" is more widely used than "gender roles," we have chosen the second usage throughout this book to avoid the risk that "sex roles" implies an underlying biological mechanism (Unger, 1979).

Sexual themes have been shown in art since ancient times. This Roman lamp, used to ward off evil spirits, and the Laksmana Temple carving, with its erotic scene, are two interesting examples.

prostitution was widespread, and sex was accepted as a straightforward fact of life.

With the advent of Judaism, an interesting interplay of sexual attitudes began to emerge. In the first five books of the Old Testament, the primary source of Jewish laws, there are rules about sexual conduct: adultery is forbidden in the Ten Commandments (Exodus 20:13), for example, and homosexual acts are strongly condemned (Leviticus 18:22, Leviticus 21:13). At the same time, sex is rec-

ognized as a creative and pleasurable force, as depicted in the Song of Songs. Sex was neither considered inherently evil nor restricted to procreative purposes alone.

In ancient Greece, however, there was tolerance and even enthusiasm regarding male homosexuality in certain forms. Homosexual relations between

gender role behavior that conveys to others that an individual is either male or female.

Oriental art has a long tradition of explicitly depicting erotic scenes, as this work from the eighteenth century shows.

an adult man and adolescent boy past the age of puberty were commonplace, usually occurring in an educational relationship where the man was responsible for the boy's moral and intellectual development (Bullough, 1976; Karlen, 1980; Tannahill, 1980). At the same time, exclusive homosexuality and homosexual acts between adults were frowned upon, and homosexual contact between adults and boys under the age of puberty was illegal. There was a strong emphasis on marriage and family, yet women were second-class citizens, if they could be considered citizens at all: "In Athens, women had no more political or legal rights than slaves; throughout their lives they were subject to the absolute authority of their male next-of-kin. . . . As everywhere else in the first millennium B.C., women were chattels, even if some of them were independent-minded ones. To the Greeks, a woman (regardless of age or marital status) was _gyne,_ whose linguistic meaning is 'bearer of children'" (Tannahill, 1980, pp. 94–95).

As Christianity developed in its early forms, there was an intermingling of Greek and Jewish attitudes toward sexuality. In contrast to Judaism, which did not distinguish physical from spiritual love, Christian theology borrowed from the Greek and separated _eros,_ or "carnal love," from _agape,_ a "spiritual, nonphysical love" (Gordis, 1977). Bullough (1976) points out that the Hellenistic era in Greece (beginning in 323 B.C.) was marked by a denial of worldly pleasures in favor of developing the spiritual. Along with the New Testament portrayal of the imminent end of the world, this led to Christianity placing a high ideal on celibacy, although St. Paul allowed that while "it is good for a man not to touch a woman . . . it is better to marry than to burn" (1 Corinthians 7:1–12).

By the end of the fourth century A.D., despite small groups of Christians whose views of sexuality were less rigid and constrained, the church's negative attitudes toward sex were dramatically presented in the writings of St. Augustine, a religious leader whose background included a vivid and varied set of erotic experiences before he renounced worldly ways. Augustine confessed in stark terms, "I muddied the stream of friendship with the filth of lewdness and clouded its clear waters with hell's black river of lust" (_Confessions,_ Book III:I). He believed that sexual lust came from the downfall of Adam and Eve in the Garden of Eden and that this sinfulness was transmitted to children by the inherent lust that separated humanity from God. Thus, sex was strongly condemned in all forms, although Augustine and his contemporaries apparently felt that marital procreative sex was less evil than other types.

Eastern Thought

Elsewhere in the world, sexual thinking varied remarkably from that just described. In particular, Islamic, Hindu, and ancient Oriental sexual attitudes were considerably more positive. Bullough states that "almost anything in the sexual field received approval from some segment of the Hindu society" and that in China "sex was not something to be feared, nor was it regarded as sinful, but rather, it was an act of worship" and even a path toward immortality (Bullough, 1976, pp. 275, 310). The _Kama Sutra,_ compiled at about the same time Augustine was writing his _Confessions,_ is a detailed Indian sex manual; in ancient China and Japan, similar manuals, which were abundant, glorified sexual pleasure and variety. These divergent patterns continued, al-

The ancient Kama Sutra from India is one of the best-known sex manuals surviving from early times.

though our focus for now will remain with the history of sex in the Western world. Other cultures are examined in later chapters.

Medieval and Renaissance Thought

The early Christian traditions regarding sexuality became more firmly entrenched in Europe during the twelfth and thirteenth centuries as the Church assumed greater power. Theology often became synonymous with common law, and there was a generally oppressive "official" attitude toward sex except for the purpose of procreation. There was, however, a certain hypocrisy between professed Church policies and actual practices: "religious houses themselves were often hotbeds of sexuality" (Taylor, 1954, p. 19).

During this era, a new style of living emerged among the upper classes that brought about a drastic separation between actual practice and religious teachings. This style, called courtly love, introduced a new code of acceptable behavior in which women (at least high-ranking women) were elevated to an immaculate plane and romanticism, secrecy, and valor were celebrated in song, poetry, and literature (Tannahill, 1980). Pure love was seen as incompatible with the temptations of the flesh, and sometimes this concept was tested by lovers lying together in bed naked to see if they could prove the fullness of their love by refraining from sexual intercourse. Needless to say, it is unlikely that courtly love was always the unconsummated romantic ideal portrayed in story and verse.

Not too long after the era of courtly love began, chastity belts made their appearance. These devices allowed husbands to lock up their wives just as they would protect their money; while they may have been originally designed to prevent rape, they also served to guard "property":

> The belt of medieval times was usually constructed on a metal framework that stretched between the woman's legs from front to back. It had two small, rigid apertures that allowed for waste elimination but effectively prevented penetration, and once it was locked over the hips the jealous husband could take away the key. (*Tannahill, 1980, p. 276*)

The rebirth of humanism and the arts that subsequently engulfed Europe in the sixteenth and seventeenth centuries was accompanied by a loosening of sexual restrictions as well as less adherence to the formulas of courtly love. The Protestant Reformation, led by Martin Luther, John Calvin, and others, generally advocated less negative attitudes toward sexual matters than the Catholic church did. For example, although Luther was hardly liberal in his sexual attitudes, he thought that sex was not inherently sinful and that chastity and celibacy were not signs of virtue. At the same time, Europe was caught in a massive epidemic of syphilis—possibly imported from the Americas—that might have worked to limit sexual freedom.

The Eighteenth and Nineteenth Centuries

When we speak of the attitudes of a historical era, we must keep in mind that there was variance among different countries, levels of society, and religious groups. Although evidence can be cited to show a rather broad tolerance toward sexuality in England and France in the 1700s (Bullough, 1976), the Puritan ethic reigned in colonial America. Sex outside marriage was condemned, and family solidarity was exalted; those giving in to the passions of adultery or premarital sex, if discovered, were flogged, put in pillories or stocks, or forced to make public confessions. Some readers may be familiar with Nathaniel Hawthorne's *The Scarlet Letter*, which presents an account of sexual attitudes in colonial times.

In America, the Puritan ethic was carried over into the nineteenth century with a curious schism. As American frontiers expanded and as large cities took on a more cosmopolitan flair, there was a corresponding loosening of notions about sexual propriety, and prostitution became commonplace. This new development was met by the formation in the 1820s and 1830s of several groups whose primary mission was to combat the social evils of prostitution and rescue the "fallen women" who plied this trade (Pivar, 1973). Despite the organized resistance of such groups as the American Society for the Prevention of Licentiousness and Vice and the Promotion of Morality and the American Society for Promoting the Observance of the Seventh Commandment, prostitution flourished. During a three-year period in the 1840s, the government prosecuted 351 brothels in Massachusetts alone, and by the eve of the Civil War, a guidebook listing fashionable brothels in big cities described 106 establishments in New York, 57 in Philadelphia, and dozens of others in Baltimore, Boston, Chicago, and Washington, DC (Pivar, 1973).

By the mid-1800s, as the Victorian era began, reserve and prudery emerged once again in Europe, although this time less connected to religious edict. The spirit of Victorianism was sexual repression and a strong sense of modesty necessitated by the presumed purity and innocence of women and children. Taylor points out, "So delicate did the sensibilities of the Victorians become, so easily were their thoughts turned to sexual matters, that the most innocent actions were taboo in case they might lead to lurid imaginings. It became indelicate to offer a lady a *leg* of chicken." Clothing styles, showing not even a glimpse of ankle or bare neck, mirrored this conservatism (Taylor, 1954, pp. 214–215). The prudishness of this period is astonishing to us today: in some Victorian homes, piano legs were covered with crinolines, and books by authors of opposite sexes were not shelved side by side unless the authors were married to each other (Sussman, 1976).

In America, although the influence of Victorianism was strongly felt, crosscurrents sent the mainstream of moral thinking into a dizzying spin. For example, in 1870 the St. Louis City Council found a loophole in state law that allowed it to legalize prostitution, causing an uproar across the nation. Groups were again formed to combat sexual immorality and managed to find allies in other organizations dedicated to the cause of temperance (abolishing the sale of alcoholic beverages). This movement achieved several legislative successes. In 1886, for example, 25 states fixed the age of consent at 10 (thus permitting child prostitution to flourish), but by 1895, only 5 states retained this low age, and 8 states had raised the age of consent to 18.

Although the mainstream of Victorianism was antisexual—pornography was first banned by law in this era—there was another side to the times. A sexual "underground" of pornographic writings and pictures was widely read (Marcus, 1967). Prostitution was common in Europe, and in the 1860s it was legalized and regulated by an act of the British Parliament. Furthermore, Victorian prudery in sexual behavior and attitudes was not standard for all social classes (Gay, 1983). The middle and lower classes did not practice the sexual pretensions of the upper class. Indeed, it was the abject poverty of the lower classes that forced many young women into prostitution, and the middle classes—despite the ideal of the docile, sexless Victorian lady—not only had sexual feelings and desires but acted on them in much the same way women do today. Victorian women had (and enjoyed) marital sex and occasionally had torrid love affairs, as seen in a number of diaries which detailed the number and quality of their orgasms (Gay, 1983). In fact, a female sex survey conducted by a woman named Clelia Duel Mosher in 1892 has recently come to light, providing additional evidence that viewing the Victorian period as strictly antisexual is incorrect. In addition, an interesting viewpoint has been advanced about female sexuality in Victorian times:

> Although it is obvious that many Victorians suffered from sexual repression, it appears on closer observation that those women who contributed to the concept of prudishness were far closer to today's feminists than most are willing to admit. . . . The Victorian woman sought to achieve a sort of sexual freedom by denying her sexuality . . . in an effort to keep from being considered or treated as a sex object. Her prudery was a mask that conveniently hid her more "radical" effort to achieve freedom of person. *(Haller and Haller, 1977, p. xii)*

Science and medicine reflected the antisexualism of the era thoroughly. Masturbation was variously branded as a source of damage to the brain and nervous system and a cause of insanity and a wide range of other illnesses (Bullough and Bullough, 1977; Haller and Haller, 1977; Tannahill, 1980). Women were thought to have little or no capacity for sexual response and were viewed as inferior to men both physically and intellectually. In 1878, the prestigious *British Medical Journal* printed a series of letters in which a number of physicians offered evidence supporting the idea that the touch of a menstruating woman would spoil hams. And even as eminent a scientist as Charles Darwin, the father of the theory of evolution, wrote in his *Descent of Man and Selection in Relation to Sex* (1871) that "man is more courageous, pugnacious, and energetic than woman, and has a more inventive genius" and that "the average of mental power in man must be above that of women."

In the latter part of the nineteenth century Richard von Krafft-Ebing, a German psychiatrist, undertook a detailed classification of sexual disorders. The impact of his *Psychopathia Sexualis* (1886), which went through 12 editions, was profound and influenced subsequent public attitudes and medical and legal practice for more than three-quarters of a century (Brecher, 1975). There were positive and negative aspects to this influence: on the one hand, Krafft-Ebing advocated sympathetic medical concern for the so-called sexual perversions and reform in laws dealing with sex criminals, while on the other hand his book seemed to lump sex, crime, and violence together. Much of his attention was devoted to aspects of sexuality he considered abnormal, such as sadomasochism (sexual arousal from inflicting or experiencing pain), homosexuality, fetishism (sexual arousal by an object rather than a person), and bestiality (sexual contact with animals). Because he frequently used lurid examples (sexual murders, cannibalism, and intercourse with the dead, to name just a few) which he presented in the same pages with less frightening sexual variations, many readers were left with a general loathing for almost all forms of sexual conduct. Nevertheless, Krafft-Ebing is often considered the founder of modern sexology.

The Twentieth Century

By the turn of the new century, sexuality began to be investigated in a more objective manner. Although Victorian attitudes still prevailed in many circles, the work of serious scientists such as Albert Moll, Magnus Hirshfeld, Iwan Bloch, and Havelock Ellis combined with the dynamic theories of Freud to initiate a striking reversal in thinking about sex.

Freud

Sigmund Freud (1856–1939) was a Viennese physician who, more successfully than any figure before or since, demonstrated the central importance of sexuality to human existence. Today Freud's genius is recognized as partly a matter of original discovery and partly a reflection of his ability to synthesize emerging ideas into a cohesive and persuasive theoretical framework (Sulloway, 1979). Freud believed that sexuality was both the primary force in the motivation of all human behavior and the principal cause of all forms of **neurosis,** a mild form of mental disorder in which anxiety is prominent and coping skills are distorted although a sense of reality is maintained. He clearly described the exis-

tence of sexuality in infants and children, expanding views expressed by other sexologists between 1880 and 1905 (Kern, 1973; Sulloway, 1979), and formulated a detailed theory of psychosexual development discussed in Chapter 8.

Freud devised many innovative concepts related to sexuality. The best known, the **Oedipus complex,** refers to an inevitable sexual attraction of the young male child to his mother accompanied by an ambivalent mixture of love, hate, fear, and rivalry toward his father. Freud also believed that boys were concerned about the possible loss of their penis as a terrible form of punishment (**castration anxiety**) and that girls felt a sense of inadequacy and jealousy at not having a penis (**penis envy**). Freud saw these situations as operating primarily at the unconscious level—a level of the personality deeper than conscious awareness. From the rich theoretical tapestry of his thought, Freud wove a clinical method called psychoanalysis for assessing and treating the unconscious conflicts that lead to psychological problems. Although many modern sexologists disagree with Freud's formulations, as we will discuss in subsequent chapters, psychoanalysis remains a widely used method of treatment today.

Ellis

At about this same time, an English physician named Havelock Ellis (1859–1939) was publishing a six-volume series called *Studies in the Psychology of Sex* (1897–1910). Ellis anticipated much that Freud later wrote about childhood sexuality and had remarkably modern views in certain areas. For

neurosis a psychological disorder usually characterized by anxiety and/or tension. In contrast to more severe forms of psychological problems, called psychoses, with a neurosis a person's sense of reality is not greatly altered.

Oedipus complex (ed' i pus) in Freudian theory, the sexual attraction of a young boy toward his mother, accompanied by a mixture of fear and rivalry toward his father.

castration anxiety (ka strā' shun) according to Freud, the unconscious fear in boys about the possible loss of their penis as a terrible form of punishment.

penis envy in Freudian theory, the girl's unconscious sense of inadequacy and jealousy at not having a penis.

Havelock Ellis, through his prolific writings, became one of the most influential early sexologists.

example, he recognized the common occurrence of masturbation in both sexes at all ages, took exception to the Victorian idea that "good" women had no sexual desire, and emphasized the psychological rather than physical causes of many sexual problems. His writings also focused on the varied nature of human sexual behavior and provided an important balancing influence to Krafft-Ebing's view of sexual variations as diseases (Brecher, 1969, 1975).

1920–1950

By the end of World War I, massive social changes were emerging in both Europe and America that differed drastically from Victorian practices. Influenced by increasing social and economic freedom for women and the availability of the automobile, sexual attitudes became increasingly less inhibited in the Jazz Age and were accompanied by corresponding changes in fashion, dance, and literature. Women had become involved professionally in the sexual revolution that was brewing. Margaret Sanger was a leader of the birth control movement in America. Katherine Davis conducted a survey of

the sex lives of 2200 women which was published initially as a series of scientific articles between 1922 and 1927 and then as a book (Davis, 1929). An Englishwoman, Marie Stopes, wrote an explicit marriage manual that sold well on both sides of the Atlantic.[3] By 1926, when a gynecologist named Theodore van de Velde published *Ideal Marriage*, providing specific details about a wide range of sexual techniques and endorsing such practices as oral–genital sex, his book became an instant international best-seller.

The Roaring Twenties came to a sudden end in 1929 with the stock market crash. In the Great Depression that followed, concern for sustenance, shelter, and survival seemed to take precedence over sex.

As Britain and America were drawn into World War II, the enormity of the conflict and its life-and-death drama provided a backdrop for wholesale changes in patterns of sexual behavior on both sides of the Atlantic. Women, who were enthusiastically enlisted in the workplace and in the armed forces, suddenly enjoyed a newfound economic freedom and personal independence but were also thrust into a confusing atmosphere of hasty marriages, anxious separation, loneliness, and fear. While their boyfriends or husbands were overseas, many turned to clandestine affairs, just as the male troops generally availed themselves of sexual opportunities near training camps, in overseas assignments, and on leave. As one social historian observed, "The lives and moral attitudes of many millions of people had undergone an extensive emotional trauma, and in the unsettled conditions of wartime many social inhibitions had lost their restraining force. Making the best of the present without thinking about the future had led to pleasure-seeking and increased promiscuity" (Costello, 1985, p. 258).

The postwar era, which was unsettled both for its burgeoning divorce rate and for the upheaval

[3]It is interesting to note that Stopes, who had obtained a doctorate and was an accomplished scientific researcher, was very much a victim of Victorian prudishness about sex. Six months after her marriage to another scientist, Dr. Reginald Ruggles Gates, she "began to feel instinctively that something was lacking," and went to the British Museum to try to discover what it was. Finding out that her marriage had not been consummated, she successfully sued for divorce and later undertook the writing of her book to help others avoid such problems (Harrison, 1977).

resulting from pushing women out of factories and offices back to their "rightful" place in the home, was also notable because it brought instant notoriety to another sexologist who was to leave an indelible mark on scientific history.

Kinsey

Alfred C. Kinsey (1894–1956), a zoologist at Indiana University, had been asked to participate in teaching a noncredit college course on marriage in the summer of 1938. Struck by the lack of scientific data about human sexual behavior, he used this opportunity to administer questionnaires to some of his students for the purpose of gathering information about their sexual histories. Soon thereafter, Kinsey decided that personal interviewing was a more promising technique for obtaining such case history material since it permitted greater flexibility and detail, and he embarked on a course of action that eventually led to interviews with thousands of men and women across the country. Joined by his coauthors and colleagues, Wardell Pomeroy and Clyde Martin, Kinsey published the monumental *Sexual Behavior in the Human Male* on January 5, 1948. Five years later, with Paul Gebhard, they published the companion volume, *Sexual Behavior in the Human Female* (Kinsey et al., 1953).

The Kinsey reports were based on extensive face-to-face interviews with 12,000 people from all segments of the population and the findings were often startling. For instance, 37 percent of American men were reported to have had at least one homosexual experience to the point of orgasm after the age of puberty; 40 percent of husbands had been unfaithful to their wives; and 62 percent of the women studied had tried masturbation.

The publication of *Sexual Behavior in the Human Male* instantly catapulted the Kinsey research into the public eye. By mid-March more than 100,000 copies had been sold, and the book remained on the best-seller list for 27 weeks.

Although Kinsey and his colleagues attempted to describe how people behave sexually without moral or medical value judgments, their work was severely criticized on methodological and moral grounds. Prestigious *Life* magazine called it "an assault on the family as a basic unit of society, a negation of moral law, and a celebration of licentiousness" (Wickware, 1948). Margaret Mead criticized Kinsey for dealing with sex "as an impersonal, meaningless act" (*The New York Times*, April 1, 1948), a charge that was echoed by many critics, including one professor from Columbia University who stated that "there should be a law against doing research dealing exclusively with sex" (*The New York Times*, April 1, 1948). However, the Kinsey report was also praised as having "done for sex what Columbus did for geography" (Ernst and Loth, 1948).

All in all, the reception of Kinsey's first volume was fairly positive (Palmore, 1952), but the same cannot be said for his second book, *Sexual Behavior in the Human Female*. Many newspapers denounced this report in editorials and refused to give it coverage in their news columns. For example, the *Times* of New Philadelphia, Ohio, justified this decision by saying, "We believe it would be offensive to a large portion of our readers" (August 20, 1953). Church leaders and educators called Kinsey's findings amoral, antifamily, and even tainted with communism.

Kinsey died in 1956, embittered and disillusioned, but the impact of his energetic investigations was to be strongly apparent in the years ahead. In addition to the cultural and scientific legacy he left behind, he and his colleagues formed the Institute for Sex Research at Indiana University, which continues as a major center today.

The 1950s

In the aftermath of Kinsey's studies there was an era marked by quite a bit of sexual confusion in the United States. Premarital sex became more com-

Alfred Kinsey brought boundless enthusiasm to his career in sex research despite the considerable controversies that his methods and findings provoked.

monplace than it had been before, although it seems to have been restricted mainly to engaged couples. Popular descriptions of sex began to appear in books (such as the then-steamy *Peyton Place*) and movies (mostly imported from overseas), and even popular music began to present sexual themes. One observer, horrified by what he heard and saw, sourly noted that the "sexualization" of music made it "naked, seductive, . . . lusty and perverse," with performers whose "bleating is underscored by their gyrations, contortions, and bodily rhythms all too clear in sexual innuendo and undisguised meaning" (Sorokin, 1956).

At the same time, the 1950s were a time when females were expected to be glamorous but brainless creatures—something along the lines portrayed by Marilyn Monroe in her movies—whose primary ambitions should be directed toward marriage and motherhood. *Harper's Magazine* (January 1950) noted: "If an American girl wears plain, unadorned eyeglasses, instead of highly colored and fancifully shaped specs, she might just as well be dead, for all the dating it will get her." And *See* magazine (January 1950) solemnly advised readers: "It is quite legitimate for a girl to use falsies and not to tell her husband about them before marriage."

Albert Ellis (1959) succinctly summarized the prevailing mores of the times this way: "The fundamental law underlying all our sex, love, and marriage attitudes can be stated with absolute and appalling clarity in two simple statements: (a) if it's FUN you mustn't do it; (b) if it's DUTY you must" (p. 227).

The 1960s

In the early 1960s, several factors influenced the start of a sexual revolution that was more visible than any America had previously seen. These in-

cluded (1) the availability of birth control pills, (2) the protest movement among adolescents and young adults, (3) the reemergence of feminism in modern form, and (4) great openness in discussions and displays of sex. While it isn't possible to render any final historical judgment on the relative importance of each of these factors in fueling the sexual revolution, it appears certain that each had a strong influence.

The pill made premarital sex considerably safer and permitted millions to think of sex as relational or recreational rather than procreative, as we have already noted. Indeed, the availability of the pill provided a sense of freedom for many women and probably contributed more to changing sexual behavior than has generally been imagined. The protest movement among the young, which began with the civil rights movement and expanded with the growing disillusionment with the Vietnam War, led teens and young adults to challenge their parents' generation ("the establishment") in every way imaginable. This challenge was expressed not only in the younger generation's clothing, long hair, and music but also in their recreational drug use and their support of sexual freedom ("Make love, not war").

With their consciousness raised at many levels to political and social injustices, young adults in the sixties also embraced the women's movement with enthusiasm. Since the pill had given women a new degree of control over their sexual destinies, it is not surprising that female sexuality was increasingly accepted as a natural fact of life.

In society at large, the initial reactions to the sexual revolution were mixed. While some sought to join the movement enthusiastically, many others seemed to regard it as a passing phase that would

BLOOM COUNTY   **by Berke Breathed**

Bloom County by Berke Breathed. © 1987 Washington Post Writers Group. Reprinted with permission.

eventually fade away. And it's probably safe to say that a sizable segment of the population watched this upheaval with great distaste and alarm, concerned that the moral fabric of American society was disintegrating before their eyes. Nevertheless, sexuality became more talked about, shown, and studied, and the sixties saw the advent of "topless" bars, nudity in Broadway shows (first with *Hair*, later with *Oh! Calcutta!*), and the publication of a revolutionary study of human sexual function.

Masters and Johnson
Kinsey and his collaborators had investigated the nature of human sexuality by interviews designed to find out how, when, and how often people behaved sexually. Since then, sex research has expanded in various directions in an attempt to answer questions that had not previously been resolved. Among the first and most significant departures from Kinsey's methods were those used by William H. Masters and Virginia E. Johnson, a physician and a behavioral scientist at Washington University Medical School in St. Louis.

Masters and Johnson believed that to understand the complexities of human sexuality, people must understand sexual anatomy and physiology as well as psychological and sociological data. Unsatisfied with the relevance to humans of information gathered by studies of sexual response in animals, Masters and Johnson decided that only a direct approach to the problem would be illuminating. They began a laboratory investigation in 1954 to observe and record the physical details of human sexual arousal. By 1965 more than 10,000 episodes of sexual activity by 382 women and 312 men had been observed, and the report that followed, *Human Sexual Response* (Masters and Johnson, 1966), drew rapid public attention. Although some health-care professionals quickly grasped the importance of these findings, others were shocked by the methods employed. Amid the accusations of "too mechanistic an approach" and the cries of moral outrage, relatively few people recognized that the physiological information was not an endpoint but was instead a foundation on which a treatment method for people with sexual problems could be based.[4]

The 1970s and 1980s
In the 1970s and 1980s, the new openness about sexuality was readily apparent. In 1970, Masters and Johnson published *Human Sexual Inadequacy*, a landmark book that described a startlingly new approach to the treatment of sexual problems that had previously required lengthy treatments without very high rates of success. With a two-week treatment program and only a 20 percent failure rate, this work was soon to give rise to an entirely new profession—sex therapy—with the eventual proliferation of thousands of sex therapy clinics across the country before the end of the decade, and the development of other therapy approaches by doctors such as Helen Kaplan and Jack Anon.

Other, less technical books about sex were published by the dozens, with Alex Comfort's *The Joy of Sex* (1972) probably being the most accomplished and certainly the most successful (with sales of over nine million copies). Television became a notable force in the sexual revolution, too, as a number of programs tackled previously taboo sexual themes. Not to be outdone, movies became more sexually explicit, and, in the early days of the home video market, pornographic films were the single best-selling category.

A number of other trends occurred during this time that affected the ways Americans viewed sexuality: (1) the practice of nonmarital cohabitation—living together—began to assume increasing importance as a stage preceding marriage; (2) the legalization of abortion by the U.S. Supreme Court in 1973 made it possible to obtain safe abortions but also provoked considerable controversy about the morality of this practice; (3) the 1974 decision by the American Psychiatric Association to remove homosexuality from classification as a mental disorder set the stage for advances to be made in the gay rights movement; (4) a growing awareness of the significance of all forms of sexual victimization—in part an outgrowth of the women's movement and in part a result of the work of scientists and scholars who effectively showed that rape is a crime of violence rather than a crime of passion (e.g., Burgess and Holmstrom, 1974; Brownmiller, 1975; Metzger, 1976)—led to major legislative changes aimed at modernizing procedures for trying rape cases as

[4]It is noteworthy that all of medical science is based on understanding normal anatomy and physiology before meaningful advances can be made in treating abnormalities. In 1966, when *Human Sexual Response* was published, many physicians seemed to forget this fact, which would have been unquestionable in the study of heart disease or skin disorders. Our files from that year contain many angry letters written by physicians criticizing the physiology work because of its impropriety and departure from traditional medical "respectability."

The Antioch Policy: A Sign of the Times?

Many couples have difficulty talking about sex (Barbach, 1982; Zilbergeld, 1992; Hatfield and Rapson, 1993; Masters, Johnson, and Kolodny, 1994), especially in the early stages of a sexual relationship. Even so, that doesn't mean you should have to put up with awkward, frustrating, or coercive sexual patterns. The skill of clearly expressing your desires (what you want and what you don't want) can be learned, and this skill is one that is very much on the minds of students on campuses all over the United States today as part of the growing awareness of the acquaintance rape issue.

In 1993, Antioch College in Yellow Springs, Ohio, developed a controversial but thought-provoking "Sexual Offense Policy" which mandates that "it isn't enough to ask someone if she'd like to have sex. . . . You must obtain consent every step of the way. . . . The goal is 100% consensual sex. . . ." (Newsweek, October 25, 1993, p. 54). This policy was developed in order to avoid misunderstandings about sex that could lead to accusations of sexual coercion of one sort or another. However, such a rigid guideline has the potential to alter the "sensual" in consensual sex for some participants, making it too cerebral, too predictable, and too wordy. Another concern is that such a policy inadvertently continues the gender stereotype of women as people who must be courted and treated with kid gloves by men who are the sexual initiators. In that scenario, women are relegated to playing out a role of being recipients of male ardor.

Obviously, all sexual encounters do not follow Antioch's suggested guidelines. Although the goal of 100 percent consensual sex is admirable, it doesn't account for the times in which one person thinks, perhaps on the basis of body language, that he or she has the consent of the other but doesn't. It also doesn't fit situations where one person's sexual needs are greater than the other's and the person who isn't really "in the mood" is still willing to have a quickie or fool around without feeling the pressure to be totally involved mentally or physically in the sexual encounter. Many people who are in long-term relationships will explain that a willingness to make some sexual compromises from time to time is not synonymous with a coercive sexual situation. In fact, they will say that it is just the opposite—it is based on trust and understanding and can only happen if each partner is self-confident and sure of the other person's concern and affection. So, the ability to make the decision to compromise is based largely on the ability to talk about one's sexual needs and on the ability to listen to a partner without shame, blame, or guilt coloring what you hear.

Nevertheless, the intentions behind Antioch's policy are good. The idea is to be sure your partner agrees to what you want to do in order to avoid unintentional coercion of any sort. This calls for clarity in communication as well as thinking about your behavior and its impact on your partner, which is not necessarily bad even if it requires some attention to detail.

well as the rapid growth in rape crisis centers across the country; (5) the appearance of new reproductive technologies encompassing the birth of the world's first "test-tube baby" in 1978 (with more than 75,000 babies conceived by similar means now alive) has proceeded to even more startling techniques, such as embryo transfer methods and the controversial surrogate mother practice.

The late 1970s and early 1980s were also a time for a backlash against what some perceived as overpermissive, even immoral sexual practices. The Moral Majority sought to block sex education in public schools and campaigned against "promiscuous" sexual behavior, which seemed to include anything other than marital sex. The right-to-life movement challenged the legality of abortion and unsuccessfully tried to pass a constitutional amendment that would have banned abortion under all circumstances. In 1983, the Reagan administration tried to implement a policy requiring

notice to the parents of teenagers requesting contraceptives; this proposal, which became derisively known as the "squeal rule," fortunately never got off the ground.

Particularly alarming to some was the appearance in the late 1970s and early 1980s of seemingly new epidemics of sexually transmitted diseases: genital herpes, primarily among heterosexuals, and AIDS (acquired immune deficiency syndrome), which in America first affected homosexual and bisexual men but soon spread to involve heterosexuals as well. (AIDS results from infection with a virus that cripples the body's immune system, leading to a variety of severe infections, cancers, and neurologic disorders.) The AIDS epidemic—which has been likened by some to a modern-day plague—is particularly frightening because the disease now seems to be invariably fatal and because there are currently thought to be as many as 2 million Americans infected with the AIDS virus. Since cures were not available for either genital herpes or AIDS and since the two diseases seemed to be linked incontrovertibly to promiscuous sexual behavior, some observers suggested that they were a form of punishment from God for sexual transgressions.

With an avalanche of media publicity about AIDS and the realization that prevention cannot be guaranteed short of sexual abstinence or sexual monogamy with an uninfected partner, millions of people seem to have shifted their patterns of sexual behavior, with some choosing celibacy and others becoming more selective in their choice of sex partners (Kolodny and Kolodny, 1987; Stevens, 1987; Winkelstein et al., 1987). Others haven't changed their sexual practices at all or have simply added

some cautionary steps to their sex lives (e.g., using condoms).

The 1990s

Although it is true that there are few abrupt shifts from one decade to another in the ebb and flow of history, there has been a definite new dimension to public awareness of sexual themes in the 1990s. Notably, it has not come in the form of any major change in personal behavior in the broad population as a result of the HIV/AIDS epidemic (Ehrhardt, Yingling, and Warne, 1991; Masters, Johnson, and Kolodny, 1994). What has happened, instead, is that a series of famous (and infamous) court cases and government investigations have captured public attention with an eerily familiar ring. Think about this partial list: the Clarence Thomas–Anita Hill confrontation in 1991 involving allegations of sexual harassment; the U.S. Navy's Tailhook scandal of the same year and the subsequent attempts at covering up what had happened during the Navy's investigation; the William Kennedy Smith rape trial (resulting in acquittal); the Mike Tyson rape trial (putting the ex-heavyweight champion of the world in prison); the strange case in 1993 of the Spur Posse in Southern California, involving a group of teenage boys who coerced girls as young as age 10 into having sex so they could score "points" for their club. To these high visibility cases we should also add the innumerable instances of charges of child sexual abuse filed against priests, school teachers, and day-care workers, which have seemed to come with increasing frequency in the recent past, as well as soaring rates of date and acquaintance rape reported on college campuses across the country, and surprisingly large numbers of prominent people going public with accusations of childhood sexual traumas. This recounting of some of the ways sex has been prominently in the news in recent years suggests a shift may be occurring in our society's attitudes toward sexual behavior.

We cannot know, of course, if the changes and trends we see as significant today will have any lasting impact on our sexual behavior over time. Nor can we be certain that a century from now, historians won't label our era with a single word (like "Victorian") and reduce the many complexities of our sexual attitudes to a single notion. The only thing we can be sure of is that our attitudes and behaviors will continue to change—what directions

Sex has been featured more prominently in the news in the 1990s than ever before.

those changes will take, however, is impossible to predict with any accuracy.

SUMMARY

1. Human sexuality is a multidimensional phenomenon having biological, psychosocial, behavioral, clinical, moral, and cultural aspects. No single dimension of sexuality is universally dominant.

2. History teaches us that sexual attitudes and practices vary considerably over time and place. For more than 2000 years, religion has been a principal force in shaping sexual thought. In the past century, the advent of sexology as a science—from the early approaches of Krafft-Ebing, Havelock Ellis, and Sigmund Freud to the dramatic research studies of Kinsey and Masters and Johnson—has greatly influenced contemporary attitudes toward sex and sexuality.

3. We must guard against interpreting sexual behavior too simplistically. For instance, although the Victorian era was certainly a time of sexual prudishness in many respects, it was clearly also a time when prostitution flourished, pornography was widely read, and the middle and lower classes paid scant attention to the sexual pretensions of the upper class.

4. In our recent past, many observers have pointed to the 1960s as a time when a sexual revolution began. Four factors contributed to this phenomenon: the availability of birth control pills, the protest movement among teenagers and young adults, a renewed interest in feminism, and a greater openness to discussion and displays of sex.

5. Alarm over new epidemics of sexually transmitted diseases—especially AIDS (acquired immune deficiency syndrome)—along with a growing trend toward conservatism seems to have brought the sexual revolution to a grinding halt. Millions of people are now adopting a more cautious attitude toward sexual behavior, with further changes likely to occur if the AIDS epidemic worsens.

6. Predicting the changes in sexual thinking and behavior that will occur in the future is difficult at best. All we can be sure of is that our attitudes and behaviors *will* change in one way or another.

Thought Questions

1. The authors state that "There is no sexual value system that is right for everyone and no single moral code that is indisputably correct and universally applicable." Do you agree with this assertion? Or are there some sexual values that are indisputably and universally right or wrong?

2. The text states that sexuality has biological, psychological, and social dimensions. However, many individuals and some religions take the position that only procreation justifies engaging in sexual activities. How would our attitudes toward proper sexual expression change if this were true? What kind of sex would be prescribed by society and what kind would be proscribed?

3. Some people regard Freud, Kinsey, and even Masters and Johnson as being "dirty old men" because of their interest in doing sexual research. How common is this perception and is it justified? What would motivate individuals to base a lifetime career on the study of sex?

4. "Make love, not war" was a slogan of the 1960s. Is there a relationship between these two activities? Is sexual repression somehow connected to war and sexual freedom to peace? Or is this slogan a catchy but meaningless piece of advice?

5. Has there been a true sexual revolution during the last few decades, or is this a myth? Does our society seem to be moving toward more or less diversity and freedom regarding sexual expression?

6. According to the text, prostitution and pornography flourished during Victorian times. Is there a cause and effect relationship here? Does sexual repression encourage an underground-type of sexual expression? Also, Victorian repression affected the sexes and the social classes differently. What might be the explanation for this?

Suggested Readings

Brecher, Edward. *The Sex Researchers.* Boston: Little, Brown, 1969. A collection of biographical sketches of the most influential sex researchers from Krafft-Ebing to Kinsey to Masters and Johnson.

Bullough, Vern, and Bullough, Bonnie. *Sin, Sickness and Sanity—A History of Sexual Attitudes.* New York: New American Library, 1977. A provocative study of how past attitudes to certain aspects of sexuality (e.g., masturbation, homosexuality, prostitution, pornography) have affected present sexual theorizing.

Costello, John. *Virtue Under Fire.* Boston: Little, Brown, 1985. A nicely done social history of the impact of World War II on sexual attitudes and behavior in America and Britain.

D'Emilio, J., and Freedman, E.B. *Intimate Matters: A History of Sexuality in America.* New York: Harper & Row, 1988. A lively historical survey of American sexual behavior, courtship etiquette, and public attitudes toward a broad spectrum of sexual matters.

Gay, Peter. *The Bourgeois Experience: Victoria to Freud.* Vol. 1, *Education of the Senses.* New York: Oxford University Press, 1983. An in-depth reassessment of sexuality during the Victorian era that shows why viewing this period as a strictly antisexual time is incorrect.

Tannahill, Reay. *Sex in History.* New York: Stein and Day, 1980. A lively, opinionated survey of sexual customs and attitudes from prehistoric to modern times.

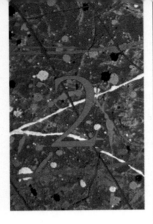

Sex Research: An Overview

Is it possible for a man to be raped by a woman? Does alcohol stimulate or inhibit sexual response? Is it normal to have sex fantasies while making love with your spouse? Do homosexuals differ from heterosexuals in the physiology of their sexual responses? Questions like these have always caused lively discussions and generated a number of answers, but, until recently, the answers that were given were simply opinions—in other words, guesses that had not been proved right or wrong. In the past two decades, these and many other questions about human sexuality have been approached in more scientific ways by professionals in the field of sex research.

Sex research is surrounded by an aura of mystery because it explores areas that are often considered forbidden, private, controversial, and exciting. But instead of being the titillating pastime the public imagines it is, research in human sexuality is like other types of scientific research. It involves hard work, long hours, careful attention to detail, and rigorous examination and evaluation of the information obtained.

Because so much is published about sex and sexuality, it can be difficult to distinguish research-based fact from one person's opinion or from an account of personal experiences. The distinction between a literary or journalist report about some facet of sex and a sex research report is often blurred. Even when a fact is based on a research study, it should not always be taken at face value. Thus, it is important to understand how sex research is conducted—including its drawbacks and limitations—in order to intelligently evaluate its findings and apply them to our own lives. This chapter describes a variety of sex research methods, discusses the designs of some major sex research reports, and provides guidelines for analyzing the reliability and significance of such studies.

GENERAL ISSUES IN SEX RESEARCH

Sampling Strategy

Researchers are almost never able to study the entire population of people that fit a category being investigated. Studies of female sexuality could not possibly include all women in the world, nor could they realistically expect to include all women in one country, state, city, or even school. Time, cost, and some individuals' unwillingness to participate in such studies are the key restraints. As a result, scientists choose a group of people (a **sample**) from a larger group with a particular characteristic (a **population**). This process is called **sample selection.** The degree to which the sample is similar to or different from the population from which it is taken has important implications about the research results.

If the sample closely matches the characteristics of the population, the research findings will also apply to the population. Applying the research findings from a sample to a larger group—either the population from which the sample was taken or a related population—is called **generalizing.** For example, if you studied a group of rape victims in Michigan, the results would probably apply to rape victims in other states. However, if your study involved drug use patterns in Southern California, your findings might not describe what was happening in the Midwest.

The size of the sample is another important factor in the confidence that can be placed in the research results. A very small sample, even if representative of the larger population, is an unreliable basis for major conclusions. Would you feel comfortable with a report on the attitudes of American college students toward premarital sex if the study involved a sample of only a dozen stu-

dents? What would your reaction be if the sample size was 25? 100? 1000? When other aspects of two research designs are equivalent, the larger sample usually provides greater reliability. However, the more alike the members of a population are—a condition statisticians call **homogeneity**—the more the sample size can be reduced while still being representative of the population.

The sample is more likely to represent the larger population from which it is drawn if it is a **random sample,** chosen so that each person in the population has the same chance of being selected. Very few sex research studies have been conducted on national probability samples, which are random samples drawn systematically from the entire U.S. population (or the segment of the general population being studied, such as married women). This is unfortunate, since a true national probability sample provides the strongest possible basis for reaching conclusions about the generalizability of a study's findings.

Methods of Obtaining Data

In addition to making decisions about sampling, the researcher must consider how to obtain information required to elucidate the problem under study. Research data may be gathered by questionnaire, personal interview, direct observation, indirect observation (e.g., use of videotapes, film, or a remote microphone), examination of case records, laboratory testing, experimentation, and other techniques. Deciding which method (or methods) is most suitable for a given study is not always easy.

sample in research, the portion of a larger population chosen to study.

population in research, the overall group being studied from which a smaller sample is drawn.

sample selection the process of choosing a sample.

generalizing applying the findings of research from a sample to the population from which the sample was taken, or the other, similar populations.

homogeneity the degree to which individuals in a population are alike.

random sample a sample in which each member of the population has an identical chance of being selected.

Sometimes ethical considerations preclude certain research approaches. For example, it would hardly be ethical to study incest by asking families to try it in order to observe its effects. Instead, questionnaires, interviews, or examination of case records would probably be used to study this controversial subject. Another factor that influences the choice of research method is the availability of reliable techniques for achieving a particular objective. For example, before the late 1960s, there was no way of accurately measuring sex hormones in the human body. Once these methods were developed, entirely new types of research were undertaken using analysis of blood samples to shed light on a wide range of sexual problems and behavior. A third set of influences on choosing a method of gathering data is matters of practicality: how much time and expense are involved, how likely is it that the method will produce useful information, and how likely is cooperation from the potential subjects? The advantages and disadvantages of various methods in sex research are discussed shortly.

Measurement or Classification of Data

Scientific research generally requires quantification—turning observations into numbers. Certain types of data are easy to quantify (e.g., height, age, number of sexual partners) or to classify (marital status, occupation, type of contraception used). Measuring other types of data is much more complex: how does one quantify love, fear, happiness, or sexual satisfaction? The researcher must devise specific strategies for quantifying or classifying information in order to process it or use it to make comparisons between groups. This is often done by constructing a scale or set of scales ("rate your sexual satisfaction on a scale from 0 to 10"), which is not quite as simple as it sounds. The adequacy of a measurement procedure depends on its **reliability,** or consistency and freedom from error, and its **validity,** the degree to which it measures what the researcher is looking for. The complex ways of testing the reliability and validity of measuring techniques are beyond the scope of our discussion.

Data Analysis

After research information has been collected, it must be evaluated. This is usually accomplished by the use of statistics. Although a detailed discussion of statistical methods is unnecessary for our purposes, several points must be made. First, statistics may be used in a purely descriptive sense (e.g., "43 percent of the men and 55 percent of the women studied were married" or "the average frequency of sexual intercourse was 2.6 times per week"). Second, statistics also may be used to draw inferences. The inferences, or predictions, that statistical tests allow to be made about sets of data are not absolute but are simply probability statements. That is, inferential statistics lead to scientific guesses (sometimes very *good* guesses) about the likelihood that a particular set of observations could have occurred by chance alone. If you studied 100 high school girls taking a sex education course and 100 girls from the same high school who did not take this course and found that only 2 in the first group had unwanted pregnancies compared with 20 in the latter group, this difference would be statistically significant. That is, it is unlikely that the pregnancies could have occurred by chance alone, and you could thereby infer that sex education courses reduce unwanted teenage pregnancies. However, inferential statistics cannot *prove* this conclusion, and some artifact in the study of which you were not aware may have determined its outcome. Third, statistical methods can also be used to examine the relationship among several variables: correlational statistics and factor analysis help researchers sort out some aspects of the problem of how one variable interacts with another but do not allow researchers to determine cause and effect.

Ethical Concerns

When conducting any type of research, investigators have a strong responsibility to respect the welfare and dignity of their subjects, a responsibility that involves attention to the following:

1. *Informed Consent.* The purposes, procedures, and potential risks and benefits of participation in a research project should be explained to all potential subjects in an understandable manner. Prospective subjects must be free to choose whether or not to participate (without any coercion, force, or deceit) and once the study has begun, participants should be free to withdraw from participation at any time without being penalized in any way.

2. *Confidentiality.* Sex researchers must take every possible precaution to protect the confidentiality of their research subjects. In some cases, information provided by research subjects could be legally incriminating (e.g., information about use of illicit drugs or illegal sexual practices), while in other instances a breakdown in confidentiality could expose participants to embarrassment, ridicule, or negative effects on their personal relationships. (Imagine, for instance, how you and your partner might feel if he or she learned because of your participation in a sex research project that you have been involved in an incestuous relationship with your sister for several years.)

Sex researchers follow a number of procedures to ensure confidentiality, including collecting data in ways that protect anonymity, such as assigning code numbers for identification and storing a master list linking the code numbers with names in a secure place, such as a bank vault; restricting access to research data to one person; and destroying all identifiable research information as soon as a study has been completed.

3. *Honesty.* While deception may occasionally be necessary as part of a research design, we believe that it is appropriate only if subjects have previously consented to being deceived (although they do not need to know the exact nature of the deception) and if the risks of deception are minimal. Whenever deception is used by researchers, they have a major responsibility to correct the situation by describing the deception to each subject in a debriefing session after the experiment so that he or she can learn about the results of the study and pose questions about the experience.

A detailed code of ethical guidelines for sex research has been developed (Masters et al., 1980) and similar codes govern research ethics for psychologists, psychiatrists, and other scientists. Most American colleges and universities now have committees known as Institutional Review Boards or Human Subject Committees that must evaluate all research planned within the institution before it is begun. If this committee discovers ethical problems in the study plan (e.g., inadequate attention to obtaining informed consent), it will make recommendations for improving the project's attention to eth-

ical matters and will withhold its approval of the research until the deficiencies are corrected.

PROBLEMS AND PITFALLS IN SEX RESEARCH

Sex research, like other forms of research, does not always provide a definitive answer to the question being addressed. Understanding the limitations of sex research methods can assist you in deciding how applicable a particular set of findings may be to your own life and can help you critically evaluate the quality of a given study.

Scientists often speak about **bias** in research, meaning that factors other than those being studied may affect the information collected and how the information is used to draw conclusions. Bias implies a systematic source of error that reduces objectivity.

Sampling Problems

One of the most frequent types of bias is **sampling bias,** which may take several forms. The size of the sample may be too small to deal with the number of variables being studied. Kinsey's research was criticized on these grounds, even though his surveys included 12,000 people. Even with a sample of adequate size, lack of similarity between the sample and the larger population it was selected to represent severely limits the research findings. An illustration of this type of sampling bias exists in studies of homosexuality prior to 1957. These studies usually involved subjects who were psychiatric patients or prisoners, thus leading to the faulty conclusion that homosexuals were maladjusted and mentally ill. Is it likely that valid conclusions about the nature of homosexuality would be drawn

reliability in research, the consistency of repeated measurements with the same procedure.

validity the soundness of the theoretically defined meaning of a measure or set of data.

bias a highly personal and unreasoned distortion of judgment; prejudice.

sampling bias frequent type of bias which may take several forms, including a sample of too small a size to deal with the number of variables, or lack of similarity between the sample and the population it is to represent.

from these samples? Would studies of heterosexuals who were psychiatric patients or prisoners be useful in reaching conclusions about personality patterns in all heterosexuals? More recently, better sampling techniques in studies on homosexuality have avoided this systematic error (Hooker, 1957; Saghir and Robins, 1973; Bell and Weinberg, 1978).

Another sampling problem is that of **volunteer bias,** meaning that there are often specific differences between people who agree to participate in a sex research project and those who decline. Statistically, a random sample is the ideal method of minimizing sampling biases because it avoids subjective errors the researcher might make in selecting study subjects. Unfortunately, truly random samples are seldom possible because of the ethical need to obtain informed consent: volunteer bias is thus automatically present. Although volunteer bias affects all methods of sex research, it is particularly evident in observational studies (Farkas, Sine, and Evans, 1978; Wolchik, Spencer, and Lisi, 1983). Would you agree to participate in studies requiring observations of your sexual behavior? People who agree probably have different attitudes toward sexual privacy from those who do not, and this unquestionably influences representativeness.

Erroneous Answers

Another source of research bias is the truthfulness of answers study subjects give. Questionnaires have an advantage if they are completed anonymously, since the respondent is relatively free from embarrassment. But questionnaires do not usually have a mechanism for checking to see if the subject understands each item; some answers may therefore be incorrect due to misinterpretation. Personal interviews usually allow explanation of questions and permit the gathering of more extensive data, but the presence of the interviewer may affect some of the answers. Certain people brag about or exaggerate their sexual experiences, while others may try to hide an embarrassing or uncomfortable fact.

Intentional falsification of answers may occur with either questionnaires or interviews, although the interviewer may be able to detect this phenomenon more easily. Lack of accuracy also occurs commonly because of faulty recall. Even in regard to recent events—those in the past month, for example—it may be difficult to remember how many times you felt a certain way or participated in a given activity. Recall of distant events (or feelings) is sometimes even more difficult. For instance, you may not be able to recall with certainty how old you were when you first learned "the facts of life." Try to remember the first time you masturbated or when your adolescent growth spurt occurred. Often, when married couples are interviewed separately about various aspects of their sexual relations, there are wide discrepancies in their answers about when, how often, and what they do. In such cases, how can an interviewer decide which person is being factually correct? If only one spouse is interviewed, how can an interviewer be certain that his or her answers are accurate?

Other sources of bias in sex research are examined as we describe the various types of sex research and discuss specific studies that exemplify these methods. While it may seem that we are occasionally being repetitious in pointing out some of these limitations, we do so to emphasize that they are recurring problems that must be kept in mind in analyzing and interpreting a particular study's usefulness. Since the findings of these studies are discussed frequently in later chapters, it is important to be aware of their strengths and weaknesses.

METHODS USED IN SEX RESEARCH

There are several different methods that can be used in sex research. Since each method has particular advantages and disadvantages, it is not usually possible to say that one approach is "best." Most often, the appropriateness of the method is determined by the nature of the subject to be studied. As we discuss each general method of sex research (surveys, observational research, case studies, clinical research, and experimental research) we look at actual studies that used these methods and examine the strengths and limitations of these investigations.

Survey Research

Surveys are used to gather information about a sample of a population by interviewing people or by having them fill out a questionnaire. Since the modern era of sex research was ushered in by the pioneering surveys of Kinsey and his colleagues, it is no surprise that this method has been the most commonly employed approach to the study of human sexual behavior. Furthermore, surveys offer many advantages compared with other research methods: they are comparatively economical, they permit flexibility in sampling, and they are generally free of significant risks to participants.

Given these facts, it is easy to understand why hundreds of sex surveys have been done. Unfortunately, many of these studies are of little use in reaching broad conclusions about human sexuality because of inadequate design, and even the better surveys must be interpreted with caution. In the following discussion of a number of major sex research surveys, we point out some of the elements that can be used to evaluate the value of survey research.

The Kinsey Reports: 1948 and 1953

The two broad-based surveys published by Kinsey and his colleagues probably have been more widely discussed and criticized than any subsequent sex research studies. Aside from acknowledging their historical significance, it is instructive to review the manner in which these studies were carried out.

Kinsey's team gathered data solely by face-to-face interviews. They used highly sophisticated techniques for gaining the confidence of each volunteer subject and avoiding the use of leading questions. At the same time, they had to code answers and detect falsification or inconsistencies in the participants' histories. Since the basic interview used by the Kinsey team involved approximately 300 questions, with the exact number of questions partially dependent on the material uncovered as the interview progressed, considerable skill was required to do each survey. Details of the interview process have been thoughtfully described by Wardell Pomeroy, one of Kinsey's original collaborators, in a recent book called *Taking a Sex History* (Pomeroy, Flax, and Wheeler, 1982).

Even though the interviewing technique of the Kinsey team stands out as a model of excellence for other researchers to follow, the interview itself (originally designed for college students) was not updated and expanded sufficiently to keep up with new developments in the research. Paul Gebhard, another early Kinsey team member, points out that Kinsey was reluctant to change the interview partly out of concern for consistency with the case histories already gathered and partly because of the time factor. The more complex the interview

grew, the longer it would take; longer interviews cost more and fewer could be done each day (Gebhard and Johnson, 1979, p. 12).

Although the interview itself had minor problems—for example, extramarital sex activity was not routinely queried about "until well into the 1940s" (about five years after the research began), according to Gebhard—the major methodological criticisms of the Kinsey surveys were leveled at their sampling techniques. Despite the extensive size of the Kinsey samples (5300 males were interviewed for the first study, while 5940 females formed the sample for the second report), these samples were far from representative of the entire U.S. population. Data gathered from blacks were simply not published in the original studies because the black samples were comparatively small (this situation was rectified by Gebhard and Johnson in 1979); the samples heavily overrepresented prisoners, college graduates, and Protestants while underrepresenting the elderly, people living in rural communities, and the poorly educated.

Kinsey said that he avoided any attempt at obtaining a random sample because he felt that such an effort would be doomed to failure. Instead, he tried to compensate in two ways. First, he hoped eventually to obtain a sample of 100,000 interviews that would be such a monumental mountain of data that it would overwhelm any and all objections to the sampling techniques. (While illustrating Kinsey's optimism, this belief did not reflect well on his understanding of the importance of sampling in the behavioral sciences.) His second way of getting partially around the problem of being unable to obtain a random sample was to devise a method he called "100 percent sampling," which involved getting virtually all the members of groups such as organizations, clubs, and college classes to agree to be interviewed. While he succeeded in getting about one-fifth of his subjects in this manner, it did not quell subsequent criticisms of his sample, as he had hoped.

On the other hand, the Kinsey team should be commended for choosing straightforward statisti-

volunteer bias a type of sampling bias in research in which the sample does not reflect the characteristics of the population because individuals with a certain characteristic or pattern of characteristics are more (or less) likely to volunteer to be studied.

cal methods that led to a fairly clear presentation of data. Although many quibbled about the statistical validity of their research (in what can now be seen as largely an attempt to discredit the credibility of Kinsey's "shocking" findings), a blue-ribbon committee of the American Statistical Association reviewed the Kinsey team's work and gave a critique that stated "our overall impression of their work is favorable" (Cochran, Mosteller, and Tukey, 1953, p. 674).

The Hunt Report: 1974

One of the first large-scale sex surveys conducted in the post-Kinsey era was commissioned by the Playboy Foundation early in the 1970s. An independent research organization was hired to design and perform the study, with the primary objectives being to update Kinsey's data on sexual behavior and to improve on Kinsey's sampling technique. The results were written about by Morton Hunt in a series of articles in *Playboy* magazine and subsequently published in book form as *Sexual Behavior in the 1970s* (Hunt, 1975). Since this research was not a magazine survey or actually conducted by *Playboy* magazine, it is often referred to as the Hunt report.

Hunt's sample was obtained by random selection from telephone book listings in 24 American cities. Twenty percent of those contacted agreed to participate in small, private group discussions of trends in sexual behavior in America; after the discussions, participants were asked to complete a self-administered questionnaire on their sexual attitudes and experiences. Virtually all the people who had taken part in the small-group discussions completed the questionnaire, giving a final sample of 982 males and 1044 females aged 18 and over. Although Hunt's sample mirrored the makeup of the national population in many ways (10 percent of participants were black, 71 percent were married, and the urban–rural mix was a close approximation of the actual distribution of the U.S. population), the sample has been faulted both for volunteer bias and for the more minor problem of underrepresenting people who are not listed in telephone directories (e.g., college students, institutionalized persons, people who don't have telephones, and people with unlisted phone numbers). Since it is uncertain how similar the 20 percent of people contacted who agreed to be in the study were to the 80 percent who declined participation, Hunt's findings must be interpreted with some caution. Nevertheless, this study provides valuable data that can be compared with that of Kinsey and his colleagues.

Magazine Surveys

One of the more intriguing trends in research about sexuality in the past decade has been the proliferation of surveys conducted by major national magazines. Various surveys of this sort have been done by *Psychology Today* (e.g., Athanasiou et al., 1970; Rubenstein and Shaver, 1982; Rubenstein, 1983), *Redbook* (Levin and Levin, 1975; Tavris and Sadd, 1977; Sarrel and Sarrel, 1979), *Ladies' Home Journal* (Schultz, 1980), *Cosmopolitan* (Wolfe, 1980), and *Consumer Reports* (Brecher and the editors of *Consumers Union Report*, 1983). Generally, these surveys produce samples far larger than those obtained in other sex research studies, sometimes drawing over 100,000 responses.

While it can certainly be useful to examine the sexual attitudes or experiences of such large numbers of people, it is important to realize that each sample consists of only a small fraction of the total number of readers of these magazines and cannot be considered to be representative of Americans in general. Since it's not likely that the profile of the average *Redbook* or *Cosmopolitan* reader is the same as the profile of the average reader of *Family Circle* or *Good Housekeeping* and since magazine readers as a group are probably more affluent and better educated than nonreaders, it is easy to see why findings of these surveys are somewhat skewed. In addition, there is no way to tell why certain people have filled out these questionnaires while others have not. For instance, a distorted picture of sexuality might emerge if people who feel comfortable about their sexuality are more likely to respond to such surveys than people who are having sexual problems. Furthermore, there is no way to tell whether people have answered the questionnaires truthfully. In some cases, magazine readers who are annoyed or upset by seeing a sex survey in their favorite publication may vent their wrath by sending in intentionally false answers so as to interfere with the results of the study. How large an impact this source of distortion (and others, such as faulty recall) has on the conclusions of such reports is difficult even to guess at.

The Hite Reports: 1976, 1981, and 1987

Shere Hite conducted three surveys that have achieved best-seller status and provoked considerable controversy in the field of sex research. The first of these, *The Hite Report* (1976), was a study of female sexuality based on questionnaire responses from 3019 women. The second study, *The Hite Report on Male Sexuality* (1981), described the replies of 7239 men to an essay-type questionnaire similar to the one in the first study. The third study, *Women and Love* (Hite, 1987), analyzed responses from a sample of 4500 women. It was particularly noteworthy for concluding that 84 percent of women are deeply dissatisfied with their husbands or male lovers and that 70 percent of women married five years or more "are having sex outside of their marriages."

Hite's research methods have been roundly criticized by a number of observers, with much of the criticism directed at her sampling technique. Despite the seemingly large number of people who completed her questionnaires, her actual response rates were quite small—only 3 percent in the 1976 study, 6 percent in the male study, and 4.5 percent in the 1987 study—making it unlikely that her samples were representative of the population at large. However, Hite makes a special point of the diversity of her sample, which was—for the male volume—accomplished in part by seeking out elderly respondents and others who statistically supplemented her main body of subjects. As Apfelbaum (1982) notes, "This is a perfectly acceptable way to broaden one's pool of respondents, but to claim, as Hite does, that the result is proof of representativeness is a bit like passing a blood test by adding a few red cells to your sample" (p. 85). Additional evidence of the nonrepresentative nature of Hite's samples is shown in her first female study, in which only 35 percent of participants were married (a rate approximately half that in the population at large).

Hite's books are also handicapped by the failure to present data in clear, quantitative terms and the absence of a valid statistical analysis of her findings (Gould, 1981; Robinson, 1981; Smith, 1989). Thus, these studies are basically anecdotal impressions, which makes it difficult to judge the significance of her findings. However, this shortcoming also provides Hite's work with one of its major strengths: readers encounter a rich lode of narrative descriptions of sexual thoughts and practices that are typically missing from more scientific studies. Thus, Hite's work can be seen as at least partly humanizing issues of sexuality rather than simply reducing them to numerical equations.

Another troublesome criticism of Hite's studies is that they frequently pose questions in a leading way. For instance, question number 132 of the male questionnaire asks: "Do you feel there is something wrong with your 'performance,' technique, or sensitivity if the woman does not orgasm from intercourse itself? That you're 'not *man* enough,' or at least that you did not do it right?" Most sexologists would shudder at this form of question, which is apt to elicit exactly the type of answers that characterize much of Hite's findings. (It would be preferable to ask the question in a more neutral manner, such as "How do you feel if the woman you're with doesn't have an orgasm from intercourse?" Then follow-up questions could be asked to see if the man feels that he's at fault or that it's his partner's problem, and so on.) Thus, for a variety of reasons, the findings of the Hite reports must be interpreted and applied very cautiously.

Blumstein and Schwartz: 1983

One of the most intriguing and sophisticated surveys of sexuality in relationships was conducted by two sociologists, Philip Blumstein and Pepper Schwartz, from the University of Washington. They recruited participants in a variety of ways, depending heavily on the use of newspaper, radio, and television announcements about their research to attract volunteers. Eventually, questionnaires were distributed to about 11,000 couples, with a return rate of about 55 percent. Their final sample consisted of 4314 heterosexual couples, including more than 650 cohabiting, unmarried couples, plus 969 gay male couples and 788 lesbian couples. In addition to analyzing the data provided by these questionnaires, Blumstein and Schwartz also conducted personal interviews with 129 heterosexual couples, 98 gay male couples, and 93 lesbian couples randomly chosen from their overall sample. Eighteen months later, they sent follow-up questionnaires to all the people who were interviewed and to more than 40 percent of their original sample.

The strengths of this study, which was published in 1983 in a book called *American Couples*, lie in four major areas: (1) a large, diverse national sample was obtained; (2) the research design allowed careful comparisons to be made between married couples, cohabiting heterosexual couples, gay male couples, and lesbian couples in a way that had not been done previously; (3) a well-planned questionnaire allowed the researchers to gather information about many nonsexual areas of relationships (e.g., work and money) that shed light on sexual attitudes and behavior; and (4) follow-up studies were included in the research plan. The principal short-coming of the study lies in the fact that the sample—despite its size and diversity—is not random or representative: the elderly, racial minorities, and working-class people were notably underrepresented, and couples who live apart were not studied at all. In addition, the research can be criticized for obtaining relatively superficial information in some areas and no information in other areas that might be considered important. For instance, no data were obtained about the use of sex fantasies by couples or about sadomasochistic practices or about rates of sexual dysfunctions. Nevertheless, the Blumstein and Schwartz study must be regarded as one of the most ambitious—and most successful—sex research studies yet carried out.

National Survey of Young Adult Men

A survey of the sexual behavior and condom use of men between the ages of 20 and 39 in the United States was recently conducted by workers at the Battelle Human Affairs Research Centers using a nationally representative sample of 3321 subjects (Billy et al., 1993; Tanfer et al., 1993). The data were drawn from the National Survey of Men, which employed a sophisticated sampling technique and study design, including the deliberate oversampling of black men to ensure their adequate representation in the final sample, combined with face-to-face interviews and follow-up contact names intended to provide a means of recontacting subjects to conduct future surveys in order to gather longitudinal data in the future (Tanfer, 1993).

In addition to the fact that this is one of the few investigations of sexual behavior using a true national probability sample, one of the major strengths of the Battelle survey was an interview response rate of 70 percent, which compares very favorably to other surveys of sexual behavior, and is especially noteworthy for research involving a face-to-face, rather than telephone, interview. The study was particularly timely because many projections and assumptions about how the HIV/AIDS epidemic will evolve for the rest of this century and beyond require data about sexual behavior, and before the availability of findings that could be regarded as methodologically reliable, public health experts and other scientists were forced to rely on projections made from much older survey information, including a heavy reliance on the clearly outdated Kinsey surveys of the 1940s.

Among the key findings of the Battelle survey (which we will discuss in detail in Chapter 10 and 16) were: (1) Almost a quarter of American men aged 20 to 39 report having had vaginal intercourse with 20 or more partners in their lives. (2) Twenty percent of never-married or formerly married men ages 20 to 39 have had four or more partners in the past 18 months. (3) In this same age group, black men are more likely than white men to use condoms (38 to 25 percent). (4) About one-fifth of American men between the ages of 20 and 39 have ever had anal intercourse. (5) Only 2 percent of sexually active men aged 20 to 39 reported having sex with another man in the past 10 years, and only 1 percent said they were exclusively homosexual for this same time period.

The last finding cited above led to some criticism of this report because many members of the gay community saw it as a sizable underestimate of the gay male population. This raises a key question about this (and almost any) sex behavior survey. How can we be sure that study subjects are telling the truth? The answer, of course, is that there is no exact test for determining rates of underreporting certain personal sexual behaviors. For this reason, the Battelle survey data on the prevalence of homosexuality should be taken as the lower limit of the number of practicing homosexuals in the general population, since it is very likely that some men who had had same-gender sexual encounters didn't disclose this to their interviewers because of personal embarrassment. In fact, certain people are more truthful in telephone interviews than with face-to-face interviews due to embarrassment (Turner, Miller and Moses, 1989; Catania et al., 1991), although face-to-face interviews have certain advantages, as well, such as permitting the interviewer to assess body language and a respondent's personal discomfort more accurately.

The National AIDS Behavioral Survey

Researchers at the University of California at San Francisco's Center for AIDS Prevention Studies recently conducted a well-designed survey that incorporated many key methodological features in gathering data about HIV risk factors among heterosexuals in the United States (Catania et al., 1992; Dolcini et al., 1993). For example, the study involved a large national sample (a total of over 10,000 people) that permitted detailed analysis by age, gender, race or ethnicity, social class, and marital status. Second, the study utilized sophisticated sampling techniques to ensure that sufficient numbers of older persons, blacks, and Hispanics were interviewed, and special arrangements were made to have interviews conducted in Spanish for those who preferred. Third, a substantial portion of the sample was drawn from 23 cities in the United States with the highest prevalence of AIDS cases. Another notable feature of this study was that a 70 percent response rate was obtained from the national sample. Overall, 9 percent of the heterosexuals in the national sample and 12 percent in the high-risk cities reported having sex with more than one partner in the preceding 12 months. In the same sample, men were more than twice as likely as women to have had two or more sex partners in the year before the survey, and condom use was low among both men and women with multiple partners.

The National Health and Social Life Survey: 1994
The most ambitious survey of American sexual behavior since Kinsey's day was carried out over an eight month period in 1992. Based on a national probability sample with an excellent 79 percent response rate, staff members of the National Opinion Research Center at the University of Chicago conducted 90-minute interviews with 3,432 people 18 to 59 years of age. The results of this survey—published in a book for general readers, *Sex in America* (Michael et al., 1994), as well as a heavily statistical version called *The Social Organization of Sexual Behavior* (Laumann et al., 1994)—were startlingly mundane, suggesting that Americans are fairly conservative in their sex lives. For example, men and women seem to engage in marital infidelity far less often than had been believed, only 2.8 percent of men and 1.4 percent of women say they are gay, and the average American woman has only had two sex partners since age 18 (while the average man has had 6).

The overall design of the NHSLS survey was commendable, with attention quite appropriately focused on statistical methods and obtaining a high response rate from those selected. However, the existence of some serious deficiencies in design cast doubt on the reliability and the generalizability of the results. First, the survey questionnaire was constructed in such a way that it could be covered in a 90-minute period. While this was necessary for

practical reasons, it did not provide an opportunity for in-depth exploration of numerous topics, and experienced sex researchers are well-aware that answers given in first time, face-to-face interviews may not be as candid as they are when a series of interviews are conducted over time. Second, the research team inexplicably allowed 21 percent of the interviews to be conducted in the presence of the respondent's spouse or children. Since not too many people would be honest in recounting details of their marital infidelities or same-sex liaisons under these circumstances, it is difficult to accept the findings in these and many other areas as fully accurate. Third, the interviewers for this survey were not actually experienced sex researchers; they were only given three days of training in the administration of a very complex questionnaire, and this could hardly have allowed them to develop adequate skills in recognizing when people are uncomfortable with sexual topics or how to get around such discomfort. Finally, the design of the study did not permit the inclusion of men and women living in any type of institutional setting, from college dorms to the military, prisons, nursing homes, or similar arrangements. Since there are millions of people living in these circumstances, it is erroneous to consider this survey a truly random national probability sample.

Surveys of Special Populations
A number of studies have targeted particular research topics that are less broad than those of the surveys discussed above. We consider several of these surveys both because of their innovative approaches to research design and because they are referred to in later chapters.

Two Studies on Homosexuality
The Kinsey Institute returned to national prominence in 1978 with the publication of a major survey conducted by psychologist Alan Bell and sociologist Martin Weinberg in a book called *Homosexualities: A Study of Its Diversities Among Men and Women*. Several years later, a subsequent volume called *Sexual Preference: Its Development in Men and Women* (Bell, Weinberg, and Hammersmith, 1981) was published based on data collected in the same survey.

Working over nearly a decade with the financial support of the National Institute of Mental Health,

Bell and Weinberg recruited a sample of homosexual men and women in the San Francisco Bay area through newspaper announcements, notices posted in gay bars and baths, mailings to membership lists of gay organizations, and similar strategies. From an initial pool of 4639 people, they were able to conduct in-depth face-to-face interviews with 979 persons: 575 white homosexual males, 111 black homosexual males, 229 white homosexual females, and 64 black homosexual females. The researchers also interviewed a comparison group of 477 heterosexuals matched to their corresponding homosexual sample for age, race, gender, and education.

Each of the interviews, which were conducted in 1970, took from two to five hours to complete and covered 528 separate questions. Meticulous attention was devoted to training a team of interviewers so that the information gathered would be as reliable as possible. In addition, a substantial number of interviews were repeated six months after the original interview as a further check on accuracy.

While the Bell and Weinberg survey has many strengths, it is important to recognize that their sample is not very representative of homosexuals in America. By choosing to conduct their study in San Francisco, which is far more accepting of homosexuality than most other cities in the country, Bell and Weinberg made a deliberate trade-off between the possible unrepresentativeness of their sample and the relative ease (and, presumably, lower expense) in locating and recruiting subjects that San Francisco provided. Thus, their sample overrepresented homosexuals with liberal attitudes and a proclivity toward political activism while it largely overlooked those who are secretive about their sexual orientation. Furthermore, compared with homosexuals in other regions of the country, it is likely that this San Francisco–based sample was—at the time of the survey—more heavily involved in experimentation with illicit drugs, raising the possibility of unaccounted variables that might have distorted the research.

Two Surveys on Sexuality in Late Adulthood

We conclude this survey of surveys by briefly considering two different studies of the sexuality of elderly adults. *The Starr–Weiner Report on Sex and Sexuality in the Mature Years* (Starr and Weiner, 1981) was based on a rather haphazardly gathered sample of 800 adults over the age of 60. Most of the subjects were recruited after hearing the authors of the study give a lecture; others were recruited by word of mouth, by referral from a colleague, or by other miscellaneous methods. While the findings of this study are of some interest because of the paucity of reliable data available on sex and the elderly, the poor sampling procedures and weak statistical analysis of this survey make it scientifically far from ideal. A particular problem of their sampling method was that subjects who heard them lecture may have been influenced to give answers that supported Starr's and Weiner's already stated-views and to keep quiet about things that didn't match their philosophy.

In contrast, a more reliable survey of sexuality in middle and later life was also published in 1981 by George and Weiler. These researchers correctly pointed out that a true understanding of the effects of aging on sexuality would have to be based on longitudinal data. Thus, they surveyed a group of several hundred men and women chosen from a local health insurance program every two years over an eight-year period, and they reported on 278 individuals who remained married throughout the study period. The findings of their research, which are discussed in Chapter 10, have considerably more validity than most studies of sex and aging because of the unique strategy they chose: using a longitudinal design.

Observational Research

Observational research involves the use of a human observer or an instrument to record the events being studied. Thus, it provides a means for avoiding dependence on subjects' self-reports. It can be done either in a laboratory setting or the natural environment of study subjects. The latter technique is called **field study** and is a method commonly used by anthropologists and sociologists. Field studies can be done in almost any setting: sex research has been done on South Sea islands, in gay bars, at massage parlors, and on college campuses, to name just a few possible locations. Neither field studies nor other types of observational research require random samples for validity as long as they involve a reasonably diverse sample. A related type of research is the **participant–observer method,** in which the scientist is involved in the social setting while recording events. Two well-known examples of the participant–observer method can be found in studies of swinging (mate-swapping) done by Bartell (1971) and of impersonal homosexual sex in public places (Humphreys, 1970).

The Masters and Johnson Studies of Sexual Physiology

As mentioned in the preceding chapter, *Human Sexual Response* (Masters and Johnson, 1966) was the first study to describe laboratory observations of the physical details of human sexual arousal. Masters began his research by interviewing 118 female prostitutes and 27 male prostitutes to gather background information about the nature of sexual response. Next, a physiology laboratory was equipped with standard testing devices such as an electrocardiogram (to measure heart rate and rhythm) and an electromyogram (to measure muscle tension and contractions during the sexual response cycle). In addition, special devices were prepared such as the so-called artificial coital equipment, which consisted of a clear plastic penis-shaped object that permitted observation and filming of changes inside the vagina during sexual stimulation that simulated intercourse. This device was designed so that a woman using this equipment could control the depth and tempo of thrusting herself. Masters and Johnson then tested their equipment on a small group of male and female prostitutes who served as their earliest research subjects.

Since they realized at the initial stages of their work that observing sexual responses among prostitutes would not suffice for a description of the physiology of a normal population, Masters and Johnson began to recruit their actual research sample from the local academic community.[1] Over time, as news of the research quietly spread through the community, they obtained a broader array of volunteers, with the final sample consisting of 382 women (ranging in age from 18 to 78) and 312 men (from 21 to 89).

It is important to realize that the people who volunteered to be watched and measured during sexual activity in a laboratory were certainly atypical in their willingness to be in such a study, and they may have been atypical in other ways as well. Both to guard against this factor as a major problem to the research and to protect the welfare of their subjects, Masters and Johnson conducted extensive interviews on several occasions with each potential subject in order to assess his or her psychological stability, motivations for volunteering, and other factors pertinent to the nature of the research.

Subjects were assured that all possible precautions would be taken to protect their confidentiality and anonymity, and as news spread around the medical center where the work was being done, these precautions proved to be of considerable importance. Physicians and nurses began to congregate in the corridors near the research suite in an attempt to catch sight of those entering and leaving, and some even tried listening to what was happening inside by putting a stethoscope to the outer wall of the research area. Masters and Johnson had fortunately foreseen the need for stringent security measures and had thoroughly sound-proofed their laboratory, but they were forced to switch many of their studies to evening hours to bypass traffic jams from curiosity seekers who "just happened to be passing by."

Once a couple was accepted for the study, and following the completion of their interviews, they were given one or more opportunities to become acclimated to the laboratory setting. This involved experimenters first showing them the equipment and testing room and then asking them to have sexual activity in the laboratory without observers present or being hooked up to any machines. This "practice session" was used to help eliminate nervousness and discomfort, although admittedly a "practice session" was not exactly the same as the real thing.

Once actual participation began, subjects were measured in a broad range of sexual activities (including self-masturbation, genital stimulation by a partner, oral–genital stimulation, and intercourse), with most subjects studied on dozens of occasions to identify degrees of variability in their response patterns. Overall, over 10,000 orgasmic sexual response cycles were studied.

[1]Prostitutes were unlikely to have had completely normal sexual anatomy because of frequent sexually transmitted infections and because many of the female prostitutes had had several abortions (at a time when abortions were both illegal and often unsafe). Furthermore, the high frequency of their sexual activity raised the possibility that their sexual physiology would have differed from other persons', much as the cardiovascular responses of trained athletes differ from those of nonathletes.

field study research conducted in the natural environment of study subjects instead of in a laboratory.

participant–observer method a form of research in which the researcher takes an active part in the situation being studied.

PERSONAL PERSPECTIVES

Reflections on Being in a Sex Research Project

The following passages are excerpted from a journal kept by a 22-year-old woman who participated in a study investigating the effects of the menstrual cycle on female sexual arousability.

I'm not sure what I got myself into today. As I was leaving the library, I saw a notice posted on the bulletin board asking for female volunteers for a sex research project. I guess it piqued my curiosity or something, because I wrote down the phone number and the information and then spent the next two hours trying to decide whether I should call. The problem was partly that I wasn't sure about what they'd want me to do, but since the study was being done at the medical school, I was pretty sure it was reputable and safe. So I finally called and made an appointment to go in tomorrow afternoon to hear a description of the project and fill out a couple of questionnaires. It was kind of simple at that—pretty much like making an appointment at the dentist's.

Last night I sort of tossed and turned in bed before I fell asleep wondering about the project I had applied for. What'll I do if they ask me to try out, like an audition for the cheerleader squad, I thought. What's this project going to involve any-

way? (They didn't say much about it on the phone yesterday—was that being secretive or professional?) Then I started thinking, what if I'm rejected? The ultimate putdown! Finally, I managed to fall asleep, but I woke up real early, and I must admit that as I write this—it's an hour before I go in for my appointment—I'm nervous as can be.

Well, it was a big relief to get that appointment over with. As it turned out, there wasn't really much to be nervous about. First, after I got there, I filled out a brief questionnaire giving some identifying information about myself. Then I met with a woman connected with the research team (not the tall, dark doctor I fantasized about last night) who explained what the project involves and let me ask questions about it. Then I signed a consent form, agreeing to be in the project, and spent 45 minutes filling out a questionnaire about my health, my menstrual patterns, and my sex life.

It seems that the project will involve my being tested on four different days, at various phases of my menstrual cycle. I'll have to abstain from drinking or having sex for at least 48 hours before each test, and as far as I can tell now, the test seems to involve masturbating in a private

---

Although some critics have contended that Masters' and Johnson's physiology research was flawed because their sample did not consist of a good cross section of the population, most research on medical physiology assumes that normative processes (e.g., natural body functions such as vision, digestion, and so forth) do not require such a sample, as long as the sample is both diverse and healthy. Thus, exercise physiologists don't worry too much about getting random samples to study the physiology of muscle, and physicians interested in the physiology of breathing aren't concerned with having a random sample to identify the anatomic events and physiologic details of respiration.

Another criticism leveled at Masters' and Johnson's work is that the artificial setting of the labo-

ratory may have distorted subjects' responses. Although there is no way of proving or disproving this criticism directly, the applicability of their findings to such areas as sex therapy, contraceptive technology, infertility counseling, and sex education weakens such criticisms.

Case Studies

Case studies are in-depth examinations of one or more people with a particular condition (such as alcoholism) or a specific characteristic (such as being a victim of sexual assault). Unlike survey interviews, which are usually done in a matter of hours, most case studies require weeks or months of assessment. The case study method was widely

room while I'm hooked up to a machine that measures sexual arousal with a small probe inside the vagina. I saw the machine today and didn't think it looked too complicated. I'll also be paid $100 for this experiment if I complete all the steps. That seemed like a classy touch.

Well, tomorrow's the big day. My first "study day," as they call it. I'm not exactly nervous about it, but I find myself wondering about a lot of things. What if I can't have an orgasm because I'm trying too hard? Will that probe interfere with my arousal? What if I don't even get aroused because of being uncomfortable? I guess that these sorts of jitters are pretty natural to have, but I hope that I won't run into any problems.

It was interesting to me that Larry got a little upset tonight because we couldn't have sex. I had told him weeks ago about the project, and he was really encouraging, but now he seems annoyed at the inconvenience factor. I'm not sure that's completely true, as I think about it, though—maybe he's jealous in some fashion (of the machine?) or just trying to be protective.

IT WAS A SNAP! After I got there, my nervousness was very apparent. My palms were sweaty, my heart was kind of racing a bit, and I was a little jumpy—especially when I was undressing in the testing room. I thought to myself, "Now's your chance to get out of this if you want to," but the research assistant was so easygoing and reassuring that I thought, why not give it a try. So I found myself lying there on a bed, listening to some soft music, with this small probe that I inserted inside my vagina (they showed me how to do this using a plastic model of a pelvis). Then I pushed a button to indicate that I was going to start masturbating. For a minute I wondered if they had a secret camera and were all watching me (making lewd jokes about my body or my masturbatory technique), but I quickly got into a favorite fantasy scene in my mind and I became really quite aroused. In fact, I was quite pleased with myself, because it was all so easy. I guess I masturbated for three or four minutes, had a nice orgasm, lay on the bed relaxing for a few minutes, and then got dressed. I came out in the hall, went to another room to fill out a few short questionnaires, made an appointment to come back in a week (around the time I'll be ovulating), and left. All in all, and despite my preliminary worries, it was much easier than I even imagined it would be.

employed in the early days of sexology, as Krafft-Ebing, Ellis, and Freud made extensive use of this method. Even today, case studies are frequently published, although they are often of limited scientific value. In fact, a single, unreplicated case usually tell us nothing but an interesting story. Another problem with case studies is that not only is the accuracy of the subject's self-reports open to question but the researcher's own biases strongly influence what he or she "sees" in the case. In addition, it is not uncommon for a patient to learn what type of information the researcher is most interested in and selectively cultivate this material so as to gain his or her praise. The researcher's biases may influence case reports in another way, as shown in the following example: a psychologist doing an in-depth study of the cause of erectile difficulties in a 28-year-old man spent many hours administering psychological tests and conducting interviews with the subject, his wife, and other family members but neglected the medical side of the evaluation since this was not his major interest. The man's sexual dysfunction eventually turned out to be due to multiple sclerosis, and the psychologist had to withdraw a paper he had submitted on the case.

Clinical Research

Clinical research usually consists of studies that test a type of treatment for a specific problem and assess how that treatment changed the underlying condition. This type of clinical research, which is sometimes known as an **outcome study,** is frequently done in conjunction with the use of a **control group** of subjects who receive no treatment. Clinical research also includes **epidemiological studies** that focus on the pattern of distribution of a phenomenon (such as the spread of a sexually transmitted infection or the prevalence of sexual dysfunctions in a population) as well as studies of a series of cases of an illness to evaluate its natural (untreated) history, to gather diagnostic information about the illness, or to uncover information about what causes it.

One of the best-known examples of clinical research in the field of sexology is *Human Sexual Inadequacy* (Masters and Johnson, 1970), a report that described the results of sex therapy in 790 cases, with many of the cases followed for a five-year period after the conclusion of therapy. Although this study has been criticized on methodological grounds (Zilbergeld and Evans, 1980), it is accepted by most sexologists today as a major research accomplishment.

Experimental Research

Experimental research involves use of a method in which the investigator varies one factor under carefully controlled conditions to isolate its effect. In a sense, researchers using this approach create the specific situation they want to investigate. Among the many strengths of this research method is that it permits conclusions about cause–effect relationships which cannot generally be proved by any other means.

Experimental research has been used to study many aspects of sexual behavior and response, including the effects of viewing erotic materials (discussed in Chapter 23), the effects of alcohol on sexual arousal (discussed in Chapter 22), and the effectiveness of various forms of sex therapy. The experimental method has also been used to evaluate gender-role effects on behavior, the nature of the premenstrual syndrome, the effects of sex education on rates of unintended teenage pregnancy, and factors that might prevent people from developing sexual difficulties.

Although the experimental method can be used to study many situations, it has a number of disadvantages as well. One of the primary limitations of this method is that laboratory experiments often involve artificial situations, so their findings may not apply to spontaneous behaviors and feeings in real life. Another problem is that of volunteer bias. Finally, researchers can't always be sure that they have implemented proper controls over all the variables that influence the phenomenon they are studying. For example, if an experiment to study sexual arousal patterns in men in response to an erotic movie is inadvertently conducted in a room where the air conditioner is blasting away, the results will likely be influenced by the temperature. If the researcher does not realize this problem, the conclusions reached on the basis of the actual results obtained will clearly be inaccurate.

Research Limitations Revisited

Biases in sex research (and research in general) come from many sources. The treatment success in an uncontrolled clinical trial may be due to the attention paid to subjects and the power of positive suggestion—scientifically known as the **placebo effect**—rather than to the treatment itself. The attitudes and preconceptions of the researcher influence the study methods, the specific questions asked, and the interpretation of data. Researchers may fail to "see" events that do not match their theoretical view of the problem or they may "see" nonexistent events that neatly fit their model of thought (Barber, 1976).

Individual characteristics of the researcher—personality, appearance, friendliness, age—may cause distortions in the data. For instance, a study of sexual function in young spinal cord–injured men used female nurses as interviewers (Bors and Comarr, 1960), thus giving rise to the possibility that subjects might have exaggerated their reports of sexual ability to impress the nurse or not embarrass themselves. It is possible that different information might have been obtained if the interviews were male. Another example: subjects interviewed by black experimenters give different answers to questions about racial prejudice than do subjects interviewed by white experimenters (Summers and Hammonds, 1966).

Questionnaires are useful from the viewpoints of economics and time efficiency. However, they have several limitations. They can be used only with subjects who can read and write; they must be constructed in such a way that respondents do not lose interest or become fatigued; and there is no opportunity for in-depth examination of the meaning or nuance of answers (Labovitz and Hagedorn, 1976). Survey studies in general—whether done by questionnaire or interview—share another limitation: the questions asked usually elicit opinions, attitudes, or *perceptions* of behavior, but these do not necessarily reflect the *actual* behavior under study. There is nothing wrong with studying attitudes or perceptions, but scientific accuracy is not served by confusing fact and feeling.

Observational and experimental studies are usually more expensive and time-consuming than surveys. In both of these methods, the setting of the study may influence the observed behavior. Even after subjects become acclimated to a laboratory environment and the equipment used to monitor or measure their responses, it is unlikely that they will be as relaxed and spontaneous as if they were at home. All observational research in which subjects know that they are being observed exerts some influences on subsequent behavior. The same is true for experimental research: subjects may try to respond in ways they believe the experimenter "wants" them to or in ways dictated by how they want the experimenter to perceive them. The change in people's behavior caused by knowing they are in an experiment is called the **Hawthorne effect.**

Significance and Replication

Although a detailed discussion of appropriate methods of statistical analysis is beyond the scope of this book, one point is important. Many reports use statistical tests of significance, with **significance** in this instance meaning a result not likely to have happened by chance. Most commonly, a probability level of 5 percent or less ($p \leq .05$) is chosen to define significance: this means that the probability of the research findings arising from chance alone is 1 in 20 or less. Although this formulation sounds impressive, results showing statistical significance are not infallible and absolute. More important than such statistics alone are the questions of whether the research design is appropriate, the types of bias minimized, and whether the findings have been

independently replicated. When research findings are closely duplicated by a separate investigator using similar methods, it is much safer to conclude that the findings are valid.

One cautionary note about replication is important, however. If two independent researchers use the same methods and perpetuate the same biases, the conclusions they come to may be identical but may still be wrong. We already discussed research on homosexuality before 1957: by repeatedly studying poorly selected samples (prisoners and psychiatric patients), researchers concluded that homosexuals were often maladjusted and sick. Later studies, without the same sampling bias, came to very different conclusions about homosexuals.

There are many other potential pitfalls in research, but an exhaustive catalogue is not likely to be useful for our purposes here. It is helpful to remember that the research perspective is just one way of looking at the world—not the only way and not necessarily the best way. Remember, research is only an approximate way of getting at facts. Studying sex research can be informative but so is knowledge gained from clinical situations, personal experiences, literature, art, and culture. No single perspective on human sexuality has a monopoly on truth.

outcome study a form of clinical research that evaluates the effect of one or more treatments on a particular condition, such as a disease.

control group individuals in an experiment who are monitored but do not receive the experimental variable; in a treatment study, this group either receives no treatment or a placebo.

epidemiological studies research focusing on patterns of the prevalence and spread of a condition or disease, especially infectious diseases and epidemics.

placebo effect the results observed in an experiment when people report various changes (e.g., sleeping better) from use of a placebo, or chemically inert drug; the effect is due to expectations of improvement.

Hawthorne effect the change in people's behavior that often occurs when they know they are being studied as part of a research project.

significance statistically, the determination that the observed result was not a matter of chance alone.

SUMMARY

1. Sex research, when properly conducted, follows the general scientific principles that also apply to research in other fields. These include paying adequate attention to obtaining a proper sample and to employing the appropriate methods for obtaining and analyzing data.

2. Responsible sex research is conducted in an ethical manner, protecting the rights and welfare of the research subjects. This requires obtaining the informed consent of potential study subjects and taking precautions to protect the subjects' confidentiality.

3. Various types of bias (extraneous influences on the research) can affect the validity of any sex research study. Common examples of the types of bias that must be considered are volunteer bias, erroneous answers, sampling problems, the placebo effect, and biases of the researcher.

4. The most popular method of sex research has been the survey, which can be done with either questionnaires or personal interviews. While questionnaires are more economical and anonymous, interviews allow for a greater depth of material to be obtained. Surveys, however, are frequently troubled by such difficulties as obtaining a proper sample (e.g., very few studies have succeeded in obtaining true national probability samples), which may limit the generalizability of the survey findings. In addition, surveys are affected by the accuracy of information provided by subjects in answering questionnaires or interviewers' questions.

5. The original Kinsey studies, published in 1948 and 1953, exemplify both the problems and the strengths of the survey method. Despite having had very large sample sizes, their two samples were not random or representative, leading some to question the validity of their reported findings. Many sex researchers have subsequently improved the survey sampling techniques of Kinsey and his co-workers.

6. Observational research involves the use of a human observer or an instrument to record the events being studied. The landmark study using this method was conducted by Masters and Johnson, who observed and recorded the physical patterns of sexual response in a laboratory setting. Field studies and participant–observer studies have also been conducted by sex researchers. Observational research enables researchers to bypass their total dependence on the accuracy of subjects' self-reports. However, volunteer bias and the question of artificiality (i.e., whether subjects would respond the same way in their home environment as they do in a laboratory setting) also pose some uncertainties and limitations on this method.

7. Case studies are in-depth examinations of one or more people having a particular condition or characteristic. These studies are usually not a good source of scientific "proof" because they are handicapped by the biases of the researcher probably more than in other forms of research.

8. Clinical research usually involves studies that test a type of treatment given for a specific problem and can include case studies, surveys, and experimental studies. Clinical research must be examined carefully to be certain that improvement is really a result of the treatment rather than a reflection of either the placebo effect or the passage of time. Clinical research done without the benefit of a control group must be viewed with a high degree of skepticism.

9. Experimental research permits scientists to isolate the specific variables that affect a condition or behavior and may allow them to draw conclusions about cause and effect. Experimental research, however, is apt to be difficult and expensive to perform, and is not completely free of error. Volunteer bias, experimenter effects, and the artificiality of the experimental situation may limit the validity of this type of study.

10. In evaluating the overall quality of any sex research study, it is useful to look at such fundamental methodological issues as the size and nature of the sample, the means by which data were collected, the type of data analysis that was done, and the researcher's discussion of the study's limitations. In addition, it is useful to see whether a study has been replicated by others, since independent verification of a set of research findings is one of the most powerful tools science can offer for confirming the validity of a study.

Thought Questions

1. Kinsey was reported to have died an "embittered and disillusioned man." If you could interview Kinsey today, what would you tell him about the long-term value of his work?

2. Are the conclusions from sex research as valid and reliable as those from other areas of social science? How should one respond when sex researchers come up with findings that are different from one's own sexual experiences?

3. A college student wants to do research on a sexual topic for a required class project. Should his or her instructor encourage this research interest in this situation? What advice should the instructor give the student?

4. What would motivate a person or a couple to volunteer to be a participant in a study such as Masters' and Johnson's, in which sexual activities would be observed and recorded by others? Can you imagine yourself volunteering for such a study? What if your partner wanted to participate and asked you to join with him or her? How would you respond?

5. Recently, the federal government refused to fund a major nationwide survey of sexual behavior on the basis that such a survey would be too controversial. A purpose of the survey was to help scientists predict the degree to which HIV infection (i.e., the AIDS virus) is being transmitted in our population. Do you agree that such a survey would be "too controversial" in the 1990s? Could an American administration fund such a study without paying a political price? Why or why not?

6. Surveys have been done regarding adolescent sexuality, but almost no research has been done on the frequency of pre-adolescent sexual behavior. Should such research be done? Would it be valuable to our society to have more objective knowledge about children's sexual activities?

Suggested Readings

Abramson, Paul. "Sexual Science: Emerging Discipline or Oxymoron?" *Journal of Sex Research* 27:147–165, 1990. A thoughtful paper on the need for rigor in sex research. Includes discussion of measurement issues and suggestions for future research topics.

Gebhard, Paul, and Johnson, Alan. *The Kinsey Data: Marginal Tabulations of the 1938–1963 Interviews Conducted by the Institute of Sex Research.* Philadelphia: Saunders, 1979. Expanded data from the original Kinsey studies, reorganized to include data from blacks and other special groups, such as a delinquent population. Although this book consists almost entirely of numerical tables, it is a valuable compendium of data for anyone interested in sex research.

Green, Richard, and Weiner, Jack (eds.). *Methodology in Sex Research.* Rockville, MD: U.S. Department of Health and Human Services (Publication Number [ADM] 80–766), 1980. A comprehensive, sophisticated "state-of-the-art" review. Difficult reading but filled with useful ideas.

Miller, Heather G.; Turner, Charles F.; and Moses, Lincoln E. (eds.). "Methodological Issues in AIDS Surveys" In *AIDS: The Second Decade.* Washington, D.C.: National Academy Press, 1990, pp. 359–471. A detailed discussion of the ins and outs of surveys of sexual behavior, with particular attention to how this applies to studying the AIDS epidemic.

Pomeroy, Wardell; Flax, Carol; and Wheeler, Connie. *Taking a Sex History: Interviewing and Recording.* New York: Free Press, 1982. An invaluable guide to the interviewing methods used in the original Kinsey research, updated to apply to contemporary sex research. Particularly fascinating for revealing the intricate coding system used by the Kinsey team.

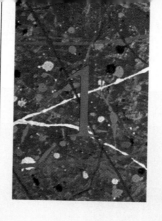

PART 1

Biological Perspectives

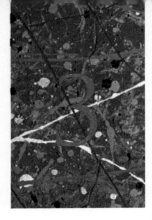

Sexual Anatomy

Karen is a 20-year-old college junior who generally avoided dating because she felt her breasts were too small. She wrote: "I hate looking in a mirror or wearing a bathing suit because I see how flat I am. I would be *mortified* to let a guy touch or see my breasts." *(Authors' files)*

Brad is an athletic 17-year-old who quit his school's basketball team because his breasts were large. He told us that his teammates kidded him mercilessly in the locker room and showers about when he was going to get a bra. He was afraid he might "turn into a woman." *(Authors' files)*

A married couple in their mid-twenties who were sex therapy patients said they frequently used stimulation of the clitoris as part of making love. When asked to identify the clitoris during a physical exam, the husband pointed to a large freckle on the lower part of his wife's left labia majora. *(Authors' files)*

A class of 80 college sophomores was given a brief test on sexual anatomy the first day of their course on sexuality. The average student had more mistakes than right answers. *(Authors' files)*

As these examples show, many of us have inaccurate information or negative feelings about our sexual anatomy. This should not be surprising for a variety of reasons: we are taught to keep our sex organs covered by clothing; we are scolded or punished for touching our "private parts"; we are not likely to be told the correct terminology to describe our sexual anatomy; we are discouraged from conversations or questions about sex; and the sexual images we are exposed to in movies and magazines are likely to present almost unattainable standards to measure ourselves against. It is no wonder that our sexual anatomy can be a source of anxiety, shame, guilt, mystery, and curiosity, as well as a source of pleasure.

The mixed feelings we have about our sexual body parts are mirrored in the words we use to talk about them: some words are "clean" and "proper," while others are "dirty" or "impolite." These differences are a result of how we interpret words, not an innate property of the words themselves. Consider, for example:

> In Nigeria, the moral taboos of sex were taught by missionaries and administrators who used only clean words. These were the words that became taboo. The dirty words used as part of the vernacular of sailors, traders, and the like, became part of Nigerian vernacular English, with no taboo attached. In consequence, today it is as forbidden to say sexual intercourse, penis and vagina on Nigerian television as it is to say fuck, cock, and cunt on the national networks in the United States. In Nigeria, the latter terms are considered normal and respectable. (*Money, 1980, pp. 50–51*)

In this book we do not use slang terms about sex because they convey a negative message to some people. As a matter of convenience, however, slang terms that describe sexual parts of the body are listed in Table 3.1. Sex organs in the pelvic region—in females the outer sexual structures and the vagina, in males the penis, scrotum, and testes—are customarily called the **genitals.**

People of all ages have common concerns about sexual anatomy: What is the normal size of the penis? Is something wrong if one breast is smaller than the other? Does circumcision lessen sexual pleasure? Do large breasts indicate a passionate woman? Is it abnormal if one testicle hangs lower than the other? Where and what is the clitoris? The answers to such questions begin with learning about sexual anatomy. The basis for understanding the way our bodies function sexually is discussed in the next chapter.

Table 3.1   Some Sexual Terminology: Science and Slang

Proper Name	Slang Terms
Vulva	Pussy, snatch, crotch
Pubic hair	Beaver, bush, pubes
Mons veneris	Love mound
Clitoris	Clit, button, joy button
Labia	—
Hymen	Cherry, maidenhead
Urethral meatus (urinary opening)	Peehole
Vagina	Cunt, box, pussy, hole, snatch, slit, twat, honeypot
Anus	Asshole
Breasts	Boobs, tits, knockers, bazooms
Buttocks	Ass, rear end, bottom, buns
Penis	Prick, cock, peter, tool, organ, meat (rod, boner, and hardon usually refer to erect penis only)
Testes	Balls, nuts, jewels

FEMALE SEXUAL ANATOMY

> We are encouraged to feel as if our bodies are not ours. Our "figure" is for a (potential) mate to admire. Our breasts are for "the man in our lives" to fondle during lovemaking, for our babies to suckle, for our doctors to examine. The same kind of "hands-off" message is even stronger for our vagina. (*Boston Women's Health Book Collective, 1976, p. 24*)

Anyone who has been around young children knows that baby girls play with their genitals just as they touch and explore all parts of their body. Although this activity seems pleasurable and interesting, most girls are quickly taught that it's "not nice" or "dirty," a prohibition that is probably reinforced during toilet training when the two- or

genitals (jen' i tulz) sex organs in the pelvic region. Customarily refers to the penis, the testes, and scrotum in the male and the vulva and vagina in the female.

three-year-old girl is urged to "wipe carefully" and "be clean." The sex-negative tone of these early childhood messages is consistently reinforced for most girls as they grow up, commonly creating anxieties and inhibitions about sex in general and their sexual anatomy in particular (Hite, 1976; Long Laws, 1979; Barbach, 1980). These difficulties are compounded by many people's perception of the female sex organs as unattractive and unclean.

Menstruation is one source of such negative attitudes: menstrual periods are sometimes called "the curse," menstrual flow is contained by "sanitary" napkins (which suggests an underlying condition of uncleanliness), sex during menstruation is often avoided by men and women because it may be messy, and in some societies there are strong taboos surrounding menstruating women that isolate them so they will not contaminate food, plants, or people (Delaney, Lupton, and Toth, 1977). In our cosmetic-conscious society laden with perfumes, deodorants, and aftershave lotions, women have been told that their vaginal odors are unpleasant and should be hidden. As a result, "feminine hygiene deodorant sprays" were widely used until it became apparent that they frequently caused vaginal irritation and itching.

Many women have not taken a direct look at their own genitals or cannot accurately name and identify the parts of their sexual anatomy. While we cannot imagine a person unable to distinguish between eyes, nose, mouth, and chin, many men and women have no idea of the locations of the female urethra, clitoris or hymen.

The Vulva

The external sex organs of the female, called the **vulva** (meaning "covering"), consist of the mons, the labia, the clitoris, and the perineum (Figure 3-1). Although the vagina has an external opening (the **introitus,** or entrance), it is principally an internal organ and discussed separately.

The Mons

The **mons veneris** (Latin for mound of Venus; Venus was the Roman goddess of love) is the area over the pubic bone which consists of a cushion of fatty tissue covered by skin and pubic hair. Since this region has numerous nerve endings, touch and/or pressure here may lead to sexual arousal. Many women find that stimulation of the mons area can be as pleasurable as direct clitoral touch.

Figure 3.1   The Vulva

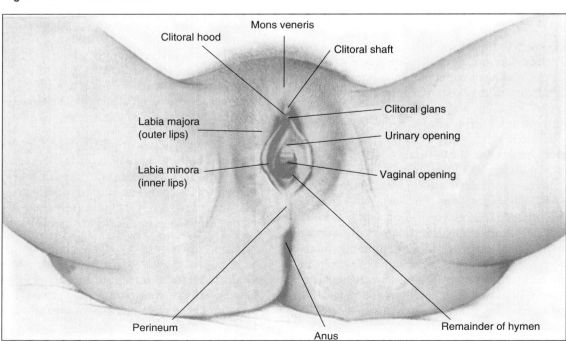

Figure 3.2   Some Variations in the Appearance of the Female Genitals

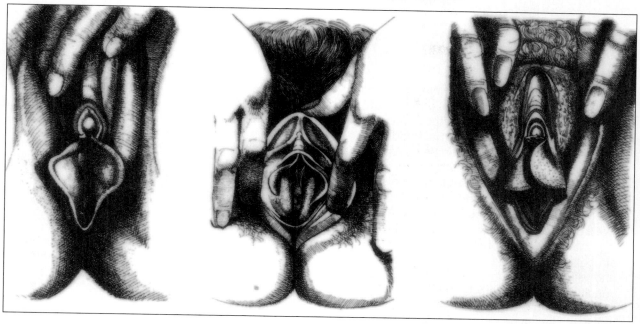

Betty Dodson's drawings of the female genitals reflect not only her artistic perspective but also the feminist view of the importance of women accepting their sexual anatomy as a positive attribute and a source of pleasure rather than shame.
Source: *Betty Dodson,* Selflove & Orgasm *(1983), Box 1933 Murray Hill Station, New York, N.Y. 10156, $5.50 pp.*

The Labia

The outer lips (**labia majora**) are folds of skin covering a large amount of fat tissue and a thin layer of smooth muscle. Pubic hair grows on the sides of the outer lips, and sweat glands, oil glands, and nerve endings are liberally distributed in them. In the sexually unstimulated state, the outer lips usually are folded together in the midline, providing mechanical protection for the urethral (urinary) opening and the vaginal entrance.

The inner lips (**labia minora**) are like curving petals. They have a core of spongy tissue rich in small blood vessels and without fat cells. The skin covering the inner lips is hairless but has many sensory nerve endings. The inner lips meet just above the clitoris, forming a fold of skin called the **clitoral hood** (see Figure 3.1). This portion of the inner lips is sometimes referred to as the female foreskin.

The labia are an important source of sexual sensations for most women since their many nerve endings serve as sensory receptors. When the skin of the labia is infected, sexual intercourse may be painful, and itching or burning may occur.

Women's external genitals may vary greatly in appearance. There are differences in the size, shape, and color of the labia (a few examples are shown in Figure 3.2), in the color, texture, amount, and distribution of pubic hair, and in the appearance of the clitoris, vaginal opening, and hymen.

vulva (vul' vuh) the external sex organs of the female: the mons, labia, clitoris, and vaginal orifice.

introitus the opening of the vagina.

mons veneris (mōnz ven' e ris) the area over the pubic bone of the female which consists of a cushion of fatty tissue covered by skin and pubic hair. Also called mons pubis or mound of Venus.

labia majora (la' bē uh muh jor' uh) the two outer folds of skin on either side of the inner lips, the clitoris, and the urethral and vaginal openings.

labia minora (la' bē uh mi nor' uh) the two inner folds of skin enclosing the urethral and vaginal openings.

clitoral hood the fold of skin covering the clitoral shaft. Sometimes referred to as the female foreskin.

Genital Mutilation and Female Puberty Rites

In many African countries, females reaching puberty must undergo operations that mutilate their genitals as part of the ritual "rites of passage" that mark the transition to womanhood. These operations, which are sometimes mistakenly referred to as "female circumcision," are actually quite different from male circumcision as we know it in the Western world. In most cases, the operations are performed in poor circumstances: by illiterate older women with no medical training, without the use of anesthesia, with the struggling child held forcefully on the ground, and with no sterile precautions. Given these conditions, it is not surprising that numerous medical complications occur as a result of these practices, including many hundreds of deaths each year.

According to some estimates around 100 million African women have undergone these mutilative genital operations (Toubia, 1994). There are actually three different operations that are performed:

1. *Sunna circumcision*—"sunna" is the Arabic word for tradition, and in this traditional operation the hood of the clitoris is removed along with the excision (cutting off) of the glans of the clitoris.

2. *Excision/clitoridectomy*—the removal of the entire shaft and glans of the clitoris along with much of the surrounding labia minora.

3. *Excision/infibulation*—the excision of the entire clitoris and labia minora, after which the two remaining sides of the vulva are scraped raw and then sewn together so that they fuse with scar tissue during the healing process and block the opening to the vagina. After marriage, the sealed opening is reopened to permit intercourse, impregnation, and delivery. After birth, the woman is sometimes (but not always) reinfibulated.

Here is a more detailed description of the practice as it is performed in Egypt today.

> On the night before the operation [the girl] is adorned with gold and dressed in new clothes. . . . With little fanfare or preparation, the midwife quickly performs the operation. As several women spread her legs, a bowl is placed beneath the girl to catch the blood, and the clitoris, labia minora, and part of the labia majora are excised with a razor or knife. The women meanwhile chant, "Come, you are now a woman," "You became a bride," "Bring her a penis, she is ready for intercourse," etc. . . .

Sexual anatomy varies just as much as facial anatomy differs from one person to another.

Bartholin's glands lie within the labia minora and are connected to small ducts that open on the inner surface of the labia next to the vaginal opening. Although they were once thought to play a major role in the production of vaginal lubrication, it is now clear that the few drops of secretion usually produced by these glands during sexual arousal are not important contributors to vaginal lubrication, although they may slightly moisten the labia.

The Clitoris

The **clitoris,** one of the most sensitive areas of a female's genitals, is located just beneath the point where the top of the inner lips meet. The only directly visible part of the clitoris is the head or **cli-toral glans,** which looks like a small, shiny button. This head can be seen by gently pushing up the skin or clitoral hood that covers it. The clitoral hood also hides the **clitoral shaft,** the spongy tissue that branches internally like an inverted V into two longer parts or **crura.** The crura lead to the bony pelvis (see Figure 3.3). The clitoris is richly endowed with nerve endings that make it highly sensitive to touch, pressure, and temperature. It is unique because it is the only organ in either sex whose only known function is to focus and accumulate sexual sensations and erotic pleasure (Masters and Johnson, 1970).

The clitoris is often regarded as a miniature penis, but this notion is sexist and incorrect. The clitoris has no reproductive or urinary function and does not usually lengthen like the penis when stim-

According to some informants, this chanting and shouting serves partially to drown the screams of the child. . . . After the ordeal, the mother and nearest female relatives serve dates, candy, popcorn and tea to the visiting women, and the hostess sprinkles them with perfume. . . . Sometimes the child's legs remain tied together for 40 days. More typically she is regarded as healed 7 to 15 days after the operation. This healing process generally provides the scar tissue for complete closure of the vulva except for a small urination orifice which is kept open by a match or reed tube (Kennedy, 1970).

Infibulation is practiced in order to make sexual intercourse impossible. In certain African societies a serious male suitor often insists upon seeing the fused genitals of his potential wife before finalizing a marriage contract so that he can be assured of her virginity. In addition, these operations reduce female sexual responsivity and, especially in the case of infibulation, often cause painful sexual intercourse.

Although the primary rationales for continuing these procedures are that they are required for morality and are a custom decreed by ancestors, the operations have provoked great controversy in Western nations as their damaging effects and widespread use have become known. For instance, fatalities have occurred as a result of uncontrolled bleeding and infection from such operations, and subsequent long-range health consequences have included urinary disturbances due to chronic infection, possible infertility, and problems with childbirth. In fact, for women who have been infibulated, unless someone cuts away the scar tissue, vaginal delivery may be impossible for, or fatal to, the mother and baby.

Despite these health risks and the fact that these operations may seem barbaric or sexist to us, we should realize that they are seen in a completely different light in the societies that continue their use. Suggestions made by some Westerners to ban such operations entirely have been decried as a form of cultural imperialism— that is, our attempting to make others see things (and do things) *our* way. Nevertheless, Sweden and England have banned all forms of female circumcision, and a similar law has been introduced in the U.S. by the Congressional Women's Caucus (Toubia, 1994). What are your feelings on this issue?

ulated, although it does become engorged. The clitoris and the penis, however, are derived embryologically from the same tissue.

The size and appearance of the clitoris vary considerably among women, but there is no evidence that a larger clitoris provides more intense sexual arousal. Contrary to the opinion of some physicians, masturbation rarely causes enlargement of this organ.

Clitoral circumcision—surgical removal of the clitoral hood—has been said to improve female sexual responsivity by exposing the clitoral glans to

Bartholin's glands (bahr' tō linz) small glands adjacent to the vaginal opening. Although they produce minimal amounts of lubrication, their function is unknown.

clitoris (klit' o ris) part of the external genitals of the female, situated at the anterior meeting of the labia minora and made up of two small erectile bodies, a glans and a hood. Its only known function is to focus and accumulate sexual sensations and erotic pleasure.

clitoral glans (klit' o rul) the tip or head and the only visible part of the clitoris, resembling a small button.

clitoral shaft part of the external female genitals; two small erectile bodies enclosed in a fibrous membrane and ending in a glans. Corresponds to the **corpus cavernosa** in the penis.

crura (kroo' ruh) The internal branches of the clitoral shaft and the corpus cavernosa attached to the bony pelvis.

Figure 3.3　　Anatomy of the Clitoris

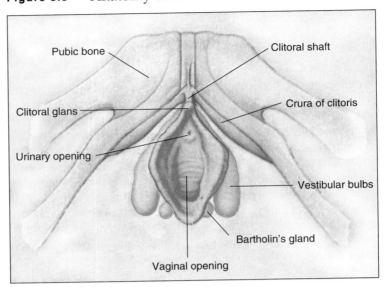

more direct stimulation. We believe, however, that this procedure is rarely useful since it has two major drawbacks: (1) the clitoral glans is often exquisitely sensitive to direct touch, to the point of pain or irritation (in this sense, the clitoral hood serves a protective function),[1] and (2) during intercourse the thrusting of the penis indirectly stimulates the clitoris by moving the inner lips of the vagina, causing the clitoral hood to rub back and forth across the clitoral glans (Masters and Johnson, 1966). A less drastic procedure than circumcision is advocated by several sexologists to improve some women's sexual responsiveness. A probe is used to loosen adhesions or thickened secretions (**smegma**) between the clitoral hood and clitoral glans (Graber and Kline-Graber, 1979). We have seen very few cases that required such an approach and remain skeptical about the use of this procedure on a routine basis.

The Perineum

The **perineum** is the hairless area of skin between the bottom of the labia and the anus (the opening for evacuation of the bowels). This region is often sensitive to touch, pressure, and temperature and may be a source of sexual arousal.

---

[1]In masturbation most women stroke areas around the clitoral glans but avoid its direct stimulation for this very reason. Apparently, the advocates of clitoral circumcision (usually men, oddly enough) have overlooked this finding.

The Hymen

The opening of the vagina is covered by a thin tissue membrane called the **hymen.** The hymen, which has no known function, typically has perforations in it that allow menstrual flow to pass from the body at puberty. The hymen usually stretches across some but not all of the vaginal opening and may vary in shape, size, and thickness, as Figure 3.4 reveals.

Historically, it has been important for a woman to have an intact hymen at the time of marriage as proof of her virginity. In some societies, a bride who does not have an intact hymen is returned to her parents, subjected to public ridicule, physically punished, or even put to death (Ford and Beach, 1951). Even in modern Japan and Italy, plastic surgeons are kept busy reconstructing the hymens of many engaged women to create "neovirginity" for those who wish to conceal their sexual histories from future husbands.

Contrary to the fears of some females, a doctor cannot usually tell if they are virgins by conducting a pelvic examination. The presence or absence of an intact hymen is not an accurate indication of prior sexual behavior. The hymen may be broken or stretched at an early age by various exercises or by inserting fingers or objects in the vagina. Some females are born with only a partial hymen or none at all. In addition, intercourse does not always tear the hymen; instead, it may simply stretch it. Under

Figure 3.4   Variations in the Hymen

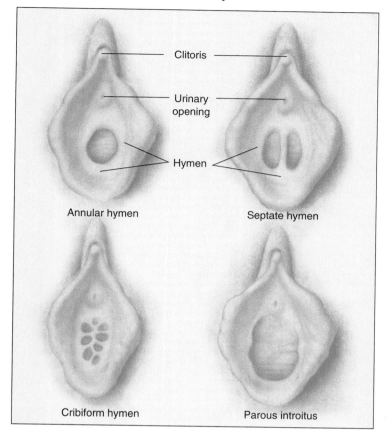

Clitoris

Urinary opening

Hymen

Annular hymen

Septate hymen

Cribiform hymen

Parous introitus

The annular hymen forms a ring around the vaginal opening; the septate hymen has one or more bands of tissue that cross the diameter of the vaginal opening; and the cribiform hymen stretches completely across the vaginal opening but has many small perforations. The parous introitus is the opening of the vagina in a woman who has previously given birth to a child by vaginal delivery; only small remnants of the tissue of the hymen are visible.

most circumstances, the first intercourse experience for a girl or woman is not painful or marked by a great deal of bleeding. The excitement of the moment is usually enough so that the pressure of the hymen is barely noticed.

The Vagina ↰

The **vagina** is a muscular internal organ that tilts upward at a 45° angle diagonally pointed toward the small of the back (Figure 3.5). In the sexually

unstimulated state, the vagina's walls are collapsed. In a woman who has never had a child, the back wall of the vagina averages 8 centimeters (about 3 inches) in length, while the front wall is approximately 6 centimeters (2 1/2 inches) long.

The vagina functions as a potential space that, like a balloon, can change shape and size. It can contract and expand, accommodate the passage of a baby during childbirth, or adjust in size to fit snugly around a finger.[2]

smegma (smeg' muh) Glandular secretions, dead cells, dirt particles, and bacteria that accumulate under the foreskin of the penis or the hood of the clitoris.

perineum (per i nē' um) The hairless area of skin between the vagina and anus in the female and between the scrotum and anus in the male.

hymen (hī' mun) a thin tissue membrane covering the opening of the vagina.

vagina (va jī' nuh) the canal in the female that receives the penis in copulation, existing as a potential space capable of contration and expansion. The opening is called the vaginal introitus.

[2]Despite its ability to contract, the human vagina cannot "clamp down" on the penis during intercourse and make physical separation impossible. In dogs, there is a type of intravaginal "locking," but it occurs primarily because of expansion of the bulbar portion of the shaft of the penis.

Figure 3.5   Internal Side View of the Female Reproductive System

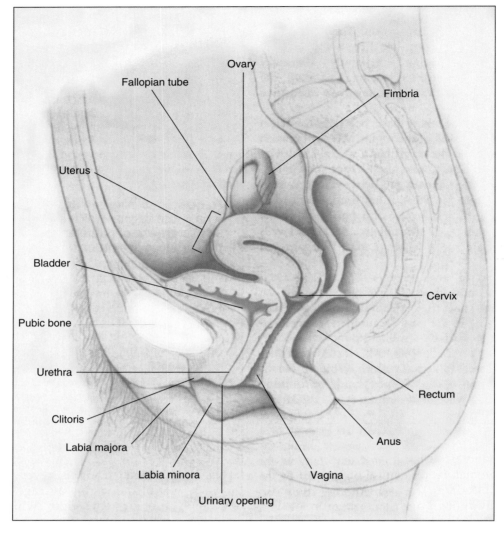

Many people wonder about the relationship between vaginal size and sexual gratification. Since the vagina adjusts equally well to a large or small penis, it is unusual for size differences between male and female sex organs to lead to sexual difficulties. Following childbirth, the vagina usually enlarges moderately and loses some degree of elasticity. Exercises to strengthen the muscles supporting the vagina are thought by some authorities to improve this condition and foster sexual responsiveness (Kegel, 1952; Kline-Graber and Graber, 1978).[3]

The inside of the vagina is lined with a surface similar to the lining inside the mouth. This **mucosa** is the source of vaginal lubrication. There are no secretory glands in the vagina, but there is a rich supply of blood vessels. The vagina has relatively few

[3]The "Kegel exercises" are done by contracting the pelvic muscles that support the vagina (most notably, the *pubococcygeus* and *bulbocavernosus* muscles). These same muscles are used when a woman stops the flow of urine or tightens the vagina against an inserted object such as a tampon, a finger, or an erect penis. The muscles are contracted firmly for one or two seconds and then released; this is repeated in a series of ten contractions several times a day for maximum results. In addition to strengthening muscular contractions, these exercises can improve a woman's sense of self-awareness. Whether they really improve sexual responsivity is less certain at present.

sensory nerve endings except near its opening. As a result, the inner two-thirds of the vagina are relatively insensitive to touch or pain.

In the last decade, there have been claims that a region in the front wall of the vagina midway between the pubic bone and the cervix has a special sensitivity to erotic stimulation. Called the **G spot** (or Gräfenberg spot, for the German physician who first suggested its presence in 1950), it has been described as a mass of tissue about the size of a small bean in the unstimulated state. When stimulated, the tissue swells to the size of a dime or larger (Ladas, Whipple, and Perry, 1982).

Ladas, Whipple, and Perry (1982) state that examinations of more than 400 women identified the "G spot" in each one; they explain that it has generally been overlooked in the past because "in its unstimulated state, it is relatively small and difficult to locate, especially since you can't see it." This explanation does not fit a research project in which Whipple herself participated in which the "G spot" could be found in only 4 out of 11 women (Goldberg et al., 1983), nor does it coincide with our studies at the Masters & Johnson Institute, where less than 10 percent of a sample of over 100 women who were carefully examined had an area of heightened sensitivity in the front wall of the vagina or a tissue mass that fit the various descriptions of this area. Another study also was unable to find evidence supporting the existence of the "G spot" (Alzate and Londono, 1984), although many of the women studied showed signs of erotic sensitivity in the front wall of the vagina. A more recent report concluded that "evidence for the existence of the G spot . . . in an appreciable minority of women, let alone the majority of them, is so far inconclusive" (Alzate and Hoch, 1986). Thus, at the present time it seems that additional research is needed to establish whether the "G spot" exists as a distinct anatomic structure or whether, as Helen Kaplan (1983) says, "the knowledge that many women have erotically sensitive areas in their vaginas which contribute to pleasure and orgasm is not new or controversial." As one recent report noted, the greater sensitivity of the anterior vaginal wall does not seem to be restricted to one specific spot, so that it may be "part and parcel of the female's clitoral/vaginal sensory arm of the orgasmic reflex" (Schultz et al., 1989).

FOCUS IN BRIEF

Douching

Concerns about vaginal cleanliness have led many women to practice **douching** (using a liquid to flush out the vagina) on a regular basis as part of their personal hygiene, and commercial preparations of douching solutions are now even advertised on television. However, there is mounting evidence of negative health effects from douching.

- Frequent douching can destroy beneficial bacteria in the vagina, which sometimes leads to an overgrowth of pathological microorganisms that produce symptomatic vaginal infections.
- Frequent douching also reduces the acidity of the vagina, which can make a woman more susceptible to vaginal infections.
- Frequent douching is a risk factor for pelvic inflammatory disease (*Forrest et al., 1989; Wolner-Hanssen et al., 1990*), a serious infection involving the inner reproductive organs in females (see Chapter 19).
- Self-diagnosing and self-treating vaginal burning, itching, discharge, or odor by douching is ill-advised, since douching may mask the presence of a serious infection such as gonorrhea and thus delay the start of appropriate medical therapy (*Covington and McClendon, 1987*).

In short, while there is probably no major health risk associated with infrequent douching (once or twice a month or less), we consider it wisest to avoid this practice unless it has been medically recommended to a woman.

mucosa (mew kō′ suh) mucous membrane. The membrane lining of the body openings, especially of the vagina, kept moist by the secretions of various types of glands.

G spot (Gräfenberg spot) a proposed region of the front wall of the vagina claimed by some researchers to have a high degree of erotic sensitivity.

Figure 3.6   Front View of the Internal Female Reproductive System

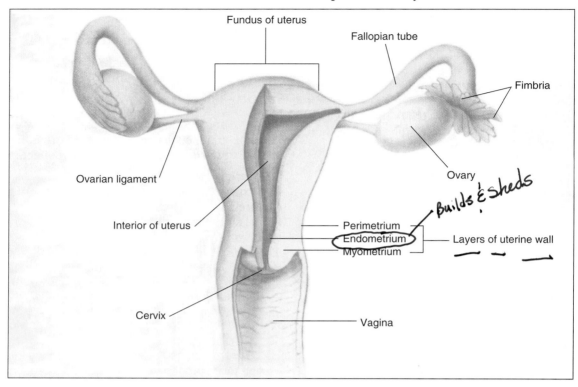

Fundus of uterus

Fallopian tube

Fimbria

Ovarian ligament

Ovary

Builds & Sheds

Interior of uterus

Perimetrium

Endometrium

Myometrium

Layers of uterine wall

Cervix

Vagina

The uterus and vagina in this figure are shown partially cut away.

The Uterus

The **cervix** is the bottom part of the uterus that protrudes into the vagina. Through the vagina, the cervix of a woman who has never been pregnant looks like a smooth pink button with a rounded face and a small central hole. At the mouth of the cervix (the **cervical os**), sperm cells enter the uterus and menstrual flow passes into the vagina. The **endocervical canal** (a thin tubelike communication between the mouth of the cervix and the cavity of the uterus) contains many secretory glands that produce mucus. The consistency of cervical mucus varies during different phases of the menstrual cycle in response to changing hormonal stimulation: just before or at the time of ovulation (when the egg is released from the ovary), cervical secretions become thin and watery; at other times, these secretions are thick and form a mucous plug that blocks the entrance to the cervix.

The cervix has no surface nerve endings, so it experiences little in the way of sexual feelings. If the cervix is removed surgically, there is no loss of sexual responsivity.

The **uterus** (womb) is a hollow muscular organ shaped like an inverted pear somewhat flattened from front to back. It is about 7.5 centimeters (3 inches) long and 5 centimeters (2 inches) wide. Anatomically, the uterus consists of several parts (Figure 3.6). The inside lining of the uterus (the **endometrium**) and the muscular component of the uterus (the **myometrium**) have separate and distinct functions. The inner lining changes during the menstrual cycle and is where a fertilized egg implants at the beginning of a pregnancy. The muscular wall facilitates labor and delivery. Both aspects of uterine function are regulated by chemicals called **hormones,** which also play a part in the growth of the uterus during pregnancy.

The uterus is held loosely in place in the pelvic cavity by six ligaments. The angle of the uterus in relation to the vagina varies from woman to woman. Ordinarily, it is relatively perpendicular to the axis of the vaginal canal, but in about 25 percent of women, the uterus is tipped backward, and in approximately 10 percent, it is tilted farther forward. If the uterus is rigidly fixed in position by scar tissue or inflammation, it may be a source of pain during sexual activity, requiring surgical correction.

The Fallopian Tubes

The **Fallopian tubes,** or oviducts, begin at the uterus and extend about 10 centimeters (4 inches) laterally (Figure 3.6). The far ends of the Fallopian tubes are funnel-shaped and terminate in long fingerlike extensions called **fimbria,** which hover near the ovaries. The inside lining of the Fallopian tubes consists of long, thin folds of tissue covered by hairlike **cilia.** The Fallopian tubes pick up eggs produced and released by the nearby ovary and then serve as the meeting ground for egg and sperm.

The Ovaries

The **ovaries,** or female gonads, are paired structures located on each side of the uterus. About the size of unshelled almonds (about $3 \times 2 \times 1.5$ centimeters or $1.2 \times 0.8 \times 0.6$ inches), they are held in place by connective tissue that attaches to the broad ligament of the uterus. The ovaries have two separate functions: manufacturing hormones (most notably, estrogen and progesterone) and producing and releasing eggs.

Before a baby girl is born, development of future eggs begins in her just-forming ovaries. About halfway through her mother's pregnancy, the girl's ovaries contain 6 or 7 million future eggs, most of which degenerate before birth. About 400,000 immature eggs are present in the newborn girl, and no new eggs are formed after this time. During childhood, continued degeneration reduces the number of eggs still further. The immature eggs are surrounded by a thin capsule of tissue forming a **follicle.**

When puberty arrives and girls begin to have menstrual cycles (see Chapter 9), each cycle is marked by a process of maturation in which some immature eggs divide twice, splitting their genetic material in half. Through this process, called **meiosis,** each young egg divides into four cells, only one of which is a mature egg (**ovum**). A mature egg is about 0.135 millimeter (1/175 of an inch) in diameter and is surrounded by a zone of jellylike material called the **zona pellucida** (Figure 3.7). A human egg is just barely visible, appearing as a speck smaller than the period at the end of this sentence. The other three cells, called **polar bodies**

---

cervix (ser' viks) the cylindrical part of the uterus that protrudes into the vagina. The point where sperm cells enter the uterus and menstrual flow exits is called the cervical os.

cervical os (ser' vi kul oss') the mouth or opening of the cervix.

endocervical canal (en' dō ser' vi kul) the tubelike connection between the mouth of the cervix and the uterine cavity containing numerous secretory glands that produce mucus.

uterus (ū' tur us) a hollow, pear-shaped muscular organ, part of the female internal genitals, in which the fertilized egg becomes embedded and the embryo and the fetus are nourished. Sometimes called the womb.

endometrium (en' dō mē' trē um) the inner lining of the uterus in which the egg implants and which is partially shed during menstruation.

myometrium (mī' ō mē' trē um) the muscular component of the uterus, important in labor and delivery.

hormone chemical substance secreted by the endocrine system into the bloodstream to be carried directly to the tissue on which it acts.

Fallopian tubes (fuh lō' pē un) the tubes that transport eggs from the ovaries to the uterus. Also called oviducts.

fimbria (fim' brē uh) long, fingerlike extensions at the entrance to the Fallopian tubes.

cilia (sil' ē uh) the hairlike filaments in the inside of the Fallopian tubes that propel the egg along to the uterus.

ovaries (ō' vur ēz) paired structures located on each side of the uterus that contain and release eggs and secrete hormones such as estrogen and progesterone. The female gonads.

follicle (fol' i kul) a thin capsule of tissue surrounding immature eggs.

meiosis (mī ō' sis) the process by which each immature egg divides into four cells, only one of which is a mature egg.

ovum (ō' vum) a mature egg cell that can, after maturation and fertilization, become another member of the same species.

zona pellucida (zō' nuh pe lew' sē duh) the jellylike material surrounding the mature egg.

polar bodies cells that arise in the development of the ovum during meiosis.

Figure 3.7   Photomicrograph of a Human Egg in a Secondary Follicle

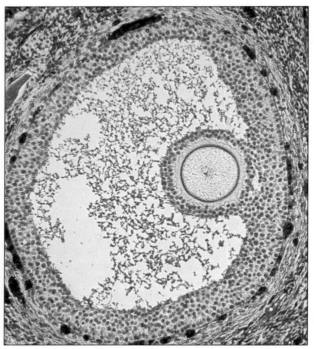

(Figure 3.8), have no known function and eventually degenerate.

Although a number of different follicles begin growing in each cycle, usually only one develops to the point where it moves to the surface of the ovary and ruptures, releasing the egg in a process called **ovulation.** For every follicle that ovulates, about a thousand undergo various degrees of growth and then degenerate. Fewer than 400 follicles are usually involved in ovulation during the female's reproductive years.

After the release of the egg, the **granulosa cells** that ade up the capsule of the follicle begin to enlarge, forming a structure called the **corpus luteum.** The corpus luteum produces hormones and is destined to degenerate within two weeks if pregnancy does not occur; with conception, the corpus luteum continues to develop and provides important hormonal support during early stages of pregnancy.

The Breasts

Although the breasts are not reproductive organs, they are clearly part of the sexual anatomy. In American society, the female breasts have a special erotic allure and symbolize sexuality, femininity, and attractiveness. Prominent attention is devoted to the breasts in clothing styles, men's magazines, advertising, television, and cinema. This attitude is not universal by any means, and in some cultures little or no erotic importance is attached to the breasts. For example, in Japan women traditionally bound their breasts to make them inconspicuous. Today, however, the westernization process has brought about changes in Japan and the breasts have become rather fully eroticized.

As the big-breasted female has become an almost universal sex symbol—the image used to promote everything from car sales to X-rated films—men and women have been bombarded daily with the not very subtle suggestion that a woman with large breasts has a definite sexual advantage. This has led to a number of harmful misconceptions. For example, men and women alike have come to believe that the larger a woman's breasts are, the more sexually excitable she is or can become. Another fallacy, still firmly subscribed to by many men, holds that the relatively flatchested woman is less able to respond sexually and actually has little, if any, interest in sex.

There is absolutely no evidence to suggest that breast size bears any relation to a woman's level of sexual interest, to her capacity for sexual response, or to the ease with which she attains orgasm. Actually, many women experience very little sexual sensation when their breasts are fondled or caressed, and this is as true of those with large breasts as it is of those with small ones. Furthermore, the woman who does become sexually excited when her breasts are stimulated does so regardless of their size.

For all their erotic significance, breasts are actually just modified sweat glands. The female breasts undergo changes in size and shape during puberty, gradually becoming conical or hemispherical, with the left breast usually slightly larger than the right (DeGowin and DeGowin, 1976). Each breast contains 15 to 20 subdivided lobes of glandular tissue arranged in a grapelike cluster, with each lobe drained by a duct opening on the surface of the nipple (Figure 3.9). The glandular lobes are surrounded by fatty and fibrous tissue, giving a soft consistency to the breast.

The **nipple** is located at the tip of the breast and mostly consists of smooth muscle fibers and a network of nerve endings that make it highly sensitive to touch and temperature. The dark wrinkled skin of the nipple extends 1 or 2 centimeters onto the

Figure 3.8   Development of Sperm Cells (upper diagram)
and Ovum (lower diagram)

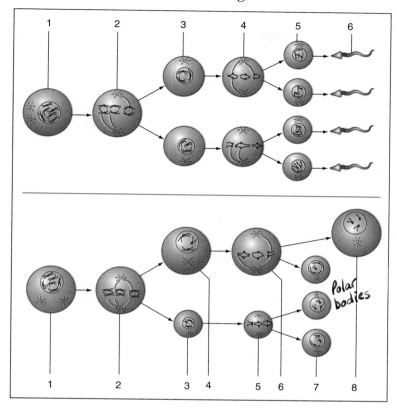

Source: "Development of Sperm Cells and Ovum" from Behold Man by Lennart Nilsson with Jon Lindberg. Copyright © 1973 by Albert Bonniers Forlag. English translation copyright © 1984 by Albert Bonniers Forlag. Reprinted by permission.

Development of sperm cells (upper diagram)
Stages 1 and 2: Primitive germ cell no. 1, the primary spermatocyte. At stage 1, the chromosomes in the nucleus double lengthwise. At stage 2, the chromosomal pairs are arranged in a plane for meiotic division. This will give rise to two new cells, each with half the normal complement of chromosomes.
Stages 3 and 4: Primitive germ cell no. 2, the secondary spermatocyte. At stage 3, the chromosomes in the nucleus again double longitudinally. At stage 4, the chromosomes are aligned in a plane for ordinary cell division, not meiosis.
Stage 5: Four sperm cell precursors, or spermatids, are produced from the original spermatocyte.
Stage 6: Mature sperm cells.
Development of an ovum (lower diagram)
Stages 1 and 2: The primitive germ cell, or the primary oocyte. At stage 1, the chromosomes in the nucleus double lengthwise. At stage 2, the chromosomes are aligned in a plane for meiotic division. This gives rise to a secondary oocyte and the first polar body, each with half the number of chromosomes.
Stages 3 and 5: First polar bodies. At stage 5, the chromosomes of the first polar body are arranged for ordinary cell division.
Stages 4 and 6: The second primitive germ cell, or the secondary oocyte. At stage 4, the chromosomes in the nucleus double longitudinally. At stage 6, the chromosomes are aligned in a plane for ordinary cell division, not meiosis.
Stage 7: Three secondary polar bodies are produced.
Stage 8: Mature ovum.

surface of the breast to form the **areola,** a circular area of dark skin with many nerve fibers and with muscle fibers that cause the nipple to stiffen and become erect.

The sexual sensitivity of the breast, areola, and nipple do not depend on breast size or shape (Figure 3.10). Personal preference, learned habit, and biology all contribute to their responsiveness. Nevertheless, the American male's fascination with female breasts leads many women who consider themselves "flat-chested" or "underdeveloped" to

seek to improve their sexual attractiveness and self-esteem by the use of exercises, lotions, or mechanical devices such as suction machines to enlarge their breasts. These methods, though widely advertised, do not work. For this reason, so-called breast augmentation surgery has become popular. In the past, liquid silicone was injected directly into the breasts to increase their size, but this technique proved to be highly unsatisfactory as it led to many medical complications. Subsequently, soft thin plastic pouches filled with silicone gel were im-

ovulation (ōv you lā′ shun) the second phase of the menstrual cycle; the release of the egg from the ovary.
granulosa cells (gran′ ū lō′ suh) the cells lining the ovarian follicle that enlarge and form the corpus luteum.
corpus luteum (kor′ pus lew′ tē um) part of the capsule of the ovarian follicle left in an ovary

after an egg is expelled. It secretes hormones and, if pregnancy does not occur, degenerates.
nipple protuberance located at the tip of the breast consisting principally of smooth muscle fibers and a network of nerve endings and containing in the female the outlets of the milk ducts.
areola (a rē′ o luh) the circular area of dark skin around the nipple.

Figure 3.9   External and Internal Anatomy of the Female Breast

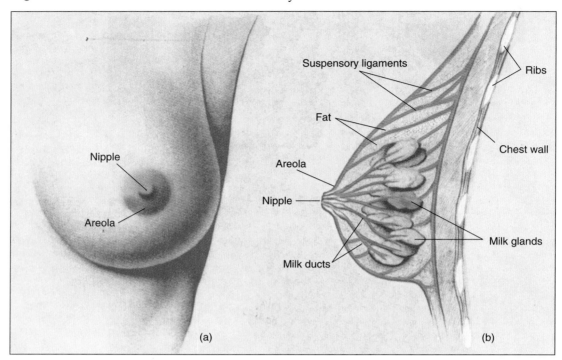

(a)   (b)

Figure 3.10   Variations in Appearance of the Female Breast

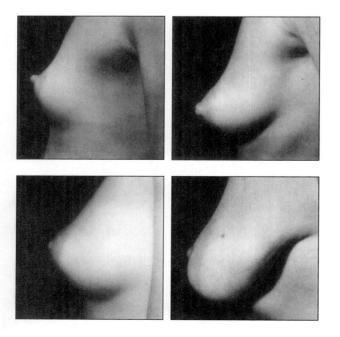

planted to increase breast size while retaining a natural-appearing and soft-feeling breast. Unfortunately, these devices tended to rupture or leak with time, causing local inflammatory reactions and possibly severe immune-related or connective tissue diseases. This problem led the Food and Drug Administration (1992) to recommend that all such implants be stopped, with the sole exception being women enrolled in research studying breast reconstruction required after mastectomy or breast injury. The FDA also recommended that women who already have silicone breast implants should not consider having them removed unless they are causing problems, such as hardening or discoloration of the breasts, or symptoms related to autoimmune diseases such as joint swelling and pain, redness of the skin, swollen glands, unusual fatigue, and swelling of the hands and feet.

Conversely, some women are troubled by breast that are too large. This condition, called **mammary hyperplasia** or **macromastia,** can be treated by reduction mammaplasty, a fairly simple operation to reduce breast size and weight. Other common breast problems include **inverted nipples** (the nip-

Self-Examination of the Breasts

It is important for women to examine their own breasts regularly because most breast lumps are self-discovered rather than found by a doctor or nurse. Although some people feel uncomfortable about this type of self-exam, two specific facts should be noted: (1) about nine out of ten breast lumps are *not* cancer and (2) women who examine their own breasts monthly have significantly higher survival rates after breast cancer than women who do not (Foster et al., 1978). The best time for a breast self-exam is right after your period ends because estrogen levels are low. Women who do not have periods should still examine their breasts once a month. The following technique should be used.

1. *Stand in front of a mirror with good lighting.* Inspect your breasts visually in the mirror, with your arms relaxed at your sides. Then raise your hands above your head. Finally, put your hands on your hips and push down. Look for flattening or bulging in one breast but not the other, puckering of the skin, dimpling or redness, or one nipple being unusually drawn up into the breast. Squeeze each nipple gently to see if there is any discharge.
2. *Lie flat on your back, with a pillow or folded towel underneath your left shoulder, and*

your left arm behind your head. Imagine that your breast is divided into four quarters, as shown in the diagram.
3. *With the fingers of your right hand held together, press firmly but gently (using the flat part of your fingertips) to feel the inner, upper quadrant of your left breast.* Move your hand in small circles so the breast tissue slides underneath the skin. Start at the breast-bone and work towards the nipple.
4. *Repeat step 3 for each of the remaining quadrants of your left breast.* Cover the entire area and also feel over the ribs to the side of the breast.
5. *Bring your left arm down to your side and feel under your left armpit for swellings.*
6. *Repeat steps 2 to 5 using your left hand to examine your right breast.*
7. *Repeat steps 2 to 6 in the sitting or standing position.* The position change redistributes the breast tissue and may allow you to feel a lump that was hidden when you were lying down. You may want to do this in the bath or shower, since hands glide more easily over wet skin.

Sources: Boston Women's Health Book Collective, *1976; Stewart et al., 1979, American Cancer Society, 1980.*

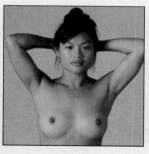 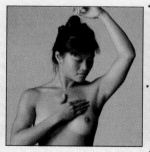 

ples are pushed inward), a harmless anatomical variation that usually does not interfere with nursing, and **extra nipples,** which are minor errors of development that have no adverse health consequences but may be a source of embarrassment. Breast self-examination is discussed above.

mammary hyperplasia or macromastia abnormally large breasts.

inverted nipples congenital condition in which the nipples are not protuberant.

extra nipples more than two paired nipples; about one person in 1000 has this condition.

MALE SEXUAL ANATOMY

It is not much of an exaggeration to say that penises in fantasyland come in only three sizes—large, gigantic, and so big you can barely get them through the doorway. . . .

Accepting your own merely human penis can be difficult. You know it is somewhat unpredictable and, even when functioning at its best, looks and feels more like a human penis than a battering ram or a mountain of stone. But you do have one small advantage. You are alive and can enjoy yourself whereas the supermen of the

model with the gigantic erections are unreal and feel nothing. *(Zilbergeld, 1978, pp. 23, 26)*

The male sex organs are more visible and accessible than the female sex organs. Unlike the clitoris or vagina, the penis is involved directly in the process of urination so that boys become accustomed to touching and handling their penises at a relatively early age. The sexual aspects of the male organ are hard for a boy to miss. He learns about them by watching, touching, and playing with his penis as it becomes erect (a pleasurable experience) or by hearing stories and jokes that graphically portray the sexual and reproductive purposes of the penis.

Figure 3.11   Anatomy of the Penis

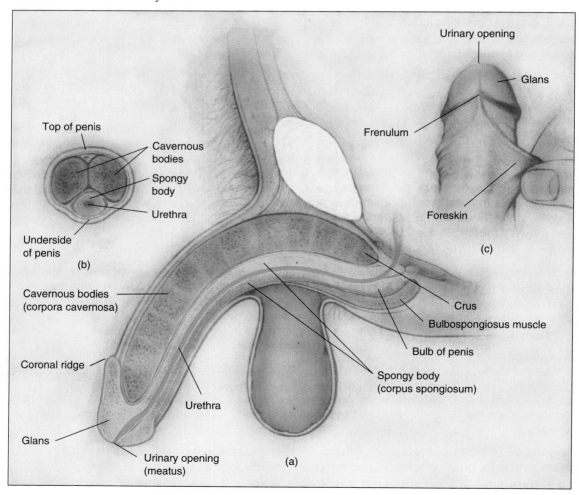

(a) Internal side view of the penis. (b) A cross section of the penis. (c) A view of the underside of the penis showing the location of the frenulum.

Despite such exposure, many males are not fully informed about the details of the anatomy and function of the sex organs.

The Penis

The penis is an external organ that consists primarily of three parallel cylinders of spongy tissue bound in thick membrane sheaths (Figure 3.11). The cylindrical body on the underside of the penis is called the **spongy body (corpus spongiosum)**. The **urethra** (a tube that carries urine or semen) runs through the middle of the spongy body and exits at the tip of the penis via the **urinary opening (urethral meatus)**. When the penis is erect, the spongy body on the underside looks and feels like a straight ridge. The other two cylinders, called the **cavernous bodies (corpora cavernosa)**, are positioned side by side above the spongy body. All three consist of irregular sponge-like tissue dotted with small blood vessels. The tissue swells with blood during sexual arousal causing the penis to become erect.

Internally, beyond the point where the penis attaches to the body, the cavernous bodies branch apart to form tips (**crura**) that are firmly attached to the pelvic bones. The penis has numerous blood vessels, both inside and apart from the cylindrical bodies; a pattern of veins is often visible on the outer skin of the erect penis. The penis also has many nerves, making it highly sensitive to touch, pressure, and temperature.

The tip of the penis, the **glans** or head, consists entirely of corpus spongiosum. This region has a higher concentration of sensory nerve endings than the shaft of the penis and is thus particularly sensitive to physical stimulation. Two other areas particularly sensitive to touch are the rim of tissue that separates the glans from the shaft of the penis (the **coronal ridge**) and the small triangular region on the underside of the penis where a thin strip of skin (the **frenulum**) attaches to the glans (Figure 3.11). Many males find that direct stimulation of the glans may become painful or irritating and prefer to masturbate by rubbing or stroking the penile shaft.

The skin that covers the penis is freely movable and forms the **foreskin** or prepuce at the glans. Inflammation or infection of the foreskin or glans may cause pain during sexual activity. Sometimes the foreskin sticks to the underlying glans when smegma, a naturally occurring substance of cheesy consistency made up of oily secretions, dead skin cells, dirt particles, sweat, and bacteria, is not regularly washed away from underneath the foreskin. This type of problem occurs only in uncircumcised men and is one argument in favor of routine circumcision.

Circumcision is the surgical removal of the foreskin. As a result of this minor operation, usually done shortly after birth, the glans of the penis is fully exposed. Circumcision is sometimes a religious practice, as in Islam or in Judaism, where it symbolizes the covenant with God made by Abraham. In the United States, it is often done routinely for nonreligious reasons, whereas is is less common in Canada and Europe.

The advantages of circumcision are primarily related to hygiene and health: smegma does not collect, the glans of the penis is easier to clean, conditions of inflammation or infection are less likely to occur, and cancer of the penis is far less frequent.

corpus spongiosum (kor′ pus spon′ jē o⁻′ sum) the cylinder of erectile tissue along the underside of the penis containing the urethra. The distal portion expands to form the glans. Also called spongy body.

urethra (u rē′ thruh) a tube beginning at the bladder and ending at the urethral meatus, carrying urine in the female and urine or semen in the male.

urethral meatus (u re′ thral mē a′ tus) the urinary opening.

corpora cavernosa (kor′ po rhu kav ur no⁻′ suh) the two parallel cylindrical bodies of erectile tissue that make up the larger part of the shaft of the penis and the clitoris. Also called cavernous bodies.

crura (kroo′ ruh) The internal branches of the clitoral shaft and the corpus cavernosa attached to the bony pelvis.

glans (glanz) the tip or head of the penis or clitoris.

coronal ridge (kor′ o⁻ nul) the rim of tissue that separates the glans from the shaft of the penis.

frenulum (fren′ u⁻ lum) a small, triangular fold of skin on the underside of the penis connecting the glans with the foreskin.

foreskin (for′ skin) the freely movable skin that covers the penis. Also the hood of the clitoris.

circumcision (sur′ kum sizh′ un) surgical removal of the foreskin of the penis.

Penis Size

We have already mentioned that many males are somewhat anxious about the size of their penis. More specifically, this concern is a comparative one: "How does *my* penis stack up against what others have?" This interest in penis size has several different components. First, it shows a concern for being "normal"—the same as everyone else. Second, it is related to a wish to be sexually adequate. Our society generally believes that "biggest is best," and the notion that a "big" penis will provide more sexual satisfaction to a woman is widespread. Actually, penile size has little physiological effect for the woman (although it may have positive or negative psychological significance) since the vagina accommodates its size equally well to an erect penis that is relatively smaller or larger in circumference. The length of the penis, which determines the depth of vaginal penetration, is also relatively unimportant, since the inner portion of the vagina and the cervix have few sensory nerve endings. Third, there is often an element of status-seeking in wishing to have a large penis. Finally, some males feel that a larger penis would make them more sexually attractive. Most of these points apply to both heterosexual and homosexual males.

In art and in the media (particularly erotic books, male magazines, and movies) there is a tendency to portray male genital size in "bigger than life" dimensions. This distortion reflects the triumph of anxious perception versus reality, literary and cinematic license (e.g., the use of particular camera angles or close-up shots), and the deliberate selection of male subjects whose genital proportions are decidedly larger than average. Male readers should remember, too, that there is a visual difference between the view you get of your own genitals (they appear shortened because of your viewing angle) and the view you get of someone else's penis size in the locker room or on the movie screen.

A team of Canadian researchers studied the psychological impact of penis size on sexual

"Doris, I thought you told me size wasn't important!"

Source: Playboy, *April 1983, p. 182. Reproduced by special permission of* Playboy *Magazine; Copyright © 1983 by* Playboy.

arousal. They found that reading erotic passages that differed only in the description of the size of the penis produced no differences in the levels of arousal of male or female undergraduates (Fisher, Branscombe, and Lemery, 1983). Thus, they concluded that "penis size may be as unimportant on a psychological level as it appears to be on a physical level."

There is a rare medical condition called *micropenis* in which the penis is formed properly but is miniature in size. This condition is marked by a penis length of less than 2 centimeters (approximately ¾ inch) and sometimes is due to a treatable deficiency of testosterone. In other circumstances, there is no means of increasing penis size by drugs, creams, gadgets, hypnosis, or hormones although there are advertisements for such "treatments" which exploit the myth that bigger is necessarily better.

Men who are preoccupied or extremely anxious about the size of their penis appear to be more likely to develop sexual difficulties than other men. These difficulties range from the avoidance of potentially sexual relationships because of embarrassment or worry to difficulty in obtaining or maintaining an erection due to poor self-confidence, tension, and anxiety. Fortunately, this type of problem can usually be overcome by brief sex counseling or therapy (see Chapter 21).

Figure 3.12   Some Variations in the Appearance of the Male Genitals

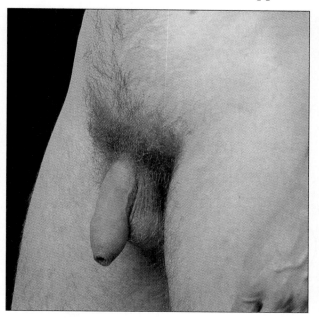
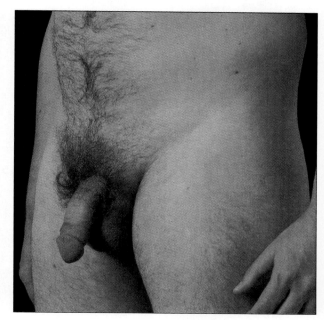

The photo on the left shows an uncircumcised penis.

Although the rate of cancer of the cervix is considerably lower in the spouses of circumcised men (Green, 1977, p. 403), it is not certain that this is a cause–effect relationship (Poland, 1990). In addition, urinary tract infections are many times higher in uncircumcised male infants than in those who are circumcised (Wissell et al., 1987; Herzog, 1989; Schoen, 1990). Urinary tract infections are also far more common in young adult men who haven't been circumcised than in those who have (Spach, Stapleton, and Stamm, 1992). More importantly, circumcision provides some protection against infection with HIV (the AIDS virus) (Quinn et al., 1988; Marx, 1989; Schoen, 1990). Circumcision also lowers the risk of infection with the human papilloma virus and many other forms of sexually transmitted disease (Goldenring, 1990).

Opponents of routine circumcision see no clear reason for this operation and suggest that removing the skin protecting the glans weakens the region's sexual sensitivity since it constantly rubs directly against clothing. Others believe that circumcision increases the risk of premature ejaculation (this is probably not true, since the foreskin of the erect uncircumcised penis retracts, exposing the glans, and researchers have not found a difference in the rates of premature ejaculation in circumcised versus uncircumcised men). We are not aware of any believable evidence demonstrating that circumcision affects male sexual function one way or the other. On the other hand, uncircumcised men who practice routine hygienic care are unlikely to be at any major health disadvantage simply because their foreskin is intact.

Although it might sound surprising, a small number of men who were so dissatisfied with having been circumcised as infants have undergone a complicated series of operations to reconstruct the foreskin. While the results were reported as uniformly pleasing to these men (Greer et al., 1982), it was also noted that the reconstructed foreskin (which was taken from the scrotum) has a noticeable difference in skin texture, color, and contour from the skin on the shaft of the penis. The series of operations takes up to a year to complete.

The appearance of the penis varies considerably from one male to another. These variations are due to differences in color, size, shape, and the status of the foreskin (circumcised or uncircumcised). Some examples of different male genitals are shown in Figure 3.12.

Concerns about penile size are common in males of all ages. Although the size of the nonerect penis differs widely from one male to another (the average length is approximately 9.5 centimeters, or just under 4 inches), in adulthood this variation is less

Figure 3.13 Internal Side View of the Male Reproductive System

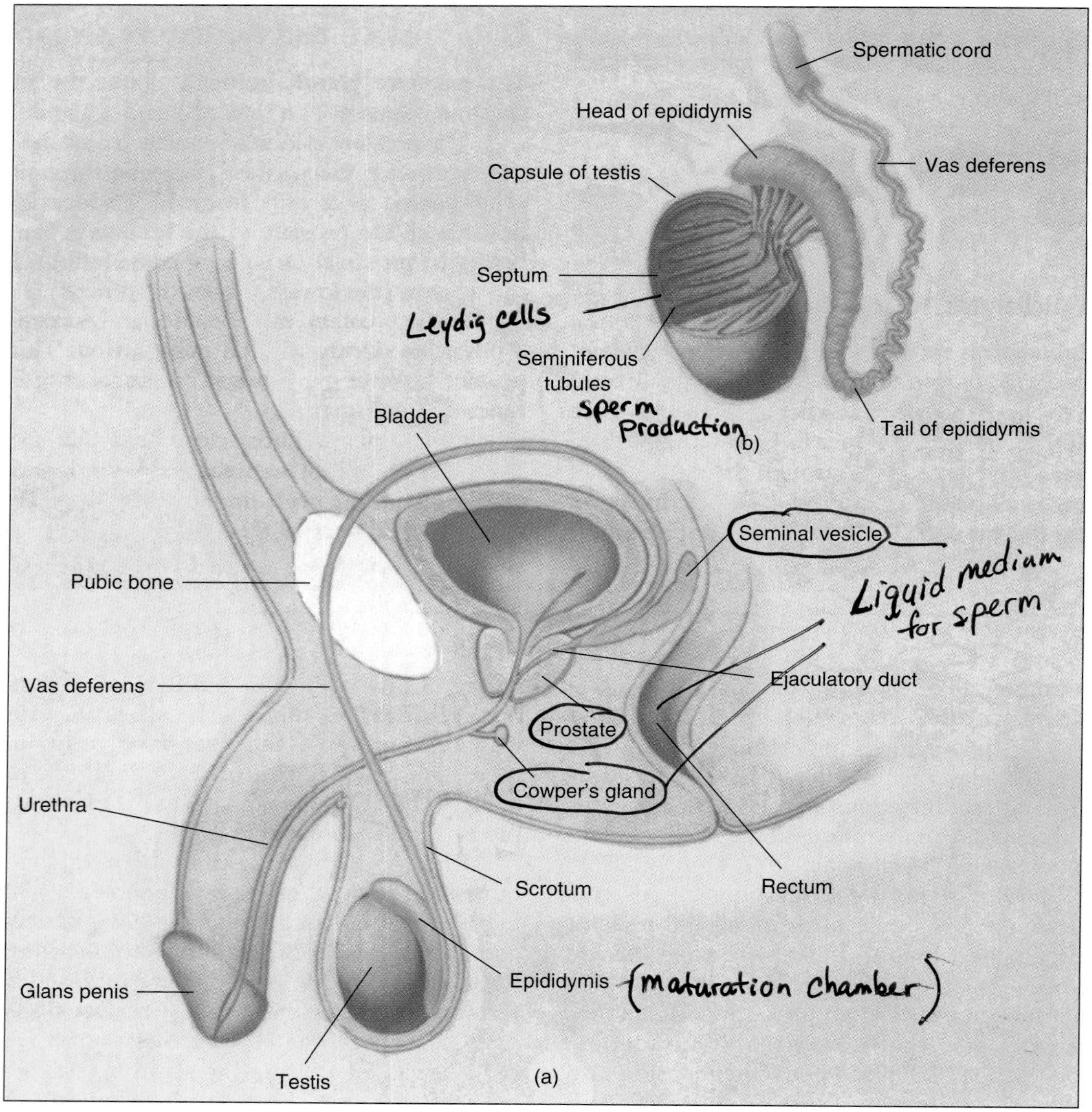

(a)

(b)

Labels in figure (b): Spermatic cord, Head of epididymis, Capsule of testis, Vas deferens, Septum, *Leydig cells*, Seminiferous tubules, *sperm Production*, Tail of epididymis

Labels in figure (a): Bladder, Seminal vesicle, *Liquid medium for sperm*, Pubic bone, Ejaculatory duct, Vas deferens, Prostate, Cowper's gland, Urethra, Rectum, Scrotum, Glans penis, Epididymis *(maturation chamber)*, Testis

apparent in the erect state. Erection can be thought of as "the great equalizer" since men with a penis that is smaller when flaccid (nonerect) usually have a larger percentage volume increase during erection than men who have a larger flaccid penis (Masters and Johnson, 1966; Jamison and Gebhard, 1988).

The Scrotum

The **scrotum** is a thin loose sac of skin underneath the penis that is sparsely covered with public hair and contains the testicles (testes). The scrotum has a

layer of muscle fibers that contract involuntarily as a result of sexual stimulation, exercise, or exposure to cold, causing the testes to be drawn up against the body. In hot weather, the scrotum relaxes and allows the testes to hang more freely away from the body. These reflexes of the scrotum help to maintain a stable temperature in the testes, an important function because sperm production (occurring in the testes) is impaired by heat or cold. In response to cold, the scrotum lifts the testes closer to the body to provide a warmer environment. In hotter conditions, the scrotum loosens, thereby moving

FOCUS IN BRIEF

Examination of Testicles

After a 29-year-old film projectionist showed a movie about testicular self-examination to a group of doctors, he decided to take the film's recommendations and found a bean-sized lump in his right testicle. This simple act probably saved his life because he had a fast-growing cancer that required immediate surgery (P.C. Smith, 1980).

Men are not usually told about the importance of self-examination of the testes even though women are advised about checking their own breasts. This may partly reflect that cancer of the testis is statistically infrequent, with fewer than 5000 cases annually (Silverberg, 1981). It is the most common cancer in men between the ages of 20 and 34, however, and in many cases it does not produce pain or other symptoms.

The self-examination procedure is a simple one. After a warm bath or shower, when the scrotum is relaxed and loose, each testis should be felt individually. The surface on each testis should be covered, using the fingertips and thumb to feel for lumps, irregularities, hardening, or enlargement. If any suspicious areas are found, see your physician *immediately*.

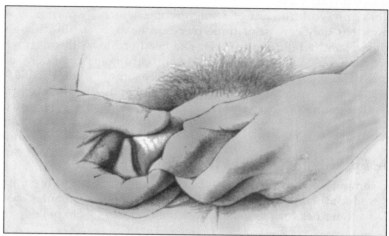

The testes away from the body and providing a larger skin surface for the dissipation of heat. Tightening of the scrotum with sexual arousal or physical exercise may be a protective reflex that lessens the risk of injury to the testes.

The Testes

The **testes** (the male gonads) are paired structures usually contained in the scrotum (Figure 3.13). The two testes are about equal in size, averaging $5 \times 2 \times 3$ centimeters ($2 \times 0.8 \times 1.2$ inches) in adults, although one testicle generally hangs lower than the other. Most often, the left testis is lower than the right one, but in left-handed men the reverse is usually true. There is no significance attached to the relative height of the testes within the scrotal sac, but if one testis is considerably larger or smaller than the other there could be a medical problem and a doctor should be seen.

The testes are highly sensitive to pressure or touch. Some men find that light caressing or stroking of the scrotum or gentle squeezing of the testes during sexual activity is arousing, but many others are uncomfortable with touching in this region.

The testes have two separate functions: hormone and sperm production. The cells that manufacture hormones—most importantly, **testosterone,** which controls male sexual development and plays an im-

scrotum (skro͞' tum) the thin, loose sac of skin that contains the testes and has a layer of muscle fibers that contract involuntarily.

testes (tes' tēz) the paired male reproductive glands contained in the scrotum. The male gonads.

testosterone (tes tos' tur ōn) the most important hormone in sexual function, present in both sexes. Often called the male hormone, it is secreted by the testes and adrenals in the male and the ovaries and adrenals in the female.

portant part in sexual interest and function—are called **Leydig cells.** Sperm production occurs in the **semi-niferous tubules,** tightly coiled tubes of microscopic size that collectively measure almost 500 meters (more than a quarter mile) in length. The entire process of sperm production takes 70 days. Unlike the female who creates no new eggs after birth, the male produces sperm from puberty on, manufacturing billions of sperm annually.

A mature spermatozoon is considerably smaller than the size of a human egg, being about 0.06 millimeter (1/500 of an inch) in length and thousands of times smaller than the egg in volume. Sperm are visible only with the aid of a microscope, which shows that they consist of three pieces: a head, a midpiece, and a tail (Figure 3.14). The head of the spermatozoon contains genetic material (**chromosomes**) and a chemical reservoir (the **acrosome**). The midpiece contains an energy system that allows the spermatozoon to swim by lashing its long tail back and forth.

The Epididymis and Vas Deferens

The seminiferous tubules (the tubes where sperm are produced) empty into the **epididymis,** a highly coiled tubing network folded against the back surface of each testis (Figure 3.13). Sperm cells generally spend several weeks traveling slowly through the epididymis as they reach full maturation. From here, sperm are carried into the **vas deferens,** long tubes (approximately 40 centimeters, or 16 inches) that leave the scrotum and curve alongside and behind the bladder. Both the right and left vas deferens are cut when a vasectomy is done (see Chapter 6).

The Prostate and Accessory Organs

The **prostate gland,** normally about the size of a chestnut, consists of a muscular and a glandular portion. The prostate is located directly below the bladder and surrounds the urethra (the tube through which urine passes) as it exits from the bladder. The relationship of the prostate to the urethra is like a large bead (the prostate) on a string (the urethra). Because the **rectum** (the lowest part of the bowels) is directly behind the prostate, the prostate can be examined by a physician during a rectal examination. This is important because the prostate can become infected or cancerous (Chapter 22).

The prostate produces clear fluid that makes up about 30 percent of **seminal fluid,** the liquid that is expelled from the penis during ejaculation. The

Figure 3.14   The Human Sperm

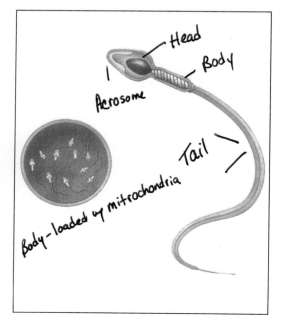
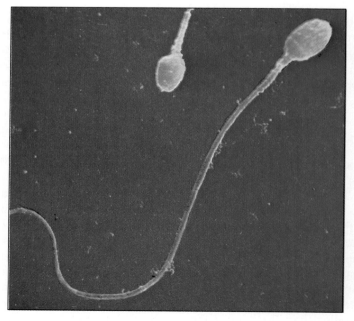

The insert shows live sperm as seen under a microscope, where their active swimming motion is apparent. The photograph of human sperm is taken with a scanning electron microscope.

other 70 percent of seminal fluid comes from the **seminal vesicles** (Eliasson and Lindholmer, 1976; Spring-Mills and Hafez, 1980). These two small structures lie against the back portion of the base of the bladder and join with the ends of the vas deferens to form the **ejaculatory ducts.** These ducts in turn join the urethra, thereby creating a continuous tubing system that leads to the end of the penis.

On the average, there are 3 to 5 milliliters (5 milliliters equal about 1 teaspoonful) of semen (seminal fluid plus sperm) per ejaculate. Although the concentration of sperm is highly variable, depending in part on the frequency of ejaculation, a count of 40 to 120 million per milliliter is considered normal. This means that there may be 120 to 600 million sperm in a single ejaculate.[5]

Seminal fluid ranges in color from whitish to tones of yellow or gray and has a creamy, sticky texture. Right after ejaculation, seminal fluid is rather thick but then liquefies quickly. It consists of water, mucus, and a large number of chemical substances that include sugar (providing an energy source for sperm), bases (for neutralizing the acidity of the male urethra and the female vagina), and prostaglandins (hormones that cause contractions in the uterus and Fallopian tubes, possibly aiding upward transit of sperm).

Cowper's glands are two pea-sized structures connected to the urethra just below the prostate gland. They produce a few drops of fluid which sometimes appear at the tip of the penis during sexual arousal but before ejaculation. Some men never notice this pre-ejaculatory fluid, while others may produce a teaspoonful or more of this slippery secretion. Although this pre-ejaculatory fluid may buffer the acidity of the urethra, there is no certainty about its function. Occasionally, the pre-ejaculatory fluid contains a small number of live sperm cells, accounting for at least some of the "failures" of withdrawal of the penis before ejaculation as a method of birth control.

The Breasts

The male breasts have a nipple and areola but have little underlying glandular tissue or fatty padding. The male nipple and areola seem to be less sensitive to touch and pressure than the same structures in adult females (Robinson and Short, 1977). Nevertheless, some males find that having their breasts or nipples stroked or licked is sexually arousing. Others do not notice any erotic pleasure from such practices.

Sometimes one or both of a male's breasts become enlarged. This condition, called **gynecomastia,** occurs in 40 to 60 percent of boys during puberty but usually disappears within a year or two (Lee, 1975; Kolodny, Masters, and Johnson, 1979). In adulthood, it may be caused by alcoholism, liver disease, thyroid disease, drug ingestion, or certain

Leydig cells (lī′ dig) the cells in the testes where hormone production occurs.

seminiferous tubules (sem′ i nif′ ur us tū′ bewls) microscopic tube-shaped structures in the testes where sperm is produced.

chromosomes (krō′ muh sōmz) the genetic material in the nucleus of every cell in the body. Sperm and eggs each have 23 chromosomes; all other cells normally have 46.

acrosome (ak′ ro sōm) chemical reservoir in the head of the spermatozoon.

epididymis (ep′ i did′ i mis) the tightly coiled tubing network folded against the back surface of each testis in which sperm cells spend several weeks maturing.

vas deferens (vas def′ ur enz) one of two long, tubelike structures that convey spermatozoa from the testes.

prostate gland (pros′ tāt) gland located directly below the bladder, surrounding the urethra as it exits the bladder. It secrets part of the seminal.

rectum (rek′ tum) the lower part of the large intestine.

seminal fluid (sem′ uh nul) the thick white, yellow, or gray liquid portion of the male ejaculate.

seminal vesicles (sem′ uh nul ves′ e kulz) in the male, paired pouchlike bodies that empty into the ejaculatory ducts and provide the major part of fluid in the ejaculate.

ejaculatory ducts (ē jak′ you luh tō′ rē) paired tubelike structures that carry sperm from the vas deferens and fluid from the seminal vesicles into the prostatic urethra.

Cowper's glands (kow′ perz) two pea-sized structures connected to the urethra just below the prostate gland. They produce fluid before ejaculation but otherwise have no known function.

gynecomastia (jīn′ e kō mas′ tē uh) enlargement of one or both male breasts.

---

[5]After a vasectomy, although there are no longer sperm in the ejaculate, the amount of fluid in the ejaculate remains the same.

forms of cancer. When gynecomastia is so severe that it creates major psychological problems, it can be corrected by relatively simply surgery.

The male breasts can also become enlarged if a man takes estrogen over a period of time. As we shall discuss in Chapter 11, most male-to-female transsexuals undergo such treatment. We have also seen a case in which a man unwittingly took birth control pills for several months, causing the same result.

OTHER EROGENOUS ANATOMY

Many parts of the body besides those involved in reproduction are potential sources of sexual arousal in both sexes. Surprisingly, the largest sensory organ for both females and males is the skin itself. The insides of the thighs, the neck, and the perineum are often sources of sexual pleasure. In our genitally oriented society, where sex is often thought of as synonymous with intercourse, it is easy to overlook the importance of touching and body-to-body contact as a form of intimacy and gratification. Stroking, caressing, and massage can be forms of nonverbal communication, sensual pleasure, or invitations to further sexual activity.

Some people are well aware of the erotic sensations they can experience from touch, while others pay little attention to this component of their sexual arousal. However, there are wide differences from person to person in such matters: for some, the skin outside the genital region has relatively little sexual input or may actually dampen sexual feelings (what would happen to your level of arousal if a touch felt persistently ticklish or irritating?); at the other extreme, we have seen one woman who could be aroused to the point of orgasm by having the small of her back rubbed without any other stimulus (Masters and Johnson, 1966). (However, the likelihood of being or encountering a female capable of reaching orgasm by back rubbing alone is probably less than one in a million.)

The mouth, including the lips and tongue, is an area of high erotic potential. Kissing is one practice that uses the sensitivity of this region in a sexually stimulating fashion. In addition to the sensory signals activated by kissing, it is also an act of intimacy that can symbolize passion and penetration (think of the form of kissing called "French kissing" or "soul kissing" in which one partner's tongue enters the other's mouth). Oral–genital contact—stimulation of one person's genitals in a licking or sucking fashion by the partner's lips or tongue—is another common form of sexual stimulation.

The anus, rectum, and buttocks are also potentially erogenous areas. The anus is highly sensitive to touch and the insertion of a finger, object, or penis in the anus and rectum is part of some people's sexual activity. Anal intercourse is often thought to be primarily an act of male homosexuals. However, numerically, far more heterosexual couples engage in this activity than homosexuals and many homosexual men have not had experience with this type of sexual behavior (see Chapters 15 and 16 for a more detailed discussion).

The buttocks are regarded in some cultures as symbolic of female sexuality in much the sense that our society regards the female breasts. The buttocks are bulky groups of muscles covered by fat and skin, with a relatively sparse distribution of nerves sensitive to touch. The underlying muscles are important in the mechanical process of pelvic thrusting during sexual intercourse. As a target for spanking, the buttocks are sometimes provocative for those of both sexes who find this activity erotically arousing. As a visible part of the anatomy, the buttocks (especially when displayed in tight jeans, swim trunks, bikinis, or similar apparel) commonly serve as a form of sexual enticement.

Many other parts of the body can also have erotic allure. For instance, hair can be sensual or sexual: some women are turned on by their partner's hairy chest and some lovers like to stroke each other's hair. Well-developed muscles make males more attractive to some females, whereas others are less impressed or actually turned off by this "he-man" appearance. Nibbling an earlobe, caressing the face, and touching fingertips can all be part of a sexual encounter and all may be a source of excitation. Our attempt here is not to provide an exhaustive catalogue but to demonstrate the wide range of what can be sexual.

We each have a unique appearance to our sexual anatomy and an even more individual experience of sexual feelings and interactions. As we have repeatedly stressed, the variations—even anatomically—from one person to another are considerable. Unfortunately, some people are preoccupied with the notion that "biggest is best" and others believe that sexual satisfaction is mainly a matter of "pushing the right buttons." Instead, we believe that a mechanical view of sex often leads to a mechanical experience, whereas a view of sex as a matter of comfort, mood, and feelings combined with physical sensations and response is more likely to be fulfilling and fun.

SUMMARY

1. Sexual anatomy includes the organs of reproduction and the parts of the body that are potential sources of sexual pleasure. Accurate knowledge about sexual anatomy can help people distinguish between fact and myth and can lead to a better understanding of one's self and one's partner.

2. The female vulva consists of the mons, the inner and outer labia, the clitoris, and the perineum. The clitoris is not a miniature penis. It is a unique organ, richly endowed with sensory nerves, that serves solely as a receptor and transformer of sexual sensations.

3. The opening of the vagina is partially covered by a membrane called the hymen, which is sometimes mistakenly thought to be a foolproof indication of female virginity. The vagina itself is an internal organ, capable of expanding and contracting, with relatively few sensory nerve endings except near its opening. The vaginal lining is similar to that found inside the mouth, and vaginal lubrication originates from this surface. There is currently considerable controversy over the possible existence of the "G spot," which is claimed by some to be an anatomic area in the front wall of the vagina that has a high degree of erotic sensitivity.

4. The uterus is a hollow muscular organ, part of which (the cervix) protrudes into the vagina.

5. The male sex organs include the penis, scrotum, testes, and various internal structures. The penis is made up of three cylinders of spongy tissue with a rich network of blood vessels. There is great variation from male to male in the size of the nonerect penis; but with erection, size differences tend to diminish.

6. The glans, or head, of the penis is covered by foreskin in the uncircumcised male but is exposed in a male who has been circumcised. Circumcision has not been proved to have any effect, positive or negative, on sexual feeling or responsivity.

7. The scrotum is a sac of skin underneath the penis that contains the testes. Muscle fibers in the scrotum move the testes closer to or farther away from the body in response to temperature changes or exercise in order to facilitate sperm production.

8. Sperm made in the testes are carried by a long tubing system (the epididymis and vas deferens) inside the body. Sperm are mixed with seminal fluid from the prostate gland and seminal vesicles to make up semen.

9. The breasts are basically modified sweat glands, but in our society the female breasts have assumed major sexual importance. Not all women find that breast stimulation is a sexual turn-on, and many women are concerned about the size (or lack of size) of their breasts.

10. The mouth, tongue, lips, thighs, buttocks, anus, and skin are other parts of the body often involved in sexual activity and can be a source of erotic arousal.

Thought Questions

1. How do you think children should be taught about sexual anatomy? When should this teaching begin? Should children be encouraged to use the correct terms, or are slang words good enough? If slang words are used, are some more appropriate than others?

2. In what ways are females in our society often given negative messages about their anatomies? Are males also given such messages?

3. Compare the clitoris and the penis in terms of function, value, implications, and so on. The penis has at times been given a prominent role in myth, art, literature, and even scientific ideas (such as Freud's). Why not the clitoris?

4. Operations for breast enlargement or reduction are common in our society. Are these medically justifiable (and thus properly paid for by Medicaid and insurance), or are they primarily done for purposes of vanity?

5. Is the uncircumcised male at a disadvantage in our culture? Why or why not? Apart from religion, what other factors might contribute to parents deciding whether or not to have a baby boy circumcised?

6. The text states that "Under most circumstances, the first intercourse experience for a

girl or woman is not painful or marked by a great deal of bleeding." What is your experience in this respect? What is it like "the first time" for both sexes?

Suggested Readings

Ayalah, D., and Weinstock, I. J. *Breasts.* New York: Summit Books, 1979. An informal and informative look at how women of all ages react to their breasts.

Boston Women's Health Book Collective. *The New Our Bodies, Ourselves.* New York: Simon & Schuster, 1984. A readable and practical collection of facts and insights into female sexuality and reproduction, updated extensively from an earlier edition.

Diagram Group. *Man's Body: An Owner's Manual.* New York: Paddington Press/Two Continents Publishing Group, 1976. Although there are no really good books on the subject of male sexual anatomy, this straightforward book includes some interesting material and diagrams.

Federation of Feminist Women's Health Centers. *A New View of a Woman's Body.* New York: Simon & Schuster, 1981. A profusely illustrated guide to female anatomy and health care. Excellent color photos of the cervix and vulva.

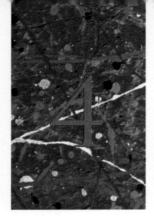

▼

Sexual Physiology

An orgasm is like a rocket ride. First the ascent, then the blackout, and after that the burst of light as the golden apple turns into the golden sun and azure skies with a slow parachute until the earth appears below, streams and meadows or a city street. You slowly touch and bounce up again. . . . Then you slowly touch once more, and then the afterglow and the deep refreshing sleep. *(Berne, 1971, p. 233)*

Orgasm can be a very mild experience, like a ripple or peaceful sigh; it can be a very sensuous experience where our body glows with warmth; it can be an intense experience with crying out and thrashing movements; it can be an ecstatic experience with momentary loss of awareness. *(Boston Women's Health Book Collective, 1976, p. 45)*

Sometimes I think orgasms are overrated. Getting there is more than half the fun. *(Comment by a 23-year-old woman, Authors' files)*

People interpret their sexual responses in various ways, as these quotations show. But the basic details of how the body responds to sexual arousal are identical whether the stimulation comes from touching, kissing, intercourse, masturbation, fantasy, watching a movie, or reading a book. This statement does not imply that sex is just a mechanical process, any more than dancing or playing the violin are "only" mechanical because certain parts of the body are involved in these activities. Human sexual response is multidimensional, with input from feelings and thoughts, learning and language, personal and cultural values, and many other sources combining with our biological reflexes to create a total experience.

To understand the complexities of human sexuality, it is helpful to become familiar with the details of sexual physiology (the functions of our sexual anatomy). Learning about the various responses of the body during sexual arousal and about the forces that regulate them will increase your awareness of your own and your partner's responses and may clarify many misconceptions, myths, and questions about sex. It is also important to understand sexual physiology to comprehend many sexual disorders discussed later in the book.

SOURCES OF SEXUAL AROUSAL

When people talk about sexual arousal, they frequently say they are "turned on," "revved up," or "hot." Each phrase likens sexual arousal to an energy system, and, as a starting point, this comparison is useful. From a scientific perspective, sexual arousal can be defined as a state of activation of a complex system of reflexes involving the sexual organs and the nervous system. The brain itself, the controlling part of the nervous system, operates with electrical and chemical impulses "wired" to the rest of the body through the spinal cord and peripheral nerves. Signals from other parts of the body (like the skin, genitals, breasts) are integrated and focused in the brain, for without sexual thoughts, feelings, or images, sexual response is fragmentary and incomplete. At times, sexual arousal may be largely a cerebral event: that is, a person may be aroused while no visible physical changes are occurring elsewhere in the body. On other occasions, genital sensations can be so intense that they block out awareness of almost everything else.

Sexual arousal can occur under a wide variety of circumstances. It may be the result of voluntary actions such as kissing, hugging, reading a sexy book, or going to an erotic movie. Sexual arousal can also be unexpected, unwanted, or even alarming. Consider, for instance, the following situations:

(1) a 12-year-old boy gets an erection while taking a shower in a crowded all-male locker room at school; (2) a female college student who is an ardent feminist becomes sexually aroused while watching a rape scene in a movie; (3) a female medical student is sexually excited when she examines an elderly male patient; (4) a male lawyer is sexually aroused by discussions with a female client who hires him to help her obtain a divorce. These people may be embarrassed or uncomfortable temporarily, but unexpected sexual arousal is normal and happens to most of us occasionally.

The sources of sexual arousal are also varied. The process of getting "turned on" may be triggered by direct physical contact such as a touch or a kiss or may be activated by a verbal invitation ("let's make love"), a nonverbal message (body language), or a visual cue (such as nudity or a particular clothing style). It may also spring from fantasies or the most everyday occurrences—clothing rubbing against the genitals, the rhythm of a moving vehicle, or taking a bath or shower. Sexual arousal occurs in all age groups, from infants to the elderly, and it occurs when we are asleep as well as when we are awake. Men have about a half dozen erections during a night's sleep (the erections usually last five to ten minutes), and women have similar episodes of vaginal lubrication during sleep (Masters and Johnson, 1966; Abel et al., 1979). These reflex responses occur automatically and are not controlled by the specific content of dreams.

THE SEXUAL RESPONSE CYCLE

Before the 1960s, relatively little was known about the way the body responds during sexual arousal. Scientists were not convinced by Kinsey's claims that some women had more than one orgasm at a time (Pomeroy, 1966), and it was thought that vaginal lubrication was produced by glands in the cervix and Bartholin's glands. The mechanisms controlling erection and ejaculation in the male were incompletely understood. As a matter of propriety, sexual response was studied in animals, not people. In this climate, the results of an investigation of sexual physiology based on direct laboratory observation of more than 10,000 episodes of sexual activity in 382 women and 312 men first appeared (Masters and Johnson, 1966).

The findings of this study indicated that human sexual response could be described as a cycle with four stages: **excitement, plateau, orgasm,** and **resolution.** These stages correspond to varying levels of sexual arousal and describe the typical responses people have during sexual function. Although it is convenient to use the cycle as a model for descriptive purposes, remember that the stages are arbitrarily defined. They are not always clearly separated from one another and may vary considerably both in one person at different times and between people. Bear in mind also that the physiological processes of sexual response are not simply mechanical movements detached from thoughts or feelings but are part of the sexual involvement and identity of the whole person.

Although the sexual response cycle usually follows a consistent pattern of progression, the sim-

plified schematic patterns of sexual response may vary widely, as Figure 4.1 reveals. Sometimes excitation is rapid and leads quickly to orgasm. On other occasions, excitement mounts slowly over a period of hours—while having a romantic, intimate meal, for example—and the rest of the cycle may seem brief in comparison. The plateau stage may not always lead to orgasm as the high levels of arousal that characterize this phase may dissipate; and a person may slip back to the excitement phase. If sexual stimulation stops, a person may also drift back into an unaroused state.

There are two basic physiologic reactions during human sexual response. The first is **vasocongestion,** an increased amount of blood concentrated in body tissues in the genitals and female breasts. The second is increased **neuromuscular tension** or **myotonia.** Here, tension does not refer to a negative

Figure 4.1   The Sexual Response Cycle

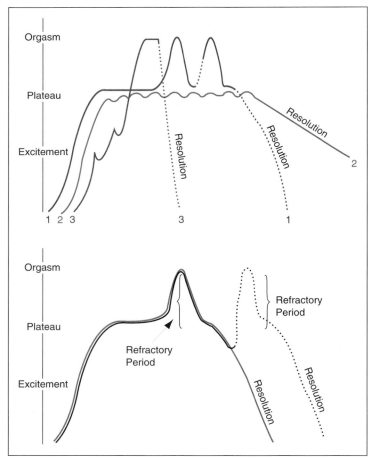

(a) Three representative variations of female sexual response. Pattern 1 shows multiple orgasm; pattern 2 shows arousal that reaches the plateau level without going on to orgasm (note that resolution occurs very slowly); and pattern 3 shows several brief drops in the excitement phase followed by an even more rapid resolution phase.
(b) The most typical pattern of male sexual response. The dotted line shows one possible variation: a second orgasm and ejaculation occurring after the refractory period is over. Numerous other variations are possible, including patterns that would match 2 and 3 of the female response cycle.

Source: *From William H. Masters and Virginia E. Johnson,* Human Sexual Response. *© 1966 by William H. Masters and Virginia E. Johnson. Reprinted by permission of Little, Brown and Company.*

physical state ("feeling tense") but to a buildup of energy in the nerves and muscles. Myotonia occurs throughout the body in response to sexual arousal, not simply in the genital region.

Although there are some differences in male and female sexual response, many details are similar. The physiology of sexual response is also the same for heterosexuals and homosexuals (Masters and Johnson, 1979).

Before we discuss the specific details of sexual response, a note of caution is in order. It is often tempting to equate the speed, size, and strength of sexual responses (such as erection, vaginal lubrication, or muscular contractions during orgasm) with the gratification a person experiences or with his or her proficiency as a lover. This is like saying that a bowl of chili is "better" than sirloin steak simply because chili causes a faster and larger secretion of digestive juices than steak. In both cases ("better" digestive response, "better" sexual response), the degree to which one experience is "better" than the other depends on your perspective *and* on your personal satisfaction.

Excitement

Excitation results from sexual stimulation, which may be physical, psychological, or a combination of the two. Sexual responses are like other physiological processes that may be triggered not only by direct contact but by vision, smell, thought, or emotion. For example, thinking about food, smelling fresh baked goods, or watching a television commercial may prompt salivation and gastric acid production; and fear may activate a complex set of reflexes including sweating, a faster pulse rate, and increased blood pressure.

Female

The first sign of sexual excitation in the female is the appearance of vaginal lubrication, which starts 10 to 30 seconds after the onset of sexual stimulation. Vaginal lubrication occurs because vasocongestion in the walls of the vagina leads to moisture seeping across the vaginal lining in a process called **transudation.** Beads of vaginal secretion first appear as isolated droplets which flow together and eventually moisten the entire inner surface of the vagina. Early in the excitement stage the quantities of fluid may be so small that neither the woman

nor her partner notices it. As vaginal lubrication increases, it sometimes flows out of the vagina, moistening the labia and the vaginal opening, but this depends on the woman's position and the type of sexual play going on.

The consistency, quantity, and odor of vaginal lubrication varies considerably from one woman to another and also varies in the same woman from time to time. Contrary to commonly held beliefs, the amount of vaginal lubrication is *not* necessarily indicative of the woman's level of sexual arousal, and the presence of vaginal lubrication does not mean the woman is "ready" for intercourse. Vaginal lubrication makes insertion of the penis into the vagina easier and smoother and prevents discomfort during intravaginal thrusting.

excitement phase first phase of the human sexual response cycle caused by physical and/or psychological stimulation. It is characterized by increasing levels of myotonia and by vasocongestion.

plateau phase the phase of human sexual response following excitement, in which a leveling off of sexual tensions occurs. This phase can be short or long prior to reaching levels required to trigger orgasm.

orgasm (or' gas um) the third and shortest phase of the human sexual response cycle. A total body response involving the sudden discharge of accumulated sexual tension.

resolution last phase of human sexual response following orgasm or maximum excitement in which the body returns to an unaroused state.

★ **vasocongestion** (vas' o kun jes' chun) an increased amount of blood concentrated in body tissues, especially in the genitals and female breasts during sexual arousal. In the male it causes erection and in the female an increase in the size of the clitoris and transudation of fluid in the vagina.

★ **neuromuscular tension** (new' rō mus' kew lur) buildup of energy in the nerves and muscles sometimes caused by sexual arousal.

★ **myotonia** (mī' ō tō nē uh) involuntary contraction of muscle.

transudation (trans' ū dā' shun) the passing of a fluid through a membrane, especially the lubrication in the vagina during sexual arousal.

Figure 4.2   Internal Changes in the Female Sexual Response Cycle

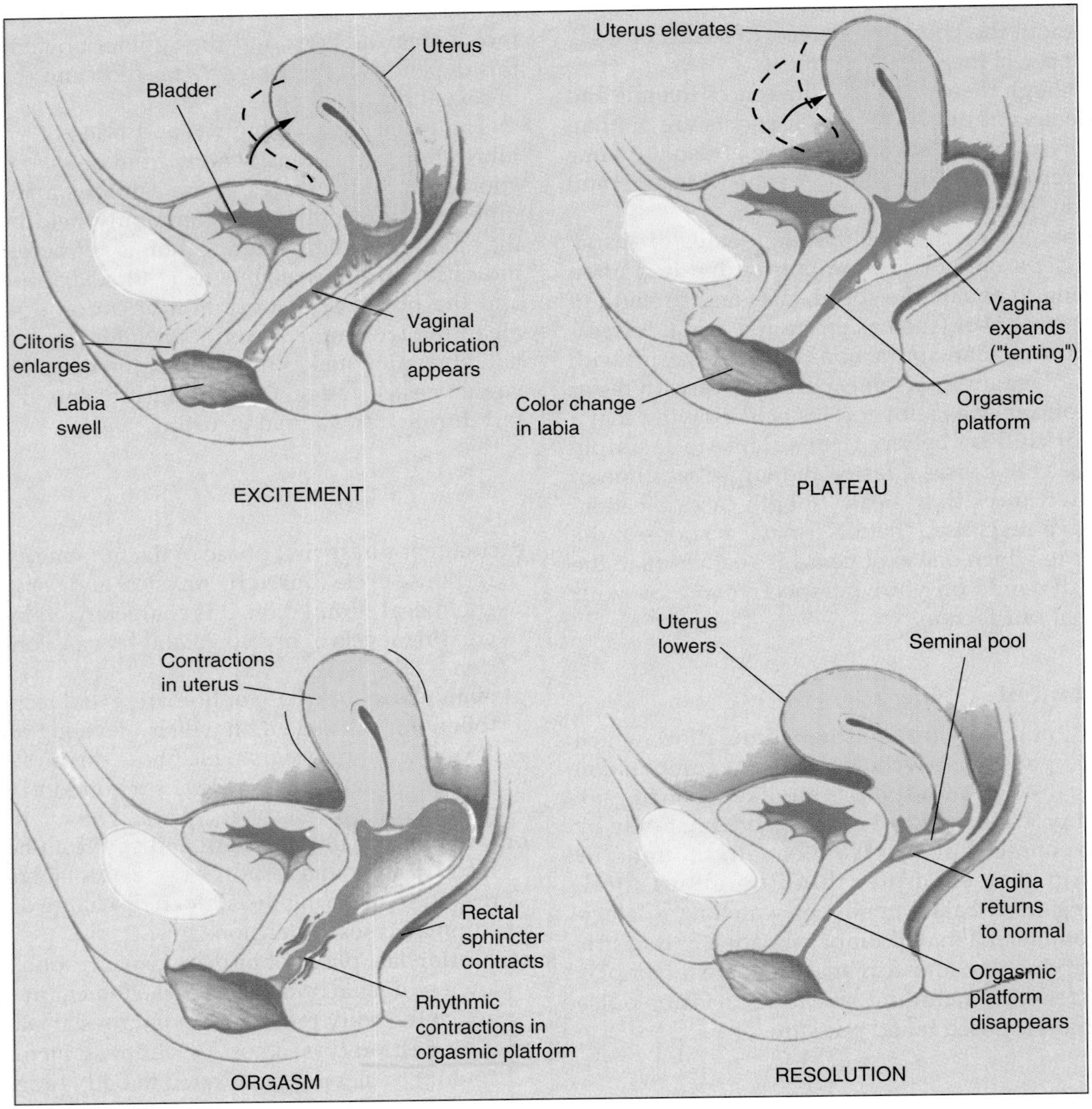

Other changes also occur in women during the excitement phase. The inner two-thirds of the vagina expand, the cervix and uterus are pulled upward, and the outer lips of the vagina flatten and move apart (see Figure 4.2). In addition, the inner lips of the vagina enlarge in diameter, and the clitoris increases in size as a result of vasocongestion. A woman's nipples typically become erect during the excitement phase as a result of contrac-

tions of small muscle fibers. Late in the excitement phase (again as a result of vasocongestion), the veins on the breasts become more visible and there also may be a small increase in breast size.

Male

The most prominent physical sign of sexual excitation in men is erection of the penis, which usually occurs within a few seconds after sexual stimula-

Figure 4.3   External and Internal Changes in the Male Sexual Response Cycle

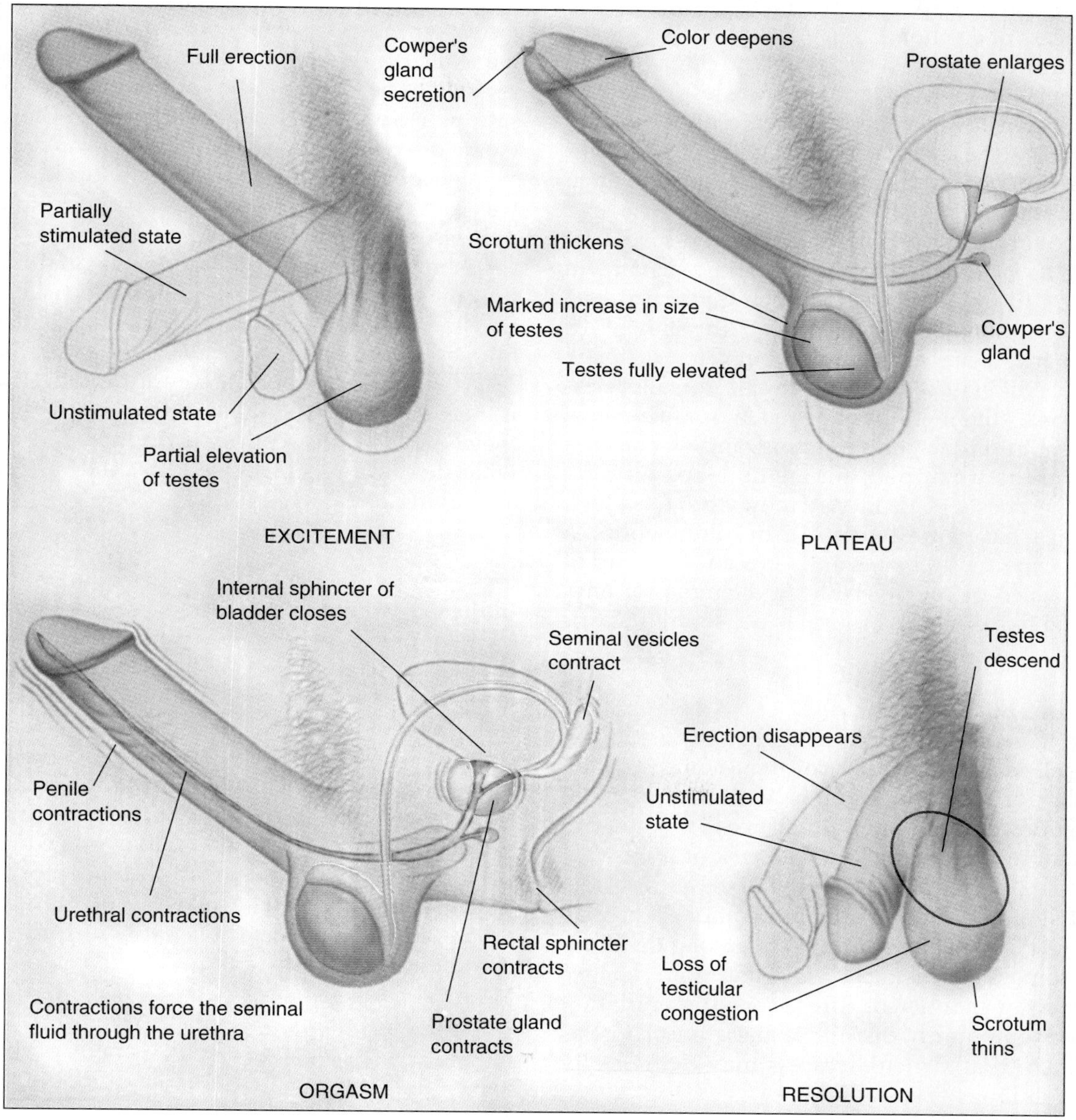

Full erection

Cowper's gland secretion

Color deepens

Prostate enlarges

Partially stimulated state

Scrotum thickens

Marked increase in size of testes

Cowper's gland

Unstimulated state

Testes fully elevated

Partial elevation of testes

EXCITEMENT

PLATEAU

Internal sphincter of bladder closes

Seminal vesicles contract

Testes descend

Erection disappears

Unstimulated state

Penile contractions

Urethral contractions

Rectal sphincter contracts

Loss of testicular congestion

Scrotum thins

Contractions force the seminal fluid through the urethra

Prostate gland contracts

ORGASM

RESOLUTION

tion starts (Figure 4.3). Although this response may seem very different from vaginal lubrication, they are parallel events that both occur because of vasocongestion. Erection results from the spongy tissues of the penis rapidly filling with blood. It is not certain at present whether engorgement occurs because the veins that drain the penis cannot keep up with this rapid filling or if special structures called "polsters" in the blood vessels of the penis limit outflow. Whatever the exact mechanism, the increased size and firmness of the erect penis are due to increased fluid pressure: erection can thus be viewed in simplest terms as a hydraulic event. Despite this seeming mechanical simplicity, a man may be physically and/or psychologically aroused and not have a firm erection, particularly under conditions of anxiety or fatigue. Contrary to some common misconceptions, there is neither a bone in the human penis (although erections are sometimes called "boners") nor a penis muscle that controls the process of erection.[1]

In addition to erection, the skin ridges of the scrotum begin to smooth out and the testes are partially drawn toward the body. Late in the excitement phase, the testes increase slightly in size. Nipple erection occurs during excitation for some men but not others.

Although many people think of male sexual response as nearly instantaneous and constant, in real life it does not always happen this way. Literary descriptions of a "pulsating," "throbbing," or "steel-hard" penis are common but often fictional. As Zilbergeld (1978) observes, in our unrealistic expectations, "the mere sight or touch of a woman is sufficient to set the penis jumping, and whenever a man's fly is unzipped, his penis leaps out. . . . Nowhere does a penis merely mosey out for a look at what's happening" (p. 24). In other words, a man is expected to be instantly erect at the drop of a bra, which of course creates a dilemma for anyone who finds that his arousal is not so dramatic or visible.

Variations in Excitement

As we have seen, the physical changes of the excitement phase are neither constant nor always increasing for men and women. Mental or physical distractions can and often do decrease the buildup of sexual tension that is the hallmark of excitation. A honking horn, a knock on the door, an inopportune telephone ring, a shift in position, a muscle cramp, or a growling stomach are among the innumerable possible distractions. In addition, changes of tempo or manner of direct sexual stimulation can also temporarily disrupt sexual arousal, just as too much of a particular caress may temporarily cause a dulling of sensations.

Some people become upset or worried if their initial sexual arousal does not build steadily to a shattering peak. If a man's erection recedes even briefly, he may think, "I'm losing it" or his partner

may wonder, "What am I doing wrong?" If a woman's vagina seems to get dry or her nipples lose their erection, she (or her partner) may have the same concerns. As a result, sexual spontaneity is likely to be lessened and awareness of body sensations is reduced. In such situations, the initial worry often becomes a self-fulfilling prophecy.

Vasocongestive mechanisms of sexual arousal wax and wane in everyone, just as most biological processes fluctuate a bit. An erection may be diminishing in firmness or size, or vaginal lubrication may seem to cease, although physical sensations and neuromuscular tension indicate that the man and woman are clearly nearing the plateau phase of the sexual response cycle. In this example, if the partners become alarmed or give up because they "see" that their physical response is less than what they want or expect it to be, they are not really giving themselves a chance.

Plateau

In the excitement phase, there is a marked increase in sexual tension above baseline (unaroused) levels. As Figure 4.1 shows, in the plateau phase, high levels of sexual arousal are maintained and intensified, potentially setting the stage for orgasm. The duration of the plateau phase varies widely. For men who have difficulty controlling ejaculation, this phase may be exceptionally brief. In some women, a short plateau phase may precede a particularly intense orgasm. For other people, a long, leisurely time at the plateau level is an intimate and erotic "high" that may be a satisfying end in its own right.

Female

During the plateau phase in women prominent vasocongestion in the outer third of the vagina causes the tissues to swell. This reaction, called the **orgasmic platform,** narrows the opening of the vagina by 30 percent or more (Figure 4.2). One reason penis size is not so important to a woman's physical stimulation during intercourse is that her outer vagina or orgasmic platform "grips" the penis if plateau levels of arousal are reached.[2] Dur-

---

[1]Many animals have a penis bone (**os penis**). The late Dr. Francis Ryan, a zoologist who taught a popular course on comparative anatomy at Columbia University, delighted in waving a large, baseball bat–sized bone in the air and asking, "Does anyone know what this is?" After no response from his all-male class, he would declare, "This, gentlemen, is the *os penis* of the Arctic Whale." He would pause then for effect before saying, "Life in the Arctic is a stiff proposition."

[2]As we mentioned in Chapter 3, some women may find a large penis to be important for *psychological* stimulation, and some women claim to receive more physical stimulation from a large penis. As someone once said, "Different strokes for different folks."

Figure 4.4   The Clitoris and Labia in the Female Sexual
Response Cycle

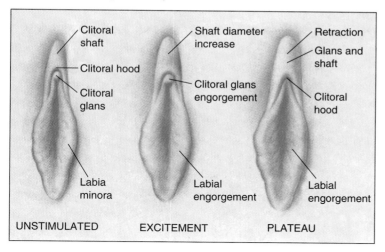

In the plateau phase, the clitoris seems to disappear
beneath its hood, but it is actually quite engorged. The
orgasmic phase is omitted because of lack of information.

ing the plateau phase, the inner two-thirds of the
vagina expand slightly more in size as the uterus
becomes more elevated in a process known as
"tenting." The production of vaginal lubrication
often slows during this phase compared with excitation, especially if the plateau phase is prolonged.

The clitoris pulls back against the pubic bone
during the plateau phase. This change, coupled
with the vasocongestion occurring in the vaginal
lips, hides the clitoris (Figure 4.4) and partially protects its head from direct touch. No loss of clitoral
sensation occurs during these changes, however,
and stimulation of the mons or the labia will result
in clitoral sensations.[3]

The inner lips enlarge dramatically as a result of
engorgement with blood, doubling or even tripling
in thickness. As this happens, the inner lips push
the outer lips apart, providing more immediate access to the opening of the vagina. Once this reaction
has occurred, vivid color changes develop in the
inner lips. The inner lips of women who have never
been pregnant range from pink to bright red, while
those in women who have been pregnant range
from bright red to a deep wine color because of
greater vascular supply delivering more blood flow
to this area. Masters and Johnson (1966) noted that

if effective sexual stimulation continues once this
"sex skin" color change appears, orgasm invariably
follows. In more than 7500 cycles of female sexual
response, an orgasm never occurred without the
preceding color change of the inner lips.

Late in the excitement phase, the areola of the female breast begins to swell. During the plateau
phase, swelling continues to the point that the earlier nipple erection usually becomes obscured (Figure 4.5). Increases in breast size during the plateau
phase are striking in women who have not breast-
fed a child, averaging 20 to 25 percent above baseline levels. For women who have previously
nursed a child, this increase is much less pronounced or nonexistent because of their more developed venous drainage. However, this does not
reduce erotic sensations in the breasts.

Late in the excitement phase or early in the
plateau phase, a reddish, spotty skin color change
resembling measles develops in 50 to 75 percent of
women and about one-fourth of men. This **sex
flush** generally begins just below the breastbone in
the upper region of the abdomen and then spreads

os penis penis bone present in some animal species
    but not in humans or other primates.
orgasmic platform the narrowing of the vagina
    during sexual excitement due to vasocongestion.
sex flush a temporary reddish, spotty, rashlike
    color change sometimes developing during sex-
    ual excitement. Usually on the abdomen and
    breasts, it can spread to any areas of the body.

---

[3]Marriage manuals in the 1950s all seemed to instruct the
male that finding and stimulating the clitoris was the key
to female sexual responsiveness. We wonder how many
men panicked when this phase of clitoral retraction
made the clitoris seem to disappear.

Figure 4.5   Breast Changes During the Female Sexual
Response Cycle

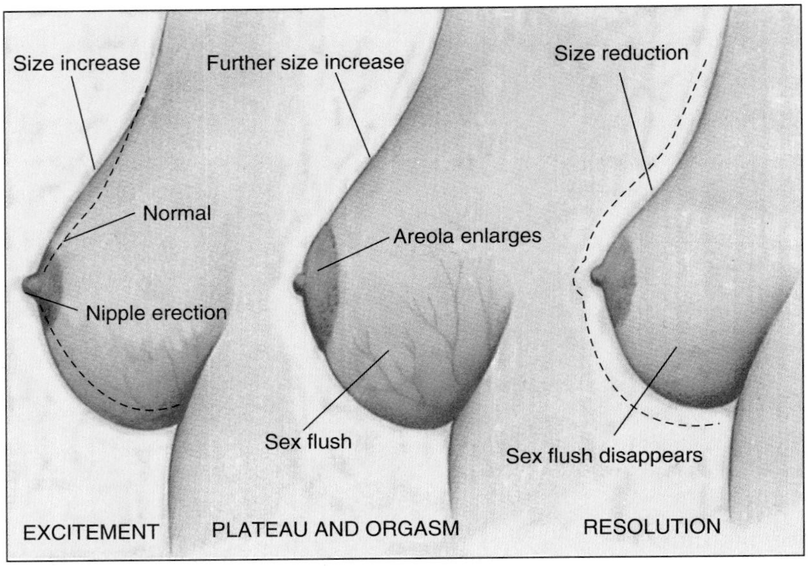

After orgasm, the rapid reduction in swelling of the areola often makes it appear as though the nipple has again become erect.

rapidly over the breasts and front of the chest. It may also appear on other parts of the body, including the neck, buttocks, back, arms, legs, and face. The sex flush results from changes in the pattern of blood flow just below the surface of the skin.

Male

During the male's plateau phase (Figure 4.3), the diameter of the head of the penis near the coronal ridge increases slightly. This area often deepens in color due to pooling of blood. Vasocongestion also causes the testes to swell, and they become 25 to 50 percent larger than in the unstimulated state.

As sexual tension mounts toward orgasm, the testes not only continue to elevate but also begin to rotate forward so that their back surfaces rest in firm contact with the perineum (the area between the scrotum and the anus). Full elevation of the testes indicates that orgasm is imminent. In some men, particularly over age 50, the testes elevate only partially. Incomplete elevation of the testes during the plateau phase is frequently associated with reduction of ejaculatory pressure during the male's orgasmic experience (Masters and Johnson, 1966).

Small amounts of clear fluid may sometimes appear from the male urethra during the plateau phase. This fluid is thought to come from Cowper's glands and, as mentioned in the previous chapter, occasionally carries live sperm. Many men experience a sensation of internal pressure or warmth during the plateau phase that corresponds to vasocongestion in the region of the prostate gland and seminal vesicles.

In addition to the sensations and changes just described, men and women experience several changes throughout their bodies during the plateau phase. A generalized increase in neuromuscular tension is particularly apparent in the buttocks and thighs. The heart rate increases, sometimes leading to a prominent awareness of heart thumping inside the chest. Breathing also becomes faster and there is a small increase in blood pressure, too.

Orgasm

If effective sexual stimulation continues late in the plateau phase, a point may be reached where the body suddenly discharges its accumulated sexual tension in a peak of sexual arousal called **orgasm.** Orgasm is sometimes called climax or coming. Eric Berne (1971) observed, "Climax started off as a decent enough word, but it has been so overworked on the newsstands that it now sounds like the moment when two toasted marshmallows finally get stuck to each other" (p. 3). We also prefer the word *orgasm*. Biologically, orgasm is the shortest phase of the sexual response cycle, usually lasting for only a few seconds during which rhythmic muscular contractions produce intense physical sensations followed by rapid relaxation. Psychologically, orgasm is usually a time of pleasure and suspended thought—the mind turns inward to enjoy the personal experience.

Orgasms vary not only for one person at different times but also for each individual. Sometimes orgasm is an explosive, ecstatic avalanche of sensations, while at other times it is milder, less intense, and less dramatic. While "an orgasm is an orgasm is an orgasm," one orgasm may differ from another just as a glass of ice water tastes better and is more satisfying if you are hot and thirsty than if you are cool and not thirsty at all. Different intensities of orgasms arise from physical factors such as fatigue and the time since the last orgasm as well as from a wide range of psychosocial factors, including mood, relation to partner, activity, expectations, and feelings about the experience.

For all these reasons, trying to define or describe orgasm is a difficult task because each individual's subjective experience includes a psychosocial as well as physiological dimension. Measuring intense muscular contractions during one orgasm does not mean that it is necessarily perceived as "better than" another orgasm with less intense bodily changes. A milder physiological orgasm may be *experienced* as bigger, better, or more satisfying than a physiologically more intense one.

Female

Until the mid-twentieth century, many people (including some medical authorities) believed that women were not capable of orgasm. This belief undoubtedly reflected a cultural bias: sex was seen as something the man did *to* the woman for his own gratification. Women were told for centuries to "do their wifely duties" by making themselves available to their husbands for sex yet were also cautioned that "proper" women did not enjoy sex. Since a sign of physical pleasure or orgasm was thought to be "unladylike," it followed that women were not able to have orgasms. In other words, females were told, "You can't have any physical sexual release, and even if you can, you shouldn't." It

is now clear, however, that orgasm occurs in both sexes.

Orgasm in the female is marked by simultaneous rhythmic muscular contractions of the uterus, the outer third of the vagina (the orgasmic platform), and the anal sphincter (Figure 4.2). The first few contractions are intense and close together (at 0.8-second intervals). As orgasm continues, the contractions diminish in force and duration and occur at less regular intervals. A mild orgasm may have only 3 to 5 contractions, while an intense orgasm may have 10 to 15.

Orgasm is a total body response, not just a pelvic event. Brain wave patterns show distinctive changes during orgasm (Cohen, Rosen, and Goldstein, 1976), and muscles in many different body regions contract during this phase of sexual response. In addition, the sex flush achieves its greatest intensity and its widest distribution at the time of orgasm.

Women often describe the sensations of an orgasm as beginning with a momentary sense of suspension, quickly followed by an intensely pleasurable feeling that usually begins at the clitoris and rapidly spreads throughout the pelvis. The physical sensations of the genitals are often described as warm, electric, or tingly, and these usually spread throughout the body. Finally, most women feel muscle contractions in their vagina or lower pelvis, often described as "pelvic throbbing."

Despite a popular misconception, most women do not ejaculate during orgasm. The erroneous belief that women ejaculate probably stems from descriptions in erotic novels of fluid gushing from the vagina as a woman writhes and moans at the peak moment of sexual passion. Such descriptions may sell books but are not particularly accurate.

There is conflicting opinion about whether a different form of female ejaculation occurs. Various workers have claimed that some women expel semen-like fluid from the urethra at the time of orgasm (Grafenberg, 1950; Sevely and Bennett, 1978; Belzer, 1981; Perry and Whipple, 1981). It has been theorized that this fluid may come from a "female prostate," rudimentary glands (Skene's glands) around the urethra near the neck of the bladder that derive embryologically from the same tissues

orgasm the third and shortest phase of the human sexual response cycle. A total body response involving the sudden discharge of accumulated sexual tension.

PERSONAL PERSPECTIVES

Describing Orgasm

Previous research has shown that expert judges were unable to reliably distinguish between written reports of male and female orgasms (Proctor, Wagner, and Butler, 1974). The sex of the person describing orgasm in the following examples from our files may surprise you.

1. Like a mild explosion, it left me warm and relaxed after a searing heat that started in my genitals and raced to my toes and head.

2. Suddenly, after the tension built and built, I was soaring in the sky, going up, up, up, feeling the cool air rushing by. My insides were tingling and my skin was cool. My heart was racing in a good way, and breathing was a job.

3. Throbbing is the best word to say what it is like. The throbbing starts as a faint vibration, then builds up in wave after wave where time seems to stand still.

4. When I come it's either like an avalanche of pleasure, tumbling through me, or like a refreshing snack—momentarily satisfying, but then I'm ready for more.

5. My orgasms feel like pulsating bursts of energy starting in my pelvic area and then engulfing my whole body. Sometimes I feel like I'm in freefall, and sometimes I feel like my body's an entire orchestra playing a grand crescendo.

6. An orgasm feels like a dive, magnified many times over. First I feel my muscles tensing, then there's a leap into a cool lake, a sense of suspension and holding my breath, and then my whole body feels relaxed and tingling.

7. Exhilaration is the best word I can find. I feel all pumped up and then, instead of exploding, I am one big wave of happiness and whooshing feelings.

8. Some orgasms feel incredibly intense and earth-shattering, but other times orgasms feel like small, compact, self-contained moments.

9. I feel like a cork popping out of a champagne bottle.

10. There is a warm rush from my toes to my head, with a strong, pulsing rhythm. Then everything settles down like a pink sunset.

1.M   2.F   3.M   4.F   5.F   6.M   7.F   8.M   9.F   10.M

that develop into the prostate gland in males. In fact, some suggest that this "female prostate" is the anatomical site of the "G spot," but this idea—although stirring considerable controversy and conjecture—has not yet been proved scientifically (Bohlen, 1982; Kaplan, 1983). And, while a report on one woman with this ejaculation-like phenomenon indicated that the fluid was not urine (Addiego et al., 1981), a more detailed study of six other women who "ejaculated" showed that the fluid they expelled was indistinguishable from urine (Goldberg et al., 1983).

Further confusion in this area is caused by uncertainty over the number of women who have this ejaculation-like response. Perry and Whipple (1981) initially claimed that "perhaps 10 percent of females" had this response but later reported that they were finding "closer to 40 percent" of women "had ever experienced" female ejaculation (Ladas, Whipple, and Perry, 1982, p. 60). A more recent questionnaire survey also found that 40 percent of the women queried reported having experienced ejaculation at the moment of orgasm (Darling, Davidson, and Conway-Welch, 1990). In our own studies, a survey of approximately 300 women aged 18 to 40 revealed only 14 who claimed to note any gushing or expulsion of fluid at orgasm. However, we *have* observed several cases of women who expelled a type of fluid that was not urine (Masters, 1982).

Although it is clear that at least *some* women experience this ejaculation-like response, it should be realized that a number of these cases represent a condition called **urinary stress incontinence** in which urine is expelled from the urethra due to physical straining such as occurs with coughing, sneezing, or sexual arousal. Since this condition is usually correctable either by the use of Kegel exercises or minor surgery, medical evaluation is warranted if a woman is bothered by such a response.

Male

Orgasms in men, unlike those in women, occur in two distinct stages. In the first stage of orgasm, the vas deferens (the two tubes that carry sperm) and the prostate and seminal vesicles begin a series of contractions that force semen into the bulb of the urethra (Figure 4.3). The man experiences a sensation of **ejaculatory inevitability**—that is, the feeling of having reached the brink of control—as these contractions begin. This sense of inevitability is quite accurate because at this point the ejaculatory process cannot be stopped.[4] In the second stage of the male orgasm, contractions of the urethra and penis combine with contractions in the prostate gland to cause ejaculation, the spurting of semen out of the tip of the penis.

During ejaculation, the neck of the urinary bladder is tightly shut to ensure that semen moves forward and to avoid any mixing of urine and semen. The rhythmic contractions of the prostate, perineal muscles, and shaft of the penis (creating the physi-

cal force that propels semen on its journey) occur initially at 0.8-second intervals, just as in women, and account for the spurting of the semen during ejaculation. After the first three or four contractions of the penis, the intervals between contractions become longer and the intensity of the contractions tapers off.

Male orgasm and ejaculation are not one and the same process, although in most men and under most circumstances the two occur simultaneously. Orgasm refers specifically to the sudden rhythmic muscular contractions in the pelvic region and elsewhere in the body that effectively release accumulated sexual tension and the mental sensations accompanying this experience. Ejaculation refers to the release of semen, which sometimes can occur without the presence of orgasm. Orgasm without ejaculation is common in boys before puberty (Kinsey, Pomeroy, and Martin, 1948) and can also occur if the prostate is diseased or with the use of some drugs. Ejaculation without orgasm is less common but can occur in certain cases of neurological illness.

In **retrograde ejaculation,** the bladder neck does not close off properly during orgasm so that semen spurts backward into the bladder. This condition occurs in some men with multiple sclerosis, diabetes, or certain types of prostate surgery. There are no harmful effects, but infertility results and the man may have a different sensation during ejaculation.

The subjective experience of orgasm in men starts quite consistently with the sensation of deep warmth or pressure (sometimes accompanied by throbbing) that corresponds to ejaculatory inevitability. Orgasm is then felt as sharp, intensely pleasurable contractions involving the anal sphincter, rectum, perineum, and genitals, which some men describe as a sensation of pumping. A differ-

---

[4]Women do not have a consistently identifiable point of orgasmic inevitability that corresponds to the stage of ejaculatory inevitability in the male response cycle. Distractions can interrupt women's orgasms, whereas if the male has reached "inevitability," orgasm occurs no matter what.

urinary stress incontinence a condition in which urine leaks from the urethra during coughing, laughing, and/or sexual arousal.

ejaculatory inevitability the first stage of orgasm in men, a feeling of having passed the point where ejaculation can be controlled as the vas deferens, seminal vesicles, and prostate start contracting.

retrograde ejaculation condition in which the semen spurts backward into the bladder during orgasm because the bladder neck does not close off properly. It occurs in men with multiple sclerosis and diabetes and following some types of prostate surgery.

ent feeling, sometimes called a warm rush of fluid or a shooting sensation, describes the actual process of semen traveling through the urethra. In general, men's orgasms tend to be more uniform than women's, although all male orgasms are certainly not identical.

During the orgasmic phase in both sexes, there are high levels of myotonia evident throughout the body. Late in the plateau phase or during orgasm, the myotonia is often visible in facial muscles, where a grimace or frown may be seen. While this expression is sometimes viewed by a partner as an indication of displeasure or discomfort, it is actually an involuntary response that indicates high levels of sexual arousal. Muscle spasms or cramps in the hands or feet may also occur late in the plateau phase or during orgasm, and at the peak of orgasm the whole body may seem to become rigid for a moment.

Controversies About Female Orgasm

While many controversies about the nature of female orgasms exist, several deserve special mention. The first controversy originated with Freud, who believed that there were two types of female orgasm, a clitoral and a vaginal orgasm. Freud stated that clitoral orgasms (those originating from masturbation or other noncoital acts) were evidence of psychological immaturity, since the clitoris was the center of infantile sexuality in the female. Vaginal orgasms (those deriving from coitus) were "authentic" and "mature" since they demonstrated that normal psychosexual development was complete. In his essay "Some Psychological Consequences of the Anatomical Distinction Between the Sexes," Freud wrote that "the elimination of clitoral sexuality is a necessary precondition for the development of femininity." Many women were considered neurotic or were pushed into psychoanalysis because of this view (Schulman, 1971; Sherfey, 1972; LoPiccolo and Heiman, 1978).

Physiologically, all female orgasms follow the same reflex response patterns, no matter what the source of sexual stimulation. An orgasm that comes from rubbing the clitoris cannot be distinguished physiologically from one that comes from intercourse or breast stimulation alone (Masters and Johnson, 1966). This does not mean that all female orgasms feel the same, have the same intensity, or are identically satisfying. As discussed earlier, feelings and intensity are matters of perceptions, and satisfaction is influenced by many factors.

Some women prefer orgasms that occur as a result of intercourse, while others prefer masturbatory orgasms. Those who prefer coital orgasms often say that the overall experience is more satisfying, but the actual orgasm is less direct and intense. One study notes that many women find masturbatory orgasms to be more satisfying than coital ones, perhaps because the woman is not affected by her partner's style, needs, or tempo (Hite, 1977). In other reports, attempts have been made to differentiate between "vulval orgasm," "uterine orgasm," and "blended orgasm" (Singer and Singer, 1972), or other classifications of orgasmic types (Fox and Fox, 1969; Clark, 1970; Fisher, 1973; Bohlen et al., 1982). Ladas, Whipple, and Perry (1982) have claimed that stimulation of the "G spot" produces a completely different type of orgasm than does stimulation of the clitoris: one in which no orgasmic platform forms, and in which the uterus, instead of elevating and expanding the inner portion of the vagina, "seems to be pushed down and the upper portion of the vagina compresses." However, data to support these claims have not yet been published. Despite the continued controversy about "types" of female orgasms, the idea that one type is immature or less good than another has generally been discarded (Masters and Johnson, 1966; Sherfey, 1972; Hite, 1977; Barbach, 1982).

A second controversy about female orgasm is the question of whether or not all women in good health are able to experience a coital orgasm without any other type of simultaneous stimulation. While Masters and Johnson (1966) and others (Sherfey, 1972; Barbach, 1980) believe all women have this ability, some sexologists believe that there may be a group of women who do not. Helen Kaplan (1974) seems to favor the latter view when she says "this pattern may represent a normal variant of female sexuality, at least for some women" (p. 374). And various studies show that the number of women who experience orgasm regularly during intercourse is about 40 to 50 percent (Kinsey et al., 1953; Fisher, 1973; Hite, 1977; Wilcox and Hager, 1980). Many authorities believe that lack of coital orgasm is usually caused by factors such as anxiety, poor communication between partners, hostility, distrust, or low self-esteem. However, if certain females are incapable of experiencing a sexual reflex due to physiological factors (Brindley and Gillan, 1982), it would have implications in diagnosing and treating some women's sexual problems, as discussed in Chapter 21.

Another controversial area has to do with the role of the muscles surrounding the vagina in orgasm. Both Arnold Kegel (a surgeon who was the inventor of the "Kegel exercises") and other workers (Perry and Whipple, 1981; Ladas, Whipple, and Perry, 1982; Graber, 1982) claim the condition of the pubococcygeus muscle (PC muscle) is an important determinant of the occurrence of orgasms in women. However, other studies fail to document any correlation between PC muscle strength and female orgasmic responsiveness (Sultan and Chambles, 1982) and have also found that using the Kegel exercises did not improve orgasmic responsivity in nonorgasmic women (Trudel and Saint Laurent, 1983).

Finally, although many researchers believe that most women don't feel that orgasm is a necessity for sexual satisfaction, a study by Waterman and Chiauzzi (1982) found that "orgasm consistency was significantly related to sexual satisfaction in females but not in males." While this doesn't mean that women who have the most frequent orgasms are happiest sexually, it does imply that not having orgasms (or not having them very often) may correlate with sexual dissatisfaction.

Resolution

There is a major difference between male and female sexual response immediately following orgasm. Generally, females have the physical capability of being **multiorgasmic:** that is, they can have one or more additional orgasms within a short time without dropping below the plateau level of sexual arousal (Figure 4.1a, pattern 1). Being multiorgasmic depends on both continued effective sexual stimulation and sexual interest, neither of which is consistently present for most women. For this reason, some women never experience multiple orgasms, and others are multiorgasmic in only a small fraction of their sexual experiences. It is unusual for a woman to have multiple orgasms during most of her sexual activity.

Interestingly, multiple orgasm in females seems to occur more frequently during masturbation than intercourse. This may reflect several factors: (1) the relative ease of continuing sexual stimulation, (2) the lack of distraction by concerns about one's partner, and (3) the more frequent use of sexual fantasy by women during masturbation than during intercourse.

Men, on the other hand, are not able to have multiple orgasm if it is defined in the same way. Immediately after ejaculation, the male enters a **refractory period** (Figure 4.1b), a recovery time during which further orgasm or ejaculation is physiologically impossible. A partial or full erection may be maintained during the refractory period, but usually the erection subsides quickly. There is great variability in the length of the refractory period both within and between individual males, and it may last anywhere from a few minutes to many hours. For most males, this interval usually gets longer with each repeated ejaculation within a time span of several hours. In addition, as a man gets older, the refractory period gets longer. In 1978, Robbins and Jensen reported on 13 men who said thay had multiple orgasms by withholding ejaculation (only one of whom they studied in the laboratory), but their claims have not yet been fully substantiated. However, it does appear that at least a few men have the capacity to have multiple orgasms before a true refractory period sets in, although it should be stressed that this usually does not happen once ejaculation has occurred. However, Dunn and Trost (1989) have reported that in a small number of men, multiple nonejaculatory orgasms sometimes occur following an initial orgasm with ejaculation.

The period of return to the unaroused state is called the resolution phase. In this phase, which includes the refractory period in men, the anatomic and physiologic changes that occurred during the excitement and plateau phase reverse. In females, the orgasmic platform disappears as the muscular contractions of orgasm pump blood away from these tissues. The uterus moves back into its resting position, the color changes of the labia disappear, the vagina begins to shorten in both width and length, and the clitoris returns to its usual size and position (Figure 4.2). If the breasts enlarged earlier in the response cycle, they decrease in size at this

multiorgasmic (mul' tē or gaz' mik) the potential ability of women to have a series of identifiable orgasmic responses without dropping below the plateau level of arousal. Men do not share this capacity.

refractory period in the male, the period immediately following ejaculation during which further orgasm is physiologically impossible. This period is not present in the female response cycle.

time, and their aureolar tissue flattens out faster than the nipples themselves, giving the impression that the nipples are again erect (Figure 4.5). Stimulation of the clitoris, the nipples, or the vagina may be unpleasant or irritating during the postorgasmic phase.

In males, erection diminishes in two stages. First, as a result of orgasmic contractions that pump blood out of the penis, there is a partial loss of erection. In the slower, second stage of this process, genital blood flow returns to baseline (unaroused) patterns. The testes decrease in size and descend into the scrotum, moving away from the body, unless sexual stimulation is continued (Figure 4.3).

As both men and women return to their unaroused state, the "sex flush" disappears and prominent sweating is sometimes noticeable. A fast, heavy breathing pattern may be present just after orgasm, accompanied by a fast heartbeat, but both recede gradually as the entire body relaxes.

If there has been considerable excitement but orgasm has not occurred, resolution takes a longer time. Although certain changes occur quickly (such as disappearance of the orgasmic platform in women and the erection in men), there is sometimes a lingering sensation of pelvic heaviness or aching that is due to continued vasocongestion. This may create a condition of some discomfort, particularly if high levels of arousal were prolonged. Testicular aching ("blue balls") in men and pelvic congestion in women may be relieved by orgasms that occur during sleep or by masturbation. Although **nocturnal emissions** ("wet dreams") in young males are well known, females also can experience orgasm during sleep (Kinsey et al., 1953).

COMMON MYTHS ABOUT SEXUAL RESPONSE

In the preceding chapter, we discussed a number of misconceptions related to sexual anatomy and sexual satisfaction (e.g., a bigger penis always provides more stimulation to the female during intercourse). In light of the physiologic responses just considered, we can now debunk some other common myths about sex.

One commonly held belief is that males have a greater sexual capacity than females. The reverse is actually true. From the viewpoint of physical capability, females have an almost unlimited orgasmic potential, while men, because of the refractory period, are unable to have a rapid series of ejaculations. (While women do not have a true refractory period, orgasmic potential is undoubtedly restricted by fatigue. There may be other physiologic limitations not known at present.) Many males also find it difficult to obtain another erection shortly after ejaculation. From a mechanical perspective then, their capacity to participate in repeated intercourse usually does not match that of the opposite sex.

Another misconception about sexual response is that the male can *always* tell if his female partner had an orgasm. At times, the male may be unaware of his partner's orgasm because he is caught up in his own feelings of arousal or because he doesn't recognize the physical signs of female orgasm. This may occur either because his expectations are inaccurate, because he doesn't know what to expect, or because the accuracy of his sense of vision is lessened during high levels of sexual excitation. Some males are fooled by a partner who "fakes" orgasm by means of loud moans and groans, intense pelvic thrusting, heavy breathing, and voluntary contractions of the outer portion of the vagina.[5]

The notion that all orgasms are intense, earth-shattering, explosive events is another widespread sexual misconception that can probably be traced to the literary imagination. Although the reflex mechanisms of orgasmic response are fairly uniform, some orgasms are mild, fluttery, or warm, while others are blockbusters. These differences arise from variations in a person's physical state such as being tired, tense, having a sore throat or headache, or from variations in the emotions that accompany the sexual experience. The sensations of any physiologic process—drinking a glass of water, eating a meal, breathing, urinating, or sex—vary in different times and circumstances.

In the 1950s, the idea that "mutual orgasm" (both partners experiencing orgasm at the same time) was the ultimate peak in sexual pleasure became popular and was advocated enthusiastically in numerous marriage manuals. Many people tried

---

[5]Men also sometimes resort to sexual fakery. For both women and men, this may be motivated by the wish to please their partner. For a fuller discussion, see Chapter 21.

to "fine-tune" the timing of their responses, but working at sex usually resulted in a loss of spontaneity and fun. While mutual orgasm can be exhilarating, each person can be so wrapped up in his or her own response that the experience of the partner's orgasm cannot be fully appreciated or can even be missed completely.

HORMONAL REGULATION OF SEXUAL FUNCTION AND BEHAVIOR

The physiologic processes of sex are not only vascular and neuromuscular. An important part of sexual physiology is under the control of the endocrine system, which consists of ductless glands that produce chemical substances called hormones. Hormones are secreted directly into the bloodstream where they are carried to tissues on which they act. Some hormones, such as cortisol (made in the adrenal glands, which lie just above the kidneys), are necessary for life itself and influence a wide range of body functions. Other hormones are required for reproduction or sexual development. Here, we consider the hormones that influence our sexual function.

The Sex Hormones

The most important hormone in sexual function is testosterone. This hormone, sometimes called the male sex hormone, is actually present in both sexes. In a normal man, 6 to 8 mg of testosterone are produced per day, with more than 95 percent manufactured in the testes and the remainder in the adrenal glands. In a woman, approximately 0.5 mg of testosterone is made daily in the ovaries and the adrenals.

Testosterone is the principal biologic determinant of the sex drive in both men and women. Deficiencies of testosterone may cause a drop in sexual desire (Bancroft, 1978; Masters, Johnson, and Kolodny, 1994), and excessive testosterone may heighten sexual interest. In men, too little testosterone may cause difficulty obtaining or maintaining erections, but it is not certain whether testosterone deficiencies interfere with female sexual functioning apart from reducing sexual desire. However, there is no evidence whatsoever to suggest that because women have less testosterone than men, they have lower sexual interest. Instead, it seems that men and women have different levels of behavioral sensitivity to the effects of this hormone, with women actually being more sensitive to small quantities in their circulation (Persky et al., 1978; Kolodny, Masters, and Johnson, 1979; Bancroft, 1984).

Estrogens, sometimes called female hormones, are also present in both sexes and are made primarily in the ovaries in women and in the testes in men. In women, they are important from a sexual viewpoint in maintaining the condition of the vaginal lining and in producing vaginal lubrication. Estrogens also help to preserve the texture and function of the female breasts and elasticity of the vagina. In men, estrogens have no known function. It does not seem that estrogens are important determinants of female sexual interest or capacity, since surgical removal of the ovaries does not reduce the sex drive in women or lessen sexual responsivity. Too much estrogen in males, however, dramatically reduces the sexual appetite and can cause difficulties with erection and enlargement of the breasts.

Progesterone, a hormone structurally related to both the estrogens and testosterone, is also present in both sexes. The effects of progesterone on sexual behavior and function have been studied primarily in animals, where it appears that large amounts suppress sexual interest. Some authorities speculate that it may also act as a sexual inhibitor in humans (Bancroft, 1984).

nocturnal emissions involuntary male orgasm and ejaculation during sleep (sometimes called wet dreams).

testosterone (tes tos' tur ōn) The most important hormone in sexual function, present in both sexes. Often called the male hormone, it is secreted by the testes and adrenals in the male and the ovaries and adrenals in the female.

estrogens (es' tro jinz) hormones present in both sexes, but primarily considered female. Produced in the ovaries and adrenal glands in the female, they maintain the lining of the vagina and produce breast growth. Also important in controlling the menstrual cycle.

progesterone (prō jes' tur ōn) a hormone present in both sexes, but primarily known as a female hormone. Present in high levels during pregnancy.

Regulatory Mechanisms

Two decades ago, it was thought that the "master gland" of endocrine function was the **pituitary,** an acorn-sized structure lying beneath the brain. It is now clear that the regulatory role of the pituitary is more like a relay station and that a portion of the brain itself—the **hypothalamus**—has primary control over most endocrine pathways.

The hypothalamus produces a substance called **gonadotropin releasing hormone (GnRH)** that controls the secretion of two hormones made in the pituitary gland which act on the gonads (ovaries and testes). **Luteinizing hormone (LH)** stimulates the Leydig cells in the testes to manufacture testosterone; in the female, LH serves as the trigger for ovulation (release of an egg from the ovary). **Follicle stimulating hormone (FSH)** stimulates the production of sperm cells in the testes; in the female, FSH prepares the ovary for ovulation.

The hypothalamus acts much like a thermostat in regulating hormonal function (Figure 4.6). Instead of reacting to temperature, as a thermostat does, the hypothalamus reacts to the concentra-

tions of hormones in its own blood supply. For example, in adult males the amount of testosterone "registers" in the hypothalamus. If the amount is high, production of GnRH is turned off, leading to a drop in LH secretion by the pituitary. The decrease in LH in the bloodstream quickly results in reduced production of testosterone in the testes, and therefore lower amounts of testosterone are secreted into the blood. When the amount of testosterone reaching the hypothalamus drops below a certain level, it triggers the secretion of GnRH into the pituitary. The pituitary responds to this signal by sending more LH into the circulation, where it will soon reach the testes and cause an increased rate of testosterone production. Testosterone also affects the pituitary gland, although the precise mechanism involved is unclear.

Hormones and Sexual Behavior

It is tempting to try to understand sexual behavior in terms of hormones. In many animal species, patterns of sexual interaction are tightly regulated by

Figure 4.6   Endocrine Regulation in Adults

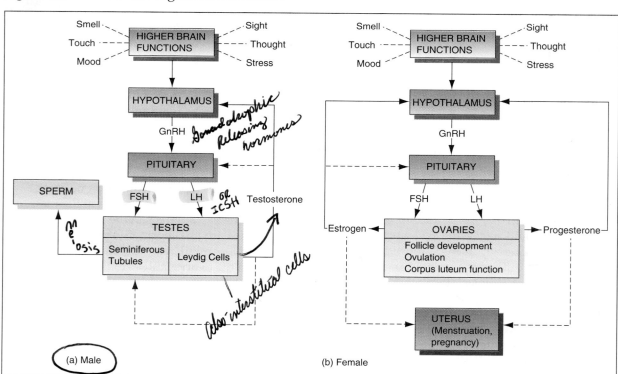

hormonal events that control both the sexual receptivity of the female (her willingness to mate) and sexual interest (courtship behavior) of the male, as well as male mounting and penile thrusting (Hutchison, 1978). Testosterone and estrogen have been found in mammals, birds, reptiles, amphibians, and fish: in all these groups, actions of sex hormones on the brain appear to be important determinants of sexual behavior (Kelley and Pfaff, 1978).

In humans, however, there is a more complicated relationship between hormones and sexual behavior. Although a marked testosterone deficiency usually reduces sexual interest in men or women, there are cases where this effect is not seen. Similarly, although many men with subnormal testosterone levels have difficulty with erection, others continue to have completely normal sexual function. Women who have low amounts of estrogen in their bodies do not usually lose their ability to be sexually aroused or to have orgasms. People's sex hormone levels do not "predict" their sexual behavior or interest.

Although there is no simple one-to-one relationship between sex hormones and human sexual behavior, fascinating questions about the role of hormones in sexuality abound. Later chapters will address such questions as: How do hormones influence sexual development (Chapter 8)? Do hormones "cause" homosexuality (Chapter 15)? What kinds of sexual disorders are caused by hormone imbalance (Chapter 22)? We now consider the hormonal patterns of the menstrual cycle and see whether they influence sexual behavior in women.

MENSTRUATION

Menstruation is a flow of blood that occurs about once a month in most women from approximately age 12 to 48. Although menstruation is a normal part of the female reproductive cycle, it is a subject of considerable misunderstanding and taboo. In ancient times, a menstruating woman was regarded as unclean and liable to pollute foods she handled or as contagious and liable to cause illness or even death in others (Delaney, Lupton, and Toth, 1977). In the modern era, menstruation is sometimes seen as a physical and emotional handicap that makes women "inferior" to men (Koeske, 1976; Frieze et al., 1978; Sherif, 1980). Whether menstruation is called the "curse," "the monthlies," or "being on the rag," it is often referred to in negative terms. In this section, we discuss the physiology of the menstrual cycle and consider the effects of menstruation on emotions and physical well-being.

Physiology of the Menstrual Cycle

The menstrual cycle is traditionally described as starting with the first day of menstrual flow (cycle day 1) and ending the day before the next menstruation begins. The length of the cycle varies, normally ranging from 21 to 40 days and averaging about 28 days (Vollman, 1977). Very few women are so regular that they can accurately and consistently predict the length of each cycle on the basis of their past pattern of cycle lengths.

The menstrual cycle consists of three phases, which we describe in terms of an "average" 28-day cycle (Figure 4.7). The **follicular phase** is the first

pituitary (pi tew' i ter' ē) an acorn-sized gland at the base of the brain which, at the direction of the hypothalamus, secretes several hormones important to sexual development and function. Once believed to control most of the endocrine system, it is now known to act only as a relay station.

hypothalamus (hī' pō thal' uh mus) the portion of the brain that has primary control over most endocrine pathways. It reacts to the level of hormones in the blood supply which regulate many sexual responses and directs their production.

gonadotropin releasing hormone (GnRH) (gō nad' ō trō' pin) a substance produced by the hypothalamus that controls the production and release of LH and FSH by the pituitary.

luteinizing hormone (LH) (lū' tē in īz' ing) produced by the pituitary gland, LH triggers ovulation and stimulates the Leydig cells to manufacture testosterone.

follicle stimulating hormone (FSH) a substance produced in the pituitary gland that prepares the ovary for ovulation and stimulates the production of sperm cells in the testes.

menstruation (men stroo' ā' shun) a flow of blood from the lining of the uterus occurring about once a month in females from puberty until the late forties or early fifties.

follicular phase (fol ik' ū lar) the first phase of the menstrual cycle, in which ovarian follicles begin to mature as a result of stimulation by FSH.

Figure 4.7   Hormone Changes During a Typical Menstrual Cycle

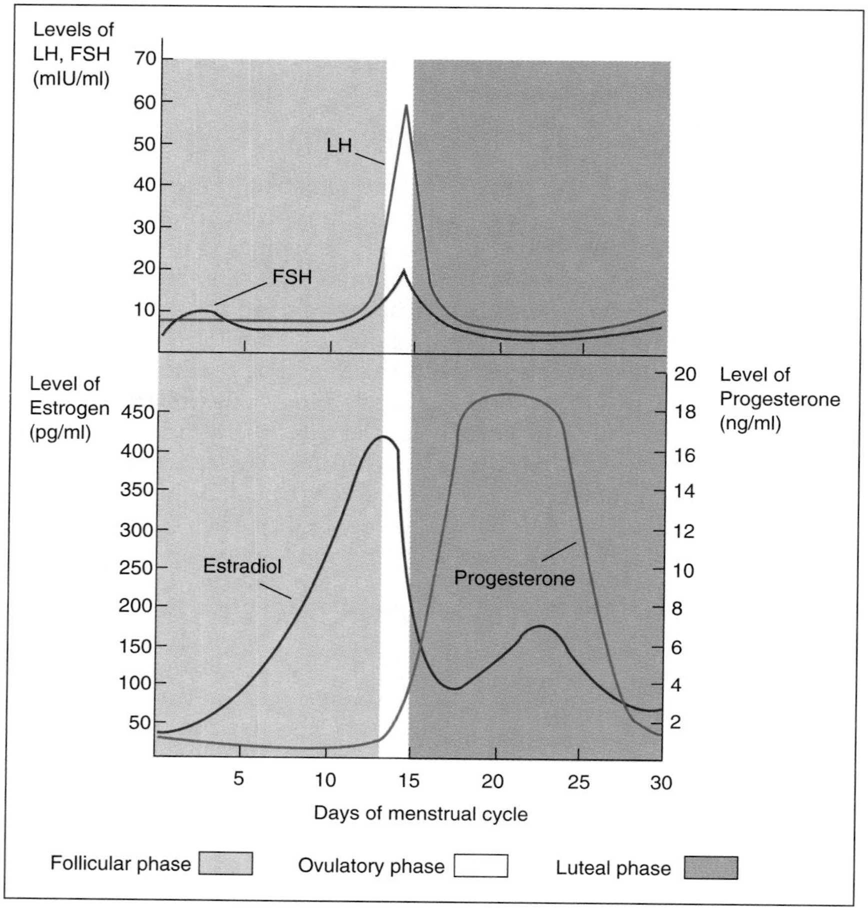

Source: *Reproduced, with permission, from Benson, R. C. (editor),* Current Obstetric and Gynecologic Diagnosis and Treatment, *3rd ed. Copyright 1980 by Lange Medical Publications, Los Altos, California*

portion of the menstrual cycle. Ovarian follicles, oval arrangements of cells around a young egg, begin to mature as FSH stimulates them. At the start of this phase, estrogen and progesterone levels are quite low and the uterus sheds its lining, resulting in three to six days of menstrual flow. Menstrual flow consists of a small amount of blood combined with tiny bits of tissue from the lining of the uterus, and the entire amount is usually only 2 or 3 ounces (4 to 6 tablespoons).

Midway in the follicular phase (around cycle days 7 to 10), estrogen output from the ovaries increases, which acts with FSH to prepare the developing follicle for ovulation. Estrogen also causes the lining of the uterus to thicken, or proliferate, due to growth of glands, connective tissue, and blood vessels. Just before ovulation, estrogen levels reach a broad peak, which acts on the hypothalamus to trigger the surge of LH and FSH released from the pituitary a day or two afterwards.

Ovulation, release of the egg from the ovary, typically occurs at about the fourteenth cycle day in most 28-day cycles. However, we have studied cycles in which ovulation ranged from the ninth day to the nineteenth day of a cycle of this length, and in some menstrual cycles ovulation does not occur at all (see Chapter 5). Ovulation usually follows the LH peak by 12 to 24 hours. The ovulatory phase is the shortest phase of the menstrual cycle.

The third portion of the menstrual cycle is the **luteal phase,** which encompasses the time from immediately after ovulation until the start of the next cycle. This phase is named for the corpus luteum, the mass of cells left in the ovary after the follicle ruptures during ovulation. The corpus luteum produces huge amounts of progesterone and estrogen, leading to increased levels of these hormones in this portion of the menstrual cycle (Figure 4.7). The progesterone causes the small blood vessels in the thickened endometrium to develop and produces coiling in the endometrial glands, changes that prepare the uterus to receive a fertilized egg if pregnancy occurs. The progesterone also registers in the hypothalamus, where it shuts off output of GnRH, resulting in a rapid decline in LH and FSH from the pituitary. Unless the egg is fertilized, the corpus luteum degenerates 10 to 12 days after ovulation, and its hormone production drops drastically. The next menstrual flow occurs as the lining of the uterus sheds in preparation for regrowth in the next cycle. Menstruation is thus the result of abrupt withdrawal of hormone stimulation.

Menstrual Cycle Effects

Brief comments from three women who participated in studies of the menstrual cycle at the Masters & Johnson Institute show the great diversity in how women feel about menstruation:

> I have a tough time with my periods. First, I get irritable and depressed a day or two before my period starts—nothing seems to go right. Then, I have real bad cramps for two days. I have to stay in bed; it's sheer agony.

> A few days before my period, my breasts get swollen and tender, and I usually get a headache. Once my period starts, everything is back to normal.

> Menstruation is no big deal. One time when I was 13 or so I had some cramping, but I really don't have any problems at all.

Mirroring this diversity, there is also considerable scientific controversy about the physiological and psychological effects of the menstrual cycle. In 1931 an American physician reported that estrogen causes "varying degrees of discomfort preceding the onset of menstruation," including "increased fatigability, irritability, lack of concentration, and attacks of pain" (Frank, 1931). High doses of x-rays were sometimes prescribed to knock out the ovaries in severe cases of the condition, which

Frank called *premenstrual tension*.

More recently, Dr. Katharina Dalton conducted an extensive series of studies on the subject, reporting that female criminal acts, accidents, hospital visits, poor judgments, and suicides are more common in the premenstrual and menstrual phases than at other times (Dalton, 1959, 1960, 1964, 1966, 1968, 1970, 1980). Numerous reports also indicate that the menstrual and premenstrual phases are associated with negative moods (Moos, 1969; Golub, 1976; May, 1976; Rossi and Rossi, 1977).

These findings, however, are not universal or interpreted in the same way by all scientists. For example, Persky (1974) found that mood was fairly consistent in college-aged women at three different points in the menstrual cycle. Dan (1976) noted that mood changes were very similar in women and their husbands over time regardless of the menstrual cycle. Webster, Bauman, and Kolodny (1978) noted that "menstrual or premenstrual symptoms" were unrelated to hormone levels and occurred with some frequency throughout the cycle, even around the time of ovulation. Another research group found no evidence of menstrual cycle effects on academic performance as shown by examination grades (Walsh et al., 1981). Many investigators have suggested that social expectations and stereotypes seem to influence the occurrences of menstrual or premenstrual distress. For example, some observers note that the title of one of the questionnaires most frequently used in menstrual cycle research, the Menstrual Distress Questionnaire, is inherently biased, as are the preponderance of questions asked.

> If the questionnaire were called the *Menstrual Joy Questionnaire*, if the majority of items asked for responses such as "happiness" or "feeling great" or "able to plot effective strategy" or "increased creativity," the end results would inevitably be different. (*Delaney, Lupton, and Toth, 1977, p. 84*)

Others in the field point out the problems associated with a person's attempts at remembering

ovulation (ōv you lā′ shun) the second phase of the menstrual cycle; the release of the egg from the ovary.

luteal phase (lū′ tē ul) the third phase of the menstrual cycle, after ovulation. The corpus luteum produces large amounts of progesterone and estrogen, which prepare the uterus to receive the fertilized egg.

past events (including the exact timing of the onset of menstruation) months after they have happened, although this type of retrospective self-reporting has been a mainstay of much of Dalton's research (Sherif, 1980). And, as Ruble, Brooks-Gunn, and Clarke (1980) have noted, cultural factors influence both the anxiety about or acceptance of a biological event like menstruation. "If a woman believes that women normally experience a variety of premenstrual symptoms, she may report such symptoms in part to make herself appear normal" (p. 234).

While it is clear that women are not ruled by their monthly hormone cycles, two kinds of menstrual problems are very common: **dysmenorrhea** (painful menstruation) and the **premenstrual syndrome (PMS).**

Dysmenorrhea

Dysmenorrhea, or painful menstruation, is usually marked by pelvic or lower abdominal cramping, backache, headache, and a feeling of being bloated, sometimes accompanied by diarrhea, nausea, or vomiting. These symptoms generally start in the 24 hours before menstrual flow begins and disappear spontaneously within 48 to 72 hours after menstruation starts.

There are two types of dysmenorrhea. Primary dysmenorrhea is defined as the group of symptoms mentioned above without the presence of any pelvic abnormalities. Secondary dysmenorrhea is diagnosed when a specific pelvic abnormality is found in the presence of the same symptoms. Common causes of secondary dysmenorrhea include endometriosis (the occurrence of the type of tissue lining the uterus in locations outside the uterus), pelvic inflammatory disease (scarring of fallopian tubes, usually resulting from a sexually transmitted disease), ovarian cysts, and tumors of the uterus. Primary dysmenorrhea usually begins in adolescence and reaches its peak incidence and severity around age 25, whereas secondary dysmenorrhea tends to occur in women in their thirties and forties.

Although primary dysmenorrhea was once thought to be a psychosomatic condition, it is now clear that it has a biochemical basis. The trigger mechanism is an excess release of prostaglandins from the uterus. Various drugs, such as aspirin, naproxen (trade name Naprosyn), naproxen sodium (trade name Anaprox), ibuprofen (trade name Motrin), and mefenamic acid (trade name Ponstel), are highly effective in inhibiting prostaglandin production, so that they effectively prevent or relieve the discomfort associated with dysmenorrhea. If these drugs do not work, birth control pills can be used as an alternative, since they relieve dysmenorrhea in more than 90 percent of cases (presumably by indirectly affecting prostaglandin production). In addition, some women find that being orgasmic relieves the discomfort of dysmenorrhea by reducing pelvic heaviness (Masters and Johnson, 1966).

PMS: The Premenstrual Syndrome

The premenstrual syndrome is a transient, recurrent condition occurring in the two to three days before menstrual flow begins marked by emotional and physical symptoms such as tension, irritability, or anxiety (Reid, 1991; Margolis and Greenwood, 1992). Depression and anxiety severe enough to become panic-like have also been found to be common (Schmidt, Grover, and Rubinow, 1993). Other variable findings include feeling sluggish, impatient, dizzy, nervous, and indecisive, as well as having physical symptoms such as breast tenderness, constipation, headache, bloating, and alcohol intolerance.

It is uncertain how many women have such premenstrual difficulties (estimates range from 20 to 75 percent). Of American women 5 to 10 percent reportedly have PMS that is severe enough to be temporarily disabling (Osofsky, 1990; Reid, 1991). For this reason, the American Psychiatric Association recognized the existence of such problems by inventing the cumbersome term, "late luteal phase dysphoric disorder" for inclusion in the Appendix to its *Diagnostic & Statistical Manual of Mental Disorders, third edition, revised,* giving it less than official status as a psychiatric diagnosis but still giving it a more than passing lip service. There do not appear to be any major differences in the premenstrual symptoms experienced by blacks and whites (see Table 4.1), although most women seeking help at PMS centers are white (Stout et al., 1986).

The specific cause of the premenstrual syndrome is unclear, although some researchers think it relates to the estrogen–progesterone ratio, the adrenal hormones controlling water retention, or chemical substances in the brain influencing mood (see Table 4.2 on p. 94). Furthermore, as Reid (1991,

Table 4.1 Premenstrual Symptoms in Black and White Women from a Community, Nonpatient Sample

	Black Women (N = 321)	White Women (N = 462)
Feeling depressed, sad, or blue	29%	27%
Having wide mood swings	26%	21%
Feeling under stress	16%	18%
Having cravings for certain foods	25%	17%
Having decreased energy	29%	23%
Being irritable	28%	31%
Feeling unable to cope	10%	10%

Source: *From Stout, A. L., et al. "Premenstrual Symptoms in Black and White Community Samples,"* American Journal of Psychiatry *143: 1436–1439, 1986. Copyright 1986, the American Psychiatric Association. Reprinted by permission.*

p. 1208) points out:

A contradictory body of research on PMS, which contains few definitive answers, has raised legitimate questions among skeptics about whether PMS is a true medical entity or merely a social phenomenon. A complex interplay of cultural beliefs, socialization factors, actual experiences, and concomitant life stress is thought to influence attitudes toward menstruation and premenstrual behavior.

The numerous controversies over PMS present a particularly complex issue, with biomedical, social, political, legal, and economic ramifications. Most researchers feel that Dalton's studies are not credible (Koeske, 1983; Fausto-Sterling, 1985), yet her findings have been used in various court cases: for instance, in Brooklyn, New York, attorney Stephanie Benson decided to defend a client who was accused of beating her four-year-old daughter by claiming that the woman was a victim of hormonal imbalances associated with her menstrual cycle. Although the idea of using PMS as a legal defense was eventually dropped in this case as part of a plea-bargaining agreement, in at least two murders in England the so-called PMS defense was used successfully to claim mitigating circumstances (*American Medical News*, Nov. 26, 1982, p. 14).

While some lawyers appear interested in pursuing this line of legal ground-breaking, many feminists feel they are uncomfortably caught in a paradoxical situation. On the one hand, as Susan Edmiston (1982) points out, "Throughout the 1970s, the feminist attitude toward menstruation was to deny that it made a difference and to minimize any effects women feel. . . . The reasoning was that to admit that menstruation mattered was to open the door to charges of biological inferiority." Now, however, increasing numbers of women (including many feminists) have become concerned about the realities of PMS, which they realize can be addressed only by open and intensive study. To

dysmenorrhea (dis men′ or ē′ uh) painful menstruation, usually including backache, headache, cramps, and a bloated feeling.
premenstrual syndrome fatigue, irritability, depression, and bloated feeling some women experience a few days before menstruation. Physical, psychological, and social causes are debated.

© 1990 Gail Machlis

Table 4.2   Proposed Causes and Treatments of PMS

Causes

Psychosomatic
Abnormality of brain neurotransmitters
Hormonal
    Estrogen excess
    Progesterone deficiency
    Antidiuretic hormone excess
    Aldosterone abnormality
    Hormone allergy
Vitamin A deficiency
Vitamin B deficiency
Low blood sugar (hypoglycemia)
Fluid retention

Treatments[a]

Exercise
Diet changes (especially restricting sugar and salt)
Birth control pills
Progesterone
Vitamin supplements
Diuretics
Dietary supplements (minerals, herbs, etc.)
Tranquilizers
Counseling

[a]*There is no current evidence that suggests that any of these treatments is superior to a placebo in producing improvement in women with PMS.*

pretend that PMS doesn't exist or that it affects only a tiny fraction of women, they believe, is going to slow much-needed research and make women who suffer from PMS feel lonely and abnormal. But, as well-known politician–lawyer–feminist Elizabeth Holtzman has pointed out, the PMS defense could backfire to harm women in divorce proceedings and custody battles and might even be used to justify violence against women (Allen, 1982).

The problem is an especially complicated one since researchers seem surrounded on all sides by disagreement, methodological difficulties, and uncertainty over what their findings mean. According to a news report in the *Journal of the American Medical Association* (June 3, 1983), scientists attending a PMS workshop sponsored by the National Institute of Mental Health agreed that PMS existed but "were hard-pressed to define the disorder precisely." Instead, noting that PMS doesn't seem to

have a single pattern, they suggested using the plural term "premenstrual syndromes" rather than the singular form.

Disagreement in PMS research seems to apply up and down the line. While some workers such as England's Dr. Katharina Dalton champion the notion that progesterone deficiency causes PMS, no studies have actually measured this deficiency in a way that shows a cause-and-effect relationship. Although one research team claims that even in its severest forms, PMS is *not* a form of depression (Haskett et al., 1980), others say that exactly the opposite is true (Shuckit et al., 1975; Halbreich, Endicott, and Nee, 1983). Worst of all, research on the treatment of PMS—which now includes literally hundreds of studies on dozens of different approaches—is often surprisingly slipshod, poorly designed, and difficult to interpret. As researcher Judith Green says, "No one approach has yielded consistent results, and no single agent has stood out as consistently useful."

Uncertainty among researchers is magnified, in a sense, by the large numbers of women who have read or heard about PMS and are now demanding treatment. Since progesterone use is not approved for treatment of PMS in the United States, many physicians are unwilling to prescribe it, particularly since it has been reported to cause cancer in animals. In addition, many of the most knowledgeable physicians in this field are aware that controlled, double-blind studies (in which neither the test subjects nor the investigators know whether a subject is taking progesterone or an inert look-alike pill called a placebo) have not been able to show that progesterone works better than a placebo in reducing premenstrual symptoms (Blume, 1983). In fact, the largest, most carefully designed study using the doses of progesterone recommended by Dalton and her colleagues recently found no difference in symptom clusters or individual symptoms in women while using progesterone compared to while using a placebo (Freeman et al., 1990). Other attempted treatments, such as the use of antidepressants, vitamins, or diuretics have also not shown any indication of providing a uniformly effective result (Schmidt, Grover, and Rubinow, 1993).

Despite this uncertainty, scores of PMS clinics have sprouted all over the country, with most of them offering progesterone therapy. Predictably, perhaps, they've been greeted by an avalanche of patients, partly because they've done a good job of selling American women on the idea that almost *any* symptom during the premenstrual week is a sign of PMS (Allen, 1982). In addition to offering the experimental hormone treatments, most of these clinics also prescribe dietary changes (e.g., avoiding salty foods, refined sugar, chocolate, and caffeine; eating six small meals a day), and they perform blood tests of dubious value. Not surprisingly, many of these centers charge high fees. The bottom line here seems to be "Let the buyer beware"—at least until the research community can provide better documentation for the causes and cures of this elusive but troublesome disorder.

Sex and the Menstrual Cycle

As part of our evolutionary heritage, there is some basis for assuming that women should be most interested in sex around the time of ovulation, when pregnancy can occur. In most animal species, the female follows this pattern of behavior rather exclusively, avoiding sexual contact at all other times. Some studies document a pattern of increased sexual activity around the presumed time of ovulation and do not find such a "peak" in women using birth control pills, which block ovulation (Udry and Morris, 1968, 1970; Adams, Gold, and Burt, 1978), but these findings appear to have been a result of imprecise determination of when ovulation occurred (James, 1971; Kolodny and Bauman, 1979). Other reports find no evidence of heightened female sexual interest during ovulation (James, 1971; Persky et al., 1978; Bancroft, 1984).

A well-designed study by Schreiner-Engel and co-workers (1981) found objective laboratory evidence of higher levels of vaginal vasocongestion during the follicular and luteal phases of the menstrual cycle. Subjective reports of sexual arousal were also higher at these times than during the ovulatory phase, providing further confirmation that an ovulatory peak in female sexual responsivity is unlikely. Another study confirmed that female sexual activity and sexual interest peak in the follicular phase well before ovulation (Bancroft et al., 1983). Nevertheless, individuals differ in unique ways, so that some women may well find themselves feeling sexier at midcycle while others are most interested in sex earlier or later in their cycles.

Taboos about sexual intercourse during menstruation are still a part of everyday life for many people. In some cases, avoiding sexual contact is a matter of religious practice. For example, Orthodox Jews are supposed to abstain from sex for seven days after the end of menstrual flow, and sex is resumed only after the woman has immersed herself in a ritual bath, called the *mikvah.* In other cases, abstinence seems to stem from cultural and psychological sources: "A man is as likely to be sexually aroused by a woman when she is menstruating as he is at any other time. But the blood of the menstruating woman is somehow dangerous, magical, and apparently not something he wants to get on his penis" (Delaney, Lupton, and Toth, 1977). The following comments illustrate the broad range of feelings people have about sexual activity during menstruation:

> I often find that I feel sexiest when I'm having my period, so making love is particularly enjoyable then. (*Author's files*)

> I somehow feel like it's not right to have sex when my girlfriend is menstruating. I don't know why, but I just feel funny about it. (*Authors' files*)

> Jill and I love to have sex during her periods. It's a particularly passionate time because we don't need to use any birth control then. (*Authors' files*)

> In a word, I'm embarrassed about it. I feel like I'm not completely clean when I'm flowing, and tampons make me dry inside, so I really prefer waiting until my period is done. (*Authors' files*)

The notion that sexual activity, including intercourse, is "dangerous" to either partner during menstruation has no basis in fact (Masters and Johnson, 1966). Yet some people feel that intercourse is messy during menstruation and restrict their sexual experiences to noncoital options. It appears as though attitudes toward sex during menstruation are beginning to change, however, since younger people seem to be less affected by the negative attitudes concerning such activity than their parents' generation (Paige, 1978).

SUMMARY

1. Sexual physiology describes the functions and reflexes of sexual response. Sexual arousal is the activation of a complex network of reflexes that involves the sex organs and sensory, cognitive, and hormonal pathways in the brain.

2. The sexual response cycle of both sexes consists of four basic stages: excitement, plateau, orgasm, and resolution. The primary physical changes that occur during the cycle are a result of vasocongestion and the accumulation of neuromuscular tension.

3. Vaginal lubrication in the female and penile erection in the male are the most prominent signs of the excitement phase. This phase is also marked by internal vaginal expansion and nipple erection.

4. In the plateau phase of high sexual arousal, the outer portion of the vagina swells, forming the orgasmic platform, and the labia thicken and undergo a prominent color change. In the male, the testes increase in size and are pulled tightly against the body, and a preejaculatory fluid may appear. A measles-like rash called the "sex flush" is seen in the majority of women and in about 25 percent of men.

5. Orgasm is a highly pleasurable reflex discharging neuromuscular tension via a total body response. In both sexes, a series of muscular contractions occur initially at 0.8-second intervals and then diminish in intensity and rapidity. In females, orgasm includes contractions of the outer portion of the vagina, the uterus, and the anal sphincter. In males, orgasm begins with contractions in the prostate and seminal vesicles, which initiates the process of ejaculation.

6. The resolution phase is a period in which the foregoing changes reverse, with a return to the unaroused state.

7. The male is limited in terms of physiologic response capacity by a refractory period immediately after ejaculation during which he cannot ejaculate again. Females do not have a refractory period. While women have the capacity to be multiorgasmic, this pattern of response has been noted in only a small number of men.

8. The old notion that there are two types of female orgasm—vaginal and clitoral—has been disproved. The physiologic patterns of female orgasm are identical no matter what the source of sexual stimulation.

9. The sex hormones—principally testosterone, estrogens, and progesterone—are present in both sexes and are controlled by the hypothalamus and pituitary gland. Testosterone is an important influence on sexual drive in males and females, but sexual behavior in humans cannot be thought of as tightly controlled by the sex hormones.

10. The menstrual cycle consists of three phases: the follicular phase, ovulation, and the luteal phase. The length of the entire cycle and its effects on mood and physical symptoms vary considerably.

11. Dysmenorrhea (painful menstruation), which is marked by cramping, backache, and feeling bloated, is now thought to be due to excessive release of chemicals called prostaglandins; it can usually be controlled by drugs that inhibit these substances.

12. PMS (premenstrual syndrome) affects a substantial number of women, typically causing irritability and tensions in the few days before the period begins. Many theories abound about the causes of PMS, but there is little agreement on this or on the proper treatment.

Thought Questions

1. Which stage of the human sexual response cycle allows for the greatest experience of intimacy between the two partners? Which allows for the least? Do you have a favorite part of the cycle? Which part, or when?

2. The text indicates that excitement, plateau, and orgasm are brought on by "effective sexual stimulation." What does "effective sexual stimulation" mean to you?

3. Researchers believe that only 40 to 50 percent of women regularly experience orgasm during intercourse. How do women who don't have orgasms during intercourse feel about it? How would men feel if they didn't regularly have orgasms during intercourse? Are the sexes different in how necessary they think it is to have an orgasm?

4. The text states that in ancient times a menstruating woman was regarded as unclean and dangerous and that, even today, many couples avoid having intercourse while the woman is menstruating. What are the reasons for these negative values? How do you feel about having sex during menstruation?

5. Do you think that men typically prefer to have intercourse during certain phases of a woman's cycle, rather than other phases?

Suggested Readings

Brecher, R., and Brecher, E. *An Analysis of Human Sexual Response.* New York: New American Library, 1966. A readable and accurate examination of Masters' and Johnson's physiology studies, with additional social and historical perspectives.

Delaney, J., Lupton, M. J., and Toth, E. *The Curse: A Cultural History of Menstruation.* New York: New American Library, 1977. A lively and authoritative account of taboos, myths, rituals, and contemporary research about menstruation and the menstrual cycle.

Hite, S. *The Hite Report.* New York: Dell, 1977. A detailed analysis of women's views of their own sexual responsivity, lacking in scientific precision but useful for women's descriptions of their sexual feelings.

Hite, S. *The Hite Report on Male Sexuality.* New York: Alfred A. Knopf, 1981. The male companion piece to the original *Hite Report;* unscientific but clearly showing the great diversity of male sexual feelings and fears.

Norris, R. V., and Sullivan, C. *PMS: Premenstrual Syndrome.* New York: Rawson Wade, 1983. An opinionated and not too scientific approach, but with some useful pointers.

Sherfey, M. J. *The Nature and Evolution of Female Sexuality.* New York: Random House, 1972. A detailed discussion integrating sexual physiology with female psychology. Heavy reading in parts, but a classic.

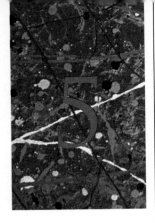

Human Reproduction

This chapter continues our look at sexuality in a biological perspective by focusing on one special aspect: how life begins. We start our discussion of reproduction by examining the process of conception (the union of egg and sperm) and then explore what happens during pregnancy, childbirth, and the first days of infancy. We conclude with a look at problem pregnancies and difficulties that prevent conception.

THE DYNAMICS OF CONCEPTION

In humans, pregnancy can result only when sperm meets egg. For this to happen, sperm must be deposited in the vagina close to the time of ovulation. In general, sperm retain their capability to penetrate the egg for 24 to 72 hours.

Figure 5.1   Human Egg and Sperm

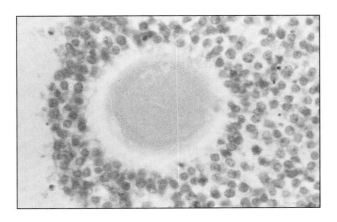
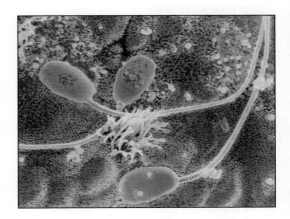

(a) Photomicrograph showing a section of a human ovary with an egg (large pink circle) about to be released. (b) Scanning electron micrograph (SEM) of human sperm.

Although it may seem as though pregnancy happens almost instantaneously, fertile couples who are trying to have a baby or who have intercourse regularly without contraception take an average of 5.3 months for pregnancy to occur (Shane, Schiff, and Wilson, 1976). Only 25 percent of women conceive after one month of unprotected intercourse. Sixty-three percent conceive by the end of six months, and by the end of one year, 80 percent become pregnant. Clearly, even when intercourse in fertile couples is timed to be near ovulation, there is an element of luck in whether a pregnancy occurs.

The Union of Sperm and Egg

After ovulation, the egg (Figure 5.1a) is gently drawn from the surface of the ovary into the Fallopian tube, where it is propelled toward the uterus by movement of cilia (tiny hairlike outgrowths). If fertilization occurs, it is usually in the upper portion of the Fallopian tube, not in the uterus.

After ejaculation in the vagina, healthy sperm (Figure 5.1b) swim rapidly into the female reproductive system in an arduous race that has few survivors. Although 200 million or more sperm are in the vagina, only a few thousand get to the Fallopian tubes and only about 200 actually get near the egg. Most sperm never reach the cervix because they spill out of the vagina or are immobilized by clumping together. Other sperm are damaged along the way, and about half the sperm that swim into the uterus take a wrong turn and enter the eggless Fallopian tube (except in rare circumstances, ovulation occurs on only *one* side each month). The difficult journey is nature's way of making sure that only the healthiest sperm have a chance to fertilize the egg.

Fertilization

Sperm spend several hours in the female reproductive tract undergoing a poorly understood process called **capacitation,** which enables them to penetrate the egg. Some sperm can reach the egg in an hour, but they must still wait to undergo this process. The race to penetrate the egg then is not always won by the swiftest; in fact, usually there are about 40 sperm clustered about the egg at fertilization (Figure 5.2a). After capacitation, sperm secrete a chemical that dissolves the **zona pellucida,** the jellylike coating around the egg.

The egg is not just a passive participant in this process. The egg actually embraces the sperm by

capacitation (kuh pas' i tā' shun) the process by which sperm become capable of penetrating an egg.

zona pellucida (zō' nuh pe lew' sē duh) the jellylike material surrounding the mature egg.

Figure 5.2   Fertilization

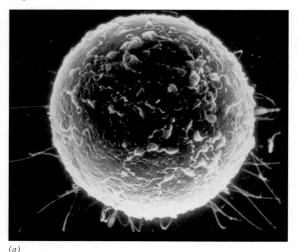

(a)

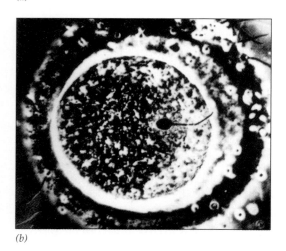

(b)

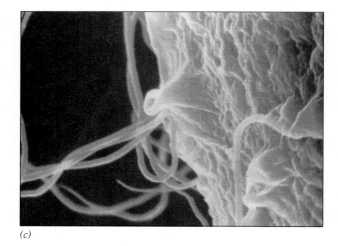

(c)

(a) SEM of many sperm attempting to penetrate an egg. Note the relative size of sperm and egg. (b) Close-up of sperm and egg. The sperm in the middle of the picture has penetrated the egg. (c) Human egg being fertilized. Note that only one sperm has penetrated the egg; the tails of many other sperm are visible at the border of the egg, where they have been blocked.

extending tiny outgrowths called microvilli up from its surface (Figure 5.2b). Then, to avoid penetration by more than one sperm, the egg first produces a brief electrical block on its surface (lasting only about 30 seconds), followed by a hard outer protein coat. Schatten and Schatten (1983, p. 32) describe it this way: "The successful sperm is held down on the egg membrane in the tight grip of microvilli, while the coat rises above it, pushing all other sperm away. It is rather as if the egg had opened an umbrella, holding the crowd of spermatozoa at a distance." Next, the egg pulls the sperm inside itself and moves its nucleus to meet that of the sperm. Once a sperm cell enters the egg, the zona becomes impenetrable (Figure 5.2c).

Fertilization is a complex process that typically lasts for 24 hours or longer, so it is not biologically correct to speak of "the moment of fertilization" (Jones and Schrader, 1989). The process of fertilization begins with the first contact of the sperm with the zona pellucida of the egg and is generally considered to be completed when genetic material from sperm and egg combine.

This marks the start of the **pre-embryo stage,** which lasts until biologic individuation occurs—the establishment beyond any doubt of one and only one biologically unique individual from the developing fertilized egg (Grobstein, 1988). The pre-embryo stage lasts for 14 days, when the start of the **embryo stage** coincides with the appearance of the **primitive streak** (a thickened linear band that will ultimately develop into various types of tissue, including portions of the spinal cord and part of the heart) (Jones and Schrader, 1989).

Fertilization produces a single cell called the **zygote** (Figure 5.3). This cell contains 23 **chromosomes** (strands of genetic material) contributed by the sperm and 23 chromosomes from the egg. These 46 chromosomes provide programming for inherited characteristics such as blood type, height, skin color, and so forth. Two of the chromosomes, called the sex chromosomes, combine to determine the sex of the developing zygote. All eggs and half of the sperm cells contain an X sex chromosome,

Figure 5.3   Early Development After Fertilization

✱ *Know this*

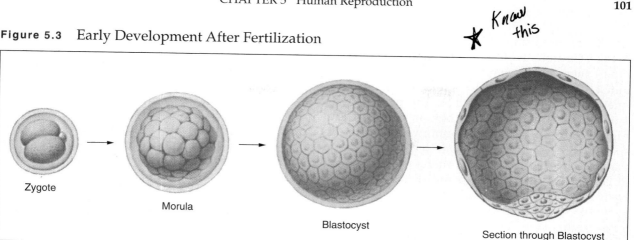

Zygote

Morula

Blastocyst

Section through Blastocyst

The blastocyst implants in the lining of the uterus.

while the remaining sperm have Y sex chromosomes only. A zygote with two X chromosomes will become a female, and a zygote with one X and one Y will become a male.[1] Since eggs always have X chromosomes, the sex of the baby is determined by the contribution of the father, whether it be an X or a Y chromosome.

Despite this biological reality, some men mistakenly believe that the woman is responsible for determining the baby's sex, and in some cultures divorces have occurred when a wife "couldn't" produce a male heir for her husband.

Sex Preselection

The desire to choose the sex of a baby before conception is probably as old as written history. In some cultures, folklore provides advice about various ways of selecting a child's sex: for instance, wearing boots to bed will produce boys, or eating sweet foods improves the chances of having a girl. In an age of greater scientific sophistication, most Americans are unlikely to believe these sorts of notions, yet interest in predetermining the sex of a child is so high that numerous other methods have been advanced with a more "plausible" scientific ring to them but without much more value than the boots or sweets theories.

One popular set of ideas proposed by Shettles and Rorvik (1970) suggested that having intercourse as close as possible to the time of ovulation,

increasing the alkalinity of vaginal secretions by douching with a baking soda solution, using deep penetration during intercourse, and having the woman be orgasmic before the male ejaculates all favor conceiving boys. These suggestions—which were each rationalized on detailed scientific grounds—have not yet been supported by any secure research data; in fact, one well-designed study of 3658 births actually found that the proportion of male births was <u>higher</u> when intercourse occurred <u>two days</u> or <u>more after ovulation</u> than when it occurred at or near ovulation (Harlap, 1979). The absence of supporting data after two decades has led several recent reviewers to conclude that Shettles' and Rorvik's methods are not only unproven but should be regarded with skepticism (Carson, 1988; Zarutskie et al., 1989).

pre-embryo stage the interval from the completion of fertilization until the appearance of a single primitive streak.
embryo (em' brē ō) the unborn child from the pre-embryo stage until eight weeks after fertilization.
primitive streak an embryonic structure that appears on about the fourteenth day of development, eventually degenerating and disappearing.
zygote (zī' gōt) the single cell created by the penetration of an egg by the sperm. An organism produced by the union of two gametes.
chromosomes (krō' muh sōmz) the genetic material in the nucleus of every cell in the body. Sperm and eggs each have 23 chromosomes; all other cells normally have 46.

[1]Some exceptions and complications of this process of sex determination are discussed in Chapter 8.

A more promising but still unproven method of sex preselection involves separating X and Y sperm in test tubes by passing them through liquid albumin, a protein found in blood that is similar to the thick material of an egg white. The faster-swimming Y sperm migrate to the bottom of the tube in higher numbers than the somewhat slower X sperm, permitting their ultimate recovery and use via artificial insemination to increase the chances of conceiving a male (Glass and Ericsson, 1982). However, sperm separation has not yet been shown to work, despite the fact that it is no longer a new technology. The current scientific consensus is that "albumin separation cannot be proved to separate X-from Y-bearing sperm" (Carson, 1988, p. 18).

If a sex preselection method is eventually found to work reliably, experts predict that it will lead to a substantially higher percentage of male births and possibly an overall decline in family size. One study of college students in Texas showed that 62 percent wanted their firstborn to be a boy, while only 6 percent wanted a firstborn daughter; furthermore, American couples often continue having children after giving birth to a girl, but stop after having a baby boy, both of which suggest a clear preference for male children in our society (Konner, 1987). In other countries, especially Japan, China, India, and elsewhere in the Orient and Africa, there is even a stronger bias toward having male children, which undoubtedly reflects socioeconomic factors (e.g., males earn more than females, and in some countries families must provide a dowry in order for their daughters to marry) and other cultural differences (Carson, 1988).

Some people are concerned about the ethics of using sex preselection techniques, which have been termed "one of the most stupendously sexist acts in which it is possible to engage" (Powledge, 1981). While many would disagree with this statement—including, for instance, couples who have several sons and would like to have a daughter, as well as couples trying to avoid the transmission of sex-linked genetic disorders—there is little question that past history strongly suggests that this practice might just become another form of discrimination against women.

Transport and Implantation

The single-celled zygote starts to divide about 30 hours after the process of fertilization begins. It splits initially into two cells, then these two cells split into four cells, eight cells, and so on. As this division occurs, the size of each cell becomes progressively smaller. This collection of cells, resembling a mulberry, is called a **morula** (Figure 5.3). During the three or four days after fertilization, the morula travels down the Fallopian tube and enters the cavity of the uterus. The morula now has a hollow inner portion containing fluid and is called a **blastocyst** (Figure 5.3).

The blastocyst undergoes further growth inside the uterus, receiving oxygen and nourishment from secretions of the lining of the uterus (the **endometrium**). After a few days, the blastocyst begins to attach itself to the lining of the uterus in a process called **implantation.** The endometrium of the uterus thickens and becomes richly endowed with blood vessels as a result of hormone secretions in the second half of the menstrual cycle. If fertilization does not occur, this hormonal stimulation ceases abruptly and the thickened tissue is shed during menstruation. However, if fertilization does occur, the thickened, spongy endometrium becomes a "bed" for the blastocyst, which usually attaches to the upper portion of the back wall of the uterus. If implantation occurs outside the uterus (e.g., in the tubes or in the abdomen), an **ectopic** (misplaced) **pregnancy** results.

Implantation is completed about 10 to 12 days after fertilization. These are no physical sensations that accompany implantation, so it is impossible to know just when it has occurred. In some women, implantation is accompanied by bleeding that may be confused with a menstrual period. As a result, women sometimes miscalculate when pregnancy began, leading to a wrong estimation of the expected date of delivery.

PREGNANCY

The average pregnancy lasts for 266 days. As a matter of convenience, the events of pregnancy are usually described in terms of three-month periods or **trimesters.** The first trimester includes the first three months after conception, the second trimester spans the fourth to the sixth month, and the third trimester ranges from the seventh month to delivery. As we have already noted, the first 14 days after fertilization is the pre-embryo stage; by definition, the embryonic stage lasts from this point until

Figure 5.4   First Trimester

  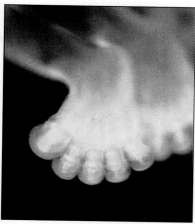

(a) Human embryo at 4–5 weeks. (b) Human fetus at 6 weeks. The fetus (left) is connected to the placenta (right) by the umbilical cord. It is enveloped in the fetal membranes and suspended in the amniotic fluid. (c) Close-up of feet of human fetus at 8 weeks.

the end of eight weeks after fertilization. After that comes the period of fetal development.

First Trimester

Embryonic and Fetal Development

Parts of the tiny, spherical blastocyst that implants in the lining of the uterus develop into the **placenta** and the **fetal membranes.** The placenta is the organ through which the embryo and fetus receive nourishment and oxygen from the mother's circulating blood. Waste products from the fetus are also passed through the placenta. The fetal membranes, an inner **amnion** and outer **chorion,** are thin sacs of tissue that enclose the developing fetus. The fetus is suspended in a liquid called **amniotic fluid** that keeps the temperature constant and serves as a shock absorber to protect the fetus against physical injury.

At the time of implantation, the blastocyst/pre-embryo is less than 1 millimeter (0.04 inch) in diameter. By the end of the first trimester, the fetus will be 9 centimeters (3.5 inches) long. This phenomenal rate of growth is accompanied by intricate patterns of organ formation that transform a small, undifferentiated mass of cells into an unmistakably human appearance.

By the end of the first month (Figure 5.4a), the embryo has a primitive heart and digestive system, and the beginnings of the brain, spinal cord, and nervous system have been established. The outlines of eyes can be seen on the large head, but distinct facial features have not appeared. In the fifth week, arm and leg buds become visible, the jaws

morula (more' u lah) a spherical mass of cells resulting from cleavage of the fertilized egg.

blastocyst (blas' tō sist) a spherical mass of cells with a hollow inner portion containing fluid produced by the cleavage of the fertilized egg.

endometrium (en' dō mē' trē um) the inner lining of the uterus in which the egg implants and which is partially shed during menstruation.

implantation the attachment of the blastocyst to the lining of the uterus.

ectopic pregnancy (ek top' ik) a misplaced pregnancy. The implantation of the blastocyst occurs outside the uterus, for example in the tubes or abdomen.

trimester a three-month period; generally used to describe the progression of pregnancy in three such periods.

placenta (pluh sen' tuh) the organ attached to the wall of the uterus that performs the functions of nutrition, respiration, and excretion for the unborn child. It is also an endocrine organ secreting large amounts of several hormones.

fetal membranes two thin sacs of tissue, the inner amnion and the outer chorion, that enclose the developing baby.

amnion (am' nē on) the inner of the thin sacs of tissue (fetal membranes) that enclose the developing fetus.

chorion (kor ee on') the outer sac of tissue that encloses the developing fetus inside the uterus.

amniotic fluid (am' nē ot' ik) the liquid in which the developing fetus is suspended. It keeps the temperature constant and cushions shock.

begin to form, and indentations are seen in the region where the ears will develop. The **umbilical cord,** which contains two arteries and a vein connecting the embryo to the placenta, becomes a distinct structure.

In the sixth and seventh weeks (Figure 5.4b), the eyes and ears develop more fully, and teeth and facial muscles begin to form. A distinct neck becomes visible, and bone formation begins as well. Testicular tissue appears in male embryos at this point, but in a female embryo formation of the ovaries has not yet begun. Before this time, male and female embryos are anatomically indistinguishable (see Chapter 8). By eight weeks, the embryo has distinct hands and feet, and all major blood vessels are forming. At this point, the embryo weighs about 1 gram (0.04 ounce) and is 3 centimeters (1.2 inches) in length (Figure 5.4c).

In the third month, fetal development proceeds with the appearance of fingernails, toenails, hair follicles, and eyelids. The limbs become more properly proportioned in relation to the rest of the body, and recognizable male and female genital organs are seen. By the end of the twelfth week, all the major organs are differentiated, although they are not all completely formed.

The Mother

Early pregnancy is experienced in different ways by different women. Some have a strong sense of energy, radiance, and well-being even before they know they are pregnant. Others find that the first months of pregnancy are marked by fatigue, loss of appetite, or humdrum emotions.

Being tired is such a typical feature of the first trimester that it is considered a symptom of pregnancy. Another frequent symptom is nausea or vomiting, which usually begins around the end of the first month. This "morning sickness" can occur at any time of day and usually disappears spontaneously a month or two after it begins. Frequent urination, irregular bowel movements, breast swelling and tenderness, and an increased amount of vaginal secretion are among the other physical changes that may be noticed by the pregnant woman in the first trimester. However, the woman cannot feel the changes going on inside her uterus during this time.

Missing a period is not a sure sign of pregnancy (periods can be skipped because of stress or illness, among other reasons), but it raises a question in most women's minds. To find the answer, a woman can purchase a kit for a self-administered home pregnancy test and then have the results confirmed by a physician, at a medical laboratory, or at a clinic.

In the past, biological tests using laboratory animals such as frogs, rabbits, or mice were employed to check for pregnancy, but these were cumbersome, time-consuming, expensive, and relatively inaccurate. Now there are many immunological tests that allow a diagnosis to be made in as short a time as 2 minutes. They work by detecting the presence of HCG (human chorionic gonadotropin), a hormone secreted by the placenta. A drop of urine is placed on a glass slide (or in a tube) and is mixed with several chemicals. If HCG is present, the mixture does not coagulate and the test is said to be positive, indicating pregnancy. These tests

Focus In Brief

Dealing with Morning Sickness

Many women can find relief from morning sickness by trying these tips:

- Eat five or six small meals throughout the day, rather than two or three large ones.
- Keep your protein consumption low and stress carbohydrates instead.
- Avoid fried foods and fatty dishes.
- Drink plenty of fluids to help neutralize stomach acids and to prevent dehydration from vomiting.
- Sucking on hard candy—lollipops, lemon drops, and so on—may help control feelings of nausea.
- Chewing on small pieces of ice or licking ice-pops (including the kind you can make yourself from natural fruit juices) is a good way to minimize problems for many women.
- Eat a snack at bedtime to help alleviate morning nausea the next day.

Source: *Modified from Todd and Tapley, 1988, Table 7.1. Reprinted from* The Columbia University College of Physicians and Surgeons Complete Guide To Pregnancy *by permission of Crown Publishers, Inc. Copyright © 1988 by the College of Physicians and Surgeons of Columbia University.*

offer 99 percent accuracy as early as one week after conception when performed properly.

At-home pregnancy tests that do not require a prescription and are simple to perform are also available. Based on a technology using monoclonal antibodies—made-to-order proteins that latch onto HCG in urine in very small amounts—these tests give results within 5 to 10 minutes with a high degree of accuracy. The First Response Pregnancy Test Kit, which can be used as early as the first day after a missed period, gives its results—a simple color change from clear to pink—in only 5 minutes. Other monoclonal antibody pregnancy test kits currently being sold are called Advance, Daisy 2, Fact Plus, Q Test, and Answer Plus. Each kit typically costs $10 to $15. Recent research shows that home pregnancy tests, when performed and interpreted by laypersons, are almost 10 percent less accurate than testing done by qualified laboratory personnel (Hicks and Iosefsohn, 1989), so it is important for a woman to have a home test result confirmed before concluding whether or not she is pregnant.

A negative pregnancy test, no matter what method is used, is *not* foolproof, and a repeat test done a week or two later may be in order. Women need to have an early knowledge of their pregnancy to begin proper health care (such as good nutrition and avoidance of cigarettes, alcohol, and drugs of all kinds—prescription, nonprescription, and illegal). Early diagnosis is also important so that those who want to terminate pregnancy can have an abortion in the first trimester, when this procedure is safest and simplest.

Pregnancy can also be detected in other ways. During a pelvic examination, a physician can note (1) a softening of the cervix, (2) a bluish color of the vagina and cervix, (3) a softening of the uterus just above the cervix, or (4) an irregular increase in the size of the uterus. These signs of pregnancy may be present at about the sixth week but are quite variable. The most conclusive physical signs of pregnancy—finding a fetal heartbeat, feeling the fetus move, and identifying the fetus by sound-wave tests—usually cannot be done before the second trimester.

One interesting fact to keep in mind is that many pregnancies end naturally before they reach the point where they are detected clinically. In one recent study which used highly sensitive testing for HCG, 22 percent of all pregnancies detected just after implantation (before the first missed period was noticed by the woman) failed to survive to the point at which they would be recognized clinically (Wilcox et al., 1988). (Overall, the total rate of pregnancy loss was 31 percent.) While the causes of early pregnancy loss are not well understood at present, some experts believe that it may be nature's way of eliminating pre-embryos that are defective in one way or another.

Once a woman knows that she is pregnant, she may be happy, proud, ambivalent, fearful, angry, depressed, or any combination thereof. Her reaction reflects many things—her age, marital status, economic resources, career objectives, personal values, and expectations of parenthood. Most of all, her reaction will depend on whether or not she wanted to be pregnant and how she feels about herself.

Negative feelings about a pregnancy, even when it is planned, are similar to the second thoughts we all have after taking a major step in our lives. Did I choose the right college? Is this really the person I wanted to marry? Why did I buy this car when that other one looks so good? Our initial uncertainties and hesitations do not necessarily predict how we will feel later on. The psychological impact of bringing a child into the world is immense and requires time for thought and acceptance.

At the same time, many women (especially those who have not yet had children) experience particularly vivid dreams about their pregnancy that are sometimes distressing to them. These dreams typically are full of anxiety: the baby has been born with a birth defect, for instance, or the baby was born but somehow was kidnapped from the nursery. Since dreaming seems to be a way in which the mind can deal with concerns that it doesn't want to think about consciously, such disturbing dreams are entirely normal (Todd and Tapley, 1988).

The Father

While often neglected as a participant in the experience of pregnancy, men also have important feelings about this event. The man's initial reaction on learning of his partner's pregnancy may be elation, joy, surprise, uncertainty, or concern. Until he has

umbilical cord the cylindrical structure connecting the fetus to the placenta. It contains two arteries and a vein.

time to adjust to the idea of pregnancy as a reality, he is likely to be somewhat ambivalent toward his partner. He may be anxious about her well-being and the developing baby's health until he can see his partner's bulging abdomen or feel the baby's movement (Grossman, Eichler, and Winickoff, 1980). His anxieties may also relate to the additional responsibilities (financial and emotional) that the pregnancy presents. Some men even have morning sickness along with their pregnant partners, perhaps a sign of their anxiety and wish to share in the pregnancy experience. In fact, one study recently found that 23 percent of a group of American expectant fathers had a condition called the **couvade syndrome,** in which husbands experience physical symptoms that are related to their wives' pregnancies and are not explained by other medical factors (Lipkin and Lamb, 1982).

Many men are uncertain about the effects of sex during pregnancy (see p. 113) and believe that the woman must refrain from exercise or vigorous work so the baby will not be injured. Other men do not understand why a pregnant woman seems so sleepy and may become upset, especially if they imagine that this tiredness will progress relentlessly through the months ahead. Both partners are likely to react to pregnancy in a more relaxed fashion if they have already had a child and have some idea of what to expect.

In the early months of pregnancy, many couples draw closer together, both emotionally and physically. Pregnancy can be a very concrete manifestation of commitment and sharing, and a first pregnancy in particular provides good reason to plan and dream about the future.

Second Trimester

Fetal Development

In the fourth month, the fetus develops lips, fingerprints, and hair on its head. Sucking motions begin, and the fetus swallows small amounts of amniotic fluid. The fetus moves and turns very actively within the amniotic sac (Figure 5.5). During the fifth month, the fetal heartbeat can be heard and the body becomes covered with tiny, downy hair. The fetus also responds to sound and spends part of its time being quite active and some being still. In the sixth month, the fetus opens its eyes and has long hair on its head. By the end of the second trimester, the fetus is 30 centimeters (12 inches)

long and weighs 600 to 700 grams (1.3 to 1.5 pounds). If born at this time, the fetus has poor chances for survival.

The Mother

The second trimester is a time of many physical changes for the pregnant woman. Her waist begins to bulge, her abdomen protrudes, her bustline expands, and her regular clothes no longer fit very well. She may be troubled by these changes in her figure, or she may be happy with her body and anxious to let the whole world know that she is pregnant.

Late in the fourth month (between the sixteenth and eighteenth weeks), the woman can usually feel the fetus moving (**quickening**). This is often an exciting event and a moment of relief because the developing fetus "signals" that it is doing well. As the kicks and twists become more vigorous in the following weeks, the novelty and wonder may wear off and the sensations may become annoying. The mother may alternate between feeling love and tenderness and feeling resentment at being controlled by the fetus.

In the second trimester, the uterus grows considerably larger and pushes up inside the abdomen. This commonly leads to indigestion and constipation. The skin over the abdomen becomes stretched, and pink or reddish stretch marks may appear on its surface. The breasts increase prominently in size, the nipples become larger and more deeply pigmented, the areolae become broader, and **colostrum,** a thin yellowish fluid which is a precursor of milk, may drip out of the nipples. These changes are a result of the hormones produced by the placenta and prepare the breasts for later milk production.

Other physical changes may lead to minor problems. Varicose veins in the legs and hemorrhoids can start to form or be worsened because of the pressure of the growing uterus. Nose bleeds may occur because of a larger blood volume. Fluid retention can cause **edema,** swelling of the hands, wrists, ankles, or feet. On the other hand, the morning sickness of the first trimester usually disappears and the woman's appetite is apt to become hearty.

Psychologically, the second trimester is often a time of relative tranquility and confidence. Most women have adjusted to being pregnant and feel more energetic than they did in the first few months. Heightened sensuality at this time is often

Figure 5.5   Second Trimester

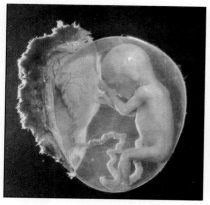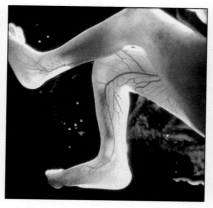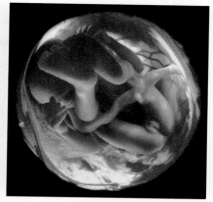

(a) Fourteen-week human fetus in amniotic sac attached by umbilical cord to placenta. (b) Human fetus (16 weeks) showing legs and feet. At this stage of development, although most major organs have formed, the fetus is unable to survive if born prematurely because its lungs are immature. (c) Five-month-old female fetus.

a pleasant bonus; it is not unusual for some women to first experience orgasm in the middle months of pregnancy (Masters and Johnson, 1966).

The Father

With birth still far away, the father is likely to be drawn more closely into the experience of pregnancy in the second trimester. He is able to see obvious changes in his partner's body, but these changes occur gradually and give him time to adjust. Feeling the fetus kick or turn is likely to give him a greater sense of identification. His partner's renewed energy is also reassuring and gives the couple more time together—a pleasant interlude that will be gone all too soon when a newborn infant arrives. His earlier anxieties about the fragility of the developing fetus in the first trimester have been generally put to rest.

One of the more sensible developments of recent years has been a trend for fathers to become more involved in their partners' pregnancies in a variety of ways. For example, the father might attend prenatal checkups to get to know the nurse-midwife or physician before the actual delivery and to ask questions that might otherwise go unanswered. As a bonus, if ultrasound testing is done during such a checkup, the father gets to see an image of the developing fetus on the ultrasound monitor, which is often an exciting experience. Men can also be more active participants in the pregnancy if they read some of the books or articles their partner reads, so they can discuss them together, and if they prepare themselves by talking with other men about their experiences during childbirth.

In some instances, it may be possible for men to arrange for paternity leave so they can be at home with the mother and newborn baby once the big day comes. As a practical matter, if this seems like a desirable possibility, we suggest that the father-to-be begin inquiries about paternity leave at work during the second trimester, if he hasn't done so earlier. Even if your employer says that there is no official company policy on paternity leave, if you're persistent you may be able to make an arrangement that will work for you or you might actually get a new policy started—with you as the first beneficiary! If this attempt fails, you may be able to arrange for a paid vacation for a week or two after the baby's arrival, which can create a perfect opportunity for sharing in the baby's care from the earliest possible time.

Early Pregnancy Classes

One of the newer developments to gain popularity in the last five years is the availability of early pregnancy classes that are typically held during the first three to six months of pregnancy. These classes

couvade syndrome (koo vahd') a condition in which a male experiences symptoms mimicking pregnancy and/or childbirth.

quickening the time during pregnancy when a woman can first feel the fetus moving.

★ **colostrum** (kohl ah' strum) a thin, watery fluid secreted by the breasts late in pregnancy as a precursor to breast milk.

edema (e dē' muh) swelling due to fluid retention.

Both early pregnancy classes and later child-birth preparation classes, such as the Lamaze class shown here, help couples talk about their feelings and familiarize them-selves with what's ahead.

are different from childbirth classes, which are usu-ally offered later in pregnancy to help a couple pre-pare for labor and delivery. Early pregnancy classes focus, instead, on the couple's emotional adjust-ment to pregnancy, provide education about the physical changes affecting the mother, and help the couple prepare for the change from couple to fam-ily. Typically, these courses meet at a YMCA or community center and involve a group leader and four to eight pregnant couples meeting for three or four weekly sessions.

One of the main benefits of such a class is that the group setting helps couples talk about their feelings. Here is what one expectant father said about a course he attended:

> I wasn't too interested in going to this class at first, thinking it was just going to be a bunch of lectures. But it turned out, instead, to be more of a discussion group . . . and that gave me a chance to hear what a few other men who were in my same position were feeling. It was good to find out that many of the concerns I had were not that uncommon, and it was also useful to hear how other couples were dealing with these issues. The end result was that the classes brought me closer together with my wife. *(Authors' files)*

You can usually find out where and when early pregnancy classes are offered from a midwife, an obstetrician, a childbirth center, or your local hospi-tal. If none exists in your community, you might consider recruiting a group leader to start one.

Third Trimester

Fetal Development

During the seventh month, the brain and nervous system complete the major steps of their develop-ment, fatty tissue grows under the skin, and the downlike hair on the fetus disappears in most places. A baby born prematurely at the beginning of the seventh month has a 20 percent chance of survival, but by the eight month this increases to 85 percent (Pernoll and Benson, 1987). In the eighth month, the baby's skin has lost its wrinkled ap-pearance and is pink in color. If it has not done so earlier, the baby is likely to assume a head-down position in the uterus. In the ninth month, the fetus usually is less active than it has been, partly be-cause of its size and cramped quarters. Its eyes are blue, because other eye colors develop only after a period of exposure to light. The fetus has acquired antibodies from its mother that will help protect it against infection during early infancy. The average full-term baby is 50 centimeters (20 inches) long and weighs 3100 to 3400 grams (6.8 to 7.5 pounds).

The Mother

The increasing size and firmness of the uterus are quite obvious. When the woman stands, it pushes forward, altering her center of gravity. To balance this, she may walk with her head and shoulders thrust backward and chest protruding, a position that can result in backache, a common occurrence in the last months of pregnancy. The enlarged uterus also puts pressure on the blood vessels in the lower part of the body, which may partly explain the common discomfort of leg cramps. Other problems caused by pressure changes include a frequent need to urinate because of pressure against the bladder and shortness of breath since the diaphragm is pushed upward against the lungs.

Many women have difficulty controlling their weight gain during pregnancy, especially during the third trimester. Physicians generally suggest that weight gain be limited to about 25 pounds because larger increases in weight increase the odds of medical problems. On the other hand, too little weight gained is potentially harmful to the fetus, since a gain of almost 20 pounds can be expected from normal physiological changes. This gain includes the weight of the baby (7½ pounds), placenta and membranes (1½ pounds), and amniotic fluid (2 pounds) as well as increases in the weight of the uterus (2½ pounds), blood (3½ pounds), and breasts (1 pound). Normal fluid retention is likely to account for another 2 or 3 pounds of weight gain.

In the last months of pregnancy, the uterus has more frequent **Braxton-Hicks contractions,** painless short episodes of muscle tightening that are not a sign of labor. In women who have not had a baby before, the head of the fetus lowers into the pelvis in the last few weeks of pregnancy. When the largest diameter of the head has settled firmly into position against the pelvic bones, it is engaged. **Engagement** (also called "dropping" or "lightening") usually occurs during labor in women who have had children.

The end of the last trimester is apt to be a time of physical discomfort and awkwardness. Each day may seem longer than the last. Sleeping is frequently interrupted by trying to find a comfortable position, by fetal movements, and by trips to the bathroom. Energy levels are low, irritability high. The first-time mother, especially, is likely to have anxieties about pain or problems with labor and delivery and may worry considerably about her baby not being normal. Her self-esteem may be on the wane as she seems, for now, to be at the mercy of the requirements of a body that does not seem really hers.

The Father

The last trimester is not without its tribulations for the male. His partner's changing shape and physical discomforts may lead to a loss of his sexual desire for her, or his continued interest may not be matched by hers. Masters and Johnson (1966) found that for these reasons the last trimester is a time some men seek extramarital sex. Men may also feel aloof for other reasons. For example, the pregnant woman may become quite close to her own mother during pregnancy, with more discussions and time spent together as delivery nears. His partner's relation to her physician may also be a source of feeling "left out." Social events, recreation, and other details of everyday living are typically altered now, and the man may be understandably anxious for things to return to "normal."

At the same time, most men feel a strong sense of loyalty, closeness, and gratitude toward their very pregnant partner. They are usually glad not to be pregnant themselves, are concerned with making their partner comfortable, and, if a home delivery has not been chosen, are more than a little nervous about driving to the hospital once labor is under way. If this is their first child, and they have been asked to be present at the delivery, they may be queasy and unsure of "how they will do."

Prenatal Care and Planning

Most pregnancies progress smoothly for the mother and unborn child, but problems can also occur. **Prenatal** (prebirth) **care** not only increases the mother's chances of staying healthy but also protects the well-being of her developing fetus. Although most people think of prenatal care as something done by a doctor or nurse-midwife, it is a

Braxton–Hicks contractions painless short episodes of muscle tightening sometimes mistaken for the onset of labor.

engagement the settling of the fetal head into position against the pelvic bones for birth. It usually occurs during the last few weeks of pregnancy in women having their first child and during labor with subsequent pregnancies. Also called dropping or lightening.

prenatal care the combined efforts of doctor, nurse, and mother to see that the pregnant woman stays healthy and the unborn child has everything needed to grow and develop.

joint venture in which the mother and her physician or nurse collaborate. The mother's responsibilities are really more important than the health-care provider's, since she lives with the pregnancy day in and day out. Prenatal care is mainly a means for preventing problems; secondarily, it is a way to detect complications as early as possible in order to minimize their impact.

Nutrition

Good nutrition during pregnancy is an essential part of prenatal care. The mother requires more calories and extra nutrients such as vitamins and minerals to meet the needs of her body and her developing baby. Poor maternal nutrition can lead to slower fetal growth, premature delivery, and low-birth-weight babies. Prematurity and low birth weight both cause higher infant death rates, and malnourished babies with low birth weights may have brain damage and retardation.

Obviously, the woman's nutritional state before pregnancy is an important consideration. If previous dietary habits were poor, special steps must be taken to provide extra amounts of needed nutrients. Even when this is not a problem, pregnant women need about 300 extra calories and extra amounts of protein, calcium, iron, and vitamins A, B, C, and D compared to their ordinary daily intake. Protein (found in meat, fish, eggs, and dairy products) is important for the growth of the placenta, uterus, and the blood supply in the pregnant woman's body. Calcium (obtained mainly from dairy products and vegetables) is necessary for growth of the fetal skeleton and tooth buds; too little calcium can also cause muscle cramps for the mother. Iron (found in red meats, dried fruits, eggs, and enriched cereals) is needed for the manufacture of red blood cells to prevent maternal anemia; folic acid (found in leafy green vegetables) also helps prevent anemia. Necessary vitamins are usually provided by a balanced diet that includes milk, bread, fresh fruits, and vegetables.

Drugs

Almost every drug used by a pregnant woman will cross the placenta and enter the circulation of the developing embryo or fetus. Because it is not always clear which drugs will have damaging effects, it is vital that drug use be restricted to situations of medical necessity, even for drugs that seem safe for the mother. Drugs that produce malforma-

tions in the embryo or fetus are called **teratogens.** The kind of effect a toxic drug produces depends partly on when it is used. Certain drugs act selectively on the formation of a particular organ in the embryo or fetus and do not cause damage after its formation is complete. For this reason, drug use in the first half of pregnancy is particularly likely to damage the fetus, since this is when organ formation occurs. The effects also depend on the duration and amount of drug use—taking a single pill is unlikely to be harmful, while repeated use may be a problem.

Medications

A wide variety of medicines can affect the fetus, including some that might surprise you. For instance, aspirin can cause fetal bleeding and, if used with large amounts of caffeine and phenacetin (in pills called APCs which are used to treat headache or pain), can lead to low birth weight, prolonged pregnancy, anemia, and lower infant survival rates after birth (Collins and Turner, 1975). Tranquilizers have also been reported to cause a variety of fetal malformations, including cleft palate (Valium) and heart defects (Librium and Equanil). Thalidomide, a tranquilizer widely used in Europe in the early 1960s (but no longer in use), resulted in severe malformations of the arms and legs of the fetus when taken during early pregnancy. Anticonvulsants, drugs used to control epilepsy, also can cause birth defects if they are used during pregnancy (Jones et al., 1989).

Hormones are also frequently teratogenic. Birth control pills used during pregnancy have been found to cause heart defects (Nora and Nora, 1973; Heinonen et al., 1977) and abnormalities of the limbs, spinal column, windpipe (trachea), and kidneys (Janerich, Piper, and Glebatis, 1974). Progesterone or testosterone can cause masculinizing changes in a female fetus and progestins or estrogens can cause improper formation of the penis in a male fetus. A form of estrogen called diethylstilbestrol (DES), which many mothers took to prevent miscarriage, may cause cancer of the vagina in girls whose mothers used this drug during pregnancy (see Chapter 22).

A drug used to treat severe acne, isoretinoin (trade name Accutane), is especially dangerous during pregnancy because it is likely to cause spontaneous abortions or major birth defects affecting the skull and face, the heart, the thymus, and the brain (Lammer et al., 1985). Medications that can damage the fetus are listed in Table 5.1.

Drug Abuse

Pregnant women who use drugs like cocaine, heroin, barbiturates, and amphetamines expose the fetus to a large number of problems. Low birth weight and prematurity are characteristic of such pregnancies. The fetus also may become addicted, in which case its first days as a newborn are likely to be a painful time of withdrawal symptoms. Convulsions and depressed breathing are commonly seen just after birth in infants born to addicted mothers. In addition, the mother's health may be compromised by poor nutrition, infections (particularly hepatitis B), and other medical difficulties caused by drug addiction or abuse. It is estimated that as many as 375,000 infants may be affected each year by maternal drug abuse during pregnancy (Silverman, 1989). In fact, one recent study found that 15 percent of pregnant women tested positive for substance abuse during pregnancy (Chasnoff, Landress, and Barrett, 1990). In many cases, the woman doesn't realize that her drug use poses a danger to her developing fetus.

Recent research shows that cocaine use in pregnancy, which had previously not been studied, has a number of major effects (Chasnoff et al., 1989; Zuckerman et al., 1989). Not only are the risks of miscarriage, premature birth, and stillbirth increased, maternal cocaine use impairs growth of the fetus. In addition to being small for their age, cocaine babies, as they are called in many hospitals, tend to have smaller heads than other babies; they also have a higher rate of malformations affecting their genitals or urinary tract (kidneys, ureters, bladder, and urethra). They are more prone to seizures than other babies and lag noticeably in development, showing increased jitteriness and irritability, abnormal sleep patterns, decreased interactive behavior, and poor organizational responses (Spear, Kirstein, and Frambes, 1989).

Researchers have not yet collected much data on the long-term effects of maternal drug use during pregnancy on children as they grow up, so little can be said on this matter. However, what is particularly distressing to some experts is that the overall effects of using combinations of drugs, which is common among drug abusers, may be even worse than the effects of using a single drug, which are bad enough to begin with.

Focus In Brief

Warning Signs During Pregnancy

If pregnant women have any of the following problems, they should see a trained nurse-midwife or doctor immediately:

- Unusually heavy or smelly vaginal discharge.
- Very bad headaches, dizziness or blurred vision, persistent fatigue, or trouble breathing.
- Bleeding from the vagina.
- Swollen hands and face (especially in late second or third trimester).
- No signs of labor more than one day after membranes rupture.
- Seizures or blackouts.
- Marked decrease in urine output.
- Severe, unexplained pain in the shoulder.

Sources: *Modified from* Population Reports, *Series L, Number 7, September 1988, and Todd and Tapley, 1988, Table 8.1. Reprinted from* The Columbia University College of Physicians and Surgeons Complete Guide To Pregnancy *by permission of Crown Publishers, Inc. Copyright © 1988 by the College of Physicians and Surgeons of Columbia University.*

Smoking

Dozens of studies show that cigarette smoking during pregnancy is associated with lower birth weights, shortened pregnancies, higher rates of spontaneous abortions, more frequent complications of pregnancy and labor, and higher rates of perinatal mortality (death of the fetus or newborn near the time of the birth) (see detailed reviews by Coleman, Piotrow, and Rinehart, 1979; and Rush and Callahan, 1989). In a more recent study, it was found that the link between maternal smoking during pregnancy and preterm delivery was especially strong, with a 60 percent increase in the risk of delivery before 33 weeks' gestation in women smoking at least a pack a day (Shiono, Klebanoff, and Rhoads, 1986).

teratogen (teh rat' ō jin) a substance, such as a drug or chemical, that causes birth defects.

Table 5.1   Medications That May Affect the Fetus if Taken During Pregnancy

Drug	Fetal Effect
Antibiotics (used to treat infections)	
Chloramphenicol	Vomiting, respiratory problems, circulatory collapse in newborns
Streptomycin	Deafness
Tetracycline	Stained teeth (common), cataracts (rare)
Anticancer drugs	
Aminopterin, Busulfan, Chlorambucil, Cyclophosphamide, Mercaptopurine, Methotrexate	Abortion, various malformations
Anticoagulant drugs (blood thinners)	
Dicumarol	Fetal bleeding or death
Warfarin	Facial deformities, mental retardation, fetal death or bleeding
Anticonvulsant drugs (used to treat epilepsy)	
Dilantin	Cleft palate, heart defects
Carbamazepine	Minor facial deformities, developmental delays
Paramethadione	Growth retardation
Trimethadione	Multiple defects
Phenobarbital	Bleeding
Hormones (various treatments)	
Birth control pills	Limb defects, genital malformations, possible heart or windpipe defects
Progestins	Masculinization of female fetus
Estrogens	Genital defects in male fetus
Diethylstilbestrol (DES)	Delayed effects: vaginal cancer in adolescent and young adult women; reproductive tract abnormalities in men
Testosterone	Masculinization of female fetus
Miscellaneous drugs	
Aspirin	Bleeding
Lithium	Heart defects
Tranquilizers (Librium, Valium, Equanil)	Various defects
Quinine	Deafness
Isoretinoin (Accutane)	Facial abnormalities, heart defects, nervous system abnormalities.

Source: *Data primarily from Wilson, 1977; Benson, 1978; Kalter and Warkany, 1983, and Jones et al., 1989.*

A study involving 28,000 children found that children of mothers who smoke heavily during pregnancy have almost twice the risk of having hyperactive-impulsive behavior at age seven than children born to nonsmoking mothers; such children also have lower IQs, grade placement, and motor skills (Dunn et al., 1977).

The effects of marijuana smoking on fetal development are not clear. The active chemical ingredients of marijuana are known to cross the placental barrier (Harbison and Mantilla-Plata, 1972), and some animal studies have shown fetal damage and miscarriages with heavy marijuana use. However, these studies may not be applicable to humans. Be-

cause chronic, frequent marijuana smoking has been found to lower blood prolactin levels in women (Kolodny et al., 1980), it is possible that nursing might be affected by marijuana use. While data obtained on newborns during the first 30 days after birth have shown that prenatal marijuana exposure may "subtly depress the normal rate of development of the central nervous system," follow-up studies at one and two years of age did not demonstrate any negative effects (Fried, 1989).

Alcohol

Heavy use of alcohol by a pregnant woman can cause considerable damage to the developing baby.

The **fetal alcohol syndrome** includes growth deficiencies before and after birth, damage to the brain and nervous system, and facial abnormalities, especially affecting the eyes (Ouellette et al., 1977; Clarren and Smith, 1978; Dorris, 1989). Mental retardation is sometimes found in the children of alcoholic mothers. There are also behavioral effects of the fetal alcohol syndrome, with irritability noted in infancy and hyperactivity in later childhood (Smith, 1979). Recent studies have shown that these major behavioral handicaps, including long-term deficits in academic achievement, last into adolescence and adulthood (Streissguth, Sampson, and Barr, 1989; Spohn, Willms, and Steinhausen, 1993).

Moderate use of alcohol and "binge" drinking by pregnant women are viewed by some scientists as risky, although the evidence here is not complete. In 1984, in a study of almost 32,000 pregnancies, Mills and his co-workers found that having "at least one to two drinks a day was associated with a substantially increased risk of producing a growth-retarded infant" (p. 1875). It seems safest for pregnant women to abstain completely from alcohol. The less you drink during pregnancy, the better.

Physical Activity

Pregnancy should not be regarded as a time of incapacity and fragility. In healthy women, patterns of work and play do not usually need to change significantly during pregnancy. Many women continue working and engaging in some sports activities until the last month of pregnancy, when fatigue and discomfort may make such activity difficult. Common sense is the best guide to follow, since avoiding excessive fatigue is largely a matter of self-judgment. Activities that might be physically dangerous (skiing, diving, roller skating, mountain climbing, and so on) must be considered carefully by each woman in terms of her health and the length of her pregnancy. Proper amounts of sleep are also important but vary considerably from person to person. Women with health complications during pregnancy such as high blood pressure or vaginal bleeding will find that these conditions respond best to rest.

Sexual Activity During Pregnancy

Pregnancy has no uniform effect on sexual feelings or function. For some women, pregnancy is a time of heightened sexual awareness and sensual pleasure, while for others no changes are noticed or sexual feelings decline. Some couples find that late in pregnancy the awkwardness of a bulging belly and concern about the baby lead to voluntary abstention from sex. For others, adjustments in sexual positions or the use of noncoital sex play solves these problems fairly easily. It's important to remember that sex is not just intercourse: oral sex, sensual massage, and mutual masturbation are among the options for noncoital sex play that can be highly gratifying and can help keep a couple's sense of intimacy alive and well.

Masters and Johnson (1966) found marked variations in patterns of sexual behavior in the first trimester of pregnancy. Not surprisingly, women with morning sickness and high levels of fatigue reported losing interest in sex and a lower frequency of sexual activity, but other women experienced just the opposite effects. In the second trimester, however, 80 percent of the women noted heightened sexuality in terms of both desire and physical response. In the last trimester, there was a pronounced drop in the frequency of intercourse. The women thought this was because they were less physically attractive, but their husbands generally denied this explanation and instead voiced concern about injuring the fetus or their wife.

These findings have been verified in other studies that also showed an increased frequency of sexual activity in the second trimester (Falicov, 1973; Tolor and DiGrazia, 1976).

A few practical guidelines about sex during pregnancy are in order. Women with a history of previous miscarriages or whose pregnancy is in danger of miscarriage should abstain from any type of sexual activity that might result in their having orgasms, since contractions of the uterus during orgasm could be risky. If vaginal or uterine bleeding occurs during pregnancy, it is also wise to avoid all forms of sexual activity until receiving a medical okay. Air blown forcefully into the vagina during oral-genital contact can be dangerous for the pregnant woman, if it causes air embolism (air bubbles in the bloodstream). Cunnilingus *without* air blown into the vagina is not risky. If the membranes have ruptured, intercourse or cunnilingus

fetal alcohol syndrome the effects on the unborn child of heavy use of alcohol by the pregnant woman, including growth deficiencies, nervous system damage, and facial abnormalities.

should be prohibited because of the danger of fetal infection. Aside from these few cautionary notes, sex during pregnancy is quite safe for the fetus and the mother.

A few doctors have voiced concern about orgasms causing premature delivery. While it is possible that uterine contractions resulting from orgasm late in the third trimester may start labor in a small number of pregnant women (or that the prostaglandins contained in semen may trigger the same response), one report documents no statistical correlation between orgasm or intercourse and premature birth (Perkins, 1979). In fact, being orgasmic by intercourse or masturbation was associated with lower rates of prematurity.

BIRTH

Preparing for Childbirth

For the woman who has never had a baby, the process of childbirth may seem mysterious and frightening. Much of the mystery and fear can be relieved by attending childbirth classes held in hospitals or clinics and by obtaining accurate information from readings and discussions with her physician. Because friends and family are as likely to recite gruesome stories or incorrect "facts" as they are to be informative, what is heard from these sources must be taken with a large grain of salt. To get the most out of the experience, the pregnant woman and her husband or partner should attend childbirth classes together whenever possible.

Childbirth classes usually combine lectures and discussions with movies or slides showing a typical delivery. Participants are familiarized with medical terminology, labor room routines, and the operation of the hospital nursery. Most classes take a guided tour of the maternity ward and the nursery as well, so these rooms and their equipment will not seem unfamiliar to them during their labor, delivery, and hospital stay. In addition, most courses provide instruction in specific types of physical exercises designed to make labor and delivery easier.

If the decision has been made to have a home delivery, it is important to do some careful planning to assure that all necessary preparations have been made well in advance. Labor doesn't always begin exactly on schedule, and a baby's arrival can certainly come a week or two before the anticipated due date. While a few doctors are willing to participate in home deliveries, it is more typical to arrange for the services of a nurse–midwife or a lay midwife for the special event.

Lay midwives, known in some states as licensed midwives, come from varied backgrounds; some have graduate degrees, but others have little or no formal education. Nurse–midwives, in contrast, are all registered nurses with extensive health-care backgrounds. While nurse–midwives are legally permitted to perform deliveries throughout the country, lay midwives are legal in only 10 states, including Arizona, New Mexico, and Washington, and banned by law in 10 others, including California. In 21 states, there are no laws governing the practice, while in the remaining states lay midwifery is severely restricted but not banned entirely.

No matter who you choose to assist in an at-home birth, be sure to consult with them about what supplies should be on hand and about any special arrangements that might be required. For instance, many midwives suggest alerting a pediatrician to the impending birth so that he or she can visit the newborn infant shortly after its arrival.

Advocates of home birth feel that it provides a more natural, loving environment for the birth experience and allows women to exercise greater control over the process of having a baby. In addition, many couples believe that a home delivery allows for more personal sensitivity than a hospital birth (e.g., you don't have to deal with the bureaucracy) as well as a better system of social support from family and friends. But not all couples are willing to forego the extensive backup services that a hospital offers if something goes wrong, recognizing that in an emergency, precious time may be lost getting the mother and baby to a facility for necessary medical care.

Labor

Labor consists of rhythmic, regular contractions of the uterus that result in delivery of the child, the placenta, and membranes. Labor is usually preceded by several related events. As already mentioned, a few weeks before labor begins, women who are pregnant for the first time experience lightening. **Effacement,** or thinning of the cervix, and **dilatation,** opening of the mouth of the cervix, are also likely to begin about two weeks before the onset of labor. A very dependable sign of imminent labor is "show" (or "bloody show"), the discharge of a small amount of blood-tinged mucus.[2] Generally, labor begins a few hours or a few days after this occurs. About 10 percent of women experience a premature rupture of their membranes (the amniotic sac or "bag of waters") before labor starts. Warm fluid may trickle or gush from the vagina either running down their legs (if standing) or wetting the bed (if lying down). Labor typically begins within a day after this occurs. If it does not, it may be desirable to start labor artificially to protect the baby from infection since it is no longer isolated from the outside world.

How Labor Begins

The exact biological forces that start labor are not clearly understood. For many years, it was thought that a rapid drop of progesterone at the end of pregnancy might stimulate the beginning of regular contractions of the uterus, but recent studies in humans do not support this explanation. **Oxytocin,** a hormone made in the pituitary gland, has been thought to play a role, but women whose pituitaries have been surgically removed are still capable of normal, spontaneous labor. At present, evidence indicates that prostaglandins may be involved because (1) they can cause strong uterine contractions at any time during pregnancy, (2) the fetal membranes have high concentrations of the substances necessary for the manufacture of prostaglandins, and (3) drugs such as aspirin that inhibit prostaglandin formation can delay the onset of labor (Cunningham, MacDonald, and Gant, 1989).

The Stages of Labor

For descriptive convenience, labor is divided into three stages. The length and experience of these stages vary from woman to woman and for different pregnancies of the same woman.[3]

The **first stage of labor** begins when uterine contractions are strong enough, long enough, and frequent enough to begin effacement and dilatation of the cervix. In first pregnancies, complete effacement occurs before dilatation starts; in later pregnancies, the two occur simultaneously.

When the cervix is completely effaced, its thickness has decreased from about 2 centimeters (0.8 inch) to the thickness of a piece of paper. This process is measured in percentages. If the doctor tells a pregnant woman that she is 50 percent effaced, that means the thickness of the cervix is about 1 centimeter (0.4 inch).

When the opening of the cervix is 10 centimeters (4 inches), a width that must be reached for a baby to be born, dilatation is complete. Dilatation is caused by pressures from uterine contractions pushing the amniotic sac or the baby's head in wedgelike fashion into the cervix.

The first stage of labor is by far the longest: in first pregnancies, it averages 13 hours, and in later pregnancies, 8 hours. Early in first-stage labor, when dilatation is minimal, contractions are mild (lasting 20 to 40 seconds) and far apart, occurring at intervals of 10 to 20 minutes. The woman is usually comfortable and can be out of bed if she wishes. In fact, one study found that walking during early labor (instead of staying in bed) makes mothers more comfortable and less in need of pain

labor the processes involved in giving birth, especially uterine contractions.

effacement (e fāce′ munt) the thinning or flattening of the cervix during labor.

dilatation (dil′ uh tā′ shun) opening of the mouth of the cervix in preparation for birth.

oxytocin (ahk′ sē to′ sin) a hormone made in the posterior pituitary thought to play a role in uterine contractions and lactation stimulation.

first stage of labor the early portion of labor in which cervical effacement and dilatation occurs.

false labor irregular contractions that do not become regular. They are felt mainly in the lower abdomen and groin in contrast to true labor, which is felt in the back and abdomen.

---

[2]"Show" is not a reliable indication of labor if a pelvic exam was done in the preceding day or two, since this may have caused a slight amount of internal bleeding and disrupted the mucous plug guarding the cervix.

[3]**False labor,** contractions that are simply an exaggeration of Braxton–Hicks contractions, may mimic the start of true labor. Although false labor can be convincing enough to result in a trip to the hospital, it can usually be differentiated from true labor. Its contractions tend to be irregular, the interval between them does not shorten, and the woman feels discomfort mainly in the lower abdomen and groin. True labor produces back and abdominal pain. Furthermore, false labor does not result in progressive effacement and dilatation.

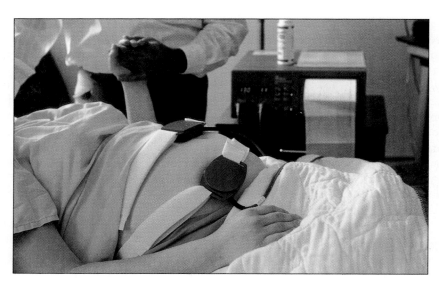

Monitoring the progress of labor and the heartbeat of the unborn child.

relief (Lupe and Gross, 1986). Walking also causes stronger labor contractions, which may shorten the overall time until delivery.

In the first stage of labor, a woman may be discouraged by the length of time it takes to get even a little dilatation, but once she has gotten to 4 or 5 centimeters she has usually completed more than half of the time in this stage. At this more active part of the first stage, contractions are typically 30 to 60 seconds long and occur every 2 to 4 minutes.

The woman may obtain treatment to help deal with pain at this time, since medications given any earlier might slow the progress of labor. Various types of pain relief are available (see Table 5.2), and the woman should become familiar with them and discuss her options with her midwife or doctor well before labor starts. Although all medications have potential risks—including some negative effects on the baby—careful use under medical supervision can be important in allowing the mother to go through labor and delivery with less discomfort. This relief can have obvious psychological and physical benefits. Regrettably, some women feel guilty if they want pain relievers during childbirth. They may feel inadequate for needing such help, especially if a friend or relative had an easy delivery *without* drugs and is sure everyone else's experience should be the same. Others have been told that the medical "establishment" pushes medications primarily for its own convenience and income. While some doctors do this, most have the welfare and comfort of their patient and her baby uppermost in their minds.

The last part of the first stage of labor (8 to 10 centimeters dilatation) is usually the most uncomfortable. The woman's contractions last 45 to 60 seconds or longer, are only about 2 minutes apart, and are very strong. In first pregnancies, this part of labor usually lasts about 40 minutes and in later pregnancies it averages 20 minutes. Most often, the membranes rupture at this time. The first stage of labor ends when dilatation of the cervix is complete.

The **second stage of labor,** which goes from full dilatation to birth of the baby, is shorter (average length, 80 minutes in first pregnancies, 30 minutes in others) and is usually less stressful for the mother. She can now assist the baby's descent by pushing down with her contractions.

Once the baby's head is delivered, blood and mucus are wiped off and the nose and mouth are suctioned to aid breathing.[4] As soon as the rest of the baby is out (a process that is surprisingly quick in an uncomplicated birth), the newborn is held below the level of the mother's body and suctioning of the mouth and nose is repeated. The umbilical cord is clamped and cut about 3 centimeters (1¼

---

[4]The baby's head is the first part to be delivered in about 95 percent of pregnancies. These are called **occiput, vertex,** or **cephalic presentations. Breech presentations** occur about 4 percent of the time. In this position, the buttocks or feet are delivered first. In the rarer cases, called **transverse positions,** the baby lies across the uterus and a shoulder or arm will present first. Breech or transverse presentations require either turning the baby or performing a cesarean section.

Table 5.2 Medications for Pain Reduction in Labor and Delivery

Analgesics	Effects on Mother	Effects on Fetus
Tranquilizers Valium, Vistaril, Sparine	Physical relaxation and reduced anxiety; takes the edge off pain but does not eliminate it entirely	Minimal
Barbiturates Nembutal, Seconal, Amytal	Drowsiness and reduced anxiety; may slow the progress of labor	Can depress nervous system and breathing
Narcotics Demerol, Dolophine, Nisentil	Reduce pain and elevate mood but may inhibit uterine contractions and cause nausea or vomiting	Can depress nervous system and breathing
Amnesics Scopolamine ("Twilight")	Does not reduce pain but causes the woman to forget her experience after it is over; may cause physical excitation and wildness	Minimal

Anesthetics	Effects on Mother	Effects on Fetus
Local Paracervical	Blocks pain in the uterus and cervix, but relatively short-lasting and ineffective late in labor; can lower mother's blood pressure	Causes a slowing of fetal heartbeat in about 20 percent of cases
Pudendal	Blocks pain from the perineum and vulva in about 50 percent of cases	Minimal
Regional Spinal, epidural, caudal	Blocks pain from the uterus, cervix, and perineum; highly effective but can cause serious drop in blood pressure or seizures	Generally does not affect fetus but requires forceps delivery more often than other methods
General Nitrous oxide (laughing gas), Halothane, Thiopental	Usually used only in the last few minutes of labor to eliminate pain completely but may cause vomiting or other complications and is a leading cause of maternal death	Can depress nervous system and breathing

inches) from the baby's body (the stub dries up in a few days and falls off, leaving the navel behind as a souvenir). Although often shown in movies or television dramas, midwives or doctors rarely have to spank a baby to induce crying and breathing, since this usually happens spontaneously. As the baby takes his or her first breaths, the skin will become pink unless there is a medical problem.

The baby is shown to the mother and usually given to her to hold. To prevent eye infections after the passage through the vagina, the baby is almost always given eye drops (usually silver nitrate) or

second stage of labor the portion of labor from full cervical dilatation to delivery of the baby.

occiput presentation the childbirth presentation in which the back part of the baby's head is the first part to pass through the birth canal.

vertex presentation (vur' teks) the childbirth presentation in which the crown of the baby's head is first to be seen at the opening of the vagina.

cephalic presentation (se fal' ik) the childbirth presentation in which the baby's head is the first part of the baby's body to pass through the birth canal.

breech presentation the childbirth presentation in which the buttocks or feet are the first part of the baby to pass through the opening of the vagina.

transverse position the childbirth presentation in which the baby lies across the uterus and a shoulder or arm is first to be seen at the opening of the vagina. A cesarean section is often necessary if the baby cannot be turned.

an antibiotic ointment. The baby is also given a vitamin K shot to prevent bleeding, since this vitamin cannot be manufactured in newborns immediately after birth. Finally, if the delivery has been conducted in a hospital or birthing center, the baby is given an identification bracelet, footprints are taken, and a medical exam is done to check for birth defects or other health problems.

The **third stage of labor** follows the baby's birth. At this point, the placenta separates from the wall of the uterus, and the placenta and membranes (the "afterbirth") are delivered. This usually requires only 10 to 12 minutes. If even small pieces of the placenta or membranes are retained in the uterus, bleeding problems may result.

Delivery

Over the years, many different schools of thought have emerged concerning the details and style of labor and delivery, and pregnant women and doctors are often bombarded with information "proving" that one way is undeniably the best. Usually, it is a matter of personal preference (or health considerations) between a woman and her midwife or doctor. Increasingly today, choices about the setting and style of delivery are made by the woman and her spouse or partner rather than leaving these up to the health-care professional's choices alone. Here, we discuss some of the more popular methods of delivery.

Hospital Delivery

A hospital delivery usually begins once the first stage of labor is under way. A nurse or doctor asks a series of questions to outline the history of the pregnancy and the sequence of events near the time of labor, and a vaginal examination is done to see how much dilatation and effacement have occurred. A blood sample and urine specimen are usually taken for a general health check, and a physical exam is performed to evaluate the mother's condition and that of the baby.

After this point, hospital procedures vary considerably. In many hospitals, sophisticated electronic equipment is used to check the progress of the baby (**fetal monitoring**) as well as the frequency, intensity, and duration of the mother's contractions. Watching the fetal heart rate is particularly important because a sustained change in rate may indicate fetal distress.

In some cases, a woman may be admitted to the hospital at, near, or past her due date to have labor started artificially. This procedure, called **induction** or **induced labor,** is usually done so that a well-rested woman can begin labor under planned conditions with her doctor present; this technique is also used in certain types of problem pregnancies where it can protect the health of the mother and child alike. Labor is usually induced by giving the mother oxytocin. Inducing labor is not without risk to the mother and fetus, but most physicians feel that the benefits outweigh the risks substantially. Some observers have claimed that the issue is really a matter of medical chauvinism, however, believing that induction is mainly done for the doctor's convenience (Hahn and Paige, 1980).

The woman's husband or partner is usually encouraged to be present during labor and delivery so that he can share the experience, give encouragement and support, and help make her comfortable. In the past, most hospitals did not permit other family members to be present. Fortunately, this situation is now changing rapidly, as many hospitals have altered their policy on this matter. Regardless of which members of the family are present, obstetrical nurses can provide close, continuing attention and information.

Doctors sometimes rupture the membranes to stimulate the progress of labor. An intravenous solution of sugar and water may be started to prevent dehydration and to allow for rapid administration of anesthesia or blood transfusions if something goes wrong. During the delivery, the baby's head may be assisted out of the vagina by the use of forceps if there is fetal distress, if the umbilical cord is wrapped tightly around the baby's neck, if the cord is being compressed so that the blood supply to the baby is cut off (**prolapsed cord**), or if anesthesia interferes with the mother's ability to push out her baby.

At the time of **crowning** (the first appearance of the baby's head at the opening of the vagina), many American physicians routinely perform an **episiotomy** to enlarge the opening for the baby's head. An episiotomy is an incision made through the skin and muscle of the perineum, the area between the vagina and the anus (see Figure 5.6). The episiotomy has several purposes: (1) it reduces the pressure against the baby's head, lessening the trauma of delivery; (2) it reduces the risk of tearing the perineum, which might cause more extensive tissue damage and might be ragged-edged and difficult to repair; and (3) it permits the use of forceps or vacuum devices if needed to assist in delivering the baby's head. Most women do not feel the incision being made because the perineum is numbed from the pressure of the baby's head.

Some people are opposed to routine episiotomies, noting that fewer than one-third of deliveries in Europe use this technique (Arms, 1975; Lake, 1976). Furthermore, they point out that the vaginal opening has the capacity to stretch widely without tearing in most circumstances and suggest that episiotomy should be done only in selected cases (Boston Women's Health Book Collective, 1984).

Although 80 percent of deliveries are straightforward and uncomplicated, there are specific advantages to hospital delivery. Sophisticated equipment is available for rapid diagnosis of problems affecting either mother or child, facilities for surgery are close at hand if emergency cesarean section is needed, blood is available for transfusion if maternal bleeding cannot be controlled, and the personnel and equipment of the nursery are specially geared to problems of the newborn infant. While some problems of labor and delivery are detectable in advance (e.g., breech presentation, transverse lie, maternal illness), others are not discovered until labor is far along.

Figure 5.6 An Episiotomy Done During Labor

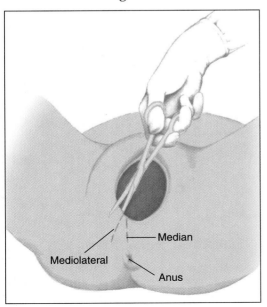

Mediolateral

Median

Anus

A generation ago, a new mother would remain in the hospital for about a week after a simple, uncomplicated delivery in order to give her time to rest and recuperate. Today, the normal pattern is for a mother to enter the hospital, have her baby, and return home again in 48 hours or less. (Even someone who has had a caesarean section can expect to be home 72 hours after the surgery.) This change reflects both economic pressures to cut the costs of childbirth (especially since those insurance policies that have obstetrical benefits usually have strict limitations on the length of hospital stay that will be covered) as well as a shift in medical attitudes that is linked to viewing women as less fragile and in need of coddling than in the past.

Natural Childbirth

Natural childbirth refers to a method described by a British obstetrician, Grantly Dick-Read, in 1932 in a book titled *Childbirth Without Fear.* He objected to much of the medical intervention in delivery and believed that culturally imbued fear and tension were the principal causes of pain and difficulty in the childbirth experience. He felt that fear and anticipation of pain led to psychological and muscular tension, which opposed dilatation of the birth canal and became, in effect, a self-fulfilling prophecy.

To break the fear–tension–pain reaction, Dick-Read suggested eliminating fear through education and reducing tension by the use of relaxation techniques such as breathing and physical exercises. Prenatal classes were used to stress the positive side

third stage of labor the period immediately following delivery of the baby, concluding with separation and expulsion of the placenta.

fetal monitor electronic equipment used during labor to check the progress of the baby, especially its heartbeat, and the duration, frequency, and intensity of uterine contractions.

induced labor labor started artificially, usually by infusing oxytocin into a vein.

prolapsed cord condition whereby the umbilical cord is compressed to the point where the blood supply to the baby is cut off.

crowning in childbirth, the appearance of the baby's head at the opening of the vagina.

episiotomy (e piz′ ē ot′ uh mē) during a vaginal delivery, the incision in the mother's perineum that gives the baby's head more room to emerge.

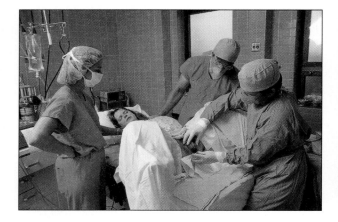
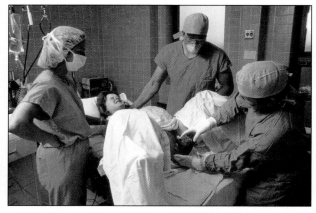
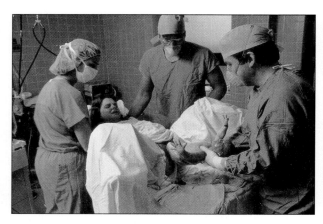
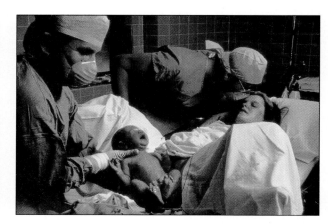
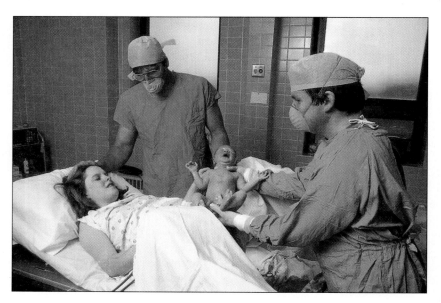

This sequence of photos of a hospital delivery shows the baby's head emerging, the doctor clearing mucus from the baby's mouth and nose, and the baby just delivered (and still connected to the mother by the umbilical cord). The bottom photo shows Mom taking her first good look at her baby, while a proud Dad looks on.

of childbirth and to teach exercises to increase elasticity in the pelvic muscles, flexibility in the joints of the pelvis and back, and improve circulation. Special breathing patterns to reduce pain and increase the effectiveness of contractions were taught.

Although some consider childbirth to be truly "natural" only if no painkilling medications are used at all, Dick-Read felt that painkillers were permissible but were to be avoided if possible.

Lamaze

A similar approach to that of Dick-Read was advocated by Fernand Lamaze, a French obstetrician who traveled to Russia to study obstetrical practices. The Lamaze method, first publicized in this country in a book called *Thank You, Dr. Lamaze* (Karmel, 1959) and later described in *Painless Childbirth* (Lamaze, 1970), also depends on education and exercises to allow a woman to gain control over her labor.

The Lamaze method, taught in prenatal classes to both the wife and the husband (or to the woman and another friend acting as her "coach" if she is not married or her husband is not available), shows women how to relax all the muscles in their bodies and how to position themselves and breathe during different stages of labor. Other techniques are used to distract the woman from awareness of pain: these include **effleurage**, a light, circular stroking of the abdomen used when active labor begins, pressure on the front of the hip bones to reduce abdominal discomfort, and massage techniques to lessen backache. Both the coach and the mother are active participants in the labor, with a prearranged set of exercises to follow.

Neither natural childbirth nor childbirth by the Lamaze method is completely painless. Both approaches depend on personal awareness through education to reduce fear of the unknown and physical relaxation techniques that reduce tension and the anticipation of pain. In both methods, there is some distraction from the perception of pain, but pain is not eliminated.

Cesarean Section

Cesarean section (C section) is an operation to remove the fetus through an incision in the walls of the abdomen and uterus. Cesareans are done when the woman cannot deliver vaginally without endangering her or the baby's life or health. Among conditions that usually require cesarean delivery

are (1) a size difference between the baby's head and the mother's pelvis that makes it difficult or impossible for the baby to pass through the birth canal, (2) transverse position of the baby or another difficult presentation, (3) fetal distress from any cause (e.g., prolapsed cord), (4) premature separation of the placenta or abnormal positioning of the placenta so it blocks the opening to the cervix from within the uterus, and (5) long, difficult labor that is not progressing properly.

In the last 15 years, the cesarean birth rate has quadrupled, from 5.5 to 23.5 percent (Myers and Gleicher, 1988; Centers for Disease Control, 1993a). In 1991, of approximately 4,111,000 live births, an estimated 966,000 were by cesarean delivery, with about 35 percent of this number done in women who had had a previous cesarean section (Centers for Disease Control, 1993a). In fact, in many suburban hospitals, cesarean births now account for 30 to 35 percent of all deliveries and it has been predicted that, without a change in obstetrical trends, the national cesarean section rate could reach 40 percent by the end of this century (Placek, Taffel, and Liss, 1987).

This development has alarmed many medical experts and health-care consumer advocates, who contend that overuse of cesarean births reflects improper medical practice and that physicians who perform unnecessary cesareans are motivated by the higher fees they charge for this procedure as well as by the desire to avoid lawsuits (Danforth, 1985; Queenan, 1988; Gould et al., 1989; Goyert et al., 1989). After all, if obstetricians routinely perform cesareans in problem pregnancies, an attorney can legitimately ask why one wasn't done in a specific case. As an editorial in the *Journal of the American Medical Association* recently put it: "In our current litigious environment where patients expect a perfect obstetric outcome and physicians using available knowledge are eager to try new technologies to improve that outcome, is it surprising we have seen an escalation of cesarean delivery rates to a level that now appears unreasonable? (Jonas and Dooley, 1989, p. 1513)."

Rosen and Thomas (1989) point out that there are three assumptions that doctors and the public share that have also contributed to the torrent of

effleurage (ef' lu razh') the circular stroking movement used in massage of the abdomen during labor in the Lamaze method.

cesarean births: cesareans are safe, they are required in a broad range of cases, and they produce healthier babies. The reality is quite different.

Although cesarean births have a low rate of complications, the maternal death rate (1 in 10,000) is double the rate for vaginal deliveries. In addition, a cesarean increases the risk of blood loss or infection during childbirth, and these complications may have long-term ramifications. Finally, there is no evidence that cesarean babies are healthier overall than those born by vaginal delivery (Gould et al., 1989; Rosen and Thomas, 1989): in fact, the opposite may be true (Battaglia, 1988).

In light of these facts, it is interesting to note that a 1980 task force sponsored by the National Institutes of Health recommended that many women who had cesarean deliveries can safely have subsequent normal vaginal deliveries, although in the past, 99 percent were automatically given cesareans for future childbirth (Kolata, 1980a). Confirming this, one study found that approximately two-thirds of women who had previously had a cesarean were able to have successful vaginal deliveries (Weitz, 1985). Furthermore, in a number of other countries, including Norway, Scotland, and Hungary, more than one-third of women who have had cesareans have vaginal births later on (Notzon, Placek, and Taffel, 1987).

The questions raised by the high rates of cesarean sections do not alter the need for this procedure as the proper treatment for certain obstetric problems, such as abnormal positioning of the placenta or fetal distress. But overuse of surgical delivery is part of the widespread American notion that doctors deliver babies, not that women give birth. In fact, one of the complaints that obstetricians have is that some women demand a cesarean—especially if they've had one before—which may reflect their feeling that a cesarean is an "easier" experience on the mother. As one 29-year-old woman explained it (Authors' files):

> I had heard a lot of stories from my friends about how painful vaginal delivery was, and to tell you the truth I'm not a person who's really good at dealing with pain. So I thought to myself, if you can have a C-section and be anesthetized so you don't feel anything at all, that's for me. So I just shopped around for a doctor who was willing to agree in advance to do it that way, and I was more than delighted with the result.

On the other hand, some couples who were not expecting a cesarean birth may feel cheated or disappointed by not going through labor and delivery as they had prepared for it, especially if they feel it is a somewhat artificial, depersonalized kind of birth experience.

While it is possible to have a cesarean section while the woman is fully awake (using spinal anesthesia), if the operation is done on an emergency basis the woman is almost always put under general anesthesia. One final point about cesarean sections is a practical matter: there is usually a longer (and more expensive) hospital stay involved—four to five days, versus the two-day stay now common for uncomplicated childbirth.

Home Delivery and Birthing Rooms

Not everyone views the hospital, with its authoritative atmosphere, complex rules, impersonality, and association with illness, as an ideal setting for childbirth. In some countries, such as France and Holland, some women go to special childbirth centers that are separate from hospitals (there are about 200 in the United States). The services of childbirth centers are usually covered by health insurance plans that include obstetrical benefits. In many societies, home delivery supervised by a midwife is common (Cavero, 1979). While two decades ago there were only 300 nurse–midwives in the United States, there are now more than 3000, with several hundred new nurse–midwives graduating annually from certified training programs. Although many work in hospitals, others are in private practice either in association with physicians or independently.

Nurse–midwives generally emphasize prenatal counseling, family-centered childbirth, and a limited degree of intervention in the natural process of labor and delivery. Unlike most physicians, nurse–midwives typically stay with a woman throughout her labor and often encourage the woman to get up out of bed and move around through most of her labor. Today, a number of states (including New York, Pennsylvania, Alaska, Maryland, Mississippi, New Mexico, and Utah) have laws requiring that insurance companies provide coverage for the services of certified nurse–midwives who work under the guidance of physicians or hospitals, but in other states there is considerable resistance to the use of nurse–mid-

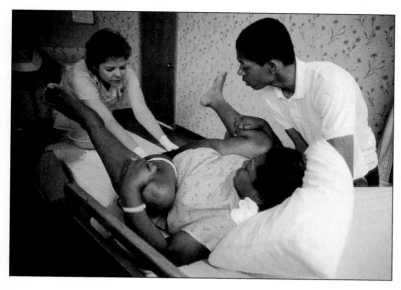

Birthing rooms have been added at many hospitals to provide a more homelike environment for labor and delivery while permitting the entire family to participate in the experience.

wives, especially those who practice independently of hospitals. Only about 10 percent of certified nurse–midwives do home deliveries.

Having a baby at home offers a chance for a more relaxed experience in familiar surroundings, freedom from hospital routines, contact with the whole family (including children who can share in the process), and a less expensive medical bill. In addition, there is preliminary evidence that home delivery may be as safe as hospital delivery for uncomplicated pregnancies (Wertz and Wertz, 1977; Hahn and Paige, 1980).

Although many doctors are opposed to home births, some are willing to cooperate and a few are even enthusiastic about the practice. In any case, careful prenatal screening must be done to identify potential problem pregnancies or difficult deliveries, provisions must be made for appropriate supervision by an experienced midwife or doctor, and emergency access to a hospital must be available since prenatal screening is not infallible.

A relatively recent compromise designed to overcome the image of hospital austerity is the opening of birthing rooms at hundreds of hospitals across America. In these rooms, which are typically furnished in a comfortable, homelike fashion but are also equipped with oxygen and anesthesia, labor and delivery are possible in a more relaxed climate in which other family members, including children, can be part of the childbirth experience. In addition, the woman does not need to be moved from a labor room to a separate delivery room. If something goes

wrong, however—for example, if a blood transfusion is needed—all necessary resources are at hand to take care of the emergency, thus circumventing what many see as the primary risk of home delivery. This is important because even among women who are prescreened to be at low risk for problems during childbirth, about one in five actually experience complications that require being transferred to the hospital (Petravage, 1983). Use of these birthing rooms usually costs about the same as a more traditional delivery in the hospital.

A recent survey of 11,814 deliveries at 84 freestanding childbirth centers involving women with a lower-than-average risk of a poor outcome of pregnancy found that one woman in six was transferred to a hospital but that overall birth centers offer a safe, acceptable alternative to hospital delivery (Rooks et al., 1989).

Psychological Aspects of Childbirth

Each woman brings her own personality style and ways of dealing with a new experience to the process of childbirth. Her initial anxieties may reflect concerns for her safety and the status of her baby, fear of the unknown, uncertainty about her capacity to love and care for a child, and a host of other questions (How will my husband react? What if the baby is not normal? Will I make a fool of myself?). The childbirth experience is also colored by the woman's relationship with her doctor, her feelings about the use of medications, the support she receives from her husband or partner, and the expectations she has of what it will be like. The relatively high rate of cesarean deliveries and other obstetrical complications means that childbirth is frequently not the experience it is expected to be (Grossman, Eichler, and Winickoff, 1980). No wonder it is difficult to talk about a "typical" experience.

In some cases, a woman may sacrifice personal choice about aspects of childbirth to medical routine or philosophical principles. For example, a woman may prefer to be given painkillers but may not allow herself to take them if friends or relatives discourage this practice. Certainly, competent obstetrical service must be available, but it should not preclude personal expression in having a baby. Childbirth is an intensely personal experience. The culmination of pregnancy in labor and delivery is ideally a time of intimacy, sharing, and fulfillment.

THE POSTPARTUM DAYS

The postpartum period, the time after the baby's birth, requires many adjustments for all concerned. Physical changes occur as the mother's body adjusts to no longer being pregnant. Both parents must also psychologically adjust to the new baby, parental roles and responsibilities, changes in family relationships, and looking ahead to the future. This is a complex time of ups and downs, new experiences, frustrations, and joys.

Physiologic and Anatomic Processes

After delivery, the uterus shrinks back to its normal size gradually, going from about 1000 grams (2.2 pounds) just after delivery to 50 to 70 grams (1.8 to 2.5 ounces) at the end of the sixth postpartum week. Once the placenta separates from the uterus, the levels of certain hormones in the mother's body (most notably, estrogen and progesterone) decline abruptly. It usually takes the woman several weeks to adjust to this rapid change, and some authorities believe that the emotional ups and downs of the early postpartum period are related to this phenomenon.

Immediately after childbirth, the cervix is collapsed and flabby but it quickly regains its tone, tightening so that by a week after delivery there is an opening of less than 1 centimeter (0.4 inch). During the first few postpartum weeks, as the lining of the uterus regrows, there is a discharge called lochia that changes in color from dark red to pinkish-brown to yellowish-white. The vagina, which was stretched considerably during birth, gradually gets smaller but usually does not return to the exact size it was before childbirth.

Psychological Reactions

The first day or two after childbirth is often a time of happiness and relief. The woman enjoys a feeling of accomplishment, family and friends congratulate her, and people around her attend to her needs without great demands on her time and energy. By the third or fourth day after delivery, many women experience a turn in their mood—feeling "down," being tearful, or having frightening thoughts or dreams—a phenomenon called "baby blues" or **postpartum depression.**

The irritability and vulnerability that also mark this emotional letdown probably stem from many sources: the hormonal changes previously mentioned, the effects of fatigue and physical stress, a sense of loneliness and separation, the strangeness of being in the hospital, and mixed feelings about the mother's role and viewing herself in a new light. In most cases, postpartum depression lasts for only a few days.

One study questions whether the unique mood changes that occur in both women and men during the postpartum period are actually depression at all (Quadagno et al., 1986). Husbands and wives in 21 couples completed daily questionnaires for 10-day periods during the third trimester, the postpartum period, and six months after birth. The moods that were experienced the most strongly during the postpartum period were not the ones usually associated with depression, such as feeling depressed, sad, discouraged, or pessimistic. Instead, the moods that were strongest during the postpartum days, for both men and women, were those related to anxiety and concern with coping ability (nervous, worried, helpless, anxious) and those associated with positive emotions (enthusiastic, happy). The authors of this study remarked, "Individuals may be nervous and worried about their ability to cope with the demands of a new infant, but yet, at the same time, they seem to feel very positively about the experience" (p. 1021). On the other hand, several recent reports find little difference between postpartum depression and other types of depression not associated with pregnancy (O'Hara et al., 1991; Whiffen and Gotlib, 1993).

Some women may feel guilty or troubled in the early postpartum period. Not all pregnancies result in normal children, and the mother of an infant with a birth defect or serious illness (as well as a woman whose child was stillborn) may try to "explain" what happened on the basis of something she did wrong. Women might also worry over their partner's welfare, over particular decisions such as nursing versus bottle-feeding, or over their ability to care for their child. For other women, there may be a personal sense of failure if, for example, they were unable to deliver vaginally and required a cesarean section. A woman who has previously decided to put her child up for adoption may have second thoughts at this time or may have a profound sense of loss even though she feels she's doing the right thing.

A new set of circumstances and a new set of adjustments occur immediately after leaving the hospital. The demands of the new infant (nighttime feedings, diaper changes, and so on) are thrown into the demands of everyday living. Older children and husband want attention, friends and family want to visit and talk, and the mother is apt to feel fragmented, confused, and exhausted. Some women receive considerable help during this time from their own mother, another relative, a friend, or someone they have hired. Husbands can help out, too, but do not always have the time, the interest, or the experience to be a major source of reliable assistance. The postpartum adjustment beyond the first week or two is primarily a reflection of the adjustment to parenting, a process that is now considered.

Parenting

The first days after delivery can play a critical role in the development of an emotional link between parent and child, a process called **parent–child bonding.** Physical contact, cuddling, cooing, and eye contact in this period of the infant's life seem to have a major impact on the child's later behavior and psychological health (Trause, Kennel, and Klaus, 1977). One experiment showed that babies who received more early postnatal contact with their mothers were more attentive to them at four weeks of age (Klaus et al., 1972). Another study demonstrated that newborns were able to recognize differences in adult voices and to show a preference for their mother's voice within the first three days of life (DeCasper and Fifer, 1980).

Father–child bonding in the early postpartum period is also thought to be important. For one thing, fathers who have been present during birth and who have cuddled the newborn and spent some time talking or just making "goo-goo" noises to it do not seem to experience the sense of alienation that is often found among "waiting room fathers"; furthermore, research shows that the fathers who have bonded with the baby tend to spend more time with it later on (Todd and Tapley, 1988).

As already mentioned, arriving at home with a new baby is apt to be a trying time. Adjusting to the state of parenthood, with its restrictions on freedom, privacy, and self-indulgence, is not easy. No one can be the perfect parent—always patient, never angry, constantly available, forever exercising good judgment, and never making a mistake—but new parents often need a while to gain this perspective.

Nursing

Milk production (**lactation**) occurs two or three days after birth, replacing the colostrum previously secreted by the breasts. The breasts are prepared for lactation by large amounts of prolactin secreted by the pituitary during the second half of pregnancy. In response to the stimulus of suckling, which further increases prolactin secretion, the breasts become more distended until finally there is a milk flow reflex (ejection of milk from the breast), which is controlled by oxytocin. In the first day or two of nursing, the breasts may be uncomfortable because of congestion; the nipples may also be sore because the hungry baby's sucking grip is surprisingly powerful. This soreness can sometimes be limited if steps are taken to condition the nipples in the two months prior to childbirth.

Nursing has a number of advantages over bottle-feeding. Breast milk has natural ingredients that

postpartum depression the letdown many women experience after giving birth. They are tearful and depressed and may have frightening dreams. Also called baby blues.

parent–child bonding the process of attachment and identification that usually occurs during early infancy.

lactation (lak tā′ shun) the production of milk by the breasts, usually beginning a few days after birth.

strengthen the baby's resistance to disease, is instantly available, does not require sterilization or heating as bottles do, and is self-replenishing. Nursing also provides a closeness that has psychological benefits for both child and mother. On the negative side, drugs and medications taken by the mother are usually secreted in her milk, breast-feeding may be inconvenient if the mother works outside the home, and in some cases, if milk flow does not prove adequate to meet the baby's nutritional needs, the mother may experience a sense of failure.

Women often become sexually aroused during nursing; some women even have orgasms in this fashion. Erotic arousal in this context can create reactions ranging from pleasure to guilt or fear. Interestingly, Masters and Johnson (1966) found that women who breast-feed their babies have considerably higher sexual interest in the first three postpartum months than women who do not.

Despite clear-cut recognition of the proven benefits of breast-feeding, the proportion of breast-feeding mothers in the United States has declined somewhat since the early 1980s (Freed, 1993). Highly educated, relatively affluent mothers are most apt to nurse their babies; the rates for breast-feeding among blacks are less than half those for whites or Hispanics (Ryan, Lewandowski, and Krieger, 1991). According to data from the La Leche League, 62.2 percent of white mothers nursed their babies while in the hospital, compared to 50.6 percent of Hispanic mothers and 24.9 percent of black mothers (Leary, 1988). In addition, black mothers tend to stop nursing sooner than whites do (Kurinij, Shiono, and Rhodes, 1988).

The individual woman's decision to nurse or to bottle-feed is influenced by many different factors. Jelliffe (1976) identified several social biases in this decision-making process: the Western world's tendency to overvalue manufactured products, overemphasis on the sexual rather than nurturing role of breasts, the changing role of women in terms of work outside the home, and pressures from the food industry via advertising. On the other hand, in recent years the arguments of breast-feeding advocates have often made women feel that bottle-feeding is a crime against nature and is a shirking of their duties as "good" mothers. Our suspicion is that if breast-feeding is undertaken out of a sense of obligation, the emotional benefits to mother and child probably diminish considerably.

Bottle-feeding allows both parents to interact with the baby more freely and can certainly foster a close, loving relationship just as breast-feeding can.

Returning to Sexual Interaction

Most doctors advise women to abstain from coitus for a number of weeks after childbirth to allow healing of the episiotomy and restoration of the vagina and uterus. The exact timing of when sexual intercourse can be resumed is an individual matter, influenced by both medical factors (e.g., persistent bleeding, fatigue) and psychological considerations (e.g., postpartum depression). By three to four weeks after delivery, most women find their sexual desire returning and can comfortably resume sexual activity. In circumstances where intercourse is still uncomfortable, alternative means of sexual expression can be used until full recovery takes place.

PROBLEM PREGNANCIES

Not all pregnancies go as planned or as described in textbooks. There are several common problems, which we discuss here.

Prematurity

A premature baby is one born any time before the thirty-sixth week of pregnancy. Babies born prematurely are more likely to have health difficulties than full-term babies; as a result, prematurity is a leading cause of newborn death. "Preemies" have a high rate of respiratory problems, seizures, and infections, which may lead to brain damage or other long-range handicaps. Premature births are associated with maternal illness, malfunction of the placenta, heavy smoking, and pregnancies in young teenagers, but in many cases no underlying cause can be found. Modern methods of caring for premature infants have significantly improved survival rates from just a few years ago (Working Group, 1990). Today, close to 50 percent of premies born weighing 500 to 750 grams (about 1 pound, 2 ounces to 1 pound, 10 ounces) can survive with appropriate neonatal intensive care, although the majority will have neurological damage (Rosenthal, 1991). Slightly heavier premature babies have an excellent chance of survival with little or no long-term health effects thanks to today's near miraculous medical technologies.

Toxemia

Toxemia of pregnancy is a disease marked by the sudden appearance of high blood pressure, severe edema, and protein in the urine after the twentieth week of pregnancy (**preeclampsia**), which in some cases progresses to convulsions and coma (**eclampsia**). Although 6 percent of pregnancies have this complication, its cause is not known. Toxemia is most frequent in first pregnancies, especially in the very young or in women over the age of 35. In later pregnancies, it may be associated with diabetes or vascular disease. Toxemia is most commonly found in women of low socioeconomic standing, and some evidence suggests that a tendency to this disorder is inherited. Untreated, toxemia can cause maternal or fetal death, but if properly treated it can usually be controlled.

Recent research on toxemia of pregnancy suggests that it may be prevented in many cases by the use of low doses of aspirin in the third trimester of pregnancy (Benigni et al., 1989; Schiff et al., 1989). Aspirin seems to work by suppressing the production of a prostaglandin-like substance from platelets (a type of blood cell) that causes spasms of the blood vessels and can lead to increases in blood pressure (Cunningham and Gant, 1989).

Birth Defects and Their Detection

Birth defects occur in approximately 3 percent of all live births and at a substantially higher rate in miscarried pregnancies. About 20 percent of birth defects are inherited, 3 to 5 percent reflect chromosome abnormalities, 2 to 3 percent are due to infections, and 5 percent are due to maternal drug use or exposure to environmental chemicals; but in the majority of cases no specific explanation can be discovered (Wilson, 1977).

Only two examples of birth defects will be mentioned here. **Down's syndrome** (also called trisomy 21 or mongolism) is a chromosome disorder that causes severe mental retardation and defects of the heart, kidneys, and intestines. Its incidence increases with advanced maternal age (see Table 5.3). In about 95 percent of cases, the extra chromosome is maternal in origin (Antonarakis et al., 1991). Maternal infection with the virus that causes German measles (**rubella**) can also be dangerous to the developing baby. German measles causes serious defects in about half of exposed embryos during the first month of pregnancy, but this rate decreases to 25 percent in the second month and less than 15 percent in the third month. The fetal damage caused by rubella includes deafness, cataracts, heart defects, mental retardation, and retarded growth. While the number of cases of German measles in the United States dropped dramatically—from 58,000 reported cases in 1969 to only 2 cases in 1989 (Centers for Disease Control, 1991)—there has recently been a sharp resurgence in the number of cases of congenital rubella syndrome (Lee et al., 1992).

Having a child with a birth defect can be frightening and disheartening. Our society emphasizes success and physical appearance, and the parents of a child with a defect may see their baby as a sign of a defect within themselves or as "punishment" for something they did wrong. Some parents react by rejection and denial, while others cope by bringing extra love and care to their newborn and accepting the infant as a full-fledged family member. Some families find new strength and closeness after the birth of a child with a defect.

Fortunately, there are now several ways of detecting the presence of certain types of defects in the developing fetus. In the procedure called **amniocentesis** (Figure 5.7), a sample of amniotic fluid

toxemia a complication of pregnancy marked by sudden increase in blood pressure, edema, and protein in the urine.

preeclampsia (prē′ e klamp′ sē uh) a condition occurring during the latter half of pregnancy characterized by high blood pressure, edema, and protein in the urine. May progress to eclampsia.

eclampsia (e klamp sē uh) a condition occurring during the latter half of pregnancy marked by high blood pressure, edema, protein in the urine, and convulsions, sometimes resulting in coma or death. Also known as toxemia of pregnancy.

Down's syndrome a chromosome disorder that causes mental retardation and defects of the heart, kidneys, and intestines. Also known as trisomy 21 or mongolism.

rubella (roo bel′ uh) German measles. If the virus crosses the placental barrier to the fetus, it can cause serious malformations including deafness, eye problems, and mental retardation.

amniocentesis (am′ nē ō sen tē′ sis) procedure used to obtain a sample of amniotic fluid from the uterus of a pregnant woman to be analyzed for a variety of genetic disorders and biochemical abnormalities in the fetus.

is obtained by inserting a needle into the uterus after first deadening the abdominal wall with a local anesthetic. Analysis of the fluid can identify a variety of genetic disorders (e.g., Down's syndrome and muscular dystrophy) as well as the sex of the fetus. If a serious abnormality is uncovered, the parents can consider terminating the pregnancy by abortion if this choice is consistent with their personal values. There is about a 1 percent risk that amniocentesis may result in loss of the fetus, but this risk must be balanced with the benefits of a highly reliable means of identifying serious genetic problems (see Table 5.4 for a list of indications for prenatal diagnosis).

A newer technique, called **chorionic villi sampling (CVS)** is seen by some authorities as having even greater usefulness. This method, which involves insertion of a thin catheter through the vagina and cervix into the uterus (see Figure 5.8), takes a small sample of tissue from the chorionic villi—tiny threadlike protrusions on the chorion membrane that surrounds the fetus. But unlike amniocentesis, which cannot be done until the sixteenth week of pregnancy, CVS can be done at the eighth week—almost as soon as a woman knows she's pregnant. Furthermore, the results from CVS are available in two days, whereas it usually takes three to four weeks to get the results of an amniocentesis. Thus, if a birth defect is detected, a first-trimester abortion can be done, which is much safer than an abortion after 20 or more weeks of pregnancy. There is one drawback to CVS, however: there is about a 2 to 3 percent rate of spontaneous abortion after it is done (Hogge, Schonberg,

Table 5.3   Risk of Chromosomal Abnormalities in Live Births, by Mother's Age

Maternal Age	Risk of Down's Syndrome	Risk of All Chromosome Abnormalities
20	1/1667	1/526
30	1/952	1/385
33	1/602	1/286
35	1/378	1/192
38	1/173	1/102
40	1/106	1/66
42	1/63	1/42
45	1/30	1/21

Source: *American College of Obstetricians and Gynecologists, 1989.*

Table 5.4   Indications for Prenatal Diagnosis

General risk factor

Maternal age ≥ 35 years at the time of delivery
Elevated or reduced maternal serum alpha-fetoprotein concentration
Results of triple screening: elevated or reduced maternal serum alpha-fetoprotein, human chorionic gonadotropin, and blood estrogen measurements

Specific risk factors

Previous child with a structural defect or chromosomal abnormality
Previous stillbirth or neonatal death
Structural abnormality in the mother or father
Balanced translocation in the mother or father
Inherited disorders: cystic fibrosis, metabolic disorders, sex-linked recessive disorders
Medical disease in the mother, diabetes mellitus, phenylketonuria
Exposure to a teratogen: ionizing radiation, anticonvulsant medicines, lithium, isotretinoin, alcohol
Infection: rubella, toxoplasmosis, cytomegalovirus

Ethnic risk factors

Disorder	*Ethnic or Racial Group*
Tay-Sachs disease	Ashkenazi Jewish, French Canadian
Sickle cell anemia	Black African, Mediterranean, Arab, Indian and Pakistani
Alpha- and beta-thalassemia	Mediterranean, Southern and Southeast Asian, Chinese

Source: *D'Alton and DeCherney, 1993, Table 1.*

and Golbus, 1986; D'Alton and De Cherney, 1993). Since this rate is approximately the same as the spontaneous abortion rate found in women who do not undergo CVS (and have pregnancies of comparable lengths), it is not yet certain how many of these pregnancies would have aborted even if the procedure had not been done. A recent study of CVS done in more than 2200 women at seven different hospitals reported an excess rate of fetal loss of less than 1 percent compared to a group of women who underwent amniocentesis (Rhoads et al., 1989). Based on this difference, it appears that amniocentesis is slightly safer, but with the disad-

Figure 5.7   Amniocentesis

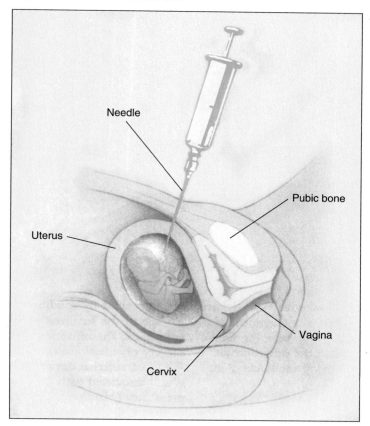

Needle

Pubic bone

Uterus

Vagina

Cervix

Amniocentesis involves removing a small amount of amniotic fluid from inside the pregnant uterus. The fluid is then analyzed in a laboratory to provide information about many types of birth defects or genetic conditions that may affect the fetus.

vantage of the delays involved, CVS will be the procedure of choice for many couples.

Another technique used to detect many birth defects (although it does not check for most genetic diseases that can be detected by amniocentesis or CVS) is the use of ultrasound examination. Ultrasonic waves are used to form a picture of the fetus. If a birth defect is detected it can sometimes be treated while the baby is still developing within the uterus, or this information may be used to plan for early delivery so the baby can receive corrective treatment (D'Alton and DeCherney, 1993). Ultrasound can also be used to evaluate the growth of the fetus, to determine if there is multiple pregnancy (twins, triplets, etc.), and to aid in the diagnosis of certain types of medical problems affecting the mother or baby.

Although ultrasound studies are now done in more than half of all pregnancies (both for diagnostic purposes and to check the sex of the developing fetus), some have questioned the use of the procedure since there are few long-term data proving the safety of this technique. Addressing this issue, Salvesen and co-workers (1992) found no difference in school performance of children at ages 8 and 9 comparing those who had undergone in utero ultrasonagraphy to those who had not. However, it is also true that routine ultrasound screening does not produce better birth outcomes as compared with targeted ultrasound use based on clinician's judgments (Ewigman et al., 1993). Since screening costs about $200 per scan, unnecessary use of ultrasound screening clearly adds a sizable sum to the overall costs of pregnancy.

chorionic villi sampling (CVS) a method for diagnosing defects in the developing fetus; done by inserting a catheter through the vagina and cervix to take a small piece of tissue from the edge of the chorion, the membrane surrounding the fetus.

Figure 5.8 Chorionic Villi Sampling

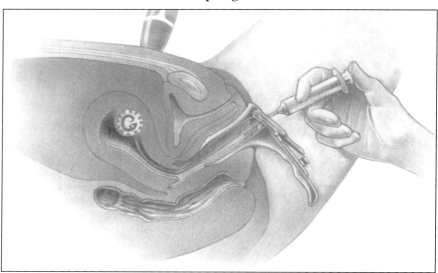

Ectopic Pregnancy

Ectopic pregnancy (a pregnancy occurring outside the cavity of the uterus) occurs approximately once in every 62 pregnancies (Centers for Disease Control, 1992b). In 1989, an estimated 88,400 U.S. women were hospitalized for this condition. The number of ectopic pregnancies in the United States more than quadrupled from 1970 to 1989 (Figure 5.9), which probably reflects both improved diagnostic methods and an increased incidence of scarring of the Fallopian tubes as a result of pelvic inflammatory disease (see Chapter 19). The highest rates of ectopic pregnancy are in women 30 years of age or older and in nonwhite women, who have an overall rate of ectopic pregnancies some 32 percent higher than that for white women (Centers for Disease Control, 1992b).

About 97 percent of ectopic pregnancies occur in the Fallopian tubes (tubal pregnancy); in the remainder of cases, the fertilized egg implants in the ovary, the abdomen, or the cervix. Ectopic pregnancies are usually caused by conditions that block or slow the passage of the fertilized egg into the uterus such as anatomical abnormalities, scar tissue resulting from surgery or infections, or tumors. The presence of an IUD (intrauterine device, a means of contraception) is also associated with an increased chance of ectopic pregnancy (Marchbanks et al., 1988).

Most ectopic pregnancies abort at a relatively early stage, but when growth of the embryo, placenta, and membranes occurs, there is a substantial risk of rupture and bleeding. Because it is difficult to diagnose this condition, ectopic pregnancy is the seventh leading cause of maternal death. The recurrence rate of an ectopic pregnancy in subsequent pregnancies is about 20 percent.

Until recently, ectopic pregnancies were treated by surgery requiring hospitalization (Ory, 1989). The surgery either involves making a small slit in the Fallopian tube to remove the ectopic pregnancy or excising the part of the tube containing the pregnancy. Now it has been found that some cases can be managed medically, on an outpatient basis, using injections of a drug called methotrexate (generally used to treat cancer) that causes the developing embryo to be resorbed before it gets large enough to rupture the Fallopian tube (Stovall, Ling, and Buster, 1989; Carson and Buster, 1993). While this treatment approach is still in the experimental stages, it may prove useful since newer medical procedures, such as ultrasound, often lead to the earlier diagnosis of ectopic pregnancy than in the past.

Rh Incompatibility

Rh incompatibility refers to a condition in which antibodies (proteins that fight off foreign substances that invade the body) from the mother's bloodstream destroy red blood cells in the fetus, causing fetal anemia, mental retardation, or death. This problem occurs only when a mother whose blood does not have the Rh factor (Rh negative) has a fetus with the Rh factor (Rh positive), a combination that can occur only if the father is Rh positive. Even in this circumstance, the risk is usually not in the first pregnancy (since antibodies have not yet formed in the woman's circulation to the Rh factor) but applies to later pregnancies with an Rh positive fetus.

The development of Rh sensitivity can be prevented by the use of a medication called Rho-GAM, which neutralizes antibody formation. This must be given within 72 hours after delivery (or abortion) of an Rh positive fetus to an Rh negative mother. If sensitivity is already present, either from a blood transfusion or an earlier pregnancy, the fetus can be given a special blood transfusion while still inside the uterus.

Figure 5.9 Ectopic Pregnancy Rates, by Year—United States, 1970–1987

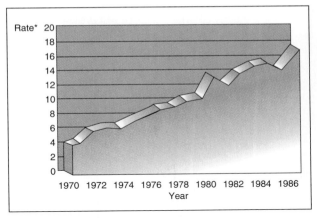

Per 1000 reported pregnancies.

Source: *Center for Disease Control*, MMWR *39: 401, 1990.*

INFERTILITY

People usually assume that reproduction happens almost automatically, but 10 to 15 percent of couples trying to have a baby do not succeed after a year or more without the use of contraception. This condition, known as **infertility,** has been greatly misunderstood. Often the source of considerable anguish and embarrassment, it rarely poses a direct threat to nonreproductive health or longevity.

Causes

Although the woman typically seeks medical help first, both partners in an infertile couple often have conditions that contribute to their inability to conceive. Thus, it is important that both the man and woman be seen by a physician, since proper treatment and an optimal chance for pregnancy depend on accurate testing. In about 85 percent of couples with infertility, a specific cause can be found.

Female Infertility

The two major causes of female infertility are failure to ovulate and blockage of the Fallopian tubes. Lack of ovulation (or infrequent ovulation) can be caused by ovarian disorders, hormone abnormalities, certain types of chronic illness, drug addiction or abuse, and poor nutrition. Rarely, ovulation is blocked by psychological stress.

Failure to ovulate may be detected by the use of **basal body temperature (BBT)** charts, hormone testing, or scraping the lining of the uterus to examine tissue under a microscope. The BBT chart is obtained by the woman's daily measurement of her temperature immediately after awakening and before getting out of bed. During the first portion of the menstrual cycle the BBT is low, but as progesterone production in the ovary increases just after ovulation, the temperature shifts upwards and remains higher for 10 to 16 days (Figure 5.10). BBT increases just after ovulation; if no temperature shift is seen, it is an indication that ovulation did not occur.

Although keeping BBT charts was, until recently, the primary method used for predicting the timing or presence of ovulation, new do-it-yourself urine tests allow users to monitor levels of **luteinizing hormone (LH)** in their urine to identify the LH

Rh incompatibility condition in which antibodies from the mother's bloodstream destroy red blood cells in the fetus, causing anemia, mental retardation, or fetal death.

infertility the inability of a couple to achieve pregnancy, usually defined after a year or more of sexual intercourse without pregnancy.

basal body temperature (BBT) temperature taken immediately after awakening and used to predict ovulation.

luteinizing hormone (LH) (lū′ tē in īz′ ing) produced by the pituitary gland, LH triggers ovulation and stimulates the Leydig cells to manufacture testosterone.

Figure 5.10   Basal Body Temperature (BBT) Patterns

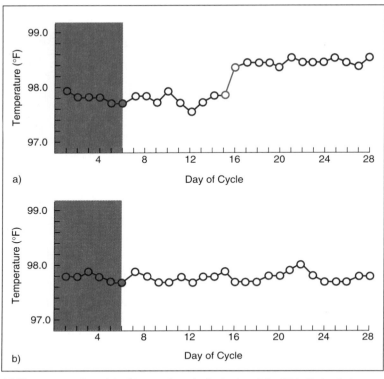

(a) The pronounced, sustained temperature rise beginning at day 16 indicates that ovulation occurred. (b) The absence of a sustained temperature rise suggests that ovulation did not occur in this cycle. (Days of menstrual flow are shaded.)

Source: *From Robert C. Kolodny, William H. Masters, and Virginia E. Johnson,* Textbook of Sexual Medicine, *© 1979 by Robert C. Kolodny, William H. Masters, and Virginia E. Johnson. Reprinted by permission of Little, Brown and Company.*

surge that precedes ovulation by 12 to 24 hours. Based on the same sort of monoclonal antibody technology used in some at-home pregnancy test kits, the LH tests are marked under trade names such as First Response, Ovutime, and OvuStick. While the tests must be done on four to six consecutive days for best accuracy and are expensive (usually costing $40 to $60 for a kit that permits testing for one month), they are much more precise than BBT patterns in identifying whether and when ovulation occurs (March, 1985).

Blocked Fallopian tubes may be caused by scarring after an infection in the pelvic tissues or abdomen. Blocked tubes can also result from **endometriosis,** a common disorder in which endometrial tissue (the tissue lining the uterine cavity) grows outside the uterus in other pelvic or abdominal organs, often leading to scar formation.

Endometriosis is usually diagnosed by inspecting the female reproductive organs through a procedure called **laparoscopy,** in which a thin, lighted telescope-like tube is inserted into the abdomen through a small incision next to the navel. If endometrial implants or cysts are found, a small piece of the abnormal tissue can be removed and thoroughly analyzed under a microscope.

The Fallopian tubes can be checked for obstruction by either **Rubin's test,** which involves inserting carbon dioxide into the uterus and seeing if this gas passes into the abdomen, or by x-rays of the uterus and tubes using a dye that outlines these structures. The x-ray method is preferred by most physicians because it is more accurate.

Other less frequent causes of female infertility include abnormal cervical mucus that impedes the passage of sperm, birth defects of the reproductive organs, tumors, infections (see Chapter 19), and allergy to sperm. In some cases, not having intercourse close to the time of ovulation may be a problem, and in other instances, the use of artificial lubricants like Vaseline or K-Y Jelly may be killing the sperm (but these preparations should not be considered as spermicides for birth control purposes).

Male Infertility

The primary cause of male infertility is a low sperm count. Less than 40 million sperm per cubic centimeter is below normal, but pregnancy is often possible with sperm counts of 20 million per cubic centimeter. With lower counts, the changes of impregnation are considerably reduced. Other factors that determine male fertility include the ability of sperm to swim, the number of abnormal sperm, and the volume of seminal fluid.

Low sperm counts can be caused by testicular injury, infection (especially mumps occurring after childhood, when it can spread to the testes), radiation, endocrine disorders, varicose veins in the scrotum, undescended testes, and birth defects. Drug use can also impair sperm production, with alcohol, cigarettes, narcotics, marijuana, and some prescription medications potential sources of such a problem (Kolodny, Masters, and Johnson, 1979). Some reports indicate that long-distance bicycle riding or tight-fitting underwear can lower sperm counts (Shane, Schiff, and Wilson, 1976). Since sperm production is sensitive to temperature, prolonged and frequent use of saunas, hot tubs, and steam baths may have a negative effect. A high frequency of ejaculation can also lower the sperm count (but not enough to be reliable as a contraceptive method!).

In the male, just as in the female, the reproductive tubing system may be blocked as a result of infection or birth defect. If the blockage is complete, no sperm will be in the ejaculate, even though sperm production in the testes is normal. Infertility can result if the male is unable to ejaculate, if he ejaculates outside the vagina, or if he is unable to have intercourse because of erectile difficulties. These conditions are discussed in Chapter 21.

Treatment

Women who do not ovulate can frequently be helped by treatment with clomiphene, a pill that induces ovulation by stimulating the pituitary to secrete LH and **follicle stimulating hormone (FSH)**. About half of the women given this medication become pregnant. There is a modestly increased chance of having a multiple pregnancy (twins, triplets, etc.), which occurs about 8 percent of the

time with clomiphene compared to 1.2 percent in routine pregnancies. Women who do not achieve a pregnancy with clomiphene may be treated with HMG (human menopausal gonadotropins), which is given in a series of injections. This medication acts directly on the ovaries, bypassing the pituitary gland, and induces ovulation in more than 90 percent of women with functioning ovaries. Pregnancy is achieved by 60 to 70 percent of women receiving this treatment, and 20 percent of these pregnancies are multiple (15 percent are twins, and 5 percent are triplets, quadruplets, quintuplets, or sextuplets). Neither clomiphene nor HMG causes a greater risk of abortion or birth defects than in naturally occurring pregnancies. These drugs, however, can overstimulate the ovaries, causing them to enlarge (sometimes to the size of grapefruit) and to leak fluid into the abdomen. This condition, which is more common with HMG than with clomiphene, usually requires hospitalization because there is a danger that the ovaries may rupture.

Blocked Fallopian tubes can sometimes be treated by microsurgery. Using a microscope for visual guidance, a surgeon removes the obstruction and then sews together the healthy portions of the tubes with tiny needles and suture material. Microsurgery is successful in only 30 to 50 percent of women with tubal problems at the present time (Jacobs et al., 1988). Women who have tubal damage beyond surgical repair or women without Fallopian tubes now have the possibility of being treated by *in vitro* fertilization, the dramatic "test-tube baby" procedure, which we discuss shortly.

When endometriosis is the cause of infertility, it is usually treated by surgery. One promising development is the use of laser technology, in which the surgeon focuses a laser beam to burn away en-

endometriosis the occurrence of endometrial tissue in locations other than the uterus; a frequent cause of female infertility.

laparoscopy an exploratory visualization of the pelvic and abdominal organs using a tubelike instrument.

Rubin's test a procedure to check for obstructed Fallopian tubes. Carbon dioxide is inserted into the uterus to see if it passes into the abdomen.

follicle stimulating hormone (FSH) a substance produced in the pituitary gland that prepares the ovary for ovulation and stimulates the production of sperm cells in the testes.

dometrial implants or adhesions. Since the laser beam actually seals off small blood vessels in the surgical area as it burns away diseased tissue, there is very little blood loss with this procedure. Pregnancy rates after laser laparoscopy are in the 40 to 65 percent range (Berger, Goldstein, and Fuerst, 1989). Endometriosis can also be treated with drugs such as danazol.

The treatment of male infertility is considerably less developed. Surgical repair of varicose veins in the scrotum can improve the sperm count substantially, but most other conditions respond poorly to treatment. The use of testosterone to achieve a "rebound effect" after first suppressing sperm production is sometimes useful, but the results obtained from using clomiphene in men have been inconclusive. Proper medical management of infections, anatomical defects, or hormonal disorders is definitely helpful, but such cases are relatively few. In men with borderline sperm counts, daily ejaculation can actually lower fertility by reducing the number of sperm, and the chances for a pregnancy can be improved by decreasing the frequency of ejaculation to a minimum of 48 hours from one time to the next.

Two Canadian studies raise some important questions about the results currently attained in treating infertility. In the first, a two- to seven-year follow-up of 1145 infertile couples showed that the pregnancy rate in the treated couples (41 percent) was just slightly better than that in untreated couples (35 percent) (Collins et al., 1983). The second study showed that the cumulative pregnancy rate in untreated couples with unexplained infertility was 65 percent (Rousseau et al., 1983). Thus, since many cases of infertility achieve pregnancy spontaneously, it appears important for physicians to perform careful diagnostic testing to determine whether, and if, treatment is required. Likewise, couples contending with infertility should realize that pregnancy is quite possible in many cases even if medical treatment initially doesn't seem to be effective.

Artificial Insemination

Artificial insemination means placing semen in the vagina or uterus by a means other than sexual intercourse. There are two basic types of artificial insemination: using semen from the husband (AIH) or using semen from a donor. For either method, the woman's fertility status must be relatively normal.

AIH can be tried if the husband's count is low but not zero. For practical reasons, successful AIH is infrequent if the count is less than 10 million per cubic centimeter or if the sperm motility is low. AIH is best done by inserting a fresh semen specimen in the vagina at the mouth of the cervix. Using frozen, thawed specimens reduces sperm motility, and combining several frozen specimens does not seem to improve the outcome. Injecting the semen into the uterus causes severe cramping and poses a risk of infection. AIH works by concentrating the husband's sperm at the mouth of the cervix; with coitus, only a small fraction of sperm get to this location.

Donor insemination is used when the husband's sperm count is zero or very low. A donor, selected on the basis of excellent health, good intelligence, and closeness of physical characteristics to the husband, provides a masturbated semen specimen (for which he is paid). The donor's identity is unknown to the couple. The legal status of donor insemination is uncertain in many states, although in California once the husband signs a consent form agreeing to use of a donor, he is the legal father of the baby. The pregnancy rate for donor insemination is about 60 percent using frozen semen obtained from a sperm bank.

The decision to undergo donor insemination must be made jointly by husband and wife; clearly this type of treatment is not psychologically right for everyone for whom it might be used. Some people equate this procedure with adultery, others have conflicts with their religious values, and some fear that the husband will reject or dislike the baby because it is not "his." Despite the latter concern, almost all couples who achieve a pregnancy using donor sperm find that the experience brings them very close together and that the husband's excitement at fatherhood is genuinely felt. In some locations, donor insemination is also being used by single women who want to become pregnant.

IVF: *In Vitro* Fertilization

Late in the evening of July 25, 1978, a slightly premature 5 pound, 12 ounce baby girl was born by cesarean section to Lesley and John Brown of Oldham, England. They named their healthy, normal baby Louise, and since then her name and picture have made the pages of nearly every major newspaper in the Western world. The sperm and egg that united to conceive Louise met not in Lesley

Brown's Fallopian tube, but in a test tube, *in vitro*, outside the mother's body. Louise Brown was the first baby ever born from *in vitro* fertilization techniques (see Figure 5.11).

The British doctors responsible for this remarkable achievement were Patrick Steptoe and Robert Edwards. Steptoe had been experimenting with ***in vitro* fertilization (IVF)** for more than a decade before meeting Lesley Brown, who was unable to conceive because of blocked Fallopian tubes. She had undergone surgery to unblock the tubes before coming to Steptoe. The surgery was not only unsuccessful, but when Steptoe did his exploration of her reproductive organs, he found the tubes so badly damaged ("mere remnants," he said) that they were removed.

Lesley was first given hormones to stimulate the maturation of eggs in her ovaries. Steptoe and Edwards then made a small incision near her navel and by using an instrument that magnifies and illuminates the tiny ovum, they withdrew a ripe egg and placed it in a laboratory dish. The dish contained a carefully mixed culture of nutrients designed to resemble the environment of the Fallopian tubes. As quickly as possible, John Brown's sperm (obtained through masturbation) were added to the culture, and the doctors waited for one of the sperm to impregnate the egg. Meanwhile, Lesley was given more hormones to ensure that her uterus would accept a fertilized egg. After the sperm and egg united in the laboratory dish and the pre-embryonic cells began to divide, the blastocyst (a hollow sphere of 60 separate cells) was inserted into Lesley's uterus. In about a week, the doctors knew the pre-embryo attached itself to a wall of the uterus and Lesley Brown was pregnant.

Steptoe and Edwards had made more than 30 attempts to implant eggs fertilized outside the mother before their success with the Browns. Two pregnancies had resulted, but both were spontaneously aborted—one because the membrane around the embryo ruptured and the other because of a genetic abnormality. This second case is a cause of concern by doctors working in this area. Who is responsible for a child born with genetic damage? Did the damage result from handling the pre-embryo outside the uterus, or would it have occurred even during normal fertilization? Is destroying a fertilized egg in a test tube abortion?

Since the initial breakthrough by Steptoe and Edwards, a large number of IVF clinics have opened around the world, including more than 200 clinics in the United States alone. More than 15,000 babies conceived *in vitro* had been born as of 1990, including 2627 live deliveries in 1988 in America (Medical Research International and Society for Assisted Reproductive Technology, 1990) and 3600 babies born in France in 1987 (*The New York Times*, April 11, 1989, p. C5). Aside from a higher rate of multiple pregnancies and a very high cesarean rate (50 to 60 percent in many clinics)—reflecting both older maternal ages and the "premium" nature of such pregnancies—the overall obstetrical experience with IVF is largely comparable to that expected in a similar group of women who had conceived by natural means (Andrews et al., 1986; Seibel, 1988). Particularly notable are several studies that show that there is no increased risk of birth defects or developmental difficulties for IVF children (Seibel, 1988; Moran et al., 1989).

The best candidates for IVF are women younger than 35 who have normal menstrual cycles and a husband with a normal sperm count (Berger, Goldstein, and Fuerst, 1989). (About 50 percent of IVF programs will treat women 40 or older, and most will also proceed if the sperm count is mild to moderately reduced; if the sperm count is very low, or zero, then the couple can consider IVF using donor sperm.) IVF can overcome many of the causes of infertility, including blocked or absent Fallopian tubes, severe endometriosis, and immunologic infertility that in the past were almost insurmountable obstacles to pregnancy for hundreds of thousands of couples.

Like any complicated medical procedure, there are some drawbacks. For one thing, IVF is expensive, generally costing $4000 to $6000 for each attempt at pregnancy. This has led to charges of commercialism (especially directed at private, for-profit clinics) as well as some rancor toward health insurance companies that refuse to pay for such procedures. Another problem is that not all IVF clinics have comparable results: in fact, some have never had a successful pregnancy resulting in a live birth (Raymond, 1988). Since the IVF "industry" is es-

***in vitro* fertilization** a procedure involving removing eggs from a woman's body and fertilizing them with sperm in a laboratory. After successful fertilization, the embryo is surgically implanted in the woman's uterus.

Figure 5.11   The Steps Involved in the *In Vitro* Fertilization Process

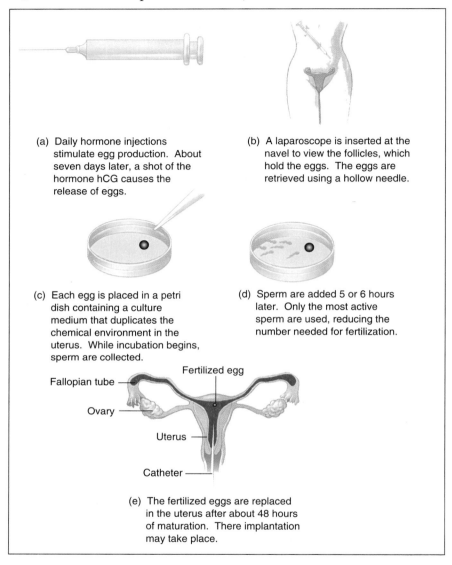

(a) Daily hormone injections stimulate egg production. About seven days later, a shot of the hormone hCG causes the release of eggs.

(b) A laparoscope is inserted at the navel to view the follicles, which hold the eggs. The eggs are retrieved using a hollow needle.

(c) Each egg is placed in a petri dish containing a culture medium that duplicates the chemical environment in the uterus. While incubation begins, sperm are collected.

(d) Sperm are added 5 or 6 hours later. Only the most active sperm are used, reducing the number needed for fertilization.

Fertilized egg

Fallopian tube

Ovary

Uterus

Catheter

(e) The fertilized eggs are replaced in the uterus after about 48 hours of maturation. There implantation may take place.

sentially unregulated, even physicians involved in the field have been worried that there may be misleading claims and practices that may confuse, or even bilk, the public. This is especially troublesome since couples turning to IVF are often emotionally overwrought as a result of their lengthy efforts to have a child, so they are not apt to be as objective as consumers shopping for a new car. (A checklist of questions to ask to help you evaluate an IVF program can be found on page 138.) In addition, since live deliveries result from only about 12 percent of IVF stimulation cycles, it is clear that not every couple going through this physically and emotionally arduous procedure will wind up with a baby.

[Some experts believe that ultimately only half the couples attempting IVF will be successful, with this success usually coming in the first four cycles in which IVF is attempted (Seibel, 1988; Seibel, Ranoux, and Kearnan, 1989).] Data from England show that for women up to age 34, almost 55 percent will become pregnant using IVF and 45 percent will have a live birth within five cycles of treatment (Tan et al., 1992). At age 40 or above, results are considerably less favorable, with only 20 percent becoming pregnant and under 15 percent actually having a baby. However, improving technology offers the hope for substantial gains in these numbers (Winston and Handyside, 1993).

To put all this in perspective, it is helpful to remember that despite the expenses and problems involved, IVF is in many ways a miracle come true. As one happy father said:

> We had basically given up on ever getting pregnant after more than ten years of treatment. When an IVF program opened up at the university nearby, we decided to give it one more shot. Now we have two-year-old twins who are a testimonial to the skill of the team at the clinic. What better reward could persistence ever have? (Authors' files)

Other Assisted Reproductive Techniques
A number of related procedures have been developed as outgrowths of IVF. These are briefly summarized here.

1. **GIFT (Gamete Intrafallopian Transfer)** involves the direct placement of a mixture of sperm and eggs into the Fallopian tube. Fertilization takes place naturally, in the Fallopian tube, rather than in the laboratory, as it does with IVF. A woman must have at least one normal Fallopian tube to be a candidate for GIFT, but this procedure generally has somewhat higher success rates than IVF: an overall 21 percent live delivery rate was reported for 135 clinics in the United States in 1988, with some centers having rates of 30 percent or more (Medical Research International and Society for Assisted Reproductive Technology, 1990). GIFT is particularly useful in dealing with endometriosis, unexplained infertility, and cervical factor infertility (where the chemical environment of the cervix seems to kill sperm). It ensures that the ovum and a large number of motile sperm reach the physiologic fertilization site—the Fallopian tube. [GIFT can be combined with donor insemination if the male has a poor sperm count; this method has a high rate of success (Cefalu et al., 1988).]

2. **ZIFT (Zygote Intrafallopian Transfer)** combines IVF with GIFT. The wife's eggs are fertilized by her husband's sperm in vitro. The zygote (the fertilized egg) is then transferred to the Fallopian tube within 24 hours. The advantage to this procedure is that the medical team can be certain that fertilization has occurred. If fertilization doesn't take place, then the couple can decide if they want to try donor insemination.

3. **Egg donors** are used in some programs for women who are unable to ovulate or who don't have ovaries. Egg donation—although only recently undertaken—is somewhat like sperm donation. The donor in some programs is completely anonymous but matched for physical characteristics with the recipient (Kennard et al., 1989). In other programs, only donors selected by the woman wishing to conceive are used (Sauer et al., 1989). Most commonly, a sister or close relative is the egg donor, but personal friends and sometimes people paid for the egg donation serve as donors. Egg donation may be particularly useful for women who want to avoid passing on a genetic disorder in the wife's family, like hemophilia, to their children. Once the eggs are obtained from the donor, fertilization with the husband's sperm is usually done in the laboratory; the fertilized egg can then be placed by ZIFT into the Fallopian tubes or handled as a straightforward IVF procedure. (The recipient must be prepared by hormonal stimulation so her uterus is ready to accept a pregnancy.) Just as with sperm donation, ethical and religious concerns about egg donation abound, as might be expected with a relatively new technology of this sort; we discuss them in Chapter 24. Results obtained with egg donation are about the same as with assisted reproductive techniques using the wife's own eggs.

4. **Embryo transplant** is a more controversial method that uses the husband's sperm to artificially inseminate a woman who is not his wife. Five days later the embryo is flushed out of the

gamete intrafallopian transfer (GIFT) the direct placement of a mixture of sperm and eggs into the Fallopian tube as a treatment for infertility.
zygote intrafallopian transfer (ZIFT) a technique of assisted reproductive technology in which the woman's eggs are fertilized *in vitro,* after which the zygote is placed in the Fallopian tube.
egg donors women who volunteer to provide their eggs for the purposes of treating anovulatory infertility or avoiding the transmittal of a genetic disorder in another woman.
embryo transplant a method of treating female infertility that involves artificially inseminating a donor female, then removing the pre-implantation pre-embryo and transplanting it to the infertile woman's uterus.

Questions to Ask About an IVF/Gift Program

With any medical treatment, patients should ask questions to determine how appropriate the treatment is for them, how qualified and experienced the personnel are in providing the treatment, what to expect in terms of costs and time, and perhaps most important, how successful the treatment may be. When it comes to highly technical procedures such as those involved in IVF or GIFT, the importance of these queries cannot be stressed enough when it comes to gathering the information needed to make an informed decision.

The following list provides 11 key questions to ask when evaluating an IVF/GIFT program. As a practical matter, if you don't get straight answers to these questions, or if the doctor or program director you're discussing them with seems annoyed at your inquisitiveness, it is usually wisest to find a different program.

1. When was your program started?
2. When did the program perform its first IVF (or GIFT) procedure?
3. How many babies have been born as a result of this program's IVF (or GIFT) procedures? How many babies have been born in the last two years in this program from IVF or GIFT?
4. What is your clinical pregnancy rate per IVF (or GIFT) procedure? What is your clinical pregnancy rate for couples our age with our particular type of problem?
5. Do you freeze eggs or embryos as part of your program? If so, what is done with them after we've had a baby?
6. Do you offer an egg donation program? If so, do we provide the donor or do you?
7. Does your program report its results to the IVF Registry?
8. Are any of your doctors board certified in Reproductive Endocrinology?
9. How much does the entire procedure cost per cycle, including the cost of drugs?
10. Do we need to pay in advance? (If so, how much?)
11. Do you have an age limit for patients?

donor's uterus, where it is in the earliest stages of implantation, and transplanted into the wife's uterus. If it implants successfully, a normal pregnancy typically ensues. (A key element to this procedure is synchronizing the recipient's menstrual cycle with the donor's by hormone injections so that the recipient's endometrium is properly "primed" to accept the transferred embryo and to allow it to implant.) Potential problems with this method include the need to be certain of the donor's health and guaranteeing that she abstain completely from using drugs or alcohol during the cycle in which she conceives. There may also be legal difficulties in some states, so couples should check with an attorney before undertaking this approach to having a baby.

5. **Embryo freezing** is another very recent development; the first human birth from a frozen embryo (actually, a frozen pre-embryo) was in 1985 (Fugger, 1989). One of the major reasons for freezing pre-embryos is to reduce the risk of multiple pregnancy when the woman has "superovulated"—produced a large number of eggs—in response to the hormonal stimulation given in an egg retrieval cycle as part of IVF. In addition, freezing the extra pre-embryos cuts down the costs of future treatment cycles, since it isn't necessary to retrieve more eggs. Prior to 1989, approximately 2000 patients had a total of more than 7000 eggs and pre-implantation embryos frozen at 25 clinics across the country, and 48 live births have already occurred after thawing (Fugger, 1989). However, thawing doesn't always work; there are still some concerns that freezing and thawing might damage the fertilized egg, with unknown consequences; and ethical and legal questions abound. For instance, who "owns" the pre-em-

bryo if a couple divorces or if the couple dies? Who determines when, or if, to destroy the frozen pre-embryo? These issues are also addressed in Chapter 24.

Surrogate Motherhood

Some couples composed of an infertile wife and a fertile husband have hired a woman to act as a "surrogate mother." Such a stand-in is artificially inseminated using the husband's sperm and carries the pregnancy to term, at that point giving the baby for adoption to the couple who had hired her. In at least one case, a surrogate mother was implanted with an ovum from an infertile woman that was fertilized *in vitro* by sperm from the infertile woman's husband (Utian et al., 1985). The infertile woman had previously undergone surgical removal of her uterus and Fallopian tubes and so was unable to carry her own pregnancy, but she still had functioning ovaries, which allowed one of her own eggs to be used for transfer to the surrogate mother after IVF.

It is currently estimated that hundreds of surrogate mothers have contracted with couples to bear a child for them for pay (ranging from $2000 to $20,000), with legal fees in the neighborhood of $5000.

In January 1983, the public's attention was drawn to this previously little-known practice by headlines announcing "Surrogate Infant Left Unclaimed." As the complicated story unraveled, what became clear was that the 26-year-old surrogate mother, Judy Stiver of Michigan, had given birth to a deformed and probably mentally retarded baby, only to have 46-year-old Alexander Malahoff of New York, who had contracted for the child, reject the child on the grounds that he was not the father. Although medical tests eventually supported Mr. Malahoff, the entire episode was an unsavory one in many respects, including a tasteless, prearranged television confrontation between the Stivers and Malahoff in which accusations seemed more important than the welfare of the child. Although the Stivers eventually agreed to keep the baby, who may need to be institutionalized, this case raises a number of difficult issues about the ethical implications of our new reproductive technologies.

What would have happened if Malahoff, or some future Malahoff, had proved to be the infant's father? Could he, as one journalist suggested, try to send the child back and demand a refund?

Technological parenthood may have the trappings of a business, but it is not a business; it is the answer to someone's most personal prayers. So it should be seen and handled. If the answer to a particular prayer happens to emerge deformed, it is no less the prayer's answer; and, as so many parents of such "damaged goods" have discovered, they sometimes give more contentment to a family than whole and healthy children and thus provide answers to different prayers entirely. (*Rosenblatt, 1983, p. 90*)

This viewpoint seems laudable, but in the real world people don't always behave in kindhearted ways. What will become of deformed children born not only to surrogate mothers but to unmarried women using the services of a sperm bank? If a baby conceived by *in vitro* methods turns out to be defective, will lawsuits follow and financial repercussions ensue? Or are we on the verge of an era of government regulation of reproductive decisions along the lines envisioned by George Orwell in *1984* or Aldous Huxley in *Brave New World*?

Another twist in the surrogate mother story occurred in 1986, when Mary Beth Whitehead of Brick Township, New Jersey—who had contracted to bear a child for William and Elizabeth Stern, using Mr. Stern's sperm for artificial insemination—decided after the birth of a baby girl that she didn't want to give her up to the Sterns. Mrs. Whitehead and her husband fled to Florida with the baby, but in a much-publicized trial in 1987, a New Jersey court awarded custody to the Sterns and upheld the legality of the contract Mrs. Whitehead and the Sterns signed. Both the trial and the judge's decision provoked a great deal of controversy, with many observers feeling it was improper to enforce a contract that required Mrs. Whitehead to give up her baby.

A number of states have now passed legislation barring the practice of surrogate motherhood. But there is also a growing acceptance of the practice among the public, physicians, and attorneys. A representative of the American Bar Foundation noted:

The movement has to be seen in the perspective of the strong autonomy our society puts on the

embryo freezing a technique of freezing pre-embryo (usually zygotes or blastocysts) for use in subsequent menstrual cycles so as to reduce the risk of multiple gestations and reduce the cost of treating infertility.

child-bearing decision. Legislation banning surrogate motherhood would be held unconstitutional, infringing on a couple's procreative autonomy under the right of privacy. So, we have
to think about a public policy to make the experience a better one for everyone involved. We
can't take an ostrich-like approach to this anymore. *(Lawson, 1986, p. C18)*

On the other hand, a report from an expert panel
on ethics and reproduction from the American Fertility Society raised a number of questions about
the ethical propriety of permitting surrogate motherhood (see Chapter 24).

Adoption and Infertility

Adopting a child is another way of becoming a
parent, although this option is far less available
today than it was 25 years ago because of legalized
abortion. Adoption is the only route to having a
child if both partners are infertile. It is a common
misconception that many women of infertile couples conceive shortly after adopting a child—presumably because the couples' pressure to reproduce is lessened (Lamb and Leurgans, 1979). While
the conception certainly attracts attention, such
couples were obviously not infertile.

The Impact of Infertility

Infertility is rarely an expected problem. Not being
able to have a child when you want to can be frustrating, confusing, and depressing. Pressures may
be felt from peers and family, spouses may blame
each other for the failure to conceive, and sex may
become work rather than fun as a couple "tries
harder" to achieve a pregnancy. Many women feel
empty and unfulfilled as they deal with a situation
of infertility, and men often experience anxiety or
depression because they incorrectly equate virility
with the ability to father a child. Many men are so
unwilling to deal with the issue of possible infertility (or afraid of what might be discovered) that
they refuse to participate in medical testing. It is no
wonder that marital tensions often flare up in this
situation.

Being treated for infertility is frequently a source
of sexual problems, since there are time pressures
("the doctor says to have intercourse Monday,
Wednesday, and Friday this week"), restrictions
("not tonight, dear, I have to have my sperm count

checked tomorrow"), and pressures to perform
("I'm ovulating today and we *have* to have intercourse. *Why* can't you get an erection?"). When sex
becomes highly focused on the goal of reproduction, couples often dispense with aspects of sexual
play that they previously enjoyed in an effort to
"get down to business," thereby creating a hurried,
unimaginative, and often emotionally detached experience. Under these circumstances, it is not surprising that sexual pleasure and responsivity both
diminish.

SUMMARY

1. Conception occurs when sperm and egg meet
   in the Fallopian tube. This leads to a single fertilized cell called the zygote, which has 46
   chromosomes, including two sex chromosomes
   (XY = male, XX = female). The zygote divides
   into a blastocyst that implants in the uterus.
2. The development of the embryo or fetus depends on the placenta, which transmits nourishment and filters wastes between the
   mother's body and her unborn child's. The embryo is protected by two membranes (the amnion and chorion) and the amniotic fluid. In
   the first trimester, all major organs develop in
   the fetus; in the second and third trimesters,
   these organs mature and the fetus undergoes
   considerable growth.
3. Early pregnancy is usually marked by missing
   a period, nausea, breast tenderness, and fatigue. Pregnancy tests, which are 95 to 98 percent accurate, depend on detecting human
   chorionic gonadotropin (HCG) in urine. The
   emotional reactions to pregnancy vary considerably from person to person, and even when a
   pregnancy is wanted it may be a source of uncertainty or worry.
4. The second trimester is a time of prominent
   physical changes for the pregnant woman: the
   uterus enlarges, making the abdomen bulge,
   and quickening occurs. It is usually a time of
   emotional tranquility and heightened sexual
   interest.
5. Physical discomfort becomes prominent in the
   third trimester, as the abdomen is occupied by
   a growing "resident" who kicks and turns a lot.
   Backache, leg cramps, shortness of breath, and
   frequent urination are common.

6. Proper prenatal care is important to the health of mother and fetus alike. This includes regular medical check-ups, proper nutrition, avoidance of unnecessary drugs, and prompt treatment of pregnancy complications such as toxemia. Attendance at childbirth classes and appropriate reading can help familiarize the parents-to-be with what lies ahead.

7. Sexual activity during pregnancy usually is possible without difficulty or risk. Although controversial, one study shows that sexual activity may reduce the frequency of premature labor.

8. Labor is divided into three stages. In the first (and longest) stage, the cervix effaces and dilates as a result of regular contractions of the uterus. In the second stage, the baby passes through the birth canal, and in the third stage, the placenta and membranes are delivered.

9. Different styles of childbirth are possible, including hospital or home delivery, induction of labor versus spontaneous labor, and use of natural childbirth or Lamaze techniques. None of these methods can guarantee a "painless" childbirth. In certain situations, cesarean section may be required to protect the child's or the mother's health.

10. The postpartum period, marked by an abrupt drop in hormone levels, is a time of adjustment. Postpartum depression is common but usually transient; adjusting to parenthood takes a while longer. Early parent–child bonding is thought to be of special significance to the child.

11. Lactation occurs because of hormone actions on the breasts. Breast-feeding provides an opportunity for a satisfying psychological experience as well as health benefits to the newborn child, but bottle-feeding has advantages of convenience and flexibility.

12. Problem pregnancies—prematurity, toxemia, birth defects, improper implantation, and Rh incompatibility—were outlined briefly.

13. Approximately one out of seven couples is affected by infertility, with the majority of cases due to failure to ovulate and blocked Fallopian tubes in women and low sperm count in men. While treatment with drugs can often induce ovulation, treating the other two problems is less successful at present. Artificial insemination using a donor's semen may be done if the husband's sperm count is poor; *in vitro* fertilization techniques (including egg donation and the use of frozen embryos) are now being used increasingly to treat women with infertility due to blocked Fallopian tubes; and hiring a surrogate mother is also sometimes done.

Thought Questions

1. Should a woman be prosecuted for child abuse if she uses an illegal substance during pregnancy? What if she drinks alcohol? Smokes cigarettes?

2. Is it correct to refer to an embryo as an "unborn baby"? "Unborn child"? "Unborn teenager"? "Unborn senior citizen"? Where do you draw the line, and why?

3. How would our society change if parents could reliably choose the sex of their children? Would most people do this? Ultrasound can tell the parents what the sex of the fetus is. Do most parents want to know? Would you?

4. How does having a first baby typically affect a couple in terms of their romantic relationship and their sex lives? Do their roles tend to change from "lovers" to "parents"? What can be done about this? Should anything be done about this?

5. What is the source of the commonly experienced let-down feeling following childbirth—the so-called postpartum blues? Do you think it is primarily physiological in nature or more a result of the increased workload that a baby represents? How can family and friends best help new parents?

6. Since amniocentesis and chorionic villi sampling are expensive procedures that are not totally without risk, should they be available for women who would be unwilling to have an abortion? Why would a woman have amniocentesis or CVS for the purpose of discovering if her fetus has a genetic defect, if she believes abortion is morally wrong?

Suggested Readings

Ashford, Janet. *The Whole Birth Catalog: A Sourcebook for Choices in Childbirth.* Trumansburg, NY: The Crossing Press, 1983. A most impressive collection of material about the various options for different styles of childbirth available today. Lots of diagrams, lists of suggested readings, and practical pointers throughout.

Berger, G. S.; Goldstein, M.; and Fuerst, M. *The Couple's Guide to Fertility: How New Medical Advances Can Help You Have a Baby.* New York: Doubleday, 1989. This is an outstanding resource book for any couple contending with infertility, explaining with great clarity the technical side of the latest medical advances and also offering many practical pointers regarding consumer awareness, legal issues, and costs. As a bonus, it has an extensive directory of leading fertility specialists and clinics.

Brown, Judith. *Nutrition for Your Pregnancy.* Minneapolis: University of Minnesota Press, 1983. A well-done, practical guide to nutrition during pregnancy and in the first three months of postpartum months. Answers almost every imaginable question in a readable but authoritative style.

Chesler, P. *Sacred Bond: The Legacy of Baby M.* New York: Times Books, 1988. A carefully thought through analysis of the Baby M surrogate mother case along with reflections on the social, legal, and ethical ramifications of surrogate parenthood and related issues.

Cunningham, F. G.; MacDonald, P. C.; and Gant, N. F. (eds.) *Williams Obstetrics,* 18th ed. East Norwalk, CT: Appleton and Lange, 1989. This is the definitive medical textbook on obstetrics. We wouldn't call this easy bedtime reading, but it has all the facts as well as many detailed drawings that are useful. (Please note: Because this text has lots of information about problem pregnancies, it is not for worry-prone readers!)

Gilman, Lois. *The Adoption Resource Book.* New York: Harper & Row, 1987. A thorough overview of the process and options in adoption, including ample attention to the emotional aspects of raising adopted children. Includes useful discussion of international adoptions.

Grad, Rae; Bash, Deborah; Guyer, Ruth; Acevedo, Zoila; Trause, Mary Anne; and Reukauf, Diane. *The Father Book: Pregnancy and Beyond.* Washington, DC: Acropolis Books, 1981. A fine forum for answering questions and clearing up uncertainties for the expectant father.

Messenger, Maire. *The Breastfeeding Book.* New York: Van Nostrand Reinhold, 1982. The best book we've ever seen on this topic.

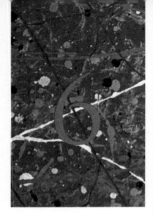

Birth Control

Men who have sex while using alcohol or drugs are less likely than others to use condoms. (*Weinstock et al., 1993*)

Highly effective emergency contraceptive measures are now available to use if your primary form of birth control fails, but these measures are woefully underemployed because of lack of knowledge of their existence. (*Trussell et al., 1992*).

Condom breakage or condoms slipping off are not just theoretical issues but real life problems for many users. (*Russell-Brown et al., 1992; Trussell, Warner, and Hatcher, 1992; Tanfer et al., 1993*)

A recent report concluded that the instructions contained in oral contraceptive pill packages are often confusing, incomplete, or inadequate. (*Williams-Deane and Potter, 1992*)

The contraceptive sponge is much less effective for women who have had children than for women who haven't. (*Speroff and Darney, 1992*)

Improvements in how vasectomies are done have simplified this procedure greatly and led to its increased popularity both in the U.S. and on a world-wide basis. (*Liskin, Benoit, and Blackburn, 1992*)

The findings listed above show that the topic of contraception is a complex one. New birth control methods have been introduced in recent years, new discoveries have been made about older methods, and the options available for men and women today are considerably more complicated than they were in the past. Nevertheless, methods for preventing unwanted or unintended pregnancy either are not used, are misused, or are used sporadically by many people. Those who rely on "faith" and "hope" as their primary contraceptives are playing a risky form of reproductive roulette, as many discover to their surprise. Others depend on unreliable contraceptive techniques like douching, using Saran wrap, or using tampons. Contrary to common misbelief, female orgasm is not a requirement for conception, and making love while standing up or crossing your fingers doesn't prevent sperm from reaching the egg.

Not too long ago, contraceptive products could not be displayed or sold in certain states, abortions were illegal, and birth control methods were not very reliable. (The landmark case of *Griswold* v. *Connecticut* that established the legality of selling contraceptive products occurred in 1965.) Although times have changed remarkably, people are now faced with a vast number of birth control products or methods, each with its own advantages and disadvantages (Table 6.1). In trying to make a personal choice, people may have a number of questions: Why use contraception? How does each method work? How well does it work? What are the medical risks? How might each method affect my sexuality? What possibilities do I have if I'm already pregnant? In the following pages, we examine the currently available methods of birth control in an effort to answer some of these questions.

Table 6.1   Patterns of Current Contraception for Women Aged 18 to 44, 1992

Method	Percentage
Pill	39
Sterilization	
Female	19
Male	12
Condom	25
Withdrawal	8
Rhythm	4
Diaphragm	4
Sponge	3
Suppository	3
Douche	3
IUD	1
Foam	1
Cream/jelly	1
Implant (Norplant)	1
Cervical cap	<0.5

Source: *Modified from Forrest and Fordyce, 1993, Table 3.*

WHY USE CONTRACEPTION

An individual's or couple's decisions about birth control depend on many factors including age, future plans, marital or relationship status (including trust and cooperation), finances, religious beliefs, sexual attitudes, health, and prior experiences. *Not using birth control if you are sexually active is a specific kind of personal decision*, just as choosing to use birth control, whatever the reason, is a personal decision.

The main reason for using birth control is to prevent an unwanted pregnancy. Not only is an unwanted pregnancy likely to cause emotional turmoil and health risks, it also may present financial burdens. Often, unwanted pregnancies occur in young teenagers or women over 35, times when health risks during pregnancy are highest. The social and economic costs may also be high at these same ages.

Of the 1.2 million teenagers who become pregnant in the United States each year, more than 400,000 obtain abortions (Henshaw and O'Reilly, 1983). Many others drop out of school and enter into hasty marriages where the odds of divorce are high, the chances of getting a good job are low, and ending up on welfare is common (Furstenberg, 1976; Fielding, 1978). Others try to raise a child alone or with assistance of relatives, but this plan often proves more difficult than it might seem. An unplanned pregnancy at any age may also disrupt career plans, and economic costs are created by terminating the pregnancy or raising the child. There is also an emotional cost to an unwanted pregnancy. Feelings of foolishness, guilt, anger, or helplessness may strain or break a relationship ("It was *all your fault!*") or may create later sexual problems.

Of course, there are other reasons for using contraception, including the wish to space pregnancies, limit family size, avoid potential genetic disorders or birth defects, protect the mother's health, and allow women more control over planning their lives. Contraception also permits people to enjoy a sexual relationship without making commitments to marriage or parenthood. Limiting reproduction also has major social and philosophical consequences in a world of limited natural resources where overpopulation exerts political and psychological effects and environmental issues are of prominent concern.

Finally, there is a compelling health reason today for many people to consider using certain forms of contraception—condoms and spermicides—for a purpose that has nothing at all to do with birth control. The reason is that these contraceptive products offer some protection against the risk of many sexually transmitted diseases, including protection against infection with HIV, the AIDS virus.

EVALUATING CONTRACEPTIVE EFFECTIVENESS AND SAFETY

The decision to use contraception and the choice of one method over another depend primarily on two practical matters: how well it works (its effectiveness) and its health risks (its safety).[1] Evaluating these two issues is complicated. *No one contraceptive is always best or safest.*

When evaluating effectiveness and safety, remember that information from various sources may be biased. The popular media, for instance, are eager to report the latest "news" about the real or suspected hazards of a contraceptive method. Yet the story is usually condensed to a few paragraphs in the news-

[1]The choice of method may also depend, in individual cases, on factors such as cost, availability without a prescription, aesthetic preferences, and sometimes even the ease of concealment.

paper or is crammed into less than 60 seconds of TV or radio broadcast time. Scientific accuracy or caution is often lost in a process of oversimplification, misinterpretation, and unwarranted conclusions. In addition, much of the research on the effectiveness and safety of birth control methods is funded by the drug companies that manufacture them. These companies have an obvious interest in presenting their merchandise in a way that will boost sales. Finally, all scientific studies are not equivalent in their applicability to *you.* In general, studies about people close to your age, cultural background, and socioeconomic status are more meaningful than studies about other groups. For example, if you are a 22-year-old single American woman, you cannot put much faith in the findings of a study about 35-year-old married women in China.

Understanding some other aspects of evaluating effectiveness can also be helpful. First, it is important to distinguish between two factors: theoretical versus actual effectiveness. The **theoretical effectiveness** of a particular method is how it *should* work if used correctly and consistently, without human error or negligence. The **actual effectiveness** is what occurs in real life, when inconsistent use or improper technique ("user failure") combines with failures of the method alone ("method failure"). For example, if a couple runs out of condoms on a week-long camping trip yet continues to have intercourse, the woman's subsequent pregnancy is not counted as a method failure. But if she conceives even though she has used a contraceptive foam exactly according to instructions each time she had intercourse, her pregnancy qualifies as a method failure.

Second, for most types of contraception, the longer a person uses a particular method, the more effective it becomes. That is, with practice and experience, the actual failure rate decreases and becomes closer to the theoretical failure rate. (Actual effectiveness rates for the first year of use of the most common methods of birth control are shown in Table 6.2.)

Third, effectiveness rates for almost every nonsurgical contraceptive method vary depending on whether a couple uses the method to *prevent* pregnancy or to *delay* (space) pregnancy. Failure rates are generally 50 to 100 percent higher for delay compared to prevention, since there seems to be less consistency in method use (Ryder, 1973).

There are other difficulties in assessing the safety of contraceptive methods. First, there are

Table 6.2 **Actual Contraceptive Failure Rates During First Year of Use[a]**

Pill	7.3%	Rhythm	31.4%
Condom	15.8%	Spermicides	30.2%
Diaphragm	22.0%	IUD	6.0%

[a]*These figures are standardized by age, race, and marital status and are corrected to allow for underreporting of abortion.*
Source: *Modified from Jones and Forrest, 1992, Table 1.*

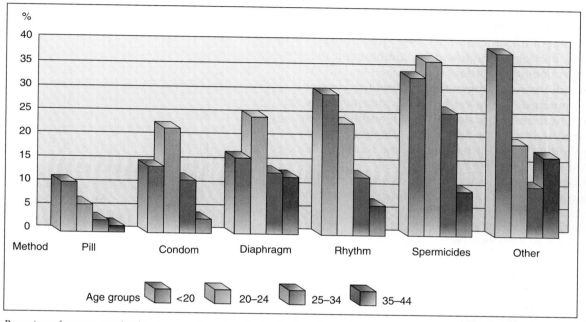

Percentage of women experiencing contraceptive failure during the first 12 months of use, by age and method, standardized by race and marital status.

often wide differences in the frequency of side effects reported by different investigators. Their results reflect differences in research design, choice of control groups, different characteristics in the populations studied (such as age, health, socioeconomic status), and the methods investigators use to identify a problem (self-administered questionnaire, personal interview, laboratory testing). Second, there are some relative aspects to the safety question. How important is avoiding pregnancy? Are the side effects of a contraceptive method more or less serious than the risks of pregnancy and childbirth? How do the risks of a contraceptive method compare with other health risks (such as the risk of getting cancer or having high blood pressure) or with risks of everyday life? These questions are addressed in more detail as we review the safety and side effects of each method of contraception.

HORMONAL METHODS OF CONTRACEPTION

Birth Control Pills (Oral Contraceptives)

The introduction of birth control pills in 1960 revolutionized contraceptive practices around the world. Millions of women turned enthusiastically to this convenient and effective method of preventing pregnancy, but within a decade reports of serious side effects of the pill began to appear and the popularity of this method declined substantially.

theoretical effectiveness the ideal effectiveness of a contraceptive method when used correctly and consistently.

actual effectiveness the observed effectiveness of a contraceptive method in real life, including user failures and method failures.

Now, after more than 30 years of observation, what are the facts about the pill?

There are two types of oral contraceptives currently in use: a **combination pill,** which contains a synthetic estrogen and a progesterone-like synthetic substance called progestogen, and a **minipill** with progestogen only in low dosage. This discussion focuses on combination pills (unless otherwise specified) because they are the most commonly used.

The most popular pill used today, accounting for 85 percent of the oral contraceptives used in America and Europe, is the low-dose combination pill. This has one-fourth or less the estrogen and about one-tenth the progestogen that earlier birth control pills contained. The lower hormone concentrations cause fewer annoying side effects; in addition, it is believed that they are less likely to cause serious complications than earlier, higher-dose forms of the pill (Mishell, 1989; Hatcher et al., 1994).

Among the numerous types of low-dose combination pills on the market are some that have a constant dose of hormones in each pill and some that are *multiphasic,* meaning that the amount of hormones in each pill varies at different times in the monthly cycle. In biphasic pills, for example, the amount of progestogen increases around mid-cycle; in triphasic pills, the amount of hormones is changed three times. Women using the multiphasic pills should note that taking their pills in an incorrect sequence may lessen contraceptive effectiveness considerably.

How Birth Control Pills Work

Birth control pills prevent pregnancy primarily by blocking the normal cyclic output of **follicle stimulating hormone (FSH)** and **luteinizing hormone (LH)** by the pituitary, thus preventing ovulation (Figure 6.1). In addition, the progestogen makes implantation difficult by inhibiting the development of the lining of the uterus and also thickens the cervical mucus, decreasing the possibility that sperm can get through.

Use and Effectiveness

Birth control pills are taken one per day for 21 days beginning on the fifth day of the menstrual cycle (i.e., 4 days after a period begins). Some brands of birth control pills are packaged with seven inactive pills (usually of another color) that the woman takes on a daily basis to complete the cycle,

Figure 6.1   Serum Gonadotrophin Levels During the Menstrual Cycle

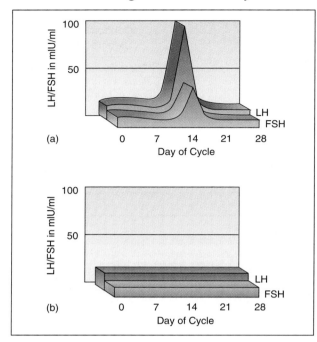

(a) Women not using oral contraceptives.
(b) Women using combination oral contraceptives.

whereas with other brands the woman must remember to resume her pills one week later. Multiphasic pills come in several different colors within each monthly packet, with each color corresponding to a different dose of hormones.

If a pill is missed, two pills should be taken the next day. If two pills in a row are missed, the woman should take two pills as soon as she realizes it and take two pills again the next day; after that, she should continue to take one pill each day. Since it is likely that birth control pills will not work properly in such a cycle, an *alternative* form of contraception must be used to prevent pregnancy. If a woman misses more than two pills in a row, or misses pills three or more times during one cycle, she should stop taking pills entirely and use another method of contraception for the rest of the cycle. She can begin a new cycle of oral contraceptives at the start of her next period. If her period is late, she should continue using her other contraceptive method and get a pregnancy test before resuming birth control pills.

Birth control pills are the most effective nonsurgical method of contraception. Among women who use the pill consistently, only one pregnancy will occur among 200 women during a year. Among all women using the pill—including those who sometimes forget to use it—3 or 6 pregnancies will occur in 100 women annually.

The minipill, which is taken every day, even during menstruation, is less effective than the combination pill. If used perfectly, 1 or 2 pregnancies will occur in 100 women during a year. In actual conditions—including the occasional forgotten pill—5 to 10 pregnancies occur in 100 women using the minipill for a year.

Side Effects and Safety

Birth control pills have now been used by more than 180 million women around the world and have probably been studied more intensively than any other medication in history. Despite scare stories that appear regularly in the press, the evidence shows that the pill has more health benefits than risks for many users. For example, there is no reliable evidence that birth control pills cause cancer (Kols et al., 1982; Speroff and Darney, 1992; Hatcher et al., 1994), and they actually protect against cancer of the ovaries (Newhouse et al., 1977; Centers for Disease Control, 1983) and of the uterine lining (Weiss and Sayvetz, 1980; Kaufman et al., 1980; Centers for Disease Control, 1983a).[2] Furthermore, women who use birth control pills are only one-fourth as likely to develop benign (noncancerous) breast tumors as nonusers, one-fourteenth as likely to develop ovarian cysts, one-half as likely to develop rheumatoid arthritis, and two-thirds as likely to develop iron deficiency anemia (Ory, Rosenfeld, and Landman, 1980).

Other beneficial effects of the pill have also been noted. Many women find that the pill reduces the amount of menstrual flow and produces more regular cycles with less menstrual cramping (Mishell, 1989). Acne can be improved by the pill (although sometimes it is worsened), premenstrual tension can be reduced, and pelvic inflammatory disease—a serious cause of infertility—is

---

[2]Two points should be made: (1) An earlier type of birth control pill, the sequential pill, was banned because it *was* found to cause cancer of the uterus. (2) As it may take decades for certain types of cancer to develop, it cannot be concluded that the combination pill *does not* cause cancer. However, more than 2000 cases of endometrial cancer are prevented each year by use of the pill (Centers for Disease Control, 1983a).

FOCUS IN BRIEF

Health Benefits of the Pill

- Reduced risk of ovarian cancer.
- Reduced risk of endometrial cancer.
- Reduced risk of benign breast tumors.
- Reduced risk of ovarian cysts.
- Reduced risk of pelvic inflammatory disease.
- Reduced risk of iron deficiency anemia.
- Reduced risk of rheumatoid arthritis.
- Reduced risk of ectopic pregnancy.
- Increased bone density in the spine.
- Often relieves premenstrual symptoms.

only half as common in pill users as in nonusers (Wharton and Blackburn, 1988). In addition, the pill seems to cause an increased bone density in the lumbar spine, which may help to prevent the thinning out of bone called osteoporosis that occurs in many women after the menopause (Mishell, 1989).

The most common bothersome side effects of the pill mimic those encountered in pregnancy: nausea, constipation, breast tenderness, minor elevations in blood pressure, edema (swelling), and skin rashes (including brown spots on the face called **chloasma**). Other relatively minor side effects include weight gain or loss, an increased amount of

combination pill a birth control pill containing both estrogen and progesterone.

minipill a contraceptive pill containing only synthetic progesterone in low dosage.

follicle stimulating hormone (FSH) a substance produced in the pituitary gland that prepares the ovary for ovulation and stimulates the production of sperm cells in the testes.

luteinizing hormone (LH) (lū′ tē in īz′ ing) produced by the pituitary gland, LH triggers ovulation and stimulates the Leydig cells to manufacture testosterone.

chloasma (klō as′ muh) brown pigmented spots, usually on the face, caused either by birth control pills or hormones produced naturally during pregnancy.

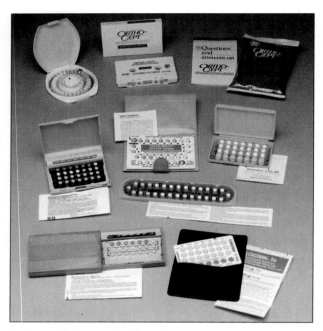

Birth control pills come in different brands and packages, each accompanied by a package insert describing their use and potential side effects.

(lower estrogen dose = lower rates of complication) applies to the other two forms of circulatory disorders linked to use of the pill, heart attacks and stroke. Earlier studies found that oral contraceptives increased the risk of heart attacks in women who smoked and/or women over age 35 (Mann and Inman, 1975; Jick et al., 1978; Rosenberg et al., 1980). A heightened risk of stroke (bleeding into the brain, or blockage of blood flow in the brain) was also found in early studies of pill users.

Based on data from these early studies, the pill was not usually prescribed for women over age 35. More recent research indicates that use of low-dose combination pills by healthy, nonsmoking women up to age 45 does not cause any increased risk of serious cardiovascular disease (Mann et al., 1986; Mishell, 1989; Upton, 1990).

One potentially serious side effect of oral contraceptives is that pill use may increase a woman's susceptibility to infection with HIV, the AIDS virus (Plummer et al., 1991; Cates and Stone, 1992a). It is ostensibly for this reason that Japan has retained its longtime ban on the pill (*The New York Times*, March 19, 1992, p. A3).

For several decades, there has also been a persistent concern that the pill may cause an increased rate of breast cancer. Most studies have not identified any link between birth control pills and breast cancer. For example, one extensive investigation found no evidence that use of oral contraceptives, even over many years, increased the risk of subsequent breast cancer in women with a family history of the disease (Murray et al., 1989). Likewise, a ten-year study of a total of 118,273 female nurses concluded, "overall past use of oral contraceptives is not associated with a substantial increase in the risk of breast cancer" (Romieu et al., 1989). Other studies have been inconsistent, however (Kay and Hannaford, 1988; Miller et al., 1989).

An FDA panel convened in 1989 to examine all of the available evidence concluded that there was no need for recommending changes in the use of birth control pills or in their warning labels (*The New York Times*, January 6, 1989, pp. A1 and A13). The panel noted that the small number of studies suggesting a heightened risk of breast cancer in women who have used the pill are inconsistent with each other and plagued with methodological problems. More recently, a prestigious committee of the National Academy of Sciences and Institute of Medicine concluded:

vaginal secretions, and an increased susceptibility to vaginal infections.

Less common but more troublesome problems caused by the pill include high blood pressure, diabetes, migraine headaches, and, rarely, jaundice or liver tumors (Mishell, 1989). In addition, if taken during pregnancy, the pill may cause birth defects (Nora and Nora, 1978; Kasan and Andrews, 1980).

The most serious risks to women using birth control pills are disorders of the circulatory system. Three different types of circulatory problems are involved. The most common is the formation of a blood clot in a vein (usually in the legs), which typically results in only minor discomfort caused by inflammation and swelling. Infrequently, a piece of the clot may break off and circulate to the lungs or the brain, where it can cause serious damage or death. These problems, called thromboembolic diseases, were two to four times more common among pill users than other women in the 1960s and 1970s (occurring in about 1 out of 1000 pill users in a year) but are thought to occur less often today with the considerably lower dose of estrogen contained in the pills currently being used (Wharton and Blackburn, 1988). The same observation

Oral contraceptives, as they have been used to date, have caused little or no overall increase in the risk of breast cancer in women in developed countries. Risks in women of all ages combined have not been appreciably enhanced by more than a decade of exposure or after a potential latent period of up to two decades. (*Committee on the Relationship Between Oral Contraceptives and Breast Cancer, 1991, p. 136*)

Nevertheless, because the risk of breast cancer occurring long after use of the pill (20 years or more) has not yet been conclusively examined, the final word on a possible relationship between the pill and breast cancer cannot be given at this time. As a practical precautionary matter, we suggest that people whose mothers or sisters have had breast cancer should probably avoid use of the pill until more conclusive studies have been completed.

Despite these health concerns, it is clear that today's low-dose birth control pills are safer than they have ever been by a considerable margin (Wharton and Blackburn, 1988; Mishell, 1989; Speroff and Darney, 1992). However, women who rely on the pill for contraception should recognize that it provides no protection at all against HIV, so any pill user who is not in a strictly monogamous relationship should also use condoms for maximal protection against HIV and other sexually transmitted diseases.

Sexual Effects

Evaluating the effects of birth control pills on sexuality is tricky. Older research generally noted that long-term use of the pill had negative sexual effects (Masters and Johnson, 1970; Herzberg et al., 1971), but later studies do not support this view (Bragonier, 1976; Gambrell et al., 1979). There is no research available as yet on the sexual effects of today's low-estrogen pills.

There are many individual reasons that the pill helps or hinders a woman's sexual feelings and function. Some reasons are biological: a woman who develops a vaginal infection may have sexual problems as a result, or a woman who has less premenstrual and menstrual cramping may feel better physically and thus may be more sexually receptive and responsive. Some reasons are psychological. If a woman expects to have sexual side effects from the pill, her prophecy becomes self-fulfilling. Some women may feel guilty about using the pill because of religious beliefs or conflicts between

wanting children and using contraception. Alternatively, the psychological security of using a highly effective method of contraception reduces the fear of pregnancy and may therefore improve sexual interest and enjoyment (after all, it is harder to enjoy something when you are afraid). One woman told us, "After switching to the pill, I found that sex became more fun. I had my first orgasm during intercourse less than two months later" (*Authors' files*). Since the pill also requires no interruptions at the time of sexual activity, it permits a degree of spontaneity and intimacy that other methods may not.

Most women using oral contraceptives today do not report significant changes in sexual interest, behavior, or enjoyment. Approximately 10 percent experience improved sexuality, which is about the same as the percent who note decreased sexual interest or responsiveness.

The Norplant System

In December 1990, the Food and Drug Administration approved the first subdermal implantable contraceptive, the Norplant System, for marketing in the United States. Norplant consists of implantable capsules containing a hormone called levonorgestrel, a synthetic progestin which has been widely used in birth control pills for years. The Norplant System had been in widespread use in Europe, Asia, and Latin America for some years prior to being approved in the United States, and has now been used by more than half a million women.

The Norplant System consists of six flexible, closed, tubular capsules each about the size of a fat match (see Figure 6.2). The capsules are inserted beneath the skin of the upper arm in a procedure that takes about 10 minutes, after which they gradually release the hormone they contain for at least five years. Once they are in place they rarely cause discomfort, although they can be felt just under the surface of the skin and are often visible to the naked eye as bulges under the skin, especially in thin women. (The implants occasionally cause minor local itching or pain in the first month or two after insertion, but less than 1 percent of women stop using Norplant because of this problem.)

Norplant works by inhibiting ovulation (Faundes et al., 1991; Siegel et al., 1991) and by thickening cervical mucus, making it difficult for sperm to

Figure 6.2   The Norplant System

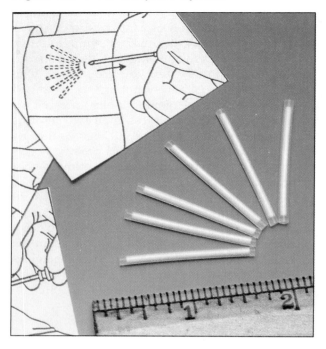
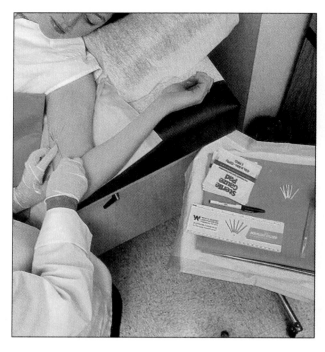

gain access to the Fallopian tubes. The effectiveness of the Norplant System is excellent: the failure rate is a low 0.3 to 0.6 percent for one year, with a total failure rate of only 1.1 percent for five years.

Despite its high level of effectiveness and its convenience, there are several drawbacks for users. The most common one is that Norplant often produces abnormal menstrual bleeding (Darney et al., 1990). This can take the form of very irregular periods (seen in about 40 percent of users), spotting or bleeding between periods (32 percent), or more frequent periods (25 percent). One woman in ten reports having consistently heavier periods while using Norplant, while 12 percent stop having periods entirely. It appears that many of these problems lessen after the first year of use, but there are no guarantees that this will occur. Other side effects of Norplant include headaches, acne, weight changes, increased growth of facial and body hair, uterine cramping, and breast discharge.

There are a few other drawbacks to Norplant. For example, it is important to recognize that it provides no protection whatsoever against HIV or other sexually transmitted diseases. Another problem is that discontinuing the use of Norplant requires a minor surgical procedure to remove the implants. While this may be an inconvenience (as well as a source of physical discomfort), the good

news is that fertility is rapidly restored after the system is removed.

Since Norplant doesn't contain any estrogen, many of the risks associated with combination birth control pills do not apply to this contraceptive method, which is one of its biggest advantages. However, Norplant should not be used by women with undiagnosed abnormal genital bleeding, known or suspected pregnancy, active thromboembolic (blood clotting) disorders, acute liver disease or liver tumors, or past or present history of breast cancer. In addition, women with high blood pressure or heart disease should not use this product (with few exceptions best decided by a woman and her physician). Furthermore, other methods of birth control are apt to be more suitable for women with a history of ectopic pregnancy, clinical depression, gallbladder disease, or severe migraine headaches. In addition, Norplant is not a good choice for women who weigh more than 154 pounds (70 kg). The reason is that the concentration of levonorgestrel, the hormone contained in Norplant, in the blood is partly proportional to body weight, so that after the first year or two of use, blood concentrations of the active contraceptive ingredient may fall to unacceptably low—hence, ineffective—levels in heavier women (Speroff and Darney, 1992).

Most women who have used Norplant experienced no sexual changes. Of those who reported a change in their sex lives, almost two-thirds said that it had improved (usually because they were less worried about pregnancy and/or because sex had become more spontaneous). Only 11 percent of users found that their sex life had gotten worse, with some women indicating that this was because of menstrual changes, and a small fraction of women reporting that their sexual interest was lower (Darney et al., 1990).

Depo-Provera

Another version of hormone-based contraception was approved for use in the United States in 1992, although it was already in widespread use in more than 90 countries around the world well before then. Depo-Provera, a long-acting, injectable synthetic form of progesterone, is given by injection once every three months and has an effectiveness rating comparable to the combination pill. Despite its high level of effectiveness, Depo-Provera has been the source of some controversy because of concerns that it might be linked to an increased risk of breast cancer or cancers of the liver or cervix. However, a recent large-scale study found no evidence of a significant long-term risk of breast cancer, suggesting that this method is both safe and reliable (WHO Collaborative Study, 1991). Side effects with Depo-Provera include irregular menstrual bleeding, breast tenderness, weight gain, and depression.

IUDs

The IUD, or **intrauterine device,** is a small plastic object that is inserted into the uterus through the vagina and cervix and then is continuously kept in place. As of early 1990, there were only two models of IUDs available in the United States: a progesterone-releasing device (called Progestasert) and a copper-containing device (called the Copper T380A). These are shown in Figure 6.3.

In the mid-1980s, major IUD manufacturers withdrew from the U.S. market because of a substantial number of lawsuits over infections in the upper part of the female genital tract—especially infection of the Fallopian tubes, known as salpingitis or pelvic inflammatory disease (PID)—which is particularly serious because it can cause permanent sterility, increases the chances of having an ectopic pregnancy, and can cause abscesses around the ovaries that may require surgery to be corrected (Mishell, 1985). The older IUD devices have now been replaced by substantially safer versions, but their popularity in the United States is considerably lower than it was a decade ago.

While IUDs became popular in this country only in the last 25 years, they are a modern application of an ancient concept. For centuries, Arab and Turkish camel drivers put a large pebble into the camel's uterus for contraceptive purposes, since a pregnant camel on a long desert trek would not be very helpful. The first IUD designed for humans, a ring made of silkworm gut, did not gain much attention when introduced in 1909. In the late 1920s a ring of gut and silver wire was developed by Grafenberg, a German physician, and enjoyed some popularity. Early models of the IUD, however, were condemned because of the risk of pelvic infection and fell into disrepute.

By 1978 about 6 percent of married women of reproductive age in America used the IUD, while about 20 percent did in Scandinavia and approximately half of all women using contraceptives adopted it in China (Piotrow, Rinehart, and Schmidt, 1979). However, as a result of negative publicity about the risk of infection linked to IUD use, the popularity of this device plummeted in the United States during the 1980s, and today only 1 percent of American women use this method. On a worldwide basis, approximately 60 million women use the IUD.

How IUDs Work

The exact way the IUD works is not known. In the past, it was thought that the major effect was by interfering with the implantation of the fertilized egg in the lining of the uterus by a local inflammatory reaction. Now it appears that IUDs also act to block sperm from fertilizing the egg (Alvarez et al., 1988; Treiman and Liskin, 1988; Mishell, 1990). This spermicidal action is thought to be a result of white blood cells engulfing or damaging sperm before they reach the egg as well as because of chemical reactions caused by enzymes in the Fallopian tubes. IUDs containing progesterone also alter the

intrauterine device (IUD) (in truh ū′ ter in) a small object, either plastic or metal, placed inside the uterus for birth control.

Figure 6.3   The IUD

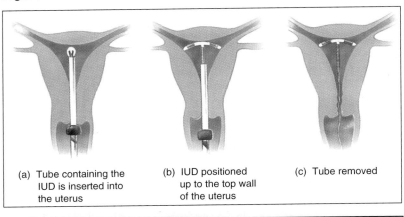

(a) Tube containing the
    IUD is inserted into
    the uterus

(b) IUD positioned
    up to the top wall
    of the uterus

(c) Tube removed

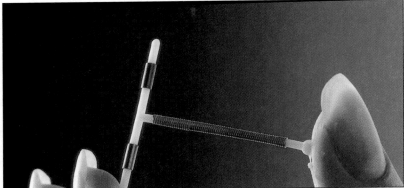

*Insertion of an IUD (a–c) and photograph of the Paraguard (Copper T380A) IUD currently
in use in the United States.*

development of the lining of the uterus so that implantation is unlikely.

Use and Effectiveness

The IUD must be inserted into the uterus (Figure 6.3) by a trained health-care professional after determining that the woman is not pregnant and does not have chlamydia, gonorrhea, or other pelvic infections. Inserting an IUD can cause abortion in a pregnant woman and can push bacteria from an infection into the uterus or Fallopian tubes. Insertion is usually done during a menstrual period, since it is a fairly reliable sign that the woman is not pregnant, but it can be done at other times.

Inserting an IUD usually causes only brief discomfort, but some women prefer to be given a short-acting painkiller. Taking two or three aspirin tablets about an hour before insertion provides some pain relief and may theoretically decrease cramping because it blocks release of prostaglandins. The woman must be shown how to check the plastic thread that comes through the mouth of the cervix to be sure the IUD is in place. If this thread cannot be located, or if it seems longer than it was before, the woman must return for a check-up, because contractions of the uterus can push the IUD downward, causing it to be partly or completely expelled from the uterus. Expulsion rates for the copper- or progesterone-containing IUDs are about 7 per 100 women during a year, with most of the expulsions occurring in the first three months after insertion (Treiman and Liskin, 1988; Cole, 1989). Expulsion rates are higher in younger women and in women who have never had children.

Even though they may be expelled, IUDs are highly effective. A number of studies show fewer than 1 pregnancy occurring in 100 women using the Copper T380A for one year, while the Progestasert IUD has a pregnancy rate of about 3 per 100 women in one year (Cole, 1989). (Adjusting the effectiveness data for abortions resulted in an actual failure rate of 6 percent in the first year of use, as shown in Table 6.2.) The Progestasert device must be replaced after one year of use because its progesterone supply is depleted by that time; the Copper T380A is currently approved for eight years of continuous use.

Side Effects and Safety

Perforation of the uterus (puncturing the wall of the uterus) is the most serious risk of using an IUD. If it occurs, it is almost always at the time of insertion. This problem, which occurs in about 1 in 1000 insertions, can cause sudden pain and bleeding or, more rarely, may be without immediate symptoms. Perforation usually requires surgery to prevent damage to the intestines, since the IUD usually perforates through the uterus into the abdomen. Inserting an IUD while a woman is breast-feeding causes a tenfold increase in the risk of perforation of the uterus (Merz, 1983), so it seems advisable to choose a different method of birth control during this time.

The most common side effects of the IUD are increased bleeding from the uterus and cramping pain. Menstrual periods are typically heavier and longer (except in women using IUDs with progesterone, which decreases menstrual flow), and there is more likely to be spotting between periods. This increased blood loss can cause anemia. Cramps and bleeding can be serious enough to have the IUD removed (about 10 percent of women find this necessary) but usually lessen after the first three months.

IUD users have about a four times higher risk of pelvic infection than other women. This risk is present not only at the time of insertion but also with continued use of the device. Bacteria, viruses, or fungus infections may enter the uterus by "climbing" the tail of the IUD, and there is a chance that such an infection will spread to the Fallopian tubes and ovaries, which can cause permanent scarring and infertility (Vessey et al., 1981; Beerthuizen et al., 1982). However, it should be noted that for women in monogamous sexual relationships, IUDs pose little risk of infection except in the first few months after they are inserted (Lee, Rubin, and Borucki, 1988).

If a pregnancy occurs in a woman with an IUD, there is about a 5 percent chance that the pregnancy will be ectopic (misplaced) (Cole, 1989). This is because IUDs protect better against intrauterine pregnancies than against ectopic ones. Since pregnancies are infrequent in IUD users, the rate of ectopic pregnancy is relatively low: less than 1.5 ectopic pregnancies per 1000 woman-years of use (Treiman and Liskin, 1988), about one-tenth the rate of ectopic pregnancies overall.

If a uterine pregnancy occurs in an IUD user, approximately half will abort spontaneously (usually in the second trimester) unless the IUD is removed. There is no evidence, however, that IUDs cause birth defects.

The IUD is well suited to women who want a highly effective contraceptive method that requires no active participation on their part and is easily and promptly reversible. It may be particularly appropriate for women who cannot use birth control pills for medical reasons and for the mentally retarded who may not be able to remember to take a pill or use a mechanical method of birth control. IUDs should not be used by women who are pregnant or who have active pelvic infection, bleeding disorders, anatomical abnormalities of the uterus or cervix, or abnormal pelvic bleeding. Women who have had an ectopic pregnancy, severe menstrual disorders, or any disease that suppresses normal immunity to infection should not use IUDs. Likewise, women who have multiple sexual partners or who have had repeated genital infections should not use IUDs.

Sexual Effects

Like birth control pills, the IUD is effective in preventing pregnancy and does not interfere with sexual spontaneity or mood. Yet the IUD can cause pain during intercourse. The woman may experience pain if the IUD is not in the right position or if there is a pelvic infection or inflammation; the man may have pain at the tip of the penis or along the shaft because of irritation from the tail of the IUD in the vagina. Both abdominal cramping and persistent bleeding can lessen a woman's interest in sexual activity, but these side effects occur in only about 10 percent of users. Infrequently, women who use IUDs find that orgasm may cause intense, unpleasant cramping because of uterine contractions around the IUD.

Anyone using an IUD should also realize that it provides no protection against infection with HIV, the virus that causes AIDS.

BARRIER METHODS

Diaphragms

The **diaphragm** is a round, shallow dome of thin rubber stretched over a flexible ring (Figure 6.4). After a spermicidal (sperm-killing) jelly or cream is applied inside the dome and around the inner part of the rim, the diaphragm must be inserted inside the vagina and positioned so that it completely covers the cervix. Before the introduction of birth control pills, the diaphragm was the most widely used method of contraception, and it is still popular today.

How Diaphragms Work

The diaphragm is a mechanical barrier that blocks the mouth of the cervix so that sperm cannot enter. Because this blocking effect is not very reliable by itself, the use of a spermicide is required to kill sperm that manage to swim inside the rim of the diaphragm.

Use and Effectiveness

Diaphragms come in different sizes and must be properly fitted by a trained health-care professional to match the anatomy of the user. The size and position of the cervix and the size and shape of the vagina must be taken into account to achieve a proper fit; the actual fitting is done using a set of graduated flexible rings to select the right size. After the fitting, the woman is shown how to insert the diaphragm either manually or with a plastic inserter (see Figure 6.4). Some clinicians recommend that a woman be refitted if she gains or loses 10 pounds. However, one study found that more women whose weight was stable needed refitting (Fiscella, 1982), so the matter is not a clear one. We recommend that women be refitted for a diaphragm after a pregnancy or annually. If there is a weight change of 15 pounds or more, it also may be advisable to be refitted.

The diaphragm can be inserted up to two hours before intercourse and should remain in place at least six hours afterward. If it is worn for more than two hours before intercourse, the effectiveness of the spermicide may drop. For this reason, a second, full application of spermicidal jelly, cream, or foam should be placed in the vagina before intercourse in these circumstances. If the diaphragm is removed less than six hours after intercourse, it is possible that live sperm in the vagina may reach the cervix and swim up into the uterus.

Although failure rates as low as 2 percent have been reported among highly motivated couples

Figure 6.4   The Diaphragm

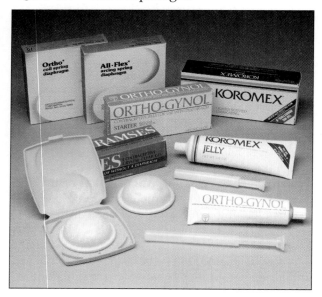 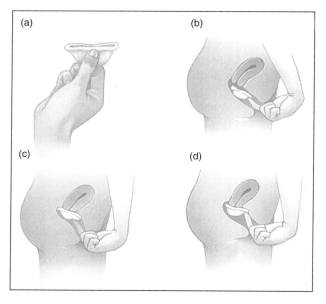

Proper use of a diaphragm: (a) After inserting spermicidal jelly or cream, the rim of the diaphragm is pinched between the fingers and thumb. (b) The folded diaphragm is gently inserted into the vagina and pushed downward and backward as far as it will go. (c) To check for proper positioning, feel the cervix to be certain it is completely covered by the soft rubber dome of the diaphragm. (d) A finger is hooked under the forward rim to remove the diaphragm.

using a diaphragm consistently and correctly, the method is generally not so effective. A failure rate of 8 to 12 percent among experienced users is more typical. During the first year of use, the actual failure rate for diaphragm use is 22 percent (see Table 6.2). The majority of failures are due to inconsistent or improper use of this method, including couples who sometimes gamble on the chance of getting pregnant by having sex without using the diaphragm. However, there are several specific problems with the diaphragm that can cause failures no matter how consistently it is used.

For example, the diaphragm may slip out of position during sexual play because of improper insertion, a poor fit, or expansion of the inside of the vagina and movement of the uterus during excitation. Johnson and Masters (1962) found that even a well-fitted and properly inserted diaphragm can become dislodged during intercourse when the woman is on top of the man or if the penis is removed and reinserted into the vagina during plateau levels of arousal. Even a tiny hole in the dome of the diaphragm will permit sperm to enter, so it is important to inspect it carefully and to avoid use of Vaseline or similar products on it, since this can cause deterioration of the latex. Despite these problems, there are some advantages, too. The diaphragm seems to offer protection against cervical cancer (Wright et al., 1978) and against some sexually transmitted diseases (Sherris, Moore, and Fox, 1984). Another benefit of the diaphragm is that it offers considerable protection against damage to the Fallopian tubes from infection (Cramer et al., 1987). Furthermore, if consistently used in combination with a condom, the rate of effectiveness is comparable to that of birth control pills.

Side Effects and Safety

The only potential side effects of diaphragm use are (1) possible allergic reactions to the rubber in the diaphragm or to the spermicide itself and (2) the chance of introducing infection into the vagina if the diaphragm is not clean. Both problems are infrequent. In addition, it is not advisable to wear a diaphragm for more than 12 hours at a time because this seems to cause an overgrowth of bacteria in the vagina and cervix that is linked to the toxic shock syndrome (see Chapter 22). The diaphragm has no effects on hormones or physical processes of the body and poses no danger to later fertility.

Women who have pelvic disorders affecting the vagina or cervix or who do not like to touch their genitals should not use the diaphragm.

Sexual Effects

The primary sexual difficulty with use of the diaphragm is inconvenience. For example, either partner may experience loss of sexual arousal while the woman takes time to insert and check the diaphragm if she did not insert it before sex play began. Some couples solve this problem by making the insertion of the diaphragm a part of their sexual play preliminary to intercourse. Either partner may find the diaphragm or the process of its insertion messy and unaesthetic. (Some users are annoyed by the "gloppiness" after removal of the diaphragm, when the spermicidal jelly may drip out of the vagina for several hours.) In addition, a diaphragm that is too large may cause pain during intercourse and some men complain that intercourse feels "different" with the diaphragm in place. For people who don't like to have intercourse during menstrual periods, the diaphragm can be used to provide a "reverse barrier" that contains flow during sexual activity.

The Cervical Cap

A device related to the diaphragm is the **cervical cap,** which fits snugly over the cervix and stays in place by suction (see Figure 6.5). After enjoying considerable popularity for the past three decades in Europe, the device was finally approved for use by the U.S. Food and Drug Administration in 1988 (*The New York Times*, May 24, 1988, pp. A1 and C8).

There are several types of cervical cap, although only one—the Prentif cavity-rim cap—has been approved by the FDA so far. This thimble-shaped version is made of soft, pliable latex and is a bit less than half the size of a diaphragm. Other types are made of a harder plastic material.

diaphragm (dī′ uh fram) a dome-shaped rubber contraceptive device that is positioned inside the vagina so that it blocks the cervix; it must be used with a spermicide to be effective.

cervical cap (ser′ vi kul kap) a small plastic or rubber contraceptive device worn on the cervix to provide a barrier to sperm.

Figure 6.5   Cervical Caps

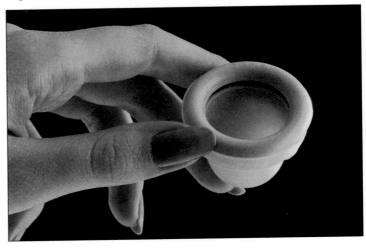

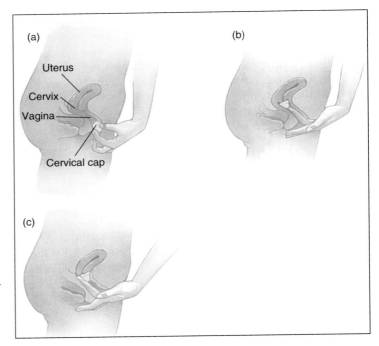

This photo of a cervical cap gives an idea of its relative size. The drawings show: (a) Initial placement of the cap inside the opening of the vagina. (b) The cap must be positioned snugly over the cervix, the way a thimble fits over your finger. (c) Removing the cap.

How the Cervical Cap Works

Like the diaphragm, the cervical cap is a mechanical barrier that blocks the mouth of the cervix so that sperm cannot enter. In fact, this blocking action is more efficient than that of the diaphragm because the cervical cap fits on the cervix more tightly than the diaphragm.

Use and Effectiveness

The Prentif cap is made in four different sizes and must be fitted properly in order to be effective. It is somewhat more difficult for the user to learn how to insert the cap correctly than it is to learn how to use a diaphragm (Mishell, 1989). At the present time, the FDA has approved the cap for only 48 hours of continuous wear, although data suggest it can safely be worn for longer periods of time (Klitsch, 1988).

The FDA recommends that a spermicide should always be placed inside the cap before use, but this is apt to only be an effective "back-up" for the first six hours of use; after that, the sperm-killing action of spermicides decreases considerably (Masters, Johnson, and Kolodny, 1982a). In fact, members of the National Women's Health Network, which led the drive to obtain approval for the device, believe that spermicide is unnecessary for the cap's effectiveness (Klitsch, 1988).

The effectiveness of the cervical cap seems to be generally comparable to the diaphragm. In several different studies, pregnancy rates ranged from 8 to 20 per 100 woman-years (Boehm, 1983; Cagen, 1986; Powell et al., 1986). In the largest U.S. study of the cap, involving around 1500 women who were randomly assigned to either the cap or a diaphragm, one-year pregnancy rates were roughly the same for both devices—17.4 per 100 women using the cervical cap, compared to 16.7 per 100 diaphragm users (Bernstein et al., 1986).

Side Effects and Safety

There is only one major questionmark about potential adverse effects of the cervical cap. The cap has been linked to abnormal Pap smears in a small number of users. In one study, for instance, 4 percent of women who used the cervical cap for three months developed changes in their Pap smears, an incidence about twice as high as in diaphragm users (*The New York Times,* May 24, 1988, pp. Al and C8). It is unclear if these cervical abnormalities are minor microscopic changes resulting from inflammation or if they may be precancerous.

There is also a small risk that if the cap is worn too long it may cause an overgrowth of bacteria linked to toxic shock syndrome (see Chapter 22). As with the diaphragm, very infrequently women may have an allergic reaction to the latex in the cap.

One of the principal safety advantages of the cap is that it does not influence a woman's hormone production or cause any changes in the functioning of a woman's body.

Women who have abnormal Pap smears or anatomical abnormalities of the cervix should not use the cervical cap.

Sexual Effects

Most women who have switched to the cervical cap after experience with a diaphragm say that it is advantageous in two ways: it permits more sexual spontaneity and it is considerably less messy (Klitsch, 1988). In a small number of cases, the cap has been reported to cause discomfort to the male during intercourse, but in our experience, this problem is quite infrequent. On the other hand, about one out of five women complains of vaginal odors caused by the cervical cap (probably the result of a backup of cervical secretions), which can be embarrassing. One other drawback is that the cap can be dislodged from the cervix, especially during deep penile thrusting (Masters and Kolodny, unpublished observation). In one large study, this occurred at least once in 40 percent of women using the cap (Bernstein et al., 1986).

Condoms

The condom (also called a rubber, safe, or prophylactic) is a thin sheath of latex rubber or tissue from a lamb's intestine that fits snugly over the penis. Currently, it is the only effective nonsurgical birth control method for males, and it does not require a prescription. Condoms can be purchased in drug stores, by mail order, at family planning clinics, and, in some locations, from coin-operated vending machines in men's rooms of bars and gas stations. In addition, many colleges now provide condom dispensers in dormitories and student health centers.

Condoms are usually rolled up into plastic or foil packets (Figure 6.6) and come in different styles. Some are lubricated, some come in a variety of colors, and some have tiny ribs or bumps on their surface that supposedly provide more stimulation to the female as intravaginal thrusting occurs. One of the more recent innovations in condom design is the introduction of a condom coated with a spermicide combined with a lubricant. Condoms are designed with either a round end or a reservoir end, a small receptacle to catch the semen.

Although condoms were somewhat ignored in the 1960s and 1970s because they were viewed as cumbersome and old-fashioned, there has been a marked increase in their popularity in the past few years for several different reasons. First, the condom's effectiveness as a barrier to the spread of the AIDS virus (as well as to the spread of other bacteria and viruses that cause sexually transmitted diseases) has brought it into the spotlight. This focus on the condom's usefulness as a preventive health measure (as well as a birth control device) has been the main reason for a resurgence of its use. Second, in addition to the positive publicity about condoms contained in the U.S. Surgeon General's Report on AIDS (Surgeon General, 1986) and similar sets of recommendations by other governmental and scientific groups, condom manufacturers have increased their advertising of this product, generating additional consumer awareness and interest. One interesting by-product of these changes is that several brands of condoms are now being marketed primarily to women, and condom sales to women surged by an estimated 300 percent between 1980 and 1989 (in one ad for Lifestyles condoms, a young woman proclaims, "I'll do a lot for love, but I'm not ready to die for it"). Finally, increasing attention to the role and responsibilities of teenage males in the high rates of unintended pregnancy in America has led to a greater emphasis on recommending condom use as a relatively inexpensive, accessible, nonprescription form of birth control that is safe and effective if properly used.

Use and Effectiveness

The condom, which works by preventing sperm from entering the vagina, must be unrolled onto the erect penis shortly before intercourse. If it is put on too early, it may tear if rubbed against the sheets (or dirt, sand, or car seat) or it may be accidently punctured by a fingernail. If put on shortly before ejaculation, some drops of pre-ejaculatory fluid containing live sperm might have already entered the vagina. If a round-end condom is used, a little extra space should be left at the tip to catch the ejaculate. After ejaculation, the condom should be held at the base of the penis so it does not slip or spill while being withdrawn. If leakage occurs for any reason, it is wise to put a spermicidal foam or cream in the vagina immediately. A condom should not be tested before use by inflating, stretching, or being filled with water. It is impossible to detect microscopic holes that would be large enough to allow sperm to pass through, and you *may* inadvertently damage the condom while you are trying to check it.

An important aspect of condom use that has received relatively little attention is that latex condoms deteriorate rapidly and are liable to break if they are in contact with oil-based lubricants such as Vaseline, baby oil, vegetable oil, many hand creams, or some of the exotic massage oils sold in sex shops. In one recent experiment, it was found that exposure of the condom to such products for just ten minutes at body temperature causes a significant weakening in the strength of the condom—a weakening that is pronounced enough to be

Figure 6.6   The Condom

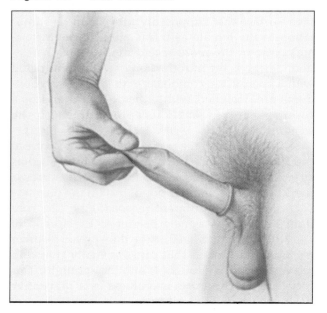
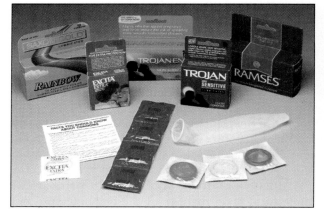

The photo shows an assortment of condoms and their packages. The drawing shows the proper method of pinching the tip of the condom without a reservoir end to leave some room for the semen.

Guidelines for Use of Condoms

1. Latex condoms should be used rather than natural membrane condoms because they offer greater protection against HIV and other viral STDs.
2. Condoms should be stored in a cool, dry place out of direct sunlight.
3. Condoms in damaged packages or those that show obvious signs of age (e.g., those that are brittle, sticky, or discolored) should not be used, since they may be defective.
4. Condoms should be handled with care to prevent punctures or rips.
5. Condoms should be put on before any genital contact to prevent exposure to fluids that may contain infectious agents.
6. Only water-based lubricants should be used. Petroleum or oil-based lubricants such as Vaseline, cooking oils, shortening, and most lotions should not be used because they weaken the latex and may cause breakage.
7. Use of condoms containing spermicides may provide some additional protection against STDs. However, vaginal use of spermicides along with condoms is likely to provide even better protection.
8. If a condom breaks, it should be replaced immediately. If ejaculation occurs after condom breakage, the immediate use of spermicide may be of some utility.
9. After ejaculation, care should be taken so that the condom does not slip off the penis before withdrawal; the base of the condom should be held throughout withdrawal. The penis should be withdrawn while still erect.
10. Condoms should never be reused.

Source: *Centers for Disease Control*, MMWR *38:S-8, Table 2, 1989.*

"likely to cause the product [the condom] to fail during use" (Pugh, 1989). Voeller (1989) reported that a large fraction of college-educated men who reported having condoms break on more than 10 percent of the occasions they used them mistakenly believed that these types of sexual lubricants were water-based because they washed off easily with water. (True water-based lubricants include K-Y Lubricating Jelly, Today Personal Lubricant, and Corn Huskers Lotion.)

In theory, the condom is a very reliable method of birth control—when used properly and consistently. Fewer than 5 pregnancies should occur in 100 couples using condoms for a year. Furthermore, if condoms are consistently used in combination with a vaginal spermicide, the theoretical effectiveness is even better, becoming almost as good as the pill. In actual practice, however, couples using the condom as their only method of contraception often have unwanted pregnancies: overall failure rates of 10 to 20 per 100 couple-years are commonly reported. The main problem is not defective condoms (they must meet rigorous testing standards of the Food and Drug Administration[3]) or improper use, but *inconsistent* use. Many people using this method sometimes "take chances" instead of using condoms during every act of intercourse.

One other aspect of condom use that is increasingly important today is that latex condoms provide considerable protection against many sexually transmitted diseases. Condoms made of natural membranes sometimes have pores large enough to allow viruses such as hepatitis B or HIV (the AIDS virus) to pass through (Minuk, Bohme, and Bower, 1986; Goldsmith, 1987).

[3]In 1987, the FDA reported that one out of five sample lots of latex condoms failed the stringent standards that they employ in testing: in other words, they leaked (*American Medical News,* September 4, 1987, p. 37). While the failure rate was highest in brands of imported condoms, roughly one out of 10 domestically manufactured condom batches were defective. (The March 1989 issue of *Consumer Reports* contains a ratings guide to latex condoms that includes data on their failure rates.)

Common Sense and Condom Sense

Many people find that one of the more delicate aspects of negotiating the ground rules of a sexual relationship with a new partner can be how to discuss the use of condoms. While plain talk is sometimes all it takes to reach agreement on the importance of condom use as a means of minimizing the risk of exposure to sexually transmitted diseases, many times a prospective sex partner is hesitant about condom use or reacts defensively, as though the request is tantamount to an accusation of uncleanliness or worse. Here are some practical responses to various objections a partner may voice about condom use.

If Your Partner Says:	*Your Response Can Be:*
"I hate condoms; they make sex clumsy and artificial."	"We can still have great sex if we let ourselves get into it."
"Condoms just turn me off."	"Sexual infections are an even worse turn-off. Let's see if we can't generate enough heat to get us both soaring."
"Using a condom ruins all the romance."	"Romance is a state of mind. If you let yourself get used to it, you'll see that we can get so caught up in each other that you'll hardly realize it's there."
"You don't have to worry about infections; my doctor told me I'm absolutely healthy just last week."	"That's great. My last check-up was all clear, too. The thing is, a condom can protect each of us from infections we may not realize we have."
"If you really loved me, you wouldn't use a condom."	"Loving you means wanting to be absolutely certain we're both safe."
"When I try to use a condom, I lose my erection."	"Not the way I'll put it on for you!"
"There's no reason to use a condom. I take the pill."	"The pill is great for birth control but a condom will protect us both from sexual infections."
"You're so insulting! What gives you the right to think I might have a disease?"	"Caring about our health isn't a put-down. If we're going to have a relationship, doesn't it make sense to be safe instead of sorry?"
"A condom blocks my sexual sensations; it's like wearing a raincoat in the shower."	"Even if you lose a little sensation, you'll still have plenty left when you make love with me!"
"I'm a virgin."	"I'm not. This way we'll both have protection."
"I don't have a condom."	"I do." or "Then let's make love this time without having intercourse."

Source: *Modified from Grieco, 1987.*

In general, latex condoms effectively block the transmission of HIV (Rietmeijer et al., 1988). However, one recent laboratory study showed that small numbers of HIV can leak through an intact condom during sexual intercourse (Carey et al., 1992). However, such leakage was estimated to total only about 0.01 percent of the volume of the ejaculate, so that—compared with not using a condom—condom use would still reduce exposure to viruses by a factor of 10,000.

Figure 6.7   The Female Condom

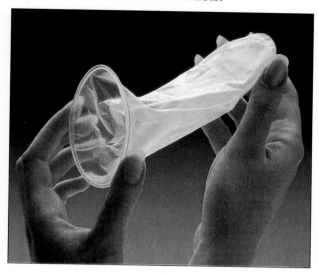

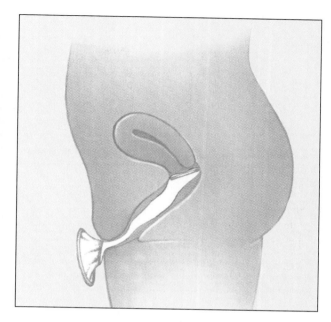

Side Effects and Safety

Very infrequently, the material the condom is made from can cause burning or irritation to the genitals. Otherwise, condoms have no health risks at all.

Sexual Effects

There are several sexual disadvantages to using condoms. Putting the condom on may interrupt sexual spontaneity, although some couples make this a shared moment of sexual play. Many men complain of lessened sensations in the penis while wearing a condom (one student told his class, "It's like playing the piano wearing mittens"), and some men have difficulty maintaining an erection while trying to put on the device. The condom is a poor contraceptive choice for a man having problems with erection, since it calls attention to the degree of erection and may seriously increase "performance anxiety" (see Chapter 21). Also, unless the penis is removed from the vagina soon after ejaculation, loss of erection makes spillage of semen more likely. This can certainly interfere with the intimacy and mood of the moment.

There are also some sexual advantages to the condom. The female may be pleased because her partner is not leaving the responsibility for birth control to her. Lubricated condoms can make intercourse more comfortable if vaginal lubrication is a problem. There is little or no postcoital drippiness

for the woman whose partner uses condoms. And use of a condom may help many men who have difficulty controlling the rapidity of ejaculation.

One of the most notable sexual benefits of condom use is that it can help give a person a sense of security about protection from sexually transmitted diseases such as genital herpes or HIV infection in a new sexual relationship. For this reason, many women who use other methods of birth control such as the pill or an IUD insist that their partners use condoms for greater personal safety.

The Female Condom

A relatively new method of contraception, a condom for women, was approved for use in the United States on May 10, 1993. Currently being marketed under the tradename Reality (to suggest the reality of females needing to have control over their own reproductive destinies), this device is also sometimes called a vaginal pouch. The 6½-inch pouch is made of thin polyurethane that is anchored by two flexible plastic rings, one at the cervix and one outside the opening of the vagina (see Figure 6.7). The female condom, which is intended for one act of intercourse, is coated inside with a silicone lubricant.

In theory, the female condom acts as a barrier to prevent sperm from reaching the mouth of the

Figure 6.8 Vaginal Spermicides

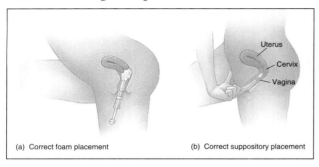

(a) Correct foam placement   (b) Correct suppository placement

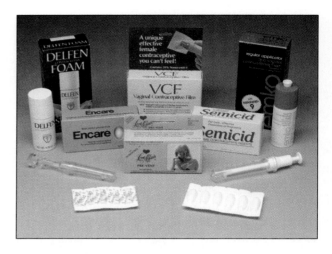

Use of vaginal spermicides: (a) When contraceptive foam is inserted with a plastic applicator, it must be placed well within the vagina so it completely covers the cervical mouth. (b) Spermicidal suppositories must be removed from their wrapper and inserted high in the vagina; the manufacturer's instructions on the timing of intercourse must be followed carefully since these products may require up to 10 minutes to dissolve.

cervix. Unfortunately, in their limited use in the past few years, female condoms have proven generally to be less effective contraceptives than other barrier methods, and are considerably less effective than male condoms—their overall failure rate is more than 25 percent per year of use (Leary, 1993). While there is hope that female condoms will protect against various sexually transmitted diseases (especially HIV), there are few data available documenting such an effect. Furthermore, the device has many esthetic drawbacks. The majority of women we interviewed who have used this product have called it cumbersome or clumsy, and 17 out of 20 said they would never consider using it as their primary birth control method. Similarly, in Great Britain, a study found that 56 percent of women stopped using the female condom after a short period of time because they found it "unacceptable" (Bounds, Guillebaud, and Newman, 1992).

Spermicides

Spermicides, or vaginal chemical contraceptives, come in many varieties, including foams, jellies, creams, and tablets or suppositories. They do not require a prescription and are available at drug stores and family planning clinics. Spermicides should not be confused with feminine hygiene products, often displayed beside them, which have no spermicidal effectiveness.

How Spermicides Work

Spermicides work in two ways: their active chemical ingredient kills sperm, while the material containing this ingredient provides a mechanical barrier that blocks the entrance to the cervix.

Use and Effectiveness

Because of the individual differences in the many products on the market, the manufacturer's instructions regarding use and effectiveness must be consulted. This information is given in the package insert that comes with each product. *These products are not identical in how they are used or in their reliability in preventing pregnancy.* In general, foams and suppositories are much more effective than creams or jellies, which should be used only with another method of birth control such as a diaphragm or condom. All spermicides require proper placement in the vagina, as shown in Figure 6.8. If used properly and regularly, some spermicidal products can be very effective. In several studies, less than 5 pregnancies occurred for every 100 couples using these methods for one year (see Coleman and Piotrow, 1979). Failure rates tend to be about three to six times higher than this in actual practice as a result of inconsistent use of the method and improper following of the manufacturer's instructions. Failures occur when a couple inserts the spermicide in the vagina incorrectly, has intercourse a second time without using more of the product, or overlooks the time limits of product effectiveness. In addition, failures can occur if the spermicide has become outdated; for this reason, users should check the expiration date stamped on the spermicide package prior to use.

Side Effects and Safety

Burning or irritation of the vagina or penis occurs in about 1 in 20 people using spermicides, but this problem can often be alleviated by changing to a different product. There are no other adverse side effects, which is one of the major advantages spermicides offer.

Despite earlier concerns, spermicides do not cause birth defects (Shapiro et al., 1982; Bracken, 1985; Watkins, 1986; Louik et al., 1987). However, it appears that women who use spermicides after becoming pregnant are more likely than other women to have miscarriages (Scholl et al., 1983).

On the positive side, there is mounting evidence that spermicides provide some protection against sexually transmitted diseases such as gonorrhea and also protect against pelvic inflammatory disease (Jick et al., 1982; Cates, Weisner, and Curran, 1982; Sherris, Moore, and Fox, 1984). Another positive is that spermicides reduce a woman's risk of developing certain types of vaginal infections (bacterial vaginosis and trichomoniasis, conditions discussed in Chapter 19) (Feldblum, Bernardik, and Rosenberg, 1988). Perhaps most important of all is early laboratory evidence that spermicides containing nonoxynol-9 offer some protection against infection with HIV, the AIDS virus (Hicks et al., 1985).

Sexual Effects

The use of spermicides may require interrupting the spontaneous flow of sexual activity, but insertion can be made a part of sexual play. With spermicidal suppositories, unlike aerosol foams, 10 to 15 minutes must elapse before vaginal distribution of the product has occurred (depending on the brand) and intercourse is "safe"—so these should not be used if you are in a hurry! Vaginal chemical contraceptives may discourage cunnilingus (oral stimulation of the vulva and vagina) because most products do not have a very pleasant taste. Finally, some people find that these products are messy and provide too much vaginal lubrication (one woman described the sensation as "sloshy").

The Contraceptive Sponge

The newest type of birth control device to become widely available (approved by the Food and Drug Administration in April 1983) is a soft, disposable contraceptive sponge that is inserted into the vagina. Now sold exclusively under the Today brand name, the 2-inch-by-1-inch round product is made of polyurethane permeated with the commonly used spermicide nonoxynol-9 (see Figure 6.9). The contraceptive sponge is sold over the counter in drugstores and doesn't require a prescription or need to be fitted by a physician. Its early reception by consumers was enthusiastic.

How the Sponge Works

There are three different ways in which the sponge functions. First and most important, it carries the spermicidal effect of nonoxynol-9 (which is the active chemical ingredient in many contraceptive creams, foams, and gels). Second, the sponge also functions as a mechanical barrier, partially preventing sperm from entering the mouth of the cervix. Finally, the sponge is also thought to trap and absorb sperm, although the importance of this action is uncertain.

Use and Effectiveness

The contraceptive sponge is inserted into the vagina before intercourse. The sponge is first dampened with about 2 tablespoons of water and then squeezed gently until foam appears (this activates the spermicide in the sponge). Many users report that it is considerably easier to insert than a diaphragm or a cervical cap and, since it can be inserted up to 18 hours before intercourse, it is convenient as well. (Insertion can be done either manually or with an applicator.) As another major advantage, the sponge retains its contraceptive effectiveness for 24 hours without any need for the reapplication of spermicide, so it provides contraceptive protection regardless of how many times the user has intercourse. The sponge is removed by pulling on a small ribbon attached to one of its sides. It should be kept in place for at least 6 hours after insertion, with a maximum time of insertion of 30 hours.

One of the major disadvantages of the sponge is a relatively high actual failure rate of 17 percent during its first year of use (Strickler and Vaughan, 1993). However, as women become more experienced with this method, the actual failure rate de-

Figure 6.9   The Contraceptive Sponge

Proper insertion of the sponge: (a) Remove the sponge from the inner pack and hold with dimple side up. The loop should dangle under the sponge. (b) The sponge will feel slightly moist. Wet it further with a small amount of clean water (about 2 tablespoons). (c) Squeeze the sponge gently to remove excess water. It should feel moist and soapy, but not dripping wet. (d) Fold the sides of the sponge upward with a finger along each side to support it. The sponge should look long and narrow. Be sure the string loop dangles underneath the sponge from one end of the fold to the other. (e) From a standing position, squat down slightly and spread your legs apart. Use your free hand to spread apart the lips of the vagina. You may also stand with one foot on a stool or chair, sit crosslegged, or lie down. The semisquatting position seems to work best for most women. Slide the sponge into the opening of the vagina as far as your fingers will go. Let the sponge slide through your fingers, deeper into the vagina. Now use one or two fingers to push the sponge gently up into your vagina as far as it will go. Be careful not to push a fingernail through the sponge. Check the position of the sponge by sliding your finger around the edge of the sponge to make sure your cervix is not exposed. You should be able to feel the string loop.

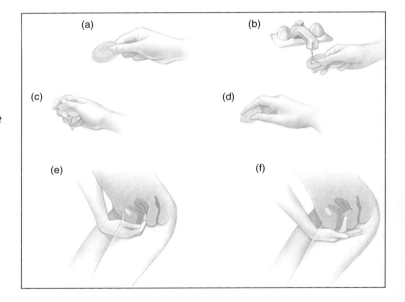

clines dramatically: in one study, it was reported to be as low as 5 percent (North and Vorhauer, 1985). As with the diaphragm or spermicides, many of the failures are due to improper use—such as removing the sponge less than six hours after intercourse—and lack of consistent use. The risk of failure is considerably higher for women who have given birth vaginally than for those who have not (20 compared to 10 percent) (Strickler and Vaughan, 1993). (This probably means that the sponge is too small for a woman whose birth canal has been enlarged by vaginal delivery.)

Women who have used the sponge report a number of distinct advantages over use of the di-

aphragm. In addition to mentioning how easy it is to insert (which is nearly a universal reaction), many women are pleased to have an inexpensive, disposable contraceptive method that is unobtrusive, tasteless, and odorless and lasts for 24 hours. In addition, the sponge reportedly isn't as messy or drippy as some spermicidal products.

Side Effects and Safety

A common side effect of the sponge is mild irritation of the vagina or penis, which occurs in about 3 to 5 percent of users. Another 8 percent of users complain of vaginal dryness, soreness, or itching (Speroff and Darney, 1992). The only serious health risk is the extremely rare occurrence of toxic shock syndrome (TSS) in a few women who used the sponge (Faich et al., 1986). While one benefit of the sponge is that it protects women against infection with chlamydia and gonorrhea, which are two of the most common sexually transmitted diseases (Rosenberg et al., 1987; Niruthisard, Roddy, and Chutivongse, 1992; Cates and Stone, 1992), the sponge does *not* protect against infection with HIV (Kreiss et al., 1992).

Sexual Effects

Because the sponge can be inserted either hours before sexual activity or at the last moment before intercourse, convenience makes it especially advantageous from a sexual viewpoint. In addition, men and women who have tried the sponge almost invariably say they don't feel it during intercourse, and many couples also report that it doesn't interfere with cunnilingus. But the sponge's most noticeable sexual benefit may be that once it is inserted, it provides protection for multiple acts of intercourse. As one woman told us, "That means we can make love at night and then again in the morning without my having to get up and get ready all over again."

RHYTHM

Rhythm methods of contraception depend on periodic abstinence from intercourse during times of the menstrual cycle when fertility is most likely. These methods are the only methods of birth control approved by the Roman Catholic church, which considers them "natural" rather than "artificial."

The Calendar Method

The **calendar method** involves identifying "safe days" in the menstrual cycle (days where intercourse will not lead to pregnancy) based on the lengths of previous cycles. The underlying assumption is that ovulation will occur approximately 14 days before the start of the next menstrual period. Careful hormone studies of the menstrual cycle, however, indicate that this assumption is not always correct (Kolodny and Bauman, 1979).

To calculate the "unsafe" (fertile) period, a record must be kept of the length of each menstrual cycle for a minimum of six months. The first day of the unsafe period is determined by subtracting 18

from the length of the shortest cycle, and the last day of the unsafe period is found by subtracting 11 from the number of days in the longest cycle. For example, if a woman's shortest cycle is 26 days and her longest is 32 days during her "record-keeping" time, she must abstain from intercourse beginning on cycle day 8 (26 − 18 = 8) and continue abstention until day 21 (32 − 11 = 21). Thus, the unsafe days would be days 8 to 21, inclusive, a time of 14 days when intercourse would not be permitted.

The Temperature Method

The **temperature method** involves daily recording of the basal body temperature (BBT) to pinpoint the time of ovulation. Intercourse is not allowed from the day menstrual flow stops until two to four days after the temperature rises. (If no temperature rise is detected in a full menstrual cycle, which sometimes happens, users of this method must observe total abstinence from sexual intercourse.)

The Ovulation Method

The **ovulation method,** also known as the Billings method or as "natural family planning," depends on changes in cervical mucus to indicate the probable days of fertility during the menstrual cycle. The start of the fertile time is signaled by the appearance of a mucus discharge within the vagina which

calendar method a technique of determing the days in the menstrual cycle when the risk of pregnancy is low; a form of the rhythm method.

temperature method a technique of determining the part of the menstrual cycle when pregnancy is likely to occur so that intercourse can be avoided then. Involves daily recording of basal body temperature to pinpoint ovulation. Intercourse is not allowed from the day menstrual flow stops until two to four days after a temperature rise. Failure rate is high.

ovulation method a method that depends on changes in the cervical mucus thought to indicate the time of ovulation. The mucus changes from cloudy, white, and tacky to clear and stretchy at the time of ovulation. Intercourse is thought to be safe four days after the ovulatory mucus begins and when the mucus has returned to a cloudy, tacky consistency. Failure rate is high.

Why the United States Lags in Contraceptive Development

Since the pill and IUD came on the market, no fundamentally new form of birth control has been introduced in the United States. In fact, research related to new contraceptive methods has slowed. The following factors help explain why this is so:

• All but one major U.S. pharmaceutical company have fled the field of contraceptive research because of lawsuits (some of which have wound up with multimillion dollar verdicts) and a difficult regulatory climate that makes contraceptive testing very time-consuming and expensive.
• Foundation support for contraceptive research, which has traditionally been a major source of funding in this area, has declined noticeably in the past decade, and federal support has languished, barely keeping pace with inflation.
• Economic factors are stacked against private industry playing a more major role, since the market for a successful contraceptive vaccine or a "once-a-month" pill is not large enough to make it a big moneymaker.
• Drug companies are also hesitant about entering the contraceptive market because of the political and economic clout of the anti-abortion movement, including the threat of consumer boycotts.

What can be done to change things? In addition to the obvious solution—more federal and foundation grants for innovative contraceptive research—a joint committee of the National Research Council and the Institute of Medicine has proposed two vital steps (Mastroianni, Donaldson, and Kane, 1990):

1. The FDA should streamline its procedures for evaluating new contraceptive products and "should be prepared to approve a contraceptive drug or device even if that drug or device presents a risk, if it can be shown that the new contraceptive also offers a safety advantage for an identifiable group of users."
2. A new federal product liability law should be implemented that would give contraceptive manufacturers protection against large liability claims if they met all the FDA requirements in developing and testing a new drug or device and if they provide proper warnings for consumers.

A similar law has already been passed to protect manufacturers of vaccines given to children to prevent diseases like measles and mumps. But because contraception is a political "hot potato," it is not very likely that such a measure will be put in place in the foreseeable future.

A special summary of the committee's overall report concluded by saying: "Unless immediate steps are taken to change public policy, the choice of contraceptives in the United States in the next century will not differ appreciably from what it is today" (Mastroianni, Donaldson, and Kane, 1990, p. 484). That is a sad state of affairs for a country that boasts the world's most sophisticated medical and scientific technology.

Sources: *Committee on Contraceptive Development, 1990; Mastroianni, Donaldson, and Kane, 1990.*

is whitish or cloudy and of tacky consistency. A day or two before ovulation, greater amounts of mucus are produced in a clear and runnier form with a stretchy consistency very similar to egg white. Intercourse is thought to be "safe" four days after the clear mucus begins, when the mucus has returned to a cloudy color.

Effectiveness of the Rhythm Methods

The overall effectiveness of the rhythm methods leaves a great deal to be desired. The calendar method is unquestionably the least reliable among this group (failure rates are approximately 15 to 45 per 100 woman-years; Ross and Piotrow, 1974), and unless the woman's cycle is very regular, long periods of abstinence from intercourse will be required. Temperature methods are inaccurate because they are difficult to interpret (Lenton, Weston, and Cooke, 1977; Bauman, 1981), and in about 20 percent of ovulatory cycles, the BBT chart does not indicate ovulation (Moghissi, 1976; Bauman, 1981). The World Health Organization (1978) found that the ovulation method was "relatively ineffective for preventing pregnancy" based on carefully designed studies done in five different countries, with an overall failure rate of 19.4 per 100 woman-years. This is probably because many women have difficulty noting the cyclic changes in their cervical mucus, and women who have a vaginal infection (which may itself create a discharge) usually cannot use this method. In another study of 725 women, an overall failure rate of 22.3 per 100 woman-years was noted (World Health Organization, 1981).

To keep these data in perspective, it should be noted that the standardized actual failure rate of women using the rhythm method (31.4 per 100 woman-years) is almost identical to the failure rate for spermicides (see Table 6.2). However, a recent report points out that couples who do not use the rhythm method properly—taking risks on occasion—actually have an 86 percent chance of pregnancy (Trussell and Grummer-Strawn, 1990). On the other hand, conscientious users may have much better success (Hatcher et al., 1994).

The availability of a number of home-use ovulation detection kits, based on identifying the pre-ovulatory LH surge in urine, may eventually be shown to increase the effectiveness of periodic abstinence as a method of birth control, but research documenting this type of use has not yet been conducted (Corsan, Ghazi, and Kemman, 1990).

Sexual Effects of the Rhythm Methods

Most couples using the rhythm methods do not experience major sexual difficulties. However, some couples may develop sexual problems because the need for abstinence creates unusual pressures to have intercourse on "safe" days regardless of whether they feel like it or not. Fear of pregnancy may also lead to sexual difficulties.

STERILIZATION

The highest degree of contraceptive protection currently available short of absolute abstinence is found in the use of **sterilization,** surgical proce-

dures to prevent pregnancy. The popularity of these operations for both men and women has increased considerably in America in the last 20 years. One estimate indicates that among all married American couples, about one-quarter will use sterilization within two years after the birth of their last wanted child; by ten years after their last child, more than half will undergo sterilization (Westoff and McCarthy, 1979).

Sterilization procedures are appealing because they are safe, effective, and permanent. Their permanence can be a drawback, however, if there is a change in feelings or circumstances (e.g., death of a child or spouse, divorce) that leads a person to want more children. Although there is some possibility of reversing the sterilization, these procedures are far from guaranteed. Anyone thinking about sterilization as a method of birth control should assume that it will not be reversible. One way of retaining the option to reproduce after male sterilization is to use a sperm bank to store several samples of frozen semen produced before sterilization. If reproduction becomes desirable at a later time, the semen samples are thawed and used in artificial insemination.

Female Sterilization

More than 100 different types of operations can be used to achieve female sterilization. Almost all block the Fallopian tubes to prevent the union of sperm and egg. **Tubal ligation** (tying the tubes) is rarely done by itself today, since it is not as effective as other methods that also cut, clip, or otherwise block the tubes (Figure 6.10). Many of these operations are still called "tubal ligation" even though more is done.

Tubal ligation is frequently achieved by using a laparoscope, a tubelike instrument with lights and a viewer that is inserted through the abdominal wall. The tubes are cut and cauterized (burned) through this instrument. If laparoscopy can be done through the navel, no scar is visible; as only a 1-inch incision is required for this operation, it is

sterilization surgical procedure performed on men (vasectomy) or women (tubal ligation; hysterectomy) to prevent union of sperm and egg.

tubal ligation (tū′ bull lī gā′ shun) literally, tying the tubes—cutting, cauterizing, and blocking the Fallopian tubes to prevent conception.

Figure 6.10   Two Types of Tubal Ligation

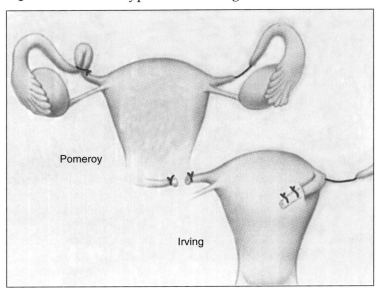

often called "Band-Aid sterilization." A similar instrument can be inserted through the back end of the vagina or through the vagina and uterus to perform a tubal ligation.

Laparotomy, an operation involving a 4- or 5-inch incision through the abdomen, can also be used to perform a tubal ligation. It is rarely used for sterilization unless there is another reason for abdominal surgery, a technical difficulty, or a danger to the woman because of a medical problem. Female sterilization also results from **hysterectomy** (removal of the uterus) or **ovariectomy** (removal of the ovaries), but these operations are generally done for other reasons with sterility occurring as a by-product.

Female sterilization by most techniques offers almost foolproof protection against pregnancy. In rare instances, the cut ends of the tubes may rejoin, leading to a pregnancy, but the most common cause for "method failure" is when the woman is already pregnant (but no one knows it) when the operation is performed (Hatcher et al., 1994). Side effects are infrequent (less than 5 percent) and are usually limited to the first few days after surgery, when infection or bleeding may be a problem.

Most women have no sexual difficulties after sterilization, which affects neither their hormones (since their ovaries are intact) nor their sexual anatomy. A few women may run into problems. If a woman undergoes sterilization involuntarily (e.g., if it was a decision she was pushed into by her husband or by health or economic circumstances), she may develop a reduced interest in sex for psychological reasons. Some women find that after sterilization they no longer feel the same way about sex (or have lowered sexual responsiveness) because they feel "incomplete" or "less than a woman." This reaction is particularly possible in a woman whose religious background considers sex unnatural or sinful if it is separated from its reproductive potential. On the other hand, some women show increased sexual interest after sterilization due to no longer fearing pregnancy.

Vasectomy

Vasectomy is a surprisingly neglected form of birth control considering that it is one of the safest and most effective methods available. However, in the United States it has enjoyed some popularity as IUDs and birth control pills fell out of favor in the 1980s. Today, as a result of improvements in surgical procedure, vasectomy usually takes no more than 10 to 15 minutes in a doctor's office, which gives it a marked advantage over female sterilization procedures both in terms of safety and expense.

Vasectomies in the United States are typically done in one of two ways. The conventional ap-

Figure 6.11   Vasectomy

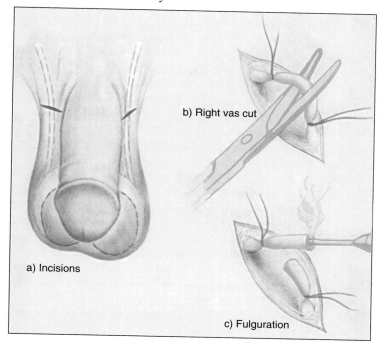

a) Incisions

b) Right vas cut

c) Fulguration

A vasectomy must completely prevent sperm from traveling out of the scrotum higher into the male reproductive system. Drawing (a) shows the site of the small incision in the scrotum used to perform a vasectomy; (b) shows the vas being cut with surgical scissors; and (c) shows the cut end of the vas being burned with a controlled electric current so that scar tissue forms to block the passage of sperm.

proach (Figure 6.11) involves making a small incision (about 1 to 2 cm) in the skin of the scrotum to provide access to each **vas deferens,** the paired tubes that carry sperm from the testes to the prostate gland and seminal vesicles. The newer approach, called a no-scalpel vasectomy, substitutes a small (less than 1 mm) puncture for the incision, which lessens postoperative pain and complications. Both procedures are done using local anesthesia and involve blocking the passage of sperm through the vas deferens by mechanical means, such as tying the tubes after cutting out a small section, the use of electrocautery (burning the tissue with a carefully controlled electric current), or the use of clips. Following either type of procedure, the man is able to get up and go home without any major restrictions on his activities. Many men return to work the following day, although for those whose jobs involve considerable physical exertion, an additional day or two of rest may be in order.

Complications from either type of vasectomy are few. Bleeding or infections occur in about 3 percent of cases done by conventional methods, while with the no-scalpel procedure the rate of complications is substantially under 1 percent (Liskin, Benoit, and

Blackburn, 1992). Minor swelling and localized pain (usually treated by ice packs and use of an athletic supporter), along with temporary skin discoloration, while more common, usually resolve within a matter of a few days.

Vasectomy does not stop sperm production; it blocks the passage of sperm from the testes to the upper part of the vas deferens. Sperm then accu-

laparotomy (lap uh rot' uh mē) any operation involving an incision through the abdominal wall. Now used for sterilization only if other surgery is required in the abdomen.

hysterectomy (his' tur ek' tuh mē) partial or total removal of the uterus.

ovariectomy (ō vuh' rē ek' tuh mé) surgical removal of the ovaries.

vasectomy (vas ek' tuh mē) surgical procedure for sterilization of the male consisting of cutting and tying each vas deferens. The operation does not stop sperm production but blocks its passage from the testes.

vas deferens (vas def' ur enz) one of two long, tubelike structures that convey spermatozoa from the testes.

mulate in the **epididymis** (a mass of tubes at the back of each testis), where they are engulfed and destroyed by cells called phagocytes. Some sperm appear to leak out into the scrotum, where they disintegrate. Following a vasectomy, it generally takes six to eight weeks—or about a dozen ejaculations—to clear out sperm that have already moved above the blockade that has been put in the vas deferens. Because this is a time where most postoperative failures occur, it is important to use a different method of birth control until at least two separate semen exams have shown that there are no sperm in the ejaculate. Very rarely, vasectomies fail even after one semen exam has been negative (Alderman, 1988).

Effectiveness

Vasectomies are highly effective, with a failure rate of 0.15 percent, or 1 in 665 procedures. The most common failures involve not using another form of contraception during the weeks after surgery before the ejaculate is truly sterile. Apparently, some men just don't believe that after having had a vasectomy they are not completely foolproof and ready to go. Other men play a form of "post-vasectomy roulette" in which the woman turns out to be the loser if her partner is not firing blanks. Other less common causes of vasectomy failure stem from errors in performing the procedure or from spontaneous rejoining of the separated ends of the vas.

Side Effects and Safety

In the 1970s, there was some concern that vasectomy might lead to later health problems, especially in light of research in monkeys that showed that vasectomy produces hardening of the arteries years after the operation (Clarkson and Alexander, 1980). But several more recent large-scale studies provide convincing evidence that vasectomy does not lead to any long-term health problems in humans. Massey and his colleagues (1984) studied more than 10,000 vasectomized men and a matched nonvasectomized control group. They found that vasectomized men had fewer cancers, fewer cancer deaths, lower rates of heart disease, and fewer deaths from heart attacks or strokes than the men in the control group who had not had vasectomies. Perrin and co-workers (1984), in a

study with an average follow-up interval of 15 years, also found no indication that vasectomy predisposes to arteriosclerosis or heart disease. And a 1992 study conducted at Harvard Medical School involving more than 14,000 men who had undergone vasectomy compared to a control group of nonvasectomized men found that vasectomy was actually associated with a lower overall death rate and a reduced rate of death from cardiovascular disease (Giovannucci et al., 1992).

Now, in what seems to be a case of deja vu, concerns have been raised once again over a possible increased long-term risk of prostate and testicular cancer in men who have had vasectomies (Cale et al., 1990; Mettlin, Natarajan, and Huben, 1990; Rosenberg et al., 1990). However, the scientific evidence on this matter is quite weak, and an expert group convened by the World Health Organization concluded that "any causal relation between vasectomy and risk of prostate or testicular cancer was unlikely" (Noticeboard).

Vasectomies should be thought of as permanent, but improvements in modern microsurgery have in fact permitted vasectomy reversal to be successfully accomplished in a large number of cases, with pregnancy rates above 50 percent. However, reversal surgery is costly, complicated, and unpredictable, and the success rate declines considerably over time. Nevertheless, in an age where divorce and remarriage is commonplace, it is reassuring to some men to have the option of attempting to have a vasectomy reversed if their family situation changes drastically.

Sexual Effects

Less than 1 man in 20 reports decreased sexual pleasure after a vasectomy, while close to half claim increased pleasure, and about a quarter report an increased frequency of intercourse (Wortman, 1975). In fact, many couples find that sex is more spontaneous and fun after a vasectomy since they don't need to worry about becoming pregnant. Men with a history of sexual problems are not always good candidates for vasectomy since they may be prone to developing psychological impotence or other difficulties after surgery. Occasionally, a man who has been well adjusted to a vasectomy may develop temporary erectile problems if he divorces and then remarries, particularly if he and his new wife would like to have children.

OTHER METHODS OF CONTRACEPTION

Withdrawal (coitus interruptus) is the removal of the penis from the vagina before ejaculation occurs. This is a difficult form of birth control in which even perfect timing (which is not always possible) does not give perfect results. If ejaculation occurs before the penis is withdrawn completely, or if drops of semen spurt into the opening of the vagina, pregnancy can occur. Because live sperm can also be in the pre-ejaculatory fluid long before ejaculation (or even if the male doesn't ejaculate), this method of contraception is chancy at best, with a failure rate of 20 to 25 percent. This method can also be a frustrating form of birth control for both parties, who may find that it seriously interrupts the spontaneity of sexual interaction. However, it is clearly better than not using any contraceptive when nothing else is available.

Douching, using a liquid to flush the vagina, is a poor method of contraception, since sperm can quickly penetrate the cervical mucus, where they are unaffected by douching. The failure rate is more than 40 percent.

Breast-feeding inhibits ovulation in some women (possibly via the effect of high prolactin levels on the ovaries), but this method of birth control is very unreliable. Women who do not want to become pregnant soon after childbirth should begin using a more effective means of contraception right away. Some studies of nursing mothers not using any other method of birth control indicate pregnancy rates of over 50 percent (Buchanan, 1975).

Abstinence from intercourse is, needless to say, a highly effective way to prevent pregnancy if practiced consistently. Some couples voluntarily limit their sex lives to noncoital acts, but this does not seem to be a very popular choice for most heterosexual couples.

POSTCOITAL CONTRACEPTIVE METHODS

There are many situations in which a woman is exposed to the possibility of an unintended pregnancy. Examples include unplanned lapses in contraceptive use (e.g., having sex when neither partner had a contraceptive available or not stopping the action to use a birth control device even if one is at hand), many cases of rape, and all instances of failure of the woman's primary contraceptive method, from condom leakage to a diaphragm slipping out of position to coitus interruptus inadvertently becoming coitus *non*interruptus. In any of these cases, the woman's risk of subsequent pregnancy depends on where she is in her menstrual cycle. (The most fertile period being in the middle two weeks of the woman's cycle.) Today, several different methods of postcoital contraception are available to deal effectively with such circumstances.

Emergency Contraceptive Pills

Several different types of hormones can be used on an emergency basis within 72 hours after unprotected intercourse to effectively prevent pregnancy. Although these methods have collectively been referred to as the "morning after" pill, this is a misleading name, because there is no need to wait until the morning after to begin treatment, and there is actually some evidence that the sooner such regimens are begun, the more effective they are (Speroff and Darney, 1992; Trussell et al., 1992). Furthermore, the term "morning after" pill suggests that this is just another variety of birth control, whereas these methods should not be considered anything other than one-time protection.

The simplest and most widely used approach is to use birth control pills marketed under the trade name Ovral in the United States, taking two pills as soon as possible after unprotected intercourse and then taking two more pills 12 hours later. (This method has replaced the older use of high doses of

epididymis (ep′ i did′ i mis) the tightly coiled tubing network folded against the back surface of each testis in which sperm cells spend several weeks maturing.

withdrawal the removal of the penis from the vagina before ejaculation occurs. When used as a birth control method, failure rate is high.

douching (dūsh′ ing) using a liquid to flush the vagina.

abstinence the act of voluntarily not engaging in some act, such as sexual intercourse. A highly effective method of birth control if practiced consistently.

DES [diethylstilbestrol] because it is just as effective but is safer and has fewer side effects.)

An alternate approach is to use three 200 mg. tablets of Danazol (danocrine) within 72 hours of unprotected intercourse and to repeat this 12 hours later. Danocrine has a lower rate of nausea, vomiting, and breast tenderness than Ovral when used in this manner (Webb, Russell, and Elstein, 1992).

Other postcoital treatment regimens include the use of ethinyl estradiol 2.5 mg. twice a day for five days (started within 72 hours after unprotected intercourse) or intravenous injections of conjugated estrogen (50 mg. per dose) on two consecutive days.

The exact mechanisms by which emergency contraceptive pills work are not fully understood. The major action which results from the short, strong burst of hormone exposure these pills provide is interference with implantation by altering the lining of the uterus. The overall effectiveness of these methods is 98 to 99 percent, with better results the sooner treatment is begun. Safety is excellent overall; the primary side effects are nausea (sometimes accompanied by vomiting), breast tenderness, and brief alterations in the menstrual cycle. *Women who are already pregnant should avoid use of emergency contraception pills because there is a small but real risk of damage to the developing embryo.*

A related version of the emergency contraceptive pill is the controversial pill RU-486, or mifepristone, which is not yet available in the United States. RU-486 is discussed in detail in the next chapter.

Other Postcoital Contraceptive Methods

A second type of postconception birth control is less widely used. This involves inserting a copper IUD into the uterus within four to five days after unprotected intercourse. The IUD prevents implantation with a very high degree of efficiency (99+ percent) but of course will not prevent an ectopic pregnancy. This method generally should not be used for rape victims because of the risk of infection.

Another approach is the technique called menstrual extraction, which has been pioneered by the women's self-help movement. Just when a period is expected, a thin, flexible plastic tube is inserted through the cervix into the uterus, and suction (using either a syringe or a pump) is applied to draw out the endometrial lining. If the woman is

pregnant, the tiny embryo is easily withdrawn. There may be mild cramping, but no anesthetic is usually used. Menstrual extraction should not be performed more than eight weeks after a missed period because complete evacuation of the embryo and its support system (the placenta) is more difficult after this point.

Although further research is required, there do not seem to be any major side effects when done under proper conditions by a health-care professional. In some instances, however, when menstrual extraction has been done as a self-help procedure by women without proper health-care training, there have been complications such as uterine perforation, infection, or incompletely extracted uterine contents, requiring subsequent surgery (Perrone, 1990).

SUMMARY

Table 6.3 summarizes the various contraceptive methods that we have discussed in this chapter.

Thought Questions

1. Describe your idea of an ideal contraceptive method. What are the most essential criteria? What are additional desirable features? Do any methods exist which approximate this ideal?

2. Do most men behave as if they have as great a responsibility as women do regarding the consistent and careful use of birth control techniques? Do they in fact have an equal responsibility? Why is there essentially only one reliable method for reversible male contraception (i.e., the condom)?

3. The IUD is a convenient and effective method of birth control that is safe for most women. However, fear of litigation has been acknowledged as causing companies to be unwilling to market them. Is this fair to American women? What could be done about this problem? Or should market forces control the availability of contraceptive devices like they control other commodities in our society?

4. Do most men and women respond negatively to using condoms during sex? Do you have any advice as to how condoms can be made more attractive to those who say they would rather not use them?

5. Is there a realistic possibility that some women will feel pressured to use the implant, Norplant, even though they cannot stop using the method on their own? (Remember, it requires surgical removal.) Do you think this method is an appropriate choice for a 17- or 18-year-old? Why or why not?

Suggested Readings

Committee on Contraceptive Development. *Developing New Contraceptives: Obstacles and Opportunities*. Washington, DC: National Academy Press, 1990. An important look at the political and policy issues involved in contraceptive research and development in the United States.

Djerassi, C. *The Politics of Contraception*. New York: Norton, 1979. One of the inventors of the pill provides an authoritative look at the ethical, social, and political sides of birth control.

Hatcher, Robert A., et al. *Contraceptive Technology* (16th ed.) New York: Irvington Publishers, 1994. Comprehensive plus, loaded with practical information, and filled with tables and references, this is the best book available on contraception and related topics.

Population Reports. Published by the Population Information Program, Johns Hopkins University, Hampton House, 624 North Broadway, Baltimore, Maryland 21205. A series of in-depth review articles on all aspects of contraceptive technology and policy, with major subjects updated annually.

Shapiro, Howard I. *The New Birth-Control Book: A Complete Guide for Women and Men*. Englewood Cliffs, NJ: Prentice-Hall, 1988. One of the most thorough and understandable guides to current contraception methods available for consumers.

Interested persons may also find useful literature at any Planned Parenthood office.

Table 6.3   Summary of Contraceptive Methods

Method	Effectiveness Rating	Ideal Failure Rate	Actual Failure Rate
Birth control pills (combination)	Excellent	1%	3–6%
Norplant	Excellent	0.5%	0.6%
Depo-Provera	Excellent	0.5%	0.5%
IUD	Excellent	1–3%	5–6%
Diaphragm and cream or jelly	Good to very good	3%	15–20%
Cervical cap	Good	3%	10–20%
Condom	Very good	3%	15%
Female condom	Poor to fair	5%	25–30%
Spermicides	Poor to fair	3%	20–30%
Sponge	Good	3%	15-20%
Rhythm	Poor to fair	13%	20–40%
Vasectomy	Excellent	0.15%	0.25%
Tubal ligation	Excellent	0.40%	0.40%
Withdrawal	Fair	9%	20–25%
Douching	Poor	?%	40+%
Breast-feeding	Poor	15%	50+%

Source: *Based on data from Jones and Forrest, 1989; Speroff and Darney, 1992; and* Population Reports *research reviews (see Suggested Readings).*

Advantages	Disadvantages
Highly reliable; coitus independent; has some health benefits	Side effects; daily use; continual cost
Highly reliable; coitus independent; safe	Irregular periods; requires surgery to insert and remove; expensive
No serious side effects; highly reliable	Irregular periods; breast tenderness
No memory or motivation required for use; very reliable	Cramping, bleeding, expulsion; risk of PID
No major health risks; inexpensive	Aesthetic objections
Can wear for weeks at a time; coitus independent; no major health risks	May be difficult to insert; may irritate cervix
Protects against STDs; simple to use; male responsibility; no health risks; no prescription required	Unaesthetic to some; requires interruption of sexual activity
Protects against STDs; simple to use; no health risks	High cost; poor acceptability
No major health risks; no prescription required	Unaesthetic to some; must be properly inserted
24-hour protection; simple to use; no taste or odor; inexpensive; effective with several acts of intercourse	Aesthetic objections
No cost; acceptable to Catholic church	Requires high motivation and periods of abstinence; unreliable
Permanent and highly reliable	Expensive; relatively irreversible; possible complications
Permanent and highly reliable	Expensive; relatively irreversible; possible complications
No cost or health risks	Reduces sexual pleasure; unreliable
Inexpensive	Extremely unreliable
No cost; acceptable to Catholic church	Extremely unreliable

Abortion

Few issues in contemporary society are as hotly debated as **abortion,** the termination of a pregnancy before the fetus can survive outside the uterus. Yet a surprising number of men and women on both sides of the abortion issue—or somewhere in between, where the vast majority of Americans cluster—have never read the key legal opinions that govern our nation's abortion laws, have little idea of who actually *gets* abortions, and have meager knowledge about abortion procedures and their safety and side effects.

In this chapter, after reviewing the legal background of the abortion issue in the United States, we present material that focuses on practical and personal aspects of abortion as a matter of sexual and reproductive health. A detailed discussion of ethical and religious aspects of abortion can be found in Chapter 24.

LEGAL ASPECTS OF ABORTION

Historical Background

Although abortion has been common from ancient times on, legal attitudes toward abortion have varied considerably in different eras and different places. The Anglo-Saxon legal precedents that established the common-law right to terminate a pregnancy can be traced back to the fourteenth century (Terkel, 1988). The first restrictions on abortion in England were implemented in 1803 in a statute called the Lord Ellenborough Act, which made abortion illegal after quickening (the time of pregnancy at which the women first feels fetal movement). The justification for the Lord Ellenborough Act was not to protect the fetus, though; it was designed to protect the life of the woman, since the drugs that were used to induce abortion at that time were highly toxic.

In the United States, abortion was permitted without legal limitations in colonial times because the colonies followed the British common-law tradition. Although it is unclear why women's rights to abortions were not mentioned in the U.S. Constitution, many legal and historical scholars believe it was because this right was not a controversial issue at the time: it was "commonly accepted and fairly widespread" (Faux, 1989).

The first legislative limitations on abortion in America came between 1820 and 1841. These laws were enacted primarily at the urging of physicians who were trying to establish the medical profession as the sole provider of health-care services in the United States. At the time, midwives and pharmacists were the primary providers of abortions or abortion-inducing drugs. Thus, the restrictive abortion laws that were passed at that time did not really ban abortions but regulated who could perform them. As a result, the laws were aimed only against illegal practitioners; women who obtained abortions could not be charged with a crime. In addition, none of these laws placed limitations on abortions done before quickening. This may have been partly because there were no reliable pregnancy tests at the time to establish definitively that a woman was pregnant and partly because most abortions performed early in pregnancy were advertised as "menstrual regulation."

When the American Medical Association was founded in 1847, an anti-abortion campaign became one of its earliest focal points, and over the next half century, physicians were among the staunchest advocates of anti-abortion legislation. Public opinion was also mobilized by three other developments: a Papal decree in 1869 that declared abortion sinful and banned it entirely for Catholics, an extensive newspaper campaign that provided readers with shocking details of cases in which women died from abortions, and a "morality campaign" led by Anthony Comstock, which was directed mainly against obscenity but had a certain amount of spillover into other areas dubbed as evil.

The result was not surprising. By 1900, every state in the Union except Kentucky had adopted bans on abortion which were far more restrictive than those passed several decades before. As a result, in many states women could be charged as criminals if they tried to get an abortion, although actual convictions were few in number.

Despite the legal ban, women continued to obtain abortions, but were forced to go to illegal (and unregulated) practitioners. To say that there were many unsavory abortionists often more concerned with their money than with their "patient's" welfare is a great understatement. Many illegal abortionists were butchers who worked in unsanitary conditions, causing many deaths among their clientele.

By the middle of this century, concern over the large numbers of women experiencing serious complications or death from illegal abortions began to mount both among the medical community and the public. Since legal abortions had become especially safe as a result of improved techniques and the development of antibiotics (legal abortions were generally permitted when necessary to save the mother's life), many physicians and nurses began campaigning for a liberalization of abortion laws. They were particularly interested in broadening the reasons that would permit legal abortions to be done—for instance, allowing abortions in instances of rape or incest, or when pregnancy posed a serious threat to the woman's emotional or physical well-being.

In actual practice, so-called therapeutic abortions were done in many non-Catholic hospitals across the country if they were approved by special committees, although such approval was typically difficult to receive. Many women had to travel outside the United States to seek abortions (in Japan and Sweden abortions were relatively easy to obtain) which meant that as a practical matter, poor women needing abortions were discriminated against by existing laws. In addition, the first stirrings of the women's rights movement would soon

abortion termination of a pregnancy before the fetus can survive outside the uterus. *Spontaneous* abortions occur naturally due to medical problems; *induced* abortions are done intentionally.

The Roe v. Wade *Story*

In August 1969, Norma McCorvey was a 21-year-old divorcee down on her luck. Already the mother of a 5-year-old daughter, she was supporting herself by selling tickets to a carnival, only to have her belongings stolen by her roommates. Penniless, forced to call a friend to wire her money for busfare to return to her hometown of Dallas, she had just managed to find a job as a waitress when she discovered she was pregnant again.

McCorvey asked her doctor about getting an abortion, but he bluntly informed her that under Texas law, abortions could only be done if her life was in danger—which it was not. He suggested she go to California, where the laws were more relaxed, but she didn't have the money to make this trip. Depressed, bitter, and more than a little frightened at her bleak prospects—including the likelihood that she would be fired when her pregnancy became apparent—she made up a story about being gang raped, thinking it might improve her chances of getting help. (Ironically, the fact that she lied about how she had gotten pregnant didn't come out until 1987, but the rape

Norma McCorvey (left) with her attorney, Gloria Allred, outside the Supreme Court.

story played no material part in subsequent legal developments.)

McCorvey was introduced to two young Dallas attorneys, Linda Coffee and Sara Weddington, who were looking for a woman to be the plaintiff in a legal challenge to the strict Texas abortion law. McCorvey readily agreed to this. When they filed their lawsuit, which asked for an injunction preventing Henry Wade, the District Attorney of Dallas County, from enforcing the state's abor-

put a spotlight on the abortion issue from yet another perspective.

Attention was particularly riveted on the campaign to liberalize abortion laws when an epidemic of German measles struck San Francisco in 1966. Because women who come down with German measles early in pregnancy have a very high chance of having babies with serious birth defects, a number of San Francisco physicians had performed abortions for this situation even though they knew it was against the law. When the state's attorney general indicted 21 of these physicians, it provoked an intense public outcry and mobilized support from the medical community across the nation.

By the late 1960s, several states changed their abortion laws as a result of legal challenges and public pressure. Colorado and California were among the first to do so, but only four states—New

York, Hawaii, Washington, and Alaska—had legalized all abortions, regardless of the reason, during the first trimester. In another dozen states, abortion bans were liberalized considerably, although not to the point sometimes called "abortion on demand." The result was that the number of legal abortions done in the United States increased from an estimated 10,000 each year in the early 1960s to 750,000 legal abortions being done annually by 1972. The stage had been set for a pivotal shift on the legal front, the background of which we briefly chronicle in the boxed item above.

Roe and Beyond

The Supreme Court startled many observers with its ruling in *Roe v. Wade* (1973) that legalized abortion on a nationwide basis. By a 7 to 2 vote, the Court

tion law as well as a declaration that the law was unconstitutional, they used the pseudonym, "Jane Roe," to protect McCorvey's identity, so the suit became designated as *Roe v. Wade.*

The case was heard initially in Federal Court in Dallas. On June 17, 1970, the Court handed down a decision ruling that the Texas abortion law was unconstitutional. However, the Court refused to issue an injunction, which as a practical matter allowed District Attorney Wade to announce that his office would crack down even harder on illegal abortions. Eventually, the State of Texas appealed the decision, and the case went all the way to the U.S. Supreme Court.

While the entire legal process was slowly inching its way forward, Norma McCorvey turned down an offer from her attorneys to pay for a California abortion since she didn't want to do anything that might jeopardize their case. However, she had relatively little contact with Weddington and Coffee, mostly watching their legal skirmish from afar. When she had her baby, she immediately put it up for adoption.

The case was initially argued before the Supreme Court in December 1971, and as in many cases, McCorvey wasn't there. Weddington presented her side smoothly, despite her nervousness and youthful appearance, and while waiting for the Court's decision, entered the political arena by running for the Texas state legislature. Then, in a dismaying (but not unheard of) twist, the Court asked to have the case reargued. This was done in October 1972, a time when two new Justices had arrived on the Court, adding to everyone's confusion.

When the long-awaited decision was finally handed down, on January 22, 1973, it was bumped from the front pages of most newspapers by coverage of the death of former President Lyndon Johnson on the same day. When Norma McCorvey read about the landmark decision in her evening newspaper, she burst into tears. A friend who was with her at the time said, "Don't tell me you knew Lyndon Johnson?" "No," McCorvey responded, "I'm Roe."

held that the decision to have an abortion in the first trimester of pregnancy is strictly up to the woman and her doctor. This landmark decision also noted that the fetus is not a person and thus is not entitled to Constitutional protection, while it defended the woman's right to an abortion in order to prevent a "distressful life and future." Other key points established in *Roe v. Wade* were the following:

• The right to have an abortion is grounded in privacy rights established by earlier judicial decisions as well as in the Ninth and Fourteenth amendments to the Constitution.

• States can impose certain regulations on second trimester abortions in order to protect the woman's health.

• In the third trimester, because the fetus may be viable, states may ban abortions except when

they are necessary to preserve the mother's life or health.

Notably, the Court did not address all areas that concerned both sides of the abortion rights issue. Here is a telling excerpt from Justice Blackmun's majority opinion (*Roe v. Wade,* 1973):

We need not resolve the difficult question of when life begins. When those trained in medicine, philosophy, and theology are unable to arrive at any consensus, the judiciary, at this point in the development of man's knowledge, is not in a position to speculate as to the answer.

On the same day that the *Roe v. Wade* decision was handed down, the Supreme Court ruled on a second case involving abortion rights. This case, known as *Doe v. Bolton,* challenged a Georgia statute that required that abortions could only be done in hospitals after approval by a hospital committee. In overturning such restrictions on a woman's right to an abortion, the Supreme Court was careful to make clear that it was not endorsing abortion on demand: it was still permitting states to play a role in regulating abortions done beyond the first trimester. This ruling would later serve as the basis for attempts made by many states to limit the circumstances in which abortions could be done.

For the better part of the next two decades, the *Roe v. Wade* decision governed more or less undisturbed over national abortion law. Nevertheless, there were numerous attempts by individual state legislatures to narrow the scope of abortion rights. In a few instances, these statutes were upheld by the Supreme Court. In 1979, for example, the Court implied that states are able to require a pregnant, unwed minor to get consent from her parents before obtaining an abortion as long as there is also an alternative procedure available, such as getting approval from a judge (*Bellotti v. Baird*). In 1980, the Court ruled that the U.S. government and the individual states have no obligation to pay for abortions for women on welfare (*Harris v. McRae*). More frequently, though, abortion cases that reached the Supreme Court were decided in a way that seemed to preserve, rather than narrow, the *Roe v. Wade* ruling. For example, husbands were denied veto power over their wives' abortion decisions (*Planned Parenthood v. Danforth*, 1976), doctors were given extensive discretion in deciding when a fetus can live outside the uterus (*Colautti v. Franklin*, 1979), and regulations requiring that all abortions after the first trimester be done in hospitals were overturned (*City of Akron v. Akron Center for Reproductive Health*, 1983; *Planned Parenthood of Kansas City v. Ashcroft*, 1983).

This trend was brought to an abrupt halt on July 3, 1989, with a decision handed down by the Supreme Court in a Missouri abortion case known as *Webster v. Reproductive Health Services*. Here, in a closely contested 5 to 4 vote, the Court unraveled much of the substance of *Roe v. Wade* without actually overturning the decision. It did so by giving states the right to place sharp new restrictions on abortions, including: (1) banning use of public facilities to perform abortions (even if the woman pays for the abortion herself); (2) prohibiting public employees (including doctors and nurses) from performing or assisting at an abortion unless it is required to save the woman's life; (3) requiring that medical tests be done on any fetus thought to be 20 weeks old in order to determine its viability; and (4) discarding the rigid trimester system suggested in *Roe v. Wade*.

The Court also upheld the language of the preamble to the Missouri law that declared that life begins at conception, while noting that the way in which this was written had no meaningful impact on the implementation of the legislation.

The majority opinion of Chief Justice Rehnquist noted (*Webster v. Reproductive Health Services*, 1989):

> Nothing in the Constitution requires States to enter or remain in the business of performing abortions. Nor . . . do private physicians and their patients have some kind of constitutional right of access to public facilities for the performance of abortion.

> Both appellants [the state of Missouri] and the United States [government] . . . have urged that we overrule our decision in *Roe v. Wade*. . . . The facts of the present case, however, differ from those at issue in *Roe*. . . . This case therefore affords us no occasion to revisit the holding of *Roe* . . . and we leave it undisturbed. To the extent indicated in our opinion, we would modify and narrow *Roe* and succeeding cases.

In a dissenting opinion, Justice Harry Blackmun—the man who had written the majority opinion in *Roe v. Wade*—poignantly asserted:

> I fear for the future. I fear for the liberty and equality of the millions of women who have lived and come of age in the 16 years since *Roe* was decided. . . . [T]he plurality discards a landmark case of the last generation, and casts into darkness the hopes and visions of every woman in this country who had come to believe that the Constitution guaranteed her the right to exercise some control over her unique ability to bear children. . . . To overturn a constitutional decision is a rare and grave undertaking. To overturn a constitutional decision that secured a fundamental personal liberty to millions of persons would be unprecedented in our 200 years of constitutional history.

As *The New York Times* observed in an editorial about *Webster v. Reproductive Health Services*, the decision "produced remarkably little new law" (July 4, 1989, p. 28). But the real judicial test seemed to lie shortly ahead, as four Supreme Court Justices signalled their intention to rapidly overturn *Roe* at the first available opportunity. However, many

pro-choice observers considered *Webster* a significant setback as it opened the doors for state legislatures to pass new laws regulating abortion (Dionne, 1989).

Another setback came on May 23, 1991, in the case of *Rust v. Sullivan.* By a 5 to 4 vote, the Supreme Court upheld federal regulations that bar employees of federally funded family planning clinics from all discussion of abortion with their patients, ruling specifically that such a restriction did not unconstitutionally infringe on First Amendment free speech rights. Even if a woman asked about abortion, physicians, nurses, or other clinic employees could only say that "the project does not consider abortion an appropriate method for family planning and therefore does not counsel or refer for abortion" (Gianelli, 1991). Although the constitutional status of abortion was not being contested in this case, pro-life supporters received the decision enthusiastically, and pro-choice advocates were dismayed, claiming the decision seriously eroded the doctor–patient relationship.

The following month, Louisiana (over the veto of its governor) passed the nation's strictest abortion law, banning virtually all abortions except those to save the life of a pregnant woman or, in limited conditions, when the pregnancy is a result of rape or incest. Under the new Louisiana law, physicians convicted of performing illegal abortions could be imprisoned for ten years and fined up to $100,000. While this law has been legally challenged and thus has not yet been implemented, as it works its way up the ladder toward a possible

Supreme Court hearing, it has had a chilling effect on abortion rights advocates across the nation, providing a glimpse of a nation that may be neither kinder nor gentler toward pregnant women in the future.

In the aftermath of *Webster v. Reproductive Health Services,* and in the shadow of the Louisiana law, legislation enacted by Pennsylvania took center stage on the Supreme Court's docket as the federal government, filing an *amicus curiae* (friend of the court) brief, once again asked to have *Roe* overturned. Several provisions of Pennsylvania's Abortion Control Act were at issue: (1) a requirement that a woman seeking an abortion give her informed consent and be provided with certain information, including information about the risks of the procedure and the probable gestational age of the "unborn child," at least 24 hours before the abortion is performed; (2) a parental-consent provision for unmarried minors; (3) a requirement that a married woman notify her husband of her intent to have an abortion; and (4) certain technical reporting requirements for clinics or other facilities that provide abortion services.

On June 29, 1992, in a somewhat surprising decision, the Court found that "the essential holding in *Roe v. Wade* should be retained and once again reaffirmed" (*The New York Times* June 30, 1992, p. A16). While preserving the notion of a woman's constitutional right to abortion prior to fetal viability, the Court's decision allowed room for the creation of new state laws creating procedural obstacles to abortion. Notably, the Court once again discarded

The Abortion Attitude Scale

One of the most controversial issues involving sexuality today is the abortion issue. If you are interested in seeing where you stand on this matter, complete the exercise below.

The self-administered, self-scored scale below is not a test. There are no right or wrong answers to any of the statements, so just answer as honestly as you can. The statements ask you to tell how you feel about legal abortion (the voluntary removal of a human embryo or fetus from a mother during the first three months of pregnancy by a qualified medical person). Tell how you feel about each statement by circling one of the choices beside each sentence. Here is a practice statement:

Abortion should be legalized. SA A SLA SLD D SD
(SA = Strongly Agree; A = Agree; SLA = Slightly Agree; SLD = Slightly Disagree; D = Disagree; SD = Strongly Disagree)
   Answer each statement and circle only one response.

1. The Supreme Court should strike down legal abortions in the United States.
   SA   A   SLA   SLD   D   SD

2. Abortion is a good way of solving an unwanted pregnancy.
   SA   A   SLA   SLD   D   SD

3. A mother should feel obligated to bear a child she has conceived.
   SA   A   SLA   SLD   D   SD

4. Abortion is wrong no matter what the circumstances are.
   SA   A   SLA   SLD   D   SD

5. A fetus is not a person until it can live outside its mother's body.
   SA   A   SLA   SLD   D   SD

6. The decision to have an abortion should be made by the pregnant mother.
   SA   A   SLA   SLD   D   SD

7. Every conceived child has the right to be born.
   SA   A   SLA   SLD   D   SD

8. A pregnant female not wanting to have a child should be encouraged to have an abortion.
   SA   A   SLA   SLD   D   SD

9. Abortion should be considered killing a person.
   SA   A   SLA   SLD   D   SD

Roe's trimester framework that severely restricted a state's power to regulate abortion in the early stages of pregnancy, saying that it was permissible to regulate abortion at any point during pregnancy as long as it doesn't impose an "undue burden" on a woman's right to end her pregnancy. Under this newly defined "undue burden" principle, the Court rejected Pennsylvania's provision for marital notification, but upheld the 24-hour waiting period, the parental notification requirement, and the record-keeping requirements on clinics that perform abortion. As one legal expert noted:

The Pennsylvania requirements for obtaining informed consent are based on the supposition that women who decide to have abortions do not think much about the decision and that if they had some additional information about the procedure and the development of the fetus, as well as 24 hours to think about it, many would continue their pregnancies to term. This view is extraordinarily patronizing to pregnant women, it is supported by no empirical data, and the consent requirements apply to no other medical procedure. *(Annas, 1992)*

While *Southeastern Pennsylvania v. Casey* clearly indicates that abortion laws as restrictive as Louisiana's will be overturned, this decision watered down the force of *Roe v. Wade* considerably, especially since Roe had held that the right to an abortion was "fundamental."

10. People should not look down on those who choose to have abortions.
    SA   A   SLA   SLD   D   SD

11. Abortion should be an available alternative for unmarried, pregnant teenagers.
    SA   A   SLA   SLD   D   SD

12. Persons should not have the power over the life or death of a fetus.
    SA   A   SLA   SLD   D   SD

13. Unwanted children should not be brought into the world.
    SA   A   SLA   SLD   D   SD

14. A fetus should be considered a person at the moment of conception.
    SA   A   SLA   SLD   D   SD

Score your answers in the following way:

Step One:

For items 2, 5, 6, 8, 10, 11, and 13:
SA = 6 points
A = 5 points
SLA = 4 points
SLD = 3 points
D = 2 points
SD = 1 point

For items 1, 3, 4, 7, 9, 12, and 14:
SA = 1 point
A = 2 points
SLA = 3 points
SLD = 4 points
D = 5 points
SD = 6 points

Step Two:

Total your points for all 14 items.

Step Three:

Use the following scoring scale to interpret your results.

0–15	Strong pro-life
16–26	Moderate pro-life
27–43	Unsure
44–55	Moderate pro-abortion
56–70	Strong pro-abortion

Source: *"Abortion Attitude Scale," L. A. Sloan. This article is reprinted with permission from* Health Education, *1983, pp. 41–42.* Health Education *is a publication of the American Alliance for Health. Physical Education, Recreation and Dance, 1900 Association Drive, Reston, VA, 22091.*

WHO HAS ABORTIONS: POPULATION PATTERNS

In 1988, there were approximately 1.6 million legal abortions performed in the United States (Henshaw, 1992).[1] This corresponded to a national abor-

---

[1]Official U.S. government statistics, which are reported by the Centers for Disease Control, provide estimates of annual numbers of abortions in the United States that are consistently about 200,000–250,000 below estimates developed by the Alan Guttmacher Institute, which we have cited here. For a comparison, see National Center for Health Statistics, *Health, United States, 1990,* Hyattsville, Maryland, U.S. Public Health Service, 1991, Table 10, p. 62 [DHHS Pub. No. PHS 91-1232].

tion rate of 27.3 abortions done per 1000 females aged 15 to 44. The national abortion ratio, which is stated in terms of the number of abortions per 1000 live births, was 286 in 1988. Since 1972, the abortion ratio has declined for all age groups (Centers for Disease Control, 1991), partly reflecting higher rates of childbearing for women in their thirties as well as better use of contraception by teenagers and young unmarried adults.

According to national data reported by the Alan Guttmacher Institute (Figure 7.1), teenagers had 25.6 percent of all legal abortions in 1988 (Henshaw and Silverman, 1988; Henshaw, 1992; Henshaw and Van Vort, 1992). Women 20 to 24 years old accounted for about one-third of abortions, while women aged 25 to 29 had about 22 percent and women 30 or over had nearly 20 percent of the abortions that were performed that year.

Only 18.5 percent of women who had abortions were married. Close to two-thirds had never been married, while the balance were either separated (6.4 percent), divorced (11.2 percent), or widowed (0.6 percent). According to U.S. government figures, the abortion ratio was 11.7 times higher for unmarried women than for married women in 1988. A disproportionately high percentage of women who obtained abortions had family incomes of under $11,000 a year, while abortions were far less common among women whose family income was $25,000 or more.

Figure 7.1 Selected Characteristics of Women Who Have Abortions

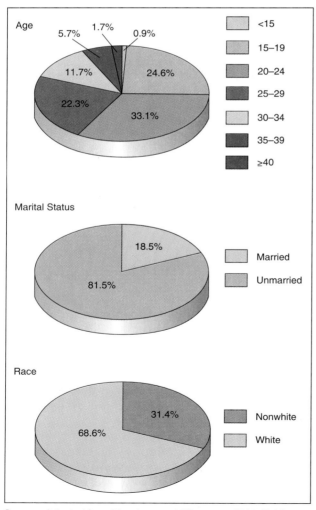

Source: *Adapted from Henshaw and Silverman, 1988, Table 1.*

Approximately two-thirds of the women who obtain legal abortions are white. However, the abortion ratio is much higher among minority women than for white women: 489 versus 259 abortions per 1000 live births in 1988 (Centers for Disease Control, 1991). In addition, black women tend to have later abortions than white women, although age is a more dominant influence than race, especially for women who have abortions at 16 weeks of pregnancy or beyond. For all racial groups, the proportion of women having an abortion done at 8 weeks or less increased with age, while the proportion obtaining late abortions decreased with age. Educational level is also linked to the timing of abortion: college-educated women are more likely to have early abortions than women who have only completed high school.

Although 88 percent of legal abortions are performed in the first 12 weeks of pregnancy (Centers for Disease Control, 1991), second trimester abortions are often chosen because of difficulty in coming up with the money for the procedure, which may partly explain why teenagers tend to have later abortions than older women. Ironically, the later abortion is not only less safe but also more expensive and may require that the woman take more time off from work or school. Second-trimester abortions may be necessary under other circumstances, of course. For instance, women with irregular periods, who frequently go for months without any menstrual flow, may not realize they are pregnant until well into the second trimester. Women who take birth control pills don't always realize when they become accidentally pregnant, especially since the pill produces side effects that mimic symptoms of pregnancy. Similarly, women with IUDs in place also may not recognize the early stages of pregnancy because they think they are adequately protected by their contraceptive method; it may take months before they suspect something is amiss. Finally, there are also many instances in which a teenager simply refuses to admit the possibility that she might be pregnant, as well as other cases in which the teenager's worries about her parents' reactions lead her to hide her pregnancy. In such cases, teenagers either hope it will somehow disappear on its own or actively try to miscarry by exercise, self-injury, or the use of drugs purported to cause abortions.

Looking at the religion of women who had legal abortions in 1987 reveals that 42 percent were Protestant, 32 percent were Catholic, 1 percent were Jewish, 3 percent were adherents of other religions, and 22 percent indicated that they had no religious affiliation (Henshaw and Silverman, 1989). This is of some interest since it shows that many Catholic women are willing to disregard the Church's teachings that prohibit abortion.

Another notable point made by the Alan Guttmacher survey was that half of all females who had abortions in 1987 said that they were practicing contraception during the month in which they conceived. This is in sharp contrast to the idea that most women who have abortions are either uninformed about contraception or unwilling to make an effort at practicing birth control, as the following comment makes clear:

A 23-year-old female graduate student: When I was a college junior I was involved in a live-in relationship with a guy I cared a lot about. We had a great sex life, but we were careful about it, with me using a diaphragm and him using a condom. You can imagine our shock—and dismay— when I turned out to be pregnant. We had never "forgotten" to use birth control; in fact, we were using two separate kinds of birth control. Still, when I told my best friend about it, she insisted that there must have been one time we slipped up and forgot. "Maybe," she said, "you were both drunk and you don't remember it." I really resented that attitude and realized how easy it is to make assumptions about people's behavior that just may not be true. *(Authors' files)*

As Table 7.1 shows, the majority of women who had an abortion in 1988 had never had a live birth. Likewise, most had never previously had an induced abortion. Less than 1 in 20 women who have abortions have had three or more abortions in the past. This last statistic strongly suggests that very few women rely on abortion as a means of birth control, although some who are opposed to legalized abortion claim that this is a common practice.

Many people seem to believe that most abortions are what are derisively termed "abortions of convenience," but these are tricky to define. As Anna Quindlen (1990) put it, "Semantics alone make it sound like a pregnancy ended because a woman wanted a child who was a Leo, not a Capricorn." If a 13-year-old is impregnated by her seventh-grade boyfriend and has an abortion, is it fair to call this an abortion of convenience? If an unmarried, unemployed 24-year-old woman who is

FOCUS IN BRIEF

What Happens to Unintended Pregnancies?

When an unintended pregnancy occurs, there are three possible outcomes: birth, abortion, or miscarriage. The following data show the percentage of unintended pregnancies that fall into each of these three categories for American women in different age groups.

Age	Birth	Abortion	Miscarriage
15–19	41.7%	45.4%	12.9%
20–24	44.8%	42.0%	13.2%
25–29	43.5%	43.5%	13.0%
30–34	45.0%	41.8%	13.2%
35–39	38.0%	49.5%	12.5%
40–44	17.3%	72.0%	10.7%

It is interesting to note that the percentage of women choosing abortion is remarkably similar over the 20-year span from age 15 to 34.

Source: *Jacqueline Darroch Forrest and Suschella Singh, "Public Sector Savings Resulting from Expenditures for Contraceptive Services."* Family Planning Perspectives, *volume 22, number 1, January/February 1990) p. 9. Copyright © 1990 The Alan Guttmacher Institute. Reprinted by permission.*

struggling to feed her four children with her meager welfare check becomes pregnant again and wants an abortion, is this also an abortion of convenience? Convenience often lies in the eyes of the beholder in these situations.

In any event, what is certainly clear is that the 1.6 million women who have abortions each year in America (and the 37 million women around the world) come from extraordinarily diverse backgrounds. While some are poor, undereducated women on welfare, others are law students, physicians, ministers, architects, housewives—women from virtually all walks of life. No matter how we view abortion as a moral issue, we should guard against prejudging these women and their situations based on stereotypes about who they are.

Table 7.1   **Percentage Distribution of Reported Legal Abortions, by Number of Previous Live Births and by Number of Previous Induced Abortions, U.S., 1988**

Previous Live Births						
0	1	2	3	4	Unknown	Total
% 51.0	22.8	15.6	5.5	2.5	2.6	100

Previous Induced Abortions					
0	1	2	3	Unknown	Total
% 56.4	26.2	10.2	4.8	2.5	100

Source: *Modified from data in* Morbidity and Mortality Weekly Report *40: SS-2, Tables 10 and 11, July 1991.*

ABORTION METHODS

There are a number of different procedures used to perform abortions. The optimal method for any pregnant woman usually depends on the length of time she's been pregnant. In general, abortions are simpler and safer the sooner they are done during a pregnancy.

The commonest form of first-trimester abortion (one performed during the first three months of pregnancy) is a method known as **vacuum aspiration** or *suction curettage* (illustrated in Figure 7.2). This technique, which is usually done on an outpatient basis (not requiring hospitalization) under local anesthesia (a paracervical block) or with no anesthesia at all,[2] now accounts for about 75 percent of all abortions in the United States and is in widespread use on a worldwide basis. The procedure involves first dilating (stretching) the opening of the cervix either by metal probes or by the use of small sticks of dried, sterilized seaweed (called *laminaria* tents) placed in the cervical canal a day before the abortion. As the *laminaria* sticks absorb moisture, their swelling causes the cervical canal to dilate gradually, which is often more comfortable than instrument-produced dilation. (Some women

notice pressure or mild cramping with *laminaria,* but many others experience no discomfort at all.) When the *laminaria* is removed, or when the cervix is dilated with instruments, a small plastic tube called a cannula is inserted through the dilated cervical canal into the cavity of the uterus. The tube is connected to a pump called a vacuum aspirator; as a result of the gentle suction provided by the pump, the contents of the uterus are quickly and easily removed. Most of the time, scraping the lining of the uterus (curettage, as in "D & C," for dilation and curettage) is not a necessary part of this procedure, and the entire process takes only 10 or 15 minutes.

In most abortion clinics, the woman would remain in the recovery room for about an hour while her blood pressure and pulse were monitored to be sure she was not hemorrhaging or having a reaction to the local anesthetic, if one had been used. Once discharged, she would be advised to rest quietly until the next day, when she can resume virtually all her everyday activities except for sexual intercourse or douching, both of which should be avoided for approximately two weeks. Normal periods usually resume four to six weeks after abortion.

First-trimester vacuum aspirations abortions are generally very safe (see Table 7.2). There are no adverse effects of first-trimester abortions on subsequent fertility, subsequent pregnancy outcomes, or the risk of subsequent ectopic (tubal) pregnancy (Schoenbaum et al., 1980; Stubblefield et al., 1984; Darling et al., 1985; Hogue, 1986; Marchbanks et al., 1988).

[2]Some women are so tense under local anesthesia that they require the use of a sedating drug such as valium (diazepam) or a painkiller such as demerol (meperidine) by injection during the procedure. If this is done, the recovery period is prolonged slightly in order to be sure the drug effects have worn off.

Figure 7.2   Vacuum Aspiration Abortion

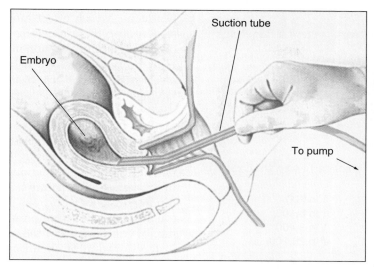

Vacuum aspiration for abortion involves suctioning the embryo and membranes within the uterus.

Dilation and curettage (D & C) is the other method occasionally used for first trimester abortions, although because this procedure requires general anesthesia and entails a greater risk of blood loss and other complications, it has distinct disadvantages. In a D & C, which is the same surgical procedure used as a diagnostic tool in cases of abnormal uterine bleeding or for removing uterine polyps, a sharp metal instrument called a curette is used to scrape the lining of the uterus rather than suctioning out the uterine contents.

The techniques of vacuum aspiration and D & C are combined in the method generally used for abortions during the late first trimester and early part of the second trimester. This method, called **dilation and evacuation (D & E),** requires dilating the cervix more than for an earlier abortion because larger instruments must be used inside the uterus. (*Laminaria* sticks are frequently used for this purpose, since they expand by five times their dry size when they absorb moisture from cervical secretions. When needed, metal dilators are used to enlarge the cervical opening even further after the *laminaria* has been removed.) Following dilation of the cervix, a blunt curette is used along with a forceps and suctioning to remove the uterine contents. A drug called *oxytocin* is sometimes given to help the uterus contract after a D & E is done in order to slow down the amount of bleeding that occurs. The whole procedure, not counting the preliminary use of *laminaria*, usually requires only 15 to 30 minutes. However, since the uterus is softer and its walls thinner after the first trimester than earlier, D & E is a technically more demanding surgical procedure with an increased risk of complications such as bleeding or perforation of the uterus.

After the fifteenth week of pregnancy, abortions are usually performed by causing the uterus to contract enough to expel the fetus and placenta in a manner resembling natural labor and delivery. Such abortions are called *induction abortions*. Induction abortions can be thought of as chemically induced miscarriages; however, these procedures are

vacuum aspiration the method usually chosen for abortion during the first trimester. The cervix is dilated and the contents of the uterus are removed through a plastic tube connected to a pump.

dilatation and curettage (D & C) (kyur e tazh') process involving dilating the cervix and then gently scraping the lining of the uterus with a metal instrument. Sometimes used as a form of abortion.

dilatation and evacuation (D & E) a method for abortion involving widening the mouth of the cervix, followed by removing the products of conception by a combination of suction and scraping.

Table 7.2   Various Complications of First-Trimester Abortions

Major Complications (Hospitalization Required):	
Retained tissue	1 in 3,600
Severe infection	1 in 4,700
Uterine perforation	1 in 10,600
Hemorrhage	1 in 14,200
Incomplete abortion	1 in 28,300
Tubal pregnancy	1 in 42,500

Minor Complications (Managed as an Outpatient):	
Mild infection	1 in 200
Cervical stenosis	1 in 6,100
Cervical tear	1 in 9,400
Convulsion	1 in 25,100

Source: *Modified from Hakim-Elahi, E., Tovell, H. M., and Burn-hill, M. S., "Complications of First Trimester Abortion: A Report of 170,000 Cases,"* Obstetrics & Gynecology *76: 929, 1990.*

riskier and more expensive than D & E's (Speroff and Darney, 1992). Although they were intially done with a hypertonic saline (salt) solution which was injected through the abdomen into the amniotic sac after first withdrawing a small amount of amniotic fluid—called **saline-induced abortion**—it is now more common to use hormones called prostaglandins to induce contractions of the uterus (**prostaglandin-induced abortion**). Prostaglandins can either be injected into the uterus directly through the abdomen or can be infused through the cervix into the gap between the lining of the uterus and the amniotic sac. Solutions of urea (either alone or in combination with prostaglandins or oxytocin) have also been used for the same purpose, and prostaglandins can also be delivered in the form of vaginal suppositories.

No matter which method is used, second-trimester abortions are considerably riskier than abortions done during the first trimester: in fact, the complication rate ranges from 5 percent for D & E's to as high as 20 percent for induction abortions in some institutions (Tatum, 1987). Among the most serious, though infrequent, complications with saline abortion are excessive salt levels in the blood, heart failure, and a condition of widespread bleeding throughout the body. Cervical lacerations and uterine bleeding are more common, though less serious, problems.

Common side effects of prostaglandin-induced abortion include nausea, vomiting, diarrhea, and headache, which affect more than half of women undergoing this procedure. Serious complications of prostaglandin abortion include a heightened risk of hemorrhage, a slight risk of seizures, and a risk of cervical laceration; in addition, the chances of having an incomplete abortion (requiring an immediate D & C) are somewhat higher with this method than with saline abortion. One other problem is that induction abortions don't always work: about 8 percent of prostaglandin inductions and 2 percent of saline inductions don't succeed on the first attempt and require a second injection. In addition, induction abortions take a much longer time (on average, about 24 hours), both in terms of waiting for contractions of the uterus to begin and then in the duration of chemically induced labor. One other problem with this method is that it may produce greater emotional stress for many women, particularly if they are awake when the fetus is expelled and the fetus is well-formed enough to have a very lifelike appearance.

Hysterotomy, which is an operation cutting into the uterus, is an infrequently used method for performing abortion. In addition to carrying heightened medical risks to the mother, there is a chance that a live fetus will be delivered if this technique (which is essentially the same as a caesarean section) is used on an advanced pregnancy.

Hysterectomy, or surgical removal of the uterus, is possible until the twenty-fourth week of pregnancy without first evacuating the contents of the uterus. This is an infrequent method of abortion that is generally reserved for women with large tumors (myomas) of the uterus that might interfere with other types of midtrimester abortion or for women who require a hysterectomy for other medical reasons. It is, of course, an irreversible procedure: not only is the current pregnancy terminated, no subsequent pregnancies will be possible.

One last form of abortion will be mentioned briefly. A small number of medical centers now perform an unusual type of abortion that is not aimed at ending fetal life, but preserving it. This seemingly paradoxical situation arises when women are pregnant with more fetuses than they can safely carry to term—a situation that occurs with some frequency when women have been given drugs to help them ovulate. For example, in one case a woman was carrying octuplets, which led her doctors to tell her that all would die unless something was done. With her consent, the doctors performed what is called a selective abortion, eliminating six of the fetuses, thus reducing the number of fetuses to two. The woman was able to continue her pregnancy and gave birth to healthy twins.

The selective abortion is performed using ultrasound to allow a miniature needle to be inserted into the chest cavity of a fetus when it is still smaller than a thumb. A chemical is injected through the needle that causes the fetal heart to stop beating. The dead fetus is eventually absorbed into the woman's body.

This octuplet case seems to offer few problems to most observers—after all, it is clear that all of the fetuses would have died if the octuplets were left undisturbed. But there have also been cases involving selective abortions as a matter of convenience for a couple—for example, reducing quadruplets to twins. [Ironically, these cases have sometimes arisen because of the practice of implanting multiple embryos as part of a GIFT procedure (discussed in Chapter 5), which is done very commonly on the theory that most of the implanted embryos will not survive.] If this is an ethically permissible practice, some wonder, where do you draw the line? What if a woman attending an IVF (*in vitro* fertilization) program conceives twins and then decides she only wants one baby—is it morally correct to abort one of the developing fetuses? What if a woman carrying twins or triplets wants to abort the female fetuses and give birth only to a male? These are matters of some moral importance in today's high-tech world of medicine.

THE ABORTION PILL

The newest chapter in the abortion story involves a pill developed in France that can safely and simply induce abortions in early pregnancy. Known scientifically as mifepristone but more commonly referred to as RU 486, the name assigned to it during its developmental stages, this abortion pill has been approved for sale in France and China since 1988 and in Sweden and Britain since 1991 but is banned in the United States. It is usually given in combination with a prostaglandin, which can either be administered vaginally, as an injection 48 hours after the RU 486 is taken, or in the form of a pill (Peyron et al., 1993). Most often, abortion occurs within hours of the administration of the prostaglandin.

RU 486 works by opposing the action of progesterone, a hormone critical to implantation of the fertilized egg in the uterus and the maintainence of pregnancy. Although the exact mechanisms of its actions are not fully understood, it causes the lining of the uterus to slough off, shedding the small embryo and amniotic sac present in early pregnancy (Baird and Glasier, 1993). It also blocks progesterone's calming action on the muscular walls of the uterus, which leads to contractions that help to dislodge the embryo (Klitsch, 1989; Grimes and Cook, 1992). In addition, the combination of RU 486 and prostaglandin opens and softens the cervix.

The utility of RU 486 has been widely confirmed, with complete success in 96 percent of pregnancies of seven weeks' duration or less (Baulieu, 1989; Lader, 1991; Goldsmith, 1991; Peyron et al., 1993). The incidence of side effects such as headache, nausea, and pelvic pain is very low. Less than 1 percent of women who have used the drug have experienced heavy bleeding and even fewer have developed infections of the uterine lining. In cases where there is incomplete expulsion of the contents of the uterus, RU 486 is followed by surgical termination of the pregnancy.

There are some situations in which RU 486 should not be used: a suspected ectopic pregnancy (since the drug is not effective in terminating pregnancies that are outside the uterus), any coexisting medical problem requiring use of hormone medications such as cortisone or prednisone (since RU 486 intereferes with the action of these steroids), and any conditions that might make the use of prostaglandins unsafe, such as asthma or severe high blood pressure.

The inventor of RU 486, Dr. Etienne-Emile Baulieu, now spends much of his time engaged in a political campaign to increase the acceptance of this controversial drug. Although it currently is

saline-induced abortion evacuation of the contents of the pregnant uterus produced by infusion of a salt solution into the amniotic fluid.
prostaglandin-induced abortion evacuation of the contents of the pregnant uterus produced by infusion of prostaglandins.
hysterotomy (his tur ot' uh mē) incision of the uterus. Infrequently used for abortion during the second trimester.
hysterectomy partial or total removal of the uterus.

often called the "abortion pill," Baulieu objects to this label, saying that the word abortion is automatically negative; instead, he suggests calling it a "contragestive"—a phrase he has coined to denote blocking gestation.

Although there are no indications of when, or whether, RU 486 will become available in the United States, it is important to realize that the drug has potential for many uses other than for abortion (Rosenfeld, 1993). In addition to potential medical uses such as in treating breast cancer, Cushing's syndrome (overactive adrenal glands), and certain brain tumors (Regelson, Loria, and Kalimi, 1990), RU 486 may also prove to be a highly effective contraceptive in the conventional sense. Taken during the first part of the menstrual cycle, RU 486's anti-progesterone action may be effective in blocking ovulation, which might eventually prove to be its most important use (Cherfas, 1989; Grimes and Cook, 1992; Baird and Glasier, 1993). Furthermore, use of this medication as a form of "morning after" pill may be one of the most effective ways of limiting the number of induced abortions on a worldwide basis.

However, it is clear that the most intense interest in RU 486 is focused on its use as an abortion pill. The relative simplicity and safety of using RU 486 in combination with a prostaglandin pill raises the possibility that abortions will become private matters between a woman and her personal physician, not even requiring a trip to an abortion clinic, where she may be harassed and intimidated by anti-abortion demonstrators. However, even under these circumstances (which would require legalization of the drug in the United States), because many women do not decide to end a pregnancy while they are in its early stages, when RU 486 is effective, many surgical abortions will continue to be done.

THE SAFETY OF ABORTION

Although all surgical procedures have associated risks, deaths from legal abortion are very rare. According to U.S. government figures, the overall death rate for legal abortions for 1980–1985 was 0.7 per 100,000 abortions, which compared with a maternal mortality rate of 9.1 per 100,000 live births for the same time period (National Center for Health Statistics, 1991, Table 10; Koonin et al., 1991). Abortions done during the first eight weeks

of pregnancy are even safer: for these early abortions, the death rate is less than 0.2 per 100,000 procedures, or less than one in a half-million. Overall, 88 percent of abortions in the United States are done in the first trimester; death rates and rates of other complications for these abortions are approximately one-tenth those for abortions done after the twelfth week of pregnancy (Speroff and Darney, 1992).

There are several different reasons why the risks of later abortions increase. For one thing, second-trimester abortions often require general anesthesia, which carries its own risks, separate and apart from the abortion itself. In addition, later abortions are more difficult surgical procedures, with a greater chance of uterine hemorrhage and other major complications, including serious postoperative infection. Furthermore, the longer a pregnancy progresses, the more likely the woman is to develop associated medical problems that may interfere with having an abortion. Despite these factors, second-trimester abortions are still three times as safe as carrying a pregnancy to term. Furthermore, there are no indications that a woman's age has any effect on abortion safety, although increased age carries a definite risk of higher maternal mortality.[3]

A woman who undergoes a single vacuum aspiration abortion—the method used in more than nine out of ten abortions in the United States today—has no greater risk of subsequent infertility than a woman who carries her pregnancy to term. Similarly, a single vacuum aspiration abortion doesn't increase the subsequent risk of miscarriage, stillbirth, birth defects, or major complications during future pregnancies or deliveries (Gold, 1990). And women who have had several induced abortions are no more likely than women who have never had an abortion to give birth to an underweight baby (Mandelson, Maden, and Daling, 1992).

There has only been one death reported with the use of RU 486 and prostaglandin as of the end of 1992, which makes it seem to be a particularly safe procedure. However, it may be too early to be certain of the relative safety of this drug combination compared to other methods of early abortion, espe-

---

[3]For women between the ages of 30 to 34, the maternal death rate is 11.8 per 100,000 live births. This rises to 23.0 for women aged 35 to 39 and increases even further, to 55.9, for women in their forties (Koonin et al., 1991).

cially since it is not yet clear under what terms and conditions RU 486 will be permitted in the United States in its present form.

PSYCHOLOGICAL RESPONSES TO ABORTION

For most women, the decision to have an abortion is reached only after considerable thought, anguish, and ambivalence. In some situations—for example, when prenatal testing reveals a condition such as Down's syndrome or a severe hereditary disease—this anguish may be heightened by the fact that the pregnancy was desired, not unintended. In other circumstances, even when the choice seems clear-cut and necessary for the man and woman involved, it may still provoke considerable guilt and turmoil.

Despite the fact that the decision to have an abortion is often accompanied by intense emotions, the emotional benefits of abortion outweigh the psychological risks for most women (Nadelson, 1978; Shusterman, 1979; Burnell and Norfleet, 1987; Zabin, Hirsch, and Emerson, 1989; Adler, 1990). Except for case studies, which usually involve problem abortions, none of the scores of studies of women following abortion reveal a high degree of psychiatric distress (Holden, 1989). In fact, serious psychological problems after abortions are far less common than postpartum depression. As the prestigious *Comprehensive Textbook of Psychiatry* puts it, "The emotional distress that is experienced by some women after abortion is usually mild and self-limited. Serious adverse sequelae are rare" (Belsky, Wan, and Douglas, 1985, p. 1054).

Not surprisingly, many women report considerable relief after an abortion. As one woman explained to us, "When I found out I was pregnant, I felt like there was a dark cloud over my future. Once I had my abortion, I could feel the sunlight again." Nevertheless, short-lived feelings of guilt, sadness, and loss are common in women who have had abortions (The Boston Women's Health Collective, 1984; Winn, 1988; Bonavoglia, 1991). Pre- and postabortion counseling are usually effective in helping women deal with these reactions.

The right-to-life camp was dealt a serious and unexpected setback when U.S. Surgeon General C. Everett Koop (who personally opposed abortion) issued a letter to President Reagan on the health effects of abortion that failed to identify serious psy-

chological aftereffects. Koop (1989) wrote that "at this time, the available scientific evidence . . . simply cannot support either the preconceived beliefs of those pro-life or pro-choice." Koop's basic position was that because of methodological flaws such as the absence of control groups, very low follow-up rates, and nonrepresentative samples, good scientific evidence is not available on the psychological or physical effects of abortion. However, it later became known that Koop's actual report had been more favorable in its conclusions about the relative safety of abortions, but had been censored by higher government figures.

The Human Resources and Intergovernmental Subcommittee of the House of Representatives investigated this matter and noted (1990):

> In his private meetings with Right-to-Life advocates, Dr. Koop expressed concern about the poor quality of their research evidence and told them that they would have to provide better proof if they wanted a Surgeon General's report consistent with their point of view. . . . In his public statements, he talked about how PHS [Public Health Service] scientists were asked to review the major articles and found them all to be flawed; in fact, however, written reviews were only requested for the National Right-to-Life Committee's "White Paper." No reviews were requested for the articles showing that abortion was psychologically safer than childbirth.

Partly for this reason, the American Psychological Association organized a blue-ribbon panel to review studies on the psychological responses of U.S. women after legal abortions. The panel concluded: "The weight of the evidence from scientific studies indicates that legal abortion of an unwanted pregnancy in the first trimester does not pose a psychological hazard for most women" and that "severe negative reactions after abortion are rare" (Adler, 1990).

Certainly, a woman's psychological reaction to an abortion doesn't occur in a vacuum. To an important degree, it depends on the social context in which the abortion occurs and the amount of emotional support she receives from significant others in her life. A woman who is made to feel guilty, as though her pregnancy was more important than she is, is more likely to have a difficult time in her postabortion adjustment. In addition, an unpleasant abortion experience involving unfeeling, judgmental clinic or hospital staff or social or religious disapproval by family or close friends will be likely to have a similar effect. On the other hand, caring family and friends can be of tremendous importance in helping a woman over the turmoil of the abortion experience.

SUMMARY

1. Legal attitudes toward abortion have varied considerably in different times and countries. In the Anglo-Saxon legal tradition, the right to abortion can be traced back to the fourteenth century, and in colonial America, following this tradition, abortion was permitted without restriction.

2. Laws regulating abortions began to appear in the United States in the mid-1800s as part of an attempt to restrict nonphysicians from carrying out medical procedures. Following a Papal decree in 1869 that declared abortion sinful and newspaper campaigns publicizing the cases of women who died from botched abortions, many states passed laws banning abortions entirely. Unfortunately, since women continued to seek help in terminating unwanted pregnancies, this spawned a large number of illegal abortion practitioners, many of whom had no medical training at all.

3. Although several states liberalized their abortion laws in the late 1960s, the landmark case legalizing abortion in the United States was *Roe v. Wade* (1973). While there have been many legislative attempts to overturn this ruling in the last decade, none have seriously undermined the legal right to abortion.

4. There are approximately 1.6 million abortions performed in the United States annually. (Worldwide, the figure is 37 million.) Teenagers account for one-quarter of all legal abortions in the United States; women 20 to 24 account for another one-third; and women 30 or over have approximately one-fifth of the abortions in America. More than 80 percent of women obtaining abortions are single, and a disproportionate number have low incomes.

5. Eighty-eight percent of legal abortions are performed in the first 12 weeks of pregnancy, but teenagers tend to have later abortions than older women. The timing of abortion is also tied to

educational level: college-educated women are more likely to have early abortions than women who only have a high school education.

6. The method most commonly used for first-trimester abortion is called vacuum aspiration or suction curettage. Usually done on an outpatient basis, this procedure involves first dilating the opening of the cervix by the use of *laminaria* tents (sticks of dried, sterilized seaweed that swell as they absorb moisture) or by using a metal probe. A small plastic tube is then threaded through the cervical canal into the uterus and the contents of the uterus are evacuated by gentle suction from a pump called a vacuum aspirator. Vacuum aspiration abortions are especially safe and have no effect on subsequent pregnancies.

7. Vacuum aspiration is combined with dilation and curettage (D & C) in the abortion method used either late in the first trimester or in the first portion of the second trimester. This approach, known as dilation and evacuation (D & E), involves more risk of complications such as uterine bleeding or perforation of the walls of the uterus.

8. Abortions done later in the second trimester typically are induction abortions, in which prostaglandins are injected into the uterus or used as vaginal suppositories. Complications are more common with this method than with those previously mentioned, and induction abortions take a longer time than earlier abortions, as well.

9. RU 486, the so-called abortion pill, is currently in use in France, China, and England, but not in the United States. This pill, which is administered in combination with a prostaglandin pill or injection, works by blocking the action of progesterone. It is effective in terminating more than 96 percent of pregnancies of up to seven weeks duration, and the incidence of side effects is strikingly low. The simplicity and safety of this abortion method may eventually alter the nature of how abortions are performed around the world quite dramatically.

10. There is absolutely no scientific evidence that freely chosen abortions are psychologically risky for most women. While individual women may certainly react to the strains of both their decision-making process and the fi-

nality of the abortion itself, most women report considerable emotional relief from ending an unwanted pregnancy. Understandably, the decision to terminate a pregnancy may be fraught with feelings of guilt and dismay, as well as feelings of intense personal religious conflicts, but women who receive warm support from their family and friends usually bounce back from the abortion experience without lasting psychological turmoil.

Thought Questions

1. If you were a Supreme Court Justice hearing a case in which a state sought to overturn *Roe v. Wade,* what would be the most important arguments that would persuade you to decide for or against this position?

2. In your experience (among your friends and acquaintances), to what extent is abortion used as a method of birth control? That is, how widespread is the practice of not using contraception because "You can always get an abortion?"

3. Do you believe that it is proper to require a pregnant 16-year-old to obtain parental consent (or a judge's permission) before getting an abortion? What if the requirement of obtaining parental consent means that she delays the abortion until it is much riskier than it would have been originally? In thinking about this matter, also consider it from the parents' viewpoint. Would you want *your* pregnant 16-year-old to get an abortion without your knowledge?

4. Do you believe that RU 486—the so-called abortion pill—should be legalized in the United States? Why or why not?

5. If RU 486 is legalized in the United States, do you think its use should be restricted to abortion clinics or hospitals or that it should be available as a prescription item for a woman to use in the privacy of her own home?

6. You have been asked to serve on a committee to design a study to document the emotional impact of abortion on women. Propose at least three different ways in which you could assess this issue. What sort of control group (or groups) should be included in your study design, and why?

Suggested Readings

Bonavoglia, A., ed. *The Choices We Made: Twenty-Five Women and Men Speak Out About Abortion.* New York: Random House, 1991. Personal glimpses into the emotions and experiences of people dealing with the abortion issue.

Faux, M. *Roe v. Wade.* New York: Mentor Books, 1989. The definitive history of the landmark case that legalized abortion in the United States in 1973, complete with a careful analysis of the courtroom drama, the role of the media, and the historical context of abortion laws and practices.

Henshaw, S. K., and Van Vort, J. *Abortion Services in the United States.* New York: Alan Guttmacher Institute, 1988. The most complete national, state, and local information on abortion practices available anywhere. Loaded with statistical tables, as well as discussions of survey methodologies.

Lader, L. *RU 486: The Pill That Could End the Abortion Wars and Why American Women Don't Have It.* Boston: Addison-Wesley, 1991. A provocative discussion of the history of RU 486 and its scientific potential, with particular attention to the political side of this story.

Interested persons can also find useful literature on abortion methods at any Planned Parenthood office. Updated statistics on U.S. abortions can be found regularly in *Family Planning Perspectives,* a journal published by the Alan Guttmacher Institute.

Developmental Perspectives

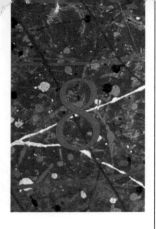

Childhood Sexuality

Sexual development is a complex process that starts at conception and continues throughout the life cycle. Before birth, in the **prenatal period,** sexual development is controlled mainly by biological forces. But from the moment the doctor says, "It's a girl" or "It's a boy," the rest of our sexual development is profoundly influenced by psychosocial factors interacting with our biological heritage.

In this chapter, we consider developmental sexuality from both biological and psychosocial viewpoints.

PRENATAL DEVELOPMENT

At the moment of conception, the combination of genetic material from each parent starts a process called **sexual differentiation** that leads to the specific physical differences between females and males. The process of prenatal sexual differentiation is largely controlled by genetic and hormonal mechanisms. We examine these mechanisms and the events they control in two ways. First we examine normal development patterns of prenatal sexual differentiation, and then we consider several examples of altered or abnormal development that can occur.

Table 8.1   Homologous Sex Organs

Male	Female
Testes	Ovaries
Penile glans	Clitoral glans
Penile shaft	Clitoral shaft
Foreskin	Clitoral hood
Scrotum	Labia majora
Underside of penile shaft	Labia minora
Cowper's glands	Bartholin's glands

Note: _Homologous structures are those that develop from the same embryonic tissue._

Normal Prenatal Differentiation

At fertilization, when the male sperm and female egg unite to form a zygote, the initial programming for sexual differentiation is set in place. Remember that the sperm carries an X or Y sex chromosome while the egg always has an X chromosome. When the 23 chromosomes of the sperm combine with the 23 chromosomes of the egg, the zygote has a total of 46 chromosomes. Under ordinary circumstances, a 46,XX chromosome pattern is the genetic code for a female and a 46,XY pattern programs for a male.

Regardless of the genetic coding, during the first weeks of development male and female embryos are anatomically identical. Two primitive gonads form during the fifth and sixth weeks of pregnancy, first as ridges of tissue and then as more distinct structures. At this point, the gonads are bipotential, meaning that depending on events to come, they can differentiate into either testes or ovaries (Table 8.1). There are also two paired primitive duct systems that form in both male and female embryos during this time, the **Müllerian ducts** and the **Wolffian ducts** (Figure 8.1).

For the testes to develop, there must be one further step in genetic control. The H-Y antigen, a chemical substance of uncertain identity (controlled by the Y chromosome), starts the transformation of the primitive gonads into testes. If this testis determining factor is not present, the primitive gonads will always develop into ovaries.

From this point on, sexual differentiation occurs at three different levels—the internal sex structures, the external genitals, and the brain—and is largely controlled by hormones. Even if the sex chromo-

some pattern is 46,XY, without enough testosterone produced at the right time anatomic development will be female rather than male (Jost, 1953; Jost, 1972; Money and Ehrhardt, 1972; Wilson, George, and Griffin, 1981).

Internal Sex Structures

If the embryo is a male, the newly formed testes begin secreting two different products by the eighth week after conception. A chemical called Müllerian duct inhibiting substance causes the Müllerian ducts to shrink and practically disappear instead of forming female internal sex organs. At the same time, testosterone is also produced, stimulating the development of the Wolffian ducts into epididymis, vas deferens, seminal vesicles, and ejaculatory ducts (Figure 8.1). In addition, testosterone is converted in some tissue to another form, called **dihydrotestosterone,** which stimulates development of the penis, scrotum, and prostate gland (Imperato-McGinley and Peterson, 1976). Testosterone and dihydrotestosterone are both **androgens,** hormones that cause masculinization.

prenatal period the time from conception to birth.

sexual differentiation the process that begins at the moment of conception to create a normal male or female.

Müllerian duct (mew ler' ē un) one of two pairs of embryonic genital ducts. In females, this duct system develops into the Fallopian tubes, uterus, and inner part of the vagina. In males, a substance secreted by the embryonic testes causes the Müllerian duct system to shrink and practically disappear.

Wolffian duct (wool' fē un) one of two primitive duct systems in the embryo. Develops in the male to form the epididymis, vas deferens, seminal vesicles, and prostate; it shrinks in the female to nonfunctioning remnants.

dihydrotestosterone (dī hī drō tes tos' ter ōn) a hormone similar to testosterone that stimulates development of the penis, scrotum, and prostate gland in the embryo.

androgens (an' dro jinz) hormones such as testosterone that develop and maintain secondary sex characteristics in males and, if in large quantities, promote masculinization in females.

Figure 8.1   The Stages of Internal Fetal Sex Differentiation

Y chromosome causes change into Wolffian ducts

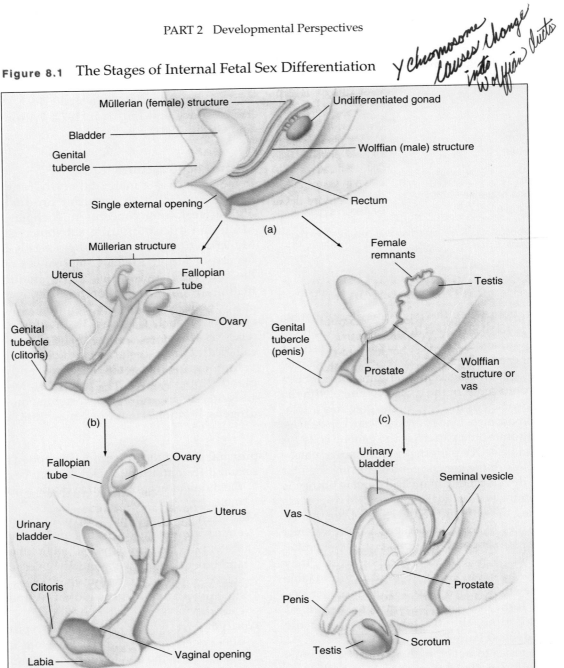

a) The undifferentiated stage at approximately 6 to 7 weeks of development. (b) The pattern of female internal differentiation at approximately 14 weeks. (c) Male differentiation at approximately 14 weeks. (d) Female differentiation at approximately 40 weeks. (e) Male differentiation at approximately 40 weeks.

In contrast, female sexual differentiation does not depend on hormones. Ovaries generally develop at about the twelfth week after conception, but even if they do not, the Müllerian duct system will proceed to develop into the uterus, Fallopian tubes, and inner third of the vagina (Money and Ehrhardt, 1972). Without high amounts of testosterone to stimulate its growth, the Wolffian duct system in the female shrinks into tiny remnants. By the fourteenth week of development, there is a clear difference in the internal sex structure of a male and female fetus (Figure 8.1b, c).

Figure 8.2 The Stages of External Fetal Sex Differentiation

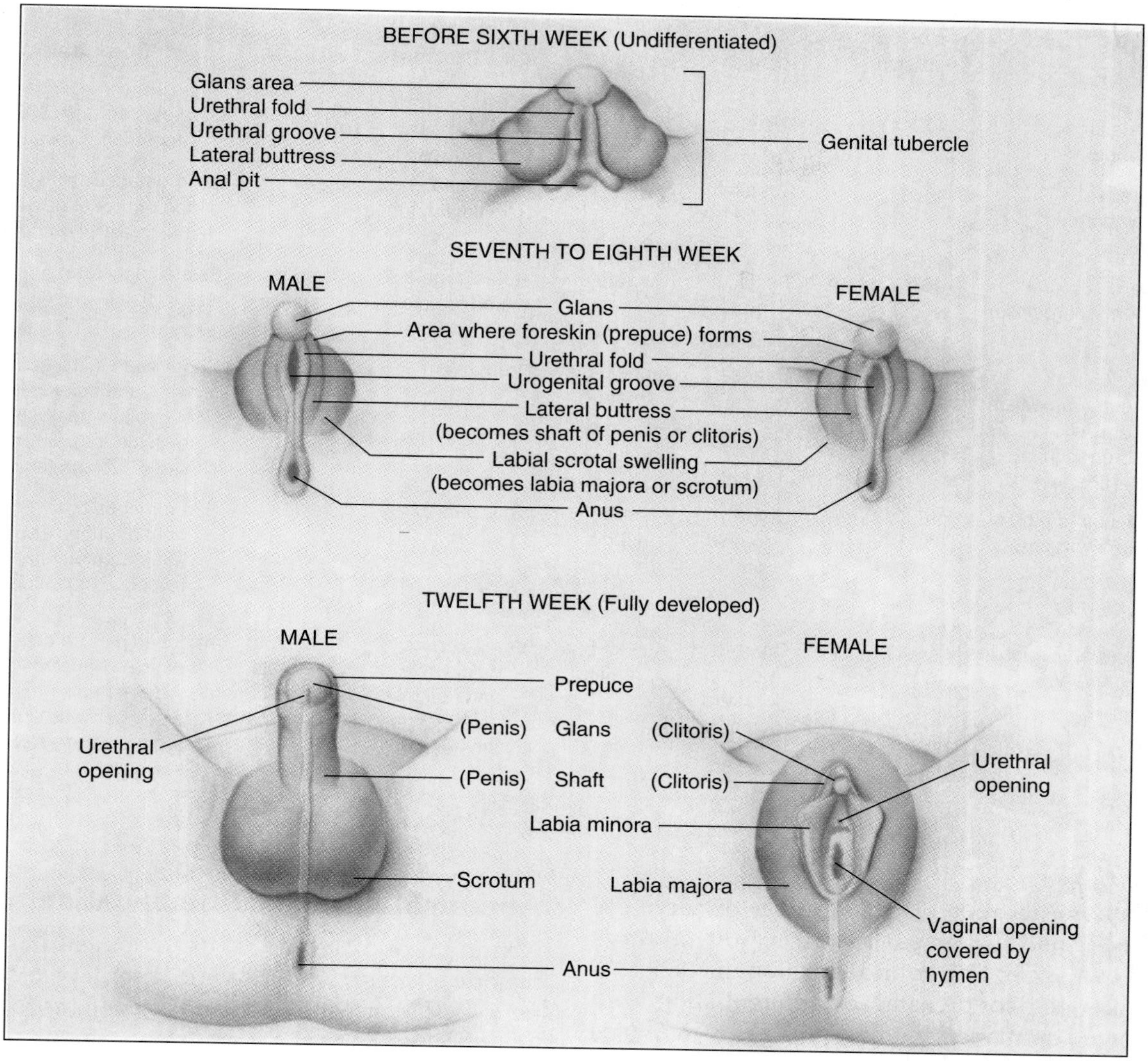

BEFORE SIXTH WEEK (Undifferentiated)

Glans area
Urethral fold
Urethral groove
Lateral buttress
Anal pit
Genital tubercle

SEVENTH TO EIGHTH WEEK

MALE   FEMALE

Glans
Area where foreskin (prepuce) forms
Urethral fold
Urogenital groove
Lateral buttress
(becomes shaft of penis or clitoris)
Labial scrotal swelling
(becomes labia majora or scrotum)
Anus

TWELFTH WEEK (Fully developed)

MALE   FEMALE

Prepuce
(Penis)   Glans   (Clitoris)
Urethral opening
(Penis)   Shaft   (Clitoris)
Urethral opening
Labia minora
Scrotum   Labia majora
Vaginal opening covered by hymen
Anus

External Genitals

In the seventh week of development, the external genitals look the same in both sexes. If there is little androgen present, as we expect in a female embryo, a clitoris, vulva, and vagina will form in six to eight weeks (Figure 8.2). In the male, androgen stimulation causes the folds that would develop into the inner vaginal lips in the female to grow together, forming the cylindrical shaft of the penis. The genital tubercle, which develops into the clitoris in the female, becomes the glans of the penis in the male. The labioscrotal swellings differentiate into the outer vaginal lips in the female and the scrotum in the male.

Both ovaries and testes first develop inside the abdomen during fetal life. Later, the ovaries move into the pelvis and the testes migrate down into the scrotum.

Brain Differentiation

Intriguingly, hormones in the blood of the fetus also affect the development of the brain and pituitary gland. The best-documented structural differences between male and female brains are in the

Table 8.2   Summary of Abnormalities of Prenatal Sex Differentiation

(handwritten margin notes: "1 in 500 males" and "1 in 2500 females")

	Chromosome Pattern	Gonads	Genitals	Internal Sex Structures	Fertility	Comments
Klinefelter's syndrome	47,XXY	Testes	Male	Normal male	Sterile	Low testosterone (80%), impotence is common
Turner's syndrome	45,X	Streak ovaries	Female	Uterus and Fallopian tubes	Sterile	No spontaneous menstruation or breast development due to estrogen deficiency
True hermaphroditism	46,XY or 46,XX	Testes and ovaries	Variable	Variable male and female combinations	Usually sterile	Exceedingly rare
Pseudo-hermaphroditism; Female adrenogenital syndrome	46,XX	Ovaries	Ambiguous male	Normal female	Fertile	Requires medical management and surgical revision of genitals; tomboy pattern in childhood; increased rate of lesbian fantasy
Testicular feminization syndrome	46,XY	Crypt-orchid testes	Female (short vagina)	No uterus or tubes; no prostate	Sterile	Spontaneous breast development at puberty but no menstruation; female psychosexual orientation
Dominican Republic syndrome	46,XY	Crypt-orchid testes	Ambiguous female	Vas deferens, epididymis, and seminal vesicles, but no prostate	Fertile but unable to in-seminate	At puberty, voice deepens, muscles develop in male pattern, penis grows, testes descend and enlarge, male gender identity is assumed

number and location of certain types of nerve cell connections (synapses) in the **hypothalamus** (Goldman, 1978; Carter and Greenough, 1979). As in other aspects of prenatal sex differentiation, with androgen stimulation the brain develops in a male pattern; without it, the brain develops in a female direction (Plapinger and McEwen, 1978; McEwen, 1981; MacLusky and Naftolin, 1981). This prenatal hormone programming determines the pattern of function of the hypothalamus and pituitary gland during and after puberty. As a result, girls have cyclic sex hormone production and menstrual cycles, while boys have a relatively constant level of sex hormone production. Female fertility is also cyclic whereas male fertility is not. Prenatal hormone effects on the brain may also influence later behavior patterns, including sexual behavior and aggressiveness, but the exact nature of these effects remains uncertain (Reinisch, 1974; Hutchison, 1978; Rubin, Reinisch, and Haskett, 1981).

Abnormal Prenatal Differentiation

Abnormal prenatal sexual development has three major causes: sex chromosome disorders, other genetic conditions, and exposure of the fetus to drugs given to the mother. A complete catalogue of such abnormalities would require an entire book, so we briefly discuss only a few conditions that illustrate important principles of sexual development. Table 8.2 is a summary.

Sex Chromosome Disorders

We have already pointed out that normally there are 46 chromosomes, including two sex chromosomes (XX or XY). Sometimes, however, a person may be born with extra sex chromosomes or one sex chromosome may be missing. These conditions have variable effects on a person's physical appearance, health, and behavior. Two of the most common sex chromosome abnormalities are described below.

Klinefelter's syndrome occurs when a genetic male has an extra X chromosome (a 47,XXY pattern). This condition occurs about once in every 500 live male births but is usually not detected until adulthood. As a result of the extra X chromosome, the microscopic structure of the testes is abnormal and no sperm production occurs, leading to infertility. Testosterone production is also usually reduced. These men tend to be tall and may have poor muscular development and enlarged breasts. Low sexual desire and impotence are common in this condition but are likely to improve if the man is given regular injections of testosterone (Kolodny, Masters, and Johnson, 1979). Of particular interest is the observation that men with Klinefelter's syndrome tend to be passive and have relatively low ambition or drive, which may be related to their testosterone deficiency.

Turner's syndrome is an example of a missing sex chromosome: the pattern is 45,X. Because one X chromosome is missing, the ovaries of a woman with Turner's syndrome never develop properly. The external genitals, however, are normal. The usual features of Turner's syndrome, which occurs in about one in 2500 live female births, include shortness, absence of menstruation, infertility, and a variety of abnormalities that may involve facial appearance and internal organs such as the heart and kidneys. Girls with Turner's syndrome who do not have any physical limitations usually develop normally as children. Yet when other girls begin to menstruate, develop breasts, and have an "adolescent growth spurt," these girls do not because of their nonfunctioning ovaries. Although menstruation and breast development can be induced by hormone treatment, the problems of height and infertility cannot be solved by any currently known approach.

Genetic Conditions

A true **hermaphrodite** is a person born with both testicular and ovarian tissue. In some cases, there is one ovary and one testis; in others, the gonads are mixtures of ovarian and testicular tissue. In this rare condition, a uterus is almost always present. There is either a Fallopian tube on one side of the body and a vas deferens and/or epididymis on the other, or male and female duct systems are on both sides. The **pseudohermaphrodite** is born with gonads that match their sex chromosomes but a geni-

tal appearance that resembles the opposite sex. A female pseudohermaphrodite has ovaries, a uterus, Fallopian tubes, and a 46,XX chromosome pattern but masculinized genitals. The appearance of the genitals can range from mild enlargement of the clitoris to the formation of a penislike phallus, and the labia may be fused together, looking like a scrotum. Sometimes the genitals seem so obviously male that the gender of the newborn child is misidentified by the physician.

The most common cause of female pseudohermaphroditism is the **adrenogenital syndrome (AGS),** an inherited disorder in which excessive amounts of androgens are produced during fetal development. Although babies with this condition may look like boys, their internal sex structures are completely female, with normal fertility potential.

hypothalamus (hī′ pō thal′ uh mus) the portion of the brain that has primary control over most endocrine pathways. It reacts to the level of hormones in the blood supply which regulate many sexual responses and direct their production.

Klinefelter's syndrome a sex chromosome abnormality marked by an extra X chromosome in a genetic male, giving a 47, XXY pattern. Most of these men tend to be tall with poor muscular development and small testes. Sexual desire is often low and impotence common.

Turner's syndrome a sex chromosome abnormality caused by a missing chromosome. The individual has a 45, X chromosome pattern and may appear fairly normal until puberty, when nonfunctioning gonads prevent development of the secondary sex characteristics and the adolescent growth spurt. May also be accompanied by webbing of the neck, heart defects, and other abnormalities.

hermaphrodite (hur maf′ rō dīt) a person with both testicular and ovarian tissue.

pseudohermaphrodite (sue′ dō hur maf′ rō dīt) an individual born with gonads matching the sex chromosomes but a genital appearance that resembles the opposite sex.

adrenogenital syndrome (a drē′ nō jen′ i tul) an inherited disorder involving an enzyme block in the adrenal glands. Females born with this condition frequently have masculinized genitals because of excess androgen exposure prenatally. In males, genital appearance is usually unaffected.

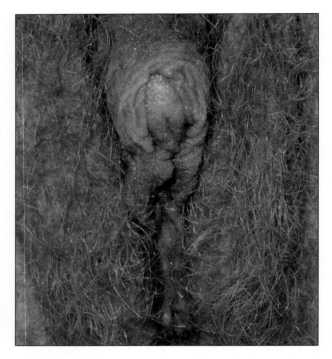

Untreated female with adrenogenital syndrome. This severe case has resulted in the fusion of the labia and marked enlargement of the clitoris.

When proper medical treatment is begun in early childhood, the abnormal androgen output of the adrenals can be brought under control, and plastic surgery can correct the appearance of the genitals.

There is some evidence that girls with AGS treated at an early age show a high rate of tomboyishness, a preference for having boys instead of girls as playmates, and little interest in doll play, grooming, attractiveness, caring for infants, or rehearsing adult roles of mother or wife (Money and Ehrhardt, 1972). (Of course, many girls *without* AGS would also rather climb trees or play ball than play house or mother.) Girls with AGS, however, are not at all ambivalent about their female gender identity. In adolescence, their dating behavior is often delayed and they commonly have difficulty in forming close erotic relationships (Money and Schwartz, 1977). In addition, there are reports that bisexual and lesbian fantasy or experience is relatively common in this syndrome (Ehrhardt, Evers, and Money, 1968; Money and Schwartz, 1977). However, it is not clear whether these findings are solely the result of prenatal androgen effects on the brain.

Male pseudohermaphrodites have testes and a 46,XY chromosome pattern but female genitals. The most common form of this disorder is the **testicular feminization syndrome,** an inherited condition in

which testosterone and other androgens have no effect on body tissues. Thus, even though normal levels of testosterone are produced, differentiation proceeds as if no androgen were present at all: a clitoris, labia, and vagina develop. Yet since the fetal testes also produce Müllerian duct inhibiting substance (which is not impaired in this syndrome), the Müllerian ducts shrink and no uterus or Fallopian tubes develop. Because the inner third of the vagina normally is formed from the Müllerian system, the vagina in this syndrome is short and ends in a blind pouch.

A newborn baby with testicular feminization looks like a normal baby girl unless the testes have descended into the labia or can be felt in the groin. These children are raised as girls and their development proceeds in a normal feminine pattern. This condition is usually not diagnosed until age 16 or later, when the lack of menstrual periods is investigated medically. Interestingly, at puberty female breast development occurs because some testosterone is broken down into estrogen (as it is in all males). Although there is a male chromosome pattern, normal testes, and no ovaries or uterus, these girls are quite feminine in appearance and behavior (Money and Ehrhardt, 1972). Their sexual behavior is also that of a normal female, although fertility is not possible.

In cases of complete testicular feminization, the child must be raised as a girl even if the diagnosis is made at birth. Neither surgery nor hormone treatment can create a functioning penis or alter the female appearance of the body. This syndrome is contrasted with another type of male pseudohermaphroditism in the Research Spotlight, "The Nature–Nurture Argument" (pp. 206–207). The comparison raises some intriguing questions about prenatal hormone effects.

Prenatal Drug Exposure

Hormones given to a pregnant woman for medical reasons cross the placenta and enter the circulation of the developing fetus. Depending on when in the pregnancy the drug is taken and how much is taken, such hormones may affect sexual anatomy. As examples, androgens can enlarge the clitoris, creating a condition very similar to AGS, and synthetic female hormones can cause malformation of the penis (Aarskog, 1979). Research interest at present, however, centers on the behavior of children exposed to synthetic hormones during their prenatal development.

One report found that teenage boys born to diabetic mothers who had received estrogen and progesterone during pregnancy were rated as lower in general masculine behavior, assertiveness, and athletic ability than other boys of the same age (Yalom, Green, and Fisk, 1973). In another study, adolescent males 16 to 19 years old who had been exposed prenatally to high levels of progesterone were found to have less physical activity and participation in heterosexual activity than control group subjects (Zussman, Zussman, and Dalton, 1975, 1977). Another study investigating adolescents who received lower hormone doses did not find such effects (Meyer-Bahlburg, 1978). And in girls exposed prenatally to estrogens or progesterone, there seems to be a mild "enhancing effect" on femininity (Ehrhardt, Grisanti, and Meyer-Bahlburg, 1977).

Although these studies are far from conclusive, they suggest that in certain cases prenatal hormone exposure may influence later patterns of behavior. The relative importance of such prenatal influences is still a matter of controversy (Ehrhardt and Meyer-Bahlburg, 1981; Rubin, Reinisch, and Haskett, 1981).

INFANCY AND CHILDHOOD

From birth on, learning is ordinarily more important than biology in shaping sexuality. However, it is impossible to completely separate learning and biology. For instance, a baby "learns" about the physical sensations of various body parts, but this type of learning is impossible without biological responses. For any learning to occur, events and their meanings must register in the brain, where they are probably coded and stored in chemical form (Money, 1980; Parsons, 1980). Individuals grow and change throughout their lives in a fashion determined by an interaction between biology and experience.

There is a surprisingly full range of physical sexual responsiveness in the first year of life. Kinsey and his colleagues reported orgasm during masturbation in nine baby boys under a year old, describing the physiological changes as "development of rhythmic body movements with distinct penis throbs and thrusts, an obvious change in sensory capacities, a final tension of muscles . . . a sudden release with convulsions, including rhythmic contractions—followed by the disappearance of symp-

toms" (Kinsey, Pomeroy, and Martin, 1948, p. 177). Orgasm has also been noted in girls during infancy and childhood (Kinsey et al., 1953; Bakwin, 1974). Although boys do not ejaculate prior to puberty, it appears that all other mechanisms of sexual response are present from infancy on.

There are only minor hormone differences between young girls and boys. In childhood, the gonads are relatively nonfunctional, and the major source of testosterone and estrogen is the adrenal glands. Because the adrenals are the same in both boys and girls, sex hormone production is the same too. The pituitary gland is, sexually speaking, not yet active because it receives no major signals from the hypothalamus.

In approximately 3 percent of newborn males (and 30 percent of premature male babies), the testes have not descended into the scrotum and are said to be **cryptorchid** (hidden). In most cases, descent occurs automatically within the first few months of life. If this does not happen, medical treatment with hormones or corrective surgery is advisable, since prolonged positioning of one or both testes in the abdomen can damage their sperm-producing capacity and creates an increased risk of cancer (Lattimer et al., 1974).

GENDER IDENTITY

Trying to understand developmental sexuality from a biological viewpoint alone is like trying to understand music solely in terms of sound waves: while the information available to you is factual, it is also incomplete. To complement the information on the biology of sexual development just presented, this chapter next examines the psychological and social factors that influence our sexual development during childhood.

In the preceding section we saw that from a biological viewpoint, the sex of an individual is determined by sex chromosomes, sex hormones, sexual anatomy (both external and internal), and secondary sex characteristics. These biological aspects of being male or female merge in important ways

testicular feminization syndrome an inherited condition in which tissues are insensitive to the effects of testosterone. The individual is born with a 46, XY chromosome pattern (male) but with female genitals.

cryptorchid (krip tor' kid) undescended testes.

RESEARCH SPOTLIGHT

The Nature–Nurture Argument

Scientists have argued for years about the relative importance of nature (biological forces) versus nurture (learning and the environment) in controlling human development. The complexity of this issue can be highlighted by reviewing two fascinating situations.

The first is one of the most famous cases in the annals of modern sexology, which was reported by John Money (Money and Ehrhardt, 1972; Money, 1975). When identical twin brothers underwent circumcision at 7 months of age, an operating error led to the loss of the penis of one twin. After considerable anguish and consultation with various medical experts, the parents were finally referred to Johns Hopkins University, and a joint decision was made that the twin missing a penis would be raised as a girl. At 17 months, the child's name, clothing, and hairstyle were changed, and four months later the first of a series of surgical procedures designed to reconstruct the genitals as female was started. Family members were provided with the best available advice about ways of coping with this gender reassignment.

The parents took great care to treat their twins as son and daughter even while knowing that both were biologically male. As a result, the daughter quickly began to prefer dresses to slacks and showed other "typical" signs of femininity, such as a desire for neatness. When the twins were 4½, the mother remarked: "One thing that really amazes me is that she is so feminine. . . . She just loves to have her hair set; she could sit under the drier all day long to have her hair set" (Money, 1975). The twins were encouraged to develop play patterns and interests in toys along traditional lines—dolls for the girl, cars and tools for the boy. The mother also reported that her son and daughter imitated their parents' behavior differentially, the son following his father's example and the daughter imitating what the mother did. According to Money, these two children achieved normal (and different) gender identities and roles although they both had identical chromosomal, anatomic, and hormonal sex during prenatal development and for the first seven months of life.

The case subsequently took a new twist, however, and the "girl" twin's adjustment to a female gender identity may not be as straightforward as Money previously suggested. According to interviews with the girl's psychiatrist conducted by the British Broadcasting System, she is having many problems as a teenager and is so unfeminine in appearance and behavior that classmates taunt her by calling her "cave-woman" (Diamond, 1982). While a final picture of her psychosexual development has not been reported as yet—and while her problems as a teenager may have reflected a need to adjust her estrogen dose properly—it is now difficult to use this case to support the position

with psychological and social factors that begin to operate at birth and continue throughout life. **Gender identity** is an individual's private and personal perception of being male or female. **Gender role,** by contrast, is an individual's outward expression of maleness or femaleness in social settings. Gender role is discussed more fully in Chapter 11.

Gender identity formation occurs early in childhood and influences sexual development in many ways. As the preceding section stated, there is some controversy as to the forces that shape gender identity. Here, we briefly summarize several current viewpoints.

Learning Theory

Learning theory suggests that gender development is shaped by personal models and cultural influences to which the young child is exposed. In a

that gender development depends primarily on learning.

Another research study claims to support just the opposite conclusion. In 1974, 38 male pseudohermaphrodites were discovered in four rural villages of the Dominican Republic. Although these subjects have normal sex chromosomes, an inherited enzyme defect causes improper formation of the external genitals, even though prenatal testosterone production is normal. The testes and internal sex organs are completely male. But at birth, the affected babies have an incompletely formed scrotum that looks like labia, a very small penis that looks like a clitoris, and a partially formed vagina. As a result, many of them are raised as female. Then, during puberty, normal male testosterone production starts, and definite masculine changes occur. The voice deepens, male-pattern muscles develop, the "clitoris" grows into a penis, and the testes descend into the scrotum. Normal erections occur and intercourse is possible.

Of the 18 genetically male children with this condition who were raised as girls, 17 changed to a male gender identity and 16 of 18 shifted to a male gender role during or after puberty (Imperato-McGinley et al., 1979). The authors of this report believe that these findings show that when sex of rearing is contrary to the biological sex, the biological sex will prevail if normal hormone production occurs during puberty.

So far it all sounds very neat and convincing. Biology is "obviously" more important than learning, since these "girls" seem to easily discard the gender roles they learned in the first 10 or 12 years of life in order to become boys. A closer look at some of the reasons that may be behind this switch may give us a different message, however.

First, girls in these rural areas have to stay at home after age 7 and do chores, while boys have "freedom to romp and play." After age 11 or 12, the boys can go to bars or cock fights, which girls are not permitted to do. Adult women are also supposed to stay home and be faithful, while men can seek entertainment and enjoy the services of prostitutes. Given these social restrictions, why wouldn't a young teenager with a choice choose to be the free and fun-seeking male? In addition, people usually define who or what they are by the reality of their physical appearance. Seeing a penis grow and a scrotum form and knowing that other such cases have occurred in the same village, the child would probably choose to live as a male. If he were to continue to live in a female role, he probably would not attract any male sex partners. Thus, this study does not "prove" anything about nature versus nurture, except that our sexual development is probably determined by an interaction of the two.

child's earliest years, parents are the most important models for the child to observe and imitate. The child learns to model the same-sex parent's behavior because imitation of that parent is rewarded. In addition, it is known that parents treat boys and girls differently from the moment of birth because of different expectations of them. This process, known as **differential socialization,** is thought to influence both gender identity and gender roles (Kagan, 1976; A. C. Petersen, 1980).

gender identity the inner sense a person has of being male or female.

gender role behavior that conveys to others that an individual is either male or female.

differential socialization the ways in which parents and others react differently to boys and girls and reinforce different behaviors for the two sexes.

Cognitive–Developmental Theory

According to this viewpoint, gender development parallels the intellectual development of the child (Kohlberg, 1966). Very young children have an oversimplified view of gender that corresponds to an oversimplified view of the world at large. Just as a 3-year-old may think there is a man inside a TV set, a 3-year-old is likely to believe that by putting on a wig and dress, a man "changes" into a woman. A 3-year-old girl, when asked what she wants to be when she grows up, may say "a daddy." It is only at ages 5 or 6, when children understand that gender is constant, that they are able to form a firm gender identity. Once this consistent self-concept is developed, children learn by observation and imitation that certain behaviors are appropriate for each gender. Cognitive–developmental theory, contrary to learning theory, proposes that children mimic adult behavior *not* to gain rewards but to achieve self-identity (Kaplan and Sedney, 1980).

Biosocial Interaction

Many researchers view the child's emerging gender identity as an interaction between biological and psychosocial factors. In other words, prenatal programming, psychology, and society's norms all influence subsequent patterns during childhood and adolescence. The extent to which prenatal programming determines gender development is controversial. Milton Diamond (1977) believes that prenatal hormones organize sex differences in the brain that are important determinants of later behavior. John Money and his colleagues agree that prenatal programming of sex differences occurs but emphasize that for most individuals, gender development is mainly influenced by social learning (Money and Ehrhardt, 1972; Money, 1980; Money and Wiedeking, 1980). The basic pathways from conception to adulthood that these workers see as contributing to gender development are summarized in Figure 8.3.

In general, the biosocial viewpoint stresses that there are certain critical periods in the overall process of sexual development. Just as there is a critical period for fetal androgen action (weeks 6 to 14 of pregnancy), Money believes there is a critical period for the formation of gender identity. He and his colleagues have found that in most instances, "core" gender identity—the fundamental establishment of a sense of one's self as male or female—is set in place by age 3. After this time, the gender identity gate seems to be tightly closed and locked and attempts at changing a child's gender orientation are thought to be fraught with psychological difficulty.

Money and his co-workers believe that the most important influences on gender development are learned rather than biologically controlled (Money and Ehrhardt, 1972; Money and Ogunro, 1974; Money, 1980). This conclusion results from their studies of matched pairs of **pseudohermaphrodites** (people with ambiguous external genitals). To briefly summarize, they found that if two babies with the same biological sex (as shown by their chromosomes and gonads) were assigned opposite sexes at birth so that one was raised as a boy and the other was raised as a girl, in almost all cases the sex of assignment proved dominant over the biological sex in determining gender identity and gender role. In other words, biologically female babies brought up as boys thought of themselves as boys, played with boys' toys, and preferred boys' sports and clothing styles. Similarly, biologically male babies raised as girls developed female gender identity and gender role. The extensive evidence Money and his colleagues gathered suggests that the biological programming of prenatal development and the control of genetic forces are usually not enough to overcome the impact of postnatal learning.

More recently, Money (1988) has devised the *lovemap theory* to explain how erotic orientation develops. A lovemap is "a developmental representation or template in the mind and in the brain depicting the idealized lover, the idealized love affair, and the idealized program of sexuoerotic activity projected in imagery or actually engaged in with that lover" (Money, 1988, pp. 209–210). Money believes that a person's lovemap—which you can think of as a brain-based blueprint for an individual's psychological and physiological patterns of love and eroticism—is formed in childhood, between ages 5 and 8 (Brody, 1990). Furthermore, if the lovemap becomes distorted by traumas such as incest, physical abuse, or severely negative parental attitudes toward sex, it may ultimately lead to atypical patterns of sexual behavior (Money and Lamacz, 1989) (discussed in more detail in Chapter 17). Money's lovemap theory supplements his earlier work on the core formation of gender identity. He still believes in the interactionist view but stresses: "Overall, it would appear that the most important formative years for homosexuality, bisexuality, and heterosexuality are those of late infancy and prepubertal childhood" (Money, 1988, p. 124).

Figure 8.3   Development of Gender Identity and Gender Role

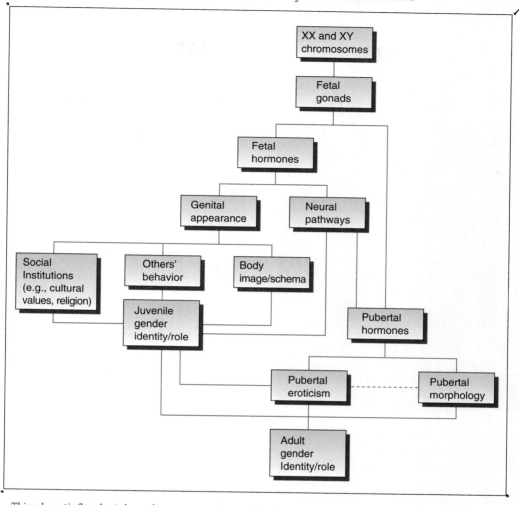

This schematic flowchart shows the sequence and cumulative interrelations of important factors in the development of gender identity/role.

Source: *Modified from Money and Wiedeking, "Gender Identity/Role: Normal Differentiation and its Transpositions," in* Handbook of Human Sexuality, *ed. By Benjamin Wolman and John Money, (c) 1980, p. 270. Reprinted by permission of Prentice-Hall, Inc., Englewood, N.J.*

This is a very interesting body of research, but its actual relevance to the question of what controls gender identity development for normal people is unclear. It might be that only those individuals who experience the unusual biological development of pseudohermaphrodites have the flexibility to accept equally the gender identity of either sex. When all the measures of biological sex are in the same direction, it may be that learning cannot successfully reverse the gender identity programming that has occurred prenatally. The fact that the identical twin who was reassigned to be reared as a girl apparently has not made a suc-cessful personal or social adjustment is supportive of this possibility (see pp. 206–207).

Today, it is no longer useful to think of sexual development as rigidly controlled by "nature" (biology) or "nurture" (learning). Biological processes do not unfold in a cultural vacuum, and learning does not occur without the biological apparatus of the brain itself. Although additional research is

pseudohermaphrodite (sue' dō hur maf' rō dīt) an individual born with gonads matching the sex chromosomes but a genital appearance that resembles the opposite sex.

Freud's Theories of Sexual Development

Freud was one of the first theorists to recognize that sexuality exists throughout the life cycle. Freud believed that the sex drive, or *libido,* an instinctual striving for sensual pleasure, was one of the key forces motivating behavior. Although Freud asserted that libido existed from infancy on, he did not say that infantile or childhood sexuality was identical to sexuality in adults. Instead, he proposed that early unfocused sexual feelings pass through a predictable series of developmental stages that are necessary for the formation of mature adult personality and behavior. He saw this development occurring in five stages.

In the first year of life, called the **oral stage,** the mouth is the primary focus of sexual energy and sensual gratification. Infants not only get obvious pleasure from sucking but also put things (*any* things) into their mouths to explore them, to see what they are like.

In the **anal stage,** from age 1 to 3, sensual pleasure shifts to the anal region. In the process of toilet training, the child has his or her first real opportunity to assert some independence from parental control. Deliberately holding back bowel movements or letting them go produces both physical and psychological pleasure, but gradually the child learns to follow socially acceptable behavior regarding bathroom functions.

In the **phallic stage,** from about age 3 to 5, erotic interest shifts to the genitals. Here, Freud suggested separate developmental pathways for boys and girls. As a boy experiences erotic pleasure from masturbation, he develops fantasies of possessing his mother sexually. (This is quite understandable, since his mother is likely to be already loved and loving.) This fantasy wish leads to the **Oedipus complex** (named after the Greek story in which Oedipus unknowingly killed his father and married his mother); the boy becomes jealous of his father whom he sees as a rival for his mother's affection. At the same time, the boy fears the anger of his powerful father and becomes especially afraid that his father will punish him by removing his penis. This **castration anxiety** is supported by two bits of logic in the young boy's mind: (1) he expects that his

---

oral stage in Freudian theory, the first year of life, in which the sexual energies are focused in the region of the mouth.

anal stage according to Freud's theory of psychosexual development, the stage that occurs from about ages 1 to 3 when a child's sexual energies are focused on the anal zone and eliminative functions.

phallic stage in Freudian theory, the period from about 3 to 5 years of age when the child's sexual energies are focused on the genitals.

Oedipus complex (ed' i pus) in Freudian theory, the sexual attraction of a young boy toward his mother, accompanied by a mixture of fear and rivalry toward his father.

castration anxiety (kas trā' shun) according to Freud, the unconscious fear in boys about the possible loss of their penis as a terrible form of punishment.

penis will be "punished" because it is the source of his pleasure and guilt, and (2) he knows by now that girls do not have penises, and this suggests that a penis can be taken away. The problem is resolved by a creative compromise. The boy gives up his sexual desire for his mother and his hostility toward his father and instead identifies with his father. In this way he tries to become as much like him as possible so that he too will one day be powerful and able to satisfy his sexual cravings.

The female counterpart of the Oedipus complex (the **Electra complex,** named after a Greek legend about a princess who helped kill her mother) is more complicated. Essentially, it is based on the view that after discovering that she does not have a penis, the girl feels envious and cheated. This so-called **penis envy** results in the girl's wanting to possess her father and to replace her mother, whom she blames for her dilemma. Freud believed that this situation is less adequately resolved than the Oedipus complex because the girl is not so powerfully motivated by fear: after all, she has already "lost her penis." Freud thought that this less successful resolution of a childhood conflict led women to be less mature psychologically than men because penis envy persists throughout life.

After the resolution of the Oedipus or Electra complex, which is usually achieved by age 6, the child enters a **latency stage** where sexual impulses presumably recede in importance. Here, the child becomes involved in nonsexual interests such as intellectual and social pursuits. This stage ends at the time of puberty when the **genital stage** is activated by internal biological forces. The adolescent gradually learns to focus his or her sexual interest on heterosexual relations in general and sexual intercourse in particular, finally expressing mature adult genital sexuality.

A brief outline of Freud's theories of sexual development does not adequately explain the richness of his work or the complexity of his viewpoints. The Freudian influence on modern sexology has been profound and continues to be felt today. Several criticisms of Freud's ideas, however, are relevant to our discussion here. First, many authorities (including some of Freud's own followers) believe that he largely overlooked the importance of cultural input on sexual development. For example, it has been suggested that the anal stage is really a result of our culture's emphasis on bowel training rather than a reflection of erotic pleasure (Marmor, 1971). Similarly, cross-cultural anthropology provides evidence that the Oedipus complex is not encountered universally and that latency is primarily a function of a sexually restrictive society rather than determined by inner psychological forces alone. Second, many critics have suggested that Freud's views on female sexuality were extremely biased (Millett, 1970; Sherfey, 1972; Tennov, 1975; Frieze et al., 1978). Finally, Freud himself acknowledged that many of his ideas were incomplete and indicated that they should be revised as new knowledge became available.

Electra complex in Freudian theory, the sexual attraction of a young girl toward her father, usually accompanied by hostility toward her mother.

penis envy in Freudian theory, the girl's unconscious sense of inadequacy and jealousy at not having a penis.

latency stage in Freudian theory, the period from about 6 years to puberty when sexual impulses are quiescent and are sublimated into nonsexual behaviors and interests.

genital stage in Freudian theory, the last stage of sexual development, which begins at puberty owing to internal biological forces. Characterized by growing independence and a final transition into adult genital sexuality.

needed to clarify details of the process, it appears that the biosocial interaction theory is the most comprehensive way of looking at all phases of sexual development.

CHILDHOOD SEXUALITY

Childhood has been called "the last frontier in sex research" (Money, 1976) because there is little reliable data about sexual behavior during this formative time. Studies based on interviewing adults about what they did or how they felt during childhood are distorted by faulty recall, exaggeration, and omissions due to embarrassment or the wish to seem "normal." Attempts to interview children or administer questionnaires to them about their sexual attitudes and behavior have often been thwarted by community outrage about "putting nasty ideas in children's minds" and accusations of undermining the moral fabric of our society. Except for some limited cross-cultural data from primitive societies in which childhood sex play is permitted and data from a few instances of direct observation, we are forced to rely on guesswork and inference in this important area.

Prior to the work of Freud and some early sexologists around the turn of the century, childhood sexuality was seen as either nonexistent or as something to be repressed because of its sinful and dangerous nature (Sulloway, 1979). These contradictory views still exist, but at least some parents today have come to regard the developing sexuality of their children in a more matter-of-fact, accepting way. Other parents are uncomfortable with any form of sexual interest or behavior in their children for several reasons. They worry that it is abnormal; they are uncertain about how to deal with it; or they are dealing with sexual conflicts within themselves.

By learning about the typical patterns of sexual development during childhood, parents (or prospective parents) can become more effective in helping their children learn about sexuality in a comfortable, unthreatening way.

Sex in Infancy

Ultrasound studies have provided clear evidence that reflex erections occur in developing baby boys for several months before birth, while they are still within the uterus (Masters, 1980; Calderone, 1983). Many newborn baby boys have erections in the first few minutes after birth—often even before the umbilical cord is cut. Similarly, newborn baby girls have vaginal lubrication and clitoral erection in their first 24 hours (Langfeldt, 1981), so it is clear that the sexual reflexes are already operating at the very start of infancy and probably even before birth.

An important phase of infantile sexuality comes from the sensuous closeness of parent and child through holding, clinging, and cuddling (Higham, 1980). As mentioned in Chapter 5, this parent–child bonding begins at birth and extends to include nursing, bathing, dressing, and other physical interactions between parents and their newborn child. A child who is deprived of warm, close bonding during infancy may experience later difficulties forming intimate relationships or, more speculatively, in being comfortable with his or her sexuality (Ainsworth, 1962; Harlow and Harlow, 1962; Trause, Kennell, and Klaus, 1977; Money, 1980).

Very young infants respond quite naturally to a variety of sources of physical sensation with signs of sexual arousal. For example, it is common for baby boys to have firm erections while they are nursing. While this is alarming to some parents, who see it as somehow abnormal or perverse, the fact is that the sensation of cuddling close to the warmth and softness of the mother's body and the intense neurological stimulation of suckling (the lips are well endowed with sensory nerve endings) combine to send messages to the brain that are interpreted as pleasurable and that activate sexual reflexes. Clitoral erection and vaginal lubrication in baby girls also occur commonly during nursing, indicating that this pattern is not restricted to one gender (although penile erection is more visible and thus more likely to be noticed). Similar signs of reflex sexual activation may occur when babies are bathed, powdered, diapered, or playfully bounced around. It is important to recognize, however, as Martinson points out, that "the infant is too young to be consciously aware of the encounter, and therefore no sociosexual erotic awakening can be said to occur" (1981, p. 26). How parents respond to observing these sexual reflexes during infancy may be part of the child's earliest sexual learning. The parent who is shocked or disapproving is apt to react in a manner that conveys discomfort, while parents who react calmly give children a message of acceptance regarding sex.

In the first months of life, parent–child bonding is an important way the child learns about intimacy.

As any observant parent knows, baby boys and girls begin to touch or rub their genitals as soon as they develop the necessary motor coordination. As we noted earlier, Kinsey and others reported that this sometimes leads to orgasm in infants less than one year old. The question is, what meaning does this behavior have? Is the infant simply exploring his or her body, with an equal likelihood that equally accessible parts (elbow, tummy, genitals) will be touched? Or is there a sexual component to such behavior, with a genuine sense of pleasure leading to repeated self-stimulation?

Although infants cannot answer these questions for us, the evidence seems to support the latter view. Helen Kaplan notes that babies "express joy when their genitals are stimulated" (1974, p. 147). Bakwin points out that "infants show extreme annoyance if efforts are made to interrupt them" during masturbation and adds that self-stimulation is done "many times during the day" (Bakwin, 1974, p. 204). By the third or fourth month of life, genital stimulation is accompanied by smiling and cooing (Martinson, 1980). By one year of age, genital play is commonly observed when the infant is naked or bathing. Genital play is more common in infants reared in families than in infants reared in nurseries (Spitz, 1949), suggesting that parent–child bonding plays a major role in the development of subsequent sexuality.

The parents of very young children react to these displays of sexual behavior in a variety of ways. Some are amused, some are surprised, and some are alarmed—particularly if they do not realize that this is a completely normal developmental pattern.

Sex in Early Childhood (Ages 2 to 5)

By age 2, most children have begun to walk and talk and have established a sense of being a boy or girl. There is unquestionable curiosity about body parts, and most children discover (if they have not already) that genital stimulation is a source of pleasurable sensations. Genital play first occurs as a solitary activity and later in games like "show me yours and I'll show you mine" and "doctor." In addition to rubbing the penis or clitoris manually, some children stimulate themselves by rubbing a doll, a pillow, a blanket, or some other object against their genitals.

Conversations with 3-year-old boys and girls indicate that they are well aware of the sensual feelings of genital stimulation, although these feelings are not labeled by them as erotic or sexual (concepts the child does not yet understand). The following comments from our files illustrate this point:

A 3-year-old girl: When I rub my 'gina it's nice and warm. Sometimes it tickles. Sometimes it gets real hot. [This child referred to her entire genital area as her "'gina" and was specifically describing manual rubbing of the mons and clitoris which she practiced at least a half-dozen times a day. From age 2½ to age 3½, she preferred to go bottomless so she could have easy access to her genitals and frequently took off her underpants to achieve this goal.]

A 3-year-old boy: Look at my wiener! I can make it stand up. I rub it and it stands up and it feels good. Sometimes I rub it a lot and it feels very, very good. [This boy was proud of his "wiener," which he liked to show to visitors. His parents told us that he stimulated his penis "several times a day" that they knew of and were pretty certain that he also pursued this activity in private.]

At about this same time, children also become aware of parental attitudes of disapproval of genital play and may be confused by parents who encourage them to be aware of their bodies but exclude the genitals from such awareness. While it is important for parents to educate their children about socially appropriate behavior (e.g., it is not acceptable to show or fondle your genitals in public places), some parents try to stop all forms of their child's sexual experimentation by saying, "That's not nice" or "Don't touch yourself down there," or by nonverbal communications such as pushing the child's hand away. The negative message that the child gets in such situations may be among the earliest causes of later sexual difficulties (Masters and Johnson, 1970; Calderone, 1978; Money, 1980). This attitude is compounded by many children's assumption that their genitals are "dirty" from messages received during toilet training. The emphasis on cleanliness in the bathroom ("wipe yourself carefully," "wash your hands after you go") conditions the child to see genital function in negative terms, even though it actually represents a legitimate health concern of parents.

Although it may run contrary to your instincts, most experts feel that the first thing parents should

do when they see their young child involved in sexual self-exploration is to simply relax (Feitel, 1990). As noted psychologist Selma Fraiberg (1959, p. 229) put it:

> How a child feels about himself, how he values himself, will also be tied up with his feelings about his own body. The child who discovers that his sex play arouses disgust in his parent may come to feel that his body is bad and that he, as a person, is bad.

Since children can sense a parent's negative reaction from voice tone, facial expression, or other body language, it is best for parents to react calmly when it comes to matters of sexual curiosity (Renshaw, 1988). This point applies not just to instances of discovering a child's sexual play, but to other situations with sexual connotations as well. For example, if a 3-year-old walks into the bathroom while a parent is just climbing out of the shower, overreacting by either harshly reprimanding the child ("Get out of here, can't you see I'm undressed!") or by grabbing for a towel as though covering up was a matter of life and death is inappropriate. This sort of reaction tells a child that a parent is uncomfortable about his or her body and is more likely than not to spur the child into repeating the intrusion.

Likewise, since young children commonly fondle themselves at times that are uncomfortable for parents, it's helpful for parents to be prepared in advance for such situations. For example, if you're in a department store when little Susie pulls up her dress and begins to rub her crotch, instead of telling her "No, don't do that," simply hand her a package to carry. Distracting a child from what is for you a socially awkward moment has the advantage of changing the behavior without making a big deal out of it or creating the impression that you're upset.

By age 4, most children in our society begin asking questions about how babies are made and how birth occurs (Martinson, 1980). Some parents respond with matter-of-fact answers, while others are obviously uncomfortable and reluctant to discuss this information at any length. Children have a pretty good idea of what bothers mommy or daddy, so they may react either by not asking such questions at all *or* by bombarding one or both parents with questions to see them squirm.

Four-year-olds generally have vague and somewhat magical notions about sex. They often believe the "stork brings the baby" explanation without any further questioning or, if given a more accurate explanation of reproductive facts, interpret them in unique ways. For example, 4-year-olds are quite literal in thinking that the mommy's egg from which a baby grows is just like the eggs bought by the dozen in the grocery store. Similarly, some 4-year-olds presented with a "daddy plants a seed in mommy's body" explanation of conception and pregnancy are convinced that there is a patch of dirt inside the mother's body that must be periodically watered and weeded for the baby to grow. This way of viewing sexual matters reflects the 4-year-old's concrete, literal view of the world in general.

Children who attend nursery school or day-care centers before reaching school age are apt to confront many situations with sexual overtones. For instance, Billy and Peter, each 4 years old, have to be told repeatedly that it's not appropriate to kiss each other while they're playing. In the same nursery class, Gerry amuses himself by sneaking up behind a girl and pulling up her skirt ("So I can see her underpants," he explains with a lot of giggling). Both girls and boys express considerable interest in bathroom functions and bathroom etiquette, and both sexes are very willing to try out new "dirty" words, a common practice that tends to alarm parents more than teachers.

◤ *Learning Theory and Sexual Development*

In contrast to the Freudian viewpoint, later theorists have developed the position that learning is the primary determinant of behavior. Learning occurs as a result of the interaction of a person with his or her environment.

The origins of modern learning theory may be traced back to the turn of the century when Ivan Pavlov (1849–1936), a Russian physiologist, elucidated the principles of classical conditioning. In studying the digestive responses of dogs, Pavlov found that a natural reflex (salivation in response to food) could be produced by an unrelated stimulus, such as a musical tone, if the sound repeatedly occurred just before the presentation of food. Once this pairing took place a number of times, the dog learned to associate the sound with the food, and the sound alone (the conditioned stimulus) would produce salivation (the conditioned response) even when the food was not present.

Pavlov's model of classical conditioning does not take us very far in understanding human sexual behavior. People may be "conditioned" in the Pavlovian sense to respond with sexual arousal when smelling a perfume or aftershave lotion their sex partner always wears or when a particular recording they usually play during sex. Such stimulus–response connections, however, are not powerful enough in most cases to override other influences on sexual behavior such as mood, needs, and circumstance. But learning theory was broadened considerably through the work of several American psychologists, including Edward Thorndike, John B. Watson, and B. F. Skinner, who showed the importance of positive or negative consequences in shaping later behavior. According to the principles of operant conditioning, behavior followed by a reward or pleasurable result, or the removal of an unpleasant stimulus, is likely to be repeated, while behavior followed by unpleasant consequences or the removal of rewarding stimuli is likely to become less frequent.

Positive reinforcement has an obvious and direct effect on sexual behavior. For example, children who find that rubbing their genitals produces pleasure are likely to engage in this behavior again and again. Punishment also influences sexual behavior. Consider, for example, a person who has pain during sexual intercourse. If this happens repeatedly, the person will learn that coitus leads to pain and will be

---

At age 5, when most children enter kindergarten, the opportunity to relate to age-mates in a structured environment leads to modesty, and sex games decrease in frequency (Martinson, 1980). Children of this age become fascinated with learning words about sexual parts that they have not heard before, and jokes about sex and genital function begin to make their rounds, often heard first from a slightly older child and then repeated. The 5-year-old may not understand the joke but laughs heartily (sometimes at the wrong line) to cover this up. As Money (1980) observes, when frank, direct information about sex is not available to a child, sexual jokes become the most important source of sex education for both girls and boys. Since even young children quickly learn the difference between a "clean" and "dirty" joke, this leads to the attitude that sex is dirty.

At this age children also begin to form ideas about sex based on their observations of physical interactions between parents: seeing mommy and daddy hugging and kissing, and obviously enjoying it, is a pretty good advertisement for the pleasures of physical and emotional intimacy. On the other hand, seeing parents constantly fighting or hearing one tell the other "don't touch me" can have just the opposite effect on the child's view of intimacy.

Sex and the School-Age Child

Six and 7-year-old children have usually acquired a clear understanding of basic anatomic differences between the sexes and typically show a strong sense of modesty about body exposure. Parental attitudes and practices regarding nudity in the home undoubtedly influence the child's self-conscious-

likely to avoid the behavior or engage in it less frequently. Punishment has been used in treating sex offenders such as child molesters. The treatment process, called aversion therapy, might involve showing a child molester pictures of children and, if he becomes sexually aroused, giving him an electric shock (Barlow, 1973). This treatment process is carried out over a series of sessions until the undesired response (sexual arousal to children) is eliminated.

Negative consequences are usually a less powerful influence on behavior than positive consequences. Punishment is not as likely to eliminate a behavior as it is apt to lead to secrecy and attempts to avoid punishment. This is particularly true when there is a conflict in a given situation between positive and negative consequences (an approach–avoidance conflict). The threat of punishment may actually heighten pleasure: the forbidden becomes more exciting so that the threat becomes part of the positive reinforcement.

Learning theory has been expanded into a still broader framework by Albert Bandura (b. 1925) in a model called social learning theory. Bandura believes that people model their so-

cial behavior according to their observations of others. What is learned depends in part on the prestige or power of the other person: a 5-year-old might imitate a 7-year-old brother or sister but not a younger one. People tend to identify with and imitate others they admire or respect. Television or movies can therefore be an important source of learned behavior or a source of learned attitudes, just as social learning also occurs from friends, teachers, and parents.

Social learning theory has many direct applications to psychosexual development. Children develop their sexual attitudes not only from what their parents say to them about sex but also from what attitudes they see expressed in their parents' behavior. Later attitudes or behaviors are strengthened or inhibited by observations of classmates, older friends, and nonfamily members. Watching a torrid seduction scene in a movie may provide a form of observational learning for a young, sexually inexperienced teenager who "learns" about how other people behave in such a situation. Social learning is also undoubtedly important to the development of gender identity and gender role.

ness, but at the same time the natural curiosity of childhood is likely to emerge in games like "hospital" or "playing house" that permit sexual exploration. These games may involve simply inspecting each other's genitals or may include touching, kissing, rubbing, or inserting objects into the rectum or vagina.

Sexual experimentation includes activities with children of the same sex and the opposite sex. One purpose of this behavior is seeking knowledge: "How different am I from others who are like me?" and "How different are members of the opposite sex from me?" Another purpose is testing the forbidden to see what happens: who finds out, how they react, what can I get away with, and so on. These two components are interrelated, since forbidden knowledge is usually more alluring than easily available knowledge.

Childhood participation in such games is probably nearly universal, although available studies (mainly based on recall data) give much lower estimates. For example, Kinsey found that about 45 percent of adult women recalled participating in some form of sex play by age 12, and 57 percent of adult males recalled similar experiences (Kinsey, Pomeroy, and Martin, 1948; Kinsey et al., 1953). More recently, 61 percent of a sample of college students reported having had some form of sexual experience with another child before age 13 (Greenwald and Leitenberg, 1989).

Childhood sex play is not psychologically harmful under ordinary circumstances and is probably a valuable psychosocial experience in developmental terms (Jensen, 1979; Money, 1980; Renshaw, 1988). However, psychological harm *can* come from harsh parental reaction. When children are discovered in sex play, ei-

RESEARCH SPOTLIGHT

Childhood Exposure to Nudity and Sleeping in the Parents' Bed

Many experts have offered opinions on the potential long-range effects of children seeing their parents nude and/or sleeping in bed with their parents, but until now these opinions have been based largely on assumptions, not facts. Recent research examining how these childhood experiences affect adult sexual adjustment sheds some much-needed light on this topic.

Lewis and Janda (1988) administered a questionnaire assessing recollections about childhood sexuality to 77 males and 133 females recruited from undergraduate psychology classes. The questionnaire obtained information about (1) the frequency of sleeping in bed with parents between 0 and 5 years and between 6 and 11 years; (2) the frequency of seeing parents, as well as others, naked between ages 0 and 5 years and between 6 and 11 years; (3) parental attitudes toward sexuality; (4) the subject's comfort level in talking about sexuality with parents; and (5) perceptions of parental discomfort regarding sexuality. Subjects also were asked about their current sexual adjustment and behavior.

There was no indication that childhood exposure to parental nudity led to any later sexual problems. Males who were exposed as young children to parental nudity were more comfortable about physical contact and affection as young adults. Exposure to parental nudity during ages 6 to 11 was positively related only to a tendency to engage in casual sexual relationships.

Females exposed to parental nudity as young children showed an increased frequency of sex compared to others, but no evidence of sexual difficulties of any sort. As with the males, exposure to parental nudity during ages 6 to 11 correlated only with a tendency to have casual sex, but the significance of this finding was uncertain.

Males who had slept in bed with their parents when they were 5 years old or younger had higher levels of self-esteem, more frequent sex, and a greater tendency to have casual sexual relationships than other males. Females who had slept in bed with their parents at a young age showed less discomfort about physical contact and affection than other females. There was no indication of any negative long-term impact from a child's sleeping in bed with his or her parents, suggesting that people who say that this practice may cause problems because it sexually stimulates the child are unnecessarily alarmist.

While the Lewis and Janda study cannot be considered the final word, especially since findings from a sample of college students may not apply to the broader population, it has opened the door for future systematic research in the area of childhood sexuality that until now has been neglected.

---

ther solitary or with others, negative parental reaction may be difficult to understand but easy to perceive. From the child's viewpoint, play is play, but for the parent who discovers a child masturbating or engaging in sex play with others, SEX in capital letters flashes across the scene. The parent who reacts with ominous predictions or threats that continuing such "bad" behavior will lead to dire consequences is frightening the child. The parent who says "that's dirty" may be interpreted very literally by the child, sowing the seeds of an attitude that may persist into adulthood.

Parental reactions to the discovery of sex play in school-age children frequently operate on a double standard. Girls are often cautioned strongly against sexual play, especially with boys. Boys, on the other hand, tend to get mixed messages from their parents; they may be warned or even punished for such activity, but there is a hint of resignation or even pride in the attitude that "boys will be boys." One father described the sexual escapades of his 7-year-old son and a female classmate by saying, "Good for him, he's getting an early start." The unspoken permission for boys to follow their sexual curiosity (except in homosexual situations, where parents consistently react in a negative way) is only rarely found directed to school-age girls in American society. With the arrival of puberty, parents seem to react with even more of a double standard toward the sexual behavior of their sons and daughters.

Freud's concept of a period of sexual latency during late childhood—a time when sexual interests and impulses are diverted into nonsexual behaviors and interests—is no longer accepted by many sexologists. Money (1980) says that this is a time of sexual prudery when participation in sex play simply goes underground. Cross-cultural studies clearly show that if a society is not repressive toward childhood sex rehearsals, such play continues and may even be more frequent during the preadolescent years (Ford and Beach, 1951; Marshall and Suggs, 1971; Currier, 1981). Kinsey's data also show that sexual experimentation does not stop or even slow down during this period (Kinsey, Pomeroy, and Martin, 1948; Kinsey et al., 1953). A detailed study of childhood sexuality involving interviews with over 800 children aged 5 and over in Australia, North America, Britain, and Sweden also provides no indication of a phase of childhood development where sexual development is suspended (Goldman and Goldman, 1982). In fact, these researchers note: "Discrediting Freud's latency period theory, overwhelming evidence was produced which reveals children from age five to fifteen to be increasingly interested in exploring sexual topics in linear progression with age" (Goldman and Goldman, 1982a, p. 7). Perhaps the available evidence is best summed up in the following passage:

> Children pursue the course of their psychosexual development in blithe disregard of an expected sexual latency. Their only nod in the direction of the theoretical expectations is that they have learned to play according to adult rules. They learn to fulfill the letter of the law, even as they proceed secretly in their own ways. (*Gadpaille, 1975, p. 189*)

The sexual experiences of older children may be infrequent and less important than other events in their lives but may include the entire range of possible sexual acts, including attempts at intercourse that are sometimes successful. Masturbation occurs in private as well as in heterosexual or homosexual pairs or groups; sexual play with animals and objects has been noted; and oral or anal sex has been reported (Gadpaille, 1975; Martinson, 1976, 1980, 1981). By age 8 or 9, there is little question that children have awareness of the erotic element of such activities, and it is no longer accurate to think of these as "play" only. Sexual arousal is more than a by-product of these deliberate activities and is willfully sought, not just an accidental happening. Erotic arousal may be accompanied by sexual fantasies, and in some instances falling in love occurs (Gadpaille, 1975; Tennov, 1979; Money, 1980). These encounters can help children learn how to relate to others, with important consequences for their adult psychosexual adjustment (Broderick, 1968; Gadpaille, 1975; Martinson, 1976; Money, 1980).

Many parents are unaware that homosexual play among children, as well as heterosexual play, is a normal part of growing up. Homosexual play does *not* usually lead to adult homosexuality, although many parents worry unnecessarily on this point.

CALVIN & HOBBES   by Bill Watterson

Sibling Sex

Another common form of childhood sexual behavior is sexual contact between siblings. While technically such behavior may be called **incest**—sexual activity between relatives—it seems unnecessarily pejorative to label the "look–see" games of a 5-year-old boy and his 6-year-old sister in so heavy-handed a fashion. Nevertheless, it can be difficult to decide when factors such as age differences between siblings, aggressive components of the sexual behavior, or exploitive or coercive elements should lead sexual contacts between siblings to be viewed as innocent play, a form of childhood learning, or a matter for parental action.

One report provides some interesting information on this topic. Greenwald and Leitenberg (1989) found that 17 percent of a sample of 526 college students reported having a sexual experience with a sibling during childhood before age 13. The average age of such sexual contact was 8 years, and parents were aware of it only 18 percent of the time. Greenwald and Leitenberg found no evidence that preadolescent childhood sexual encounters between siblings had a harmful impact on later sexual adjustment even among the group where some genital contact—as opposed to just looking—had occurred. In addition, they found a very low rate of coercion involved in sibling sex: only 2 percent of the incidents involved force, and only 6 percent involved any form of threat.

Somewhat different findings emerged from an earlier set of studies on sex between siblings (Finkelhor, 1980, 1981), which provides the most detailed nonclinical sample available. In brief, he found that 13 percent of college students surveyed admitted to childhood sexual activity with a brother or sister (a figure he considered an underestimate). Approximately three-quarters of these relationships were heterosexual (brother–sister), while one-quarter were homosexual (brother–brother or sister–sister). Additional findings from this survey included the following.

1. Sexual contact between siblings was not restricted to young children only; 73 percent of the experiences reported occurred when at least one sibling was over age 8.

2. The most common type of sexual activity between siblings was genital touching; only 4 percent included intercourse. Among younger children, looking at one another's genitals was the primary form of sex play.

3. There was considerable variability in the duration of these activities. One-third were single occurrences, while 27 percent continued off and on for at least one year.

4. In one-quarter of the experiences, some type of force was involved (with girls being victimized most often).

5. Almost one-quarter of the experiences involved siblings who were at least five years apart in age.

These findings suggest that it may be necessary for sexologists to rethink previous notions about sexual contact between siblings as an innocent form of play. A situation where one sibling is much older than the other (by four years or more) or where force is used (which may be much more common than previously realized) is almost invariably exploitive and thus is cause for concern. However, parents must use their judgment in dealing with such situations. One episode of genital touching between an 11-year-old girl and her consenting 7-year-old brother is not the same as a pattern of forced sex between siblings. Furthermore, it is important to realize that parental displays of alarm and horror on learning of their children's incestuous activities are not only inappropriate but may sometimes be harmful to the children. Finally, if an exploitive incest situation is discovered, obtaining psychological counseling for the victim may be advisable.

Since there is now considerable evidence that incest victimization often has negative long-term psychological consequences, including sexual problems in adulthood, parents may want to consider ways to minimize the risk of such an occurrence. For example, it may be helpful to discourage siblings who are more than two years apart from bathing together, and it is also advisable to avoid having an older sibling share a bedroom with a much younger one. A more detailed discussion of incest, including information about parent–child incest, appears in Chapter 18.

As long as aggressive or coercive behavior is not involved, it is unlikely that isolated instances of childhood sexual activity are abnormal. It is not very helpful for parents to react to the discovery of childhood sex play with alarm or punishment. A matter-of-fact approach that includes understanding and age-appropriate sex education (while maintaining the parents' right to set limits) is likely to be more effective than threats and theatrics in helping the child undergo healthy psychosexual growth.

SEX EDUCATION

In the last decade, there has been an unusual amount of controversy on the topic of sex education. While almost everyone seems to agree that teaching children about sex is necessary, there is much disagreement about what should be taught, *where* it should be taught, and who should do the teaching.

In the middle of this confusion, a point many people seem to miss is this (Ehrenberg and Ehrenberg, 1988, p. 28):

> Although we may not like it, children are born as sexual beings, and parents, whether or not they are aware of it, are constantly providing lessons in sex education. The way parents respond to a child's innate sexuality and allow it to unfold is the core of a child's sex education. *This response does more to mold that child's mature sexual behavior than all the information or misinformation parents may provide.*

Ehrenberg and Ehrenberg (1988) have also described four basic ways in which parents relate to sexuality in their home, which they call Sex Repressive, Sex Avoidant, Sex Obsessive, and Sex Expressive. (Generally, according to the Ehrenbergs, the sexual attitudes of spouses coincide, but this is not always the case.)

- *Sex Repressive* parents send a strong message to their children that sex is evil and dirty. They typically forbid dirty words, dirty jokes, and nudity, and often rear children in line with traditional gender-role stereotypes. Their efforts at sex education can be summed up in two phrases: "it's dangerous" and "wait until you're married."

- *Sex Avoidant* parents are more tolerant intellectually of the notion that sexuality is healthy, rather than evil, but their intellectual viewpoint is counterbalanced by an embarrassed inapproachability when it comes to the subject of sex. Although they are not negative about sex, they tend to avoid direct discussions about sex or turn such discussions into lectures. By stressing the "here's how the plumbing works" approach, they inadvertently leave out the warm, human, loving side of sexuality, an omission their children quickly recognize, but that they never seem to see.

- *Sex Obsessive* parents see sex as something healthy and good but go beyond this in making sex a focal point of family life. They are ultra-liberal in their attitudes toward sex, sometimes pushing their own sex lives onto center stage in a way that can be embarrassing or overwhelming to their children. (For example, they may talk openly about their affairs or their collection of X-rated videos.) Children often feel that sex obsessive parents are intrusive and may feel pressured by all the attention given to sex—for instance, when Dad makes it a point to show 8-year-old Johnny his *Playboy* magazine each month, Johnny may feel more uncomfortable than enlightened.

- *Sex Expressive* parents manage to integrate sex into their family life in a balanced way. They approach sex matter-of-factly, dealing with sexual topics openly whenever appropriate, but setting reasonable limits on sexual behavior for their children—just as they set rules for all behavior. They present sex as healthy and positive, but not something that you've got to rush into just because it's there.

A number of studies indicate that only a minority of parents provide meaningful quantities of sex education for their children. American teenagers, for example, report that they learned most of what they know about sex from their friends, not their parents (Gebhard, 1977; Kirby, Alter, and Scales, 1979; Kallen, Stephenson, and Doughty, 1983). Until relatively recently, this problem seemed to polarize communities into two groups: those who favored sex education in schools to prevent lack of knowledge and those who insisted that sex education in the schools was unnecessary and unwise. Opponents of sex education in the schools argued that (1) exposing children to information about sex would liven their sexual curiosity and draw them prematurely into sexual behavior; (2) teaching about sex is so closely linked to moral and religious values that it should be done at home or in a religious setting; and (3) the quality of materials and teaching in public school sex education was uneven at best and quite poor in many cases.

Today, although opposition to sex education in the schools continues, its tone is somewhat muted. Seventy-seven percent of American adults believe sex education should be taught in schools, and

incest sexual activity between close relatives.

Practical Pointers on Educating Your Children About Sex

Despite the fact that some parents are vigorously opposed to sex education for children, parents don't really have a choice about whether their children get sex information: they can only choose whether or not to participate in the sex education that is already taking place. Realizing this, and wanting to do a good job in providing sex education at home, many parents approach this task with great trepidation, being at once unsure of how to begin, uncertain of what to say, and worried that they'll frighten a child with inappropriate detail.

The truth of the matter is that teaching children about sex need not be different from teaching them about lots of other things; you don't need to have a Ph.D. in agriculture to teach children about gardening, for example. And just as you wouldn't wait for a child to ask you about the alphabet before exploring the ABCs, don't wait to talk about sex, either: take the initiative in talking about this topic.

Here are some straightforward suggestions for parents to keep in mind when it comes to sex education:

1. When you discuss sex with your child, try to do it in a matter-of-fact manner, the way you'd talk about anything else.

2. Avoid lecturing about sex. While it may relieve your anxiety to cover the whole topic in a 15-minute talk, young children don't usually have a long enough attention span for this approach and also need to ask questions about what they're learning.

3. Be sure that your discussions include more than just biological facts. Children need to learn about values, emotions, and decision making, too.

4. Don't worry about telling a child "too much" about sex. Children will almost always tune out what they don't understand; in most cases, it will go over their heads.

5. When your child uses four-letter words, calmly explain their meaning and then explain why you don't want him or her to use those words. For example, you might say, "Other people get upset if they hear those words" or "I don't think that's a very good way of explaining how you feel." Remember that laughing or joking about your child's four-letter words will usually encourage repeat performances.

6. Try to use correct terminology for sexual body parts instead of using terms like "pee pee" for penis or "bottom" for vagina.

7. Even preschool-age children should know how to protect themselves from sexual abuse. This means that you need to let them

when courses are given, fewer than 5 percent of parents ban their children from attending (Kirby, Alter, and Scales, 1979; Alan Guttmacher Institute, 1981; Gordon and Gordon, 1983). An increasing number of school systems have some form of sex education (often called "Family Life Education") offered in the curriculum, and 23 states as well as the District of Columbia now require it (de Mauro, 1989/1990). In 1986, when U.S. Surgeon General C. Everett Koop called for sex education in public schools at an early age to warn children about AIDS, it was a particularly compelling argument for why sex education does belong in the classroom.

Despite these signs of progress, there are still a number of problems with sex education today. Certainly one of the most pressing dilemmas is that relatively few American fathers play an active role in providing their children with age-appropriate sex information. Another aspect that requires attention is the fact that sex education, beyond the most rudimentary "birds and bees" facts of anatomy and reproduction, is often ignored by parents and schools alike until a child reaches adolescence. Since children are exposed to a great deal of information about sex at an earlier age—through television shows, movies, books, and a host of other

know that it's okay to say no to an adult. Here's a good example of how this might be discussed with a 4- or 5-year-old:

You know, there are big people out there who have a hard time making friends with other big people. So sometimes they make friends with kids. And that's OK, but sometimes they ask kids to do things big people shouldn't ask kids to do. Like they ask them to put their hands down their pants, or to touch each other sexually. I love you a lot, and if anyone ever asks you to do that, or asks you to do something you think is funny and asks you to keep it a secret, I want you to say "No" and come tell me right away. (Sanford, 1982, p. 13)

8. Don't wait until your child hits the teenage years before discussing puberty. Physical changes like breast development, menstruation, and wet dreams commonly occur before age 10.

9. Be sure to discuss menstruation with boys as well as girls, and be sure that girls understand what an erection is. Also, don't leave topics like homosexuality and prostitution out of your discussions. Most children see and hear these subjects mentioned on television and read about them and have a natural curiosity about what they are.

10. Be direct in bringing up the topic of AIDS (as well as other sexually transmitted diseases). But try to do this in a way that is sensitive to how a child will react. After all, there's little sense in frightening a 5- or 6-year-old by telling him or her that AIDS is always fatal. On the other hand, ignoring this issue until your child reaches adolescence is not doing the child a favor. Even school-age children need to learn about what AIDS is and how it is transmitted.

11. Help your child feel comfortable in coming to ask you questions about sex. Don't embarrass a child or tell him or her "you're too young to understand that now." If a child is old enough to ask questions, he or she needs to understand it at some level.

12. If you don't know the answer to a question your child has asked, don't be afraid to say so. Then either look it up or call on someone, such as your family doctor, who can help you with the necessary facts.

13. After you've tried to answer your child's question, check to see if your answer is understood. Also see if you've told him or her what he or she really wanted to know and give a chance to ask more questions that may arise from the answer you've provided.

sources—parents run the risk of allowing children to interpret what they see as accurate depictions of what sex is all about, which may have unfortunate consequences. Put another way, this is education by default.

Another particularly disturbing problem is that, with all the attention given to sexual abuse of children and the AIDS epidemic in the last few years, young, impressionable children may get the idea that sex is dangerous and bad—an attitude that they may retain as they grow up, with unknown psychological consequences. Thus, it is particularly important for those who plan school curricula to

do so in a sensitive, balanced manner and for persons teaching sex education courses to not make it seem like sex is primarily a matter of illness and abuse. Sex education should cover the problems surrounding sexuality, but it should also discuss such aspects of sex as love, intimacy, and interpersonal responsibility.

Even when schools provide reasonably comprehensive sex education courses, it is important for parents to play an active role in providing sex education at home. This shared responsibility allows parents to convey their personal values about sexuality to their children, as well as facts,

Talking with Your Children About AIDS

Deciding what to tell children about AIDS and how to tailor your discussion to different ages presents most parents with a daunting task. The following advice is from a booklet published by SIECUS (Sex Information and Education Council of the U.S.), one of the most respected authorities on sex education in the country.

Talking with Preschool Children (3–4 Years)

Children at this age are learning about their bodies and the basic facts of life. They learn about the world through play. They begin to ask questions about where babies come from and they can understand simple answers. They do not understand abstract ideas or adult sexual behaviors. They can learn simple things to do to be healthy, such as bathing, brushing their teeth, eating good foods, and napping. They can begin to accept the need for privacy. The best thing a parent can do at this age is to create an atmosphere in which children will feel free to ask questions about their bodies, health, and sexuality. Children then will learn that sex is one of the things that can be talked about in their home.

Talking with Young Children (5–8 Years)

Children at this age are able to understand more complex issues about health, disease, and sexuality. They are interested in birth, marriage, and death. They have probably heard about AIDS from TV, their friends, or adults. They may have questions or fears about AIDS. They need to know that they do not have to worry that either you or they will get AIDS. They need to know that people do not get AIDS from being bad. Children can understand basic answers to their questions based on concrete examples

their lives. For example, if your child cuts his/her finger and blood appears, this is a good time to explain how germs (things that make you sick) can get into the blood system from cuts in the body. They can understand that they should never take drugs or medicine without your approval. If they are in school with a child infected with HIV, they need to know that they cannot get AIDS from playing, studying, or talking with that child.

Talking with Preteens (9–12 Years)

Children at this age are going through all the changes of puberty. They are concerned about their bodies, their looks, and what is normal. For some preteens, this time marks the start of dating, early sexual experience, and trying drugs. Because of the strong social pressures which begin at this age, it is important that you talk about AIDS, regardless of what you know about your children's sexual or drug experiences. As a concerned parent, you must make sure your children know about prevention NOW. During the changes of puberty, preteens are very curious about sex and need to be given basic, accurate information. They need to know what is meant by sexual intercourse, homosexuality, and oral and anal sex. Preteens need to be told that sex can have consequences, including pregnancy and HIV infection. They should be told why sexual intercourse is not healthy for children, and why it is a good idea to wait to have sex. They need to know how HIV is transmitted, how it is not transmitted, and how to prevent transmission, including talking about condoms. This may seem like a difficult task, but it will give you a chance to teach your children the values that you hope they will adopt in their lives. It is also time to let your children know that they can come to you with their questions about AIDS or sex.

and improves the odds of their children growing into sexually responsible teenagers and adults. Practical pointers to assist in this task are provided in the boxed item on pages 222–223. A particularly important aspect of the entire process is that parents should strive to be "askable"—able to talk to their children comfortably about sex—instead of trying to deliver lectures on the subject.

We believe that waiting until a child's teenage years to provide him or her with sex education is waiting too long. Educating *all* children in an age-appropriate fashion about sexuality will ultimately help them make informed, responsible sexual choices in their lives and play an important role in the long-term prevention of sexual problems.

SUMMARY

1. Sexual development begins before birth and continues throughout the life cycle. Sex chromosomes (XY = male, XX = female) provide the initial programming for sex differentiation.

2. Growth of the testes begins at about the sixth week after conception. The testes then produce testosterone (stimulating growth of the Wolffian ducts) and Müllerian duct inhibiting substance, which causes the structures that would develop into a female reproductive system to shrink. *For male sexual differentiation to occur, both the testis determining factor and testosterone must be present in adequate amounts at the right time of development.*

3. Female sexual differentiation does not require hormone stimulation. The ovaries develop at the twelfth week of pregnancy, and the Müllerian duct system gives rise to the uterus, Fallopian tubes, and inner third of the vagina.

4. Prenatal sex differentiation in both sexes involves the genitals, the internal reproductive structures, and the brain itself.

5. Disorders of prenatal sex development include sex chromosome problems (47,XXY = Klinefelter's syndrome; 45,X = Turner's syndrome), conditions of male or female pseudo-hermaphroditism (such as adrenogenital syndrome and the syndrome of testicular feminization), and problems caused by hormones given to a pregnant woman.

6. In infancy and childhood, the sexual reflexes for males and females are all present except for the ability of the male to ejaculate. Sex hormone levels are low.

7. Gender identity is usually shaped by an interaction between biological and psychosocial forces in the first few years of life.

8. Erections occur in the later months of fetal development. Together with data showing that newborn babies of both sexes show signs of sexual responsivity, this indicates the innate naturalness of sexuality from the very beginning of life. It is also common to see young babies rubbing or stroking their genitals and responding to such self-stimulation with coos and smiles of pleasure.

9. Children typically show considerable curiosity about sexual matters and are likely to engage in sexual games with others at one time or another. (These activities may include same-sex contacts or sexual contacts between siblings.) Although some parents are upset by such behavior, it is unlikely to be harmful as long as it is not exploitive.

10. Many sexologists have rejected Freud's notion of a period of sexual latency during late childhood, particularly in light of cross-cultural studies showing that, in some societies, childhood sexual play increases in frequency during the preadolescent years.

11. While most parents think of sex education in terms of lectures about the "birds and bees," sex education is actually an ongoing process that depends as much on the models parents provide for their children and how they respond to the growing child's unfolding sexuality as it does on the provision of factual information. Sex education taught at home is an important way for parents to provide a valid framework to their children that will hopefully carry over into responsible adolescent sexual behavior.

Thought Questions

1. The parents of the identical twin boys decided on the best advice available to reassign the damaged twin to be a girl. They decided it would be better to raise the child as a girl who would need surgeries, hormones, and be unable to have children, rather than as a boy without a penis. Setting aside the outcome in this particular case, do you agree with the val-

ues expressed by this decision? Why or why not? What problems would the child and the parents have had if the twin without a penis had been raised as a boy?

2. The trend in our society has been to reduce the stigma associated with birth defects and to accept with sympathy rather than horror that some babies are born with defects that may or may not be correctable. However, if the defects involve the sex organs, people seem still to regard such errors as embarrassing and shameful. Do you agree that this is true, and, if so, can you explain why?

3. Children who are born with the "Dominican Republic syndrome" are reported to change their gender identity from female to male when the penis grows at puberty. Why might this be so, when, in general, other pseudo-hermaphrodites are reported to maintain the gender identity of their sex of rearing, regardless of bodily changes at puberty?

4. How should parents respond when they become aware that their children are playing doctor or engaging in sexual activities with their playmates? What if the playmates are siblings? Does that make a difference in how parents should respond?

5. Eric Berne, who developed Transactional Analysis, made this statement about toilet training: "The demon in the bathroom becomes the demon in the bedroom." What did he mean? What mistakes do parents make during toilet training their children, and how can they be avoided?

6. The text reports that babies experience sexual pleasure and apparently may even masturbate to orgasm. What do you suppose this signifies? How should parents respond if their baby shows extreme annoyance if efforts are made to interrupt his or her masturbation or if such self-stimulation is done many times during the day?

7. Is it possible to tell children too much about sex when they ask questions? Should all questions be answered, or are there some things that children should not be told until they are older?

Suggested Readings

Calderone, Mary S., and Johnson, Eric. *The Family Book About Sexuality* 2nd ed. New York: Harper & Row, 1989. A comprehensive book about sexuality that can make the task of sex education at home considerably easier.

Constantine, Larry, and Martinson, Floyd, (eds.). *Children and Sex: New Findings, New Perspectives.* Boston: Little, Brown, 1981. A multidisciplinary collection of essays and research reports on childhood that is uneven in its coverage in spots, often highly opinionated, and controversial. Nevertheless, it is highly informative reading that is generally presented without too much technical jargon.

Ehrenberg, Miriam, and Ehrenberg, Otto. *The Intimate Circle: The Sexual Dynamics of Family Life.* New York: Simon & Shuster, 1988. A thorough discussion of the sexual dynamics of family life, including useful information on styles of sex education and children's sexual development.

Goldman, Ronald, and Goldman, Juliette. *Children's Sexual Thinking.* Boston: Routledge and Kegan Paul, 1982. An impressive study of the sexual thinking of over 800 children in four different countries, based on direct interviews. Although parts of the book are sometimes dry and bogged down in statistical detail, the conclusions are quite fascinating.

Gordon, Sol, and Gordon, Judith. *Raising a Child Conservatively in a Sexually Permissive World*, rev. ed. New York: Simon & Shuster, 1989. The title conveys the contents accurately. Written in understandable, jargon-free language by two of the nation's preeminent sex educators, the book is replete with useful advice, from how to be an "askable" parent to the questions children ask most often about sex.

Money, John. *Lovemaps.* New York: Irvington Press, 1986. A wealth of new theories on the origins and dynamics of sexual development. Money's prose is often turgid and technical, but as one of the world's leading sexologists, his command of clinical material in combination with his original thinking makes this an important book.

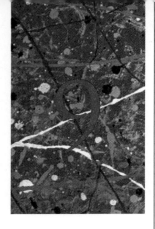

Adolescent Sexuality

Adolescence, the period from ages 12 to 19, is a time of rapid change and difficult challenge. Physical changes are only one part of this process; adolescents face a wide variety of psychosocial demands as well: becoming independent from parents, developing skills in interacting well with their peers, devising a workable set of ethical principles, becoming intellectually competent, and acquiring a sense of social and personal responsibility, to name just a few. At the same time this complex set of developmental challenges is being met, the adolescent must also cope with his or her sexuality by learning how to deal with changing sexual feelings, deciding whether to participate in various types of sexual activity, discovering how to recognize love, and learning how to prevent unwanted pregnancy. It is no wonder that the adolescent sometimes feels conflict, pain, and confusion.

On the other hand, adolescence is also a time of discovery and awakening, a time when intellectual and emotional maturation combine with physical development to create increasing freedom and excitement. Adolescence is not simply a period of turmoil, as older theory states, but is just as likely to be a time of pleasure and happiness as a turbulent, troubled passage to adulthood (Offer and Offer, 1975). The paradoxical nature of adolescence is particularly visible in the sexual sphere.

OVERVIEW

When we think about adolescent sexuality, the image that comes to mind is neatly captured in this dialogue:

FATHER: "I think it's time we had a talk about sex."
SON: "Sure, Dad. What do you want to know?"

The message is, however, a little out of touch with reality: teens don't really know everything there is to know about sex, even though many of them act as if they do. In addition to possessing incomplete, inaccurate, or misinterpreted information about sex, many adolescents also lack personal comfort with sexual matters. Fourteen year olds are apt to worry about the "right" way to French kiss, or how to deal with a date's unbridled physical passion; 16-year-olds may be uncertain about how to "do" oral sex; almost all teens are concerned with the question, "Is my sex life normal?" The teenager's outward posture of sexual sophistication often hides an underlying sense of personal anxiety and confusion.

As adolescents grapple with their developing sexuality, a number of distinct themes come into play. These include:

1. The links between pubertal development, body image, and self-image.

2. The task of learning about one's body and its sensual and sexual responses and needs.

3. Forging an identity, which includes dealing with issues of socially dictated gender role expectations and developing comfort with and certainty about one's sexual orientation.

4. Learning about sexual and romantic relationships, including learning about sexual negotiation, intimacy, and commitment.

5. Developing a personal sexual value system.

As we discuss each of these themes, keep in mind that all adolescents are not alike. Observations about the sexuality of 13-year-olds will not apply precisely to 17- or 18-year-olds. And not all 13-year-olds are alike: just as some are more physically mature than others, there also is considerable variation in their emotional maturity. In addition, teenagers in different communities (or even in different neighborhoods within the same community) are often subjected to strikingly different cultural values, peer group pressures, and social expectations, which combine with other variables—including socioeconomic and religious factors and gender role models—that shape the emergence and expression of their developing sexuality.

1. The Links Between Pubertal Development, Body Image, and Self-Image.

Teenagers are especially concerned with personal attractiveness, which is very closely linked to the way they see their own bodies—their body image. For better or for worse, we live in a society that often measures personal worth in terms of personal attractiveness, and, influenced by movies and television, teens grasp this basic fact very quickly.

Whether you are male or female, if you think back to your early and middle teenage years you will probably recall many times when you stood in front of a mirror inspecting your face for pimples, checking out your body's physique from different angles, or worrying about your height, weight, or body shape. It's a sad but true fact that, for most of us, concerns about our physical attractiveness— Am I too short? Too fat? Too gawky? Too plain-looking?—have a lot to do with how we feel about ourselves.

For teenagers, these concerns seem to be magnified out of proportion to reality. The 15-year-old teenage boy who hasn't yet started his adolescent growth spurt, and so is 6 inches shorter than the average girl in his class, or the 14-year-old girl who is 5'3" and 160 pounds are both likely to feel personally inadequate as well as selfconscious. The teenager's concern about physical appearance is usually of more importance to them than it is to other people. As Siegel (1982, p. 538) observes:

> Virtually any and all physical characteristics receive extraordinary attention and examination during this phase. This is a time when being different is to be avoided at almost any cost and when undesirable physical characteristics put the adolescent at risk for teasing, ridicule, or exclusion.

One reason for this central focus on body image is that the teenager hasn't yet identified a clear sense of his or her own identity as a person, so that, to the teenager, "what I look like" and "how others see me" equate very strongly with "who I am." Another reason is that most younger adolescents haven't yet developed a broad enough sense of self-esteem, based on their accomplishments, personal characteristics, and relationships with others, to counterbalance their perceptions of their unattractiveness.

The adolescent's concern with body image is made even more complex by the fact that his or her body is going through an odyssey of its own, changing size, shape, and other characteristics almost inexplicably as part of the process of puberty. Teenage girls are acutely aware of their breast development not only in personal terms but in comparative terms too: how do they stack up next to other girls in their grade or in their group of friends? (Teenage boys also notice—and sometimes rate—the girls' breast development; partly for this reason, being too well-endowed can be just as embarrassing as being underdeveloped.) Teenage boys are less subject to sexual scrutiny on the basis of appearance, because their primary sex development is less visible; but their physical masculinity is rated by themselves and by others in terms of height, muscularity, the appearance of facial hair growth, and the development of lower-pitched voice. Slow-to-mature teenage boys are all too familiar with the terrors of the boys' locker room, where they must undress—and display themselves—in front of other boys, who make fun of them for not yet having pubic hair or not having adequately developed genitals. Concerns like these lessen over time for most people as psychological maturation and physical development progress, but in the first half of adolescence these matters are understandably of central importance (Simmons and Rosenberg, 1975). And since there is a positive relationship between physical attractiveness and social acceptance during adolescence (Kleck, Richardson, and Ronald, 1974; Daniel, 1982; Chernin, 1985), the concern with body image has some logic.

2. The Task of Learning about One's Body and Its Sensual and Sexual Responses and Needs.

In addition to focusing on outward appearance, teenagers also have to learn about their own bodies. This is not as easy as it seems because there are many aspects of puberty which no one bothers to discuss with them and this lack of information creates predictable sources of anxiety. For example, most adolescent girls don't realize that the increased levels of circulating estrogen in their bodies typically produce a perfectly normal vaginal discharge and they often feel embarrassed or worried when they notice their panties stained by the dis-

charge. Boys may react similarly to their first wet dreams if no one has explained that these are perfectly normal body responses. And the frequent occurrence of sudden erections at exactly the most inopportune moments—going to the blackboard to do an algebra problem, skinny-dipping with a bunch of guys, or even during the sermon at church—also creates an almost universal experience of confusion, embarrassment, and anxieties about normality for teenage boys. Here's how one college student described his most embarrassing moment:

> I made the varsity swim team in my freshman year, which was a great accomplishment. The whole team wore these specially tight-fitting, low-cut racing trunks to cut down our resistance in the water. The only problem was, when I had to get up on the victory stand to receive my medal at the state meet, I got a gigantic boner. While I stood there at attention as the school victory song was being played, my crotch bulged out of my swimming trunks like there was an oversized cucumber inside. (Authors' files)

One of the primary ways adolescents learn about their bodies is by physical inspection and exploration. Many young teenagers spend hours examining the intricacies of their genitals, sometimes aided by a hand-held mirror, sometimes (for boys especially) with the aid of a tape measure or ruler to check on exact dimensions. Young teenage girls are apt to inspect their breasts in great detail, worrying about size discrepancies between the two breasts, the presence or absence of hair around the areola, the prominence of their nipples, and the shape and size of these organs. Physical inspection typically extends to physical exploration, with teenagers of both sexes experimenting with how various types of touch feel and what sorts of responses they produce. As one 18-year-old girl put it:

> When I was 13 or 14, I would see what it felt like to put baby oil or hand lotion on my genitals, rubbing or stroking the surface with my hand or with various other objects, like a feather or a fuzzy stuffed animal. I didn't think of this as masturbation, and I wasn't trying to have an orgasm. I'm not even sure I knew what an orgasm was, back then. But I remember playing with my nipples, touching them real lightly one minute, pinching them, dripping warm water on my

For Better or For Worse®   **by Lynn Johnston**

breasts, sometimes touching my clitoris at the same time I rubbed a nipple. It was like I was trying to find the right recipe—only I didn't know the recipe for what. (*Authors' files*)

This type of learning eventually leads to more deliberate attempts at producing sexual arousal. Teenagers want to discover just how aroused they can become how quickly, how to integrate fantasy with their physical response, how long they can stay aroused, how quickly they can regain their arousal after letting it flag, what orgasm feels like, and what it feels like to be aroused but not have orgasm. These are partly a form of rehearsal for later interpersonal sex and partly a form of self-discovery and becoming comfortable with one's own body and its responses. In general, since we are comfortable with things that are familiar to us, repeated explorations lead to more familiarity and more comfort.

The process of learning about one's body is not the same for all teenagers, but there are probably few teenage boys who haven't, at one time or another, tried to put on a condom while they were in the privacy of their own room—just to "see what it's like." Similarly, the majority of teenage girls have probably tried to insert an object into their vagina to see what it felt like. Curiosity and a desire to "act grown up" are both normal components of early adolescence.

Learning about one's body doesn't only occur when teenagers are by themselves: it also occurs with touching or being touched, kissing or being kissed, undressing or seeing someone else undressed. Early adolescents, for example, usually don't plunge abruptly into sex but instead spend a lot of time holding hands, snuggling together (with

the boy's arm around the girl's shoulder, slowly—perhaps over weeks—and casually dipping down toward its first "accidental" brush against the girl's breast). Later in adolescence, the ground rules may have changed considerably: for some 17- or 18-year-olds, oral sex on the first date is a distinct possibility.

3. Forging an Identity.

Noted psychologist Erik Erikson (1968, 1985) believed that the search for identity and the conquest of identity confusion are the central developmental issues of adolescence. This search is made more difficult for the teenager by a number of potential roadblocks, including rigid gender role expectations (cultural stereotypes about the appropriate traits and behaviors of males and females) and the related issue of sexual orientation. Adolescents who have no trouble fitting the "quarterback/cheerleader" expectations, in which males are supposed to be athletically inclined, emotionally controlled, and willing to take physical risks, while females are supposed to be attractive, bubbly, and supportive, usually have an easier time of it than those who don't fit these stereotypically defined roles. A teenage boy who is more interested in ballet than in baseball, or a girl who is a talented shotputter, may be unfairly labeled as a "weirdo" or worse unless he or she is able to establish firm proof of their masculinity or femininity in other ways.

Much of the sexual behavior in early and mid-adolescence is motivated by expectations about gender-appropriate behavior and the related desire for peer acceptance rather than by actual sexual desire (Miller and Simon, 1980; Gagnon, 1989). Teenagers "prove" their masculinity or femininity in part by being seen going through the right heterosexual rituals or talking as though they have. A 16-year-old boy who's never had a girlfriend, who doesn't talk about the great centerfold in last month's *Playboy,* and who isn't seen wrapped around a female body in some starry-eyed "close dancing" at a class party may be suspect. Similarly, a 16-year-old girl who doesn't date may be socially ostracized as an "undesirable"; this negative labeling may be even stronger if she doesn't dress in a manner that is "in" for girls at her high school or if she seems too aggressive in her nonsexual conduct.

4. Learning about Sexual and Romantic Relationships.

Learning about sexual and romantic relationships generally begins in early adolescence as boys and girls practice the necessary social skills involved in group activities ranging from hanging out at the mall to dances, parties, and group "dates" to the movies. For most adolescents, these rehearsals of what will later blossom into more "serious" relationships take the form of heterosexual pairing off (we discuss adolescents who have a homosexual orientation a little later in this chapter). Generally, the degree of emotional closeness and sexual intimacy in these relationships increases as the adolescents become older and more experienced. Most adolescents have a series of such romantic relationships throughout the teenage years (Gagnon, 1989). There is considerable variation in this pattern, however: in some cases, young teenagers fall deeply in love and become sexually intimate by age 13 or 14, while more typically, sexual experimentation doesn't progress to intercourse until the late teenage years (Sorenson, 1973; Chilman, 1979; Furstenberg et al., 1987). In some instances, sexual activity occurs outside romantic pairings: although few teenage boys have their introduction to sexual intercourse with prostitutes today (in contrast to the relative frequency of this way of losing their virginity back in the 1940s, as the Kinsey studies documented), sex is sometimes a more-or-less casual accompaniment to the use of illicit drugs or is simply "something to do" without having any romantic significance.

Despite the fact that many of the rigid, old gender-role "rules" differentiating what was acceptable sexual behavior for males and females have undergone massive change in the past 25 years (Hass, 1979; Hatcher et al., 1994), it is still true that sex is typically seen as a form of "scoring" or "conquest" by teenage males, whereas for teenage females sex seems to be most important as a means of obtaining affection, caring, and intimacy (Carrol, Volk, and Hyde, 1985; DeLamater, 1987). However, what is particularly notable is that for most adolescents today, the old "double standard" that approved sexual experimentation by males, while insisting that teenage females remain virgins, has been discarded in favor of a more egalitarian standard. Further aspects of this topic and the entire issue of gender-role socialization in adolescence are discussed in Chapter 11.

Whether in love relationships or in other social interactions, an important aspect of middle and late adolescence is learning the ground rules and the art of sexual negotiation. This includes learning how to set limits, how to communicate about sex with and without words, how to avoid misunderstandings (particularly, for females, how to avoid being considered a "cockteaser"; for males, how to avoid being too aggressive or insensitive), and how to show a partner what you like, as well as what you don't like. While many college students will already have forgotten how important these issues seemed to be at age 16 or 17, the proficiency and self-confidence that adolescents develop in such sexual negotiations become important components of later sexual feelings. For example, a female who learns as a teenager how to say no to an insistent date—or how to tactfully disengage from a guy at a party who is "all hands" when she doesn't want him to be—is apt to be much more confident in how she deals with similar situations as a young adult. On the other hand, adolescents who feel that they have been ineffective in sexual negotiations may be cautious and guarded in future intimate relationships, an approach that can prevent them from being spontaneous and enjoying themselves.

5. Developing a Personal Sexual Value System.

The process of developing a personal sexual value system is linked to the task of finding a comfortable identity. In answering the question, "Who am I?," the adolescent is also looking for answers to questions like "What do I stand for? What do I believe in? Who should I choose as role models?" Gradually devising a set of sexual values is partly an outgrowth of this important aspect of adolescence. For example, the teenager either chooses to be honest as a general way of behaving or decides that deceit is sometimes allowable in order to get something he or she wants. Similarly, teens must choose between sex as a means of expressing intimacy and affection, or as a more casual gratification with no strings attached, or as something reserved for a love relationship. These choices are not made in a moral or intellectual vacuum; family values, religious values, and the values of a teen's closest friends are undoubtedly important factors in the overall equation (Jessor and Jessor, 1977; Feather, 1980).

PSYCHOSEXUAL ASPECTS OF ADOLESCENCE

There are many links between the social and psychological reactions of adolescence and the biological side of puberty that we will discuss shortly. Here, we examine several of these psychosocial areas briefly.

Sexual Fantasies

Sexual fantasies and dreams become more common and explicit in adolescence than at earlier ages, often as an accompaniment to masturbation (Hass, 1979). One study found that only 7 percent of adolescent girls and 11 percent of adolescent boys who masturbated never fantasized, and about half reported using fantasy most of the time during masturbation (Sorenson, 1973). Fantasy seems to serve several different purposes in adolescence: it can add to the pleasure of a sexual activity, be a substitute for a real (but unavailable) experience, induce arousal or orgasm, provide a form of mental rehearsal for later sexual experiences (thus increasing comfort and anticipating possible problems just as rehearsing any other kind of activity can), and provide a safe, controlled, unembarrassing means of sexual experimentation. Each of these functions of fantasy is a forerunner of ways in which sexual imagery will continue to be used in adulthood by most people. For this reason, the adolescent's experience in and exploration of the range and uses of fantasy are important to her or his later sexual existence and confidence.

Independence

As adolescents struggle to establish a sense of personal identity and independence from parents and other authority figures, interactions with their peer group (other people of about their same age) become increasingly important. Teenagers look to each other for support and guidance, vowing to correct the mistakes of the older generations, but quickly discover that their peer group has its own set of expectations, social controls, and rules of conduct. Thus, adolescents' need for freedom is usually accompanied by a need to be like their friends, even though these two needs sometimes conflict.

Peer group pressures vary from one community to another and also reflect the ethnic and economic subcultures within each community. In one group, the code of sexual conduct may be very traditional with a high premium on female virginity and almost all sexual activity limited to "meaningful" relationships. If this code is not followed by females, they will get a "reputation" that may tarnish their futures and make them prey for boys looking for an "easy lay." In another group, sex may be viewed as a status symbol—the "uninitiated" versus "those in the know." This view often motivates members of the group to participate in sexual activity to be accepted. The suggestion has been made that a new tyranny of sexual values is emerging: teenagers are expected by their peers to become sexually experienced at an early age and those who are not comfortable with this pressure are viewed as old-fashioned, immature, or "uptight" (Chilman, 1979; Sarrel and Sarrel, 1979; Burkhart, 1981).

The teenager's sexual decision-making reflects individual psychological readiness, personal values, moral reasoning, fear of negative consequences, and involvement in romantic attachments. These personal factors are often not compatible with peer pressures and seem to be felt as limits more strongly by adolescent females than by males in our society. It appears that teenagers who engage in sexual intercourse and those who are close to doing so place a high premium on personal independence, have loosened family ties in favor of more reliance on friends, and are more apt to experiment with drugs or alcohol and to engage in political activism than their contemporaries (Jessor and Jessor, 1975; Henshaw et al., 1989).

In seeking to become free from parental or adult control, some adolescents see sex as a way of proving their ability to make independent decisions and of challenging the values of the older generation. Their freedom is not achieved so easily: adolescents manage to acquire a sizable sexual legacy from the

Young adolescents like to hang out in groups, while older teens focus more intently on one-to-one romances.

older generation complete with a persistent double standard and a strong sense of sexual guilt. Teenage *attitudes* have changed more rapidly than behavior, since an attitude of equality between the sexes is now fairly widespread; yet the old double standard persists in certain ways. The male is still expected to be the sexual initiator; if the female assumes this role, she is likely to be viewed as "aggressive" or "oversexed." Adolescents have not rid themselves of all sexual conflict, misinformation, and embarrassment; instead, it seems they have sometimes traded one set of problems for another (Sarrel and Sarrel, 1979; Gagnon, 1989).

Parental Reactions

While adults generally encourage adolescents to develop independence, our society puts teenagers in a double bind. No longer children, not yet adults, adolescents are expected to act grown-up in many ways, but this attitude usually does not extend to their sexual behavior. Many adults seem threatened by adolescent sexuality and try to regulate it in illogical ways: ban sex education in schools (it would "put ideas in their heads"), limit information about contraceptive methods ("keep them afraid of getting pregnant"), censor what teenagers read or can see in movies ("pure minds think pure thoughts"), invent school dress codes ("modesty conquers lust"), or simply pretend that adolescent sexuality does not exist.

Fortunately, not all parents adopt such a negative view of teenage sexuality, and in some instances parents take a much more liberal stance. Not only are there some parents who discuss sex very openly and assist their teenage daughters and sons in obtaining contraception, a few parents actually pres-

sure their adolescent children into becoming sexually experienced. This attitude sometimes reflects the parents' desire to relive their own teenage years through the experience of their children.

It is also important to realize that teenagers may create pressure for their parents by their sexual behavior. Most parents are concerned about the possibility of an unwanted teenage pregnancy, realizing that even if their son or daughter has access to contraception, that does not mean it will be effectively used whenever needed. Parents are also realistically worried about sexually transmitted disease. In addition, many parents are caught in a double bind of their own: they do not want to seem old-fashioned and unduly restrictive but they genuinely believe in traditional values about sexual behavior that the teenager may have a hard time understanding. Interestingly, some parents become worried if their teenage child *does not* show any interest in the opposite sex, since they interpret this as a possible sign of homosexuality.

Most parents, regardless of their own sexual lifestyles, have a tendency to be less permissive about premarital sex for their own children (I. L.

Reiss, 1967, 1980). Perhaps as a result, when parents are the primary source of sex education, adolescents have more traditional sex values and have higher rates of virginity (Lewis, 1973). In addition, research shows that teenagers who have close relationships with their mothers are more likely to have sexual attitudes and behavior that are consistent with their mothers' attitudes (Weinstein and Thornton, 1989).

PUBERTY

Puberty is a period of change from biological immaturity to maturity. In this transition, dramatic physical changes occur such as the adolescent "growth spurt," the development of secondary sex characteristics, the onset of menstruation (**menarche**), and the ability of the male to ejaculate. In addition, this is a time when fertility for both sexes is achieved and important psychological changes occur.

Some people think that puberty happens overnight—as a student put it, "One morning, you wake up with pimples"—but actually, the maturing process lasts anywhere from one and one-half to six years (Grumbach, 1980). The blueprint for the physical changes that occur during puberty was actually established before birth, when the hypothalamus and pituitary gland were programmed by hormones for a later "awakening."

Physical Growth and Development

Changes in Body Size

Everyone probably remembers a teenage friend who went away over a summer and came back much taller. This was not a result of sunshine, exercise, or clean living—it was simply the **adolescent growth spurt.** The explanation of this explosive growth rate is simple: it occurs because rising sex hormone levels in puberty temporarily cause bone growth.

The adolescent growth spurt typically occurs two years earlier in girls than in boys (on average, age 12 versus 14) (Marshall, 1977). As a result, girls are usually taller than boys of the same age from about age 11 to 14. (Remember those seventh grade dances where girls seemed to tower over their partners, especially if they wore heels?) The self-consciousness this may cause fortunately lessens by midadolescence as males "catch up" and usually go on to become somewhat taller than females.

The adolescent growth spurt does not always start at the same time in all parts of the body. For

Around age 12, girls are often taller than boys because they have an earlier adolescent growth spurt.

example, growth of the foot typically begins about four months before growth in the lower leg, so an adolescent's feet may seem disproportionately large (Marshall, 1975). Not realizing that more harmonious relative proportions will be restored, some teenagers are upset at this pattern.

There is no correlation between an "early" growth spurt and final adult height (which is partly controlled by genetics). This finding should comfort a young teenager who is the class "shrimp"; by age 16 or 17 the "shrimp" may be as tall as or taller than his or her classmates.

Sexual Maturation in Girls

The first physical sign of puberty in girls is usually the beginning of breast development, which

menarche (me nar' kē) the onset of menses.
adolescent growth spurt a period of fast bone growth usually occurring in the early or middle teens caused by the rising sex hormone levels of puberty.

Figure 9.1   Stages of Female Breast
Development During
Puberty

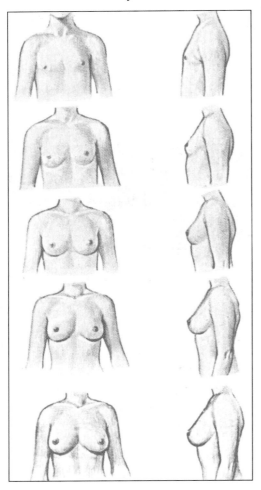

occurs as early as age 8 or as late as age 13. In the
earliest stage of breast growth, there is only a
small mound of tissue (the "breast bud"), but
gradually the nipple and areola enlarge and the
contour of the breast becomes more prominent
(see Figure 9.1). Some girls have fully mature
breasts before their twelfth birthdays, but others
do not reach this stage until age 19 or even later.
Breast growth is controlled by estrogen levels and
heredity.

The appearance of pubic hair (first lightly pigmented and sparse, gradually becoming darker,
coarser, curlier, and more abundant) usually starts
shortly after breast growth begins. By this time, the
vagina has already begun to lengthen and the
uterus is slowly enlarging. Menarche usually oc-

curs as breast growth nears completion and almost
invariably comes after the peak growth spurt (Marshall and Tanner, 1969).

In the United States, the average age at menarche is 12.8 years for whites and 12.5 for blacks (U.S.
Department of Health, Education, and Welfare,
1973). It is interesting to note that a century ago,
menstruation first occurred at an average of 16 or
older; since then, the age at menarche has been
consistently decreasing decade by decade
(Zacharias and Wurtman, 1969) (Figure 9.2). Socioeconomic factors, climate, heredity, family size,
and nutrition all influence the age of menarche.
Most recently, this decrease has leveled off, perhaps
reflecting more uniform nutritional conditions.

An interesting idea has been proposed by a research team studying the onset of menstruation.
They believe that menarche occurs only when a
minimum percentage of body fat is present (Frisch
and McArthur, 1974). In support of this theory, female long-distance runners and ballet dancers have
been noted to have delayed menarche or to actually stop having periods when they are in rigorous
training (Frisch, Wyshak, and Vincent, 1980).

The age of menarche varies widely from one girl
to another, occurring as early as age 8 and as late as
16 or later. In the first year after menarche, menstrual cycles are frequently irregular and ovulation
usually does not occur. It is possible, however, to

Figure 9.2   Declining Age of Menarche in
Various Countries

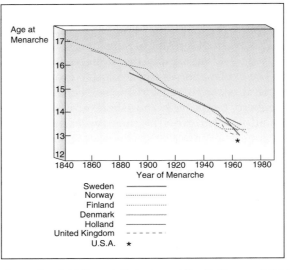

Source: *From J. M. Tanner, in* Endocrine and Genetic Diseases of Childhood and Adolescence *(L. I. Gardner, Ed.) W. B. Saunders, 1975, pp. 14–64.*

begin ovulating with the very first menstrual cycle, and young adolescents who engage in intercourse need contraception.

One other aspect of female puberty not mentioned often is that vaginal secretions are likely to increase because of the changing hormone status. Some vaginal lubrication occurs because of sexual excitation whether this results from daydreams, reading, or sexual activity. But vaginal lubrication can also appear spontaneously, without a direct connection to sexual thoughts or acts. The sensations of vaginal wetness may be curious, pleasing, shameful, or alarming to the young teenager.

Sexual Maturation in Boys

The physical signs of puberty in boys are also controlled by hormone changes, but puberty usually starts one to two years later than in girls. The earliest change during puberty is growth of the testes, resulting from LH stimulation and subsequent testosterone production. The increasing levels of testosterone also stimulate growth of the penis and the accessory male sex organs (prostate, seminal vesicles, and epididymis). Ejaculation is not possible before puberty because the prostate and seminal vesicles do not begin to function until they receive appropriate hormone signals.

Boys begin to undergo genital development at an average age of 11.6 years, and the genitals reach adult size and shape at an average age of 14.9 (Marshall and Tanner, 1970) (Figure 9.3). In some boys, genital development occurs rapidly (in about a year), while in others it may take up to five and one-half years (Tanner, 1974). Sperm production (which begins in childhood) becomes fully established during puberty so fertility is present.

There is no exact counterpart in male puberty to menarche, but wet dreams seem to have a parallel degree of psychological importance. Kinsey, Pomeroy, and Martin (1948) reported that one-quarter of 14-year-olds and nearly two-thirds of 17-year-olds had this experience, yet many pubertal boys are not told about the possibility of nocturnal emissions and are surprised, puzzled, or frightened upon discovery of the event. The ejaculatory experience itself or the resulting sensation of wetness or stickiness may awaken the boy having a nocturnal emission, and—just as uninformed girls may view their initial menstrual flow as a sign of illness—he may become anxious about disease or injury. Whether informed or not about this experience, the

Figure 9.3   Stages of Male Genital Development During Puberty

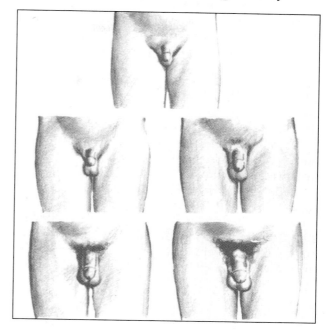

pubertal boy may attempt to "hide the evidence" of a stained sheet or pajamas to avoid embarrassment or questioning by his parents.

Growth of pubic hair begins around the time of genital development and is usually followed a year or two later by the appearance of facial and axillary hair. Facial hair growth is an important event because the earlier changes of male puberty are usually less visible than breast development in the female and beard growth is a visible sign of "becoming a man." Facial hair growth begins at the corners of the upper lip with a fine, fuzzy appearance and then spreads to form a mustache with coarser texture. Hair next appears on the upper cheeks and just below the lower lip and last of all on the chin. Body hair also appears during puberty, and chest hair continues to grow for a decade or more after this time.[1]

---

[1]The degree of facial and body hairiness in both sexes is controlled by genetic factors in addition to hormones. As a result, some people are hairier than others. This is often a source of embarrassment to women who compare themselves to the apparently "hairless" women in *Playboy* or *Vogue* or to men who are exposed to macho figures of heavily mustached men with an abundant crop of chest hair in various advertisements.

Deepening of the voice is another change of puberty and is caused by testosterone stimulation of the voice box, or **larynx.** As the larynx grows, the boy's voice may go through an awkward period of breaks and squawks, which may be a source of embarrassment. Like age at menarche, the average age of this voice change in boys has decreased, from 18 years in 1749 to about 13.5 years today (Grumbach, 1980). Transient breast enlargement or gynecomastia is commonly seen in male puberty but typically disappears a year or two after it starts.

Hormone differences between adolescent boys and girls also cause differences in body shapes. For instance, the average 17- or 18-year-old boy has a leaner body and more muscle mass than his female counterpart. This is because estrogens cause accumulation of fat under the skin, while testosterone stimulates muscle growth. The structure of pelvic bones is also different in males and females, with the wider female pelvis creating a properly sized birth canal.

Pubertal Hormones and Sexuality

During puberty, rising hormone levels contribute to an activation of sexual sensations and erotic thoughts and dreams for boys and girls. John Money has described the role of hormones as follows: "The correct conception of hormonal puberty is that it puts gas in the metaphorical tank and upgrades the model of the vehicle, but it does not build the engine nor program the itinerary of the journey" (Money, 1980, pp. 36–37).

The relationship between pubertal hormones and sexual behavior is shown in the finding that boys who undergo "late" puberty (around age 15 or 16) generally have less and later teenage sexual activity—including masturbation and intercourse—than boys who have "early" puberty (around age 12 or 13). Kinsey and his colleagues pointed out this pattern (Kinsey, Pomeroy, and Martin, 1948), and we have some preliminary data showing it is probably true. If testosterone levels of the pubertal boy increase the frequency or intensity of erections, for example, he may possibly have a heightened awareness of sexual sensations. Increased testosterone in the blood may also influence the brain itself to activate sexual feelings or thoughts or to lower the threshold for external triggers that activate such feelings or thoughts. Boys with higher testosterone levels, then, are more likely to be more physically developed and sexually active. Shorter, less-muscular, later-maturing boys may experience a social handicap. While having sexual feelings, they may feel less confident about their abilities and therefore "lag" in sexual behavior.

In parallel fashion, girls who undergo "late" puberty seem to have a lower rate of early adolescent sexual activity than girls who complete puberty at age 12 or 13. Although a lower frequency or later age of participation in sexual activity might be explained by purely psychological or social factors (e.g., less physically developed girls may be more shy or self-conscious about sex with a partner), it appears that masturbation is less frequent and occurs later in late-maturing compared to early-maturing adolescent girls. A large cross-cultural study found similar evidence. According to Udry and Cliquet (1982), data from five different countries show that girls who are younger at menarche tend to have intercourse and to give birth at earlier ages than girls with later menarche.

In contrast to the findings linking sexual activity to "early" puberty, when pubertal changes occur before age 9—a condition called **precocious puberty**—there is usually no accompanying change in sexual behavior (Kolodny, Masters, and Johnson, 1979). This is probably because the hormonal stimulation alone is not enough to initiate new behavior patterns without a state of psychosexual readiness that the younger child simply hasn't attained.

PATTERNS OF SEXUAL BEHAVIOR

If the sexual revolution is over, today's teenagers haven't heard. Despite the realities of the HIV/AIDS epidemic, soaring rates of other sexually transmitted diseases, and a continuing problem with unintended teenage pregnancy, American teens are more sexually active in the 1990s than they have been at any time in the past. The trend over the past three decades has been for participation in sexual activity to begin at ever younger ages.

Throughout all ages of adolescence, males are more likely than are females to report having had intercourse (see Table 9.1) (Bigler, 1989; Centers for Disease Control, 1992c). This is nothing particularly new, since it was true in Kinsey's day and probably in earlier decades, as well. What is new is that the gap in rates of coital experience between

Table 9.1 Never-Married U.S. Teenage Males Who Have Had Sexual Intercourse, by Age (cumulative percentages), 1988

Age	All Races	Black	White	Hispanic
13	5.4%	19.8%	2.9%	3.9%
14	11.0	34.6	7.1	6.3
15	21.1	47.8	16.2	19.4
16	37.8	63.5	33.0	37.7
17	57.5	78.4	53.0	63.2
18	67.4	84.7	69.8	60.9
19	79.0	95.8	75.9	80.5

Source: *Modified from Sonenstein, Pleck, and Ku, 1991, Table 1.*

the sexes has shrunk notably since the early 1960s (see Figure 9.4). However, males and females seem to take somewhat different attitudes toward their first experience with intercourse. As one report puts it, "Although they have equal levels of anxiety about first intercourse, girls are likely to be worried about whether they are doing the right thing, while boys are worried about whether they are doing the thing right" (Children's Defense Fund, 1988).

Boys and girls also have different motivations for becoming sexually experienced. For teenage boys, sex is first and foremost a badge of manhood: becoming sexually experienced is part of the process of achieving maturity, acquiring social status, and regarding themselves as grown up. While

Figure 9.4 The Closing Gender Gap in Unmarried Teenagers Who Have Had Sexual Intercourse

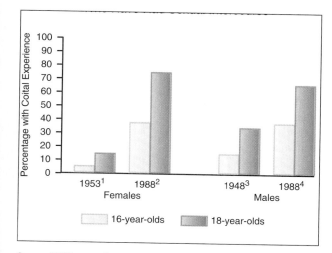

Source: [1] Kinsey et al., 1953; [2] Forrest and Singh, 1990, Table 4; [3] Kinsey, Pomeroy and Martin, 1948; [4] Sonenstein, Pleck, and Ku, 1991, Table 1.

teenage girls certainly also see sex as a marker of personal and social maturity (and thus desirable as a way of leaving childhood behind), girls are more likely than boys to view intercourse as a way of obtaining or solidifying love and commitment (Nielsen, 1991). Teenage boys don't think about love and intimacy in the same romanticized way girls do: mirroring the practice of past decades, a boy is still more likely to give a girl a line in order to convince her to have sex, and one of the most common lines still in use is, "If you loved me, you would."

Reliable data on teenage sexual activity are few and far between. This is partly a reflection of a lack of sponsorship of such research by the federal government over the past several decades and partly a result of the difficulty of obtaining scientifically valid samples. In addition, statistics from the 1970s and early 1980s are now largely outdated, especially given the impact of the HIV/AIDS epidemic. Here, we briefly summarize the findings of some recent studies to provide a snapshot of teenage sexual behavior.

- A study of 758 eighth-grade students from rural communities in Maryland surprisingly showed that 61 percent of the boys and 47 percent of the girls had already entered the ranks of nonvirgins (Alexander et al., 1989).
- A well-designed national survey of high school students recently found that 40 percent of ninth graders had had sexual intercourse; by 12th grade, this figure had risen to 72 percent (see Table 9.2).
- Data from a national probability sample revealed that by age 18 or 19, three-quarters of females had had coital experience (see Table 9.3).
- A recent survey of heterosexual students at a large midwestern university found that undergraduate males reported having, on average, 11.2 lifetime sex partners; female students reported an average of 5.6 different partners (Reinisch et al., 1992).

These eye-opening statistics drive home what is common knowledge for today's teens: in a phrase, (almost) everybody's doing it. To be sure, there are

larynx the voice box.

precocious puberty (pree koh' shus pew' burr tee) physical-changes of puberty occurring before age 8 in girls or age 10 in boys.

Table 9.2 **Sexual Experience of U.S. High School Students, 1990**

Category	Female	Male
Race/Ethnicity		
White	47.0%	56.4%
Black	60.0	87.8
Hispanic	45.0	63.0
Grade		
9th	37.0%	48.7%
10th	42.9	52.5
11th	52.7	62.6
12th	66.6	76.3
Total	48.0	60.8

Source: *Data from Centers for Disease Control, "Sexual Behavior Among High School Students—United States, 1990,"* Morbidity and Mortality Weekly Report *40:885–888, 1992, Table 1.*

still a substantial number of adolescents whose strict religious upbringing keeps them from experimenting with sex, and there are other teenagers who, due to personal value systems, shyness, lack of social skills, lack of opportunity, or assorted other reasons remain virgins. But there is also no question that the survey data referred to above represent only a portion of the sexual activity that is going on among today's adolescents, since these surveys have primarily relied on yes-no answers to a few simple questions about sex.

Because of the lack of reliable data on noncoital sexual behavior during adolescence, we can only offer a few generalizations on this topic based on our own admittedly limited studies. One such point pertains to the incidence of masturbation during adolescence. According to Kinsey and his co-workers, male adolescents were much more likely than females to engage in masturbation at any age

Table 9.3 **Percentage of Women Aged 15 to 19 Who Have Ever Had Sexual Intercourse, 1988**

	Age	
Race/Ethnicity	15 to 17	18 to 19
Non-Hispanic White	36.2%	74.3%
Non-Hispanic Black	50.5	78.0
Hispanic	36.1	70.0
Total	38.4	74.4

Source: *Modified from Forrest and Singh, 1990, Table 4.*

during the teenage years (Kinsey et al., 1953). Studies done during the 1970s continued to report a considerable male–female difference in teenage experience with masturbation (Sorenson, 1973; Arafat and Cotton, 1974; Hass, 1979). However, data that we have gathered over the last 12 years suggest that this difference is shrinking: while close to 95 percent of teenage boys experiment with masturbation, for teenage girls the incidence has now risen to almost 80 percent. This convergence undoubtedly reflects a change in attitudes about masturbation in the past 20 years in society at large. Today masturbation is more likely to be seen as a healthy form of sexual expression than as a sinful, dirty practice. On the other hand, at least one recent study in a small, nonrepresentative sample suggests that a large gender difference in patterns of masturbation persists among adolescents (Leitenberg, Detzer, and Srebnik, 1993).

Oral–genital sex is also more accepted by today's adolescents than it was in Kinsey's day. Several studies suggest that 40 to 50 percent of teenagers have tried oral–genital contact (Young, 1980; Newcomer and Udry, 1985), and our own surveys suggest that the figure may be even higher than this. Oral–genital sex serves as a good compromise for some teens who are seeking sexual gratification but want to avoid the risk of pregnancy or the moral confusion they may associate with sexual intercourse; for other teens, it is simply one of several different alternatives for sexual experimentation. As one 17-year-old girl put it, "Oral sex is a good way to take care of my boyfriend when I'm not in the mood for making love but he's really horny. I don't even have to take my clothes off and I can still get the job done."

The most notable change in adolescent sexual behavior in the past 20 years (along with the trend toward becoming sexually active at younger and younger ages) is that today's teenagers have intercourse with considerably more sexual partners than in the past. While exact statistics are not available, think about this fact for a moment: According to a recent survey, the average sexually active 15-year-old American boy has had intercourse with at least four different partners (Sonenstein, Pleck and Ku, 1991)!

The old concept of being faithful still applies for most of today's teenagers: The sexual behavior pattern for the majority of sexually active adolescents seems to be one of *serial monogamy*, that is, having only one sexual relationship at a time but not hesitating to have more than one sex partner, but the accent is on "serial" rather than on "monogamy."

Today, many teenagers have discarded the standard of being in love as a prerequisite for sex in favor of simply feeling good about their partner. However, there are still teens who continue to see sexual intercourse as something to be saved for a love relationship and, ideally, for a premarital trial with the person they feel destined to marry. Still, adolescent participation in coital activity today is not "premarital" in the sense that it once was.

> Although it does occur before marriage, only some of it is in the service of the marriage institution. If, for instance, a young person's first intercourse occurs at 15 or 16 and first marriage in the mid-20s, with a number of affectional-sexual relationships (including intercourse) in between, the first experience and many of the later ones will have been undertaken for their own sakes, not in a search for marriage partners *(Gagnon, 1989, p. 516).*

In the midst of these various changes, teens today seem to be somewhat more conscientious about using contraception than in past decades. More than three-quarters of sexually active teenagers reported using some form of contraception during the last time they had intercourse (Centers for Disease Control, 1992c). However, since many teenagers use withdrawal (a notoriously ineffective method) as their primary form of birth control, this statistic is less positive than it might seem to be if taken at face value.

GAY AND LESBIAN TEENS

In a society that programs its children and adolescents for a heterosexual world, it can be a source of considerable emotional turmoil for a teenager to discover that he or she has a sexual orientation that's "different." For one thing, we continue to live in a society that is predominantly homophobic, and this negative attitude towards homosexuality spills over into rejection, hostility, and cruelty from numerous sources—including, at times, parents, friends, and church or synagogue—that makes the gay or lesbian teenager feel like a misfit. For another thing, since peer group acceptance is vitally important to most adolescents' self-esteem—far more important than at any other phase in the life

cycle—lack of access to a readily identifiable peer group deprives the gay or lesbian teenager of an important source of external support to feeling accepted and acceptable.

As a result, many teenagers who possess a strong same-sex attraction struggle against this impulse in an effort to make themselves fit in the expected heterosexual mold. Part of this struggle may involve telling themselves they are "just going through a passing phase" or withdrawing into relative social isolation, sometimes by becoming intensely involved in hobbies that can be pursued alone, like computers or art or music.

Relatively few lesbians actually identify themselves as such with certainty during their teenage years; many women do not admit their nonheterosexual orientation to themselves until a later point in their lives—especially after a failed marriage (Zitter, 1987). And relatively few women who later identify themselves as lesbians actually have a sexual encounter with another female during adolescence.

For teenage males who feel "different," there is more variability. Many have recognized their sexual orientation since an early age and have already accepted it as a given aspect of their lives. Others experiment hesitantly with their same-sex impulses: at first, they seek out books, magazines, and films to try out their reactions and expectations (frequently using such materials as masturbatory aids). Later, especially if they connect with a friend who seems similar, they may engage in homosexual activity. (Teenage boys who live in cities with visible gay communities are usually able to make contacts and find information—and partners—more readily than their counterparts who live in more isolated suburbs, small towns, or rural areas.) Still others, who may feel attracted to girls but have also been turned on in same-sex encounters with friends, are confused and worried about their sexual identities.

Many teenage boys who feel erotic urges toward other boys fight against them in numerous ways: they may try to establish their masculinity (thereby obtaining peer acceptance) by participating in sports; they go through the motions of dating and otherwise trying to fit in to the heterosexual scene; and most of all, they desperately try to hide the side of themselves that they consider shameful or even dangerous. However, a majority of gay males have an initial sexual experience with another male during adolescence and many have a substantial number of partners by the time they graduate from high school.

Healthy psychosexual development for an adolescent who identifies himself or herself as gay is no easy task. There are no manuals, schools, institutions, or easily visible role models for guidance. In fact, the path is usually obscured by misinformation, fear, and shame. Sexual development for gay and lesbian people is a function of learning through experience, experiences that may result in contracting a fatal sexually transmitted disease (AIDS), facing social ostracism, or other harsh penalties. The development of a healthy sexual identity against such odds is a testimony to the resilience of adolescents and adults who survive the crisis of "coming out" (Remafedi, 1989).

Today, many gay and lesbian adolescents find a ready-made support network when they get to college. A substantial number of colleges and universities now have active gay and lesbian societies that organize social events, work diligently to counter homophobia, and encourage students who have not yet become comfortable with their sexual identities. Still, we suspect that relatively few gays and lesbians actually identify themselves to their families until they are young adults. The natural identity confusion of adolescence is simply too fragile to permit most homosexual or lesbian individuals to undertake such a drastic step until they have solidified their own sense of who they are.

UNINTENDED TEENAGE PREGNANCY

More than 1 million pregnancies occur each year among American teenage females, which is equivalent to one adolescent pregnancy beginning every 35 seconds. Since the majority of these pregnancies are unplanned and unwanted, it is no surprise that they frequently create considerable psychological anguish, serious economic consequences, and even health risks that are too often ignored or misunderstood.

A few background statistics can highlight the scope of this epidemic. (Alan Guttmacher Institute, 1981; Zelnik, Kantner, and Ford, 1981; Trussel, 1988; Henshaw and Van Vort, 1989; Rosenheim and Testa, 1993):

- Thirty thousand pregnancies occur annually in the United States among girls under 15 years of age.
- One out of 12 unmarried female American

teenagers becomes pregnant each year; about half of them carry the pregnancy to term.
- Less than half of teenage females use contraception the first time they have intercourse; not surprisingly, half of all first pregnancies occur within the first six months of becoming sexually active.
- Four hundred thousand American teenagers have abortions each year, accounting for more than one-third of all abortions performed in this country.
- Six out of ten teenage females who have a child before age 17 will be pregnant again before age 19.
- America's teenage birth rate is the highest in the Western hemisphere, is double the rate of Sweden, and is an astonishing 17 times higher than Japan's.
- Four out of ten girls now 14 years old will get pregnant in their teens.

In the United States, approximately 18 percent of sexually experienced teenage females aged 15 to 19 become pregnant each year, with substantially higher rates found among blacks than whites (Maciak et al., 1987; Centers for Disease Control, 1993e).

In absolute numbers, in 1990 more than 1 million teenagers became pregnant (Centers for Disease Control, 1993e). These pregnancies resulted in over half a million live births and more than 400,000 induced abortions (the rest ended in miscarriages or stillbirths).

While it is true that since 1970 the birth rate among teens has declined significantly, most of this decrease has been due to the legalization of abortion in 1973 (Lewin, 1988). In fact, teenage birth rates actually *increased* in most states from 1980 to 1990 because declines in abortion rates generally exceeded those of pregnancy rates (Centers for Disease Control, 1993e).

Teenage Mothers

The preceding statistical profile shows how widespread the problem of unintended teenage pregnancy is, but to understand *why* it is a problem, we need to examine some additional aspects of the consequences of teenage pregnancy. To begin with, there are increased health risks associated with teenage pregnancy, particularly among younger teens (those in the 13-to-16-year age

A teenage mom does her homework while tending her baby.

group). For example, babies of teenage mothers have an increased chance of being underweight and are nearly twice as likely to die in infancy as those born to women in their twenties (Smith and Mumford, 1980; McCormick, Shapiro, and Starfield, 1981). In addition, teenagers tend to have more medically complicated pregnancies—including miscarriages, toxemia, and hemorrhage—as well as a higher risk of maternal death than women in their twenties (Hatcher et al., 1994).

Possibly even more alarming than these medical risks are the socioeconomic consequences of unintended teenage pregnancy. Even though it is now illegal to expel students who are pregnant or who are mothers from public schools, in the past many teenage mothers who kept their babies dropped out of school and didn't return (Bolton, 1980; Furstenberg, Menken, and Lincoln, 1981; McGee, 1982). Largely as a result of this abrupt withdrawal from formal education, women in this group were far less likely than their peers to enter the job market or to gain regular employment (McCarthy and Radish, 1982). It is no surprise, then, that these teenage mothers are overrepresented in poverty statistics and are apt to become largely dependent on government services and support (Moore et al., 1979; Alan Guttmacher Institute, 1981; McGee, 1982).[2]

Fortunately, however, it now appears that a majority of teenage mothers are graduating from high school despite the obstacles in their paths (Upchurch and McCarthy, 1989), in contrast to the situation just a decade earlier. Family background factors, such as maternal education and parental marital stability, seem especially important positive influences on a teenage mother's school completion (Ahn, 1994).

Unmarried teenage girls who find themselves pregnant are confronted by a series of psychologically complicated choices as well. They often get little or no support—either emotionally or financially—from the father. They must decide whether to abort the pregnancy (which sometimes produces feelings of guilt and anguish) or have the baby. If they have the baby, they then must decide to keep it or put it up for adoption; today, fewer than 5 percent of unwed teenage mothers choose adoption as a course of action (McGee, 1982; Henshaw and Van Vort, 1989). In other cases, their partners or parents may pressure them to do something they don't want to, thus creating additional pressures and uncertainties. Here's how one 17-year-old described her dilemma:

> When I found out I was pregnant, my boyfriend insisted that we get married and have the baby. I had no interest in marrying him or in being saddled with an infant at age 18, so I refused. But his parents hired a lawyer to try to stop me from having an abortion, and the whole thing wound up being a nightmare for me and my parents. Fortunately, I got the abortion and dumped my so-called boyfriend, so I'll be going to college next year instead of playing mommy. (*Authors' files*)

[2]There is another way of looking at this situation, however. Evidence exists that girls who are weak academically and who come from poor families are more apt to become teenage mothers (Lewin, 1988). In a sense, this produces a self-perpetuating cycle in which poor academic preparation and poverty lead to teenage pregnancies, and the consequences of the teenage pregnancies, such as dropping out of school, limit the teen mother's future options considerably.

Some teenagers, unlike the one quoted above, find themselves rushed into unanticipated marriage as a result of a pregnancy. Unfortunately, these marriages are much likelier than most to end in divorce or desertion, and there is a suicide risk among these young women that is considerably higher than in the general population (Cvetkovitch et al., 1975; Bolton, 1980; Furstenberg, Menken, and Lincoln, 1981).

Teenage Fathers

Until recently, little was known about teenage fathers, or which adolescents were most likely to become teenage fathers. New research, admittedly still incomplete, offers some interesting findings.

Hanson, Morrison, and Ginsburg (1989) used a sample of tenth grade boys drawn from 1100 high schools across the United States in 1980, with follow-ups done in 1982 and 1984. They compared adolescents who became fathers with controls who did not and concluded that there are three major predictors of teen fatherhood: (1) being black, which was associated with an increased probability of fathering a child even when the effect of socioeconomic status was controlled for; (2) going steady, which raised the odds of becoming a teenage father by 50 percent; and (3) having nontraditional, accepting attitudes toward out-of-wedlock childbearing. They also noted that taking a sex education course in school had no relation to teenage fatherhood.

These findings were consistent with other studies that showed that being black increases the chances of teenage fatherhood (Michael and Tuma, 1985; Marsiglio, 1987).

The racial disparity, which has been noted not only in the studies cited above but in others as well, raises the difficult question of whether there is a different outlook on teenage pregnancy and childbearing in the black community. This issue is highlighted by the fact that among all American teenage males, blacks are twice as likely as Hispanics to father a child out-of-wedlock, and more than four times as likely as whites (Marsiglio, 1987). (Of course, this statistic is partly influenced by whether or not the pregnancy is ended by abortion, so it is not as clear-cut as it might first seem to be.) In addition, fewer black teenage males use effective contraception in their first intercourse experience than either whites or Hispanics (Sonnenstein, Pleck, and Ku, 1989, Table 5). While a full

discussion of this issue is beyond the scope of this text, some experts have suggested that lack of economic opportunity in the black community causes teens to develop pessimistic outlooks about their educational and occupational prospects, setting the stage for fatal-istic attitudes toward the inevitability of early parenthood (Hanson, Morrison, and Ginsburg, 1989). Others point out that black teenagers may have goals that are more compatible with early parenthood than their high school classmates (Haggstrom et al., 1981; Rosenheim and Testa, 1993). In any event, there is no convincing evidence that black teenage males are sexually or socially irresponsible, although myths about teenage fathers abound.

The general stereotype about teenage fathers is well known: they are typically portrayed as irresponsible, interested only in their personal sexual gratification, and quicker to duck out the door than to assume any financial, emotional, or familial role in caring for their offspring. New research suggests that this bleak portrait is far from accurate. Instead, it shows that many teenage fathers are choosing not to abandon their babies, opting instead to contribute financially to the care of their children and showing more than passing interest in the responsibilities of parenting.

Much of the work on this topic done during the 1980s has been summarized in a book called *Teenage Fathers* (Robinson, 1988), which identifies five common myths that have been applied to this group in the past:

1. *Super Stud Myth:* The teenage father is worldly wise and more knowledgeable about sex, and more sexually experienced, than other teens.

   Fact: While teenage fathers tend to be sexually active earlier than other teens, they are relatively unsophisticated in their sexual knowledge—especially when it comes to knowledge about contraception.

2. *Don Juan Myth:* Teenage fathers prey on unsuspecting, innocent girls with their smooth banter and sexual demands; they are sexual exploiters, more interested in conquests than consequences.

   Fact: The available evidence indicates that there is relatively little exploitation in teenage sexual relationships where pregnancies occur. Indeed, some teenage fathers feel that they were exploited, rather than the other way around, especially if the girl claimed to be using contra-

PERSONAL PERSPECTIVES

The Empathy Belly

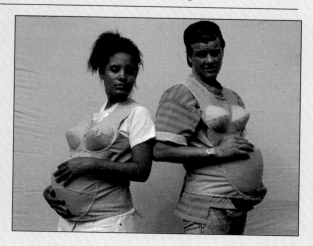

Sex educators, family planning experts, physicians, and concerned parents have searched long and hard for ways to inform adolescent males convincingly of the realities of unintended teenage pregnancy. Unfortunately, past efforts have generally failed to effectively capture the attention of teenage boys. A new educational device called The Empathy Belly may soon change the situation dramatically, if comments from early users are born out.

The Empathy Belly, shown in the accompanying photo, is a garment designed to show anyone who wears it—either male or female—what many of the physical effects of pregnancy feel like (although only in a limited way). The device consists of a vest that has various compartments which are filled with water and weights so as to produce a protruding belly, an ache in the lower back, shortness of breath, and the sensation of what it feels like to walk around with 31 pounds of extra weight that are not evenly distributed on the body.

The reaction of most males who have used it is twofold. First, after overcoming their initial sense of embarrassment, they express considerable surprise at the physical discomforts and fatigue this imitation type of pregnancy produces. "Walking up a flight of stairs was a real experience," one 16-year-old boy remarked (an understatement, as any woman who's been pregnant can tell you). In addition, males voice a mixed sense of awe and respect for the female's role as mother-to-be, often adding gratefully, "I'm glad I don't have to go through that."

Linda Ware, inventor of the device, is a childbirth educator and social worker who got the idea for The Empathy Belly years ago from a March of Dimes poster that showed a teenage boy holding his abdomen. The caption read: "Would you be more careful if *you* could get pregnant?" After years of development and field testing, and after input from many doctors, nurses, and other consultants, Ware finally brought the product to market.

The Empathy Belly, which costs about $600, quickly found acceptance as a teaching device in a variety of settings, including prenatal classes (where it helped expectant fathers empathize better with the physical complaints of their wives) as well as family life and sex education courses designed for teens. While its primary use may be to make pregnancy a vivid reality for males who have never thought about it in this physical way, it is also useful in showing a 15-year-old female that being pregnant is not a lark.

For further information about the device, write to: Birthways Inc., P.O. Box 2069, Vashon, Washington, 98070-2269 or call 1-800-882-3559.

ception—but wasn't.

3. *Macho Myth:* Teenage fathers have poor impulse control and are bent on proving their masculinity at all costs. Having sex with a girl lets them put a notch on their belt.

Fact: There is no evidence that teenage fathers

are more lacking in impulse control than other teenage males of the same age and background. Although the need to prove one's masculinity through sex may sometimes be present (as it is in many young adult and middle-aged men too), it could also be argued that teenage mothers are proving their femininity through their sexual participation.

4. *Mr. Cool Myth:* Teenage fathers typically have brief, casual sex with the girls they impregnate and have few emotional attachments to either the baby or the mother.

   Fact: In contrast to the notion of teenage fathers having brief, casual sexual relations, studies show that most have close, caring ties with their girlfriends and have strong feelings about the pregnancy.

5. *Phantom Father Myth:* Teenage fathers quickly detach themselves from the relationship once pregnancy occurs, leaving the mother and baby alone and on their own, with no support from them.

   Fact: In the past, a teenage boy who impregnated a girl often left town to avoid being forced to marry her, sometimes joining the army, sometimes just "disappearing." Today, things are different. Not only are forced marriages far less frequent, but teenage fathers frequently choose to marry the girls they get pregnant. [In one study, one-third of those responsible for a nonmarital conception married within one year, and half lived with their child shortly after the baby's birth (Marsiglio, 1987).]

Of course, exposing these myths and stereotypes doesn't mean that all teenage fathers are thoughtful, responsible individuals. Many are high school dropouts (although some may have dropped out of school *before* impregnating a girlfriend), which is apt to put them at a distinct disadvantage in the job market. By being undereducated, they limit their earning capacity, which in turn hampers their ability to contribute financially to the upbringing of their child. Other teenagers who father children become involved in drugs, gambling, or other criminal activities either in pursuit of status and adventure or in pursuit of money. And some simply don't care about the girl they've gotten pregnant or the baby.

Those who marry as teenagers are not exactly destined for a happy future. Researchers have recently identified a number of long-range repercussions on their lives, regardless of whether they married because they had gotten someone pregnant or not. In a nationally representative survey of more than 14,000 men in three different age groups, those who were married before age 19 were com-

pared to those who married later. Men who married as teenagers had lower educational attainment (completing 11.8 years of school compared to 13.1 years for men who married later), lower family incomes ($22,950 compared to $25,470), and discernibly lower occupational status (Teti, Lamb, and Elster, 1987). In addition, the men who had married as teenagers were twice as likely to get divorced as men who married later.

For the sake of completeness, it should be pointed out that the fathers of babies born to adolescent females are not always teenagers themselves. One recent study in Baltimore, which analyzed the age of fathers of children born to teenage mothers by data from birth certificates, found that 28 percent of the partners of black women and 45 percent of the partners of white women were 20 years of age or older (Hardy et al., 1989). In this study, only 16 percent of the fathers were living with or married to the mother of their child 15 months after the child's birth.

Toward Prevention

While there are no easy solutions to the problem of unintended teenage pregnancy, it appears that misinformation or complete lack of information is a key factor. At present, only one-half of American junior and senior high schools offer sex education courses, and many of those offered are remarkably incomplete (Orr, 1982; Forrest and Silverman, 1989). Since many of the sex education courses are given only to older teenagers, their preventive function is lessened considerably. Those people who believe that sex education should be taught in the home—while voicing a fine idea—overlook the reality of the situation today. Research indicates that only about 10 percent of parents discuss sexuality with their teenage children beyond simply saying "don't." On the other hand, a study by Zelnik and Kim (1982) demonstrates that among unmarried sexually active teenage women, those who have had sex education courses have fewer pregnancies than those who haven't. A more recent study has also shown the effectiveness of school-based sex education in terms of helping young teenagers postpone sexual involvement (Howard and McCabe, 1990).

Almost all authorities agree that greater responsibility for contraceptive use by the adolescent male is a major element in the effort to reduce the

Counselling <u>both</u> males and females about STDs and contraception is an important means of reducing unintended teenage pregnancies.

rate of unintended pregnancy. First, educating males about contraceptive options at an early age seems warranted since studies suggest that this information leads to better contraceptive use (Cvetkovitch and Grote, 1983). Although teenage males are generally unwilling to admit to ignorance or misinformation about sex, it is not unusual to find 15- and 16-year-old boys who believe that a diaphragm should be removed right after intercourse or who don't know the fertile days in a female's menstrual cycle. Such education need not be restricted to schools: it can be done at home, in church-affiliated programs, or as part of community projects (Carrera and Dempsey, 1988; Sandoval, 1988; Kirby et al., 1989). Education must be practical too, explaining how and where to purchase contraceptives, why it's important to discuss birth control with a partner, and why consistent contraceptive use is necessary.

Another important step is to provide males (as well as females) with a better view of how birth control practices relate to their own lives. For instance, teens must recognize how rigid sex roles or the risk of parental disapproval can influence their contraceptive behavior. In addition, teens need to be aware that the risk of contracting a sexually transmitted disease is materially reduced by use of certain contraceptive methods. This is important not only because it encourages the teenage male to use contraception but because the male's expression of interest and concern about contraception

encourages his partner to find and use an appropriate method as well (Gilgun, 1983). In addition, teenagers need incentives to engage in responsible birth control practices.

One key element in the complicated equation explaining the high rates of unintended teenage pregnancy may be the messages about sex that teenagers get from television and the movies. Television programs, from popular daytime soap operas to prime-time shows, show glamorous actors and actresses hopping into bed with one another with no discussion of birth control, responsibility, or consequences. Since the average American teenager watches more than 30 hours of television a week, it's not too surprising that this lack of effective sexual role models may translate into impulsive, over-romanticized views of what sex is all about. Despite pressure from groups such as Planned Parenthood, network executives have generally resisted balancing their programming by incorporating more realistic messages about sex into their scripts. This situation is compounded by the fact that advertisements for contraceptives have been widely banned by the national TV networks on the grounds that they are too controversial and would be morally offensive to many viewers. While there have been a small number of condom ads that have been aired on a limited basis (primarily aimed at AIDS prevention), these remain the exception rather than the rule. We can only hope that both of these situations will change in the near future.

AIDS Awareness Among Adolescents

Data on adolescent awareness of the HIV/AIDS epidemic and on the impact of such awareness on actual sexual behavior are slowly emerging. Despite clear evidence that anal intercourse and vaginal intercourse with more than one partner put a person at risk of infection with HIV and that condoms reduce the risk of transmission of HIV, many teenagers seem oblivious to the need to exercise caution.

Only a minority of sexually active adolescents consistently use condoms (DiClement, Boyer and Morales, 1988; Ku, Sonenstein, and Pleck, 1992; Reinisch et al., 1992). One report noted that 26 percent of teenage females had engaged in anal intercourse, with only one-third of them using condoms for this high-risk activity (Jaffe et al., 1988). Approximately 40 percent of sexually active teenagers have multiple sex partners each year, and those who have the largest number of partners are least likely to follow "safer sex" guidelines.

A recent survey of seventh and eighth grade students (average age, 13.2) found that 25 percent were sexually active, and that those who were sexually active tended to be less knowledgeable about HIV, less afraid of becoming infected with HIV, and more likely to engage in risky behaviors than peers who were not sexually active (Brown, DiClemente, and Beausoleil, 1992).

Even among teenage males with hemophilia —an especially high-risk group for infection with the AIDS virus—the reportedly "high level of factual knowledge" about AIDS did not seem to coincide with sensible behavior: only one of nine who were sexually active always used condoms, and 69 percent had not altered their sexual behavior because of concerns about transmitting HIV (Overby, Lo, and Litt, 1989). Remarkably, however, their knowledge of the AIDS risk did not predict whether teens would use condoms in their most recent episode of sexual intercourse.

On the other hand, data from the 1988 National Survey of Adolescent Males reported that levels of condom use rose substantially from 1979 to 1988: among 17- to 19-year-old males in metropolitan areas, condom use at last intercourse almost tripled (from 21 percent in 1979 to 58 percent in 1988) (Sonenstein, Pleck, and Ku, 1989). At the same time, it was disturbing to note that male teenagers who had used drugs intravenously or whose sex partners had done so, or who had ever had sex with a prostitute, or who had five or more sex partners in the past year had significantly lower than average condom use. Since these groups totaled some 42 percent of the men in the survey, it is clear that AIDS prevention is hardly being implemented in a risk-related manner among most teenagers. Follow-up interviews conducted with these same subjects in 1990–1991 at ages 17 to 22 showed that as they grew older, their condom use declined in tandem with less concern about getting AIDS (Pleck, Sonenstein, and Ku, 1993).

SEX EDUCATION FOR TEENS

There has been a great deal of controversy on the topic of sex education over the years, particularly on the issue of sex education in public schools. As discussed in the preceding chapter, one vocal faction made up of a small number of parents and some church groups opposes school-based sex education in any form, arguing that sex education should be done either in the home, where it can be placed in the context of family values, or in church-sponsored settings, where it can be taught within a proper moral framework. The vast majority of parents and teachers, however, believe that school involvement in sex education is both proper and necessary (Rosoff, 1989).

In recent years, there has been a definite trend toward more sex education in public schools, although it appears that AIDS education is getting more attention and funding from both the states and local school districts than sex education. Currently, all but four states support programs for

RESEARCH SPOTLIGHT

Nonvoluntary Sex Among Teenagers

Although many studies have focused attention on patterns of teenage sexual activity, particularly emphasizing the collection of data on age at first sexual intercourse, until recently there had been no major investigation of nonvoluntary sex among teenagers. A report by Moore, Nord, and Peterson (1989) remedied this situation with a detailed look at a nationally representative sample of American adolescents.

The survey they conducted involved interviews in 1987 with approximately 1100 adolescents and young adults primarily between the ages of 18 and 22. These interviews represented the third time data were collected from the same sample in a study begun in 1976 when the children were aged 7 to 11 and continued in 1981 with the same children when they were between the ages of 12 and 16. Seven percent of all respondents interviewed in 1987 gave an affirmative answer to the question:

"Was there ever a time when you were forced to have sex against your will, or were raped?" (The researchers believe that because of the sensitive nature of this question, the 7 percent figure is probably an underestimate of the true incidence of nonvoluntary sex.) Among white females, nearly 13 percent reported having been raped or coerced into sex by age 20, while 8 percent of black females reported having such an experience (see accompanying table). While the incidence of nonvoluntary sex for males was lower than for females, it is notable that it was roughly three times as high for black males as white males (6 percent versus 2 percent).

Working from a number of background variables, the researchers were able to develop a profile of a white teenage female's risk of nonvoluntary intercourse. Six risk factors proved to be important: parental heavy drinking; parental

Percentage[a] of 18- to 22-Year-Olds Who Report Ever Having Experienced Nonvoluntary Sexual Intercourse, by Age, According to Sex and Race

Age	Females		Males	
	White	Black	White	Black
14	5.8%	2.9%	0.3%	0.0%
15	6.3	3.2	0.4	1.4
16	7.5	3.5	0.4	4.8
17	9.1	5.1	0.4	5.6
18	10.8	5.6	0.4	6.1
19	11.9	6.0	1.9	6.1
20	12.7	8.0	1.9	6.1

[a]*Percentages are weighted.*
Source: *Moore, Nord, and Peterson, 1989. Table 1.*

of illicit drugs; parental smoking as a teenager; physical, emotional, or mental limitation on the part of the teenager; living apart from both parents before age 16; and childhood poverty. When none of these risk factors was present, there was a 5.7 percent risk of ever having experienced nonvoluntary sexual intercourse. With only one risk factor present, the proportion rose to 9.4 percent. But with two risk factors, there was a one out of four chance of having been raped or having been sexually coerced, and with three or more risk factors present, the odds rose to 67.8 percent that the teenager had been sexually victimized.

Moore, Nord, and Peterson note: "The data in this study illuminate one reason why some young people do not adequately protect themselves against pregnancy or disease: A small but important sub-group of children and adolescents enter sexual activity as victims forced to have sex against their will."

AIDS education, but only two-thirds of states require or encourage schools to teach about pregnancy prevention (Kenney, Guardad, and Brown, 1989). As a result, only one-third of American junior high schools and one-half of senior high

schools offer sex education courses (Orr, 1982; Kenney, Guardad, and Brown, 1989).

Unfortunately, sex education programs vary considerably from school district to school district in their timing, content, and community accept-

Educational posters are aimed at teenagers in an attempt to combat unintended adolescent pregnancies.

ance. Topics that most teachers believe should be covered by grades seven or eight, at the latest, frequently are not taught until ninth or tenth grades (or later), and many school-based sex education courses omit coverage of important topics, including sources of birth control, "safer sex" practices, and homosexuality (Forrest and Silverman, 1989). When sex education is provided only to older teenagers, its preventive function is lessened considerably. Perhaps for this reason, there is very little evidence that school sex education programs are effective when measured in terms of actual behavior such as preventing unintended pregnancies. An exception to this is the previously mentioned study by Zelnik and Kim (1982) which showed that among unmarried sexually active teenage women, those who had sex education had fewer pregnancies than those who had not.

One of a handful of school-based programs that *has* been conclusively found to be effective was conducted in inner-city Baltimore. Here, classroom teaching and individual counseling in junior high and high school settings were combined with educational, counseling, and medical services—including no-cost contraceptive services—provided in a storefront clinic located across the street from the senior high school (Zabin et al., 1988, 1988a). The clinic was open after school every day until the early evening. While this program was effective in lowering rates of unintended teen pregnancy by 30 percent over a two-year period, it is a mistake to regard it as simply a sex education program. In fact, since only 22 percent of staff–student contact occurred in the classroom, to equate the results of this program with the more commonly encountered standard classroom-only sex education course is incorrect.

Another innovative program has been designed for use by eighth graders in Atlanta schools (Howard and McCabe, 1990). The unique features of the program, which focuses on helping students resist peer and social pressures to initiate sexual activity, are (1) the use of older teenagers in male–female teams as session leaders and (2) practical exercises emphasizing skills like how to say "no" without hurting the other person's feelings. Among students who had not had sexual intercourse by the eighth grade, those who participated in this program were significantly more likely to continue postponing sexual activity through the end of the ninth grade than were students who did not participate in the program.

These two examples of successful programs highlight one of the major difficulties with current sex education curricula. There is little indication that transmitting information, by itself, alters adolescents' sexual behavior in a meaningful way, which is undoubtedly why most school-based sex education programs have not proved to be effective in reducing rates of teenage sexual activity or unintended teen pregnancies (Furstenberg, Moore, and Peterson, 1985; Dawson, 1986). Furthermore, many sex education programs are so slanted toward the notion of sexual abstinence for teens that high school students are apt to disregard them entirely (Wilson and Sanderson, 1988; Brick, 1989).

The abstinence approach might be effective with some adolescents—particularly those who are younger and sexually inexperienced—but it would probably not be realistically effective with the majority of teenagers, given today's patterns of sexual behavior in our culture. Also, such an approach runs the risk of being repressive—it is, after all, an attempt to frighten teens into abstinence—and this may produce a backlash. In any case, since it is unlikely that the majority of sexually experienced teenagers will suddenly become abstinent, it is necessary to provide teens with positive role models toward effective contraceptive use and a more effective view of the ways in which responsibility in sexual behavior is important to their welfare. This includes highlighting the possibility that teenagers can avoid casual, promiscuous sex and instead put the emphasis on sex in the context of a committed, caring relationship.

One possible approach represents a compromise position in which the role of abstinence is promoted, but not as the exclusive option available to teens. Peterson (1988) suggests this can be accomplished by:

- Encouraging teens to make healthy decisions for themselves.
- Giving straight facts about the health concerns of teen pregnancy and STDs.
- Supporting those teens who have chosen abstinence.
- Strengthening communication between parents and their children.
- Supporting comprehensive sexuality education that involves parents and community leaders.
- Offering quality counseling and medical services to those teens who call for help.

There is also solid agreement that greater responsibility for contraceptive use by the adolescent male is a major element in the effort to reduce the rate of unintended teenage pregnancy and to reduce the spread of STDs, including AIDS. Evidence suggests that educating males about contraceptive options at an early age leads to better contraceptive use (Cvetkovitch and Grote, 1983), but such education need not be confined to the classroom. Community-based programs (Carrera and Dempsey, 1988; Sandoval, 1988), direct mailing campaigns (Kirby et al., 1989), media campaigns, and church-affiliated programs may all play a role in this undertaking. But the information given must be practical, not just informative: it must explain how and where to purchase contraceptives (and how to deal with embarrassment over the purchase), why it's important to discuss birth control with a partner, and why consistent contraceptive use is necessary.

Whatever the ultimate solution, we believe that it is particularly important to realize that sex education for teens cannot be successful if it only focuses on biological facts and negative consequences. Without including coverage of intimacy, interpersonal relationships, sexual decision making, different sexual orientations, and coercive sex, to name just a few essential topics, school programs will be incomplete and, inevitably, ineffective. In addition, if sex education programs cannot acknowledge that sexual activity for adolescents is not inherently harmful, sinful, or destructive—if they cannot be honest enough to point out that sex for teenagers can be pleasurable, responsible, and caring—we are providing our teens with the wrong message.

SUMMARY

1. There are several prominent factors that are interwoven in the ordinary development of adolescent sexuality. These include the links between pubertal development, body image, and self-image; the task of learning about one's body and its sensual and sexual responses and needs; forging an identity (including dealing with gender-role expectations and sexual orientation); learning about sexual and romantic relationships; and developing a personal sexual value system. In addition, teens must learn to deal with their sexual fantasies, peer pressures, and parental reactions to their developing sexuality.

2. With puberty, as sex hormone levels are activated, there is a growth spurt, maturation of the gonads and genitals, and development of secondary sex characteristics. Girls begin menstruation and have breast and pubic hair growth; boys become able to ejaculate and have voice deepening, growth of facial and body hair, and development of muscle mass. There is great variability to the timing and duration of puberty.

3. Patterns of sexual behavior among adolescents show evidence of having changed in several ways since the Kinsey era. For one thing, there has been a convergence in the rates of sexual activity for teenage males and females, although throughout all ages of adolescence, males are still more likely to have engaged in sexual intercourse than females. In addition,

the age of first sexual intercourse has declined noticeably for teenage females in the past three decades. Although not all adolescents are sexually experienced, and about 30 percent of nonvirgins seem dissatisfied with their sex lives, a majority of American teenagers become coitally experienced by age 18 or 19.

4. Some adolescents realize that they do not fit the expected heterosexual mold, and others worry about their sexual orientation. Gay and lesbian teenagers are often confronted with hostility and homophobia from their peers and family, as well as by the lack of visible role models to follow.

5. Unintended teenage pregnancy is a major social and public health concern in America today, with more than 1 million teenage pregnancies occurring annually. These pregnancies are often problematic because of increased health risks (among younger teens) and adverse socioeconomic consequences for both the parents and the child. However, there are indications that teenage fathers are not the irresponsible thrill-seekers they have often been portrayed as; many of them choose not to abandon their babies and contribute financially to the care of their children.

6. While no easy solutions are available to resolve the problem of unintended teenage pregnancy (or the related problem of high rates of STDs among teens), new types of school-based sex education programs have been devised that appear to be more effective than the old "knowledge-based" programs were. Key challenges such programs will have to face are involvement of the male (as well as the female) in the contraceptive decision process, dealing with community opposition, and providing young teens with the motivation to postpone their sexual involvement. However, waiting until tenth or eleventh grade to offer such programs will not work, in our judgment; the most important part of adolescent sex education should begin before the teenage years arrive.

Thought Questions

1. Is there still a double standard regarding sexual activity of boys versus girls? Do teenagers still talk in terms of "nice girls" versus "sluts"? Why isn't there a term for a male counterpart to a slut?

2. Does listening to rock and roll or rap music and other popular music with explicit sexual lyrics increase the likelihood teenagers will become sexually active? Should the recording industry be required to put warning stickers on album covers to identify those with sexually explicit content?

3. Do boys and girls differ in how important "being in love" is to their becoming sexual with each other? Is the old adage true that "Boys fall in love in order to get sex, while girls give sex in order to get love"?

4. What kinds of strategies might be effective in increasing teenage boys' sense of responsibility regarding birth control, condoms, and safer sex practices?

5. Should contraceptives and birth control information be available to minors through school clinics? If so, at what age should they be available?

6. Why do you think the United States has the highest rate of unintended teenage pregnancy of all the relatively wealthy and developed countries?

Suggested Readings

Bryne, Donn, and Fisher, William (eds.). *Adolescents, Sex, and Contraception*. Hillsdale, N.J.: Lawrence Erlbaum Associates, 1983. Comprehensive discussion of teenage sexuality principally in terms of factors that govern contraceptive attitudes and behavior. Difficult reading in spots, but worth the effort for its thorough and thoughtful coverage.

Burkhart, Kathryn. *Growing into Love*. New York: Putnam, 1981. Interviews with teenagers on sexuality presented with wit, insight, and sensitivity. Although this is not a research study in the scientific sense, it is highly informative nontechnical reading.

Cassell, Carol. *Straight from the Heart: How to Talk to Your Teenagers about Love and Sex*. New York: Simon and Schuster, 1987. A practical guidebook for parents designed to help them deal with the complex issues of adolescent sexuality. The emphasis is on how to initiate discussions, how much to say, and how personal to get, rather than just a compilation of facts. This book should be on the shelf of every parent with a teenager at home!

Henshaw, Stanley K. et al., *Teenage Pregnancy in the United States: The Scope of the Problem and State Responses*. New York: Alan Guttmacher Institute, 1989. A concise summary of state-by-state statis-tics on adolescent pregnancies and their out-comes combined with an analysis of various adolescent pregnancy initiatives launched dur-ing the 1980s by many states.

Robinson, B.E. *Teenage Fathers*. Lexington, MA: D.C. Heath, 1988. A superb analysis of a much-ne-glected topic. This book exposes many myths about teenage fathers and offers a good deal of insight in an easy-to-read style.

Adult Sexuality

Traditionally, developmentalists have studied childhood and adolescence as a means of understanding adulthood. This viewpoint is useful in many ways, but it has inadvertently created the impression that development stops at a precise moment, leaving the adult a relatively static creature. Another view, which can be traced back to the writings of psychologists Carl Jung and Erik Erikson, stresses the developmental aspects of adulthood. According to this perspective, adulthood is a continuing pattern of learning, crisis, and choice. Daniel Levinson (1978) has suggested that the life cycle is a kind of journey:

> Many influences along the way shape the nature of the journey. They may produce alternate routes or detours along the way; they may speed up or slow down the timetable within certain limits; in extreme cases they may stop the developmental process altogether. But as long as the journey continues, it follows the basic sequence. *(p. 6)*

Gail Sheehy (1976) has added to the view of adult developmental stages by conceptualizing them as a series of passages through fairly predictable crises that contribute to our growth. She observes:

> During each of these passages, how we feel about our way of living will undergo subtle

changes in four areas of perception. One is the interior sense of self in relation to others. A second is the proportion of safeness to danger we feel in our lives. A third is our perception of time—do we have plenty of it, or are we beginning to feel that time is running out? Last, there will be some shift at the gut level in our sense of aliveness or stagnation. These are the hazy sensations that compose the background tone of living and shape the decisions on which we take action. *(p. 21)*

We take only an abbreviated look at adult sexuality here because the rest of this book is largely about the sexual experiences and sexual problems of adults. The notion of adulthood as a time of transition and development is a useful one to retain while reading subsequent chapters.

EARLY ADULTHOOD

The phase of early adulthood, from approximately age 20 to 40, is a time when people make important life choices (marriage, occupation, lifestyle) and move from the relatively untested ambitions of adolescence to a personal maturity shaped by the realities of the world in which they live. For most people, it is a time of increasing responsibility in terms of interpersonal relations and family life.

The Single Life

In recent years, both in the United States and abroad, there has been a definite trend toward marriage at a later age than in past decades (Sweet and Bumpass, 1987; Goldscheider and Da Vanzo, 1989; Cherlin, 1992). As a result, many young men and women face an extended period of being single after adolescence that unquestionably has changed patterns of sexual behavior from Kinsey's day. Today, most people in their twenties believe that becoming sexually experienced rather than preserving virginity is an important prelude for selecting a mate. Erikson (1968) remarks that developing the capacity for intimacy is a central task for the young adult.

The early years of adulthood are a time of sexual uncertainty for some and sexual satisfaction for others. Conflict can arise because of attitudes of sexual guilt or immorality carried over from earlier

ages. The adolescent's concern with sexual normality has not fully disappeared, and the young adult continues to worry about his or her physique, sexual endowment, and personal skill in making love. Sexual identity conflicts may not yet have been resolved, and even for those who have come to accept themselves as homosexual or bisexual, social pressures and prejudices may cause some difficulty.

Despite the existence of such problems, young adults are more sexually active today than in the past (Robinson and Jedlicka, 1982; Gagnon, 1989). A major factor contributing to this change has been the relative disappearance of the old double standard that regarded premarital sexual experience as permissible for men but not for women (DeLamater and MacCorquodale, 1979). Thus, it is not surprising to see that the gender gap in premarital sexual experience has narrowed considerably from what it used to be, as shown in Table 10.1. Another contributing factor is the increased practice of cohabitation today compared to two decades ago, which we will discuss shortly.

Although the popular notion is that being young and single automatically leads to sexual happiness, the reality may be somewhat different. In one survey of 250 college students, for instance, 43 percent stated that they were concerned about being unable to find time for sexual relations, and 40 percent had problems with lack of privacy for sex (Koch, 1982). This survey also found relatively high rates of sexual dysfunctions: 37 percent of the students had difficulty becoming vaginally lubricated or getting erections at least half of the time; 30 percent of the females had trouble reaching orgasm; and 23 percent of the males ejaculated too quickly. College students are not the only ones who have

Table 10.1 **Percentage of College Students Having Premarital Intercourse**

Year	Males		Females	
	%	N	%	N
1965	65.1	129	28.7	115
1970	65.0	136	37.3	158
1975	73.9	115	57.1	275
1980	77.4	168	63.5	230

Source: *Robinson and Jedlicka, 1982.*

these sorts of problems. A 1983 *Psychology Today* survey of young adults found that 28 percent of men and 40 percent of women complained of lack of sexual desire, while almost 20 percent of both sexes admitted to fears about sexual adequacy (Rubenstein, 1983).

Today's young adults are faced with some additional sexual conflicts that may represent a sort of backlash against the "anything goes" banner of the sexual revolution of the 1960s and 1970s. For example, while attitudes toward premarital sex have changed dramatically in the last three decades, having sex with a large number of partners is still frowned on (Robinson and Jedlicka, 1982). Furthermore, although most singles don't believe that love is necessary for good sex, some observers claim that there seems to be increasing disillusionment with casual sex or one-night stands (Simenauer and Carroll, 1982; Rubenstein, 1983).

This trend seems to be at least partly the result of increased awareness of the possibility of exposure to sexually transmitted diseases, such as AIDS and genital herpes (Mosher and Pratt, 1993; Potter and Anderson, 1993; Centers for Disease Control, 1993f). Among young adult homosexual men, who have—as a group—typically participated in casual sex much more than their heterosexual age-mates, fear of contracting AIDS has also led recently to a reduction in the number of sexual partners and more interest in establishing "monogamous" relationships. (For a more detailed discussion of this point, see Chapters 16 and 20.) Fear is not, however, the only element operating here. Many of the young adults we have interviewed are concerned with another aspect of casual sex: its relatively impersonal nature. The following remarks are typical of what we have been told:

A 26-year-old man: Having one-night stands was fun at first because there were no demands attached, no one's expectations to fulfill. But after a year or so I began to realize that something was missing from these encounters—a sense of caring about the person I was making it with, or a feeling that she cared about me. *(Authors' files)*

A 30-year-old woman: You just can't compare the quality of sex with someone you hardly know and feel nothing for with the quality of sex in a caring relationship. Casual sex is just mechanical, one-dimensional release. Sex with someone I care about is warmer and psychologically far more satisfying. *(Authors' files)*

Why are a number of young adults becoming disillusioned with having only casual sexual encounters? Peter Marin, in an article titled "A Revolution's Broken Promises" (1983) offers one interesting analysis of what may be occurring: he suggests that while loosening restraints on sexual behavior creates a climate of sexual freedom and choice, this freedom is not unequivocally positive. Sexual freedom can lead to disappointment, pressure, and conflict as well as to satisfaction, so that "to the extent that it diversifies and expands experience, it also diversifies and multiplies the pain that accompanies experience, the kinds of errors that we can make, the kinds of harm we can do to one another" (p. 53).

On the other hand, one recent study of college women showed no indication of a trend toward fewer sexual partners in this age group (DeBuono et al., 1990; Table 10.2), and most males in their twenties today would laugh at the idea of limiting their sexual experiences.

A recent survey showed that 17.9 percent of men aged 20 to 24 had had at least 20 sex partners in their lifetimes, and for men between the ages of 25 and 29, this figure rose to 20.5 percent (Billy et al., 1993). That young women are also sexually active is clear from another national study: 38 percent of 20- to 24-year-olds and 45.5 percent of 25- to 29-

Table 10.2   Sexual Activity of College Women, 1975 Versus 1989[a]

	1975 N = 486	1989 N = 132
Lifetime number of male sexual partners		
0	12%	13%
1	25	12
2–5	41	52
≥ 6	22	21
Number of male sexual partners in past year		
0	14	17
1	44	44
2	20	17
≥ 3	22	21

[a]*Figures are rounded to the nearest percent.*
Source: *"Sexual Activity of College Women, 1975 vs. 1989" from DeBuono et al., "Sexual Behavior of College Women in 1975, 1986 and 1989," New England Journal of Medicine, 322: 821–825, 1990, table 1. Reprinted by permission of The New England Journal of Medicine.*

year-olds reported at least 4 lifetime sexual partners, while one out of 10 women in their thirties had had more than 10 lifetime sexual partners (Kost and Forrest, 1992).

As Table 10.3 shows, a majority of college men and women are sexually active today. Further evidence of this trend can be seen in data from a recent survey done at a midwestern university that showed that females had an average of 5.6 sexual partners, while for males, the figure was 11.2 (Reinisch et al., 1992).

To be sure, sexual experiences in early adulthood are often warm, exciting, gratifying, and untroubled. Even casual sex can serve a number of useful purposes, psychologically as well as physically, and there is certainly no reason that having fun is to be frowned on. But the prevailing trend is clearly toward sex in the context of caring relationships, and one place this is particularly evident is in the relatively recent growth of cohabitation—unmarried heterosexual couples living together.

Cohabitation

Only 25 years ago, the typical female college student had an 11:00 p.m. curfew (extended to midnight on Fridays and Saturdays) and had to sign in and out of her dormitory. Male visitors were often not allowed above the ground-floor level, and only

a few daring campuses permitted female visitors in male dorms—usually for one or two hours per week, with the door wide open, and "monitors" to enforce these regulations. Today, many college campuses have mixed dorms (men and women living side by side) and unrestricted visiting policies.

Perhaps even more striking than these revolutionary changes is the rapid acceptance of unmarried couples living together in heterosexual arrangements formally called **cohabitation.**[1] Current estimates suggest that more than 3 million single people are cohabiting (Macklin, 1987; Bumpass and Sweet, 1989). Although cohabitation is *not* a practice limited to college students—in fact, cohabitation rates are higher among high school dropouts than among college students or college graduates—about one-quarter of college students have had the experience and another 50 percent would like to (Macklin, 1987; Bumpass and Sweet, 1989). One study found that the incidence of cohabiting before marriage increased from 11 percent among couples who married between 1965 and 1974 to 44 percent of couples who married from 1980 to 1984 (Bumpass and Sweet, 1989). And Cherlin (1992, p.12) notes: "Cohabitation is now so prevalent that a majority of the third postwar generation—the offspring of the baby boom children—likely will live with a partner before marrying."

Actually, about half of the people now cohabiting have previously been married, although the majority of cohabitants are under age 35.

What factors led to the popularity of cohabitation? One psychologist suggests that the women's movement, loosening of restrictive college housing regulations, and the radical political climate of the 1960s combined with other social changes to promote this practice (Macklin, 1978):

> The increase in divorce, and the changing conception of the function of marriage, caused many young single people and divorcees to move cautiously into that state. The increased

Table 10.3   Male–Female Similarities and Differences in Selected Recent Sexual Experiences[a] Among College Students

Type of Sexual Experience	Females	Males
Masturbation alone	71%	83%
Receiving oral–genital stimulation	71	64
Giving oral–genital stimulation	68	60
Sexual intercourse	68	68
Reading/watching pornography	37	58
Anal intercourse	10	6
Being forced to submit	6	1
Sex with a virgin	1	7
Sex with two or more people at the same time	1	4

[a]*Recent experiences were defined as those occurring in the previous three months.*
Source: *From Person et al., Journal of Sex and Marital Therapy, 15 (3), 187–198, 1982. Copyright © 1989 by Brunner/Mazel, Inc. Reprinted by permission.*

cohabitation a situation in which an unmarried heterosexual couple live together.

[1]Cohabitation is legally distinguished from common-law marriage in how the partners present themselves to the world. While cohabitants may live much as husbands and wives, they must advertise themselves as single if they do not want to take the risk of running afoul of laws pertaining to common-law marriage.

FOCUS IN BRIEF

Research on Cohabitation

- About 3 million Americans are currently cohabiting.
- The age breakdown is as follows:
  38 percent of the women and 25 percent of the men were under 25;
  36 percent of the women and 41 percent of the men were 25 to 34;
  20 percent of the women and 28 percent of the men were 35 to 64;
  6 percent of both sexes were 65 or older.
- Most cohabiting relationships either break up or get married within two years; two out of five break up within one year.
- Twenty-five percent of college undergraduates have had at least one cohabitation relationship.
- Couples who have cohabited tend to have more disagreements and less marital satisfaction in the early years after marriage than couples who haven't cohabited.
- Cohabitation doesn't seem to help people choose their mates more effectively than noncohabitants do; 36 percent of married couples who cohabited before marriage separate or divorce within 10 years, compared to 27 percent who did not live together before marriage.

Sources: *U.S. Bureau of the Census, 1989; Macklin, 1987; Bumpass and Sweet, 1989.*

acceptance of sexuality outside marriage and improved contraception made it easier for non-married persons to engage openly and comfortably in a sexual relationship. And the increased emphasis on relationships and personal growth called into question the superficiality of the traditional dating game, and led to a search for styles of relating that allowed for change, growth, and a high degree of intimacy. *(pp. 199–200)*

The majority of college students apparently believe that no long-term commitment between partners is necessary to undertake a cohabitation relationship (Macklin, 1978, Table 3; Bumpass, Sweet,

and Cherlin, 1991). Generally, there are three basic forms of cohabitation—casual or temporary involvement, preparation or testing for marriage, and substitute for or alternative to marriage. Most college students who begin cohabitation see their relationship as affectionate but uncommitted (Petty, 1975; Macklin, 1978: Cherlin, 1992). In one study, however, 96 percent of the students who had cohabited said that they wanted to marry in the future (Bower and Christopherson, 1977). Often, cohabitation serves as an added step in the courtship process. In fact, given the current trend of delaying the timing of marriage, cohabitation for a period of several years or more may be becoming something of a cultural fixture (Bumpass and Sweet, 1989).

In their study of relationships, Blumstein and Schwartz (1983) included 653 cohabiting heterosexual couples who had lived together an average of 2.5 years. They found that while cohabitants had more frequent sex than married couples, as cohabitants stayed together longer their frequency of sexual relations declined. Other key findings included:

1. As with married couples, when there were problems in nonsexual areas of the cohabitants' lives, their sex lives suffered.

2. Cohabiting women initiate sex more often than married women, but in older cohabiting couples the male often resents this.

3. Only about one-third of people who are cohabiting have sex with other people outside their relationship.

Blumstein and Schwartz (1983) believe that it will be difficult for cohabitation to become a viable permanent institution as long as the traditional marriage model exists, since "as long as marriage retains its image as the highest form of commitment, it acts as a lure to cohabiting couples who want to prove their love for each other" (p. 321.) Furthermore, family and social pressures to marry—especially before having children—are so strong in the United States that it seems unlikely, at present, that cohabitation will become accepted here as a long-term alternative to marriage (Cherlin, 1992). In Sweden, however, cohabitation without legal marriage has become a social institution that is, for many couples, a variant of marriage. While at least half of Swedish cohabiting couples eventually marry, it is usually after they have cohabited for a lengthy period, and often their children are included in the wedding party (Macklin, 1987).

One interesting study (Newcomb, 1986) looked at differences in sexual behavior between people living together (cohabitants) and noncohabitants. Not surprisingly, this study found that cohabitants were generally more sexually experienced than noncohabitants. In addition, while satisfaction with sexual intercourse and subjective orgasmic responsiveness were about the same in both groups, cohabiting women reported more frequent orgasms in all forms of sexual activity than noncohabiting women. This finding may have been related to the fact that cohabiting women were more self-assured and confident than noncohabitants, or, as Newcomb suggested, it may indicate that the broader range of sexual experience cohabiting women possessed made it easier for them to be orgasmic.

What effects does cohabitation have on the participants? Generally, cohabitants have given very positive ratings to their experience, describing it as "maturing," "fostering emotional growth and personal understanding," and "improving skills in heterosexual relationships" (Peterman, Ridley, and Anderson, 1974; Macklin, 1976, 1987). The great majority of college students surveyed who have had prior experience with cohabitation say they would never marry without living with the person first (Bower, 1975; Macklin, 1976; Kolodny, 1994). However, it should also be noted that marriages that follow cohabitation break up more often than those begun without a prior period of living together (Cherlin, 1992).

Marriage and Divorce

In contrast to single life, marriage, which is discussed in greater detail in Chapters 12 and 16, presents different sexual development patterns. For better or for worse, a majority of young adults eventually marry, which can itself create certain sexual difficulties. As the novelty of early marital bliss dissolves in the process of learning to live with one another's quirks and habits, as early dreams of conquering the world give way to a more practical focus on details of everyday life, sex is likely to become less exciting and sometimes less gratifying for one or both partners. Reflecting this, the frequency of sexual activity generally declines in the early years of marriage, as shown in Table 10.4. Parenthood leads to less privacy, more demands, and even exhaustion. It is hard to get excited about sex if you have been running after a 2-year-old all day long, just as sex is apt to lose its

attraction if you have worked a 14-hour day at the office.

For most young married adults, sex is no longer the frantic secret activity of adolescence or the stylistic tour de force of singlehood. While sexual pleasure is not sacrificed or lost, it is balanced with other needs and responsibilities—an important developmental task in this phase of the life cycle. Those who do not succeed in this process of integration are more likely to become sexually dissatisfied. As a result, they may turn to extramarital sex, professional counseling, or divorce. Each of these paths seems well-traveled at the present time.

Some couples fulfill the American dream of marital bliss by staying together, raising children, remaining faithful, and loving one another all along the way. Others live out a modified version of this script in which love disappears but the other features are retained. Still others modify the script in different ways: no children, no faithfulness, or no bliss. The appearance to outsiders and the reality within the relationship do not always match.

One concrete bit of evidence that bliss is often missing from marriages can be found in the divorce rate in our society. Since the early 1960s, the annual number of divorces has climbed steadily (Figure 10.1), reflecting the change in attitudes toward divorce (less stigmatization and sense of failure) and in divorce laws (which make it possible to obtain "no fault" divorces in most states). Projections based on statistics gathered by the U.S. Census Bureau suggest that approximately one out of five couples marrying now will divorce before their fifth anniversary, while a third won't make it through a decade of marriage (National Center for Health Statistics, 1982). Four out of ten will divorce before

Table 10.4 Frequency of Intercourse in Early Marriage

	N	Mean Frequency of Intercourse per Month
1st year	12	14.8
2nd year	10	12.2
3rd year	19	11.9
4th year	7	9.0
5th year	18	9.7
6th year	8	6.3

Source: *Modified from Greenblatt, 1983.*

Figure 10.1   Proportion of Marriages Begun in Each Year That Will End in Divorce, 1867 to 1985

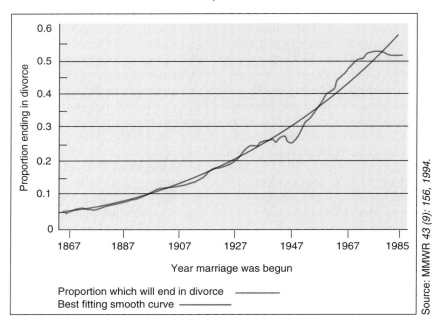

Source: MMWR 43 (9): 156, 1994.

their fifteenth anniversary. Thus, as you might infer from these projections, the majority of divorces involve spouses who have not yet reached middle age. Overall, a majority of people who marry today will probably get divorced (Cherlin, 1992).

It is not clear how frequently sexual dissatisfaction is a primary cause of divorce, but marriage counselors are well aware that sexual problems are common in couples whose marriages are troubled. Whether the sexual difficulties precede and contribute to other marital problems or whether the reverse is more typically true is simply not known.

Relatively little has been written about sexuality in the aftermath of divorce. It might be expected that the new sense of personal freedom that would follow a divorce would lead to increased rates of sexual activity, and in fact one study of 367 divorced singles has partially confirmed this (Simenauer and Carroll, 1982). The same study, however, found that 27 percent of the men and 36 percent of the women reported decreased amounts of sexual activity. Similarly, a separate survey found that lack of sexual desire was more prevalent among divorced men than among those who were married (Rubenstein, 1983).

A more recent study found further evidence of surprisingly low rates of sexual activity among divorced people: one-quarter of those surveyed had been totally abstinent, and another 9 percent had only had sexual intercourse once or twice a year (Stack and Gundlach, 1992). To understand why this divergence occurs, we should realize that the reality of life after divorce is not always one of freedom and happiness. These comments illustrate what may be going on:

A 32-year-old woman: Sure I wanted to have new sexual experiences, but someone had to take care of my kids, and the guys I met were all pretty grubby, and I spent a lot of time feeling sorry for myself. Looking back, I guess I wasn't very good company. *(Authors' files)*

A 33-year-old man: It wasn't at all what I thought it was going to be. I sort of expected to find being single again a blessing, sexually speaking. I had visions of myself living out fantasies from *Playboy,* but it didn't really work like that at all. At the beginning, I was so nervous and embarrassed I couldn't function properly; then, I got an infection from a girl I really was beginning to like. Being single is no cup of tea. *(Authors' files)*

A 26-year-old woman: Every guy who asked me out expected that because I had been married, I'd be happy to have sex with him on our first date. It just wasn't comfortable for me, but I don't think many of them cared. *(Authors' files)*

The recently divorced man or woman may be delighted with a newfound sexual freedom, but the initial thrill is likely to be dampened by one of several difficulties. Returning to the rituals of dating and courtship may be annoying or embarrassing, especially to those who have been out of circulation for a decade or longer. Self-consciousness about sex with someone who is almost a stranger may be distressing. Concerns about the adequacy of sexual performance and personal attractiveness may be combined with remorse or guilt over lack of commitment and morality. To all of this, we must also add that there is frequently a sense that time is running out: "I'd better get a partner while I can."

Statistics show that about three out of four men and about two out of three women remarry after a divorce—about half within three years—apparently deciding that a second marriage will give them a chance to do things differently (Cherlin, 1992). Often this is more illusion than reality: statistical projections suggest that more than half of *second* marriages for women born between 1945 and 1954 are expected to fail, with men trailing close behind with a projected 40 percent second marriage divorce rate (Hegger, 1983). In addition, there is no evidence that divorced persons who remarry have an increased sense of well-being compared with those who remain single (Spanier and Furstenberg, 1982).

The problems encountered in second marriages are apt to be complex, including, for example, how to deal with children of earlier marriages, the financial strain of alimony, and relations between the new spouse and the "ex." In addition, many of the same problems that plagued a first marriage tend to reappear in a second one: selfishness, alcohol abuse, lack of communication, and other similar problems don't disappear easily.

One research survey of couples in second marriages suggests that the same sexual problems often reappear as well (Kolodny, 1983). These problems are not always apparent before the remarriage since sexual problems, such as low sexual desire, may temporarily be overcome by the excitement of a new romance and by the special attentions that each partner pays to the other. When the romance dies down to a low flickering flame and sex is attempted not in romantic circumstances but after bathing three kids, washing the dishes, paying the bills, and arguing about who is going to take the garbage out, it is no surprise that sexual feelings are not at an ecstatic peak. In addition, some couples

may decide to marry even when they realize that a sexual problem is present. They may either hope that the problem will disappear with time—which is generally unlikely—or they may adopt a "who cares" attitude that deliberately deemphasizes the role of sex even before the marriage begins.

Despite the fact that the divorce doesn't always provide as neat a solution to problems as many people think it will, there are certainly many instances in which divorce is the soundest option available. Knowing when to put an end to an unpleasant or painful relationship is often a key step toward creating the chance for a new start.

By their mid- to late thirties, most married people have moved beyond the demands of early parenthood and have acquired a sense of maturity and security in their own world. Individuals who have chosen not to marry have typically worked through whatever uncertainty may have surrounded this lifestyle choice at an early age. For both men and women, this is a time of becoming one's own person (Levinson et al., 1978; Frieze et al., 1978) and making decisions about future life directions. Women with teenage children begin to look toward establishing life goals outside the home. Others who have postponed childbearing face final decisions about whether to proceed with having a family. Although this might seem to be, at last, the attainment of equilibrium and stability, it is often just the lull before the storm.

MIDDLE ADULTHOOD

At around 40, people enter a period of transition from their younger years to what has traditionally been called "middle age." It is a time when the visions and energy of youth begin to give way to hard realities and when most people first confront their own mortality and sense that time is running out. Some feel alarmed because their physique has folded and their youth "has flown the coop," never to be regained (despite attempts at fancy diets, jogging, hair dye, and facelifts). For most people, life must be reappraised in terms of goals, accomplishments, and experiences. As a result, a midlife crisis sometimes begins to take shape (Howells, 1981).

The Midlife Crisis

From a sexual perspective, the male seems to be particularly vulnerable to the midlife crisis. Since rumor has it that after age 40 a man is "over the hill" sexually, many men begin to check their sexual performance for signs of wear and tear. This is well described in the following:

> He notes that it takes more time to become aroused. Where it used to be a matter of seconds and a mere glance at the orbs of flesh colliding beneath a pair of tennis shorts, he may take minutes or more to reach erection as he gets older. He also notices, correctly, that he is slower on the comeback. In the sweet agonies of teen age he may have walked about with an erection all day, seldom completely losing it even after he made love or masturbated—a virtual prisoner of his hormones and tight-fitting pants. But now each sexual act has a definite beginning and end, and it may be a matter of hours or all day before he can reach erection again. Comparisons, stinging comparisons . . . he is not the boy he once was. *(Sheehy, 1976, p. 305)*

Once a man begins to question his sexual capabilities, the odds are that he will experience difficulty getting or keeping an erection. This, of course, "proves" the correctness of the underlying concern, and a vicious cycle is set in motion.

Some men turn to younger sexual partners to heat up their passion and others succeed, at least to a certain degree, in blaming the problem on their wives. But the middle-aged male is in a precarious position of sexual vulnerability. If he goes to a physician to discuss the problem, he may be told (as several of our patients have been), "At your age, you shouldn't worry about it anymore."

The woman's midlife crisis is less apt to include concern about her sexual capacity. For women who have chiefly been mothers, it is a time for an emerging identity, a freeing of the inner self as children reach a relative stage of greater independence. It is a bittersweet time in which a woman who has not established a career or nonfamily interests may mourn the passing of her offspring into their own maturity and may simultaneously look at available options for redirecting her talents and energy. As children leave home, the "empty-nest syndrome" may strike, causing depression and listlessness as the women tries to deal with too much unstructured time and few sources of rewarding or interesting activities (Frieze et al., 1978). Since these vulnerable feelings may be followed by or coincide with the menopausal years, it may be a particularly trying period for such women. Interestingly, some research suggests that it is not only women who may be affected by the empty-nest syndrome. Roberts and Lewis (1981) point out that men are also sometimes distressed by their children's departure from home, "discovering that their marriages and friendships had become empty shells about the same time that loved children were leaving." Of course, having children leave home can have positive effects on a marriage too: for instance, it gives couples a chance to focus on their own interaction and can create opportunities for freer, more relaxed sex as well.

There are more and more variations on the midlife transition today. Career-oriented women who postponed motherhood (and time off from work) until their mid-thirties may be anxious to reconfirm their work identity but may have trouble finding a job or getting back on the "fast track." Other mothers who refused to restructure their lives around childrearing and continued to work outside the home—either by choice or by economic necessity—may feel considerable guilt or exhaustion. Still other women find their lives complicated by divorce and face childrearing as a single parent; alternatively, if they remarry a man with children of his own, the family interactions may become particularly complex.

Of course, not everyone experiences a full-blown midlife crisis, and for some, the forties and fifties are a time of happiness and sexual satisfaction. One woman told us, "I'd never want to be 21 again—being 45 is more fun!"

Other Considerations

Most men have "discovered" their sexuality in a joyous way by their twenties, but—at least in past generations—a sizable number of women did not awaken from their socially programmed sexual dormancy until their thirties or forties. Given the traditional limits set on female sexual behavior and feelings ("nice girls don't. . .") and given the traditional division of marital responsibilities (domestic and childbearing duties are "female," career orientation is "male"), this pattern should come as no surprise. As a result, many women undergo a process of sexual self-discovery in mid-adulthood, perhaps including being orgasmic for the first time. Although not written about extensively, the woman in this phase of the life cycle is just as likely as her mate to seek out extramarital sexual opportunities: (Wolfe, 1980; Grosskopf, 1983; Heyn, 1992; Botwin, 1994).

In a survey of 160 midlife women, Rubin (1982) found that the most characteristic pattern was one of *improving* sexuality. She noted that although these women had to overcome sexual inexperience and cultural prohibitions against female sexuality when they were younger (and then had to deal with raising young children), by midlife women were better able to relate sex to their own wishes and needs rather than participating in sexual activity principally to please their partners. Thus, Rubin found that midlife women take the sexual initiative more often than they previously had done (although, paradoxically, some of these women became concerned with putting sexual pressure on their husbands or partners by initiating sex too often).

Sex can improve for people in middle adulthood for a number of different reasons in addition to those mentioned above. Certainly one of the most important is that some individuals find themselves in new relationships that meet their needs better than previous ones. Others manage to transform the nature of a long-standing relationship to one of greater intimacy, which understandably has benefits in sexual terms. A third factor also applies in many instances: after years of experience together, some couples eventually become more adept at meeting each other's needs and learning how to compromise. They may discover that what had previously been sexual stalemates can instead be turned into fulfilling, romantic occasions.

One intriguing finding has been noted about sex differences in the psychology of middle adulthood. Among those 40 to 45, men are apt to exhibit a strong sense of self-confidence and control and typically engage in behavior geared to show their power and proficiency, while women tend to be more dependent, passive, and lacking in confidence. By the late fifties, however, a decided shift occurs. Men seem to move away from their need to demonstrate power and mastery and begin to show more concern for emotional sensitivity and interpersonal relations. At the same time, women frequently begin to show more self-confidence and assertiveness, in effect reversing the earlier roles that had been observed (Chiriboga, 1981). While the implications of this observation for sexual behavior are not entirely clear, it appears to lend support to the notion that some postmenopausal women become more sexually assertive than they had been previously, while men may become more interested in sharing tenderness and affection as they become less preoccupied with career concerns.

A few additional aspects of middle adulthood deserve mention. Some people who were content with being single as young adults begin to yearn for the commitment and long-term companionship that marriage can offer. These individuals may have a difficult time finding a potential mate who fits their expectations. For many in this situation, an increasingly acceptable alternative to the singles bar scene has been the "personal classified" ad section of a newspaper or magazine.

While society has long accepted the practice of middle-aged men seeking younger women in an effort to find rejuvenation, friends and family and society in general often view a middle-aged woman's romance with a younger man as improper and shocking (Derenski and Landsburg, 1981). Today, perhaps in part because of higher divorce rates and a larger number of women gaining status and independence through career pursuits, it is no longer rare to see a middle-aged woman dating a man five to ten years or more her junior. There is, however, one typical difference between these relations and those of the middle-aged (or older) male with a younger female partner. The physical attractiveness of the older male seems to be of only minor importance to his desirability compared with his status or power, while the middle-aged woman generally needs to be relatively good-looking in order to attract a younger male.

Contrary to popular misconceptions, there has not been a sudden upsurge in the divorce rate for people in mid-adulthood. In fact, most of the boring or unhappy marriages that survive to middle age will continue to old age rather than be dissolved by a midlife crisis (Friedman, 1981). For those caught in such marital inertia, there is apt to be a decline in sexual ardor at home, which can express itself in a variety of ways. Decreased sexual desire frequently first appears at this time, as earlier pretenses of enjoying sex together are shed in favor of more behavioral honesty. Sexual dysfunctions can also appear as a reflection of marital stresses or of the pent-up hostility of one spouse for another. Extramarital involvement is another sexual possibility that can provide a sense of escape from a stagnant relationship along with the excitement of getting to know a new partner on intimate terms; this topic is discussed more fully in Chapter 16.

One study of middle-adult couples engaged in marital or sex therapy found that spouses placed little emphasis on committing time or psychological energy to their marital or sexual relations (McCarthy, 1982). In this sample, 80 percent of marriages had experienced an extramarital affair. The likelihood of stress in the marital relationship was somewhat higher when the wife was having an affair. McCarthy observed that this might be because the women in his sample tended to become more emotionally involved in their affairs than did the men, who generally focused on the sexual interaction.

Another revealing aspect of this study had to do with husband–wife differences in expectations about sex:

Men's expectations tended to be extreme, either extremely high in terms of frequent, high-intensity sex (the "every sex is dynamite" myth) or an extremely low expectation—after having sex with someone for six months there is just no excitement (the "sex is not for marriage" myth). The woman's views ran the gamut from romanticism to seeing sex as a duty. Many women had an underlying disappointment about their husband's attitudes toward marital sexuality and with their skills as lovers. Yet, the women were reluctant to initiate discussions about sexuality and even more hesitant to experiment sexually and explore with their spouses. (McCarthy, 1982, p. 10)

The sexual problems of mid-adulthood are not restricted to heterosexuals, although little attention has been given to the middle-aged homosexual population in America. Here, too, a wide variety of patterns is seen. Gay men in their forties may find that it becomes more difficult to attract younger partners on physical grounds alone. As a result, some homosexual males turn to paid male prostitutes, others become relatively celibate, and still others form long-term relationships that provide companionship and emotional support as well as sexual opportunity. Gay men who were previously in heterosexual marriages—including many who were fathers—often decide to divorce and change to an exclusively homosexual life.

It has been noted that some gay males who have put an emphasis on conquests, techniques, and the ideals of the youth culture develop much anxiety about aging (Levy, 1981). These men sometimes resort to facelifts or hair transplants to retain the illusion of their youthfulness (as some heterosexual men do too), and they often develop depression or become alcoholic as a reflection of the negative sense of self they experience as their aging becomes more apparent (Gagnon and Simon, 1973; Saghir and Robins, 1973; Harry, 1982; Smith, 1982). However, most homosexual men do not encounter such difficulties; generally, they have the same types of problems as they grow older that heterosexuals have (Berger, 1982).

Lesbians are often able to make an easier transition into middle adulthood because more of them are in lasting, one-to-one relationships (Tripp, 1975; Bell and Weinberg, 1978; Kimmel, 1978). Nevertheless, while concern over physical attractiveness may not be quite as strong an issue as it is for some gay males, there can be intense jealousy that arises in these relationships "whenever the relationship is threatened by other women who might intrude and attempt to disrupt the coupling" (Levy, 1981, p. 125).

THE MENOPAUSE

With aging, all women reach an end to their fertility. First, there is a gradual decline in female reproductive capacity from age 30 on, reflecting both a drop in fertility and a higher rate of miscarriages (Schwartz, 1982; Navot et al., 1991; American Fertility Society, 1991). In addition, abnormalities of the menstrual cycle become more frequent over 35 as the aging ovaries respond less efficiently to luteinizing hormone (LH) and follicle stimulating hormone (FSH) from the pituitary gland. After age 40, the frequency of ovulation generally begins to decrease, and around age 48 to 52, menstrual flow stops entirely in a process called **menopause.** However, since deciding when the menopause has occurred can be done only retrospectively—by convention, after one year without further menstrual flow—women who are sexually active at this stage of their lives should continue to practice birth control until it is certain they cannot become pregnant.

The timing of the menopause and the symptoms that accompany it vary greatly from one woman to another. Although the ovaries stop producing all but a minute amount of estrogen, and ovarian progesterone production ceases entirely, small amounts of these hormones are still present because of continued activity of the adrenal glands. LH and FSH levels typically become elevated after menopause.[2]

Symptoms

Although about 80 percent of women experience symptoms due to their changing hormone levels, only a minority of menopausal women seek treatment for symptom relief (Sheehy, 1992; Greendale and Judd, 1993). This is probably because the majority of symptoms are of a relatively minor nature and tend to disappear with time.

The most common symptom in the menopause is the **hot flash,** which affects 75 to 80 percent of menopausal women (Bates, 1981; Erlik et al., 1981). Typically, the hot flash appears suddenly as a feeling of warmth over the upper part of the body (very much like a generalized blushing) and is accompanied by reddening, sweating, and, occasionally, dizziness. In some women, hot flashes are infrequent (once a week or less) but others have them every few hours. Hot flashes may last just a few

seconds and be quite mild, or they may last for 15 minutes or more in the most severe cases (experienced by less than 10 percent of women). One particularly disturbing feature of the hot flash is that it occurs more often during sleep than in the daytime, in which case it is liable to awaken the woman abruptly and contribute to insomnia.

Current evidence suggests that hot flashes are due to a malfunction of temperature control mechanisms in the hypothalamus (Casper, Yen, and Wilkes, 1979; Bates, 1981; Erlik et al., 1981) but other mechanisms may be involved (Chen et al., 1993; Greendale and Judd, 1993). Although estrogen deficiency seems to be a necessary condition for hot flashes to occur, and estrogen therapy effectively combats this symptom, hot flashes generally disappear spontaneously within a few years after the menopause even without treatment. In approximately 30 to 50 percent of affected women hot flashes persist for at least five years beyond the onset (Greendale and Judd, 1993). Since this symptom is sometimes severe enough to interfere with everyday functioning and there is no test that can predict when hot flashes will disappear spontaneously, deciding whether to obtain treatment or not is very much a subjective decision for the woman.

Other changes also reflect prolonged estrogen deficiency (Sherwin, 1991; Masters, Johnson, and Kolodny, 1994). Lowered levels of circulating estrogen predispose women to shrinking and thinning of the vagina, a loss of tissue elasticity, and lessened vaginal lubrication during sexual arousal, all of which may sometimes lead to painful intercourse. Other physical changes that may occur in

menopause (men' ō paws) the period during which menstruation gradually stops, usually occurring in the late forties. Sometimes called female climacteric.

climacteric (klī mak' tur ik) syndrome experienced by about 5 percent of men over 60, marked by weakness, fatigue, poor appetite, decreased sexual drive, reduction or loss of potency, irritability, and impaired ability to concentrate. Also see *menopause,* which is sometimes called the female climacteric.

perimenopausal years (perry men oh paws' uhl) the years immediately before and after menopause.

hot flash sudden sensations of warmth, blushing, and sweating, sometimes with dizziness, that occur commonly in menopausal women.

---

[2]The term **menopause** correctly refers only to a woman's last natural menstrual period. Many people incorrectly use the word menopause to refer to a time more correctly called the **climacteric** or the **perimenopausal years,** that is, the several years immediately before and after the menopause.

the postmenopausal years include thinning of the breasts and the vulva and loss of mineral content in bones, resulting in a more brittle structure (a condition that is called **osteoporosis**).

Treatment

Although there has been considerable controversy in the past about the risks and benefits of hormone replacement therapy (HRT) in the menopause and postmenopausal years, strong scientific evidence shows that the symptoms we have discussed can be significantly alleviated by its use and that there are additional preventive health benefits from HRT as well (Barrett-Connor, 1989; Goldman and Tosteson, 1991; Henderson, Paganini-Hill, and Ross, 1991; Martin and Freeman, 1993). Specifically, HRT slows the occurrence of osteoporosis, especially when it is started immediately after menopause (Consensus Development Conference, 1991; Felson et al., 1993). [Taking extra dietary calcium also helps slow postmenopausal bone loss (Reid et al., 1993).] Furthermore, the intravaginal administration of estrogen in the form of a cream prevents recurrent urinary tract infections in postmenopausal woman (Raz and Stamm, 1993). There is also strong evidence that HRT protects postmenopausal women against the risk of certain forms of heart disease (Sullivan et al., 1990; Stampfer et al., 1991; Nabulsi et al., 1993). In fact, HRT reduces the risk of coronary heart disease by 40 to 50 percent overall in postmenopausal women (Goldman and Tosteson, 1991). And women who used estrogen for at least 15 years postmenopausally had a 40 percent reduction in the overall death rate compared to women without HRT (Henderson, Paganini-Hill, and Ross, 1991).

Despite these clear-cut benefits, there are some potential risks with HRT. For example, estrogen use increases the risk of cancer of the uterus and also appears to be associated with about a 30 percent increase in the risk of breast cancer (Steinberg et al., 1991; Colditz et al., 1990; U.S. Preventive Services Task Force, 1990), although there is some disagreement on the latter point (Greendale and Judd, 1993). For these reasons, caution is in order, and it is advisable for women with a family history of breast cancer to avoid the use of HRT (Masters, Johnson, and Kolodny, 1994). However, adding a progestin to the latter part of the estrogen cycle for at least ten days essentially prevents the risk of cancer of the uterus that arises from estrogen use alone (U.S. Preventive Services Task Force, 1990; Voigt et al., 1991; Martin and Freeman, 1993).

Most authorities caution that HRT should not be used indiscriminately and that it should be employed in the smallest effective dose for the shortest period of time compatible with the therapeutic need.

Psychological Aspects

In the past, just about every problem that could befall a woman was inaccurately attributed to the menopause. In eighteenth- and nineteenth-century Europe, for instance, physicians thought women decayed at menopause (Stearns, 1975), and "nervous irritability" was diagnosed in nine out of ten menopausal women (Ballinger, 1981). Mistakenly blaming emotional instability, depression, and other psychological problems on the hormonal changes of

For Better or For Worse®   by Lynn Johnston

the menopausal years has not just been a practice of ancient history; it is a relatively common error in modern times that continues even today.

Ballinger (1981) finds no evidence for an increased rate of depression or major psychiatric disorders in the years following the menopause and points out that "emotional symptoms at this time of life, as at any other time, are influenced by a multitude of environmental and personality factors." Others contend that menopausal discomfort has been greatly exaggerated, that the menopause may actually be an adaptive, positive event, and that "the mythology surrounding the menopause is based less on the reality of the female experience than on the sexist interpretations of the female experience" by male physicians (Alington-MacKinnon and Troll, 1981). Bart and Grossman (1978) also point out that much of the research on the menopause is methodologically flawed, particularly the portion related to psychological aspects of the menopausal years. They suggest that a woman's response to the menopause is in large part a function of her "premenopausal personality and life patterns" and note that menopausal depression (when it occurs) is far more a result of lack of meaningful roles for women and poor self-esteem at this stage in their lives than a reflection of hormonal changes.

Several recent books on the menopause suggest that there is vast individual variability in this experience, and that more than a few women have more emotional problems during this time period than has been widely recognized (Sheehy, 1992; Barbach, 1993). Part of the problem may be that physicians have been lax in recognizing the psychological accompaniments of menopause, such as mood instability, listlessness, and poor concentration as symptoms of a physiological process and so have neglected treatment options that may have helped stabilize these women's lives.

While there is some disagreement about the impact of the menopause on female sexuality, several studies suggest there is characteristically a decline in sexual interest and possibly a loss of female orgasmic responsivity in the immediate postmenopausal years (Pfeiffer, Verwoerdt, and Davis, 1972; Zussman et al., 1981; Dennerstein and Burrows, 1982). Hallstrom (1979) studied 800 women in Sweden and found considerable evidence to support this premise; for example, the prevalence of weak or absent sexual interest increased progressively from age 38 to 54, and a declining capacity

for orgasm was reported for these same ages. However, Hallstrom also found that some postmenopausal women showed increased sexual interest and capacity for orgasm. On the other hand, several reports (Masters and Johnson, 1966, 1970; Kaplan, 1974; Starr and Weiner, 1981) have noted that sexual interest may increase in the postmenopausal years. The discrepancy in these findings may be the result of inadequate research design that does not take into account factors such as the health status of study subjects and their spouses or sexual partners.

LATE ADULTHOOD

In America, sex is generally regarded as something for the young, healthy, and attractive. Thinking of an elderly couple engaging in sexual relations usually provokes discomfort in young adults. The idea of sexual partners in a nursing home seems shocking and immoral to most people. Despite these cultural myths, the psychological need for intimacy, excitement, and pleasure does not disappear in old age, and there is nothing in the biology of aging that automatically shuts down sexual function. Since the number of elderly persons in the United States almost doubled from nearly 17 million in 1960 to 32 million in 1991, and will reach a projected 51 million by 2020 (Cantor, 1991), this topic takes on a particular relevance to all of our lives.

Biological Considerations

Female Aging

Aging alone does not diminish female sexual interest or the potential of the woman to be sexually responsive if her general health is good. Specific physiological changes do occur, however, in the sexual response cycle of postmenopausal women. These changes do not appear abruptly or in exactly the same fashion in each woman (Masters and Johnson, 1966).

Typically, there is little or no increase in breast size accompanying sexual arousal, although breast sensitivity to stimulation continues. The sex flush

osteoporosis (ah stee oh pohr oh' sis) a condition in which the bones become thin and brittle due to mineral loss; a common occurrence in postmenopausal women.

"Your Frederick's of Hollywood package came today, but I didn't sign for it. Instead of the peekaboo bra and matching panties you ordered, they sent two peekaboo bras."

Source: *Reproduced by Special Permission of* Playboy *Magazine. Copyright* © *1987 by* Playboy.

occurs less often and less extensively than at younger ages, but this change has absolutely no effect on sexual feelings or functioning. Less muscle tension develops during sexual arousal, particularly in the plateau phase, which is not surprising since this corresponds to the usual decrease in muscle size and strength that occurs with aging. This reduced muscular tension may account (at least in part) for the reduced intensity of orgasm that is sometimes experienced by women in late adulthood.

While clitoral response is not affected by aging, vaginal function changes in two different ways. First, reduced elasticity in the walls of the vagina leads to less expansion during sexual arousal. Second, vaginal lubrication generally begins more slowly than at younger ages, and vaginal dryness may create some problems as the quantities of lubrication are somewhat reduced. This condition can be overcome if it causes discomfort either by estrogen replacement therapy or by the use of an artificial lubricant such as K-Y Jelly.

The decrease in vaginal lubrication in postmenopausal women is the direct result of diminished vaginal blood flow that, in turn, is caused by low estrogen (Semmens and Wagner, 1982). Leiblum and co-workers (1983) found that sexually active postmenopausal women had less shrinkage of the vagina and higher levels of androgens and pituitary gonadotropins (LH and FSH) than sexually inactive women. This suggests that regular sexual activity may provide at least some protection against the physiologic changes of aging in relation to female sexual anatomy.

Male Aging

The normal pattern of reproductive aging in men is quite different from that in women because there is no definite end to male fertility. Although sperm production slows down after age 40, it continues into the eighties and nineties. Similarly, while testosterone production declines gradually from age 55 or 60 on, there is usually no major drop in sex hormone levels in men as there is in women (Vermeulen and Kaufman, 1992).

About 5 percent of men over 60 experience a condition called the *male climacteric*, which resembles the female menopause in some ways. (Using the term "male menopause" to describe the male climacteric is incorrect since men do not have menstrual periods.) This condition is marked by some or all of the following features: weakness, tiredness, poor appetite, decreased sexual desire, reduction or loss of potency, irritability, and impaired ability to concentrate (Greenblatt et al., 1979; Masters, Johnson, and Kolodny, 1994). These changes occur because of low testosterone production, and they can be reversed or improved by testosterone injections. It should be stressed that *most* men do not have a recognizable climacteric as they age.

The physiology of male sexual response is affected by aging in a number of ways. The following changes have been noted in men over 55:

1. It usually takes a longer time and more direct stimulation for the penis to become erect.

2. Erections tend to be less firm, on average, than at earlier ages.

3. The testes elevate only partway up to the perineum and do so more slowly than in younger men.

4. The amount of semen is reduced, and the intensity of ejaculation is lessened.

5. There is usually less physical need to ejaculate.

6. The refractory period—the time interval after ejaculation when the male is unable to ejacu-

late again—becomes longer (Masters and Johnson, 1966).

In addition, the sex flush usually does not occur in aging men, and muscle tension during sexual arousal is reduced, as in women, since muscle mass and strength generally decrease with aging.

Although the changes in male sexual physiology do not usually occur abruptly or represent an impairment of function, men who are uninformed about these patterns may be frightened into thinking something is wrong with them. In other instances, a man's partner may be the one to become alarmed. For example, while many men find that they enjoy sex in their later years without ejaculating at every opportunity, partners who don't realize this may think it reflects poorly on their attractiveness or skill as lovers.

Some men have completely unrealistic expectations about what their sex lives *should* be as they age. While they wouldn't expect to run a mile as fast at age 65 as they did at age 25 (or to recuperate from their exertion as quickly), they expect to get rock-hard erections instantly in all sexual situations and are worried when they can't make love twice in one evening. The aging male, by misinterpreting these changes, is particularly vulnerable to performance anxiety.

Psychosocial Considerations

In part, our cultural negativism about sex and romance in the geriatric years is a reflection of an attitude called **ageism,** a prejudice against people because they are old, that is similar to the more familiar prejudices of racism and sexism in our society. As Butler and Lewis (1976, p. 4) point out: "The ageist sees older people in stereotypes: rigid, boring, talkative, senile, old-fashioned in morality and lacking in skills, useless and with little redeeming social value." These same authors observe that ageism in relation to sexuality is the ultimate form of desexualization: "if you are getting old, you're finished" (p. 5).

Ageism is not restricted to heterosexuals, either, as this quote from *Gay and Gray: The Older Homosexual Male* (Berger, 1982) shows:

Many older gay men believe that younger gays react negatively to them. Most older gays feel that young people sometimes take advantage of them, do not welcome their company in bars, clubs, and bathhouses, do not care to associate

FOCUS IN BRIEF

Marital Status of Population 65 and Over by Sex, 1987

Marital Status	Males 65–74	Males 75+	Females 65–74	Females 75+
Total[a]	7608	3970	9624	6773
Never married	4.7%	4.3%	4.8%	6.4%
Married, spouse present	79.7	65.9	51.0	22.4
Married, spouse absent	0.7	1.9	0.8	0.9
Widowed	9.0	23.6	36.7	67.0
Separated	1.1	1.0	1.2	0.6
Divorced	4.8	3.3	5.5	2.7

[a]Number expressed in thousands.
Source: *U.S. Bureau of the Census, 1989.*

or form friendships with them, and think they are dull company. (p. 191)

It is interesting to note that in one study, college students estimated that married couples in their sixties had intercourse less than once a month and expected that married couples in their seventies had intercourse even less often (Zeiss, 1982). As we will see, these are underestimates of actual behavior, showing that young adults are susceptible to ageism in their thinking—at least when it comes to sex.

Kinsey and his colleagues (1948, 1953) were the first to examine systematically the effect of aging on sexual behavior. Although their studies indicated that sex continued well into late adulthood, they also described a general decline in the frequency of sexual activity for both men and women across the adult age range. A number of other studies confirmed these overall trends (Newman and Nichols, 1960; Pfeiffer and Davis, 1972; Martin, 1977), with most reports suggesting that the decrease in sexual activity is partly due to diminished health and partly a reflection of cultural attitudes and expectations.

More recently, a longitudinal study done at Duke University found that patterns of sexual activity actually remained relatively stable over middle and late adulthood, with only a modest decline appearing in most individuals (George and Weiler,

ageism an attitude of prejudice against the elderly.

PERSONAL PERSPECTIVES

Sex After Sixty

Contrary to the popular notion that sexual interest and prowess disappear in aging adults, research shows that many members of the over-60 set continue to lead active sex lives. Here are some excerpts from personal observations offered in group discussions that were conducted in a retirement community after the participants saw a film on sexuality and aging.

A 68-year-old married man: I have to admit that I used to think that older people didn't have sexual relations. I never really thought about it in personal terms, though, so when I got to my sixties and found my needs were still there, I wasn't all that surprised.

A 72-year-old woman: I think that the thing that surprises people is that we even think about sex, but why shouldn't we? If sex is still fun, and doesn't cost anything, and you've got a person you love to be with, it's no sin.

A 76-year-old widow: I say that you're as young as you think you are. If you think you're over the hill, you will be in a hurry. If you leave all the fun to younger people, you'll just sit in a rocking chair feeling old.

An 81-year-old-man: To me, it's like knowing how to ride a bicycle. Once you learn, you never really forget. Even though my friends don't talk much about sex except to make jokes, I still think about sex and even have dreams about it. And a couple of years ago, when I was having trouble with my prostate, my doctor was certainly surprised when I told him I still have sex twice a week.

A 71-year-old widow: I think it's perfectly all right to stop having sex whenever you want to. When my husband was still alive, we continued to love one another long after we stopped having sex.

A 70-year-old married woman: You have to admit that sex isn't exactly the same when you get older. I enjoy myself, and I know my husband does, but the passionate responses simmered down years ago, and sometimes I think we respond more out of memory than excitement.

A 69-year-old widower: One thing that nobody ever talks about is the pressure you get from women if you're an eligible man who is reasonably healthy and secure. They flirt, they hint, they make outright propositions—and I don't always like it, although I must admit that sometimes I do. But it's embarrassing to find that you've got a willing partner and you're not capable.

Table 10.5   Sex Problems[a] in the Old Old

Men (N = 43)	%	Women (N = 20)	%
Fear of poor performance	37	Orgasms too infrequent	30
Inability to maintain erection	33	Partner's erection problems	30
Inability to reach orgasm	28	Lack of vaginal lubrication	30
Inability to achieve erection	28	Worry about nonsexual problems	25
Not enough opportunities for sexual encounters	23	Not enough opportunities for sexual encounters	25
Partner's vaginal pain or lack of lubrication	23	Low sex drive	25

[a]Problems of men and women aged 80 or older who were in good health and who had a regular sex partner or partners.
Source: Bretschneider and McCoy, 1988, Table V.

1981). For example, men who were 66 to 71 years old at the start of this study had no overall decline in sexual activity scores over the next six years, and a majority of men and women in the 56 to 65 age bracket at the beginning of the study had stable rates of sexual activity during this same time period. However, in those over age 65, 18 percent of the men and 33 percent of the women completely stopped sexual activity with their partners over a six-year period.[3]

Data regarding sexual interest and behavior in a previously neglected subgroup of the aged, the "old old," were recently collected by Bretschneider and McCoy (1988), who studied a sample of 202 healthy men and women between the ages of 80 and 102 (see Table 10.5). Sixty-two percent of the men and 30 percent of the women indicated that they were still having sexual intercourse, but for both sexes the most common form of sexual activity was touching and caressing without intercourse. Notably, the past importance and frequency of sexual activity earlier in life correlated significantly with the frequency and enjoyment of sexual intercourse and touching and caressing without intercourse in "old old" age.

Various studies of sexual behavior in late adulthood indicate that the male's declining interest seems to be the major limiting factor to continued sexual activity (Kinsey et al., 1953; Pfeiffer and

Davis, 1972; Martin, 1977; George and Weiler, 1981). This declining interest, however, may say more about cultural expectations that become self-fulfilling prophecies than about anything else. While the pattern of sexual activity among aged people varies considerably, coital frequency in early marriage and overall quality of sexual activity in early adulthood correlate significantly with the frequency of sexual activity in late adulthood (Masters and Johnson, 1966).

On the other hand, a recent report noted that 35 percent of a sample of men over 60 had difficulty getting or maintaining erections, with more than half of the married men over 70 affected by this problem (Diokno, Brown, and Herzog, 1990). Many of these cases were linked to medical difficulties. The same conclusion has been reached in several other studies (Kaiser et al., 1988; Mulligan and Katz, 1988; Mulligan et al., 1988), suggesting that the real problem is not just declining sexual interest, but declining health. Both hormonal and vascular factors appear to be frequently involved (Kaiser et al., 1988; Diokno, Brown, and Herzog, 1990). One plausible explanation is that the health problems cause erectile difficulties and that male sexual interest wanes only after the erectile problems have been firmly established.

It is interesting to note that most researchers who claim to be studying sexual activity rates in the elderly have actually restricted themselves to studying coital behavior, as though other forms of sexual activity "don't count." As Table 10.6 shows, many adults over 60 continue to masturbate (Catania and White, 1982; Bretschneider and McCoy, 1988), although these are almost entirely individuals who masturbated when they were younger. Not

[3]The George and Weiler (1981) study was particularly well designed in ways that represent an important advance over prior studies of geriatric sexuality. In addition to being longitudinal rather than cross-sectional (so that each person's behavior could be tracked over time), they also included only married subjects, since marital status is a determinant of sexual opportunity and sexual behavior in old age.

Table 10.6   Current Incidence of Masturbation in Older Adults

Age	Male	N	Female	N
60–69	52.6%	152	47.1%	281
70–79	29.5	95	49.1	161
80–91	45.8	24	34.5	29

Source: *Copyright © 1981 by Bernard D. Starr, Ph.D. and Marcella Bakur Weiner, Ed.D. from the book* The Starr-Weiner Report on Sex and Sexuality in the Mature Years. *Originally published by Stein & Day, Inc., reprinted with permission of Scarborough House/Publishers.*

surprisingly, elderly people without sexual partners tend to masturbate more frequently (Catania and White, 1982). In couples over 60, other forms of sexual stimulation continue to be utilized (e.g., oral sex and manual stimulation); they not only provide some variety but also can be a source of pleasure and closeness even if the male is unable to obtain or maintain erections (Starr and Weiner, 1981; Turner and Adams, 1988). Here is what one 78-year-old man told us:

> In my mid-sixties, I had a real problem getting it up. Sexual intercourse became impossible and I got very upset over it at first. But my wife just found other ways to excite me, and after a while—when I relaxed more, I guess—my problem disappeared. Now, even though she doesn't always want to have intercourse when I do, we still use our mouths and tongues on each other, and we plan to keep doing it, too. *(Authors' files)*

In late adulthood, the longer life span of women combined with their tendency to marry men who are their age or slightly older frequently creates a situation of widowhood. At the same time that fewer men of the same age are available as new sexual partners, younger men tend to focus their attentions on women under 40. Thus, sexual opportunities and social contacts with men are often extremely limited for these mature women who might otherwise be enthusiastic sexual partners.

In the past decade, a new trend has emerged in which not all women 60 or older who find themselves widowed or divorced are passively accepting their fate. Some women in this situation are using their ingenuity to find new partners, as shown by the following ad from the personal classified section of a well-known magazine.

Tall, handsome intelligent man sixty to sixty-five, wanted for attractive, lively sixty-two-year-old widow with fantastic figure and modern values. If you're interested in romance more than golf, send a photo and your phone.

Although a 65-year-old widow (or widower) may have an interest in sexual activity, social pressures may prevent sexual opportunities or belittle their meaning via snide jokes (e.g., only "dirty old men" are interested in sex, and "dirty old women" should "act their age"). As prolonged abstention from sexual activity in old age leads to shrinking of the sexual organs (just as a healthy arm loses strength and coordination if put in a sling for four months), the older adult is truly faced with a sexual dilemma—"use it or lose it."

An often-neglected aspect of aging in our society is that many elderly persons are relegated to nursing homes or other long-term care facilities for health reasons, to "protect" themselves, or for the convenience of their children. Although research on sexual behavior in this population is understandably sparse, a number of authorities have spoken out in favor of making provisions in such facilities (such as making private rooms available) for those who desire sexual interaction (Kassel, 1976; McKinley and Drew, 1977; D. B. Miller, 1978; Wasow and Loeb, 1979). While most nursing home administrators seem opposed to this notion, and some facilities actually insist on segregating men and women even if they're married, both ethical considerations for protecting the rights of the elderly and more practical considerations having to do with maintaining self-esteem and personal well-being lead us to advocate change in this area. However, it should be noted that permitting sexual expression in the institutionalized elderly is not the entire solution to their plight. Additional steps must be taken to overcome loneliness and boredom in the nursing home environment so that these facilities are not unintentional prisons for our older adults.

In the United States, where there is little preparation or education for aging, it is not surprising that many people are uninformed about the physiological changes in their sexual function in their sixties and seventies. They may mistakenly view these normal "slowing down" processes as evidence that loss of function is imminent. Brief preventive counseling during middle age might result in significant change in this area, but changed attitudes toward sex and aging seem even more necessary. What people must recognize is that given good health and the availability of an interested and interesting partner, there is no reason that sexual enjoyment should have to come to an end in late adulthood. Perhaps the ultimate test of whether we have lived through a sexual revolution will be if attitudes toward sexuality in old age are transformed.

SUMMARY

1. Young adults are more sexually active today than they were two or three decades ago, although there has been a general trend toward marriage at a later age. This has been accompanied by the relative disappearance of the double standard regarding premarital sexual experience and a marked upsurge in the number of cohabiting couples.

2. Young adults are not completely free of sexual problems despite this shift in attitudes and behavior. Sexual dysfunctions and low sexual desire are common, sexual pressures abound, and there are signs of a growing disillusionment with casual sex.

3. Marriage tends to complicate sexual behavior in some ways (while simplifying it in others) and requires an integration of sex with other aspects of life. However, the climbing divorce rate in our society, with divorces occurring primarily among young adults, suggests that marriage is no longer regarded as a life-long commitment. And while most divorced people remarry, they often find problems in their second marriages that are similar to those they had experienced before.

4. Middle adulthood is often initiated by a midlife crisis in which the male is particularly vulnerable in sexual terms. In some cases, the female's midlife crisis may coincide with her children leaving home and the onset of menopause. But for other women, mid-adulthood is a time of sexual self-discovery.

5. The menopause, which typically occurs around age 48 to 52, is the cessation of menstrual periods. Dramatic decreases in estrogen production in the ovaries in the perimenopausal years can cause a variety of symptoms, including hot flashes, shrinking and thinning of the vagina, decreased vaginal lubrication during sexual arousal, and osteoporosis. These symptoms can generally be prevented or alleviated by estrogen replacement therapy combined with cyclic use of progestin (to minimize the risk of cancer of the uterus).

6. Although many psychological problems have been attributed to the menopause, current research finds no evidence of an increased rate of emotional problems in the postmenopausal years.

7. About 5 percent of men over 60 have a male climacteric, marked by symptoms such as decreased sexual desire, weakness, tiredness, and poor appetite. This condition is the result of a testosterone deficiency that can be corrected by testosterone injections.

8. In late adulthood, there are a number of biological changes in the sexual response cycle, such as decreased vaginal lubrication in women and slower erectile response in men. In both sexes, muscle tension is reduced. However, these changes do not generally prevent sexual functioning.

9. Sexuality in late adulthood is profoundly influenced by ageism and other cultural stereotypes that deny the normality of sexual feelings and capabilities at this stage of the life cycle. While health problems and lack of a partner may complicate sexual functioning, there is no inherent reason most elderly persons must stop enjoying sex.

Thought Questions

1. How do the perspectives regarding sex typically differ between 20-year-olds and older adults? What sort of learning and attitude changes regarding sexuality tend commonly to occur during adulthood?

2. The text states that the double standard regarding sex has "relatively" disappeared. Do you agree? If so, which parts of the double standard situation are still prominent in our society and which no longer apply?

3. In your opinion, is it wise to marry someone with whom you have never had sexual intercourse? Is it wise to marry someone with whom you have never lived? Among your friends, has cohabitation helped or harmed their relationships?

4. Long-term marriages and sexual relationships are often characterized by sexual burnout.

What besides length of the relationship contributes to sexual burnout? Can sexual burnout be avoided? What advice might be given to long-term couples who find themselves sliding into sexual boredom?

5. Do you agree that our society has a concept of a handsome, sexy, middle-aged man but not of a beautiful, sexy, middle-aged woman? Must women, in order to be regarded as beautiful and sexy, look young?

6. Most readers of this text would probably deplore prejudice on the basis of race or sex. However, prejudice against the elderly is also very common and probably more socially acceptable in our culture. Why is prejudice against the elderly a *particularly* foolish form of prejudice? Do younger people really mean it when they say things such as "I hope I die before I get old"?

Suggested Readings

Barbach, Lonnie. *The Pause: Positive Approaches to the Menopause.* New York: Dutton, 1993. Practial advice for women who are managing difficult symptoms during the perimenopausal years.

Berger, Raymond M. *Gay and Gray: The Older Homosexual Male.* Urbana, IL: University of Illinois Press, 1982. A humanistic, thought-provoking study of a much-neglected topic.

Cherlin, Andrew J. *Marriage, Divorce, Remarriage.* Cambridge, MA: Harvard University Press, 1992. A concise study of current demographic trends and the meanings driving American marriage and divorce rates.

Fuchs, Estelle. *The Second Season: Life, Love and Sex for Women in the Middle Years.* Garden City, NY: Anchor Books, 1978. A well-written, thoughtful commentary including valuable insights on menopause, divorce, and widowhood.

Howells, John G., ed. *Modern Perspectives in the Psychiatry of Middle Age.* New York: Brunner/Mazel, 1981. A useful collection of excellent review articles on topics such as the empty-nest syndrome, divorce and middle age, and the psychology of the widow and widower.

Sheehy, Gail. *The Silent Passage.* New York: Simon & Schuster, 1992. A detailed look at the social and psychological significance of the menopause for today's women.

Silverstone, Barbara, and Hyman, Helen K. *Growing Older Together: A Couple's Guide to Understanding and Coping with the Challenges of Later Life.* New York: Pantheon, 1992. The subtitle says it all.

Starr, Bernard D., and Weiner, Marcella B. *The Starr–Weiner Report on Sex and Sexuality in the Mature Years.* New York: Stein and Day, 1981. Results of a survey of 800 people over age 60, presented clearly and nontechnically.

Gender Roles

This chapter was written by Linda H. Kolodny and Nancy J. Kolodny, M.A., M.S.W.

On a television soap opera, a self-confident, smooth-talking businessman seduces a beautiful but not too bright female secretary. A children's book describes a warm, caring, stay-at-home mother while depicting father as an adventurous business traveler. A magazine ad for women's underwear shows a waif-like female model, so slender as to be considered anorectic, lying stomach down on a couch while completely naked. MTV routinely features scantily dressed, erotically energized women in their videos. Each of these examples contains both obvious and implied stereotypes about men and women.

In American culture, the labels of masculinity and feminity have a lot of power to affect what we think, say, and do in our personal and professional lives. Our culture places masculinity and femininity at opposite ends of a spectrum as if they are mutually exclusive antagonists. But that view is being challenged by people who realize that no one is 100 percent masculine or 100 percent feminine, and by those androgynous people who are able to blend aspects of masculine and feminine traits without worrying about labels, stereotypes, or gender roles (the outward expression of maleness or femaleness).

Old patterns of sex differences, child-rearing practices, masculinity and femininity, and what society defines as "appropriate" gender-role behavior are changing. Some people are comfortable with that, others aren't. Beliefs about gender differences in traits, talents, and temperaments have influenced social, political, and economic systems throughout history. That influence has not always been positive and women have often been placed at a disadvantage. Recent trends have threatened age-old social distinctions between the sexes: today a majority of American women work outside the home, a practice that was considered unnecessary, unfeminine, and even irresponsible in earlier times. (Unfortunately, many people still have difficulty understanding and accepting changing gender-role patterns in our society as women have shifted from being housewives to being frontline tank commanders, jet pilots, or even Supreme Court justices.)

The definition of family has also changed and broadened as have perceptions of men's and women's roles in the family, especially those involving parenting. The definition of marriage has even changed: in some cities, lesbian or homosexual marriages are legal. Many fashions in hairstyles, clothing, footwear, and jewelry are unisex, and even anatomic status is not fixed because change-of-sex surgery is possible. The women's movement is becoming a powerful political voice bringing increased attention and political action on issues such as sex discrimination, sexual harassment, and domestic violence that have an impact on women's and men's personal and professional lives. There is even a men's movement that is gaining momentum, which encourages men to become aware of and comfortable with their emotions in order to better understand themselves and other men.

Because there is a continuum of types of socialization today and because men and women are not bound to behave according to stereotyped gender roles, it's important that people increase their awareness of what's happening in the arena of gender roles so positive changes will continue to occur in the relationships between the sexes. This chapter examines these issues and trends as they influence the experience of being male and female.

MASCULINITY AND FEMININITY

What does it mean to be a man or a woman? In your opinion, what traits should a typical American man and woman have? Before reading further, jot down a list of the characteristics that popped into your mind in answer to the above questions.

If you're like most people—who not only believe that men and women differ but share similar beliefs about the ways in which they differ (Broverman et al., 1972)—your "instantaneous" descriptive list probably included characteristics like strong, courageous, self-reliant, competitive, objective, and aggressive for the typical man; intuitive, gentle, dependent, emotional, connected, sensitive, talkative, loving for the typical woman. If your list did look like the one above, you are thinking—as many of us do—stereotypically.

Stereotypes are standard beliefs about an identifiable group (Fagot, Leinbach, and O'Boyle, 1992) that help you organize your thoughts about people, places, or things into acceptable, predictable patterns. These beliefs are based on inferences people make about what they see and know (Leinbach and Hort, 1989) and affect how people treat one another. Because stereotypes can be based on faulty assumptions, oversimplified evidence, or uncritical thinking, they often lead to incorrect judgments and generalizations. Because many stereotypes about sexuality are based on assumptions about the nature of masculinity and femininity, let's look more closely at them.

The social psychologist Sandra Bem (1993) refers to the assumptions as **lenses of gender:** androcentrism, gender polarization, and biological essentialism. These lenses are derived from three prevalent beliefs about males and females: (1) males and females have different psychological and sexual natures, (2) men are inherently the dominant or superior sex, and (3) both male–female difference and male dominance are natural. Thus, male centeredness and the male experience becomes the norm for the culture and the species—**androcentrism;** social life is organized around the distinction between

stereotypes standard beliefs about an identifiable group.

lenses of gender according to Sandra Bem, assumptions about the nature of masculinity and femininity that people commonly employ.

androcentrism making the male perspective and male experience the cultural norm.

male and female, has mutually exclusive scripts for being male and female, and defines any person or behavior deviating from these scripts as problematic—**gender polarization**; and androcentrism and gender polarization are inevitable consequences of the biological natures of men and women—**biological essentialism** (Bem, 1993).

These assumptions about men and women—the lenses of gender—are undergoing change in today's culture. Androcentrism isn't automatically accepted as the norm anymore. Androgyny, the coexistence of stereotypical masculine and feminine characteristics in one person, is an acceptable alternative. People who study gender have moved beyond discussion of gender polarization and have begun to talk about **gender-role transcendence** [any behavior that's appropriate and adaptive in a given situation, regardless of gender (Rebecca, Hefner, and Oleshansky, 1976)] and **gender schema** [how we use gender-based classifications to organize, internalize, and operationalize our beliefs about masculinity and femininity (Bem, 1993; Hudak, 1993)]. Gender-role researchers have also begun to examine the effects of so much discussion about masculinity and femininity. Carol Tavris (1992) warns us that although gender-polarized thinking is so ingrained in our society that many psychologists believe it is a fundamental aspect of the mind's organization, it can actually be hazardous to our personal and business relationships and social policies. For instance, although most people assume that antagonism and conflict underlie male–female relationships, Tavris believes that "nothing in the nature of women and men requires us to emphasize difference and opposition. We can emphasize similarity and reciprocity" (Tavris, 1992, p. 92).

But in another sense, masculinity and femininity refer to the degree to which a person matches cultural expectations of how males and females should behave or look. According to this perspective, it's desirable for males to be masculine and females to be feminine in part because when behavior matches cultural expectations, it seems to preserve social equilibrium and yields a certain feeling of stability in the day-to-day details of ordinary life. Researchers say it makes you feel good and lets you evaluate yourself positively if you fulfill the goals ascribed to your gender: it's no wonder men like being independent, autonomous; women like being sensitive, interdependent (Joseph, Markus, and Tafarodi, 1992). "Masculine" men and "feminine" women are thought of as relatively predictable (go back and look at your "instantaneous" list of traits if you want an indication of just how predictable "predictable" is) and seem to behave in ways that are consistent and complementary. This view implies that conformity to cultural norms indicates "adjustment" and "health."

People who don't follow the cultural script become problematic because they contradict the prevailing stereotype. Many people truly believe that straying too far from expected, stereotypical behavior patterns indicates abnormality, immorality, or even disease. It is for this reason that many people get upset by long hair and earrings on young men or tattoos on young women, or when young women are accepted into military service academies like West Point, and that the controversy about allowing homosexuals and lesbians to enlist in the military has become so hotly debated. None of these behavior patterns "fits" prevailing expectations about the sexes and all challenge standard cultural scripts.

Masculinity and femininity also refer to traits measured by standardized psychological tests that compare one person's responses to those of large groups of men and women. The traditional approach to studying masculinity and femininity looked at these traits as opposites. Terman and Miles' test (1936) assumed that either masculinity or femininity was the *core* dimension of someone's personality and that a person must be either masculine or feminine but not both (Terman and Miles, 1936; Spence and Helmreich, 1978; Bem, 1993). It was assumed that if people scored high on certain traits judged as masculine (e.g., independence, competitiveness) they would lack traits of femininity (and vice versa). Furthermore, men and women whose masculinity or femininity scores differed substantially from group averages were judged to be less emotionally healthy and less socially adjusted than others with "proper" scores. Most psychological tests designed to measure masculinity and femininity from that point on set up a single masculinity–femininity scale (Kaplan and Sedney, 1980).

Researchers began to challenge and test these assumptions and findings. Bem developed the Bem Sex Role Inventory (BSRI) in the early 1970s (Bem, 1972, 1993). Her test listed 60 attributes (20 reflected *current cultural definitions* of masculinity, 20 of femininity, and 20 were fillers) and asked the test taker to describe how well each described himself or herself. The test taker was unaware of the categories, and also didn't realize that each trait had been selected for assessing how desirable a trait it would be in American society for either a man or a woman at that time (i.e., the 1970s). Bem was attempting to "locate masculinity and femininity in the discourse of the culture" (Bem, 1993, p. 119), rather than in the individual personality, which Terman and Miles had done. Her items were scored as independent scales of masculinity and femininity, not as opposites as had been done in the Terman-Miles test, and she contrasted conventionally sex-typed people with androgynous people, challenging Terman's and Miles' idea that anything other than conventional sex-typing indicated pathology. Bem revolutionized thinking about the nature of masculinity and femininity and set the stage for the standards of mental health to be genderless. Today we don't often question the belief that a woman who is competitive can still be thought of as feminine; a man who is tender and loving may also be very masculine.

Stereotypes are being challenged today because we're realizing that masculinity and femininity (whatever they mean) don't tell us much about an individual's personality, sexuality, or lifestyle. More dynamic scientific views and research are challenging the lenses of gender, altering our definitions by showing us how masculine and feminine characteristics coexist to some degree in every individual (Spence and Helmreich, 1978; Cook, 1985; Tavris, 1992; Bem, 1993). Though it may take us a while to get there, we are moving slowly in the direction Tavris suggested: we are getting more comfortable exploring the similarities between the masculine and feminine in our culture. Let's try to keep that in mind as we discuss the ways in which people learn gender roles and examine the impact these roles have on our lives.

gender polarization mutually exclusive scripts and expectations for how males and females should act, with a person not following these scripts viewed as problematic or abnormal.

biological essentialism the view that androcentrism and gender polarization are the inevitable expression of the innate biological nature of men and women.

gender-role transcendence behavior that is functional in a particular situation without regard to whether it fits stereotypical views of masculinity and femininity.

gender schema how we use gender-based classifications to view our beliefs about masculinity and femininity and to translate them into our own behavior.

GENDER ROLES

Gender role refers to everything you say or do (not just sexually but in all aspects of life) that indicates the degree to which you are male, female, or androgynous (Nanda, 1990). Many of us have been raised with flexible attitudes toward gender roles so that we are **androgynous** (our self-concepts incorporate aspects of both masculine and feminine behavior and don't depend on cultural definitions of what men and women can or can't do or be) (Bem, 1993). Many of us have lived with people such as parents and grandparents who have struggled and succeeded in breaking away from stereotyped thinking about masculinity and femininity even though they are themselves comfortable in traditional male or female roles. Yet just as many of us still find it hard to accept that gender roles aren't clearly and completely divided into male and female categories characterized by specific behaviors and motivations for each.

We are not born knowing about gender roles. While our genetic make-up determines our biological sex, our awareness of gender is not an obvious or instantaneous "given." It develops over time and is influenced by our biological sex, age, family, school experiences, religious background, friends, and cultural factors like the media. Our ideas about what it means to be male or female and our experience of being male or female emerge from this potent brew of information.

PATTERNS OF GENDER-ROLE SOCIALIZATION

Even before a baby is born, parents are likely to have different attitudes about the sex of their child. In most societies, male children are clearly preferred over female children (Markle, 1974; Coombs, 1977), and having a son is more often seen as a mark of status and achievement than having a daughter (Westoff and Rindfuss, 1974). This preference probably stems from the belief that men are stronger, smarter, braver, and more productive than women and that "it's a man's world" (certainly true in the past)—meaning that there are more and better educational, occupational, political, and economic opportunities open to males than to females.

Birth and Infancy

Parents often try to guess the sex of their unborn child and may construct elaborate plans and ambi-

tions for the child's life. If the child is thought to be a boy, the parents are likely to think of him as sports-oriented, achievement-oriented, tough, and independent. If the child is thought to be a girl, parents are more apt to envision beauty, grace, sensitivity, artistic talents, and marriage. This sort of prenatal thinking is one form of stereotyping, as is guessing that the baby will be a boy because "he" kicks a lot inside the uterus. It is not surprising then to find that the earliest interactions between parents and their newborn child are influenced in subtle (and not-so-subtle) ways by cultural expectations.

At the moment of birth, the baby's sex ("It's a boy" or "It's a girl") is usually the first thing that's announced. These simple statements are about much more than biological sex. Each is loaded with meaning, not only for how others will relate to that baby but also for how that baby will learn to relate to others. The statements carry implicit guidelines about how the infant will develop a concept of "self" and how he or she will develop emotionally, physically, and intellectually throughout life. "It's a boy" and "It's a girl" label people at birth and categorize them so that it often seems they must follow preset patterns in order to meet social standards and norms. Every society has certain expectations for how a person is to behave as a male or a female; *socialization* is a process by which a child learns about those expectations and either behaves in accordance with them or varies somewhat from the standard.

Let's look at the chain of events that either "It's a boy" or "It's a girl" sets in motion, such as assigning a pink or blue identification bracelet, choosing a name, selecting a wardrobe, and decorating the baby's room, each of which involves making distinctions between males and females.

As friends, relatives, and parents discuss the newborn's appearance, gender stereotypes are everywhere: "Look at his size—he'll be a football player, I bet." "She has beautiful eyes—she's a real doll." "See how intelligent he looks!" "She's got great legs already! You'll have to work to keep the boys away." Informal banter about the child's future is also likely to be gender-linked: if friends remark, "You better start saving for the wedding," you can bet they are not talking about a baby boy.

Parents of newborn infants describe daughters as softer, smaller, finer-featured, and less active than sons, although no objective differences in appearance or activity level were noted by physicians (Rubin, Provenzano, and Luria, 1974). In early infancy, boys receive more physical contact from their mothers than girls do, while girls are talked to and looked at more than boys (Lewis, 1972)—a difference in treatment which tends to reinforce a female's verbal activities and a male's physical activity. Walum (1977) reports an exploratory study in which two groups of young mothers were given the same six-month-old infant dressed either in blue overalls and called Adam or wearing a pink frilly dress and called Beth: the results showed that "Beth" was smiled at more, given a doll to play with more often, and viewed as "sweet" compared with "Adam." Another study confirms that both mothers and fathers behave differently toward unfamiliar infants on the basis of perceived sex, although the parents were unaware of this differential treatment (Culp, Cook, and Housley, 1983).

Parents respond differently to infant boys and girls in other ways. They react more quickly to the cries of a baby girl than a baby boy (Frieze et al., 1978) and are more likely to allow a baby boy to explore, to move farther away, or to be alone, thus fostering independence. In contrast, the baby girl seems to be unintentionally programmed in the direction of dependency and passivity (Weitzman, 1975; Long Laws, 1979).

Gender differences in socializing children occur for reasons that are complex and not fully understood in spite of continuing scientific interest and an enormous body of research that has accumulated during the past several decades. The tendency is to want to determine which is the most powerful influence: biology or culture? The trouble is that science hasn't found the answer. We really don't know, but we make a lot of inferences. For example, one study found the likelihood that sex differences in physical aggression and rough-and-tumble play is caused by biology (Maccoby and Jacklin, 1974) while another found that sex differences in aggression are caused by differential treatment of the two sexes (Fausto-Sterling, 1985). Bem (1993) suggested that if females were assigned "warrior" roles in childhood and practiced activities directly related to fighting, killing, strength testing, and proving physical courage, then sex differences in aggression might not occur at all.

Parents are often unaware of the extent to which their actions and interactions with their children differ depending upon the child's sex. Some researchers believe that differential socialization seems to occur even in parents who are philosophically committed to the idea of avoiding gender stereotyping (Scanzoni and Fox, 1980). Others believe that traditional and nontraditional parenting strongly affect a child's gender-role development (Fagot, Leinbach, and O'Boyle, 1992).

Either way, both boys and girls learn about nurturing (a gender quality associated with being female) from being nurtured themselves, usually by their mothers. In learning how to be nurturing individuals, children learn to be aware of and respond to others' needs and begin to develop a sense of morality and expressiveness. But children learn the gender distinctions about the male–female aspects of gender role (wife role, husband role) through interactions with their fathers. Small children learn early on that the husband and father roles have implications of power that the mother and wife roles don't. Numerous studies have found that fathers are more concerned than mothers with the male–female distinctions of gender roles, tend to interact differently with sons than daughters, and have more gender-stereotyped attitudes from the time the children are newborns. Fathers talk and interact more with their toddler boys than with their toddler girls and maintain more frequent contact with sons than with daughters as their children grow up. Fathers reinforce gender-stereotypical behavior more than mothers do, and seem to give more encouragement to sons than daughters to be intellectually competent (see Stockard and Johnson, 1992, pp. 200–225).

How Do Children Process All the Information About Gender and Learn to Use It?

It's very interesting to watch children as they process the information that leads them to make judgments about gender and cues them about how people behave in gender-appropriate ways. In 1932, the Swiss psychologist Jean Piaget proposed that the organizing principle of children's thought processes is gender-based. He believed that between the ages of 18 months and 7 years when the ability to think and reason hasn't yet fully developed, children are rigid gender traditionalists. For these children, a person has to both look and act male or fe-

gender role everything a person says or does that expresses his or her masculinity, femininity, or androgyny.

androgynous behavior that expresses aspects of stereotypical masculine and feminine characteristics by the same person either simultaneously or sequentially

Examples of typical and nontypical gender play.

male to actually be male or female (Bem, 1993). Kohlberg (1966) believed that very young children seek regularity and look for patterns in their worlds, and that each child will *spontaneously* develop a self and set of social rules consistent with the patterns they see around them.

Researchers have found that the ability to assign male or female gender labels to activities and people varies in young children, but it usually begins between 2 and 3 years of age (Fagot, Leinbach, and O'Boyle, 1992). Though toddlers may not be able to express the knowledge, they sense the scope and importance of gender stereotypes (Leinbach and Hort, 1989). Bem (1981) says such children intuitively know there's more to this male–female business than just learning about what a man or woman does and has. Let's look at how such distinctions become ingrained during early childhood.

Early Childhood (Ages 2 to 5)

Eighty percent of American 2-year-olds can distinguish male from female on the basis of cues such as hairstyle and clothing (Bem, 1993) and many can sort clothing into different boxes for boys and girls (Thompson, 1975). However, 2-year-olds don't usually apply correct gender labels to their own photographs with any predictable consistency: this ability usually appears around 2½ years. Furthermore, as many as 50 percent of 3- and 4-year-olds can't make a male–female distinction if they're asked to judge on the basis of natural, biological cues like genitalia and body physique (Bem, 1993).

How do children acquire the ability to label? Fagot, Leinbach, and O'Boyle (1992) found that by the age of 27 months, early-labeling girls (those who correctly made male–female distinctions) spent more time communicating with adults and showed less aggression than late-labeling girls and late- or early-labeling boys. Furthermore, moms and dads of early-labeling toddlers reacted more emotionally (whether positively or negatively) when their own children engaged in sex-typical (i.e., stereotypical, gender "appropriate") behavior. The mothers of these early labelers were more positive about sex-typed play and initiated sex-typical toy play more often (i.e., played dolls with girls, trucks with boys), and, interestingly, initiated less opposite-sex toy play with sons. As a group, the mothers of early labelers were more traditional in their attitudes about so-called appropriate behavior for women and about sex roles within the family. This study, then, points to the style of parenting as an important variable in the development of a child's ability to use gender labels.

Bem (1993) suggests that male–female differences interest children because they see evidence of it all the time in their communities as well as at home, and contends that the transfer of gender information from culture to child is "nonconscious" so the child is virtually unaware of how much he or she is actually learning about gender. That's why children make gender-based classifications without even realizing it. Bem calls this the ability to be gender schematic.

Core gender identity (the personal sense of being male or female) seems to solidify by age 3 (Money, 1988). This process is probably aided by the acquisition of verbal skills with which children identify themselves and others in terms of gender. Toddlers frequently apply pronouns such as "he"

or "she" to other people and things, as if testing their awareness of gender and checking out their ability to label. They are trying to make sense of the ways in which the outward expression of maleness or femaleness (gender roles) fit in with the world as they know it, particularly within their own families. While it might seem as if toddlers form very sketchy impressions of gender roles at first— "Mommies don't wear ties" or "Daddies don't wear lipstick"—their understanding is much more complex than their ability to express it. For instance, preschoolers have gender-stereotypic beliefs about specific emotions which are similar to those held by adults: they both perceive anger as characteristic of males, sadness as characteristic of females (Karbon et al., 1992).

Children also listen with much greater intensity to what their parents say and how they say it than most of us realize. One of the ways they learn about gender appropriate behavior is by mimicking the speech patterns of their parents. Psycholinguist Jean Berko Gleason (1987) found that fathers *command*—they issue command statements to their children more frequently than the mothers do, and fathers' commands are issued more often to sons than to daughters. Perhaps this is why preschool girls and boys have such different styles of initiating play. Boys (like their fathers) usually give commands ("We're going to play army!") while girls are more likely to begin by saying, "Let's . . ." ("Let's build a fort.") (Goodwin, 1990; Sachs, 1987).

Play patterns are a mirror and training ground for practicing and understanding gender. The serious business of young childhood is play, so by examining the objects used in play activities we may be able to learn something about gender-role socialization. Walk through the toy department of a large store and you will quickly see the principle of differential socialization at work. Boys' toys are action-oriented (guns, trucks, spaceships, sports equipment) while girls' toys reflect quieter play, often with a domestic theme (dolls, tea sets, "pretend" makeup kits, or miniature vacuum cleaners, ovens, or refrigerators). Where a particular toy is marketed to both girls and boys, the version for girls is usually feminized in certain ways. For instance, a boys' bicycle is described as "rugged, fast, and durable." The girls' model of the same bike has floral designs on the seat and pretty pink tassels on the hand-grips and is described as "petite and safe." A detailed analysis of the content of 96 children's rooms showed that boys were given more toy cars and trucks, sports equipment, and military toys, while girls received many more dolls, doll houses, and domestic toys (Rheingold and Cook, 1975). Many boys today play with action figure dolls, dinosaurs, monsters, Ninja turtles, and toys that tend to fall in and out of popularity based on the current hot movie or television show. While most parents of boys are comfortable with their sons' action-doll play, or play with dolls designed to look like boys such as the Ruff 'N' Tuff line of Cabbage Patch Kids, they are not so comfortable if those sons develop preferences for frilly, "feminine" dolls (Collins, 1984).

Preschool boys also play games like doctor which involve interaction with girls. But when they do, boys want to be "doctor" the majority of the time, whereas girls don't need to be the doctor all the time and are willing to play other roles in the game (Sachs, 1987; Tannen, 1990). It is interesting to note how early on gender patterns emerge and take form. As early as preschool, girls seem to exhibit more equality and inclusiveness in their play and are more willing to negotiate ("Let's...") without fussing too much about status. Boys, in contrast, seem to gravitate toward status roles, and seek power in relationships. As early as 20 to 24 months of age, children generate more restrictive gender rules for male peers than female peers, which means that so-called "sissies" are more harshly dealt with in the social world of toddlers than are tomboys (Fagot, 1977, 1986; Stoddart and Turiel, 1985; Carter and McCloskey, 1983–84).

Picture books can be another important source for learning gender roles. As Weitzman (1975) observes, "Through books, children learn about the world outside their immediate environment: they learn what is expected for children of their age" (p. 110). In the past, there was obvious gender-role bias found in award-winning books for preschoolers, with males—shown 11 times as often as females—portrayed as active, independent, and engaged in a variety of occupations and professions, while most females were consistently identified as mothers or wives and presented in passive roles (Weitzman et al., 1972). Today, this imbalanced example of gender stereotyping in books has changed, and there are wonderful nonsexist, gender-diverse choices for children, such as Stan and Jan Berenstain's various "Bears" books or the Sesame Street Children's Television Workshop books among the hundreds of others.

Television is also a powerful force in the gender-role socialization of young children because it provides an open window and instant access to the rest of the world. Yet it persists in presenting gender stereotypes. Saturday morning cartoons have a spotty record in terms of providing female heroines to balance the male heroes. Characters like Ariel in "The Little Mermaid" don't pack the same punch as the Teenage Mutant Ninja Turtles; if anyone on Saturday morning television is going to rescue anyone else from a force of evil, chances are it's still going to be a male who does the rescuing. Even "Sesame Street" is searching for a formula that balances the sexes: in late 1993 the show introduced Zoë, a new female Muppet the show's creators hope will match the popularity and impact of an Ernie or Bert.

Advertisements geared at preschoolers perpetuate gender stereotyping. Indeed, it's rare to see a toy commercial showing boys and girls playing together. Girls are shown playing with girls and "girl" toys—combing dolls' hair, bathing them, putting on makeup, whispering, giggling, and so on. Boys are shown crashing toy cars with other boys, menacing one another with toy dinosaurs, pretending to be mechanics with their toy garages rather than playing with doll houses, and so on.

The School-Age Child

> Gender is not something one passively "is" or "has"; in the phrasing of Candace West and Don Zimmerman, we "do gender" *(Thorne, 1993, p. 5)*.

"Doing gender" is a particularly important aspect of children's lives during the elementary school years. There's a certain unevenness to the business of gender during that time span: children in grades three and six have more negative reactions to gender-inconsistent behavior than do kindergarten children, and the intolerance is greater for boys than for girls (Berndt and Heller, 1986). The fact that a 7-year-old girl who likes sports and climbs trees is probably considered a cute tomboy whereas a 7-year-old boy who prefers playing with dolls and jumping rope is labeled a sissy, reflects that in the elementary school years it's more acceptable for girls to be gender inconsistent than it is for boys. In the past, child psychiatrists considered tomboyishness in girls as a "normal passing phase" (Green, 1974), whereas "effeminate" boys were said to need treatment to prevent later sexual problems or homosexuality (Lebovitz, 1972; Green, 1974, 1987; Newman, 1976; Rekers et al., 1978). Today, it's uncommon for health-care professionals to advocate treatment of an effeminate young boy to prevent potential homosexuality.

Patterns of gender-linked play continue during the elementary school years and are reinforced by peer group interactions. Boyish and girlish play increases and is relatively entrenched by fourth grade when it's common to see group games with many rules dominating boys' play and parallel, constructive play and peer conversations dominating girls' play (Moller, Hymet, and Rubin, 1992). Boys are expected to show masculinity by demonstrating physical competence and competitive spirit in sports, the primary focus of boyhood play. Rewarded for bravery and stamina, criticized for showing fear or frustration ("Big boys don't cry"), the gender role assigned boys in our culture seems to demand that they like and partake in rough-and-tumble play. Children whose play preferences don't match the majority's are considered "weird" and may be the butt of jokes or name calling; for example, boys who play with girls in games of jump rope or gymnastics are seen as immature, girlish, or "fags" (Thorne, 1993). So, there is powerful motivation to behave like everyone else and not cross over into play with the opposite gender in order to have friends and be accepted by a group.

Just because girls aren't expected to maintain a stiff upper lip in play doesn't imply that they are stuck in a time warp in which boys only play team sports and girls take ballet or music lessons after school. This aspect of gender stereotypes has changed radically during the past two decades. Girls in elementary school learn the fundamentals of soccer, swimming, field hockey, ice hockey, lacrosse, basketball, t-ball, and baseball, and by the time they reach high school girls exhibit as much interest, skill, team spirit, and passion for their sports as the boys do for theirs. In this one respect, then, girls seem to have fared better than boys: gender stereotypes regarding sports participation have altered for girls, broadened their options, and changed the stereotyped expectations that girls be quiet, neat, clean, and physically passive. Studies of children of both genders and all racial–ethnic groups have found that involvement in team sports increases their friendship networks (Thorne, 1993).

However, girls are disadvantaged by their gender in other ways. Girls who were comfortable at age 8 expressing their feelings about other people and situations become less comfortable over time. As they reach the conclusion of their elementary school years, 10- and 11-year-olds feel an increasing need to be "nice" in order to be well liked by peers and adults. They struggle with the discrepancies between what they *know* is going on (i.e., that so-called friends are talking about each other behind their backs) and what they're *supposed* to think and say about what's going on (i.e., that the girls are all "tight" as ever) (Brown and Gilligan, 1992). It's no longer okay to express even remotely negative thoughts and feelings because it could get people mad, and if people get mad there is a risk of being turned into a social outcast. Researchers Lyn Mikel Brown and Carol Gilligan (1992) summarize a girl's dilemma this way: "If she 'pretends' and 'agrees' and is nice when she does not feel nice, she abandons herself, her thoughts and feelings, and becomes . . . 'not really me'" (p. 61). What she becomes is a girl playing a gender-appropriate preteen role, attempting to be "perfect" while knowing, at some level, that this means squelching her truer, innermost self and creating an alternate, gender-friendly version.

Teachers' Impact on Gender Roles

The attempt to exhibit gender-appropriate behavior and adhere to gender roles is not only the result of children paying attention to the rules of their peer group. It is also a natural outgrowth of their attention to the rules of the school, the way their teachers talk to them and about them. Teachers and aides use gender to point out and control groups of students, and the phrases "big boy" and "big girl" indicate teachers' praise, especially in the lower elementary school grades. Even the way children are asked to line up, who gets to stand at the front of a line, whether lines are separated into all boys and all girls, or combined, gives the children messages about gender (Thorne, 1993).

Gender-role stereotyping in the context of what is actually taught within the classroom varies. If in use, older textbooks may still present a male-dominated view of history in which women's contributions are reduced to examples such as Betsy Ross serving the cause of the American Revolution by sewing. It is more likely, though, that stereotyping comes across these days less in the actual content of lessons than in how teachers treat boys and girls in the classroom. Old habits are hard to break, and teachers tend to assign activities to boys and girls based on the teachers' presumptions about gender-role preferences. Girls still find themselves being asked to do different classroom chores than boys (i.e., boys may be asked to carry stacks of books, girls are asked to take out the trash or straighten up the room). In one school, third grade girls were asked to draw a mural while the boys were asked to build a fort. A girl who said she'd rather work on the fort was told by the teacher, "That's not a job for young ladies." In another school, summer vacation was coming up and the children were asked if any of them wanted to take the classroom pets, a bunny and a garter snake, home for the summer. When a girl and boy each volunteered to take the snake, the teacher gave it to the boy and told the girl that "Snakes and girls don't make a good match." Who got the bunny? The girl, of course (Authors' files, 1992).

Gender and the Social Lives of Elementary School Children

What goes on around grade school lunchroom tables provides further insight about gender: boys and girls may be seated at the same table but they tend to cluster into smaller, same-gender groupings. The fact is that even when girls and boys are together, interacting in classrooms, on playgrounds, or in lunchrooms, the opposite-sex contacts don't usually evolve into friendships, whereas same-gender interactions tend to result in the kind of bonding that leads to solid and lasting friendships (Thorne, 1993).

In the world of the early to middle childhood years when major changes in thoughts about sex-role behavior occur (Moller, Hymet, and Rubin, 1992), a lot of teasing behavior occurs between the sexes. If a girl is said to like a boy or vice versa, the words may be "hurled like an insult" (Thorne, 1993, p. 53) so the possibility of being teased makes it very risky to interact with the opposite gender. One way to avoid this risk is by engaging in cross-gender chasing, the kind that occurs in games of tag, with girls most often the ones threatening to kiss boys rather than the other way around, "a ritualized form of provocation" (Thorne, 1993, p. 71) or in games of "cooties" or "cootie tag" in which girls give cooties to boys more often than the reverse (see Thorne, 1993, pp. 73–76). Thorne calls

"cooties" an example of a pollution ritual and suggests that in our culture there's an implied, out-of-place female sexuality that comes across in this children's game, a sexuality that seems somehow potentially dangerous or contaminating. (You may recall how menstruation was regarded as contaminating from Chapter 4.) Whatever the reasons, thought-provoking studies such as Thorne's make us wonder if it is either possible or desirable to cross the gender divide during the elementary school years.

The Continuing Importance of Parents

Parents continue to be an important influence on children's gender-role development even after they begin to attend school. As we mentioned earlier, children learn about nurturing mainly from their mothers and about gender typing and male–female differences more through their relationships with their fathers than mothers. Some researchers suggest that the father–daughter relationship is a prototype of adult heterosexual relationships, that it mimics the stereotypical male—dominance pattern of our society in a way that a mother–son relationship can't (Stockard and Johnson, 1992).

Adolescence

Gender-appropriate roles become straitjackets for many teenagers as they try to work their ways through the different stages of adolescence and make the necessary transitions to young adulthood. The rules seem to change, the seriousness of the behaviors increases, the results of the teen's choices have greater social, emotional, even physical impact. A child's earlier "rehearsal" of gender-appropriate roles, say by playing at being a certain kind of person by doing certain things, is transformed into the real thing during adolescence. Life seems more complicated, the penalties for being different are harsher, and future success seems pinned to the outcome of how well the adolescent fulfills those gender-appropriate roles. Sexuality becomes more and more entwined with gender definitions of masculinity and femininity, and sexual awareness, knowledge, and activity complicate teenagers' attempts to pull off what's expected of them within the frame of gender roles. In fact, by the end of adolescence, the gender segregation and polarization that our society encourages in adult roles is embedded in many teens'

minds and is imitated in their lives (Stockard and Johnson, 1992).

Gender roles for adolescent boys seem to have changed less over the past decades and remain more explicit than those for adolescent girls. Simply stated, adolescent boys have three basic rules to follow in relation to gender roles: (1) Succeed at athletics. (2) Become interested in girls and sex. (3) Don't show signs of (or admit to) "feminine" interests or traits. Boys who stick to the rules are headed down the road to acceptance and popularity; boys who stray too far from the norms may be ridiculed and ostracized.

The traditional prohibition of feminine traits in male adolescents is in part an outgrowth of the view that masculinity and femininity are opposites. In this view, if a teenage boy is to "fit" the male stereotype, he must be achievement-oriented, independent, self-confident, strong, and so on. He defines his social status in terms of his own skill and achievement, especially in sports (Eckert, 1989). For both boys and men, aggression is an important component of friendship and is actually one way that boys initiate contact with each other and indicate their interest in starting a friendship. Verbal and physical fights actually seem to facilitate male friendships (Tannen, 1990). The stereotypical male sees life in terms of contests and if feminine traits emerge, his masculinity is subject to question or ridicule.

Androgyny may not be considered an acceptable alternative. A teenage boy who exhibits feminine interests (preferring ballet to football, for instance) or traits (passivity, shyness) may actually be assumed to be homosexual. Though by now we should understand that homosexuality is a variation of human sexuality and is not something to be ridiculed or feared, that knowledge does not always translate into acceptance in our culture, so the teenage boy with feminine or androgynous traits may be socially and emotionally at risk within his peer and family groups.

As a group, girls tend to have a more difficult time juggling the demands of gender roles than do boys during adolescence. Whereas most boys and some girls derive a lot of satisfaction and status from sports, participation in sports is not usually enough to empower teenage girls to resolve the conflicting demands of gender roles during adolescence. Unfortunately, excellence in academics doesn't usually suffice, either. We've come a long way since the days when girls were forced to take home economics while boys took shop, when girls could become nurses but rarely doctors, and legal secretaries but rarely lawyers. And although it would seem that educational training and opportunities based on a gender-blind or gender-neutral basis are the rule rather than the exception for modern teens, it isn't necessarily so in practice. Boys' and girls' academic interests tend to "parallel the occupations available to males and females" (Stockard and Johnson, 1992, p. 227). However, girls *do not* usually sacrifice their academic abilities as a means to attract boys (Stockard and Johnson, 1992)—this is a myth based on gender stereotypes.

Recently "The AAUW [American Association of University Women] Report: How Schools Short-change Girls" (1992) conducted in connection with the Wellesley College Center on Research for Women noted the following facts about gender-based treatment in schools:

- Girls receive significantly less attention from classroom teachers than do boys.

- Girls who are extremely competent in math and science are less likely than male classmates to pursue careers in science and technology.

- Although differences between boys and girls in math achievement are declining, in high schools the girls are still less likely than boys to elect advanced courses and be in top-scoring math groups.

- Boys are more likely to get scholarships based on SAT scores than are girls who have equal or better grades in high school than did the boys.

Though current laws prohibit gender discrimination in school admissions policies, women are still underrepresented at prestigious colleges and in graduate schools. They even face discrimination in financing their educations—some families would rather invest their money in sons' education than daughters' based on the assumption that a male needs an occupation to ensure economic success but a female's education is seen as a route to finding a husband (who will then be the source of the female's secure future) (Stockard and Johnson, 1992).

Other researchers have found that adolescent girls in all socioeconomic groups have different orientations toward work than do boys. Girls tend to plan to interrupt whatever careers they embark upon to make allowances for family responsibilities. Gender differences in work orientation are even stronger in working-class, non-college-bound groups of teenage girls than in groups of girls from middle class backgrounds who tend to aspire to male-typed professions (Stockard and Johnson, 1992). This doesn't mean that girls cannot succeed brilliantly in school or at work, but it is clear that gender stacks the deck against many girls within the context of academic and work life. Thus it is harder for female adolescents who want to break out of stereotypical gender patterns and expectations to do so.

In the middle school/junior high years, girls' popularity and status among other girls is often a function of the girls' popularity with boys. However, boys' popularity with their male peers doesn't depend on popularity with girls (Thorne, 1993). The culture of teenage girls is largely a "cosmetic" one (Thorne, 1993). Magazines like *Seventeen, YM, Sassy* teach adolescent girls how to make themselves more attractive to boys, and although these magazines do teach about responsible sexuality, discuss controversial issues such as date rape and teenage pregnancy, how to make lifestyle choices, and how to maintain friendships, the bulk of the articles and ads tell girls how to make themselves look and seem a certain way: pretty, sexy, cute, available, sharp, and maybe—once in a while—smart. You don't find articles announcing "Snowboard Chic" or "How to Lose 30 Pounds in 30 Days" in magazines geared to males, like *Sports Illustrated* or *Esquire*. Adolescent girls learn very quickly that looks count in all contexts (Brown and Gilligan, 1992).

Gender Roles and the Norms of Teenage Sexual Behavior

Both boys and girls use their sexuality to test and practice gender roles. Obviously, the physical changes that occur during adolescence (see Chapter 9) alter how teens feel about themselves and how others react and relate to them. The norms of sexual behavior vacillate tremendously in spite of the dangers of sexually transmitted diseases (STDs), AIDS, and greater public awareness and disapproval of coercive sexual encounters. In some groups the traditional double standard persists, saying males can have premarital sexual experiences but females really should remain virgins before marriage. This double standard assigns responsibility for being the sexual expert to the male who is to initiate sex, control its timing and tempo, select the appropriate activities to arouse his partner, and bring her to orgasm. It turns sex into something a male does "for" a female (which is an improvement on the even older idea that sex is something a male does "to" a female for his own release because a "good" woman has no sexual feelings). It doesn't encourage sharing or flexibility in playing sexual roles, may compel a male to make sexual advances to prove his masculinity (even if he's not in the mood or particularly attracted to his companion). The double standard implies that a female shouldn't let herself "get into it" sexually or should set sexual limits for herself even when she doesn't want to, reducing her potential for sexual pleasure.

Teenage boys who decide to have sex and are "responsible" (i.e., they use condoms, ask their partners "Is this okay with you" as they ease themselves into their lovemaking) are applauded by society. In contrast to boys, sexually active female teenagers face a broader range of reactions to their sexual choices. Unfortunately, they still run the risk of being labeled "sluts" if they're too sexually adventurous or overt about their interest in being sexual (Thorne, 1993) or even if they're sexually responsible and mature about relationships but have the misfortune of being the subject of teenage gossip or parental overreaction. It can be hard to figure out the relationship between femininity and sexuality.

The traditional message about sexual behavior has been "nice girls don't" or that they should feel guilty if they do. But nice girls "do" today, and that flies in the face of convention. In some groups of teenagers, girls flaunt their sexual experiences as often as boys do, as a badge of honor, proof of power, a sign of belonging to a group, or a mark of physical and emotional maturity, proof of sexual desirability. The traditional double standard's sexual script disappears here, and girls become assertive and aggressive in dating and intimacy situations. Some *try* to become pregnant yet aren't interested in marrying their boyfriends, disregard the risks of STDs or AIDS, talk about having babies in much the same way as boys might talk about how many girls they'd "nailed." So it's clear that gender roles for female sexual behavior is shifting for some teens.

In many ways, the old predictable "quarterback-cheerleader" ideas of adolescent masculine and feminine gender roles were easier for teenagers to deal with. Everything was decided in advance, the boundaries were in place, and the risks of crossing them were pretty clear. Today's culture offers more options for teens but forces them to answer many more questions: What am I really getting into? Is this safe? Is this what I want? Is this what my partner wants? Is this appropriate? How will this make me look to other people?

Where do my decisions fit into my parents' beliefs? Precisely because male and female gender roles are changing and sexual norms are in flux, it is that much more important to take the time to pose these kinds of questions and to answer them honestly.

Adulthood

Adulthood is a time for honing, practicing, juggling, and struggling with gender roles. In the past, gender roles were cut-and- dried and everyone knew what was expected of him or her—women became wives, mothers, and homemakers; men became husbands, fathers, and breadwinners; men led, women followed; men gave orders, women asked permission; women's lives were rooted in the home, men's lives didn't necessarily have to be rooted at all; women were dependent, men independent; men were allowed to be sexually adventurous or promiscuous, women weren't. In American society today, these distinctions have become less important for many men and women. How much they've faded depends upon a number of variables. Biological sex, age, family philosophy, family configuration (e.g., intact, divorced, single-parent family, extended/blended family, gay or lesbian parents), socioeconomic status, ethnicity, geographic location, educational opportunity and achievement, religious and political orientation, job availability, life stage (Stockard and Johnson, 1992; Brok, 1992) are some of the variables that produce the experience that molds your personal concept of gender roles and teaches you how they are to be played out.

A person's gender-role orientation is not set in concrete once he or she hits adulthood. Today's culture practically demands that a person be flexible to meet the changing challenges of modern gender roles. Gender roles for adults in American society are less clearly defined and less rigidly enforced than they have ever been before, yet men and women still differ in how they view themselves playing certain gender roles, possibly because of the different requirements each must meet in order to be considered "good" members of their gender groups (i.e., women must still be loving and caring people, men must still be good providers) (Joseph, Markus, and Tafarodi, 1992).

As we've noted elsewhere, men's roles tend to require that they be individualistic, independent, and autonomous people (Markus and Kitayama, 1991) who are able to fulfill these and other gender goals by being better than others (Markus and Cross, 1990). When men tell stories about themselves that pertain to gender roles, for example, they often speak of how they sacrifice their lives to their careers (Tavris, 1992). Tavris challenges the validity of the gender role of "empathic caretaker" that American culture assigns to women and suggests it isn't necessarily due to some inborn ability of the female sex. The expression of empathy (compassion, understanding, kindness) is a learned skill that men can easily master and that women don't always succeed at. In effect, critics of our gender-role-dominated culture challenge Americans to eliminate "gender caricatures" (Bem, 1993, p. 194). But to eliminate them, however, we must understand what these are.

Gender Roles in The Workplace

For women to adhere to cultural gender norms means they must be sensitive, attuned to, and interconnected with other people (Markus and Cross, 1990), possibly because women's relative powerlessness in society demands they be constantly responsive to others (Miller, 1986). As Stewart and Lykes (1985) point out, the norms of being a so-called "good" woman and being a "good" person may be at odds for women in some situations such as business. Today, for example, three-fourths of married women with school-age children are employed outside the home and that figure is higher for divorced women (Stockard and Johnson, 1992). At work, a woman may have to function in terms of gender roles as a stereotypical man would; for instance, she might need to drop the pretense of being "connected" and instead be interested in being "better than" her competitors.

However, Brenda Major's and her co-worker's research (1984) found that when men and women worked at the same jobs, with the same level of prestige, they tended to behave similarly, valued the same things, expected the same pay, and strove with equivalent energy for promotions. Rosabeth Kanter (1977) challenged the gender-role stereotype about women's focus on "connectedness" in the workplace. She found that when men worked in tedious, blue-collar jobs with little opportunity for advancement they behaved and reacted more like the female-gender stereotype in terms of work orientation. That is, the men sought pleasure and

satisfaction outside of their work environment and were more involved in peer groups and social activities than they were in their work. Kanter's study contradicted traditional gender-role beliefs by proving that it was the *conditions of the job*, not the qualities of the person, that determined what people valued about work. In order to understand adult gender roles, we must distinguish between the *theories* about them and what we observe about how gender roles are played out by men and women in everyday life. Let's look at some more examples and see if we can come to any conclusions about adult gender roles today.

It used to be said that men were best suited for jobs that involved working with money but women were best suited for jobs that were people-oriented (Tavris, 1992). Gender roles in the workplace have changed for both sexes, although the experience of being accepted within the workplace has changed less for women than men. For instance, men who have entered professions that used to be virtually all female (the people-oriented jobs Tavris alluded to)—nursing, preschool and elementary school teaching, office jobs of a secretarial nature, and so on—are usually accepted in those contexts, and are rarely subjected to harassment.

Women who cross over the workplace gender divide are not always so lucky. In a wide variety of jobs, they are harassed because of gender and only rarely do such cases come to public attention. Four out of ten women in supervisory positions have experienced sexual harassment from men at their places of work; only one of eight of these women ever report the incidents (Morrison, 1992).

Gender-role stereotyping creates other problems for women in the workplace. Women who are employed in what were formerly and traditionally all-male industries (e.g., steel, autos) may find themselves the targets of name calling, given the silent treatment, or excluded from office social functions by male co-workers who are angry that women "took" jobs that men could have had. Economically, women in many occupations are still penalized for their gender by being paid lower wages than men [for the same jobs women's salaries are 70 percent of men's salaries (Tavris, 1992)], getting fewer benefits, and facing more obstacles to career advancement on the job. If women and men have identical training, they are usually hired for different jobs and paid different wages (Stockard and Johnson, 1992). If women are successful in their achievements at work, the results are more likely to be attributed to luck than to skill, dedication, or effort (Walum, 1977; Heilman, 1980).

Sex discrimination can be found in a variety of contexts. A research study asked 360 college students, half of them male and the other half female, to evaluate academic articles presented to them as written by "*John T. McKay*" or "*Joan T. McKay*." Though the same articles were used for the evaluations (just the first name of the author changed), the articles supposedly written by "John" were more favorably evaluated by both sexes than the articles supposedly written by "Joan" (Paludi and Bauer, 1983). A recent murder trial that seized the attention of the American public and press provided another instance of sex discrimination. Leslie Abramson, the female criminal defense lawyer who defended Erik Menendez when he was on trial with his brother for killing their parents, was warned by the male judge to act like a professional, not like a "nursemaid" or "surrogate mother"; she responded in an interview by saying that one of the myths of our culture is that "if you're a woman, you get emotionally attached to your clients, but if you're a man, you don't" (*People*, October 11, 1993, p. 53). Chances are, if she had been a man, equally attentive to his client as she seemed to be to hers, the judge's comment would not have been made. It's clear that a giant chasm still divides male and female gender roles and influences how they can be played out within the workplace.

Gender Roles in The Family

Is it possible to fulfill both masculine and feminine gender-role expectations as an adult? Perhaps it is—and with more ease and acceptance for men—within the context of family. LaRossa (1989) suggests we make a distinction between the *culture of fatherhood* (society's beliefs about and the values it places on fatherhood) and the *conduct of fatherhood* (what fathers really do). In part because of the demands of dual-career family life, single-parent families, and families with same-sex parents, stereotypical gender-role distinctions are fading. Many household tasks and family roles that were previously considered "women's work" are being done by men (although usually men still do only about one-third of the amount done by wives, whether or not the wives are working outside the home) (Pleck, 1985; Douthitt, 1989; Wainrib, 1992). Fathers who opt for paternity leave when their children are

Gender Differences in Couples' Conflicts

Buss (1989) has found that dating couples and married men and women agree on certain traits in their partner that are bothersome to them. For instance, unfaithfulness and abusiveness bother men and women equally. But some interesting differences in sources of conflict between the sexes emerged; these are summarized below.

What Bothers a Woman About a Man

- *Sexual demands:* being too aggressive sexually, making her feel sexually used; pushing for sex without regard to her feeings.
- *Condescension:* treating her as stupid or somehow inferior ("the weaker sex"); disregarding or belittling her opinions because she is a woman.
- *Emotional constriction:* keeping his feelings hidden so as not to appear weak or vulnerable.
- *Behavioral excesses:* drinking too much; getting into arguments or fights too easily; smoking.
- *Neglect:* spending too little time with her; forgetting to call her when he had promised he would; not saying "I love you" to her; being unreliable.

What Bothers a Man About a Woman

- *Sexual rejection:* saying no to sex too often; being unresponsive to his sexual overtures; being a sexual tease.
- *Self-absorption:* being preoccupied with her appearance; spending too lavishly on clothes; worrying about her weight, her hairdo, and her makeup too much.
- *Being too moody:* being too controlled by her emotions; acting "bitchy" unpredictably.

born are applauded in our culture and no one criticizes or blames them when they have to return to work, and it is gradually becoming more acceptable for men to choose to be house-husbands while their wives go off to work. While married men—as a group—are physically and mentally healthier than single men (Gurman and Klein, 1980; Scanzoni and Fox, 1980; Weissman, 1980), married women have higher rates of mental and physical problems than do single women (Walker et al., 1985; Gotlib and McCabe, 1990). This contrast suggests the relative ease with which men can blend what might be considered stereotypic male and female gender roles into their lives, and the relative difficulty women have trying to do the same thing.

Men usually do not have to blend, separate, and juggle roles (worker, parent, caregiver) to the same degree women do. Men spend more time and emotional energy taking stock of their position in the work world: figuring out how well they've accomplished the goals they set for themselves in earlier years, assessing the status they've achieved at work (Stockard and Johnson, 1992). In contrast, most women have to function at peak efficiency in both the work world and the family domain. Unlike men, women who go back to work after the birth of children may be looked upon with some blame, as if they're abandoning their children, "choosing" one domain over the other even if it is purely a choice based on economic necessity. In spite of fading gender-role stereotypes, married working women still bear the brunt of the home and child-care responsibilities. In terms of choosing which gender roles to concentrate upon, the so-called choice for women is illusion. Approximately 30 percent of working women say they expect to work full time as soon as their children become preschoolers (O'Connell, Betz, and Kurth, 1989), but this implies that they know they'll have to make adjustments in their work schedules for the first two or three years of the child's life. As Bem (1993) says, the United States has yet to construct a cultural environment in which any woman who decides to have a child can "easily step outside the role of child care" (p. 33)—unless she is in an economic situation that lets her hire full-time help. Gender-role conflict for women is practically a given in American culture, and Bem says the stress of this conflict may result in poor physical and mental health for some women.

Older Adults

There is some convergence of gender roles as adults age. That convergence is partly a result of retirement from work, which all but eliminates the necessity for a man to play the role of breadwinner. Because children are grown, the man no longer has to play the role of authoritarian father. Instead, both males and females who become grandparents tend to slip easily and comfortably into nurturing roles in their interactions with their grandchildren. But when researchers examined the issue of nurturance and caregiving as it applied to looking after aging parents or ill spouses, they discovered that women felt it more stressful to be caretakers (the feminine gender role) than did men. Interestingly, this result has to do with sex-stereotyped behaviors. Men delegate responsibility and seek outside help while women try to do everything themselves (Belsky, 1992). Another study that looked at aging men across cultures found that as they age men become more passive but not necessarily androgynous. They stay gender identified as male, but lose some of their "sexual and aggressive behavioral interests" (Brok, 1992, p. 174 referring to a 1987 study by D. L. Guttman).

Gender roles being what they are, it seems impossible to expect that women's and men's lives can ever be made equivalent. They may be comparable in some realms of life, but to date, there are just as many situations in which gender roles don't easily blend. True gender-role equality will take into account the need for parental leave and child care, organizational flexibility at work or school, and fairly valuing and compensating "women's work." As Tavris suggests, we ought to "ask how to achieve equality *despite* gender differences, not how to achieve equality by getting rid of (or pretending to ignore) gender differences" (Tavris, 1992, p. 125). The challenge is there for us to accept and fulfill.

ANDROGYNY

In spite of the fact that our culture is divided into male–female gender camps (gender polarization), no person is 100 percent "masculine" or 100 percent "feminine" in terms of gender traits. When we say that gender roles for adults are less rigidly enforced than they have been before or that men and women should be flexible in terms of how they fulfill gender roles, we are actually making a strong case for the value of androgyny.

Androgyny refers to the combined presence of both feminine *and* masculine characteristics in one person (Kaplan and Sedney, 1980). The word itself comes from two Greek roots: *andro,* meaning male, and *gyn,* meaning female. An androgynous person incorporates cultural definitions of masculinity and femininity without depending on or caring too much about cultural definitions of gender appropriateness (Bem, 1993). Androgyny does *not* refer to economic equality between the sexes, the absence of gender-role differentiation, bisexuality, or biological conditions of hermaphroditism (when a person has both testicular and ovarian tissue).

Some researchers like Pleck (1975) think the capacity to become androgynous is a skill which evolves in some children after they pass through two other stages of gender-role development paralleling the developmental stages of cognitive thinking (which we discussed in the section about toddlers earlier in this chapter). At stage one, children are unorganized about their sense of gender and gender roles. At stage two, they become very rigid in their concepts. They reach stage three, androgyny, when they are able to be flexible about their notions of male–female gender roles.

Other researchers like Hyde and her colleagues (1991) challenge the assumption that androgyny is a developmental phenomenon and suggest, instead, that androgyny can be best explained as a function of and reflection of society's values about sex roles.

What exactly does it mean to be androgynous in daily actions and reactions? As with masculinity and femininity there's no single, fixed profile or definition that all researchers and commentators agree on. Some like Kaplan and Sedney (1980) described androgyny as the coexistence of feminine and masculine traits that can be expressed at different times. For example, a person could disagree about a work-related matter with a colleague in a forceful and aggressive way (a stereotypical masculine reaction) but be very caring later on when discussing that colleague's personal problem (a stereotypical female reaction). Another perspective says feminine and masculine traits can exist in a fully integrated way within one person. Rather than alternating between feminine and masculine traits, the individual blends the characteristics together. So, a woman may initiate sexual activity (a traditionally masculine role) but do so in a style that is warm and sensitive (traditionally considered feminine traits).

Therefore, androgyny doesn't require a person to lose the qualities associated with his or her gender and take on those associated with the opposite

sex. Instead, androgyny gives a person options and freedoms to blend masculine and feminine temperaments and behaviors without having to feel constrained by stereotypical gender role "shoulds" (Bem, 1993). Androgyny is not always uniformly positive—it's possible for an androgynous person to combine the negative elements of masculinity and femininity, such as being domineering and nagging, or being harsh and weak (Cook, 1985).

Recent research about androgyny has yielded some interesting information. Parents and teachers of younger children don't mind encouraging androgyny in girls but are less comfortable doing so with boys. However, encouraging androgyny all but evaporates in adolescence when the leeway tightens for girls and they are more or less expected to slip into the polarized female gender roles of the adult world (Thorne, 1993). Hudak (1993) questioned whether men's perceptions of themselves influenced their perception of women and found that androgynous men, in contrast to masculine men who see women as stereotypically feminine, perceive American women as significantly more androgynous. Peters and Cantrell (1993) compared groups of feminist lesbian women and heterosexual women and found that "overall, it appears that androgynous individuals fare best with regard to relationship quality" (p. 381), regardless of sexual preferences. In a study of work environments and how professional people are evaluated within their occupations, Arkkelin and O'Connor (1992) found that along with the bias that favors masculine traits in general, androgynous traits are viewed as equally desirable.

LOOKING BEYOND ANDROGYNY

The flush of excitement about androgyny that researchers felt in the 1970s and early 1980s made it seem as though androgyny led to or enhanced self-esteem, social competence, achievement orientation (Spence and Helmreich, 1978); flexibility in behavior patterns (Bem, 1972, 1975; Bem, Martyna, and Watson, 1976); and lower incidence of psychological problems (Burchardt and Serbin, 1982). Later research found that androgyny carried with it the potential for some negative consequences. Cook (1985) found (1) some androgynous people were anxious and moody due to social pressures resulting from their androgyny; (2) some had trouble balancing their masculine and feminine traits and couldn't effectively direct their behavior; and (3) in romantic relationships disappointment might result if the androgynous person's partner wasn't androgynous or if that partner expected a partner with more traditional gender-role behavior.

Depending on how one measures self-esteem, different results have been obtained in studies of androgyny (Dorgan, Goegel, and House, 1983), so there is some confusion about the connection between androgyny and self-esteem. Bem herself (1993), author of the Bem Sex Role Inventory, which helped define androgyny, later recognized some problems inherent in the concept of androgyny: (1) it still used the male as the ideal against which a female was compared, so the androgynous person was initially considered as a "perfect *man*"; (2) the concept of androgyny is too gender neutral and doesn't acknowledge the historical reality of gender inequality; (3) by focusing so much on the individual, it ignores the political implications of gender inequality; (4) it assumes that masculinity and femininity are "givens," implies that heterosexuality is the norm, and therefore replicates gender polarization by focusing on male–female distinctions (Bem, 1993, pp. 121–127).

Bem switched the focus of her research (circa 1978) from androgyny to *gender schematicity,* which refers to how people internalize the awareness of gender polarizations that exist in their culture and then go on to define masculinity and femininity for themselves—often without realizing that's what they're doing—so that they'll know how to behave and react in the context of their culture (1981; 1993, p. 125). Rebecca, Hefner, and Oleshanksy (1976) suggested going beyond androgyny to *gender transcendence,* a way of behaving in appropriate ways without worrying about or conforming to gender roles. Whether you agree or disagree with any of these researchers, androgyny is part of the spectrum of gender-role behaviors we can choose from.

THE PSYCHOLOGY OF SEX DIFFERENCES

The controversy over the psychological differences between the sexes has long been steeped in myth. Some of the early researchers who determined which sex possessed "superior" skills are now being accused of using sloppy methods and male bias to ensure that the results affirmed male superiority. Times have changed, and a landmark study published in 1974 dispels many of these myths by concluding that the sexes are more alike than different.

Eleanor Maccoby and Carol Jacklin spent three years compiling and reviewing over 2000 books and articles on sex differences in children to find which beliefs were backed by hard evidence and which had insufficient experimental support. Their study did not try to explain why these differences and similarities exist; Maccoby and Jacklin wanted only to describe the present state of the research—without bias.

To rate your own biases, take the following true/false quiz:

T F   1. Girls are more social than boys.
T F   2. Boys have higher self-esteem than girls.
T F   3. Girls are better than boys at simple, repetitive tasks.
T F   4. Boys have greater mathematical and visual–spatial abilities than girls.
T F   5. Boys are more analytical than girls.
T F   6. Girls have greater verbal ability than boys.
T F   7. Boys have a stronger motivation to achieve.
T F   8. Girls are less aggressive than boys.
T F   9. Girls can be persuaded more easily than boys.
T F   10. Girls are more alert to auditory stimulation; boys are more alert to visual stimulation.

The answers, based on the Maccoby and Jacklin research, are surprising.

Question 1: There is no evidence to suggest that girls are more social than boys. In early childhood, both sexes choose to play in groups with equal frequency, and neither sex is more willing to play alone. Boys do not prefer inanimate objects over playmates, and at certain ages boys spend more time with playmates than girls do.

Question 2: Psychological tests show that girls and boys are very similar in self-esteem throughout childhood and adolescence, but they pick different areas in which they feel they have greatest self-confidence. Girls believe they have more social competence; boys see themselves as dominant and powerful. These beliefs have no experimental support and probably spring from early social learning rather than an accurate assessment of their own abilities.

Questions 3 and 4: Both sexes perform equally well at simple, repetitive tasks. Boys excel in mathematical ability from about age 12 and have an increased ability to perceive relationships among objects in space. Boys, for example, are better able to mentally rotate a picture of an object and to correctly describe its hidden side. This difference is not evident until adolescence, suggesting it may arise either from environmental factors (perhaps boys are given more opportunities to perfect their skill) or from hormonal influences.

While some authorities have questionend whether male mathematical superiority is a by-product of cultural expectations (Kolata, 1980), the evidence seems to be somewhat divided. A study by researchers at the University of Chicago found no sign of sex differences in the ability to solve geometry problems among 1366 tenth graders. Two other reports suggest, however, that biological influences may be important. In one study, researchers found that men with severe lifetime androgen deficiency had impaired spatial abilities compared to men with normal hormone levels or men who developed androgen deficiencies after puberty (Hier and Crowley, 1982). In another study, researchers have found additional evidence linking exceptional mathematical talent to hormonal status, suggesting that prenatal programming of the brain by androgens may predispose to later sex differences that may be magnified at the time of puberty by rising levels of the male hormone (Kolata, 1983). It is important to realize, however, that the sexes overlap considerably in their mathematical abilities, so this minor sex difference should not be used to counsel boys or girls in regard to courses or careers. Furthermore, some experts question whether there is any innate difference at all, citing evidence that girls are given less encouragement to study math by parents and teachers than boys are and are also given less individual instruction in math by teachers (Fausto-Sterling, 1985). Furthermore, girls get better grades in math courses than boys do, raising the possibility that boys may simply do better on standardized tests (Kimball, 1989).

Question 5: Boys are not more analytical than girls. To analyze, one must be able to recognize the important information in a situation uninfluenced by context or surroundings. Both boys and girls are as likely to respond to the unimportant elements in analyzing a problem.

Question 6: Girls' verbal abilities mature more rapidly than boys'. Boys and girls remain about equal from infancy to early adolescence, but in high school and possibly beyond, females take the lead. Girls score higher on tests requiring the understanding of complex language, creative writing, analogies, fluency, and spelling. As with the boys' greater mathematical abilities, the girls' later increase in verbal ability may result more from socialization encouraging girls to perfect language skills.

Question 7: Boys and girls can be equally motivated to achieve but by different factors. Girls are motivated to achieve when neither competition nor social comparison is stressed. Boys need direct appeals to their ego and a sense of competition to reach the girls' level of motivation.

Question 8: Girls are less aggressive than boys, a difference exhibited as early as age 2, when social play begins. Boys are more aggressive physically and engage in mock fighting and verbal forcefulness. Their aggression is usually directed at other male playmates rather than at the less aggressive girls. There is no evidence, however, that parents encourage boys to be more aggressive than girls: they actually discourage aggression in both sexes.

Question 9: Boys and girls are both as likely to be persuaded by others and to imitate the behavior of people around them. Both sexes are equally affected by social pressure to conform. The only verifiable difference is that girls are slightly more likely to adapt their own judgments to those of the group, while boys are able to accept peer group values without changing their own values even when the two conflict.

Question 10: Male and female infants respond alike to aspects of their environment that require hearing and sight. They are similarly skilled in identifying speech patterns, various noises, objects, shapes, and distances. This equality persists throughout adulthood.

An alternative approach for detecting differences between the sexes is the "brain-based" study. Neurologists and psychologists measure brain size and use tests such as the electroencephalograph (the "brain wave" test) to measure the brain's electrical response to stimuli. These studies reduce the possibility of experimenter bias because they do not rely as heavily on interpretations of observed behavior.

Major findings of these brain-based studies (published after the Maccoby and Jacklin research) point toward a neurological basis for some sex differences. Dianne McGuinness and Karl Pribram (1978), using an approach similar to that of Maccoby and Jacklin, summarized the findings of a majority of these studies. They found that women have more sensitive taste, touch, and hearing. A woman's hearing in the higher ranges is so much better than a man's that a sound at 85 decibels seems twice as loud to her as to him. McGuinness and Pribram also concluded that women have better manual dexterity and fine coordination, are more interested in people, and are more attentive to sounds as infants. Since evidence is beginning to emerge showing some structural anatomic differences between the brains of men and women (Lacoste-Utamsing and Holloway, 1982), it seems that more brain-based studies will be required to clarify the current controversies in this area.

There is also a large body of research data showing that in virtually every mammalian species studied, from rodents to monkeys to humans, there are significant anatomical sex differences (Gibbons, 1991). In humans, for example, men's brains are on average about 15 percent larger than women's brains, which is about twice the difference in average body size between the sexes. Furthermore, the corpus callosum—the bundle of nerve fibers connecting the right and left hemispheres of the brain—is larger in men, which might explain a phenomenon such as women's greater use of both sides of the brain for language skills in comparison to men. In contrast, another connecting region of the brain, the anterior commissure, is larger in women than men. And specific regions of the hypothalamus, the portion of the brain that controls key hormonal events in the body, are 250 percent larger in men than women.

It is undeniable that males and females differ physically and that biology has some degree of influence on gender differences in human life. You see the impact of biology on nurturance and aggression (which are considered psychological traits), on social roles (such as child care), and physical distinctions (such as the male's superior visual–spatial ability, the female's greater resistance to disease, the male's greater strength). However,

no matter how great the biological distinctions are between males and females and in spite of the fact that studying the psychology of sex differences is enhanced by an awareness of the biological underpinnings, biology alone doesn't explain the higher value placed on men's activities than on women's in our society and cross-culturally (Stockard and Johnson, 1992; Bem, 1993).

THE TRANSSEXUAL PHENOMENON

In 1953 the world was startled to learn about Christine Jorgensen, an American ex-Marine who underwent surgery in Denmark to convert his anatomical appearance from male to female. Since then transsexualism has achieved considerable notoriety. Jan Morris' autobiography, *Conundrum*, provides some fascinating details into her own transsexual odyssey. Renee Richards, an accomplished eye doctor and tennis player as a male, provoked quite a stir when she insisted on joining the woman's pro tennis circuit as a converted female.

Transsexual individuals persistently feel an incongruity between their anatomical sex and gender identity. They frequently describe their dilemma as "being trapped in the wrong body." Their psychological sense of existence as male or female (their gender identity) does not match the appearance of their genitals and secondary sex characteristics. Looking and being biologically male, the male transsexual wishes to change to female anatomy and live as a woman. Conversely, looking and being biologically female, the female transsexual wishes to change to male anatomy and live as a man.

Precise statistics on the prevalence of this gender identity disorder are not available, but one estimate suggests the figure as 1 in 100,000 for male transsexuals and 1 in 130,000 for female transsexuals (Pauly, 1974). Among persons who contact gender identity clinics and request change-of-sex surgery, there are many more men than women (American Psychiatric Association, 1980). Although there has been considerable speculation about the possible cause(s) of transsexualism (Benjamin, 1966; Green and Money, 1969; Stoller, 1972, 1975; Green, 1974; Hunt, Carr, and Hampson, 1981), there is little agreement on this matter among researchers in the field. Both biological and psychological factors have been suggested as causes. No convincing evi-

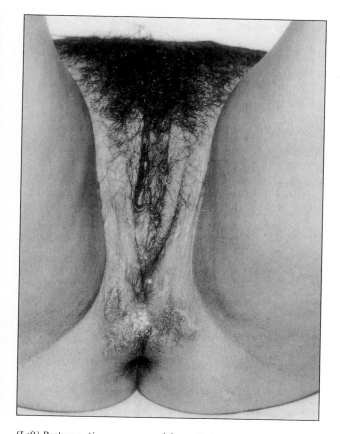
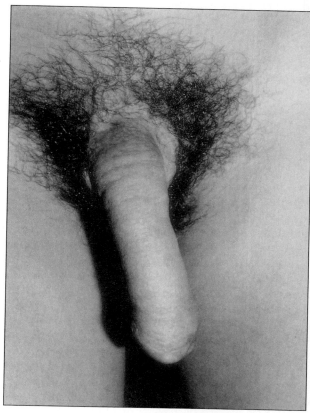

(Left) Post-operative appearance of the genitals in a male-to-female transsexual. (Right) Post-operative appearance of the genitals in a female-to-male transsexual.

dence of biological causes of transsexualism have been documented, however (LeVay, 1993). As Green (1992, pp. 102–103) puts it, "It remains a sexual science mystery why some males and females are transsexual. No psychological or physiological explanation has proven satisfactory."

In the best-defined cases of transsexualism, the person has a lifelong sense of being psychologically at odds with his or her sexual anatomy. Typically, this psychological discomfort is partially (but only temporarily) relieved by pretending to be a member of the opposite, desired sex. Many transsexuals describe having had great interest in cross-dressing (i.e., wearing clothes of the "other" sex) during childhood or adolescence. Transsexuals, however, should not be confused with **transvestites,** who cross-dress to become sexually aroused but usually do not want permanent change of anatomy or appearance (see Chapter 17). In at least some cases, discovery of transsexual impulses does not occur until adulthood.

Psychotherapy has been generally unsuccessful in resolving the transsexual's basic distress of feeling trapped in the wrong body (Tollison and Adams, 1979). As a result, those judged to be authentic transsexuals have been treated in programs designed to lead to change-of-sex surgery—in effect, redoing the body to match the mind. Since such surgery is irreversible, responsible practitioners take a cautious approach and require a one- to two-year trial period beyond the initial evaluation during which the transsexual patient lives in a cross-gender role (Meyer and Hoopes, 1974; Money and Wiedeking, 1980). During this time, the trans-

transvestite (trans ves′ tit) an individual who receives sexual gratification and release from anxiety by dressing in the clothing of the opposite sex. Unlike transsexuals, transvestites are not interested in becoming a member of the opposite sex.

sexual begins living openly as a person of the opposite sex, adopting hairstyles, clothing, and mannerisms of that sex, and also assuming a name that "matches" the new gender.

The transsexual male is given estrogens on a daily basis to produce a certain degree of anatomic feminization: breast growth occurs, skin texture becomes softer, and muscularity decreases, for example. However, treatment with estrogens does not remove facial or body hair (electrolysis is required) or raise voice pitch (some male-to-female transsexuals take voice lessons to learn to speak in a more feminine fashion). Estrogen therapy also reduces the frequency of erections and causes the prostate gland and seminal vesicles to shrink.

Transsexual women are treated with testosterone to suppress menstruation, increase facial and body hair growth, and deepen the voice. Surgery is required to reduce breast size. For both male and female transsexuals, hormone treatments are given throughout the trial period of cross-dressing and adjusting to a new set of gender roles. At the same time, the patient's progress is periodically evaluated by a psychiatrist or psychologist. Attention is also directed to achieving legal recognition of the sex change and to personal matters, such as family or religious counseling.

If all goes fairly smoothly in the trial period and the transsexual is judged to be psychologically stable and able to adjust socially to the conversion, the final stage of treatment is surgery to change the sexual anatomy. At present, it is much simpler to perform male-to-female conversion surgery than the reverse. The male-to-female operation requires removing the penis and testes and creating an artificial vagina and female-appearing external genitals. The more difficult female-to-male procedure involves creating a "penis" from a tube made from abdominal skin or from tissue from the vaginal lips and perineum. While the artificial vagina created in the male-to-female transsexual often looks authentic and may allow a fairly full range of sexual response (e.g., vaginal lubrication and orgasm have both been claimed but not scientifically verified), female-to-male transsexual surgery creates an artificial penis that cannot become erect or feel tactile sensation.

In female-to-male transsexual surgery, it is sometimes possible to attain a degree of sexual function by implanting a mechanical inflatable device inside the penis to produce an artificial erection. Experience with this method is limited at present, and in any event, ejaculation is not possible. Many female-to-male transsexuals choose to have hormone therapy and surgical removal of their breasts and uterus but do not opt for an artificial penis.

In one recent study, Lief and Hubschman (1993) queried 14 male-to-female transsexuals and found that after surgery 8 out of 10 lost their capacity for orgasm entirely, while 2 who were previously nonorgasmic began to experience orgasms with intercourse. Overall, 2 of the 14 individuals were better from the viewpoint of their sexual functioning, while 4 were unchanged and 8 were worse. Female-to-male transsexuals fared considerably better. Six out of 9 individuals in this category studied by Lief and Hubschman reported having been nonorgasmic before surgery, but postoperatively 7 out of 9 reported having orgasms.

Follow-up studies on transsexualism are unfortunately small in number. Lundstrom (1981) noted that male-to-female transsexuals have poor postoperative sexual adjustment. Sorenson (1981) found that about one out of five people who underwent sex reassignment surgery later regretted their decision. In a more recent report, which involved intensive follow-up interviews with 13 male-to-female transsexuals an average of 12 years after their sex-change surgery, it was found that "only one-third of the patients where a vaginal construction was carried out had a functioning vagina," and a majority of patients (8 of 13) were found to be psychologically unchanged despite having had the surgery (Lindemalm, Korlin, and Uddenberg, 1986). In contrast, a study of 22 female-to-male transsexuals found that generally these individuals and their spouses reported "good and mutually satisfying interpersonal relationships" (Fleming, MacGowan, and Costos, 1985). An overview of eleven different follow-up studies involving some 350 postoperative transsexuals concluded that 87 percent of male-to-female transsexuals have a satisfactory outcome, with this number rising to 97 percent for female-to-male transsexuals (Green and Fleming, 1990).

Transsexual surgery is not a cure for this disorder but is only a procedure that may foster a sense of emotional well-being. In fact, the wisdom of surgery for transsexuals has been questioned by researchers who claimed to find no significant psychological benefits in patients who had undergone such operations compared to those who did not (Meyer and Reter, 1979). The matter is unresolved at present, although several prominent medical

Between Man and Woman: The Hijras of India

An intriguing example of people who fill alternate gender roles involves the *Hijras* of India. They are emasculated, impotent men whose job in society is a ritualized one, that of conferring fertility blessings on newborn males and on newlywed couples. As performers and dancers, they are thought to transmit the power of the Mother Goddess who transforms them from merely impotent men into powerful forces of generativity. They are considered to be "neither man nor woman" (Nanda, 1990, p. 10) but ascetics who have an important alternative gender role in Indian society.

Surgical removal of the genitals is at the heart of the social identity of Hijras. They say they are in between male and female, "man minus man" or "not man" (Nanda, 1990, p. 15). Impotence is central to the definition of "not man" and Hijras are not the equivalents of homosexuals because by becoming Hijras a man removes himself from the category of effeminate male or that of passive partner in a homosexual relationship [however, many Hijras are homosexual prostitutes, which may undermine their respect in society but doesn't seem to negate their importance as performers of ritual functions (Nanda, 1990, p. 10)]. Once castrated and healed from the surgery, Hijras dress in women's clothes, wear their hair long, wear traditional feminine jewelry, and place the bindi (the colored dot that all Hindu women who aren't widowed wear on their foreheads) on their own foreheads. They take female names, use female kinship terms for each other, and adopt female behavior. Hijras are "also not women, though they are 'like' women" (Nanda, 1990, p. 17).

Interestingly, the Hijras wield considerable power within Hindu Indian society and have a very "positive, collective self-image" (Nanda, 1990, p. 12). People who, in Western cultures such as ours, would be differentiated into diverse categories such as eunuchs, transsexuals, homosexuals, hermaphrodites, and transvestites, seem to come together in this role of Hijras, because it "is a magnet that attracts people with many different kinds of cross-gender identities, attributes, and behaviors" (Nanda, 1990, p. 19). Sexual ambiguities are not really ambiguous, then, when a culture can accommodate them, give them power and meaning, and tolerate and embrace sexual contradictions and gender variations (Nanda, 1990, p. 23). Looking at alternative gender roles in other cultures helps us to question and even alter how we interpret "the nature and assumptions" (Nanda, 1990, p. 129) that form the basis of our own gender systems.

centers stopped doing transsexual surgery in 1980 because of the lack of solid evidence that the surgery is beneficial. On the other hand, Pauly and Edgerton (1986), who claim that the vast majority of sex-reassignment cases have a satisfactory outcome, point out that there are approximately 40 centers in which interdisciplinary teams provide evaluation and treatment for transsexual patients.

GENDER ROLES AND SEXUAL BEHAVIOR

In most societies, there are strong connections between gender roles and existing sexual attitudes and behavior although it is hard to tell which comes first: the behavior and attitude or the gender role? In spite of the advances American society has made on loosening the rigidity of gender roles in many areas of everyday life (e.g., work, school, parenting) stereotypes about gender roles and sexual behavior persist. These stereotypes suggest that males are innately more interested in sex than females, that males characteristically assume an active role in sex while females are characteristically passive, and that male sexual arousal occurs quickly and automatically while female sexual arousal takes longer, is more precarious, must be coaxed from a woman, and may not be as intense or explosive as a man's. The behavioral consequences of such sexual stereotypes can cause a man to try to "measure up" to the gender role, turning him into a macho man who ignores or misreads his female partner's cues or who makes it difficult for any sexual encounter to be much more than a "he does it to her or for her" event.

The consequences of the masculine stereotype can create tremendous sexual performance anxieties for a man, making him wonder if he can possibly be as "manly" as the gender stereotype says he should be. These anxieties may cause him to withdraw emotionally from intimacy, or avoid sexual contact altogether.

A woman may react to her gender-role stereotype by accepting the notion that from a sexual viewpoint she is a second-class citizen. She may consistently ignore her own needs for her own physical gratification and say that things are fine sexually as long as and because her "man" is satisfied. She may be afraid to ask for or demand from a partner the kind and amount of sexual attention that is pleasing to her on the mistaken impression that to do so is inappropriate, that it doesn't fit the feminine gender role in the sexual arena. The worse-case scenario is that a woman who is bound by belief to this male-dominant, female-submissive gender role, subjects herself to physical and emotional abuse within sexual situations because she doesn't really think she has the right to stand up for herself.

GENDER ROLES, CROSS-CULTURALLY

Sometimes we need to look at very different cultures to see just how limiting the stereotypes of our own culture can be. There are many cultures with expectations about sexual interactions that are startlingly different from our own. When considering these other cultures, keep in mind the definition of gender—the psychological, social, and behavioral aspects of being male and female—and how we apply the terms "masculine" and "feminine" when we speak of gender. Remember, too, that in American culture gender identity and gender roles tend to be polarized, that is, divided into either masculine or feminine categories.

In Mangaia, a tiny Polynesian island in the South Pacific, the cultural message is that sexual pleasure is for everyone. As a result, "Less than one out of a hundred girls, and even fewer boys—if, indeed, there are any exceptions in either sex—have *not* had substantial sexual experience prior to marriage" (Marshall, 1971, p. 117). Female sexual passivity is frowned on among Mangaians, and sexual intimacy does not require prior establishment of personal affection. Girls are expected to learn to be orgasmic at a young age, and although their first sexual experiences are likely to be with boys of their own age, older and more experienced partners soon become desirable because they can give more sexual pleasure (Marshall, 1971). One particularly interesting observation: "upon hearing that some American and European women cannot or do not achieve the climax, the Mangaian immediately asks (with real concern) whether this inability will not injure the married woman's health" (Marshall, 1971, p. 162). On Mangaia, all women are expected to learn to be orgasmic.

Other cultures have *third gender roles* usually played by men. In Islamic Oman, on the Saudi Arabian peninsula, the *Xanith* are born as males, remain anatomically male, have masculine names, male's rights, support themselves economically, but do women's work at home. They are judged in appearance by standards of feminine beauty, are classified with women for many social purposes (i.e., they're the only men who are allowed to see a bride's face on her wedding night). The Xanith are "not men" because in Oman, the definition of "man" centers on his sexual potency and his ability to consummate a marriage. The Xanith act as male homosexual prostitutes. They are not considered women, because women are "pure" and obviously, as prostitutes, the Xanith aren't pure. However, Xanith can *become* men if they choose to by marrying and proving their ability to penetrate their female partners (Nanda, 1990).

In Tahiti, a third gender role is *Mahu*. Each district has one Mahu, a cultural role filled voluntarily by a man who is willing to take on the dress of a woman as well as her activities. As with the Xanith of Oman, it is possible to stop being a Mahu (Nanda, 1990). A similar third gender role exists among the Burmese, where males with cross-gender behavior are referred to as *acaults* and are respected for their roles as shamans and seers (Coleman, Colgan, and Gooren, 1992).

In older Native American cultures, neither anatomy nor sexual potency define masculinity or femininity. People born male who publicly engaged in women's work or wore women's dress, and in some cases, who assumed the woman's role in sexual intercourse, were thought of as having adopted a new gender status. Male transvestite homosexuals called *Alyha* were part of Mohave culture and were not ridiculed for their behaviors. It was thought that they couldn't help having their inclinations to behave as they did and they were actually thought to be powerful shamans (healers) who were very effective in curing STDs like syphilis [G. Devereux (1937) cited in Nanda, 1990].

For another example of an alternate gender role played by males in India, see the boxed item on page 299.

IN CONCLUSION

We've seen a lot of evidence in this chapter about the power of gender roles. We've explored how gender roles develop and what they mean for men and women in all aspects of their lives. Having looked at gender roles across the stages of life, from the viewpoints of masculinity, femininity, and androgyny, from various cultural perspectives, it seems clear that in the United States, at least, we are headed in the right direction. We are moving away from rigid role definitions to more flexible standards that allow people to experiment with a broad range of gender-role choices that suit them best at varying points in their lives. When the definitions of gender "roles" are expanded so they bypass the stereotypical notions of male–female options, men and women are more likely to be satisfied emotionally, physically, psychologically, and economically. When gender roles operate flexibly, there is a better chance that each partner will have equal opportunity to play his or her role of choice at a particular time, and that the decision-making process will have included some mutual interaction between partners.

SUMMARY

1. It's hard to concisely define masculinity and femininity but we can say that it pertains to how closely a person's behavior or appearance conforms to cultural expectations of males and females. American culture tends to place masculine and feminine traits at opposite ends of a spectrum, as if they are mutually exclusive of one another. This way of thinking, which makes it seem as if masculinity and femininity are antagonists, is being challenged. It's more accurate to say that no one is 100 percent masculine or 100 percent feminine and that masculine and feminine traits coexist in each of us. People in whom masculine and feminine traits are comfortably blended are androgynous.

2. Gender-role socialization occurs as girls and boys are exposed to different role models and learn what is appropriate for each gender. This process starts at birth when parents are the initial gender-role teachers. It continues in the preschool years and by the age of 3 or 4 children have the roles down pat. They learn the roles and the "rules" of the roles almost unconsciously. As they grow, children learn more from toys, books, television, play groups, and school—all of which provide important and potent input into their socialization.

3. By adolescence, socially dictated gender-role distinctions can prove problematic. Girls who are achievement-oriented, outspoken, self-confident, competitive in academics and sports, sexually adventurous and assertive, androgynous, may find themselves locked in a struggle with social group expectations that they follow more stereotypical paths based on the sexual double standard and traditional gender-role standard (i.e., a woman's first priority and responsibility is to family, husband, children). Many females are still taught that achievement detracts from femininity and popularity.

   The gender role for teenage boys make it clear that they are expected to "achieve," whether in school, sports, or sexually. Males are still conditioned to equate masculinity with sexual proficiency and experience, though many boys try to express their more sensitive "feminine" sides and behave in androgynous ways.

4. Gender-role expectations affect every aspect of adult life. The distinctions between male and female roles are fading and sometimes blend in family life and in the working world, but careful analysis shows that stereotypical masculine and feminine roles persist. Even when women work, they are still largely responsible for child care and housework. Big discrepancies between men and women still exist in terms of the kinds of jobs they typically are hired for, the pay each gender receives, the benefits each gets, and the opportunities for advancement each has. Women lose out on all counts.

5. Cross-cultural studies have found evidence that the two-gender, polarized lens through

which our culture looks is supported and encouraged by adherence to stereotypes. Many male–female "givens" that we accept as gender-role-based are challenged by studying cultures that allow for "third genders" and understanding how they incorporate people with third-gender traits into their societies, empowering them and valuing them.

6. Studies in the psychology of sex differences show that males and females are far more similar than different, although there are also some specific areas in which consistent differences emerge. Differences in the anatomy of the brain between males and females may account for some of these findings.

7. The transsexual has a persistent, life-long feeling of being trapped in the "wrong" body. The cause of transsexualism is unknown. Currently, there is disagreement about whether change of sex surgery is the optimal treatment for this, although if it follows a rigorous one- to two-year trial of living in a cross-gender role it is more likely to work well.

Thought Questions

1. Is it easier to live with the male or the female sex role? What are the relative advantages and disadvantages?

2. If most people in our society suddenly became androgynous, how would our society change? How would sexual relations change? Do you think this would be a good thing for our society?

3. Without encouragement from society, would little boys still want to play with guns or war toys? Are the gender differences in choice of toys and style of play primarily due to the culture or to biology?

4. Can you imagine what it would be like to believe that you are a woman born into a male body or vice versa? Why do you suppose transsexualism is more characteristic of biological males than females? What do you think of nontranssexual men and women who fall in love with people who have had sex-change surgery?

5. At what stage of the lifespan do you think gender roles are the most rigid? The least rigid?

6. The text refers to research which concluded that married men are mentally healthier than single men, while married women are less mentally healthy than single women. Does your experience generally agree with this finding? If so, do you agree with the reasons given in the text as explanations for this finding?

7. In a culture where boys and girls are reared in a truly egalitarian fashion, do you think there would still be major gender role differences? If so, which differences do you think would ve most visible and persistent?

8. Today, with many professional women having attained prominent roles in the workplace, it is quite common to find men who have women as their bosses. Does this reversal of "traditional" power dynamics usually present problems for either party? Why or why not?

Suggested Readings

Bem, Sandra L. *The Lenses of Gender: Transforming the Debate on Sexual Inequality.* New Haven, CT: Yale University Press, 1993. A thoughtful analysis of the gender bind our culture places on women, its impact on men, alternatives to change the situation, and why a feminist awareness can be helpful without scaring off the men.

Gilmore, David D. *Manhood in the Making.* New Haven: Yale University Press, 1990. An analysis of the meaning of masculinity and how it is "earned" or "proved" in a variety of societies, from contemporary America to rural Spain and the jungles of New Guinea.

Maccoby, Eleanor E., and Jacklin, Carol. *The Psychology of Sex Differences.* Stanford, CA: Stanford University Press, 1974. This definitive work on gender roles is tough reading but has exhaustive coverage. Maccoby and Jacklin are frequently cited in current research and they continue to work in the field.

Pleck, Joseph H. *Working Wives/Working Husbands.* Beverly Hills, CA: Sage Publications, 1985. An interesting discussion, chock full of statistics, about how men and women in two-career families deal with their gender-role expectations and the practicalities of daily life.

Stockard, Jean, and Johnson, Miriam M. *Sex and Gender in Society,* 2nd ed. Englewood Cliffs, NJ:

Prentice Hall, 1992. From cross cultural analysis to in-depth coverage of gender in America, the authors provide everything from psychological to symbolic to political and practical analyses of sex and gender. The chapters on biology and life cycle issues are particularly well done.

Tannen, Deborah. *Gender and Disclosure.* New York: Oxford University Press, 1994. A psycholinguistic scholar explores the conversational styles of males and females in a variety of contexts, from childhood to adulthood, to demonstrate how gender differences in linguistics influence power balances in relationships.

Tannen, Deborah. *You Just Don't Understand: Women and Men in Conversation.* New York: William Morrow and Company, 1990. Fascinating, important insights into why men and women seem to speak different languages and often walk away with different impressions of the same conversation. This easy-to-read, crystal-clear book was a major national best-seller, and we recommend it heartily for all readers.

Tavris, Carol. *The Mismeasure of Woman.* New York: Simon & Schuster, 1992. All the reasons gender polarization should be challenged can be found in this readable, thought provoking analysis. The author suggests masculinity and femininity ought not to be considered antagonistic traits set in cultural stone.

Thorne, B. *Gender Play: Girls and Boys in School.* New Brunswick, NJ: Rutgers University Press, 1993. A detailed analysis of gender roles and how they are expressed in elementary school children by a researcher with a keen analytical eye.

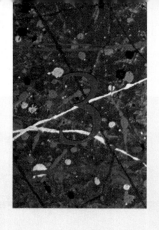

PART

Psychosocial Perspectives

Loving and
Being Loved

When William James wrote his classic *Principles of Psychology* in 1890, he devoted only two pages to "love." While noting the connection between love and "sexual impulses," James observed "these details are a little unpleasant to discuss" (James [1890], 1950, vol. 2, p. 439). D. H. Lawrence, the English novelist, was much less timid in dealing with this topic. In *Lady Chatterley's Lover* (1962), he suggested that love depends on being uninhibited in all respects, as illustrated in this bit of dialogue between Lady Chatterley and Mellors, her lover:

> "But what *do* you believe in?" she insisted.
>
> "I don't know."
>
> "Nothing, like all the men I've ever known," she said.
>
> They were both silent. Then he roused himself and said: "Yes, I do believe in something. I believe in being warm-hearted. I believe especially in being warm-hearted in love, in fucking with a warm heart. I believe if men could fuck with warm hearts, and the women take it warm-heartedly everything would come all right. It's all this cold-hearted fucking that is death and idiocy." *(p. 266)*

Until very recently, the topic of love was more in the province of writers, poets, and philosophers than in the minds of psychologists and scientists. Even though it has been said that "love makes the world go round," few sexologists (including ourselves) have addressed this subject in any detail. Nevertheless, we have all felt love in one way or another. Many of us have dreamed of it, struggled with it, or basked in its radiant pleasures. It is also safe to say that most of us have been confused by it too. In this chapter, we focus our attention on the complicated relationships between love, sex, and marriage in an effort to reduce at least some of this confusion.

WHAT IS LOVE?

Trying to define love is a difficult task. Besides loving a spouse or boyfriend or girlfriend, people can love their children, parents, siblings, pets, country, or God, as well as rainbows, chocolate sundaes, or the Boston Red Sox. Although the English language has only one word to apply to each of these situations, there are clearly different meanings involved.

When we talk about person-to-person love, the simplest definition may be one given by Robert Heinlein in the book *Stranger in a Strange Land:* "Love is that condition in which the happiness of another person is essential to your own" (Heinlein, 1961, p. 345). This is certainly the love that Shakespeare described in *Romeo and Juliet*, that popular singers celebrate, and that led Edward VIII to abdicate the throne of England to marry the woman in his life.

In any type of love, the element of caring about the loved person is essential. Unless genuine caring is present, what looks like love may be just one form of desire. For example, a teenage boy may tell

his girlfriend "I love you" just to convince her to have sex with him. In other cases, the desire to gain wealth, status, or power may lead a person to pretend to love someone to reach these goals.

Because sexual desire and love may both be passionate and all-consuming, it may be difficult to distinguish between them in terms of intensity. The key feature is the substance behind the feeling. Generally, sexual desire is narrowly focused and rather easily discharged, and love is a more complex and constant emotion. In pure, unadulterated sexual desire, the elements of caring and respect are minimal, perhaps present as an afterthought, but not a central part of the feeling. The desire to know the other person is defined in only a physical or sensual way, not in a spiritual one. The end is easily satisfied. While love may include a passionate yearning for sexual union, respect for the loved one is a primary concern. Without respect and caring, our attraction for another person can only be an imitation of love. Respect allows us to value a loved one's identity and integrity and thus prevents us from selfishly exploiting them.

The importance of caring and respect was central to the thinking of Erich Fromm, whose classic book *The Art of Loving* (1956) influenced all subsequent study of this subject. Fromm believed that people can achieve a meaningful type of love only if they have first reached a state of self-realization (being secure in one's own identity). Thus, Fromm defined mature love as "union under the condition of preserving one's integrity, one's individuality," and noted that the paradox of love is that "beings become one and yet remain two" (p. 17). In speaking about the respect inherent in all love, Fromm suggested that a lover must feel, "I want the loved person to grow and unfold for his own sake, and in his own ways, and not for the purpose of serving me" (pp. 23–24).

Fromm's insistence that people must be self-realized before having a "meaningful" type of love overlooks that love itself can be a way of attaining self-realization. We believe that people have a great capacity to learn about themselves from a love relationship, although we also agree with psychologist Nathaniel Branden's observation that love cannot be a substitute for personal identity (Branden, 1980).

Peele and Brodsky (1976) have an interesting view-point on what happens when respect and car-

ing are missing from a love relationship. They be-lieve that some relationships of this variety serve the same needs that can lead people to alcohol abuse or drug addiction. The resulting "love" is re-ally a dependency relationship:

> When a person goes to another with the aim of filling a void in himself, the relationship quickly becomes the center of his or her life. It offers him a solace that contrasts sharply with what he finds everywhere else, so he returns to it more and more, until he needs it to get through each day of his otherwise stressful and unpleasant existence. When a constant exposure to something is neces-sary in order to make life bearable, an addiction has been brought about, however romantic the trappings. The ever-present danger of with-drawal creates an ever-present craving. *(p. 70)*

Peele and Brodsky suggest specific criteria for dis-tinguishing between love as a healthy relationship with growth potential versus love as a form of ad-diction:

1. Does each lover have a secure belief in his or her own value?
2. Are the lovers improved by the relationship? By some measure outside of the relationship are they better, stronger, more attractive, more accomplished, or more sensitive individuals? Do they value the relationship for this very reason?
3. Do the lovers maintain serious interests out-side the relationship, including other mean-ingful personal relationships?
4. Is the relationship integrated into, rather than being set off from, the totality of the lovers' lives?
5. Are the lovers beyond being possessive or jealous of each other's growth and expansion of interests?
6. Are the lovers also friends? Would they seek each other out if they should cease to be pri-mary partners? *(pp. 83–84)*

These questions are not listed to suggest that there is only one "right" way to love. While most people in love probably cannot answer "yes" to all six questions, thinking about these issues may give you some ideas for present or future relationships.

Once Peele and Brodsky identified an undeni-ably negative type of love with their "love as ad-diction" concept, others extended the focus. In fact, several books dealing with problematic love rela-tionships made it onto the national best-seller lists in the mid-1980s—for example, *Women Who Love Too Much* (Norwood, 1985) and *Smart Women/Fool-ish Choices* (Cowan and Kinder, 1985). As a result of this shift in emphasis, many people began to real-ize that not all love relationships are the idealized, perfect unions we'd like them to be. In reality, some are exploitive, desperate, or simply unfulfilling (Peele, 1988).

Before we move on to discuss additional theo-ries about love, we have to point out that it is often difficult to draw a line between liking and loving. Although various researchers have tried to measure love (Rubin, 1970; Pam, Plutchik, and Conte, 1975; Dion and Dion, 1976; Hatfield and Sprecher, 1986; Sternberg and Barnes, 1988), not everyone agrees on whether love is a distinct, sep-arate entity. Some psychologists believe that "the only real difference between liking and loving is the depth of our feelings and the degree of our in-volvement with the other person" (Walster and Walster, 1978, p. 9). On the other hand, Berscheid (1988, p. 369) has observed that "it seems quite clear that more and more liking for another does not, in the end, lead to romantic love; more and more liking just leads to a lot of liking." After much thought on the subject, we have come to be-lieve that liking and loving, while interrelated, are distinct phenomena.

GLOBAL THEORIES OF LOVE

Sternberg's Triangular Theory of Love

Psychologist Robert J. Sternberg has devised a three-part theory of love that can be shown in the form of a triangle (see Figure 12.1). The three components of love, according to this theory, are intimacy, passion, and a component called "deci-sion/commitment." Briefly, here is a summary of what these components encompass (Sternberg, 1988, 1988a). (Before you read any further in this section, you may want to take a few minutes to complete the self-administered questionnaire on pages 310-311 that will allow you to compute your own "love triangle scores.")

The intimacy component includes giving and receiving emotional support to and from the loved one, as well as other behaviors that foster a feeling of warmth in a loving relationship. These include communicating openly and honestly, sharing, experiencing happiness together, understanding each other, and valuing the loved one.

The passion component includes both sexual passion and other needs that elicit a passionate response. For instance, needs for self-esteem, affiliation with others, dominating others, or being dominated by others may be more of a source of passion than plain old sex for some people. Consider the following example that Sternberg (1988a, pp. 43–44) provides:

> Debbie grew up in a broken home, with no extended family to speak of, and two parents who were at constant war with each other and eventually divorced when she was an adolescent. Debbie felt as though she never had a family, and when she met Arthur, her passion was kindled. What he had to offer was not great sex but a large, warm, closely knit family that welcomed Debbie with open arms. Arthur was Debbie's ticket to the sense of belongingness that she had never experienced but had always craved, and his ability to bring belongingness into her life aroused her passion for him.

The decision/commitment component of love has two parts. The short-term part is the decision that a person loves someone. The long-term part is the person's degree of commitment to maintaining that love. If you think about it, you will realize quickly that the short-term decision to love someone doesn't always go hand in hand with a major long-term commitment, although there are certainly times when the two are absolutely linked together.

Comparing the involvement of each partner in a love relationship can be done by seeing how closely the two people's love triangles fit each other, as shown in Figure 12.2. In well-matched involvements, the two triangles can almost be superimposed. In mismatched relationships—where one person's needs greatly exceed the other's, or where the two partners' needs are in widely divergent directions—the triangles are far from being congruent. These two dimensions of love can be termed the intensity and the balance of the relationship.

Figure 12.1
Sternberg's Triangle of Love

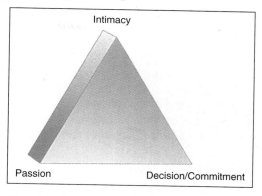

The assignment of components to vertices is one of convenience; it is essentially arbitrary.

Source: The Triangle of Love: Intimacy, Passions, Commitment *by Robert J. Sternberg. Copyright © 1988 by Basic Books, Inc. Reprinted by permission of Basic Books, Inc., Publishers, New York.*

Sternberg suggests that it is both the match between the two partners' real love triangles and the match between each individual partner's real love triangle and his or her ideal love triangle that determine satisfaction in a love relationship. For example, whenever there is a substantial mismatch between a person's ideal love triangle and the triangle that actually describes a current love relationship, the person is apt to be dissatisfied. Likewise, if there is a major discrepancy in the love triangles of the partners in a love relationship, it implies that the partners are out of phase with each other and probably have difficulty in reciprocating each other's needs.

Love triangles are neither static over time nor independent of the loved one's behavior and feelings (Sternberg, 1988a). For example, passion tends to peak fairly quickly in a love relationship and then settles down to a lower level, in what can be called the habituation phase (Figure 12.3). With habituation, a partner is no longer as stimulating as he or she once was. (This is similar to the habituation that occurs with regular use of many substances such as caffeine, alcohol, or cigarettes. Once habituation occurs, even increased amounts of the substance do not stimulate the arousal that occurred at first.) Likewise, it would be a mistake to neglect the influence one partner has on the other in a love relationship. Since each person's needs may change from time to time, it is important to be flexible in

The Sternberg Triangular Love Scale

The blanks represent the person with whom you are in a relationship. Rate each statement on a 1-to-9 scale, where 1 = "not at all," 5 = "moderately," and 9 = "extremely." Use intermediate points on the scale to indicate intermediate feelings.

1. I am actively supportive of _____'s well-being.
2. I have a warm relationship with _____
3. I am able to count on _____ in times of need.
4. _____ is able to count on me in times of need.
5. I am willing to share myself and my possessions with _____.
6. I receive considerable emotional support from _____.
7. I give considerable emotional support to _____.
8. I communicate well with _____.
9. I value _____ greatly in my life.
10. I feel close to _____.
11. I have a comfortable relationship with _____.
12. I feel that I really understand _____.
13. I feel that _____ really understands me.
14. I feel that I can really trust _____.
15. I share deeply personal information about myself with _____.
16. Just seeing _____ excites me.
17. I find myself thinking about _____ frequently during the day.
18. My relationship with _____ is very romantic.
19. I find _____ to be very personally attractive.
20. I idealize _____.
21. I cannot imagine another person making me as happy as _____ does.
22. I would rather be with _____ than anyone else.
23. There is nothing more important to me than my relationship with _____.
24. I especially like physical contact with _____.
25. There is something almost "magical" about my relationship with _____.
26. I adore _____.

order to let love continue to flourish. As Sternberg notes (1988, pp. 137–138):

> Perhaps the most important use of the triangular theory is to help people recognize that relationships are, almost inevitably, dynamic. "Living happily ever after" need not be a myth, but if it is to be a reality, the happiness must be based upon different configurations of mutual feelings at various times in a relationship. Couples who expect their passion to last forever, or their intimacy to remain unchallenged, are in for disappointment. The theory suggests that we must constantly work at understanding, building, and rebuilding our love relationships. Relationships are constructions, and they decay over time if they are not maintained and improved. We cannot expect a relationship simply to take care of itself, any more than we can expect that of a building. Rather, we must take responsibility for making our relationships the best they can be.

Sternberg's theory has not yet been tested by others. However, some critics have claimed that the triangle image is overly simplistic, failing to distinguish between various nuances of passion, commitment, and intimacy, and not taking into account the influence of third parties—or the real world—on a love relationship (Levinger, 1988; Williams and Barnes, 1988). In fact, Stanton Peele (1988), who originated the "love as addiction" concept mentioned earlier in this chapter, notes:

> Evaluating a love relationship in the larger framework of a couple's psychological functioning and connection to their environment often yields a picture different than that of an idyllic

27. I cannot imagine life without _____.
28. My relationship with _____ is passionate.
29. When I see romantic movies and read romantic books I think of _____.
30. I fantasize about _____.
31. I know that I care about _____.
32. I am committed to maintaining my relationship with _____.
33. Because of my commitment to _____, I would not let other people come between us.
34. I have confidence in the stability of my relationship with _____.
35. I could not let anything get in the way of my commitment to _____.
36. I expect my love for _____ to last for the rest of my life.
37. I will always feel a strong responsibility for _____.
38. I view my commitment to _____ as a solid one.
39. I cannot imagine ending my relationship with _____.
40. I am certain of my love for _____.

41. I view my relationship with _____ as permanent.
42. I view my relationship with _____ as a good decision.
43. I feel a sense of responsibility toward _____.
44. I plan to continue my relationship with _____.
45. Even when _____ is hard to deal with, I remain committed to our relationship.

Items 1 to 15 are for measuring the intimacy component; 16 to 30, for the passion component; and 31 to 45 for the decision/commitment component. In order to obtain your score, add up your rating for each of the component subscales in the space below and divide the total by 15. This will give you an average rating for each item. (As generally administered, the scale items appear in random order, rather than clustered by component as they are here.)

Source: The Triangle of Love: Intimacy, Passions, Commitment by Robert J. Sternberg. Copyright © 1988 by Basic Books, Inc., Reprinted by permission of Basic Books, Inc., Publishers, New York.

love affair. What is most lacking in the ostensibly social–psychological perspective is this sense of context, so that the research focus on the intensity of the lovers' experience of each other supports the notion that love can be isolated from the rest of the lovers' lives. *(p. 170)*

Love As Attachment

An unusual theory views adult love relationships as remarkably similar to attachment behavior between an infant and its parent (Shaver, Hazan, and Bradshaw, 1984, 1988). Common dynamics found in both love pairings include reliance on the loved one to fulfill basic emotional and security needs, fear of rejection, distress at separation, powerful empathy between the two people in the relationship, and a great deal of nonverbal communication.

According to Shaver, Hazen, and Bradshaw, all love relationships in a person's life, including those with lovers and spouses, mimic the type of attachment found in early mother–infant relationships. However, not all mother–infant relationships are perfect. If a mother is consistently slow in responding to her infant's cries, or if she regularly interferes with the infant's spontaneous actions, the baby often becomes anxious (Ainsworth et al., 1978). And if a mother ignores her baby's attempts to have physical contact with her by cuddling, or touching, or other similar behaviors, the baby will probably learn to avoid her (Ainsworth et al., 1978).

Shaver, Hazan, and Bradshaw use precisely the same categories to describe adult love relationships. They differentiate between *secure* lovers, who don't worry about being abandoned or about having someone get too close to them, and *avoidant*

Figure 12.2   Relations Between Involvement of Two Individuals in a Relationship

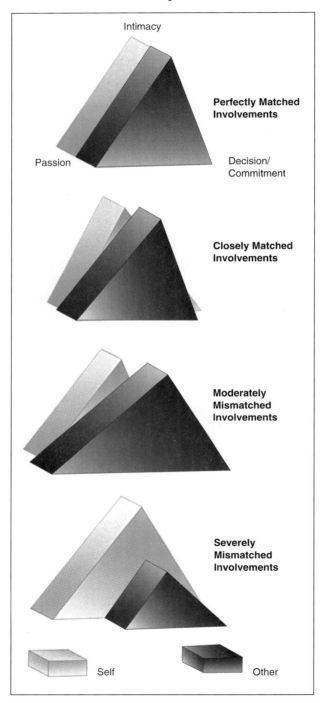

or *anxious/ambivalent* lovers. Avoidant lovers are uncomfortable being too close to someone else and have trouble trusting a lover completely. Anxious/ambivalent lovers, on the other hand, are insecure about their relationships. They tend to worry that their partners don't really love them or won't want to stay with them; they are often so intense and overbearing in their love that they scare partners away.

Shaver, Hazan, and Bradshaw (1988) analyzed 620 responses to a questionnaire they published in a Denver newspaper. They found that a little more than half of adult love relationships could be categorized as secure (see Figure 12.4), while one-fourth were avoidant relationships and 19 percent were anxious/ambivalent ones. Similar results were obtained in a later replication study in a university population, which is intriguing because these numbers match reasonably well with the proportions reported in the Ainsworth et al. (1978) study of mother–infant attachment. In addition, there were no sex differences found in any of these studies.

Some psychologists believe that the attachment theory of love is an exciting new development (e.g., Sternberg, 1988a). Elaine Hatfield (1988) even notes that nonhuman primates seem to demonstrate this same attachment behavior in infancy, implying an evolutionary imperative for this theoretical viewpoint. Others, however, are more critical. For one thing, believing that the nature of adult love relationships is determined largely by events during

Figure 12.3   The Course of Passion as a Function of Duration of Relationship

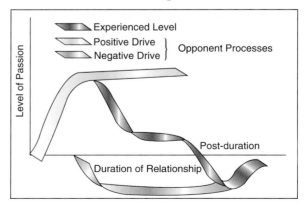

Figure 12.4   The Frequency of Various Adult Attachment Types in Love Relationships*

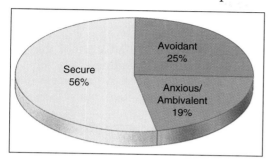

* Adapted from Shaver, Hazan, and Bradshaw, 1988, from data in Table 4.2.

infancy ignores the pivotal development of thinking patterns, moral and social responsibilities, and experiential input during childhood, adolescence, and adulthood (Peele, 1988). In a sense, if the attachment theory is right, we are more or less doomed (or at least, preordained) as to our love-style before we are even out of diapers, which sort of pushes the concept of free will right out the window. (On the other hand, many psychoanalytic thinkers would be fairly comfortable with such a deterministic notion; it is very much in keeping with their view of behavioral causation.)

Another problem with attachment theory is that it doesn't adequately explain cross-cultural observations about love and love relationships that are very different in India or Japan or the Fiji Islands from the patterns we take for granted in America. Nevertheless, despite such criticisms, attachment theory offers an interesting opportunity for long-range study. What seems to be needed to evaluate this theory properly is a prospective longitudinal study that initially evaluates mother–infant attachments in a large sample and then determines the love-styles of infants once they have grown up 20 or more years down the road.

ROMANTIC LOVE

The great loves of fiction and verse have been romantic loves marked by a whirlwind of emotions from passion to jealousy to anguish. In romantic love, unlike any other type of love, we immerse ourselves almost completely in another person (Pope, 1980). When Chaucer wrote that "love is

blind," he was acknowledging that the intensity of romantic love distorts our objectivity. In our craving for our loved one, we may overlook flaws, magnify strengths, and lose all sense of proportion.

The puzzles and paradoxes of romantic love are many. We address them by first discussing some psychological theories about the nature of romantic love and then presenting a conceptual model of the romantic love cycle.

Psychological Perspectives

It should be no surprise that there is little agreement among psychologists on a valid definition of romantic love. Branden (1980) says that it is "a passionate spiritual–emotional–sexual attachment between a man and woman that reflects a high regard for the value of each other's person." Since we believe that romantic love is not restricted to heterosexual relationships, this definition is too restrictive. Fromm did not define romantic love specifically, but it appears that he used the term "erotic love" to mean the same thing. In contrast, other definitions of romantic love do not include a sexual component as a requirement, as shown in this example:

> A preoccupation with another person. A deeply felt desire to be with the loved one. A feeling of incompleteness without him or her. Thinking of the loved one often, whether together or apart. Separation frequently provokes feelings of genuine despair or else tantalizing anticipation of reuniting. Reunion is seen as bringing feelings of euphoric ecstasy or peace and fulfillment. (Pope, 1980, p. 4)

Psychologist Dorothy Tennov (1979) coined the word **limerence** to describe the particularly powerful form of romantic love in which a person is said to be "love-struck" or "head-over-heels" in love. Limerence is marked by preoccupation with thoughts of the loved one and the certain knowledge that only this person can satisfy your needs. The limerent lover's mood depends almost totally on the actions of the loved one; that person's every gesture or word is doted on in hope of approval and in fear of rejection.

limerence word coined by Dorothy Tennov to describe a blind, intense kind of love outside a person's rational control.

Limerence, like other forms of romantic love, is an affliction as well as a joy because it is almost completely outside rational control. The consuming emotional ups and downs of limerence can interfere with other relationships, reduce the capacity for work or study, and disturb a person's peace of mind. According to Tennov, many people never experience limerence (although they may experience love), while other people pass through a series of limerent episodes.

The Romantic Love Cycle

Research on romantic love has not been exhaustive, but we summarize the current data and present our clinical observations in terms of a "romantic love cycle." The model shown in Figure 12.5 does not imply that all romantic loves are identical or that each romantic love passes through the phases of this cycle in a predictable, sequential fashion. Instead, it gives us a way to organize our thinking about romantic love.

Love Readiness

Although there is no certifiable proof that people can be in a state of love readiness, we believe that such a state of mind exists. Love readiness does not always result in falling in love, but it does seem to increase its probability.

Love readiness consists of several different elements. First, love is seen as something that is desirable and rewarding rather than as troublesome or encumbering. People who look at romantic love as a sign of weakness or as a distraction from career development are unlikely to permit themselves to fall in love (as far as anyone can control such emo-

Figure 12.5   The Romantic Love Cycle

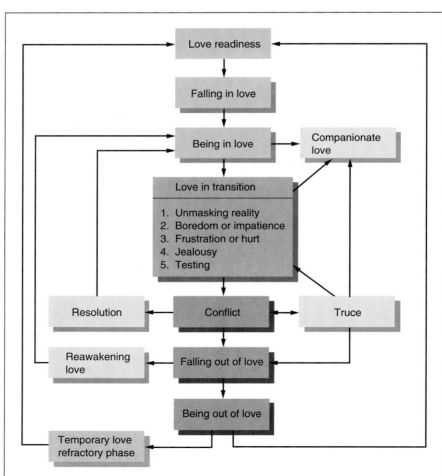

tions). But people who believe that love is ennobling and brings out their best may actively search for a suitable love object. Second, there is a longing for interpersonal intimacy and companionship. This longing may be motivated by loneliness, jealousy for someone else's love relationship, or a desire to replace a past love. Third, sexual frustration often contributes to the state of love readiness (Walster and Walster, 1978). This frustration may result from sexual deprivation or from a wish for sex as part of a passionate, committed relationship. Casual sex may be accessible but less fulfilling. Finally, love readiness may reflect the hopefulness people have about being loved; if this is so, the frequency of romantic love may decline as people get older because their expectations of having their feelings returned are reduced (Tennov, 1979).

Some people always seem to be in a state of love readiness but never succeed in getting any further. While they may eventually make concessions and enter into relationships that don't really qualify as romantic love, their mental quest doesn't seem to end. Other people never experience love readiness or pass beyond it after a brief time. In trying to evaluate love readiness, remember that no one has ever measured it and that it's not unusual for people who don't match the description given here to find themselves falling in love. As we said before, love is neither rational nor completely predictable.

Falling in Love

> Like everybody who is not in love, he imagined that one chose the person whom one loved after endless deliberations and on the strength of various qualities and advantages. *(Marcel Proust, Cities of the Plain, C. K. Scott Moncrieff, trans. New York: Random House, 1970)*

What triggers love is still the subject of guesswork. But the process of experiencing romantic love begins with a stage of falling in love that ranges from the instantaneous "love at first sight" to a gradual process that requires months or years of development.

A sudden flash of love is unlikely to occur unless a person is in a state of love readiness. In real life, instantaneous love is the exception, not the rule, and falling in love is a process that can start out in many ways. Dating provides an opportunity for discovering if two people like each other, are compatible, and can meet one another's needs. Being physically near a person is another pathway: by

close association, you can come to some preliminary conclusions about a person's desirability without announcing even the possibility of a romantic interest. Friendships sometimes blossom into love, although it may be difficult to pinpoint exactly when the falling in love occurs. The trusting atmosphere of an intimate friendship may make passion seem out of place, and love, if it develops, may be a low-keyed rather than fiery emotion.

Two aspects of falling in love are particularly likely to ignite passion—the excitement of getting to know someone intimately and the excitement of sex (Walster and Walster, 1978; Berscheid, 1988; Sternberg, 1988). Both types of arousal intensify the push toward love by positive reinforcement.

Being in Love

Being in love, like falling in love, can occur whether or not love is returned. If there is no indication that reciprocal love might develop, the probability of a person's staying in love begins to decrease rapidly. But a person who has reached the "being" phase of romantic love is usually inventive, hopeful, and willing to accept even the flimsiest signs of reciprocation.

The romantic lover at this stage may be head over heels in love (caught in the grips of limerence) or in a more tranquil, self-satisfied, secure, and objective state. Sexual attraction is almost invariably strong, although it may not lead to action because of shyness, sexual problems, or moral constraints (Tennov, 1979). In some situations, people may try to defuse their sexual impulses by masturbation or strenuous exercise either to keep their love "pure" of if their loved one shows no interest in a sexual relationship. Whatever form being in love assumes, it is usually a passing phase, lasting an average of one or two years (Hill, Rubin, and Peplau, 1976; Tennov, 1979). Most of the time, romantic love either changes into another form called companionate love or gradually dissolves because of conflicts, boredom, or disinterest.

Love in Transition

The transitional phase of romantic love is a pivotal time. Here, the initial excitement of getting to know someone and the passion of a new sexual relationship begin to lessen and the thrill is going if not gone. Lovers begin to notice imperfections in each other that were previously unobserved or ignored, and boredom or impatience begins to set in. Frustration occurs when love does not measure up to

our fantasies, when we realize that all our problems are not "cured," or when we discover that the ecstasy cannot go on forever without intermissions.

Characteristically, lovers in this transitional phase begin to test one another—and the presumed strength of their love—in various ways. Each lover is likely to try to force or trick the other into becoming what they were thought to be or what he or she would like them to become. Power struggles and competitive strivings emerge (Coleman, 1977). Testing becomes a means of making a rational decision about the future of the relationship: "Do I want to stay with this person, or should I get away now, while I can?" Jealousy may rear its ugly head, anger may erupt, and conflict is almost unavoidable.

The transition stage of love is basically a time for testing reality. In a sense, love pulls its head down from the clouds, and the conflicts and doubts that arise may lead to a stage of falling out of love or measures may be taken to push the relationship into a temporary state of truce. The truce may either lead things back to the "love in transition" stage (with the probability being high that further conflicts will occur) or lead directly to a companionate love relationship.

If, on the other hand, given the ingredients of motivation, flexibility, cooperation, and a little bit of luck, the conflicts are resolved, the relationship returns to the "being in love" stage. If this occurs, the new version of the relationship may actually be stronger, strengthened by the ability to successfully survive its conflicts. Mutual trust is no longer just a matter of faith but a by-product of experience.

Falling Out of Love

Just as people falling in love delight in learning everything about their partners and revealing much about themselves, people falling out of love are less open, intimate, and interested in their partners. Concern for the partner's happiness becomes a second priority rather than a guiding light and eventually becomes an incidental thought. Communications may be strained because the two lovers are no longer "on the same wavelength," and whatever troubles occur at this point in the relationship hardly seem worth the effort to overcome.

Love relationships come apart in different ways, most of which are painful. Only about 15 percent of love relationships end by mutual consent (Hill, Rubin, and Peplau, 1976). Many times one person pulls out of a love relationship while the other is still "in love." Here, the falling out of love stage occurs at different times for the two lovers. The heartbreak and sorrow of the deserted lover are sometimes very similar to the reactions of someone who

"When I fell in love with you, suddenly your eyes didn't seem close together. Now they seem close together again."

Source: The New Yorker, *March 15, 1976, p. 28. Drawing by Wm. Hamilton;* © 1976 The New Yorker Magazine, Inc.

has experienced the death of a spouse or close friend. As in a grief reaction, the lover may pass through a period of tearful mourning and shock followed by a time of persistent, haunting memories before there is a return to happiness. At other times, the jilted lover becomes angry, vengeful, or determined to avoid future love at any cost.

Being Out of Love

Once having fallen out of love, some people quickly revert to a state of love readiness, no worse for wear and perhaps even wiser and wealthier for their love experience. There is a kernel of truth to the notion that a person "on the rebound" may be more open (and more vulnerable) to a new love relationship. On the other hand, there often seems to be a "refractory period" early in the "being out of love" phase during which it simply is not possible to fall in love again.

COMPANIONATE LOVE

It is rare for the passion and excitement of a romantic love relationship to last for more than a few years. Usually, romance is replaced (except for occasional brief flickers) by another kind of love which comes to a new state of equilibrium. This is

called companionate love, which can be looked at as a steadier love based on sharing, affection, trust, involvement, and togetherness rather than passion.

Companionate love is not just a sorry substitute for romantic love, although it can deteriorate into drabness and routine if not sustained by continued caring and respect. Many companionate love relationships include an exciting, satisfying sexual side, and in many ways the partners may find that their pleasure in each other increases. Companionate love is less turbulent and more predictable than romantic love, so many people find it to be a soothing, secure kind of relationship.

Companionate love is most characteristic of marriage and other long-term committed relationships. Because it is less possessive and consuming than romantic love, it allows two people to carry on their lives—working, raising children, having hobbies, relaxing with friends—with a minimum of interference. It is a reality-based and steady love, as opposed to romantic love, which is all too often based merely on ideals and fantasies.

THE BIOLOGICAL SIDE OF LOVE

So far we have discussed love as though it is solely a product of the mind. Some scientists suggest that there may be a biological component as well. Two types of evidence can be cited in favor of this idea.

First, evolutionary biologists point out that reproductive success may be at least partly linked to love. Hundreds of centuries ago, successful reproduction hinged on two factors: (1) genetic diversity to ensure the health of offspring, and (2) the man's closeness to his sexual partner during pregnancy and the infancy of their newborn child to provide protection and food and to help in child rearing. Love might have created more stable attachments than sexual attraction could accomplish by itself (E. O. Wilson, 1978; Rizley, 1980). Love also drew genetically unrelated persons together to engage in mating, thus diversifying the gene pool and contributing to the survival of the species. Thus, as Buss (1988, p. 115) notes, "The existence of love acts may be traced ultimately to the reproductive advantages conferred on those performing such acts effectively."

A second type of evidence that may shed light on the biological side of love also relates to sex. In 1964 psychologist Stanley Schachter devised a theory based on the physiological responses that accompany many emotions—a pounding heart, sweaty palms,

Researchers on Love

No one is completely certain about what causes the feeling of love. Although the image of Cupid practicing his archer's skills is clearly not a satisfactory explanation, no good alternative has really been proposed. Much of the research on love has addressed this issue from the perspective of social psychology, looking at interpersonal attraction as a possible source for some answers. Let's see what findings from these studies might apply.

Physical appearance seems to be an important element in determining how attracted one person is to another. Nursery school children (Dion and Berscheid, 1974), teenagers (Dion, Berscheid, and Walster, 1972; Dermer and Thiel, 1975), and adults (Adams and Huston, 1975) all regard good-looking people with more favor than their less attractive peers. People tend to be more socially responsive and more willing to provide help to attractive individuals (Barocas and Karoly, 1972; Benson, Karabenick, and Lerner, 1976). There is fairly solid evidence that despite sayings like "you can't tell a book by its cover" or "beauty is only skin deep," the physical attractiveness of females has a strong influence on their dating frequency—a finding that is far less true for males (Berscheid et al., 1971; Krebs and Adinolfi, 1975).

In a thought-provoking experiment, Dion, Berscheid, and Walster (1972) found that physical attractiveness also influences our expectations about other people's personalities and behavior. On the basis of photographs, both men and women rated good-looking people as more sexually warm and responsive, interesting, poised, sociable, kind, strong, and outgoing than less attractive people. The group judged as physically attractive was also seen as more likely to attain high occupational status, to make better husbands or wives, and to have happier marriages than the less attractive group. And a recent study involving college-age couples matched by computer found that both sexes reacted most positively to their dates if they were good-looking; intelligence, personality, and social charm had little to do with the romantic chemistry.

heavy breathing, and so on. According to Schachter, how we distinguish between love, anger, jealousy, nervousness, and other emotions is not based on our bodily reaction only (since the responses may be identical) but rather on the way we interpret or label what we are experiencing. In Schachter's sense, love is a matter of physiological arousal interpreted in a certain way. Recent studies have shown, however, that Schachter's theories are only partly correct. It now appears that there are some specific differences in the reactions of the autonomic nervous system to various types of emotions (Ekman, Levenson, and Friesen, 1983), raising the possibility that the feeling we call love may be accompanied by a unique set of physiological responses.

One plausible explanation is suggested by psychiatrist Dr. Michael Liebowitz, who contends that the excitement and arousal of romantic love are a direct result of surging levels of two neurotransmitters, dopamine and norepinephrine, that carry chemical messages that bridge the gap between the nerve cells in the brain. In his 1983 book *The Chemistry of Love,* Liebowitz argues that these neurotransmitters are activated by visual cues—noticing someone who fits our ideal of attractiveness, for example—and then bathe the pleasure center of the brain in a sea of chemical messages. Liebowitz also believes that intense, transcendent love experiences may involve a separate neurotransmitter called serotonin, which can produce an almost psychedelic high, while companionate love may rely more on the brain's production of narcotic-like substances called endorphins that give a sense of tranquility. In addition, in Liebowitz's view, the emotional crash that follows the breakup of a passionate love relationship may be analogous to the withdrawal period a drug addict experiences: in both situations, deprivation of the chemical source of pleasure leads to a period of emotional pain and irritability.

Physical attractiveness seems to be more important for females than for males in affecting interpersonal relationships. A man's occupational status or financial success is generally more important in rating his "social desirability" (Rubin, 1973; Walster and Walster, 1978). Physicians, lawyers, and other professionals are consistently rated by women as more desirable dates or marriage partners than men with low-status occupations such as janitor or waiter.

Here are a few other salient findings by "love researchers":

1. The notion of "love at first sight" may in many cases be only a myth that fulfills our need for instant acceptance and rationalizes our feelings of sexual arousal by giving them a "dignified" label (Murstein, 1980), but in some cases it proves to be real (Solomon, 1981, 1989). Unfortunately, only the passage of time will show which is which.
2. The old bit of folklore that men prefer "hard-to-get" women just is not true (Walster et al., 1973).
3. College-age women fall in love more frequently than college-age men (Dion and Dion, 1973, 1975), but college-age men fall in love more quickly (Hill, Rubin, and Peplau, 1976).
4. Among college men and women, more than 80 percent say they would not consider marrying someone they aren't in love with (Berscheid, 1988).
5. Men hang on longer in a dying love affair than women (Walster and Walster, 1978), and women end more romances than men (Hill, Rubin, and Peplau, 1976).

Although research on love has become more fashionable in recent years, the following observation by a prominent psychologist still applies: "So far as love or affection is concerned, psychologists have failed in their mission. The little we know about love does not transcend simple observation, and the little we write about it has been written better by poets and novelists" (Harlow, 1958, p. 673).

LOVE AND SEX

The relationship between love and sex in our society is complicated. Traditionally, females were taught that love is a requirement for sex, while males were urged to obtain sexual experience whether or not love was present. Gradually in the 1960s and 1970s, premarital sex became more acceptable for females, at first if they were engaged to be married and later if they were involved in a "significant relationship" (one usually defined by love). Today, although restrictions have loosened even more for some, many heterosexual couples still need a statement of love before they feel morally comfortable with the idea of "going all the way."

Sex Without Love

It is tempting to categorize sex involving people who are not in love as casual sex, distinguishing it from relational sex. But people who do not love one another can have a strong relationship, and lovers can sometimes have casual sex in the sense that there's not much thinking about it or interpersonal communication going on. Sex can be mechanical, impersonal, and hurried whether or not two people love each other.

There is nothing inherently bad about impersonal sex if it is clearly consented to by all parties. Under certain circumstances and for some people, impersonal sex may be enjoyable in its own right. Others are offended or distressed by impersonal sex and could never consider participating in a group sex scene or having sex with a stranger or prostitute.

Some people enjoy a more personal, intimate brand of sex, hoping that it may develop into love. There are no guarantees that this will happen, so if this is the only reason for sexual participation, these people are liable to feel disappointed, cheated, or angry. It is probably easier for those who engage in casual sex to view sex without love as an experience valued for its own pleasures and unique returns. If nothing more is expected, disappointment is less likely.

Some moralists would be happier if it could be proved that sex without love does not work. There is no evidence, however, that sex is usually better if you are in love. We have worked with hundreds of loving, committed relationships where the sexual interaction was in shambles and with hundreds of people who deeply enjoyed sex without being in love.

Another aspect of this topic deserves mention. A love relationship, unless it's on the rocks, offers some protection against being used sexually. As we pointed out earlier, love is marked by caring and respect that buffers this risk. Sex without love is probably more likely to create misunderstandings and involves a greater risk of being used for the purposes of your partner without much regard for your own feelings and needs. It is harder to gauge the trust in a nonloving relationship, so "proceed at your own risk" (Figure 12.6).

Love Without Sex

There are a variety of circumstances in which a love relationship exists without sex. Parent–child love, brotherly love, and so-called platonic (friendly, nonsexual) love are some obvious examples. There are also forms of romantic and companionate love in which there is no sexual component. In the purest forms of love without sex, both partners agree to abstain from physical intimacies. They may make this choice because of religious beliefs, a disinterest in sex, or a desire to wait until marriage. This comment from a 25-year-old man shows another motive for abstaining from sex:

> My partner and I became so caught up in our sexual activity that the rest of our relationship was neglected. After we decided not to have sex, we found more time and energy to love each other in ways that meant more to us. (*Authors' files*)

There are also unavoidable circumstances that may prevent or limit sexual interaction in a love relationship, such as serious illness or geographic separation. Sometimes the decision is one-sided rather

Figure 12.6   Feelings About Sex Without Love

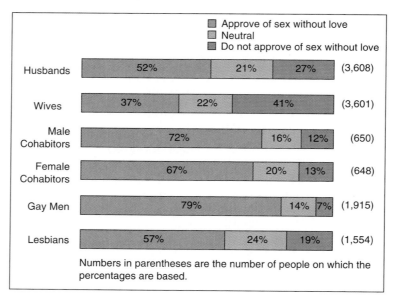

Numbers in parentheses are the number of people on which the percentages are based.

American adults' attitudes toward the propriety of sex without love are shown in this survey. Note that married women are least approving of this practice.

than mutual, in which case one lover may be left in a sexually frustrating situation.

Personal Values and Sexual Decisions

Many people are troubled by questions about what's "right" and "wrong" sexually. Adolescents and young adults are often uncertain about the pros and cons of premarital sex. Others are puzzled about the morality and propriety of extramarital sex. When love is added into the equation, even more complex questions arise: Does sexual attraction to someone other than your lover mean that love is dying? Does "extrarelational" sex undermine the quality of love or trust in a primary love relationship? Should the presence or absence of love be the major determinant of our sexual decisions?

There is no simple formula for answering such questions. Each person approaches sexual decision making from a framework of personal values, beliefs, and experiences that tip the balance one way or another. Some love relationships will wither and die if sex is "off limits." In other relationships, premature leaps toward the bedroom may jeopardize the foundations of love. For one person, abstaining from premarital sex is a matter of deep moral conviction, with potentially negative consequences if these convictions are set aside. For others, the same act of abstention prevents them from learning that there is a poor sexual compatability with their future mate, creating a difficult problem to be faced early in marriage.

The dimensions of sexual decision-making can be appreciated better if we recognize some of the sources of potential conflict. It is easy to see how our society encourages us to adhere to a particular set of sexual values. Our religious beliefs—and the strength of these beliefs—may also guide us. But at the personal level of decision making, we must deal with the tensions between our various needs. For instance, there is a built-in conflict between the following pairs of values: commitment versus freedom, privacy versus intimacy, sexual novelty versus permanence, independence versus sexual fidelity (Meyners and Wooster, 1979). A person's sexual decisions are outgrowths of how she or he judges the relative importance of such personal values.

Sexual decisions are unfortunately sometimes made on the basis of guilt, ignorance, or impulse. This creates a different kind of decision-making process that is more likely to be second-guessed later on. Since we must live with our sexual decisions, we should take an active role in making sexual choices instead of just letting the choices "happen."

LOVE AND MARRIAGE

To discuss love without discussing its relationship to marriage would be like discussing free enterprise with no mention of money. Love and marriage are certainly not synonymous, but they are linked in important ways.

While marriage, unlike love, can be defined in legal terms, its psychosocial dimension is most closely related to love. We do not believe that marriage is the only way to go, the "best" choice, or a perfect solution to life's problems. We recognize that some couples who live together without a marriage certificate are more meaningfully wedded, more committed to each other, than other couples whose marriages are legally sanctioned. But we agree with the following idea:

> For all the books and preaching and counseling and psychological knowledge we have today, for all our new ideals of freedom and our emphasis on personal growth and fulfillment, marriage is still basically two people trying to love each other and answer each other's needs. *(O'Neil, 1978, p. 4)*

Selecting a Mate

Our culture is unique in the emphasis it places on love *before* marriage (I. L. Reiss, 1980). Unlike societies in which marriages are traditionally arranged by parents, with courtship following tightly controlled etiquette, we are led to believe that "love conquers all" and live our lives accordingly. In India, China, Japan, and parts of Africa and the Arab world, arranged marriages are common. Often these matches preserve social and economic order and create a stable setting for family living. The partners in an "arranged" marriage—who may be "pledged" to each other during childhood—are not expected to begin their marriage *because* of love. Instead, devotion and responsibility are expected to grow as the marriage develops, and love may or may not occur.

Paradoxically, in America, where our strong sense of freedom and democracy carries over into mate se-

RESEARCH SPOTLIGHT

The Role of Arousal

Some men believe that taking a date to an emotionally evocative event, like a horror movie or a boxing match, or a ride on a topsy-turvy rollercoaster, will stir up the woman's romantic feelings toward them. There is now some experimental evidence that such an arousal effect does indeed occur.

The best-known example of this effect is a study by Dutton and Aron in which they compared reactions of young men crossing two bridges at a scenic tourist spot in North Vancouver. One bridge was a 450-foot long, narrow, wobbly structure that swayed back and forth 230 scary feet above a rocky gorge. In contrast, the second bridge was a solid, safe, immobile structure not very high off the ground. Male test subjects were randomly assigned to walk across one bridge or the other. As they completed their walk, they were met by an attractive college woman who was an assistant of the psychologists conducting the study. The woman explained that she was conducting a class project and asked each man to answer a few questions and write a brief

story in response to a picture. After this was done, the woman offered to explain her project in more detail and wrote her telephone number on a piece of paper so the man could call her at home if he wanted more information. Intriguingly, the researchers found that the highest level of sexual imagery in the stories the men wrote was provided by the men who had crossed the anxiety-provoking suspension bridge. In addition, 9 of the 33 men who had crossed the suspension bridge called the research assistant later on, whereas only 2 of the men who had crossed the solid bridge called her.

While it is possible to interpret these results in several different ways—for instance, perhaps the men who called the female research assistant may really have been interested in her project—the most plausible explanation is that emotional arousal seems to trigger sexual attraction.

A second experiment by Dutton and Aron also explored the role of fear in provoking sexual arousal. College-age men were recruited for

lection processes, we have an extraordinarily high rate of divorce. This may tell us something about the lack of love education we receive while growing up. We are expected to recognize love and to select a marriage mate "till death do us part" largely on the basis of love. The odds are strong, however, that most of us have gotten more training in learning how to drive than in learning how to love.

Those caught in the throes of romantic love are drawn to thoughts of marriage like moths to light. The desire to be one with your loved one, especially when the love is mutually felt, fits neatly into our expectations of marriage as a form of intimate, lasting romance. But the irrational nature of romantic love often causes us to overlook potential problems and to minimize what will happen when and if the passion dies down.

This doesn't mean that you must adopt a scientific, calculating analysis of likely marriage candidates. Despite the success some computer dating

services claim in finding the "perfect" match, no one has succeeded in devising a foolproof formula for marital success. Like many things in life, the process of selecting a mate is largely a matter of common sense combined with an element of luck.

At the commonsense level, it helps to realize that men and women tend to be happiest in equitable relationships. People feel most comfortable when they are getting from a relationship what they believe they deserve: too much or too little (inequity) leads to discomfort and dissatisfaction (Murstein, 1976; Walster, Walster, and Berscheid, 1978). Research on "equity theory" shows that men and women generally marry someone with similar physical attractiveness, intelligence, and attributes (Walster and Walster, 1978). Marrying someone with a markedly different socioeconomic, educational, or cultural background is likely to be riskier than marrying someone more closely

a learning experiment. When they arrived at the testing facility, they found that the partner they were going to be working with was an extremely attractive young woman. At the same time, they were informed that the experiment they were about to begin was designed to test the effects of electric shock on learning. Some of the men were deliberately told that they would receive strong, painful electric shocks as part of the experiment. Others were told that they were assigned to a control group and would receive very weak electric shocks which would barely cause a tingling sensation. (None of the subjects actually received any shocks. The shocks were mentioned just to cause anxiety in some of the men as part of the real experiment going on.)

Before the sham experiment was supposed to begin, one of the investigators spoke with each man in private and asked him about his feelings toward the attractive young woman who was assigned to be his partner. Not surprisingly, the men reacted just as the researchers predicted

they would: men who were terrified found the woman much sexier than the calmer men did and were much more interested in dating her.

Now it has become evident that other types of arousal, including intense physical exercise, can fan the flames of passion—at least to a limited degree. In one experiment, running in place for 2 minutes intensified the reactions of male subjects to viewing videotapes of either an attractive or an unattractive woman (White, Fishbein, and Rutstein, 1981). Men who had exercised vigorously found the pretty woman to be even more appealing then men who had only exercised for 15 seconds, while they had more intensely negative reactions to the unattractive female than the men who had not become physiologically aroused. (There may be a message in here about coed gyms or health clubs as a place to find a lover, but we're fairly certain the reality is quite a bit more complicated than the experiments described above.) Other studies also support the concept that emotionally neutral physiological arousal can stir up passion (Zillman, 1984).

matching your own characteristics, but this is where personal choice comes into play. A general set of statistics is not an infallible guide, and sometimes you're better off following your heart than your head. Since people tend to change over the years, even the most impressive statistics may be invalid ten years later.

One way of assessing someone's marriage potential is to stay in a long-term relationship to see what happens. After the initial luster of love wears off, you can see how problems are solved, how interactions change in times of stress and with the passage of time, and if boredom or dissent become commonplace. You can be fairly certain that premarital problems are likely to intensify rather than disappear once the honeymoon is over. One way of accomplishing this type of assessment is by living together, a route chosen by about one-quarter of United States undergraduates in the 1980s (Macklin, 1989).

One last note on mate selection. While sex is not the most important ingredient in most marriages, it does help to know if you and your spouse-to-be are sexually compatible or have considerable difficulty getting things together sexually. This doesn't mean that you should rush into a sexual relationship (again, your own values must be applied here) or that you need to have a performance checklist (a tactic that could boomerang in unexpected ways), but you do need to decide how to deal with the sexual side of your relationship and to think about how important sex is (or isn't) to *you*.

Love in Marriage

Marriage is rarely a faithful replay of the fairy-tale ending "and they all lived happily ever after." Living in a marriage and making it work are no easy matter. It's easier to be loving when you aren't awakened by kids at 3:00 a.m., when you're not squabbling with the in-laws, or when your sexual advances aren't repelled by a headful of curlers, a facial mask, cigar breath, or Monday night football.

In the real world, few marriages maintain a perpetually loving relationship. Even companionate love shifts its intensity from time to time as a married couple reacts to the ordinary stresses and strains of life together. At any given moment, a husband and wife may dislike each other or even hate each other, yet still spring back into a love relationship.

Researchers have found that marital dissatisfaction tends to increase the longer people have been married (Wills, Weiss, and Patterson, 1974; O'Neil, 1978; Gottman, 1994). While it is possible to speculate on its many causes—lessened sexual interest, the responsibilities of parenting and occupation, failure to share time together, poor communications, and changes in personal attractiveness, to name just a few—many marriages suffer from a kind of benign neglect that relegates the relationship to a low priority, thus removing the elements that usually sustain love.

To maintain love or help it grow, marriage partners must invest emotions and energy on a continuing basis. Spouses who succeed in "giving" to one another—in communications, physical warmth, shared interests, and shared responsibilities—are also likely to succeed in staying in love.

While some marriages succeed quite well in keeping love alive, others evolve into business relationships or a sort of "roommate" status in which love fades away completely. Partners in marriages that become strained over time may stay together to protect the children or to adhere to a philosophy that simply will not allow for separation or divorce. Although these marriages may be loveless, they are not necessarily "bad." Even good marriages are susceptible to a disappearance of love.

In an essay called "The Future of Marriage," Morton Hunt (1977) observed: "Formal promises to love are promises no one can keep, for love is not an act of will; and legal bonds have no power to keep love alive when it is dying." The nature of marriage in the 1990s may have changed considerably from earlier times, but the nature of love has not. A major challenge facing any marriage is to preserve the spark of love—a task that requires hard work and creativity.

Source: *Reproduced by Special Permission of* Playboy *Magazine. Copyright ©* 1987 by Playboy.

SUMMARY

1. Interpersonal love can be defined as a state in which someone else's happiness is essential to your own. The elements of caring and respect are important aspects of love and can help one distinguish between love as a growth relationship and love as a form of addiction or dependency.

2. Openness and sharing and desire (sexual or otherwise) are usually part of but not the same as love. The degree to which each of these characteristics is found in any love relationship is highly variable and does not define which love is automatically "best."

3. Sternberg's Triangular Theory identifies three key components of love: intimacy, passion, and

decision/commitment. Sternberg contends that you can compare the involvement of two people in love by seeing how well their love triangles match; a major misfit is a sign of imbalance or potential problems.

4. Attachment theory has been applied to adult love relationships by the recent claim that all love relationships mimic the type of attachment found in early mother–infant interactions. This approach categorizes love relationships as either secure, avoidant, or anxious/ambivalent.

5. Romantic love is the dramatic, passionate form of love that has been celebrated in story and verse throughout history. Tennov coined the word *limerence* to describe the most intense forms of romantic love.

6. The romantic love cycle often, but not always, begins with a stage of receptivity toward love, or *love readiness*. The *falling in love* stage usually flows into a stage of being in love, marked by optimism, elation, and a sense of permanency. This stage is usually short-lived, giving way to a *transitional period* in which lovers first notice imperfections and faults, encounter boredom, impatience, or frustration, and begin testing each other. This phase generates conflict, which may be resolved (maintaining the relationship), temporarily shelved (in an uneasy truce), or cause a *falling out of love*.

7. Companionate love is a reality-based love without the passions of romantic love but with a better durability.

8. Love may have some biological basis as shown by evolutionary evidence and the interaction between physiological arousal states and emotions; but love is most importantly a psychosocial phenomenon.

9. In our culture, love is closely linked to sex and marriage, but either can exist without love. Sex without love isn't necessarily less good than sex with love, just as love without sex is most comfortable for some people. Personal decisions about sex are best made on the basis of individual values and beliefs, including examining and establishing a priority between two values that may conflict.

10. Love is not an automatic accompaniment to marriage, nor is marriage an automatic outgrowth of love. Our society has an unrealistic set of expectations about love in marriage (possibly because we do not think about education to prepare for love or being loved), and people are often disappointed or surprised when their own relationship does not hold its love in an effortless fashion. Keeping love alive requires active participation from two people: in order to "get" love, it helps to start by "giving."

Thought Questions

1. Do you agree with the contention that passionate love is a form of addiction? Why or why not?

2. Is it possible to have great sex without love? To have passionate love without great sex? Is there any common denominator between love and sex, or do they rely on primarily different sorts of impulses?

3. According to the 1960s rock song, "Breaking Up Is Hard To Do." What factors make breaking up difficult? Is it easier if you are the person who initiates the break-up? If you are thinking about breaking up with your partner, what steps can you take to lessen the psychological blow?

4. Is it true that you can judge the intensity of someone's love for you by their jealousy toward others who show an interest in you? Is it possible for someone to be so confidently in love that he or she is beyond feeling jealousy?

5. Although we live in a society that puts a premium on love before marriage, are there any circumstances that might lead you to consider marrying someone you didn't love? If you did marry someone you didn't love, do you think that love would eventually develop in your relationship? Why or why not?

6. Is it possible to be in love with two people at the same time?

Suggested Readings

Fromm, Erich. *The Art of Loving*. New York: Harper & Row, 1956. Although a bit dated, this short, classic book was the bible of love for many Americans.

Liebowitz, Michael R. *The Chemistry of Love*. Boston: Little, Brown, 1983. A provocative look at the biological mechanisms possibly involved in the feelings and experience we call "love."

Pope, Kenneth S. (ed.). *On Love and Loving*. San Francisco: Jossey-Bass, 1980. A comprehensive, balanced set of essays on the nature of romantic love from a wide variety of theoretical perspectives. Particularly useful is its life-cycle approach to the study of love.

Solomon, Robert C. *About Love: Reinventing Romance for Our Times*. New York: Touchstone, 1989. In a modern version of Erich Fromm's classic, *The Art of Loving*, philosopher Solomon illuminates many aspects of loving that have been overlooked or misinterpreted by others.

Sternberg, Robert J. *The Triangle of Love*. New York: Basic Books, 1988. A lively presentation of Sternberg's theories about love in practical, down-to-earth language, with a helpful critical discussion of other love research.

Sternberg, Robert J., and Barnes, Michael L. (eds.). *The Psychology of Love*. New Haven: Yale University Press, 1988. A detailed compendium of various theoretical viewpoints on love that provides an exceptional overview of current thinking on this topic.

Tennov, Dorothy. *Love and Limerence*. New York: Stein and Day, 1979. A fast-paced book that will hold your attention from start to finish. Tennov's theories present important ideas on the many faces of love.

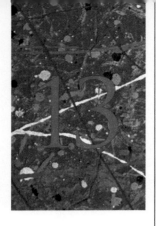

13

Intimacy and Communication Skills

Intimacy. We hunger for it, but we also fear it. We come close to a loved one, then we back off. A teacher I once had described this as the "go away a little closer" message. I call it the approach-avoidance dance. *(L. Rubin, 1983, p. 65)*

The search for intimacy is a familiar part of our lives, yet finding and sustaining satisfying intimate relationships seem to be difficult undertakings for many people. This might be surprising at first, since the benefits we derive from sharing warm, trusting relationships—like enjoyment, acceptance, comfort, support, and companionship—have an obviously self-fulfilling role in our lives. Yet despite most people's agreement that intimacy is desirable, there is no clear-cut path to follow for establishing an intimate relationship, and preserving intimacy, or helping it grow, seems to be a major problem today if we consider current divorce statistics or the tens of thousands of couples seeking marriage counseling.

Understanding the nature of intimacy—what it is, how to achieve and sustain it—while also recognizing the potential pitfalls and problems of intimacy is the subject of this chapter. In addition, since effective communications are, in many ways, essential to developing and maintaining intimacy, we also discuss communication skills as they apply to intimate relationships.

INTIMACY AND INTIMATE RELATIONS

The word *intimacy* comes from the Latin *intimus*, which means "innermost" or "deepest." Intimacy can be defined as a process in which two caring people share as freely as possible in the exchange of feelings, thoughts, and actions (Levinger and Raush, 1977; Macionis, 1978; Hatfield, 1982). As we use the term in this discussion, intimacy is generally marked by a mutual sense of acceptance, commitment, tenderness, and trust.

This definition allows us to see that intimacy is not precisely the same as romance or even strong affection. Friends may work or play together and enjoy each other's company but have little or no exchange of their inner thoughts and feelings, and a person may fall in love with someone without expressing that feeling to the loved one.

In much the same way, intimacy as a temporary condition (in contrast to an ongoing process) is sometimes situation-bound: it is defined by a particular set of circumstances that leads to openness with no commitment or tenderness necessarily present (Wong, 1981). For example, two people sitting next to each other on a long flight might engage in a very personal conversation, but if they later meet accidentally at a cocktail party, they might be quite uncomfortable about their disclosures. In much the same way, two people who have engaged in casual sex together without any real exchange of feelings may have "been intimate" sexually but they have not experienced the sharing and caring of intimacy as we have defined it.

Thus, we can see that there is much variety and complexity in intimate relations; they are not all alike by any means. In particular, we can expect that intimacy without romance or sexual interaction (where this status is agreeable to both persons involved) is apt to be quite different from the intimacy that accompanies love or romance or sexual passion. But before we go on to examine the nature of interpersonal intimacy in more detail, it is helpful to take a brief look at another component of intimacy that undoubtedly influences a person's relationships with others: intimacy with self.

Intimacy with Self

I used to think that intimacy was something I'd get, like a present, when I met "Mr. Right," but now I realize intimacy begins within me. *(Authors' files)*

A number of psychologists have stressed that a person's ability to form intimate relationships with others depends in part on having a firm sense of self based on realistic self-knowledge and a reasonable degree of self-acceptance (Erikson, 1963; Rogers, 1972; Levinger and Raush, 1977; Wolf, 1982). Such self-awareness helps us to identify our needs and feelings and thus enables us to share them with others. Self-acceptance is also an important building block for interpersonal intimacy because it allows people to be themselves without pretending to be something other than who and what they are.

People who don't like themselves very much or who feel ashamed of who they are often have a difficult time establishing and maintaining intimacy because they are preoccupied with trying to prove themselves to others or with trying to gain recognition or respect. Even if they are successful in these efforts, their feelings about themselves usually don't change in a lasting way. Others who are anxious or depressed about themselves may deal with these feelings in ways that block self-awareness: by using drugs (including alcohol) for escape, by sitting passively in front of a television set to distract themselves from themselves, or by becoming immersed in their work. Still others who are unhappy with themselves try to find personal satisfaction in relationships in which someone else cares for them, protects them, provides for them, or entertains them, but this is often only a short-term solution.

This does not mean that a person must be totally happy with himself or herself to be capable of intimacy with others. When we look within ourselves, we may not always like what we see. Generally, we separate what we like from what we don't like and use this process to try to change. If we are honest in our self-appraisals, the intimate knowledge we develop helps us relate to others. At the same time, a person who *never* looks inward (whether out of fear, laziness, or self-hatred) has such distorted self-perceptions that it is unlikely he or she can contribute fully to a relationship with someone else.

One useful caution should be added here. It is important to retain our sense of self even while involved in an intimate relation with another and not to become so preoccupied with a relationship that we lose touch with our sense of self. An intimate relationship that absorbs most of your time and emotional energy can be exhilarating, but it can also leave you little time for knowing yourself. Such an all-absorbing relationship can be draining or damaging rather than fulfilling. In contrast, intimate relations that enhance your self-acceptance and self-knowledge are likely to be positive elements in your life.

Components of Interpersonal Intimacy

A 22-year-old single woman: What I really want most from a relationship is the privilege of being honest all the time. I don't know if that's possible, though. (*Authors' files*)

A 29-year-old married man: To me, intimacy means sharing. You share the good and the bad, the joys and the pain, and through all the sharing you know your partner cares about you. (*Authors' files*)

A 35-year-old single woman: It comes as a shock to some people to realize that lesbians can have committed, lasting relationships, but that's exactly what Sallie and I have. To us, that commitment is a lifetime bond. (*Authors' files*)

Because the joys of intimacy are numerous and varied, it is a mistake to think of it as a single, unchanging condition. Not only does intimacy exist in various degrees of intensity and in different types of relationships—between friends, between lovers, between family members, and so on—intimacy as a process fluctuates within any given relationship over time. This is partly because each partner's expectations and hopes influence how he or she evaluates what he or she is getting from the relationship (Stuart, 1980; Margolin, 1982). People who feel that an intimate relationship is consistently unfair or one-sided generally are more likely to end the relationship (or look for another to take its place). In contrast, those who view their relationships as equitable and balanced are likely to be happiest and stay together for longer times (Walster, Walster, and Berscheid, 1978; Hatfield, 1982). In addition, the intensity of intimacy in a particular relationship is influenced by external circumstances, such as geographic separation or work pressures, which can temporarily divert a person's energy and attention from the relationship to other aspects of his or her life.

To better understand the process of intimacy, we examine its basic components: caring, sharing, trust, commitment, honesty, empathy, and tenderness. To get the most out of this discussion, however, it is important to recognize that these components do not usually exist separately from each other but instead are blended in a unique amalgam in which each strengthens and solidifies the others.

Caring and Sharing

Caring is an attitude or feeling you have for another person that is generally related to the intensity of your positive feelings toward him or her. Although you might have positive feelings about someone with whom you have no personal involvement—on the basis of good looks alone, for instance, you might feel positively about a person sitting across the table from you in the library—the mutual caring characteristic of intimacy occurs only when two people share and interact together.

The sharing of thoughts, feelings, and experiences that accompanies the growth of intimacy requires spending time together to learn about each other without the ordinary barriers with which people protect their privacy. Thus, one of the key steps in developing an intimate relationship is self-disclosure, the willingness to tell another person what you're thinking and feeling. Because there is no certainty that the other person will be interested in what you have to say, and because it takes some time to establish the trustworthiness of the other person, most people begin the process of self-disclosure gradually. Instead of revealing their fondest dreams and deepest fears all at once, people generally develop personal openness in a relationship as they find it reciprocated and as they see signs of the other person's continuing interest (Altman, Vinsel, and Brown, 1981).

This process of intimate sharing is not limited to superficial or pleasant things alone but should extend across a broad spectrum. According to noted psychologist Carl Rogers, saying "'I want to share myself and my feelings with you, even when they are not all positive,' almost guarantees a constructive process to communications" (1972, p. 203). Sharing uncertainties, worries, and other personal problems with an intimate partner is essential for the growth of intimacy.

Although sharing thoughts and feelings is important to intimacy, it is important that experiences be shared also. Research has shown that people

The sharing and caring of intimacy are not lessened by disability.

who share mutually rewarding experiences are most likely to develop and sustain a warm, caring relationship (Gottman, 1979; Hatfield, 1982). Such shared experiences can include many things. Sharing hard times and good times, sharing child rearing or a dual career, sharing recreational activities, or sharing in planning for the future are all examples of how intimate couples interact.

Sharing experiences does not necessarily mean that intimate partners should do everything together. Although such a system might work well for a few couples, most people would find total sharing difficult. This is partly because a particular activity or experience doesn't always provide equal rewards to each partner. You might love jogging, for instance, while your partner prefers to play bridge. Forcing each other into activities that are *not* mutually enjoyable just for the sake of togetherness is unwise. Furthermore, constant and complete sharing is not necessarily a measure of a couple's intimacy. Indeed, maintaining an identity independent of an intimate relationship is also important to the longevity of the relationship (Laurence, 1982). Pursuing individual interests and maintaining a circle of friends give a person a

chance to process the feelings generated in intimate interactions. Such efforts help to prevent partners from becoming psychologically overloaded with too much one-to-one togetherness. In addition, such independence allows people to bring new experiences and thoughts to their primary relationship, which can also help it grow.

Trust

The process of self-disclosure doesn't occur in a vacuum but depends on the degree to which you trust the person to whom you are making disclosures about yourself. Thus, trust is another necessary ingredient for intimacy, and, like caring and sharing, trust develops over time. While people trying to form an intimate relationship usually have to make some initial assumptions about trusting each other, trust solidifies when a partner's behavior matches his or her words. If he promises to help and be there and his behavior confirms those words, she comes to trust him. If she promises never to laugh at his personal secrets and she doesn't, he comes to trust her. Once trust grows strong, two people are able to share even more information about their thoughts and feelings without fear that this will be used against them in some way.

FOCUS IN BRIEF

Eight Common Myths About Intimacy

1. Intimacy means being able to read each other's mind.
2. Romance is an essential part of intimacy.
3. Unless intimacy develops automatically and effortlessly, it isn't authentic.
4. Sex = intimacy.
5. Intimacy requires knowing everything about each other.
6. True intimacy only occurs if you and your partner have the same interests and enjoy the same activities.
7. Intimacy means always being in agreement.
8. Intimacy is always a source of happiness.

Commitment

Another component of intimacy, commitment, is generally an outgrowth of the caring, sharing, and trust that develop in the early stages of an intimate relationship (Levinger and Raush, 1977). Commitment requires both partners to work willingly to maintain their intimacy through periods of crisis, boredom, frustration, and fatigue, as well as through times of joy, prosperity, and excitement. Intimacy that surfaces only when life is on the upswing is a fleeting, unreliable form of closeness rather than the more encompassing interaction most people would like it to be. Here, too, Carl Rogers has nicely captured the essence of the commitment of intimacy: "We each commit ourselves to working together on the changing process of our present relationship, because our relationship is currently enriching our love and our life and we wish it to grow" (1972, p. 201).

Realistically, it is important to recognize that the degree of one's commitment to an intimate relationship may change over time. Those who pledge themselves to each other "forever and ever" on the basis of a passionate relationship that has lasted only a few weeks may find that as they get to know each other better their desire to stay together lessens. Even couples who have shared years of satisfying intimacy may find that they later grow apart or develop problems that undermine their relationship. Thus, commitment should be regarded as an attitude that states current intentions without being an irrevocable guarantee of the future. Nevertheless, commitment that is backed up by a willingness to work to overcome problems that might develop in a relationship is an important ingredient for a durable future.

Other Components of Intimacy

Honesty is another necessary part of intimacy, although total honesty in the sense of full self-disclosure is not necessarily good for a relationship. Too much honesty can be devastating to any relationship if it is not tempered with an understanding of how a given message might affect one's partner. But there is a decided difference between keeping some things private—that is, setting limits on the self-disclosure that occurs—and deceit. When deliberate deception occurs in friendships or romances, it generally undermines the quality of information exchange that can occur and therefore undermines intimacy. In-

Intimacy is not bound by time or place.

deed, the presence of deceit in a relationship usually is a warning sign that manipulation of one form or another is occurring.

If a person engages in deceit in an intimate relationship, even with the best intentions, the discovery of that deceit almost inevitably leads to a loss of trust. Thus, telling lies (a sin of commission) is usually more harmful to intimacy than keeping something private (a sin of omission). This means that if your partner asks about something that you don't feel you can discuss truthfully, you can always say, "I don't want to discuss this particular subject" without violating your partner's trust. Of course, putting too many topics "off limits" can lead your partner to wonder what you're hiding and may also result in your partner's pulling away from openness too; as in most aspects of intimate relations, partners tend to parallel each other's behavior.

Empathy is the ability to understand and relate to another person's feelings and point of view. For self-disclosures to occur between intimate partners, each must feel that he or she is listened to and understood (or at least accepted) by the other person. Such empathy enables each person in an intimate relationship to act in ways that support and help the other and to avoid or limit destructive, irritating, or alienating attitudes.

One of the most neglected aspects of intimacy is the expression of tenderness, which can be achieved either by spoken messages or by physical contact (e.g., hugging, cuddling, holding hands) as well as by direct behavior. This ingredient of intimacy often seems to be particularly difficult for men, who have been socialized to be purely rational, action-oriented beings: they seem bewildered by tenderness or afraid that it is an "unmanly" way of acting. On the other hand, some of these men are able to be physically tender but lack comfort or familiarity with the verbal side of tenderness. Both components—verbal and physical tenderness—are usually necessary for romantic intimacy. In fact, much of the time that people complain about intimacy disappearing from their relationships they are actually acknowledging that the amount of tenderness they receive from their partners has noticeably declined. Thus, paying attention to ways to express your tenderness to your partner, by both words and actions, is one of the best ways of keeping intimacy fresh and satisfying over time.

Finally, it is important to recognize that unless intimate partners are willing to set aside many of the ordinary defenses they use in everyday life, it can hardly be said that the intimate relation is a special one. It is hard to be intimate with a person who continually denies the reality of his or her inner feelings (e.g., someone who always pretends that everything's great). It is equally difficult to have satisfying intimacy with a person whose behavior is based on pretense (e.g., a partner who is always looking for "status" and ways of impressing others). On the other hand, people who are able to relinquish such defenses in favor of being themselves, authentically and spontaneously, are apt to find intimacy more rewarding.

A cautionary note about intimacy has been sounded recently. Psychiatrist Carol Anderson points out, for example, that we may set expectations for intimacy in our relationships at such a high level that it becomes unattainable (Hiebert, 1987). Anderson notes that this may be related to our searching for intense forms of intimacy while assigning less value to forms of intimacy such as loyalty, steadiness over time, and a sense of family. She traces this trend, in part, to the emphasis that arose in the 1960s in the encounter group movement on "getting in touch with feelings" and then expressing these feelings verbally. The implication is that too much emphasis on verbal intimacy as the "premium" or most meaningful variety can make it difficult for a person who cannot easily verbalize to be accepted as a caring, committed partner in an intimate relationship. Wynne and Wynne (1986) also note that if intimacy is demanded or expected constantly, it is likely to diminish. In fact, they believe that intimacy occurs most reliably "when it emerges spontaneously within a context of basic, well-functioning relational processes" (Wynne and Wynne, 1986, p. 383).

Sex Differences in Intimacy

A 28-year-old woman: Whenever I go out with a guy, it seems like all he's interested in is sex. We sleep together once or twice and suddenly he disappears. I think all the men I know are afraid of a really intimate relationship. *(Authors' files)*

A 25-year-old man: It's sad to hear women condemning men for being unwilling to get into close, loving relationships. Many of my friends value intimacy highly, although admittedly it's not easy to find. *(Authors' files)*

The two opinions quoted above about sex differences in intimacy highlight a much-debated topic. Currently, there aren't any reliable data on whether men and women have different levels or types of motivations for intimacy. Thus, the best we can do is review current research evidence on sex differences in particular aspects of intimate behavior, such as self-disclosure.

A number of studies show that women seem more adept at self-disclosure than men (Markel, Long, and Saine, 1976; Hatfield and Rapson, 1993) and that girls and women disclose more intimate information to their friends than do boys or men (Rivenbark, 1971; Chelune, 1976; Fischer and Narus, 1981; Tannen, 1990; Bem, 1993). In addition, girls tend to have more intimate friendships than boys, and women show a higher correlation between friendship and intimate disclosures than men (Rubin and Shenker, 1978; Bell, 1981; Tannen, 1990). Furthermore, women have an easier time building "genuine, deep, loyal, noncompetitive" friendships with other women than men do with other men (Sheehy, 1981).

However, the research evidence does not uniformly support the view that there are major sex differences in self-disclosure. Rubin and his coworkers (1980), who conducted a study of 231 dating college couples, found few differences in the levels of self-disclosure that men and women made to each other. Fifty-seven percent of each sex had made full disclosure of their previous sexual experiences to their current partner, 73 percent of the men and 74 percent of the women had fully disclosed their feelings about their sexual relationship together, and 48 percent of the men and 46 percent of the women had given their partner their honest views on the future of the relationship. Although some differences were found (e.g., women revealed more about their greatest fears, their feelings toward their parents, and their feelings about their closest friends, while men revealed more about the things they were proudest of, the things they liked best about their partners, and their political views), the researchers noted that, overall, their sample of college students generally adhered to a norm of "full and equal disclosure." Other studies have also found that men confide more in their girlfriends than in anyone else (Komarovsky, 1976) and that sex differences in self-disclosure are minimal (Hacker, 1981).

Other research indicates that intimacy is somewhat easier for women than men and/or that intimacy is more rewarding to or ingrained in women. For example, lesbians are more likely to pair off in intimate relationships than gay men (Saghir and Robins, 1973; Tripp, 1975; Bell and Weinberg, 1978; Peplau and Gordon, 1982). Similarly, sex therapists have noted that fear of intimacy is relatively common in men but less frequent in women (Sager, 1977; H. S. Kaplan, 1979; Schwartz, 1983). Furthermore, men seem to want "instant intimacy" more often than women, an attitude that indicates a fundamental misperception of how intimacy actually develops.

How can we explain such differences? First, we should realize that the existing research focuses on intimacy in only a limited way, particularly emphasizing verbal self-disclosure. This approach necessarily avoids a more comprehensive view of intimacy as an ongoing experience in which time together, physical contact, and shared activities may outweigh the importance of the verbal exchanges that occur. Thus, it is possible that with more sophisticated studies, male–female intimacy differences would prove to be minor or nonexistent. However, it may be that early differences in the socialization of males and females in our society (discussed in detail in Chapter 11) account for later differences in intimacy skills. Generally, females in our culture have been socialized to show their feelings, while males have been taught to keep their feelings hidden and to show no signs of weakness or fear. [As Kate Millett (1970) succinctly put it, "Women express, men repress."] In addition, females tend to be touched more during infancy and early childhood than males (Montagu, 1977), something that might lead to later sex differences in intimacy. Similarly, the competitive, aggressive behaviors that are generally encouraged in males in our society do not, in turn, encourage intimacy, while the nurturance and sensitivity usually encouraged in females do enhance intimate behavior.

Whatever differences in intimacy preparation exist because of childhood socialization, men are certainly fully *capable* of intimacy: some of them simply seem to need a while to learn how to find it. In fact, men seem to become increasingly concerned with intimacy form age 40 on (Sheehy, 1981), although many men certainly develop a great deal of intimacy at much earlier ages. Perhaps the real dilemma of the sex differences in intimacy problem has been aptly described by Rubenstein and Shaver (1982), who point out that although "men and women need intimacy to the same degree . . . fewer women than men get their needs met, despite women's expertise, because so many men are intimacy-takers rather than givers."

Intimacy Problems

Although most people readily express a need for intimacy in their lives, it often seems to be elusive. In this section, we examine several different types of problems people have with intimacy, including common barriers to intimacy, fear of intimacy, and pseudo-intimacy.

Barriers to Intimacy

Some people seem to be able to forge close relationships easily, while others have a difficult time getting past the "social acquaintance" stage. The fortunate few who can comfortably develop closeness and rapport with others in a seemingly effortless way are a distinct minority. Most of us have to work at developing intimacy, and most of us, at one time or another, find that our intimacy overtures are ignored or rejected. Here is a list of common reasons for difficulty initiating or maintaining intimate relations.

1. *Shyness.* People whose shyness causes them to avoid social interactions or to isolate themselves in social settings are unwittingly restricting their opportunities for intimacy. Paradoxically, shy people often long for intimacy and companionship in their lives, but they seem unwilling or unable to take the risks necessary to overcome their shyness.

2. *Aggressiveness.* People who behave aggressively often scare others away or cause them to adopt a defensive posture. The typical concern seems to be "I'll be overpowered by this person," and few people look for relationships in which they'll be dominated by someone else. Toning down aggressive language and behavior can improve a person's chances for intimacy.

3. *Self-centeredness.* Being preoccupied with one's self commonly turns others off. We all know people who insist on being center-stage all the time, who ignore the needs of others (not out of malice but because of lack of awareness), who monopolize conversations, and who are generally unwilling to do what a partner wants unless it coincides with their own needs. These people frequently initiate intimacy by telling others a great deal about themselves, but they tend to have a more difficult time maintaining long-term relationships.

4. *Selfishness.* Going beyond self-centeredness, selfishness is apt to be far more damaging to the development of genuine intimacy. Selfish people are often manipulative and try to gain a tactical advantage over others to get their own way. The selfish person doesn't care much about what's best for the relationship or best for the other person; instead, he or she seeks to exert control for personal gain.

5. *Lack of empathy.* The person who is unwilling or unable to accept and understand another's views, thoughts, or feelings has a difficult time in intimate relationships. Often, these people

Source: *From "Common Errors in Times of Intimacy." First printed in* Esquire *magazine, February 1984.*

seem to have difficulty listening: either they block out what their partner says or they fail to internalize the message and look at the situation from the partner's point of view. Empathetic people do not just sympathize with the feelings and needs of others, they try to respond to these feelings and needs as well.

6. *Conflicting or unrealistic expectations.* Many people are so idealistic about intimacy that they expect the impossible, creating a situation that frequently leads to disappointment, frustration, or, possibly, to giving up. In other intimate relationships, the partners' goals may be so different that the relationship fails. For instance, if one person is looking primarily for companionship and entertainment in a friendship while the other is looking for a deeply philosophical, intellectual relationship, they are not likely to find a pleasing intimacy together.

7. *Trying to force intimacy along.* When people try too hard to share things together, to reveal their innermost feelings and thoughts, and to demonstrate tenderness toward each other in direct response to the partner's repeated requests, there is always the danger that the whole effort collapses under its own weight. When intimacy is turned into a homework assignment, to be successfully completed under the threat of getting a failing grade, it's little wonder that its spontaneity and effervesence are apt to be missing, and whatever closeness occurs may seem counterfeit or forced.

There is another sort of intimacy problem that crops up with some frequency in newly formed relationships. We call this "intimacy impatience" (Masters, Johnson, and Kolodny, 1994). Because intimacy has so much cachet these days—because it has come to be seen as the ultimate marker of authenticity, commitment, and honesty—there is an understandable push for developing intimacy sooner rather than later as a relationship is getting started. (We are not referring to sexual intimacy here, but rather intimacy in its broadest nonsexual sense.) This has a number of ramifications, including a definite tendency to end some relationships prematurely if a suitable amount of intimacy isn't forthcoming early on—without regard to how comfortable both partners are with self-disclosure, moving towards intense levels of personal vulnerability, and being willing to make an emotional commitment to the other.

Another outgrowth of intimacy impatience is the practice of "rating" your partner on some imaginary intimacy scale to judge how well he or she is measuring up to your expectations (as well as how much long-term relationship potential you can hope to discover). Just as it may not be wise to rate your partner's sexual skills too early in a relationship, for a variety of reasons, trying to judge someone's intimacy potential too quickly doesn't make allowances for important situational elements (e.g., is she just getting over the breakup of a long-term relationship with someone else), personality differences (e.g., is he proceeding cautiously because he's shy), and other variables that may have no predictive value at all for the long haul.

Needless to say, this is not a complete list of all possible barriers to intimacy. There are other conditions, such as depression, drug abuse, or severe physical illness, that may make intimacy extremely difficult even when the other ingredients seem to be in place. But it is also important to realize that intimacy is often extraordinarily resilient, making its own way in the face of unforeseen obstacles. Perhaps that's one reason why so many of us are concerned with finding and keeping intimacy in our lives.

Fear of Intimacy

Fear of intimacy is a common problem. People with such a fear are typically anxious about intimacy because of distrust, fear of rejection, and fear of losing control. In addition, many people who fear intimacy have negative self-images; they believe that they have nothing of value to bring to an intimate relationship and doubt the judgment of someone who seems interested in them because they consider themselves unworthy and uninteresting.

People who are untrusting and fear rejection sometimes avoid forming intimate relations entirely, preferring to have many superficial relationships instead of a relationship that calls for taking risks and making a commitment to someone else. These people guard themselves from hurt, but they also isolate themselves emotionally. Others enter into intimate relations but protect themselves by regulating the degree of closeness. Whenever the relationship threatens to become too intimate, they pick a fight, become distracted, or bury themselves in work; in short, they construct a buffer against the demands of the relationship and thus calm their fears by keeping the intimacy under control. Helen Kaplan notes that sometimes *both* partners in a relationship have intimacy conflicts:

> Such couples long for closeness with each other, but when they achieve a certain point of contact they become anxious. Then one or the other will behave in such a manner as to create distance. When distance reaches a certain point, anxiety and longing for closeness will be evoked in the couple. They miss each other and move closer to each other again—but not too close. Then the see-saw will move in the other direction. *(Kaplan, 1979, p. 184)*

In some cases, fear of intimacy is a life-long condition. Sometimes such a fear reflects traumatic relations with parents during early childhood; in other cases, it develops after a painful experience in an intimate relationship in which a person was not only hurt but intensely disappointed. While most of us survive the breakup of intimate relationships none the worse for wear, this isn't true in all cases—and if the emotional scars are thick enough, the fear of intimacy is most understandable.

Pseudo-Intimacy

It is possible to distinguish between genuine intimacy, which is a positive, self-enhancing process, and pseudo-intimacy, which is more pretense than openness, more manipulation than sharing. The latter form of intimacy is marked by the following features, which, while far from comprehensive, convey the key elements of pseudo-intimacy:

1. One person looks to the other to meet most or all of his or her needs rather than taking the responsibility to meet these needs.

2. There is a big gap between what is said and what is done.

3. Mutual trust is missing from the relationship or has been deliberately and repeatedly violated by one of the partners.

4. The commitment in the relationship is either one-sided or illusory.

5. One person in the relationship persistently acts in a selfish fashion and shows little interest in giving.

6. Communication is one-sided (one partner monopolizes the talking or has little to say).

7. One or both partners order each other about and criticize each other for not following these demands.

8. Conflicts and arguments consume much of the time and energy of the partners with little or no resolution of key issues typically occurring.

This doesn't mean that genuine intimacy is present only if there is perfect tranquility and affection in a relationship. Commitment to a relationship and caring about one's partner do not ensure that intimacy always produces positive, happy feelings or mutual agreement on all issues. People who are very much in love, for instance, can have moments when they hate each other just as people who feel tenderness toward each other sometimes act in cruel ways (Tennov, 1979; Stuart, 1980; L. Rubin, 1983). This variation of feelings doesn't mean that

a couple doesn't have a meaningful intimacy: it simply shows that intimate relationships are highly complex. And in the final analysis, it is exactly this complexity that gives intimacy its greatest value—the strength that bonds us together, one to one, in a unique relationship of mutual giving and getting.

COMMUNICATIONS

When you read the heading "Communications," are you aware of how many ways that one word can be interpreted? If you look in a thesaurus for synonyms, you will find terms like *relationship, friendship, intimacy, rapport, union, knowledge, data, disclosure, exchange, expression, information, news,* and *notification* among the various meanings of communications. Being aware of the complexity of communications is an important first step in learning how to become an effective communicator in real life and is also crucial to understanding how and why people may have difficulty sharing and expressing needs and emotions as they try to communicate with one another.

As we said in the introduction to this chapter, it is through effective communication that intimacy is established and can grow. Thus, understanding how to communicate effectively is a cornerstone of interpersonal and sexual relations, yet few of us are taught the skills of intimate communications. In schools we learn to write essays and term papers and sometimes even the fundamentals of public speaking or debate, but when it comes to developing intimate communication skills, we are left alone. The following discussion provides some practical, commonsense suggestions for developing your ability to communicate effectively in personal relationships. In the process, you will also become aware of gender differences in communication styles that may have hindered you in the past but that you can learn to alter to suit your personal needs within a variety of relationship contexts.

The Communication Process

Communication usually begins with the intent to convey information to someone else. The sender must convert the intent into an actual message that is presented to the intended recipient. The message

The Difficulty of Saying No

According to traditional sexual scripts, males initiate sexual behavior and females set the limits. While this pattern can lead to a perfectly enjoyable sexual encounter when both partners are interested and willing participants, there are also many times in which one partner is eager to have sex but the other isn't. What happens at these times has been virtually ignored as a topic of sex research.

To shed light on this situation, we conducted interviews with three different samples. The first group consisted of 75 couples (all in first marriages) who had been married between 5 and 20 years. The average age of the husbands in this sample was 34.2 years, while the average age of the wives was 31.7 years. The second group consisted of 75 never-married, cohabiting heterosexual couples who had been living together for at least one year. The mean age of the men in this group was 28.5, while for the women it was 27.1 years. The third group consisted of 75 heterosexual couples who were involved in a committed romantic relationship but not cohabiting. The mean ages in this group were 22.9 for males and 22.0 for females.

In each sample, we conducted interviews to find out the frequency with which unwanted sexual intercourse occurred. For the purpose of this study, unwanted intercourse was defined as a situation in which one partner had a strong preference for not participating in sex but acquiesced reluctantly to accommodate his or her partner's desire.

The results were interesting. First, the frequency of unwanted intercourse in the year preceding the interviews was highest in married couples, accounting for almost one-quarter of all coital episodes for wives and 15 percent for husbands. In the cohabiting couples, unwanted intercourse was much less frequent: for females, only 1 out of 10 sexual encounters was unwanted, while for males, the self-reported figure was 8 percent. (An intriguing footnote emerged here: among couples who had been cohabiting for four years or longer, the rates of unwanted intercourse were about double the rates of the other cohabiting couples. This suggests that the more time a couple lives together, the more sporadic sexual desire becomes.) Among dating

---

may be verbal (words, sounds) or nonverbal (consisting of a look, a touch, or an action). The recipient must not only receive the message but also understand and interpret its meanings. If you think that's easy or automatic, think again. At each one of these seemingly simple steps, things can and do go wrong. The reasons why things go wrong for many heterosexual couples—and why they go wrong so frequently—are often linked to differences in the way males and females use conversation and language and the styles in which they are comfortable communicating. While situational factors certainly influence the communication process (e.g., where you are, who you are with), our focus here is specifically on one-to-one communicating in intimate relationships.

As we discussed in Chapter 11, there are vast differences in the way males and females are socialized and acculturated. In many ways these differences are so great that talk between males and females is what linguist Deborah Tannen calls a type of cross cultural communication (Tannen, 1990). As you may recall, different styles of communicating emerge as early as the preschool years, when children's play patterns show girls tending to say "Let's" and trying to be inclusive, while boys experiment with issuing commands (see Chapter 11). These stylistic differences continue through life and can be the cause of many communication problems between males and females (Gray, 1993). The ways women speak to and with one another, such as gossiping, being apologetic, playing down

couples in our sample, unwanted intercourse was reported to occur infrequently: about 6 percent of the time for females and only 1 percent of the time for males.

The explanations given by our subjects for what conditions generally led to not wanting to participate in sex were surprisingly uniform across all three of our samples and between male and female respondents. Being tired was the primary reason cited for not wanting to have sex. This was followed (in descending order for all groups) by not feeling well physically, by being tense or preoccupied, and by being angry at one's partner. Surprisingly, very few of the people interviewed said that sexual boredom or dissatisfaction was a major reason for not wanting to make love when their partner did.

Finally, we tried to find out what prompted people to acquiesce to their partner's desire in these sorts of circumstances. What emerged was that generally when people agreed reluctantly to have sex when they didn't want to, one of three dynamics applied. Many people saw it as a form of compromise that they believed their partner would view as a "gift" or "good deed," which would in turn give them an advantage in making later choices or decisions—the "you owe me one now" philosophy or the "sex is a bargaining chip" approach. Others noted that it was usually simpler to give in than to cause a strain in their relationship or run the risk of starting a fight. In other words, sexual acquiescence was seen by these people as a means of keeping peace. A less frequent dynamic was the attitude that "I'll do it, but he/she will have to do all the work," which was usually accompanied by more resentment on giving in than the other patterns.

Two other findings from this study should be mentioned in closing. Perhaps predictably, in most situations of unwanted intercourse, the enjoyment level was low for both partners. Intriguingly, however, in about one-fifth of such encounters the person who was initially reluctant about having sex wound up getting quite turned on by the experience. This sort of "surprise" effect is undoubtedly one reason that people are willing to say yes to sex when they really want to say no.

their expertise, phrasing their ideas in terms of questions, and speaking at a relatively low volume, may make perfect sense in terms of female–female conversations (both one-on-one and in same-sex groups) but may make women appear very passive, self-deprecating, and almost powerless in conversations with men (Tannen, 1990).

Men's conversations with each other often seem to be negotiation sessions in which they try to avoid being put down or pushed around in an effort to preserve their status and independence. On the other hand, women's conversations often seem designed to foster emotional intimacy, allow the speakers to show support for one another, reach consensus, acknowledge friendship hierarchies, and avoid isolation (Tannen, 1990). Men favor direct, logical conversational styles; women have a "shifting sands" approach to discussion and don't usually follow a linear, A-to-Z approach to conversation. Given such differences, is it any wonder that a woman resents it when a man offers solutions to her problems instead of the empathy she is seeking? Many men don't realize that when their girlfriends or wives cry or describe a problem in considerable emotional detail, they are not asking the man to fix it, they are simply asking for a sympathetic listening ear.

To put it another way, men engage in "report talk" while women engage in "rapport talk" (Tannen, 1990, p. 77). This profound difference—action-oriented, linear male communications styles (sometimes bordering on lecturing) versus emotion-oriented, empathy-seeking nonlinear female communications—has been verified in a variety of couples situations (Fitzpatrick, 1988; Gottman and Krokoff, 1989; Gray, 1993).

Another difference in communications patterns involves how men and women talk with their friends about their partners. A man may not understand or tolerate it when a lover or wife shares intimate details of personal problems with one or more friends. Men tend to view such discussions as acts of disloyalty or betrayal, or see them as trivial, unnecessary gossip. In fact, men have a tendency to "hear any statement about women and men, coming from a woman, as an accusation" (Tannen, 1990, p. 14). But most women want and need to share these intimate secrets via "trouble talk" (Tannen, 1990, p. 59) not just to problem solve or gripe but as a way to cement friendships and maintain relationships.

Another important distinction between male and female communication styles has to do with recognizing and dealing with conflict. Men seem to enjoy conversational conflict and use it as a way to display power and status in a relationship. They like to interrupt and challenge each other, and these verbal habits actually enhance affiliation among men. Women, on the other hand, generally dislike open conflict and may misinterpret the friendly aggression expressed in men's words by confusing the words with the man's feelings and intentions. Just as men misinterpret the reasons behind women's gossip, women misinterpret the reasons behind men's adversarial communications styles (Notarius et al., 1989; Tannen, 1990; Sayers and Baucom, 1991; Gray, 1993). At the same time, many men see women as voicing too many demands and complaints, which can lead them to withdraw into a wall of silence and defensiveness. These differences can create self-perpetuating patterns of unhappiness within couples (Christensen and Heavey, 1990; Sayers and Baucom, 1991; Gottman, 1993).

Women who are comfortable or used to responding to other's remarks often wait for men to take the initiative in a conversation, but such women often don't get what they want or need sexually as a consequence of this communication pattern (Tannen, 1990; Hatfield and Rapson, 1993). In fact, women generally make more accommodations to men across the entire spectrum of communication, and this is usually "at the cost of their own preferences" (Tannen, 1990, p. 294). Unless you are aware of these very typical patterns that distinguish male and female speech and male and female behavior, the chances of misinterpretation on both sides of the gender continuum are great. Now let's consider some specific examples of communication glitches.

In many cases, the sender doesn't succeed in saying what he or she really means. Sometimes, for example, people can't find the right words to convey what they're feeling or what they need, so the messages they send are inaccurate. Even if the message has been accurately formulated, something may go wrong in the sending process so it's never received at all or is received in a garbled fashion. How often has someone missed the main point of your message, and after you explained yourself (perhaps with some exasperation) said, "Oh, that wasn't what I thought you said."

Next, the receiver may not be turned on and so may miss the message (i.e., a person may not be lis-

tening to what you're saying), or he might hear what he would like or expect to hear, rather than what is actually said.

Possibly the single greatest source of communication trouble, however, is in the way messages are interpreted by those who receive them.

MAN: I told you earlier this evening I didn't want to make love tonight.

WOMAN: I thought you just meant you didn't want to *then*, I didn't realize you meant for the whole night.

Although the seemingly simple act of communication can often be difficult and complex, there are steps we can take to ensure that our messages are sent as clearly as possible *and* that we are open to receiving messages as efficiently as we can. We examine these steps in the following sections.

Sending Signals Clearly

Effective communication begins with the message sent from one person to another. If an unclear message goes out, even an attentive listener is likely to be confused and forced to guess about the intended meaning. There seem to be three main reasons for this lack of clarity:

1. *Not saying what you mean.* When people aren't able to find the right words to express their feelings, they may not be fully in touch with their feelings. People may also avoid saying what they really mean so they won't hurt someone they care about, so they won't be embarrassed, or so they won't risk being rejected.

2. *Sending mixed messages.* Mixed messages carry contradictory meanings. This can happen when body language or a person's tone of voice contradicts the spoken words. For instance, if someone says, "That's lovely," but grimaces while speaking, the listener is apt to be confused. Likewise, a person who says "I am not upset" in a forced, slowly articulated voice is indicating just the opposite. Mixed messages also occur when there's an inconsistency in the content of a message, as when one part of the message negates the other: "I love it when you're rough with me, but I wish you'd be more gentle" or "I really don't want to worry you, but I think I may be pregnant" are examples of this type of problem.

3. *Not being specific.* Vague statements leave a listener frustrated and wondering "What did he/she mean?" For instance, being told, "We should really have more romance in our lives" by your partner might lead you to ask yourself: Does this mean there's something wrong with our relationship? Am I being criticized? Should I be doing something new? Is my partner unhappy? What does my partner want? A more specific statement such as "I'd love it if you would read me some love poems once in a while to help me feel romantic" wouldn't leave those loose ends.

Clarity in communications can be enhanced in a number of different ways. Here are some general suggestions to think about:

1. Think through what you want to say and how you'll say it, particularly if it's an important or emotionally charged message.

2. Let your partner know what your priorities are; try not to crowd in so many requests and instructions that it's difficult to grasp your key points.

3. Be concise. Long-winded discussions are more likely to confuse than clarify. On the other hand, being concise doesn't mean being simplistic or superficial. Don't leave out important information about your feelings or desires in order to be brief.

4. Don't talk at your partner. Give him or her a chance to respond and interact.

5. Try not to begin communications by criticizing or blaming your partner. Starting on a negative note puts your partner on the defensive and makes objective listening difficult.

6. Don't be afraid to put what you need to say in a letter if you're having trouble saying it face to face. Writing it down shows that you cared enough to take the time to say it carefully.

7. Ask for feedback from your partner to be sure you've been understood and to get his or her reactions.

Nonverbal Communications

After a lovemaking session one night, Cathy withdrew into a stubborn silence. When George asked her what was wrong, she said "Nothing at all," but the firm set of her lips and the way she rolled away to avoid his touch told George how to interpret these words—that in fact something *was* bothering her. With some patience and encouragement, George was finally able to find out what had upset Cathy. She hadn't had an orgasm, and she felt the reason was that he had stopped stroking her clitoris too soon. (*Author's files*)

As this example shows, the nonverbal side of communication is often at least as important as the words that are spoken. In fact, one psychologist suggests that of the total feeling expressed by a spoken message, only 7 percent is verbal feeling, 38 percent is vocal feeling, and 55 percent is conveyed by facial expression (Mehrabian, 1972). Posture and positioning (body language) also are powerful forms of nonverbal messages, sometimes saying "Keep away" and sometimes inviting intimacy and closeness (Fast, 1972). Sitting in a relaxed fashion sprawled out next to your partner usually conveys a sense of comfort and warmth, while sitting rigidly on the edge of your chair at a deliberate distance from your partner usually conveys a sense of withdrawal, annoyance, or preoccupation. Unspoken messages can also be powerfully transmitted by touch, which can suggest an attitude of caring and accessibility (Montagu, 1977).

It's important to recognize that inconsistencies between nonverbal cues and verbal content are usually resolved in favor of the former: in this sense, nonverbal messages are more "powerful" than spoken words alone (Stuart, 1980). For this reason it's useful to communicate in ways that maintain consistency between the verbal and nonverbal messages you send to your partner, taking care to avoid sending mixed messages by saying one thing with your words and something different with your body language or vocal tone. Thus, one way to improve the chances of communicating effectively is to be aware of your own nonverbal language—an aspect of communicating to which many people never pay attention. It also helps to actually practice ways of sending positive nonverbal messages that express trust, commitment, and caring rather than suspicion, rejection, or impatience. You can do this by yourself with the aid of a mirror or tape recorder or you can use your partner's help. Together you can discuss the nonverbal communication patterns in your relationship and see how they can be improved.

Not surprisingly, nonverbal messages apply in a special way to sexual interactions. At times, they indicate displeasure or resentment. For instance, if your partner's body tenses up whenever you stimulate the genital area with your tongue, you may begin to think that he or she is uncomfortable with this caress no matter what is said. Likewise, if your partner usually moans with passion as you make love together, the sudden absence of such sounds may make you feel like you're doing something wrong. At other times, nonverbal messages convey a sense of pleasure, involvement, warmth, or similar feelings. In addition, nonverbal communications during sex can help your partner see what you like without breaking the mood by words. And taking your partner's hand and guiding it on your body or showing your partner exactly how you'd like to be touched can be a true gift of sexual intimacy.

Although touch can be used as an effective means of nonverbal communication in a variety of ways, intimate partners often seem to talk too much and touch too little, missing many opportunities to convey feelings of tenderness or affection to each other. In many situations, a long, tight hug says more about the way people feel about each other than a ten-minute dialogue. Likewise, stroking a partner's hair or face, or leisurely kissing, or performing a sensual massage can convey a sense of caring and pleasure that goes beyond words. On the other hand, if people confine their touching to sexual situations, they compartmentalize the physical side of their interaction, sometimes making sex seem like a bartered commodity used to attain closeness.

Vulnerability and Trust

Communicating in an intimate relationship differs in certain ways from communicating with other people in your life. This is partly because partners in a truly committed, intimate relationship can make the very basic assumption that neither one of them deliberately intends to hurt the other, an assumption that can't always be made in our dealings with the rest of the world. While this doesn't mean that emotional hurts will never occur, it does provide a safety net of trust and support that allows each person to become uniquely vulnerable in an intimate, caring relationship.

The willingness to risk being vulnerable, which is at the essential core of intimacy, and the trust that makes it possible encourage people to say

Body language and facial expressions are important parts of the communication process.

what they're feeling or thinking. They feel free to reveal things about themselves—including fears, shortcomings, and failures—without worrying that this information will be used against them at any time. Thus, while trust and vulnerability are not methods of communication, they are necessary preconditions for intimate communications to occur.

"I" Language

One of the most direct ways to communicate clearly and to avoid mind-reading games in a relationship is to use a highly effective style of communicating called "I" language. The basic premise of this approach is that a person should take responsibility for himself or herself, since no one knows better than the individual what he or she is feeling or needs at any given moment. By beginning as many statements as possible with the pronoun "I," a person takes responsibility for his or her self-expression. "I" sentences tell what you feel, what you need, or what you want. "I'd love it if we could cuddle and kiss," "I'm feeling restless now," or "I wish we could spend more time talking to each other" are examples of "I" language. To some people, "I" language sounds selfish because we're taught from an early age that it's not polite to talk about ourselves excessively. Intimacy, however, requires that a person open up and express his or her feelings without beating around the bush.

In contrast, sentences that begin with "you" are apt to be demanding or accusatory, provoking defensiveness in the other person: "You don't kiss me much anymore" or "You don't spend enough time

talking to me" have a very different tone from that of the "I" messages previously listed.

"We" sentences are potentially problematical because they compel one person to speak for both. This requires that the person make assumptions or guesses about his or her partner's moods, preferences, and needs—and while a charming sense of togetherness may result when the "we" assumptions prove accurate, on many occasions they are actually annoyingly off target. "We" messages can also encourage imbalanced communications: one partner may monopolize the talking by speaking for both almost all the time. In this situation, the less assertive partner won't say much of anything and is liable to submerge his or her requirements beneath the flood of directives from the outspoken partner. Such lopsided communication is not conducive to close, intimate relations.

"I" language, then, provides an excellent means for one partner to put his or her emotional cards on the table in intimate dialogues instead of coyly fencing around. This openness, in turn, invites the other person to speak openly as well. Consider the following contrast in styles and content:

Without "I" Language

EILEEN: What do you want to do tonight?

JOHN: Oh, I don't know. What would you like to do?

EILEEN: Well, I wanted to do something we'd both enjoy.

JOHN: Don't you have any ideas? (The conversation is apt to continue in this wheel-spinning mode for a while, since Eileen and John are trying not to pressure or offend each other by making the first suggestion.)

With "I" Language

EILEEN: I'm feeling a bit lazy tonight, so I'd like to stay home and relax.

JOHN: I was kind of looking forward to getting out—I thought maybe we'd go dancing.

EILEEN: I don't think I'd really enjoy that the way I'm feeling. I'm just too tired to handle that right now.

JOHN: Well, there's a ballgame on TV I can watch, so maybe we'll get out this weekend.

If John and Eileen hadn't agreed on what to do, "I" language could be used to reach a negotiated solution that would be mutually satisfactory. Here's an example of how it might be achieved:

EILEEN: I really wasn't planning to go out tonight; I was hoping to stay in and take it easy. Would that bother you?

JOHN: Well, I don't have my mind set on dancing, but I certainly wanted to get out and do *something*.

EILEEN: I guess I can handle something that doesn't involve exerting much energy. How about a movie? How does that sound to you?

JOHN: Oh, that'd be great. I wanted to see that new Woody Allen flick and we could catch the nine o'clock show.

EILEEN: That's fine with me. I'll take a nap if you make dinner, and then we can get going.

JOHN: Sounds good to me. I'll wake you up in a half hour, okay?

When a satisfactory compromise can't be found via this sort of negotiation, the next step is for both partners to examine the relative strength of their different needs. Some couples find that this is easiest if each person rates the intensity of his or her needs on a quantitative scale (for instance, using a scale from −10 to +10, where 0 represents a neutral feeling). Other couples compare their needs by discussion that doesn't involve exact quantification. In either case, the basic premise of such negotiations is that it will usually be in the best interests of the relationship to go in the direction of the person whose need is greatest, as long as the other person isn't hurt by this process. It is also possible to negotiate so that each partner does something separately from the other; being in an intimate relationship doesn't mean always doing things together.

A word of caution about "I" language: phony "I" sentences, such as ones that begin "I think that you. . ." or "I feel that you. . .," are really just "you" sentences camouflaged by the addition of the "I think" or "I feel." These should be avoided since it's not the grammatical construction of the sentence that's the key; the essence of "I" language is to speak for yourself without accusing or blaming.

The most complete, functional "I" messages should not simply announce what or how you're feeling (especially if it's negative) but should go on to say what you think you need to try to maintain (or change) the feeling. This prevents your partner from the often frustrating task of having to conjure up a remedy for whatever ails you. In sexual situations, this principle is particularly true. Instead of

saying, "I don't like it when you dive for my crotch," you might rephrase the message to say, "I really get uncomfortable when I feel sex is rushed and hurried, but a slow leisurely tempo turns me on." This type of communication avoids the trap of sending half a message—what you *don't* like—by completing the message and saying what you'd prefer. Here again, by assuming responsibility for stating your own needs and preferences, you relieve your partner of having to figure out what will please you.

It is also important to realize that "I" language is not the only way of communicating effectively in an intimate relationship. In fact, since intimacy generally produces a sense of thinking about a partnership as "we" or "us" rather than simply "you" and "me" (Hatfield, 1982), there is nothing wrong with using language that emphasizes this viewpoint. Similarly, "you" sentences that offer positive rather than critical content—for example, "You're so kind and sensitive"—are certainly welcome in any relationship. Thus, "I" language should be seen as a potential way of achieving clarity in intimate communication instead of as the only correct way of communicating with your partner.

Expressing Affection

While it might seem that expressing affection in an intimate relationship ought to be the easiest thing in the world, marriage counselors and sex therapists frequently find that even loving couples often neglect this side of their relationship. Although affection is expressed in actions more meaningfully than words, never hearing words of affection can be troubling and can lead people to question whether their partners really care for them.

I know deep inside me that she really loves me, but she never says it anymore. I feel a little stupid about it, because I can't exactly say to her, "Laura, please tell me you love me"—then I wouldn't be sure if she really meant it or if she was just saying it to make me happy. (*Authors' files*)

Similarly, when affection is expressed only during sex, and not at any other time, it can lead a person to feel as though it's a limited or conditional affection—in other words, "I love having sex with you" rather than "I love you."

Some couples find creative ways of expressing their feelings for each other. These can be as varied as a note stuck inside a jacket pocket, a poem written by one person for the other, or a quick telephone call that says, "I just wanted to say how crazy I am about you." Whatever style is chosen, being sure that your intimate partner knows of your affection (as long as it's real) is an important key to the durablity of any relationship.

Responding to Criticism

Few people like to be criticized, although some forms of criticism (from a teacher, a coach, or a friend) fall into the category of constructive criticism—advice motivated by a real desire to be helpful and informed by useful, positive suggestions for change. Because unsolicited criticism usually elicits an almost automatic negative reaction, it often provokes almost automatic responses even between lovers (or would-be lovers). The problem is, many of these knee-jerk response styles are notoriously ineffective in dealing with criticism and often backfire by unintentionally leading to an escalation of critical comments in reply to the defensive comebacks people use.

Here are three examples of particularly ineffective ways of dealing with criticism.

1. *The aggressive reply.* This is the "chip-on-your-shoulder" approach to communications. If your lover says "Do you really need that second piece of cake?" (with its implied criticism of your weight and self-control), the aggressive reply is to swing back at them. "Well, at least I don't need to diet as badly as you do." Lashing out at criticism when it comes from people who are very close to you is ineffective for several reasons. First, it disregards the merits of the criticism entirely since it operates on the automatic assumption the criticism is undeserved or wrong. Second, it invites retaliation. Your partner or friend is prodded into parrying your aggressive response with his or her counterattack, which will probably prod you into escalating the arguing still further. Third, if you characteristically deal with criticism this way, it not only puts people off but also actively pushes people away from you.

2. *The passive reply:* Some people think it's easiest to deal with criticism by avoiding a fight at any cost. Their answer to any critical comment is likely to be along the lines of, "Yes, you're right. That is a problem I need to deal with" or "Geez, I didn't realize I was doing that. I'll try

to watch out for that from now on." Although apologies or promises to change can be a good way of avoiding fights in the short run, over the longer term these ways of reacting to criticism are problematic. For one thing, if you're always passive about criticism, you devalue yourself in your partner's eyes and you almost automatically invite your partner to come at you again . . . and again . . . and again in order to provoke a response. Another problem is that such passivity leads to a power imbalance in any intimate relationship. The person who is continually the criticizer becomes "top dog"; the passive respondent (or nonrespondent, because silence is one form of passive response) becomes the "designated loser." This almost inevitably dooms a budding romance to unhappiness even though the couple may stay together for a long time.

3. *The passive–aggressive pattern.* The hallmark of this response style is for the person being criticized to react passively at first and then to land a zinger in retaliation later on. This "duck now, fight back later" pattern is especially dangerous because it undermines the trust in a relationship and leads to anxious anticipation of when the person with the simmering resentment will try to get even. A variation of this flip-flop response pattern is the *aggressive–passive reaction* in which the initial reply to the criticism is of the "Oh, yeah? What of it?" ("Do you want to start a fight?") variety, with a delayed passive secondary component of profuse apology, admissions of error, or promises to try to overcome the fault or flaw. In either version, there is a barrier to the free flow of communication and an element of uncertainty as to which is the genuine response. Often, both the passive and aggressive components of the response to criticism become annoying and counterproductive.

Fortunately, there are more effective ways of meeting criticism directly and honestly. The underlying principle, of course, is to fit the type of response you use to the validity of the critic's premise. A corollary point is to remember who has provided the criticism: just because a bit of criticism hurts, it doesn't mean it was intended that way. Keeping these hints in mind, here are four different ways to deal with criticism effectively when it comes your way, even if it is totally unanticipated and unwanted:

1. *Agree with the criticism if it's valid.* Simpler said than done, you might think, and that is certainly true. But if the criticism is on target, saying so can disarm your critic and create an opportunity for exchanging feelings on the matter. For example, "I know I haven't been paying as much attention to you as you'd like" is a good opening, but it needs some follow-up discussion. Make a concrete suggestion or two for ways to rectify the situation and ask how your partner feels about your proposed solutions; he or she will appreciate your acceptance of the situation and your willingness to correct it.

2. *If the criticism is off target, explain why in a nondefensive manner.* Not all critical statements are accurate. Some are a result of misperception, or not having all the facts. Many of the "If you were only more like John (or Sally). . . " criticisms fall into this category. (Comparative criticisms can be especially irksome.) One effective reply might be, "Well, I know John pretty well, and while it might seem that he's always reliable, the fact is that he treats his girlfriends like dirt." Similarly, if your lover criticizes you for being late for a dinner date, you might explain, "I know that I'm late, but the reason was I got a flat and it took me a half hour to fix it."

3. *Deal with most criticism as a matter of perception, not a fact.* Many criticisms fall into the gray zone of not being completely accurate, but not being totally erroneous, either. Here, you can acknowledge the part that's valid while explaining why it isn't fully so. Consider this exchange: "Gosh, your room is such a mess. You really are a slob." "I know my room looks like a combat zone, but the reason is I had three friends sleeping here this weekend on their way to California and I haven't had a chance to clean up yet." A point to keep in mind here is that if you reserve your detailed explanations and rebuttals for the more important criticisms that come your way, rather than the trivial ones, you are less likely to be regarded by others as being unduly defensive or argumentative. After all, everyone is entitled to their own opinion, and you don't have to agree wholeheartedly with your critic even if you don't choose to make a big deal out of it.

4. *Understand how tact and diplomacy can help you deal with criticism without having to get into a fight.* Here is one example. Even when someone's criticism doesn't exactly fit, you can acknowledge the criticism without fully agreeing with it (although you may keep your disagreement to yourself). Another way to handle criticism diplomatically is to agree with it in part, but not entirely. Yet another possibility is to conditionally acknowledge the point being made without accepting it as completely applicable to you. "Yes, I agree that laziness is an unattractive trait" doesn't have to mean that you admit that *you* are lazy.

One last point to keep in mind about dealing with criticism is to reply in "I" sentences whenever possible. This provides the best chance for preventing one critical comment from escalating into a barrage of back-and-forth barbs and accusations.

Expressing Anger

Anger at its raging peak is almost certain to distort communications, and it makes any real dialogue quite difficult. Postponing serious discussions about the source of your anger and its possible solutions until you have simmered down is usually a wise thing to do if at all possible. If not, it's best for both partners to recognize that much of what is said in anger may be regretted later on, since it may not be meant (it may be said just to hurt).

We believe it is important to recognize that anger is usually not a primary emotion. In most cases anger develops from preceding feelings of hurt, resentment, or frustration. If these can be identified and discussed while they're in their early stages, *before* they grow into anger, there is a much better chance of dealing with them successfully and avoiding the harm that anger can produce. However, when anger does occur, it is often better to release it quickly, in small doses, and in appropriate ways than to let it simmer in continuing resentment and hostility until it boils over and explodes. As social psychologist Carol Tavris points out, "Couples who are not defeated by rage and the conflicts that cause it know two things: when to keep quiet about trivial angers, for sake of civility, and how to argue about important ones, for the sake of personal autonomy and growth" (1982, pp. 222–223).

Some authorities believe that an outburst of anger can help people discharge pent-up tensions and can "clear the decks" to allow for a return to a relative state of emotional equilibrium (Bach and Wyden, 1968; T. I. Rubin, 1970; Bry, 1977). Others have concluded that anger is generally "constructively motivated" (not intended to hurt someone, but to bring about a change) and have conducted research showing that anger is usually beneficial to both the person expressing the anger and the person who is its target (Averill, 1982). Thus, it is important to realize that getting angry with your partner occasionally is certainly no sign that your relationship is doomed. As Carol Tavris observes: "In the final analysis, managing anger depends on taking responsibility for one's emotions and one's actions: on refusing the temptation, for instance, to remain stuck in blame or fury or silent resentment" (1982, p. 226).

The Art of Listening

Many people have the mistaken notion that being a good listener simply means sitting back in a chair and keeping your mouth closed. But the ability to listen accurately and empathetically is actually a complex process. Here are some specific pointers about what it takes to be an effective listener:

1. *Effective listening requires your undivided attention.* Trying to listen while you're doing something else, like watching TV or reading, tells your partner that you don't think that what he or she has to say is very important. In addition, listening with "half an ear" increases the chance that you'll miss a detail or nuance of your partner's message (verbal or nonverbal) that may be crucial to its overall meaning.

2. *Effective listening is an active rather than passive process.* The best listeners show the speaker that they are involved in the communication process even though they are temporarily silent. This can be done by eye contact, nodding your head, or asking an occasional question to clarify a point without disrupting your partner's message.

3. *Effective listeners are patient in their listening style.* People don't always plunge right in to intimate discussions without first establishing that their partner is receptive and willing to talk. If they feel rushed, they'll either skip the conversation entirely (and probably feel angry about your inaccessibility) or be forced to convey their message in a choppy, incomplete version. The patient listener realizes that a bit of encouragement early in a conversation can set the stage for a more meaningful dialogue later on. At the same time, patient listeners refrain from the temptation to barge in with their own comments before the other person has completed his or her message.

4. *Effective listeners avoid putting undue emphasis on one word or phrase in a message and wait for the message to be completed before they react to it.* This is particularly true in sexual matters, where many key words (such as "orgasm" or "satisfaction") can trigger an emotional response. One man became so agitated and annoyed when his wife mentioned the frequency of their sexual relations that he missed her actual message—that she was enjoying sex now more than ever before—as he mentally rushed to defend himself from criticism.

5. *Effective listeners pay attention to what the speaker is actually saying instead of approaching conversations with preconceived notions of what might be said.*

6. *Effective listeners are attuned to their partners even when there's been no request for a discussion.* Sometimes the most important communications occur in odd, offhand moments rather than in planned, formal dialogues. Unless you're tuned in to this possibility and receptive to what is being said, you seriously cut down the chances of spontaneous communications, which are often the most valuable.

7. *You don't have to agree in order to listen—in fact, it can be useful to disagree.* The point of being a good listener is to understand what the speaker is saying; this doesn't mean that you have to endorse the message. Recognize that your partner is expressing his or her feelings, which may be very different from your own.

In addition to these points, it is also a good idea to realize that the listener's role is not a totally silent one. Most often, intimate communications invite some form of dialogue, with the listener making some acknowledgment of having heard the message, checking out any areas of uncertainty by asking for further clarification, and paraphrasing the overall gist of the message to be sure it has been correctly understood. The following exchange at the end of a longer conversation illustrates how this might be done:

DAN: I hear your concern about our sex life. I don't know quite what to say right now—it's taken me by surprise.

JANE: That's okay, I just want you to think about it a while, not to have an answer tonight.

DAN: Is the major thing that's bothering you that sex has gotten too mechanical for us?

JANE: Well, that's part of it, but I'm also getting a little bored.

DAN: So you want us both to think about how we can get more creativity and tenderness in our sex?

JANE: That's it exactly.

Notice, in this dialogue, that when Dan checks out Jane's meaning and then paraphrases her earlier comments, he doesn't use "I" language. Dan isn't talking about himself here; instead, since he's trying to clarify Jane's "I" messages, he uses sentences that are focused on her rather than himself. Part of the art of listening is deciding when to listen and when to respond.

Talking About Sex

Although communicating about sex doesn't always involve words, letting a partner know what is important or pleasing to us sexually often requires verbal statements. Yet many people are particularly hesitant when it comes to talking about sex, perhaps because of embarrassment, fear of rejection, or concern that talking about it will cause sexual spontaneity to disappear.

As children, most of us were discouraged from saying much about sex and many never learned the terminology to describe their sexual anatomy. So, part of the hesitancy people have in talking about sex with a partner is actually a carryover from these childhood taboos.

Our difficulties in talking about sex with even an intimate partner also are related to the sexual scripts our society has written, particularly the one that casts the male as the sexual expert and the female as the passive, naive participant.

I'd been dating Larry for three or four months when I finally decided that I had to talk to him about sex. I just wasn't enjoying his style, which was much too fast and rough for me. But every time I tried to bring up the topic, my vocal cords seemed to freeze and I backed off. Finally, I wrote him a letter that broke the ice, and we worked it out pretty easily. (Authors' files)

Nancy and I were having some problems with our sex life about a year after we got married, but I somehow couldn't bring myself to say anything to her about it. I figured that I was supposed to know what was wrong and how to fix it because I was the male—and because I was more experienced. It took us three years before we saw somebody who helped us straighten things out. (Authors' files)

Many couples have difficulty talking about sex (Sarrel and Sarrel, 1979; Barbach, 1982), so it's not surprising that people frequently put up with awkward or frustrating sexual patterns or don't openly express their desires. Yet talking about sex, like any other form of communication, can be facilitated by some thought and practice. Here are some pointers that may prove useful:

1. *Talk with your partner about how and when it would be most comfortable to discuss sex.* You may be surprised to find that your partner is also hesitant about sexual discussions and that simply bringing the topic out in the open provides you both with a good opportunity for defusing tensions. You may also be able to determine when it will be easiest to talk about sex. Some people prefer avoiding the "instant replay" analysis right after making love, but others feel this is the perfect time for talking since events and feelings are fresh in their minds. Whatever you decide about this, the important thing is to let your partner know that you're interested in feedback about your sexual interaction. Armed with this knowledge, your partner won't be worried that you'll react to anything that's said as though it was a criticism.

2. *Consider the possibility of using books or other media sources to initiate discussions.* This approach allows partners to discuss what they've read or seen and relate it to their personal preferences or dislikes. The advantage is that the discussion is more abstract—in effect, a discussion of sexual ideas as much as sexual action—and thus doesn't sound so much like "When you touched me here I didn't feel good." The disadvantages are that the books you read may

not fit your own styles and needs and that some of the suggestions you read about may be offensive or uncomfortable.

3. *Use "I" language as much as possible when talking about sex together, and try to avoid putting blame on your partner for your own patterns of response (or lack thereof).*

4. *Remember that if your partner rejects a type of sexual activity that you think you might enjoy, he or she is not rejecting you as a person.*

5. *Be aware that sexual feelings and preferences change from time to time.* It's very tempting, on hearing that your partner likes to have his or her earlobe licked, to do this automatically every time you make love. That way, you might think, you can't be accused of forgetting. The problem is that doing the same things over and over tends to get boring and sometimes becomes downright unpleasant. The other side of this coin is that a partner who doesn't generally like a particular form of sexual stimulation, such as oral sex, may develop a yen for that activity on a given occasion. Be flexible in translating your talks about sex into action; be prepared to change when necessary or advisable.

6. *Don't neglect the nonverbal side of sexual communications, since these messages often speak louder than words.* Don't be afraid of showing your partner just how you like to be touched: with firm or feathery stroking, with vigorous or slow rubbing, with alternating intensity to the touch, or with a consistent pattern held for some time. Since it's often difficult to express your precise preferences in words, put your hand on your partner's and demonstrate. Not only is this a perfect "I" message, it also relieves your partner of the need to guess at what you like.

7. *Don't expect perfection.* Intimate relations can stumble if partners expect that sex should always be a memorable, passionate experience. Realize that just as your mood can change, or your physical feelings ebb and flow, so too can sexual experiences range from ecstatic peaks to fizzled-out fiascos. It isn't necessary to analyze what went wrong whenever sex wasn't superlative; instead, it's useful to talk with your partner to be sure that you both have realistic expectations about sex rather than impossible

dreams that can only lead to disappointment.

It's important to realize that talking about sex with your partner isn't something to do once and then put aside. Like all forms of intimate communications, this topic benefits from an ongoing dialogue that permits a couple to learn about each other and resolve confusions or uncertainties over time.

If your partner doesn't communicate very openly about your sexual interaction, and you've tried to draw him or her into discussions a number of times only to be shut out, you need to examine your options. If you are generally happy with your sex life together, there may not be a pressing reason to talk about sex. As long as you feel that you can make your needs known, respecting your partner's silence on the subject can be the wisest course. If, on the other hand, your sex life is unsatisfactory (whatever the reason), attempting a candid conversation by stating your feelings and concerns and asking your partner to respond in kind certainly seems in order. Some couples find that a visit to a sex therapist or counselor is helpful if talking about sex together is difficult; the therapist or counselor may be able to pinpoint the source of reluctance for such discussions and suggest ways of solving this type of problem.

SUMMARY

1. Intimacy is an ongoing process in which two caring people share as freely as possible in the exchange of their feelings, thoughts, experiences, and actions in an atmosphere of mutual acceptance, commitment, and trust.

2. Developing intimate relationships with others is easier if a person first has a reasonable degree of self-knowledge and self-acceptance. (However, intimate relationships can also help people gain insights into themselves.)

3. In general, people disclose more of themselves to others as the intimacy of their relationship increases. However, too much self-disclosure or self-disclosure offered too fast can sometimes scare people away from a relationship rather than enhance intimacy.

4. The evidence available today (which may be limited somewhat by how we evaluate intimacy) generally shows that females are more

comfortable and accomplished in intimacy skills than males. However, there doesn't seem to be any difference between the sexes in the need for intimacy.

5. Intimacy can be difficult to attain because of certain types of barriers, including shyness, aggressiveness, self-centeredness, selfishness, lack of empathy, or unrealistic intimacy expectations. Fear of intimacy is another common problem in which people have difficulties forming intimate relationships entirely or need to set limits on the closeness that develops in an intimate relationship. This condition is often related to distrust of others, fear of rejection, or fear of not being in control.

6. Pseudo-intimacy masquerades as the real thing but is closely marked by manipulation, dependency, lack of commitment, deceit, or other negative elements that prevent the relationship from being satisfying to both partners.

7. Communication is essential to the development and maintenance of intimacy. Effective communication requires that a clear message be sent and accurately received. Communication includes both verbal (words) and nonverbal (touch, body language) messages.

8. Ambiguity in communications commonly arises because of not saying what you mean, sending mixed messages, and not being specific. Unclear or ambiguous messages force the listener to guess what is meant, and they often lead to erroneous conclusions.

9. Nonverbal messages such as voice inflections, facial expressions, body language, and posture are particularly powerful forms of communication. When there is an inconsistency between the spoken word and the nonverbal messages that accompany it, people typically give more weight to the nonverbal clues and discount the spoken message.

10. Communicating in intimate relationships is best done as a form of self-expression and self-responsibility. Starting sentences with the word "I" can help the communicator in keeping this focus and avoiding the pitfalls of "you" sentences, which tend to be blaming or accusatory, and "we" sentences, which are often incorrect in their content and assumptions.

11. A much-neglected aspect of intimacy is the need to express affection on a regular basis to your partner. Not hearing affection expressed can lead some people to feel that they're taken for granted, or even unloved, and can undermine the solidity of a relationship.

12. Anger is an emotion that usually grows out of hurt or resentment. While it's sometimes useful to get anger out in the open, it's often even better to prevent it from occurring by recognizing and doing something about the things that lead to the early stages of resentment or hurt. Anger generally distorts communications.

13. Being an effective listener (a large part of effective communication) depends on several different things, including giving the speaker your undivided attention, being patient, not taking something out of context, and being receptive. It isn't necessary to agree with your partner to listen effectively, but your role as a listener can be enhanced by giving feedback to your partner, checking out anything you're uncertain about, and using paraphrasing to be certain you've understood correctly.

14. While talking about sex isn't inherently different from other kinds of intimate communications, many people have a difficult time in this area because of taboos carried over from childhood, embarrassment, or other concerns. Couples in intimate relations should try to talk openly and honestly with each other about sex using whatever approaches they are most comfortable with. Through talking and nonverbal messages, couples can learn to enhance their sexual communications, which will often enhance their sexual intimacy.

Thought Questions

1. In your opinion, are there major differences in the nature of intimacy in sexual as opposed to nonsexual relationships? That is, is it easier to be intimate with a friend, rather than a lover? Or the other way around? Does the stage the love relationship is in make a difference? Explain.

2. The text states that reliable data regarding whether men and women have different levels or types of motivations for intimacy do not exist. However, in your opinion, do such differences exist? Explain.

3. If a person with high needs for verbal intimacy is in love with or married to a person who does not easily express his or her feelings verbally,

what could be done about it? Should anything be done about it?

4. Is it as easy (or as difficult) to give negative feedback to one's lover as it is to give positive feedback? Why? Would you as the lover appreciate your partner's telling you something about having sex with you that was negative or uncomplimentary? Why or why not?

5. How much of your past should a new partner know? Is it ever okay to keep important aspects of your sexuality a secret from a partner with whom you want to develop an intimate relationship? Or is honesty always the best policy?

6. The text advises you not to expect perfect intimacy in your intimate relationships. However, how should you respond if a person with whom you thought you had an intimate relationship betrays your trust? Is this to be expected once in a while and taken in stride? Or would behaving in a dishonest manner, by definition, indicate that the relationship is not truly intimate?

Suggested Readings

Branden, Nathaniel. *If You Could Hear What I Cannot Say.* New York: Bantam Books, 1983. A self-help book that uses sentence-completion techniques to help examine many of the principles of intimate communication.

Fisher, Martin, and Stricker, George, eds. *Intimacy.* New York: Plenum Press, 1982. A rich collection of papers on the nature of intimacy from a remarkably multidisciplinary group of contributors. Highly recommended reading.

Gray, John. *Men Are From Mars, Women Are From Venus.* New York: HarperCollins, 1993. An examination of why men and women seem to speak different languages when it comes to interacting in couples. Not as pithy and insightful as Deborah Tannen's book (see below), but interesting, thought-provoking reading.

O'Connor, Dagmar. *How to Put the Love Back into Making Love.* New York: Doubleday, 1989. A balanced, down-to-earth guide to keeping intimacy alive in a sexual relationship. The first part of the book deals with problems that interfere with intimacy, while the second part deals mainly with fostering sensuality in an intimate relationship.

Rubenstein, Carin, and Shaver, Philip. *In Search of Intimacy.* New York: Random House, 1982. A thought-provoking look at intimacy and loneliness based on extensive survey research. Well-written, nontechnical, and insightful.

Rubin, Lillian. *Intimate Strangers: Men and Women Together.* New York: Harper & Row, 1983. A clearly written, insightful look at the relations between men and women, including much material on intimacy and communications.

Tannen, Deborah. *You Just Don't Understand: Women and Men in Conversation.* New York: William Morrow, 1990. An absolutely superb book about male-female differences in communications and the impasses these differences commonly cause. If you only have time to read one book about communications, make it this one!

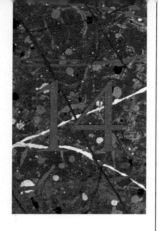

Enhancing Your Sexual Relationships

While learning about the latest research on human sexuality or various theories of sexual behavior can be enlightening, it sometimes has very limited applicability to your own life. This chapter presents practical information that addresses common problems and concerns people have about their sexuality and sexual satisfaction in their intimate relationships. If you are having problems in your relationships that are related to sex, or if you simply want to improve the sexual part of your life, there are a variety of positive steps you can take on your own to produce change.

The material in this chapter will not make you irresistable or help you find and win over a new sex partner, but it *can* help you enhance the quality of an existing sexual relationship.

DIFFERENCES IN SEXUAL DESIRE

There is a wonderful scene in Woody Allen's film *Annie Hall* in which the camera shows Woody in his psychiatrist's office while simultaneously showing his lover (Diane Keaton) in session with her psychiatrist. Both are being asked by their doctors how often they make love together.

"Hardly ever," Woody says plaintively, "maybe three times a week."

"Constantly," Diane intones, "I'd say three times a week."

In real life, actual disorders of low sexual desire are not as common as they are in sex therapy clinics. Yet, as the dialogue above shows, more couples complain about differences in sexual needs and desires than any other single category of sexual problem. On hearing this, you might wonder how such mismatched people ever got together in the first place.

The answer isn't all that complicated. When two people first become seriously attracted to each other—whether they're dating, living together, or have just gotten married—they seem to have remarkably similar appetites for sex. This is partly because people with major discrepancies in sexual desire work selectively in the courtship process to weed out mismatches, and partly because, in the early stages of a relationship, both parties are trying their best to be sensitive to their partners' needs and to be romantic, sensual, and sexy. Once this initial halo effect wears off, once the newness and excitement of sex begin to tarnish and the wish to accommodate a partner gives way to thinking about oneself (or the children) first, sex not only becomes more routine but also frequently becomes less rewarding and, for some people, more of a job. As a result of any or all of these factors, the couple's frequency of sex decreases.

When they finally reach a new steady state of sexual relations, it is possible that it will be entirely satisfactory to both partners. But for millions of couples, the new rate of sexual activity leaves one partner feeling deprived, while the other often feels put upon and even overwhelmed by the perceived voraciousness of the opposite's sexual needs. Furthermore, the dilemma often worsens because the person who feels sexually deprived typically experiences an artificial exaggeration of libido (i.e., their sexual appetite gets bigger because they feel deprived) so that it often sounds as if he or she is preoccupied with sexual thoughts and feelings. This preoccupation can have a markedly negative effect on the person whose sexual appetite is lower, because this low-appetite persons feels the partner has insatiable sexual demands.

Just as the less-interested person is convinced that his or her partner thinks about sex all the time, the more highly sexed person is convinced that the other never thinks about sex at all. Even worse, the sexually deprived person begins to feel that his or her partner is deliberately avoiding sex to torment him or her. Because he thinks about sex as often as he does (just as a starving man thinks and dreams about food), he cannot conceive of the possibility that she isn't thinking about sex, too. So when he wakes up and showers and has a little time before breakfast, he already has sex on his mind and is puzzled and upset when she isn't interested because she's busy getting dressed for work. When he calls her at her office to say he'll be home early, he has sex on his mind, whereas she hears the possibility of an early dinner and a night out at the movies. No wonder, then, that he is angered when she isn't ready to jump into bed as soon as he walks in the door at 6:00 p.m.—he's been thinking about how nice it would be if they just made love, while she's tired or preoccupied and just wants a quick dinner and a relaxing night at the movies.

As the differences in sexual desire become more problematic, the normal give-and-take with which two people make ordinary decisions ("Would you like to rent a movie tonight?" "Can we go out with the Hammonds for dinner?") becomes twisted by intense scrutiny of motivations: for instance, when she's deeply involved in reading a novel, and says, "Not now, I'm really interested in this book," he takes it as a personal rejection and replies, "Oh yeah? Well, how come you're never that interested in sex or me anymore?" The implication is, "What's wrong with you?" "Maybe tomorrow," she says hopefully. He hears this as just another put-off and resolves to get back at her for her insensitivity to his needs.

In all probability, neither person in the above example intends to hurt the other. Neither one is likely to see things from the other's point of view either. If they did (or could) the odds are that the problem would get resolved. Even though long-term relationship problems like this become so deeply ingrained that it feels like you're stuck inside a continually revolving door, the basic approach we take is to point out to people that if you just stop the door from revolving, it's easy to get out. And, to continue the revolving door metaphor, if the people trapped inside stop pushing, the door stops revolving.

Practical Pointers for Dealing with Differences in Sexual Desire

As the above examples show, when one partner wants sex more than the other on a regular basis, severe tensions are created within the relationship.

Here are some suggestions for improving the situation without having to resort to therapy:

1. *Communicate clearly.* We are amazed at how often this simple edict is ignored by so many people. More often than most couples realize, missed communications (or muddled communications) contribute greatly to the sexual stalemates that occur in their lives. Consider the case of Betty M., an attractive 37-year-old realtor married to Bill, a district sales manager for a well-known national corporation. When she wanted sex, she went through a particular ritual: taking a bubble bath, shaving her legs, and putting on what she thought was her sexiest nightgown. The trouble was that Bill often didn't respond to her overtures, leaving her feeling rejected, neglected, and incredibly crabby. After many sessions of marriage counseling, it became clear that Bill had no idea of what she was doing in the bathroom and really never noticed what nightgown she was wearing. ("They all sort of look the same to me," Bill said.) What she had interpreted as lack of interest on his part was, instead, more a case of being unaware of her sexual signals. "If you'd just tell me when you want to make love, there'd be a lot less confusion," said Bill. Once the communication problem was identified and cleared up, the frequency of their lovemaking picked up to a satisfactory level for Betty.

It's not always this simple, of course. For some people, a direct invitation to have sex makes it somehow less romantic and spontaneous. But this aspect can often be handled by developing a useful code language to transmit clearly one party's sexual interest without making it sound like a request to pass the salt. Because the code language needs to be agreed on in advance, a couple must sit down together, discuss the possibilities and decide things such as how the "invited" party can clearly turn down a sexual invitation. For example, one couple used a musical metaphor for their erotic invitations: "Do you want to go dancing tonight?" became their code phrase for bedroom activities. Another couple coded their sexual interest in the question "Can I read you some poetry?" If you pursue this path to easier communication of sexual desires, be sure to pick a code that both partners agree on and that is not likely to cause you to burst out laughing. "How would you like to wrestle tonight?" or "How about a tiptoe through the tulips?" just might set the wrong tone for many couples.

2. *Differentiate between an invitation and a demand.* With a few exceptions more in the realm of sex fantasies than reality, no one really likes to be pushed into something. When it comes to sexual interactions, it is almost always true that making demands on a partner is likely to be a turn-off: the partner of whom something is demanded (rather than requested) usually feels hassled, becomes stubborn and uncooperative, and is unlikely to respond with passion or even a nonpassionate, lukewarm compliance. Most people realize this tendency and avoid making sexual demands as demands; instead, they bargain, beg, or sweet-talk to get their partner's cooperation.

In couples with a major discrepancy in levels of sexual desire, though, this natural interaction is thrown out of kilter for two reasons. First, the person being invited to a sexual interlude often doesn't hear an invitation at all, but hears a demand. The fact that the invitation is perceived as a demand makes it seem one-sided, inconsiderate, selfish, and imposing. True invitations do not have such negative feelings attached to them because they are offered as a more genuine choice, so that the person being "invited" is not treated as a villain if the invitation is declined. Second, the tendency for the not-so-interested-in-sex person to hear an invitation as a demand is not always as unreasonable as it may sound at first. Past experience—in fact, *many* past experiences—may have told them that what is advertised as an invitation ("It's up to you") is actually a demand in the sense that if the invitation isn't accepted right then and there, the degree of disappointment and resentment that the other partner shows makes it plain that it wasn't, in fact, an invitation at all, but a poorly masked form of demand that over time becomes more aggravating exactly because it is made to seem innocent and nondemanding.

3. *Try to let sex simmer on low instead of expecting it to come to an immediate boil.* If the expectation is for sex to heat up rapidly, the not-so-interested person may tend to check his or her initial responsiveness and say, "Hmmmm, I'm not really very turned on—so that must mean I'm

not interested." That sort of "preflight inspection" turns out to be self-defeating, because it doesn't allow for the possibility that sexual feelings (and responses) can get stirred up by simply allowing oneself to be in the situation with no automatic performance checklist (or timetable) to signal success or failure.

4. *Understand the difference between rejecting an activity and rejecting a person.* Here is one of the major sources of trouble when it comes to individual differences in sexual appetites. How you turn your partner down when you're not in the mood has a great deal to do with how your partner reacts to your message. If he or she feels rejected as a person, almost invariably he or she will feel hurt or angry. If, on the other hand, you make it clear that there's a reason why sex doesn't fit your needs right now (and leave open the possibility that the situation may change soon), your partner doesn't feel as if you've just slammed the door in his or her face.

The flip side of this equation is that if your partner turns away from your preludes to making love, don't leap to the conclusion that he or she is turning away from you. If you can't help feeling rejected—especially if you have a very strong need for sexual togetherness or release—talk things out instead of just rolling over and stewing about it.

5. *Learn to employ the art of compromise.* In sexually "together" relationships, usually each partner is willing to be available sexually when the other one needs him or her. You don't have to promise to be at your most passionate peak of performance in order to make things work. In fact, often a "quickie"—not necessarily involving intercourse—may be enough to satisfy your partner's need, just as a snack is sometimes a good substitution for a bigger meal when someone is hungry. Women can almost always accommodate their partners without too much physical difficulty (assuming the absence of out-of-the-ordinary conditions such as severe PMS, a vaginal infection, or the like); anatomical reality dictates that unless a male becomes at least moderately aroused, he will have to provide sexual stimulation to his partner by some means other than a fully erect penis, and *there is absolutely nothing wrong with this!*

6. *Don't approach every lovemaking session as though it has to follow the numbers.* If you are flexible in allowing for options in your sexual togetherness, you may find it paying more dividends than you imagine. Consider the marriage of Dave and Mary L. After 14 years and three kids, Mary was chronically tired and not particularly interested in sex. Dave not only wanted sex more than Mary did, but (as so often happens in these situations) became more and more obsessed with sex the more he was stymied in his approaches.

The solution they found, after a one-hour consultation with us, was stunningly simple. Mary agreed to "service" Dave even when she wasn't particularly in the mood as long as Dave would respect her wishes to decline when she was really frazzled. But she had the option of *how* she would "service" him: by hand, by mouth, or by intercourse, which gave her more choices . . . and more control. Dave was amenable to this arrangement initially because, as he put it, "Half a loaf is better than none." He quickly discovered that the half loaf kept replenishing itself, as Mary's willingness to be available on her terms, rather than his, apparently freed up something inside her and she began gradually to find sex more interesting and inviting. At the same time, as Dave found himself with a partner who was available to him more often than before (even though not as the wildly turned-on partner he would have liked), his own sexual appetite began to become less pressing.

The moral of the story is simple: if you'll meet each other part way when there are different sexual appetites, the differences often disappear or become inconsequential. Part of the agony felt by the person whose sexual needs are not being met in a relationship is fueled by the lack of willingness to *attempt* to deal with his or her needs—no one likes to feel neglected or ignored.

7. *If you're not interested in sex at the moment your partner "invites" you, but you might be later on, convey this clearly.* If your wife is starving at 4:00 p.m. on Sunday afternoon but you don't want to eat then, there's no reason to say, "I'm not going to eat today." Why not take the same approach to sex? While you may not both be interested in

sex at exactly the same time, if you keep your options open for the possibility of more closely matching appetites later in the evening, you haven't shut her out completely. What's more, even though your wife was the one who offered the initial invitation, the opportunity is now there for either of you to flash a green light if the feelings are even mildly favorable.

8. *Expand your sexual repertoire.* If boredom is the bane of satisfying sex, following the same sexual script over and over again is not the wisest way to kindle dwindling sexual interests. In nondysfunctional couples, one reason that sex loses its allure thus creating desire discrepancies is that it simply becomes too routine. In your sex life, doing the same thing over and over again in the same way, in the same position, even at the same time of day, can become predictable and stale. The solution is straightforward: try something a little different. We're not suggesting that you run out and recruit another partner so you can have a threesome. Instead, we're suggesting that you should try to implement some changes within your present relationship. If you're used to always having a cold appetizer, try a hot one. If you always have shrimp cocktail instead of soup, once in a while, go with the soup instead. In other words, try some things you haven't done recently, or maybe never before; try varying the timing or setting for sex (a motel room, or the living room floor); consider using a vibrator or some flavored massage lotion to add a new dimension to your erotic existence.

9. *Use sex fantasies to help turn yourself on if your level of passion is only lukewarm.* Sex fantasies can really set the sexual juices flowing. However, people with low sexual desire often don't spend much time thinking about sex and don't have many sexual fantasies, either (Nutter and Condron, 1983, 1985). Anyone can change this situation by deliberately calling up erotic fantasies to enrich (and jump-start) their sex lives. And if you don't have some favorite fantasies of your own, you can find various books (such as those listed in the Suggested Readings at the end of this chapter) that will help you get started with short descriptions of many common fantasy scenarios. Sex fantasies are probably the best aphrodisiacs around—and they don't cost anything, either.

10. *Identify obstacles to your sexual opportunities and come up with practical ways to get around them.* Children are one of the principal problems when it comes to flagging sexual desire. For example, young children may tire their parents out so badly that hitting the pillow is more important than melting into your spouse's arms with passionate abandon. Even older kids have a funny way of being unintentionally intrusive just when you're trying to make some time for yourselves to have a little romance—and few things can botch up foreplay more than a 15-year-old's knock on the bedroom door just as you're beginning to get aroused. (If you live in a college dormitory or share an apartment with friends, you may already have experience with this sort of problem without being a parent.) Possible solutions to these problems are not hard to devise, but they are sadly neglected, as though putting your sexual needs before the needs of your kids might somehow damage their development. Tackle problem Number 1, wornout parents of young children, by the judicious use of a babysitter to allow you and your partner to get away, rest up, or recharge your sexual batteries. Problem Number 2, intrusive older children, can be dealt with in various ways. A "DO NOT DISTURB" sign on the bedroom door can work wonders, for example. In any event, take time with your partner to draw up a list of problems of a similar nature that interrupt or inhibit your sexual togetherness and then implement specific action plans for handling each one.

DEALING WITH AROUSAL DIFFICULTIES

One inadvertent effect of the sexual revolution has been the idea that sex is a test of adequacy. People who look at sexual activity as a hundred yard dash stress the swiftness and magnitude of physical response while ignoring the emotional or feeling side of the sexual equation. It's little wonder, then, that women who don't warm up to sex as quickly as their partners do tend to see themselves as deficient or inhibited. Likewise, men who don't get turned on as swiftly as Clark Kent transforms himself into Superman have a tendency to see themselves as sexual laggards or worse. For both sexes, however, the problem usually lies more in expectations and mind-sets than in the actual physical responses.

Excluding specific physical problems that may impair sexual arousal (see Chapters 21 and 22), perhaps the most remarkable thing about sex is how effortlessly and automatically it can happen if it isn't blocked by extraneous factors such as pressure over finishing your big term paper or financial worries that make you wonder how you're ever going to pay this month's rent or excitement over an upcoming event like a vacation or a wedding. Since so much of sex involves reflex responses over which people have no voluntary control, the natural flow of our physical responses shouldn't come as a big surprise. For this reason, dealing with difficulties in sexual arousal is often mainly a matter of identifying the obstacles that prevent it from happening spontaneously, not of concocting a recipe for instant turn-on.

Here are some specific suggestions to help identify and deal with common obstacles to sexual arousal:

1. *Don't shut off your erotic potential by locking yourself into negative predictions.* Sex is as much a state of mind as a set of physical responses. Believing there isn't going to be any pleasure or pizzazz from a sexual experience not only limits your enthusiasm, it even changes your body's receptiveness so that touches, kisses, or other acts of tenderness aren't allowed to register their sensory messages in the brain. Since pleasurable sex depends in part on the cumulative, synergistic effect of such sensual messages—much as a symphony is built of thousands of individual notes and blended harmonies—obstructing your awareness of the building blocks of sensual/sexual feelings, tactile and otherwise, almost always prevents sex from being a positive experience. To avoid such self-fulfilling prophecies and let yourself be receptive to whatever evolves doesn't mean you have to be wildly passionate or precisely in the mood: it's a matter of being a participant, rather than a self-critic, so that you can concentrate on your sensory awareness and let yourself experience the full range of physical and emotional sensations that occur during a sexual encounter.

2. *If there's something about your lovemaking style that doesn't suit you, take an active role in making a change.* Maybe the problem is that your partner rushes things or that his or her touch is too heavy or too light. Perhaps your sexual encounters always seem to unfold at 11:00 p.m., when you're so tired it's hard enough just to brush your teeth and get into bed, let alone think about participating in any kind of physical activity. This list of problems, which could be expanded by hundreds of other similar examples, makes many people feel that sex doesn't hold much for them. The key thing to realize, however, is that these problems are not insurmountable: they are minor stylistic glitches that have simple and straightforward solutions. Finding solutions won't occur magically, though. To devise solutions, you need to begin by identifying what or where the problems are, breaking the problems down into their component parts, and then addressing the question of what might be done to change things. Sometimes the process of making a change—almost any change at all—will work right away, and sometimes it takes several tries to hit on the right combination of changes. But by giving yourself a chance to do things differently *with your partner's cooperation*, you become an active agent in developing your options, which may help you view sex as more "user-friendly" than it's seemed before.

3. *Many problems with sexual arousal are a result of the tendency to think too much and touch too little.* Thinking about sex is obviously a turn-on for some people. But thinking about sex as it's happening can also lead to negative self-appraisals. For instance, a woman may think: "Did I shave my legs today?" "Maybe I should have showered again." "Am I getting excited yet?" "Am I getting HIM excited?" "Is he rushing me again?" "Are we tuned in to each other?" "What am I going to do if he wants oral sex?" A man may worry: "Why don't I have a better erection?" "What if she's been with guys who are bigger than I am?" "How can I tell if she's really turned on or if she's just faking it?" These intruding thoughts can put anyone into the spectator role at his or her own bedside, unintentionally inhibiting both physical and psychological responses. One way to combat the tendency to think too much (or to dwell on anxious thoughts) is to luxuriate in the sensations and the action of a sensual/sex-

ual encounter. As we discuss shortly, a good way to do this is to focus on a specific part of your partner's body and get lost in the sensations of stroking, touching, or holding him or her, thus taking the mental spotlight off your own response.

4. *Use fantasies to jump-start your sexual arousal or to boost your turn-on once it's underway.* Many people who are accustomed to using sex fantasies while they masturbate are hesitant to use them when they're with a partner, fearing that this is improper or immature or that it somehow detracts from the interpersonal nature of the experience. But avoiding the use of fantasy actually puts them (and their partners) at a disadvantage: without this customary stimulus, both their physical and emotional responses may lag. There is absolutely nothing wrong with using erotic fantasies as a private aphrodisiac. Fantasies can help anyone get in a particularlu sexy mood as well as intensify or accelerate arousal. Since using fantasies can aid women in becoming more responsive sex partners, and since most men are accustomed to using sex fantasies themselves, it's no wonder that most men have no objections at all to this practice. (If a woman is psychologically uncomfortable fantasizing about sex with a stranger, or sex with her old high school boyfriend, or sex with a movie star, she can usually feel very secure if she fantasies about sex with her current partner.)

5. *Emphasize the playfulness of sex instead of turning it into a chore or a mission.* Many individuals with arousal problems recall getting turned on very easily when they were teenagers necking in the back seat of a car. This was probably not some accidental happening tied to adolescent hormones or sexual innocence; it's more likely to reflect the fact that at that age they experienced sex more as a playful, unpredictable encounter than as a work assignment. Adults usually take things more seriously than teenagers do, but where sex is concerned, this can have its disadvantages. Reclaiming the playful, exploratory side of sex can help defuse performance anxieties and restore that sense of fun and adventure between partners.

6. *Don't be afraid to experiment with different types of sensual stimulation.* Many people with arousal problems become so intently focused on their difficulties that they lose sight of certain basic aspects of experiencing pleasure. One common problem is that too much sameness in sexual routines not only leads to boredom, it often triggers feelings of *deja vu* that cause someone to write off an encounter before he or she has even gotten into it. Another aspect of this problem is that many couples are reluctant to experiment with sex, feeling that if they've tried something once and didn't like it, it means they will always react to this activity the same way. Nothing could be further from the truth. Experimentation can take many different forms. Try various positions for touching one another. Sometimes if the woman gets on top of her partner *without* any attempt to have intercourse, it opens new vistas of experiencing touches and kisses. Try exploring each other's body with your lips and tongues instead of your fingertips, doing so in a way that emphasizes the sensual side of this action instead of trying to produce a specific response. Have a sensual encounter while you're both fully or partially clothed. Once again, the point of experimenting is discovery. You may be surprised at how simple changes produce new or different feelings.

Individuals with arousal difficulties (but normal sexual desire) who find that the above suggestions are of little help should consider consulting a sex therapist for further evaluation and individualized treatment recommendations, especially if their problems seem linked to fears of sex, distaste for sexual acts, or recurrent deep-seated anxieties. In general, we suggest that if you are in a long-term romantic relationship, both you and your partner should seek help together.

SEX AND SENSUALITY

If words are the currency of poetry, and color is the currency of art, touch is the currency of sex. But somewhere in the evolutionary process, modern civilization has lessened our awareness of this important fact, and sex has been recast as a type of action. This has reduced it from a sensual and sensory phenomenon to a set of reflex responses that happen to meet together occasionally. However, ignoring our sensual side inevitably lessens our sexual involvement and our sexual gratification. As the noted anthropologist Ashley Montagu put it, "Without tactile communication—what the body feels and says nonverbally—the experience of sex can only be at most incomplete (Montagu, 1978, p. 167)." When we talk about the sensual side of sex, we are primarily referring to our tactile (touching) sensations, for it is largely (although not exclusively) through skin to skin contact that we experience sex.

It's one thing to talk about sensuality in the abstract and quite another to put it into action. Some couples have an intuitive grasp of what being sensual is all about; others seem baffled, as though they've been asked to read a document in Sanskrit. From our work as sex therapists, we know very well that telling couples to just go home and touch doesn't usually do much to rekindle their sensuous cravings. In cases where passion has turned to indifference, or where a couple is having fundamental problems with unfulfilling sex, it often takes careful orchestration to get things back in tune.

One of the key approaches we have devised to accomplish this is a set of at-home exercises that virtually any couple can employ. These *sensate focus exercises*, as we call them, provide a framework for individual self-discovery as well as a vehicle for a creative reawakening of a couple's sensuous impulses and interaction. When used in the course of sex therapy, sensate focus has a number of different purposes. For example, a couple's reports about their sensate focus experiences provide important diagnostic information to the therapists. Sensate focus is a key part of the treatment for reducing or eliminating performance anxieties (which are ultimately the cause of many sexual dysfunctions). As therapy proceeds, reports of what has happened during sensate focus also help the therapists judge a couple's progress in solving whatever problems they are facing. But the utility of the sensate focus approach is much broader than these points convey. Because the sensate focus method restructures and reorients how people ordinarily approach sexual interactions, letting them move away from old, familiar habit patterns that they have fallen into, it allows any couple to reinvent the physical side of their relationship.

Sensate focus is about touching and being touched. Many couples think that this sounds about as exciting as wet sand, but the truth is that the art of touching and the art of being touched has

a lot more to it than most people realize. One of the ways of maximizing the potential of sensate focus is to begin without any preconceived notions of what you will feel, how good it will be, or how much pleasure it will produce. In other words, even if the idea doesn't seem thrilling, you need to start out with an open mind about it, because otherwise your expectations tend to color your experience and feelings.

You also need to reorient your thinking away from being judgmental and evaluative to simply being and experiencing. In sexual matters, judgmental thinking almost always boxes us in: Was it good? Was it boring? Was it ecstatic? Evaluative thinking—which we define as a form of judgmental thinking that occurs as something is happening, not after it's over—is even more self-defeating in erotic moments. Just as being a restaurant critic changes your experience of dining out, being evaluative as sex is happening invariably puts you in the position of being an observer as well as a participant. The part of your mind that is observing is blocked from experiencing, with the all-too-common result that you think too much and feel too little.

The judgmental/evaluative posture also forces us to pigeonhole what's happening in terms of loaded words and concepts. Sex gets rated as good or bad, boring or sizzling, explosive or tame in an artificial way. Remember, there is no panel of judges at your bedside ready to hold up scorecards to tell you how good or bad your performance was ("8.5 on the creative program—4.4 on the compulsories").

Part of getting into the sensate focus experience is to avoid judging or evaluating what's happening and to concentrate instead on *noticing* what's happening in terms of physical feelings. By noticing whether your partner's skin feels smooth or warm or moist, you avoid having evaluative, judgmental thoughts and simply focus on the experience.

In order to set the stage for a new type of touching that puts the emphasis on sensuality, rather than sexuality, we instruct couples to abstain from any type of sexual activity during the first step of sensate focus. This means that no matter how turned on they might become, touching the genitals (or the woman's breasts), having oral sex, having intercourse, or having any other type of sexual involvement is off limits. This prohibition is partly intended to set a clear focus on the sensual side of touching as valuable in its own right. (Of course,

FOCUS IN BRIEF

Ten Ways of Blocking Sensuality

Over the years, we've learned a bit about what interferes with the sensual side of sex. Here are the most common roadblocks we've identified. These problems, which are not listed in any particular order, are self-evident enough to require no further explanation.

1. The "wham, bam, thank you m'am" approach.
2. Children (or roommates) who pop into your room whenever they want to.
3. Time constraints, including always leaving sex for the last thing at night when you and your partner are both tired out.
4. The "it's my job to make my partner happy" attitude.
5. The notion that sex is serious business.
6. The idea that sex is solely for the man's pleasure.
7. Inattention to your partner's sensibilities, as demonstrated by cigar breath, a headful of haircurlers, or unrelenting body odor.
8. The mistaken belief that fulfilling sex is only for young and attractive people.
9. Thinking (and worrying) too much during sex.
10. Being angry with your partner, but keeping your anger to yourself.

There are obviously many other sources of sexual problems which are not included on this list. We will discuss many of them later in this book, especially in Chapters 21 and 22. But we have certainly found that if a couple manages to maintain a healthy sensuality in their relationship, it automatically provides a boost to their sexual satisfaction together.

approach is likely to be very different from the way couples usually approach touching, and this is exactly the point: it allows for new discoveries and avoids ingrained behavior patterns that may have gotten stale and unrewarding.

We will now describe a version of sensate focus that has been designed especially for you to use on your own. These exercises are slightly modified from the ones we use in sex therapy. Many couples will find that time spent on the sensate focus process can be a useful and pleasant way to reawaken their own sensual (and sexual) feelings.

We suggest that you try these exercises when you and your partner are both relaxed, well rested, and feeling comfortable about one another. (Trying to start at a time when either one of you is tense, tired, or grumpy is not advisable: the chances are that you'd just be wasting your time.) In the privacy of your own home, at a time when you won't be interrupted by telephone calls or other distractions, and when you have at least 30 to 40 minutes to yourselves, you can begin. As a practical matter, we suggest that it's best to decide in advance who will pick the time for the first touching session; after that, alternate who chooses, so you don't have to deal with the problem of "Are you ready to start touching now?" queries and unnecessary negotiations or guesswork.

Step 1: Nongenital Touching

There are two parts to this step, which we call A and B. For illustrative purposes and grammatical simplicity, assume that it is the woman who decides when to begin in this example. (Second guessing her timing isn't very useful and can get things started on the wrong foot, so don't turn down her invitation unless you're really tired, distracted, or emotionally wrung out.) From the beginning, both partners need to be completely undressed. We also suggest the removal of earrings, watches, necklaces and rings, and it also helps to be sure that you're not sweaty or dirty, so a preliminary bath or shower may be in order. It isn't necessary, however, to be obsessive about cleanliness, and it's best, too, not to pour on perfume or aftershave lotion. Note: If nudity distresses either partner, or if overwhelming hostility is a fact of life in your relationship, it is advisable to get professional help before trying these exercises.

learning to be sensual has something to do with being sexual, too.) It also serves to remove any pressures on either partner to need to respond in some particular way—getting an erection, becoming sexually aroused, or responding in a certain manner to a partner's needs. In addition, this

The person who issues the invitation to begin is the active participant in part A. Her partner lies flat on his back on the bed (or on the floor, if he likes); his role, for now, is simply to take in the sensations he is feeling as he is touched by his partner. He should not return her touch, comment on her touching, or talk about what he is feeling in any way. Remembering that the man's genitals are off limits, the woman is free to begin exploring her partner's body in any way that interests her in order to discover what she feels as she does this. Because starting can be awkward, some women prefer to begin at one spot on the man's body—say, the neck or feet—and work their way up or down from there. Other women don't need a definite plan of action and simply explore the various textures and temperatures and contours of their partner's body without any preconceived idea of how they will proceed.

Whichever way you choose, the point of this exercise, as the term sensate focus implies, is to zero in on the sensations you are experiencing as you touch. There is no right way or wrong way to do this, and the point of this touching opportunity is *not* to try to turn your partner on, or to make him feel good, or to give him a massage: the point is to try to live through your fingertips, taking in each and every physical sensation they provide, while doing whatever happens to interest you at the moment.

Some women become fascinated by the fine detail in the contours and angles on their partner's face. They may never before have taken the opportunity to trace their fingertips lightly along his lips, or to feel the difference in texture between an ear and a cheek, or to notice that the hair at the nape of his neck is softer than the hair on top of his head. Other women move from one region of the man's body to another more quickly, comparing the smoothness of the skin on his thigh to the rougher palm of his hand, or to his toes. Again, there is no right way to do this exercise other than allowing yourself the opportunity to focus on your physical awareness of sensations in a nonevaluative way. At any point during the touching, the woman can ask her partner to turn over so she can touch his back and have easier access to the backs of his legs and neck.

The man's role in part A is primarily to focus on his own sensations as he is being touched. For the moment, he is not expected to reciprocate by touching his partner. He should be noticing the sensa-

tions he is receiving not in terms of evaluating or analyzing them ("I like that," or "Why is she doing that?") but of allowing himself to *experience* them. His only responsibility is to protect his partner from doing something that makes him acutely uncomfortable, either physically or psychologically. If she is rubbing a sore spot on his back, he must tell her immediately. If her touch is so light that it tickles and he doesn't like it, he should let her know this as well. This permits the toucher to concentrate on her own feelings without having to worry about her partner's comfort.

Either partner can suggest going on to part B of this exercise. We recommend, however, that part A continue at least 15 minutes—especially since we recognize that, at the beginning, it may seem a bit awkward or unnatural, and a few minutes might be needed to get past the strangeness. On the other hand, we urge touching not to be prolonged to the point of boredom or fatigue for either partner.

Part B of this exercise simply reverses the roles of the man and woman, so that now the woman is the one who lies down and the man is the one who does the touching. Unless it's absolutely necessary—such as needing to use the bathroom—we strongly suggest not taking a break of any sort between parts A and B.

As in part A, the man is free to touch his partner's body anywhere but the genitals; in addition, he should not touch her breasts for now. His partner's only responsibility is to protect him from doing anything that makes her physically or psychologically uncomfortable. Just as her partner did, the woman now focuses on what her partner's touches feel like to her, avoiding any attempts to evaluate or judge what he's doing. (Helpful hint: Don't compare your touching style to your partner's; there's no reason for two people to take the same approach or use the same touches or sequence; each partner has his or her individual feelings and perceptions.) As the man explores his partner's body from head to toe, it is important that he not set out to try to touch her in a way that he thinks she's going to like, or in a way that he thinks she'll find stimulating. Again, the purpose of this exercise is *not* to set the erotic juices flowing; it is to let both partners get in touch with their own physical sensations in a leisurely, unstructured, non-goal-oriented manner.

Many men aren't particularly used to noticing tactile sensations deriving from textures or temperatures, so they may need a little while to become adjusted to this process. Here are some suggestions we've found helpful with regard to the various types of touching that can be explored.

- Play a texture awareness game with yourself. First, see if you can notice differences in the surface texture of skin on different parts of her body. How does the smoothness and softness of skin on her cheeks compare to the backs of her hands, her calves, or her neck? Are there areas on her face that seem silkier or more supple than others?
- Vary the firmness and tempo of your touching. Let yourself feel the difference between a long-drawn-out, feathery-light touch on your partner's arm (or face or leg) and a slightly firmer and quicker touch, using small circular motions, in the same areas. Switch to a stacatto type of rhythm for a while, and then switch back to a smoother, more lingering touch. Does changing the tempo of your touch alter your tactile sensations?
- See how touching with your whole hand feels compared to touching just with your fingertips. Notice how touching with both hands at once differs (or *whether* it differs) compared to the tactile sensations you get from just using one hand.

Let's review several points. First, the goal of this exercise is *not* to produce any kind of erotic response. Even if you find yourself becoming wildly aroused, *do not* turn this into a sexual encounter. Second, either partner can ask to end the touching session. Apart from the 15 minute minimum, as in part A, there is no need that part B has to match or exceed part A in duration; just don't touch for so long that you become worn out or uninterested. (If you start to fall asleep while you're touching or being touched, it is not apt to be a positive growth experience, is it?) Third, the point of sensate focus is not to give your partner a back rub or massage (although either may be a perfectly wonderful and romantic thing to do on another occasion) or to touch her in a way that you think will make her happy. The point is very straightforward: to allow the person doing the touching to take in a variety of sensory experiences and to notice what they feel like, without any distractions or "shoulds" lurking in the background.

Some couples enjoy repeating this version of the sensate focus exercises for several days. Often they notice things a little differently each time, and they also try out variations in technique and timing that allow them to experiment—in a nonpressured way—with their sensual perceptions. But the decision on whether to repeat this step a few times or to move on to the next step is a flexible one: there's no test to pass before you "graduate" to the next level.

Step 2: Genital Touching

In this next step of sensate focus, the prohibition on touching the breasts and genitals is dropped, but you should still abstain from attempting sexual intercourse. As with the preceding step, one person should be designated to pick the time to begin. (If you don't simply want to alternate from whoever made this choice the last time, you can always flip a coin to decide. In this example, we will have the man begin.) The background details are also the same as before: privacy, nudity, cleanliness, and so forth.

In part A of this session, the man should begin exactly as in the nongenital touching, with general touching of his partner's body. It is often advisable for the woman to start out lying face down on the bed to facilitate this process so the man doesn't become automatically fixated on her breasts and genitals as though he was a bomber pilot homing in on his target zone. *Even though the ban on touching the breasts and genitals is no longer in effect, the man should be especially careful NOT to change the nature of the touching experience by rushing immediately and single-mindedly to "sexual" touching.* In fact, it is helpful to remember that this is not a torrid X-rated movie but a *sensate* focus exercise: the point is not to try to be turned on or to make something happen to or for your partner, but to pay attention to your sensations in the context of exploring your partner's body as a sensual, sensory tactile experience.

If the impulse toward action is overwhelmingly tempting to you, take a mental step backwards and try to repeat some of what you learned in the previous step of sensate focus. Slowly feel the curve of your partner's back and compare it to the contour of her hips; trace along the edge of her spine and see how this feels compared to the softer tissue on the back of her upper arms; run your fingers through her hair as though you were feeling its texture and thickness for the first time. After you are comfortable and feeling in the rhythm of the mo-

Figure 14.1

This position is suggested for the sensate focus exercise at the stage that includes genital exploration when the man is touching his partner. Couples are urged to modify this position to whatever they find comfortable and to experiment with other positions, too.

ment, as well as feeling as if you are connecting with the sensations that are registering through your fingertips, then shift into the position shown in Figure 14.1.

If there is no headboard on your bed, a few pillows behind his back will provide support for him as he sits with his legs slightly spread in a V. The woman leans back against his chest so that her head is resting on one of his shoulders. By reaching down or around her, the man can touch most of his partner's body (although he probably cannot reach her lower legs and feet in this position).

At this juncture, as the man continues his general exploration of his partner's body, a new twist is added in the form of a special technique to enhance nonverbal communication: the woman puts her hand on top of his as he is touching (as shown in Figure 14.2). The intention of this hand-riding technique is not for the woman to suddenly take the lead in directing the action but rather to provide a simple, quick, effective way for the woman to transmit additional information to her partner as he touches her. He continues to touch for what he finds interesting, to distinguish and notice various sensations, and to do so in an open-ended, non-goal-directed manner, but she has the opportunity

of providing him with nonverbal feedback about subtle preferences of her own. Although it is not his *job* to anticipate her feelings (in fact, she may not even be able to anticipate them herself), responding to her silent messages gives him a way to integrate her reactions into his actions.

With the hand-riding technique, the woman can show her partner where she'd like a firmer touch, where she'd like him to linger a while, or where she'd like a lighter, silky sort of touch. She can show him when a slower sort of stroking might be especially sensual, or let him know when she'd like him to move from one part of her body to an entirely different spot. The man doesn't have to abide by these tidbits of information as though they were instructions from an airport control tower; with a little practice, he can learn how to combine his own feelings and needs with the messages provided by his partner. He should also recognize that a signal to move his hand is not a criticism of what he's doing; instead, it means "Right now, I think I'd like to try this."

As we mentioned earlier, the man is free to incorporate genital touching into his tactile explorations in this exercise. (In part B, which we will describe shortly, the woman will have the same op-

Figure 14.2

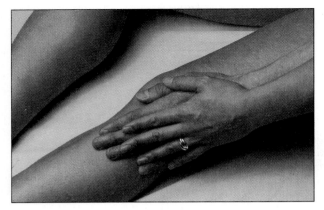

The "hand-riding" technique for conveniently giving nonverbal messages.

portunity.) But it is especially important that he does not suddenly shift the nature of his touching into a relentless assault or a feverish push to make his partner quiver and melt in his arms. This means, for example, that it is usually best to touch briefly in or around the genital area and then move elsewhere on the woman's body for a while, returning to the genitals in the natural ebb and flow of exploratory touching. (For those men who may be wondering, "a while" means longer than 3 seconds.) If a man literally pounces on his partner's genitals and then concentrates his touching there almost exclusively, without regard to her feelings, it is understandably apt to make her feel like a sex object and not much more. If, instead, the man adds gentle, light caresses of the breasts and genital area (including the lips of the vagina, the clitoris, and even the region between the vagina and the rectum) to a broader repertoire of touching that includes all of his partner's body, he extends the range of the sensual experience both he and his partner are having.

Here are a few additional pointers to keep in mind:

- The couple should feel free to move into a different position than the one we suggested at any point they would like to (although many women report feeling especially comfortable and relaxed in the position we illustrated).
- The woman should be especially careful to give her partner signals while he is touching her genital area so he doesn't need to guess at what type

of touching she prefers. It isn't necessary that she know in advance exactly what will feel pleasing or interesting, only that she provide him with feedback as he's touching her.

- So that you don't lose sight of the fact that this is a sensate focus opportunity, not just a preamble to sex, we suggest that you abstain from kissing while you are doing this exercise. Kissing often seems to push people into cruise control when it comes to sensual/sexual behavior, and what you are trying to accomplish here is to break old habit patterns, not solidify them.
- If the woman finds that her feelings are aroused enough that she wants to be orgasmic, it is perfectly appropriate to let orgasm occur either by manual stimulation from her partner (with some hand-riding guidance from her) or by using the reverse approach: letting her partner put his hand on top of hers and follow her motions and touches as she stimulates herself to orgasm. (Men: if you try either of these methods, this is *not* the time for an analytical discussion of why a particular type of touch feels a certain way. Just let it happen.) There is no point, however, in working to make orgasm happen. If the touching begins to feel like a job, either partner should call "time out."

As in Step 1 of the sensate focus exercises, either the man or woman can say "I'd like to switch." There is no specific time requirement or limitation, although once again, our general suggestion is that the touching should not last so long that either person becomes bored or tired.

The procedure for part B should parallel the steps that are outlined above. We suggest that the woman begin with a period of general body touching, permitting herself to flow into the experience by focusing on her tactile sensations. As in the previous phase of sensate focus, she should take time to notice subtle variations in surfaces and contours, textures and temperatures of her partner's body, and she should explore his body in a way that interests her, not in order to make something happen to or for him.

At some point when she is feeling reasonably comfortable and absorbed in the experience, the couple can move into the position shown in Figure 14.3. (This is not a mandatory part of the exercise,

Figure 14.3

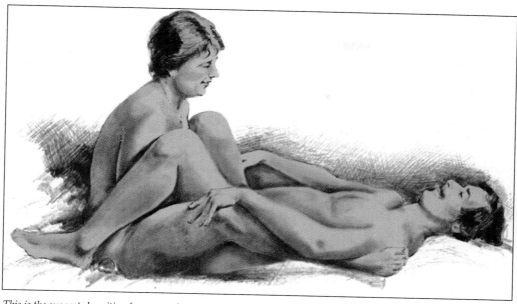

This is the suggested position for sensate focus experience with genital touching when the woman is touching her partner.

but many couples have found this to be useful.) In this position, where the man in lying on his back with his head pointed away from his partner's body, and his legs bent at the knees and draped over her waist while she is sitting close to him, she is able to easily reach forward with access to most of his body. At this juncture, the couple can again use the hand-riding technique, this time with the man's hand placed on top of his partner's as she touches and explores his body.

The woman can now extend her touching to include her partner's genital area as well as other regions. We recommend that the woman simply incorporate genital touching into her general explorations with no specific goal (such as trying to get her partner aroused) and without parking her hand indefinitely in this area. The man may or may not develop an erection, and whether he does or not is unimportant. If he does become erect, the woman should make a point of stroking the penis for a bit and then deliberately moving her hand to a different area, rather than staying focused on his sexual organ. In addition to touching or stroking the penis (whether or not it is erect), the woman might also want to use her fingertips to explore the scrotum, feeling the texture of the skin of the scrotal sac, gently cupping the testicles in her hands, and even running her fingers along the perineum,

the sensitive region of skin between the base of the scrotum and the rectum. These are not meant to be suggestions in the how-to-turn-your-partner-on mode: they are meant to provide a greater degree of awareness of your partner's body.

As this touching and exploration continues, the man can use the hand-riding technique to send subtle messages to his partner about the types of touching he finds most comfortable and pleasurable. It's important for both partners to realize that when they receive a message of this sort suggesting they move to a different spot, it doesn't mean they should never return. Both men and women find that what is comfortable or pleasing changes with time; a touch that is just perfect right now may be too much, or too little, or off target, in just a few moments. (Here's a perfect case in point. If you've ever tried to have your partner scratch an itchy spot on your back because you couldn't reach it yourself, you know how elusive getting that itch can be. One moment he or she is at exactly the right spot, but then the itch shifts just a little higher or a little lower or a bit to the left, and you've got to ask them to move a little to relieve the itch precisely.)

As the woman's exploration of her partner's body continues, the man may well find himself becoming sexually excited, which is perfectly fine and natural. The woman doesn't need to direct her attention to penile stimulation immediately, as though an erection requires emergency care, but if her partner feels that he wants to receive further penile touching and possibly go on to ejaculation, either she can provide this type of stroking for him (with his hand riding on hers to guide its tempo and firmness) or she can instead put her hand on his and follow his motions as he stimulates himself. Either choice is a matter of personal preference at the moment, not a reflection of the state of your relationship. As in part A of this exercise, if either partner starts to feel that the touching has turned into some sort of job or obligation, it's advisable to stop. (If necessary, the man can ejaculate by self-stimulation even if his partner needs to call it quits for now.)

Step 3: Adding Lotion

One of the ways of enhancing sensory awareness is to alter the medium of touch a bit. Since we don't have volume control knobs on our fingertips, the next best thing is to try the same sensate focus exercise described in Step 2 with the addition of a lotion or oil to add a slicker, silkier dimension to your touching. We suggest using a nonalcoholic, hypoallergenic lotion, but many couples find that baby oil or even suntan lotion is convenient, inexpensive, and fun.

If you try this step (which is completely optional), it's best first to warm the container of oil or lotion in a basin of hot water. Another hint to prevent the lotion from feeling chilly is never to drip it onto your partner's body. Putting some lotion in the palm of your hand and then rubbing it briefly also helps to warm it up.

Some couples like to begin touching *without* the lotion and then add the lotion partway into the experience for contrast. Other couples experiment by using the lotion on one hand and not the other, comparing and contrasting sensations between the two hands. Other couples find it easier to use the lotion from the very beginning of their touching. Whichever approach you choose (and you might want to try each option on different occasions), be sure that you don't let the lotion inadvertently turn you into a massage artist. The point of the exercise is still to focus on your sensations.

Step 4: Mutual Touching

So far, we have deliberately structured the touching exercises so that you were always in a "your turn/my turn" mode. Now, it's time to extend the scope of the touching experience by removing the artificiality of separate turns. This gives each of you the opportunity to use your newly improved sensory awareness to focus simultaneously on your fingertip sensations from touching your partner *and* on the physical sensations your body registers from being touched and held.

We suggest that the first time or two you try this version of sensate focus, you still refrain from kissing and from attempting intercourse. These simple steps help to prevent you from just reverting to your old, tried and true sexual behavior patterns. Remember, what you are trying to achieve here is a way of adding a new sensual dimension to your lives.

When you become involved in mutual touching, it's useful to view it as a continuation of the earliest sensate focus opportunities, not just another way of getting around to sex. If you decide that you are becoming too sexually (as opposed to sensually) focused, it's perfectly fine to lie back and let your partner do the touching for a while. It's also useful to direct your attention to decidedly nonsexual areas, although it's amazing how absolutely sensuous (and stimulating) your partner's hair or neck or lips can be. Another way of avoiding the problem of turning this into pure sex is to keep yourself from using sexual fantasies as the touching is going on. (While we are enthusiastic advocates of sexual fantasizing in lots of other situations, it does have a way of distracting your attention from sensual matters because your brain has to focus on your mental erotic imagery.)

One possible variation in the mutual touching opportunities is to incorporate oral–genital stimulation as part of your sensual play. This doesn't mean using oral sex to make something happen to or for your partner; it means using your lips and tongue as a way of sensually exploring your partner's body. There is a big difference in these two intentions. Especially if you've done oral sex a lot before, see how different it can be when you approach it as sensual exploration instead of a way of servicing your partner.

Another variation you might want to try is changing the scene of your sensate focus activities from the bedroom to the shower or bathtub. Some couples find that the slippery feel of warm water and soap suds (or with bath gel) gives them a special set of sensations. While this might not be an everyday event, it can provide an interesting change of perceptions.

Figure 14.4

Step 5: Sensual Intercourse

Almost everybody knows what sexual intercourse is, but have you ever thought about *sensual* intercourse? If you haven't tried it, you probably don't know what you're missing.

Sexual intercourse is often a very mechanical act, with an emphasis on thrusting and pushing toward orgasm. In this version of sensate focus, you extend the gains you have already made in emphasizing your awareness of physical sensations into the realm of penile–vaginal contact to find a stylistically different type of intercourse. Here again, there is no right way or wrong way of doing things; instead, the goal is to find out what feels interesting and pleasurable.

As with all of the previous phases of sensate focus, which build on the same foundation, we suggest starting this exercise with a period of general body (nongenital) touching. Allow yourselves to get into a comfortable rhythm and focus: be aware of what your fingertips are telling you and don't worry about whether or not you or your partner is becoming aroused.

Gradually extend the scope of the touching to include exploration of the genitals. Don't be shy about using the hand-riding technique to show your partner what you like, but don't try to be a traffic cop and direct every move he or she makes.

When you are both comfortable, move into a position where the man lies on his back and the woman moves astride him, positioning herself so that her vaginal area is close to his penis (see Figure 14.4). Once you've gotten to this point, don't rush things. Use the same principles of sensate focus you've been using all along to continue your touching, but now extend the touching so that it is not only done by your fingertips, but so your genital areas can touch each other, too. It is usually easiest for the woman to take hold of the man's penis (which, after all, is fairly easy to find) and move it against herself, rubbing it against her clitoris, or along the lips of the vagina, or playing with the penis around her vaginal opening. The man doesn't need to be a passive participant as this is happening. In addition to focusing on the sensations he is receiving through his penis, he can be actively touching the woman anywhere he finds interesting or pleasurable, whether this involves stroking her hair, fondling her breasts, running his fingers up and down her spine, or reaching up to gently trace the curves of her cheekbones.

When the woman feels ready, she can hold the erect penis at an angle of about 45 degrees (pointed toward the man's head) and slide back slowly on the penis, letting her vagina snuggle around the head of the penis without attempting to insert it any further. Once in this position, resist the urge to start thrusting right away. Instead, let the penis rub very gently and slowly in and out of the opening of the vagina, noticing the sensations you both are receiving from this type of contact. After a few minutes, the woman can slide a bit further back onto the penis, letting it come about halfway inside her. Again, instead of immediately establishing a vigorous thrusting pattern, stop to feel the sensations of warmth and contact. Hold absolutely still for a few seconds, and then the woman can squeeze her legs together (or contract the muscles around her vagina) to see what different sensations these maneuvers produce.

Here again, instead of moving right away into the old, familiar thrusting pattern, continue your sensual intercourse experience by slowly withdrawing the penis from the vagina and playing with it at the external genital area again briefly—for 20 or 30 seconds. Then the woman can slide back onto the penis, repeating any of the above steps that seem interesting or pleasurable, until either partner decides that some deeper thrusting would be a good change of pace.

Once you've tried these sorts of sensual variations, you may certainly want to move to a quicker type of thrusting, and you may also instinctively move into a deeper thrusting pattern. Some couples find that it's very enjoyable to establish a quicker, *shallower* thrusting pattern for a while. (In fact, women find this especially sensual, since nerve endings in the vagina are more heavily concentrated in the outer portion than deep inside, as we will discuss in more detail in the following chapter.) However you proceed, try to keep your focus on your sensations as much as possible, and give yourself the opportunity to enjoy your "new" way of having intercourse.

One final point: if you enjoy sensual intercourse and want to use this approach from time to time, you've got to let your partner know what you're thinking about in advance. If one person is having good old lusty sexual intercourse while the other wants a more leisurely sensual experience, it could be like playing a record at 33 and 45 rpm's at the same time.

Someone wrote us a note talking about sense aid focus (her way of spelling sensate focus) and in a way, she was absolutely right. The point of these exercises, after all, is to come to the aid of your senses: to restore the feeling side to sex.

SUMMARY

1. Differences in sexual desire are common and can be exaggerated and blown out of proportion if two people in a relationship don't devise effective means of communicating about their sexual needs and work out useful compromises.

2. Difficulties with sexual arousal (in the absence of a physical or medical problem) are often the result of extraneous pressures ranging from negative predictions, too much sexual routine, too much thinking and analyzing sexual matters, or making sex into a job. Arousal can often be boosted by the judicious use of sex fantasies as well as by emphasizing the playfulness of sex.

3. Sensate focus exercises provide a non-goal-oriented means of returning to the sensual side of sexual interaction in a nonpressured, nonevaluative way. Starting with nongenital touching, and eventually moving ahead to "sensual" intercourse, these touching opportunities can provide a welcome means of solving problems or just returning to the basic A-B-Cs of sex whenever things seem to get stale or shaky.

Thought Questions

1. How important do you think it is for sex partners to understand what turns each other on or off? Do you ever feel that protecting your privacy is more important than telling your partner exactly what your sexual cravings are?

2. Have you ever heard the Pointer Sisters' song, "(I Want a Man with a) Slow Hand"? In addition to letting sex unfold at a slow, leisurely pace, what other dimensions of sexual interaction help contribute to a gratifying sensual experience for you?

3. If you were asked to write a magazine article about sex, what points could you add to our list of "Ten Ways of Blocking Sensuality?"

4. If good sex isn't—as we contend—just a matter of what happens in bed, what factors promote good sex? To what degree do you and your partner (or partners) find that sexual pleasure is independent of other aspects of your relationship? How important is romance to sex for you?

5. For readers who have had more than one sexual partner: In your own experience, what are the main factors that distinguished between pleasing sex and not-so-satisfying sexual relationships?

6. A fundamental belief of this book is that good communication underlies the most pleasurable sexual relationships and that sex is actually a form of communication at an especially intimate level. What are the most important aspects of relationship communication for you (whether you're in a straight, gay, or nonsexual couple)?

Suggested Readings

Friday, Nancy. *My Secret Garden*. New York: Trident Press, 1973; and *Women on Top*. New York: Pocket Books, 1991. Intriguing collections of women's sex fantasies that can provide helpful blueprints for anyone having trouble with coming up with their own.

Friday, Nancy. *Men in Love*. New York: Delacorte Press, 1980. A collection of sex fantasy patterns from men. Skip the author's interpretations, but the fantasies themselves can fuel the imagination of anyone having difficulty devising his own.

Heiman, Julia R., and LoPiccolo, Joseph. *Becoming Orgasmic: A Sexual and Personal Growth Program for Women*. (Revised and expanded edition.) New York: Prentice-Hall Press, 1988. A personal growth and self-discovery guide to female sexuality written in a warm, easily understandable style.

Masters, William H.; Johnson, Virginia E.; and Kolodny, Robert C. *Heterosexuality*. New York: HarperCollins, 1994. A comprehensive guide to dealing with a broad range of sexual difficulties, from boredom to sexual dysfunctions, with a major emphasis on how to identify and solve your own problems.

Stanway, Andrew. *The Joy of Sexual Fantasy*. New York: Carroll & Graf, 1991. A comprehensive, almost encyclopedic, look at various varieties of sex fantasies. A smorgasbord for the erotic imagination.

Sexual Orientation

• On the eve of a 1993 gay and lesbian rights parade in Washington, thousands of women walked down Connecticut Avenue chanting, "Two, four, six, eight, how do you know your grandmother's straight?" (*Newsweek*, June 21, 1993).

• New research findings suggest a genetic predisposition to homosexuality, making the idea that sexual orientation is primarily a matter of choice—like choosing how to dress or where to live—scientifically unsupportable. Still, as of mid-1993, 46 percent of Americans believed that homosexuals *choose* to be gay or lesbian (*U.S. News & World Report*, July 5, 1993), a belief that leads many people to oppose civil rights for homosexuals.

• In the past few years, more and more media stars have rejected the old, "closeted" form of homosexual existence for a new public visibility. For example, country singer k.d. lang came out to *The Advocate,* a bi-weekly gay magazine, in 1992, and rock singer Melissa Etheridge publicly announced her lesbian orientation the following year (*The Advocate*, April 20, 1993, p. 77).

• Although President Clinton campaigned on a promise to end the military ban on homosexuals, staunch political resistance to this move forced him to back away from this position in the first year of his presidency.

While discussions of gay and lesbian issues have become more mainstream, both on college campuses and on TV talk shows, gays and lesbians have not become more widely tolerated: violence against homosexuals has been on the rise (Comstock, 1991) and nonviolent acts of anti-gay prejudice and discrimination—from outrageous T-shirt slogans to illegal employment bans against gays—continue to escalate unchecked. Furthermore, a clear majority of Americans still opposes same-sex marriages or "legal partnerships" for same-sex couples, and many Americans object to homosexual public school teachers, homosexual clergy, and gay or lesbian couples adopting children. Reflecting this viewpoint, in the last few years a number of anti-gay-rights ordinances were passed by various cities, counties, and states in this country on the mistaken premise that protecting the rights of gays and lesbians somehow endorses or promotes homosexuality. While Colorado's 1992 amendment overturning gay rights laws is the most prominent example of this regressive political trend (Zeman and Meyer, 1992; Stumbo, 1993), Colorado has hardly been alone. The Oregon towns of Junction City and Canby and four counties voted to prevent the enactment of any laws that would protect gays' civil rights (*Facts on File*, July 15, 1993, p. 520), but the state failed to pass a broader bill, known as Measure 9, that declared homosexuality abhorent and perverse (Sullivan, 1992).

Despite such strongly negative attitudes toward homosexuality, the last two decades have also provided a remarkable set of counterbalancing events. In 1974 the American Psychiatric Association officially decided that homosexuality was not an illness. Increasing numbers of courts began to uphold the civil rights of homosexuals on the basic premise that discriminating against people on the basis of their sexual orientation was illegal. Today, for example, gay and lesbian couples have a much better chance of adopting children than in the past (Green, 1992); some forward-minded businesses, including Lotus Corporation (a software manufacturer) and Ben & Jerry's (an ice cream producer) include coverage of employees' same-sex partners for benefits such as health care; and virtually all colleges, universities, and research centers prohibit discrimination against gay men and women in hiring practices.

If you are a heterosexual trying to understand something about the causes of sexual orientation,

Award-winning singer k.d.lang "came out" to her fans several years ago.

here are a few questions to ask yourself: (1) What do you think caused *your* heterosexuality? (2) How old were you when you first came to recognize your heterosexual impulses? (3) Do you think your heterosexuality might be a reflection of the strength of your parents' marriage? Or, if your parents have been divorced, is your heterosexuality in part a symbolic attempt to rectify the broken promise of their marriage? (4) If you've never had a same-sex erotic encounter, how can you be sure your heterosexuality isn't just a passing phase—something you'll outgrow? (5) Have you talked with a therapist about your heterosexual tendencies? Have you *really* made an effort to change?

The reason we have posed these questions (which are somewhat absurd, as we hope you noticed) is to let heterosexual readers put themselves in the position of gay and lesbian readers, who have probably been asked these questions hundreds, if not thousands, of times. We hope that everyone thinking about the origins of sexual orientation, whether gay, straight, or somewhere in between, understands how imprecise our knowledge on this matter is today.

In this chapter, we will examine a number of core issues regarding sexual orientation. For example, how do you define homosexuality, bisexuality, and heterosexuality? How many gays, lesbians, and bisexuals are there in the general population? What causes sexual orientation? Is homosexuality an illness? Are homosexuals or lesbians different psychologically from heterosexual men and women? Are all bisexuals alike? Exactly what is homophobia and why does it affect all of our lives? The reason we emphasize homosexuality and bisexuality throughout this discussion is that while sexual orientation is actually a continuum, as we will see shortly, in real life people categorize everyone into discrete entities or groups and compare them with one another. By examining certain aspects of gay, lesbian, and bisexual orientation, we come to a better comparative perspective on all of our lives.

Legal issues related to sexual orientation are discussed in Chapter 23, and religious attitudes toward sexual orientation are considered in Chapter 24.

DEFINING TERMS

The word **homosexual** comes from the Greek root *homo,* meaning "same," although the word itself was not coined until the late nineteenth century (Karlen, 1971). It can be used either as an adjective (as in a homosexual act, a homosexual bar) or as a noun that describes men or women who have a preferential sexual attraction to people of their same sex over a significant period of time. While most homosexuals engage in overt sexual activity with members of the same sex and generally do not find themselves particularly attracted sexually to people of the opposite sex, neither of these two conditions is required to fit the definition we have offered. It is clear that a person with no sexual experience whatever may still consider himself or herself homosexual; also, many homosexuals are able to be aroused by heterosexual partners or heterosexual fantasies (Bell and Weinberg, 1978; Masters and Johnson, 1979).

Bisexuals, in contrast, are men or women who are sexually attracted to people of either sex. Usually, but not always, the bisexual has had overt sexual activity with partners of both sexes.

Various other definitions of bisexuality have been offered. For instance, Klein (1978) states that a bisexual is a person "who is capable of a complex state of sexual relatedness characterized by sexual intimacy with both sexes." McDonald (1981) defines it this way:

To be bisexual means that a person can enjoy and engage in sexual activity with members of both sexes, or recognizes a desire to do so. Also, although the strength and direction of preference may be constant for some bisexuals, it may vary considerably for others with respect to time of life and specific partners.

Coleman (1987) points out that bisexuality should be measured in several different dimensions, including behavior, sex fantasy content, and emotional attachments. As these various definitions suggest, bisexuality is a complex term that can be used to describe a state of mind, a pattern of actual behavior, or a transitional bridge from one sexual orientation to another.

Heterosexuals, in contrast, are preferentially and consistently attracted sexually to people of the opposite gender.

To clarify that heterosexuality, bisexuality, and homosexuality exist along a continuum in real life, Kinsey and his colleagues (1948) devised a 7-point rating scale to describe the overt sexual experiences and the inner psychological reactions (including fantasies) of an individual (see Table 15.1). The bisexual man or woman would be rated as a Kinsey 2, 3, or 4.

THE NUMBERS QUESTION

Until recently, the most comprehensive statistics available on the numbers of homosexual men and women in the United States came from the Kinsey reports (Kinsey, Pomeroy, and Martin, 1948; Kinsey et al., 1953). These surveys indicated that 10 percent of white Americans were more or less exclusively homosexual for at least three years of their lives between ages 16 and 55 and that 4 percent were exclusively homosexual on a life-long basis. Thirty-seven percent of the white male population had had at least one homosexual experience in adolescence or adulthood that led to orgasm. In females, Kinsey's team found that by age 40, 19 percent had experienced same-sex erotic contact, but only 2 or 3 percent of women were mostly or exclusively homosexual on a lifelong basis.

More recent statistics gathered by the Kinsey Institute, based on a national probability sample surveyed in 1970 (but not published until 1989) estimated that 3.3 percent of the American adult male population had homosexual contact "occasionally" or "fairly often" after age 20 (Fay et al., 1989).

It now appears that the original Kinsey data may have overestimated the prevalence of homosexuality in the general population in part because of the nonrepresentative nature of the Kinsey samples. One of the key problems may have been the large number of prisoners included in the Kinsey male study; another difficulty was that many of the individuals interviewed by Kinsey's staff were volunteers from gay organizations.

Specifically, a carefully designed nationally representative survey of American men aged 20 to 39 conducted in 1991 found that only 2 percent of sexually active men have had any same-gender sexual contact during the past ten years, and only 1 percent reported being exclusively homosexual during this same time period (Billy et al., 1993). This finding, which contrasts sharply with the Kinsey data, is consistent with the findings of several other recent studies. For example, the 1989 General Social Survey reported that 98 percent of sexually active men 18 and older were exclusively heterosexual during the year prior to being interviewed and estimated that, "three percent [of American males] have not been sexually active as adults, 91–93 percent have been exclusively heterosexual, 5–6 percent have been bisexual and less than 1 percent have been exclusively homosexual" (Smith, 1991, p. 105). Similarly, a large national sex survey conducted recently in France found that only 4 percent of men aged 18 to 69 had ever had a same-gender sexual experience, while only 1 percent had done so in the 12 months preceding the survey (Analyse des Comportements Sexuels en France, 1992). Only 1.4 percent of the men and 0.4 percent of the women surveyed had had sex with a person of the same gender during the last five years. A recent large-scale national survey in Britain came up with remarkably similar results: 1.4 percent of the men surveyed reported having at least one homosexual contact in the preceding five years (Johnson et al., 1992). Data from surveys in Japan, the Phillipines, Thailand, Denmark, and the Netherlands are quite consistent with the findings cited above, leading Diamond (1993, p. 303) to note:

No study finds any figure reaching 10% for all respondents [sic] experiences with homosexual and bisexual activity combined. Considering the comparatively liberal attitudes toward homosexual or bisexual activity in Denmark, the Netherlands, Phillipines, and Thailand, if not in Japan,

Table 15.1 Kinsey's Heterosexual–Homosexual Rating Scale

0	Exclusively heterosexual
1	Predominantly heterosexual: only incidentally homosexual
2	Predominantly heterosexual: more than incidentally homosexual
3	Equally heterosexual and homosexual
4	Predominantly homosexual: more than incidentally heterosexual
5	Predominantly homosexual: only incidentally heterosexual
6	Exclusively homosexual

Source: *Modified from Kinsey, Pomeroy, and Martin,* Sexual Behavior in the Human Male *(Philadelphia: Saunders, 1948). Reprinted by permission of The Kinsey Institute for Research in Sex, Gender & Reproduction, Inc.*

Great Britain, or the United States, these data must be considered strongly. All these studies taken together indicate that bisexuality, and indeed homosexuality, are less common than previously considered. This appears whether the group surveyed are self-identified gays or from random samples.

HISTORICAL PERSPECTIVES

Homosexuality was clearly condemned in the earliest Jewish tradition. In the Bible we are told: "And if a man lie with mankind, as with womankind, both of them have committed abomination: they shall surely be put to death; their blood shall be upon them" (Leviticus 20:13).

Yet in ancient Greece, homosexuality and bisexuality in certain forms were widely accepted as natural in all segments of society (Hoffman, 1980). Plato's *Symposium* praised the virtues of male homosexuality and suggested that pairs of homosexual lovers would make the best soldiers. Many of the Greek mythological heroes, such as Zeus, Hercules, Poseidon, and Achilles, were linked with ho-

homosexual (hō′ mō sek shoo ul) a person with sexual preference for partners of his or her own sex.

bisexual (bī sek′ shoo ul) a person sexually attracted to both males and females.

heterosexual a person with sexual preference for partners of the opposite gender.

mosexual behavior (Boswell, 1980). Although some Greek literature and art portrayed sexual relations between two women or two adult men, most of the homosexual relations seemed to occur between grown men and young adolescent boys (Karlen, 1980). Clearly, most Greek men married; yet homosexual activity was not seen as shameful or sinful.

In the early days of the Roman Empire, homosexuality was apparently unregulated by law, and homosexual behavior was common. Marriages between two men or between two women were legal and accepted among the upper classes, and several emperors, including Nero, reportedly were married to men (Boswell, 1980).

Although most historians who have written on the subject suggest that Christianity more or less from its beginnings strongly condemned and persecuted homosexuality, this may not have been the case at all. In a book called *Christianity, Social Tolerance, and Homosexuality*, John Boswell (1980) argues that for many centuries Catholic Europe showed no hostility to homosexuality. More recently, Boswell (1994) uncovered evidence of Church ceremonies used to solemnize same–sex unions from the 11th to 16th centuries.

The primary ammunition for the Catholic church's position against homosexuality came from the writings of St. Augustine and St. Thomas Aquinas, who both suggested that any sexual acts that could not lead to conception were unnatural and therefore sinful. Using this line of reasoning, the church became a potent force in the regulation (and punishment) of sexual behavior. While some homosexuals were mildly rebuked and given prayer as penance, others were tortured or burned at the stake.

In the Middle Ages, accusations of homosexuality became one of the weapons of the Inquisition, whose dedicated investigators rarely failed to extract an appropriate "confession" from their suspect, whether guilty or not. These "confessions" were used to portray purported homosexuals not only as sexually deviant but as heretic and treasonous (Karlen, 1980).

The negative attitudes toward homosexuality that stemmed from religious beliefs dominated Western thought until the medical view of sexuality began to emerge in the eighteenth and nineteenth centuries (Bullough, 1978). This was hardly a sign of progress, however, since the medical view

simply substituted the word *illness* for *sin*. For example, Krafft-Ebing's *Psychopathia Sexualis* linked homosexuality to genetic flaws and a predisposing weakness of the nervous system. By the start of the twentieth century, it was generally agreed that homosexuality was an illness with which a person was born.

Although there is still a lively scientific debate on the origins of homosexuality, it appears that tolerance for homosexuality is once again on the upswing. In 1957 the Wolfenden Report in England recommended that laws against any form of private sexual behavior between consenting adults be repealed. In 1969 a few nights of summertime demonstrations on Christopher Street in Manhattan's Greenwich Village protesting police raids on a homosexual bar marked the beginning of an era of gay political activism that expanded into a full-fledged gay rights movement (see Figure 15.1). By 1990, many American cities, towns, and countries had enacted ordinances that banned discrimination against homosexuals in housing and jobs, although as we mentioned earlier, this produced some legislative backlash in the next few years.

The visibility of the gay community activated political and social opposition from many quarters, and even today tensions exist not only between heterosexuals and homosexuals but within the homosexual community itself.

In his book *The Homosexualization of America*, Dennis Altman (1982) pointed out:

> No longer sinners, criminals, perverts, neurotics, or deviants, homosexuals are being slowly redefined in less value-laden terms as practitioners of an alternative lifestyle, members of a new community. In a self-proclaimed pluralistic society like the United States, this is probably the most effective way to win tolerance, if not acceptance. *(p. 35)*

However, Altman's view, which was undoubtedly correct at the beginning of the 1980s, was rapidly undermined by the appearance of AIDS (for acquired immune deficiency syndrome, discussed in detail in Chapter 20). Although it is now clear that AIDS can be transmitted heterosexually, the concentration of cases early in the epidemic in gay and bisexual men gave people an excuse once again to view homosexuality as a form of disease and provided ammunition to those who want to discriminate against gays.

Figure 15.1 A Timeline of Notable Events in the Gay Rights Movement

1969 ► A police raid on the Stonewall Inn, a gay bar in New York's Greenwich Village, sets off three days of riots and demonstrations, marking the start of the gay-rights movement.

1970 ► Gay Pride parades in New York and San Francisco are held on the anniversary of the Stonewall riots, starting a national trend.

1973 ► American Psychiatric Association removes homosexuality from its list of mental disorders.

1977 ► Harvey Milk becomes the first openly gay supervisor of San Francisco.

1981 ► First cases of the disease now called AIDS, but then unnamed, reported by the U.S. Centers for Disease Control.

1982 ► Gay Men's Health Crisis is founded in New York City; first National Lesbian and Gay Leadership Conference is held in Dallas; the mysterious disease striking gay men is tentatively called GRID (Gay-Related Immune Deficiency) by some researchers.

1983 ► Representative Gerry Studds (D-Massachusetts) announces his homosexuality amid a sex scandal, becoming the first U.S. Congress member to make his homosexuality public; he was later reelected.

1983 ► As of December 19, 1983, there are 3000 reported cases of AIDS in America, with 1283 deaths.

1984 ► San Francisco bathhouses are closed during the Democratic National Convention; 100,000 march in protest.

1986 ► U.S. Supreme Court upholds states' rights to outlaw homosexual sodomy.

1987 ► Three hundred thousand people march in Washington on behalf of the Gay Rights movement; the AIDS Quilt is unfurled.

1988 ► ACT UP attains national prominence in its advocacy of people with AIDS.

1989 ► San Francisco passes an ordinance giving legal recognition to domestic partnerships of homosexuals; State Bar Association of California urges recognition of gay marriages.

1993 ► Senate Armed Services Committee holds hearings on President Clinton's plan to end the ban on gays and lesbians from openly serving in the military.

Now we will turn from our historical considerations to a view of how homosexuality exists in a number of other cultures. The premise to keep in mind is that no single pattern of homosexuality is invariably found, just as no single pattern of heterosexuality exists.

PATTERNS OF MALE HOMOSEXUALITY: A CROSS-CULTURAL VIEW *

In many societies, homosexual acts occur between members of the same sex regardless of the erotic

*This section was written by J. Patrick Gray and Linda D. Wolfe.

preferences of the individuals involved. Two men with erotic preferences for females may engage in homosexual acts without changing their erotic orientations; that is, their erotic preference remains heterosexual while their behavior is homosexual. The reverse situation can also occur. If a man with sexual preference for men engages in sexual activity with a woman, his erotic preference is homosexual, while his behavior is heterosexual. Here we refer to a person as a homosexual only if his erotic preference is homosexual.

Because erotic preferences are in the mind and may not be shown in behavior, anthropologists do not know if the frequency of homosexuality varies from society to society or from time to time within a single society. Societies do, however, vary in their attitudes toward male homosexual behavior (Whitham, 1983; Blackwood, 1986; Endleman, 1986), which can create the illusion that the frequency of homosexuality differs from one society to another. To see how this is so, consider three societies. One society has a fairly tolerant attitude toward male homosexual behavior and therefore homosexuals are fairly open about their behavior. In the second society, all males are required to engage in homosexual behavior during puberty and early adulthood. Finally, in the last society, male homosexual behavior is stigmatized and severely punished, and most homosexuals do not manifest their sexual preferences openly.

An outside observer is likely to conclude that the first two societies produce more homosexuals than the last society, but this conclusion might not be correct. In the first society, homosexuals are not stigmatized for their behavior and therefore an outsider is likely to see many indications of homosexual behavior. In the society with ritualized homosexuality, the vast majority of males engaged in homosexual behavior during puberty and early adulthood are heterosexuals performing homosexual acts. The last society may contain as many homosexuals as the first two, but their sexual preference is hidden from the public. Thus, the frequency of homosexuals could be the same in the three societies, but the frequency of observable homosexual acts may be quite different.

Factors That Affect a Society's Attitude Toward Homosexuality

Anthropologists have identified a number of factors related to a society's attitudes toward male homosexual behavior. Werner (1979) found that societies that permit at least some segment of the population to engage in homosexual behavior also tend to permit abortion and infanticide. In contrast, societies that forbid any homosexual behavior usually also bar both abortion and infanticide. Werner suggests that social attitudes toward homosexuality relate to concern about population size. In societies where population increase is desired, homosexuality, abortion, and infanticide are banned. When a society fears overpopulation, these three behaviors are permitted open expression. Werner's cross-cultural study may help explain historical changes in attitudes toward homosexuality in industrial societies.

Ira Reiss (1986) examined male homosexual behavior in a sample of 70 societies and found that societies that exhibit high frequencies of such behavior usually have a child-rearing pattern in which the father interacts very little with infants and children. Societies that raise children in this way usually define gender roles very strictly and insist on male dominance over women and children. In these societies boys may have difficulty learning how to play the masculine gender role because they have so little contact with their fathers or other adult males (Chodorow, 1978). Reiss suggests that such societies may generate high frequencies of male homosexual acts by following one of two possible paths. In those societies that forbid homosexual behavior, boys who have trouble achieving a masculine self-identity may reject the heterosexuality of the male role and turn to homosexual behavior. A second pathway is found in those societies where male dominance is based on the existence of aggressive male kin groups. In these societies the majority of men are heterosexuals, but they use homosexual behavior to create and express their common identity as males.

Reiss' (1986) work and Werner's (1979) work demonstrate some possible explanations of the variation in social attitudes toward male homosexual behavior. Another aspect of cross-cultural variation is found in the way that cultures contrast heterosexual and homosexual behaviors.

Three Contrasting Cultures

An American Pattern

The belief of much of American society is that people are born male or female and "naturally" desire sex with members of the opposite sex. Homosexual behavior is seen as an incompatible alternative to heterosexual behavior, and individuals who engage in one are seen as avoiding the other except under extraordinary conditions (e.g., imprisonment). (Although many people are aware of the concept of bisexuality, it does not currently play a major role in the concept of the relationship between homosexual and heterosexual behaviors held by most Americans.) In spite of the widespread publicity given to ideas such as the distinction between gender role and erotic preference or between transsexualism, transvestism, and homosexuality, the most common American cultural pattern holds that gender role, erotic preference, and sexual behavior will naturally be of the same orientation. Thus, a man who voluntarily engages in homosexual behavior is defined as more feminine or somewhat less masculine than men who engage in heterosexual behavior. The idea that homosexual behavior is the result of a disease or a depraved moral state is also a common belief held by Americans.

An Azande Pattern
Other cultural patterns of the relationship between homosexual and heterosexual behavior separate the elements that the American pattern defines as inseparable: biological gender, erotic preference, gender role, and sexual behavior. For example, a pattern found in many societies separates biological gender and erotic preference from sexual behavior and defines sexual behavior in relation to age or gender role. Prior to conquest by the British, the Azande of Africa illustrated this pattern (Evans-Pritchard, 1970, 1971).

In Azande society, there was a shortage of unmarried women because men could have more than one wife. As a result, some males turned to masturbation (which was not considered shameful) or homosexual behavior for sexual release. This pattern was institutionalized in organized military companies in which older men married boys aged 12 to 20. The husband paid bridewealth to the boy's parents and was expected to behave as a dutiful son-in-law. The Azande had strict rules against adultery, and if the boy slept with another man his husband could press charges for adultery. The boy performed all the household and caretaking duties appropriate to the feminine gender role. The couple slept together at night and engaged in sex, with the husband inserting his penis between the boy's thighs. Evans-Pritchard notes that the Azande expressed disgust at the idea of anal intercourse. His report does not mention oral–genital sex and leaves the impression that the boy did not reverse sex roles with his husband.

The termination of these marriages illustrates the Azande separation of sexual behavior and sexual preference. When the boy–wife matured, he became a warrior and left his husband, perhaps to marry a woman. If he could not find an eligible woman or could not afford the bride-price, he might marry a young boy. The boy's former husband might marry another boy or, if able to pay bride-price, a woman. If the older man had been a

dutiful son-in-law, his parents-in-law might replace their son with one of their daughters. Evans-Pritchard indicates that when men married women they no longer engaged in homosexual behavior.

The Azande boy–wife custom is a case in which a minority of males in a special institution engaged in homosexual behavior while having a heterosexual erotic preference (although a few might have had a homosexual erotic preference). The society did not classify these males as biologically or morally deviant, nor did it see the husbands expressing a feminine identity by engaging in homosexual behavior. The boy–wife played a feminine gender role until he became a warrior, at which point he switched to a full masculine gender role. The general attitude was that homosexual behavior was a poor substitute for heterosexual behavior, an unfortunate necessity due to the shortage of women.

In the Azande culture, men who engaged in homosexual behavior were not stigmatized, and their activities were not seen as having great significance; male homosexual behavior was nothing more than a release of sexual tension. This contrasts with the Azande view of female homosexual behavior. It was believed that females in a large polygynous household might turn to one another for sex if their husband did not have intercourse with them frequently enough to release sexual tension. Two women might enact male and female positions in intercourse, using a banana or sweet potato as a substitute for a penis. While male homosexual behavior had no consequences beyond the release of sexual tension, sex between two wives might supernaturally cause the death of their husband. Furthermore, while the Azande held that male homosexual behavior did not affect the future sexual behavior of either the husband or his boy–wife, they believed that once women engaged in homosexual activity they would continue to do so because they learned they could control their own sexual gratification.

A Melanesian Pattern
A third cultural pattern of homosexual behavior is illustrated by some Melanesian societies, in which homosexual activity is seen as necessary to prepare a man for heterosexual intercourse (Herdt, 1981, 1984). Some of these groups assume that the only way a boy can grow into a virile and active adult capable of performing the masculine role is to ac-

cept semen from older men. The idea that homosexual behavior is required to become a fully masculine adult contrasts with both the common American pattern, where homosexual behavior typically is seen as precluding both heterosexual behavior and proper fulfillment of the masculine role, and the Azande pattern, where homosexual behavior is viewed as a simple alternative to heterosexual activity that does not produce any significant changes in practitioners.

Gilbert Herdt's (1981, 1986) fieldwork from 1974 to 1976 among the Sambia of New Guinea provides the best description of a Melanesian society with ritualized male homosexual behavior. The Sambia are divided into small units that frequently war with one another. Warriorhood is the dominant component in the Sambia masculine gender role, and men view themselves as warriors with the duty to defend their unit. Sambian men see women as sexually desirable, yet they believe that sex with women weakens men and can destroy a man's ability to fulfill the masculine gender role. One reason Sambian culture exhibits intense antagonism between males and females may be that wives frequently come from enemy groups.

The key to Sambian patterning of homosexual behavior is the belief that males and females mature differently. The Sambia believe that a girl's internal organs cause her to mature much earlier than boys. These organs are present at birth and need no special help in turning a girl into a woman. In contrast, the Sambia believe that a boy is born with an internal organ that will eventually produce growth but is incapable of doing so on its own. The organ must be supplied with semen from older males if the boy is to outstrip the growth of girls and become a strong and handsome man. This organ does not use all the semen that a boy takes in to create growth. Some is stored so that the boy can engage in sexual activity as an adult. Although there are ways a man can replenish a small portion of the semen he loses when engaging in sex, the semen organ does not manufacture semen, and an adult's supply depends on how much he ingests during his period as an initiate.

Young boys begin the initiation into masculine society between age 7 and 10. They are separated from their mothers at this time and live in the men's hut for 10 to 20 years. They undergo numerous painful rites to rid themselves of the pollution they have accumulated by living with women. For example, they swallow flexible canes to induce vomiting that will expel some of the pollution, and they release polluted maternal blood from their bodies by violently jabbing sharp spears of grass up their noses. While emptying themselves of pollution, they also start filling themselves with the semen necessary to become men by performing acts of fellatio on older but not yet fully adult males. Herdt (1981) notes that these older males do not reverse positions because such an act would rob the younger boys of precious semen.

Semen transfers are governed by complex rules that suggest that erotic preference has only a minor part to play in this activity. The rules of incest governing heterosexual activity are also applied to homosexual behavior. While a boy should not take semen from his father or other close male kin, for example, it is considered best when he accepts semen from his sister's husband, who belongs to a different group. In fact, donors typically belong to groups that are potential enemies of the boy's group. Semen transfer is not a one-time ceremonial activity; after being introduced to semen ingestion at a ritual, young boys try to accept sperm every day.

After six to eight years of ingesting semen, the initiate is classified as a bachelor and becomes a semen donor to young boys in other groups. For a few years after becoming a semen donor the bachelor continues to avoid women and engages only in homosexual behavior. However, shortly after turning 16 he marries, usually a girl who has not yet undergone menarche. For one or two years the newly married man is fellated both by his bride and by boys in other groups. However, once his wife experiences menarche and he begins to engage in intercourse with her, homosexual behavior should cease. The Sambia believe that the vagina contaminates the penis and that to place the polluted organ into a young boy's mouth would be harmful.

The Sambia provide an interesting case for analyzing the development of sexual identity and erotic preference. The logic of the common American patterning of homosexual and heterosexual behavior would suggest that a stage of life during which all boys engaged in homosexual behavior would have a powerful effect on their sexual identity, turning many of them into homosexuals. Herdt (1981) argues that even though the young boys must eroticize the penis and the mouths of other males to engage in homosexual behavior, the vast majority of Sambian males have a heterosexual erotic preference as adults. He estimates that less than 5 percent of the adult males continues to prefer homosexual behavior with boys to heterosexual behavior. The other adult males look down on such men and see them as deviant.

The homosexual activity of the Sambia occurs in a set of complex cultural meanings that we can only touch on here. One area of meaning involves the nature of the sexes. A secret myth told only to initiates reveals that the first beings were androgynous. One became the first woman when s/he fellated the other, causing her breasts to swell and her penis to disappear while also reducing the breasts of the first man. Herdt (1981) notes that this myth may fuel men's concern about their masculinity since they ingest semen just as the first woman did. To deny that they are "feminized," men constantly demonstrate their masculinity in ritual and warfare.

A second area of meaning involves the idea of male control over fertility. This is a widespread concern in Melanesian societies, and different groups pattern this concern in various ways. In some groups the role of semen as an agent of growth is taken over by blood, in others by magic spells, and in others by "medicines." Thus, to understand the meaning of Sambian homosexual behavior, the Sambian ideas of growth and fertility must be compared with the ideas of groups that are concerned with growth but do not engage in ritualized homosexual behavior.

A final question of meaning concerns the potential hostility between the donors and takers of sperm. Other groups with ritualized homosexual behavior pattern this relationship quite differently. For example, the Kimam of southern New Guinea (Serpenti, 1965; Gray, 1986) have ceremonially opposed village sectors that compete in growing yams and children. A boy of one sector is initiated into adulthood when the males of the opposite sector symbolically kill and bury him. The adult males of the boy's sector provide sperm that is smeared into cuts in his arms and legs, while a slightly older boy inseminates him through anal intercourse. This semen revives him and allows him to grow into an adult. Years later he is displayed to the men of the opposite sector at a yam feast to demonstrate that the men of his sector still control growth and fertility. The Sambian boy engaged in homosexual be-

havior with a potential enemy must have a very different sexual experience from a Kimam boy who receives sperm from a male who is his social ally.

Other Patterns of Male Homosexual Behavior
Humans exhibit many other patterns of male homosexual behavior. For example, some societies permit men to adopt a gender role that might be labeled "not-men" (Callender and Kochems, 1986). These biological males take on some aspects of feminine dress and/or occupation and reject the masculine gender role. Some societies require that these not-men engage in sex with males, while others do not require it but do permit it. In other societies these not-men might marry women and father children, while also engaging in sex with males. Recent studies of the berdache, a not-men role found in many Native American societies prior to contact with European culture, emphasize that although these men adopted a feminine-like gender role, they were not always expected to engage in homosexual behavior (Whitehead, 1981). [For females who crossed gender roles in Native American societies, see Blackwood (1984).]

THEORIES ON THE ORIGINS OF SEXUAL ORIENTATION

Why do some people become homosexual? Is it a life-long condition over which a person has no control? Is it an entirely voluntary choice, consciously and deliberately made at a certain phase in life? Is it mainly a response to the role models a child is exposed to at home or at school?

Each of these questions has important implications for political, legal, and religious interpretations of homosexuality, but, unfortunately, the basic problem is that no one really knows what "causes" heterosexuality either. It may simply be that so far the wrong research questions have been asked. Nevertheless, it is useful to understand some of the viewpoints on the origins of homosexuality.

Biological Theories

Many homosexuals claim that their sexual orientation is the result of biological forces over which they have no control or choice. Several types of evidence have been examined to see if this might be so.

Genetic Factors

One investigator reported findings that supported the earlier viewpoint that homosexuality was a genetic condition (Kallman, 1952). This study examined the sexual orientations of sets of identical and fraternal (nonidentical) male twins where one twin was homosexual. Its underlying assumption was that since both twins were exposed to the same prenatal and postnatal environments, a genetic cause for homosexuality would show up as a high concordance rate among identical twins, since they have identical genes; that is, both twins would be homosexual rather than one being homosexual and one heterosexual. A lower concordance rate would be expected among fraternal twins, since their genetic makeup is different. Astonishingly, Kallman found 100 percent concordance in identical twins for male homosexuality and only 12 percent concordance in fraternal twins. This finding is astonishing because very few phenomena in biological research show 100 percent outcomes or matching. Subsequent studies largely failed to replicate Kallman's findings (Zuger, 1976; Heston and Shields, 1968; Eckert et al., 1986) and the genetic theory of homosexuality was largely discarded by scientists during the 1980s.

However, several recent studies of twins and adoptive siblings have revitalized the idea that there is a large genetic component to both male and female homosexuality, rekindling the debate. For example, psychologist Michael Bailey and psychiatrist Richard Pillard studied 115 male twins and 46 adoptive brothers of these twins and found that if one identical twin was gay, the other was almost three times more likely to also be gay than if they were fraternal (nonidentical) twins (Bailey and Pillard, 1991). Bailey and his co-workers (1993) then conducted a similar study of lesbians and found essentially the same degree of linkage. If one identical twin was lesbian, the other identical twin had a high probability of being lesbian too. Nonidentical same-sex twins were two and a half times more likely than adoptive sisters to be lesbian, but far less likely than identical twins.

The evidence for a genetic basis for a predisposition to homosexuality became even stronger with the mid-1993 publication of a study by researchers at the National Cancer Institute uncovering a region on the X chromosome that appears to contain one or more genes for homosexuality (Hamer et al., 1993; Pool, 1993). After recruiting 76 homosex-

ual men, Hamer and his colleagues traced out detailed family trees for each and determined whether any other family members were gay or bisexual. Overall, 13.5 percent of the gay men's brothers were homosexual, which was considerably higher than the rate of approximately 2 percent that these researchers found in the general population. However, perhaps the most startling finding was that there were more gay relatives on the mother's side of the family than on the father's side, suggesting that at least for some homosexual men, a biological predisposition is passed through female members of the family—an inheritance pattern that geneticists call "X-linked" (since the X chromosome in males is contributed exclusively by the mother).

The researchers then recruited 40 pairs of homosexual brothers and took blood samples from each to analyze their DNA patterns. (Current analytic methods allow scientists to map the exact patterns of DNA, comparing one person's DNA to another's to look for matching "pieces.") Hamer and his colleagues found that 33 of the 40 pairs of homosexual brothers had a shared stretch of DNA on the long arm of the X chromosome. This translated into a 99.5 percent degree of technical certainty that there are one or more genes in this region that predispose a male toward homosexuality. However, as the researchers pointed out, not all the homosexual brothers in their study showed this linkage, and it is likely that one "homosexuality gene" cannot explain all male homosexuality (Pool, 1993).

Not all scientists or geneticists have been quick to applaud the new findings, however. Ruth Hubbard, professor emeritus of biology at Harvard, believes this study is seriously flawed:

> It is based on simplistic assumptions about sexuality and is hampered by the near impossibility of establishing links between genes and behavior. . . . Also, the researchers did not do the obvious control experiment of checking for the presence of these markers among heterosexual brothers of the gay men they studied. It is surprising that the correlation found in this report warranted publication without these controls. . . . (*Hubbard, 1993, p. A15*)

Furthermore, twin studies are not always as reliable or easy to interpret as they might seem (Phillips, 1993). Byne and Parsons (1993) note that these studies are "hampered by technical flaws," including the fact that subjects were recruited by ads in homosexually oriented periodicals and are unlikely to be representative of homosexuals in the general population. The finding that a large proportion of identical twins were discordant for sexual orientation, even though they shared an identical genetic pattern, prenatal conditions, and family environment, serves as a caution about assuming that biology "causes" homosexuality in a predictable, direct manner.

Brain Factors

Recent research has also focused on brain structure and function as possible determinants of sexual orientation. For example, one team of scientists found evidence of an enlarged region of the hypothalamus in homosexual men compared to heterosexuals (Swaab and Hoffman, 1990). More of a stir was created in 1991 with the publication of a study by neuroanatomist Simon LeVay of the Salk Institute for Biological Studies. LeVay studied a portion of the anterior hypothalamus because it had been shown in other species to be involved with male-typical sexual behavior. Furthermore, previous researchers had noted that two regions of the hypothalamus are twice as large in men as they are in women. LeVay conducted autopsy studies involving microscopic examinations of the brains of men and women. Specifically, he discovered that one of the regions of the hypothalamus called INAH-3 was considerably smaller in homosexual men than in heterosexual men: that in gay men it was actually about the same size as in women (LeVay, 1991).

LeVay's study produced an avalanche of media responses, in part because it seemed to offer irrefutable proof that a homosexual orientation is something a person is born with and is not formed by choice or by social influences. This conclusion might have profound implications for religious views of a homosexual orientation, as well as far-reaching legal and social implications. However, the media excitement over this study was clearly disproportionate to the science involved. For one thing, it is not clear whether the anatomic findings are a cause or a consequence of sexual orientation (Byne and Parsons, 1993). For another, the homosexual men whose brains LeVay studied had died of AIDS, which commonly involves extensive brain disease because HIV frequently infects brain cells (Ho et al., 1989; Cohen, Sande, and Volberding, 1990). An additional problem was that there

was no certainty that the men classified as heterosexual in this study actually were; the assumption was simply made that they were heterosexual since there was no notation in their medical charts that they were gay. Finally, the sample size was very small: only 18 male homosexuals and 1 bisexual man were included, and of the 16 presumed heterosexual men studied, 6 had died of AIDS. (The brains of 6 women were also studied.) While it is possible that LeVay's research will be confirmed by others, it would be wrong to jump to the conclusion that sexual orientation is controlled by a small collection of cells in the hypothalamus.

Hormonal Factors

Several different types of research have led many to speculate on the possibility of hormonal factors causing or predisposing to homosexuality. First, it has been well documented that prenatal hormone treatments of various types can lead to male or female homosexual behavior patterns in several different animal species (Dörner, 1968, 1976; Money and Ehrhardt, 1972; Hutchison, 1978). Second, some scattered findings show that prenatal sex hormone excess or deficiency in humans may be associated with homosexuality. For example, some preliminary studies of human females with the adrenogenital syndrome—a prenatal androgen excess discussed in Chapter 7—indicate that these individuals may be more likely to develop a lesbian orientation (Ehrhardt, Evers, and Money, 1968; Money and Schwartz, 1977).

Third, a great deal of attention has focused on a comparison of hormone levels in adult homosexuals and heterosexuals. While several studies have found either lower testosterone or higher estrogen in homosexual men, and one study found higher blood testosterone in lesbians than in heterosexual women, other studies have failed to replicate these findings (Meyer-Bahlburg, 1977, 1979; Tourney, 1980). Similarly, although prior research suggested that more subtle changes in sex hormone feedback dynamics were different in homosexual and heterosexual men (Gladue, Green, and Hellman, 1984), more recent studies have failed to substantiate this claim (Hendricks, Graber, and Rodriguez-Sierra, 1989).

Another version of how hormonal factors might influence sexual orientation is known as the *maternal stress effect*. This hypothesis is based on research in rats showing that stress on a pregnant rat leads to an increased rate of atypical sexual behavior in her male offspring (although whether this atypical behavior is in any way equivalent to male homosexuality in humans is far from clear). The reason behind this effect is that the maternal stress lowers the level of testosterone in the developing male fetuses during critical periods of fetal brain differentiation (LeVay, 1993). Although arguments have been made that this mechanism may pertain to humans (Dörner et al., 1980; Ellis et al., 1988), there is little research evidence for this (Gooren, Fliers, and Courtney, 1990; Bailey, Willerman, and Parks, 1991). Although Dörner and his colleagues (1983) claimed that human prenatal maternal stress just before and during the Second World War in Germany may have led to a subsequent increase in homosexuality and transsexuality in that country, an attempt to replicate their findings was unsuccessful (Schmidt and Clement, 1990).

This body of research has major limitations. For example, treating adult homosexuals with sex hormones does not alter their sexual orientation in any way. The experimental animal models of homosexuality do not appear to be a good parallel to homosexuality in humans. The relatively rare instances of prenatal hormone excess or deficiency linked to homosexuality in humans may be special cases without much relevance to sexual development in general. And the conflicting reports on the sex hormone status of adult homosexuals leave many questions unanswered. Most notably, there may possibly be many "types" of homosexuality (and heterosexuality) which—until discovered—will confound attempts at pinpointing the biological infuences on sexual orientation (Masters and Johnson, 1979).

Despite the interest in possible hormone mechanisms in the origin of homosexuality, no serious scientist today suggests that a simple cause–effect relationship applies. Instead, the possibility that prenatal hormones may influence brain development in ways that could predispose individuals to certain adult patterns of sexual behavior is being considered.

Psychological Theories

Freud's Views
Freud believed that homosexuality was an outgrowth of an innate bisexual predisposition in all people. Under ordinary circumstances, the psycho-sexual development of the child would proceed smoothly along a heterosexual course. Under certain circumstances, however, such as improper resolution of the Oedipus complex (p. 210), normal development might be arrested in an "immature" stage, resulting in adult homosexuality. Furthermore, since Freud thought that all people have latent homosexual tendencies, he believed that under certain conditions—such as continuing castration anxiety in males—overt homosexual behavior might occur for the first time in adulthood.

Freud's views on homosexuality are difficult to pin down because he wrote relatively little on the subject. Although psychoanalysis seems to have reinforced the notion of homosexuality as a form of mental illness, Freud took a fairly neutral stance on the subject in a letter to the mother of a homosexual son:

> Homosexuality is assuredly no advantage, but it is nothing to be ashamed of, no vice, no degradation, it cannot be classified as an illness; we consider it to be a variation of the sexual development. Many highly respected individuals of ancient and modern times have been homosexuals, several of the greatest men among them (Plato, Michelangelo, Leonardo da Vinci, etc.). It is a great injustice to persecute homosexuality as a crime and cruelty, too. *(Historical Notes: A Letter from Freud, 1951)*

While it is not clear whether Freud was simply trying to reassure this distraught mother or genuinely held to the sentiments shown in this letter, it is clear that many later psychoanalysts took positions strongly opposed to homosexuality (see reviews by Karlen, 1971; Green, 1972; Tripp, 1975).

Bieber's Model
Since Freud had suggested that disordered parent–child relations might lead to homosexuality, psychoanalyst Irving Bieber and his colleagues (1962) evaluated the family backgrounds of 106 homosexual and 100 heterosexual men seen as patients. They found that many of the homosexual men they saw had overprotective, dominant mothers and weak or passive fathers, whereas this family pattern was infrequently seen in their heterosexual subjects. Bieber discarded the Freudian notion of psychic bisexuality and suggested that homosexuality results from fears of heterosexual interactions.

Further research on this apparent "cause" of male homosexuality has had mixed results. Bene (1965) found that homosexual men had relatively poorer relationships with their fathers than did heterosexual men and described their fathers as "ineffective," but there was no indication of maternal overprotection. Greenblatt (1966), however, found that fathers of homosexual men were good, generous, dominant, and underprotective, while mothers were free of excessive protectiveness or dominance. Siegelman (1974) reported that for groups of heterosexuals and homosexuals who were well adjusted psychologically, there were no apparent differences in family relationships. Likewise, Bell, Weinberg, and Hammersmith (1981) found no support for Bieber's theory in their important study discussed in the Research Spotlight on page 384.

Reviewing such findings, Marmor (1980) suggests that although there seems to be "a reasonable amount of evidence that boys exposed to this kind of family background have a greater than average likelihood of becoming homosexual," not all people who have this background become homosexual (p. 10). As Marmor also notes:

> Homosexuals can also come from families with distant or hostile mothers and overly close fathers, from families with ambivalent relationships with older brothers, from homes with absent mothers, absent fathers, idealized fathers, and from a variety of broken homes. *(p. 11)*

Pursuing this same line of research, Wolff (1971) found that among 100 lesbians compared with heterosexual women, the most prominent parental characteristics were a rejecting or indifferent mother and a distant or absent father. Thus, she believed that female homosexuality arises from a girl's receiving inadequate love from her mother—leading her to continually seek such love from other women—combined with her poor relationship with her father that prevented her from learning to relate to men. To these observations we must add that many homosexuals come from perfectly well-adjusted family backgrounds (Tripp, 1975; Gagnon, 1977; Masters and Johnson, 1979). Unfortunately, many parents assume the blame for a child's turning out gay and agonize over "What did we do wrong?" The present evidence simply does not show that homosexuality only or usually results from improper parenting.

Behavioral Theories

Psychosocial theories emphasize that homosexuality is primarily a learned phenomenon (McGuire, Carlisle, and Young, 1965; Gagnon and Simon, 1973; Masters and Johnson, 1979). In this view, the psychological conditioning associated with the reinforcement or punishment of early sexual behavior (and sexual thoughts and feelings) largely controls the process of sexual orientation. Thus, people's early sexual experiences may steer them toward homosexual behavior by pleasurable, gratifying same-sex encounters, or by unpleasant, dissatisfying, or frightening heterosexual experiences.

Sexual fantasies can also be conditioned. A positive sexual encounter with a homosexual partner can become the raw material for fantasy during masturbation, which is positively reinforced when it is followed by orgasm. In addition, a variety of other factors may influence a person's early sexual conditioning. Currently, attention has focused on children who show atypical gender-role behavior ("sissy" boys and "tomboyish" girls) who may have a greater likelihood of becoming homosexual (Green, 1974, 1987; Hockenberry and Billingham, 1987; Zuger, 1984, 1989).

The behavioral view also suggests why some heterosexuals change to homosexuality in adulthood. According to Feldman and MacCulloch (1971), if a person has unpleasant heterosexual experiences combined with rewarding homosexual encounters, there may be a gradual shift in the homosexual direction. Although some homosexuals who have "switched" after an earlier period of heterosexual life do not fit this picture exactly, it is common to find many who do (Masters and Johnson, 1979). The observation that some female rape victims shift to lesbianism also supports this viewpoint (Grundlach, 1977).

A Concluding Note on "Causes"

There is certainly no agreement among scientists about what "causes" heterosexuality or homosexuality or bisexuality. This may be partly because these terms encompass such a broad range of individuals, behaviors, and mind-sets that they cannot be defined or analyzed as uniform entities. Also, when we discussed a few of the best-known theories, we cautioned in almost every instance that the data are not complete and that current thinking must be left open, subject to better stud-

RESEARCH SPOTLIGHT

How Sexual Preference Develops

Tackling the complex question of how people become heterosexual or homosexual is not an easy task. A new level of methodological sophistication in approaching this topic was shown by Bell, Weinberg, and Hammersmith in a two-volume study entitled *Sexual Preference: Its Development in Men and Women* (1981). The sample that they examined consisted of 686 homosexual men, 293 homosexual women, 337 heterosexual men, and 140 heterosexual women, all of whom underwent an extensive face-to-face interview requiring three to five hours to complete.

In addition to developing what is probably the most extensive collection of data in existence on such a sizable sample, Bell and his co-workers were careful to draw on a variety of different theories about the "causes" of homosexuality in order to examine their validity. Thus, they gathered information that might support the psychoanalytic viewpoint of how homosexuality develops as well as information that might "prove" the social learning theory view or tie in with various sociological theories.

The researchers tested their data by using a complicated statistical method called "path analysis" that attempts to fit the observed findings in a study to a causative chain of linked events or conditions in a given theoretical model. On the basis of their analyses, they reached the following conclusions:

1. There is little evidence that male homosexuality is caused by a dominant mother and a weak or inadequate father.
2. There is no support for the theory that female homosexuality is caused by girls choosing their fathers as role models.
3. The stereotype that homosexuality is frequently caused by being seduced by an older person of the same sex is untrue.
4. Sexual preference is strongly established by adolescence; sexual feelings rarely undergo major directional changes in adulthood.
5. As children and adolescents, homosexuals have as many heterosexual experiences as their heterosexual counterparts, but they find these encounters ungratifying or less gratifying.
6. Gender nonconformity (e.g., boys avoiding sports like baseball and football while enjoying more "girlish" activities like playing house, hopscotch, or jacks) in childhood is a significant (but not absolute) predictor of the later development of homosexuality.

The most surprising conclusion of this study was the researchers' speculation that since they could not find solid support for any of the theories they tested, there is probably a biological basis for homosexuality. In fact, Bell, Weinberg, and Hammersmith say that hormonal influences during the prenatal period could produce patterns consistent with the data they found. However, since they conducted no hormone or genetic studies of their subjects and made no attempt to gather information concerning their mothers' pregnancy histories (e.g., drug use, illness), it seems that their research leaves us pretty much back at square one in understanding homosexuality. And their contention that homosexuality is probably biological in its origins requires that further research must be done if we hope to understand more fully how sexual preference develops.

ies and research methods. Neverthless, the findings from the past few years which indicate that biological factors are more important than previously thought in shaping sexual orientation are impressive. As noted neuroanatomist Simon LeVay puts it:

Believing in a biological explanation for sexual orientation is not the same thing as insisting that sexual orientation is inborn or genetically determined. Our entire mental life involves biological processes. We know that our sexual orientation, like our tastes in music and our memory of our last vacation, is engraved in some morphological or chemical substrate in the brain. *(LeVay, 1993, p. 108)*

Although it is likely that biological factors play a role in shaping sexual orientation, we do not think they are the only things that determine whether one is heterosexual, homosexual, or bisexual. Whatever genetic or hormonal conditions exist in a person, sexual orientation will inevitably be influenced by psychological, cultural, and experiential factors in a complex formula that will most likely still be undeciphered many years from now.

THE PSYCHOLOGICAL ADJUSTMENT OF HOMOSEXUALS

Through most of the last hundred years, the prevailing notion was that homosexuality was an illness. Recalling Krafft-Ebing's belief that homosexuality resulted from hereditary defects and the psychoanalytic notion that homosexuality resulted from incapacitating fears of castration, it is not difficult to see how this viewpoint was so logically accepted.

Further "proof" of the psychological maladjustment of homosexuals was provided by a number of enterprising scientists. Some who conducted studies of homosexuals in prisons concluded, not surprisingly, that these individuals were less emotionally healthy than heterosexuals chosen from everyday life. By the 1950s, the trend was to select homosexuals being seen by psychiatrists, ignoring the basic sampling error this strategy introduces: since people usually go to psychiatrists because of emotional difficulties, it was almost certain that this type of sampling would lead to the unwarranted conclusion that homosexuals are mentally ill.

Fortunately, a more sophisticated line of research was undertaken by psychologist Evelyn Hooker (1957). Hooker selected a group of 60 men—30 homosexuals and 30 heterosexuals—who were neither psychiatric patients nor prisoners and who were matched for age, education, and IQ. She gave them all personality tests, obtained detailed information about their life histories, and then had a group of expert psychologists evaluate the tests without knowing which belonged to the homosex-

ual or heterosexual men. The results showed that the raters could not distinguish between the two groups, providing the first objective indication that homosexuality is not necessarily a form of psychological maladjustment.

In an important series of studies Saghir and Robins (1973) extended the work begun by Hooker. They not only chose nonpatient populations but also decided to compare male and female homosexuals to unmarried heterosexuals, since the rate of certain psychiatric illnesses is higher in single persons. Their overall conclusion was straightforward: the majority of homosexuals studied were well-adjusted, productive people with no signs of psychiatric illness. Relatively few differences were observed between the homosexual and heterosexual groups, although an increased rate of alcoholism was found in lesbian subjects.

For the last 20 years, many research studies have evaluated the performance of homosexuals and heterosexuals on a variety of psychological tests. A review of data from dozens of these studies concluded that there are no psychological tests that can distinguish between homosexuals and heterosexuals and there is no evidence of higher rates of emotional instability or psychiatric illness among homosexuals than among heterosexuals (B. F. Reiss, 1980).

These results do not imply that homosexuals are *always* emotionally healthy any more than similar results could prove that heterosexuals never get depressed or become anxious. But the underlying fact is that homosexuality, by itself, is not a form of mental illness nor is it typically associated with other signs of mental illness (Green, 1972; Hoffman, 1977; Marmor, 1980a; American Psychiatric Association, 1987).

HOMOPHOBIA

The hostility and fear that many people have toward homosexuality is called **homophobia.** Because this term has been rather loosely applied to a broad range of feelings, beliefs, attitudes, and behavior toward homosexual individuals (or people suspected of being homosexual), some experts have suggested that it might be more useful to restrict this term to

homophobia obsessive hostility and fear toward homosexuals.

apply to circumstances that are clearly phobic—that is, those involving an irrational fear (Blumenfeld, 1992). Haaga (1991) suggests using the term "anti-homosexual prejudice" to describe prejudiced attitudes and discriminatory behavior that are separate from a phobic reaction. Anna Pelligrini (1992) prefers the plural term "homophobias" be used to indicate that there are different tiers of reactions organized along gender lines: (1) homophobia directed by men toward men; (2) homophobia of men toward lesbians; (3) the homophobia of women toward lesbians; and (4) homophobia directed by women toward men. The term "heterosexism" has also gained currency as a means of describing cultural attitudes that promote heterosexuality as the norm and stigmatize any other sexual orientation as less desirable, less healthy, and less valid. (Heterosexism is usually used to indicate the assumption that male sexuality is the dominant form and that female sexuality is somehow subservient or inferior to the male version.)

The most extreme example of homophobia is in overt acts of physical violence against lesbians and gay men, which occur with a frightening frequency in modern American society (Comstock, 1991). But homophobia occurs in a variety of situations with a broad range of results. For example, homophobia affects the athletic decisions of both heterosexual and lesbian women. Lesbians are often afraid to take scholarships at high-profile colleges, while straight women drop out of sports because they fear being mislabeled as lesbians (Heaton, 1992). Homophobia takes a toll on business productivity in a variety of ways. For instance, some men are afraid to choose nontraditional occupations such as nursing because of worries that they will be labeled as gay; and homophobic attitudes in the workplace affect hiring and promotion decisions and the ways workers interact effectively together (Blumenfeld, 1992).

The origins of homophobia are just as uncertain as the origins of homosexuality, but some psychologists believe that it is partly a defense that people use to insulate themselves from something that is too close to home. Thus, in cases of brutal beatings or murders of homosexuals—perhaps the ultimate expression of homophobia—the motivation may be partly to stamp out any inherent homosexual impulses that may lurk in the attacker's heart. Most attacks against homosexuals are committed by adolescents who seem to be trying to prove how "macho" they are to their peers (Greer, 1986). In ad-

dition, physical attacks against homosexuals have risen as an outgrowth of the activities of organized hate groups, including the Ku Klux Klan and the neo-Nazis (Gutis, 1989).

Whitam and Mathy (1986) describe the phenomenon of homophobia in its broadest social sense as follows:

> Not only are homosexuals criminalized, victimized, and labeled pathological, they are also regarded by some religious groups as sinners deserving to be put to death, a view reminiscent of the Inquisition. . . . There are very few, if any, groups in American society which evoke more hostility than homosexuals. (p. 180)

In support of this observation, it seems that violence against homosexuals has risen dramatically in the past decade, as homosexuals have lobbied very visibly over civil rights issues and have also been thrust into the harsh spotlight of publicity because of the AIDS epidemic (Greer, 1986; Gutis, 1989). And many homosexual groups expressed outrage at a 1986 statement from the Vatican which said that "when civil legislation is introduced to protect behavior to which no one has any conceivable right" people should not be surprised when "irrational and violent reactions increase" (The New York Times, October 31, 1986, p. A17).

Homophobia is expressed in many ways in our society. Homosexuals are ridiculed by jokes or by derogatory terms like "fairy," "faggot," or "queer." Parents are fearful that any "feminine" interest shown by a boy may lead to a homosexual life, so they are quick to provide footballs, toy guns, and model airplanes even if their son is not very interested in those items. Police use a variety of techniques to apprehend men engaging in homosexual acts, including entrapment (having a policeman pose as a willing homosexual partner) and use of hidden cameras in public restrooms; if these forms of law enforcement were to be directed at heterosexual activity, the objections would be deafening!

Homosexuals have been banned from the military and the ministry (although not in all denominations). Homosexuals have been denied housing, jobs, and bank loans. To many people, the homosexual is seen as a sick or even "contagious" individual who may "infect" others and so propel them to a life of homosexual depravity.

In light of such homophobia, it is not surprising that much of the straight world thinks homosexuals should be treated to convert them to heterosexuality. While such treatment is sometimes possible with homosexuals who are highly motivated and desire such a change (Hatterer, 1970; Masters and Johnson, 1979; Marmor, 1980), it is unwarranted and unethical for homosexuals who have no wish to *be* converted.

PERSPECTIVES ON HOMOSEXUAL ORIENTATION

Although it is just as foolish to suppose that all homosexuals are alike as it would be to imagine that all vegetarians behave the same way, dress similarly, and fit a general personality profile, many people make just such an assumption. The resulting stereotypes tell us that we can identify a homosexual by appearance (e.g., the limp-wristed, lisping, mincing male or the short-haired, "butch" female), by profession (the male hairdresser or interior decorator), by personality (maladjusted, overemotional, and impulsive), and by lifestyle (unmarried men or women over 30 are "suspect"; if they live with another person of the same sex, they are *doubly* suspect).

These stereotypes are largely inaccurate. While it is true that a small number of homosexual men carry themselves in an effeminate way, this group amounts to no more than 15 percent of the homosexual population (Voeller, 1980). There are also many men who are totally *heterosexual* who speak in an effeminate voice or whose other mannerisms appear effeminate. The number of gay women who have a "masculine" appearance is also very small, and a woman who looks "masculine" is not necessarily homosexual. Similarly, there are homosexual doctors, lawyers, truck drivers, professional athletes, and politicians as well as gay hairdressers or designers. No occupational group is purely heterosexual or homosexual.

There is no evidence that most homosexuals are emotionally maladjusted—a fact that is particularly remarkable when one considers the anti-homosexual prejudices of our society. Finally, there is no such thing as a "homosexual lifestyle" that would accurately describe how most gays live. This is not surprising, since there are people who are exclusively homosexual on a life-long basis while others are exclusively homosexual for just a few years. There are also "closet" homosexuals who try to

pass as straight in the everyday world (including many homosexuals who are in heterosexual marriages) and others who have openly announced their homosexuality. There are militant homosexuals and more conservative ones; there are homosexuals who remain in long-term, committed relationships while others prefer independence and a more casual approach to sex: there are endless examples of homosexual diversity.

Recognizing these facts, it is nevertheless possible to discuss certain common aspects of homosexual behavior as they apply to the lives of many gay people just as we examined heterosexual behavior patterns.

Discovering Homosexuality

Some homosexuals say that they were aware of being gay as early as age 5 or 6, while others don't make the discovery until sometime in adulthood. However, it is not very likely that the young child has a real sense of homosexual orientation. The sense of being "different" during childhood that some homosexuals recall as adults is not always an accurate barometer of later sexual orientation, since many "straight" adults also feel "different" as children. Furthermore, adult recollections of childhood feelings and behaviors may possibly be influenced by social expectations of what homosexuals "should" have felt (Ross, 1980).

Most of the available research of self-discovery of a homosexual identity suggests that this process is most likely to occur during adolescence for males and at a somewhat later time for females (Dank, 1971; Weinberg, 1978; Cass, 1979; Stanley and Wolfe, 1980; Troiden and Goode, 1980). At earlier ages, the child is exposed to role models that are exclusively heterosexual (at least in a visible sense) whether at home, at school, on television, or in children's books. This fact, combined with the automatic assumption in our society that everyone is heterosexual unless "proved" otherwise, means that children are almost invariably conditioned to think of themselves as heterosexuals destined to live a heterosexual life.

How do people "discover" that they are homosexual? No single pattern fits everyone. Many gay males report having first had some type of sexual contact with another boy as young teenagers which led them to initially suspect that they were homosexual. Only after a period of identity confusion

Are You Homophobic?

If you're interested in getting a better sense of whether you're homophobic or not, the Index of Homophobia (IHP) self-administered questionnaire reproduced here can give you an opportunity to find out. This questionnaire is not a test, so there are no right or wrong answers. Answer each item using the following scoring to indicate how you feel: 1 = strongly agree, 2 = agree, 3 = neither agree nor disagree, 4 = disagree, and 5 = strongly disagree.*

1. I would feel comfortable working closely with a male homosexual. _____
2. I would enjoy attending social functions at which homosexuals were present. _____
3. I would feel uncomfortable if I learned that my neighbor was homosexual. _____
4. If a member of my sex made a sexual advance toward me I would feel angry. _____
5. I would feel comfortable knowing that I was attractive to members of my sex. _____
6. I would feel uncomfortable being seen in a gay bar. _____
7. I would feel comfortable if a member of my sex made an advance toward me. _____
8. I would be comfortable if I found myself attracted to a member of my sex. _____
9. I would feel disappointed if I learned that my child was homosexual. _____
10. I would feel nervous being in a group of homosexuals. _____
11. I would feel comfortable knowing that my clergyman was homosexual. _____
12. I would be upset if I learned that my brother or sister was homosexual. _____
13. I would feel that I had failed as a parent if I learned that my child was gay. _____

14. If I saw two men holding hands in public I would feel disgusted. _____
15. If a member of my sex made an advance toward me I would be offended. _____
16. I would feel comfortable if I learned that my daughter's teacher was a lesbian. _____
17. I would feel uncomfortable if I learned that my spouse or partner was attracted to members of his or her sex. _____
18. I would feel at ease talking with a homosexual person at a party. _____
19. I would feel uncomfortable if I learned that my boss was homosexual. _____
20. It would not bother me to walk through a predominantly gay section of town. _____
21. It would disturb me to find out that my doctor was homosexual. _____
22. I would feel comfortable if I learned that my best friend of my sex was homosexual. _____
23. If a member of my sex made an advance toward me I would feel flattered. _____
24. I would feel uncomfortable knowing that my son's male teacher was homosexual. _____
25. I would feel comfortable working closely with a female homosexual. _____

*Items 3, 4, 6, 9, 10, 12, 13, 14, 15, 17, 19, 21, and 24 must be reverse scored. Then total your scores for the 25 items. A score of 75 or less indicates no homophobia, 76–87 indicates mild homophobia, 88–99 indicates moderate homophobia, and 100 or more shows a high degree of homophobia.

Source: *Questionnaire from "A Strategy for the Measurement of Homophobia," by Hudson and Ricketts,* Journal of Homosexuality *vol. 5, pp. 357–372, 1980. Reprinted by permission of The Haworth Press, Inc., Binghamton, New York.*

Some older gays are not only out of the closet, but proud of it, too.

did they begin to actually think of themselves as homosexual, to seek out other homosexuals, and to devise ways of dealing with their homosexuality in a heterosexual world (Cass, 1979).[1] Others suspect that they may be homosexual *before* having any same-sex sexual activity and confirm their suspicion by positive responses to sexual experiences with male partners or by feeling more comfortable with homosexual friends than heterosexual ones (Weinberg, 1978). For some homosexuals, the process of self-discovery occurs only after much effort is spent trying to fit the expected heterosexual mode but finding that it just isn't comfortable.

Although some lesbians come to a firm discovery of their sexual identity in adolescence, more typically whatever homosexual feelings they have during this time are pushed aside as "a passing phase" (Stanley and Wolfe, 1980). There may be close emotional attachments formed with other females that never progress to the stage of physical contact, or specifically sexual experiences may not be labeled as homosexual. A large number of lesbians do not adopt this sexual orientation until after a heterosexual marriage.

There is, of course, a big difference between *discovering* homosexuality and *accepting* it. Some gay

men and women have no difficulty at all in this sphere, but much more often there is conflict and uncertainty over the implications of being homosexual in a heterosexual society. Some who have labeled themselves as homosexual seek therapy to "cure" themselves of this self-perceived problem; others feel enthusiastic and even energized by their homosexuality. Although only 1 out of 20 homosexual men and women studied by Bell and Weinberg (1978) expressed a great deal of regret over being homosexual, approximately 1 in 3 had considered giving up their homosexual activity. These authors also noted that gay men are more likely than lesbians to have difficulty accepting their homosexuality, which they speculated might be because homosexuality is more often seen by males "as a failure to achieve a 'masculine' sexual adjustment," whereas lesbians "more often experience their homosexuality as a freely chosen rejection of heterosexual relationships" (Bell and Weinberg, 1978, p. 128).

Coming Out

"Coming out" is a process in which homosexuals inform others of their sexual orientation. It can be a long process of self-disclosure that begins cautiously with telling a best friend (and waiting to see the reaction), then progresses to include a group of close friends, and finally—in its most complete form—lets family members, colleagues at work, and more casual acquaintances know as well. Com-

[1]It is important to remember that homosexual and heterosexual experimentation is very common in childhood or adolescence. The fact that someone finds pleasure in a sexual act with another person of the same sex does *not* necessarily mean that he or she is homosexual.

ing out can also be accomplished in a remarkably brief time, although a great deal of thought and planning may have gone into the decision.

Many homosexuals find that it is considerably easier to come out in the gay world than to their heterosexual friends and family. They may choose to live a life of "passing" as heterosexual to avoid social disapproval, economic repercussions, or other potential problems while they are still known to other gays as "out of the closet" in a limited sense. Here is what one 26-year-old homosexual man said about this issue:

> Philosophically, I'd love to announce my gay-ness to the world. But it'd probably cost me my job, and it would cause so many problems for

my family (especially my father, who's a minis-ter) that I just don't see the point. I lead one life at night and another during working hours or family get-togethers, and it's really no big deal. *(Authors' files)*

Others consider such a solution unsatisfying, dishonest, or lacking in trust and conviction. How-ever, coming out to a hostile world can create tremendous agony in a person's life. On the other hand, finding support from family and friends can be reassuring and gratifying, as this explanation from a 24-year-old woman makes clear:

> For my whole college career I was afraid to let my parents know I was gay. I talked about com-

For Better or For Worse®   by Lynn Johnston

The topic of homosexuality has been treated far more openly and sympathetically in many different forms of media, as these examples from a widely-read family-oriented comic strip appearing in 1993 show.

Privacy and the Gay Community

Throughout most of the 1980s, the gay community put a high premium on protecting privacy rights, especially when there was potential conflict between widespread testing for infection with the AIDS virus (e.g., testing all patients admitted to hospitals, or testing marriage license applicants). In addition, privacy was a particularly touchy issue since the threat of disclosing a gay person's sexual orientation had sometimes been used for purposes of blackmail. Now, however, there is a movement in the gay community that many people view as adopting the opposite tactic: publicly unmasking famous people who are claimed to be secretly gay (Johnson, 1990).

In the past, gay leaders and journalists generally agreed that homosexuals who chose to keep their sexual orientation secret had every right to do so (Shilts, 1990). Recently, however, a number of gay activists and newspapers have begun to employ a highly controversial tactic called "outing"—a term derived from "out of the closet"—in which they identify public figures, such as politicians, as gay.

Advocates of outing say that the practice provides positive role models for other gays and that outing can help reduce the stigma associated with homosexuality (Johnson, 1990). Those who favor outing also say that it can help wake the country up to the threat of AIDS by showing that "lesbians and gay men are to be found among the most respected public figures in every field of American society" (Shilts, 1990).

Critics of the practice, including many members of the gay community, are dismayed by the fundamental rift in their own ranks, especially since the right to privacy had been enshrined as one of the most crucial protections that gays relied upon. A spokesman for the Human Rights Campaign Fund, the largest lobbying group for gay rights, pointed out: "We believe privacy is a fundamental tenet of what the gay and lesbian movement is all about" (Johnson, 1990).

Others who oppose outing not only lament the erosion of personal privacy that is a direct result of this ploy but acknowledge its considerable potential for abuse. For example, what's to prevent a group from threatening to go public with false information about a politician's supposed gay proclivities in order to get his vote on a pivotal issue? Respected gay journalist Randy Shilts (1990) admits that "outing threats are political blackmail." In addition, what about cases in which a person isn't homosexual, but has had a single same-sex encounter—perhaps when he or she was drunk—wouldn't outing be a distortion of the truth?

The controversy over outing is perhaps most sharply focused on the inconsistency of claiming that sexual orientation and sexual actions should be protected by the constitutional shield of privacy, while at the same time declaring that when it may be politically expedient, outing is appropriate and ethically correct. As one gay scientist told us: "If outing is used as a weapon, we'd better be careful before that weapon is turned against those it's intended to help."

ing out, and worried about it tremendously, but I couldn't really bring myself to do it. Then, just before I graduated, something clicked in my head that said I had to come out *NOW*. I just couldn't believe how accepting my parents were. It certainly helped me feel better about myself. (*Authors' files*)

"Coming out" doesn't usually work out this easily, however. Most parents are terribly upset at finding out that their son or daughter is homosexual, and many of them urge the child to seek therapy to "correct the problem." In some cases, parents refuse to see or speak to a gay child; in other cases, while taking a less severe attitude of re-

Long-term relationship are far more common for homosexual men and lesbian women than many people realize.

proach, parents (or other family members) clearly remain very uncomfortable with the idea of having a homosexual relative.

One study of the relations between 93 gay men and their parents (Cramer and Roach, 1988) made the following points:

1. Most relationships between gay sons and their parents are strained immediately after the son comes out, but this initial turmoil eventually gives way to improved relations—in many cases, better than they were prior to disclosure of the son's sexual orientation.

2. Many gay men who do not disclose their homosexuality to their parents are worried about hurting or disappointing them; fear of parental rejection or abuse is cited far less often as a concern.

3. The most frequently mentioned reasons for coming out to parents are a desire to share one's personal life with them, being tired of hiding the truth, wanting to have more freedom, and hoping for greater intimacy with the parents.

4. Parental reaction to a son's homosexuality seems to be about the same whether the son comes out voluntarily or whether the parents learn about their son's homosexuality from someone else, from asking him, or by accident.

For many lesbians, coming out to one's mother poses certain unique problems. As Zitter (1987) points out, the mother's response is frequently negative, which may reflect her feelings of rejection as well as her sense of betrayal at giving up her dreams of her daughter's marriage, the joys of being a grandparent, and simply "fitting in" to the heterosexual expectations of family and society. Zitter (1987, p. 190) also notes:

> Often, disclosure can be followed by parental hopes for a "cure" and well-meaning offers to pay for therapy. A daughter who is unsure of her lesbianism and looking for external validation may feel her anxieties and ambivalences raised by this reaction. One who is sure of her lesbianism may become enraged at a mother's suggestion of a "cure," and the event of disclosure can end in a full-scale conflict that closes off communication for a time.

On the more positive side, not all mothers (or fathers) react negatively to a lesbian daughter's disclosure of her sexual identity. In fact, once a daughter comes out to her parents, it can help relieve many tensions in the family: for example, it may eliminate parental nagging about "why don't you find a nice guy to marry?" and stop repeated attempts to fix the daughter up with promising young men. However, unless the parents have suspected a daughter's lesbianism for years, or unless they are particularly open-minded, the process of moving from their initial negative reaction to an eventual point of acceptance is likely to be long and somewhat painful (just as it is apt to be for parents of gay males). In fact, coming out can cause a grieving process in the mother that is very similar to mourning for someone who has died (Zitter, 1987). This also has a potentially positive side, because "if this mourning process is allowed to take place, a mother may eventually be able to accept a daughter as a lesbian, opening the way for mother and daughter to establish a different kind of relationship" (Zitter, 1987, p. 184).

Despite a current push for homosexuals to "come out of the closet" to indicate pride in their sexual orientation and to work for political gains, most homosexual men and women keep their sexual orientation a private matter. It appears that homosexuals with lower social status are somewhat more likely to be open about their sexual orientation, while those who are better educated or who have more income are more likely to keep their homosexuality hidden (Bell and Weinberg, 1978).

A Typology of Homosexuals

Bell and Weinberg (1978) studied 979 homosexual men and women who were recruited by personal contacts, public advertising, use of mailing lists, and special recruitment cards distributed in gay bars, in gay baths, and by gay organizations. Although their sample was neither truly cross-sectional nor representative of all homosexuals in America, it provided a broad-based opportunity for analyzing important information about homosexual feelings and behavior. One of the more interesting findings to emerge from this study was the existence of a typology of sexual experiences that allowed for comparisons between groups. Approximately three-fourths of their sample could be assigned to one of these types on the basis of statistical criteria (Table 15.2).

Close-coupled homosexuals lived in one-to-one same-sex relationships that were very similar to heterosexual marriages. They had few sexual problems, few sexual partners, and infrequently engaged in cruising (deliberately searching for a sexual partner).

Open-coupled homosexuals lived in one-to-one same-sex relationships but typically had many outside sexual partners and spent a relatively large amount of time cruising. They were more likely to have sexual problems and to regret their homosexuality than close-coupled homosexuals.

Functional homosexuals were those who were not "coupled," who had a high number of sexual partners and few sexual problems. These individuals tended to be younger, to have few regrets over their homosexuality, and to have high levels of sexual interest.

Dysfunctional homosexuals were not "coupled" and, while scoring high in number of partners or amount of sexual activity, had substantial numbers of sexual problems.

Asexual homosexuals were low in sexual interest and activity and were not "coupled." They tended to be less exclusively homosexual and more secretive about their homosexuality than others.

These types also proved to have important connections to a person's social and psychological adjustment. In general, close-coupled homosexuals tended to be at least as happy and well-adjusted as heterosexual men and women. The dysfunctionals and asexuals, on the other hand, tended to be worse off psychologically than heterosexuals and had considerable difficulty coping with life. Male dysfunctionals were "more lonely, worrisome,

Table 15.2 Percentage of Homosexuals in Each Group[a] of the Bell–Weinberg Typology

	Close-Coupled	Open-Coupled	Functional	Dysfunctional	Asexual
Male homosexuals	10%	18%	15%	12%	16%
Lesbians	28	17	10	5	11

[a] Twenty-nine percent of male homosexuals and 28 percent of lesbians could not be classified into one group or another.

Source: *Data from Alan P. Bell and Martin S. Weinberg,* Homosexualities. *Copyright © 1978 by Alan P. Bell and Martin S. Weinberg. Reprinted by permission of Simon & Schuster, Inc. and Mitchell Beazley Pub., Ltd., London.*

paranoid, depressed, tense, and unhappy than any of the other men," and dysfunctional lesbians were more likely than other women "to have needed long-term professional help for an emotional problem" (Bell and Weinberg, 1978, p. 225). The asexuals were generally loners who, despite being lonely, had little interest in becoming involved with friends or socializing in the gay community. Asexual homosexual men had the highest incidence of suicidal thoughts.

The existence of these homosexual types "proves" nothing: there are probably corresponding "types" of heterosexuals that could be identified, with some showing better social and psychological adjustment and others being more troubled. The point we want to reinforce is that all homosexuals are not alike; there is just as much diversity among homosexuals as among heterosexuals.

The Gay World

The gay world, like the heterosexual world, is not simply or easily described in a few paragraphs. In large urban areas, the gay community may exist as a full-fledged entity, complete with places for social and sexual contacts such as bars, gay merchants, gay churches, gay clinics, and gay recreational groups. In other areas, there is no organized homosexual community, and sexual contacts may be hurriedly made in public restrooms, parks, and pick-up bars.

Although in the past homosexuals were often forced to go to gay bars or to "cruise" in certain designated locations, today there are mushrooming numbers of homosexual organizations that provide new meeting grounds without the stigma of "being on the prowl." Other organizations aim to provide various forms of counseling services for homosexu-

Gay parenting has become more commonplace in the past decade.

als ranging from religious advice to help in dieting to finding nonjudgmental medical care. On many college and university campuses, gay students have formed groups to provide peer support and acceptance. Homosexually oriented newspapers and magazines, both national and regional, provide additional information about the homosexual subculture in America and also carry personal advertisements that allow interested parties to get together for sexual purposes.

One of the notable trends in the gay community over the past decade has been an upsurge in the number of homosexual men and women raising children. Adoption by openly homosexual people is now relatively commonplace; gay men and women are increasingly gaining custody of their children in divorce proceedings as their heterosexual marriages are dissolved; and lesbian women often turn to artificial insemination to become biological mothers (Salholz et al., 1990).

Concerns that growing up in a household with openly gay parents will produce conflicts or confusion in sexual identity development have been shown to be unwarranted (Harris and Turner, 1986; Bozett, 1988, 1989; DiLapi, 1989). In fact, a parent's homosexuality seems to create few long-term problems for their children and generally proves of little importance in the overall parent–child relationship (Bozett, 1989; Huggins, 1989).

The Impact of the HIV/AIDS Epidemic

In America, the gay male community has borne the brunt of the HIV/AIDS epidemic more strongly than any other group. First felt by the gay male populations in New York and San Francisco, where the majority of cases of AIDS were clustered in the first few years of the epidemic, this impact— which is at once physical, emotional, social, and economic—has now spread to cities across the country.

At the most immediate level, the realization that AIDS was a deadly disease that differed from other sexually transmitted diseases in both its fatal outcome and its typically prolonged incubation period (on average, there are eight to ten years between the initial infection and the appearance of symptoms) led to widespread panic. Male homosexuals who were not in exclusive, long-term monogamous relationships wondered, as one man described it, "whether I'm a walking time-bomb" (Authors'

FOCUS IN BRIEF

Gay Fathers

- Gay men who father children are no more masculine than gay men who do not father children.
- Most gay fathers are not content in their marriages.
- Gay fathers have more difficulty acknowledging their homosexuality than lesbian mothers do.
- Gay fathers find it harder to come out to their children than lesbian mothers do.
- Most children's reactions to their gay father's coming out to them is tolerant and understanding.
- A father's homosexuality creates few lasting problems for his children, although there may be temporary problems with a child's peers if the father's sexual orientation has been openly disclosed.
- Most gay fathers report positive relationships with their children, although relatively few have physical custody of them.

---

files). This undoubtedly led many homosexual men to change their patterns of sexual behavior drastically—cutting out sex with anonymous partners, for instance, and using condoms during all sexual contact that involved the potential exchange of body fluids—but in hundreds of thousands of cases, this was already too late. Infection with the AIDS virus had already occurred.

The social and emotional effects on the gay community have not simply been changes in sexual lifestyles. Many gay men in New York and San Francisco have watched scores of their friends die. (In fact, the carnage has been compared by some to the Vietnam War.) In many instances, partners have stayed together so that one could nurse the other during his terminal illness. In other instances, long-term relationships have broken up as a side effect of AIDS anxieties. Indeed, some gay men have at least temporarily opted for celibacy until a cure or vaccine is found for AIDS.

Notably, the gay community responded to the crisis in bold and far-reaching ways. One of the earliest organizations formed to combat the epidemic was New York City's Gay Men's Health Crisis, a group that has conducted highly effective public education campaigns and organized networks to provide people infected with HIV with an extensive range of services, including information hotlines, treatment bulletins, medical referrals, home care programs, and legal consultants. Similar organizations now exist in many large cities and include many heterosexual volunteers among their workers. As one observer notes (Clark, 1987, p. 13):

> Though gay men did not invent or give this disease to the world, along with the lesbians of our community and the non-gay people who love us, we *have* given the world a model of how to care for one another in a crisis, even when governments shockingly fail to fulfill their responsibility, and bigots freely attack. We have managed to retain our sanity and remember that neither sex nor homosexuality per se are evil. We have been able to demonstrate that it is not necessary to yield to selfish fear and run from people in need.

Another noteworthy group that was born in response to the AIDS epidemic is ACT UP (the AIDS Coalition to Unleash Power), an activist organization that has staged a number of public demonstrations to shock more complacent establishment groups into action. ACT UP demonstrated on the floor of the New York Stock Exchange to protest the expense of drugs used to treat AIDS, forced the FDA to adopt new rules to permit more rapid testing of experimental drugs that may be useful in fighting the epidemic, and disrupted mass at St. Patrick's Cathedral in New York to call attention to the Catholic church's refusal to endorse the use of condoms as a means of preventing the transmission of HIV. While ACT UP's attention-grabbing tactics have created some tensions in the gay community, most gay leaders applaud its results-oriented agenda (*Newsweek*, March 12, 1990, pp. 21–22).

There have also been direct and indirect economic ramifications on gays from AIDS. For example, several insurance companies have tried to stop writing life insurance policies for unmarried males in certain high-risk regions unless applicants undergo blood tests to show that they aren't infected with the AIDS virus. (The legality of insurance companies' requiring such a test, or even asking questions about lifestyles, is being contested in the courts in several states.) Military recruits and personnel who have positive blood tests for AIDS antibodies have been summarily dismissed by the armed forces as a matter of policy, whether or not there is any evidence that they are ill. And in many instances, homosexuals with AIDS or HIV infection have been fired from their jobs as soon as their illness became known to their employer (although recent court decisions make this discriminatory practice illegal). In addition, there have also been numerous court cases in which parents of gay men who died from AIDS have contested their wills, so as to prevent a homosexual lover from inheriting the deceased's estate. Other cases have been brought by long-term partners of men who died with AIDS and didn't leave a will; the partners have tried to assert their claim to receiving at least a partial inheritance. This issue is particularly knotty because in some cases, a couple has used up a sizable amount of their joint savings to pay for the costs of hospitalization and treatment for the AIDS victim.

Many gays are concerned that if widespread blood testing for HIV infection becomes mandatory, concerns for confidentiality will become secondary and a real witch-hunt will begin. In this sense, many gay leaders believe that homosexuals are already being used as scapegoats to "blame" for the outbreak of a deadly communicable disease that was spreading elsewhere in the world (as in central Africa) as much by heterosexual transmission as by gay contacts.

These observations are necessarily based on the impact AIDS has had on the gay community over a relatively short time span. If this epidemic continues to run unchecked, even more profound changes will undoubtedly take place, and the number of lives directly touched by AIDS will become truly staggering. Even now, when the American public is coming to realize that AIDS is not just a disease affecting homosexuals, homosexuals continue to be most harshly affected by this modern scourge.

BISEXUALITY

Although homosexuality has been extensively studied and written about in the last 15 years, bisexuality has received far less attention. It is difficult to estimate the incidence of bisexuality in our society today. Kinsey and his co-workers (1953) found that 9 percent of single 30-year-old women could be classified between 2 and 4 on the hetero-sexual–homosexual rating scale while about 16 percent of single 30-year-old men fit the same description. However, these numbers may exaggerate the active incidence of bisexuality, which we suspect is actually less than 5 percent in our society if it is defined in terms of sexual activity with male and female partners in the past year. Partial support for this view comes from data finding that only about 2 percent of married American adult men reported same-gender sexual contact in the preceding year (Fay et al., 1989). The most extensive survey to date of sexual behavior in the general American population found that only 2.4 percent of men and 1.3 percent of women identified themselves as homosexual or bisexual (Laumann et al., 1994).

The lack of reliable data on the actual incidence of bisexuality can be seen by considering the results of a survey of psyhiatrists and sex therapists: about 5 percent of both groups of experts estimated that the incidence of bisexuality was less than 1 percent, while more than one-quarter of psychiatrists and 36 percent of sex therapists estimated the incidence at 11 percent or more (Hill, 1989). Judd Marmor (1989), a former president of the American Psychiatric Association, has noted:

> There are some who deny that . . . [bisexuality] exists at all, and who believe that all bisexuals are really closet homosexuals taking refuge behind a heterosexual facade. Counterposed to this point of view are those who claim that all people are bisexual but that the original alternative impulses have been repressed, either by societal pressures (in heterosexuals) or by certain early life experiences (in homosexuals). *(p. 211)*

Bisexuals are sometimes called "AC/DC" (based on terminology used to describe two types of electric current), "switch-hitters" (borrowed from baseball lingo for a person who bats from either the right or left side of home plate depending on who's pitching), or people who "swing both ways" (this too is a baseball phrase that might also relate to "swinging" as a type of sexual behavior). In the late 1970s, bisexuality became stylish in certain circles where it was regarded as a sign of sexual sophistication and being "open-minded." By the mid-1980s, however, bisexuality became decidedly less fashionable as a result of its clear association with AIDS. In fact, many males who previously enjoyed occasional same-sex contact (while living a predominantly heterosexual life) have now dropped

their bisexual activity as a result of fear of exposure to the AIDS virus (Weinberg, Williams, and Pryor, 1994). Bisexuality among women does not seem to have been affected by this concern, however, which is in keeping with the fact that same-sex female contact does not seem to be an important means of spreading AIDS, although it can theoretically be a mode of transmitting HIV infection.

Gagnon (1977) proposes five different categories of bisexual behavior: young people who are experimenting to discover their sexual preferences; persons in transition from homosexual to heterosexual orientation, or vice versa; prostitutes (of either gender) who participate in same-sex activity for pay; people who are responsive to sexual stimulation no matter what its source; and people who have a definite preference for sexual activity with both genders. As we shall see, there are some additional categories that can also be described.

People move into bisexuality in a number of different ways. For many, it is a form of experimentation that adds spice to their sex lives but doesn't become the main course. For others, it represents a deliberate choice that permits participation in whatever feels best at the moment. Some men and women seem to alternate their choice of sex partners randomly, depending on availability and circumstances to dictate which gender is involved at a particular time. Most often, whichever of these patterns applies, people with bisexual experience have a decided preference for one gender, but this is not always true.

Money (1988) points out that some bisexuals are not ordinarily sexually responsive to partners of both genders; they require special circumstances to become physically aroused with the gender that is less attractive to them. For instance, a male who is predominantly heterosexual by preference may engage in bisexual acts in a sexual threesome with another man and woman. As another example, a woman who is predominantly lesbian might have sex with a man if she first gets high on cocaine.

Masters and Johnson (1979) described a subgroup of bisexuals they called **ambisexuals** who were men or women who had no preference whatsoever over the gender of their sex partners, had

ambisexual (am' bē sek shoo ul) term used by Masters and Johnson to refer to men or women who have no preference about the gender of their sex partners and who accept or reject sexual opportunities based on their own physical need.

Bisexuals and Gays in Heterosexual Marriages

Many gay or bisexual people choose to enter conventional heterosexual marriages. Although precise data are not currently available, various research surveys have found that about one-fifth of homosexual men and one-third of lesbians have been married at least once (Bell and Weinberg, 1978; Masters and Johnson, 1979), and the number of bisexuals who are married probably measures in the millions (Gochros, 1989; Hill, 1989).

Although understanding how marriage might appeal to a bisexual person is not difficult, many people cannot envision why some homosexual men and women choose to enter heterosexual marriages. It appears that there are several explanations that are almost universal in their applicability. First, our society pushes people toward marriage as an expected condition of responsible adulthood. Parents and other relatives often exert strong pressures on their young adult children to "marry and settle down," and people with same-sex preferences are not immune to these pressures. In addition, singlehood may be a handicap in certain business situations, where married people are often judged to be more stable and responsible than their nonmarried peers. Second, most of the homosexuals or bisexuals who choose to marry have negative feelings about "gay life" (Coleman,

1981/82). Not wanting to be labeled homosexual and not wanting to be part of a life they consider sordid or sinful, they turn to marriage as "proof" that they're really not gay.

On the positive side, most of the homosexual men or women who marry genuinely love their chosen spouse and many of them want to have children (Coleman, 1981/82; Bozett, 1989; Gochros, 1989). In addition, it is important to realize that some of these individuals marry without consciously seeing themselves as bisexual or homosexual, only coming to recognize this orientation at a later time. As Clark (1987, pp. 199–200) points out: "Most of us were taught . . . that if one has both heterosexual and homosexual feelings and there is love in the heterosexual feelings that the homosexuality is just a phase. . . . At worst, we were told, we were delayed in growing up or a bit confused, but a good heterosexual marriage should take care of all of that."

Relatively few of the people who are aware of their same-sex feelings prior to marriage disclose them to their prospective spouse (Gochros, 1989; Hays and Samuels, 1989). While some marriages seem on the surface to be none the worse for this situation—at least in terms of the sexual relationship and overall marital satisfaction—others are strained by sexual

never become involved in a committed sexual relationship, and had frequent sexual interaction with both men and women. The ambisexuals accepted or rejected any sexual opportunity primarily on the basis of their physical need, with the personality or physical attractiveness of a potential partner having much less to do with their choice.

In some instances, the bisexual has had a long-term heterosexual relationship which is then followed by a long-term homosexual relationship (or vice versa). After such a sequence, the person involved may develop new views on traditional notions that limit sex-object choice

(Blumstein and Schwartz, 1976). In other instances, the late emergence of homosexuality in sequential bisexuality may be linked to recovery from a long-term illness (e.g., alcoholism) that had masked or blocked the homosexual potential (Money, 1988). However, the majority of bisexuals start by establishing their heterosexuality and add same-sex contact later on (Weinberg, Williams, and Pryor, 1994).

Another pattern sometimes seen is concurrent involvement in heterosexual and homosexual relationships, as described in this comment from a 23-year-old woman:

problems and other types of interpersonal difficulties, including problems with trust.

Recently, Hays and Samuels (1989) studied a sample of heterosexual women who were or had been married to bisexual or homosexual men and who had children by them. All the women went through a painful grief reaction, including feelings of anger, shame, fear, guilt, and physical stress, when they learned of their husbands' sexual orientation. Their reactions were generally aggravated by feeling stupid or deceived for not having figured out the truth on their own. The majority of the wives indicated that they would not have gotten married had they known about the situation before marriage.

In a book called *When Husbands Come Out of the Closet,* Gochros (1989) notes that women who marry bisexual or homosexual men are basically no different from other women and acknowledges that many marital breakdowns occur in the "complex crisis-prone situation" of discovery or disclosure. Gochros claims that women tend to cope with learning of their husbands' homosexual needs "remarkably well . . . showing understanding [and] flexibility" (p. 254), but points out that her interviews were done before there was much awareness of the AIDS epidemic. There is much less acceptance and understanding shown today by women who have been exposed to the risk of HIV infection by husbands who have concealed their same-sex activities from them (Kaplan, 1987; Masters, Johnson, and Kolodny, 1988).

At a practical level, Clark (1987) makes two useful points for couples in this situation. The first is that staying married for the sake of the children isn't generally a good idea: "If this is the only factor keeping the marriage going, it . . . creates enough tension to make life worse for the children than divorce or separation would" (Clark, 1987, p. 201). The second point, which we can verify from our experience counseling scores of couples where the husband was gay or bisexual, is that promises to maintain sexual monogamy generally don't work out. As Clark puts it: "It is very difficult to be Gay and remain monogamous in a heterosexual marriage." Thus, a couple that includes a gay or bisexual spouse that wants to maintain their marriage needs to work out the groundrules for how sex will be handled, which is often no easy matter. Nevertheless, a genuinely committed, mutually loving couple can certainly overcome these obstacles if each partner is willing to compromise and communicate—which is, in the final analysis, exactly what it takes for most marriages to flourish.

I had been dating a guy I was very friendly with for about a year with a good sexual relationship. Then I suddenly found myself making it with my roommate, who slowly but expertly introduced me to how two women can make love. I really enjoyed both kinds of sex and both personal relationships, so I continued them for some while until my graduate school career was over and I moved to a new town. *(Authors' files)*

Research on female bisexuality has shown that some women who identify themselves as bisexual say that they have different emotional needs, some of which are best (or exclusively) met by men and others by women (Blumstein and Schwartz, 1976). We have occasionally come across this same explanation from bisexual men, but much more often the male bisexual explains his sexual lifestyle in terms of a need for variety and creativity. Some bisexuals of either gender say that their sexual openness is a sign that they aren't biased against homosexuality and that they aren't sexist.

Three different sets of circumstances seem to be particularly conducive to bisexuality (Blumstein and Schwartz, 1977). Sexual experimentation in a relationship with a close friend is quite common among women and can also occur with two male friends or with a male homosexual who develops a casual but friendly relationship with a woman. Group sex is another avenue for bisexual experimentation; while males usually initiate the group activity, females often feel more comfortable engaging in same-sex contact. Finally, some people come to adopt a bisexual philosophy as an outgrowth of their personal belief systems. For instance, some women who have been active in the women's movement find that they are drawn closer to other women by the experience and translate this closeness into sexual expression. This same process can be a form of subtle coercion, however:

> I was an ardent feminist but also as straight as I could be. As I worked extensively with women's groups, I began to feel more and more pressure to "try" a sexual experience with another woman, with the implication being that if I didn't, I really wasn't into sisterhood and was enslaved by male cultural propaganda. I finally gave in to this pressure and had an awful time. Shortly after that, I began drifting away from the movement because it hit too raw a nerve in me. *(Authors' files)*

A few other circumstances of bisexual behavior are notable because they are usually not labeled as bisexual by the participants. Under conditions of prolonged sexual segregation, heterosexual people often turn temporarily to same-sex experiences. This is true of both male and female prisoners (Kirkham, 1971; Giallombardo, 1974; Money and Bohmer, 1980) and members of the military. Similarly, many men who participate in brief sexual encounters in public restrooms (called the "tearoom trade") are heterosexually married and do not think of themselves as bisexual (Humphreys, 1970). Young male prostitutes who cater to a homosexual clientele generally see this as a detached, depersonalized act done "for the money"; thus their self-perception remains strongly heterosexual (A. J. Reiss, 1967; Allen, 1980).

One facet of bisexuality that has received very little attention is same-gender sexual contact in minority populations. In a recent paper, de la Vega (1990, p. 6) notes: "Within many Latino cultures, there are many self-labeled male heterosexuals who manifest private bisexual behavior." According to de la Vega, bisexual activity for some Latino men only emerges when they are under the influence of alcohol or drugs; but in other instances,

men are forced by harsh cultural gender-role expectations among Latino people to live outwardly as heterosexual, while keeping their homosexual/bisexual contacts hidden and private. Furthermore, the strong undercurrent of **machismo** encourages males to be sexually dominant over people who are more feminine (either feminine females or feminine males), thus sometimes promoting bisexual behavior.

There are four different types of bisexual behavior that de la Vega identifies among Latino males:

1. *Closeted, self-identified homosexual Latinos* engage in same-gender sex only in private. They are often married as a result of pressures from their families or from the community, but they typically prefer sex with other men—when they can do so privately and discreetly.

2. *Closeted, latent-homosexual Latinos* see themselves as heterosexual, but have persistent erotic attractions to men, which humiliate and anger them. These men participate in bisexual acts only when they are intoxicated, which gives them an excuse for this "strange" behavior. Often, such men are strongly homophobic in their public pronouncements, using their derision of homosexuality as a form of psychological protection.

3. *Supermacho heterosexual Latinos* will sometimes have sexual intercourse with homosexuals because they don't view them as real men: they see them instead as "pseudo-females."

4. *Poverty-induced bisexual behavior in Latinos* occurs when otherwise heterosexual males engage in bisexual prostitution in order to support themselves or their families. In a related manner, drug addiction sometimes leads otherwise heterosexual Latinos into bisexual prostitution to support their drug habits.

There are almost undoubtedly similar patterns of bisexual behavior in other minority populations, but they have not been studied in detail up until now.

Bisexuals face a number of problems in our society, as Coleman (1987) points out. There is a general lack of public acceptance for their situation, with no organizational support to parallel various gay liberation groups. Bisexuals also have to deal with numerous myths about their orientation. For instance, some people think bisexuals are incapable of meaningful love, while others view them as oversexed or highly neurotic. Bisexuals also may have a tougher time in marriages than heterosexuals do (Coleman, 1982, 1985). In addition, bisexuals are often rejected or looked down on by homosexuals as well as by heterosexuals. Coleman (1987) explains this as follows:

> The threat appears to be similar to "homophobia" for heterosexual people. The existence of an "opposite" sexual orientation can be threatening to an individual with a fragile and insecure sexual identity. So, too, "biphobia" exists in individuals who are easily threatened and the underpinnings of their sexual orientation is tenuous and shaky. *(p. 231)*

Finally, as mentioned earlier, bisexuality has become strongly stigmatized today as an outgrowth of concern over the AIDS epidemic.

Despite facing such problems, there is no indication that bisexuals have poorer pyschological adjustment than heterosexuals or homosexuals. For example, a study comparing bisexual, heterosexual, and homosexual women on various psychological characteristics found no significant differences between these groups (LaTorre and Wendenberg, 1983). A similar study of males has reached the same conclusion (Klein, 1978).

The nature of bisexuality remains very much a puzzle at the present time. There are no good leads on what "causes" bisexuality, and the varied pattern of bisexual biographies wreaks havoc with many theories about the origins of sexual orientation. It is very possible that as more is learned about this subject our understanding of the complexities of human sexuality will be improved.

SUMMARY

1. Although attitudes toward homosexuality in the past have varied from acceptance to strong condemnation, homosexuals in our society today are clearly a minority faced with social, religious, and legal prejudices. Homophobia—a fear of homosexuality—is widespread and difficult to reduce in light of prevailing stereotypes.
2. There are many theories about the "causes" of homosexuality. Some suggest biological origins such as genetic factors, prenatal hormone exposure, or a hormone imbalance. Others stress faulty childhood development, such as Freud's idea that homosexuality arises from a fixation at an immature stage of psychosexual development or Bieber's theory that male homosexuality results from having a weak, passive father and a dominant, overprotective mother. According to learning theory, sexual orientation is partly dependent on the nature of early sexual experiences. There is no firm support for any of these theories, perhaps because there are different types of homosexuality, each of which originates in a different way.
3. Homosexuality is neither an illness nor a form of poor psychological adjustment. Much of the early research that attempted to show that homosexuals were "sick" suffered from poor research design, and more research studies have generally shown that homosexuals are as well-adjusted as properly matched groups of heterosexuals. Recognizing this, the American Psychiatric Association no longer considers homosexuality an illness.
4. In general, self-discovery of homosexuality in males occurs at an earlier age than in females. The decision on whether or when to "come out" is a difficult one for many homosexuals, regardless of their age.
5. Homosexuals are not usually recognizable by their appearance, mannerisms, or occupational choice. The diversity of homosexual lifestyles is considerable, but most homosexual men are more active sexually (i.e., engage in sex more frequently) than lesbians and have more sex partners than lesbians or heterosexuals. However, many gay men and women have lasting committed same-sex relationships.
6. The gay world has its visible and invisible components. Today, in addition to gay bars and baths, there are also gay churches, organizations, newspapers, and—in larger cities—full-scale gay business and social communities. But homosexuality is not always "gay": there is a less pleasant side to homosexuality, with impersonal, hurried sex, fear of police entrapment, high rates of sexually transmitted disease, alcoholism, and personal guilt or fear of discovery. Reflecting this, mounting fear of

macho aggressively male. The adjective form of **machismo,** which describes a set of masculine attitudes and behaviors originally from South American and Mediterranean cultures.

AIDS has led to major changes in sexual behavior within some segments of the gay male community.

7. Bisexuality is a form of sexual experimentation or a deliberately chosen sexual style. Relatively little research has been done on this subject, but it appears to be a comfortable option for some people while being unthinkable to many others.

Thought Questions

1. Some prominent politicians are homosexuals in the closet who consistently vote against bills that would benefit gays and lesbians. Some homosexuals think these people should be exposed—that is, "forced out of the closet." What do you think? Should gays who know that an apparently homophobic politician is actually homosexual in his behavior respect his privacy? Or should gays act against powerful but hypocritical members of their own group and make the "coming out" choice for them?

2. Does the Freudian explanation that most homophobia in our culture is a reflection of fears of latent homosexuality account for most homophobics in our culture? Or are there other reasons why Americans are homophobic?

3. To what degree should the homosexuality of a parent play a role in a child custody case?

4. The term "homosexual" was actually coined before the term "heterosexual." Why do you think this was true? What lesson does this teach us?

5. Is a person who admits to a homosexual orientation but who never engages in partner sex a homosexual? Can there be a distinction between a person's homosexual identity and his or her homosexual behavior?

6. A newspaper headlined a story about a 12-year-old boy who was abducted and sexually abused, using the term "homosexual rape." However, the rapist turned out to be a married man who was known locally for his avid homophobia. Was this a homosexual rape?

7. Scientific attempts at estimating the prevalence of homosexuality and bisexuality in various societies have generated considerable political heat in the past few years. Gay groups have, in general, claimed that various surveys have seriously *underestimated* the number of homosexuals in America, while many conservatives are happy to accept lower estimates. What are the ramifications of this controversy? For example, do lower estimates of the prevalence of homosexuality make it easier to stigmatize gays and lesbians? Would higher estimates encourage larger appropriations for HIV/AIDS research and treatment?

8. The recent discovery of a possible genetic basis for homosexuality raises a number of different ethical questions. For example, would it be ethically permissible for an employer to screen job candidates for possible homosexuality by doing DNA analysis on blood samples ostensibly taken for other purposes? Should the military—or the FBI—be permitted to do such testing? Why or why not? If there IS a genetic predisposition to homosexuality, does this mean it would be the *main* determinant of adult sexual orientation, or is it more likely to be just one among a number of different factors that influence a person's sexual orientation and behavior?

Suggested Readings

Blumenfeld, Warren J. (ed.). *Homophobia: How We All Pay the Price.* Boston: Beacon Press, 1992. A superb collection of essays showing how homophobia casts its shadow broadly across our lives, in both personal and societal terms.

Bozett, F. W. (ed.). *Homosexuality and the Family.* New York: Harington Park Press, 1989. An outstanding collection of papers on the family dynamics of homosexuality, focusing particularly on reactions of family members to coming out and on gays and lesbians as parents.

Clark, D. *The New Loving Someone Gay.* Berkeley CA: Celestial Arts, 1987. A sensitively written guide for gay people and their families and friends that debunks many myths about homosexuality and offers practical advice on a wide range of topics, from coming out to dealing with the threat of AIDS.

Comstock, Gary David. *Violence Against Lesbians and Gay Men.* New York: Columbia University Press, 1991. An eye-opening analysis of the extent of and reasons for physical violence towards homosexual men and women in modern America. Reading this book will help you understand why homophobia should not be tolerated in our society.

Faderman, Lillian. *Odd Girls and Twilight Lovers: A History of Lesbian Life in Twentieth-Century America*. New York: Penguin Books, 1991. A very readable analysis of how lesbian culture evolved as we know it now. Interesting explanations of its nineteenth-century origins in "romantic friendships," how and why those friendships fell out of favor, and the cultural stereotypes that both decried and now allow the flourishing of lesbian community.

Gochros, J. S. *When Husbands Come Out of the Closet*. New York: Harrington Park Press, 1989. A profile of heterosexual wives married to gay or bisexual men that explores the ways in which the wives cope and what happens to such marriages.

Hill, I. (ed.). *The Bisexual Spouse*. New York: Harper & Row, 1989. An easy-to-read collection of personal interviews with couples where one spouse is bisexual, augmented by a sexuality survey on homosexuality and bisexuality. While this book doesn't provide definitive answers, it does ask a lot of provocative questions.

LeVay, Simon. *The Sexual Brain*. Cambridge, MA: MIT Press, 1993. A clear description of current knowledge of the biological basis of sexual development and sexual behavior written by one of the world's leading neuroanatomists. Especially strong chapter on "Sexual Orientation and Its Development."

Marmor, Judd (ed.). *Homosexual Behavior*. New York: Basic Books, 1980. A thought-provoking group of essays on homosexuality by a well-balanced group of experts in fields such as law, history, sociology, anthropology, psychology, psychiatry, and religion.

McWhirter, David, and Mattison, Andrew. *The Male Couple*. Englewood Cliffs, NJ: Prentice-Hall, 1984. An intriguing look at the ways in which gay male relationships develop and stabilize over time.

Shilts, Randy. *Conduct Unbecoming: Gays and Lesbians in the U.S. Military*. New York: St. Martin's Press, 1993. The definitive history and social analysis of homosexual men and women in the military. This 784-page book is fast-paced, thoughtful, and a sample of hard-hitting investigative journalism at its best.

Weinberg, Martin S., Williams, Colin J., and Pryor, Douglas W. *Dual Attraction: Understanding Bisexuality*. New York: Oxford University Press, 1994. An interesting survey of the relationships and backgrounds of bisexual men and women.

Sexual Behavior

Even though sexual behavior is the subject of most of this book, there are certain aspects of common forms of sexual behavior that deserve particular attention. First, we discuss solitary sexual behavior, including masturbation and sexual fantasies, and explode some common myths about these practices. Second, we turn our attention to the various techniques of heterosexual lovemaking as well as gay and lesbian sex. The final portion of the chapter examines various aspects of interpersonal sexual behavior in a variety of contexts: premarital, marital, extramarital, and nonmarital.

MASTURBATION

Masturbation can be defined as sexual self-pleasuring that involves some form of direct physical stimulation. Most often, masturbation is done by rubbing, stroking, fondling, squeezing, or otherwise stimulating the genitals, but it can also be carried out by self-stimulation of other body parts such as the breasts, the inner thighs, or the anus. The term *masturbation* refers to the act of self-stimulation without regard to the outcome; that is, sexual self-stimulation need not lead to orgasm to be masturbation.

In this book, we have deliberately used the term *masturbation* to refer only to sexual *self*-stimulation. Stimulation received from a partner, although similar in many ways, involves an interactional element that makes it helpful to maintain this distinction. While masturbation can occur as part of sexual activity with a partner, our focus in this chapter is primarily on masturbation as a private act.

As we have already pointed out, masturbation often begins during childhood and occurs commonly in both males and females throughout the life cycle. Masturbation is also found elsewhere in the animal kingdom. Ford and Beach (1951) noted that many species of apes and monkeys "form habits of self-stimulation," and other mammals also practice masturbation:

> Sexually excited male porcupines, for example, walk about on three legs while holding one forepaw on the genitals. . . . Male elephants sometimes manipulate their semi-erect penis with the trunk. . . . Male dogs and cats regularly lick the phallic organ, often showing convulsive pelvic movements which indicate the stimulatory value of the resulting sensations. . . . One [captive] male [dolphin] had a habit of holding his erect penis in the jet of water intake, and other [dolphins] characteristically rubbed the tumescent organ against the floor of the tank. *(p. 160)*

Despite this apparent "naturalness" of masturbation from an evolutionary viewpoint, Ford and Beach noted that most human societies consider masturbation by adults to be undesirable. For an understanding of how a negative attitude toward masturbation developed in our own society, a glimpse back in history is revealing.

Historical Perspectives

The origins of the word *masturbation* are not entirely clear, although it seems to have been coined in Roman times. While it was previously thought that the term derived from the Latin *manus* (hand) and *stupro* (to defile), scholars now believe it has a Greek root, *mezea* (genitals), with the original meaning "to arouse the genitals" (Bullough and Bullough, 1977).

The ancient Greeks and Romans were relatively silent on the subject of masturbation, although Hippocrates (a Greek physician commonly regarded as the Father of Medicine) believed that excessive loss of semen caused spinal consumption (Haller and Haller, 1977). Even though the Bible has no clear-cut prohibitions against this sexual activity, both traditional Judaism and Christianity generally regarded masturbation as sinful. [The story of Onan (Genesis 38:9–11), which had been thought of as an edict against masturbation, is now thought by modern scholars to describe coitus interruptus, a very different act. Nevertheless, masturbation was referred to as "onanism" well into the twentieth century.]

Masturbation was sometimes referred to as an "unnatural act" by church leaders because it had no reproductive goal, but later it was described as "self-abuse," "defilement of the flesh," and "self-pollution." In large part, the credit for giving masturbation such a bad reputation belongs to a Swiss physician, S. Tissot (1728–1797), who brought the matter into the scientific arena and transformed masturbation from a simple sin to an illness that had to be cured.

Tissot believed that all sexual activity was dangerous because it forced blood to rush to the head, leaving too little in the rest of the body, so that nerves and other vital tissues slowly degenerated. In keeping with the scientific knowledge of his time, he was certain that this form of nerve damage caused insanity. Tissot was convinced that masturbation was a particularly "dangerous" form of sex because it was convenient and could be started during the vulnerable years of childhood and because the masturbator's guilt over his or her sinfulness further irritated the nervous system and made it more susceptible to damage.

The "proof" of Tissot's theory could be seen in mental asylums, where patients were either observed in the process of, or openly admitted to, masturbating. By the time Tissot's notions had crossed the Atlantic to America, the average doctor was quite willing to believe that masturbation caused insanity, epilepsy, acne, weight loss, decreased mental capability, weakness, lethargy, and—the ultimate punishment—early death.

"WHY DO THEY CALL IT SELF-ABUSE? I HAPPEN TO LOVE IT."

Source: Playboy, *March 1984, p. 174. Reproduced by special permission of Playboy* Magazine; Copyright © *1984 by* Playboy.

Parents searched desperately for ways to keep their children from being stricken. Physicians were happy to oblige; after all, it was the conscientious doctor's duty to put an end to masturbation. Much energy and money were spent on cures ranging from elaborate belts, locks, and cages—to protect the genitals from roving hands—to surgical "cures" which left little for the patient to fondle.

The nineteenth-century medical profession in America attacked masturbation with zest. The battle was fought on two main fronts, diet and physical constraint. Gravies, alcohol, oysters, salt, pepper, fish, jelly, chocolate, ginger, and coffee were forbidden to masturbators (both male and female) since it was thought that they irritated the nerves and increased sexual desire.

Other doctors blamed tight britches, the friction of sheets, handling of the genitals during urination, and the touching of children's genitals by nursemaids or parents during bathing. If "irritants" were removed from the diet and tight britches removed from the wardrobe but masturbation still continued, drastic steps became necessary. Doctors prescribed such remedies as dressing the child in straightjackets at bedtime, wrapping the child in cold, wet sheets to "cool" desire, and tying the hands to the bedposts. The U.S. Patent Office granted several patents to variations of the medieval chastity belt

that shielded the genitals from fondling. Parents could padlock their children into these elaborate "genital cages" and tuck away the key (Figure 16.1). By the early part of this century, metal mittens were being sold to deter the evil wanderings of little children's hands as well as an alarm that rang in the parents' bedroom if their child's bed was moving (LoPiccolo and Heiman, 1978).

For those seeking a more permanent solution to their problem (cages, belts, and metal mittens had to be removed for bathing, leaving the wearer vulnerable to temptation), doctors prescribed other treatments: leeches could be applied to the genital area to suck away blood and relieve the congestion that caused sexual desire; cautery (burning of genital tissue by an electric current or hot iron) was believed to deaden the nerves and decrease feeling and desire. The extreme cures—castration and removal of the clitoris—were most popular in the 1850s and 1860s. American medical journals of the mid-1800s also reported that castration was often a successful treatment of insanity.

Slowly, beginning in the early 1900s, the American medical community began to realize that masturbation caused neither acne nor insanity. A few brave doctors even recommended that females masturbate to relieve hysteria and that males masturbate instead of picking up prostitutes (and venereal disease). As recently as 1930, however, a medical authority continued to warn of the dangers of "onanism" that could lurk in activities like rope climbing, bicycle riding, or running a sewing machine. He argued that "the path leads to imbecility and premature senility," "loss of spirit, weakness of memory, dependency," "apathy," "languor, irritability, headaches, neuralgias, dimness of vision," and so on (Scott, 1930, p. 424).

Contemporary Attitudes

By the time of the Kinsey reports (1948, 1953), both public and professional thinking about masturbation had shifted significantly from that of the early part of the century. But carryovers remained: even today, some people half-jokingly believe that masturbation will lead to "hair on the palm of your hand" or misshapen genitals, while others are convinced masturbation causes sterility, sexual dysfunction, fatigue, or memory loss.

A number of studies in the last 20 years indicate that attitudes toward masturbation have relaxed

Figure 16.1 Antimasturbation Devices of the Nineteenth Century

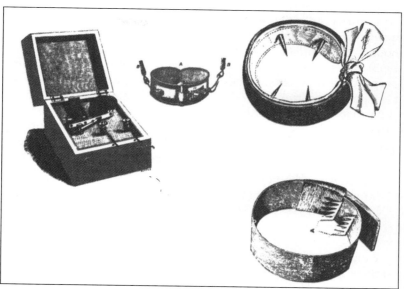

considerably compared with earlier times. Morton Hunt (1975), reporting on the *Playboy* survey of sexual attitudes and behavior, found that only one out of six men or women between the ages of 18 and 34 felt that masturbation is wrong. In the 45 and over age groups he studied, approximately one-third of the women and men viewed masturbation as wrong. Arafat and Cotton (1974), reporting on a questionnaire administered to 230 college males and 205 college females, found that most of those who did not masturbate refrained due to lack of desire. Of the nonmasturbators, 32 percent of the males versus 14 percent of females thought of masturbation as a waste of energy, as immoral, and as producing cheap feelings. Only a small fraction of those who did not masturbate cited guilt, inhibition, or religious beliefs as their reasons. However, Atwood and Gagnon (1987) reported that 40 percent of the college students they surveyed who did not masturbate said they refrained because they felt masturbation was immoral.

Today masturbation is a more accepted form of sexual behavior than it has ever been in the past, but there are still some lingering doubts. These doubts center on the following sorts of issues:

1. *Masturbation is sinful.* This, of course, is a matter of moral or religious conviction that each person must deal with in his or her own way. Several studies have found that people who are strongly religious masturbate less often than those who are not religious or who have less strongly held religious beliefs (DeMartino, 1979).

2. *Masturbation is unnatural.* The logic of this statement is hard to grasp. If naturalness refers to what occurs in nature, then this statement is incorrect since masturbation has been observed in many animal species. Furthermore, the numerous reports of masturbation during infancy or early childhood also refute the notion that it is unnatural.

3. *Masturbation may be a part of growing up, but adults who masturbate are psychologically immature.* Freudian theory generally supports this viewpoint, suggesting that adult masturbation is a symptom of psychosexual immaturity except when it is used as a substitute for heterosexual intercourse when no partner is available (Marcus and Francis, 1975). Today most authorities believe that adult masturbation is a legitimate type of sexual activity in its own right (e.g., see Hite, 1977; Peters, 1988; Calderone and Johnson, 1989). The tension between these two positions is created by differ-

ent theories of psychological maturity; yet no studies show that adults who masturbate are less mature than those who do not. Some experts believe that masturbation is "immature" only when it is *exclusively* and *compulsively* practiced even though other outlets are easily available (Ellis, 1965). Nevertheless, many college students disapprove of masturbation because they feel it is a poor substitute for having sex with a partner—in other words, sort of a "nerdy" thing to do.

4. *Masturbation tends to be habit-forming and may prevent the development of healthy sexual function.* Virtually all sexologists and psychotherapists see this claim as a throwback to nineteenth-century thinking. Nancy Friday (1991, p. 34) expresses current opinion well: "By teaching ourselves what excites us, we become more orgasmic and better sexual partners, responsible for our share, capable of giving pleasure, better able to give direction in what it is that excites us." Learning about masturbation is also a central feature of many sex therapy programs (Heiman and LoPiccolo, 1988; Leiblum and Rosen, 1989; Zilbergeld, 1992; Masters, Johnson, and Kolodny, 1994). Furthermore, masturbation is associated with higher self-esteem and enhanced marital and sexual satisfaction for women (Hurlbert and Whittaker, 1991).

In addition, it is now clear that masturbation may have a number of additional benefits. For example, it can provide a viable (and pleasurable) sexual outlet for people without partners, including the elderly. It can also be beneficial to persons whose sex drives are greater than their partners' at a particular moment. In the era of AIDS, it is one of the principal means of practicing safer sex (Kaplan, 1987; Money, 1988a). Finally, it is often a gratifying way of releasing tension, thus helping a person relax.

Techniques of Masturbation

People use a wide variety of methods of sexual self-pleasuring. For some, a single approach to masturbation, with only minor variations on the theme, is used over and over again. Other people experiment with a number of different masturbatory methods, sometimes selecting a few favorites for consistent use, and sometimes preferring continued inventiveness to repeat performances.

Masters and Johnson (1966) noted that no two women they studied had been observed to masturbate in exactly the same way. Even if the general pattern of physical self-stimulation was similar, the timing, tempo, and style of each individual's approach were unique. While men, in general, have less diversity and more "sameness" in their masturbation patterns, individual embellishments or idiosyncrasies exist here too.

A complete catalogue of the varieties of techniques used in masturbation could fill a full-length book and would probably be boring reading. Thus, we restrict our discussion to common patterns of masturbation with brief mention of a few interesting variations.

Female Masturbation

The most common form of female masturbation is to stimulate the clitoris, mons, or vaginal lips by stroking, rubbing, or applying pressure by hand (Masters and Johnson, 1966, 1979; Fisher, 1973; Hite, 1977). Clitoral stimulation may be accomplished by rubbing or stroking the clitoral shaft or may result from applying pressure to the mons or tugging on the vaginal lips. The clitoral glans, or tip, is rarely rubbed directly during masturbation because of its sensitivity. If clitoral stimulation is concentrated in one area for a long time, or if intense stimulation is applied to one spot, pleasurable sensations may lessen because the area can become partially numb (Masters and Johnson, 1966).

Interestingly, only a few women masturbate by inserting a finger or object into the vagina: Kinsey and his associates (1953) found that about 20 percent of women used this approach, and Hite (1977) found that only 1.5 percent of women masturbated by vaginal insertion alone. Similarly, only a small percentage of women routinely include breast stimulation as a part of masturbation (Kinsey's group found that 11 percent of women who masturbate incorporate breast play into self-stimulation).

Most women masturbate while lying on their backs, but some prefer a standing or sitting position. Hite (1977) found that 5.5 percent of her sample usually applied clitoral/vulval stimulation lying face down, with a hand placed between their legs. Other women prefer to masturbate by rubbing their genitals against an object such as a pillow, chair, bedpost, or doorknob. (A few years ago, one of our research subjects insisted on bringing her

Female masturbation.

own pillow to our offices for a study involving masturbation since she couldn't masturbate without it.) In variations on this theme, the woman may rub her genitals with fur, velvet, silk, or any soft material.

About 3 percent of women usually masturbate by pressing their thighs together rhythmically (Hite, 1977), and some women prefer to masturbate using some form of water massage of the genital region or perineum. The use of oils or lotions during masturbation is a fairly common practice but is usually only a secondary part of the masturbatory experience.

As women have become more informed and liberated in their attitudes toward masturbation, they have increasingly used hand-held vibrators to enhance sexual sensations. Almost half of the young women in our studies who masturbate have tried a vibrator at least once, and one-quarter of these women prefer the vibrator over other methods of self-stimulation (see Table 16.1). Vibrators come in many sizes, shapes, and styles. Some are cylindrical or shaped to anatomically resemble a penis, and others have changeable attachments that permit different types of stimulation. A few are discreetly designed and are sold in fashionable stores without any hint of their possible sexual utility.

Vibrators are usually applied to the external genitals, but some women prefer to insert the vibrator into the vagina and move it slowly in and out. Other objects may be inserted into the vagina during masturbation, including dildos (artificial penis-shaped objects usually made of rubber), benwa balls (two metal balls that are put inside the vagina and provide stimulation as they roll against each other), and a variety of other objects such as candles, soda bottles, and cucumbers. Among little-used but novel approaches to this type of female masturbation we've encountered are an electric toothbrush, a dildo made of ice, and a lucky rabbit's foot.

Male Masturbation

Most males masturbate by rubbing, stroking, or pumping the shaft of the penis with one hand (see Table 16.2). Scrotal stimulation or direct stimulation of the head of the penis is relatively infrequent (Masters and Johnson, 1966, 1979), although men sometimes stroke the whole penis in an up-and-down motion. A few men focus their self-stimulation on the raised area (the frenulum) just below the head on the underside of the penis, and a few masturbate primarily by pulling their foreskin back and forth.

The typical male masturbatory episode begins with a comparatively slow, deliberate touch. As sexual arousal increases, the tempo also increases, and by the time of impending orgasm, the stroking motion becomes as rapid as possible

Table 16.1   Preferred Types of Female Masturbation[a]

Manual stimulation of clitoral/vulval area	48%
Vibrator stimulation of clitoral/vulval area	26
Vaginal insertion	10
Rubbing against an object	6
Thigh pressure	4
Water massage	4
Miscellaneous methods	2
Breast stimulation only	0

[a]Data from 265 women, aged 18 to 35, who completed a detailed sex history questionnaire and personal interview as part of the screening process for a research project at the Masters & Johnson Institute. Data collected from 1977 to 1980.

Table 16.2   Preferred Types of Male Masturbation[a]

Manual stimulation of the penis	82%
Lying on stomach, rubbing against bed	15
Thigh pressure	1
Water massage	0.5
Self-fellatio	0.5

[a]Data compiled from The Hite Report on Male Sexuality by Shere Hite, p. 1106. Copyright © 1978, 1981. Reprinted by permission of Alfred A. Knopf, Inc.

(Masters and Johnson, 1966). During ejaculation, penile stimulation is variable: some men slow down, others grip the penis firmly, and others stop all stimulation.

A relatively small percentage of males employ some type of friction against an object such as a bed or a pillow as a preferred form of masturbation (Kinsey, Pomeroy, and Martin, 1948). Other "hands-off" varieties of male masturbation depend on thrusting the penis into something—the neck of a milkbottle, a cored apple, or modeling clay, for example—in a form of simulated coitus.

Gadgets assisting male masturbation abound and are widely advertised in sex tabloids, magazines, and direct mail catalogues. They include numerous models of "artificial vaginas" made of rubber or other soft, pliable material; "inflatable life-size dolls" variably equipped with vagina, breasts, open mouth, and anus; suction devices (manually and electrically operated) that promise to deliver the ultimate forms of sexual ecstasy for the male without a partner. These devices can be used with lubricating lotion or cream and may also have features that add vibration or heat to the experience.

It should be pointed out that these devices are not always carefully manufactured and may pose some physical risk if they go haywire. Some cases of severe penile injury have been caused by inserting the penis into a vacuum cleaner hose (Mannion, 1973).

Statistically rare varieties of male masturbation include the two or three males per thousand who perform oral sex on themselves (Kinsey, Pomeroy, and Martin, 1948) as well as males who masturbate

by inserting objects into the urethra or the anus. Breast stimulation is rarely included as a regular feature of male masturbation.

Separating Fact from Fiction

Data about masturbation are a bit tricky to interpret. You may recall that Kinsey and his colleagues (1948, 1953) found a wide discrepancy in the incidence of masturbation between male and female adolescents, but more recent studies suggest that this difference may be narrowing (see Chapter 9). A similar trend may also be occurring in regard to masturbatory behavior in adulthood.

There are several possible explanations for the rise in female masturbation:

1. Negative attitudes toward female masturbation seem to have softened, although some women continue to feel guilty or ashamed of this activity.

2. Women have learned about masturbation at an earlier age and in more explicit detail than in the past, primarily through the media (books, magazines, movies). As a result, masturbation is less likely to be discovered only accidentally.

3. Both men and women have become more aware that sexuality is a positive aspect of being female. Acting upon sexual feelings is thus a legitimate activity for women, who are sometimes encouraged to first try masturbation by a sexual partner.

Although the number of females who masturbate seems to be increasing, research data do not suggest that females as a group masturbate as often as males. While there is wide individual variability and some females masturbate several times a day,

Male masturbation.

FOCUS IN BRIEF

Masturbation During College

- During the freshman year of college, 76.8 percent of males masturbate, compared to only 31.8 percent of females.
- By the senior year of college, more than four-fifths of males masturbate, while for females only two out of five do so.
- Overall, males masturbate more frequently during high school than they do in college, while for females the frequency stays about the same.
- Only 3 percent of male college students masturbate daily; another 19 percent masturbate at least twice a week. In one large survey, no female college students reported masturbating daily, and only 7 percent reported masturbating at least twice a week.
- For college students who do not masturbate, the most common reasons reported are not having the urge to do so and believing masturbation to be immoral.

Source: *Atwood and Gagnon, 1987.*

it appears that males masturbate about twice as often as females (Sorenson, 1973; DeMartino, 1979; Atwood and Gagnon, 1987; Michael et al., 1994).

Kinsey and his colleagues (1948) found that among individuals who masturbate, the average frequency for single 16- to 20-year-old males was 57 times a year, dropping to 42 times a year in the 21- to 25-year-old group. In contrast, the average frequency for single females aged 18 to 24 was about 21 times a year (Kinsey et al., 1953). The *Playboy* survey suggests a contemporary increase in female masturbatory activity: the 18- to 24-year-old sample comparable to Kinsey's had an average masturbatory frequency of 37 times a year (Hunt, 1975). However, the most recent data available indicate that while more than 30 percent of males aged 18 to

34 masturbate once a week or more, less than 10 percent of females of the same age masturbate this frequently (Laumann et al., 1994, Table 3.1).

Many people assume that once someone has married, his or her use of masturbation should all but disappear. This generally doesn't happen, though: in the *Playboy* survey, 72 percent of young married husbands masturbated, with an average frequency of about 24 times per year, and 68 percent of young married wives were actively involved in masturbation, averaging approximately 10 times per year (Hunt, 1975). The *Redbook* survey came up with similar findings. Even among older married couples, masturbation continues as a common type of sexual behavior (Masters and Johnson, 1966; DeMartino, 1979).

Most of the old myths about masturbation causing health problems have now been laid to rest. Physical tolerance for masturbation (or any sexual stimulation) in fact has a built-in safety valve: once the system has reached a point of overload, it temporarily shuts down and does not respond to further stimulation. There is no evidence that masturbation causes physical problems other than the rare cases of genital injury stemming from overvigorous stimulation.

Nevertheless, a few authorities caution against "excessive" masturbation although they rarely define the term. Men almost always see "excessive" masturbation as somewhat more than their own rate (Masters and Johnson, 1966). Very few people we have seen either as research subjects or as patients feel they masturbate too much. Of those who do, the concern is often "It's excessive because I'm married" or "It's excessive for my age." Rather than count masturbatory episodes, it is probably more useful to consider whether masturbation involves anxiety, conflict, guilt, or an overwhelming compulsiveness. If it does, a person may benefit from professional help, but if masturbation leads to satisfaction and pleasure, it's unlikely to be a problem.

At the opposite end of the spectrum, in the rush to legitimatize masturbation, there is often a built-in implication that everyone *should* masturbate. People who have *never* masturbated, while in a statistical minority, should certainly not be made to feel abnormal. People who choose not to masturbate—whether or not they've tried it, whether or not their choice is based on religious conviction, personal preference, or some other consideration—have every right to their decision without being made to feel guilty or strange by self-proclaimed experts in sexual health. Sexual decisions, in the final analysis, must be personal.

SEXUAL AROUSAL AND SLEEP

We have already mentioned that sexual reflexes function in a rhythmic fashion during sleep (see Chapter 4). In addition to having sleep-associated erections or vaginal lubrication, people can experience orgasm during sleep. While it may not be entirely accurate to call this a type of sexual behavior, this form of solitary sex deserves discussion too.

Nocturnal Ejaculation

Kinsey and his co-workers (1948) found that 83 percent of males experience nocturnal ejaculation at one time or another, with the highest incidence and frequency of this phenomenon occurring during the late teens. The average frequency of about once a month during this period declines substantially during the twenties, and few men over the age of 30 continue to ejaculate during sleep. Kinsey's group pointed out, however, that several cases of nocturnal ejaculation in older males up to age 80 had been verified.

Nocturnal ejaculation provides a physiologic "safety valve" for accumulated sexual tension that has not been released in another fashion. Men who have reached high and sustained levels of sexual arousal without ejaculating, no matter how the arousal came about, are thus able to discharge this physiologic tension in a completely natural reflex.

Female Orgasm and Sleep

Kinsey's group (1953) also found that women can experience orgasm during sleep. They noted: "As with the male, the female is often awakened by the muscular spasms . . . which follow her orgasms" (p. 192). Thirty-seven percent of their sample reported orgasm during sleep by age 45, but only about 10 percent of females had such an experience in any given year. Eight percent of their sample had sleep-associated orgasms more than five times per year and only 3 percent averaged more than twice a month.

In a more recent survey of 245 women from a large midwestern university, 30 percent reported having had orgasms during sleep in the preceding year (Wells, 1986). Among the findings in this study, several points deserve mention. (1) The frequency of a woman's sexual dreams did not seem to be related to whether or not she experienced sleep-associated orgasms. (2) The frequency of participating in various types of sexual activity was not predictive of whether a woman would have orgasms during sleep. (3) Whether a woman masturbates or not did not appear related to whether she had sleep-associated orgasms.

We have found that almost all women who report sleep-associated orgasms have previously been orgasmic by other means. A small number of women are distressed by orgasms occurring during sleep because they fear they either may have been unknowingly masturbating or are "oversexed." One married woman told us:

One month I was awakened by orgasms four or five different times. I have a good sex life with my husband, and I hardly ever masturbate, so I couldn't figure out why this was happening to me. I started to think that perhaps I was becoming a nymphomaniac, a person who could never get enough sexual satisfaction. Fortunately, I was able to discuss this with a woman who's a psychiatrist, and she set my mind at ease.

Until more people become aware of the natural occurrence of female orgasms and periodic vaginal lubrication during sleep, it is likely that similar reactions will occur.

Sexual Dreams

Explicitly sexual dreams, like wakeful sexual fantasies, are quite common. Seventy percent of females and nearly 100 percent of males have erotic dreams (Kinsey et al., 1953). The content of sexual dreams may sometimes be alarming because behavior is depicted that might be objectionable as an actual event. While most people realize that dreams are not equivalent to action, others are distressed because they fear the impulse that the dream represents. Persistently disturbing sexual dreams may in some cases be a sign of an underlying sexual conflict that might benefit from professional counseling.

SEXUAL FANTASY

From childhood on, most people have sexual fantasies that serve a variety of functions and elicit a broad range of reactions. Some are pleasant or exhilarating; others are embarrassing, puzzling, or even shocking. For purposes of clarity in this discussion, we restrict our use of the term "sexual fantasy" to refer only to wakeful thoughts as distinguished from sleep-associated dreams.

Facts About Fantasies

Although every child learns that pretending is an important type of play, sexual fantasies after childhood are usually not thought of as playful. This attitude may exist because sex is usually regarded as a serious matter, even in the imagination. Furthermore, some religious traditions regard a thought as equivalent to an act; thus, a person who has "immoral" sexual daydreams or desires is as sinful as a person who acts on those impulses. Fantasies have

also been viewed as having implications for mental health. Psychoanalysts were the only group for half a century to study fantasy in any depth. They viewed "deviant" sexual fantasies—those portraying anything other than heterosexual acts that led to intercourse—as immature expressions of the sex drive and as blocks to the development of more mature sexuality (Hollender, 1963). Many psychoanalysts also believed that such fantasies were likely to be forerunners of "deviant" sexual behavior (Eidelberg, 1945; Freud, 1946; Yalom, 1960).

Generally, imagination, creativity, and playfulness are part of the act of fantasizing. However, if a fantasy becomes a controlling force in a person's life, the play element may be completely eliminated. This situation isn't very different from that of a person who becomes addicted to gambling (which also begins as a form of play) or of the person who gets so caught up in a competitive sport, such as long-distance running, that the playful side of the activity is lost.

At times, it may be difficult to distinguish sexual fantasy from sexual desire. Just as your awareness of hunger and thinking about what kind of food you'd like to eat may blend together, your sexual appetite may merge with thoughts about how sexual satisfaction may be obtained. Although a fantasy may be valued strictly as a piece of fiction as opposed to a preview of an expected reality, this distinction does not always hold. In some cases, a sexual fantasy expresses sexual desire, while in others in *provokes* sexual desire that does not necessarily require the fantasied act for fulfillment.

The Context of Sexual Fantasies

Sexual fantasies occur in an astonishingly wide variety of settings and circumstances. Sometimes these imaginative interludes are intentionally called forth to pass the time, to enliven a boring experience, or to provide a sense of excitement. At other times, sex fantasies float into our awareness in a seemingly random fashion, perhaps triggered by thoughts or feelings of which we have little awareness.

Preferential Patterns

Among the most common varieties of sexual fantasies are those that can best be described as old familiar stories. The origin of such a fantasy, if it can be traced at all, might have been a book, a movie scene, or an actual experience. The person using this fantasy finds it to be particularly pleasing and comfortable as well as quite effective in producing arousal and returns to it again and again.

How a particular fantasy comes to be preferred and repeated over and over again is not entirely clear. Sometimes the primary fascination with this sort of fantasy lies in its sexual arousal, while at other times the pleasure may be more related to the "director's role"—being able to control the scene, plot, and actors. In many instances, the complexity of this fantasy makes it more suitable for use in solitary situations than during sexual activity with a partner.

In another form of the preferential fantasy pattern the person repeatedly uses a particular *type* of fantasy—group sex, for example—but no characters or story line connect one fantasy to another. The first pattern described is like playing a specific record again and again, while this pattern is more like playing a certain type of record—country and western or classical music—repeatedly.

There are at least two situations in which preferential fantasies may become troublesome. For some people, the repeated and exclusive use of such a fantasy may lead to a situation in which the fantasy becomes necessary for sexual arousal. The person no longer responds sexually to his or her partner since sexual arousal depends on the fantasy alone. Infrequently, preferential fantasies can become obsessions that may interfere with thinking or behavior. Obsessional fantasies are discussed more fully in Chapter 17.

Solitary or Shared?

Many people regard their fantasies as private property and keep them to themselves. However, it has been suggested that sharing fantasies between partners fosters intimacy and understanding. The implication is that not sharing your sexual fantasies may be selfish or immature. Those who believe in sharing fantasies point out that after a long time in a relationship, many couples discover that they each have fantasies about the same activity (e.g., having anal intercourse). Fearing that their partner may be embarrassed, offended, or unwilling to "play," many couples do not share their fantasies. Sometimes the fantasies of two people in a relationship are quite complementary, as when one person wants to be spanked during

sexual activity, while his or her partner fantasizes about spanking someone.

People who suggest that keeping fantasies private reflects immaturity do so for a number of reasons, some of which are at least partially incorrect. They believe that being embarrassed or ashamed of one's fantasies is in and of itself a mark of immaturity. They also feel that intimate relationships should have no barriers to communication because open communication is a mark of maturity and commitment. A third reason they give to "prove" that sharing sexual fantasies is best is that sharing fosters a deeper degree of understanding between partners and so is likely to improve the relationship. Finally, they often point out that sexual fantasies are more likely to be kept private by people who are sexually inhibited or "uptight." By bringing these fantasies out into the open, a person can become less inhibited (therefore, more "mature") and may attain more sexual satisfaction.

Such arguments are oversimplified in many ways. To begin with, there is nothing wrong or immature about having private thoughts or feelings. If private fantasies give a distorted view of a person's preferences, sharing the fantasy with a partner may result in misperception of what that person needs or wants instead of better understanding. For instance, if a woman occasionally fantasizes about being raped and enjoys the fantasy, this does not mean that she wants to be raped or would enjoy being raped. The same can be said of a person who fantasizes about robbing a bank: he or she can

This block print by Harunobu, done in the late 1760s, shows a young girl fantasizing about her lover while she masturbates.

hardly be said to have a criminal mind or to be "dangerous" because of this type of fantasy.

A partner may not only misunderstand a fantasy but may also believe that he or she is in some way expected to play it out in real life. Although the partner can say no, there may be a subtle pressure, whether intentional or unintentional. Having learned that your partner is turned on by a particular sexual fantasy, do you agree to try it, even if it is a bit uncomfortable, in order to be open-minded and sensitive to your partner's needs? What if you mistakenly decide to "try out" the fantasy when your partner doesn't really want to? Sometimes, once a fantasy has been shared with a partner, it provokes jealousy, guilt, or self-doubt. This is particularly true when one partner assumes that the other's fantasy indicates dissatisfaction or a desire to try someone else.

Many people find that after telling a partner about their most highly charged sexual fantasy, the turn-on value of the fantasy fizzles. While this does not always happen—sometimes the erotic stimulus of the fantasy increases—it is a potential pitfall. Unfortunately, there is no way of knowing beforehand if partners will benefit from sharing details of their sexual fantasies or if problems will result.

Intruding Fantasies

Not all sexual fantasies are willfully conjured up or pleasing. Some fantasies recur over and over again

"I think you're being silly. Would you like it better if I was thinking of you and sleeping with Robert Redford?"

Source: Playboy *November 1977. Reproduced by special permission of* Playboy Magazine; *Copyright © 1977 by* Playboy.

despite being unwanted; other fantasies flood into a person's awareness in a frightening fashion, producing inner turmoil, guilt, or conflict. Fantasies of this sort either may result in sexual arousal or may be so distressing that they shut off sexual feelings.

Usually, intruding fantasies that depict sexual situations or conduct that the fantasizer considers abnormal or bizarre (yet also arousing) include some imagined form of punishment or injury as the price to be paid for the sexual indulgence. The punishment within the fantasy may range from physical afflictions (such as venereal disease or cancer) to being discovered by others in the midst of sexual activity, being arrested and jailed, or being deprived of sexual satisfaction via one calamity or another. Other intruding fantasies may result in real-life problems such as avoidance of sexual activity, profound sexual guilt, or sexual dysfunction.

It is not difficult to imagine how distressing it might be for a 40-year-old married woman with conservative religious and sexual values to find that during sexual activity with her husband she repeatedly has fantasies about having sex with a group of men. Similarly, a man who prides himself on his macho image and is strongly anti-homosexual may be alarmed to find himself fantasizing about performing oral sex on another man. If distressing fantasies recur regularly, counseling may be required. Psychologists, psychiatrists, or sex therapists can help a person troubled by such fantasy patterns learn how to "switch the channel" (as you would switch from a disturbing TV show to a more pleasant one) or can teach thought-blocking techniques to deal with the situation (Wolpe, 1969; Abel and Blanchard, 1974).

Functions of Sexual Fantasy

Our use of the sexual imagination is quite varied. Fantasies function at many different levels to boost our self-confidence, provide a safety valve for pent-up feelings, increase sexual excitement, or let us triumph over the forces that prove troublesome in the everyday world, to mention just a few. Some of the most common functions of sexual fantasies are now described.

Inducing or Enhancing Arousal

We have already said that fantasy and sexual desire often merge together. People with low levels of sexual desire typically have few sexual fantasies (H. S. Kaplan, 1979; Kolodny, Masters, and Johnson, 1979; Nutter and Condron, 1983, 1985) and will often benefit from treatment that helps them form positive fantasies (Leiblum and Rosen, 1988).

Many times, sexual fantasies are used to induce or enhance sexual arousal, and while fantasies are often combined with masturbation to provide a source of turn-on when a partner is not available, fantasies are also extremely common during sexual activity with someone else (Friday, 1973, 1980; Hunt, 1975; Hariton and Singer, 1974; Lunde et al., 1991). For instance, one study of 212 married women found that sex fantasies helped many women achieve sexual arousal and/or orgasm during sexual intercourse (Davidson and Hoffman, 1986).

For some, the use of fantasy provides an initial boost to getting things under way. Others use fantasy to move from a leisurely, low-key sexual level into a more passionate state. One of the most frequent patterns we have encountered is the use of a particularly treasured fantasy to move from the plateau phase of arousal to orgasm. Some men and women report that they are unable to be orgasmic unless they use fantasy in this way.

Sexual fantasies can enhance both the psychological and physiological sides of sexual response in many ways: counteracting boredom, focusing thoughts and feelings (thus avoiding distractions or pressures), boosting our self-image (in our fantasies we can assume our desired physical attributes and need not worry about penis size, breast size, or body weight), and imagining an ideal partner (or partners) who suits all our needs.

Safety with Excitement

Sexual fantasies also provide a safe, protected environment for engaging the imagination and letting our sexual feelings roam. They are safe because they are private and fictional: privacy ensures that fantasies are undiscoverable, while the fictional makeup of our fantasies relieves us of personal accountability.

If you consider that most sexual fantasies involve situations, partners, and/or behavior that might be judged improper or illegal if they were real, the importance of safety as a backdrop for excitement becomes apparent. A mild-mannered, genteel college professor can fantasize about orgies with the three attractive coeds in the first row of his classroom without risking his tenure or reputation. A young woman lawyer can fantasize about raping one of her clients without jeopardizing her standing before the bar. A teenage boy can construct elaborate sexual fantasies about ravishing his best friend's mother without risking parental punishment or losing a friend. Clearly, the element of safety ensures the appeal and power of these erotic images.

Releasing Anxiety or Guilt

Fantasies of all types function as psychological safety valves that discharge inner tensions or needs in a relatively painless way (Byrne, 1977). In our fantasies, we can get even with others for real or imagined injustices, conquer fears by carefully controlling the action and emotions, and compensate for any personal shortcomings that are troublesome in real life. Consider the following examples from our files:

A 32-year-old married woman: My husband and I had a lousy sex life for years, and it mirrored a lousy relationship. During this time, my sex fantasies almost always involved making it with other men while he was forced to watch me with great humiliation. It was sweet revenge, I guess. . . .

Once we started marriage counseling, things began to improve. We learned how to talk together, and our sex life improved too. The interesting thing was, my fantasies began to change. I guess I no longer had a need to retaliate.

A 22-year-old unmarried male medical student: I've always been very uptight about sex. I suppose one reason is that I'm embarrassed about the size of my penis, which seems very small. In my fantasies, the woman I'm with always remarks on how big my penis is and seems in awe of its power. I found that if I used this fantasy while I was really with someone, I was much less nervous. It sounds silly, but I really felt better about myself.

Since we live in a society with a strong tradition of sexual restrictions and taboos and we learn not to discuss sexual behavior, fantasy often provides an important means of clarifying and dealing with sexual conflicts or confusion.

Controlled Rehearsal

For most people, fantasy provides a way to preview an anticipated experience and to prepare themselves for what to expect and how to act.

While this function of sexual fantasies may be most prominent during adolescence or with any people who have only limited sexual experience, it is very important. The opportunity to visualize oneself in a certain form of erotic activity—oral–genital sex, for example—allows one to anticipate some problems that may occur. By replaying a scene several times, fantasizers can develop a better idea of how to minimize difficulties and can also partially desensitize themselves to feelings of awkwardness, embarrassment, or surprise. Of course, if and when the fantasy is transformed into fact, the actual event may be considerably different from the imagined one in feelings, tempo, and other details. Nevertheless, a sense of comfort usually results from using fantasy as rehearsal.

Fantasy and Sexual Values

Many people misunderstand the nature of sexual fantasy and think that it expresses an actual desire to participate in or experience a given situation. This is like saying that a person who daydreams about being a war hero wants to go to war or that a person who fantasizes about having children is ready or willing to be a parent. Professionals are not immune to confusing the issues still further, as Lonnie Barbach (1980) explains:

> I worked with a group of feminist therapists who argued that it is sexist to derive pleasure from rape fantasies or fantasies that portray male domination. It was difficult for them to separate the sexual pleasure the fantasy provided from its political interpretation. I also knew a lesbian therapist who nearly panicked when she found herself having heterosexual fantasies, fearing that she might be a "latent heterosexual." (p. 119)

In an ongoing study of sexual fantasies being done at the Masters & Johnson Institute, we have found that most women who are aroused by fantasies that portray "unusual" sex practices such as rape, incest, sex with animals, or sadomasochistic sex indicate that they have no interest whatsoever in acting out the fantasy. In contrast, men appear to be somewhat more adventuresome. About two-thirds of the men we have interviewed who have such fantasies declare that they would be willing to try them under the right circumstances.

A study of the sexual fantasies of married women during intercourse with their husbands stressed that fantasy content does not indicate sexual problems, psychological problems, or personality flaws (Hariton and Singer, 1974). Masters and Johnson (1979) have shown that most people with recurrent sexual fantasies feel neither the desire nor the need to act on them in real life. They also found that the content of the most common fantasies of heterosexuals and homosexuals are remarkably similar. Homosexuals frequently fantasize about heterosexual situations and heterosexuals commonly fantasize about homosexual encounters (see Table 16.3).

While most people realize that a fleeting fantasy is not an in-depth revelation of the inner psyche, it is tempting to assume that a favorite fantasy theme says important things about our psychological makeup. There are no research data showing that this is true for all people (although it may be true in individual instances). Our sexual and personal values may differ considerably from our fantasy lives, just as an actor's true identity may vary greatly from the dramatic roles he plays. Nevertheless, some people feel guilty about having sexual fantasies. Cado and Leitenberg (1990) found that people who report the most guilt about having fantasies during intercourse have higher levels of sexual dissatisfaction and dysfunction than those who are relatively guilt-free.

Fantasy as Fact

Although many people say that they have no wish to transform their sexual fantasies into reality, for some the opposite is true. What motivates a person to lean one way or the other is uncertain, but some of the relevant factors may be (1) how powerful an erotic turn-on is involved, (2) how receptive, trustworthy, and understanding the partner is perceived to be, (3) how a person feels about himself or herself, and (4) how unusual or bizarre a fantasy appears.

Reliable statistics on how many people act out their sexual fantasies in real life are not available. For some couples, the acting out involves a limited dramatization, playing roles in a carefully controlled way—a rehearsal of the fantasy instead of the entire experience. For example, a woman who fantasizes about being spanked may ask her partner to give her a gentle spanking which is more symbolic than real, or a man who fantasizes about having sex with a young teenage girl may ask his

Table 16.3   Comparative Content of Fantasy Material by Frequency of Occurrence[a]

Heterosexual male
1. Replacement of established partner
2. Forced sexual encounter with female
3. Observation of sexual activity
4. Homosexual encounters
5. Group sex experiences

Heterosexual female
1. Replacement of established partner
2. Forced sexual encounter with male
3. Observation of sexual activity
4. Idyllic encounters with unknown men
5. Lesbian encounters

Homosexual male
1. Imagery of male sexual anatomy
2. Forced sexual encounters with males
3. Heterosexual encounters with females
4. Idyllic encounters with unknown men
5. Group sex experiences

Homosexual female
1. Forced sexual encounters
2. Idyllic encounter with established partner
3. Heterosexual encounters
4. Recall of past sexual experience
5. Sadistic imagery

[a]*Data from interviews with 30 persons in each group collected between 1957 and 1968.*

Source: *Based on Table 9-1 in William H. Masters and Virginia E. Johnson,* Homosexuality in Perspective. *© 1979 by William H. Masters and Virginia E. Johnson. Reprinted by permission of Little, Brown and Company.*

partner to dress and act like a 13-year-old. In such situations, the fantasy comes to life in the sense of being "in the flesh" rather than imaginary, but it is still not the real thing. The limited dramatization form of acting out fantasies is particularly appealing to many people because of its safety and control, but it is often less psychologically satisfying than the purely imaginary fantasy since it is "only an act."

Some people go further in transforming a sexual fantasy into real life. A married couple may respond to an ad in a "swinger's magazine" to try out a fantasy of switching partners. A person with fantasies about being tied up (bondage) may convince his or her partner to do so. In some cases, the fantasy becomes more fulfilling, more meaningful, and a part of the continuing sexual relationship. Very often, however, the result is less than ex-

pected: sexual fantasies that are tried in real life often turn out to be disappointing, unexciting, or even unpleasant. Nancy Friday, who has studied male and female sex fantasies for well over a decade, says: "I think that for every person who has written to me about the joys of performing their sexual dreams in reality, there have been three or four who knew in advance that it wouldn't work, or who tried it and were disappointed" (Friday, 1975, p. 280). Our research also indicates that for many people, transforming fantasy to fact is unsatisfactory, resulting at times in a complete loss of the erotic value of the fantasy. A 22-year-old female college student told us:

> I used to have one particular fantasy that never failed to work. It was almost an electric thing, like flipping a switch and then "Zowie." I almost always had my best orgasms, and most exciting sex, when I flashed this fantasy through my mind. Then, unfortunately, I decided to try it out with my partner. We were both interested in this, I wasn't embarrassed or uptight, but it just didn't click together for me. After we had tried it two or three times, the fantasy itself became less exciting and less reliable and finally just didn't work at all. It was like losing a best friend.

A similar point is made by Karen Shanor in a book called *The Fantasy Files* (1977):

> Often when a fantasy is finally acted out, it does not occur again with any frequency as a fantasy. Only if the acting-out experience is amazingly good does the thought remain prominent. . . . Most of the time reality does not live up to the excitement of the fantasy, and the fantasy is therefore modified or significantly lessened in its importance *(pp. 162–163).*

TECHNIQUES OF HETEROSEXUAL ACTIVITY

There is always a danger that any discussion of sexual technique will sound like a mechanical checklist that implies that good sex is simply a matter of pushing the right buttons at the right time. Fortunately, sex usually involves more than mechanical coupling. It draws on feelings, moods, desires, and attitudes that are expressed in the physical interaction and that contribute significantly to the quality of the shared experience. At the risk of saying the obvious, there is not just one way of having good sex: sexual technique is, as much as anything else, a matter of communication between partners in which each person conveys to the other a sense of what feels good and what doesn't. As we discuss sexual techniques with some attention to their physical (and practical) details, keep the preceding thoughts firmly in mind.

Noncoital Sex Play

Many people describe all sexual activity between partners other than intercourse by the term "foreplay," which implies that these acts are (or should be) preliminary to intercourse, making intercourse the "main event." However, foreplay is a misleading term because intercourse is not always the focal point of sex; some people prefer other forms of sexual activity instead of coitus. Furthermore, if coitus is first and other sexual acts follow, should these then be called "afterplay?" To avoid such problems, we prefer to discard the term *foreplay* entirely and talk instead about noncoital sex play.

Touching and Being Touched

Touching can be many different things. At one level, it is primarily a wordless way to communicate a willingness, a wish, or a demand to make love. At another level, while touching serves the same communicative purpose, it is valued and enjoyed for its sensual pleasures almost as much as intercourse or orgasm. At still another level, touching is a source of comfort and security—an affirmation of togetherness, commitment, and trust. Touching can also be a mechanical, unemotional way of manipulating another body. In this approach, the essence of sexual interaction seems to be in knowing how to move a hand, where to place a mouth, or when to use a tongue in a joining of separate, almost disembodied anatomical parts. This mechanical kind of touching turns persons into objects, regardless of gender.

Touching need not involve the hands only. Many varieties of skin-to-skin contact lead to feelings of warmth, tenderness, and closeness. Kissing is a fine example of a touch that can be immensely sensual or more important as a symbol of affection and intimacy. Some people enjoy passionate, almost continuous kissing during sex, while others prefer only an occasional kiss or no mouth-to-mouth kissing at all. Psychiatrist Marc Hollender (1971) theo-

rizes that women have a greater need for being held and cuddled than men do, although he emphasizes that this does not mean that sex is less important to women. He does speculate, however, that sometimes a woman's need to be held leads her to participate sexually in exchange for cuddling and affection from her partner.

The act of touching can be unstructured and exploratory, or it can be focused in a more stimulative fashion. While touch as a vehicle for sexual arousal will be discussed in some detail in just a moment, it is also relevant to point out that many people find that touch in the form of a massage—with or without sexual stimulation—permits them to relax and to develop an awareness of their bodies that enhances the quality of a sexual experience.

Touching the Genitals

Many forms of genital stimulation can result in sexual pleasure and arousal. The genital regions in both sexes are highly sensitive to touch, and this sensitivity tends to increase as erotic excitation mounts. A touch that might be unarousing or even uncomfortable to a person who is not sexually excited can be pleasurable or electrifying as physical passion rises; conversely, a touch that is "just right" in the beginning moments of sexual play may be "too little" or "too slow" or otherwise out of sync at a later moment.

During genital touching, many people presume that their partner would like just the same type of stimulation they enjoy. As a result, men often stimulate the clitoris vigorously, mimicking the rapid, forceful stroking typical of male masturbation (Masters and Johnson, 1979). In contrast, women are often worried about stroking the penis too vigorously or touching or squeezing the scrotum too roughly, not wishing to hurt their partner. In addition, men and women often rely on erroneous assumptions about what would or would not turn their partner on; probably the most common example is that many men routinely insert a finger or fingers deeply into the vagina early in genital play although relatively few women find this arousing and some find it distracting or uncomfortable (Masters and Johnson 1966, 1979).

These observations underscore the importance of clear communication between sexual partners not only to enhance sexual pleasure but to protect your partner from making you uncomfortable physically or psychologically. One person can't know with any real accuracy what another is feeling or wants at a given moment without some form of communication. Since none of us is an infallible mind reader, it is helpful to develop open lines of information exchange. But since words may disturb a beautiful mood, nonverbal messages—conveyed by a touch, a sigh, a move, a look—are often best suited to the occasion unless they don't succeed in getting the message across, in which case words become necessary.

Not only does the type of genital play that a woman prefers vary from one woman to another, the same woman may have different preferences at different times. Many women enjoy firm, sustained rubbing of the shaft of the clitoris (as we mentioned earlier, direct stimulation of the tip of the clitoris is frequently uncomfortable), while others prefer clitoral stimulation alternated with caresses of the vaginal lips, the mons, or the perineum. Some women enjoy insertion of a finger into the mouth of the vagina, or gentle, teasing stroking just outside the vaginal opening. Deep vaginal penetration is usually not pleasurable unless a woman is highly aroused and even then she may get little out of this form of stimulation, permitting it to occur primarily because she feels that it excites her partner (Masters and Johnson, 1966, 1979; Hite, 1977). There are wide individual differences in this matter, as the following comment from a 24-year-old woman shows:

> The thing that I like best of all about sex is when I'm really turned on and Tom is finger-fucking me. If he can get three or four fingers crammed inside, I have my biggest and best orgasms. (Authors' files)

The tissues of the vulva and vagina may be irritated by too much touching or too much pressure if there is not enough lubrication present. Since the clitoris and the vaginal lips have no lubrication of their own, bringing some lubrication from the vagina to these areas is often helpful. Saliva or artificial lubricants such as K-Y Jelly, hypoallergenic lotions, or baby oil can also be used to reduce friction and to provide another dimension to genital touching.

A vibrator can be incorporated into partner sex as well, but it is important to talk this through together. Some men feel that the vibrator is a kind of mechanical intruder; others worry that the vibrator is desired only because they can't do the job properly; yet many men are perfectly happy to share in a variety of sexual stimulation that increases their partner's pleasure. Some couples have made their vibrator an integral part of their sex lives, even taking it with them on vacations, while others use it only from time to time.

There are many similarities between male and female sexuality, as we have noted before, and genital touching preferences are no exception. Men do not want only one kind of touch, and there is variability between men and in the same man at different times regarding the genital touches that create pleasure or arousal.

When the penis is not erect, most men prefer a light, playful stroking or caressing of the penis, the inner thighs, and the scrotum. If touching is restricted to the penis (or if penile stimulation is too vigorous) while the penis is flaccid, it is unlikely to be very arousing and may actually be somewhat threatening since the man may begin to worry that he isn't responding swiftly enough. Once erection begins to occur, the firmness of touch applied to the penis in stroking or squeezing motions can be comfortably (and arousingly) increased. One of the most common complaints we have heard from men is that their female partners don't grasp the penis firmly enough once it is erect (Masters and Johnson, 1979). Men usually prefer an up-and-down stroking of the penis with the fingers encircling the shaft; direct manual stimulation of the head of the penis may be uncomfortable or irritating.

Some men enjoy having the scrotum gently squeezed or lightly stroked or cupped in their partner's hand, while other men prefer not receiving any direct scrotal stimulation. If the testes are "rubbed the wrong way," it may be quite uncomfortable and a real dampener to sexual feelings. Many men enjoy some form of tactile stimulation focused at the frenulum (the small fold of skin just below the coronal ridge on the underside of the penis), although relatively few women seem to be aware of this fact. Men may also enjoy having saliva, lotion, or oil applied to the penis to enhance their arousal. Care should be taken (in either sex) that the lotion or oil applied to the genitals is not too cold or too hot and that it contains no alcohol, since alcohol tends to irritate the male urethra and female genital tissues.

It may be surprising, but relatively few heterosexual men and women have taken the time to show their partners how they like to have their

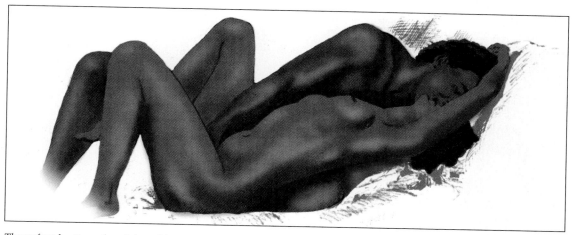

The preferred pattern of genital touching varies considerably from person to person and from time to time.

genitals touched (Masters and Johnson, 1979). Of course, this can be accomplished partly in conversation alone ("I really liked how you did that tonight—would you try that again another time?"). But conversation sometimes leaves a few doubts ("What does he mean by a firmer touch?"), and a "hands-on" demonstration is often the simplest way of conveying an accurate message. One person can place a hand on top of his or her partner's hand, showing what he or she means by "firm" and "light" or just *where* to stroke, since small differences in positioning may make all the difference in the world.[1] You can also show your partner exactly what you like by doing it yourself in his or her view. For a variation on this theme, ask your partner to put his or her hand on top of yours to actually feel the rhythm of the movement.

Oral–Genital Sex

Stimulation of the male genitals by the use of the tongue, lips, and mouth is called **fellatio,** and oral stimulation of the female genitals is called **cunnilingus.** Fellatio or cunnilingus can be used to induce or heighten sexual arousal or to produce orgasm. Either form of oral–genital sex can be done with one partner stimulating the other individually or with simultaneous reciprocal stimulation (the si-

multaneous version is sometimes called "69" because the inverted, side-by-side position of the numbers is similar to the position commonly used for this form of sex play).

There are a vast number of techniques and combinations of techniques for oral–genital stimulation that can be pleasurable and arousing. No one way is the "right" way to do it. Licking, sucking, kissing, and nibbling can feel good anywhere on the genitals; the pressure (light, firm, or in-between), speed (fast, slow, or changing), and type of motion employed can be varied considerably to attain different effects. The moistness and warmth of oral–genital contact is highly erotic for many people. Some enjoy a teasing, stop–start approach; others prefer a more direct, sustained type of stimulation. Here too, finding out what your partner likes is a matter of open communication.

In cunnilingus, many women are highly aroused by oral stimulation of the clitoris. This can take the form of gentle tongue movements over the shaft and tip of the clitoris, more rapid, focused licking, or sucking the clitoris either gently or in a rougher fashion. During high levels of arousal, a few women enjoy having the clitoris bitten gently. Other techniques some women enjoy are oral stimulation of the clitoris combined with manual stimulation of the vagina; oral stimulation of the minor lips (the area just outside the vagina); having the tongue

---

[1]This point is readily apparent to those who have had an itch on their back that they couldn't reach themselves. Trying to direct someone else to just the right spot—"A little higher . . . to the left . . . now up a little . . . no, back down a little lower and toward the middle . . ."—can be terribly frustrating. Just the same is sometimes true of telling someone in words what feels good sexually.

fellatio (fe lā′ shē ō) stimulation of the male
    genitals by oral contact.
cunnilingus (kun′ i ling′ gus) stimulation of the
    external genitals of the female by oral contact.

Simultaneous oral–genital stimulation in the "69" position.

thrust in and out of the vaginal opening; having the clitoris stimulated manually (either by their partner or by themselves) while oral stimulation is directed at other parts of their genitals; and having their partner blow into the vagina or on the clitoris.

In fellatio, methods of stimulation include sucking the glans or shaft of the penis by engulfing it in the mouth, licking various parts of the penis or scrotum, and nibbling or kissing anywhere along the genitals. Although fellatio is often referred to as a "blow job," most men don't enjoy a real blowing motion (it's not like playing a saxophone). The frenulum is often particularly sensitive to oral stimulation and most men find that the glans of the penis is also exquisitely sensitive to warm, moist caresses. Many men enjoy having the scrotum lightly stroked during fellatio and the area just beneath the scrotum is often quite sensitive to manual or oral massage.

Some women are uncomfortable with fellatio because they have a sensation of gagging if they take the erect penis into their mouth. This sensation is often due to a reflex response called the "gag reflex," which can be triggered by pressure at the back of the tongue or in the throat; it is a real physiologic event, not an imaginary happening. Even when a woman can comfortably accommodate part of the penis in her mouth, if her partner thrusts in the throes of his own excitement, it may push the penis so far in that the gag reflex takes over. There are two solutions to this problem. First, the woman

can grasp the shaft of the penis so that she has full control over the depth of penile penetration into her mouth, preventing sudden thrusts or jabs. Second, the gag reflex can be fairly easily reconditioned in most people by gradually inserting the penis a bit more deeply over a number of occasions until the reflex is minimized, or even practicing by inserting a cylindrical object (or some fingers) into the mouth.

Another difficulty a woman may have with fellatio is not wanting the man to ejaculate in her mouth. A couple can agree in advance that the man will withdraw before ejaculation; alternatively, many women have found that with a little experience they can overcome this concern. Some women prefer to rinse the ejaculate out of their mouth promptly because they don't like the taste of semen; others don't mind it much; and still others swallow the ejaculate. While there are no health risks to swallowing semen, it is unlikely that this has beneficial health effects (preventing acne or preserving youthfulness) either.

While many people are enthusiastic about the pleasures of oral–genital sex, others consider it "dirty," perverted, sinful, embarrassing, or simply unappealing. Among those with such reservations about this type of sexual activity, many find that with a little effort (and practice) they can easily develop a personal comfort level for oral–genital sex. This comment from a 28-year-old man illustrates some of the dilemmas:

At first, when I thought about oral sex on a woman I was scared—scared that I would be turned off by the smell and the flavor, and scared that I wouldn't know how to do it right. I was also into this trip where I didn't think it was a very "manly" thing to do, although I can't really remember where I got that idea. But then I got involved with a beautiful woman who sort of eased me into it, helping me take my time and all. After just a few tries, my fears disappeared and I sort of threw myself into the action. *(Authors' files)*

Although many people have been taught to think of the genitals as unclean, routine bathing or showering that includes carefully washing the genitals with soap and water will ensure cleanliness, although it will not prevent exposure to sexual infections, which can all be transmitted by this form of sexual contact. From a scientific viewpoint, oral–genital contact is no less hygienic than mouth-to-mouth kissing. The natural secretions of the genitals are relatively clean, and each person's genital odors partly reflect the type of food he or she eats. Many couples like to shower or bathe together before engaging in oral sex, and some people who consider oral sex the most intimate form of sex will engage in this activity only with a partner to whom they are particularly close. For others, oral sex is a stopping point to prevent the intimacy (and reproductive risk) of coitus, as shown by this comment from a 22-year-old woman:

> While I was in high school I learned that if I gave a guy a good blow job he wouldn't pressure me into screwing. So I stayed a virgin—except for my mouth—for five years of a very active sex life. Everyone was happy! *(Authors' files)*

One last word about oral–genital sex: some people incorrectly think that fellatio or cunnilingus are homosexual acts, even if experienced by heterosexual couples. While many homosexuals engage in oral–genital sex, so do a majority of heterosexual couples. The activity itself is neither homosexual nor heterosexual.

Anal Sex

Stimulation of the anus during sexual activity can be done in several different ways: manually, orally, or by anal intercourse. Although anal sex is sometimes thought of as a strictly "homosexual" activity, a large number of heterosexual couples occasionally incorporate some variety of anal stimulation into their noncoital sexual play.

Anal stimulation can be the primary focus of sexual activity or an accompaniment to other types of stimulation. For instance, many couples sometimes include manual stimulation of the anus (either lightly rubbing the rim or inserting a finger into the anus) during coitus, and others use this technique during oral–genital sex. Anal sex in any of its forms can be highly arousing and lead to male and female orgasms. But many people have strongly negative attitudes toward anal sex, an act which they may regard as being unclean, unnatural, perverted, disgusting, or simply unappealing. Concerns about the riskiness of anal intercourse as a means of transmitting the AIDS virus have added to these negative attitudes in the past decade.

Although anal intercourse can be pleasurable, it can also be a source of discomfort in both a physical and emotional sense. The anal sphincter tightens ordinarily if stimulated, and attempts at penile insertion may be distressing even if done slowly and gently. If the penis is forced into the anus, injury is possible. To minimize risk, it is wisest to use an artificial lubricant liberally and to dilate the anus gently by manual stimulation before attempting insertion.

It should also be realized that the lining of the rectum is very thin and delicate and thus is relatively easily torn (Agnew, 1986). Such breaks or tears in the rectal mucosa (even when small and painless) can provide a means of entry into the bloodstream for a variety of infectious microbes, including the virus that causes AIDS, the bacterium that causes gonorrhea, and the organism that causes syphilis. For this reason, many authorities now recommend the routine use of condoms for heterosexual anal intercourse as a means of reducing the risk of transmitting the AIDS virus (see Chapter 20 for a more detailed discussion).

One final note about anal stimulation. Anything that has been inserted into the anus should not be subsequently put into the vagina unless it has been thoroughly washed. Bacteria that are naturally present in the anus can cause vaginal infections, so moving from anal intercourse (or finger insertion) to vaginal intercourse (or finger insertion) is unwise.

Coital Sex

For many people, the hallmark of heterosexuality is penile–vaginal intercourse, or coitus. Hundreds of marriage manuals have offered instruction in the

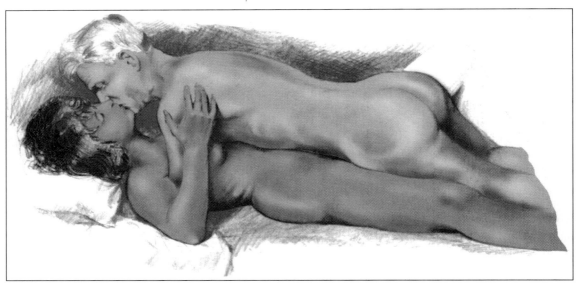

Man-on-top, face-to-face intercourse position.

how-to's of coital connection; although many of these books speak of "making love," they usually wind up conveying the message that the best sex is attained by following their mechanical blueprints. As Germaine Greer put it in *The Female Eunuch* (1972):

> The implication that there is a statistically ideal fuck which will always result in satisfaction if the right procedures are followed is depressing and misleading. . . . Real satisfaction is not enshrined in a tiny cluster of nerves but in the sexual involvement of the whole person. *(p. 37)*

We have talked about the individuality of sexual responsivity in many places in this book. Each person is a unique sexual being with personal preferences and idiosyncrasies molded by past experiences, current needs, mood, personality, and a host of other variables. Each of us may also find that our body responds in different ways at different times, even if external circumstances are almost the same. When we add a partner into this equation, it's no wonder there is no way of describing the ideal type of coitus. We discuss selected aspects of techniques of coital sex first in terms of coital positions and then in terms of styles.

Man on Top, Face to Face

The most common coital position in the United States is with the woman lying on her back, legs spread somewhat apart, with the man lying on top of her. This position, which is sometimes called the "missionary position," offers a relative degree of ease of penile insertion and also permits as much eye contact and kissing as desired. If the woman wishes, she may raise her legs in the air or wrap them around the man's back or shoulders, which causes deeper penetration of the penis in the vagina. This position also gives the best chance of conception, since the semen pools in a position in the vagina closest to the mouth of the cervix.

Despite its popularity, the man-on-top position has some disadvantages. Many women feel "pinned" underneath the weight of their partner and find it difficult to do much pelvic movement. The woman also has little control over the depth of penetration, and if her partner is lying against her body it may be difficult for either person to stimulate the clitoris manually. While the man has maximum freedom of movement, he may find it tiring to support his weight on his elbows and knees and, as his muscles fatigue, he may "tense up" physically. In addition, men tend to have less control over ejaculation in this position than in many others. This position is also apt to be uncomfortable if the man is considerably heavier than the woman or if the woman is in the later stages of pregnancy.

Woman on Top, Face to Face

Another popular coital position is for the woman to be on top. In this position, the woman either can be sitting up to a degree or can lie down against

Variations of the woman-on-top, face-to-face intercourse position.

her partner. In contrast to the man-on-top position, in this position the woman has considerable control over coital movements, thrusting, and tempo. The woman is free to caress her partner's body with her hands, and the man has his hands available for stroking her breasts, genitals, or other body parts. The visual stimulation of this position and the man's freedom from supporting his weight may encourage his stroking. The woman-on-top position is generally the best one to use for a man who

wants to gain greater control over ejaculation and is also the position used most often in sex therapy when a woman has difficulty reaching orgasm, since either partner can stimulate the clitoris manually in this position. It is also well suited to the later stages of pregnancy.

A few drawbacks to the woman-on-top position should be mentioned. Some couples feel uncomfortable with this position because they believe the man should "always" be on top. Since the woman may seem to be the "aggressor" by being above the man and since she has greater control over pelvic movements, a few men feel that their masculinity is threatened in this position. At a more practical level, some men find it difficult to engage in pelvic thrusting in this position.

When the woman-on-top position is used, it is important to insert the penis properly. The woman should never hold the erect penis at a 90 degree angle to the man's body and try to sit down on it, as this can be uncomfortable to either partner. Instead, the penis should be held at a 45 to 60 degree angle (pointed in the direction of the man's head) since this matches the angle of the vagina when the woman is in a forward-leaning position; the woman can then slide back onto the penis. With a little bit of practice, this maneuver becomes simple.

Rear Entry

In rear-entry positions, the man faces the woman's back and the penis is placed into the vagina from behind. Coitus can be accomplished with the woman on her hands and knees in the "doggy style"; the woman may lie face down with her hips propped up by a pillow; or the couple may lie on their sides, with the man's front to the woman's back in the "spoon position." Rear entry can also be done in a sitting or standing position. In most of these positions, the man can usually reach around his partner's body to stimulate her clitoris or breasts, but mouth-to-mouth kissing is difficult and eye contact is lost. Many couples feel that rear-entry coitus is less intimate for these latter reasons, and some couples object to this position because it seems too much like anal intercourse. However, the sensations of thrusting against the buttocks can be pleasurable, and when the woman's legs are close together more stimulation of the penis is possible.

Side to Side, Face to Face

In this position, the partners are facing each other but lying on their sides. Since neither person is burdened by the other's weight, this is often a relaxed position where a lot of leisurely caressing and cuddling can be included. Both partners have at least one free hand. The primary drawback of this posi-

Rear-entry intercourse, "doggy style."

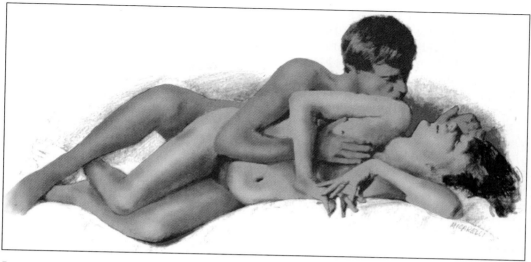

Rear-entry intercourse, "spoon position."

tion is that inserting the penis in the vagina can be tricky. Thus, many couples begin in a different face-to-face position and then roll onto their sides. There are two other disadvantages in the side-by-side position: first, the penis is a bit more likely to slip out of the vagina than in other positions, and second, there is less mechanical leverage to achieve vigorous pelvic thrusting.

Timing, Tempo, and Other Themes

Above and beyond the countless embellishments in coital positioning that are possible, many stylistic variations affect coital sex. The surroundings chosen for a sexual encounter can range from a bedroom to an automobile to an outdoor setting.

People can make love in the dark, with dim lighting, or in broad daylight. Some people like to have background music for sex, others like to use a water bed or lots of pillows, and still others prefer sex in a hot tub or in front of a crackling fire.

Timing and tempo are also important ingredients. Just as a person's appetite for food can be met in a variety of ways—a quick snack, an elegant gourmet meal, or a simple, satisfying steak—sexual appetite can also be served by a "quickie," by a long, leisurely episode of lovemaking, or by a technically straightforward sexual encounter. One version is not always better than another: its quality and enjoyment depend on the needs and responses of the people involved.

Side-to-side, face-to-face intercourse position.

Many heterosexual couples approach coitus in a businesslike fashion: sex is always at the same time (usually late at night), with the same "routines," the same position, and sometimes identical dialogue. Although this can lead to boredom for some people, for others it is a perfectly comfortable and satisfying situation: predictability is not always a liability. On the other hand, many couples enjoy a more creative approach to their sex lives, varying not only the positions and stimulatory techniques they use but also the time when sex occurs, the setting, and who plays the most active role.

We cannot conclude this section about sexual techniques without stressing again that sexual enjoyment usually relates less to mechanical proficiency than to how two people relate to one another. This does not mean that good sex requires a meaningful long-term relationship, but it most often depends on effective communications between partners. Working at sex—trying to develop erotic artistry through diligence, practice, and having a single-minded purpose—is more likely to interfere with the spontaneous enjoyment of sexual experiences than to produce a memorable sexual encounter.

TECHNIQUES OF LESBIAN AND GAY SEXUAL ACTIVITY

The sexual techniques used by homosexual men and women generally mirror those of heterosexual partners, but homosexuals seem to be more willing to experiment and to be more attentive to style. This is partly because heterosexuality is more subject to convention and partly because heterosexual variations are regarded as "abnormal" by many people; since *no* techniques of homosexual stimulation are socially approved, there are fewer automatic restrictions that limit the behavior of homosexual partners (Tripp, 1975).

One other fact can be helpful as you read further in this section. It has been shown that the physiological responses of homosexual men and women are no different from those of their heterosexual counterparts (Masters and Johnson, 1979). Laboratory observation of the sexual responses of 94 homosexual men and 82 homosexual women in more than 1200 sexual response cycles involving masturbation, partner manipulation, and oral–genital sex

showed that more than 99 percent of these cycles resulted in orgasm. This percentage almost exactly matches the earlier observations of heterosexual men and women studied under identical conditions. Of course, equivalent physiology does not suggest equivalence in all other ways, but it is helpful to realize that the ways in which our sexual responses work are not controlled by our individual sexual orientation, whether it is homosexual or heterosexual.

Lesbian Sex

Kinsey and his co-workers (1953) found that two-thirds of homosexual women had orgasms in 90 to 100 percent of their lesbian contacts, while only two-fifths of women in their fifth year of marital intercourse had this high a rate of orgasmic frequency. They also found that among women with extensive lesbian experience, 98 percent had used genital touching, 97 percent had manually stimulated the breasts, 85 percent had orally stimulated the breasts, 78 percent had experience with cunnilingus, and 56 percent had used a genital apposition technique (rubbing the genitals together).

Manual stimulation of the genitals is the most widespread and frequent form of lesbian sex. Bell and Weinberg (1978) noted that approximately 80 percent of their sample had used this technique in the past year, with more than 40 percent reporting a frequency of once a week or more.

In contrast to married heterosexual couples—where the "action-oriented" man seems to hurriedly reach for the breasts or move directly to genital stimulation—committed lesbian partners usually share full body contact, with holding, kissing, and general caressing for some while before they make a specific approach to breast or genital touching (Masters and Johnson, 1979). Furthermore, when a committed lesbian couple begins breast play, the two women usually give it lengthier and more detailed attention than do heterosexual couples. The lesbian caressing her partner's breasts seems to do so with more attention to her partner's responses, while men often approach heterosexual breast stimulation more for their own arousal than for their partner's pleasure. This concern is also shown by the fact that lesbian lovers realize that breast touching can be painful just before a period, while many men seem oblivious to this fact.

During genital stimulation in lesbian couples, the clitoris is rarely approached first, in contrast to the pattern shown in marital sex, where direct clitoral stimulation was the first form of genital contact in about half of the observed episodes (Masters and Johnson, 1979). Besides starting with more relaxed genital play, lesbians do not usually insert a finger deeply into the vagina. When vaginal stimulation occurred, it was usually in the form of play around or just inside the mouth of the vagina. In spite of the common belief that lesbians usually use a dildo or object inserted in the vagina to simulate heterosexual intercourse, a distinct minority of lesbians employ this technique (Kinsey et al., 1953; Saghir and Robins, 1973).

Two patterns of genital play are most common in lesbian encounters: (1) a prolonged, nondemanding approach of repeatedly bringing the partner to a high level of arousal which is then allowed to recede, in a "teasing" pattern used repeatedly before reaching orgasm; and (2) stimulation involving more continuity and rapidly increasing intensity until orgasm is reached. Although these two approaches are sometimes combined, most lesbian couples seem to prefer and consistently use one or the other (Masters and Johnson, 1979).

Cunnilingus is the preferred sexual technique among lesbians for reaching orgasm (Bell and Weinberg, 1978; Califia, 1979). Lesbians generally are more effective in stimulating their partners via oral–genital sex than heterosexual men are and usually involve themselves with more inventiveness and less restraint than heterosexual couples (Masters and Johnson, 1979). This is probably because a woman is more apt to know what feels good to another woman on the basis of her own personal experiences; lesbian lovers may also be less embarrassed about genital tastes and odors than their heterosexual counterparts. In keeping with these points, it was noted that committed lesbian couples characteristically used a leisurely, less demanding approach to cunnilingus than married heterosexuals.

While lesbians who have oral sex most frequently seem happiest with their sex lives and their relationships, about one-quarter of lesbians say they rarely or never use this form of stimulation (Blumstein and Schwartz, 1983).

Body-rubbing techniques involving total body contact and specific genital-to-genital rubbing are also enjoyed by some lesbians but seem to be a less important source of attaining orgasm (Bell and Weinberg, 1978; Califia, 1979). Relatively few lesbians use techniques of anal stimulation.

One survey that included 772 lesbian couples and 3547 married heterosexual couples found that lesbians had genital sexual activity considerably less often than married heterosexuals (Blumstein and Schwartz, 1983). However, another study that involved individuals rather than couples found that lesbians had sex more often than heterosexual women and also had more frequent orgasms, a greater number of partners, and a higher degree of sexual satisfaction (Coleman, Hoon, and Hoon, 1983).

Gay Male Sex

Like their lesbian counterparts, male homosexuals in committed couples tend to take their time with whatever form of sexual interaction they are involved in instead of hurrying along in a goal-oriented effort. Male homosexuals also tend to deliberately move more slowly through excitement and to linger at the plateau stage of arousal, using more freeflowing, inventive styles of sexual play than married heterosexuals. This general description has its exceptions. Some committed homosexual couples are completely goal-oriented and push ahead with the sexual action at a frenzied pace while some married heterosexuals enjoy a much more leisurely, unstructured pattern of sex. But the overall contrast between the two groups is striking (Masters and Johnson, 1979).

In the initial stages of sexual interaction, most committed homosexual male couples begin with a generalized approach of hugging, caressing, or kissing. Nipple stimulation—either manually or orally—is frequently incorporated into the early touching, almost invariably leading to erection for the men being stimulated. (Interestingly, few wives stimulate their husbands' nipples as part of sexual play.)

A "teasing" pattern of genital play is frequently used in gay male sex. This often involves selective attention to the frenulum of the penis and the use of a variety of touches or caresses to enhance erotic arousal. Many of the men in committed homosexual relationships studied by Masters and Johnson said that they stimulated their partners the way they liked to be stimulated. Others said that they had discussed genital stimulation techniques directly with their partners and had learned in this fashion what was most pleasing.

There are no major differences in the techniques used for fellatio between homosexual or heterosexual couples, presuming that there are equivalent amounts of experience with this type of sexual play. Fellatio seems to be the most common form of gay male sexual activity, with more than 90 percent having experience in giving and receiving such stimulation (Saghir and Robins, 1973; Bell and Weinberg, 1978).

Anal intercourse is another common male homosexual practice. Saghir and Robins (1973) found that 93 percent of the homosexual men they studied had experienced anal intercourse with a male partner. However, Bell and Weinberg (1978) found that 22 percent of the gay white males in their study had not performed anal intercourse in the preceding year, and the frequency of anal intercourse was considerably less than for fellatio. Today, because of concerns over the high-risk nature of anal sex in terms of HIV transmission (discussed in more detail in Chapter 20), it appears that anal intercourse may be becoming a less frequent sexual outlet for many homosexual men (Richwald et al., 1988; Connell and Kippax, 1990).

Some authorities have suggested that male homosexuals be classified as "active" or "passive" depending on whether they prefer to be the "insertor" or the "insertee" in anal intercourse. The fact is, most gay men who participate in anal sex enjoy both roles; other gay men find the idea of anal sex discomforting or repulsive.

In the late 1970s, another form of anal sex became popular in certain gay communities. This practice, known as "fisting" or "handballing," involves the insertion of the hand into the rectum (usually after prior cleansing with an enema) followed by movement geared at producing sexual stimulation (Morin, 1981; Lowry and Williams, 1983). While this type of sexual activity is not unique to homosexual males, having been reported also in both heterosexuals and lesbians, it appears to be predominantly a practice of the gay male community. Devotees of this form of sexual stimulation, which is often combined with the use of illicit drugs, point out that it requires considerable trust, slowness, and gentleness, and sometimes describe it as an ecstatic, transcendent experience (Lowry and Williams, 1983). There are substantial health risks associated with "fisting," including the risk of damaging the anus or rectum (which may pose an increased risk of HIV infection) and the risk of contracting hepatitis B.

PERSPECTIVES ON SEXUAL BEHAVIOR

Now we shift our attention from matters of sexual technique to an examination of sexual behavior and attitudes toward such behavior. As we have pointed out, the descriptive information about sexual behaviors and attitudes available from various survey studies has methodological shortcomings. Nevertheless, it is useful to become acquainted with some of the findings of these surveys as long as we recognize that they are all approximations of the actual patterns of behavior they seek to measure.

Premarital Sex

Premarital sex is often talked about as synonymous with premarital intercourse, but people can be sexually active prior to marriage without having coital experience. Another problem with the term "premarital sex" is its implication that marriage is the goal of each and every person in our society.

There is no question that premarital intercourse among women is more widespread today than it once was and that the age of first intercourse is declining (for additional observations on these points, see also Hopkins, 1977; Barrett, 1980; Wolfe, 1980; Zelnik and Kantner, 1980; Bigler, 1989; and Laumann et al., 1994).[2]

Despite this, it appears that approval of premarital coitus for many teenagers and young adults is still restricted to love relationships or relationships with strong caring and affection (Hunt, 1975; I. L. Reiss, 1980). Recreational or casual sex, as opposed to relationship sex, is far less common, although it is written about so extensively that many young adults are convinced that most of their contemporaries have "freer" sexual attitudes than they do. The fact that most young adults see premarital coitus as justified when it occurs in a legitimate, committed relationship but less so when it is purely casual and sensuous shows that older cultural values have not been discarded but have changed (Hunt, 1975; Hopkins, 1977; Reiss, 1991).

---

[2]Although the trend toward having premarital sex with multiple partners is clear-cut and cuts across virtually all socioeconomic and demographic lines, Tanfer and Schoorl (1992) found that Catholic women and women who attend religious services once a week or more have the fewest number of sexual partners of all groups in the United States.

A number of other notable changes have occurred in premarital sexual behavior in the last four decades. First, relatively few young men today are sexually initiated by prostitutes or have premarital intercourse with prostitutes (Hunt, 1975; Sarrel and Sarrel, 1979), although Kinsey and his colleagues (1948) found that more than one-quarter of college-educated men who had not married by age 25 and 54 percent of high school-educated men had premarital intercourse with a prostitute. Second, use of oral–genital sex among young unmarried men and women has increased dramatically compared with Kinsey's day (Gagnon and Simon, 1987), with the percentage of people using fellatio more than doubling and the percentage trying cunnilingus rising from 14 to 69 percent (Hunt, 1975). Third, there is more premarital sexual experimentation in recent years compared to Kinsey's time. People are more willing to try a wider range of coital positions, drugs (especially marijuana) to enhance sexual and sensual feelings, and anal intercourse (Hunt, 1975; Levin, 1975; Hite 1977; Reinisch, 1990; Reinisch et al., 1992). The trend toward experimentation is also shown by evidence that women are having premarital sex with more partners than in the past (Levin, 1975; Wolfe, 1980; Wyatt, Peters, and Guthrie, 1988a, 1988b; DeBuono et al., 1990).

That trends do not describe everyone's experience can be seen from the following statistics taken from the National Health and Social Life Survey (referred to from now on as the NHSLS) (Laumann et al., 1994): 18 percent of American men and 30.2 percent of American women born between 1963 and 1974 who subsequently married were virgins when they took their wedding vows.

Gay and Lesbian Partners and Relationships

Not all homosexuals engage in sexual activity on a frequent basis, but in general homosexual men tend to be more sexually active than homosexual women (Figure 16.2). Most research has also shown that homosexual men tend to have many more sexual partners than lesbians (Table 16.4) or heterosexual men and women (Saghir and Robins, 1973; Bell and Weinberg, 1978; Turner, Miller, and Moses, 1989; Laumann et al., 1994).

While many homosexual males engage in quick, impersonal sex with strangers, others prefer to enter into long-term affectionate homosexual rela-

tionships. Tripp (1975) suggests that these ongoing homosexual relationships seem to be rare because they are far less visible than either long-term heterosexual relationships or short-lived homosexual liaisons. Bell and Weinberg (1978) note that the relative instability of long-term homosexual relationships may be partly because they are not encouraged socially or sanctioned legally. However, some observers believe that one effect of the recent AIDS epidemic has been to encourage monogamy and close-coupled relationships among gay men.

The most extensive studies done to date of male homosexuals in long-term relationships were conducted by McWhirter and Mattison (1984), who studied 156 couples who had been together for a mean of 8.9 years. On the basis of numerous interviews and observations of the interactions of these couples, McWhirter and Mattison proposed that such relationships typically passed through six stages. Stage one (the "blending" stage), which usually occurred in the first year of the relationship, was marked by high levels of sexual activity, merging of personal interests, strong feelings of love and attraction, and forging an identity as a partnership. Stage two (the "nesting" stage), which generally occurred in the second or third years of being together, put an emphasis on homemaking and finding personal compatibility. The sense of being head over heels in love generally cooled off in this stage, and while sexual activity continued on a frequent basis, it declined somewhat from stage one levels. Ambivalence and doubt about the relationship also sometimes affected couples at this point in their interaction. Stage three (the "maintaining" stage, usually years 4 and 5 of a relationship) was a time in which each partner began to reassert his individuality. This stage was also marked by the need to deal with conflicts as well as by considerable time and energy spent in establishing traditions.

Stage four (the "building" stage), typically occurring in years 6 through 10 of a male homosexual relationship, was a time of collaboration, increasing personal productivity, establishing independence, and developing a solid sense of dependability between the partners. Stage five (years 11 to 20, the "releasing" stage) was marked by trusting, merging of money and other assets, and beginning to take each other for granted, as well as a noticeable drop in the frequency of sexual contact. Stage six ("renewing"), which went beyond 20 years of

Figure 16.2 Frequency of Sexual Activity in Various Groups of American Couples

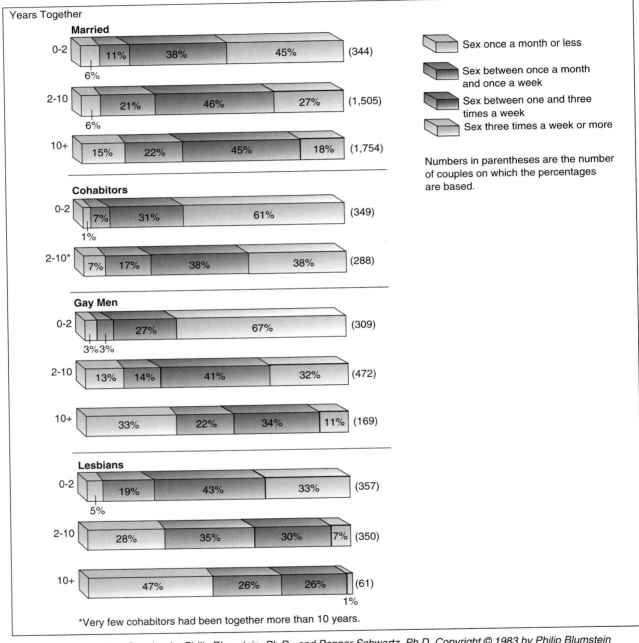

*Very few cohabitors had been together more than 10 years.

maintaining a relationship, was characterized by achieving security, shifting personal perspectives, restoring the sense of partnership, and remembering shared experiences and good times.

McWhirter and Mattison found that when one partner moved more rapidly or more slowly than the other through a particular stage, it was likely to create difficulties for the relationship. This should not be too surprising, since similar observations have been made pertaining to heterosexual couples in long-term relationships (Blumstein and Schwartz, 1983; Wolman and Stricker, 1983).

Table 16.4   Sexual Partnerships Among Homosexuals

	Homosexual Males		Homosexual Females	
	White (N = 574)	Black (N = 111)	White (N = 227)	Black (N = 64)
Lifetime number of homosexual partners				
1	0%	0%	3%	5%
2	0	0	9	5
3–4	1	2	15	14
5–9	2	4	31	30
10–14	3	5	16	9
15–24	3	6	10	16
25–49	8	6	8	11
50–99	9	18	5	8
100–249	15	15	1	2
250–499	17	11	1	2
500–999	15	14	0	0
1000 or more	28	19	0	0
Proportion of partners who were strangers				
None	1%	5%	62%	56%
Half or less	20	43	32	38
More than half	79	51	6	6
Proportion of partners with whom sexual activity occurred only once				
None	1%	4%	38%	41%
Half or less	29	59	51	55
More than half	70	38	12	5

Source: *Adapted from Alan P. Bell and Martin S. Weinberg,* Homosexualities. *Copyright © 1978 by Alan P. Bell and Martin S. Weinberg. Reprinted by permission of Simon & Schuster, Inc. and Mitchell Beazley Pub., Ltd., London.*

Coleman (1981/82) believes that male homosexuals are at a disadvantage in learning intimacy and relationship skills because they have few role models to follow and because there has traditionally been "a lack of public support for these relationships." He also points out that "lingering negative attitudes about homosexuality can sabotage efforts to establish or maintain a relationship." Extending this view, McCandlish (1981/82) states that "society's homophobia and resulting social isolation" and lack of family support often produce such stresses on stable relationships that "what might have been minor and even growth-producing difficulties, instead overwhelm the couple and force a premature end to the relationship."

Another perspective on this topic can be gained by recalling the differences in socialization that typically affect males and females in Western society. As Bell and Weinberg (1978) suggest, socialization tends to orient males (straight or gay) to sexual variety, whereas females (straight or gay)

are more oriented to monogamy. As a result, many young males want a number of sexual partners, while most females want the intimacy that they are more likely to find in a one-to-one relationship. When heterosexual males form relationships with females, they are socialized by the female to become more monogamous (Gagnon and Simon, 1973), but this is less likely to happen for males in homosexual relations. Thus, many gay males are promiscuous because they've had few social learning experiences to help them develop intimacy skills.

Studies of lesbian relationships have suggested that the very intimacy that would seem to provide the perfect backdrop for sexual desire often has the opposite effect. Many lesbian couples "exist happily for years with little or no genital contact in their relationships . . . [but] continue to define themselves as lovers" (Nichols, 1988, p. 392). Nichols theorizes that this situation may occur for three basic reasons: (1) too much closeness in the relationship so that individual differences are ignored, discouraged, or denied; the closeness—called *fusion*—may reduce the mystery and unpredictability needed to maintain sexual tension and desire; (2) sex-negative attitudes that put many sexual practices (such as S/M) "off-limits" by labeling them as "bad" or "unacceptable"; and (3) too much dependence on only one trigger—limerence [the "head-over-heels-in-love" state described by Tennov (1979)]—for sexual desire. The findings from the Blumstein and Schwartz study (1983) generally support Nichols' thesis. For instance, only about one-third of lesbians in relationships of two years or longer had sex once a week or more (Figure 16.2), and 47 percent of lesbians in relationships that had lasted a decade or longer had sex once a month or less often.

Marital Sex

More than 90 percent of Americans have married by their early thirties. By age 45 to 54, only about 4 percent of women and 6 percent of men in the United States have never been married (Cherlin, 1992). In this section, we examine patterns of marital sex behavior in terms of coital frequency, orgasm, techniques, and satisfaction in traditional marriages and then look briefly at the sexual implications of alternative marriage styles.

Frequency of Marital Coitus

The average American married couple has intercourse two or three times per week in their twen-

ties and thirties, after which the frequency slowly declines (see Figure 16.3). Past age 50, coital frequency averages once a week or less. The survey data that provide the basis for this overview (Kinsey, Pomeroy, and Martin, 1948; Kinsey et al., 1953; Bell and Bell, 1972; Hunt, 1975; Levin and Levin, 1975; Trussell and Westoff, 1980; Laumann et al., 1994) are less than precise because of methodological limitations.

"Average" frequencies do not tell the whole story, however. In each study on the frequency of marital coitus, a broad range of individual variation was found. Some young married couples have no coital activity, while other couples have intercourse several times a day. While, in general, coital frequency rates decline with the length of marriage, some couples clearly develop better sexual relationships as time goes by and may be more coitally active after 15 to 20 years of marriage than they were early in their marital lives.

There is also a category of sexually inactive marriages, which can reflect a wide variety of factors ranging from health problems to personal values. Although this group has not been studied in any detail, Donnelly (1993, p. 171) observes "although sexually inactive marriages are not uncommon, they are not happy, stable marriages in which the partners simply do not have sex. Lack of sexual activity may be a danger signal for many marriages."

Orgasm

Although Kinsey, Pomeroy, and Martin (1948) reported that men reached orgasm in essentially all

Figure 16.3   Frequency of Intercourse

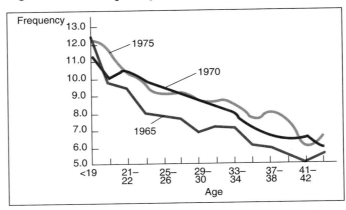

The average frequency of intercourse in the four weeks before interview for married American women, by age.

Source: *From Trussell and Westoff, 1980, p. 248. Reprinted with permission from Family Planning Perspectives, Volume 12, Number 5, 1980.*

of their marital coitus, Hunt (1975) found that 8 percent of husbands in the 45 and older age group did not have orgasm anywhere from occasionally to most of the time, and 7 percent of the 24- to 44-year-old married men did not have orgasm in at least one-quarter of their coital experiences. These statistics do not mean that a man who doesn't ejaculate during intercourse necessarily has a problem: in some cases, the man may have already ejaculated in another type of sexual play, and in other cases, the man simply may not feel the need.

Kinsey and his co-workers (1953) reported that marital coital orgasm had not been experienced by one-quarter of women after one year of marriage, but by the end of 20 years of marriage, this figure had fallen to 11 percent. In the same study, it was found that 45 percent of wives reported orgasms in 90 to 100 percent of coital experiences in their fifteenth year of marriage. Hunt (1975) found that 53 percent of wives reported coital orgasms "all or almost all the time" in marriages of 15 years median duration. In the *Redbook* survey, 63 percent of wives reported coital orgasms all or almost all of the time, and only 7 percent had never experienced coital orgasm.

While lack of orgasmic responsiveness in coitus can be a major problem for some couples, for other couples, lack of female coital orgasm poses no problem or threat, as a 31-year-old woman explained:

I've never had an orgasm during intercourse, but that's never really bothered me. In fact, I think my husband was more concerned about it than I was. I enjoy the closeness and touching of sex, and I get aroused, too—it's just the orgasm that's missing. If I need the release of an orgasm I can masturbate, but orgasm just isn't the most important part of sex for me. (*Author's files*)

Sexual Techniques

Marital sexual techniques have undergone some remarkable changes in the last 40 years if data from available surveys are to be believed. For example, while oral–genital sex was avoided by large numbers of the married men and women who participated in the Kinsey studies, a majority of married people today include fellatio and cunnilingus in their sexual repertoires (Table 16.5). Eighty-seven percent of wives in the *Redbook* survey reported using cunnilingus often or occasionally, and 85 percent reported fellatio with a similar frequency (Tavris and Sadd, 1977). The NHSLS reported that 80 percent of married American men participate in both fellatio and cunnilingus, while 71 percent of married women have experience with fellatio and 74 percent have tried cunnilingus (Laumann et al., 1994). Similarly, although Kinsey and his colleagues did not report statistics on anal intercourse in marriage in their initial volumes, an updated report (Gebhard and Johnson, 1979) showed that less than 9 percent of married respondents had experience with this type of sexual act. In contrast, nearly one-quarter of the married women in Hunt's study (1975) and 43 percent of the wives in the *Redbook* survey (Levin, 1975) had tried anal intercourse. (Most women indicated, however, that this was the least liked type of sexual activity.)

Data on experience with heterosexual anal intercourse is relatively scanty, with most estimates

Table 16.5   Oral–Genital Activity in Marital Sex Relations

	Percentage of Marriages Using Fellatio			Percentage of Marriages Using Cunnilingus		
	1938–1946 (Kinsey)	1972 (Hunt)	1994 (Masters, Johnson, and Kolodny*)	1938–1946 (Kinsey)	1972 (Hunt)	1994 (Masters, Johnson, and Kolodny*)
High school males	15%	54%	66%	15%	56%	61%
College males	43	61	82	45	66	73
High school females	46	52	74	50	58	63
College females	52	72	84	58	72	77

*1994 date based on written questionnaire responses from 2200 married couples.

Source: *Data from Kinsey, Pomeroy, and Martin (1948), Kinsey et al., 1953; Hunt, 1974; and Masters, Johnson, and Kolodny, unpublished data, 1994.*

ranging from 10 to 20 percent for the broad population (Voeller, 1991; Billy et al., 1993). However,
several surveys have identified higher rates than
this. For example, Reinisch and her co-workers
(1992) reported that 22.2 percent of the undergraduate heterosexual females they surveyed at a
large midwestern university had ever had anal intercourse. However, for those engaging in this activity, the frequency was quite low: on average,
less than twice in the preceding year. A startling
higher figure was presented by Wyatt (1988), who
found that 43 percent of white females and 21 percent of Afro-American women reported having
had anal intercourse at least once in their lives.
[Billy et al. (1993) also noted a lower rate of anal
intercourse among Afro-American males (14 percent) compared to whites (21 percent)]. The
NHSLS found that 26 percent of men and 20 percent of women between the ages of 18 and 59 had
tried anal intercourse; in the preceding year, 10
percent of men and 9 percent of women had engaged in this form of sexual activity (Michael, et
al., 1994).

The other major changes in marital sexual technique include an increased amount of time in sexual
play and the use of a wider variety of coital positions. While Kinsey and his co-workers found that
precoital play was often limited to a few kisses
among those with a grade school education and averaged about 12 minutes among the college-educated, Hunt found that at both educational levels the
time spent in sexual play before intercourse averaged 15 minutes. Similarly, while Kinsey believed
that three-fourths of married men ejaculated within
2 minutes after inserting the penis in the vagina,
Hunt's data indicate that marital coitus now lasts an
average of 10 minutes. This change may reflect a
greater awareness of married men and women
today that women are likely to enjoy sex more and
to be more orgasmic if intercourse is unhurried. Although the NHSLS didn't gather specific information on the duration of marital coitus, it did find that
the last episode of sex with a partner had lasted
more than 15 minutes for 84 percent of men and 86
percent of women (Michael et al., 1994, Table 10).

Greater use of a diversity of coital positions in
marriages today may be due to an increased awareness that the "missionary position" often limits the
sexual options available to the woman. Table 16.6
shows the percentage of married couples using
other coital positions on a frequent basis.

Sexual Satisfaction

How does the quality of a couple's marriage contribute to their sexual satisfaction? And how does
the nature of a married couple's sex life relate to
their overall marital satisfaction? Since relatively
little research has been done on these subjects,
these questions can only be partially answered.

The original Kinsey reports did not evaluate
the relationship between sexual adjustment and
marital happiness, but a later analysis of the data
led Gebhard (1966) to conclude that women were
much more likely to be orgasmic in "very happy"
marriages (rated by self-report) than in other
marriages. It is not clear whether the very happy
marriages led to a better sexual climate or vice
versa.

The *Redbook* survey (Levin, 1975) found a strong
correlation between the frequency of intercourse
and satisfaction with marital sex for women. It also
noted that 81 percent of the women who were orgasmic all or most of the time in marital coitus
rated the sexual side of their marriage as good or
very good, while only 52 percent of women who
were occasionally orgasmic and 29 percent of
women who were never orgasmic (or who did not
know if they were) felt that their sexual relationship was good. A strong correlation was also found
between a wife's ability to communicate her sexual
desires and feelings to her husband and the quality
of marital sex.

More recently, Blumstein and Schwartz (1983)
also found a correlation between the frequency of
marital sex and sexual satisfaction (Figure 16.4).
Among those having sex three times a week or
more, 89 percent of husbands and wives were satis-

Table 16.6   Marital Coital Positions

Position	Kinsey et al.[a]	Hunt[b]	
		18–24 (age)	35–44 (age)
Female on top	16%	37%	29%
Side by side, face to face	12	21	15
Rear entry	4	20	8
Sitting	—	4	2

[a]*Kinsey data adapted from Gebhard and Johnson (1979), showing frequent use among college-educated, white, married couples.*

[b]*Hunt data adapted from Hunt (1975), Table 33, for white, mar-ried sample reporting the frequency of using a specific coital po-sition as "often," given for two different age groups.*

Figure 16.4

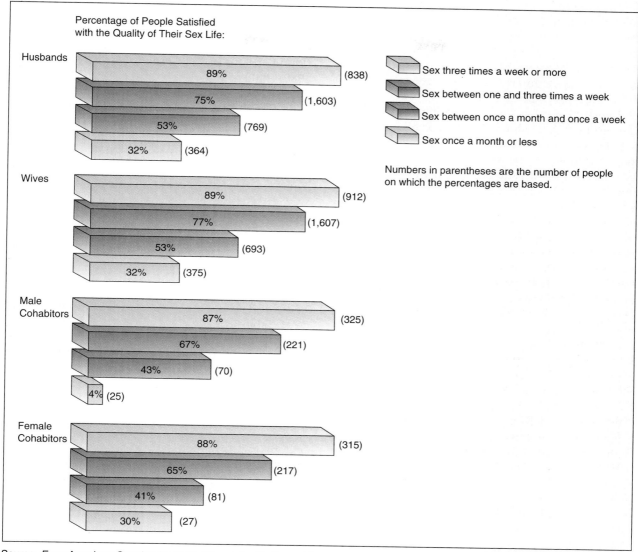

Percentage of People Satisfied
with the Quality of Their Sex Life:

Husbands
- 89% (838)
- 75% (1,603)
- 53% (769)
- 32% (364)

Wives
- 89% (912)
- 77% (1,607)
- 53% (693)
- 32% (375)

Male Cohabitors
- 87% (325)
- 67% (221)
- 43% (70)
- 4% (25)

Female Cohabitors
- 88% (315)
- 65% (217)
- 41% (81)
- 30% (27)

- Sex three times a week or more
- Sex between one and three times a week
- Sex between once a month and once a week
- Sex once a month or less

Numbers in parentheses are the number of people on which the percentages are based.

Source: *From* American Couples *by Philip Blumstein, Ph.D., and Pepper Schwartz, Ph.D. Copyright © 1983 by Philip Blumstein and Pepper Schwartz. By permission of William Morrow & Company and International Creative Management.*

fied with the quality of their sex lives, while only 53 percent of those having sex between once a week and once a month were satisfied. In marriages with a sexual frequency of once a month or less, the satisfaction rate dropped to only 32 percent. Another important factor that was linked to sexual satisfaction was equality in initiating or refusing sex. Eighty percent of husbands and wives who reported that sexual initiation in their relationship was equal were satisfied with the quality of their sex lives, versus 66 percent of those who said

that sexual initiation was one-sided. Similarly, 80 percent of married men and women who reported being able to refuse sex on an equal basis were satisfied with the quality of their sex lives, compared with 58 percent of husbands and 61 percent of wives who reported that sexual refusal was not equal.

Intriguingly, it appears that heterosexual men who receive and give oral sex are happier with their sex lives and with their relationships than those who do not (Blumstein and Schwartz, 1983).

Performing or receiving oral sex, however, does not seem to be linked to sexual satisfaction for heterosexual women, possibly because many of them see both fellatio and cunnilingus as a form of submissiveness or degradation. Instead, it appears that intercourse is more essential to sexual satisfaction for heterosexual women than for heterosexual men (Blumstein and Schwartz, 1983).

Research surveys are not the only way of elucidating the relationship between sexual and marital satisfaction, and attempts to categorize just what satisfaction is may be misleading. One person may be satisfied with a marriage that provides economic security and freedom from major conflict, while another person considers that kind of marriage as tolerable but unsatisfactory. Likewise, one person may judge how satisfying a sexual relationship is primarily in terms of coital frequency, while to someone else a variety of forms of sex play and the quality of both partners' sexual responses may be the basis for making a judgment. If both spouses largely agree on what they require for sexual and marital happiness, the chances seem to be higher that they will be able to attain it. On the other hand, many marriage counselors and sex therapists can attest to the fact that many marriages are troubled by some major form of sexual distress (Masters and Johnson, 1970; Kaplan, 1974; Frank, Anderson, and Rubinstein, 1978; LoPiccolo and LoPiccolo, 1978). It has also been suggested that the high prevalence of extramarital sex may relate to a lack of marital sexual satisfaction since, as I. L. Reiss (1980) says, if other things are equal, "the more marital sexual satisfaction, the less the desire for extramarital relationships."

Extramarital Sex

Extramarital sex can be defined as any form of sexual activity between a married person and someone other than his or her spouse. Although considered sinful, criminal, or immoral through most of the history of the Western world—and sometimes punished by whippings, fines, brandings, and even death (Murstein, 1974)—the practice has both persisted and become fairly commonplace.

In 1948 Kinsey, Pomeroy, and Martin estimated that half of all married males in their sample had had extramarital coitus (this figure was approximate because many men were reluctant to discuss this area openly). Kinsey's group (1953) also noted

that by age 40, 26 percent of married women had had extramarital sex. In 1975 Hunt believed that these estimates were still accurate, but the *Redbook* survey found that among 35- to 39-year-old wives, 38 percent had extramarital sexual experience (Levin, 1975). In the *Cosmopolitan* survey (Wolfe, 1980), half of married women 18 to 34 years old and 69.2 percent of married women 35 or older had had extramarital sexual activity. While some other recent surveys have also reported higher figures for extramarital sex—for example, Hite (1981) found that two-thirds of the married men in her sample had extramarital experience, and the *Playgirl* survey found a 43 percent incidence in married women (Grosskopf, 1983)—these numbers contrast sharply with the data of Blumstein and Schwartz (1983), which show that only 26 percent of husbands ($N = 3591$) and 21 percent of the wives ($N = 3606$) they studied had any form of extramarital sex involvement. The NHSLS also found low rates of extramarital affairs for both men (24.5 percent) and women (15 percent) (Laumann et al., 1994, Table 5.15).

Unfortunately, much of the research on extramarital sex is methodologically limited and the reasons that motivate people to engage in extramarital sex are only poorly understood at present (Moultrop, 1990; Gloss and Wright, 1992; Masters, Johnson, and Koladny, 1994).

The Extramarital Experience

While most people believe that extramarital sex is always wrong (Pittman, 1991), there has been a traditional double standard that rationalizes to a certain degree extramarital sex for men while more strongly condemning it for women. In some European countries, for instance, having a mistress is regarded as a privilege of wealthy married men. Similarly, many societies permit female heterosexual prostitution (a sort of temporary "rent-a-mistress") as a means of providing for a presumed male need for sexual variety while protecting against destruction of the bonds of matrimonial relationships. Since prostitution is seen by most people as extramarital sex at a purely physical level, it is not as threatening as other types of extramarital sex that carry the risk of emotional involvement that might eventually lead to the breakup of a marriage.

Perhaps for this same reason, some married people feel most comfortable with extramarital sex that is purely and directly aimed at physical pleasure:

Table 16.7   Reasons Given by Women for Having an Extramarital Affair

Reason	Percentage
Emotionally dissatisfied with husband	72
Sexually dissatisfied with husband	46
Seduced by lover	39
Feel naturally polygamous	39
Found out husband had an affair	35
To gain revenge against husband	23
Have an open marriage	14
Don't know why	30

Source: *Modified from data in Grosskopf (1983), p. 195; based on replies from 516 married women.*

Table 16.8   Reasons Given by Married Men for Having an Affair

Reason	Percentage
To find more sexual excitement	74
To counteract sexual boredom	67
To provide better sex	65
To have greater sexual frequency	59
To receive a particular type of sexual stimulation that the wife refuses to provide	31
To have a more attractive (or younger) partner	28
To deal with a sexual dysfunction	12
To deal with wife's physical incapacity	2
To have sex with another male	2

Source: *Masters, Johnson, and Kolodny, 1994.*

the "one-night stand." The background circumstances that lead to this brief encounter of extramarital sex vary tremendously—a lonely businessman on an overnight trip, a bored housewife who feels the walls are closing in on her at home and makes the rounds of the city bars, men or women trying to prove to themselves that they're not really getting old or that they still have sex appeal—the list could go on indefinitely. The extramarital one-night stand is often so impersonal that the participants don't know each other's names. No commitment is made and none is intended; it's really sex with "no strings attached." Although this is a risky undertaking in the age of AIDS, there is no evidence that such behavior has suddenly stopped (Gagnon, 1989).

How do people react to having such an experience? Some people find exactly what they're looking for: a release of pent-up tension, a means of getting even with their spouse for something, a way of satisfying their curiosity, a change of pace from their ordinary sexual diet, or a temporary form of escape. Others find the experience to be empty, guilt-provoking, awkward, or frightening. These comments illustrate the types of reactions we've frequently heard:

A 31-year-old woman: I'd been married for almost ten years and had always been faithful, but I kept wondering what it would be like to have sex with someone else. One night I was out with some friends, and we met a few guys who bought us drinks and talked with us awhile. One of them was real good-looking and flirting with me, and I sort of flirted back. We went off

to a motel for three or four hours, and it was beautiful sex, fantastic sex, just like in a novel. But that was the end of it, and it just felt good to know that I'd had the experience. I never told my husband and I don't plan to. *(Authors' files)*

A 36-year-old man: My wife and I have very old-fashioned values and we both took our marital vows seriously, meaning no screwing around with anyone else. I never worried about it too much, since I wasn't the type to be running around anyway. But one night when I was working late a secretary asked me for a ride home, and then invited me in for coffee, and I was perfectly happy to oblige. But it was a stupid thing to do—not much fun, and lots of guilt about it afterwards—and I don't think I'd do it again. *(Authors' files)*

The extramarital affair contrasts sharply with the one-night stand in that there is a continued sexual relationship over time. The affair may be relatively short-lived (a few weeks) or may go on for years. An extramarital affair can be mainly for sex or it can blossom into a relationship on its own with sex playing a relatively minor part and companionship and conversation being more important (see Tables 16.7 and 16.8).

Affairs are probably less frequent than one-night stands for both practical and personal reasons. Unless a person's spouse knows about, and approves

extramarital sex sexual activity involving a married person and a partner who isn't his or her spouse.

of, a continued extramarital liaison (a statistically unlikely possibility at present), the partners in the affair must create time to be together, find a place to meet (and preserve their anonymity), and explain their absence to their spouses.[3] For these reasons, many affairs involve secretive (and hurried) get-togethers during the day, since it may be easier to get an hour or two away from work than a similar time away from home at night.

At the personal level, many people feel that having an affair is like "playing with dynamite." Although it may be sexually satisfying and emotionally fulfilling, they are cautious about letting the affair take over their lives or pose a threat to their marriage. Many people who have had affairs state that they loved their spouse during the time of their extramarital involvement and did not want to jeopardize that relationship.

Many married women find, much to their surprise, that an affair brings them a sense of empowerment that was previously lacking from their lives. This boost to their self-esteem stems from at least four separate sources. First, the element of active choice replaces the sex-as-duty dullness that tarnishes many marriages. Second, and far more powerful, the married woman involved in an affair is likely to be treated with attentiveness and affection that kindles a feeling of being special and being wanted that is reminiscent of her courtship days. Third, an affair almost inevitably endorses a woman's sense of attractiveness and desirability. (When affairs come to an end, of course, there may be a backlash of this phenomenon, with the woman winding up feeling unattractive and undesirable especially if she did not want the affair to end.) Finally, affairs give married women an alternate reality in their lives—a way of combating roles they have found unsatisfying and replacing them, even if only fleetingly, with new ways of self-expressiveness and different patterns of behavior.

Another source of self-empowerment for some married women in affairs is the discovery that they

[3]Extramarital sex between a married man and a single woman or a married woman and a single man is likely to offer greater convenience than an affair between two married persons. They have a place to go (the single partner's residence) and less of a scheduling problem, since the single partner is not as likely to be tied down by home and family responsibilities. But these types of affairs can create their own brand of problems: the single person may press the married one to divorce and remarry, for example.

are more sexually responsive than they had imagined. This is sometimes the case for women who enter affairs out of a feeling of sexual dissatisfaction in their marriages: the "is this all there is?" syndrome. Given the numerous reasons for a woman's sexual dissatisfaction—including having a sexually dysfunctional or inhibited mate, having a spouse who is clumsy or inconsiderate in bed, or having a husband who has little appetite for sex—it is not surprising that this category is larger than many men would imagine.

Although extramarital sex offers excitement, variety, and the thrill of the forbidden, the available data show that the overall pleasure of extramarital sex is somewhat lower for men and women in general than their overall sexual pleasure in their marriages (Hunt; 1975; Blumstein and Schwartz, 1983; Pittman, 1991). While extramarital sex may release sexual inhibitions for some people and help them to become fully responsive for the first time in their lives, it may lead other people to sexual problems (Masters, Johnson, and Kolodny, 1994).

The major problem for American women when it comes to affairs is guilt (Botwin, 1994); in contrast, American men are not generally guilty about their extramarital dalliances. In fact, most of the men we've interviewed about their affairs seem to be proud of them rather than ashamed in any way. The major exception to this observation is the subcategory of men from strongly religious backgrounds who have had extramarital involvements. Although these men speak more contritely about their extramarital activities than most others do, it often sounds forced and formulaic. In fact, it often sounds like their guilt has more to do with being caught than with regret about their extramarital conduct.

Female guilt about extramarital sex is such a strongly felt emotion that in perhaps a quarter of cases it leads women to break off an affair even when it is physically pleasurable and psychically energizing. In these cases, the guilt and ambivalence the woman experiences (usually cast in terms of a sense of betraying her husband) eventually overcome any positive returns, and she ends the affair as a matter of conscience. At times, it seems that the woman's pleasure, both sexually and psychologically, becomes the very source of guilt. In America, women often feel guilty about feeling good, as many feminist writers have acknowledged.

RESEARCH SPOTLIGHT

Nonmonogamy

In *American Couples,* Blumstein and Schwartz (1983) use the term "nonmonogamy" to describe sexual activity outside a couple's relationship so that they can examine such behavior in married couples, cohabiting heterosexual couples, and homosexual and lesbian couples. Here is a summary of their major findings:

1. Monogamy is strongly held as a moral ideal even by those who don't practice what they preach.
2. Sex differences in monogamy are most apparent among homosexual women and men (82 percent of gay men versus 28 percent of lesbians are nonmonogamous), but while similar numbers of husbands and wives have had extramarital sexual experiences, the men have had more partners.
3. Couples can never be completely sure their relationships will remain monogamous even after they've been together a decade or longer.

4. One episode of nonmonogamy doesn't mean that a person has begun a "career" of infidelity: in fact, for some people an act of sex outside the relationship may be more to satisfy curiosity than anything else.
5. Men are more likely to seek casual sex outside their relationships, while women seek to form emotional attachments.
6. People who attend church or synagogue regularly are as likely as anyone else to have extramarital sex.
7. Heterosexuals who have nonmonogamous sex are just as happy with their relationships as monogamous people, but they are somewhat less sure their relationships will last.

Source: *From American Couples by Philip Blumstein, Ph.D., and Pepper Schwartz, Ph.D. Copyright © 1983 by Philip Blumstein and Pepper Schwartz. By permission of William Morrow & Company and International Creative Management.*

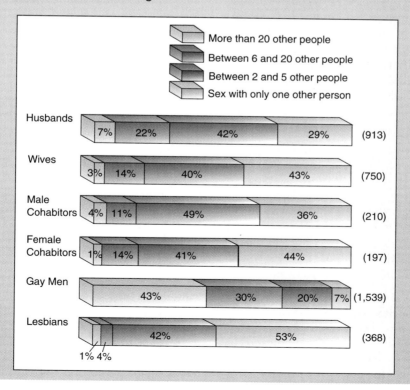

Relatively few men act in a similar vein. When men end affairs for reasons other than becoming bored or finding a new extramarital partner, it is typically because they are worried that their wife is about to discover their secret or because they are having problems meeting the demands of the extramarital relationship. Guilt rarely enters the picture: men find dozens of ready explanations to justify their behavior. "It makes me feel younger." "It helps to keep my marriage together." "It helps me deal with stress." "My lover does things my wife won't do." Indeed, many men regard casual extramarital flings as having about the moral equivalence of stopping for a pizza if they're hungry.

Now an additional factor may be influencing people's willingness to participate in extramarital sex: the reality of the HIV/AIDS epidemic. Although no systematic research is available yet to show a decrease in extramarital liaisons as a result of widespread publicity about AIDS, our impression from hundreds of interviews with married couples from 1986 to 1993 is that rates of extramarital involvement have dropped somewhat—perhaps by about 25 percent (although admittedly the people we have interviewed don't represent a random sample). This reduction in extramarital sexual activity is more prominent in casual sexual contacts—the so-called one-night stands—and not particularly noticeable in long-standing affairs. But it does seem that many people who have previously had extramarital sexual activity are rethinking the wisdom of continuing such practices, as this comment from our files aptly puts it:

A 38-year-old woman: I used to go to the bars a lot at night when my husband was out of town, and I probably slept with five or six men a year that I met in those circumstances. It didn't seem like a big deal at all—after all, I knew my husband was probably doing the same thing I was. But now I'm just afraid to have sex with anyone but him, and I've told him in no uncertain terms that I expect him to toe the line, too. Life's too much fun to risk it all for an instant of passion.

Consensual Extramarital Sex

When two spouses agree that one or both of them is free to engage in extramarital sexual activity, there may be many reasons behind the decision. They may be looking for a way to preserve their personal freedom, hoping to improve the quality of their marriage, seeking to live by a particular personal philosophy, or simply trying to add variety and excitement to their lives.

Both partners may be interested in extramarital sex or one person may agree to let the other do as he or she pleases without any intention of participating themselves. For one couple, talking about the extramarital experience in vivid detail may be a source of turn-on, while another couple decides that extramarital sex is okay for them only if they don't discuss it together.

Consensual (i.e., with consent) extramarital sex can take many forms. In 1972, Nena and George O'Neill wrote a best-selling book called *Open Marriage* in which they suggested that traditional marriages often presented few options for choice or change. Their "open marriage" concept—as opposed to the "closed," or traditional, marriage—envisioned a flexible relationship in which both spouses were committed to their own and their partner's fulfillment and growth. The O'Neills stressed that an open marriage involved a willingness to negotiate change and to discard the expectations of a closed marriage, particularly the idea that one partner is able to meet all of the other's needs (emotional, social, economic, intellectual, and sexual). The O'Neills emphasized role equality and flexibility between spouses, but many people presumed that their book was primarily an endorsement of consensual extramarital sex as a growth experience. However, the O'Neills later wrote:

> While some benefits were noted, it was observed that by and large these [extramarital sex] experiences did not occur in a context where the marital partners were developing their primary marriage relationship sufficiently for this activity to count as a growth experience. Frequently it obscured relationship problems, became an avenue of escape, and intensified conflicts. *(O'Neill and O'Neill, 1977, p. 293)*

Nevertheless, the open-marriage approach to discarding the notion of sexual exclusivity and restrictiveness seems to work well for some couples. It should be noted, however, that an open marriage does not need to involve outside sexual relationships (Knapp and Whitehurst, 1978).

One study followed a matched sample of 82 married couples from 1978 to 1983 to see if there were major differences in the rates of marital stability between sexually exclusive marriages and sexually open marriages (Rubin and Adams, 1986). Although there was a higher rate of marriages breaking up among the open-marriage couples than among the sexually exclusive couples (32 percent versus 18 percent), this difference was not statistically significant. Of particular interest was the fact that jealousy didn't appear to play much of a role in the open marriages that were studied. Rubin and Adams (1986) noted: "Among those in the open [marriage] group for whom jealousy did become a serious debilitation, those couples usually did not separate but rather chose to stop having sex outside the relationship (or, in some cases, to stop being open about it)" (p. 317).

Swinging is another form of consensual extramarital sex. Here, married couples exchange partners with other couples, with all parties agreeing to the arrangement. Most surveys indicate that only 2 to 4 percent of married couples have ever engaged in swinging, and less than half of these couples have done it on a regular basis (Spanier and Cole, 1972; Athanasiou, 1973; Hunt, 1975; Murstein, 1978a).

The husband usually first brings up the idea of swinging, and the wife's reaction is typically one of shock (Murstein, 1978a). Only a few couples who discuss the idea ever attempt to put it into reality, and many get cold feet and don't go through with their plans at the last minute.

Although a couple will occasionally be introduced to swinging by people they already know, this is generally an "underground" activity. The interested couple usually must turn to swingers' magazines or sexually explicit newspapers to either answer an ad or place one themselves. Here are several examples of ads from swingers' publications:

Attractive Couple. He, mid-30s, muscular, virile. She, mid-20s, shapely, sexy. Desire open-minded couples under 35 for relaxed get-togethers.

Sensual Black Couple, male 32 and hung, female 28 and 36–24–36. Into partying and fun. Photos required for reply.

Super Attractive Couple—she bi, 28, beautiful, natural redhead; he, 30, 6'1", 175 lbs., handsome and good build. Seeking extremely attractive couples for friendship and fun. Both educated, sincere, gentle, with sense of humor. Photo, phone a must.

Swingers may either get together for a two-couple "party" or may meet in groups with many couples. There are usually drinks served and pornographic movies may be shown to get people in the mood. The sexual activity may take place entirely in heterosexual twosomes, with each couple retreating behind a closed bedroom door ("closed swinging") or, if the door is left open, it's a signal for anyone who wishes to come in and join the fun (Murstein, 1978a). While "open swinging" commonly involves two women having sex together, male homosexual contact is less frequent and in some groups of swingers it is entirely barred. Several factors account for female homosexual relationships among swingers: most men are hardly matches for sexually aroused multiorgasmic women. While the men rest, they often experience sexual restimulation if they watch women make love to each other. Presumably the sight of other men making love to their spouses (while they are not similarly occupied) can be too ego-threatening, while the sight of two women making love usually is not.

In the 1970s, variations on the swinging theme included group sex in private clubs such as the now defunct Sandstone in California (Talese, 1980) or in clubs that charged admission, such as Plato's Retreat in New York City. In an era of increasing awareness of sexually transmitted diseases, though, sex clubs like these have largely disappeared. Swinging can also be an activity with a prominent social side: groups of swingers occasionally vacation together, organize picnics, or go for a day at the beach.

Different studies have defined the backgrounds and personalities of swingers in different ways. In some studies, swingers appeared to be conservative, traditional, and religious (Bartell, 1971; Walshok, 1971). In others they were portrayed as liberal, nonreligious (or even antireligious), and antiestablishment (Gilmartin, 1974). All studies agree that swingers as a group tend to have more premarital experience, more premarital partners, and more (and earlier) interest in sex than "nonswingers" (Murstein, 1978a). Although there is no evidence that swingers have abnormal personalities, two studies found that swingers are more likely to have had counseling or psychotherapy

swinging a form of consensual extramarital sex in which married couples switch partners with one or more other couples.

than nonswingers (Smith and Smith, 1970; Gilmartin, 1974).

The positive side of swinging includes having a shared activity that truly eliminates the double standard. Couples may feel pleased by having a variety of sexual partners without deceiving each other; some couples find that their own sex lives are improved. But the other side of the coin bears examining too, especially since most couples withdraw from swinging after brief experimentation (Murstein, 1978a). They may find that swinging has led to jealousy, feelings of inadequacy, guilt, rejection, and even to sexual dysfunction and divorce (Masters and Johnson, 1976).

Nonmarital Sex

Despite the popularity of marriage in our society, there are still many people who remain single by choice or by lack of marital opportunity. Current statistics indicate, for example, that almost 3 million Americans are now living in cohabitation relationships (see Chapter 10). Others become single after once having been married by divorce or death of a spouse. Although largely neglected by researchers, these individuals also have sexual needs which they act on in various ways.

The Never-Married Single

Although in the past it was often presumed that a man or woman who reached age 30 without marrying was flawed in one way or another, today it is clear that many people choose to be single as a creative option in their lives. The choice may be a rejection of the restrictions and responsibilities of marriage or it may be based on other factors, such as economic independence. Increasing numbers of women are placing career objectives ahead of marriage as a goal today (Frieze et al., 1978; Cherlin, 1992), and men are also reconsidering whether being married is really the way they want to live. Some of these people decide to marry after a long period of singlehood while others remain single throughout their lives.

Relatively few people choose to be single to preserve a particular sexual lifestyle, but the image of the "swinging singles scene"—freely accessible sex with little or no interpersonal responsibility beyond the requirements of the moment—has been burned into the public mind by the media. While singles bars continue to flourish in many locales, many people dislike the impersonal nature of sexual shopping around, as these two comments reveal:

A 28-year-old woman: I spent much of last year making the rounds at the singles bars looking for fun. After a while, the "lines" and faces all blurred together—every guy claimed he was a doctor, a lawyer, or a corporate vice president—and the deceptiveness got to be too much. Even the sex wasn't very good . . . it certainly wasn't worth the agonies of trying to find someone to make it with. *(Authors' files)*

A 34-year-old-man: I tried the dating bars for a month or so, but I couldn't really bring myself to continue. Sure there was lots of sex available—by 11:00 at night a lot of gals got desperate—but it was all a phony scene, one that had no real humanity to it. *(Authors' files)*

On the other hand, some people find the freedom and variety of the singles bars exciting and fulfilling.

A 29-year-old woman: I'm a lawyer, and all day long I've got to think, to use my brain. Sometimes at night I just like to throw away that identity and go out for a good time. If I meet an attractive guy, I invite myself to his place—that way I don't have to worry about throwing *him* out, I can get up and leave when I'm ready. And sometimes it just feels good to make contact with someone else, with no commitments or obligations. *(Authors' files)*

The singles bars are populated by several different groups of people. The under-25 singles are generally in a "premarital" stage. Most of the over-thirties are divorced people and married men or women on the prowl for extramarital sex. The 25- to 30-year-olds include both the not-interested-in-marriage-now group, the younger divorced crowd, and some people looking for the perfect mate.

Other nonmarried singles choose different approaches to satisfying their sexual needs, meeting prospective partners at work, through their families, or in other social settings. In recent years, computer dating services have become a popular means of trying to meet someone with similar interests where a sexual opportunity may develop. Some nonmarried people form relatively exclusive long-term sexual relationships in which neither partner has marriage as an objective. Others maintain nonexclusive long-term sexual relationships with a small number of partners whom they see on a rotating basis. Others avoid lasting relationships in favor of a series of one-night stands, and others choose celibacy as best for themselves.

The Previously Married Single

People who have been married and then become single through divorce or death of a spouse remarry at extraordinarily high rates, as we mentioned in Chapter 10. Most divorced men and women become sexually active within a year following their divorce (Hunt, 1975), although older divorced people are somewhat slower in this regard than those under age 40.

Since almost half of all marriages end in divorce, there is less stigma toward divorce now than in the past. The divorced woman is no longer viewed as "used goods" by men, and people are not regarded as being "failures" if their marriages don't last forever. The person who becomes divorced, however, may find it somewhat difficult at first to adjust to the idea of nonmarital sex, to work out the specific details of how to meet people, and to handle the logistics of sexual activity (where to go, what to tell the kids, and so on).

Widowed men and women sometimes choose to abstain from sexual activity after their spouse's death but a large majority of widowers and 43 percent of widows engage in postmarital coitus (Gebhard, 1968; Hunt, 1975). The widow over 60 is sometimes handicapped by a lack of available male partners. Interestingly, the widower at any age is likely to have a wider selection of partners as women outlive men and men are relatively free to choose from women of all ages. Widows, conversely, are expected to choose partners close to their own age or older. As previously stated, many people think that the elderly have no sexual needs or feelings, but this is far from true: sexual interest is often maintained and sometimes improves with age. Among divorced or widowed persons, it is common to hear that postmarital sex is more pleasurable and fulfilling than in their prior marital experience.

SUMMARY

1. Masturbation, or sexual self-pleasuring involving some form of direct physical stimulation, is a normal form of sexual behavior in people of all ages. Although negative views of masturba-

tion can be traced to religious viewpoints that condemned sexual pleasure as sinful as well as to a historical legacy that was preoccupied with the mistaken notion that masturbation causes illness and insanity. In actuality, masturbation is a healthy act that helps people learn about their bodies and their sexual responses, as well as being a helpful tension-reducer and a way of dealing with situations where sex with a partner is not possible.

2. Sexual fantasies begin in childhood and serve important functions in our lives, such as providing or enhancing excitement, releasing inner tensions, and permitting safe, imaginary rehearsals of untried behavior. A person's use of a particular type of fantasy does not necessarily mean that he or she wishes to act it out.

3. Sexual activity is not just a matter of good technique; interpersonal communication is usually an important component of the sexual experience. Finding out what your partner likes and dislikes and informing your partner about your own stylistic preferences are important aspects of any sexual relationship.

4. Among the many varieties of physical stimulation couples can use during lovemaking, certain practices such as oral–genital sex or anal stimulation can be anxiety-provoking for some people while acceptable and highly arousing for others. In one recent survey, it was found that almost 90 percent of married couples had oral–genital sex often or occasionally.

5. There are an almost infinite number of positions for intercourse, but most are variations on four basic methods: man on top, face to face (the "missionary" position); woman on top, face to face; rear entry; and side by side. Although the missionary position is most commonly used, other positions can offer the woman more freedom of movement and some people enjoy changing positions from time to time for variety's sake alone.

6. The sexual techniques of gay men and lesbians are generally similar to heterosexual techniques, but homosexuals in committed relationships seem more attuned to their partner's responses and somewhat less goal-oriented than most heterosexual married couples.

7. In general, men and women today are less bound by old sexual stereotypes that limited the woman's role initiating or participating ac-

tively in sex. More traditional views on other aspects of sexual behavior—particularly premarital sex—have also undergone substantial change in the last 30 to 40 years.

8. There is solid research evidence that premarital sex is more common among women today than in the past, but for most people it still occurs in the context of an affectionate or love relationship.

9. Most Americans marry and have coitus two to three times a week during their twenties and thirties, after which the average coital frequency declines. There are wide individual differences in the frequency of marital sex and the activities that married couples include in their sexual interaction. The amount of time spent in noncoital play and the average duration of intercourse among married couples both seem to have lengthened since Kinsey's day.

10. There is no simple one-to-one relationship between good sex and good marriage, but marriages that are most satisfying sexually tend to stay together longer and have less extramarital sex than marriages marked by sexual dissatisfaction. Communication between partners seems to be a key element influencing the quality of a couple's sexual relationship.

11. Although extramarital sex has been strongly condemned in the past, many people seem to be doing it today. In the last few decades, more married women have become involved in this behavior as a result of shifting attitudes (e.g., a fading double standard, the advent of women's liberation), contraceptive availability, and more time spent outside the home.

12. Extramarital sex can take many forms: secretive versus consensual, one-night stands versus long-term affairs, recreational or relational, and so on. Although swinging is a relatively infrequent type of extramarital involvement, it is similar to other varieties in that all these behaviors can lead to pleasure or distress. It is not clear at present how often marital infidelity contributes to divorce, but our guess is that it is a fairly important factor in many cases.

13. Nonmarital sex includes the sexual behavior of the never-married single, the widowed, and the divorced. There is relatively little research about this area, but it generally appears that there are no major surprises. Sexual behavior is not all that different inside or outside marriage.

Thought Questions

1. What kind of variations do you observe in people's attitudes toward oral sex? How many find it a preferred activity? How many have an aversion to it? Why are some people willing to give but not receive oral sex, and vice versa? Are there sex differences in this respect? What factors do you think might account for these variations in attitudes and behaviors?

2. What percentage of people do you think desire to have anal sex? Do men and women differ in this respect? Is anal sex more stigmatized than other variations of sexual intercourse? How do you think most men feel about women who enjoy anal sex? Are men's feelings of love or respect for a woman affected by whether she consents to anal sex or whether she refuses?

3. Do men really want women to initiate sex, to take the lead in "orchestrating" the activities of a sexual encounter, and to take responsibility for their own orgasms? Or would most men be made nervous by a woman who behaved this way?

4. Sex researchers have concluded that an incident of extramarital sex is unlikely to harm most otherwise strong relationships, particularly if the partner never learns about it. However, assume that one member of a committed-monogamous pair "falls off the wagon" and has sex outside the relationship. Does he or she have a responsibility to tell the partner, in this day and age of concern about transmission of the AIDS virus? Must marriage evolve new standards regarding frankness about extra-marital sex because of the AIDS risk?

5. Social scientists have made the case that a major reason why extramarital sex by wives has been so strongly condemned is the need to assure the husband that in fact he is the father of the children he will help raise. If this is true, why don't more people establish marriages characterized by consensual extramarital sex now that birth control is more reliable and sterilization more common? Would it be possible

for such arrangements ever to become generally acceptable in our society? Would such acceptability be desirable?

6. Is a lifetime being single a viable option now, or are never-married people still considered to be social failures in our society?

Suggested Readings

Blumstein, Philip, and Schwartz, Pepper. *American Couples.* New York: William Morrow, 1983. A monumental study of American couples—married, cohabiting, and homosexual—that includes unique data on sexual relations. One of the best research studies of the last 30 years.

Comfort, Alex. *The New Joy of Sex.* New York: Pocket Books, 1991. A revised edition of Comfort's aptly described "gourmet guide to lovemaking," this book includes many drawings and photos as well as warm-hearted advice.

Friday, Nancy. *My Secret Garden.* New York: Trident Press, 1973. A nonscientific but intriguing collection of women's sexual fantasies, showing the diversity and inventiveness of the erotic imagination. A classic.

Friday, Nancy. *Men in Love.* New York: Delacorte Press, 1980. A compilation of sex fantasy patterns from men that provides provocative reading if you disregard the author's interpretations of their "meanings."

Friday, Nancy. *Women on Top.* New York: Pocket Books, 1991. Fascinating transcripts of women's sexual fantasies. The editorializing is not quite as useful as the diversity of fantasies themselves.

Karlen, Arno. *Threesomes.* New York: Beech Tree Books, 1988. This is a major study of the nature of sexual triads that is simultaneously well-written and fascinating. There is simply no other book that comes close to its wealth of detail or insightful observations on this much-neglected topic.

Michael, R.T., et al. *Sex in America: A Definitive Survey.* Boston: Little, Brown, 1994. The results of a national survey on American sexual practices, presented in a readable form.

Moultroup, D. J. *Husbands, Wives, and Lovers: The Emotional System of the Extramarital Affair.* New York: Guilford Press, 1990. A thoughtful look at the dynamics of affairs and their impact on marriages.

Silverstein, Charles, and Picano, Felice. *The New Joy of Gay Sex.* New York: Harper Collins, 1992. A counterpart to Alex Comfort's book (see above): a gourmet guide to gay lovemaking.

Stubbs, Kenneth R. *Erotic Massage: The Touch of Love.* Larkspur, CA: Secret Garden, 1989. A beautifully illustrated book covering the techniques of massage, with a particular emphasis on how massage unlocks sensuality.

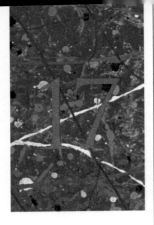

Sexual Variations

Sexual behavior, like human behavior, is varied and complex and defies simple schemes of classification. In this chapter, we shift our focus from the more common patterns of sexual behavior considered in the last three chapters and look at the diversity shown in less typical sexual variations. Considering these variations can be intriguing and instructive: besides learning more about the nature of sexuality, we also increase our tolerance for others, including those who are different from us and, in some instances, those who are hurt by such "different" behavior. To accomplish these goals of learning and tolerance in a reasonably objective manner, we start by discussing the concepts of normality, labeling, and stigmatization.

DEFINING NORMALITY

It isn't very difficult to decide that a person who is sexually aroused only when riding a camel is abnormal or that a couple whose sex life consists primarily of intercourse several times a week at night in the privacy of their bedroom seems almost "too normal." Most people believe they know intuitively how to rate sexual behavior as normal or abnormal. Nevertheless, trying to define what is sexually normal and what is not is one of the more perplexing problems in sexology today. Let's see where the difficulties arise.

Most dictionary definitions of "normal" say that it is primarily a matter of conforming to a usual or typical pattern. What is unusual or atypical not only varies from culture to culture but also varies over time, as we have noted throughout this book. But there is still more complexity in establishing a definition of what is normal. From a sociological perspective, behavior that falls outside the accepted customs and rules of a particular society is considered deviant. From a biological viewpoint, normality implies natural and healthy. A psychological view of abnormality stresses that it produces a personal, subjective sense of distress—such as excessive nervousness, depression, or guilt—or that it interferes with a person's ability to function adequately in ordinary social and occupational roles. Statistically, normality becomes a matter of numbers: what is rare is abnormal, what is common is not.

The point we are making is twofold: first, defining normality is not as simple as it seems; second, the distinction between normal and abnormal is somewhat arbitrary because it generally involves value judgments of one type or another. Thus, it is important to note that in many instances there is no clear-cut separation between normal and abnormal. While it is easy to say that a person who masturbates twice a week is not exhibiting abnormal sexual behavior and that a person who compulsively masturbates a dozen times a day *is*, where do we draw the line? Once a day? Three times a day? Six times a day? Is the behavior abnormal only if it is compulsive? Is it abnormal only if it continues persistently over time?

Given these potential difficulties in determining just what normality means, we suggest that you be aware of your own feelings about the topics we'll be discussing and try to determine how those feelings color your reaction to understanding these different forms of sexual behavior.

LABELING AND STIGMATIZATION

Using words like *normal* or *abnormal* to describe people or behavior, or using other word combinations that may sound scientific or "official" (such as healthy, well-adjusted, and law-abiding versus diseased, pathological, deviant, sick, or criminal) is called *labeling*. Labels affect how we view other people and how they view us in return; labels may also affect how we feel about ourselves. In general, labels that identify a person as "different" are likely

to lead people to cautiously distance themselves from or perhaps reject that person; labels that indicate sameness or familiarity (in association with something viewed as "normal" or "good") tend to foster acceptance.

Stigmatization refers to the negative effects labeling can produce, such as social, legal, and economic consequences that can result from branding people as undesirable or discrediting them in various ways. For instance, people labeled as forgers may be picked up by the police as suspects if bad checks are being passed in their community even if they have reformed completely. A veteran with a dishonorable discharge may have a hard time getting a job. Stigmatization operates very strongly in terms of sexual labels too: how would you react to being told that someone was a child molester? Or even that someone was *suspected* of being a child molester?

In the past, some of the forms of sexual behavior discussed in this chapter were called sexual deviations, perversions, or aberrations. These labels inevitably led to stigmatization and were also applied in a somewhat arbitrary fashion, since their underlying concept was based on a notion of cultural conformity (Tallent, 1977). To avoid these problems as much as possible, we prefer to speak about sexual variations and to use the relatively neutral term *paraphilia*—derived from Greek roots meaning "alongside of" and "love"—to describe what used to be called sexual deviations. While this strategy serves our purpose fairly well at this time, it is possible that in the future this term will also become a source of stigmatization and a new, unstigmatized alternative will be needed.

THE PARAPHILIAS

A **paraphilia** is a condition in which a person's sexual arousal and gratification depend on a fantasy theme of an unusual sexual experience that becomes the principal focus of sexual behavior. A paraphilia can revolve around a particular sexual object (e.g., children, animals, underwear) or a particular act (e.g., inflicting pain, making obscene telephone calls). The nature of a paraphilia is gen-

paraphilia (par'uh fil'ē uh) a condition in which a person's sexual gratification is dependent on an unusual sexual experience (or fantasy). A neutral term for sexual alternatives that have been called deviant.

FOCUS IN BRIEF

The Paraphilias

Essential features:
- Recurrent, intense sexual urges and sexually arousing fantasies usually involving either (1) nonhuman objects, (2) the suffering or humiliation of oneself or one's partner, or (3) children or other nonconsenting persons.

Associated features:
- People with paraphilias may select an occupation or develop a hobby or volunteer work that puts them in contact with the desired erotic stimuli; for example, selling women's shoes or lingerie in fetishism, or working with children in pedophilia.
- Sexual dysfunctions such as erectile dysfunction or inability to ejaculate are common in attempts at sexual activity without the paraphilic theme.
- There may be other coexistent problems, including alcohol or drug abuse, intimacy problems, and personality disturbances (especially emotional immaturity).

Criteria for judging severity:
- *Mild:* The person is markedly distressed by the recurrent paraphilic urges but has never acted on them.
- *Moderate:* The person has occasionally acted on the paraphilic urge.
- *Severe:* The person has repeatedly acted on the paraphilic urge.

Source: *American Psychiatric Association*, 1987.

---

types of sexual activity outside the boundaries of the paraphilia generally lose their turn-on potential unless the person supplements them with the paraphilic fantasy.

While some of the paraphilias may seem so foreign to you that it's hard to see how they could be arousing to anyone, paraphilic acts, often in watered-down versions, are commonly used by sex partners wishing to add a little variety to their ordinary techniques. For example, some people get turned on by very explicit sexual language, others want to be bitten, scratched, or slapped during sex, and others find that watching their partners undress is highly arousing. Each of these innocuous acts if magnified to the point of psychological dependence could potentially be transformed into a paraphilia.

With this general background, we now discuss some of the major types of paraphilias.

Fetishism

In **fetishism,** sexual arousal occurs principally in response to an inanimate object or body part that is not primarily sexual in nature. The fetish object is almost invariably used during masturbation and is also incorporated into sexual activity with a partner to produce sexual excitation. Fetishists usually collect such objects and may go to great lengths, including theft, to add just the "right" type of item to their collection. One man we encountered who had a fetish for women's high-heel shoes had gradually accumulated a hoard of more than a thousand pairs, which he catalogued and concealed from his wife in his attic.

Among the long list of objects that have served as fetishes, the most common are items of women's clothing such as panties, brassieres, slips, stockings or pantyhose, negligees, shoes, boots, and gloves. Other common fetish objects include specific materials such as leather, rubber, silk, or fur or body parts such as hair, feet, legs, or buttocks. While a few fetishists are aroused by drawings or photographs of the fetish object, more commonly the fetishist prefers or requires an object that has already been worn. This object, however, does not function as a symbolic substitute for a person (the former owner). Rather it is *preferred* to the owner because it is "safe, silent, cooperative, tranquil and can be harmed or destroyed without consequence" (Stoller, 1977, p. 196). In the great majority of cases,

erally specific and unchanging, and most of the paraphilias are far more common in men than in women (Money, 1988). In some instances, however, the paraphilic preferences occur only episodically—for example, during periods of stress (American Psychiatric Association, 1987).

A paraphilia is distinguished from sporadic sexual experimentation just as drug dependence is different from episodic, recreational drug use. The person with a full-blown paraphilia typically becomes preoccupied with thoughts of reaching sexual fulfillment to the point of being seriously distracted from other responsibilities. In addition, the person with a fetish poses no danger to others and pursues the use of the fetish object in private.

In some cases, the fetishist can become sexually aroused and orgasmic only when the fetish is being used. In other instances, sexual responsiveness is diminished without the fetish but not completely wiped out. In the second set of circumstances, the fetishist often engineers sexual arousal by fantasizing about the fetish. For a small number of fetishists, the fetish object must be used by a partner in a particular way for it to be effective: for instance, the genitals must be rubbed by silk, or a partner must wear black garters and high-heel shoes.

There is a thin line of distinction between fetishism and certain types of sexual preferences. A person is not described as a fetishist if sexual arousal is dependent on having an attractive partner; a man who is turned on by a woman in black, lacy lingerie is also not labeled as a fetishist as long as this is not the primary focus of his arousal. Deciding exactly when individual preference blends into too much dependency is not always easy.

Transvestism

A **transvestite** is a heterosexual male who repeatedly and persistently becomes sexually aroused by wearing feminine clothing (cross-dressing).[1] Although many transvestites are married and are unremarkably masculine in everyday life, their cross-dressing may be accompanied by elaborate use of makeup, wigs, and feminine mannerisms in a masquerade that sometimes can fool even the most skilled onlooker.

Transvestism must be distinguished from male transsexualism, where the person wants an anatomical gender change and wants to live as a woman (see Chapter 11). Transsexuals usually are not sexually aroused by cross-dressing, but in a few cases transvestism may evolve into transsexualism (Wise and Meyer, 1980; American Psychiatric Association, 1987; Money, 1988). Transvestites can also be distinguished both from female impersonators (who are entertainers) and from male homosexuals who occasionally "go in drag" (cross-dress). These types of cross-dressing are not associated with sex-

[1]It is interesting to note that women who cross-dress (wear male clothing) are often regarded as fashionable and are not diagnosed as transvestites. While cross-dressing among women is not rare, it has not generally been associated with sexual excitement.

ual arousal, and there is no psychological dependence on wearing feminine clothing as a form of tension release.

Cross-dressing usually begins in childhood or early adolescence, with the histories of many transvestites indicating that as children they were punished by being dressed in girl's clothes (American Psychiatric Association, 1987). In one of the cases we have seen, a 6-year-old boy was deliberately "taught" to cross-dress by his transvestite father, who in turn had been guided into this behavior by his father when he was a child. In adulthood, most transvestites confine their cross-dressing to the privacy of their own homes, although a few may wear women's panties under their usual masculine clothing throughout the day. In many cases, the transvestite's wife is fully aware of her husband's cross-dressing and may actually help him perfect his use of makeup or select attractive clothing styles (Stoller, 1977). In other cases, the wife may be confused and upset by discovering her husband's passion for cross-dressing and may insist that he seek treatment or may simply file for divorce. In couples where the man has disclosed his transvestism to his wife or partner, more than half point to this paraphilia as "the biggest problem in our relationship" (Brown and Collier, 1989). Other wives reluctantly tolerate the cross-dressing but don't give it their approval, as this 42-year-old woman explains:

> I can't really understand why John enjoys this bizarre business, and I live in constant fear that he'll be discovered by our children. But he doesn't hurt anyone with his dressing up, and it doesn't take anything away from our love, so I really can't complain too much—I just have to accept things as they are. (*Authors' files*)

While most transvestites are exclusively heterosexual (the majority of married transvestites have

fetishism (fet' ish iz um) a condition in which sexual arousal occurs principally in response to an inanimate object or body part rather than a partner.

transvestite (trans ves' tīt) an individual who receives sexual gratification and release from anxiety by dressing in the clothing of the opposite sex. Unlike transsexuals, transvestites are not interested in becoming a member of the opposite sex.

PERSONAL PERSPECTIVES

A Man of Fashion

The following letter was written by a 38-year-old married man seeking help because of his wife's growing discomfort with his cross-dressing activities.

I am asking for your help for only one reason—I'm afraid Sally will leave me if I don't take action now to deal with what she calls "The Problem." But "The Problem" isn't really a problem to me, it's a "Problem" only in how my passion for dressing up in feminine clothes has become a matter of conflict between us.

It wasn't always this way. When we became engaged more than 15 years ago, I realized that I needed to be open about my turn-on with Sally so she wouldn't discover my secret later on. After a lot of agonizing over it, I handed her a "True Confessions" letter one night. Although she was more than a little confused about the whole thing, she also seemed reasonably accepting. That is, she was as accepting as a woman in love could be, figuring that either she would change me eventually or that I would grow out of this obsession. I also realize that she was so touched by my embarrassment at making this disclosure to her that she misinterpreted my dilemma (should I tell her or keep it secret?) as an inclination to put this stuff behind me.

I never had any intention of abandoning my private passion; I simply wanted her to share in it. I knew that many other men had convinced their wives to be accomplices in their dressing up, even helping her husband put on makeup, select appropriate underwear, etc. I also had a strong desire to have sex with Sally while I was dressed up, because this was when I was the most aroused. And for many years, while Sally wasn't exactly enthusiastic in these circumstances, at least she went along with it, which was enough for me.

After we started our family, things slowly began to change. Sally began to nag me more and more about "The Problem," urging me to give it up—as though it was just some passing hobby of mine, like bowling, that I wouldn't miss much if I just found a substitute. Only after I convinced her that I was unable and unwilling to quit, after I did try a number of times to cut way down on my dressing up and just found myself becoming irritable and depressed and preoccupied with daydreams about what I was missing, did she start on her new tack: go get help.

So that's where we are now. Admittedly, it's been four or five years since she started pushing for me to go for help. Admittedly, I don't want help that is going to put an end to my private passion. It is simply too much a part of me to give up. The only kind of help I want is help to resolve the distance between us over "The Problem"—in other words, what I really want is to have you help Sally to learn to live with who I am and what I do as a legitimate form of sexual expression.

Although the man who wrote this letter and his wife came for therapy, it was quickly apparent that there was such an impasse between them that no real "treatment" was possible. Instead, the therapists helped this couple find a compromise solution: the husband agreed to limit his cross-dressing to not more than twice a month in return for his wife's agreeing to stop nagging him to give up an activity that was intensely gratifying and not really harming anyone else. Considerable attention was also devoted to teaching the wife how to be more assertive by expressing her own needs and feelings in the relationship without making all of her happiness dependent on her husband's moods and actions.

Source: *Authors' files.*

children), a small percentage cross-dress while cruising heterosexual bars or social clubs. Their prospective male partners may be completely unaware that a masquerade is going on and may become involved in limited varieties of sexual activity. The transvestite, for example, may perform

Many men who are cross-dressers prefer to do so in private, but these men appear to be enjoying the attention they are receiving.

fellatio on them or masturbate them manually, claiming to be genitally "indisposed" because of menstruation or some other reason. Obviously, the "truth-in-advertising" laws are not being met here, or to paraphrase a Flip Wilson line, "What you get is not exactly what you see."

Voyeurism

In our society, looking at nude or scantily clad women is an acceptable male pastime, as shown by attendance at topless bars, Las Vegas revues, and the binoculars that are trained on the Dallas Cowboy cheerleaders instead of the action on the football field. There is a corresponding phenomenon among women who can view the nude or seminude male in "women-only" clubs that feature attractive male go-go dancers or in women's magazines that show male frontal nudity. The social acceptance of such interests illustrates our earlier point about the continuum between normality and abnormality because the pleasures of "looking" can be transformed into another form of paraphilia.

The **voyeur,** or Peeping Tom, is a person who obtains sexual gratification by watching others engaging in sexual activity or by spying on them when they are undressing or nude. *Voyeur* comes from the French verb meaning "to see." Peeping Tom comes from the legendary nude ride of Lady Godiva; Tom the Tailor was the only townsman who violated Lady Godiva's request for privacy by "peeping." In **voyeurism,** "peeping" (or fantasizing about peeping) is the repeatedly preferred or exclusive means of becoming sexually aroused. While women may be "voyeuristic" in the sense of becoming sexually excited by seeing others nude or watching others in sexual acts, cases of female dependency on voyeurism for sexual response are very rare.

Voyeurism is found mainly among young men and often seems to burn out by the middle-age years. Voyeurs frequently have a great deal of trouble forming heterosexual relationships (Tollison and Adams, 1979), and many have limited amounts of heterosexual experience. In fact, being a voyeur allows such a man to avoid social and sexual interaction with women; many voyeurs confine their sexual activity to masturbation while peeping or while fantasizing about previous peeping escapades.

The voyeur prefers to peep at women who are strangers, since this confers a novelty and forbidden quality on the act (Gebhard et al., 1965). The voyeur is often most sexually excited by situations

voyeurism (voi yur' iz um) a sexual variation in which a person (voyeur) obtains sexual gratification by witnessing the sexual acts of others or by spying on other people who are undressing or are nude.

in which the risk of discovery is high, which may also explain why most voyeurs are not particularly attracted to nudist camps, burlesque shows, nude beaches, or other places where observing nudity is accepted (Tollison and Adams, 1979).

While it might be thought that peepers are harmless individuals because they avoid personal contact, this is not always the case. Some voyeurs have committed rape, burglary, arson, or other crimes (Yalom, 1960; Gebhard et al., 1965; MacNamara and Sagarin, 1977).

Exhibitionism

Exhibitionism is a condition in which a person repeatedly and preferentially exposes the sex organs to unsuspecting strangers to obtain sexual arousal. While exhibitionism is found almost exclusively in males (Stoller, 1977; American Psychiatric Association, 1987), a few cases of female exhibitionism have been reported (Evans, 1970; Hollender, Brown, and Roback, 1977; Grob, 1985). Many exhibitionists are impotent in other forms of heterosexual activity and seem to be pushed by an "uncontrollable urge" which leads to their impulsive behavior.

Exhibitionism usually starts before age 18 and has its peak occurrence in the twenties, with relatively few cases after age 40 (American Psychiatric Association, 1987.) According to one study, the typical exhibitionist is married, above average in intelligence, satisfactorily employed, and without evidence of serious emotional problems (Smukler and Schiebel, 1975). Most exhibitionists also tend to be passive, shy, and sexually inhibited men. In many instances, a particular episode of exhibitionistic behavior is triggered by a family conflict or a run-in with an authority figure (Tollison and Adams, 1979).

Although an act of exhibition usually produces sexual excitation in the performer, it is not always accompanied by erection or ejaculation even if the man masturbates while exposing himself. For some men, the primary intent of exhibitionism is to evoke shock or fear in their victims; without such a visible reaction, they derive little pleasure from the act. Apparently such men are trying to "prove" their masculinity by an unmistakable anatomical display.

More exhibitionists are caught by the police than are persons in any other category of paraphilia. The need to risk being caught may be an important ele-

" You don't often see a real silk lining, these days ... "

Source: © Punch—Spencer/Rothco.

ment of the turn-on (Stoller, 1977), leading some exhibitionists into behavior almost guaranteed to result in arrest. The exhibitionist may repeatedly "perform" at the same street corner or use a parked car (which can be easily identified) as the theater for his "act."

It is generally agreed that the exhibitionist is unlikely to rape or assault his victims (Tollison and Adams, 1979; American Psychiatric Association, 1987), but there are apparently a few exceptions to this finding (Gebhard et al., 1965; MacNamara and Sagarin, 1977). In one case, an exhibitionist who was unsatisfied with his victim's response slapped her in the face; in another instance, an exhibitionist became so enraged at being ignored by his victim that he ran after her, dragged her into an alley, and forced her to perform fellatio (Authors' files).

Just as observing nudity or sexual activity is relatively acceptable in our society under certain conditions, displaying one's body in sexually provocative garb (low-cut dresses, open-necked shirts, "see-through" blouses, tight-fitting pants) is acceptable too.

Obscene Telephone Calling

Twentieth-century technology has contributed at least one new type of paraphilia through the widespread availability of the telephone: some people repeatedly make obscene telephone calls as a means of obtaining sexual excitement.

The obscene telephone caller is almost always male and typically has major difficulties in interpersonal relationships. The relative safety and one-sided anonymity of the telephone—the caller usually knows the name and phone number of the person to whom he is speaking—allows an idealized masturbatory experience with no need to worry about a face-to-face confrontation.

There are three different types of obscene telephone calls. In the first (and probably most common), the caller boasts about himself and describes his masturbatory action in explicit detail. In the second type, the caller directly threatens his victim ("I've been watching you," "I'm going to find you"). In the third type, the caller tries to get the victim to reveal intimate details about her life. This is often done by the caller claiming to be conducting a "telephone research survey" about a subject such as women's lingerie, menstruation, or contraception. More than a few obscene telephone callers announce themselves to their victims as sex researchers.[2]

Sometimes the obscene telephone caller repeatedly calls the same victim; more often, unless the "victim" shows a willingness to stay on the phone and play his game (and a surprising number of women do), the caller moves on to other victims. The compulsive obscene phone caller must be distinguished from the adolescent who occasionally indulges in the same activity as a prank without giving much thought to the distress caused to others (MacNamara and Sagarin, 1977).

Women who have received obscene phone calls sometimes feel that they somehow mishandled the situation—an example of blaming themselves for their own victimization (Warner, 1988). The judgments of others that the woman tells about the situation, including friends, family members, police, or telephone company personnel, can also have a negative impact on the woman, putting her on the defensive about her own behavior.

The victim can report obscene phone calls to the telephone company and the police, but the chances of catching the caller are fairly low unless the call can be traced by keeping the caller on the line or the caller can be trapped into "meeting" the victim under police supervision. The recent introduction in some areas of telephones with automatic caller identification capabilities or automatic call tracing by computer at telephone company headquarters will undoubtedly be a major step forward in combating obscene phone calls, but these advances can be countered by callers who use public pay telephones for their illicit calls. Obtaining an unlisted phone number may help stop obscene telephone calls, and some women prefer to list their names in the phone book with last name and first initial only to make themselves a less-obvious target.

Sadism and Masochism

Sadism is the intentional, repeated infliction of pain or humiliation on another person to achieve sexual excitement. It is named after the Marquis de Sade (1774–1814), a French author who wrote extensively about cruelty as a means of obtaining sexual gratification. **Masochism** is a condition in which a person derives sexual arousal from being hurt or humiliated. It is named after an Austrian novelist, Leopold Baron Von Sacher-Masoch (1836–1905), whose *Venus in Furs* (1888) gave a detailed description of the pleasure of pain.

The exact incidence of sadism and masochism (sometimes abbreviated as S & M) is not known, but several surveys indicate that 5 to 10 percent of

exhibitionism a condition in which a person repeatedly and preferentially exposes the sex organs to unsuspecting strangers to obtain sexual arousal.

sadism (sā′ diz um) the intentional infliction of pain on another person to achieve sexual excitement.

masochism (mas′ ō kiz um) the need for experiencing pain and humiliation to achieve sexual gratification.

[2]We have had many complaints over the years from women who received phone calls inquiring about their sex lives from men who claimed to be representatives of the Masters & Johnson Institute. Incredibly, many of these women talked at great length to the bogus "interviewer" and had second thoughts only after the call was completed. Readers should be aware that *no* legitimate sex research is conducted by telephone surveys.

men and women describe such activities as sexually pleasurable on an occasional basis (Kinsey et al., 1953; Hunt, 1975; Barbach and Levine, 1980). One study, which was conducted by placing questionnaires in two publications and advertising in an S & M magazine, found that 72 percent of the respondents were male and 28 percent were female (Breslow, Evans, and Langley, 1985). In this group, which had a mean age of 36.2 for men and 33.4 for women, more than half were married. The men averaged 25 different sadomasochistic encounters in the year preceding the study, while the women averaged 53 different S & M encounters. The preferred types of S & M acts for both sexes are shown in Table 17.1.

Many of the people who have occasionally tried S & M have probably engaged in mild or even symbolic sadistic or masochistic behavior, with no real physical pain or violence involved. Judging from our research, sadomasochism is only infrequently a full-fledged paraphilia. Giving or receiving physical suffering is thus infrequently the preferred or exclusive means of attaining sexual excitement. And, contrary to the mistaken notion that most women are masochists, both sadism and masochism occur as paraphilias predominantly in men.

Forms of sadism run the entire gamut from "gentle," carefully controlled play-acting with a willing partner to assaultive behavior that may include torture, rape, or even lust-murder. Some sadists require an unconsenting victim to derive pleasure; others become sexually aroused with a consenting partner only if the suffering is obvious.

Similarly, masochism can range from mild versions to extremes. In the mild forms of masochism, activities like bondage (being tied up for the purpose of sexual arousal), being spanked, or being "overpowered" by physical force are mainly symbolic enactments under carefully controlled conditions with a trusted partner. At the opposite end of the spectrum are genuinely painful activities such as whippings, semistrangulation, being trampled, and self-mutilation. The masochist who desires "heavy" pain or bondage may have great difficulty in finding a cooperative partner. For this reason, some masochists resort to inflicting pain on themselves in bizarre ways, including burning themselves, hanging themselves, or searching out the services of a prostitute who will provide the necessary stimulation.

Although sadomasochistic activities in their extreme forms can be physically dangerous, most

Table 17.1   Preferences of S & M Activities for Men and Women in the S & M Subculture

Interest	Male (%) (N = 130)	Female (%) (N = 52)
Spanking	79	80
Master–slave relationships	79	76
Oral sex	77	90
Masturbation	70	73
Bondage	67	88
Humiliation	65	61
Erotic lingerie	63	88
Restraint	60	83
Anal sex	58	51
Pain	51	34
Whipping	47	39
Rubber/leather	42	42
Boots/shoes	40	49
Verbal abuse	40	51
Stringent bondage	39	54
Enemas	33	22
Torture	32	32
Golden showers	30	37
Transvestism	28	20
Petticoat punishment	25	20
Toilet activities	19	12

Source: *From Breslow, N., Evans, L., and Langley, J., "On the Prevalence and Roles of Females in the Sadomasochistic Subculture,"* Archives of Sexual Behavior *14:303–317, 1985. Reprinted by permission.*

people who try these varieties of sex do so with a commonsense understanding of the risks involved and stay within carefully predetermined limits. The allure of sadomasochistic sex, for many people, seems to lie in its erotic nature and its sense of "breaking the rules" of ordinary sexual conduct. In sharp contrast is the relative handful of people whose sexual arousal is dependent on sadomasochism, whose preoccupation with pleasure derived from giving or receiving pain becomes almost all-consuming. As one man told us, "In the heat of my sexual passions, I would stop thinking about the real world and its consequences" (*Authors' files*).

The psychological meaning of sadomasochism is unclear at present. Noting that many masochists are men who occupy positions of high status and authority (such as executives, politicians, judges, and bankers), some experts theorize that private acts of submissiveness and degradation provide the masochists with an escape valve from their rigidly controlled public lives (Leo, 1981). In an ex-

CASE STUDY

A Marriage on the Rocks

A 26-year-old female law student was referred from the student health service of her university to a sex therapist because of sexual and marital problems. She had been married for four years to a college classmate; he was attending business school at the same university.

For as long as she could remember, she had only become sexually aroused if she were treated roughly, or if she fantasized about being ravished and abused. While her husband had initially been willing to go along with her requests to provide her with rough sex, he eventually found it both tiresome and demeaning. She felt cheated by his attitude and often tried to get him angry enough to hit her. When he more or less withdrew from her sexual demands, she began picking up men at off-campus bars and having sex with them in the backseats of their cars or in grungy motel rooms as long as they would agree to spank her or slap her around as part of the sexual activity. While she was ashamed of her conduct, especially since she had hidden it carefully from her husband, she also was unwilling to stop because it was, as she put it, "the most intense, ecstatic feeling I've ever had."

Her history revealed that her first orgasm occurred at age 8 or 9 when she was being spanked by a neighbor as part of an "initiation" into a secret club. As a young teenager, she whipped herself with a leather belt while she masturbated, using her vivid imagination to construct detailed fantasy scenarios of torture and punishment that drove her to peaks of sexual excitement. By the time she got to college, she had acquired a large box full of pornographic books about spanking, whipping, and other S & M activities and noticed that unless she fanta-

sized about being sexually punished or brutalized she was unable to be orgasmic. She was particularly attracted to her husband because when they first met he showed considerable interest in her collection of erotica and seemed to enjoy acting out many of these fantasy scenes in their sex lives together.

Although she wanted to save their marriage, she was reluctant to disclose her extramarital sorties to her husband and insisted that treatment could only begin if the therapist agreed to keep this information confidential. After attending just a few therapy sessions, her husband announced that he was leaving her; they divorced shortly thereafter.

Comment: This case of masochism illustrates several points about the paraphilias. First, virtually all the paraphilias have their origins in a person's early sexual history. Second, the "victimless" paraphilias rarely create interpersonal problems if the sex partner is willing to cooperate with the required source of arousal. (For instance, a rubber fetishist may actually have a highly intimate, gratifying marriage if his wife participates enthusiastically in the wearing of appropriate paraphernalia during sex.) But when one party tires of the relatively exclusive focus on one form of sex—in the case above, the S & M component—then the relationship typically gets on much rockier terms. Third, in a true paraphilia the preference for the specific act or object is so strong that it invariably leads to repeated clandestine acts if the spouse or partner objects to it; in fact, in many cases, the person with the paraphilia will sacrifice a marriage in order to continue to pursue the pleasure-producing activity.

tension of this thesis, Baumeister (1988) suggests that masochism may be a means of escaping from a high degree of self-awareness by reorienting a person's focus to an immediate concern with body sensations. Seeking sexual pain or humiliation may also be a way of atoning for sexual pleasure for a person who was raised to believe that sex is sinful and evil. Conversely, sadists either may be seeking a means to bolster their self-esteem (by "proving" how powerful and dominant they are) or may be venting an internal hostility that they cannot discharge in other ways.

An entire industry has evolved in support of sadomasochistic sex. There are equipment supply catalogues that advertise shackles, whips, nail-studded chains, mouth gags, and other devices of torment. There are magazines with picture spreads on S & M activities and detailed how-to articles. On-line computer services often feature interactive "chat rooms" with S & M themes. In some large cities, S & M bars have opened, and "private" clubs featuring dungeons and regular "social" hours exist. Sexually explicit newspapers usually carry ads like these:

"Mistress Alexandra"—I was born to dominate men. My perfect, young sensuous body brings men to their knees. . . . Slaves desire so much to please me that they will submit to penis torture, nipple discipline, rectum stretching, enemas, whichever entertains me. I will, if necessary, enforce obedience with my cat-of-nine-tails or other dungeon devices. Mon.–Sat. Noon 'til 10 p.m. Call _____.

MISTRESS INGA'S WORLD—Come visit her dungeon room built out of 7" solid stone, equipped with everything from a whipping post to a suspension system. Call _____.

"Submissive Cherry"—Most girls grow up needing to be touched gently "like China dolls." Ever since I was a little girl I wanted to be dominated and put in my place. Now I am a big girl with a luscious bottom that needs to be spanked. I would like to be your total body slave. Reasonable Rates. Call _____.

As we pointed out in Chapter 16, sadomasochistic fantasies are very common, but most people who find such fantasies arousing have no desire to have the real-life experience.

Some S & M practitioners—particularly those who are frightened by the intensity of their impulses to hurt others or to be hurt—seek help in changing their sexual behavior. While it is relatively easy to help such people add new, nonsadomasochistic behaviors to their sexual patterns, attempts to eliminate the erotic attraction of sadomasochistic acts are usually only temporarily successful at best (Moser, 1988).

Zoophilia

Engaging in sexual contact with animals is known as **bestiality;** when the act or fantasy of sexual activity with animals is a repeatedly preferred or exclusive means of obtaining sexual excitement, it is called **zoophilia.**

Kinsey and his colleagues (1948, 1953) found that 8 percent of the adult males and about 4 percent of the adult females they studied reported sexual contact with animals. For the females, this usually involved sexual contact with household pets, while for males, this often involved farm animals such as sheep, calves, or burros (animal sex contacts were two to three times as common in rural males as in city dwellers, according to Kinsey's findings). Male bestiality generally included vaginal intercourse, while female bestiality was more likely to be limited to having the animal perform cunnilingus or masturbating a male animal. A few adult women have trained dogs to mount them and regularly engage in intercourse with their pet.

Bestiality usually involves curiosity, a desire for novelty, or a desire for sexual release when another partner is unavailable (Tollison and Adams, 1979). Zoophilia sometimes involves sadistic acts that may harm the animal.

Pedophilia

Pedophilia (literally, "love of children") describes adults whose preferred or exclusive method of achieving sexual excitement is by fantasizing or engaging in sexual activity with prepubertal children (American Psychiatric Association, 1987). While some authorities state that pedophilia occurs only in males (Stoller, 1977), there are specific cases of women having repeated sexual contact with children (Kolodny, Masters, and Johnson, 1979; Tollison and Adams, 1979; Finkelhor, 1984). About two-thirds of the victims of pedophiles are girls (most commonly between ages 8 and 11).

The pedophile, or child molester, is a complete stranger to the child in only 10.3 percent of cases (Mohr, Turner, and Jerry, 1964), showing that the popular stereotype of the child molester as a stranger who lurks around schools and playgrounds with a bag of candy is generally incorrect. In about 15 percent of reported cases, the pedophile is a relative, making the sexual contact a form of incest. The actual percentage of cases involving relatives may be higher than this, since fewer cases of this type may be reported to the police out of concern for "protecting" the family member. (Incest is discussed in more detail in

Chapter 18). Most pedophiles are heterosexual and many are married fathers; a substantial number have marital or sexual difficulties and problems with alcohol (Finkelhor, 1984; Crewdson, 1988).

However, MacNamara and Sagarin (1977) caution that it is hard to know how often pedophiles who have been caught say they were drunk as an excuse to reduce the stigma and lessen the chances of punishment: "By claiming drunkenness, a man is saying in effect that he is not the sort of person who in a sober state would become involved in an act of this type" (p. 73). Thus, he may convince others that instead of needing punishment, psychiatric care, or rehabilitation, he simply needs to stop getting drunk.

There are three distinct age groups where pedophilia is common: over age 50, in the middle-to-late thirties, and in adolescence.[3] Strictly speaking, the person who has only isolated sexual contacts with children is not a pedophile (American Psychiatric Association, 1987) and may be expressing sexual frustration, loneliness, or personal conflict.

Several different types of pedophiles have been distinguished. According to Cohen, Seghorn, and Calmas (1969), the most common is the *personally immature pedophile*—a person who has never succeeded in developing interpersonal skills and is drawn to children because he feels in control of the situation. His victims are usually not strangers and the sexual contact is not impulsive, often beginning with a drawn-out "courtship" in which he befriends the child with stories, games, and disarming companionship. In contrast, the *regressed pedophile* usually has developed strong heterosexual relationships without much difficulty; during some point in adulthood, however, he begins to develop a sense of sexual inadequacy, has problems dealing with everyday stresses, and often becomes alcoholic. His sexual contact with children is apt to be impulsive and with strangers, sometimes reflecting a sudden, uncontrollable urge that comes over him. The *aggressive pedophile* (the least-common version) often has a history of antisocial behavior and may

[3]Although there are no empirical data on this point, it is likely that the apparent age gap from 20 to 35 where pedophilia seems to diminish in prevalence is something of an illusion. The pedophile probably does temporarily give up sexual contact with children (at least in many cases) once he marries. In some instances, of course, he then goes on to molest his own children, but incest is usually not "counted" as pedophilia.

FOCUS IN BRIEF

Behavior Patterns of Child Molesters

Child Victims

4%
Both Sexes

26%
Male

70%
Female

Frequency of Behaviors, by Gender of Victim

Behavior	Percentage of Offenses	
	Male Victim	Female Victim
Vaginal contact	—	42
Anal contact	33	10
Oral–genital, by offender	41	19
Oral–genital, by victim	29	17
Fondling by offender	43	54
Fonding by victim	8	7

Source: *Modified from Erickson, Walbek, and Seely, 1988, Table III.*

feel strong hostility toward women. He is most likely to assault his victims and may cause severe physical harm.

According to psychologist Nicholas Groth (1979), who works extensively with sex offenders, 80 percent of pedophiles have a history of having been sexually abused when they were children. Exactly why these men who were themselves sexually

bestiality (bes' tē al' i tē) engaging in sexual activity with an animal.

zoophilia (zō' uh fil' ē uh) a sexual variation in which a person prefers sexual activity with animals.

pedophilia (ped ō fil' ē uh) a sexual variation in which the preferred or exclusive method of achieving sexual excitement is by fantasizing or engaging in sexual activity with children.

victimized should in turn victimize others is uncertain at present, but the tendency may relate to defects in personality development partly caused by the trauma of sexual victimization.

Finkelhor and Araji (1986) proposed a four-factor model to summarize the various theories about why some adults become sexually interested in and involved with children. The four factors they identified, which are shown in Table 17.2, are emotional congruence, sexual arousal, blockage, and disinhibition. *Emotional congruence* describes reasons an adult may have an emotional need to relate sexually to children. This may arise from an adult's arrested psychological development, which leaves the adult with childish emotional needs, or from a pedophile's generally poor self-esteem, which is improved by being able to exert power and control over a child. Another aspect of emotional congruence is a concept called "identification with the aggressor," which refers to adults who were themselves the victims of sex abuse as children. By "turning the table" when they get older, these adults become the powerful victimizer not only to gain revenge but to combat their sense of having been victimized. In the same manner, fantasies about pedophilic sex can provide a symbolic mastery of the trauma that was felt by someone who was sexually abused as a child, helping that person to purge the sense of shame and powerlessness he felt when he was unable to do anything about it.

Sexual arousal theories try to explain why an adult finds children sexually stimulating. Among the possible explanations Finkelhor and Araji cite are that many pedophiles may have had early sexual experiences that condition them to be aroused by children later, when they are adults. These experiences may have been traumatic ones, perhaps becoming more indelibly conditioned because of the psychological pain associated with the experience, or they may have been incorporated into the child's fantasy life so that the scene of sex with a child was repeatedly used during masturbation, which would tend to reinforce (strengthen) the conditioning. Early modeling by others—that is, having as a role model a person who finds children sexually arousing—may also play a part in the origins of pedophilia. Another possible explanation is misattribution of arousal, which Finkelhor and Araji (1986) explain as follows: "perhaps certain socialization experiences or subjectively felt sexual deprivation may

prompt individuals to label any emotional arousal [e.g., affection, paternal feelings] as a sexual response. Once having labeled a response as sexual, they may find ways to reinforce it through repetition and fantasy and thus come to have a much more general sexual arousal to a child in particular or children in general" (p. 152). Finkelhor and Araji also note that it is possible that as yet undiscovered biological factors may prove to be important in this area, too.

Another group of theories are put in the category called *blockage*, the phenomenon in which some adults seem to be blocked in having their sexual and emotional needs met in more conventional adult–adult sexual relationships. Such gratification and fulfillment can be blocked as a result of poor social skills in adult heterosexual relationships, anxiety about sex, unresolved Oedipal conflicts, the unavailability of or conflict with a committed partner (such as a spouse), as well as repressive social–sexual norms.

The final group of factors are called *disinhibition*. These refer to the reasons that our conventional inhibitions against sexual contact with children fail to operate in pedophilic adults. Disinhibiting factors include mental retardation, dementia, senility, psychosis, poor impulse control, drug or alcohol abuse, severe situational stress, and failure of usual incest-avoidance mechanisms (such failure can occur, for example, between a stepfather and adolescent stepdaughter; because the stepfather was not in the family while the girl was an infant and young child, the ordinary inhibitions that would exist between father and daughter did not develop over time).

While the Finkelhor–Araji four-factor model of pedophilia does not offer a precise explanation of the dynamics of each case, it does provide us with a useful way of organizing our thinking about this problem. By allowing for the interaction of various factors, both individual and societal, that contribute to this type of behavior, we may be able to get closer to an eventual solution.

There is no single pattern of sexual activity that fits all pedophiles. While fondling the child's genitals or having the child touch his own genitals may be the most common pedophilic act, there are many instances of intercourse, fellatio, and other varieties of sexual stimulation. Both incest offenders and nonfamily pedophiles have sexual penetration with their victims in more than half of the

Table 17.2   The Four-Factor Model for Explaining Pedophilia

Theory Type	Level of Explanation	
	Individual	**Social/Cultural**
Emotional congruence	Arrested development Low self-esteem Symbolic mastery of trauma Identification with aggressor Narcissistic identification	Male socialization to dominance
Sexual arousal	Arousing childhood experience Traumatic childhood sexual experience Operant conditioning Early modeling by others Misattribution of arousal Biological factors	Child pornography Erotization of children in advertising
Blockage	Oedipal conflict masturbation, Castration anxiety Fear of adult females Traumatic experience with adult sexuality Inadequate social skills Marital disturbance	Repressive norms about extramarital sex
Disinhibition	Impulse disorder Senility Alcohol abuse Psychosis Situational stress Failure of incest-avoidance mechanism	Cultural toleration Pornography Patriarchal prerogatives

Source: *From Finkelhor, D., and Araji, S., "Explanations of Pedophilia: A Four-Factor Model."* The Journal of Sex Research 22:145–161, 1986. Reprinted by permission.

cases and use physical force, such as beatings, in 89 percent of cases—a degree of violence that is notably higher than previously suspected (Stermac, Hall, and Henskens, 1989). As Erickson, Walbek, and Seely note (1988, p. 84): "Younger children appear to serve largely as impersonal masturbatory aids for the perpetrator, whereas older ones are treated more like sexual partners, albeit unwilling ones." However, they also observe that "injuries to child victims are usually the result of impulsive violence rather than deliberate plan" (p. 85).

Most societies take a dim view of pedophilia, and laws against sexual contacts between adults and children are strongly enforced. But the sexual abuse of children has become another "big business" today, with numerous instances of children being pushed into prostitution or being used for the production of pornography. Even more recently, charges of child sexual abuse have been leveled at school and day-care personnel in various parts of the country (including some women as well as men). A strong public outcry against such practices has occurred in the past few years as the dimensions of this problem have become more widely publicized.

Other Paraphilias

There are a number of other paraphilias that are relatively rare and about which fairly little is known. **Apotemnophilia** refers to persons with a sexual attraction to amputations, who may sometimes try to convince a surgeon to perform a medically unnecessary amputation on them to increase their erotic satisfaction (Money, Jobaris, and Furth, 1977). Persons with this type of paraphilia seek out sexual partners who are amputees.

apotemnophilia sexual excitement preferentially or exclusively from visualizing or touching an amputation, either in the person with this paraphilia or in his or her partner.

Coprophilia and **urophilia** refer, respectively, to sexual excitement deriving from contact with feces and urine. **Klismaphilia** is sexual excitement preferentially or exclusively resulting from the use of enemas. **Frotteurism** is sexual arousal that results from rubbing the genitals against the body of a fully clothed person in crowded situations such as subways, buses, or elevators (see the Case Study on page 463 for a fuller discussion).

Necrophilia is sexual arousal from viewing or having sexual contact with a corpse. This bizarre paraphilia has sometimes led people to remove corpses from cemeteries or seek jobs in morgues or funeral homes (Tollison and Adams, 1979).

Causes and Treatment of the Paraphilias

There is very little certainty about what causes a paraphilia. Psychoanalysts generally theorize that these conditions represent "a regression to or a fixation at an earlier level of psychosexual development resulting in a repetitive pattern of . . . sexual behavior that is not mature in its application and expression" (Sadoff, 1975, p. 1539). In other words, an individual repeats or reverts to a sexual habit arising early in life. Castration anxiety and Oedipal problems are seen as central issues. According to Robert Stoller (1975a, 1977), these conditions are all expressions of hostility in which sexual fantasies or unusual sexual acts become a means of obtaining revenge for a childhood trauma usually related to parents inhibiting their child's budding sexuality by threats or punishment. The persistent, repetitive nature of the paraphilia is caused by an inability to completely erase the underlying trauma.

Behaviorists, instead, suggest that the paraphilias begin via a process of conditioning. Nonsexual objects can become sexually arousing if they are frequently and repeatedly associated with pleasurable sexual activity (most typically, masturbation). Particular sexual acts (such as peeping, exhibiting, bestiality) that provide an especially intense erotic response (often heightened because of their "forbidden" nature) can, under certain circumstances, lead the person to prefer this sexual behavior. However, this is not usually a matter of conditioning alone: there must usually be some predisposing factor, such as difficulty forming person-to-person sexual relationships or poor self-esteem (Tollison and Adams, 1979).

The "vandalized lovemap" theory, originated by Dr. John Money, traces the development of paraphilias to the period in early childhood when the first links between sex, love, and lust are formed. In Money's view, the formation of the child's lovemap, the brain's highly personalized blueprint for what produces erotic arousal and what produces love (a concept discussed in Chapter 8), is traumatized or distorted in such a way that a paraphilic orientation is made more likely to occur (Money, 1988; Money and Lamacz, 1989). This distortion typically involves a break in the natural link between romantic love and sexual lust during childhood, so that by adulthood the individual is unable to unite "pure" love and "dirty" lust in his (or her) sexual and romantic behavior. As a result of the inability to integrate love and lust, the lust is often expressed through highly specific paraphilic behaviors that are kept completely separate and apart from affection or intimacy.

Money cites the following situations as examples in which severely negative parental reactions to signs of sexuality in a child can inadvertently tip the child's lovemap in a paraphilic direction.

1. Parents who humiliate and punish a small boy for strutting around proudly with an erect penis, boasting and showing off to the females who watch him, do not realize that they are exposing the child to the risk of developing a lovemap of exhibitionism.

2. A pedophile who sexually abuses a young boy in an involuntary relationship in which the boy has no way of escaping creates a high probability of traumatizing the boy's lovemap so that he may repeat the pedophilic behavior when he becomes an adult.

3. As we have already mentioned, many transvestites report so-called "petticoat humiliation"—being dressed in frilly girls' clothes as a form of parental punishment—during childhood. According to Money's vandalized lovemap theory, this form of negative conditioning about sex produces a tendency toward transvestism by affecting an individual's developing lovemap at a particularly vulnerable age. Money clearly acknowledges, however, that not everyone punished in this way winds up with a paraphilic lovemap.

Whatever the cause, it is apparent that paraphilics rarely seek treatment unless they are trapped into it by an arrest or discovery by a family member. Most of the time, the paraphilia produces such immense pleasure that giving it up is unthinkable (Money, 1988). Among paraphilics in therapy,

C A S E   S T U D Y

Underground Sex

Charles was 45 when he was referred for psychiatric consultation by his parole officer following his second arrest for rubbing up against a woman in the subway. According to Charles, he had a "good" sexual relationship with his wife of 15 years when he began, 10 years ago, to touch women in the subway. A typical episode would begin with his decision to go into the subway to rub against a woman, usually in her twenties. He would select the woman as he walked into the subway station, move in behind her and wait for the train to arrive. He always prepared in advance for these excursions by putting plastic wrap around his penis so as not to stain his pants after ejaculating while rubbing up against his victim. As riders moved on the train, he would follow the woman he had selected. When the doors closed, he would begin to push his penis up against her buttocks, fantasizing that they were having intercourse in a normal noncoercive manner. In about half of the episodes, he would ejaculate and then go on to work. If he failed to ejaculate, he would either give up for that day or change trains and select another victim. According to Charles, he felt guilty immediately after each episode but would soon find himself ruminating about and anticipating the next encounter. He estimated that he had done this about twice a week for the last 10 years and thus had probably rubbed up against approximately a thousand women.

During the interview, Charles expressed extreme guilt about his behavior and often cried when talking about fears that his wife or employer would find out about his second arrest. However, he had apparently never thought about how his victims felt about what he did to them.

Comment: Recurrent rubbing up against a nonconsenting person for the purpose of sexual arousal and gratification is called frotteurism. No cases of this paraphilia have ever been reported in females.

Charles's behavior is typical of that seen in this disorder. A crowded place where there is a wide selection of victims is selected (e.g., subway, sports event, mall). In such a setting the initial rubbing of the woman may not be immediately noticed; the victim usually does not protest because she is not absolutely sure what has happened. This probably explains why Charles has only been arrested twice.

As with many paraphilias, frotteurism is in a sense a substitute for authentic sexual interactions. Its appeal seems to come as much, if not more, from its illicit nature and the simultaneous feeling of risk and power as from its actual sexual content.

Source: *Spitzer et al., 1989, pp. 106–107.*

there may be deliberate attempts to lull the therapist into believing the behavior has been eradicated when it continues in full force.

The literature describing treatment approaches is fragmentary and incomplete. Traditional psychoanalysis has not appeared to be particularly effective with the paraphilias and generally requires several years in treatment. Therapy with hypnosis has also had poor results. Current interest is focused primarily on a number of behavioral techniques that include (1) *aversion therapy*, which attempts to reduce or extinguish behavior by conditioning: for example, giving electric shocks to a person while he views

coprophilia sexual excitement deriving from contact with feces.

urophilia sexual excitement deriving from contact with urine.

klismaphilia sexual excitement preferentially or exclusively resulting from the use of enemas.

frotteurism sexual arousal that results from rubbing the genitals against the body of a fully clothed person in crowded situations such as subways, buses, or elevators.

necrophilia sexual arousal from viewing or having sexual contact with a corpse.

photographs of the undesired behavior; (2) *desensitization procedures,* which neutralize the anxiety-provoking aspects of nonparaphiliac sexual situations and behavior by a process of gradual exposure; (3) *social skills training,* generally used in conjunction with either of the other approaches and aimed at improving a person's ability to form interpersonal relationships (Abel et al., 1992): for example, coaching a man in how to talk with women, how to overcome his fear of rejection, and how to express affection; (4) *orgasmic reconditioning,* wherein a person might be instructed to masturbate using his paraphilia fantasy and to switch to a more appropriate fantasy (e.g., intercourse with his wife) just at the moment of orgasm. With the reconditioning process, the person is gradually taught to become aroused by more acceptable mental imagery, and other appropriate techniques, such as fading or satiation, are used to reduce substantially the arousal of the undesirable fantasy (Schwartz and Masters, 1983).

Other behavioral techniques appear useful in some cases of paraphilia. For instance, *satiation* can be accomplished in one of two forms. *Verbal satiation* requires the patient to verbalize detailed descriptions of deviant fantasies for lengthy time periods until the fantasies stop becoming arousing and start losing their interest. *Masturbatory satiation* involves having the patient masturbate to orgasm using nondeviant sexual themes and then switch to his favorite paraphilic fantasies while he continues masturbating. The premise is that the postorgasmic masturbation to the paraphilic fantasies is rendered unarousing and even annoying (Laws and Marshall, 1991).

Another approach is through a method called Relapse Prevention (RP), which is a self-control program designed to teach paraphilics how to anticipate dangerous situations or feelings that may trigger their deviant behavior patterns and give them coping skills to handle tension and stress. Abel et al. (1992) describe the program as having two major parts: assessment and treatment. The assessment process in RP focuses on helping the individual recognize key feelings and environmental situations that are likely to precede the unwanted behavior. Treatment is designed both to help prevent lapses and to avoid letting a single slip-up snowball into a full-blown relapse. Treatment procedures include the following: (1) Identifying offense precursors—the subtle decisions and feelings that lead to high risk situations; (2) stimulus control by means such as avoiding or removing situations that put the individual at high risk; (3) programmed coping responses, which a person learns through role playing and repetitive rehearsal, that allow him to deal automatically with high risk situations; (4) escape strategies that give a paraphilic a means of physically withdrawing from risky situations; and (5) specific skills for coping with unwanted sexual urges, anger, stress, and feelings of being out of control.

Drugs called antiandrogens that drastically lower testosterone temporarily have been used in conjunction with these various forms of treatment (Money, 1987; Bradford and Pawlak, 1993). The antiandrogens lower sex drive in males and also reduce the frequency and intensity of deviant sexual fantasies. Thus, these drugs usually lessen the compulsiveness of the paraphilia, allowing concentration on counseling without as strong a distraction from paraphilic urges (Abel et al., 1992; Bradford and Pawlak, 1993a). MPA (medroxyprogesterone acetate, also known by its trade name, Depo-Provera) has been the main antiandrogen used in this country.

Despite more than a decade of experience with these treatment programs, most workers in the field are not convinced that they have a high degree of success (Laws, 1989). Furthermore, because some cases involve severe abuse, many people would prefer to lock up the sex offender than to have him out in the community in a treatment program or on parole after the treatment program has been completed.

HYPERSEXUALITY

People with extraordinarily high sex drives, which are insistent and persistent but rarely lead to more than fleeting gratification or release despite numerous sex acts with numerous partners, are considered to be **hypersexual,** or "oversexed." In women, this condition has been called **nymphomania;** in men, it is called satyriasis or **Don Juanism.**[4]

There has been little scientific study of these conditions, which often seem to be considered

hypersexual having an extraordinarily high sex drive; "over-sexed." Sometimes called **nymphomania** in women and **satyriasis** or **Don Juanism** in men.

[4]The satyrs were half-human, half-animal creatures in Greek mythology; they led carefree, lusty lives with orgies and other types of partying perpetually occupying their attention. Don Juan was a fictional character who seduced women in prodigious numbers without regard for their feelings and without obtaining real satisfaction from these brief encounters.

Treating Sex Offenders

Psychiatrist Gene Abel of Emory University has long been regarded as one of the world's innovators in treating sex offenders. He has been the only researcher in this field thus far to receive a government certificate of confidentiality that exempted him and members of his research team from any requirement to report his patients for sex crimes. This allowed him to get self-reports from sex offenders in his treatment program that were far more honest than other researchers might obtain, since the offenders knew that he wouldn't have to report parole violations to which they might confess. In addition, his treatment has been remarkably successful: 85 percent of 199 paraphiliacs were cured by his approach.

The essence of Abel's approach is a form of behavioral conditioning that teaches sex offenders how to eliminate their sexual arousal resulting from illegal behaviors. He does this by using a technique called satiation, which he contends breaks the connection between deviant sexual fantasies and orgasms.

Satiation is achieved in a somewhat controversial part of Abel's program that patients carry out in the privacy of their own homes on a daily basis. The patient must describe a nondeviant sexual fantasy scene aloud, while talking into a tape recorder at the same time as he masturbates to orgasm. (The use of the tape recorder permits Abel to check each tape to be sure that patients are following his treatment instructions.) Immediately after their orgasm occurs, they must begin describing one of their favorite paraphilic fantasies aloud into the tape recorder and they must continue masturbating while they do this. The result, of course, is that with their sexual responsivity at low ebb after the first orgasm, the paraphilic fantasy is far less effectively arousing than it would be on its own. Eventually, in fact, when this type of masturbatory reconditioning is carried out for 20 hours or so over a period of many weeks, the paraphilic fantasies that were once such a turn-on become boring and unrewarding, both physically and mentally. The result is that they get discarded, having lost their erotic appeal.

Abel uses other types of reconditioning exercises to help cut down on the erotic fulfillment offenders get from their favorite paraphilic fantasies. For instance, he may pair exciting paraphilic fantasies with thoughts of negative consequences (being caught by the police, catching AIDS) or with whiffs of a noxious odor like ammonia. Together with other standard components of treatment, such as cognitive therapy (to help counteract the distorted beliefs that supported the sex-offending behavior), such treatment methods are now becoming more widely available.

Abel has also pioneered the use of an unusual way to evaluate the effectiveness of his treatment program. Recognizing that sex offenders will often lie about their use of fantasies and even their behavior, Abel uses direct measurement of his patients' erections in response to audiotaped descriptions of paraphilic and nonparaphilic sexual acts. If he is able to consistently extinguish physical arousal in response to paraphilic stimuli, while arousal is present with nonparaphilic stimuli, Abel believes he has reached a successful outcome.

Abel's work is not perfect, of course. For one thing, there are no guarantees that a patient can't "fake" his nonresponsiveness to deviant fantasies. (He might, for instance, distract himself mentally while listening to a tape so that the fantasy doesn't really register in his mind.) Another problem is that there is no guarantee that patients who seem to be cured won't subsequently relapse. Yet, Abel says, punishing sex offenders by putting them in prison only makes their problems worse by providing them with an almost unlimited time to focus on their deviant fantasies. Isn't it more sensible, he asks, to let them participate in treatment that has a good chance of rehabilitating them rather than worsening their condition?

more of a joke than anything else. There are no absolute criteria for defining hypersexuality. Most cases studied exhibit the following central features: (1) sexual activity is an insatiable need, often interfering with other areas of everyday functioning; (2) sex is impersonal, with no emotional intimacy; and (3) despite frequent orgasms, sexual activity is generally not satisfying.

To many men, the idea of a woman with a greater sex drive than their own is somewhat threatening, so they may use the label nymphomania to preserve their own egos: the label "proves" that the woman is abnormal. Similarly, men with sexual dysfunction sometimes accuse their wives or partners of being "over-sexed" in an effort to hide their own fears and sense of inadequacy, just as some women who do not enjoy sex or object to the frequency of their husband's or partner's amorous desires accuse him of being oversexed. In our society, a man who is highly sexed and who has many sexual partners is generally (often enviously) called a "stud," while a woman with the same characteristics is often called a "nympho," which carries a negative connotation.

SEXUAL ADDICTIONS: FACT OR FAD?

In the last decade, a number of clinicians have suggested that compulsive sexual behavior is actually an addiction, like alcoholism, drug dependency, or compulsive gambling. The key features are (1) a lack of control over sexual impulses; (2) harmful consequences from the behavior, although this is characteristically denied by the addict; (3) unmanageability in other areas of life; (4) escalation in frequency over time; and (5) withdrawal symptoms with cessation (Carnes, 1983; Schwartz and Brasted, 1985; Kasl, 1989).

Earle and Crow (1989) have described the overall pattern as follows:

All of our sexually addicted patients get from sex the same things drug addicts get from drugs and alcoholics get from drinking: an intensely pleasurable high, comparable to nothing else in their lives; a means to anesthetize painful feelings such as sadness, anger, anxiety, or fear; and a way to escape the pressures and problems of daily living. The urge to escape and repeatedly recapture the high is extremely powerful, so powerful, in fact, that sex addicts, like alcoholics

and other addicts, are virtually helpless to resist it. They *want* to stop. Time and again, they *promise* to stop. They even *try* to stop, but they cannot. *(p. 13)*

Most sex addicts are men, and sexual addiction often involves unusual forms of sex, such as the paraphilias, but it can also include uncontrolled promiscuity, compulsive masturbation, homosexuality, rape, or incest, as well as more usual sexual conduct taken to extreme levels of ritualistic frequency. In the case of one couple who came to the Masters & Johnson Institute, the husband insisted on having intercourse at least four times a day with his wife; the wife gave in to his demands because he threatened to have sex with prostitutes if she didn't "take care of his needs." Carnes (1983) described another typical case: a married lawyer who had multiple affairs (often two or more at the same time), who habitually visited massage parlors for paid sex, and who also hung out in adult bookstores where he would have homosexual encounters with strangers in the private movie booths.

In women, sexual addiction is most likely to appear as "frequent dangerous sexual encounters with strangers" (Schwartz and Brasted, 1985). The sexually addicted woman, seeking a sense of personal power and self-worth, as well as an escape from pain and loneliness, uses sex as a way to feel in control and to grab for a momentary high, as described in the book *Women, Sex, and Addiction* (Kasl, 1989, p. 50):

Sexually addicted women get caught up in a cycle in which their primary source of power is sexual conquest, and they fulfill their need for tenderness and touch through the sexual act. Beneath their addiction is a burning desire to escape feelings of worthlessness and shame. These women become addicted to seduction, to the hunt, to the feeling of having made a conquest. They long to bond but they don't know how.

No matter what the specific type of sexual behavior, it is the element of compulsion and the utter disregard for consequences that make the sexual behavior an addiction. For this reason, it is important to realize that not all Peeping Toms or transvestites would be classified as sex addicts, although some of them (those most uncontrollably driven to peep or to cross-dress) would be.

Carnes (1983) identifies four core beliefs that characterize many male sex addicts' negative views of themselves. (1) I am basically a bad, unworthy person. (2) No one would love me as I am. (3) My needs are never going to be met if I have to depend on others. (4) Sex is my most important need.

Kasl (1989) identifies a similar list of core beliefs of female sex addicts. (1) I am powerless. (2) I'll always be alone or lonely. (3) I'll always be abandoned. (4) My body is shameful/defective/repulsive.

These core beliefs lead, in turn, to operational beliefs that affect how the sex addict acts. For example, the core belief that "No one would love me as I am" leads to the mistaken concept that equates sex with love: "I am loveable if someone wants me sexually" or "Having sex with someone proves I am loveable." And a woman's core belief that she'll always be abandoned is operationalized in the belief that "I won't be abandoned if I'm good at seduction."

Most treatment programs designed to help sex addicts and their partners are based on the Twelve Steps recovery program of Alcoholics Anonymous. Groups such as Sexaholics Anonymous (SA), Sex and Love Addicts Anonymous (SLAA), and Sex Addicts Anonymous (SAA)—whose addresses and telephone numbers are listed in the Appendix on page 466—provide a self-help support network. Many experts believe that professional therapy—whether individual, couple, or group—is also needed to deal with the addiction. Among the central tasks of such therapy are learning to alter the negative core beliefs that fuel the addiction, recognizing that there are alternatives for dealing with anxiety or stress besides sex, and learning improved social skills. Better social skills help recovering sex addicts reduce their loneliness and isolation by successfully forming new relationships or by repairing the damage done to pre-existent ones.

Not all experts have embraced the sexual addiction model enthusiastically, however. Levine and Troiden (1988) claim that the definitions of sexual addiction and compulsion are "conceptually flawed" and that the criteria used to diagnose these conditions are "subjective and value laden." They point out, for example, that sexual behavior that had been legitimitized in the 1970s was reclassified in the 1980s as abnormal by "medicalizing" morality—giving it a scientific-sounding label (such as "sexual addiction") and thus declaring it to be a disease. In this way, the mental health experts who advocate the sexual addiction model are functioning as "social control agents"

by enforcing conformity to the sexual standards of the majority of people in our culture. Levine and Troiden claim that this push for conformity has been a result of the health threats associated with genital herpes and AIDS, as well as with the rise of politically powerful right-wing groups morally opposed to nonrelational sex. Furthermore, Levine and Troiden note that there are no true physiologic withdrawal symptoms (e.g., diarrhea, convulsions) when the "addictive" behavior is stopped.

A related criticism of the sex addiction concept has come from Stanton Peele, author of *Love and Addiction* and a number of other books about addiction. Peele (1988, p. 16) observes:

> The more psychologists and attorneys dismiss forms of behavior as uncontrollable compulsions, the less people are held accountable for their actions—even when they have harmed others. Often, the only penalty for gross, even criminal misconduct is undergoing counseling in a treatment center. Creating a world of addictive diseases may mean creating a world in which anything is excusable, one that must inevitably slide into chaos.

Finally, it should be pointed out that no research has proved that sex addiction is a valid or distinct diagnostic category. While this certainly doesn't mean that there is no reality to the concept—since it is entirely clear that there are people desperately driven by sexual compulsions—the main issue is whether labeling certain people as sex addicts provides a useful way of diagnosing or treating problematic sexual behavior or whether it is just another type of stigmatization.

CELIBACY

A very different form of sexual behavior is **celibacy,** or abstention from sexual activity with a partner. Celibacy can be a conscious and deliberate choice, or it can be a condition dictated by circumstance (poor health, unavailable partner, etc.).

---

celibacy (sel' uh buh sē) abstention from sexual intercourse. The state of remaining unmarried, as some members of the clergy do.

In some religions, a vow of lifetime celibacy is expected of those who join the clergy.[5] Various religions also exalt the purity and holiness of celibacy for their lay members. Celibacy can also be practiced on a temporary or periodic basis, where it can allow some people to have more of a sense of control over their lives, to devote more attention to nonsexual aspects of their relationships, or to take a "rest" from the pressures of sexual interaction.

In the last decade, celibacy has become more talked about as a sexual alternative. In 1980 a book appeared entitled *The New Celibacy: Why More Men and Women Are Abstaining from Sex—And Enjoying It,* suggesting:

> Celibacy is a way of breaking boundaries, old patterns of behavior that exist between mind and body, between the self and others. It enables one to be free of sexuality in order to evaluate and experience the joys of life without sex. If the results of being celibate for some time lead to becoming sexual once again, fine; it will be bringing about an even more sexually alive state than before. If one chooses to remain celibate because other nonsexual experiences turn out to be very fascinating, then too there will be clear benefits resulting from the celibate exploration. *(Brown, 1980, p.29)*

The massive publicity surrounding the AIDS epidemic has also led a number of people to choose celibacy as the only sure means of preventing this dreaded infection. The following comments from our files point up the reasoning behind such a choice:

A 28-year-old man: As a confirmed homosexual who has no interest at all in trying to become straight, I'm caught between a rock and a hard place. I know three men whom I'd had sex with who died of AIDS. Finally I came to the realization that it's best not to be suicidal—so I've switched to a life of abstinence until there's an effective vaccine to prevent this disease.

A 22-year-old woman: I made a deliberate choice in my life that fits my psychological needs. I'd rather be a somewhat sexually frustrated woman than an AIDS statistic, and I'd rather be happy-go-lucky instead of worrying about AIDS all the time. When I get ready to marry, I'll insist that my husband-to-be join me in taking a blood test for AIDS before we have sex together, and I'll also be sure to marry someone who agrees with my belief that being faithful to each other is the only way to have safe sex in this day and age.

For people who get no pleasure out of sex, celibacy may be a welcome relief, like being released from imprisonment. Others may choose celibacy even though they enjoy sex because they find that abstinence rejuvenates their lives or creativity. Of course, some people find celibacy to be a frustrating and unfulfilling choice and may quickly reject it.

There are no health risks known to result from celibacy. As mentioned in Chapter 16, if physical sexual tensions mount to a critical level, they are discharged by orgasms during sleep. But it is clear that while celibacy is a positive sexual alternative for some people, it is not right for everyone.

PROSTITUTION[6]

Prostitution is difficult to define since humans have always used sex to obtain desirables such as food, money, valuables, promotions, and power. For practical purposes it is best to define a prostitute as a person who for immediate payment in money or valuables will engage in sexual activity with any other person, known or unknown, who meets minimal requirements as to gender, age, cleanliness, sobriety, ethnic group, and health. Some societies lack prostitution while in others, particularly urban societies, prostitution is tolerated or exists in spite of efforts to eliminate it.

The major reason for the existence and extraordinary persistence of female prostitution is that it is an easy solution to the problem faced by economically disadvantaged women. Virtually all the prostitutes in Europe and America today entered their occupation for economic reasons; they were not captured by "white slavers" or motivated by pathological sexual needs. Some needed money for an emergency or a drug habit, others drifted into it through accepting gifts and finally money from boyfriends who gradually became more numerous

---

[5]The vows are not always followed, however. In an interesting research study, it was shown that a sizable number of Catholic priests and nuns engage in sex (Halstead and Halstead, 1978).

[6]The original version of this section on prostitution was written in collaboration with Paul Gebhard, Ph.D., formerly Director of the Institute of Sex Research at Indiana University.

and less known; some were beguiled by a pimp's promises; and still others simply realized—as one said—"I was sitting on a fortune."

Here are two different stories that show how a woman finds her way into "the life."

A 19-year-old call girl: I was one of six children in a poor family with nowhere to go. I was having sex regularly by the time I was 13, and at age 17 I realized I might as well get paid for it. Everyone knew who the pimps were, and I just connected with a guy who set me up in his stable. Now I make plenty of money and help my family out. *(Authors' files)*

A 24-year-old massage parlor attendant: I was divorced at twenty-one with a kid and no talent. The only legitimate work I could find was at the minimum wage and that was the pits. A friend told me about this place, and now I get about $500 a week for locals [masturbating the male customer] and blow jobs. If a guy wants to get laid, that'll cost him $50 extra. In another couple of years I'll quit this job, but I'll have some money saved. *(Authors' files)*

Female prostitutes can be classified as house girls who work in brothels, street girls who solicit in public, B-girls who meet their clients in bars, and call girls who accept appointments, usually via telephone and often only with recommended clients. To this list, one must now add massage parlors and other not-so-subtly-disguised cover-ups such as "escort services." Many, but by no means all, have pimps with whom they share their income. The pimp provides affection and protection, arranges for bail, is available for an occasional loan, and often helps obtain customers. A pimp generally (depending on one's viewpoint) is supported by, or manages, several prostitutes.

There are no solid data on the number of female prostitutes in the United States and the length of time they spend working as prostitutes. However, data obtained over two decades (starting in 1970) in Colorado, when extended to the entire nation, suggest that about 84,000 women worked as prostitutes annually in the United States during the 1980s (Potterat et al., 1990). This estimate ignores the growing number of women who trade sex for drugs in and around crack houses (see Chapter 22), so it is probably an underestimate. Potterat and his colleagues also found that the typical pros-

titute remains in prostitution for about four to five years.

Female prostitutes seldom have orgasm in their business contacts but are normally orgasmic in private life. (But also see the "Focus in Brief" on p. 470.) Some will engage in certain sexual techniques with a customer but never with a husband or boyfriend and vice versa. Prostitution may be a regular occupation or an occasional source of extra income, but age ultimately reduces attractiveness and forces retirement.

The detrimental side of female prostitution is not the sexual activity itself but the evils that often accompany prostitution: exploitation by organized crime and/or pimps, sexually transmitted disease, drug addiction, the physical risks of "kinky" sex or assault by a customer, and the inability to save money for future needs. These evils can be eliminated or at least minimized, as in Denmark where organized prostitution and pimping are strictly prohibited and where the prostitutes are required to have regular employment in addition to their prostitution. Most nations, however, content themselves with futile attempts to wholly suppress prostitution or to confine it to specific areas.

In the era of HIV infection, considerable attention has been focused on prostitutes for several public health reasons. For one thing, many prostitutes are intravenous drug users and in this group, rates of being infected with HIV are sometimes quite high: in one survey, 26.2 percent of prostitutes in Miami and more than half of IV drug using prostitutes in New Jersey tested positive for the AIDS virus (Turner, Miller, and Moses, 1989, Table 2-8). In addition, since having sex with multiple partners is now recognized as a risk factor for acquiring HIV infection (as discussed in Chapter 20), prostitutes may be at heightened risk for becoming infected with HIV in this manner. Furthermore, since many prostitutes do not insist that their clients use condoms (Leonard et al., 1989), there is some concern that HIV-infected prostitutes may transmit this infection to both their paying customers and their own sex partners (Masters, Johnson, and Kolodny, 1988; Freund, Leonard, and Lee, 1989). This matter has not been thoroughly researched as yet, so it is not clear how serious a public health problem is involved.

While female prostitution is almost exclusively heterosexual (men paying women), male prostitu-

FOCUS IN BRIEF

A Few Facts About Female Prostitution

- Although prostitutes usually come from lower socioeconomic strata and minority populations, their clients come from all classes and racial groups (Turner, Miller, and Moses, 1989).
- For streetwalkers, approximately half of their sexual contacts are with repeat clients. A typical streetwalker works five days per week, has four to five clients a day, and usually performs oral sex on her clients; less than one-quarter of client–prostitute contacts involve penile–vaginal intercourse (Freund, Leonard, and Lee, 1989).
- Contrary to popular misconceptions, many prostitutes enjoy their sexual contacts with clients. In one survey of streetwalkers in Philadelphia, 39 percent reported enjoying intercourse all or most of the time with their customers, while 57 percent reported enjoying giving oral sex to their customers most of the time and 70 percent reported enjoying receiving oral sex from their customers all or most of the time (Savitz and Rosen, 1988).

tion is almost exclusively homosexual (men paying men). In male prostitution, there are no pimps; large-scale organization is absent; the price is much less; male brothels are extremely rare (although call boys exist); and the relationship with the customer is not the same. In the United States the male prostitute often presents himself as a "straight" (heterosexual) male who has orgasm as a result of the customer's activities and who often does nothing to the customer. Elsewhere in the world, the male prostitute is active rather than passive and seeks to provide the customer with an orgasm.

Male prostitutes are often known as "hustlers" since "hustling" (by male or female prostitutes) is the act of soliciting a prospective customer. As with female prostitutes, customers are referred to as "Johns," "scores," or "tricks." Male prostitutes

sometimes assault and rob their customers knowing that there is almost no likelihood their crime will be reported to the police. One study found that about seven out of ten young male prostitutes are only "part-timers" who continue to pursue conventional educational, vocational, and social paths while earning money by selling sex (Allen, 1980). Male prostitutes who sell their services to women are generally known as gigolos. However, gigolos primarily cater to wealthy, older women.

Prostitution exists primarily because men are willing to pay for sex. Men seek out prostitutes for a variety of reasons. Some men are temporarily without sexual partners because they are traveling or in military service; others with a physical or personality handicap cannot easily obtain partners. In some societies sex with nonprostitutes is very difficult to arrange. Some males seek special techniques that their usual partner will not provide; others do not want to invest the time, emotion, and money in an affectional relationship and simply prefer to buy physical sex. While the increase in nonmarital sexual intercourse in the United States has diminished the prevalence of prostitution, there will always be some customers such as the men just described.

SUMMARY

1. Defining abnormal behavior consists of several different components: social deviance, frequency and persistence, psychological dependence, and the behavior's effect on psychosocial functioning. Labeling something as abnormal affects how we view ourselves and others; stigmatization refers to the negative effects labeling can produce.

2. The paraphilias (previously called "sexual deviations") are conditions where sexual arousal becomes dependent on an unusual type of sexual behavior or fantasies of that behavior. The paraphilias are much more common in men than in women and often do not cause any sense of personal distress.

3. Specific examples of paraphilia include fetishism (inanimate objects), transvestism (cross-dressing), voyeurism (peeping), exhibitionism (displaying the sex organs), obscene telephone calling, sadism (pleasure from inflict-

ing pain), masochism (pleasure from experiencing pain), zoophilia (sex with animals), and pedophilia (sexual contact with children by an adult).

4. The origins of paraphilias are obscure at present. Many different treatment approaches have been tried, but none of them works in a completely satisfactory way.

5. Hypersexuality (nymphomania in females, satyriasis in males) is also of obscure origins and is difficult to define. The core features seem to be an insatiable sexual appetite, fairly impersonal sex, and low or nonexistent sexual satisfaction.

6. The validity of the concept of sexual addiction has not yet been established, but many clinicians find the addiction model useful in understanding and treating certain types of compulsive sexual behavior.

7. Celibacy, or sexual abstinence, is a viable choice for some people but an unappealing option for others.

8. Prostitution—engaging in sex for pay—takes many different forms, from the lowly street walker to the more stylish call girl. Most prostitutes choose "the life" for economic reasons. While female prostitution is almost entirely heterosexual, male prostitution is primarily homosexual. Today, the HIV epidemic puts prostitutes at especially high risk.

Thought Questions

1. Women are allowed to feel sexy when dressed in silks, lace, and frilly lingerie. Why shouldn't men be allowed to feel sexy when dressed this way? Is this prohibition strictly cultural, or is there a biological basis for it?

2. Is the term *paraphilia* appropriate to all the variations discussed in this chapter, or should some of them be regarded as true perversions? To what degree should paraphiliacs be regarded as expressing a normal variation, as handicapped or limited individuals, or as creeps, weirdos, or sinners?

3. Some researchers believe that it is usually not the experience itself which psychologically injures the molested child, but the parents' reaction to the event. What do you think? How should parents best react? What did your

parents tell you to protect you from child molesters?

4. Is the choice of a long-term and unnecessary sexual abstinence normal, or is it a reverse form of a paraphilia?

5. Why is it that paraphilias are generally so much more common in males than in females?

6. If a person is compulsively driven to commit illegal sexual acts, do you think he or she should be imprisoned or put in an outpatient treatment program?

Suggested Readings

Allen, Donald M. "Young male prostitutes: A psychosocial study," *Archives of Sexual Behavior* 9:399–426 (1980). A comprehensive report based on personal interviews with 98 male prostitutes.

Brown, Gabrielle. *The New Celibacy*. New York: McGraw-Hill, 1980. The whys and wherefores of abstinence as a sexual option.

Earle, R., and Crow, G. *Lonely All the Time*. New York: Pocket Books, 1989. A readable presentation of the many facets of sex addiction. No research is cited here, and the tone occasionally gets strident and repetitive, but the book is filled with numerous examples of compulsive sexual behavior and practical advice on how it can be overcome.

Finkelhor, David. *Child Sexual Abuse*. New York: Free Press, 1984. An outstanding, important book. Must reading for someone interested in this area.

Kasl, C. D. *Women, Sex, and Addiction*. New York: Ticknor & Fields, 1989. This book explores the nature of female sexual addictions and sexually codependent behavior, taking the view that many women use sex and romance as a high or as a way to feel in control—much like an alcoholic uses alcohol. While you may not agree totally with Kasl's main thesis, this is a thought-provoking, well-written book.

Laws, D. R. (ed.). *Relapse Prevention with Sex Offenders*. New York: Guilford Press, 1989. A detailed, state-of-the-art survey of the various means of treating sex offenders. The best single book we know of on this important topic.

Money, J., and Lamacz, M. *Vandalized Lovemaps*. Buffalo, NY: Prometheus, 1989. A study showing how lovemap distortions during childhood can lead to later paraphilias. The detailed case histories and insightful theorizing make for fascinating reading.

Sheehy, Gail. *Prostitution: Hustling in Our Wide-Open Society.* New York: Delacorte Press, 1973. A journalistic look at many sides of prostitution, including the role of the pimp.

Stoller, Robert J. "Sexual Deviations." In Beach, Frank A. (ed.), *Human Sexuality in Four Perspectives*, pp. 190–214. Baltimore: Johns Hopkins University Press, 1977. A psychoanalyst–sex researcher presents his ideas on the paraphilias concisely and readably.

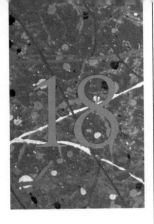

18

Coercive Sex: The Varieties of Sexual Assault

In the past few years, sexual victimization has received far more publicity than previously because of a cluster of high-visibility cases.

•Clarence Thomas's confirmation hearings before the U.S. Senate in 1991 awakened much of the nation to the issue of sexual harassment in the workplace.
•A sensitized public was further educated by the lessons of the U.S. Navy Tailhook scandal and accusations of sexual harassment made against Senator Robert Packwood in 1992 and 1993.
•The William Kennedy Smith trial involving allegations of acquaintance rape and the Iron Mike Tyson trial, pitting the world's former heavyweight boxing champion against the accusations of Desiree Washington, a teenage beauty contest contestant who he had forcibly raped, similarly opened many eyes about the legal issues involved in cases of sexual assault.
•A number of highly publicized cases involved athletes, including accusations of rape against various professional baseball players, the trials of high school athletes in Glen Ridge, New Jersey, accused of sexually assaulting a mentally retarded teenage girl, and the lacrosse players at St. John's University accused of sexually assaulting a classmate they had gotten drunk.

The photos (clockwise, from left) show Anita Harris and Clarence Thomas at Senate confirmation hearings in 1991 where allegations of sexual harassment were raised, and Woody Allen and Mia Farrow, who were embroiled in court proceedings over child sexual abuse.

- The infamous Spur Posse in California—teenage boys from an affluent community who competed with one another to have sex with the most girls, sometimes resorting to raping girls as young as age 10 in order to "score"—were ridiculed in the press and on national TV, but may have been just a symptom of the attitudes in our society that condone male sexual aggressiveness under the "boys will be boys" banner that one parent invoked in explaining their behavior.

- The Amy Fischer–Joey Buttafuoco story seemed like a long-running public soap opera. Eventually, this case of shootings, statutory rape, prostitution, and pimping was turned into three made-for-TV movies as well as several books.

- Finally, in one of the most startling examples of all, in 1993, a women who claimed to have been raped by her husband cut off his penis with a knife. (His penis was reattached surgically and he was acquitted on charges of rape).

All these cases riveted the national attention on various types of sexual assault in a concentrated way rarely seen previously.

These cases only represent the most visible tip of the iceberg, however. The FBI reports that between 1972 and 1991, there was a 128 percent increase in the number of reported rapes in the United States, with an estimated 1.5 million female survivors of forcible rape or forcible rape attempts in this country alone (Buchwald, Fletcher, and Roth, 1993). The FBI itself admits that these statistics are very conservative because rape remains one of the most underreported crimes of all (Koss, 1992). Thus, the fact that according to the National Crime Victimization Survey there are some 469 rapes each day of the year—1 rape every 3.5 minutes—as well as more than twice as many instances of child sexual abuse (Buchwald, Fletcher, and Roth, 1993) just begins to suggest the magnitude of the problem our nation faces. Add to this the tens of thousands of women who are sexually harassed at work or at school, the teenagers pushed into prostitution, and the wives who are beaten if they are not ready for sex when their husbands demand it, and the true dimensions of coercive sex become even more apparent. This chapter provides some historical, legal, social, and psychological perspectives about coercive sex. Additional discussion of certain legal aspects of these topics can be found in Chapter 23.

RAPE

Rape is an emotion-laden subject surrounded by myths and misunderstandings. While it is defined as a sexual act, it is primarily an expression of violence, anger, or power. Its victims can be male or female, very young or very old, rich, poor, mentally retarded, disabled, or able-bodied. The victimizers—those who rape—are also a diverse group that defies neat classification or description.

Historical Perspectives

The word *rape* comes from a Latin term (*rapere*) that means to steal, seize, or carry away (Warner, 1980). In ancient times, rape was one way to procure a wife: a man simply overpowered a desirable woman and then brought her into his tribe. The man then had to protect his property and his honor by preventing others from seizing or raping his wife. This appears to have provided the origins for the first laws against rape in which rape was viewed as a crime against property or honor but not against women (Brownmiller, 1975).

According to the Code of Hammurabi, a set of laws established in Babylonia about 4000 years ago, a man who raped a betrothed virgin was to be put to death. If a man raped a married woman, however, both the rapist and his victim were regarded as guilty and were executed by drowning. A similar distinction with a slightly different twist was found in biblical injunctions about rape (Deuteronomy 22:22–28): a married woman who was raped was seen as a willing accomplice, so she and her rapist were killed; a virgin was considered guilty only if she was raped in the city, since it was assumed that her screams would have led to her rescue. In contrast, a virgin who was raped in a field outside the city walls was spared, since no one could hear her screaming. If she was betrothed to someone, her rapist was stoned to death—if not, he

had to marry her (whether or not she liked this arrangement didn't seem to matter).

Later laws against rape continued to specify varying circumstances by which rape was judged as more or less serious. Penalties were higher if the woman was a virgin or of high social class. Under William the Conqueror (1035–1087), a man who raped a virgin of high social standing was punished by castration and blinding. Guilt, however, was determined by trial by combat, so unless the victim had a champion willing to risk his life by fighting the accused rapist, she had no way of establishing her case.

By the twelfth century, jury trials replaced combat as a means of determining guilt or innocence. Yet all were not equal in the eyes of the law: a nobleman or knight could easily blame a rape he committed on one of his men and save his vision and chances for fatherhood. At the end of the thirteenth century, two additional changes appeared in English law concerning rape: the distinction between raping a virgin or a married woman was dropped, and the old custom of penitence through marriage was permanently banned (Brownmiller, 1975). The essential elements of defining rape and its punishment had fallen into place. Seven centuries later, not too many changes have been made.

Despite the legal system, rape has not always been regarded as bad. In wartime, from thousands of years ago until today, victorious soldiers have raped enemy women. In literature, rape has sometimes been presented in heroic terms, as Ayn Rand did in *The Fountainhead*. In society, rape has often been practically defined in terms of the social positions of victim and victimizer: in the 1940s and 1950s, for example, a white male was rarely charged with raping a black woman in the South, but a black male charged with raping a white woman was dealt with swiftly and harshly. Even today, in most jurisdictions, a man is unlikely to be charged with raping a prostitute, and forced intercourse between husband and wife does not "count" as rape in the majority of American states.

The last decade and a half have seen a great increase in public awareness of rape. The women's movement played a major role in this process, raising issues and demanding improvements in services to rape victims. Today, almost all metropolitan police departments have specially trained teams (including policewomen) to work with rape victims; there are thousands of rape hotlines and rape crisis centers for emergency and long-term assistance; many hospital emergency rooms have developed special procedures for treating rape victims; and trial procedures and laws about rape have been changed in important ways.

Myths About Rape

The most devastating myths about rape have cast women in the role of being responsible for the rapist's act (Gager and Schurr, 1976; Metzger, 1976). According to this view, women secretly "want" to be raped and really enjoy the experience. This nonsensical notion has led at least one rapist to give his name and phone number to his victim so she could "get together" with him again. His stupidity led to his immediate arrest. Lurking beneath the surface of this myth are some commonly held misconceptions: women find overpowering men irresistible; women's rape fantasies indicate a real-life sexual desire; and women dress and act provocatively to "turn on" men, who somehow are the hapless victims of their own reactions to this deliberate provocation.

Closely allied to this view of the woman as instigator is the idea that "she was asking for it, and she got what she deserved." Susan Brownmiller (1975) comments on this "explanation" of rape:

> The popularity of the belief that a woman seduces or "cock-teases" a man into rape, or precipitates a rape by incautious behavior, is part of the smoke screen that men throw up to obscure their actions. The insecurity of women runs so deep that many, possibly most, rape victims agonize afterward in an effort to uncover what it was in their behavior, their manner, their dress that triggered this awful act against them. (pp. 312–313)

Most research shows that rapists look for targets they see as vulnerable (e.g., women walking by themselves, appearing unfamiliar with where they are) rather than women who are dressed in a certain way or who have a particular manner of appearance (Grossman and Sutherland, 1982/83). The "provocation" myth loses its believability when it is recognized that many rape victims are elderly women or young children (Burgess et al., 1978; Davis and Brody, 1979). Furthermore, it is a little

like believing people should dress in old, worn-out clothes in order to prevent being mugged, thus misplacing responsibility from the criminal to the victim.

Despite this, the victim is still frequently "blamed" for being raped. This view is based not only on her possible role as instigator but on the incorrect notion that a woman who resists *cannot* be raped. According to two old saws: "A girl can run faster with her skirts up than a man can with his pants down" and "You can't thread a moving needle." These bits of attempted "commonsense" humor completely overlook the terror of the rape victim, her fear of physical injury, mutilation, and death, and her shock and disbelief. Even when no weapon is in view, can a woman be certain that one is not hidden? In rape situations, many women hope that by seeming to cooperate with their assailant, they can avoid injury and get it over with more quickly (Burgess and Holmstrom, 1976). But, in an irony of our legal system, this intelligent way of coping with a violent assault is penalized: the case against her attacker depends in part on "proving" her physical resistance by cuts, bruises, and other signs that she put up a struggle. No such evidence is required to "prove" that a robbery occurred.

The last myth we mention here (although there are many others) is the idea that women frequently make false accusations of rape. While there have certainly been cases where a false cry of rape was made for some ulterior motive, the belief that most women are capable of such an act is the ultimate view of women as emotional, vengeful "bitches." Yet the law in some states quietly upholds this view: unlike cases of assault or robbery, where the victim's word and evidence are enough to prove that a crime occurred, in rape cases another person's testimony or evidence—called *corroboration*—is required as proof (Gager and Schurr, 1976; Lasater, 1980).

Rape Patterns

Forcible rape is far and away the most common form of rape reported. Here, the act of penile penetration is achieved by force or the threat of force. Several subcategories of forcible rape can be distinguished, although most of these are not legally defined terms. The *solo rape* is carried out by one man, acting alone. The *pair rape* or *gang rape*—a particularly terrifying form of rape—involves either two men or a group of men, sometimes with a female accomplice, who take turns raping the victim. An apparently rare form of gang rape involves several women raping a man (Groth, 1979; Sarrel, 1980; Sarrel and Masters, 1982). In another, more common version, a group of men rape another man rectally. This rape of men by men is infrequent among homosexuals and usually involves heterosexual men in prison (Groth, 1979; Braen, 1980). Two other types of forcible rape, *date rape* and *mate rape*, are distinctive enough that we will discuss them in greater detail.

Date and Acquaintance Rape

A survey of acquaintance rape on 32 college campuses conducted by *Ms.* magazine showed that one out of ten women had been raped in the previous year, and one in six had been the victim of an attempted rape (Warshaw, 1988). Fifty-seven percent of the actual rapes occurred on dates, and in 84 percent of the cases, the victims knew their assailant. Other studies suggest that women are four times more likely to be raped by someone they know than by a stranger (Parrot and Bechofer, 1991; Koss, 1992).

The following account given by a 21-year-old woman is typical of the experience:

> I was out on my second date with Jerry and we'd been drinking and dancing and having fun. I agreed to go back to his apartment with two other couples. We drank some more, and the other people left, and we were messing around a little on his bed. When I said I had to get home, it was late, he got mad and pushed me down and raped me. I wasn't really hurt, but I was forced to do something I didn't want to. But I couldn't see that anything would be gained by reporting it. *(Authors' files)*

Other statistics show a comparable incidence of date rape. For example, a survey of 500 students at Brown University conducted in 1984 found that 16 percent of the women had been raped either by men they knew or by men they were dating, and 11 percent of the men surveyed admitted that they had forced a woman to have intercourse (Sherman, 1985). A more encompassing survey that included more than 7000 students at 35 colleges showed that 1 out of 16 women had been a victim of date rape (Sweet, 1985). An interview survey at the University of South Dakota found that 1 out of 5 women had been physically forced by a man to have sexual intercourse on a date, with these findings being quite similar to those obtained in studies at Kent State University, the University of Rhode Island, and St. Cloud State University (*American Medical News*, June 21, 1985, p. 8).

Although there is no significant difference among college men and women in rates of inflicting or suffering from *physical* abuse in dating relationships, men inflict four times as much sexual abuse as women do according to one study (Burke, Stets, and Pirog-Good, 1988). Another finding of particular interest from this same source is that *less masculine* males were more likely to be sexually abusive toward their dating partner(s). In other words, contrary to the macho myths, "masculine" men are not the most likely to abuse women sexually.

Most cases of date rape are never reported to the police. In fact, many of the women who have been victimized are not even sure that a crime has been committed. One reason for this is that weapons are almost never employed in date rape, and direct verbal threats are frequently not made. In addition, it's hard for many women to define what's happened as rape, since the stereotyped image of a rapist is a stranger wearing a stocking mask and grabbing a woman as she walks by a dark alley. Victims of date rape also tend to put a lot of the responsibility for what happened on their own shoulders, questioning their own judgment, rather than placing the blame where it belongs—on the rapist.

If any common denominator among victims of date rape exists, it may be a lack of sophistication about men and dating. College women may be especially vulnerable to date rape because they are away from home—often for the first time—and may be uncertain of how to handle themselves in new situations. They may also be too trusting of males they are dating, assuming almost automatically that a fellow student wouldn't want to hurt or exploit them. This is particularly evident in cases where a college woman goes to her date's room and fails to recognize the sexual intentions likely to be present in such a situation.

Men Who Commit Date Rape

There has not been much research on men who commit date rape. Some seem to be driven by a traditional view of the male's role as sexual aggressor,

RESEARCH SPOTLIGHT

Rape of Men by Women

To fully examine the spectrum of coercive sex, we must acknowledge that men can be rape victims too. That males can be raped by other males—in the form of anal rape—has been reported as occurring in community settings (Groth and Burgess, 1980) and, more commonly, in prisons (Sagarin, 1976; Money, 1981; Scacco, 1982). Until very recently, however, not many realized that men could actually be raped by women.

Sarrel and Masters (1982) documented 11 cases in which men were sexually assaulted by women, including a number of cases in which the men were forced to have intercourse by the female rapists. Here are brief descriptions of several of these cases:

- A 23-year-old medical student was tied up and then forced to have intercourse with a woman who threatened him with a scalpel.
- A 37-year-old white married man was forced to have intercourse by two black women who accosted him at gunpoint. The man was terrified during the entire experience.
- A 27-year-old truck driver who fell asleep in a motel with a woman he had just met in a bar awoke to find himself gagged, blindfolded, and tied to the bed. He was forced to have intercourse with four different women who threatened him with castration if he didn't perform properly—he could feel the blade of the knife being held against his genitals—and he was held captive and repeatedly assaulted for more than 24 hours.

In many ways, of course, these cases mirror the circumstances in which women are raped by men. One of the more notable findings to emerge from these case examples is that even though these males were extremely frightened—indeed, in a near panic state—they were still sexually responsive. This may shed some light on the fact that some women who are raped respond with signs of physical sexual arousal (e.g., vaginal lubrication, orgasm). In either case, the physical response does not mean the victim is enjoying the experience: yet victims who respond physically during a sexual assault are apt to feel tremendous guilt.

Another similarity between male and female rape victims is that the males had a postrape trauma reaction, and most of them also developed sexual difficulties after the traumatic sexual experience. Understandably, perhaps, given the lack of information on this type of rape, most of these victims also saw themselves as abnormal for responding in the circumstances of assault and thought of themselves as inadequate in their masculinity.

Because men who have been raped by women may be embarassed by what happened to them or convinced that the police won't believe their stories, few cases of this type of violent crime are ever reported. While some of these men seek treatment for ensuing sexual problems, others harbor their feelings of guilt and anguish, which is why we believe it is important for the public to become more aware of this form of sexual assault.

---

which leads them to misinterpret cues (even direct, verbal statements) from the woman. Others are simply intent on "scoring," believing that male–female relations are a sort of game and that the woman "owes" them sex. These comments from three men we've interviewed who all had committed date rape on at least three occasions provide some additional information into the variety of motivations and reasoning that can be operating.

A 22-year-old man: I never thought of what happened as rape. We were just going out, having fun, and when it came to sex these girls were just a little inhibited—and I helped them loosen up and relax. I really think they all liked it, too—but it was no big deal. I'm no criminal.

A 19-year-old man: Before we went out, I had already decided I was going to nail her. I brought some pot along for us, and once she started

smoking a joint with me, I knew it was a done deed. When she told me to stop, I was already turned on and didn't care much about her. But I never thought that I was raping her—it wasn't like I dragged her into my room from off the street.

A 20-year-old man: I guess that I probably forced five or six women into having sex with me on dates. While I was doing it, I never saw it as rape. It was just the game that males and females play, and I was the winner. When Sara reported me to the campus cops, I laughed about it at first. After all, how could she say that I raped her after the way she'd been flirting with me in the library? How could she prove anything, you know? But now I realize that what I did was wrong, even though it didn't feel wrong to me then. It just made me feel strong and pow-

erful. I never really thought about how the girls felt, though. I guess I sort of thought it was a game for them, too.

Many males make the assumption that they have never raped a female because they mistakenly view rape as a physically violent act committed by a stranger (Parrot, 1988). They are often so caught up in their misperception that they don't realize that coercing a partner into sexual intercourse is a crime, no matter what the circumstances. Some of these males who are certain they have never committed rape are quick to admit that they have tricked a date into having sex by getting her drunk, or by getting her high on drugs, or by putting her in a frightening situation. Some say that they have "scored" with a girl by getting "a little" rough with her (e.g., twisting her arm or holding her down on the bed), which they do not consider to be violence.

Some managed to have sex with a date by threatening her verbally ("You led me on—now it's time to pay up"). All these males in the examples above have committed rape even though they may not realize it.

According to a survey of almost 3000 college men by *Ms.* magazine, these males had committed 187 rapes and 157 attempted rapes in the preceding year (Warshaw, 1988). In fact, 1 in 12 had raped a woman (or attempted to) at some point since age 14. While these findings are alarming, they are not surprising. After all, males in our society have been socialized to view sex as a kind of contest in which they win by "scoring" even if their partner isn't particularly involved or satisfied. In fact, in the scripted role of "macho" male—that is, the role predominating in our society (Mosher and Tomkins, 1988)—violence and aggression are clearly protrayed as manly and callous sexual attitudes are the norm.

In the *Ms.* survey mentioned above, 85 percent of the men who had committed rapes knew the women they victimized, and more than half of the sexual assaults occurred during dates. Furthermore, 84 percent of the men who had committed rape stated unequivocally that what they did was *not* rape. What accounts for this perception gap—not recognizing rape as rape—is not fully understood at present but at least partly depends on the male myths about rape that we discussed previously (see p. 477 and Garrett-Gooding and Senter, 1987; Margolin, Miller, and Moran, 1989). Combined with this perception gap is the male attitude that a date should know she's getting into a potential sexual situation, so she must be consenting in advance to sex—otherwise she wouldn't be there. This is borne out by a number of studies showing that males find more sexual intent in social situations than females do (Abbey and Melbey, 1986; Muehlenhard and Linton, 1987). In addition, both males and females tend to see date rape as a situation in which the female fails to set limits, rather than a situation in which the male becomes aggressive (Bridges and McGrail, 1989).

Another study of college males reveals the underpinnings of male sexual aggression on campuses today. Greendlinger and Byrne (1987) found that 91 percent of male college undergraduates agreed with the statement, "I like to dominate a woman," while 86 percent agreed that "I enjoy the conquest part of sex," and 84 percent agreed "Some women look like they're just asking to be raped." These Neanderthal attitudes do not tell the whole

story, however, because attitudes don't automatically translate into behavior.

There are certainly instances in which the male believes he is talking his partner into consenting sexual activity, but the female's consent comes only because she feels frightened or threatened (Estrich, 1987; Gordon and Riger, 1989). For instance, a normally unintimidating guy who's acting a little tipsy from three or four tequilas may think he's sweet-talking his date into a state of lustful abandon, while she feels terribly intimidated by his physical size, his bravado, and his iron-clad grip on her wrist. If she gives in and has sex with him, is this date rape or consensual sex?

Consider another example with somewhat different circumstances: a couple dated regularly during their sophomore year of college, with passionate sex a prominent part of their relationship. When they came back to school for their junior year, their relationship cooled down a little. They went to the Homecoming Dance together and returned to the male's apartment after the dance, and as they sat around listening to music, the woman agreed she wanted to have sex. Once in bed, however, the woman changed her mind and told her date to stop. He thought she was joking, and before she could say anything more—since she wasn't resisting physically—he was inside her. She decided not to push him off, but she felt used.

As these examples show, there may be murky circumstances in certain situations involving sexual behavior. It's no fairer to expect the inebriated male in the first example above to be able to read the intimidation in his date's mind than it is to expect her to realize that he's actually a nice guy who wouldn't dream of hurting her. And in the second example, it's easy to see where the confusion arose. Deciding who's at fault in this case is not such an easy matter; in fact, some observers would feel that both partners played a part in the confusion. (Advice for both sexes on how to reduce such confusion and handle situations like this effectively is given later in this chapter.)

One of the primary problems of date rape is that many males believe the idea that women are so coy and illogical that "when they say no they mean maybe, and when they say maybe they mean yes." Thus, the male rejects his date's messages about sex partly because he wants to interpret them his way, rather than in their literal meaning. Furthermore, the male is often primed into forcing himself sexually on his date through the prior use of alcohol, which lowers his ordinary social inhibitions and may increase his sense of urgency to "score" and fulfill his "macho" self-image without recognizing that what he is doing is actually a form of criminal behavior. In fact, in a study of 71 college males who had committed date rape, it was found that 76 percent attempted to seduce the woman by using alcohol and/or marijuana, whereas only 23 percent of a control group of age-matched college men who had never raped had tried to seduce their dates in the same way.

Of particular interest in date rape research is a study that disproves the notion that males who coerce their dates into intercourse do so because they are otherwise unable to find willing sex partners. In 1985, sociologist Eugene Kanin found that men who admitted to having committed date rape actually had averaged almost twice as much heterosexual activity over the year preceding their rape as an age-matched group of controls. Kanin concluded that date rapes are largely a result of a process of sexual socialization in which some males develop an exaggerated sexual impulse and put a premium on attaining sexual "conquest." If they find themselves aroused by noncoital sexual involvement with a date but frustrated in their ultimate goal of "scoring," their high expectancy of success drives them to disregard the female's limit setting as not genuinely meant, so they push on by any means available to attain their goal without regard for their date's feelings or wishes. Thus, in a sense the date-rapist behaves as he does to "prove" how good he is at getting what he wants.

In addition, some men think they've paid for sex by picking up the tab on a date: they see women who refuse their sexual advances as backing down from their side of the bargain.

Gang Acquaintance Rapes

Not all acquaintance rapes are committed by a single assailant. Gang acquaintance rapes, sometimes called party rapes because they often occur at parties, are a little spoken of but relatively frequent form of sexual assault, especially on college campuses across the country.

One typical setting for a campus gang acquaintance rape is a fraternity party where a good deal of drinking has already taken place. The men involved don't usually think of it as rape; to them, they've found a "nympho" who knew exactly what she was getting into. The same group spirit that values fraternal loyalty often debases women, although, fortunately, some national fraternities have organized educational programs for their members in order to cut down on this problem. Pi Kappa Phi has put out a poster that proclaims, under a scene in a painting of soldiers raping women, "TODAY'S GREEKS CALL IT DATE RAPE. Just a reminder from Pi Kappa Phi. Against her will is against the law."

Another trouble spot for campus gang acquaintance rapes involves members of athletic teams who are often housed together in a "jock" dormitory. One university president, asking to remain anonymous, explained it this way to us:

> Star athletes get special treatment on many college campuses. In fact, they're sometimes treated like they're gods. As a result, they get a warped sense of what's right and wrong, and quickly come to think of themselves as invincible. It's no wonder, then, that they think they don't have to take "no" as an answer in sexual situations, and that they sometimes assume that all college coeds are team groupies—sort of group property just hanging around for their personal use.

In these sorts of situations, the female is often at a major disadvantage in pressing charges with the university or with local law enforcement agencies. This is partly because the teammates typically band together in an "it's her word against ours" defense and partly because school officials may bring pressure on the victim to drop her charges (Carmody, 1989).

Males as Date Rape Victims

There is another, generally overlooked, side to the date/acquaintance rape picture. Males are sometimes the victims, even though this pattern doesn't seem to fit prevailing stereotypes that are applied to this crime. While instances in which *physical* force used by females against males to obtain sex are probably few in number, it is not unusual to find that a male has been victimized by female coercion or threats, as shown in the following example:

> Larry was a sophomore at a large Midwestern university. He was not very sexually experienced, which stemmed in large part from his strong religious up-bringing. In fact, he believed that it was wrong for him to have intercourse with anyone unless they were on the verge of marrying, so he was still a virgin. Although he

Another View of Date Rape

Virtually every college freshman orientation program now features seminars about personal safety, including frank and often frightening discussions about the frequency of date and acquaintance rape on campuses today. While everyone agrees that coercive sex is deplorable, some observers have a different view of its actual prevalence and consider all the attention given to this topic a matter of near hysteria.

Katie Roiphe, a recent college graduate herself, has written a thought-provoking and controversial book, *The Morning After: Sex, Fear, and Feminism on Campus* (1993) challenging the current perception that date rape is so commonplace that one in four women are victims of such abuse. Instead, she says that the "rape crisis movement" merely recycles an old model of sexuality in which women are portrayed as passive, weak, even silent individuals who are unable to protect themselves from harm, and that many cases of date rape are in fact women who consented to sex and later changed their minds.

Roiphe is concerned that because the current definitions of coercive sex include such a wide spectrum, from emotional pressure to sexual harassment, too wide a net is cast to really catch those who commit contemptible acts. For instance, she doesn't think it's right to include someone glancing down your shirt in a definition of a sexual harasser, noting that "not nice is a different thing than against the rules . . . [against] the law . . . [or] oppressing women" (p. 99). In her version of sexual reality, in order to "find wanted sexual attention, you have to give and receive a certain amount of unwanted sexual attention" (p. 87).

Roiphe believes that every generation has "stock plots" people turn to for self-definition and direction, and she deplores her generation's plot. Why? She says it is one of a sexually harassed sensitive female "pinched, leered at, assaulted daily by sexual advances, encroached upon, kept down . . . by harsh reality" (p. 172). Males have all the power in that scenario, which makes them implicitly dangerous. They are suspect since the

male gender is the source of sexual harassment and sexual assault (see pp. 87–100). Roiphe disagrees with the notion that being male gives anyone the right to bypass social convention, to grab something he wants and run with it, and points out that most college men are not power-grabbers or potential date rapists, although you wouldn't know it from reading some of the literature of the rape crisis movement.

To Roiphe, the problem with defining every man as a potential date rapist is that very assumption of guilt. It makes it hard for the college student to balance a natural, acceptable, normal drive for sexual experience against the drive to avoid sexual contact because of fear. It creates an aura of generalized anxiety about all things sexual. She is troubled by the current emphasis on explicit mutual consent—the "explicit yes" (p. 62)—in sexual matters because in her mind this implies that "women, like children, have trouble communicating what they want" (p. 62) and that unspoken, subtler forms of consent become unworkable. "In this era of Just Say No and No Means No, we don't have many words for embracing experience. Now instead of liberation and libido, the emphasis is on trauma and disease. . . . The possibility of adventure is clouded by the specter of illness. It's a difficult backdrop for conducting one's youth" (p. 12). And since the end of adolescence and the beginning of young adulthood tends to be the time in which our self-definitions move from the realm of intellectual "what ifs" and "maybes" to behavioral realities, sexual experimentation is a big part of that transition. But today, Roiphe says, it is hard to explore those aspects of self without anxiety. It is not a rape crisis per se that our campuses are facing but a crisis that is deeper, one about sexual identity which pushes women into passive roles. "The idea that women can't withstand verbal or emotional pressure infantalizes them . . . allowing verbal coercion to constitute rape is a sign of tolerance toward the . . . stance of passivity" (pp. 67–68). What do you think?

dated only sporadically, he didn't give it much thought, since his main focus was on his studies. He had been dating Sandra every few weeks during the fall semester and had just gotten comfortable with her when he found himself in a puzzling situation. One night in her dorm room, Sandra began pushing him to have sex, and when he told her no, she began taunting him with accusations that he was gay. The more he protested, the more she insisted that he "prove" he wasn't gay. Finally, he gave in after she threatened to tell all of his friends that he was really a closet homosexual. *(Authors' files)*

Males who have been the victims of date or acquaintance rape are even less likely than female victims to report the crime to campus authorities or to the police due to embarrassment (Struckman-Johnson and Struckman-Johnson, 1994). Internalizing the trauma, and being unable to even discuss it with friends, can lead some male victims to severe bouts of depression. This is even more true when the male has been victimized by another male, or a group of males, in a homosexual rape (Braen, 1980a). And any male rape victim is apt to find it difficult if he does report the crime, because most law enforcement officers have such a stereotyped view of masculinity that they find it hard to believe that the victim wasn't in some way a willing participant (Grossman and Sutherland, 1982/83).

Preventing Date Rape: The Female Perspective

There are many steps that can be taken to reduce the chances of being victimized by date or acquaintance rape. However, it is important to remember that since some acquaintance rapes are largely unavoidable, it is wrong to blame yourself for the rape if you are—or have been—victimized.

These suggestions apply to males as well as females, since they too can be sexually assaulted by someone they know. (Given the fact that females are victimized far more often than males, though, this discussion is written stylistically from the female's point of view.)

1. *Communicate your sexual limits directly to your partner.* It's your right to be uninterested in sex, or to choose not to have sexual intercourse, but unless you convey this clearly to your partner, he may be uncertain of what your desires are. Being or acting uncertain in this situation isn't feminine, mysterious, or playful: such behavior only asks your partner to guess about what

you want, and he may not make the right guess.

2. *Avoid people who treat you badly or try to control you.* Rape counselors agree that certain categories of men are more likely to force themselves sexually on women. The following danger signs can alert you to avoid being alone with a man:
   - He's bully who throws his weight around.
   - He enjoys being cruel to people, taunting them, insulting them, or frightening them.
   - He's reckless and inconsiderate.
   - He's physically violent in any way.
   - He drinks a lot or uses illegal drugs.
   - He's prone to outbursts of anger or jealousy, especially if he doesn't get his way.
   - He frequently berates women and treats them like sex objects.
   - He disregards your limits, whether related to sex, drinking, curfews, or any other areas.
   - He thinks laws are made to be broken (whether he shows this by cheating, running red lights, or ripping off the phone company).

3. *Sobriety and a clear head are your allies when it comes to your personal safety.* As Warshaw (1988, p. 155) notes, "Your best chance for staying in control is not to lose touch with what's happening around you." Many people who are planning to rape a date go about it by trying to ply them with alcohol or other drugs. They feel that it will make you "less inhibited," but the reality is that being drunk, tipsy, or stoned simply sets you up to be victimized. Your reaction time is slowed, your ability to communicate is reduced, and you may wind up inadvertently sending the wrong signal to your partner—a signal that you are acquiescing to his or her seduction plan.

4. *Steer clear of places that give a would-be rapist the advantage.* Experts agree that certain situations are obvious red flags. These include isolated spots in the countryside, deserted beaches at night, or going alone to the apartment of someone you don't know very well. In fact, most acquaintance rapes occur in the victim's or assailant's home (Parrot, 1988). (If you invite a date to come up to your apartment or home and there's no one else there, he may take it as an automatic invitation for sex.) If you're in any of these situations and you see signs of danger brewing, get away as fast as you can.

5. *Plan your defense BEFORE any problems develop.* Defense can take many forms, from attending a woman's self-defense course (now offered on many campuses and at most YWCAs) to being sure you have money with you to pay for cab fare or bus fare if you need to leave your date abruptly. Defense also includes planning where you'll be and how to get away if necessary.

6. Don't give mixed messages about sex. Here's some solid advice from Dr. Andrea Parrot, a Cornell University expert on date rape:

> When you have decided what you want sexually, you must communicate that clearly, giving the same message with your words and your body language. If you really don't want to have sex with him, don't tell him that you just want to be friends while you let him unbutton your blouse. Don't tell him that you don't want to have sex because you don't have any means of birth control; he may have a condom in his wallet. If you don't want to have sex, make that clear with time parameters, such as, "I don't go to bed on the first date," or "I want to wait until marriage." If you say, "I don't want to have sex right now," he may think that five minutes later will be all right. *(Parrot, 1988, p. 91)*

7. *Most of all, trust your instincts.* If you're getting bad vibrations from a man on your first date—if he's pawing you without regard to your objections, or if he's acting too "macho" or wild for your taste—don't wait to see what will develop because you may be very unpleasantly surprised. Being a little cautious—ending the evening with whatever excuse you can muster or joining a group of friends where you can be certain you'll be able to get a ride if you leave your date—can pay solid dividends in terms of your personal safety.

Preventing Date Rape: The Male's Perspective
Here are guidelines for men to help them avoid even inadvertently committing date or acquaintance rape (Parrot, 1988; Warshaw, 1988).

- *Never force yourself sexually on a female*—even if you think she is leading you on, even if she has had sex with someone you know, and not even if she has previously had sex with you.
- *Whenever a sex partner says "No," stop what you're doing.* If you're unsure of the exact intent of the message (she says "No" but keeps kissing you), ASK her directly—don't guess.
- *Don't pressure your partner into having sex.* What seems like a smooth, persuasive line to you may be threatening to her. If she gives in because she feels powerless and frightened, even if you don't mean it to be like this, it is certainly coercive, nonconsenting sex.
- *Don't make "scoring" your top priority.* Keeping score is for golf or football, not for human relations. Looking at sex as some kind of contest, with a winner and a loser, may be a good tip-off that you're closer to committing date rape than you might think.
- *Sex is not a commodity.* You don't have a "right" to sex as some sort of payback for a good time. Your partner DOES have the right to decide for herself if and when she wants to experience sexual intimacy.
- *An intoxicated woman cannot give a legally binding consent to having sex.* So if you believe the myth that a drunk woman is asking to be raped, you're absolutely wrong. Likewise, someone who's stoned on drugs cannot consent to having sex in a legally meaningful way.
- *Drunkenness or being high on drugs is no legal defense against rape.* Being out of control because of substance abuse doesn't mean that you're not responsible for what you've done both in terms of criminal and civil liability, just as it wouldn't absolve you for responsibility for hitting someone with your car or committing a robbery.
- *Don't make the mistake of "joining in" automatically if a friend asks you to have sex with his partner.* Unless you can be sure his partner is giving her full and free consent to your participation, you may actually be joining in the commission of a crime. It's better to be safe and certain than to be on the receiving end of a criminal indictment.
- *Ignorance of the law is no excuse.* Not realizing that you've committed a rape doesn't get you off the hook legally or morally, and certainly doesn't change the impact you've had on your partner's emotions. Be aware of the consequences of *all* your sexual behavior.

Mate Rape
Mate rapes are probably even more common than date rape but can be charged in only a minority of states at present because rape laws generally ex-

empt a husband from raping his wife on the assumption that their marriage provides firm evidence of her consent to sexual relations. It is interesting to note that marriage does not exempt people from conviction for other acts of physical violence against spouses.

Marital rape is estimated to be a far more common form of family violence than had previously been realized. In one study, rape by a husband reportedly occurred more than twice as often as rape by a stranger, with one out of eight married women saying that they had been victimized in this manner (Russell, 1982). Other researchers suspect that the real incidence of mate rape is much higher, noting that many women either are unwilling to report being forced to have sex by their husbands or don't think of this as a "real" form of rape. While some cases of forced sex in marriage might not qualify as rape according to a court of law, in other instances the victim (usually, but not always, the wife) is beaten and battered or otherwise abused. A recent study of marital rape found that there is little evidence that wives who have been raped by their husbands provoke these assaults by refusing reasonable sexual requests. Instead, it appeared that the husbands liked violent sex and used physical force to intimidate and control their wives (Frieze, 1983).

One of the most troublesome aspects of mate rape, of course, is that the victim not only must live with the memory of her traumatic experience but also must live with her rapist, never being sure when she will be assaulted again. One 33-year-old woman described it in this way:

> If he's mad at me, he loves to drag me into the bedroom and force me to have sex. It's a punishment session, he says. I learned a long time ago that physically resisting just goaded him on and left me bruised and bloody. So I don't fight back now, but I don't see how anyone could call this violence a form of making love. (*Authors' files*)

Statutory Rape

In addition to forcible rape, there is also a somewhat smaller category of nonforcible rape. Included here is **statutory rape**, defined as intercourse with a girl below the age of consent (even if she agreed to or initiated the sexual contact). While a woman could theoretically be charged with statutory rape, cases of intercourse between a woman and an underage boy are generally prosecuted

under charges such as "contributing to the delinquency of a minor" or "carnal abuse." Also included in the category of nonforcible rape are rapes where the woman's capacity to consent is impaired because of mental illness or retardation, drugs or alcohol, or deceit. Other varieties of nonforcible rape involve some form of coercion: a blackmailer who extracts sexual payment, a professor who demands sex in return for a better grade, a sex therapist who "diagnoses" or "treats" his female patients by having sex with them, a prospective employer who makes it clear that a job offer depends on sexual submission.

Rape Survivors

> Rape is an act of violence and humiliation in which the victim experiences overwhelming fear for her very existence as well as a profound sense of powerlessness and helplessness which few other events in one's life can parallel. (*Hilberman, 1976, p. 437*)

> Rape is a crime against the person, not against the hymen. (*Metzger, 1976, p. 406*)

> You have to stop being a victim of the rape. The person who raped you didn't do it for sexual pleasure; he did it to have power over you. And if you let him have power over you for the rest of your life, he's really won. A lot of women remain victims the rest of their lives. (*Anonymous rape victim, quoted in the* St. Louis Globe-Democrat, *March 20, 1983*)

According to the National Crime Victimization Survey, there were 171,420 rapes reported in the United States in 1991 (Buchwald, Fletcher, and Roth, 1993). Most researchers and law enforcement authorities believe that reported rapes are only a small fraction of actual rapes, so it is likely that the number of annual rapes is over three-quarters of a million (Koss, 1992). Various estimates suggest that one woman in five or six will be the victim of an attempted rape in her lifetime (Warshaw, 1988; Koss, 1992; Becker and Kaplan, 1991). In light of these statistics, it is particularly important to understand the effects of rape on the survivor.

Medical Considerations

The rape victim, whether female or male, young or old, emotionally composed or in a terrified state of shock and disbelief, needs careful medical atten-

Nancy Ziegenmeyer astounded readers of the Des Moines Register *in 1990 by voluntarily going public with a detailed story about being raped. Most U.S. newspapers do not report the names of women who have been raped in order to preserve their privacy, but some claim this practice encourages a "blame the victim" attitude and treats rape differently than other crimes.*

tion. Physical injuries are common—and not always visible or obvious—and some are so serious that they present a life-threatening emergency.

In addition to the detection and treatment of physical injuries, the survivor should be provided with information about testing for and possibly treating sexually transmitted diseases to which she or he may have been exposed. Female rape survivors who could become pregnant should also undergo a pregnancy test and should be informed of the pregnancy prevention options available to them. These include the use of estrogen, insertion of an IUD (which prevents implantation), menstrual extraction, and abortion.

Finally, if the survivor consents, the medical examination may be used to gather evidence for possible legal proceedings. For this reason, it is advisable that the woman not bathe or shower (or otherwise clean herself up) before being examined if she wants to report the rape to legal authorities.

Legal Considerations

For many rape survivors, a major question is whether to report their rape to the police or not. While reporting a rape may seem logical, many women have hesitated or decided against it for any or all of the following reasons: (1) fear of retribution by the rapist who may get out on bail; (2) an attitude of futility—"the police probably won't catch him, and even if they do, he'll probably get off"; (3) fear of publicity and embarrassment; (4) fear of being mistreated by the police or trial lawyers; (5) pressure from a family member against reporting; and (6) occasionally, unwillingness to ruin a friend's or relative's life by sending him to prison. In addition, the survivor of a date rape may be afraid of facing the adverse judgment of mutual friends if she reports the incident, and the marital rape survivor may fear the social and economic consequences if her husband is convicted and sent to jail.

These concerns are, by and large, founded in fact. In the past, police often scoffed at a woman's story and asked humiliating questions like "Did you enjoy it?" or "Do you like sex a lot?" As Gager and Schurr (1976) comment, "Such questions have little to do with finding the rapist and much more with human curiosity or satisfying the officer's vicarious sexual urges" (p. 68). Similarly, in many instances a report of rape never gets to trial, even if the rapist is identified: the district attorney can simply decide that the case is unfounded or unprovable (Brownmiller, 1975; Gager and Schurr, 1976).

Even when reporting a rape leads to identification and arrest of a suspect, the trial itself may be an anguishing ordeal for the survivor. Typically, the woman is made to feel that *she* is on trial rather than the accused man. The defense lawyer may try to show that she consented to sexual activity; if she waited for more than a few hours to report the rape, her motivation and truthfulness may be questioned; if she showered or changed her clothes, there may be insufficient evidence; and in some instances, her past sexual behavior may be questioned on the presumption that a woman with many sexual partners is likely to have consented rather than to have been raped (Slovenko, 1973; Brownmiller, 1975).

Fortunately, there have been some major advances in police investigations of rape cases

statutory rape intercourse with a female below the legal age of consent.

(Moody and Hayes, 1980) as well as in the legal process (Lasater, 1980). In many states, for example, it is no longer permissible for a defense attorney to introduce the woman's past sexual behavior into the trial, and women are not required to "prove" that they attempted to resist the rape by signs of physical injury. Police have also generally improved their sensitivity toward dealing with rape survivors. In most American cities, police departments now have specially trained teams for dealing with victims of sexual assault.

Unfortunately, despite these advances, the outcome of rape trials is still a far too subjective matter. Recent research funded by the National Center for Prevention and Control of Rape, a division of the National Institute of Mental Health, shows that American juries are far more likely to believe that a female has been raped if she appears chaste and has a traditional lifestyle. In this study, which involved interviews with 360 jurors in sexual assault trials immediately after they were over, Barbara Reskin, a professor of sociology at the University of Michigan, and her colleagues found that if the jurors questioned the survivor's "moral character" they were far more likely to vote against convicting the defendant. Rape survivors were most likely to be believed by jurors if they were married and were assaulted in their own homes. Conversely, if the rape victim was portrayed as sexually active or morally "loose," having had an illegitimate child or using marijuana, for example, the jurors were apt not to take her testimony seriously. Furthermore, while jurors were relatively biased against defendants who seemed to be losers or who had a scruffy appearance, those who were good-looking and could show that they had sexual access to a woman were likely to get the jury to side with them more easily. Despite the fact that many states now prohibit defense attorneys from questioning rape survivors about their sexual histories, women continue to be put through a major ordeal on the witness stand in such cases, with attorneys often asking questions that they know will be objected to simply to plant a seed of doubt in the minds of the jury. In one trial attended in Reskin's study, "a woman who was raped in her own home at 2 a.m. while she was sleeping was asked by the defense attorney if she had been wearing a bra."

The Aftermath of Rape

The psychological impact of rape can be profound from the first moments of the attack and for years afterward. The rape survivor reacts initially with a sense of isolation, helplessness, and a total loss of self (Metzger, 1976; Hilberman, 1978). How the survivor handles the severe stress of this crisis usually falls into a recognizable pattern (Sutherland and Scherl, 1970; Burgess and Holmstrom, 1974; Notman and Nadelson, 1976; Warner, 1980).

The acute reaction phase usually lasts for a few days to a few weeks. The survivor typically reacts with shock, fear, disbelief, and emotional turmoil. Guilt, shame, anger, and outrage are commonly seen in those women who are able to talk about their feelings. Other women, who adopt a more controlled style, have an apparent calmness that may indicate that they are forcing an attitude of control or are denying the reality or impact of the experience.

This phase is usually followed by a post-traumatic "recoil" phase, which can last weeks or months. The survivor undergoes a limited degree of coming to grips with herself and her situation. Superficially, she may seem to be over the experience. She tries to relate to her family and friends. She returns to everyday activities and tries to be cheerful and relaxed. But deep down inside, she has not really grappled with her fears, her self-doubts, and her feelings about the experience.

The final phase, a long-term regrowth and recovery process, varies considerably depending on the survivor's age, personality, available support systems, and the treatment of her by others. Frightening flashbacks and nightmares are common. Fears about being alone, suspicious men, and sexual activity surface with distressing frequency. Proper counseling or psychotherapy may be needed to deal with these fears and the depression that often occurs.

One study of women interviewed an average of 22 months after being raped found that three-quarters of the women reported changes in their lives that they directly attributed to the rape experience (Nadelson et al., 1982). Almost half of the women reported some form of fear, anxiety, or symptoms of depression; many also had trouble sleeping, feelings of vulnerability, and fear of walking alone, even during the day. The most common symptom still present in these women almost two years after the rape was generalized suspicion of others. Notably, acquaintance rape is just as psychologically devastating to the victim as rape by a stranger (Koss et al., 1988; Parrot and Bechofer, 1991; Muehlenhard, Harney, and Jones, 1992).

A distraught rape victim at a rape crisis center.

After a rape, some women avoid any type of involvement with men in sexual or social situations. Other women take just the opposite approach, with mixed results.

> After I was raped, I had intercourse with my husband as a ritual gesture. (I had learned as a child to get back on my bike after falling, lest I never mount again.) Intercourse was easy. It didn't matter. I was an abandoned house. Vacated. Anyone or anything could enter. *(Metzger, 1976, p. 406)*

Women who have been raped may face a number of sexual problems as a consequence (Becker et al., 1983, 1986; Becker and Kaplan, 1991). Sexual aversion and vaginismus are the most dramatic responses to the trauma of rape, but some women also have difficulty with decreased sexual desire, impaired vaginal lubrication, loss of genital sensations, pain during intercourse, and anorgasmia

(Masters, Johnson, and Kolodny, 1994). One study indicates that even though rape victims may have the same *frequency* of sexual activity one year after their rape as nonraped women, their sexual satisfaction is significantly reduced (Feldman-Summers, Gordon, and Meagher, 1979). Another study found that more than half of a group of 372 women who were survivors of either rape or incest had postassault **sexual dysfunctions,** with fear of sex, lowered sexual desire, and difficulty becoming sexually aroused accounting for the majority of problems (Becker et al., 1983, 1986). Becker and Kaplan (1991) note that response-inhibiting sexual problems (such as low or absent sexual desire) were three times more common in her survey than problems with orgasm, suggesting that the rape victim sees all sexual stimuli as anxiety-provoking even years after the assault. The husband or sexual partner of the rape survivor may also encounter sexual difficulties. Erectile dysfunction is not unusual, and *his* sexual desire may be affected by anger or disgust.

The male partner of a rape survivor often experiences a psychological crisis too, in which shock, blame, and a sense of guilt emerge (Orzek, 1983). This may cause him to become overprotective or to try to take charge of the legal and medical decisions that his partner faces. In some instances, the male may become preoccupied with thoughts of vengeance as a means of dealing with his own turmoil and discomfort. In other cases, the male may try to show that his love for his partner is still intact by pushing for sexual intimacy, not recognizing that the woman needs to be the one to decide—based on her own feelings and reactions—when to resume sexual activity (Burgess and Holmstrom, 1979).

What is most helpful is a willingness on the male's part to allow for open communication, giving his partner a chance to express her anger, anxieties, or other feelings in an atmosphere of acceptance and empathy. This openness should also include his being able to accept her silence, if this is what she re-

sexual dysfunction conditions in which the ordinary physical responses of sexual excitement or orgasm are impaired. Can be classified as psychosocial (caused by psychological, interpersonal, environmental, and cultural factors) or organic (caused by physical or medical factors such as illness, injury, or drugs).

quires. In addition, if the couple has children, they also will be likely to sense that something significant has happened. As Grossman and Sutherland (1982/83) point out: "What children imagine is usually more frightening to them than knowing the facts. It is helpful if they are given the opportunity to deal with their feelings" (p. 32).

As the couple adjusts to the postrape period, the male may benefit from counseling too. In fact, the long-term process of recovery from rape often can be facilitated by counseling for the couple, since there is some evidence that in stable, committed relationships, the male is a prime source of support for his partner (Crenshaw, 1978; Orzek, 1983).

How a rape survivor resolves all these problems is not well understood at present. For many, the counseling experience provides a useful opportunity for working through feelings of anger, worthlessness, depression, or fear. Others seem to handle things most comfortably on their own, although until more information is available, it is not certain that their adjustment is as satisfactory.

The Rapist

Information about men who commit forcible rape almost exclusively depends on studies of convicted rapists. The information obtained from these studies cannot be applied to all rapists because the less intelligent, less affluent rapist is most likely to be arrested and found guilty. Many of these studies are also done many months or even years after the rape was committed, and the rapist may not be accurate in recalling the details of his act.

Summarizing findings from a number of sources (Amir, 1971; Rada, 1978; Groth, 1979; Wolfe and Baker, 1980; Kruttschnitt, 1989), we can outline some general facts about convicted rapists:

- Eighty-five percent have a prior criminal record.
- Eighty percent never completed high school.
- Seventy-five percent are under 30 years old.
- Seventy percent are unmarried.
- Seventy percent are strangers to their victims.
- Sixty percent are members of racial minorities.
- Fifty percent were drinking heavily or drunk when they committed the rape.
- Thirty-five percent have previously been convicted of rape.

However, convicted rapists are not all alike. Their motivations for raping vary considerably, and their

methods of finding a victim, overpowering her, and sexually tormenting her are not the same. In some cases, the rapist methodically commits a long string of carefully planned assaults. Other rapists act impulsively, with no apparent premeditation of their act.

One of the key advances in studying rapists has been the realization that rapists are not oversexed men and that rape is usually an expression of power or anger and not an act of sexual desire (Burgess and Holmstrom, 1974; Brownmiller, 1975; Hilberman, 1976; Groth, Burgess, and Holmstrom, 1977). Notably, most rapists do not lack available sexual partners (Groth, 1979; Estrich, 1987). This is not to say that rape has no sexual meaning or motivation; in most rapes, however, the aggressive components are so predominant that the sexuality of the act becomes secondary (Tollison and Adams, 1979).

Groth, Burgess, and Holmstrom (1977)—a psychologist, nurse, and sociologist—studied 133 rapists and 92 rape victims to better understand the dynamics of the rape situation. They found that forcible rape could be classified as either power rape or anger rape. None of their rape cases showed sex as the dominant motive. According to these researchers, power rape occurs when the rapist tries to intimidate his victim by using a weapon, physical force, and threats of bodily harm. The power rapist is usually awkward in interpersonal relationships and feels inadequate as a person. Rape becomes a way for him to reassure himself about his strength, identity, and sexual adequacy.

In anger rape, the rapist brutalizes his victim and expresses rage and hatred by physical assault and verbal abuse. The motive behind this type of rape is often revenge and punishment against women in general and not the victim specifically. The anger rapist usually gets little or no sexual satisfaction from the rape and may have difficulty getting an erection or being able to ejaculate during the assault.

Groth, Burgess, and Holmstrom later described a third pattern, sadistic rape, where sexuality and aggression are fused and the suffering of the victim is the primary source of the rapist's satisfaction (Groth, 1979). The victim of a sadistic rape may be tortured or deliberately injured by cigarette burns, bites, or whipping. Sex murders, with grotesque mutilations of the victim's body, are extreme cases of sadistic rape. Groth (1979) estimates that about 5 percent of rapes are sadistic rapes, 40 percent are anger rapes, and 55 percent are power rapes.

Two separate studies shed additional light on the psychological makeup of the rapist (Abel et al., 1977; Barbaree, Marshall, and Lanthier, 1979). In each study, a group of rapists was compared with a group of nonrapists in terms of erection measurements while listening to taped descriptions of rape and mutually consenting sexual scenes. Both studies showed that rapists developed erections while listening to descriptions of rape, but nonrapists did not. In response to descriptions of mutually consenting intercourse, the erection responses of rapists and nonrapists were similar. Interestingly, the rapists did not show greater sexual arousal to forced or violent sex than to consenting sex. These findings suggest that nonrapists may have internal controls, such as fear or empathy for the victim, that inhibit their sexual arousal to descriptions of rape situations, while rapists either lack such internal controls or have learned to overcome them. It should be noted, however, that these studies involved only a small group of rapists, and it is uncertain if these findings apply more widely. Barbaree and Marshall (1991) point out that different patterns of sexual response are found in different groups of rapists, so that not all rapists should be thought of as being triggered by the same cues or motivations.

It is also not clear if the patterns described above apply to the motivations and dynamics of date rape. In date rape situations—which may actually be the most common form of rape—the sexual anticipation component may be a primary factor, although the power issue is also involved. Further research is required in this area.

Recently, a biosocial theory of rape was proposed by Ellis (1991), who bases his thinking partly on evolutionary biology. Ellis believes that "raping tendencies may be seen as resulting from an increased sex drive, a desire to possess and control multiple sex partners, and an insensitivity to adverse consequences of one's actions" (Ellis, 1991, p. 638). He suggests that this is not a learned process but rather reflects prenatal and postnatal androgen exposure levels that may act on the brains of certain men to predispose them to rape. To date, there has been no substantiation of this theory, and we think it is very unlikely that such an explanation will prove accurate.

Male Sexual Dysfunction During Rape

A fascinating study of 170 convicted rapists showed that sexual dysfunction during rape attempts is a frequent occurrence (Groth and Burgess, 1977). After eliminating 69 cases where no data were available or where an evaluation of sexual function was inapplicable because of successful resistance by the victim, an interrupted assault, or no attempt made at penile penetration, 101 cases were left. Of these cases, erectile difficulties occurred in 27 men, premature ejaculation occurred in 5 men, and ejaculatory incompetence was seen in 26 cases.

These findings have two important implications. First, they confirm the view that rape is not primarily an act of sexual desire. Fifty-eight percent of the rapists in this study were sexually *dysfunctional*, indicating that either desire or arousal had gone awry. Ejaculatory incompetence is a particularly infrequent male dysfunction in the general population, and its high rate of occurrence in rapists may signify that their preoccupation with expressing power or anger inhibits their sexual responsiveness. Second, a very practical point arises from this study. In some rape cases, the woman's testimony has been discredited if no sperm were detected on her body. Now two new findings will prove useful in prosecuting rapists who in the past may have been acquitted: many men do not ejaculate during rape and others may ejaculate prematurely before touching their victim.

Treatment of the Rapist

Since rape is a crime, rather than a medical diagnosis, most convicted rapists are sent to prison. Often, there is little attempt at rehabilitating the rapist; instead, the prison term is regarded purely and simply as punishment. Given this practice, it is not surprising that approximately three-quarters of convicted rapists become repeat offenders.

Various attempts to provide psychological counseling to men convicted of rape have not improved the situation very much. One of the problems with these "psychotherapy only" programs has been that they have not succeeded, by and large, in quelling the inner compulsion to rape that some of the rapists claim they feel. This problem has been approached (in a limited number of cases) by the combined use of the drug medroxyprogesterone acetate (MPA; also known by its trade name, Depo-Provera) and psychotherapy. The use of MPA results in a sizable reduction in circulating testosterone, which in turn causes a marked drop in the man's sex drive and his aggressiveness. This enables psychotherapists to be more effective in helping the man to reorient his sexual and aggressive impulses, although the effect lasts only for as long as the drug is taken.

Dr. Fred Berlin of Johns Hopkins University, who has pioneered the use of MPA for rapists and other sex offenders, states that 17 out of 20 men treated with this drug were able to self-regulate their sexual behavior while receiving the medication (*American Medical News*, August 26, 1983). However, almost all the men who stopped taking the drug subsequently relapsed, and it is not yet clear how this experimental treatment could be monitored effectively even if it ultimately proves useful. Another, more compelling criticism is that MPA is hardly the answer to what is basically a crime of violence. Since there is no guarantee that MPA will prevent a man from functioning sexually or that it would reduce a rapist's hostility toward women, it is even possible that the use of MPA might make some rapists more hostile, and thus more likely to break the law, than they may have been before. In any event, it is clear that more information is required on the long-term effectiveness of the use of MPA in treating rapists before this method will be widely accepted.

INCEST

Incest (from the Latin word for "impure" or "soiled") refers to sexual activity between a person and a close relative, such as a parent, a brother or sister, a grandparent, or an uncle or aunt. Although brother–sister incest is probably most common, most cases of incest reported to the authorities involve an adult–child interaction. Therefore, we discuss this form of incest in most detail. All states require the reporting of such cases of suspected incest under child abuse laws, with the underlying assumption that a child is unable to consent in a meaningful way to sexual interaction with an adult.

The incidence of incest can only be guessed at since reported cases make up only a small fraction of the overall number. Estimates suggest that perhaps 50,000 children are abused sexually by their parents or guardians each year (Burgess et al., 1978; Finkelhor, 1978; Summit and Kryso, 1978; Crewdson, 1988), with an even larger number of victims of rape or molestation at the hands of other family members. In one study, in 32 percent of rapes involving children, the offender was a relative (Peters, 1976).

Research on incest has been plagued by the limitations of working with clinical samples (those seeking treatment) or samples drawn from prisons. One distortion that this has introduced is the idea that father–daughter incest is the most frequent pattern. In reality, father–daughter incest seems to be far less common than brother–sister incest, but sexual activity between siblings is almost never reported or brought into treatment. The Playboy Foundation survey (Hunt, 1975) found that about 4 percent of men and women had ever had sexual contact with a sibling, but only 0.5 percent of the women had sexual contact with their fathers and an even smaller percentage of men described participation in parent–child sex. The Kinsey surveys (1948, 1953) also found that brother–sister incest was far more common than parent–child sexual relations. More recent data from a sex therapy clinic confirm this finding (Renshaw, 1983).

David Finkelhor (1984), associate director of the Family Violence Research Program at the University of New Hampshire, has developed a list of the factors that appear to be important predictors of childhood sexual abuse. The single most important predictor was having a stepfather, which more than doubled a girl's vulnerability to sexual victimization. Next in importance was having a mother who was punitive or highly negative about sexual matters (e.g., scolding or punishing a child for asking sexual questions or masturbating). The other vulnerability factors Finkelhor noted were having a mother who had not graduated from high school, not having a good relationship with the mother, not receiving physical affection from the father, having a family income under $10,000, and having two or fewer close friends in childhood. In a study of 796 college students, Finkelhor (1984) found that if none of these risk factors were present in a student's background, there were virtually no reports of childhood sexual victimization. Strikingly, however, among those with five or more of these risk factors, two-thirds had been sexually abused (see Figure 18.1).

Figure 18.1   Likelihood of Girl's Sexual Victimization by Presence of 8 Vulnerability Factors in Childhood

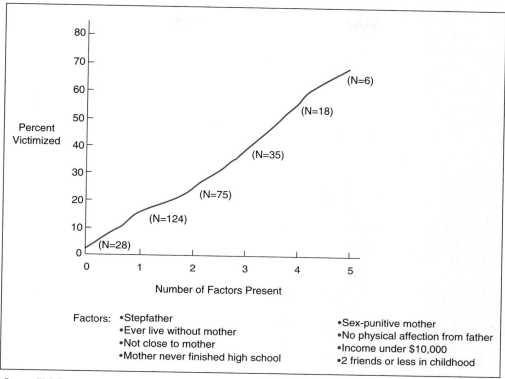

Source: *Finkelhor, 1984, p. 29.*

Myths About Incest

Several myths about incest continue to be widely believed. The origins of these myths are not entirely clear, but they continue to influence people's thinking about incest.

Myth: Incest only occurs in poor, uneducated families.
FACT: Incest is not bound by family wealth or education. While incest in middle-class or well-to-do families may be handled privately without being reported to the courts or social agencies, solid evidence shows that families in all walks of life can be affected (Meiselman, 1978).

Myth: Incest is usually committed by a father who is a sexual degenerate.
FACT: Most studies show that fathers who commit incest are neither "oversexed" nor fixated on children as sex objects (Gebhard et al., 1965; Finkelhor, 1979, 1984).

Myth: Claims of incest by a child are usually made up.
FACT: This myth can be traced back to Freud, who suggested that reports of sexual activity with a par-

ent were actually based on fantasies due to Oedipal desires (Peters, 1976). Unfortunately, most children's reports of incest—no matter how shocking and unbelievable they may seem—are likely to be true.

Patterns of Incest

Incest occurs in a wide variety of forms, and it would be foolish to regard them all as equivalent. Some cases of incest, for example, are one-time occurrences producing so much guilt or anxiety for either participant that they are never repeated. Other cases involve long-term interactions in which both parties seem to be interested (with no physical force used), one party is overtly coerced and terrorized, or multiple incest occurs, as when a father molests several daughters.

Other variables to consider when defining the incest situation include the child's age at the outset of the relationship, the openness or secrecy of the

incest sexual activity between close relatives.

activities, the types of sexual activity involved, and the impact of the interaction on family dynamics. Often, the incest behavior begins as a kind of teasing, playful activity with prolonged kissing, wrestling, and surreptitious genital touching. Over time, these activities can develop into overt genital sexuality, without any physical force being used.

> Commonly, the daughter is made to feel that the father and mother's happiness, their love for her, and the stability of the family rests on her willingness and her silence. Unlike many other forms of sexual abuse, incest often leads to very complex, ambiguous feelings in the daughter. It is not uncommon for the daughter to experience some sexual pleasure and a feeling of importance and power in her family. Often these feelings are intertwined with negative feelings such as sexual displeasure, pain, and guilt. *(Gottlieb, 1980, pp. 122–123)*

At other times, incest begins abruptly and forcefully. The father may be drunk or may have had a vicious argument with his wife, or he decides to use sex to "punish" his daughter or to "teach her what she needs to know." The child is likely to fight back and may be physically injured.

Interestingly, most men who become involved in incest are shy, conventional, and claim devotion to their families (Meiselman, 1978; Summit and Kryso, 1978; Finkelhor, 1984; Crewdson, 1988). Many profess to be strongly religious, although privately they are apt to voice scorn or disregard for ordinary taboos. However, the dissimilarities among fathers who commit incest are far more noticeable than the similarities. They may be heavy drinkers or teetotalers, construction workers or professionals, highly educated or elementary school dropouts. Although many seem to be mild-mannered, this outward appearance can be quite deceptive. While some are confirmed sociopaths, with little or no regard for others and a glib, believable explanation for everything, and others are clearly psychotics who suffer from a vastly distorted sense of reality, many incest offenders do not have a diagnosable psychiatric disorder.

This variability in the profile of male incest offenders is mirrored by the considerable variability in their incest acts. Most commonly, incest behavior begins when a child is 8 to 12 years old, but we have seen a number of cases where incest was initiated while the child was still in diapers. In some in-

cest families, the father selects only one child (usually the oldest daughter) as his victim, but it is common for several siblings to be victimized—sometimes sequentially over the years, sometimes simultaneously. Variability is also evident in the frequency of incestuous contacts (ranging from daily acts to those that occur only once or twice a year), the type of sex acts involved, and other characteristics such as whether there is an overtly sadistic element to the forced sexual encounters.

Father–son incest is considerably less common than father–daughter incest; consequently there is far less information available about this pattern. However, there are several pertinent observations that can be made about this virtually neglected form of incest.

1. In contrast to the situation with father–daughter incest, where the likelihood is that the daughter has been the sole child to be victimized, when a boy is the incest victim of his father the odds are much higher that there is at least one other sibling who also has been victimized.
2. Fathers who sexually abuse their sons are not necessarily, or even typically, homosexuals. In many cases, these fathers have never had an adult sexual experience with another man.
3. Boys who are sexually victimized by their fathers tend to be somewhat younger than daughters who are victimized.
4. A substantial number of fathers who sexually abuse their sons were themselves the victims of incest as children.

Wives of husbands who commit incest were often themselves the victims of sexual abuse as children and tend to be dependent, disenchanted women who withdraw from the family either through depression or outside diversions (Summit and Kryso, 1978; Gottlieb, 1980). The mother may actually force the daughter into assuming her role, relieved at having the daughter as a "buffer" between her and her husband and sometimes pleased to no longer have to deal with her husband's sexual advances (Browning and Boatman, 1977; Herman and Hirschman, 1977; Meiselman, 1978). Even after incest is discovered by a mother, in more than two-thirds of cases she does not try to help or protect her child (Stoenner, 1972; Herman and Hirschman, 1977). Yet the mother is not the pri-

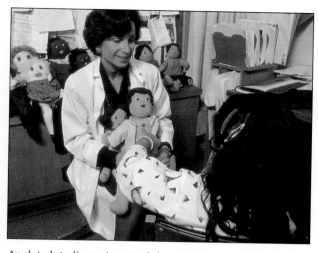

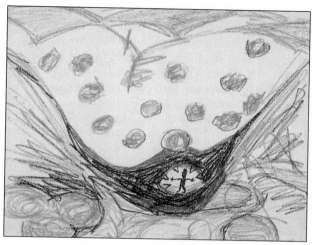

An obstacle to discovering sexual abuse is that young children lack the vocabulary to describe what happened. Using stuffed dolls, this victim of incest demonstrates for a social worker how she was abused. The extraordinary drawing on the right was done by a nine-year-old male whose mother had been sexually molesting him until he was placed in a foster home. The child drew himself as trapped inside a circular, vagina-like area surrounded by teeth.

mary culprit in most cases of incest; she may be defenseless to stop her husband, unable to control her daughter, fearful of her husband's physical retaliation, and worried about having her family break up if her husband is put in jail.

Incest is particularly common in reconstituted families, those in which remarriage occurs after divorce or the death of a spouse (Renshaw, 1983; Sager et al., 1983). Statistics gathered by researcher Diana Russell support this view: in interviews of 930 San Francisco women, Russell found that only 1 out of 40 was sexually abused by her biological father, but 1 out of 6 reared in reconstituted families had been sexually abused by a stepfather (*Sexuality Today*, Vol. 7, No. 1, October 24, 1983). The explanation for this difference may be that there is less of an incest taboo between nonblood relatives. In addition, in many reconstituted families the stepfather is thrust into close daily contact with an adolescent stepdaughter, a situation possibly contributing to sexual arousal. Lacking proper internal controls that ordinarily arise from the protectiveness of parenting a child from infancy on, the new father may find less to prevent such arousal from being translated into behavior. In fact, it appears that in at least some instances men have married divorced women primarily so they could gain sexual access to their children (Schwartz, 1983).

The incest victim, whether female or male, is subjected to a number of intense pressures that are apt to create considerable internal conflict. Almost

invariably, the father makes threats to frighten the victim into maintaining secrecy. These threats run the gamut from promises of physical retaliation against the victim or other family members to predictions of breakup of the family if the incestuous activity is revealed. At the same time, many of the fathers who commit incest provide, at least occasionally, some form of positive reinforcement to the child they are victimizing, such as gifts, monetary rewards, or special privileges. In addition, sometimes the child experiences pleasurable sensations in connection with the incestuous acts. These sensations are characteristically associated with a sense of guilt. These two factors combine to give the child victim a sense of complicity in the situation that makes disclosure seem all the more difficult. In fact, many children who are incest victims acknowledge that the fear of being blamed for instigating the forbidden acts is one of the major factors in their continuing silence. Unfortunately, it is also common to find that when a child incest victim has finally gotten up enough courage to tell an adult, the adult's reaction is one of disbelief ("Oh, that can't *possibly* be true.") (Crewdson, 1988).

There is relatively little systematic research information available on brother–sister incest. Reported cases usually involve an older brother (in his late teens or early twenties) and a considerably younger sister (Gebhard et al., 1965), but most cases probably involve siblings who are close in age (Finkelhor, 1980). The brother is usually the dominant partner in sibling incest (Meiselman, 1978), but we have seen almost a dozen cases where the reverse relationship was true. Although most cases of brother–sister incest seem to involve mutual consent, in a few instances one sibling blackmails the other into providing sexual gratification, as shown by this description of her experiences given to us by a 26-year-old woman:

> When I was 14, my older brother (who was 16) found out that I was doing drugs. Apparently he snuck around for a while and got a whole set of "evidence" together, and then he confronted me with it one night when our folks were at a movie. He told me I had two choices: either give him a blow-job, or he'd tell my parents what I was doing.

A survey of 796 college students found that of those who reported sibling incest experiences (15 percent of females and 10 percent of males), one-fourth of the experiences were categorized as exploitive (Finkelhor, 1980).

Mother–son incest is rare. In one sample of 203 cases of incest in the nuclear family (i.e., mother, father, and children—not other relatives), only 2 cases of mother–son sexual activity were described (Weinberg, 1955). According to Meiselman (1978), "In the great majority of reported cases in which the son initiates incest with his mother, the son is schizophrenic or severely disturbed in some other way prior to incest" (pp. 299–300). In cases of mother-initiated incest, the mother is usually psychologically disturbed. Mother–son incest typically involves genital fondling without intercourse if the child is young, but with boys over age 10, coitus is the most typical activity.

Mother–daughter incest seems to be the rarest form of nuclear family sex. While father–son incest is encountered more frequently, it too is exceptionally rare and accounts for less than 1 percent of cases overall.

The Aftermath of Incest

Incest and other types of childhood sexual abuse typically produce intensely damaging long-term psychological effects. Those who survive such abuse often have a tendency to get stuck in the past, fall into patterns of guilt, blaming, and shaming, and have poor self-esteem, an excessive amount of personal anxiety, and problems forming loving, trusting relationships (Bass and Davis, 1988; Cole and Putnam, 1992). If they dwell on their victimization, they may wind up "feeling so scarred and/or angered that they are unable to assume responsibility for their lives and sexuality" (McCarthy, 1992, p. 10). If, instead, they choose to view themselves as survivors, rather than victims, they can reorient their attention from the injuries of the past to the realities of the present (Bass and Davis, 1993). However, this is not an easy task.

Among the various psychological problems that affect victims of sexual abuse, subsequent sexual and relationship difficulties as adults are most characteristic (Everstine and Everstine, 1989; Wyatt et al., 1992; Frazier and Cohen, 1992). In addition to having high rates of sexual dysfunction—among male as well as female incest survivors—disorders of sexual desire are common as well (Masters, Johnson, and Kolodny, 1994). Understandably, women who were sexually victimized by their fathers often have problems forming intimate relationships with men because they expect betrayal, rejection, or punishment (Summit and Kryso, 1978; Bass and Davis, 1988; Schwartz, 1992). Drug and alcohol abuse, eating disorders, depression, suicide attempts, post-traumatic stress disorder, multiple personality disorder, and self-destructive behaviors are especially common as well (Bass and Davis, 1988; Crewdson, 1988; Goodwin, Cheeves, and Connell, 1990; Enoch, Herrman, and Walsh, 1990; Wyatt et al., 1992; Cole and Putman, 1992; Hoorwitz, 1992). Certain of these psychological disorders are associated so frequently with a past history of incest that they of particular interest. These are summarized in Table 18.1.

In addition to the effects mentioned above, some victims of childhood or adolescent sexual abuse seem unable to feel physical pain, so they mutilate themselves. Self-mutilation, such as deliberately cutting oneself on the arm or leg with a knife or razor, is poorly understood but a phenomenon that is commonly encountered among incest survivors. More common is PTSD, post-traumatic stress disorder, in which survivors of abuse live with constant and often debilitating anxiety. This anxiety may surface as recurrent nightmares, unexplained fears, flashbacks to scenes of childhood degradation or pain, and severe anxiety.

In a careful review article, Cole and Putnam (1992, p. 180) claim:

> . . . all incest victims suffer in their self- and social functioning. The severity of outcome is a

Table 18.1   Criterion and Associated Symptoms of Major Psychiatric Disorders Associated with History of Incest

Disorder	Self-Integrity	Self-Regulation	Social Problem
Borderline personality	Unstable sense of self Marked identity problems "Splitting"	Affective instability Impulsiveness Self-mutilating behavior Suicide attempts	Unstable relationships Frantic fear of abandonment
Multiple personality	Sense of separate selves Lost memories of past self Personified self-conflicts	Mood swings Panic attacks Impulsiveness Self-mutilating behavior Suicide attempts	Distrust of others Fragmentation of social roles Unstable relationships
Somatization disorder	Unfounded sense of body as ill or weak Hallucination that name has been called	Anxiety, depression Antisocial behavior Suicidal threats	Occupational, interpersonal, and marital problems
Eating disorder	Distorted body image	Binge eating and purging Intense fear of weight Self-injurious acts Depression	Avoidance of sexual relations
Substance use	Separate drug or alcohol identity	Aggressive, antisocial Mood lability Regulation of mood by drug	Social isolation, withdrawal Suspiciousness

Source: *Cole and Putnam, 1992.*

function of the timing of the interference of self and social development, as well as other contextual factors such as the child's coping ability and individual differences in temperament and the familial context, particularly whether the mother colludes in the abuse.

There are a few studies, however, that suggest incest victims may not be harmed by their experience and can become healthy, well-adjusted adults (Bender and Blau, 1937; Yorukoglu and Kemph, 1966). If such cases exist in any numbers, they would be the last to be identified or reported by traditional means. Nevertheless, it seems likely that an incestuous relationship between an adult and a child will create major conflicts for the child, even if these are eventually overcome. In addition, and perhaps more important, even in cases where incest has no demonstrably harmful effects on the child, it is still morally wrong because the child is not capable of truly giving a free and meaningful consent to such behavior. While these remarks do not apply to cases of adult–adult incest, we believe that adults are morally and ethically bound to refuse to have sexual contacts with children and that failure to follow this ethical imperative should be regarded as an act of serious consequences.

Incest Support Groups: Toward Healing

Today, virtually every community has at least one provider of incest survivor support groups, whether it is a hospital, a clinic, a church, a local rape crisis center, or a social service agency. For many individuals, such support groups provide an important beginning in the healing process. Here are several comments that are typical of the reactions we've heard in such groups.

I've learned I am lovable and loved.

There was a voice inside me that just said, You've got to connect with the present again. You've got to remake your personal reality.

It was time to come out of my shell and start living. Otherwise my father would have victimized me twice. (*Authors' files*)

Most survivors come to their first support group session nervous and frightened and unsure of what to expect. Some can't look anyone else in the face, some are unable to speak in more than a barely audible whisper. But what they have in common is the pain they have lived with for years, which has often become so intolerable that they have finally decided to reach out in their struggle to survive. As

Bass and Davis (1993, p. 10) put it, "You can't heal from child sexual abuse alone. You need to break the silence that has surrounded the abuse and reach out for support." The first-timer entering a group session to reveal himself or herself to a group of strangers as a shame-burdened incest survivor already has the comforting knowledge that each and every one of the strangers in that group carries the same hefty burden. For most participants, that awareness provides the spark for instant empathy and trust.

The key aspects of the healing process that can either be dealt with in psychotherapy or in support groups, according to Bass and Davis (1993), are:

1. Understanding that it wasn't your fault.
2. Overcoming shame.
3. Dealing with grief and anger.
4. Learning how to implement change.
5. Resolution and moving on.

To implement this process, support group sessions center on the release of long-hidden feelings, thoughts, and histories. The process can only occur in a safe and caring environment, but when it works, it often means voicing the unspeakable for the first time in a person's life. The atmosphere of warmth and understanding provided by the group—the "I've been there too, so I can relate to what you're saying and feeling"—is usually able to overcome the gut-wrenching pain and the seemingly never-ending tears and turmoil.

The process is not all gut-wrenching and distressing. There are moments of praise, applause, love, laughter and growth intermingled with group sessions, all of which facilitate the healing process. As the anger and hurt and sense of betrayal are shared, it becomes possible to triumph over the prison of one's past. While it is certainly true that this is not an easy process and that each survivor must journey on his or her own road to psychological health, each participant can gain considerable strength and courage from the support group.

There are some cautions to be considered in this matter, however. For example, Carol Tavris, a well-known social psychologist, is skeptical about how the incest-survivor industry has grown by leaps and bounds (Tavris, 1993). She points out that current research clearly shows that false memories can be introduced into people's minds by the mechanism of suggestion, and criticizes the authors of many incest-survivor self-help books by saying that their criteria for determining if you might have been a victim as a child are so broad as to be scientifically meaningless. Here is one of her most cogent points (Tavris, 1993, p. 16):

> To reach their inflated statistics, the survivor books rely on definitions that are as expandable as a hot-air balloon. In these books, the rule is: If you feel abused, you were abused. . . . It doesn't matter if no sexual contact occurred; anything that your parents did that you didn't like is a violation.

Likewise, sex therapist Barry McCarthy (1992) believes that the "new" view of as many as 70 percent of children having been sexually abused is a case of exaggeration. As McCarthy notes, "The pendulum has swung too far." He also deplores the emphasis on victimization, which he contends leads the affected individual to define his or her self-esteem based on being a victim, rather than on living in the present.

CHILD PORNOGRAPHY AND SEX RINGS

The use of children in the production of pornographic photographs, movies, or videotapes is another variety of child sexual abuse that attracted little attention until the past decade. While the number of children involved in such activities is unknown, it is certain that thousands are exploited in this fashion every year. In some instances, very young children apparently have no idea they are posing for pornographic purposes: they may actually be posed with teddy bears or dolls. In other cases, what begins as nude modeling quickly escalates to posing in nude scenes staged to resemble sexual activity to finally enacting "live" sex so that movies can be shot or photographs can become more realistic. The allure of payment for such work is usually the principal motivating factor, but in some cases "cooperation" is obtained by threats, blackmail, or kidnapping. There are also cases where an adolescent seeks out a chance to "be in the movies," where not only the money but the thirst for adventure and "stardom" comes into play.

Many of the "stars" and "starlets" for such productions come from the ranks of the estimated 700,000 to 1 million children who run away from home each year (Baker, 1980). Usually, the runaway child has no realistic plan of survival and only lim-

If You Have Ever Been Involved in Incest

Some people feel completely comfortable with a "forgive and forget" attitude and have no desire to talk about this topic with anyone. Others who feel they were in consensual, nonexploitive incest relationships may not even see a need to forgive or forget, since they may view the entire experience as a positive one. Reading about incest can stir up old, hidden memories for anyone who has been involved in sexual contact with a relative. The descriptions of incest presented here may or may not match your own feelings and experiences; for example, you might be surprised to learn that others were harmed by such involvement if you never felt you were, or you might not have realized that incest is illegal. Certainly, no two people cope with an incest experience in exactly the same way. However, since current studies show that many people who were involved in incest as children never told anyone about this situation and have residual feelings of guilt, resentment, anger, or poor self-esteem that seem to be linked to the incest experience, it may be helpful to consider the following options.

People with a background of incest who are having sexual problems or difficulty forming or maintaining intimate relationships are likely to benefit from professional help in dealing with these issues. Even though the incest may have occurred decades ago, even if it were a single episode rather than a recurring pattern, consulting a psychologist, psychiatrist, social worker, or sex therapist can help you determine whether counseling on this issue can help. In fact, in these circumstances many people discover that the opportunity to bring the incest experience and their long-range reactions to it out in the open is a key step in gaining more control over their lives.

If you fall in-between these two groups—those who are most comfortable leaving things as they are and those who seek professional help—there are two other options you can also consider:

1. Some incest survivors have felt tremendous relief in confronting the person who initiated the incest behavior years later, in adulthood, to explain how they felt and to obtain an acknowledgment or even an apology. This approach can help you feel more in control and less a victim, but it can backfire if you let anger drown out all your other feelings or if the person you confront denies your accusations or even asserts that *you* initiated the sexual contact.

2. Short of confrontation, which may not always be possible (e.g., if the other person has died or is mentally incapacitated), it can be helpful to confide in someone else—a spouse, sibling, parent, lover, best friend, or member of the clergy, for example—so that you're not forced to bottle up your feelings and carry around this burdensome "secret" for the rest of your life. In many instances, the very act of disclosure to someone you trust can be a tremendous relief. But only you can judge whether you are comfortable with this approach.

One other aspect of incest should be mentioned here. If your child ever tells you that he or she has been approached sexually by a family member, do *not* dismiss it as a "misunderstanding" or something that the child "imagined." Realize that younger children usually won't have a vocabulary to describe just what happened—so they may say something like "Uncle Joe was trying to do funny things to me." All children should be taught that they have the right to say no to adults who ask them to do something they don't want to do; they should also know that any form of genital contact with adults is strictly off limits.

ited financial resources; lacking friends, family, lodging, and the ordinary restraints of everyday routine, such children are perfect victims for the porn recruiters and pimps who prowl bus depots and hamburger stands looking for their victims. In addition to money, drugs are often provided as enticement or pay. One of the unpleasant ironies of this situation is that many runaways flee their homes because of sexual abuse, only to find themselves further entwined in coercive sex once they're on their own.

Recently, additional information has come to light suggesting that sex rings in which adults exploit children—often, but not only, for purposes of producing pornography—are far more common than previously imagined. In an important study published in the *American Journal of Psychiatry*, Ann Burgess and her colleagues (1984) described 11 such rings that involved 66 children aged 6 to 16. The 14 adults who led these sordid activities included a scout leader, a school bus driver, a respected coach, a teacher, and a grandfather. Both solo sex rings, in which one adult was sexually involved with small groups of children, and syndicated rings, in which several adults formed an organization for recruiting children, producing pornography, and providing direct sexual services to a network of adult customers, were noted. Children were sometimes recruited for these rings by their siblings or friends and were often given drugs by the adult ring leaders to "reward" them for their participation. The adult leaders simultaneously frightened children into not revealing their involvement by threats; they maintained the children's participation by convincing them that such activities were normal. In addition, the children themselves typically exerted pressure on their fellow group members to maintain secrecy.

Burgess and her co-workers noted that "the sexual abuse of the children by the adult is compounded by the adult's supporting the children's exploitation of each other." Often, the older, stronger children abused the younger, smaller ones on a regular basis, mimicking the sadistic, humiliating practices of the adult ringleaders. In all the sex rings studied, adult pornographic books and magazines were shown to the children to "instruct" and "educate" them. Not surprisingly, three-quarters of the children had identifiable patterns of problems with psychological and social adjustment

after their involvement was discovered. While no systematic studies have yet been done on the long-term effects of the exploitation of children by such sex rings, clinical observation suggests that the impact may be profound.

The effects of participation in child pornography are serious and lasting. A psychoanalyst warns: "Children who pose . . . begin to see themselves as objects to be sold. They cut off their feelings of affection, finally responding like objects rather than people" (*Time*, April 4, 1977, p. 56). As with other victims of sexual coercion, they are prone to sexual problems as adults. Worst of all is that "sexually exploited children tend to become sexual exploiters of children themselves as adults" (Baker, 1980, p. 304). In 1982, a government report recommended the following legislative steps to combat the problem of child pornography:

1. Require film processors and laboratories that receive what appears to be child pornography to turn the material over to local law enforcement bodies or to the state's attorney.

2. Require photographers wishing to film a child nude or seminude to receive and maintain possession of a signed release from the child's parent or guardian authorizing such photography.

3. Amend the civil code to provide for licensing of all children used in commercial modeling or performing, with carefully worded prescriptions and substantial sanctions against the use of such children in sexually explicit activities (General Accounting Office, 1982).

Unfortunately, these steps will not do much to deter the activities of the sex rings. These are more likely to be combated effectively by educating children and parents about sexual exploitation by adults rather than pretending "it can't ever happen to *my* child."

SEXUAL HARASSMENT AT WORK

Many women who work outside the home have been victimized by another sort of sexual coercion. Although sexual harassment at work is less shocking to most people than rape or incest, it is a social problem of considerable size. Traditionally joked about or viewed as trivial, it has now become an important issue of sex discrimination in both a legal and a practical sense. Although there has been relatively little research on the subject, cases of male sexual harassment at work have also come into view. In fact, more than 200 men file sexual harassment charges each year with the EEOC (*The Wall Street Journal* October 18, 1991, p. B3). Overall, since the Clarence Thomas–Anita Hill confrontation in 1991, federal sexual harassment complaints have almost doubled, from 6,892 in 1991 to 12,537 in the first ten months of 1993 (*Time,* November 22, 1993, p. 46).

What makes sexual harassment fundamentally different from other forms of coercive sex is that actions that might simply be annoying or embarrassing outside the workplace—such as a man whistling at a woman as she walks down the street, or a woman making a comment about a man's body—take on a different meaning at work. The reason is that exiting from an uncomfortable (or even threatening) situation isn't so easy when the harasser is the person's boss or colleague, someone with whom he or she is in contact almost every day.

Sexual harassment at work can appear in a number of different forms. One version is in the attempt to seek employment. Here, the prospective employer makes it clear that hiring the applicant depends on her sexual availability—and a "sample" is requested as a sign of "good faith." Jokes about the "Hollywood casting couch" as a means for aspiring starlets to gain entry to the world of entertainment are based on fact. Even with far less glamorous jobs, the person doing the hiring has economic power to assist him in making such a request. To a woman who has been unable to find a

job and needs to support her family, economic realities may make giving in the simplest and most logical thing to do.

A more common situation for sexual harassment occurs when a boss or supervisor makes sexual compliance a condition for keeping a job, getting a promotion, or obtaining other work-related benefits. Again, the person who does the hiring and firing has economic power. The coercion is even stronger than the preemployment situation because if the woman is fired for her unwillingness to cooperate sexually, her boss will have to make up a reason "for the record," and this may hurt her chances for future employment. In some situations, the request for sexual interaction is direct, blatant, and threatening. In other cases, while the sexual invitation may be direct, the threat is unspoken: the woman is left to decide what will happen to her if she refuses to play along.

Other, less severe types of verbal harassment can also occur. For example, there can be subtle pressures or advances in which the target or goal is somewhat ambiguous, such as double entendre statements, or "wishing out loud" comments ("I really need some TLC," or "God, I'm feeling horny today"), or inappropriate personal questions ("Would you ever date a married man?" "Have you ever had an affair?") (Gruber, 1992). These sorts of comments (and other comments made in a joking manner) may not be bothersome once or twice, but if they become repetitive, day after day after day, they can certainly become threatening (Webb, 1991).

At an entirely different level are actual instances of sexual assault: the harasser fondling a woman's buttocks, or ripping off her blouse, or trying to push his tongue into her mouth. Less flagrant instances of sexual touching, such as a pinch or a grab, are no less sexual harassment than more offensive actions, even though they seem to be less serious. A related type of harassment occurs with sexual posturing, including violations of personal space and attempts to have physical contact by following someone closely, trying to corner them, leaning up against them, or trying to peer down the front of a woman's blouse.

Sexual harassment can occur in virtually any setting (Brewer, 1982). One survey of nurses found that more than 60 percent had experienced sexual harassment in the preceding year (Duldt, 1982), and surveys of female law students, medical students, and military personnel have also reported alarmingly high rates of sexual harassment (Bravo and Cassidy, 1992). A survey of 20,000 federal employees found that 42 percent of the women and 15 percent of the men reported having been sexually harassed at work in the preceding 24 months (Tangri, Burt, and Johnson, 1982). A more recent study of federal employees virtually duplicated this outcome, reporting that 42 percent of women and 14 percent of men said they had been sexually harassed at work in the two-year period from 1985 to 1987 (*The New York Times*, July 1, 1988, p. B6). (It should be pointed out that the respondents in this survey generally didn't believe that the problem was any worse in the federal government than in private business.) Only 5 percent of the workers took any formal action to deal with the harassment they experienced.

According to Catherine MacKinnon (1979), a lawyer who has written one of the landmark books on the subject, when a woman refuses the sexual advances of her boss, retaliation may come in any number of ways. She may be demoted or have her salary cut, unfavorable reports may be put in her personal file, she may be denied requests for vacations, she may be passed over for promotion, she may be given tedious or unpleasant assignments, or her work conditions may be made undesirable. In the last category,

> She may be constantly felt or pinched, visually undressed and stared at, surreptitiously kissed, commented upon, manipulated into being found alone, and generally taken advantage of at work—but never promised or denied anything explicitly connected with her job. . . . Never knowing if it will even stop or if escalation is imminent, a woman can put up with it or leave. . . . Most women are coerced into tolerance. *(p. 40)*

Although a survey by *Redbook* in 1976 answered by more than 9000 working women revealed that almost 9 out of 10 experienced some form of sexual harassment at work, the impact of this type of sexual coercion has been studied only to a limited degree. The experience seems to be a degrading, humiliating one in which the woman usually feels a sense of helplessness similar to the feeling reported by rape victims (Safran, 1976). As one woman explained:

> I'd heard before about women being told to "put out or get out." But when my boss, who was my father's age, tried to get me to sleep with him, I thought at first it was a nice compliment. Nothing too shocking, and something I assumed would pass. I wasn't prepared for his change in behavior. Suddenly, nothing I did was right. I was constantly pressured to change my mind. He began to grab at me, and one day he pulled me down on his lap. I felt cheap, confused, and used—although I hadn't done anything wrong. Later, I felt anger, and I went to see a lawyer. *(Authors' files)*

A 1981 survey of almost 2000 business executives done by *Redbook* and the *Harvard Business Review* found that men and women in top management positions disagree considerably on the extent of the problem of sexual harassment at work, with two-thirds of the men believing the scope of the problem "is greatly exaggerated" while only one-third of the women agreed with that statement (Safran, 1981). Male and female executives, however, were nearly unanimous in feeling that "unwanted sexual approaches distract people from the job at hand" and nearly three-quarters were in favor of management issuing a statement to all employees disapproving of sexual harassment. Today, in the aftermath of the Clarence Thomas hearings and in light of various estimates that sexual harassment costs American business tens of millions of dollars annually—and cost the federal governments more than $250 million between 1985 and 1987—the attentiveness of employers to this matter has changed considerably (*The Wall Street Journal*, October 18, 1991, Section B; Webb, 1991; Bravo and Cassedy, 1992).

There are many ways in which sexual harassment mirrors other forms of sexual assault, the chief one being that the sex in sexual harassment is inevitably an expression of power, not romance or fun. For example, some male harassers want to put "uppity women" in their place (Bravo and Cassedy, 1992), which is a comment many rapists make as well. And as we have seen in other categories, victims who report sexual harassment are often blamed for provoking the problem or are told they are overreacting to "harmless flirting" or that they "can't take a joke" (Webb, 1991, p. 66). Sometimes, in fact, co-workers turn their backs on the victim, because supporting her (or him) may make them feel vulnerable and may in some instances jeopardize their jobs.

SEXUAL HARASSMENT AT SCHOOL

Sexual harassment is not confined to the workplace, of course. Examples of sexual harassment are common in many situations in which there is a hierarchy of power. Even the halls of academe are not immune from this form of abusive behavior, as these examples show.

A 22-year-old woman: My economics professor kept asking me to schedule meetings with him to review the work I was doing on my senior thesis. Whenever he could, he would drape his arm on my shoulder while we were talking and he would remind me that I needed his support to get an honors grade and to get into grad school. One day, he tried to rub my breasts—and when I pulled away from him, he just came out and said, "Look, either you put out for me or I won't put out for you." When I went to the dean to complain, I was told that without proof of my accusation, nothing could be done.

A 27-year-old woman: One of my professors seemed to take a strong interest in my work and asked if I would help him grade some exam papers from his intro course. While I was working in his office, he calmly peeled off his clothes and said, "Let's take a break." I made a fast retreat, believe me, but I was shaken up by the experience. Then he called me at home to say that I shouldn't have been upset, he was only trying to be friendly. *(Authors' files)*

The scope of sexual harassment on college campuses is not known for certain, but various studies suggest that it may involve one-quarter to one-third of female undergraduates and 40 to 50 percent of female graduate students (Paludi, 1990; Marks and Nelson, 1993; Komaromy et al., 1993). (One problem in comparing various surveys in this area is that definitions of sexual harassment have varied considerably from one study to another.) Whatever the precise numbers may be, it is clear that sexual harassment is a problem of considerable magnitude.

Sexual harassment also exists in other school settings, from grade school on. For example, the American Association of University Women recently published a report suggesting that sexual harassment from boys was a pervasive problem for junior high school and high school girls across the nation (AAUW, 1993), and the Minnesota Department of Human Rights ruled in favor of a grade school girl who complained that boys as young as 6 years old had repeatedly made lewd remarks and sexual taunts to her on her school bus (*The New York Times* November 12, 1993, p. A16).

Since various studies have indicated that females are more likely than men to define incidents as sexual harassment (Adams, Kottke, and Padgitt, 1983; Kenig and Ryan, 1986; Valentine-French and Radtke, 1989), it is important to know whether this indicates that females are somehow "oversensitized" to this issue—whether in fact they are sometimes "crying wolf." One important study finds that this is not the case: the experiences students report as sexual harassment "are relatively clear and unambiguous" (Mazer and Percival, 1989, p. 145).

However, it is also true that not all cases of questionable sexual or romantic behavior on campuses are crystal clear. A number of psychologists have studied situations that might be considered by many to fall in the "gray zone"—for example, a professor who habitually tells sexist jokes in class, or a professor who flirts with his or her students—and find that except for clear-cut coercive and intrusive behaviors, there is still considerable uncertainly about just what sexual harassment actually is (Fitzgerald and Ormerod, 1991; Summers and Myklebust, 1992; Jones and Remland, 1992; Williams and Cyr, 1992).

The negative effects on anyone who is victimized by sexual harassment at school include loss of self-confidence, decreased emotional stability, less effort devoted to schoolwork, disillusionment with the male faculty, and a tendency to blame themselves as a cause of the objectionable behavior (Marks and Nelson, 1993).

DEALING WITH SEXUAL HARASSMENT

Sexual harassment can occur in other circumstances, of course. In recent years, increasing numbers of young, single women have complained about sexual harassment from landlords, for example. This type of harassment can happen when a landlord says he'll rent an apartment to a woman in return for sex or when a landlord or superintendent who has access to a woman's apartment tries to force himself on her. Sexual harassment can also occur when a professional person—such as a doctor, dentist, or lawyer—tries to take advantage of a person's vulnerability by making sexual advances.

Another study categorizes women's responses to sexual harassment (Gruber, 1989). In ascending order of how assertive the response is (from least to most assertive) and in descending order of how frequently they are used (from most to least frequent), the categories are avoidance, defusion, negotiation, and confrontation.

1. *Avoidance,* the most common response, is a passive reaction, such as ignoring the harassment or changing jobs.

2. *Defusion* is a way of putting up with the harassment without changing it and may include such actions as treating it as a joke, going along with it, or stalling the harasser by vague talk or flirting. It may also include telling co-workers or friends, who in turn may either help the victim express her feelings to them or offer useful suggestions for dealing with the harassment.

3. *Negotiation* is a more active, assertive response in which the victim shifts the focus to her needs and in effect asks the harasser to stop what he's doing or change his unwanted behavior to a more acceptable form.

4. *Confrontation,* the most assertive form of response, includes direct personal responses ranging from using forceful, insistent language to order the harasser to stop to using the organizational power structure to deal with the harassment by complaining to a supervisor or union officials or by obtaining outside legal assistance.

Deciding how to handle sexual harassment in its various forms is not an easy task. As the preceding discussion shows, victims of sexual harassment are typically in a precarious position because they have less power than the person who is harassing them. Because of this, they may worry about whether their accusations will be believed and whether the harasser will be able to get back at them in some manner. Thus, as with other forms of sexual coercion, it appears that the overwhelming majority of cases of sexual harassment are never reported, leaving the harasser free to victimize others repeatedly. Being informed about options for handling this problem can help turn things around. Here, then, are a number of practical pointers:

1. If you have been the victim of actual or attempted sexual assault or rape by a boss, su-

pervisor, or co-worker, you can file either civil or criminal charges against the offender.

2. In cases of sexual harassment that have not included an actual assault, you can confront the person who is harassing you in a number of different ways.

   a. Consider writing a letter to your harasser telling him (or her) (1) what the facts are as you see them (e.g., "On March 14, 1994, when we met in your office to go over my draft of the Smith contract, you put your arm around me and tried to kiss me, and then you asked me to come to your apartment so we could 'work more intimately together'"), (2) how you feel about what happened (e.g., "Now I am upset when I see you and worried that you won't evaluate my work objectively"), and (3) what you want to happen next (e.g., "I am willing to forget what happened if our relationship is a purely professional one from this point on").

   b. An alternative approach would be to confront the person who is harassing you, either in person or by telephone, although this is more likely to produce an emotional response than a letter is.

   c. Another possibility is to have an attorney write to your harasser for you, telling him to immediately stop such behavior or to run the risk of a subsequent lawsuit. (An attorney's letter may be more effective than your own in letting the harasser know you mean business.)

3. Keep careful documentation of each incident of harassment, including memos that include the dates, times, and specific details of offensive actions. Note the names of any witnesses, since they may be of considerable help in substantiating your case.

4. File a grievance with the appropriate person (e.g., someone at the dean's office or the personnel office at work or with a union representative, if you're a union member).

5. If confronting the offender and filing a grievance do not work, seek help from sympathetic co-workers. You may discover others who have been victims of sexual harassment at the hands of the same person. Consider forming a group to discuss and deal with issues of sexual harassment.

6. If you aren't able to remedy the situation by the above steps, or if you have been unjustly fired or discriminated against in any other way, you can file a complaint with the Equal Employment Opportunity Commission (EEOC). You may be entitled to unemployment compensation and back pay, in addition to damages.

7. Don't blame yourself or let yourself feel guilty. As Bravo and Cassedy (1992, p. 80) say,

> No matter what the outcome of your situation, you are not at fault. . . . Dealing with harassment is a process of regaining control after the harasser sought to take it away from you. . . . It's important to see your response as something *you* choose out of the options available to you. But it's also helpful to remember this: many women have not taken action against sexual harassment for fear they would be fired—and wound up being fired anyway. Sometimes the *best* protection is to speak up."

THE CULTURAL UNDERPINNINGS OF SEX VICTIMOLOGY

We live in a society that trains and encourages females to be victims of sexual coercion and males to victimize females. This statement is harsh but true, and it has important implications for what must be done to prevent sex victimization in its many forms.

Without repeating the detailed discussion of gender roles presented in Chapter 11, we can summarize the situation by saying that females are generally socialized for passivity and dependency, while males are programmed for independence and aggressiveness (Bem, 1993). This fundamental difference lies at the heart of sexual victimization, which is primarily an act of power and control.

> The fact is that families generally are given the job of socializing children to fill prescribed roles and thus supply the needs of a power society. . . . Ingrained in our present family system is the nucleus of male power and domination, and no matter how often we witness the devastatingly harmful effects of this arrangement on women and children, the victims are asked to uphold the family and submit to abuse. *(Rush, 1974, p. 72)*

The teenage boy is quick to learn that he is expected to be the sexual aggressor. For him, it is acceptable—even "manly"—to use persuasion or trickery to seduce his prey. He is also taught (by our society, if not in his home) that females do not really know what they want, that when they say "no" they mean "maybe," and when they say "maybe" they mean "yes." He may also have heard a bit of male folk wisdom that says—in reference to some "uppity" or unhappy female—"What she needs is a good lay." Given this background, it's not surprising that what men see as being an "active, aggressive (and desirable) lover" may quickly be transformed into sexual assault in its various forms.

Most women have been taught as children not only to be passive ("nice," "polite," "lady-like") but also to be seductive and coy. They are usually not trained to deal with physical aggression (unlike boys, whose play activities develop this capacity) but *are* trained to deal demurely with sexual situations. Thus, the female in a situation of sexual coercion is ill prepared to act against it. Faced with a physical threat, she often becomes psychologically paralyzed (Brownmiller, 1975). Faced with unwanted sexual demands, she is likely to question what it is about her manner, dress, or behavior that produced the attention: she blames herself and feels guilt instead of taking more positive action. This hesitancy is frequently misread by the male, who sees it as a sign of weakness and a chance that she will give in. His past experience may prove him right: how many women "give in" in various undesired sexual situations just is not known.

There are no perfect solutions that can wipe out sexual coercion, but a significant part of the problem can be addressed in two fundamental ways. First and foremost, as this discussion implies, is to change traditional gender-role socialization that puts females in the position of being vulnerable to sexual abuse. Second, in-depth attention is required to identify the conditions that push men into the "victimizer" role. Only when a clear understanding of the causes and motivations underlying coercive sex is at hand will it be possible to develop effective strategies for dealing with this problem on a large-scale basis.

In an essay titled "Raising Girls for the 21st Century," Emilie Buchwald (1993) makes the following suggestions for helping girls learn to know their strengths:

1. Tell your daughters what helped you to survive growing up.

2. Give girls your attention and approval.

3. Teach girls to be independent.

4. Encourage fathers to be active allies in remaking the culture.

5. Teach girls at an early age about their bodies and their sexuality; replace sexual ignorance (and gender-linked stereotypes) with sexual knowledge, including specific facts about sexual harassment and other forms of sexual coercion.

6. Let girls recognize that they can be part of changing our culture, and that cultures can in fact change.

7. Enlist women mentors and role models.

8. Find ways for girls to empower themselves through athletics and learning to play together.

9. Teach girls to be media critical in order to avoid the undercurrent of endorsements of sexual violence in today's movies, television shows, and even popular music.

10. Avoid reinforcing gender stereotypes.

11. Encourage girls to feel joyful, ecstatic, and alive.

Boys can be taught different sexual values and attitudes if we protect them from violent entertainment (or at least help them see how the violence in our media is not an endorsement of what should happen in real life) and teach them, from toddlerhood on, to view themselves as future nurturing, nonviolent, responsible fathers (Miedzian, 1993).

In the final analysis, the process of changing our society's attitudes toward sexual violence is not simple and will not happen quickly. But we are now in a process of recognizing the dimensions of the problem more acutely than we have in the past, which is the necessary first step along the way. Beyond this, what is really required has been stated succinctly by Miller and Biele (1993, p. 53):

> Rape will not stop until both men and women are allowed our full humanity. It is difficult, if not impossible, to harm another whom one perceives as equally human. The violence that comes from bias, hatred, and inequality can change when we figure out how to relate to one another as equals. . . .

SUMMARY

1. Coercive sex takes many different forms, with the key element being an abuse of physical or social power. Females are victimized by coercive sex far more often than males.

2. Rape is a form of sexual assault in which penile penetration of the vagina occurs without mutual consent. It affects victims from all age groups and walks of life; males can be victimized (either by women or via rectal rape by other men) as well as females. Date rape and acquaintance rape appear to be especially common forms of rape. Prevention of date rape particularly hinges on clear lines of communication.

3. Rape victims require attention to their medical needs, legal choices, and psychological reactions. Many women are reluctant to report rapes based on deficiencies in the police and legal systems. In many locations these deficiencies have been improved or overcome by the availability of "victim advocates" and specially trained police and lawyers.

4. The psychological impact of rape is usually profound; the typical rape survivor feels isolated, helpless, and frightened. Three stages of psychological reaction to rape have been described by researchers—the acute reaction phase, the post-traumatic "recoil" phase, and a long-term regrowth and recovery phase. Sexual difficulties after rape are very common.

5. Information about rapists is very incomplete because it is based mainly on studies of men convicted for this crime. These men tend to be young and poorly educated, often having a prior criminal record.

6. Rape is not primarily a sexual act. Research studies show that most rapes are an expression of power, anger, or sadistic impulses through sexual assault.

7. Incest, or sexual contact between relatives, can occur in families in all walks of life and is not usually associated with diagnosable mental illness. Father–daughter incest is most frequently reported to authorities, but brother–sister incest is probably far more common. Incest with adults is generally thought to be psychologically harmful to children, but research in this area is limited. It is clear that some incest victims have a variety of later sexual problems.

8. Sexual harassment at work or at school is a less recognized but widespread form of sexual coercion. Like the rape victim, the victim of sexual harassment may feel helpless, degraded, used,

and angry. Increasingly, this form of sexual co-ercion has led to legal action from victims.

9. As long as our culture enforces gender-role stereotypes that train females to be sexual vic-tims and program males to see sexual aggres-sion as "manly," we will probably continue to have problems with sexual coercion in its many forms.

Thought Questions

1. If a man takes a woman out and spends a great deal of money on her, does he have the right to expect sex in return? Does the woman feel that she owes him something if he spends a lot of money on their date? If misunderstandings arise over these expectations, how should the situation best be handled?

2. The text discusses the problem of sexual harass-ment by teachers. Is the policy by some colleges which bans faculty from romantic relationships with students a reasonable one? What if there is no exploitation involved and the student wants the relationship? What factors determine whether romantic or sexual relationships be-tween faculty and students are desirable?

3. The text gives an example in which a woman wants to have sex, then tells her date to stop but doesn't resist physically, then does not push him off after he enters her, but she feels "used." Does she have the right to feel used? Has she been raped? Is her date a rapist? Is the woman a tease? What circumstances define "being a tease"? If a woman has "teased" a man and he forces her to have sex, is he less of a rapist?

4. Why are so many women unclear in rejecting a date's sexual advances? Why don't they say "No, certainly not!" instead of giving mixed messages?

5. Is rape basically a sex crime? To what degree is rape an act based on sex, rather than an act based on anger, power, or hostility toward women? Do men who genuinely like women ever rape?

6. What are the pros and cons for the victim if she reports the rape and testifies against the ac-cused rapist in a trail? What if the victim were a man? Would these pros and cons change?

7. Proposals have been made to castrate sex of-fenders, including rapists. Would this help pre-vent rape? Why or why not?

8. If a daughter gives in to her father's demands for sex because he gives her money, presents, and privileges, and if the mother turns a blind eye to the situation because she doesn't want to have sex with her husband, who is the guilty party—the daughter, the mother, or the father? Are all equally guilty?

9. How can parents raise their sons so that the sons will not become rapists, particularly date rapists? How can parents raise their daughters so that their daughters will not become victims of date or mate rape?

Suggested Readings

Bass, Ellen, and Davis, Laura. *The Courage to Heal: A Guide for Women Survivors of Child Sexual Abuse.* New York: Harper & Row, 1988. A superb self-help book for women who have been in-volved in incest.

Bravo, Ellen, and Cassedy, Ellen. *The 9 to 5 Guide to Combating Sexual Harassment.* New York: John Wiley, & Sons, 1992. A detailed, readable guide to recognizing, combating, and preventing sex-ual harassment in the workplace.

Brownmiller, Susan. *Against Our Will.* New York: Simon & Schuster, 1975. One of the key books re-sponsible for shifting public attitudes toward rape, this volume is actually the definitive his-tory of rape, discussed from a strong (sometimes strident) feminist perspective.

Buchwald, Emilie; Fletcher, Pamela R.; and Roth, Martha (eds.). *Transforming a Rape Culture.* Mineappolis: Milkweed Editions, 1993. An im-portant, provocative book that examines the fac-tors that cause rape in our society and that makes some intriguing suggestions for ways to prevent sexual violence in all its forms.

Crewdson, J. *By Silence Betrayed: Sexual Abuse of Children in America.* Boston: Little, Brown, 1988. A compelling analysis of the various forms of children sexual abuse as they exist today in America, filled with sociological and psycholog-ical insights and facts.

Finkelhor, David. *Child Sexual Abuse.* New York: Free Press, 1984. A superb book summarizing current thinking on this difficult topic which also presents much important research data.

Paludi, Michelle, ed. *Ivory Power: Sexual Harassment on Campus.* Albany, NY: State University of New York Press, 1990. A detailed review of the multiple facets of sexual harassment in a college or university setting. Includes sections outlining the effects on victims of harassment, a profile of harassers, and a detailed discussion on handling complaints.

Parrot, A. *Coping with Date Rape & Acquaintance Rape.* New York: The Rosen Publishing Group, 1988. A short, practical, down-to-earth discussion of date rape, suitable for wide use on college campuses and elsewhere as part of a prevention program.

Russell, Diana E. H. *Rape in Marriage.* New York: Macmillan, 1982. An eye-opening treatment of an important but largely overlooked topic.

Warshaw, Robin. *I Never Called It Rape.* New York: Harper & Row, 1988. The most comprehensive sourcebook on date and acquaintance rape available. Includes many statistics from the *Ms.* magazine survey, as well as summaries of many other research studies, and a good resource list. A well-written, hard-hitting work.

Webb, Susan L. *Step Forward: Sexual Harassment in the Workplace.* New York: MasterMedia, 1991. A brief handbook providing essential facts and strategies for dealing with sexual harassment at work.

PART 4

Sexual Health
Perspectives

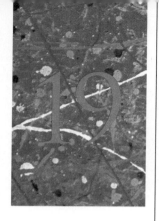

19

Sexually Transmitted Diseases and Sexual Infections

Infections that are spread by sexual contact are referred to as **sexually transmitted diseases** or **STDs.** STDs include infections that were formerly known as venereal diseases (VD)—those almost always transmitted by sexual contact—as well as various other infections that are sometimes transmitted by nonsexual routes. In addition to describing a broader category of infections, the term STD has not yet acquired the stigmatizing sound that the label VD carries. The following sections will describe the symptoms, diagnosis, and suggested treatment of sexually transmitted diseases, as well as similar information about several other types of sexual infections. Because of the complex influence the human immunodeficiency virus (HIV, the virus that causes AIDS) has had on sexuality and society in recent years, HIV infection and AIDS are discussed separately in the following chapter even though they too are STDs.

GONORRHEA ✈

Gonorrhea is the oldest and one of the most common forms of STD. In the Old Testament, Moses spoke about its infectivity (Leviticus 15); it was also mentioned in the ancient writings of Plato, Aristotle, and Hippocrates. Its modern name was coined by Galen, a Greek physician in the second century A.D. In 1879 Albert Neisser discovered the bacterium that causes it, which was named after him (*Neisseria gonorrheae*).

Although the discovery of penicillin as an effective treatment for this disease slowed its spread in the 1940s and 1950s, the incidence of gonorrhea had grown to epidemic proportions by 1980. However, there has been a relatively slow but steady decline in cases since that time (see Figure 19.1), with the one million cases of reported gonorrhea of 1980 having dropped to approximately 500,000 cases reported in 1992 (Handsfield, 1984; Centers for Disease Control, 1993q). A significant portion of this drop has been due to declines in the occurrence of gonorrhea in homosexual and bisexual men, presumably as a result of safer sex practices linked to concerns about AIDS (Judson, 1983; Holmes et al., 1990).

Gonorrhea is transmitted by any form of sexual contact, ranging from sexual intercourse to fellatio, anal intercourse, and, infrequently, cunnilingus or even kissing (Barlow, 1979; Robertson, McMillan, and Young, 1980). A woman who has intercourse once with an infected man has a 50 percent chance of getting gonorrhea (Platt, Rice, and McCormack, 1983), while a man who has intercourse once with an infected woman has a lower risk, probably around 20 to 25 percent, of becoming infected (Handsfield, 1984). The difference in risk is probably due to the woman's exposure to a larger number of infective bacteria as well as to retention of infected semen in the vagina, where the semen ordinarily pools around the cervix.

The risk of transmission is probably somewhat higher for anal intercourse (either homosexual or heterosexual), although precise data are not available on this point. Likewise, anyone performing fellatio on a male with gonorrhea has a very high risk of developing gonorrhea in the throat, although the odds of transmitting this infection by cunnilingus are small.

sexually transmitted disease (STD)   infection spread mainly by sexual contact.

Figure 19.1   Annual Number of Reported Cases of Gonorrhea, United States, 1973–1992

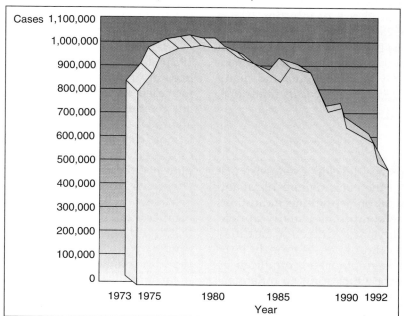

Source: *Centers for Disease Control, "Summary of Notifiable Diseases, United States, 1992,"* Morbidity and Mortality Weekly Report *41 (55), published September 24, 1993, for 1992. Data from Tables 1 and 3.*

Although there were only 500,000 cases of gonorrhea reported in the United States in 1992, most authorities agree that fewer than half of all cases are reported, so there are probably well over 1 million cases a year. Despite the fact that this underreporting undoubtedly produces distortions in what is known about patterns of gonorrhea in the general population (e.g., cases seen by physicians in private practice are far less likely to be reported than cases seen by physicians in public health clinics, introducing a socioeconomic and racial bias into the available data), several points can be made. First, gonorrhea is principally a disease of teenagers and young adults: in 1992, 73 percent of cases occurred in persons 15 to 29 years old (Centers for Disease Control, 1993q). Second, males are infected with gonorrhea more often than females (overall, the sex ratio is about 1.5 to 1) although in adolescents, the rates are higher in females (see Table 19.1). Third, African-Americans are affected disproportionately by this disease, with rates substantially higher than whites (Centers for Disease Control, 1993q). In addition, the following generalizations can be made. Gonorrhea occurs most often in persons with numerous sex partners. The risk of gonorrhea is also partly linked to patterns of contraceptive use, with women using the pill having an increased risk of this STD, while women who use spermicides or a diaphragm or sponge having a reduced risk of infection (Cates and Stone, 1992, 1992a). Finally, gonorrhea often coexists with other STDs. Fifteen to 25 percent of men and 30 to 50 percent of women with gonorrhea also have chlamydial infections, and many women also have *Trichomonas vaginalis* infections, as well.

Symptoms

Most men with gonorrhea develop a yellowish discharge from the tip of the penis (Figure 19.2a) and painful, frequent urination as the first indications of gonorrhea. These symptoms usually appear within two to ten days after infection but may sometimes start as much as a month later (Schofield, 1979). The symptoms are produced by infection in the urethra which leads to inflammation (urethritis). The puslike discharge (which often stains the underwear) is part of the body's reaction to this infection. In about 10 percent of cases in men, there may be no symptoms from the infec-

Table 19.1   Gonorrhea Rates per 100,000 Population—1991

Age Group	Males	Females
10–14	32	99
15–19	883	1,044
20–29	780	595
>30	146	48

Source: *Modified from Centers for Disease Control,* Morbidity and Mortality Weekly Report *42 (SS-3), 1993, Table 1.*

tion, which means that the man can spread gonorrhea without realizing it.

Men with symptoms from gonorrhea usually seek treatment promptly and are cured. For men who do not receive treatment, the infection may move up the urethra to the prostate, seminal vesicles, and epididymis and can cause severe pain and fever. If untreated, gonorrhea can lead to sterility (Holmes et al., 1989), but this is a relatively infrequent complication in men.

Since less than half of the women with gonorrhea have any visible symptoms, they are likely to have their infection for a longer time before treatment is begun. This delay exposes women to a greater risk of complications. In addition, symptomless women may unknowingly spread their infections to their sexual partners. Many women do not find out they are infected until their partner's penile discharge or burning appears.

Even when symptoms occur in women (Figure 19.2b), they may be very mild and tend to go unnoticed or are misdiagnosed. The symptoms include increased vaginal discharge, irritation of the external genitals, pain or burning with urination, and abnormal menstrual bleeding. In women, infection is most commonly found in the cervix (90 percent of cases) but can also be present in the urethra (70 percent), the rectum (30 to 40 percent), the throat (10 percent), or any combination of these sites.

Women who are untreated may develop serious complications. Gonorrhea commonly spreads from the cervix to the uterus, Fallopian tubes, and ovaries, causing pelvic inflammatory disease (PID). PID is the most common cause of female infertility because it can produce scarring that blocks the Fallopian tubes. The early symptoms of PID are lower abdominal pain, fever, nausea or vomiting, and pain during intercourse. Involuntary infertility occurs in 15 percent of women who have had one attack of PID

Figure 19.2   Symptoms of Gonorrhea.

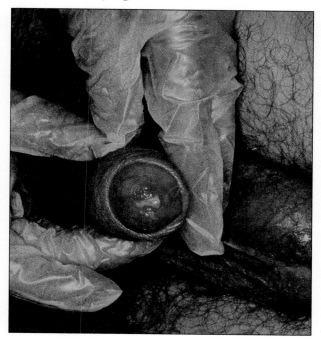

(a) Gonorrhea discharge from penis.

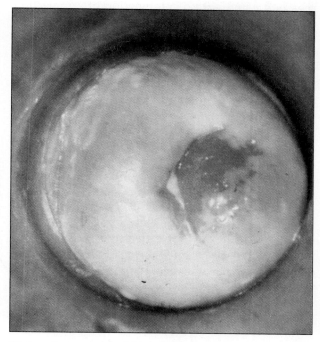

(b) Gonorrhea causing cervicitis in female.

and 50 percent of women who have three such episodes (Sperling, 1992). PID is also problematic for a different reason: it accounts for health-care costs of more than $4 billion annually in the United States (Washington and Katz, 1991). (While gonorrhea is not the only source of PID, it is certainly one of the two major causes, the other being chlamydia, an STD we discuss later in this chapter.)

In both sexes, gonorrhea can spread through the bloodstream to other organs, causing infection and inflammation of the joints (gonococcal arthritis), the heart (gonococcal endocarditis), or the covering of the brain (gonococcal meningitis). Fortunately, these complications are rare and treatable. Eye infections with gonorrhea occur (rarely) in adults, where they are caused by touching the eye with a contaminated hand. Newborn children may develop eye infections during birth if their mother's cervix is infected. Because this can produce blindness, infection-preventing drops, usually silver nitrate, are routinely put in every newborn baby's eyes.

Diagnosis and Treatment

Gonorrhea in men is diagnosed by examining the urethral discharge under a microscope after stain-ing it with a specially colored dye. As this method is only about 90 percent accurate, it may also be necessary to try to grow the infecting bacteria in a laboratory by a culture test that takes several days. Men who have had homosexual contacts should have cultures of the throat and rectum as well as the urethra.

In women, culture tests are the only reliable means of establishing the diagnosis. Swabs should *always* be taken from the mouth of the cervix *and* the rectum, even if the woman has never had anal intercourse, because a vaginal discharge may drip onto the anus and cause infection there. If the woman has experience with fellatio, a throat swab should also be taken. There is no blood test that can identify gonorrhea reliably at the present time.

The most effective treatment for gonorrhea used to be an injection of penicillin G given along with a pill called probenecid that blocked excretion of the penicillin in the urine, keeping a high concentration in the body. Unfortunately, some strains of gonorrhea that are resistant to penicillin evolved and have now become so common that they account for over 4 percent of gonorrhea cases in the United States (Handsfield et al., 1989). As a result, the U.S. Public Health Service and the CDC now recommend that nonpregnant adults with gonor-rhea be treated with a combination of an injection of an antibiotic called ceftriaxone *plus* the use of doxycycline pills. This regimen also has the advantage of simultaneously treating the chlamydial infections that often coexist with gonorrhea (see p. 519).

It is also recommended that ALL people with gonorrhea should have a blood test for syphilis and should be offered confidential testing and counseling for HIV infection. In addition, anyone exposed sexually to gonorrhea within the previous 30 days should be examined, cultured, and treated as above on the presumption that they are infected.

In *any* case of gonorrhea, it is important to abstain from sexual activity with a partner until you have been rechecked after treatment to be certain you are cured. *It is also extremely important to notify anyone with whom you had sexual contact, including the person you know or suspect gave you the infection, to insist that he or she see a doctor for proper diagnosis and treatment.*

SYPHILIS more serious than Ghonerecha

Syphilis first came to public attention at the end of the fifteenth century, when it swept across Europe, decimating armies and towns as it traveled. The source of this widespread outbreak is unclear. Some authorities believe that a particularly infectious type of syphilis was imported from America by Columbus and his crew (*The New York Times*, October 10, 1989, p. C13), while others believe that it was already present in Europe (Catterall, 1974). The spiral-shaped microorganism that causes syphilis, *Treponema pallidum*, was identified in 1905 (Figure 19.3).

Syphilis is far less common than gonorrhea today. In 1992, the overall number of reported syphilis cases exceeded 100,000 (see Figure 19.4). Most experts believe that this represents less than half of the actual cases that occur each year.

Syphilis is usually transmitted by sexual contacts, but it can also be acquired from a blood transfusion or can be transmitted from a pregnant mother to the fetus.

Symptoms

The earliest sign of syphilis in its *primary stage* is a sore called a **chancre** (pronounced "shanker")

Figure 19.3 Syphilis

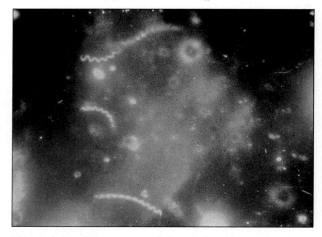

The spiral-shaped Treponema pallidum *is the microorganism that causes syphilis.*

(Figure 19.5 on p. 516). The chancre generally appears two to four weeks after infection. The most common locations for the chancre, which is painless in 75 percent of cases, are the genitals and anus, but chancres can also develop on the lips, in the mouth, on a finger, on a breast, or on any part of the body where the infecting organism entered the skin. The chancre typically begins as a dull-red spot which develops into a pimple. The pimple ulcerates, forming a round or oval sore usually surrounded by a red rim. The chancre usually heals within four to six weeks, leading to the erroneous belief that the "problem" went away.

Secondary syphilis begins anywhere from one week to six months after the chancre heals if effective treatment was not received. The symptoms include a pale red or pinkish rash (often found on the palms and soles; see Figure 19.6), fever, sore throat, headaches, joint pains, poor appetite, weight loss, and hair loss. Moist sores called *condyloma lata* may appear around the genitals or anus and are highly infectious. Because of the diversity of symptoms, syphilis is sometimes called "the great imitator." The symptoms of the secondary stage of syphilis usually last three to six months but can come and go periodically. After all symptoms disappear, the disease passes into a *latent stage*. During this stage, the disease is no longer contagious, but the infecting microorganisms burrow their way into various tissues, such as the brain, spinal cord, blood vessels, and bones. Fifty to 70 percent of people with

Figure 19.4 Annual Total Number of Reported Cases of Syphilis, United States, 1973—1992

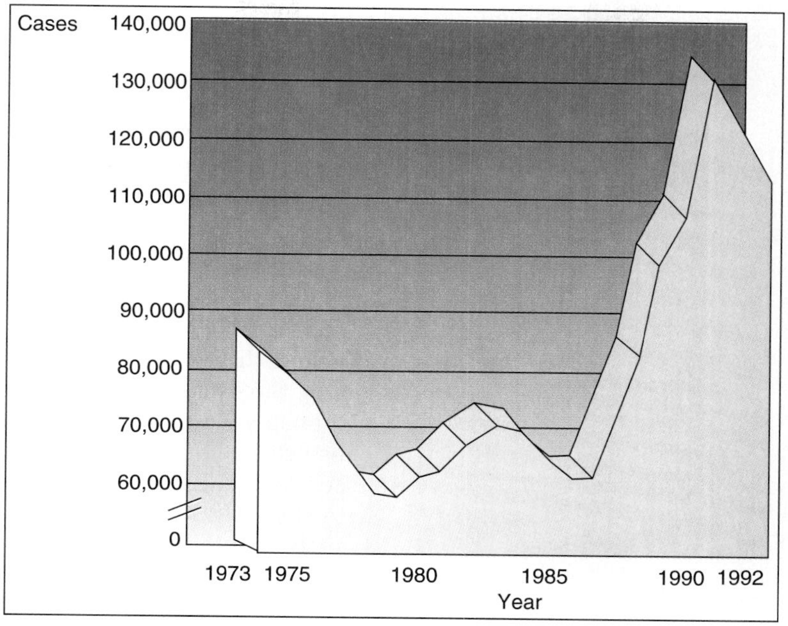

Source: *Centers for Disease Control, "Summary of Notifiable Diseases, United States, 1992,"* Morbidity and Mortality Weekly Report *41 (55), Published September 24, 1993. Data from Tables 1 and 3.*

untreated syphilis stay in this stage for the rest of their lives, but the remainder pass on to the *tertiary stage,* or late syphilis. Late syphilis involves serious heart problems, eye problems, and brain or spinal cord damage. These complications can cause paralysis, insanity, blindness, and death.

Syphilis can be acquired by an unborn baby from its mother if the infecting microorganisms are in her bloodstream, since they cross the placenta. The resulting infection, called **congenital syphilis,** produces bone and teeth deformities, anemia, kidney problems, and other abnormalities. Congenital syphilis can be prevented if a pregnant woman with syphilis is treated adequately before the sixteenth week of pregnancy (Holmes, 1980).

Diagnosis and Treatment

Syphilis is usually diagnosed by a blood test. Several different tests are available, including some that are most suitable for screening and others that are more time-consuming and expensive but also more accurate. Although none of these tests is completely fool-proof in detecting the primary stage of syphilis, secondary syphilis can be diagnosed with

100 percent accuracy. Diagnosis also depends on a carefully performed physical examination looking for signs of primary or secondary syphilis. Chancres of the cervix or vagina may be detected only by a pelvic examination, since they are usually painless. An examination under a special microscope of the fluid taken from a chancre will usually show the characteristic spiral-shaped organisms.

Syphilis can easily be treated with one injection of penicillin in its primary or secondary stages. Latent, tertiary, or congenital syphilis requires larger doses over a period of time, but the treatment is usually successful in these cases too. Patients who are allergic to penicillin can be given tetracycline or erythromycin.

Persons sexually exposed to someone with proven early syphilis should promptly be evaluated. The CDC recommends that if exposure occurred within the previous 90 days, the person

chancre (shan' ker) a painless sore that appears in the primary stage of syphilis.
congenital syphilis syphilis contracted by the fetus from an infected mother, causing various abnormalities in the unborn child.

Figure 19.5   Symptoms of Primary Syphilis

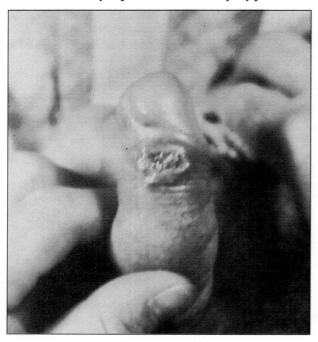

A typical chancre of the penis, the hallmark of primary stage syphilis.

Figure 19.6   Symptoms of Secondary Syphilis

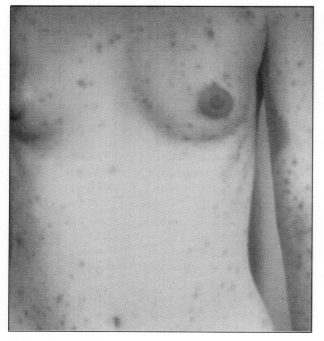

(a) Secondary syphilis in a female. One of the principal physical signs is a rash.

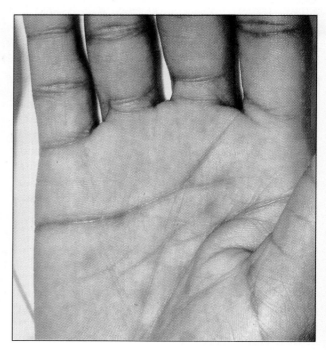

(b) Typical rash on the palms in secondary syphilis.

should be treated with penicillin even if blood tests are negative, since the person could be infected but not yet have developed a positive blood test (Centers for Disease Control, 1993r).

CHLAMYDIAL INFECTIONS

Infections caused by the bacteria *Chlamydia trachomatis* have been surprisingly overlooked until recently although they are now known to be the most common bacterial STD in the United States, with an estimated 4 million cases annually (Centers for Disease Control, 1993r). Furthermore, because it has been difficult to grow *C. trachomatis* in the laboratory, the disease often went undetected as a cause of nonspecific medical symptoms. In addition, because chlamydial infections are not reportable diseases nationally, physicians may have been lulled into thinking that they are less important or less transmissible STDs than others. Unfortunately, however, the health problems caused by chlamydial infections are serious, so being properly informed about this group of STDs is important. In fact, the U.S. Centers for Disease Control estimates that the direct and indirect cost of complications from chlamydial infections in women and newborns exceeds $2 billion annually (Centers for Disease Control, 1993r).

The number of new cases of chlamydial infections has been growing rapidly over the last decade and has now reached an alarming incidence. Data from several different surveys show the extent of this problem. Some college health services are reporting rates of chlamydial infection as high as 17 percent in undergraduate women (Goldsmith, 1986; Centers for Disease Control, 1993r). At STD clinics, an average of 20 to 40 percent of all people tested are found to have chlamydial infections (Thompson and Washington, 1983; Stamm et al., 1984; Jones et al., 1986). The prevalence of chlamydial infections in adolescents is especially noteworthy: 15 percent of teenage girls and 8 percent of teenage boys are infected with this STD (Shafer et al., 1989).

Many diseases and medical complications are caused by *C. trachomatis*. In men, about half of all cases of nongonococcal urethritis (infection of the urethra not due to gonorrhea) is caused by this organism (Stamm, 1988). This condition alone—chlamydial urethritis—has an incidence about 2.5 times that of urethritis caused by gonorrhea (Centers for Disease Control, 1985). In addition, *Chlamydia trachomatis* causes about half of the 500,000 annual cases of acute epididymitis (infection of the epididymis) in the United States. Both of these conditions are more common in younger males: chlamydial urethritis is most prevalent in males aged 15 to 24, while chlamydial epididymitis is predominantly found in males under 35 years of age. Chlamydial urethritis is only one-third as common in homosexual males as in heterosexuals, but 6 to 8 percent of homosexual males have evidence of chlamydial infections of the rectum (Centers for Disease Control, 1985). Based on current knowledge, there do not seem to be major long-term consequences to males from chlamydial infections, even if they recur or are chronic (Holmes et al., 1990). However, relatively little research has been done on this topic, so it should not be presumed that it is safe for men to ignore such an infection. Furthermore, men who are not properly treated will almost inevitably transmit their infections to their sex partners, which can have dire consequences for females.

In females, *C. trachomatis* causes a number of different problems at various levels of the reproductive tract. The female version of chlamydial urethritis is a condition called the urethral syndrome. In addition, chlamydia causes cervicitis (infection of the cervix) and accounts for an estimated 250,000 to 500,000 cases of PID (pelvic inflammatory disease) annually. If you recall that many cases of PID eventually progress to the point where they cause scarring of the Fallopian tubes, you will see why this complication is a major cause of female infertility as well as a major factor in some ectopic pregnancies (Centers for Disease Control, 1985; Sanders et al., 1986; Holmes et al., 1990). In many cases chlamydial infection also involves the endometrium (inner lining) of the uterus. In one study, it was found that 41 percent of women infected with *C. trachomatis* had chlamydial endometritis (Jones et al., 1986).

Another major problem in females is that maternal chlamydial infections during pregnancy are commonly passed to the newborn during childbirth, presumably from the infant coming in contact with infected secretions in the birth canal. Up to 50 percent of infants born to infected mothers develop conjunctivitis (a type of eye infection), and 3 to 18 percent develop chlamydial pneumonia (a lung infection) before they are 4 months old (Centers for Disease Control, 1985; Schacter et al., 1986). While chlamydial pneumonia is not usually serious, chlamydial conjunctivitis can sometimes cause chronic eye disease (Holmes et al., 1990). (This is not the same type of eye infection as trachoma, another form of chlamydial disease and a major cause of blindness in developing countries. Trachoma is spread primarily by flies, not by sexual transmission.)

Chlamydial infection can also be a cause of pharyngitis (sore throat), although the strain that causes this problem is a different one, just recently recognized, called *Chlamydia pneumoniae* (Komaroff et al., 1989).

A different strain of *C. trachomatis* also causes an STD called lymphogranuloma venereum (LGV), which is rare in North America and Europe but common in South America, Africa, and Asia. LGV is about four times as common in males as in females. Like syphilis, this disease has three stages. The primary lesion is a small, hardly noticeable ulcer or pimple on the genitals that appears after an incubation period of 3 to 12 days and then heals rapidly. While this lesion is usually painless, if it occurs in the urethra it may cause pain or burning.

The secondary stage of LGV, which occurs several months after the primary lesion, is marked by painful swelling of lymph nodes in the groin (usually on one side of the body), with accompanying fever, chills, and generalized aching. While almost all males with LGV have such a reaction in the secondary stage, only 20 to 30 percent of females do. Another one-third of women have lower abdominal and back pain. In addition, both men and women may experience symptoms of rectal infection that include a mucuslike discharge, rectal bleeding, and abscess formation. While the great majority of people recover from LGV after the secondary stage, even if untreated, late complications of this STD are serious. They include genital elephantiasis (large swellings of the genitals) and severe scarring of the rectum, sometimes leading to partial bowel obstruction.

Transmission

Chlamydial infections (except for trachoma) are most commonly sexually transmitted. As a STD, chlamydial infections follow a pattern that is quite similar to that of gonorrhea, although with a lower degree of transmissibility. In one study, male sexual partners of women who had either gonorrhea or chlamydial cervicitis were found to have chlamydial infections less often than gonorrhea: 28 percent versus 81 percent (Lycke et al., 1980). In the same study, male partners of women who had dual infections of gonorrhea and chlamydia also got chlamydial infections much less often than they got gonorrhea (28 percent versus 77 percent).

Chlamydial infections can be transmitted by vaginal or anal intercourse and (less often) by oral–genital contact. Chlamydial infections, not surprisingly, are also most common in persons with multiple sex partners (Centers for Disease Control, 1985). As with gonorrhea, women seem more susceptible to chlamydial infections. About 70 percent of the female sex partners of men with documented chlamydial infections are found to be infected with chlamydia too, while 25 to 50 percent of the male sex partners of women with chlamydia have been found to be infected (Centers for Disease Control, 1985).

Symptoms

One of the difficult problems with chlamydial infections is that, much like gonorrhea, they often do not produce symptoms in infected females. According to some estimates, half of all women with chlamydial infections are symptom-free. A smaller number of men—estimated to be about 15 to 30 percent—do not have symptoms either, but since the long-term consequences for males are not as serious as for females, this is a far less serious medical problem.

In males, *C. trachomatis* most commonly causes symptoms of urethritis after one to three weeks' incubation. The two primary symptoms of urethritis are burning with urination and a whitish or clear urethral discharge. While these two symptoms typically occur together, either can occur without the other. In most cases, these symptoms are milder than in gonorrhea (Holmes et al., 1990).

Epididymitis in men under age 35 is presumed to be due to chlamydia unless proved otherwise and is marked by swelling, pain and tenderness in the scrotum (usually on one side only), and, often, fever. There may also be an associated urethritis. The pain of epididymitis can be so severe as to interfere with walking or running, but it also can be low-grade, feeling more like an aching sensation than a searing pain. Epididymitis usually makes sexual activity quite unpleasant for the affected male partly because during sexual arousal the scrotum pulls up toward the body. Along with the vasocongestion in the testes, this creates pressure on the infected epididymis that is usually painful.

In females, chlamydial cervicitis does not generally produce symptoms. A cloudy mucous discharge from the cervix is sometimes seen but one study found this in only 37 percent of women who had *Chlamydia trachomatis* isolated from the cervix. In some cases there may be itchiness or mild discomfort in the genitals, but in most instances there are no symptoms, so the female has no way of knowing that she has an active chlamydial infection that requires treatment. The lack of symptoms is a problem because of the likelihood that the infection will move higher in the female reproductive tract, where it is apt to do more damage.

Females with chlamydial urethritis are in a similar situation. Only about one-third of these women develop pain, burning with urination, or frequent urination, and only a small percentage develop a urethral discharge or soreness at the opening of the urethra. Thus, few seek treatment. Although women with chlamydial endometritis may have intermittent vaginal bleeding, this occur only in a minority; this type of chlamydial infection is also typically without any noticeable symptoms.

In contrast, chlamydial PID is more likely to be accompanied by symptoms, including the sudden onset of lower abdominal pain, vaginal bleeding, fever, and dyspareunia (painful intercourse). Another key symptom is that pressure on the lower abdomen during a pelvic exam is painful. However, as many as half of all cases of chlamydial PID may not have any symptoms, which is especially true for those cases that represent low-grade, smoldering infections that persist over time.

Chlamydial infection can occasionally spread from the Fallopian tubes to the surface of the liver (Stamm et al, 1988). This condition, called perihepatitis, is marked by pain in the right upper quadrant of the abdomen accompanied by nausea, vomiting, and fever. There may or may not be evidence of PID when this condition becomes symptomatic.

Diagnosis and Treatment

Because *Chlamydia trachomatis* grows only intracellularly (inside living cells), it is technically difficult and expensive to culture. In addition, because it usually takes at least three days to get the result of a culture for chlamydial infections, treatment is often started on the presumption that a chlamydial infection is present, a strategy that the U.S. Centers for Disease Control (1993r) endorse. Nevertheless, a culture is the most accurate means of establishing the diagnosis.

To avoid these difficulties, several new types of antibody testing have recently become available. These tests, which can detect chlamydial infections in genital secretions with a fairly high degree of accuracy (Tam, 1984; Howard et al., 1986; Stamm et al., 1988), can generally be done within a few hours and are less expensive than cultures.

A number of antibiotics are very effective in treating chlamydial infections. Azithromycin (which can be given orally in a single dose) or doxycycline (which is taken orally for one week) is currently the drug of choice except in pregnant women (Centers for Disease Control, 1993r). Erythromycin, ofloxacin, and sulfamethoxazole are alternative possibilities that are also highly effective. (Erythromycin is the drug of choice for pregnant women.)

It should be noted that penicillin is *not* effective against chlamydial infections. Because it is com-

mon to get chlamydial and gonorrheal infections at the same time, people are often treated for gonorrhea without realizing that they have a coexistent chlamydial infection—in part because gonorrhea has a shorter incubation time and in part because gonorrhea is easier to detect in the laboratory. This creates a situation in which the gonorrhea is cured by the penicillin, but the chlamydial infection is untouched. In some instances, this leads to a new flare-up of symptoms (chlamydial urethritis is common after gonorrhea in men), but if no symptoms occur or if they are ignored and go away spontaneously, the person remains infected and contagious to others and runs the risk of additional health complications.

It is particularly important that people who are diagnosed as having a chlamydial infection (or a suspected chlamydial infection) notify any partner with whom they had sex in the 30 days prior to the appearance of symptoms so that these individuals can be evaluated and treated (Centers for Disease Control, 1993r).

CHANCROID

Chancroid is a sexually transmitted bacterial disease that until recently has been uncommon in the industrialized Western nations but is thought to be more common than syphilis on a worldwide basis (Schmid et al., 1987). Caused by *Hemophilus ducreyi*, a short, compact, rod-shaped bacterium, this disease now affects an estimated 5000 to 10,000 people annually in America, a startling increase over the fewer than 1000 cases reported annually in the United States in the 1970s (Schmid et al., 1987; Leary, 1988).

Public health officials attribute the rise in chancroid and other previously infrequent STDs during the 1980s in the United States to increased prostitution tied to female drug use, as well as to the diversion of local STD personnel and funds to the fight against AIDS (Leary, 1988). Increased international travel may also play a role in this process.

Symptoms

The incubation period after exposure is short, usually between four and seven days. The hallmark lesion is a genital ulcer (sometimes called a "soft chancre," in distinction to the "hard chancre" of syphilis) that begins as a tender pimple surrounded by a reddened area (Figure 19.7). Over one to two days, it becomes filled with pus and breaks open into a sharply demarcated ulceration with ragged edges. Approximately half of those infected have more than one genital ulcer.

In males, the ulcers are most frequently on the foreskin, the frenulum, or the coronal ridge (the area separating the head of the penis from the shaft). Although the head or shaft of the penis can be affected, this is much less typical.

In females, the ulcers are usually at or near the entrance to the vagina. They may involve the labia, the clitoris, or the area just inside the vaginal opening, as well as the region between the vagina and the rectum. The cervix can also be affected, and lesions involving the breasts, the fingers, the thighs, and the mouth have also been encountered, although with far less frequency.

The other prominent clinical finding in chancroid is painful swelling of the lymph nodes on one side of the groin (the side that drains the infected region of the genitals). Although this occurs in only about half of chancroid patients, it is often a dramatic development, as the large swollen lymph nodes, called *buboes*, can rupture and exude a thick, creamy pus.

Chancroid does not appear to cause any major health complications beyond those mentioned above. *Hemophilus ducreyi* apparently does not cause disease in babies born to mothers with this infection at the time of delivery (Ronald and Albritton, 1984).

Figure 19.7 Chancroid in the Male

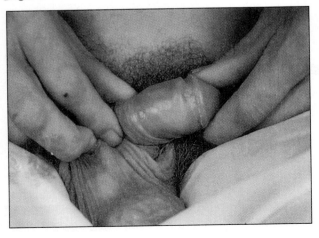

Diagnosis and Treatment

No blood test is available to diagnose chancroid, so the diagnosis is usually made on clinical grounds after a physical exam (Schmid et al., 1987).

The recommended treatment for chancroid is antibiotics—either a single oral dose of azithromycin, or erythromycin, taken in pill form for a week, or a single injection of ceftriaxone (Centers for Disease Control, 1993q). Fortunately, these treatments are highly effective; if improvement doesn't occur promptly (within a week after therapy), it is important to consider whether the diagnosis was correct, whether the person may also be infected with another STD—especially HIV—or whether the strain of *H. ducreyi* is antibiotic-resistant to the drug used.

Anyone who has had sexual contact with a chancroid-infected person within ten days preceding the onset of that person's infection or during the infection should be examined and treated whether there are symptoms or not (Centers for Disease Control, 1993q).

GENITAL HERPES

The herpes family of viruses and the infections they cause, such as chickenpox, shingles, and cold sores, are widespread today, as they have been for thousands of years. First named by ancient Greek physicians from the word *herpein*, meaning "to creep," because of the appearance of their characteristic skin rashes, and described in some detail by Roman physicians of the first and second centuries A.D., herpes infections have recently been the subject of considerable public attention.

Genital herpes currently affects some 30 to 40 million Americans, with an additional 500,000 cases occurring annually. Viewed by some as a relatively minor skin infection with annoying but brief symptoms and by others as a life-threatening disease or even a heaven-sent directive against loose morals, the genital herpes epidemic of the 1980s had received almost as much media coverage as a presidential campaign by 1983, when it began to be outshadowed in the press by coverage of the AIDS epidemic.

Genital herpes is caused by two different but related forms of the herpes simplex virus, known as herpes virus type 1 and herpes virus type 2. In the past, herpes virus type 1 was almost exclusively a cause of cold sores and fever blisters, while genital herpes infections were almost invariably caused by the type 2 virus. Today, this distinction no longer holds true: in the United States, 10 to 20 percent of cases of genital herpes are now caused by the type 1 virus (Peter, Bryson, and Lovett, 1982), while in Japan 35 percent of first episodes are due to the type 1 virus (Corey et al., 1983).

A national survey done on blood samples obtained in the late 1970s showed that 16.4 percent of the U.S. population 15 to 74 years of age was infected with herpes simplex virus type 2 (Johnson et al., 1989). The prevalence of herpes virus type 2 antibody increased from under 1 percent in the group under age 15 to 20 percent in the 30 to 44 age bracket and was significantly higher in blacks than in whites at all ages.

Genital herpes is generally transmitted by sexual contact. Direct contact with infected genitals can cause transmission via sexual intercourse, rubbing the genitals together, oral–genital contact, anal intercourse, or oral–anal contact. In addition, normally protected areas of skin can become infected if there is a cut, rash, or sore, so that infections of the fingers, thighs, or other areas of the body are also possible.

The risk of developing genital herpes in a woman exposed to an infected, symptomatic man is estimated to be 80 to 90 percent (Straus et al., 1985). A man's risk of developing genital herpes from a single sexual encounter with an infected woman is estimated to be about 50 percent.

In some cases, genital herpes can be spread by less direct means. For example, transmission of the herpes simplex virus can occur by kissing alone, and if herpes of the mouth develops, it can then be spread by autoinoculation, that is, touching your genitals after putting your fingers in your mouth. Several reports have noted that the herpes virus can live for at least several hours on toilet seats, plastic, and cloth, raising the possibility of genital herpes infection occurring by nonsexual transmission (Larson and Bryson, 1982; Turner et al., 1983; Nerurkar et al., 1983). It is unlikely, however, that this mode of transmission is very common. The herpes virus does not seem able to survive the chemical purifiers typically used in hot tubs (Nerurkar et al., 1983). Genital herpes infections can also be transmitted by artificial insemination (Moore et al., 1989), and one case report indicates that it can be transmitted by a hickey (a "love

bite") as well (del Rosario, Blair, and Rickman, 1987).

Genital herpes can be transmitted by an asymptomatic sex partner—that is, a person who has no herpes blisters and no genital burning or itching (Rooney et al., 1986; Brock et al., 1990; Mertz et al., 1992). This finding is particularly troubling because it means that someone who doesn't realize that he or she is infected with the herpes simplex virus can inadvertently infect another person. While this mode of transmission is probably not too common, even if it occurs at only one-tenth the rate of symptomatic infection, asymptomatic transmission would occur in 1 out of 20 herpes victims.

The complexity of asymptomatic transmission is compounded further by the fact that someone may have large concentrations of herpes virus present in genital secretions on an episodic basis only, so that cultures of these fluids (semen, cervical mucus, vaginal secretions) that are negative for the herpes virus on one day may be positive a week later. One possibility is for persons with genital herpes to have cultures done on three occasions at least a week apart while they are totally asymptomatic: if all three cultures are negative, they can be fairly certain they won't infect a partner in their asymptomatic phase.

Symptoms

Genital herpes is marked by clusters of small, painful blisters on the genitals (Figure 19.8). After a few days, these blisters burst, leaving small ulcers in their place. In men, the blisters occur most commonly on the penis but they can also appear in the urethra or rectum. In women, blisters appear on the vaginal lips most often, but the cervix or anal area can also be affected.

The first episode of genital herpes is accompanied by fever, headache, and muscle soreness for two or more consecutive days in 39 percent of men and 68 percent of women (Corey et al., 1983). Almost all cases are marked by painful burning at the site of blister formation. Other relatively common symptoms include pain or burning during urination, discharge from the urethra or vagina, and ten-

genital herpes (jen' i tul her pēz) painful blisters of the genitals caused by infection with the herpes virus; outbreaks typically are recurrent and are highly contagious.

Figure 19.8   Genital Herpes

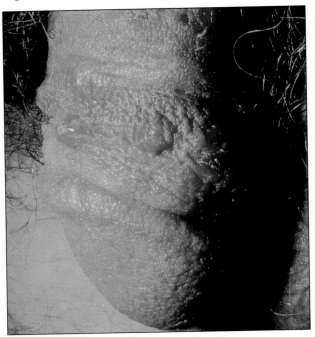

(a) Genital herpes in the male. Characteristically, the lesions are clustered and of various sizes.

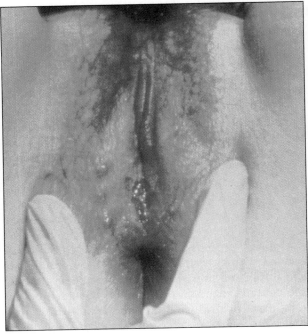

(b) External genital herpes in the female. Note the involvement in the perineal region, extending toward the rectum.

der, swollen lymph nodes in the groin, but these all tend to disappear within one to two weeks. More serious complications of first episodes, which occur more often in women than men, include the following: aseptic meningitis (an inflammation of the covering of the brain), estimated to occur in 8 percent of cases; eye infections, which occur in 1 percent of cases; and infection of the cervix in 88 percent of women with primary herpes type 2 infection (Peter, Bryson, and Lovett, 1982; Corey et al., 1983; Langston, 1983).

A typical first infection of genital herpes involves the appearance of 10 to 20 painful blisters on the genitals. If generalized symptoms such as fever or headache appear, they are usually most prominent within the first four days after the blisters occur, and then they diminish gradually over the first week of the infection. After the blisters burst, they may form larger reddish wet sores or ulcers, which usually heal in one or two weeks. Sores on the penis or on the mons become crusted before they heal, whereas those on the vaginal lips do not. Skin lesions last an average of 16.5 days in men and 19.7 days in women during first episodes of genital herpes (Corey et al., 1983), but if the sores

become secondarily infected with bacteria, healing may be somewhat delayed.

Although the blisters disappear and the ulcers heal spontaneously within one to three weeks, the herpes simplex virus invades nerves in the pelvic region and continues to live in a dormant state near the base of the spinal cord. In about 10 percent of cases there are no further attacks, but many people have recurrent episodes of genital herpes varying in frequency from once a month to once every few years.[1] Repeat attacks are sometimes brought on by emotional stress, illness, sunburn, physical exhaustion, or extreme climates, or they may occur for no apparent reason (Glaser et al., 1985; Wyngaarden, 1988; Kemeny et al., 1989). Generally, these recurrences are less severe than the original episode because the body is able to mobilize appropriate antibodies to counteract the infecting virus. Fortunately, many who suffer from herpes find that repeat attacks tend to die out after a few years (Gillespie, 1982).

---

[1]If the first episode of genital herpes is caused by the type 1 virus, recurrences occur in only 55 percent of cases (Corey et al., 1983).

Recurrences are sometimes preceded by warning symptoms that occur up to 36 hours before blisters appear. These include itching or tingling sensations in or near the genitals, tenderness or aching in the groin area, and burning or pain with urination or defecation. While these symptoms are not invariably followed by active outbreaks, and while some repeat episodes of genital herpes are totally symptom-free, when such symptoms occur they deserve attention. First, they indicate the possibility that a person may be infectious *even before blisters appear.* This is possible because live herpes virus may be carried in semen or cervical or vaginal secretions even when no rashes or blisters can be seen. Second, it may be possible to prevent a flare-up of herpes by taking steps that reduce stress (e.g., getting more sleep, eating well, and avoiding substances like alcohol or drugs that might suppress the body's immunologic response system) (Gillespie, 1982; Langston, 1983).

Scientists are still puzzled by many aspects of genital herpes, and we do not understand clearly why some people never have recurrences while others have a number of repeat attacks. Certainly no one leads a completely stress-free life, nor can most people completely avoid the types of physical illnesses—like the flu—that often trigger recurrences. It is possible that there may be different strains of the herpes type 1 and 2 viruses which differ in their virulence, partly accounting for this variability, and the individual's resistance (as determined by the body's immunologic defenses) may play a role too. However, it would be a mistake to assume that people who experience recurrences of genital herpes aren't taking care of themselves properly or are being reinfected by another sexual partner, since such things usually aren't true. It is important to realize that even if no recurrences appear, a person is still infected with this virus on a life-long basis and can transmit it to a sex partner asymptomatically.

It now appears that the pattern of recurrence is strongly influenced by the type of the infecting herpes virus (Lafferty et al., 1987). Lesions affecting the mouth or lips are very common in type 1 infections but infrequent in those with type 2, while genital recurrences are six times more common than recurrences in the mouth in people infected with type 2.

One intriguing recent finding about genital herpes is that close to half of people who were previously thought to have an "asymptomatic" infection can actually be taught to recognize genital lesions that don't have the classical appearance of herpes blisters, such as mild external irritation or itching, or small cracks in the genital skin (Langenberg et al., 1989). Recognizing such lesions as herpes is important because it permits the person to avoid sexual contact during a time of increased transmissibility.

Genital herpes presents special problems. First, like syphilis, genital herpes in a pregnant woman can cause birth defects in the developing fetus since the virus can cross the placenta. Fortunately, this is a rare occurrence. More worrisome is that the baby can be infected from the cervix or vagina during delivery, with such infections causing death or serious damage to the brain or eyes more than 50 percent of the time in those newborns who are infected (Binkin and Alexander, 1983). The rate of herpes infections in newborns has increased considerably in the last 15 years, probably mirroring the rising prevalence in the general population (Holmes et al., 1990; Cone et al., 1994). While the risk of infecting the baby may be as high as 50 percent with vaginal delivery during a first attack of genital herpes in the mother, the risk is estimated at about 5 percent during recurrent episodes (Corey et al., 1983; Prober et al., 1987). Compounding the difficulties of this situation is the fact that newborns may be infected even when the mother has no symptoms at the time of delivery. A recent study showed that cultures taken at the time of labor do not show accurately whether the infant will be exposed to the herpes simplex virus at delivery (Cone et al., 1994). For this reason, cesarean section is often recommended to pregnant women with active genital herpes (Prober et al., 1988), but this is an individual matter that each woman should discuss with her physician. In addition, infection can occur after birth if the mother or father has oral lesions or if the virus is transmitted in breast milk.

The second serious issue regarding complications of genital herpes is that there appears to be an association between the herpes simplex type 2 virus and both cervical cancer (McDougall et al., 1980; Kessler, 1979; Graham et al., 1982) and cancer of the vulva (Schwartz et al., 1981). While only some women who have genital herpes will be so affected, because these forms of cancer are easily treated if detected early, it is advisable for all women who have had genital herpes to have a Pap smear and pelvic exam every six months.

The third source of concern is that a number of recent reports suggest genital herpes may make people more vulnerable to infection with HIV, the human immunodeficiency virus that causes AIDS (Cannon et al., 1988; Holmberg et al., 1988; Stamm et al., 1988). Current thinking holds that the genital ulcerations caused by herpes may provide HIV with an easy mode of access into the body, whereas intact genital skin surfaces may be less susceptible to attack by this virus.

Diagnosis and Treatment

The diagnosis of an active infection generally can be made with accuracy by a physician on the basis of a physical examination of the genital blisters and/or ulcers. However, other STDs can mimic genital herpes, and sometimes genital blisters or ulcers are a result of inflammation rather than infection. Thus, making a proper diagnosis is not always a simple matter. Various laboratory tests can establish the diagnosis with more certainty. These include (in increasing order of accuracy) (1) Pap smears in women, (2) blood tests to measure antibodies against herpes viruses, and (3) cultures to grow the virus in the laboratory (these are usually taken by touching a cotton swab to a blister or ulcer; the procedure is generally painless).

There is no known cure for genital herpes, although much research is being done. A new drug called acyclovir is of some usefulness in lessening the severity of symptoms, especially in first attacks. When taken by mouth within five or six days after the onset of symptoms in a first episode of genital herpes, acyclovir reduced the period of viral shedding (virus being present in body fluids such as semen or vaginal secretions) by two-thirds compared with treatment with a placebo (Bryson et al., 1983; Mertz et al., 1984). In these same studies, acyclovir shortened the healing time of genital herpes lesions by four to nine days. In addition, taken on a long-term, continuous basis, oral acyclovir seems to cut down the number and duration of recurrences: in fact, in several studies, the rate of recurrence was lowered by at least 75 percent (Douglas et al., 1984; Mindel et al., 1984; Straus et al., 1984). In recurrences, acyclovir is less effective. However, this medication is quite useful in reducing the number of flare-ups of genital herpes in individuals with frequent or particularly severe attacks. In 525 patients who used acyclovir continuously for

three years after having had at least six genital herpes attacks in the year before being treated, 61 percent were completely recurrence-free in the third year of drug use, and no significant side effects were noted (Kaplowitz et al., 1991). One potential problem with long-term treatment is that some strains of herpes simplex virus have become resistant to this drug, raising concerns that overuse may lead to a situation of a more virulent strain of the virus becoming widespread (Hirsch and Schooley, 1989; Englund et al., 1990).

General measures such as taking aspirin (or an aspirin substitute) and using cold, wet compresses to relieve pain are often helpful during an initial herpes episode or recurrent flare-ups. In addition, avoiding tight underwear or clothing can reduce irritation, and keeping the genitals clean and dry by washing with warm water and soap several times a day can also be beneficial. The skin should be dried with clean towels and a patting, rather than vigorous rubbing motion, and hand-to-eye contact should be avoided after touching the genitals. Towels and washcloths should be kept separately, since they may be contagious to others. In fact, it's wisest to use a separate towel for the face to avoid inadvertent spread of the virus from the genital region to the eyes. Here are several other practical hints. Temporarily eliminate physical activities that may cause skin irritation. For instance, avoid bicycling and long-distance running, as well as types of dancing that involve intense exertion. (Once lesions have begun to heal thoroughly, these activities can be gradually resumed.) Finally, use a disinfectant spray (we suggest Betadine, which is widely used in hospitals and clinics) several times a day to prevent secondary bacterial infections in the open lesions after herpes blisters burst.

Sexual contact should be completely avoided from the time symptoms of genital herpes first begin until ten days after healing is complete (for a first attack) or until two days after complete healing in recurrent episodes. Unfortunately, a few people seem to shed virus all the time—whether or not they have visible skin lesions or symptoms—so it's impossible to guarantee that there is no risk of contagion. While use of a condom can help prevent transmission of genital herpes, it is not a foolproof method (both because it doesn't cover all lesions and because it isn't always worn from the start of genital contact) and it may actually irritate the condition.

VIRAL HEPATITIS

Viral hepatitis is an infection of the liver that can vary in severity from a completely symptomless state to mild gastrointestinal symptoms (poor appetite, indigestion, diarrhea) to an acute debilitating illness with fever, jaundice (yellowish appearance of the skin), vomiting, abdominal pain, and—occasionally—more serious medical complications, including death. There are four main types of viral hepatitis: hepatitis A, hepatitis B, hepatitis C, and delta (type D) hepatitis. All four types can be sexually transmitted.

Transmission

Hepatitis A

Hepatitis A (formerly known as infectious hepatitis) has an incubation period of 15 to 45 days. The hepatitis A virus is mainly spread by the fecal–oral route, with person-to-person transmission, food-borne epidemics (usually caused by infected food handlers), and the consumption of raw or poorly cooked shellfish from contaminated waters accounting for most cases in industrialized nations. Previous data have shown that homosexual males have a higher incidence of hepatitis A than heterosexuals (Corey and Holmes, 1980; Fawaz and Matloff, 1981). It appears that oral–anal contact is the primary explanation for this finding, so that at least within the homosexual population hepatitis A may sometimes be sexually transmitted. In 1991, there was a sudden upsurge in hepatitis A among homosexual men, suggesting that there may have been a return to unsafe sexual practices that transmit this virus (Centers for Disease Control, 1992h). Heterosexual transmission of hepatitis A is possible but does not seem to be a significant risk factor in broad-based population studies. This may be largely because oral–anal contact is unusual among heterosexual couples. There are about 30,000 cases of hepatitis A reported annually in the United States.

Hepatitis B

Hepatitis B, previously called serum hepatitis, is usually spread by blood or blood products but it can also be transmitted by saliva, seminal fluid, vaginal secretions, and other biologic fluids (Zuckerman, 1982). Many of the approximately 200,000

to 300,000 annual new cases of hepatitis B in the United States are sexually transmitted (Brandt, 1982; Alter, et al., 1989; Centers for Disease Control, 1993q), and evidence suggests that homosexual men have the highest rates of previous or current infection with this disorder (Reiner et al., 1982; Schreeded et al., 1982; Holmes et al., 1989). However, it is noteworthy that the proportion of hepatitis B cases accounted for by homosexual activity decreased by 62 percent between 1981 and 1988 (Alter et al., 1990). It is thought that trauma to the rectal mucosa from anal intercourse, manual stimulation of the rectum, or frequent use of enemas may predispose to the spread of this infection.

Studies of the prevalence of hepatitis B infection among various groups show that overall prevalence in homosexual males is 40 to 60 percent, whereas in heterosexual males it ranges from 4 to 18 percent (Alter et al., 1986). In this same report, it was found among heterosexual university students that students with three or more sexual partners in the four months before the study were much more likely to have been infected with hepatitis B virus than students with fewer than three partners in this same time period (14 percent versus 1.5 percent, respectively). Dan (1986) suggests that this result might mean that persons whose lifestyle exposes them to numerous sex partners are actually exposed to a pool of people with much higher rates of hepatitis B infection than are the group of people with few sex partners. If this view is correct, it means that a person having many sex partners has a risk of infection that is not just numerically proportional to the number of partners but is actually considerably higher since each of the partners is "riskier" from a health viewpoint—that is, more likely to be infected with the hepatitis B virus and thus more likely to be a carrier. Data from a controlled study confirmed that heterosexuals with hepatitis B were more likely to have multiple sex partners than heterosexual control subjects (Alter, et al., 1989). Anal intercourse and failing to use vaginal contraceptives may facilitate sexual transmission of hepatitis B to women (Rosenblum et al., 1992).

Hepatitis B persists in an asymptomatic carrier state in approximately 5 to 10 percent of infected

viral hepatitis infection of the liver by a virus causing a debilitating acute illness and sometimes a chronic condition.

adults, with an estimated 400,000 to 800,000 carriers in the United States and 150 to 200 million worldwide. This condition, in which the person is still infectious although not generally ill, can persist for months, years, or a lifetime. Carriers of hepatitis B have an increased risk of developing liver cancer in their lifetime.

Hepatitis C

Recently, scientists have finally succeeded in identifying the hepatitis C virus, solving a mystery of what caused the type of hepatitis previously called "non-A, non-B" (Alter and Sampliner, 1989; Davis et al., 1989; Di Bisceglie et al., 1989; Kuo et al., 1989). Currently, the CDC estimates that there are 150,000 cases of hepatitis C annually in the United States, with fewer than one-tenth resulting from transfusions (Alter and Sampliner, 1989). One percent of volunteer blood donors have been found to be carriers of antibody to the hepatitis C virus (Stevens et al., 1990). Heterosexual transmission plays a significant role in the spread of this form of hepatitis (Alter et al., 1990), although the most recent evidence suggests that such sexual transmission is much less efficient than for hepatitis B (Osmond et al., 1993; Weinstock et al., 1993; Bresters et al., 1993).

Hepatitis C currently accounts for more than 90 percent of the cases of hepatitis that develop after blood transfusions and is particularly devastating because at least half of those infected with it acutely eventually develop chronic hepatitis, which commonly leads to cirrhosis or cancer of the liver (Alter and Sampliner, 1989; Davis et al., 1989).

Hepatitis D

Delta hepatitis, also called type D hepatitis, is an unusual infection in the United States that was first discovered in the late 1970s. The hepatitis D virus requires the presence of the hepatitis B virus to multiply (Hoofnagle, 1989). In a sense, it "piggybacks" onto the hepatitis B virus, either at the same time acute hepatitis B infection occurs, or later on when it infects a chronic hepatitis B carrier. In both situations, it is often a very severe infection, with high death rates and serious permanent liver damage in many of those who survive. Unlike other forms of hepatitis, it is most likely to occur in prolonged, severe outbreaks in isolated communities. It is especially common in the Mediterranean and the Middle East, but rare in Northern Europe, the

Western hemisphere, China, and Southeast Asia. IV drug use appears to be an especially important means of transmitting the hepatitis D virus, but male homosexuals and non-IV-drug-using female prostitutes have also been found to be infected (Solomon et al., 1988; Weisfuse, 1989; and Rosenblum et al., 1992). Detailed information is lacking on additional aspects of the sexual transmission of delta hepatitis at present.

Diagnosis and Treatment

Hepatitis is diagnosed on the basis of laboratory tests (e.g., blood tests that show abnormalities in liver enzymes), and the specific type of hepatitis is determined by immunologic testing of blood samples. Treatment is generally symptomatic, with hospitalization required only in the more severe cases. In 1989, a major breakthrough occurred in treating hepatitis C, with the discovery that the drug alpha interferon can often prevent the hepatitis C virus from destroying liver cells, although relapses are common when the drug is stopped (Davis et al., 1989; Di Bisceglie et al., 1989).

Persons in intimate contact with someone with hepatitis A can obtain partial immunity by getting a shot of immune serum globulin, but as a practical matter they have often been exposed for weeks before the diagnosis has been made. A vaccine for hepatitis A was licensed in Europe in 1992 but is not yet available in the United States. Viral hepatitis B vaccines are now available that are safe and effective (Hadler et al., 1986). It is currently recommended that anyone who is at high risk of acquiring hepatitis B, such as male homosexuals or bisexuals, heterosexuals with multiple sex partners, people who inject illicit drugs, all health-care workers, and family members of hepatitis B carriers, be vaccinated (Hoffnagle, 1989a). Since hepatitis D depends on prior or simultaneous infection with the hepatitis B virus, it can effectively be prevented by the hepatitis B vaccine. There is no vaccine available for hepatitis C.

GENITAL WARTS

Genital warts (condylomata accuminata) are dry, usually painless warts that grow on or near the genitals and around the anus. According to one recent government estimate, there are 12 million

Figure 19.9   Genital Warts

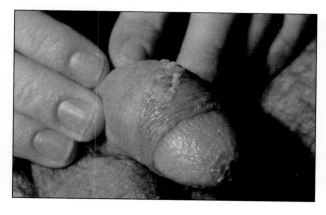
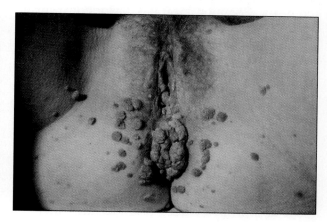

Genital warts in the male (left) and female (right).

cases of genital warts in America today, with 750,000 new cases annually (Goldsmith, 1989). They are caused by a sexually transmitted virus called the human papilloma virus (HPV) and are usually pink or grayish-white with a cauliflower-like appearance.

When epithelial cells (cells that line the outer or inner surface of the body) are infected by HPV, they undergo a transformation in which they divide continuously (Marx, 1989a), causing a buildup of abnormal tissue that eventually becomes a wart.

Although genital warts were once thought to be more of a cosmetic nuisance than a health problem, it is now clear that the virus that causes them is an important long-term cause of cancer of the cervix and other cancers of the anal and genital region, including cancer of the penis (Rando, 1988; Marx, 1989a; Reeves et al., 1989). For instance, in one large case–control study in Latin America, cervical infection with HPV types 16 or 18 was more than twice as common in cervical cancer cases as in controls (Reeves et al., 1989). While no one believes that it is the papilloma virus alone that causes such cancers, scientists are now developing theories to explain what role these fairly common viruses may play in producing malignancies and why only some infected persons develop these cancers.

HPV was found in 29 percent of pregnant women in one study (Gissman and Schwarz, 1986); in the Latin American survey cited above, 32 percent of women in the control group had cervical infection with HPV (Reeves et al., 1989). Male sexual partners of women with HPV infection are commonly infected too; in one survey, almost three-quarters of the males were found to have HPV in genital lesions (Kennedy, 1988). In addition, since genital warts commonly co-exist with other STDs, anyone with such growths should undergo thorough medical evaluation to check for the possibility of an asymptomatic case of gonorrhea, chlamydial infection, or syphilis. It is currently thought that genital warts are most likely to occur in adolescents or young adults—precisely the same age range as gonorrhea.

Approximately two-thirds of the sexual partners of individuals with genital warts develop the disease themselves. The incubation period is six to eight weeks. Although the infection is certainly transmitted by direct contact with the lesions, there is also evidence that the virus is also transmitted by semen (Inoue et al., 1992).

Symptoms

Although genital warts are, as the name implies, most often found on (or inside) the genitals, they can also be found in other locations, including the mouth, the eyelid, the lip, the nipple, and around the anus (Figure 19.9). (Genital warts, or condylomata accuminata, are not the same as ordinary skin warts, which occur on most parts of the body.)

genital warts dry, painless warts on or near the genitals or anus that are caused by a sexually transmitted virus. Sometimes referred to as venereal warts.

In males, genital warts can involve any part of the penis. Common locations include just inside the opening of the urethra (where they are apt to have a bright red appearance), on the frenulum, on the head of the penis or the coronal ridge, and on the inner surface of the foreskin, as well as along the penile shaft. The appearance of the warts can range in size from tiny, solitary dotlike growths to large, irregular, rough-surfaced masses that protrude from the penis by a half-inch or more.

In females, genital warts commonly involve the labia, the opening to the vagina, the inner third of the vagina, and the cervix. In some cases, they appear as relatively isolated patches of greyish-pink tissue tags, while in other instances, the pattern of growth is distressing because extensive wart formation virtually covers the external genitals. (Rarely, genital warts can become so large as to block the birth canal at the time of labor, requiring a cesarean delivery.) As with males, genital warts in females may grow just inside the urethra.

While the primary problem with genital warts for most people is the embarrassment they cause, if they become large they may also create some mechanical discomfort (particularly during sex). In addition, large genital warts are also more likely to become secondarily infected or to become ulcerated (often because of the rubbing of underwear against them). Infrequently, genital warts may be a source of bleeding, particularly if they are quite large.

Diagnosis and Treatment

The diagnosis of genital warts is usually obvious to a medically trained examiner. Because similar lesions can be found during secondary syphilis (these are called condylomata lata), a blood test to detect syphilis is, as we mentioned above, always in order when warts appear on the genitals. Currently, tests to detect the specific type of DNA that the HPV possesses are being performed in many centers, but it is not clear what practical influence this will have on treatment decisions at present.

According to the CDC, no therapy has been shown to actually eradicate HPV (Centers for Disease Control, 1993q). Thus, the goal of treatment is simply to remove visible or symptomatic warts. The available treatments include: (1) use of a liquid containing podophyllin, a caustic chemical that erodes the warts when applied repeatedly for short periods of time (this must be done by a qualified health-care professional, not self-administered, and it should not be used for pregnant women); (2) use of tricholacetic acid applied to the warts on a weekly basis; (3) use of carbon dioxide laser surgery to burn away the warts painlessly; (4) use of liquid nitrogen to freeze the warts, which usually destroys them in one or two visits; (5) use of a drug called interferon injected into the base of the warts. Unfortunately, recurrences of the warts can occur after any of these treatment methods and none of them eradicates the underlying HPV infection, which remains in tissues next to a wart that has been chemically or surgically destroyed.

Anyone with genital warts should use condoms during sexual activity with a partner to cut down the risk of transmitting HPV. (For safety's sake, this is advisable permanently—not just when genital warts are visible.) In addition, if your partner has been exposed, it is wise to have that person get a medical checkup to see if he or she requires treatment.

MOLLUSCUM CONTAGIOSUM

Molluscum contagiosum is caused by a pox virus that typically produces raised lesions on the external genitals or on the thighs, buttocks, or lower abdomen (Figure 19.10). The painless lesions, which usually appear three to six weeks after exposure, vary from 1 millimeter to 1 centimeter in

Figure 19.10　Molluscum Contagiosm

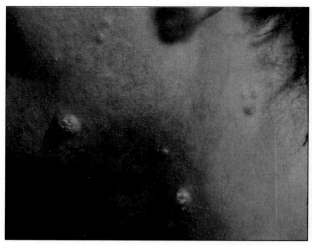

Molluscum contagiosum on the face and neck.

diameter and have a pinkish-orange color with a pearly top. If the lesion is squeezed, the cheesy plug of material within it can be expressed, much like a blackhead. Since the infection usually causes little trouble and often disappears spontaneously in about six months, treatment is not always necessary. Local applications of liquid nitrogen or frozen carbon dioxide have been used to remove the skin lesions.

PUBIC LICE

Pubic lice, or "crabs," are parasites that invade the pubic region (Figure 19.11). Although crabs are usually transmitted by sexual contact, they may also be inadvertently picked up from sheets, towels, or clothing used by an infested person. The lice attach themselves to pubic hair and require fresh blood at least twice a day to survive. Eggs laid by female lice are cemented onto the pubic hairs and cannot be washed off.

The crab louse (known officially as *Phthirus pubis* and called "papillon d'amour," or "butterfly of love," by the French) causes intense itching, which is mainly felt at night. A few people have no real symptoms; others develop an allergic rash that can be infected by bacteria after a lot of scratching. The lice can be killed by gamma benzene hexachloride, marketed in cream, lotion, or shampoo form under the trade name Kwell. Another highly effec-

tive treatment is a lotion called malathion (marketed under the trade name Prioderm). Neither of these drugs should be applied to the eyebrows or eyelashes, even if these areas are infested. Instead, infestations in these areas can usually be controlled by applying Vaseline or a similar petroleum jelly product twice a day for seven to ten days to suffocate the lice and their eggs. It is a myth that using brown soap to wash or that applying kerosene to the skin are the best ways to treat lice.

Although pubic lice can survive for only 24 hours once they leave the human body, eggs that fall off into sheets or onto clothing can survive for six days. For this reason, fresh bedding and clean clothing should always be used to avoid reinfestation.

VAGINAL INFECTIONS

Vaginitis

Vaginitis refers to any vaginal inflammation, whether caused by infection, allergic reaction, estrogen deficiency, or chemical irritation. It is helpful to realize that while vaginitis frequently is transmitted sexually, probably 30 percent of cases arise from nonsexual causes. Vaginitis can create sexual problems by causing tenderness or pain during intercourse or by causing disagreeable odors that embarrass the woman or reduce her partner's enthusiasm for intimacy. Here we consider only the most common forms of vaginal infection.

Trichomonas Infections

Trichomonas vaginitis is caused by a one-cell microorganism called *Trichomonas vaginalis,* ordinarily present in small numbers in the vagina (Holmes et

Figure 19.11   The Crab Louse

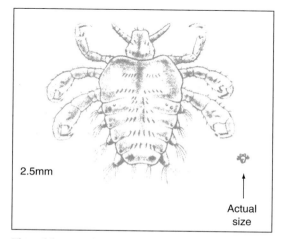

2.5mm

Actual
size

The crab louse can be transmitted by sexual or non-sexual contact and typically causes intense itching in the pubic region at night.

molluscum contagiosum a skin disease caused by a pox virus; the skin breaks out in small, bumpy lesions with a pearly top.
pubic lice parasites that invade the pubic region, often transmitted during sexual intercourse.
vaginitis (vaj in ī' tis) vaginal inflammation from infection or chemical irritation.
trichomonas vaginitis (trick o mōn' ess) an infection of the vagina caused by bacteria called *trichomonas vaginalis.* Accompanied by a frothy, thin, greenish or yellowish gray, foul-smelling discharge and burning and itching.

al., 1990). It is almost always sexually transmitted and has a high rate of infectivity. Eighty-five percent of the female partners of infected men and 40 percent of the male partners of infected women are also found to be infected (Holmes et al., 1990). While most men harboring this infection are asymptomatic (although a small percent have urethritis), trichomonal infection in females produces a vaginitis that is usually quite bothersome. The hallmark features are a profuse, often malodorous, frothy, yellowish or greyish runny vaginal discharge; intense vaginal itching; and pain with intercourse. The symptoms often begin or worsen during or immediately after a menstrual period. The diagnosis can be made by identifying the offending organism either by microscopic examination or by culture. Treatment involves the simultaneous administration of a drug called metronidazole (Flagyl) in pill form to the infected woman and her male sexual partner(s). Not treating the male increases the odds of a "ping pong" effect in which the woman is temporarily cured, only to be reinfected by her partner. It is wisest to use a condom until the infection has cleared completely.

Monilia Infections

Monilial vaginitis is a type of fungus or yeast infection caused by an overgrowth of *Candida albicans,* a microorganism normally found in the vagina. This infection, which is thought to affect three-quarters of all women at one time or another, is usually marked by vulvar and/or vaginal itching; a white, thick, curdlike, nonodorous vaginal discharge; and burning after vaginal intercourse. Sexual transmission accounts for only about 30 percent of cases. Other common factors that predispose to candidal infections are pregnancy, use of high-estrogen-content birth control pills, and diabetes. Candidal vaginitis is also common during the use of various broad-spectrum antibiotics like tetracyclines and ampicillin, and is a particular problem in women who need to take corticosteroids like cortisone or prednisone on a long-term basis. Presumably, the antibiotics alter the natural microbial balance in the vagina, reducing the number of protective vaginal microorganisms that ordinarily prevent an invasion or overgrowth of candidal forms, while the corticosteroids alter the body's immune response as well as change the microbial mix in the vagina.

The diagnosis of candidal vaginitis is made either by examining a vaginal smear microscopically

to identify the characteristic fungus filaments and spores or by vaginal culture. Treatment can be accomplished with a variety of antifungal creams, lotions, vaginal tablets, or suppositories, including miconazole (Monistat), nystatin (Micostatin), butoconazole (Femstat), clotrimazole (Gynelotrimin, Mycelex) and similar products. For mild infections, good results are usually obtained with 3 to 5 days of treatment, but for more severe or recurrent infections, longer treatment schedules of 7 to 14 days are more effective. Oral nystatin taken three times a day for several weeks may also be effective when other treatment regimens have failed.

Some promise for improved prevention may be contained in a recent study that found that eating 8 ounces of yogurt containing *Lactobacillus acidophilus* daily for six months greatly reduced the occurrence of candidal vaginitis (Hilton et al., 1992). Since all yogurt products do not contain this microorganism, it is important for a woman who wants to try this method to be sure that she is getting the proper type of yogurt, which is usually available at health food stores (not in general supermarkets).

While treatment of a woman's sex partner isn't usually indicated, in particularly recalcitrant cases this may be advisable. Because candidal species are common in the mouth, it may also be helpful to abstain from oral–genital sex temporarily to see if this is a potential source of reinfection.

Preventing Vaginitis

The vagina normally contains a number of different microorganisms. Some of these seem to play a specific role in vaginal physiology, such as maintaining the proper degree of acidity, while others can produce symptoms and infection if they multiply disproportionately. According to a review by Larsen and Galask (1982), an average of seven different species of bacteria are found in the vagina, and other microorganisms such as yeasts and viruses are also present.

Why some women develop vaginal pain or itching without having any detectable infection is unclear (Osborne, Grubin, and Pratson, 1982). It is also uncertain why many women with documented infections don't have any discharge or other symptoms. However, the fact remains that vaginitis is often an annoying condition that women and their sex partners would like to prevent if they can. Here are several suggestions for minimizing the risk of developing vaginitis:

1. Wear cotton underpants; nylon or synthetic fiber underpants or pantyhose retain heat and moisture, creating a good environment for bacteria to grow.

2. Avoid frequent douching, since this can irritate the vagina and remove important "natural" microorganisms that protect you. (Many medical authorities believe that routine douching is unnecessary and advise it only under specific conditions.)

3. After going to the bathroom, always wipe with a front-to-back motion. This way, bacteria from the rectum will not be brought forward to the vagina.

4. Avoid the long-term use of antibiotics, which can reduce the number of bacteria normally present in the vagina, allowing yeast forms to overgrow.

5. Maintain good habits of personal hygiene, including regular washing of the genital and anal regions with mild soap and water. Avoid so-called feminine hygiene sprays, which can be irritating to the skin.

6. If your partner has an infection of the genitals, avoid sexual contact. (Using a condom may be of some help in this situation.)

7. Do not put the penis in or near the vagina after anal intercourse since this can directly introduce "foreign" bacteria into the vagina.

8. Avoid forms of sexual activity that produce any vaginal discomfort.

Bacterial Vaginosis

Bacterial vaginosis is a vaginal infection that was previously known as nonspecific vaginitis or hemophilus vaginitis. The term *vaginosis* has been used in preference to vaginitis to indicate that signs of inflammation (such as redness and tenderness) are not usually present with this condition; usually in medicine, the suffix "itis" indicates inflammation. In addition the bacterial organism *Hemophilus vaginalis*, since renamed *Gardnerella vaginalis*, is now known to be only one of several bacteria that accounts for this disorder, although it can be cultured from the vagina in about 95 percent of cases (Sobel, 1989). The primary problem seems to be one in which the normal protective bacterial organisms

in the vagina decrease drastically in number while the infecting bacteria overgrow. The result of the overgrowth is a grayish-white discharge that usually has a foul "fishy" odor and is accompanied by burning or itching, although the latter symptoms tend to be much less intense than with many other vaginal infections.

Bacterial vaginosis is very common in sexually active women. It occurs in about 15 percent of women seen at a university student gynecology clinic, in 10 to 25 percent of pregnant women, and in close to 40 percent of women seen at STD clinics (Sobel, 1989; Hillier and Holmes, 1990; Lande, 1993). However, many of these infections are asymptomatic, and their long-term significance is unknown. Simultaneous infections with *G. vaginalis* are typically found in the urethras of male sex partners of women with this disorder. Treatment consists of either metronidazole (Flagyl) taken in pill form or an antibiotic called clindamycin, used in the form of an intravaginal cream. Treatment of the male partner does not appear to be necessary at present, although good data on this point are lacking. However, the male should definitely wear a condom during sexual intercourse not only to cut down the risk of his becoming infected but also to prevent transmission of other pathogens (especially gonorrhea) to which the woman with bacterial vaginosis may be especially vulnerable.

PSYCHOSOCIAL ASPECTS OF STDS

There is little question that in the 1980s our society was overwhelmed by new developments regarding STDs. First there was a tremendous amount of attention given to the still-raging genital herpes epidemic. Although the media focus on this disease was initially informative and useful, it gradually took on overtones of emotional hysteria in some quarters. This reaction may have peaked in mid-1982, but by early 1983, the public's intense fears

monilial vaginitis (mon il' ee all vaj in eye' tis) infection of the vagina caused by a fungus; usually accompanied by a thick, cheesy discharge with intense itching.

bacterial vaginosis a bacterial infection of the vagina marked by a malodorous grayish-white discharge and symptoms of burning or itching; this condition is caused by an overgrowth of various bacteria, including *Gardnerella vaginalis*.

about genital herpes were put dramatically in perspective by news coverage about AIDS.

Increased concern over AIDS has removed the spotlight from the millions of adults with genital herpes, but it has also led to a climate of fear surrounding AIDS and its contagiousness. This fear has mushroomed as it has become increasingly clear that the AIDS virus can be heterosexually transmitted.

The fear that governs many people's reactions to the AIDS epidemic is in some ways similar to the fear experienced by people when they discover that they have symptoms that *might* indicate the presence of an STD. Fear, along with a disbelief that they might have an STD, leads many people to delay a visit to a physician. They deny the reality of the situation as if pretending an infection isn't there will make it go away. This is an example of the operation of the defense mechanism called denial, in which a person simply refuses to acknowledge that a stressful or dangerous situation is real. Denial is one of the most basic means people use to deal with anxiety-provoking situations.

In the case of STDs, denial is unfortunately often reinforced, because most STD symptoms disappear within a matter of a few weeks. However, infected individuals continue to harbor the infection in their bodies and expose their sex partners to the risk of infection, as well.

A better perspective on how the denial mechanism and its conscious analog avoidance come into play when people first wonder if they have been infected with an STD can be gotten from considering the following. In a survey of 100 consecutive first visits to a college student health clinic for the purpose of being checked for an STD, only one-fifth of the students had made their appointment within three days of the onset of their symptoms (Kolodny, 1990). More than half of the students had waited for at least two weeks before getting medical attention. Since about one-third of the overall sample did not turn out to have an STD, these students went through a lot of unnecessary worrying before being tested and given a clean bill of health. And the 40 percent of students who waited for more than two weeks before being tested not only worried during most of this time about their situation but actually contributed to endangering their own health—and the health of their sexual partner(s)—by their prolonged denial or avoidance.

"HI, I'M LOU. I'M NOT A CARRIER OF HERPES, OR HEPATITUS A, OR OF AIDS, AND I USE CONDOMS. SO, WHAT'S YOUR SIGN?"

Source: *Reproduced by special permission of* Playboy *magazine. Copyright ©* 1989 by Playboy.

The fear and denial that combine to make people delay visiting a doctor or clinic to be tested for an STD are augmented by another common defense mechanism: rationalization. Rationalization is the process of generating excuses to explain one's behavior rather than accepting the actual reason for the behavior. A clear example of rationalization was given by one of the students in the research described in the preceding paragraph when he told an interviewer: "I really didn't have time to get here any sooner. I was working on a term paper and I had a big exam coming up, and on top of that I thought I was getting the flu. Besides, I've had a discharge like this once before, and it didn't turn out to be anything" (*Authors' files*). The fact that this student's girlfriend had also been having symptoms of an STD apparently didn't break through his defense mechanisms. This too is a typical pattern: common sense takes a back seat to the initial refusal to believe that something is wrong.

Some people are also reluctant to go to a physician when they have symptoms of a possible STD because they're worried about getting a lecture or they're worried about the confidentiality that will be extended to them. Although physicians are legally bound to keep information they learn about their patients confidential, there are circumstances in which physicians are obligated to act differently. For example, in some states a physician's records can be subpoenaed by a court order. In all localities, a physician is supposed to report instances of certain communicable diseases to state public health departments (although as of mid-1994, most states did not require the mandatory reporting of cases of infection with chlamydia or genital herpes). Physicians' records are often accessible to insurance companies, since patients consent to having their records examined whenever they file a health insurance claim or when they apply for a new health or life policy. For this reason, anyone who is particularly concerned about this issue needs to discuss with his or her physician the limits to absolute confidentiality that might apply to his or her case.

Just a few years ago, people were dismayed if they received a lecture from their physician that advocated traditional sexual values and pointed out the health risks of casual sex with multiple partners. Now with what our society has learned about STD epidemics in the past decade, such physicians may simply be preaching about sensible public health practices. Nevertheless, if you encounter a physician who makes you uncomfortable by giving you unwanted moralistic-sounding advice, don't be intimidated; it will generally be in your best interests to switch to another doctor with whom you feel more at ease.

What is the impact of an STD on a person's sexuality? In most cases other than AIDS, assuming the infection is properly detected and treated, there will be little if any physical effect. During the acute phase of many STDs some people have little interest in sex because it's painful, while others continue functioning sexually without noticing that anything is wrong. Even when an STD has been untreated and has become chronic, it is not likely to depress libido or interfere with sexual functioning (genital herpes is the major exception, since sex can be quite painful during flare-ups). But even though STDs don't typically interfere with the *physical* component of sexual functioning, some people find themselves having sexual difficulties due to the psychological effects of finding out they have an STD. Often, these individuals are guilty and embarrassed about what has happened. They sometimes decide that their infection was God's way of

warning or punishing them for sexual transgressions. Since they equate sex with sin, it is no wonder that such people occasionally develop subsequent sexual inhibitions.

Others develop obsessive concerns about sexual cleanliness and worry constantly about the possibility of being reinfected or catching another form of STD. Some men who fall in this category find themselves having erectile problems, while women who are exceptionally fearful about STDs may develop vaginismus as an unconscious way of protecting themselves from infection. Needless to say, such major concerns about sexual cleanliness may lead people to change their patterns of sexual behavior too—for instance, not participating in oral–genital sex.

When one partner in an intimate relationship develops an STD that the other person doesn't have, it immediately implies that the infected person has been sexually active outside the relationship. While this isn't always true, and some types of STD (such as hepatitis B) are also commonly transmitted by nonsexual means, doubt and suspicion may affect even a stable, loving relationship. If one partner infects the other with an STD, there may be even more conflict and hostility. This hostility may be expressed in sexual terms (i.e., by rejecting sexual activity with the other person) and may spill over into the entire relationship. This type of reaction can infect a relationship far more destructively than an STD. Fortunately, most people soon return to a better state of relating to their partners.

Except for AIDS, STDs are no longer as frightening as they once were, but for many people they remain somehow "different" from other infections because they are transmitted by sexual contact and generally affect the sex organs. Until people are able to think about sex as naturally as they think about breathing or eating, it is likely that this form of stigmatization will continue as a fact of life.

PREVENTING SEXUALLY TRANSMITTED DISEASES

The People's Republic of China apparently has managed to practically wipe out syphilis and many other STDs by enforcing rigid codes of sexual behavior and stopping prostitution, but most other countries must contend with the STDs as a price for social and sexual freedom. Even so, some practical guidelines can be offered to help minimize the chances of contracting an STD or spreading it once you've caught it.

1. *Be Informed*. Knowing about the symptoms of STDs can help protect you against exposing yourself to the risk of infection from a partner and help you know when to seek treatment.

2. *Be Observant*. Knowledge alone is not enough. Looking is the best way of discovering if you or your partner has a genital discharge, sore, rash, or other sign of sexual infection. (This can't be done with the lights out or in a moonlit back seat of a car.) If you see a suspicious sore or blister, don't be a hero about it: refrain from sexual contact and insist that your partner be examined. While "looking" may seem clinical and crass, you don't have to announce *why* you're looking, and often a good, close look can be obtained in the sexual preliminaries (getting undressed, giving your partner a massage). A step beyond looking is commonly used by prostitutes (and doctors) to check for gonorrhea and NSU in men. The penis is gently but firmly "milked" from its base to its head to see if any discharge is present; the "exam" is sometimes called a "short-arm inspection."

3. *Be Selective*. Having numerous sex partners greatly increases the risk of developing an STD. Likewise, anonymous sex is risky too: you don't know if you can trust your partner or who he or she has been with in the recent past. Being selective in your choice of sex partners will improve your chances of avoiding STDs.

4. *Be Honest*. If you have (or think you *may* have) an STD, tell your partner (or partners). This can avoid spreading the infection and will alert your partner to watch for her or his own symptoms, or to be examined or tested. Similarly, if you are worried about your partner's status, don't hesitate to ask. It's foolish to jeopardize your health to protect someone else's feelings.

5. *Be Cautious*. Use of a condom will significantly lower the chances of getting or spreading STDs. Using an intravaginal chemical contraceptive (foams, jellies, creams) reduces the woman's risk of getting gonorrhea. Urinating soon after sexual activity helps flush invading organisms out of the urethra and so limits risks to a small degree. *If you think you've been exposed, promptly contact your doctor for advice.* If you *know* that you've been exposed, get medical help immediately and also abstain from sexual activity until your tests show that everything is okay.

6. *Be Promptly Tested and Treated*. A quick diagnosis and an effective course of treatment will help you prevent some of the serious complications of STDs. Treatment can be obtained from your private doctor, hospital clinics, or public health service clinics. After treatment, you must be rechecked to be certain that the disease has been eradicated. In addition, be sure to urge your partner to be tested (and treated if necessary) so as to avoid reinfection.

SUMMARY

Table 19.2 (on p. 536) summarizes the key features of the sexually transmitted diseases that we have discussed in this chapter.

Thought Questions

1. A child or teenager who has never gotten close to "having sex" can come down with a herpes infection of the genitals through auto-inoculation of oral herpes. Yet the media and most people regard genital herpes strictly as a sexually transmitted disease. What advice would you give a child with this condition for dealing with the stigma of herpes? How should parents respond to statements that automatically assume genital herpes means sexual activity?

2. How does a person with genital herpes stay safely sexually active when the infection can be transmitted asymptomatically, and a condom does not protect as well against herpes as for other STDs? What advice would you give to a person with genital herpes who is seeking a sex partner, a lover, or a mate?

3. Should the justice system deal with people who knowingly infect others with an STD? If

so, should this be handled through criminal penalties or civil suits?

4. How would you respond if your partner became infected with an STD, particularly if the relationship was supposed to be monogamous? What if your partner continued to claim that he or she had not had sex outside the relationship? Should you believe your partner?

5. Regarding research priorities: Close to 30 percent of the U.S. sexually active population may have had an episode of genital warts, which is of serious concern since genital warts are associated with genital cancer. No treatment has yet been discovered which eradicates this infection, and thus infected people are advised to *always* use condoms, even in long-term, monogamous relationships. This is a huge number of people who are being adversely affected by an STD. However, relatively little funding is available to research cures and vaccines for genital warts, while AIDS, which at least currently affects far fewer people, is heavily funded for research (if not for treatment). Do you agree with these research priorities? Why or why not?

Suggested Readings

Covington, Timothy R., and McClendon, J. Frank. *Sex Care: The Complete Guide to Safe and Healthy Sex*. New York: Pocket Books, 1987. Practical, detailed information on STDs presented in an easy-to-read format, with many charts to aid the reader's grasp of material.

Holmes, King K., et al. *Sexually Transmitted Diseases*, 2nd ed. New York: McGraw-Hill, 1990. If its hefty weight (it's 1200 pages long) and technical verbiage (given that it's a highly scientific medical textbook) don't put you off, you will find this to be the definitive sourcebook on STDs. A color insert shows numerous photos of the various skin lesions caused by STDs.

Langston, Deborah. *Living with Herpes*. Garden City, NY: Doubleday, 1983. This is an exceptionally thoughtful, scientifically accurate, detailed, yet readable book on all forms of herpes. If you have herpes, or you're close to someone who does, you should make this book number one on your reading list.

The most up-to-date material on STDs (including HIV infection and AIDS) is a weekly bulletin put out by the Centers for Disease Control called *Morbidity and Mortality Weekly Report* (it is commonly referred to by the acronym *MMWR*). Included in the wealth of data it publishes is weekly information on the numbers of cases of certain reportable communicable diseases, such as syphilis, gonorrhea, hepatitis, and AIDS.

Table 19.2   Key Features of STDs

Disease	Causative Agent	Usual Incubation Period	First Symptoms
Gonorrhea	*Neisseria gonorrhea* (bacterium)	2–10 days	Males: urethral discharge, painful urination Female: often asymptomatic; vaginal discharge, pain or burning with urination
Syphilis	*Treponema pallidum* (a bacteria-like microbe)	2–4 weeks (can be as long as 90 days)	Painless chancre, swollen lymph nodes
Chlamydial Infections	*Chlamydia trachomatis* (non-bacterial microbial parasite)	1–3 weeks	Males: urethritis (discharge and burning), 15–30% symptom-free Females: mucus discharge from cervix and/or urethritis, 50% symptom-free
Chancroid	*Hemophilus ducreyi* (bacteria)	4–7 days	Genital ulcer(s), buboes (large, swollen lymph nodes)
Genital Herpes	Herpes simplex virus, type 1 or 2	2–5 days	Painful blisters on or inside the genitals, with pain, itching, painful urination, sometimes accompanied by fever, headache, and stiff neck
Viral Hepatitis	Hepatitis A, B, C, D viruses	A: 15–45 days B: 40–110 days C: 15–70 days D: 40–110 days	Fever, dark urine or jaundice, abdominal pain, poor appetite
Genital Warts	Human papilloma virus	6–8 weeks	Warts on or inside the genitals or around the anus
Molluscum Contagiosum	Molluscum contagiosum virus	2–3 months	Appearance of small, painless dome-shaped pimples in the genital area or on the thighs, groin, or lower abdomen; while mostly asymptomatic, sometimes causes itching
Pubic Lice	*Phthirus pubis* (parasite)	It takes 5 days after infestation for allergic sensitization to occur	Intense itching in pubic region
Trichomonas Vaginitis	*Trichomonas vaginalis* (flagellated protozoon)	1–2 days	Females: profuse, odorous yellow-greyish frothy vaginal discharge, usually accompanied by vaginal itching Males: mostly symptom-free; a minority of cases have urethritis
Monilial Vaginitis	*Candida albicans* (yeast)	Uncertain/not applicable in most cases	Females: vaginal itching and whitish, odorless discharge Males: usually symptom-free
Bacterial Vaginosis	*Gardnerella vaginalis* (bacteria), *Bacteroides* species (bacteria), and *Mycoplasma hominis* (bacteria)	Not applicable	Fishy-smelling vaginal discharge, sometimes with burning and itching; half of women have no symptoms

Untreated Progression	Transmission Pattern	Diagnosis	Treatment
Males: involvement of prostate, seminal vesicles and epididymis, infrequently causing sterility Females: PID, infertility Both sexes: arthritis, endocarditis, meningitis	Mainly sexual	Culture; no reliable blood test	Ceftriaxone (injection) or cefixime, ciprofloxacin, or ofloxacin pills
Primary chancre heals; secondary syphilis (marked by fever, rashes, sore throat, headaches, painful joints, hair loss, and swollen lymph nodes) develops within weeks to months, then passes to a latent (symptom-free) stage after 3–6 months; 30 to 50% then progress to tertiary syphilis, with heart, skin, and neurological problems	Mainly sexual; pregnant mother to fetus	Blood tests	Penicillin injection
Males: epididymitis, prostatitis Females: PID Both sexes: spread to liver	Mainly sexual	Cultures are most reliable but expensive and time-consuming; antibody tests less accurate but useful	Doxycycline or azithromycin pills
Healing usually occurs in 4–6 weeks	Sexual contact exclusively	Clinical examination	Erythromycin or azithromycin (pills) or ceftriaxone (injection)
Initial symptoms disappear within 2 weeks as the infection enters a latent state, which is life-long; recurrences are often less severe, but can occur at any time	Almost exclusively sexual (Note: Asymptomatic persons without any visible blisters or sores may be infectious)	Usually by clinical exam; viral cultures also available	Acyclovir pills shorten duration of initial attacks and reduce frequency and severity of recurrences, but are not curative
A: usually uneventful B: 1% develop acute liver failure; 5–10% develop chronic carrier state C: Cirrhosis or cancer of the liver, long-term D: Can be fatal in its acute stage or can lead to chronic liver disease	A: Mainly fecal-oral route B: Sexual transmission common C: Sexual transmissions occur D: Mainly in IV drug-users, but can be sexual	Specific blood tests	None
Warts may grow in size and number; HPV may play a role in subsequent development of cancer	Exclusively sexual	Clinical exam; blood test to determine type of HPV available but used infrequently	Liquid nitrogen to freeze warts; local application of podofilox, podo-phyllin, or TCA (trichloracetic acid) (Note: no cure is available)
Eventually disappears without health consequences	Both sexual and nonsexual	Clinical exam; microscopic exam of skin abnormalities	Removal of the core of the skin lesion by direct pressure or scraping; or use of liquid nitrogen to destroy the lesions
Typically resolves in 1–2 years, may be complicated by bacterial superinfection	Mainly sexual, but can be spread from infested bedding, clothing, towels, etc.	Clinical examination	Kwell (gamma benzene hexachloride) lotion, shampoo, or cream; or Lindane (shampoo)
None	Mainly sexual; can affect female babies born to infected mothers	Microscopic identification or culture	Metronidazole (pill) to woman and her sexual partner(s)
May become a chronic or recurrent condition, causing pain with intercourse, vaginal soreness, and painful urination	Sexually transmitted in a minority of cases; often a result of overgrowth of vaginal yeast during pregnancy, with broad-spectrum antibiotics or high-estrogen birth control pills, or in diabetic women	Microscopic identification of infecting organism or culture	Numerous intravaginal creams or tablets, such as miconazole, nystatin, butoconazole, clotrimazole and others
Generally none, but may predispose to infectious obstetric complications	Unclear, but thought to be sexually transmitted in part	Microscopic examination of discharge	Metronidazole or Clindamycin (either one in pill or cream form)

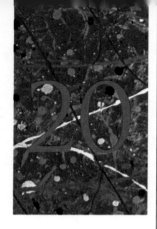

HIV Infection and AIDS

The newest and most frightening STD yet discovered was first documented in 1981. Known as **AIDS—for acquired immune deficiency syndrome**—this devastating illness is a result of infection with the *human immunodeficiency virus (HIV)*. The hallmark of AIDS is a breakdown of the immune system, the system that ordinarily protects the body against infections. Because of the collapse of the body's defenses, people with AIDS get a variety of rare infections known as opportunistic infections, usually found only in cancer or transplant patients whose resistance is lowered by medications that impair their immune responses.

Because the earliest cases of AIDS were found primarily in gay and bisexual men and intravenous drug abusers, there was a certain amount of complacency toward the HIV/AIDS epidemic in many quarters—"This doesn't involve me" (Shilts, 1987;

Presidential Commission on the Human Immunod-eficiency Virus Epidemic, 1988; Kramer, 1990). As Harvard University's noted biologist Stephen Jay Gould put it, "If AIDS had first been imported from Africa into a Park Avenue apartment, we would not have dithered as the exponential march began" (Gould, 1987, pp. 32–33). In actuality, the HIV epidemic is driven by a virus that knows no racial, sexual, or class boundaries. Today it is clear that not only are more and more heterosexuals involved in the epidemic but also that HIV infec-tion is not restricted to certain groups of people. It occurs on college campuses, in private high schools, in small towns and wealthy suburbs, and in the famous just as in the poor, the elderly, the unknown, and the homeless.

Today, HIV infection and AIDS are among the top three causes of death for males between the ages of 15 and 44 in the United States and are one of the major causes of years of potential life lost for both males and females, especially producing fatal-ities among people in their twenties and thirties (Centers for Disease Control [MMWR 38:561–563], 1989; Eckholm, 1992; Mann, Tarantola and Netter, 1992). In 1990, it was estimated that there were 212 cases of full-blown AIDS diagnosed each day in the United States and one death from AIDS every 12 minutes (Kramer, 1990); today, these numbers are substantially higher. However, because AIDS typi-cally develops seven to ten years after initial infec-tion with HIV, these numbers are only the tip of the iceberg. Since the cases of AIDS being diagnosed today are largely a result of HIV infections that occurred in the mid-1980s, the number of AIDS fa-talities will continue to grow at an alarming pace unless a scientific breakthrough occurs to help stem the tide of this epidemic. In the meantime, there are a number of measures we can each take to reduce our chances of becoming infected with HIV, which we discuss in detail.

It is misleading to focus primarily on AIDS, the disease, instead of the broader spectrum of HIV in-fection. Thus, this chapter will emphasize the entire spectrum of HIV infection in terms of its biology, its clinical course, its social and emotional aftermath, and the public policy issues that need to be consid-ered to turn the tide in one of the most serious epi-demics our country, and the world, has ever faced.

It is particularly important to be careful about the language we use to discuss HIV infection and AIDS because it is easy inadvertently to create erro-neous impressions and subtle prejudices by our choice of terminology. For example, calling AIDS a "plague" implies to some that this disease is a form of punishment for sinful behavior, whereas de-scribing it as an "epidemic" sounds more scientific and less judgmental. Likewise, if we choose to de-clare war on AIDS, we must be careful to remem-ber that the enemy is not the person infected with HIV but the virus itself.

Because new information about HIV and AIDS develops rapidly, the material presented here should not be considered the last word. Readers are urged to check with updates from other sources, especially information appearing in the publication of the U.S. Centers for Disease Control and Prevention, *Morbidity and Mortality Weekly Re-port*. The rapidity with which new discoveries are made is certainly one of the brightest rays of hope for an eventual cure for this problem: in one decade, we have learned more about HIV than about any other known virus. We have also learned a great deal about how to respond humanely to this challenge, helping set the stage for eventually overcoming what now seem like formidable obsta-cles in bringing this epidemic under control. The message that is most important to take from this chapter, however, is that this epidemic is treatable, preventable, and predictable. Each of us can play a real part in bringing it to a close.

EMERGING PATTERNS OF THE EPIDEMIC: AN OVERVIEW

According to the Centers for Disease Control, more than 400,000 cases of AIDS had been reported in the United States as of July 1994 (Centers for Dis-ease Control, 1994b). In Western Europe, AIDS is less common, but the situation appears to be much worse in many major cities in East and Central Africa, where it is estimated that 10 to 20 percent or more of the adult population is infected with HIV (Rwandan HIV Seroprevalence Study Group, 1989; Eckholm and Tierney, 1990; Palca, 1991; Berkeley, 1992). In addition, areas that had previously ap-peared to be spared from this disease are reporting

AIDS (acquired immune deficiency syndrome) A condition of increased susceptibility to unusual forms of cancer and infection resulting from dis-turbances in the body's immune defenses as a long-term consequence of infection with HIV.

Figure 20.1   Worldwide Patterns of HIV Infection as of Mid-1993

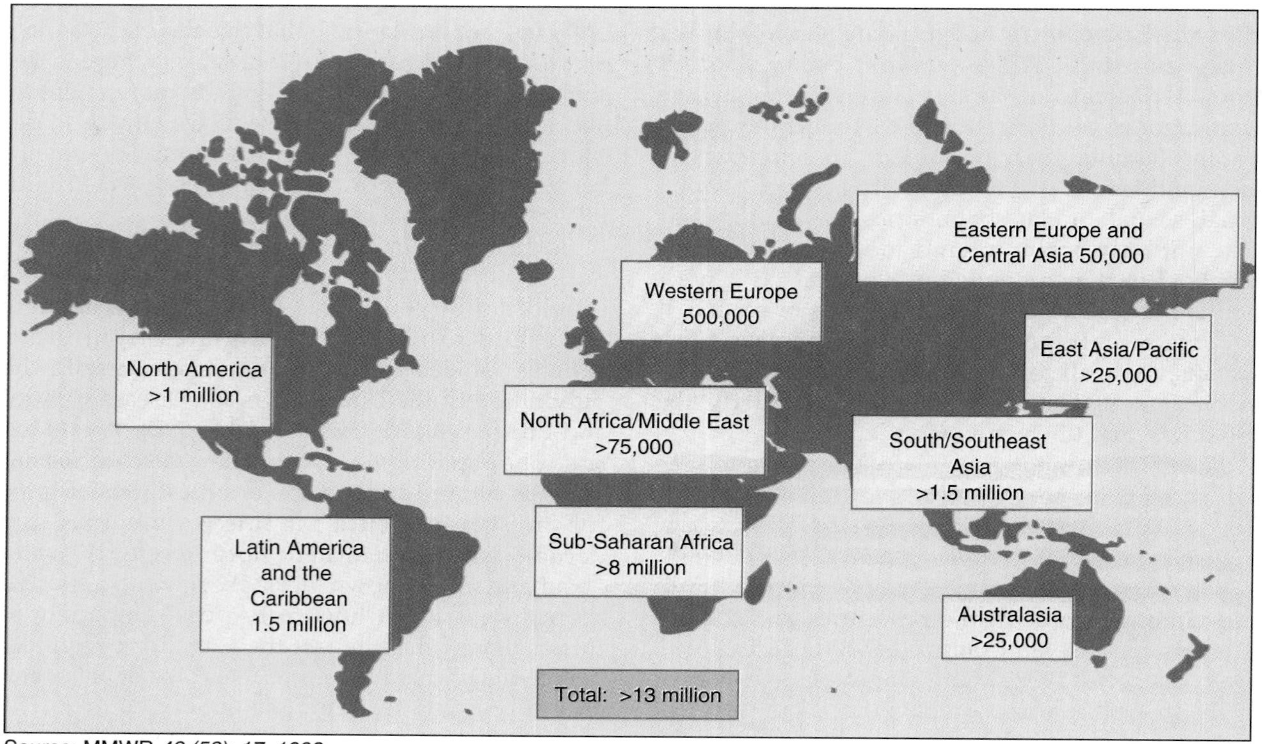

Eastern Europe and
Central Asia 50,000

Western Europe
500,000

East Asia/Pacific
>25,000

North America
>1 million

North Africa/Middle East
>75,000

South/Southeast
Asia
>1.5 million

Latin America
and the
Caribbean
1.5 million

Sub-Saharan Africa
>8 million

Australasia
>25,000

Total: >13 million

Source: MMWR *42 (53): 17, 1993.*

increased rates of HIV infection. In Thailand, for instance, HIV infection is expanding dramatically: among IV drug users in Bangkok the rate of HIV infection climbed from 1 percent in late 1987 to more than 30 percent in mid-1991, and growing numbers of female prostitutes are infected as well, endangering not only their own countrymen (and themselves) but the tens of thousands of foreign visitors who trek to Thailand for commercial sex vacations (Smith, 1990; Weniger et al., 1991). The threat of even larger epidemics is painfully evident in a number of other areas, including India and Latin America, where the epidemic seems to be establishing a strong foothold (Ramalingaswami, 1992; Goldsmith, 1992; Berkeley, 1992a; Brooke, 1993).

These numbers hardly depict the full extent of the worldwide pandemic. For one thing, even in the United States, many diagnosed cases of AIDS are never reported to government centers that are tracking the disease (Hopkins and Johnson, 1988; Laumann et al., 1989; Masterson et al., 1989; Centers for Disease Control, 1992f). In addition, in some countries statistics on the extent of the AIDS

epidemic appear to have been understated because of political and/or economic concerns such as wanting to avoid a drop-off in tourism, or just as a matter of national pride. One other contributing factor to underreporting is that in some locations many cases of AIDS are never correctly identified. Thus, while "official" reports of AIDS cases worldwide totaled about 600,000 as of year-end 1993, the World Health Organization and the U.S. Centers for Disease Control estimated that the actual number was around 2.5 million (Centers for Disease Control and World Health Organization, 1994).

Even an accurate count of AIDS cases wouldn't tell the whole story about the extent of the HIV epidemic, however, since AIDS is only the final stage of HIV infection. According to the U.S. Public Health Service, 1.5 million Americans are infected with HIV and capable of transmitting it to others but have not yet developed any symptoms (Centers for Disease Control [MMWR 38: S-4], 1989); worldwide, the figure is thought to be 12 million adults and 1 million children (see Figure 20.1) (Merson, 1993). [It is now projected that 40 to 110 million people worldwide will be infected by the

FOCUS IN BRIEF

The History of the AIDS Epidemic: A Timeline

—1981   Five cases of *Pneumocystis carinii* pneumonia in young homosexual men in Los Angeles and 26 cases of Kaposi's sarcoma in young homosexual men in New York and California are reported to the CDC, arousing attention.

—1982   New disease is named "acquired immune deficiency syndrome" (AIDS); case definition is first published by the CDC; first cases of AIDS detected in patients with hemophilia and in recipients of blood transfusions.

—1983   U.S. Public Health Service issues guidelines for the prevention of AIDS; first cases of heterosexual transmission reported.

—1984   A retrovirus, first called HTLV-III, is identified as the cause of AIDS; later, it is renamed the "human immunodeficiency virus," HIV.

—1985   Blood tests to identify antibodies to the AIDS virus become widely available and are first used routinely to screen the nation's blood supply; AZT (zidovudine) is first used in clinical trials; the news that Rock Hudson has AIDS mobilizes worldwide media attention.

—1986   *Surgeon General's Report on AIDS* is issued by Dr. C. Everett Koop; clinical testing shows that AZT can improve survival and quality of life for people with AIDS; cumulative total of AIDS cases crosses 25,000 in U.S.

—1987   FDA approves AZT for severe HIV infection; clinical trials of a vaccine against HIV begin in U.S.; President Reagan orders that all immigrants and federal prisoners be tested for HIV; the AIDS Quilt Project begins.

—1988   President's Commission on the HIV Epidemic issues broad report urging focus on HIV infection rather than just AIDS, early diagnosis, and antidiscrimination measures; aerosol pentamidine found to be effective in preventing PCP pneumonia.

—1989   National HIV prevalence study blocked by political pressures; FDA licenses aerosol pentamidine; cumulative total of AIDS cases crosses 100,000 in U.S.

—1990   Recommended dose of AZT halved by FDA; first report of a dentist who may have transmitted HIV to patients published by CDC.

—1991   Magic Johnson stuns the world by announcing that he is infected with HIV.

—1992   Reports of AIDS-like illness without the presence of HIV draw worldwide attention.

—1993   Cumulative total of AIDS cases crosses 300,000 in U.S.; heterosexually transmitted cases are the fastest growing category.

year 2000 (Mann, Tarantola, and Netter, 1992; Goldsmith, 1992; World Health Organization, 1993)].

Initially, it was hoped that only a small proportion of people infected with HIV but without symptoms would go on to develop full-blown cases of AIDS. According to current studies, however, it appears that almost all of those infected with HIV will eventually progress to AIDS if no effective treatment becomes available (Lui, Darrow, and Rutherford, 1988; Lambert, 1990). Since AIDS is, at present, almost always fatal, the implications

are staggering. The U.S. Public Health Service has predicted that there will be a cumulative total of 1 million cases of AIDS in America by 1998 (Altman, 1989). Other projections suggest that between 1 and 2 million Americans will have been diagnosed with AIDS by the turn of the century (*The New York Times* March 4, 1989, p. A20; Hopkins and Johnson, 1988; Masters, Johnson, and Kolodny, 1988).

Two different patterns of AIDS and HIV infection have been recognized around the world. In North America, parts of South America, Australia,

Figure 20.2 A Profile of the first 100,000 cases of AIDS in the United States*

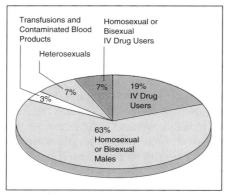

Transfusions and Contaminated Blood Products

Homosexual or Bisexual IV Drug Users

Heterosexuals

7%

3%

7%

19% IV Drug Users

63% Homosexual or Bisexual Males

*Note: The 100,000th case was reported to the CDC in July, 1989.

Source: CDC AIDS Surveillance Reports, *AMA/NET AIDS Information Service*, *September 1989*.

New Zealand, and many Western European countries, most AIDS cases have occurred as a result of homosexual transmission or as a result of IV drug abuse. In contrast, in most of Africa and in the Caribbean, the vast majority of cases appear to be due to heterosexual transmission. However, in most of Europe, in South America, and in the United States, heterosexual AIDS constitutes the fastest growing category of new cases (Ades et al., 1991; Allen, 1991; Banatvala et al., 1991; Chamberlain et al., 1991; Ellerbock et al., 1991; Forrest, 1991; Crane, 1992; Goldsmith, 1992; Berkeley, 1992a; Centers for Disease Control [MMWR 48: 899], 1992; Brooke, 1993; Centers for Disease Control, 1994a). Whether these two patterns will continue, or whether eventually most cases of AIDS will be a result of heterosexual transmission, is an unanswered question at the present time.

As shown in Figure 20.2, of the first 100,000 cases of AIDS in the United States, 63 percent involved homosexual or bisexual men who were not intravenous drug users, 19 percent occurred in heterosexual IV drug users, 7 percent occurred in homosexual or bisexual drug users, 7 percent occurred in heterosexual partners of people with AIDS or of people in high-risk groups, and 3 percent involved people who had received transfusions of contaminated blood products (Centers for Disease Control [MMWR 38:561–563], 1989). However, in Africa cases are divided almost equally

between men and women. Elsewhere in the world, as the HIV epidemic has grown, there has been a notable shift in statistics: for example, in Central and South America, where earlier reports showed three to ten times as many men as women with AIDS, this ratio has now changed substantially, and in some regions men and women are affected equally (Hilts, 1989). In fact, it is now clear that heterosexual transmission is not only common but the predominant mode of worldwide transmission—accounting for some 80 percent of all new cases, according to the World Health Organization (Forrest, 1991)—and that no one group can be singled out as "at risk" for developing this disease.

In the United States, it has become apparent that the nature of the HIV epidemic is shifting significantly from its early days, when the overwhelming number of AIDS patients were gay and bisexual men. In the past few years, AIDS has had a disproportionate impact on the poor, on blacks, and on Hispanics in inner-city populations (Figure 20.3), where the primary impetus for its spread has been needle sharing by drug addicts, followed by the transmission of HIV to sex partners of infected individuals (Altman, 1989a; Centers for Disease Control [MMWR 38: 229–236], 1989 and [MMWR 39 (SS-3):22-30], 1990). Notably, AIDS is particularly affecting women in these populations (Centers for Disease Control, 1994a). In addition, the geographic nature of the epidemic is changing. What had initially been a problem of New York and California now affects every state and territory and is not limited to large metropolitan areas alone (Curran, 1983; Laumann et al., 1989; Ellerbock et al., 1991; Centers for Disease Control, *HIV/AIDS Surveillance*, April 1993).

This evolving view of the epidemic is buttressed by newly emerging data showing that HIV is spreading rapidly among some groups of teenagers and that among adolescents, equal numbers of males and females are infected (Kolata, 1989; Vermund et al., 1989; Burke et al., 1990). A 1989 study by the Centers for Disease Control found that 1 percent of teenagers in cities like New York and Miami, where the HIV epidemic has been pronounced, are already infected with the AIDS virus (Centers for Disease Control, 1989). Disadvantaged adolescents appear to be at particularly high risk of HIV infection, with the male–female ratio in this group an alarming 1.2:1 (St. Louis, 1991). Little wonder, then, that many experts agree with Dr. Gary Strokash, a specialist in

Figure 20.3 Annual Incidence of AIDS in Women 15-44 Years of Age, by Race/Ethnicity and year of Diagnosis, 1982-1988

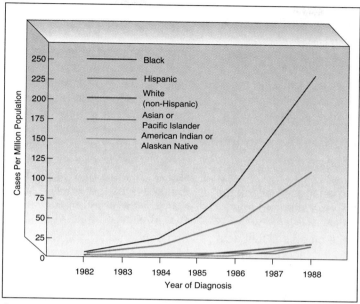

Source: MMWR *39 (55-3): 26, 1990.*

adolescent medicine, who believes that HIV infection among teenagers is "dreadful and it's going to be devastating"; in fact, he states, it "is going to be the next crisis" (*The New York Times* October 8, 1989, Section 1, p. 1).

THE ORIGINS OF HIV

Although there is no certainty at present about how the AIDS virus originated, many scientists believe that it began in central Africa (Cohen, Sande, and Volberding, 1990). One possibility is that a slightly different strain of the AIDS virus first infected monkey colonies there (Kanki et al., 1986; Essex and Kanki, 1988; Smith et al., 1988) and subsequently spread to humans. Viruses frequently cross over from animal species to humans; this is a natural part of the process of evolution that has been going on for tens of thousands of years. Today, in fact, our world offers many possibilities for exotic or previously undetected viruses to spread to new locales because of the efficiency and wide availability of modern transportation systems. It is likely that both the various types of HIV and the strains of the AIDS virus that infect monkeys arose from a common viral ancestor (Cohen, Sande, and Volberding, 1990).

Whatever the beginning may have been, one research study using long-stored frozen blood samples found evidence for the existence of HIV in central Africa in 1959 (Nahmias et al., 1986). From there, AIDS may have been carried across the Atlantic Ocean by Haitians who once lived in or visited central Africa. From Haiti, AIDS may have spread to the United States by two routes: Haitian immigrants and vacationing American homosexual males, who often traveled to Haiti. If this explanation is correct, the early clustering of AIDS cases in the United States in gay males may have been largely accidental. And if this scenario is true, it is likely that in the future far more AIDS cases in the United States will arise from heterosexual transmission.

The earliest known case of AIDS in the United States (not recognized as such at the time), based on the laboratory analysis of long-frozen blood and tissue samples, appears to have been in a teenage boy in 1968 in St. Louis (Garry et al., 1988). There have also been retrospective reports of cases of AIDS in a Norwegian family during the 1960s (Froland et al., 1988) and a fatal HIV infection in a 25-year-old British sailor in 1959 (Corbitt, Bailey and Williams, 1990).

Understanding the Immune System

The primary strike force of our immune system consists of 1 trillion white blood cells that attack and repel our microbial enemies. Although the immune process is complex and multidimensional, here is a basic summary of the system's operations. Keep in mind that the same principles apply to how our bodies fight off any type of infection, from the common cold to serious, life-threatening conditions.

When a foreign invader manages to evade the body's first lines of defense—the skin and mucous membranes—it is quickly detected by macrophages, a type of white blood cell that acts like an armed scout roaming the bloodstream to clean up debris and sound the alarm when an enemy is encountered. One of the key duties of the macrophage is to search for antigens—chains of unique proteins attached to the surface of invaders that serve as identifiers, allowing the body to recognize what is "foreign" compared to what is "self." In addition to detecting suspicious intruders and engulfing them, macrophages also activate the main portion of the immune system by secreting messenger proteins, the lymphokines. In addition, some macrophages carry a fragment of what they've ingested as a type of biochemical flag to signal another element of the immune system, the helper T cell. (This surface fragment is known as an antigen because it becomes an *anti*body *gen*erator.)

T cells are manufactured in the bone marrow, as are all white blood cells. They are programmed for their work in the thymus, a butterfly-shaped gland in the upper chest. Here, one type of T cell, the helper T cell, is prepared to respond to specific "foreign" antigens and to recognize on every cell of the body a string of molecules that identifies it as self. A separate class of T cells, called killer T cells, is special troops that attack infected cells.

When macrophages engulf invaders such as HIV, the antigen they attach to their surface acts like a distress flag that summons help. This im-munologic assistance comes first in the form of a backup army made up of helper T cells. The T cells travel through the circulation in specialized groups. Each group recognizes only a certain type of antigen. When the antigen displayed on the surface of the macrophage fits into the receptor on the T cell's surface, the two stick together. This "key-in-the-lock" phenomenon causes the macrophage to release a chemical that activates the T cells and sounds a general alarm to the immune system as a whole, particularly mobilizing the killer T cells, which multiply and concentrate their attack on the invader, following their chemical programming.

Another part of the immune system is also activated in this process. It consists of a separate class of white blood cells, called B cells, that ordinarily are stockpiled in the spleen and lymph nodes. B cells have the primary task of manufacturing antibodies, protein substances that seek out and bind tightly to specific invader antigens, marking the enemy for elimination. Many varieties of antibody are produced by B cells. Each one binds to a specific antigen. Unless you have previously been exposed to an invading microbe, the body typically requires a number of weeks to generate a measurable antibody response. But if you've been previously exposed, either through a vaccination or by fighting off the actual microbe in question, the antibody response is much quicker because the body "remembers" the invader and is biochemically programmed to manufacture antibodies with greater rapidity. When antibodies stick to the antigen surface of invading microbes, they usually prevent them from attacking other cells and make them easier targets for macrophages to capture.

With HIV infection, something in the body's immune process goes wrong. Although antibody production is stimulated quickly in most cases, the HIV antibodies that are manufactured seem to be unable to work effectively. The reduced effectiveness may be partly because HIV gets inside

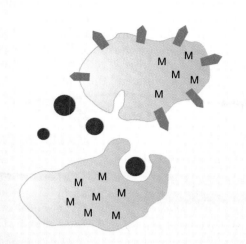

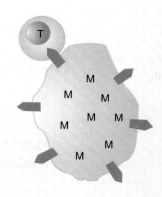

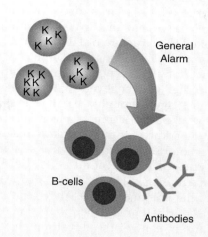

1. When infectious microbes gain entry to the body, macrophages [M] attack and engulf them. Fragments of the ingested microbes (antigens) are carried like flags on the surface of some macrophages to signal T-cells.

2. A helper T-cell [T] locks on to the surface antigen and is activated by chemical messages from the macrophage.

3. Once activated, the helper T-cell sounds a general alarm, mobilizing killer T-cells [K] and leading B-cells [B] to produce antibodies.

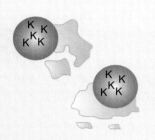

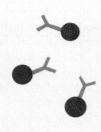

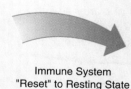

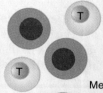

4. Infected cells are sought out and destroyed by killer T-cells, interrupting the disease-causing replication cycle.

5. Antibodies manufactured by B-cells bind to the invading microbes, inhibiting their infectiousness and targeting them for attack and destruction.

6. When the infection is controlled, an "all clear" is sent to the entire immune system via chemical signals. Specialized antigen-specific memory cells remain permanently to provide a swift response against another invasion by the same microbe.

T cells and macrophages, where it copies its own genetic code into the host cell's DNA, so that it actually becomes part of the host cell's genetic structure. In such a situation, any activation of the immune system actually stimulates production of the invading virus—the exact opposite of what should be happening. Over time—in fact, usually over a period of years—this insidious invasion wreaks havoc by destroying helper T cells, so that the body's front line of defense is seriously depleted, and as the T cell count drops drastically, the body is unable to respond appropriately to fend off the opportunistic infections and cancers that typically make AIDS a fatal disease.

THE BIOLOGY OF HIV

AIDS is caused by the human immunodeficiency virus (HIV), a virus discovered in the mid-1980s. HIV is so small that 16,000 could fit on the head of a pin. (The structure of HIV is shown in Figure 20.4.) Typically, HIV gains entry to the body by sexual contact or by intravenous drug use with a contaminated needle. (It is believed that in most cases the virus must enter through a break in the skin or other tissue, like a cut, a sore, or a tear. This is one reason that drug addicts are at particularly heightened risk of infection.) Once inside, the virus selectively attacks two types of white blood cells, **helper T cells** and **macrophages.** Helper T cells are the key coordinators of the immune system. They send out chemical signals that stimulate the production of antibodies and largely control the development of several other types of cells that make up the immune system (see "Understanding the Immune System" on pp. 544–545). Macrophages, on the other hand, roam the bloodstream as scouts with two primary missions: to detect invading substances and to capture them, removing them from the circulation. Because they literally devour intruders, macrophages are classified in a group of cells known as phagocytes, from the Greek *phagein*, to eat. Macrophages not only search for invading microbes and engulf them, they also send an alarm to the rest of the immune system by secreting messenger proteins, called lymphokines.

After attaching itself to the outer surface of the helper T cell by a biochemical process that is very much like a key fitting in a lock, HIV injects its core inside the cell, establishing a permanent infection (see Figure 20.5a). (The HIV core consists of two strands of RNA as well as a group of structural proteins and enzymes that are important for later steps in the life cycle of the virus.) Once this occurs, the virus copies its genetic information into the DNA of the host cell, actually becoming part of that cell's genetic structure.[1] In this form, it can remain inactive and hidden for years (Redfield and Burke, 1988). However, if the immune system is activated in response to another invader (such as a common "flu" virus), infected helper T cells proliferate and produce large quantities of new HIV particles that are then released from the host T cell. These new viruses attack not only other T cells but also other cells of the immune system and the brain.

HOW HIV IS TRANSMITTED

Sexual Transmission

In more than 78 percent of all AIDS cases the virus has been sexually transmitted (Mann, Tarantola, and Netter, 1992; Merson, 1993). HIV is not, however, as highly contagious as some other STDs such as syphilis, gonorrhea, and hepatitis B. Current estimates suggest that the risk of being infected with HIV from a single act of heterosexual vaginal intercourse with an infected person is 1 in 500 for a woman and 1 in 700 for a man (Turner, Miller, and Moses, 1989). The risk from a single episode of anal intercourse with an infected partner is considerably higher—probably on the order of 1 in 50 to 100 (Voeller, 1986). This risk with anal intercourse is higher because the lining of the rectum is very delicate and tears easily during anal sex, readily allowing infected white blood cells and HIV in the ejaculate to enter the tissue and bloodstream of the receptive partner (whether male or female).

Since the risk of catching gonorrhea from a single heterosexual exposure to an infected partner is 50 percent for women and 25 percent for men, and the risk of sexual transmission of hepatitis B appears to be more than eight times greater than the risk of transmitting HIV (Kingsley et al., 1990), it is clear that HIV is far less contagious. Nevertheless, anyone who engages in risky sexual activity has a small but definite chance, each time, of becoming infected with HIV—and the more chances taken and the more exposures, the greater the likelihood of infection. What's more, there have been numerous instances documented in which infection occurred with a single episode of heterosexual intercourse (Peterman et al., 1988; Haverkos and Edelman, 1988; Glaser, Strange, and Rosati, 1989), which means that even though the *average* risk may be only 1 in 500 per sexual encounter, there is still a chance that HIV can be transmitted with only one sexual contact.

---

[1]This is where the term *retrovirus* originated. Usually, the genetic material in cells is DNA, and when genes are expressed, the DNA is initially copied into messenger RNA which then functions as the model for the production of proteins. In a retrovirus, this process is essentially reversed: the RNA is converted into DNA before it can be expressed or duplicated. In other words, retroviruses reverse what had seemed to be the normal flow of genetic coding (Haseltine, W. A., and Wong-Staal, F., "The molecular biology of the AIDS virus," *Scientific American* 259 (4):52–62, October 1988).

Figure 20.4   The structure of HIV

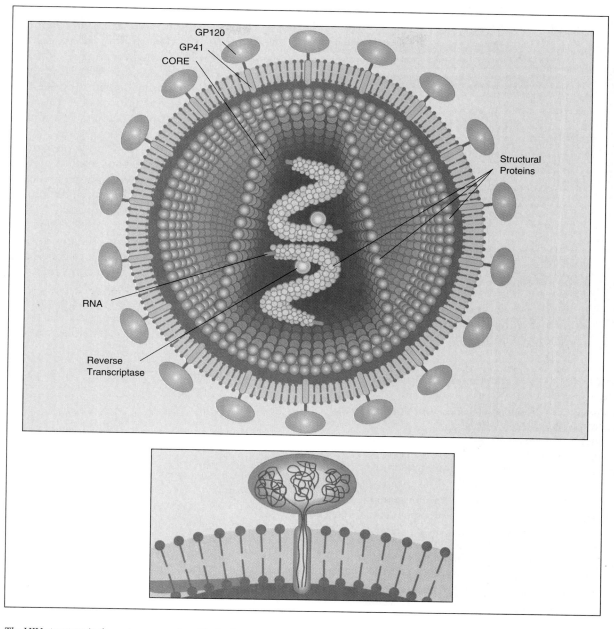

The HIV structure is shown in cross section. The knobs consist of a protein called gp120, which is anchored to another protein called gp41. The virus's core includes a protein, 2 strands of RNA (which carries the virus's genetic information) and an enzyme known as reverse transcriptase. Once the HIV core is inside its host cell, reverse transcriptase enables the virus to make DNA corresponding to the viral RNA. The DNA inserts itself into the host cell's chromosomes and remains latent until it is activated to make new virus particles.

helper T cells a type of white blood cell that responds to foreign antigens, playing an important role in activating the immune response.

macrophages white blood cells that act as scouts and scavengers in the immune system.

While it is certain that vaginal and anal sexual intercourse are the primary means by which HIV is transmitted, it is also clear that it can be transmitted by other forms of sexual activity (see Table 20.1).

Oral–genital sex, which is known to transmit every other form of STD, has now been shown conclusively to be a means of transmitting HIV (Perry, Jacobsberg, and Fogel, 1989; Spitzer and Weiner, 1989; Staver, 1990; Murray et al., 1991). Earlier difficulties in proving that oral–genital sex could transmit HIV infection primarily reflected the problem of finding people who had engaged exclusively in oral–genital contact and never in coitus or intravenous drug use. Thus, one study of 45 married couples in which one spouse had AIDS found that the frequency of oral–genital sex correlated with the previously uninfected partner's becoming infected with HIV (Fischl et al., 1987), but this was not proof of a cause–effect relationship. (Correlational studies cannot provide this type of proof.) While it does not appear at present that the risk of transmitting HIV via oral–genital sex is as high as the risk during coitus, there has been no way based on current knowledge to quantify the risk precisely.

It would certainly seem sensible in an individual set of circumstances to assume that the risk is higher if you or your partner have cuts or sores on the genitals, on the lips, or inside the mouth, but this doesn't help in determining the magnitude of risk for oral–genital sex when such conditions are not present. However, it is important to remember that oral–genital sex cannot "create" the AIDS virus if one person isn't already infected: if you are certain that both you and your partner are uninfected, there is no reason to abstain from oral sex.

There has been a great deal of skepticism about whether French kissing, or soul kissing (which involves exchanging saliva with your partner), can transmit HIV. While some reports claiming to document such transmission have appeared (Rozenbaum et al., 1988; Piazza et al., 1989), there is also evidence that saliva inactivates HIV (at least in the laboratory setting). Furthermore, the concentration of HIV is much lower in saliva than in blood or semen. On the other hand, since it is very common to have minor cuts or abrasions of the gums, lips, or inner mouth that may provide a place for the virus to enter, it is a biologically plausible possibility.

Table 20.1   Risk Estimates of HIV Transmission from Various Sexual Practices

Safer—Probably No Risk for HIV Transmission
Abstention from sexual contact
Monogamous relationship, both partners uninfected
Self masturbation
Touching, massaging, hugging, stroking
Dry kissing (social kissing)

Low but Real Risk for HIV Transmission
Anal or vaginal intercourse with proper use of intact condom
French kissing
Fellatio without ejaculation in the mouth
Genital–genital contact without penetration
Contact with urine (exclusive of contact with mouth, rectum, or cuts or breaks in the skin)

Unsafe—Moderate Risk for Transmitting HIV
Fellatio with ejaculation in the mouth
Cunnilingus (risk may be greater during menstruation when blood is present or if there are sores in the mouth)
Sharing sex toys and implements
Sex play (such as S/M activities) that causes bleeding

Unsafe—High Risk for Transmitting HIV
Numerous sexual partners
Unprotected anal receptive sex with infected partner
Unprotected anal penetration with the hand (fisting)
Anal douching in combination with anal sex
Oral–anal contact (rimming)
Vaginal intercourse with an infected partner without a condom

Source: *Modified from T. Cohen, M. A. Sande, and P. A. Volberding (eds.),* The AIDS Knowledge Base, *1990, Chapter 11.1.4.*

Figure 20.5 Cellular Details of HIV Infection

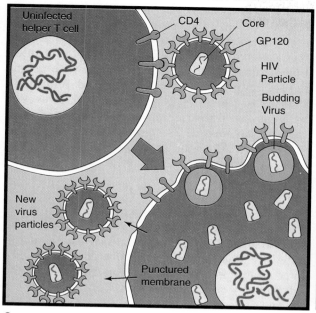

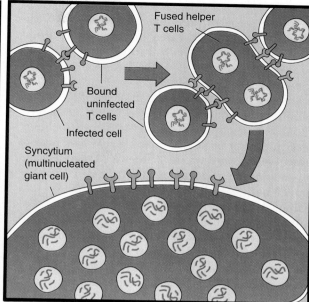

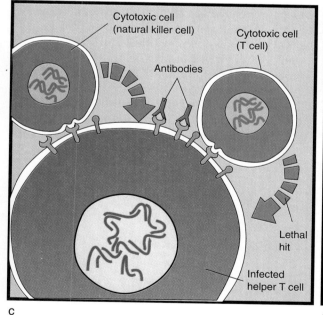

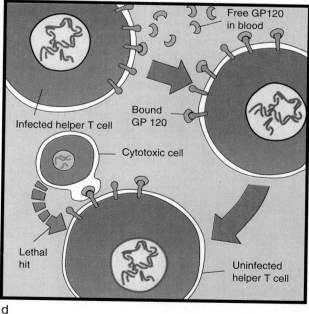

Destruction of helper T Cells, which are critical to immune defense, is the major cause of the progressive immune dysfunction that is the hallmark of HIV infection. (a) The virus is known to kill cells by replicating, budding from them and damaging the cell membrane. (b) HIV might also kill T4 cells indirectly, by means of a viral protein, gp120, that is displayed on an infected cell's surface. A molecule on T4 cells—the CD4 receptor—has a strong affinity for gp120, and healthy T4 cells can bind to the gp120 and merge with the infected cell. The end result, a giant cell called a syncytium, cannot survive, and all the once healthy cells it contains are destroyed along with the infected cell. (c) HIV can also elicit normal cellular immune defenses against infected cells. With or without the help of antibodies, cytotoxic defensive cells can destroy an infected cell that displays viral proteins on its surface. (d) Finally, free gp120 may circulate in the blood of people with HIV. The free protein may bind to the CD4 receptor of uninfected cells, making them appear to be infected and evoking an immune defensive response which destroys the healthy helper T cell, further weakening the body's immune system.

That it may be an actuality, under some circumstances, is suggested by one report that described the transmission of HIV infection from a 70-year-old woman who had been infected by a blood transfusion to her 72-year-old husband, who had had no sexual activity other than passionate kissing for many years (Illa, 1989).

Absolute, incontrovertible proof that HIV can or cannot be transmitted by French kissing is not yet available and may be extremely difficult to obtain. Nevertheless, it is clearly possible that this type of transmission could occur. While this doesn't mean you should demand a medical certificate from your partner before embarking on a first kiss, or that kissing should be reserved only for long-term relationships, it would certainly be wisest to avoid French kissing a person you know to be infected with HIV.

Substantial evidence has accumulated showing that having another STD is an important risk factor for becoming infected with HIV via sexual contacts. (Such a risk factor is often referred to as a cofactor, a condition that plays a causative role, although it is not the sole cause of the infection.) This observation was first made in Africa, where the high rate of coexistent STDs (especially those causing genital sores or ulcers) is thought to be particularly important in the large proportion of heterosexually transmitted cases of HIV infection (Mann, Tarantola, and Netter, 1992; Kreiss et al., 1992). The association between other STDs and HIV infection has been noted in the United States as well. For example, researchers in Baltimore found an association between syphilis and HIV infection in men and a similar association with a history of genital warts in women (Quinn et al., 1988). Studies have also found that the risk of HIV infection is substantially higher in people with genital herpes than in others (Deodhar and Tendolkar, 1989; Wasserheit, 1992; Altman, 1993). However, heterosexual transmission is possible even when there are no other STDs present (Turner, Miller and Moses, 1989; Allen and Setlow, 1991).

Nonsexual Transmission

Aside from sexual transmission, the major route by which HIV is transmitted is by intravenous drug users sharing needles or syringes that are contaminated by small amounts of infected blood. Once infected in this way, someone can then pass on the infection by sexual contact as well as by further sharing of needles.

Intravenous drug users may have a higher susceptibility than others to infection with HIV because their general health and nutritional status are often poor and their immune defenses may already be partly broken down by other illnesses.

The AIDS virus can also be transmitted by the transfusion of contaminated blood or blood products. In the 1990s, 2 to 3 percent of AIDS cases in the United States had fallen into this category, although the figure had previously been higher (Cohen, Sande, and Volberding, 1990; Centers for

Children with AIDS are a neglected but all-too-real part of this epidemic here and abroad.

A community-outreach condom distribution program in Austin, Texas, is one of the many ways in which the HIV epidemic is being attacked.

Disease Control and Prevention, *HIV/AIDS Surveillance Report* 5:3, 1993). The routine use since 1985 of screening tests to detect HIV antibodies in donated blood and blood products (see page 564) has substantially lessened the risk of using contaminated blood for transfusions. However, the blood supply is not completely safe because the screening tests are not foolproof, as we will discuss shortly. As a result, it is estimated that there are still about 1,000 cases a year in which the recipient of a blood transfusion is infected with HIV because of receiving a contaminated unit of blood (Ward et al., 1988; Donahue et al., 1990; Busch et al., 1991; Conley and Holmberg, 1992). To put this number in perspective, although the risk of HIV infection with a single unit of transfused blood is approximately 1 in 40,000, this is much safer than the risk of dying from general anesthesia (about 1 in 10,000).

Because of this small but real risk, some people having elective, nonemergency surgery have donated their own blood months or weeks before their surgery and have had it frozen and stored so it can be used if needed in a transfusion. This procedure has received strong endorsements from the medical community. In addition to preventing any chance of inadvertently transmitting HIV, it also has the benefit of completely eliminating the risk of other transfusion-linked infections, such as hepatitis.

It is important to recognize that there is absolutely no risk to *giving* blood as long as a sterile needle is used, which is standard and mandatory procedure throughout the United States and Canada.

HIV can also be transmitted from an infected mother to her developing child during pregnancy or childbirth. Current research suggests that 20 to 50 percent of infants born to infected mothers will be infected (European Collabortive Study, 1988; Cohen, Sande, and Volberding, 1990), although how many of these children will develop AIDS is not known at present. Because of the high risk that the baby will be born HIV-infected, women infected with HIV should not become pregnant if they can help it. Most experts also feel that a woman who is infected with HIV who becomes pregnant should consider having an abortion, although of course this is a complicated personal decision. The best solution is for women who are infected with HIV to avoid pregnancy completely.

HIV can also be transmitted from a sperm donor or an organ transplant donor to an uninfected person, although instances of this sort are rare (Chiasson, Stoneburner, and Joseph, 1990; Simonds et al., 1992). Nevertheless, the possibility of transmission in this fashion has led several states to pass legislation requiring that all sperm donors be screened for HIV.

Another type of transmission happens during breast feeding. Since HIV appears in breast milk (Levy, 1989), it can be passed from a mother to her nursing infant (Ziegler et al., 1985; Van De Perre et al., 1991, 1992; Dunn et al., 1992). Furthermore, several cases have been reported from a Russian hospital where babies who had been infected by a contaminated syringe infected their mothers during nursing. Presumably, blood from sores in the baby's mouth entered the mother's body through cracks in the mother's nipples (Pokrovsky and Eramova, 1989).

HIV can also be transmitted by needle-stick injuries, which occur when doctors or nurses giving an HIV-infected person an injection (or drawing a blood sample) accidentally stick themselves with the needle after it has been used. HIV transmission occurs in less than one-half of 1 percent of such injuries (Henderson et al., 1990; O'Neill et al., 1992). In contrast, the risk of infection with hepatitis B virus after such an exposure is estimated to be 23 to 43 percent, and the CDC estimates that more than 10,000 cases of occupationally acquired hepatitis B occur annually in the United States (Fahey and Henderson, 1990). At least one instance of HIV infection due to contaminated acupuncture needles has also been reported (Vittecoq et al., 1989).

How HIV is *Not* Transmitted

Despite the finding of a low degree of infectiousness, many people have been so frightened by the

AIDS epidemic that they worry that HIV infection might be transmitted by casual contact such as shaking hands with an infected person or coming in contact with the virus on a doorknob, toilet seat, or water fountain. Researchers agree that such fears are unfounded: there is no evidence at all that the AIDS virus is transmitted by casual contact of this sort (Liskin and Blackburn, 1986; Heywood and Curran, 1988; American Health Consultants, 1993). While HIV has been identified in blood, tears, urine, saliva, semen, and vaginal secretions (Liskin and Blackburn, 1986; Wofsy et al., 1986), many studies have shown that people in close daily contact with persons with AIDS—such as a parent caring for a child with AIDS and nurses, doctors, and dentists working closely with AIDS patients—do not develop HIV infections from these contacts (Friedland et al., 1986; Fischl et al., 1987; Heywood and Curran, 1988; Bartlett and Finkbeiner, 1991). In many instances, of course, family members share drinking glasses or eating utensils with a person with AIDS, yet transmission of HIV by such acts has never been demonstrated.

Earlier concerns that the AIDS virus might be transmitted by insects such as mosquitoes now have been put to rest. Although HIV can survive for 48 hours in mosquitoes fed on infected blood (Booth, 1987), there is no indication that the virus reproduces inside mosquitoes or any other type of insect. Furthermore, if HIV were transmitted by insect bites, there would likely be a high rate of infection in preadolescent children in Africa and other tropical areas, but there is no evidence that this has occurred.

PROTECTING AGAINST HIV INFECTION: SAFER SEX GUIDELINES

Experts are somewhat divided on exactly what constitutes "safe" sex. Complete abstinence is one solution, but this option isn't appealing to most people. Another possibility is a mutually monogamous relationship with an uninfected partner. While there is no way to tell by someone's appearance if he or she is free of HIV, a blood test can be done to detect whether or not HIV infection is present (see p. 554). If you and your partner are both tested and are found to be uninfected and you remain sexually faithful to each other, you are effectively assured that you won't get AIDS (making allowances for the slim chance of becoming infected by nonsexual

means such as a blood transfusion). If such an approach is either impractical or unrealistic in your circumstances, the following guidelines may be of some help:

1. *Completely safe sex is possible if there is no exchange of body fluids.* While this means cutting out oral sex and intercourse as options—because even without ejaculation there is a danger of transmitting HIV in pre-ejaculatory fluid and vaginal secretions—techniques such as massage, use of vibrators, and mutual masturbation can be used. In addition, any sexual practices that can cause injury or rips in tissue should be avoided.

2. *Proper and consistent use of condoms will greatly reduce the risk of transmission of HIV as a result of sexual contact.* Studies have found that the pores of latex ("synthetic") condoms are so small that even viruses cannot pass through, and thus latex condoms, used properly, can prevent the transmission of HIV (Kish et al., 1983; Minuk, Bohme and Bower, 1986; Feldblum and Fortney, 1988). (So-called natural membrane or animal skin condoms do occasionally leak virus particles, and thus are not recommended.) However, since improper use of condoms or a tear in the condom can certainly lead to leakage, this method is *not* a foolproof means of preventing infection (see Chapter 6). In fact, condoms fail more often than you might think. One survey found that 22 percent of heterosexuals and 31 percent of homosexuals had experienced condom failure in the preceding 3 months (Miller, Downer and Krueger, 1988). Remember, condoms are not perfect contraceptives, and they're not perfect barriers to HIV or other STDs, either.

3. *Use of spermicides containing nonoxynol-9 may offer additional protection.* Nonoxynol-9 kills HIV under laboratory conditions (Hicks et al., 1985), although under real-life conditions it may not provide as much protection as a condom (Kreiss et al., 1992). The best solution seems to be to use both a condom and a spermicide with nonoxynol-9 during intercourse.

4. *Be selective in choosing your sex partners.* As we've already noted, it isn't possible to judge who's infected with HIV by any symptoms, since it can take years after becoming infected for symptoms to develop. Furthermore, the

FOCUS IN BRIEF

Dishonesty In Dating

Much of the advice about protecting yourself against exposure to HIV hinges on establishing possible risk-factors of your sex partner. However, as the data from 18- to 25-year-old college students summarized here shows, sizable percentages of men and women lie about sex to their partners.

	Men (N = 196)	Women (N = 226)
Actual Experiences		
Has told a lie in order to have sex	34%	10%
Lied about ejaculatory control	38	—
Lied about likelihood of pregnancy	—	14
Sexually involved with more than one person	32	23
Partner did not know	68	59
Has been lied to for purposes of sex	47	60
Partner lied about ejaculatory control	—	46
or likelihood of pregnancy	34	—
Hypothetical Willingness to Lie		
Would lie about having negative HIV-antibody test	20	4
Would understate number of previous sex partners	47	42
Would disclose existence of other partner to new partner		
Never	22	10
After a while, when safe to do so	34	28
Only if asked	31	33
Yes	13	29
Would disclose a single episode of sexual infidelity		
Never	43	34
After a while, when safe to do so	21	20
Only if asked	14	11
Yes	22	35

Source: Cochran, S.D., and Mays, V.M., "Sex, Lies, and HIV," New England Journal of Medicine 322: 774–775, 1990.

great majority of people who are infected with HIV don't realize they're infected, so don't rely on a potential sex partner to warn you that there may be a danger of transmission. Under current conditions, it is prudent to realize that people who have had a large number of sex partners and people who inject drugs are statistically more likely to have been exposed to and infected by HIV. Similarly, males who have had same-sex experiences in the past decade are statistically more likely to be infected with HIV. Selectivity regarding a prospective sex partner can be lifesaving.

5. *Learn as much as you can about someone BEFORE you have sex together, but don't blindly trust whatever you are told.* Research shows that people often lie about how many sex partners they have had (Cochran and Mays, 1990). The *Kinsey Institute New Report on Sex* notes, "Researchers suspect people are even more likely to lie about homosexual activity, sex with prostitutes, or the use of illegal drugs" (Reinisch and Beasley, 1990, p. 45).

6. *Stay away from high-risk sexual activity with a new partner until you have developed enough trust and rapport in your relationship to know each other fairly well.* While you shouldn't necessarily refrain from all sexual contact with a new partner for a period of months, it is perfectly sensible to start out slowly and to be forthright about which types of sex you'd prefer to leave until later in the relationship.

These guidelines need to be applied with a certain amount of common sense in order to be most useful to you. For example, we don't think it's advisable to have sexual intercourse (gay or straight) with a partner you know is infected with HIV, even if you use a condom. (We are sensitive to the problems this advice poses in long-term, committed relationships, including marriages, when one partner becomes infected and the other partner is not. Still, we stand by this position: condoms may reduce the risk of transmitting HIV, but they are far from failsafe.) Likewise, if you suspect (but can't prove) that a prospective sexual partner has been an intravenous drug user, it may be most prudent to evaluate the situation cautiously, and refuse to have any sexual contact without first having blood tests done.

DETECTING HIV INFECTION

Several different blood tests can be used to detect HIV antibodies. The most widely used test is called **ELISA** (for **enzyme-linked immunoabsorbent assay**); it was developed to screen blood used for transfusions. Like all biomedical tests, ELISA is not infallible, although the accuracy of current versions of ELISA, which is very high, is improved substantially from five years ago. ELISA tests fail to detect HIV antibodies in about 0.3 percent of samples known to be positive (a mistake known as a "false negative"). In addition, this test incorrectly "finds" HIV antibodies in about 1 percent of samples (in other words, using the ELISA test alone, 1 out of 100 tests will be mistakenly called positive when it actually is not—a situation known as a "false positive") (Centers for Disease Control [MMWR 39:380–383], 1990).

Because of these inaccuracies, which may seem minor from a statistical viewpoint but which are certainly anything *but* minor if they involve *your* test, it is important to verify any positive result found by ELISA by using a different, more complicated (and expensive) test after repeating the ELISA test. This confirmatory test is called the Western blot test. When used together (ELISA test first, repeated if positive, and then confirmed by the Western blot test), the accuracy of testing for HIV antibodies is much better than most other medical screening tests, although even this method of screening is not perfect. In fact, several laborato-

ries have reported false positive rates of less than 1 in 100,000 tests using these two tests combined (Burke et al., 1988; MacDonald et al., 1989).

Testing is complicated somewhat by the fact that infrequently, a person may be infected with HIV for more than two years before antibodies become detectable by either ELISA or Western blot testing (Loche and Mach, 1988; Imagawa et al., 1989). In addition, in rare cases a person who was initially seropositive (that is, had detectable HIV antibodies) may become seronegative (have no detectable HIV antibodies in the bloodstream), even though he or she is still infected with HIV (Farzadegan, 1988). In such cases, it appears that HIV "hides" in macrophages and monocytes, where it is somehow camouflaged from the usual testing. Fortunately, the incidence of disappearing HIV antibodies is low—0.4 percent (4 out of 1,000 persons tested)—and the phenomenon is still of uncertain significance.

A false positive test result can be caused by technical error in performing the test or a clerical error in identifying the blood sample. A false positive result can also occur if some substance in the blood reacts with chemicals used in the test so that a mistaken reading is given. (False positives are more common in women than in men and may be related to previous pregnancy.)

Despite these various possibilities and problems with testing, we should stress that a confirmed positive test *is* cause for concern and should be followed up by careful long-term medical evaluation. In addition, as noted emphatically by a panel of experts, "All persons who are antibody positive for HIV, whether they are symptom free or ill, must be considered to be potentially infectious to others by sexual transmission, by sharing of drug injection equipment, by childbearing, or by donation of blood, semen, or organs" (Consensus Conference, 1986).

It is important to realize that finding HIV antibodies in someone's blood does not, by itself, mean that the person has AIDS. Until 1993, the diagnosis of AIDS was made when a major disease such as *Pneumocystis carinii* pneumonia or Kaposi's sarcoma that signals an underlying deficiency in the immune system occurred in the absence of other conditions known to be risk factors for these illnesses. AIDS could also be diagnosed if a person had a positive HIV antibody test, evidence of a suppressed immune system (for instance, a low T cell count), and at least

Photomicrograph of a T cell infected by HIV.

one disease from a list of some of the lesser infections associated with AIDS. As of January 1, 1993, however, the U.S. Public Health Service and Centers for Disease Control and Prevention revised and expanded the criteria used to diagnose AIDS to include all HIV-infected persons who have a CD4+ T cell count below 200 and to add three "AIDS-defining" conditions—pulmonary tuberculosis, recurrent pneumonia, and invasive cervical cancer—to the previously established conditions (Centers for Disease Control, 1992g and 1993c). The impact of this change will be discussed shortly.

THE STAGES OF HIV INFECTION

As we have already noted, it is important to observe the entire spectrum of HIV disease instead of simply looking at AIDS, because HIV is a slow-acting virus. People who become infected today may not have any symptoms of their infection for ten years or more, although sometimes they become ill at a much more rapid pace. Despite such variability, it is clear that HIV infection is a chronic, progressive disease (Cohen, Sande, and Volberding, 1990). Full-blown AIDS is the end stage of an infection that begins long before we can recognize that people are physically ill. Understanding this progression can help our understanding both of peo-

ple who are infected with HIV and of what we can do to avoid this infection.

Initial Infection

No matter how someone is infected with HIV, when this virus enters the bloodstream the person's immune system typically responds by producing antibodies to the invading organism. Most people have no symptoms that accompany the initial infection or the production of antibodies, but 10 to 25 percent may have a brief illness that occurs two to five weeks after the virus enters the body (Cooper et al., 1985; Tucker et al., 1985). Symptoms include fever, chills, aches, swollen lymph glands, and itchy rashes, symptoms similar to those of infectious mononucleosis, or "mono." Because of the nonspecific nature of these symptoms, which are frequent accompaniments to many types of viral infections—including the common cold—do *not* assume that a two-day bout of swollen glands, a runny nose, and fever means you've been infected with HIV! Antibodies to HIV can usually be detected within two months after the initial infection, but there are some cases in which antibodies do not appear for a year or longer (Francis and Chin, 1987; Ranki et al., 1987; Imagawa et al., 1989).

The Asymptomatic Carrier State

The infected person then passes into a phase called the **asymptomatic carrier state.** (*Asymptomatic* means symptomless.) In this phase, a person looks and feels perfectly healthy, but the infection is present and antibodies persist. Many asymptomatic carriers also have a reduced number of helper T cells in their blood. *The presence of the live virus in the asymptomatic carrier state means that such a person can infect others without realizing that he or she is infected.* It is important to understand that asymptomatic carriers do not have AIDS (the illness), although they are infected with the virus that causes AIDS.

Here, from our files, are some personal reactions that illustrate the surprise and anguish many people who are asymptomatic HIV carriers express on learning of a positive test result:

ELISA (enzyme-linked immunoabsorbent assay)
the commonest blood test used to screen for HIV infection.

asymptomatic carrier state the state of being infected with HIV but having no symptoms.

A 23-year-old married woman: I was tested for HIV when I applied for an overseas job. When the results came back, I was absolutely sure they were wrong. There was no way I could have been infected, I thought. I never messed around, I never did drugs, and I never had a blood transfusion. Plus, I had never felt better in my life. But it turned out that my husband was positive, too, and that he had a bisexual affair when he was a sophomore in college. I was devastated, let me tell you.

A 28-year-old male rock musician: I found out I was infected when I went to donate blood for a friend who was having surgery. It sounds so simple now, but I was stunned when I heard the news. The counselor at the blood bank told me, "How can you be surprised? You've got about every risk factor in the book." Now that I've come to terms with it, I guess I had led a pretty wild life, but it's tough to think that I'll be dead in a few years unless they find some cure.

A 26-year-old gay man: When someone from the public health department called to tell me that one of my sex partners from a few years back had come down with AIDS, I had nightmares every night. I kept putting off the time to go get tested, because I didn't want to get the news. And I kept saying to myself, "Relax—you feel so good; you couldn't possibly be sick." But I finally went for testing and found out just what I didn't want to hear. What do I do now about my sex life? Do I tell someone "I've got it" just before we get it on? And what do I tell the people I've been with the past few years? "Oh, hey, I got it from Larry and now I've passed it on to you?" *(Author's files)*

It is uncertain how long infected people can remain asymptomatic before they develop signs of illness. Many individuals remain in the asymptomatic carrier state for periods of five years or longer before developing AIDS or related symptoms. Current evidence suggests that about 20 percent of asymptomatic carriers will develop full-blown cases of AIDS within six years (Bachetti and Moss, 1989; Cohen, Sande and Volberding, 1990), and some data suggest that with the passage of additional time, as many as 99 percent may eventually develop AIDS (Lui, Darrow and Rutherford, 1988; Eyster et al., 1989; Vella et al., 1992; Farizo, 1992). The best long-term data now available,

based on blood samples frozen and stored as part of a hepatitis study conducted in San Francisco in the late 1970s, show that 11 years after infection with HIV, 53 percent of subjects had progressed to full-blown AIDS, and under a quarter of the subjects were still symptom-free (Bachetti and Moss, 1989; Lambert, 1990).

Much remains to be done to clarify how and when HIV infection progresses to AIDS. Different groups may have different rates of progression. For instance, homosexual men seem to develop full-scale AIDS more rapidly than hemophiliacs do (Goedert et al., 1986). Similarly, adults over age 35 who are infected with HIV have been reported to progress more rapidly to AIDS than younger adults and adolescents (Moss et al., 1988; Goedert, 1989). Such differences may be a result of various factors. For example, repeated infections with HIV may reactivate the virus when it has been relatively dormant in the body. It is also possible that persons who have current or past infections with other viruses (for instance, the hepatitis B virus) may be most at risk for developing AIDS. Another theory is that use of certain illicit drugs—most particularly, volatile nitrites like amyl nitrite ("poppers")—may somehow set the stage for developing AIDS more easily by lowering natural resistance to HIV. Whether any of these theories will prove correct is uncertain at present.

It is also important to realize that there have been only relatively brief follow-up studies done on people infected with HIV, a fact that is understandable since this infection was first identified in the early 1980s. It is possible that 15 or 20 years after infection, unless a cure or other form of treatment is found, most people will progress to full-blown AIDS or will have died from other complications of HIV infection. On the other hand, since data from the 1980s is based primarily on HIV infection in homosexual males and in IV drug users, it is possible that this pattern may not accurately predict the experience that will be found in heterosexual, non-drug-abusing populations.

Symptomatic HIV Infection

In some people, HIV infection leads to symptoms that are less serious than AIDS itself. This stage was previously known as AIDS-related complex (ARC), but this term has now been generally discarded after the recognition that it was not a specific disease entity and had no special significance for treatment or outcome. Symptomatic HIV infection should be understood as part of a continuum of effects. As HIV multiplies within the body over time, it slowly destroys immune defenses. As these defenses deteriorate, susceptibility increases to a variety of infections that the immune system normally holds in check. These include non-life-threatening infections such as *shingles* or *thrush* (a fungus infection of the mouth), as well as more dangerous infections such as tuberculosis.

Symptomatic HIV infection is also commonly marked by persistent swelling of lymph nodes in several locations in the body (for example, the neck, the armpits, just above the collarbones), which can occur alone or with other symptoms. The most common symptoms are diarrhea, weight loss, fatigue, and fever, but these tend to be episodic, not constant. In addition, neurologic problems are frequently encountered (Koralnik et al., 1990; [unsigned editorial], 1992; Porter and Sande, 1992). However, it should be emphasized that many people with symptomatic HIV infection are well enough to lead relatively normal lives much of the time, continuing to work productively, to participate in sports and other recreational activities, and to appear quite healthy. Here is how one person described it:

> *A 32-year-old male architect:* I've been infected with HIV for more than six years now. Until last year I was completely free of any symptoms, but this year I've lost 12 pounds and have started to have occasional bouts of night sweats and fevers. But I still manage to jog three miles each day, play tennis on most week-ends, and keep an active social calendar. My doctor tells me that staying in good physical condition will help my fight against this killer—and so far it has. (*Author's files*)

Unfortunately, people with symptomatic HIV infection do not always realize they are infected, either because their condition has been misdiagnosed, because they haven't gone to a doctor, or because they minimize the significance of the physical problems they are having. People in this situation may unknowingly and unintentionally expose their sex partners to HIV infection.

It is virtually inevitable that all people with symptomatic HIV infection will eventually develop AIDS (Brachetti and Moss, 1989; Goedert, 1989; Cohen, Sande, and Volberding, 1990).

AIDS and Its Symptoms

While no single pattern of signs and symptoms fits all cases of AIDS, some of the most common are similar to those of symptomatic HIV infection: progressive and unexplained weight loss, persistent fever (sometimes accompanied by night sweats), swollen lymph nodes, and slightly raised reddish-purple coin-sized spots on the skin. These skin spots often turn out to be a form of cancer of the small blood vessels, a condition called **Kaposi's sarcoma** (often abbreviated as "KS") (see Figure 20.6). Kaposi's sarcoma was unusual in the United States before the start of the HIV epidemic. However, about one-quarter of homosexual males with AIDS in the United States have been found to have Kaposi's sarcoma, although KS is relatively rare in heterosexuals IV drug users and hemophiliacs with AIDS (Beral et al., 1989).

When symptoms of AIDS first appear they may remain unchanged for many months or they may be quickly followed by one or more opportunistic infections: that is, infections that occur when immunity is broken down. One of the most common of these infections is the unusual, often-fatal form of pneumonia caused by *Pneumocystis carinii*, the presence of which established the diagnosis of AIDS in almost two-thirds of the cases seen in the United States prior to 1993.

Among other common infections in people with AIDS are severe fungal infections (including a form that spreads to the covering of the brain, causing meningitis), tuberculosis, and various forms of herpes that are more severe and recur more often than usual. Encephalitis (inflammation of the brain) is another life-threatening condition that occurs with greatly increased frequency in people with AIDS. In fact, because HIV can directly infect brain cells, a variety of neurological disturbances are seen in an estimated 30 to 65 percent of AIDS patients (Ho et al., 1989; Dina, 1991; Keating et al., 1991). These conditions include memory disturbances, psychiatric symptoms, severe mental confusion (dementia), difficulty walking, seizures, and coma. Although treatment can often temporarily fend off these infections, the typical course is for one after another overwhelming infection to occur until the victim finally dies because the depressed condition of the immune sys-

Kaposi's sarcoma purple colored skin lesions resulting from an unusual form of cancer.

Figure 20.6 AIDS Patient with Kaposi's Sarcoma

tem becomes progressively worse, leading eventually to one final infection that cannot be overcome.

The human side of these symptoms is difficult to grasp unless you have been involved personally in caring for someone with AIDS. Here is a description offered by one man who took care of his brother for the last year of the brother's life, as they both dealt with this devastating disease:

> Tom was determined to handle his affairs with dignity. While he was a realist until the very end, he was also able to look at the cards life had dealt him without bitterness or a sense of defeat. "Everyone's got to die sometime" was a phrase he used over and over again, mostly to cheer his visitors out of their dismay at his appearance. Still, once he became so weak that he was unable to walk more than a few steps at a time, we both realized things were going downhill rapidly. What worried him most of all was that he might develop AIDS dementia. Fortunately, even through three hospitalizations and a ferocious bout of shingles, Tom's mind stayed sharp until he was done living. While this was an emotionally trying time for us all, it gave me a chance to get to know my brother on a level I never would have known him before. (*Author's files*)

At present, AIDS is almost always fatal within a matter of two to four years after it is first diagnosed (Pantaleo, Graziosi and Fauci, 1993). [The median

survival for AIDS patients in San Francisco is 12.5 months, with fewer than 9 percent of patients surviving for three years (Payne et al., 1989).] Despite these statistics, many people with AIDS are able to lead relatively normal lives early in the course of their disease, although coping with the social, economic, and emotional aspects of their illness is especially difficult for many, as we discuss shortly. As more treatments are developed and become available for AIDS and for the severe infections associated with it, both the quality and length of life for people with AIDS will improve substantially.

While some people with AIDS continue their employment and usual activities for six months or more after the diagnosis is established, eventually the weight loss, constant fatigue, and multiple infections take such a toll that even ordinary movement becomes a major effort and the person becomes an invalid. (In Africa, AIDS is often called "slim" because in its late stages its victims look as if they had been starving.)

TREATMENT OF HIV INFECTION AND AIDS

Although as of late 1994 no successful cure for AIDS or HIV infection has been found, there are some definite signs of progress against this disease. Most notable has been the identification of a drug called AZT (azidothymidine or zidovudine, marketed in the United States under the trade name Retrovir), which has proved to be an effective treatment, although it has limitations as well. AZT was initially found to slow the progression of disease in patients with full-blown AIDS. Subsequent studies not only confirmed that AZT delayed the progression of disease in AIDS patients (Fischl et al., 1987) and patients with asymptomatic HIV infection (Volberding et al., 1990) but also showed that it could be effective in lower doses than were used initially (Friedland, 1990). By using lower doses, it is possible to minimize the serious side effects many people experience with this drug (Collier et al., 1990; Fischl et al., 1990), the most common of which is suppression of bone marrow function. Since the bone marrow serves to produce new blood cells, suppression of this function causes severe anemia (low red blood cell count, which causes severe fatigue) and lowering of the white blood cell count (further reducing the body's ability to fight infections).

Possible Ways To Combat HIV

The HIV life cycle is subject to attack by drugs at several stages.

1. Antibodies or chemicals could block the binding of HIV to CD4 receptors on the surface of helper T cells.
2. Other agents might keep viral RNA and reverse transcriptase from escaping their protein coat.
3. AZT and similar drugs work by blocking the reverse transcription of viral RNA into viral DNA.
4. Drugs are also being sought to block the translation of messenger RNA into viral proteins.
5. Since the newly produced viral proteins must undergo chemical and structural modifications before they can be assembled into new infectious virus, it may be possible to interfere successfully with this modification process.
6. Finally, antiviral substances such as interferon may be able to keep the new virus particles from assembling themselves and budding out of the cell.

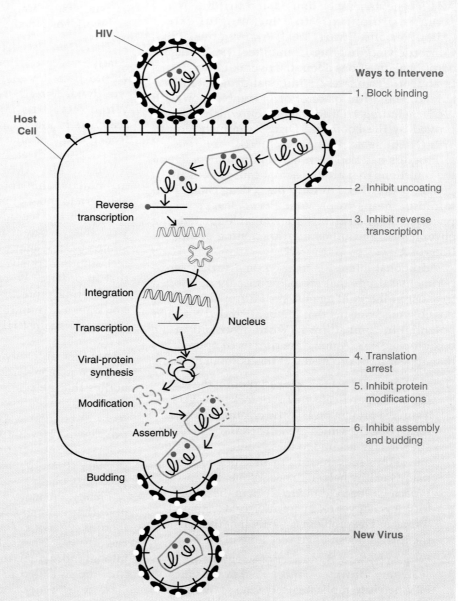

The belief that AZT can prolong life for people with HIV infection was one major reason why AIDS experts began calling for early detection and treatment (Cohen, Sande, and Volberding, 1990; Angell, 1991; Francis, 1992). However, there is evidence that some strains of HIV develop resistance to AZT when they are exposed to the drug over long time periods (Larder, Draby, and Richman, 1989; Cohen, 1993). If this resistance becomes widespread, the overall utility of using AZT would be reduced considerably. Furthermore, recent studies in Europe have found that the duration of AZT's benefits may be limited and that it may not actually prolong life to a meaningful extent (Aboulker and Swart, 1993; Anonymous, 1993; Concorde Coordinating Committee, 1994), raising additional questions about the overall utility of this treatment. Fortunately, additional drugs are available to be used in place of or in combination with AZT, including DDI (didanosine), which was approved by the Food and Drug Administration in 1991 (Nightingale, 1991; Sachs, 1992).

Progress has also been made in treating some of the infections that are the actual causes of death in people with AIDS. For example, a drug called pentamidine helps to prevent *Pneumocystis carinii* pneumonia; other drugs are available for fighting encephalitis and other life-threatening complications of AIDS.

Additional interest is focused on a variety of experimental drugs that are being rapidly developed to assist in the fight against the HIV epidemic. The possible mechanisms that are being tested for their potential in combatting HIV are described in the box on page 559. Among the dozens of approaches that appear most promising at this point in time are:

1. *Synthetic CD4.* CD4 is the receptor on the surface of helper T cells that is unlocked by gp 120, a surface protein on HIV. By creating synthetic forms of CD4, which are infused into the bloodstream, HIV is lured to these "decoy" molecules and is thus prevented from attaching to as many healthy helper T cells. While this approach has been found to work in the laboratory, it is not yet ready for full-scale testing in humans. The problem is partly that the synthetic CD4 doesn't live very long in the body.

2. *Enzyme blockers.* A number of scientists are searching for ways to block the key enzymes HIV needs to replicate itself. One of these is an enzyme called protease; if it could be blocked effectively, HIV would be unable to multiply within T cells or macrophages, and thus would be unlikely to seriously harm the immune system (Johnson and Hoth, 1993). While progress with this approach is still in its early stages, many experts feel this offers the best possibility for effective treatment.

3. *Vaccines.* Vaccines can be used either to *prevent* infection from occurring or treat an infection after it has occurred. Dr. Jonas Salk, famed developer of the first polio vaccine, tried the latter approach with some preliminary signs of success, although initial enthusiasm over Salk's work has faded considerably.

There has also been an active search for a preventive vaccine, which, if successfully developed would be a key element in actually halting the worldwide spread of HIV infection (Haynes, 1993). While there was initial excitement because researchers produced a vaccine that appeared to protect eight out of nine monkeys against simian AIDS (an AIDS-like disease caused by a retrovirus closely related to HIV) (Murphy-Corb et al., 1989), optimism about this approach has lessened considerably as a number of problems have appeared.

One of the technical difficulties in devising a workable vaccine is that there are several different strains of HIV against which the vaccine must protect simultaneously. Another practical problem is that in order to be effective, a vaccine must have long-lasting protective effects—measured in years, not weeks or months. Whether such long-lasting immunity against HIV can be devised is uncertain at present.

Another difficulty is that vaccines work by triggering a person's immune system to produce antibodies that help to kill a virus. In HIV infection, however, the antibodies that are usually produced seem to be unable to kill the virus, which is why people with HIV antibodies eventually go on to develop AIDS. Overcoming this hurdle may be the primary stumbling block in developing an effective vaccine (Cohen, 1994).

Finally, the matter of safety is also of paramount importance: in any vaccine containing killed virus, there is always a slight risk that some viral particles survive or get reactivated, so that once injected into an individual, they can cause the very disease they are intended to prevent. Despite such obstacles, development of various vaccines continues, although progress is proceeding far more slowly

Many celebrities from Elton John to Madonna, have contributed time and money to the effort to combat ignorance about HIV.

than people had hoped (Redfield and Birx, 1992; Haynes, 1993; Altman, 1993; Cohen, 1994).

Caring for People with AIDS

Because people with AIDS may have only minimal symptoms of their disease, may be struggling against acute and life-threatening infections, or may be anywhere on the spectrum between these two extremes, special care and support systems have been devised in many cities to provide a broad range of necessary services to those who need help. In San Francisco, for example, the following components exist (Cohen, Sande, and Volberding, 1990):

1. a walk-in clinic for everyone from the "worried well" to those who are dying;

2. a specialized AIDS inpatient unit for those requiring hospitalization;

3. an extensive array of community-based care, including the following services that are provided at the residence of the person with AIDS: assistance with shopping, housecleaning, meal preparation, special nursing services, legal assistance, and obtaining necessary medications;

4. volunteer organizations providing a variety of forms of support (the best-known of these groups in San Francisco is the Shanti Project, which assigns a trained volunteer counselor to every person newly diagnosed with AIDS and provides a wide range of services, from ongoing support groups to low-cost housing for those who need it);

5. a hospice program for those in the terminal stage of illness. Hospices aim to make a dying person's last weeks or months more comfortable, both physically and psychologically, by providing a broad range of services. In addition to providing care aimed at minimizing the person's distress when no cure is realistically possible, hospices generally try to deal with many aspects of the lives of their patients, including spiritual needs, family matters, and legal and financial concerns. Hospices also help family members and friends deal with grieving and loss.

Across the country, community volunteers and both families and friends of people with AIDS are learning new ways of relating and communicating—of bringing caring, compassion, and dignity as powerful tools to deal with this epidemic. While it would be a mistake to believe that this action completely counterbalances the prejudices against people with HIV infection and AIDS that exist in many segments of our society, it is certainly a much-needed step in the right direction.

PATTERNS OF THE EPIDEMIC: A LOOK AT THE NUMBERS

Regrettably, 12 years after the first recognition of AIDS and 8 years after the development of tests to detect antibodies to HIV, no national prevalence survey has been done to establish definitively the exact dimensions of the HIV epidemic in the

When Someone You Know Has AIDS

When a devastating illness like AIDS strikes a family member or friend, it is natural to feel unable to offer much help or hope and to think you can't do anything that would make a difference. Instead of giving in to these feelings, here are some concrete suggestions for what you *can* do to make a difference.

- Simply being there as often as you've been in the past (or maybe even a little more often) is one of the best ways to convey your concern and caring. But be sure to call first. Let your friend decide if he or she wants a visitor right at that time.
- Offer to help out in various ways. Washing dishes, doing the grocery shopping, or picking up the cleaning may seem like small tasks to you, but such help is likely to be greatly appreciated. Your effort is tangible proof that you care, so it is much more than "just" cooking dinner or doing a few chores.
- You should realize that dealing with a fatal disease is not simple. You can get many helpful hints from AIDS groups in your area, but recognize that they don't make you an expert on the subject. So don't try to be one—you will only create conflicts with your friend's health-care providers.
- Be aware that holidays are a time when loneliness can be particularly hard to deal with. (This is especially true if your friend is in the hospital.) A special visit that helps your friend feel included in the holiday spirit is a thoughtful act. And creative use of decorations, snacks, or gifts with the holiday theme—like a Christmas stocking stuffed with hard candies, paperbacks, and toiletries—is a concrete way of leaving a reminder of your feelings even after your visit is over.
- While it isn't useful to dwell on all the details of your friend's or relative's medical condition and treatment, don't pretend the illness doesn't exist. Questions like "How are you feeling?" are certainly appropriate (just as they would be for someone with any other type of illness).
- Include news of the outside world in your conversations to help your friend avoid feeling completely isolated and uninvolved. Tell him or her about mutual friends and what's going on at work, discuss your favorite sports teams, and bring up current events from the national and international scene.
- Reach out and touch your friend. A hug, a kiss, or an arm around his or her shoulder

United States. (Prevalence denotes the proportion of a population that is currently infected.) In fact, former Surgeon General C. Everett Koop acknowledged this problem when he said, "How many are infected? That's our whole problem—we don't know that number. We use the number of a million or a million and a half, but it could be 400,000 or it could be 4 million. We just don't know" (*The New York Times*, July 22, 1988, p. B4). Nevertheless, a substantial number of prevalence studies have been done in various segments of the population. By studying their range of results, it is possible to form a preliminary picture of the HIV epidemic as it currently exists.

Before considering these surveys, it is useful to look back at the evolution of the HIV epidemic from several different viewpoints. First, it is helpful to keep in mind that the early years of the HIV epidemic hit hardest in New York, New Jersey, and California. In fact, many scientists and politicians in the Midwest and in the South (outside of Florida) voiced doubts that AIDS would ever take much of a toll in their locales. While it is obvious today that this attitude of denial was incorrect, denial occurred in other ways as well. For example, as recently as the mid-1980s many scientists considered it unlikely that HIV could be transmitted by heterosexual intercourse, giving detailed explanations as to why the pattern in Africa and the Caribbean was somehow "different" from the United States. The AIDS epidemic was considered rather simplistically to be a problem of the gay community and of people who

means more than you probably realize.
- Don't lie to your friend about how he or she looks or how he or she is doing. You don't have to blurt out everything you're thinking— there is a place for tactful gentleness in all human relations. If you try, you can probably find something optimistic to focus on, even if the optimism has to be put in terms of hope for the future: "I bet things will be better by the weekend."
- Don't give your friend lectures if he or she isn't dealing with the illness in the way you think is best. You don't know what medical, legal, or other advice he or she has been given, and you can't know exactly what his or her feelings are.
- Realize that from time to time, your friend or relative may get angry with you even though you've tried to be helpful. When this happens, don't take it personally. Anger may be a way of venting feelings of inadequacy and help-lessness when dealing with illness. In a way, it's a compliment that your friend knows you care for him or her enough to get angry with you, knowing deep inside that such feelings won't be misunderstood.
- Try to be in touch with significant others in your friend's or relative's life. They can help you stay informed about progress (or compli-cations) on the medical front, which allows you to offer help when needed—help your friend may be embarrassed to ask for. For example, your friend's spouse or lover may need a break from nursing duties. You can offer to spell him or her for a Saturday after-noon, so he or she can get out and attend to his or her own needs for a while.
- Do not confuse acceptance of AIDS with res-ignation from living. Accepting the reality of this disease may free your friend or relative from a sense of turmoil and uncertainty. Ac-ceptance can also provide your friend with a sense of his or her own power.
- If you have been particularly close to your friend or relative, recognize your own needs for support or counseling. Many AIDS organi-zations have support groups you can join for just this purpose.

abused drugs. Even more recently, there have been many observers who contend that the epidemic is mainly a problem for minority communities—inner-city populations that are heavily black and Hispanic. This "ghettoization" of the problem also reflects a signal misunderstanding: HIV doesn't recognize skin color or social class when it invades a host.

Patterns and Trends of HIV Infection

Counting cases of AIDS only tells us what hap-pened seven to ten years ago, because that is the average length of time from initial infection with HIV to the point where AIDS is diagnosed. Thus, to identify current trends in the epidemic, it is useful to examine information about the prevalence of

HIV infection in various segments of the broader population. Here is a rundown on what is known.

Homosexual and Bisexual Males
In San Francisco and New York City, HIV infection among gay and bisexual men hovers around the 50 percent mark. Although it had previously been thought that communitywide education in these cities had resulted in careful adherence to safer sex guidelines, and thus no new cases of HIV infection were occurring in these groups, several recent studies have shown that a modest number of new infections are occurring in these groups annually (Siegel et al., 1988; Ekstrand et al., 1989; *American Medical News*, June 29, 1990, p. 3). Elsewhere in the United States, prevalence rates among homosexual

and bisexual males are somewhat lower. For instance, in Milwaukee the figure recently stood at 24 percent, whereas in Albuquerque, New Mexico, it was 14 percent (MMWR 38: S-4, 1989). Similarly, a recent survey of homosexual men in 16 small cities across the country found that 9 percent were HIV positive (Kelly et al., 1992).

Intravenous Drug Users

Among IV drug users surveyed through treatment programs, hospitals, and drug treatment centers, HIV infection rates are considerably higher on the East Coast than on the West Coast. For instance, in New York City and northern New Jersey rates are in the 50 to 60 percent range (Hahn et al., 1989; El-Sadr et al., 1992), and in Washington, D.C., one study reported a seroprevalence rate of 28 percent, which is similar to the rate reported from Baltimore. In contrast, in Los Angeles only a 3 percent seroprevalence rate was found (MMWR 38: S-4, 1989, Table 6), and in Sacramento the seroprevalence rate in IV drug users participating in a drug treatment program was 2 percent (MMWR 38: 370, 1989).

Heterosexuals

There have been relatively few studies of HIV infection in the general heterosexual population. One of the first studies (done in 1987) tested 800 heterosexual men and women in four locations (New York, Los Angeles, Atlanta, and St. Louis) and found that 5 percent of the men and 7 percent of the women with at least six sex partners a year for the preceding five years were seropositive (Masters, Johnson, and Kolodny, 1988). (Having at least six sex partners a year would be considered by many to be an operational definition for promiscuity; we should also point out that only a small portion of the general heterosexual population would meet this criterion.) In contrast, none of the women and only 1 of 200 men in strictly monogamous relationships were seropositive.

A similar study of sexually active heterosexuals with no known risk factors for HIV infection was conducted by Margaret Fischl and her co-workers in Miami. Of 346 people they studied, 5 percent were seropositive, with the only potential risk factor identified being multiple sexual partners (Fischl et al., 1988a).

The appearance of HIV infection in middle-class heterosexuals, mainly as a result of sexual contact with IV drug users, is now being documented with increasing frequency (Glaser, Strange, and Rosati, 1989).

One interesting point to keep in mind is that in women, HIV infection appears to be linked increasingly to heterosexual transmission rather than to intravenous drug use (Ellerbock et al., 1991; MMWR 40: 357–363, 1991; St. Louis 1991; Mann, Tarantola, and Netter, 1992). For example, in New Jersey, the percentage of women who gave birth to HIV-infected babies whose only apparent risk factor was heterosexual intercourse rose from 14 percent in 1982 to 1985 to 43 percent in the time period from 1986 to 1988 (Weiss, 1989).

AIDS Surveillance

AIDS cases have been reported in all 50 states, but the geographic distribution of cases—which has shifted over time—varies considerably from one region to another. In 1992, the annual incidence of reported cases of AIDS ranged from a high of 116 cases per 100,000 persons in Washington, D.C., and 46 per 100,000 persons in New York to a low of 0.9 per 100,000 persons in Wyoming (Centers for Disease Control, 1993) (see Figure 20.7.). Whereas before 1983 63 percent of all AIDS cases in the United States were reported from New York, New Jersey, and Pennsylvania, this proportion gradually dropped to below 30 percent of cases in 1992. Another notable feature of the changing nature of the AIDS epidemic in the United States is that new cases of AIDS among heterosexuals are increasing at a faster rate than any other category. In fact, according to the Centers for Disease Control, AIDS cases attributed solely to heterosexual transmission went from 1.9 percent of the national total in 1985 to 9 percent in 1993 (Altman, 1994), and this number is probably an underestimate. In 1993, heterosexual HIV transmission accounted for 6056 AIDS cases reported among women in the United States and 3232 cases in men (Centers for Disease Control, 1994a).

The U.S. Centers for Disease Control has noted that the reported cases of AIDS are underestimates because of incompleteness of reporting, delays in reporting, and the fact that not all persons with AIDS have access to adequate medical or diagnostic care, so that "reported AIDS cases may represent fewer than 80% of all cases of recognized or unrecognized severe morbidity associated with HIV infection"

Figure 20.7   AIDS Cases per 100,000 Population, United States, 1993

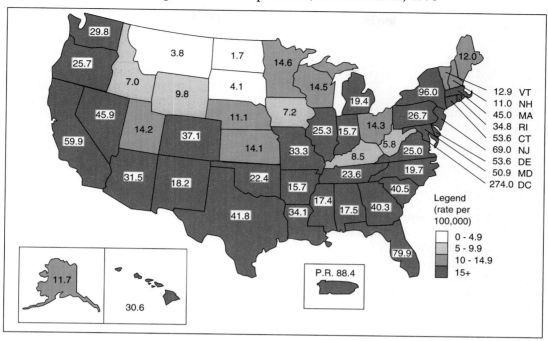

12.9 VT
11.0 NH
45.0 MA
34.8 RI
53.6 CT
69.0 NJ
53.6 DE
50.9 MD
274.0 DC

Legend
(rate per
100,000)

☐ 0 - 4.9
☐ 5 - 9.9
☐ 10 - 14.9
☐ 15+

P.R. 88.4

Source: MMWR *42 (53): 17, 1993*.

Figure 20.8   Number of AIDS cases attributed to heterosexual HIV
transmission and percentage of total AIDS—United
States, 1981-1993

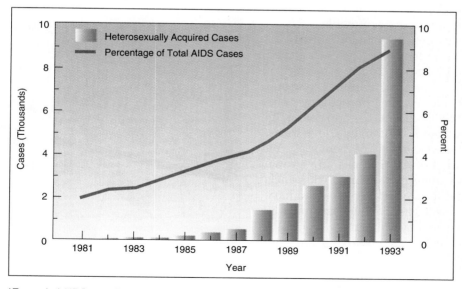

*Expanded AIDS surveillance case definition implemented.

Source: MMWR *43 (9): 156, 1994*.

(MMWR 38: S-4, 1989, p. 4). The shift in the trend of mode of transmission of AIDS cases in the United States is depicted dramatically in Figure 20.8.

PERSONAL ASPECTS OF THE HIV EPIDEMIC

The HIV/AIDS epidemic has many faces. Thus far in this chapter, we have primarily examined its biologic side. But the epidemic also has intensely personal aspects.

Social and Emotional Reactions

The impact of the HIV epidemic on our society has already been divisive and emotional. For many, the epidemic is a ready-made excuse for intensified prejudice against homosexuals, particularly among the misinformed, who think that shaking hands with a gay person or being served by a homosexual waiter could transmit a fatal infection. Some people have even suggested that everyone infected with HIV should be quarantined—a concept that is not only inhumane but also economically unfeasible since it would involve the enforced isolation for a period of many years of an estimated 1.5 million Americans now infected with HIV. Others are complacent about this major public health crisis because they mistakenly see AIDS as a problem confined to homosexuals, bisexuals, and drug users rather than a problem for American society as a whole.

Fortunately, our awareness of and sensitivity toward the HIV/AIDS epidemic has been heightened considerably in the past few years by a number of small steps that have succeeded in humanizing and demystifying the epidemic. One particularly noteworthy step in this direction was the creation of the AIDS Quilt Project, begun in 1987 by Cleve Jones. This project was started as a way of memorializing a friend who had died of AIDS. It has now grown to a giant quilt containing more than 11,000 panels sewn by friends and families of persons who have died. The Quilt Project has travelled around the country and been viewed by millions.

Other signs of increased awareness of the HIV/AIDS epidemic crop up in diverse places. In many cities, obituaries now routinely mention AIDS as a cause of death, in contrast to the situation just five or six years ago, when the topic seemed taboo. Fund-raisers for AIDS research, hosted by well-known entertainers such as Eliza-

beth Taylor and Madonna, are frequent and successful. Even television soap operas have woven AIDS-related story lines into their scripts, although the same national television networks still refuse to air condom advertisements because of worries about the sensitivities of their viewers (and concerns about boycotts by right-wing groups).

In the gay community, which was clearly most directly affected in the first decade of the HIV epidemic, the initial fear and dismay quickly gave way to highly organized educational efforts combined with compassionate caring for people with AIDS and active lobbying for more government funding, antidiscrimination legislation, and streamlined guidelines for approving new treatment methods. Recognition of the realities of sexual transmission of HIV has generally led to widespread changes in the sexual behavior of this group: most gay men now avoid the bathhouse scene entirely and a large number have cut back to having sex with only a small number of partners who are well known to them (Martin, 1987; Winkelstein et al., 1987; Turner, Miller, and Moses, 1989).

The AIDS Quilt Project has been a stark memorial to the personal dimensions of the HIV epidemic.

In addition, a large majority of gay men have adopted safer sex practices, either by avoiding anal sex entirely or by carefully using condoms for anal intercourse (Becker and Joseph, 1988; Turner, Miller, and Moses, 1989; Catania et al., 1991). As a result of these patterns, particularly the cutback in number of sexual partners, the incidence of other STDs such as gonorrhea and syphilis in gay men has also declined noticeably.

There are also some homosexual males who are so overwhelmed by fear of AIDS that they decide to be completely abstinent sexually until a vaccine or cure is found. In an occasional variation on this theme, a small number of male homosexuals and bisexuals have switched to heterosexual partners, at least temporarily. And, for reasons that are more than understandable, it is not unusual to find homosexual men who have developed such a degree of AIDS anxiety that they have become preoccupied with every minor physical ailment they experience. To these gay men, a sore throat, a skin rash, or a fever is a sign of impending doom, and they may even mistakenly tell their partners that they have AIDS before it is diagnosed. Among the very fearful it is common to see a sharp drop in sexual interest and sexual activity.

Anyone who discovers that one of his or her previous sex partners has AIDS or tests positive for HIV infection has definite reason for concern. So far in the epidemic, this situation has primarily affected gays and IV drug users, but heterosexuals are increasingly going to have to confront the same possibility as the HIV epidemic spreads into the broad population. Just how does it feel to be in such a situation?

A 28-year-old heterosexual man: I heard from a friend that a girl I used to date had come down with AIDS. At first I thought it was just a crazy story, something to try to scare me with, but when I checked it out I was horrified to discover it was true. God, I thought, we had sex together a couple of dozen times, and we never used a condom because she was on the pill. My doctor sent me for a blood test, which much to my relief came back okay, but in the 24 hours before I got that report I can only say that I had visions of a slow, agonizing death right before my eyes, and I was plenty worried. You can be sure that I'll remember this episode for a long time.

A 33-year-old divorced woman: I had been divorced for about three years when I found out my "ex"

was in the hospital with AIDS. I knew he had messed around with drugs from time to time, but I never thought of him as addicted or anything like that. So this news shook me up pretty badly. When I was tested myself and the doctor told me I was positive, I broke down on the spot and cried. I have two kids, and I'm not ready to die. So far I've been lucky. My T cell count is pretty good and I haven't had any major problems, just some minor infections and stuff. But I am still furious that he did this to me, even though I know he didn't mean to. *(Authors' files)*

For some heterosexuals, concern about AIDS is mounting as people become aware that AIDS is not just a homosexual disease. For instance, it is not unusual now for a person to ask a potential partner to have a blood test for anti-HIV antibody before beginning sexual relations. As one college-age woman told us, "It's not that I'm totally nervous about AIDS, but considering the stakes are so high, what's the purpose in pretending that everyone you'll meet will be honest? If someone doesn't care enough about me to have the test, the relationship isn't going to go anywhere anyway." But as we discuss shortly, many heterosexuals continue to demonstrate complacency about their personal risks of encountering HIV or becoming infected with it.

Immediately after learning that they are infected with HIV or that they have AIDS, most people react with shock, anger, and denial. Here is how it is described by a counselor at one HIV testing center in New York (James, 1990, p. 280):

Typical responses have included crying hysterically, going blank and numb, ranting and shouting—"I'm going to die now!"—and questioning—"Did the test tell how long I have to live?" Some clients try to bolt out of the office. . . . Some clients report that they were prepared for this and have a plan of action/treatment. Most clients, however, are "freaked out."

These are perfectly normal defense mechanisms that can initially cushion the blow of receiving such a diagnosis. In the weeks or months after the diagnosis, this initial reaction typically undergoes a transition into guilt, sadness, and resignation to one's fate—a sort of unhappy acceptance of the situation. Of course, different people react in very different ways.

People who are diagnosed as being HIV infected or having AIDS are usually young adults who have generally been healthy, so they have relatively little

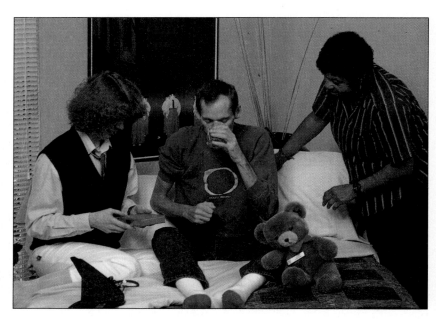

Remembering to take numerous medications at different times of day is just one of the many logistical problems facing HIV-infected people.

preparation for facing a life-threatening disease with a very bleak prognosis. As if this were not difficult enough, those who are infected, whether gay or straight, must also face a hostile and fearful society. Many are ostracized at work, rejected by their family and friends, and put in a situation of social isolation (Bartlett and Finkbeiner, 1991; Hunter and Rubenstein, 1992). It is emotionally difficult to find that your landlord wants to evict you, that your dentist refuses to take care of you any longer, or that your employer wants to fire you—all of which are uncalled-for discriminatory actions. Fortunately, federal legislation that prohibits discrimination against the disabled has been extended to apply to AIDS victims and people infected with HIV, but such legislation doesn't change people's attitudes quickly.

The scope of the emotional anguish people with AIDS must face is often even broader than the discriminatory problems just listed. Consider, for instance, the situation of a woman who knows she's dying from AIDS and has just discovered that her 6-month-old baby is also infected with HIV. Who will care for her baby after her death? How can she resolve the guilt she probably feels over transmitting this infection to her child? And who will care for her 4-year-old child who *isn't* HIV-infected? As another example, what about the personal turmoil in the life of a woman infected from a blood transfusion who has unwittingly transmitted her HIV infection to her husband?

Another problem you might expect is that people infected with HIV also are apt to have sexual difficulties. In a study of 120 gay men who were infected with HIV, Heino Meyer-Bahlburg and co-workers (1989) found that two-fifths of their sample reported decreased sexual satisfaction, two-fifths had some degree of difficulty with erectile failure, and more than half had some degree of negative feelings during sex.

In addition to the emotional anguish caused by dealing with all of these issues, AIDS victims must face the prospect of numerous medical complications and hospitalizations, deal with concerns about the economic cost of their illness, and come to terms with their own identity and emotions as part of the ultimate task of preparing for death.

Behavioral Aspects

Although it is clear that in the absence of an effective vaccine or cure massive changes will be required in patterns of sexual and drug-related behavior in order to stem the tide of the HIV epidemic, there is little evidence that such changes are occurring in the general population.

The gay community has been a major exception. It has been notably successful in implementing risk-reducing behavior since the exact nature of the AIDS epidemic became clear. While widespread changes have occurred, these changes have been "expectably incomplete" (Becker and Joseph, 1988), and concerns are now mounting that a "second wave" of HIV infections in younger gay men may be occurring (Linn et al., 1989; Ekstrand and Coates, 1990; Kelly et al., 1991; Stone, 1992; Navarro, 1993). Part of the reason for this is that widespread use of drugs and alcohol by young gay men may be altering their judgment and their planning for using safer sex practices. Another reason is that some people tire of following safer sex guidelines and relapse to risky behavior patterns (Miller, Turner, and Moses, 1990; Navarro, 1993).

For example, in a longitudinal study done in San Francisco, it was noted that between 1985 and 1986 the average number of sex partners decreased by 20 percent for those men not in a monogamous relationship, but 37 percent of the men continued to engage in sexual activities that were "probably risky" (such as ingesting semen during oral–genital sex) and 38 percent still engaged in high-risk activities such as anal sex without a condom (Stall et al., 1986). Through the end of 1987, while almost a third of the subjects changed to and maintained low-risk behaviors, 16 percent relapsed to risky sex after an initial short-term behavior change (Ekstrand et al., 1989). A similar longitudinal study done in New York showed that 48 percent of the gay men studied continued to engage in risky sex, including sex with multiple anonymous partners, and that for every two men who shifted to safer sex practices over time, one slipped back from safer sex to riskier sex (Siegel et al., 1988). Continued high rates of risky sexual behavior have been noted especially among gay men in small U.S. cities, outside the original epicenters of the HIV epidemic. For example, 40 percent of one sample of such men reported more than one male sex partner in the previous two months, and nearly one-third reported engaging in unprotected anal intercourse (Kelly et al., 1992).

A number of other studies also show, collectively, that positive behavioral changes have occurred among gay and bisexual males, but that these risk-reducing changes are far from complete (Martin, 1987; Doll et al., 1989). One review of 24 separate studies of changes in sexual behavior by gay men in response to AIDS found that, overall, approximately 20 percent had not altered their unsafe sex practices and that a portion of this resistance to change was probably due to frequent use of recreational drugs (Stempel and Moss, 1988). For example, substantial numbers of gay men continue to engage in anal sex with multiple partners—even though these men

know that they are infected with HIV (van Griesven et al., 1989). About half of these men either do not use condoms at all or use them very erratically (Masters, Johnson, and Kolodny, 1988; van Griesven, 1989; Kelly et al., 1989, Linn et al., 1989).

Among heterosexuals there seems to be considerably less concern for safe sex in terms of changed behavior, although the matter has not been investigated extensively. For example, in San Francisco among patrons of bars, single heterosexual women were less likely to engage in safe sex practices than single homosexual men were (McKusick and Hoff, 1989). In another study, it was found that only 6 of 200 heterosexual women who had at least six sex partners a year routinely asked their partners to use condoms during vaginal intercourse (Masters, Johnson, and Kolodny, 1988). Likewise, a survey of Canadian college students reported that among those with more than ten sex partners, only 21 percent of the men and 7.5 percent of the women used condoms regularly (MacDonald et al., 1990). And a recent study of women in the military found that a growing number are becoming infected with HIV "through unprotected sex with bisexual or IV [intravenous] drug-using men" even though most of them reported having only one or two sexual partners (Staver, 1990).

That lifetime monogamy is no longer the norm can be seen in data from a large national survey of U.S. women, that found that two-thirds of all women aged 15 to 44 who had ever had intercourse have had more than one partner, and 41 percent

"REMEMBER WHEN 'SAFE SEX' MEANT HER HUSBAND WAS OUT OF TOWN?"

have had four or more nonmarital partners (Kost and Forrest, 1992). A similar survey found that 23 percent of U.S. men aged 20 to 39 have had intercourse with 20 or more women in their lives (Billy et al., 1993).

Although condom sales jumped dramatically in the late 1980s as a result of the public's awareness of AIDS, regular condom use has not become very common among heterosexuals, nor have heterosexuals in general shifted to strictly monogamous sex. A survey of the general heterosexual population in the United States found that only 17 percent of people with multiple sex partners and 12.6 percent of those with risky sex partners (e.g., IV drug users, bisexual men) used condoms all the time (Catania, 1992). As a result of this complacency, rates of other STDs such as syphilis, chancroid, and hepatitis B in the United States jumped substantially in the past five years, with the rise attributable entirely to more cases in the heterosexual population. In fact, even among persons attending STD clinics, condom use is sporadic at best (MMWR 39: 685–689, 1990). And only a minority of sexually active adolescents uses condoms at all (Goodwin, 1990).

Other signs of a general lack of concern in most heterosexuals about the HIV epidemic are apparent, although no one has thoroughly studied them as yet. For instance, in most urban areas prostitution continues to thrive, despite considerable publicity about the possible transmission of HIV. (Since a majority of prostitutes are also IV drug users, there is an obvious danger of HIV infection with such sexual activity.) Furthermore, most male customers of prostitutes prefer not to use condoms; although few data are available on this point, one recent study showed that about half of the men who patronized prostitutes never used condoms, and many others used condoms erratically (Wallace, Mann, and Beatrice, 1988).

Condom use is also very low in black and Hispanic groups who are at heightened risk of exposure to HIV infection because of widespread drug use in their communities (Altman, 1989b; Miller, Turner, and Moses, 1990; MMWR 39: 685–689, 1990; Catania et al., 1992; Anderson and Dahlberg, 1992). In addition to this cultural bias, there is another relatively recent development contributing to the spread of HIV: the use of cocaine in a particularly powerful form known as "crack." The use of crack cocaine, which is highly addictive, is often done in "binges" of almost continual use over several days.

In order to support their drug habit, many female crack addicts resort to prostitution (often with as many as ten or more clients per day); since many of their clients have a history of IV drug abuse, and thus have a heightened likelihood of HIV infection, many observers believe this has become an important factor in the heterosexual transmission of HIV (Goldsmith, 1988; Kolata, 1989; Weiss, 1989; Miller, Turner, and Moses, 1990).

Even in more "traditional" settings, there are many indications that inadvertent HIV transmission is not unusual in the heterosexual world at large. Walk through a singles bar on a weekend evening, or browse through the classified personal ads in many newspapers and magazines, and you will quickly realize that heterosexuals have hardly given up on the sexual revolution. Despite lip service to the notion of safe sex, many heterosexuals continue to behave sexually much as they did in the days before AIDS, which is certainly understandable since many have been led to believe that AIDS is "just" a gay disease.

The following comments from interviews with single heterosexuals reflect this overall sense of complacency:

> *A 26-year-old woman:* I don't want to sound like a fool, but I don't know anyone with AIDS, and I doubt that the guys I would date are shooting up drugs or anything like that. Maybe if I lived in New York or San Francisco I'd be more worried, but I don't want to live my life in fear.

> *A 29-year-old man:* I think the papers made too big a thing out of the whole AIDS business. Last year I heard a government report that said the epidemic was leveling off. And even though I've had sex with five or six partners every year, I've never had a problem. *(Authors' files)*

The same lack of concern is all too apparent on college campuses today, where despite well-intended attempts at preventive AIDS education, sexual behavior patterns are not much different from those of a decade ago. Several surveys of college students bear this out, showing that relatively few students are worried about personal exposure to HIV or are consistently using safer sex practices (Baldwin and Baldwin, 1988; DeBuono et al., 1990; MacDonald et al., 1990). One of these studies, done in Southern California with a sample of 851 students, found that 66 percent had not used condoms at all in the preceding three months despite being sexually active. In addition, students with four or more sex partners annually used condoms no more than students with fewer partners per year did (Baldwin and Baldwin, 1988). Similarly, a survey of 350 students at a large East Coast university showed that most felt they had little or no risk of exposure to HIV, and also felt that they could somehow intuitively sense when a prospective sexual partner wasn't "safe." Many said that they did not use condoms at all, and "In general, students equated 'safer sex' with 'not-for-fun' sex" (Caron and McMullen, 1987).

The situation on college campuses is not unusual; in many ways, it mirrors the broader picture fairly accurately. As yet, we have not succeeded very well in implementing widespread behavioral change to fight the HIV epidemic because the American public has received mixed messages, watered-down messages, and often no messages at all about what needs to be done to turn the tide. Politicians and religious leaders have blocked many efforts at using public funds to develop educational materials about AIDS because of concerns that the materials would be too sexually explicit; school-based AIDS education programs have frequently foundered because of arguments over the "moral" way to teach about AIDS and HIV (for instance, some people claim it is permissible only to teach that abstinence is the sole way to avoid AIDS); on some college campuses, condom dispensers have been removed to avoid offending certain alumni groups. Until more effective HIV/AIDS education messages are sent to the public, this epidemic will probably continue to grow at a frightening rate.

PUBLIC POLICY ISSUES

The history of the early years of the HIV epidemic, thoroughly chronicled in Randy Shilts's book *And the Band Played On* (1987), is in many ways a story of tragic dimensions. Lives were wasted and precious time was lost in combating a deadly disease because of homophobia, complacency, and the federal government's relative inaction. As recently as 1990, Larry Kramer, founder of Gay Men's Health Crisis, has said, "I am so frightened that the war against AIDS has already been lost. It is beyond comprehension why, in a presumably civilized country, in the modern era, such a continuing, extraordinary destruction of life is being attended to

so tentatively, so meekly and in such a cowardly fashion" (Kramer, 1990, p. A15).

Today there is still considerable complacency about the epidemic. Homophobia continues to play a major role in how people view questions about HIV infection and AIDS. There is another side to our ineffectiveness in dealing with the epidemic, however. For years, more emphasis was put on protecting individual rights to privacy than protecting public health. Furthermore, much-needed research on sexual behavior and other aspects of the HIV epidemic has been stalled or killed for strictly political reasons. Implementation of several federally funded national sex research surveys—studies that many believe are essential to a successful fight against the further spread of HIV—was blocked because a handful of politicians objected to asking explicit questions about private sexual behavior (*USA Today* March 31, 1989; Marshall, 1991; Moffat, 1991).

Given this hodgepodge situation with different groups arguing for and against certain policy choices for their own self-interested reasons, it can be difficult to sort out the issues. The following discussion of a number of pivotal policy issues draws on the recommendations of the National Research Council, the Institute of Medicine of the National Academy of Sciences, the Presidential Commission on the HIV Epidemic, and the National Commission on AIDS, as well as other authoritative sources, to present consensus opinions emerging at the beginning of the 1990s on how to proceed in our efforts to control the HIV/AIDS epidemic.

Education and Research

Since it is clear that science, by itself, cannot stop the spread of this epidemic (even if a vaccine were discovered tommorrow, it would take years of testing before it would receive approval and become widely available), it is important that every effort be made to implement widespread behavioral changes in our society to control the spread of HIV. To be effective, this type of education must go beyond simply informing people about facts—it must also motivate them to modify their behavior.

We have previously recommended the following steps for development of broad educational programs in this country:

1. A comprehensive AIDS curriculum must be developed for widespread use in public

schools. In order to be effective, such a program must begin well before young people begin to engage in sexual activity and drug use, which means such programs must begin no later than fourth or fifth grade.

2. Special education programs must be targeted at specific groups whose behaviors or situations place them at high risk of being exposed to HIV. These include intravenous drug abusers and their sex partners, homosexual and bisexual men, prostitutes and their customers, and heterosexuals who have multiple sex partners. Furthermore, special programs must be developed for groups that may have unique requirements in program design, including minority populations, the blind and the deaf, and people who cannot read.

3. A broad-based, multimedia general education campaign that encourages responsible behavior should be undertaken as soon as possible. This campaign should encompass the television and movie community (where scriptwriters can incorporate warnings about HIV into their prime-time shows or movies), celebrities from the world of rock, sports stars, and other "high visibility" spokespersons who have particular credibility with adolescents and young adults.

4. All colleges and universities should provide their students with extensive educational and counseling services related to prevention of HIV infection.

5. To coordinate and implement the entire educational effort, a special office should be created in the U.S. Department of Health and Human Services and it should be given enough budgetary support and administrative power to accomplish its mission.

In addition, it is imperative that the progress that has been made in the last decade in fighting the HIV epidemic be built upon and expanded by promptly and intensively increasing behavioral and biomedical research.

Testing

Earlier in the course of the HIV epidemic, there

was considerable resistance to the idea of widespread testing for the presence of infection because of concerns about the accuracy of the blood tests that were available, concerns about privacy and confidentiality, and a sense of futility: what good did it do to know that you're infected with the AIDS virus if there was no treatment available to prolong your life? Today, there is a vastly different perspective on this issue: most experts agree that virtually anyone at risk should undergo confidential testing on a voluntary basis (Lo et al., 1989; Francis et al., 1989; Cohen, Sande and Volberding, 1990; Francis, 1992; Quinn, 1992; Janssen, 1992).

The reasons for this change are relatively straightforward. First, the accuracy of tests for HIV infection have improved significantly. Second, worries about lack of confidentiality of test results have been lessened considerably as many states have passed legislation specifically addressing this issue and as many states provide anonymous testing sites. Most important, however, early detection of HIV infection is the only way to ensure early medical treatment, and it is clear that early medical treatment can prolong life and prevent (or at least postpone) some of the serious complications of AIDS.

Widespread voluntary testing also leads to many personal benefits. For example, in many cases, people who have been tested will discover that they are *not* infected, which will not only be psychologically reassuring, but may also help them make important personal decisions about marriage, pregnancy, or other issues. On the other hand, people who discover that they are infected can: (1) protect their sexual partners from infection, (2) make arrangements for appropriate medical care, (3) avoid situations where they would have additional exposures to HIV; (4) make informed plans concerning careers, insurance, finances, and other related matters.

There are certainly some personal drawbacks to widespread testing. For one thing, positive test results may cause profound anxiety or depression. A second problem is the small chance of having a false positive result, which could certainly have a serious impact on a person's life. Another difficulty is that unless your test results are absolutely confidential (not all tests done in hospitals or doctors' offices are, especially if you sign a form authorizing the release of your medical records to an insurance company), you may find that you encounter problems. For example, military applicants who turn out to be HIV positive are denied jobs in the military. And someone who tests positive may have difficulty obtaining certain types of insurance coverage in the future.

Widespread voluntary testing also benefits the general public as well as individuals. For example, public health authorities would gain a better picture of trends in the HIV epidemic and would be better able to address broad policy issues such as educational campaigns and other prevention programs targeted at special population groups. Furthermore, this sort of information is essential to the economic planning that will be needed to deal with the epidemic in the future, as well as the planning for the delivery of health-care services.

While mandatory testing of blood, organ, and tissue donors and the military population is currently in place in the United States, attempts at mandatory premarital testing for HIV proved ineffective in Illinois and Louisiana and have now been discontinued. Routine (but not mandatory) prenatal HIV screening has been advocated by some experts but has not yet been implemented in most locales (Minkoff et al., 1988; Angell, 1991; Gwinn et al., 1991; Brandeau, 1992).

Public Health Measures

Contact tracing and notification—tracking down the sex partners of people with a reportable STD and informing them that they may have been exposed, without revealing the identity of the "index case"—has been one of the most time-tested public health strategies (Gostin, 1989; Giesecke et al., 1991; Unsigned Editorial, 1991). In fact, public health statutes usually authorize contact tracing for STDs, but in an odd quirk, most states today do not classify HIV infection as an STD. (The reason for this is that these states wish to avoid the automatic contact tracing programs that would be triggered by existing laws if HIV infection was classified as an STD.) Nevertheless, a number of states (such as Colorado and South Carolina) and cities have implemented contact tracing and notification programs, with generally good results (Jones et al., 1990; Ramstedt et al., 1990; Wycoff et al., 1991; Landis et al., 1992). A few other states, such as California, have a voluntary contact tracing program.

By focusing on people with a high probability of exposure to HIV, contact tracing is efficient in detecting those with previously unidentified infection.

This detection has important implications for prevention in two ways: (1) uninfected sex partners of an already infected person are warned that they've been exposed, which may lead them to behavioral changes that would reduce their risk of subsequent infection, and (2) identifying persons with a previously undetected HIV infection should allow them to take steps to protect their own sex partners, minimizing the risk of spreading HIV further.

There has been some controversy about the physician's role in contact tracing and partner notification. Concerns about protecting the confidentiality of HIV-infected persons have created conflicting opinions on this issue, but in many states, including New York and California, while protecting patient confidentiality is a legal obligation, there is also a responsibility to warn anyone who is in clear and imminent danger of becoming infected. This means that if an HIV-infected man refuses to inform his sex partners of his infection, a physician is authorized to disclose this information to the partners in order to protect their health and well-being.

Although public health laws in all jurisdictions in this country carry provisions for quarantine of persons with communicable diseases, and a few states have laws authorizing the compulsory isolation of persons with AIDS or HIV infection who are aware of this but continue to engage in high-risk behaviors, there is virtual unanimity among public health authorities that quarantine is unnecessary—and inhumane—in the HIV epidemic.

Another possible public health measure that has stirred considerable controversy is the use of sterile-needle and syringe-exchange programs as a means of reducing the spread of HIV among intravenous drug abusers. While such programs have been operating successfully in Europe for years, in the United States they have been primarily restricted to small-scale pilot projects in a few cities such as New York, Seattle, and Portland, Oregon. The main obstacle in America is concern that providing sterile needles and syringes to drug abusers is condoning an illegal act and might lead to more widespread drug abuse. The available evidence suggests that this isn't happening in Europe, but needle exchange programs don't eliminate HIV risk behavior, either (Miller, Turner, and Moses, 1990).

Antidiscrimination Issues

Because AIDS first appeared in this country in groups that were already stigmatized—homosexuals and IV drug abusers—society's response has been strongly shaped by bias, assignments of blame, and a disregard for the needs of those most directly affected by the epidemic. In addition, fears about casual transmission of HIV that were widespread in the early days of the epidemic (fears that have now been effectively proven to be unfounded) fueled many examples of discriminatory responses to people with AIDS or HIV infection.

For instance, office workers sometimes shunned a colleague with AIDS because of worries that they might become infected by indirect physical contact with him. Landlords tried to evict tenants with AIDS on the grounds that they had an easily communicable disease that might affect other building occupants. In some particularly sad cases, infected children have been banned from attending school on the grounds that they posed a health hazard to their classmates.

Today we have made a good deal of progress in moving beyond these discriminatory practices, but fear of discrimination is still a major stumbling block to the acceptance of potentially effective public health strategies by gay rights groups and other AIDS activists. The federal Rehabilitation Act of 1973, Section 504, prohibits discrimination against "otherwise qualified" handicapped persons, and the courts have consistently found that HIV-related conditions are covered by this—but the coverage applies only to federally funded programs. To address this issue, legislative attempts to counter HIV-related discrimination have already been passed in many states. It will probably take a growing realization that HIV infects people from all walks of life (not just gay and bisexual men and IV drug abusers) to change attitudes toward the epidemic enough so that HIV-infected persons are regarded no differently than people with cancer, heart disease or high blood pressure.

Additional Considerations

Society must face a large number of challenging issues as part of addressing the HIV epidemic. What can be done about the problem of HIV infection in the homeless? Who will care for the HIV-infected babies whose parents have died of AIDS? How can we put an end to the patterns of drug abuse that contribute in major ways to the spread of HIV infection? How will we finance the health-care requirements of the hundreds of thousands of people who are already HIV-infected? Unfortunately, it is clear that the answers to these challenges are not always easy or affordable, so choices have to be made in terms of budgets and allocation of manpower and other resources in this epic fight. One set of such recommendations is described in the section that follows.

The President's AIDS Commission.

In 1987, President Reagan created a special commission to investigate the HIV epidemic and to make recommendations that could be used to protect the public health, assist in finding a cure for AIDS, and provide care for those already infected. (As a historical note, it should be pointed out that many observers felt that the commission should have been created years earlier; furthermore, there was initially considerable controversy over the makeup of the commission, with many groups dismayed that the gay community was not adequately represented and others worried that the commission was lacking in medical and scientific expertise.) At the end of a year of hearing expert testimony from some 600 witnesses, the commission issued a widely acclaimed final report. Among its key recommendations were the following:

- Early diagnosis of HIV infection is essential both for obtaining optimal medical care and counseling and for protecting others. This requires encouragement of extensive voluntary testing.

- "HIV infection is a disability and should be treated as such under federal and state law. . . . Infected persons should be encouraged to continue normal activities, such as work or school, and live in their own home as long as they are able" (Presidential Commission, 1988, p. xviii).

- Strong measures should be implemented for protecting the confidentiality of persons who are infected with HIV. At the same time, public health authorities should immediately begin a system of confidential partner notification so that all partners who have been exposed to an HIV-infected person can be counseled, tested, and followed up.

- States should begin to require the reporting of all HIV-positive tests, not just cases of AIDS, to track the course of the epidemic more accurately.

- Prevention and treatment of intravenous drug abuse should be made a top national priority. A new policy of "treatment on demand" should be implemented (at a cost to the government of about $1.5 billion annually), since the ability to control the course of the HIV epidemic depends to a large extent on being able to curtail IV drug abuse.

The commission also called for new federal and

state funding to reverse the national nursing shortage, emphasized the need for developing comprehensive drug and alcohol education programs and "age appropriate, comprehensive health education programs" from kindergarten through grade twelve, and suggested that there is a responsibility for all citizens to treat HIV-infected persons with respect and compassion.

A Concluding Note

The HIV epidemic can be stopped in its tracks if people take personal responsibility over their behavior by abstaining from IV drug use and consistently following safer sex guidelines.

Medical science today is technologically equipped to solve the puzzles of HIV infection—although how long it will take to accomplish this is not entirely clear.

But what is clear is this: within the next few years, every single person in the United States will know someone who is infected with HIV. How we will respond to this challenge, both as individuals and as a society, cannot be known as yet. But one thing is certain: We are all in this together. As the novelist James Carroll puts it:

> Now no one is immune. Those things that have always cut us off from one another—sexism, homophobia, racism, hatred of addicts—have the additional effect of making this disease more powerful. However understandable the common impulse to blame is, however "human" it is, the fact now is that we indulge it at our common peril.
>
> The climate in which prevention thrives is marked not by blaming, but by caring. It is marked by the frank and open exchange of real information, even information that we once regarded as inappropriate for exchange. It is marked by willingness to consider, in the name of prevention, ideas and strategies that at first may offend us. We have to work constantly, in other words, at changing those attitudes that feed the infection, at keeping open minds as well as open hearts. (Carroll, 1990, pp. 20–21).

SUMMARY

1. Acquired immune deficiency syndrome (AIDS) is an illness resulting from infection with HIV,

the human immunodeficiency virus. AIDS, which was first recognized as a clinical entity in 1981, is characterized by a breakdown of the body's immune defenses, ultimately leading to susceptibility to opportunistic infections and death.

2. Although the earliest cases of AIDS in the United States were detected primarily in homosexual and bisexual men and intravenous drug users, the pattern of the HIV/AIDS epidemic in America has undergone considerable change in recent years, with increasing numbers of people infected by heterosexual transmission and a rapidly rising rate of infections among women. Similarly, although the epidemic in its earliest stages was heavily concentrated in New York and California, it now has expanded to involve the entire country.

3. As of mid-1994, there had been a cumulative total of more than 400,000 cases of AIDS reported in the United States. This was only a small fraction of the 2.5 million estimated cases around the world, with Africa being the most heavily affected region, but with surging numbers in Latin America and Southeast Asia as well.

4. HIV, a retrovirus believed to have evolved from a virus that infects monkeys in Africa, selectively attacks helper T cells and macrophages once it gains entry to the body. When HIV invades these white blood cells, it turns them into factories for manufacturing its own genetic information, in effect duplicating itself many times over. HIV particles actively attack other cells in the immune system and other parts of the body, including the brain, causing considerable damage.

5. HIV is transmitted by three primary routes: sexual contact, blood-to-blood transmission (as with needle sharing among intravenous drug users or with contaminated blood transfusions), and perinatally, from an infected mother to her infant. Anal intercourse—whether homosexual or heterosexual—is the riskiest form of sexual contact, but vaginal intercourse and oral–genital sex are also capable of transmitting HIV. HIV is *not* transmitted by casual contact (such as a handshake) or by mosquitoes.

6. Completely safe sex is only possible under a few sets of circumstances, including abstinence, restricting sexual contact only to activi-

ties that do not involve the exchange of body fluids, or sex in a mutually monogamous relationship between two uninfected partners. However, proper and consistent use of latex condoms reduces the risk of HIV transmission during sex. Limiting the number of sex partners also materially reduces the risk of exposure.

7. HIV infection can be detected by a number of different blood tests. The most commonly used screening test, the ELISA test, is only acceptable if a positive result (indicating infection) is confirmed by another more sophisticated test. The Western blot test is usually used for this purpose. Using the two tests in combination, false positives are now very unusual—according to some studies, less than 1 in 100,000.

8. HIV infection proceeds through several distinct stages. The *initial infection* is often completely unrecognized, although 10 to 25 percent of people who are infected have a brief febrile illness several weeks after the infection occurs. Initial infection is typically followed by an *asymptomatic carrier state* in which the person feels healthy but is a carrier of live HIV and is capable of infecting others. This asymptomatic period commonly lasts seven to ten years or longer. The next stage of illness is *symptomatic HIV infection*, in which destruction of the immune system begins to manifest by annoying but non-life-threatening infections such as shingles (herpes zoster) or thrush (monilia). Weight loss, swollen lymph nodes, and fatigue are other common symptoms. The last stage of HIV infection is full-blown *AIDS*, which may be accompanied by Kaposi's sarcoma (a form of skin cancer), *Pneumocystis carinii* pneumonia (a previously rare, often-fatal lung infection), and a variety of neurological disorders and other opportunistic infections.

9. While HIV infection and AIDS are not curable, they are treatable. AZT (also known as zidovudine) prolongs life for AIDS patients and slows the progression to AIDS for those infected with HIV, although viral resistance to AZT has become a common problem, and the drug is not effective for as long as scientists had once hoped it would be. Other drugs are effective in treating the opportunistic infections that occur commonly in AIDS, and currently a number of drugs are being studied as a means of combatting HIV infection. Dozens of vaccines that may be useful in treatment as well as prevention are currently being avidly pursued, although it is unlikely that a safe and effective vaccine will be available in the near future.

10. Counting cases of AIDS doesn't say a great deal about the dynamics of HIV infection today because of the long time lag from initial infection to developing full-blown AIDS. Thus, the focus has shifted to tracking patterns of HIV infection. While infection rates are around 50 percent in homosexual and bisexual men in large cities in New York, New Jersey, and California, elsewhere in the country they are generally in the range of 20 to 25 percent. Among intravenous drug users, infection rates also vary according to geography, with cities in the Northeast having rates in the 40 to 50 percent range, but rates of less than 10 percent in most of the rest of the country. In the second decade of the HIV epidemic, there has been a particularly rapid increase of infections involving women and adolescents. Worldwide, there were an estimated 12 to 14 million cases of HIV infection in 1993.

11. Although social reactions to the HIV/AIDS epidemic have been distorted by a combination of homophobia and complacency, along with unwarranted fear about the possibility of casual contagiousness, there are signs that such prejudices (and the discrimination they cause) are lessening and awareness is improving. Nevertheless, there are still countless instances of economic and social discrimination against HIV-infected persons.

12. The gay community has been remarkably successful in its campaigns to promote risk-reducing behavior and safer sex practices, resulting in a marked decline in the rate of new HIV infections in many areas. However, the response is far from perfect, as some gay and bisexual men ignore the risks as a result of drug or alcohol use and as others simply tire of being careful. Among heterosexuals, there is much less concern about the risk of contracting HIV. This is shown particularly by infrequent (or inconsistent) patterns of condom use, little (if any) reduction in number of sex partners, and participation in risky sexual acts. The link between crack cocaine and heterosexual transmission of

HIV has also been recognized.

13. There are serious gaps in our nation's current approach to public policy issues related to this epidemic which are, at least in part, a result of studied neglect by the White House through the first dozen years of the HIV/AIDS era. For one thing, there is no national leadership for comprehensive HIV/AIDS educational efforts. For another, in spite of the availability of effective treatments for people with early, asymptomatic HIV infection, we have not succeeded in getting across the message that anyone at risk for this infection should voluntarily undergo testing. Lingering concerns about the frequency of false positive test results (which are now very uncommon) and about possible breaches of confidentiality seem to be part of the problem. In addition, standard practices used in combatting STDs have not been brought into play in most locales in the HIV/AIDS epidemic because of political pressures, although measures such as contact tracing and notification appear to be efficient and effective.

Thought Questions

1. In many states, all newborn babies are tested anonymously for HIV infection in order to track the dimensions of the HIV epidemic. When an infected baby is found, it is an infallible indication that the mother is infected, too. However, most states take no action to notify the mother of her infection on the grounds that individual privacy rights supercede the need to be informed of the existence of this condition. Do you agree or disagree with this position? Could you suggest ways in which states could take action without violating the mother's rights?

2. Many cities and states have refused to initiate contact tracing and notification programs to locate, test, and counsel the sexual partners of persons found to be infected with HIV. Do you think this is a good policy? Why or why not? If someone you had sex with several years ago was found to be infected with HIV, would you want to be informed about it?

3. If you were a marriage counselor treating a couple and discovered that one of the partners was infected with HIV but refused to tell the other person despite the fact that they were having sex together, how would you proceed?

4. In some cases, people who have been infected with HIV from sexual contact have sued the person who gave them the infection if they have reason to believe this person knew that he or she was infected but didn't tell them. Do you think this type of legal action is right or wrong? What if the person who transmitted the infection didn't realize he or she was infected? Would this change your thinking at all?

5. The press often publishes stories in which famous people are identified as being infected with HIV. (Tennis star Arthur Ashe was forced to "announce" his infection publicly in 1992 after a newspaper threatened such disclosure; various rock stars and others have been in the same predicament.) The media contend that this is a legitimate function of a free press and that the public has a right to know such information, especially since it reminds them of the realities of the HIV/AIDS epidemic. But such disclosures violate the person's right to privacy and may pose problems for their families or careers, as well. How do you feel on this issue?

6. In some cities, including New York and Los Angeles, dozens of sex clubs (gay, bisexual, and straight) have sprung up in the 1990s where casual, anonymous sexual contacts occur. In the midst of a growing HIV/AIDS epidemic, do you believe such clubs pose a significant public health threat? What, if anything, do you think should be done about these clubs?

7. Many cities, both large and small, have begun condom distribution programs in high schools for teenagers as part of their effort to reduce the risk of unintended pregnancy and sexually transmitted diseases, including HIV. Now some sex educators and public health experts are calling for condom distribution to younger schoolchildren—in grades six, seven, and eight—for precisely the same reasons. How do you feel about this idea? Since research evidence makes it plain that many 12- to 14-year-olds are already sexually active, is condom distribution in public schools likely to increase this trend, or is it simply a way of making sex safer?

Suggested Readings

Bartlett, John G., and Finkbeiner, Ann K., *The Guide to Living with HIV Infection*. Baltimore: The Johns Hopkins University Press, 1991. An A to Z guide to the practicalities of dealing with HIV infection in all its stages, encompassing both physical and emotional aspects. Useful for people who are infected with HIV as well as their friends, relatives, and caregivers.

Bayer, Ronald. *Private Acts, Social Consequences.* New York: Free Press, 1989. A thoughtful analysis of the tensions between public health principles and individuals' rights in the context of the HIV epidemic.

Hunter, Nan D., and Rubenstein, William B., eds. *AIDS Agenda: Emerging Issues in Civil Rights.* New York: New Press, 1992. Compelling essays on legal and social policy aspects of the HIV epidemic, with special emphasis on discrimination and civil liberties.

Mann, Jonathan, Tarantola, Daniel J. M., and Netter, Thomas (eds.). *AIDS in the World.* Cambridge, MA: Harvard University Press, 1992. An excellent in-depth summary of global aspects of the HIV epidemic. Includes hundreds of graphs and charts, as well as projections of future trends.

Shilts, Randy. *And the Band Played On: Politics, People, and the AIDS Epidemic.* New York: St. Martin's Press, 1987. An impressive history of the early years of the AIDS epidemic that is told in vivid detail. This book is must reading for anyone wanting to understand the background of our country's early response to AIDS.

Sexual Dysfunctions and Sex Therapy

Like many other body processes, when sexual function goes along smoothly, it is usually taken for granted and given little thought. But if sexual function is a problem in one way or another, it can be a source of anxiety, anguish, and frustration that often leads to general unhappiness and distress in personal relationships.

This chapter begins with a description of sexual dysfunction—conditions in which the ordinary physical responses of sexual function are impaired. Our attention then turns to the causes of these dysfunctions. The concluding portion of the chapter discusses the methods and effectiveness of sex therapy in dealing with these problems.

MALE SEXUAL DYSFUNCTION

For most men in most societies, sexual adequacy is considered a yardstick for measuring personal adequacy. The man who does not "measure up" sexually is often embarrassed, confused, or depressed over his plight, which he regards as reflecting poorly on his manhood. The sexually dysfunctional male may change his behavior to avoid sexual situations (fearing in advance that he will fail); he may cope with his dilemma by inventing excuses (blaming the dysfunction on his partner, for example); or he may try to overcome his problem by diligently "working" at sex, which usually makes the situation worse instead of better.

Erectile Dysfunction (Impotence)

Erectile dysfunction, or **impotence,** is the inability to have or maintain an erection that is firm enough for coitus. Erectile dysfunction is classified as either primary or secondary: the male with **primary erectile dysfunction** has never been able to have intercourse, whereas the male with **secondary erectile dysfunction** has succeeded in having intercourse once, twice, or a thousand times before his dysfunction began. Secondary erectile dysfunction is about ten times more common than primary erectile dysfunction (Kolodny, Masters, and Johnson, 1979).

Erectile dysfunction can occur at any age and can assume many different forms. Total absence of erection is infrequent except in certain medical conditions. More typically, the male with erectile dysfunction has partial erections that are too weak for vaginal insertion (or anal intercourse). Sometimes firm erections quickly disappear if intercourse is attempted. In other instances, a man with erectile dysfunction may be able to have normal erections under some circumstances but not others. For example, some men with erectile dysfunction have no problem during masturbation but cannot get erections during sexual activity with a partner. Other men have solid erections during extramarital sex but only feeble erections with their spouses. The reverse of this pattern is also common: some men who have no sexual difficulty with their wives are unable to function during attempts at extramarital sex.

Isolated episodes of not having erections (or losing an erection at an inopportune time) are so common that they are nearly a universal occurrence among men. [For this reason, Masters and Johnson (1970) classified a man as secondarily impotent only if his erection problems occurred in at least 25 percent of his sexual encounters.] Such isolated episodes do *not* mean that a man has a sexual dysfunction; they may reflect a temporary form of physical stress (having the flu, being tired, having overindulged in food or drink) or may relate to other problems like tension, lack of privacy, or adjusting to a new sexual partner. If the man does not take such incidents in stride and becomes deeply upset by his "failure" to respond the "right" way physically, he may set the stage for difficulties in later sexual situations because he is worried about his ability (or inability) to perform.

One aspect of erectile dysfunction that is not widely recognized is that this problem sometimes

disappears spontaneously. In one survey, it was found that 30 percent of men with erectile problems not caused by physical conditions were functioning normally six months later without receiving any treatment (Segraves et al., 1985). While such spontaneous "cures" are most likely in males who have had erectile difficulties for relatively short periods of time—typically less than three years—we have also seen instances of an abrupt return to normal sexual functioning after ten years or more of erectile dysfunction. Although there is no simple explanation for why these instances occur, it often seems to be linked to reduction in stress levels in a man's life.

Fears of sexual performance—"Will I lose my erection?" "Will I satisfy my partner?"—are likely to dampen sexual arousal and cause loss of erection. The stronger and more insistent such fears become, the greater is the likelihood that they will become self-fulfilling prophecies, and the man will experience an actual inability to get and keep an erection. On a long-term basis, performance fears may lead to lowered interest in sex (avoidance), loss of self-esteem, and attempts to control the anxiety by working hard to overcome it (which usually reduces sexual spontaneity and causes sex to be even more of a "performance" instead of just being *fun*). In addition, fears of performance often cause one or both partners to become spectators during their sexual interaction, observing and evaluating their own or their partner's sexual response. By becoming a spectator, a person usually becomes less involved in the sexual activity because of the distraction of watching and evaluating what is going on.

The spectator role, which can affect men and women, is found not only in cases of erectile dysfunction. When a person slips into the spectator role because of performance fears, the reduced intimacy and spontaneity of the situation combined with preexisting fears usually stifle the capacity for physical response. This cycle tends to feed on itself: erectile failure leads to performance fears, which lead to the spectator role, which results in distraction and loss of erection, which heightens the fears of performance.

erectile dysfunction (impotence) the inability to have or maintain an erection firm enough for coitus. Can be classified as **primary** (always existing) or **secondary** (having functioned in the past).

Unless this cycle is broken, there is a strong possibility that sexual dysfunction will be firmly established.

Men react to erectile dysfunction in various ways, ranging from great dismay (probably the most typical response) to studied nonchalance (the least typical). While there are some men and women who see sex as more than a throbbing, erect penis and do not judge the satisfaction of a sexual encounter on the basis of having intercourse alone, for most people the practical limitations of erectile dysfunction are bothersome. One 34-year-old man relates his personal feelings in dealing with it:

> After a while, the problem becomes so predictable that you start to make excuses in advance. It's as though you lose any chance of having sexual pleasure because you become preoccupied with the notion of failure. And the failure hits you right in the gut—you don't feel like much of a man. *(Authors' files)*

The partner of a man with erectile dysfunction may blame herself for not being attractive enough to turn him on or not being skilled enough to arouse his passion, or she may fear that she is pressuring him and causing his difficulties. On the other hand, the partner may blame the man in various ways for his sexual problems. We have encountered women who accused their husbands of extramarital sex, being homosexual, or not being in love with them as explanations of erectile dysfunction. Sometimes the impact of erectile dysfunction can alter the fabric of a close relationship by introducing strain, doubt, irritability, and frustration, all of which have effects outside the bedroom.

Premature Ejaculation

Premature ejaculation, or rapid ejaculation, is a common sexual dysfunction but is difficult to define precisely. Older definitions that used a specific duration of intercourse as the dividing line ("less than two minutes," for example) or that specified a minimum number of penile thrusts before ejaculation have now been discarded. This is fortunate because some men actually tried to time themselves with a stopwatch to determine if they were normal, and others tried to hurry their thrusting ("just four more thrusts, dear") although this usually speeds up ejaculation instead of delaying it.

In *Human Sexual Inadequacy,* an attempt was made to define premature ejaculation in terms of the interaction between sexual partners, not just the male alone. (Prior to 1970, premature ejaculation had frequently been classified as a form of impotence, a belief that reflected a poor understanding of the underlying physiology.) A man was considered to ejaculate prematurely if his partner wasn't orgasmic in at least 50 percent of their coital episodes, but it was acknowledged that this definition was still lacking (Masters and Johnson, 1970). Specifically, it couldn't be applied to situations in which a woman was infrequently orgasmic or never had orgasms during intercourse, and it was an arbitrary way of estimating normality at best. Later, Helen Kaplan (1974) suggested that premature ejaculation occurred if the male didn't have voluntary control over when he ejaculated—although most sex therapists agree that total voluntary control over the timing of ejaculation is the exception rather than the rule.

The American Psychiatric Association has sidestepped this issue neatly by defining premature ejaculation in terms of "reasonable voluntary control." "The judgment of 'reasonable control' is made by . . . taking into account factors that affect duration of the excitement phase, such as age, novelty of the sexual partner, and frequency and duration of coitus" (American Psychiatric Association, 1980, p. 280). Another view suggests that premature ejaculation does *not* exist if both partners "agree that the quality of their sexual encounters is not influenced by efforts to delay ejaculation" (LoPiccolo, 1977, p. 1234).

Despite the shortcomings of these definitions (or the definitions of this shortcoming), it is usually not too difficult to decide when rapid ejaculation is problematic in a sexual relationship. Although Kinsey and his co-workers suggested that rapid ejaculation was a sign of biological competence, noting that "it would be difficult to find another situation in which an individual who was quick and intense in his responses was labeled anything but superior . . . however inconvenient and unfortunate . . . from the standpoint of [the] wife" (Kinsey, Pomeroy, and Martin, 1948, p. 580), today most sexologists disagree with this idea. Kinsey's belief may have influenced his finding that 75 percent of men ejaculated within two minutes of vaginal entry, but it now seems unlikely that this figure is accurate (Hunt, 1975). While it is certainly true that some people see sex as primarily for the male's pleasure—and some females may actually be grateful to "get it over with" quickly—these ideas, which were once widespread, seem to have been replaced today by a more egalitarian view of sexual interact-ion except among the least educated and lowest socioeconomic levels.

Clearly, the male who persistently ejaculates unintentionally during noncoital sexual play or while trying to enter his partner has a problem. While this extreme situation is found in fewer than 10 percent of cases, it is likely to be particularly distressing. More typically, the premature ejaculator is able to participate in a variety of sexual activities and only loses his ejaculatory control soon after intercourse begins. Premature ejaculation may occur in some situations and not in others. For example, a man may have this problem only during extramarital sex.

Some men are not bothered at all by ejaculating rapidly. Many others question their masculinity and have low self-esteem (Perelman, 1980; Kaplan, 1989). Fears of performance often heighten the lack of ejaculatory control and can lead to erectile dysfunction by the "fears–spectator–failure–greater fears" cycle described earlier (Masters, Johnson, and Kolodny, 1994). Erectile difficulties can also occur if a premature ejaculator struggles to control his sexual arousal by using distraction (thinking about the office or counting backwards from 1000): if he succeeds too well in distracting himself from involvement in the sexual interaction, he may lose his erection as well as the urgency to ejaculate.

While many of the female partners of men with premature ejaculation are understanding and accepting of the involuntary nature of the problem, others "feel angry and 'used,' leading them to seek professional guidance, to seek another lover, or to avoid sex" (Perelman, 1980, p. 201). Because most males have a tendency to ejaculate more quickly if it has been a long time between sexual opportunities, avoidance is likely to worsen the problem and may worsen the relationship too. Similarly, if the man tries to reduce his arousal by shortening the time of noncoital play, his tactic not only is ineffective but also may backfire by further convincing the woman of her partner's selfishness (Masters, Johnson, and Kolodny, 1994).

Although premature ejaculation is less frequent than erectile dysfunction among male patients at the Masters & Johnson Institute (Masters and Johnson, 1970; Kolodny, Masters, and Johnson, 1979), we believe it is probably the most common sexual dysfunction in the general population. We estimate that 15 to 20 percent of American men have at least a moderate degree of difficulty controlling rapid ejaculation, but less than one-fifth of this group consider it to be enough of a problem to seek help. Some men find that they can overcome premature ejaculation on their own by using a condom to cut down on genital sensations; others discover that a glass or two of an alcoholic beverage may reduce their ejaculatory quickness; and others find that controlling ejaculation is no problem "the second time around"—that is, once they have already had one orgasm and attempt intercourse within the next two or three hours. Over-the-counter creams and ointments that "desensitize" the penis deaden sensations. If they help control rapid ejaculation at all, they do so at the cost of not feeling very much or by the power of suggestion.

Ejaculatory Incompetence and Retarded Ejaculation

Ejaculatory incompetence is the inability to ejaculate within the vagina despite a firm erection and relatively high levels of sexual arousal. It must be distinguished from **retrograde ejaculation,** which is a condition where the bladder neck does not close off properly during orgasm so that the semen spurts backward into the bladder, where it is mixed with urine. **Retarded ejaculation** can be thought of as the opposite of premature ejaculation; here, although intravaginal ejaculation eventually occurs, it requires a long time and strenuous efforts at coital stimulation, and sexual arousal may be sluggish.

Ejaculatory incompetence is an infrequent disorder mainly seen in men under age 35. The most

premature ejaculation unintentional ejaculation during noncoital play, while the male is trying to enter his partner, or soon after intercourse begins.

ejaculatory incompetence the inability to ejaculate within the vagina. Can be classified as **primary** (always existing) or **secondary** (having been able to ejaculate in the past).

retrograde ejaculation condition in which the semen spurts backward into the bladder during orgasm because the bladder neck does not close off properly. It occurs in men with multiple sclerosis and diabetes and following some types of prostate surgery.

retarded ejaculation condition in which ejaculation in the vagina occurs only after a lengthy time period and strenuous efforts.

common pattern (about two-thirds of patients) is **primary ejaculatory incompetence** or never having been able to ejaculate in the vagina. **Secondary ejaculatory incompetence** refers to men who have lost the ability to ejaculate intravaginally or who do so infrequently after a prior history of normal coital ejaculation. In either the primary or secondary version of this dysfunction, ejaculation is usually possible by masturbation (about 85 percent of patients in our series) or by noncoital partner stimulation (about 50 percent of patients in our series). In about 15 percent of our cases, men with ejaculatory incompetence had never experienced ejaculation except through nocturnal emissions. Rarely, ejaculatory incompetence can be situational, occurring with one partner but not another (Munjack and Kanno, 1979).

Ejaculatory incompetence can be a source of sexual pleasure because it permits prolonged periods of coitus. A few of our patients have told us that they were regularly able to sustain an erection for one or two hours of intercourse—much to the delight of their partners, many of whom marveled at this staying power. However, once the woman discovers that her partner is unable to ejaculate intravaginally, a new reaction most likely sets in. She may assume that the man does not find her attractive, is not enjoying the experience, or is "withholding" orgasm as a sign of selfishness (Munjack and Oziel, 1980). If reproduction is a goal of the sexual partners, ejaculatory incompetence can be even more frustrating and may lead to accusations and arguments that can threaten even the best of relationships, as this example from our files shows:

> *A 27-year-old married man:* I'm sick and tired of being psychoanalyzed by my wife because of this problem we're having. I want a baby just as much as she does, but my penis doesn't seem to understand. But that's no reason to accuse me of being homosexual.

Retarded ejaculation is seen in all age groups from adolescence on and is probably two or three times more common than ejaculatory incompetence. Although it may also be a source of sexual enjoyment, sometimes the prolonged periods of coital thrusting required to bring about ejaculation are uncomfortable both physically and psychologically for the female, whose own sexual needs may have been amply met in a briefer time frame. The woman may become resentful of the sexual demands placed on

her by her partner. Her feeling corresponds to the male whose female partner needs to be stimulated coitally for a long time to reach orgasm.

Here again, it is important to distinguish between the fairly consistent pattern of sexual dysfunction and the occasional episodes when a man cannot ejaculate intravaginally or requires a long period of vaginal containment and thrusting to ejaculate. Occasional difficulty with ejaculation is *not* a sign of sexual disturbance and is often related to fatigue, tension, illness, too much sex in too short a time, or the effects of alcohol or other drugs (see Chapter 22). In addition, a male may be unable to ejaculate with a partner he's not very emotionally involved with (e.g., when he's just having sex because he feels it's expected of him).

Painful Intercourse

Painful intercourse, or **dyspareunia,** is generally thought of as a female dysfunction but it also affects males. Most typically, the pain is felt in the penis but it can be felt in the testes or internally, where it is often associated with a problem of the prostate or seminal vesicles. Causes of painful intercourse in males are discussed later in this chapter.

FEMALE SEXUAL DYSFUNCTION

Until fairly recently, it was presumed that women were less sexual than men. Females with a sexual dysfunction were therefore not seen as incomplete or "unable to measure up" as men with sexual problems were. In the past two decades, traditional views of female sexuality were all but demolished, and women's sexual needs became accepted as legitimate in their own right. But as part of this process, female sexual responsivity became something of an expected accomplishment, with women—helped along by numerous magazine articles, how-to books, and TV talk shows—suddenly put on the spot with performance pressures of their own.

As a result, females began to develop more awareness of the existence of sexual dysfunctions. The woman who sees herself as "unresponsive" in one way or another often becomes embarrassed, confused, or depressed just as men do. She too may try to cope by avoidance, inventing excuses, or studiously "working" at sex to find the "right" technique to unlock her sexual potential.

Vaginismus

Vaginismus is a condition in which the muscles around the outer third of the vagina have involuntary spasms in response to attempts at vaginal penetration (Figure 21.1). Females of any age can be affected, and the severity of the reflex is highly variable. At one extreme, vaginismus can be so dramatic that the vaginal opening is tightly clamped shut, preventing not only intercourse but even insertion of a finger. Less severe, but still considerably distressing, is when any attempts at coitus—no matter how gentle, relaxed, and loving—result in pelvic pain. In its milder versions, vaginismus may allow a woman to have intercourse, but only with some discomfort. The frequency of vaginismus in the general population is unknown, but judging from our patients, it accounts for less than 10 percent of cases of female sexual dysfunction. We estimate that 2 to 3 percent of all postadolescent women have vaginismus.

Although some women with vaginismus are very fearful of sexual activity, which may impair their sexual responsiveness, most women with this dysfunction have little or no difficulty with sexual arousal. Vaginal lubrication occurs normally, noncoital sexual play may be pleasurable and satisfying, and orgasm is often unaffected (Kolodny, Masters, and Johnson, 1979). Women with vaginismus usually have normal sexual desire and are upset by their inability to enjoy intercourse. Vaginismus can be particularly troubling to a couple who want to have children, and it is often this consideration that pushes the couple to seek help.

The male partner of the woman with vaginismus may be completely baffled about why sexual difficulties arise. Often, he has no specific knowledge of the involuntary muscle spasms involved and either thinks that he is doing something that hurts his partner or sees her as deliberately avoiding intercourse by "tensing up." If he thinks he is hurting her, he may become more and more passive in sexual situations. Erectile dysfunction may

dyspareunia (dis' puh roo' nē uh) painful intercourse.

vaginismus (vaj in iz' mus) involuntary spasms of the muscles around the vagina in response to attempts at penetration.

Figure 21.1   Vaginismus

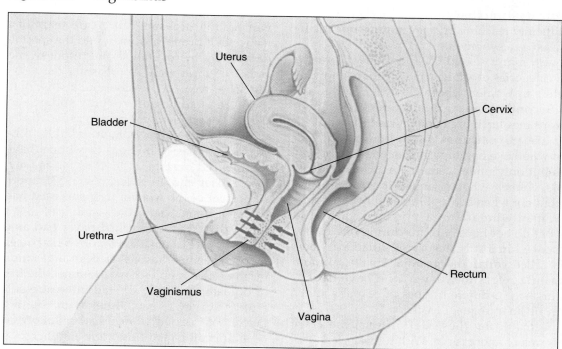

The involuntary muscular spasms of vaginismus at the outer third of the vagina are shown by the arrows.

develop, especially if he assumes the blame for the situation. If, instead, he blames the woman, he may lose patience after a while and become resentful or openly hostile or may simply seek other sexual partners.

Vaginismus may be suspected from a woman's history (e.g., the woman may have had difficulty using a tampon or a diaphragm), but identification of this dysfunction can be made with certainty only by a careful pelvic examination. Unfortunately, not all physicians are well versed in detecting sexual problems, and women are sometimes mistakenly told "everything's normal" when vaginismus is unquestionably present.

Anorgasmia

Before the publication of *Human Sexual Inadequacy* in 1970, the term **frigidity** was generally used to describe a number of female sexual difficulties ranging from not having orgasms to not being interested in sex to not becoming sexually aroused. As this term lacked diagnostic precision and was increasingly used in a negative, disparaging way, portraying women as "cold" or "rejecting," many sexologists abandoned its use. Masters and Johnson (1970) and Kaplan (1974) substituted the term **orgasmic dysfunction** to describe women who have difficulty reaching orgasm; **anorgasmia** is currently used as a synonym.

As with many sexual dysfunctions, there are several categories of anorgasmia. **Primary anorgasmia** refers to women who have never had an orgasm. **Secondary anorgasmia** refers to women who were regularly orgasmic at one time but no longer are. **Situational anorgasmia** refers to women who have had orgasms on one or more occasions but only under certain circumstances—for example, women who are orgasmic when masturbating but not when being stimulated by their partner. Women who are orgasmic by a variety of means but do not have orgasms during intercourse are described in a subcategory of situational anorgasmia called **coital anorgasmia**. Finally, **random anorgasmia** refers to women who have experienced orgasm in different types of sexual activity, but only on an infrequent basis.

As indicated by these definitions, there are many forms of anorgasmia. Within these classifications, the diversity is even greater. Some anorgasmic women get little pleasure out of sex and see it as an obligation of marriage or a means of maintaining a relationship. Other anorgasmic women find that sex is stimulating and satisfying. One woman told us: "Since I've never had an orgasm, I don't really know what I'm missing, but I certainly know when I'm having fun." Many women with orgasmic difficulties voice opinions somewhere between these extremes, as shown by these comments from our files:

> *A 22-year-old single woman:* I enjoy sex, but I keep pushing to reach for an orgasm, and the worry that it won't be there keeps gnawing away inside me. I'd feel a lot better if I knew I could come every time.

> *A 31-year-old married woman:* I've always been able to have orgasms when I masturbate, but it's never happened with my husband. After eight years of marriage this has really become a strain on our relationship—for him, because he feels he's inadequate; for me, because I'm missing a special kind of sharing.

> *A 19-year-old college student:* There's so much talk about orgasms that I've been wondering what's wrong with me, that I don't have them. I used to enjoy sex a lot, but lately it's a bad scene because I just get reminded of my own problems.

Not having orgasms can create fears of performance that propel a woman into the spectator role, dampening her overall sexual responsiveness, just as is true for a man. Anorgasmia can also lead to less self-esteem, depression, and a sense of futility.

There is some controversy today about the number of women who are orgasmic during intercourse. While some women are able to have orgasms very easily, millions of women have never experienced orgasm, at least as far as they recognize. Kinsey and his colleagues (1953) reported that 10 percent of the women they surveyed had never had an orgasm. Shere Hite's sample of 1844 women found that 11.6 percent had never had an orgasm (Hite, 1976). Fisher (1973) reported that 6 percent of married women had never been orgasmic by any means. Other studies have examined the frequency of orgasm occurring during intercourse. Morton Hunt's survey of sexual behavior found that 53 percent of married women had coital orgasms "all or almost all of the time" and another 21 percent had coital orgasms about three-quarters of the time (Hunt, 1975). Only 7 percent of the white, married women in his study either had no coital orgasms at all or very infrequent coital orgasms. Similarly, in a survey of 100,000 women, *Redbook* found that 63 percent of married women had orgasm all of the time or most of the time with intercourse, and only 7 percent never had coital orgasms (Tavris and Sadd, 1977).

Although there has been some disagreement in the past as to whether the absence of coital orgasms without accompanying manual clitoral stimulation is an abnormality per se, most sexologists today have concluded that this is not the case (Wincze and Carey, 1991). In fact, the American Psychiatric Association's definition of the diagnostic category of "inhibited female orgasm" notes that this pattern usually represents "a normal variation of the female sexual response" and does not justify a diagnosis of a sexual dysfunction unless there is a specific psychological inhibition present (American Psychiatric Association, 1987). This distinction is often of little solace to a woman who is unhappy about not having orgasms with intercourse, however, even if she is vehemently reassured that she is completely normal.

Certainly, it is easier for most women to be orgasmic during masturbation than during intercourse. The explanation for this difference is partly physiologic and partly psychological. With masturbation, a woman can focus sexual stimulation precisely where she finds it most arousing, making adjustments in the tempo, placement, and intensity of stimulation as required to give herself maximal pleasure. If she chooses, she can use a vibrator to provide an especially intense source of stimulation or take a leisurely approach to allowing her sexual tension to build to peak levels, which is not always possible with a partner. For most women, masturbation involves some form of stimulation of the clitoris, whereas with intercourse, the clitoris is only stimulated indirectly, primarily by friction from the clitoral hood. As sex therapist Lonnie Barbach notes:

In reality, the clitoris is the female sex organ. Roughly comparable in sensitivity to the penis, the clitoris serves no other function than that of providing sexual pleasure. The vagina is comparable in sensitivity to the male testicles. Therefore, if instead of sexual intercourse, which directly stimulates the male's most sensitive organ, and only indirectly stimulates the female's most sexually sensitive organ, love-mak-

ing were practiced by a male rubbing the clitoris with his testicles—then women would be orgasmic and men would be in groups of pre-orgasmic treatment! *(Barbach, 1975, p. 23)*

In contrast, unless a woman's partner is exceptionally attentive to her preferred stimulatory patterns and the subtle adjustments that augment them, there is unlikely to be as much effective physical stimulation provided to the woman during intercourse as she can produce when she masturbates. Furthermore, the interactive nature of sexual intercourse means that a woman's sexual feelings are necessarily dependent, to a certain degree, on her partner's arousal and physical proficiency as a lover. Some women are distracted from attending to their own needs by concerns about their partner (especially if he is insecure in his erectile consist-ency, or if he ejaculates rapidly). Nevertheless, many women prefer intercourse to masturbation because it gives them additional sensual benefits such as being held and being kissed and also makes them part of a spontaneous give and take. Blumstein and Schwartz (1983) call this "shared intimacy" and note that intercourse is a "central ingredient to [heterosexual] women's happiness," whereas for heterosexual men, intercourse is not always the preferred form of sexual activity.

Anorgasmia in its different forms is far and away the largest category of female sexual dysfunction, accounting for about 90 percent of cases in most large studies. Many women, however, are not orgasmic during every sexual encounter yet do *not* have a sexual dysfunction. Lack of orgasm must be viewed in terms of the individual's desires, the skill and sensitivity of her partner (as well as his attractiveness, cooperation, etc.), the circumstances of sexual activity (privacy, timing, comfort, and so on), and other factors too numerous to men-

frigidity (fri jid' i tē) an outdated term formerly used to describe female sexual difficulties.
orgasmic dysfunction (or gaz' mik) the inability of a female to reach orgasm.
anorgasmia (an' or gaz' mē uh) the inability of a woman to reach orgasm. Can be classified as **primary** (always existing), **secondary** (having been orgasmic in the past), **situational** (existing only during coitus), or **random** (existing on a frequent basis during different types of sexual activity).

tion here. A woman who sometimes has orgasms should be classified as having orgasmic dysfunction only if her orgasmic frequency is so low that it is a source of distress or dissatisfaction.

The male partner of an anorgasmic woman may feel sympathetic while also feeling threatened, since many men assume it's their responsibility to make their partner orgasmic. If he sees his role as "tutor" or "coach," he may become impatient or angry if his partner doesn't reach orgasm in response to his attentions. If he concentrates on romance and carefully orchestrated sexual technique, he may become resentful if the female does not achieve orgasm. Some men give up trying and become resigned to the situation, while others are convinced that their partners are deliberately withholding orgasm. If a man discovers that his partner has been faking orgasm, he is particularly likely to be upset or angered.

Rapid Orgasm

Although premature ejaculation in men has been widely discussed, its female counterpart—**rapid orgasm**—has been almost completely ignored by sexologists. This is probably because the condition is relatively rare. In more than three decades of our research, we have encountered only a handful of women who complained of reaching orgasm too quickly. The primary problem for these women is that once orgasm occurs they have little interest in further sexual activity and often find that it is physically uncomfortable. In contrast, most women who have rapid orgasms remain sexually interested and aroused (often going on to additional orgasms) and thus consider it an asset, not a liability. The male partner of a woman who reaches orgasm rapidly is also likely to view it in a positive light, either seeing it as a sign of a very responsive partner or giving himself a pat on the back for his lovemaking skills.

Painful Intercourse

Dyspareunia, or painful intercourse, in women can present a major stumbling block to sexual satisfaction. In this condition, which can occur at any age, pain can appear at the start of intercourse, midway through coital activities, at the time of orgasm, or after intercourse is completed. The pain can be felt as burning, sharp, searing, or cramping; it can be external, within the vagina, or deep in the pelvic region or abdomen.

The incidence of dyspareunia is unknown. We have found that about 15 percent of adult women experience coital discomfort on a few occasions per year. We estimate that 1 to 2 percent of adult women have painful intercourse on more than an occasional basis. A recent review notes that other studies have given estimates from 8 to 33 percent (Wincze and Carey, 1991).

Dyspareunia detracts from a person's sexual enjoyment and can interfere with sexual arousal and orgasm. The fear of pain may make the woman tense and decrease her sexual pleasure; in many cases, the woman may avoid coital activity or abstain from all forms of sexual contact. The partner of a woman with dyspareunia may either be very understanding and sensitive to her feelings or resentful and demanding in spite of her discomfort.

CAUSES OF SEXUAL DYSFUNCTION

It is customary to classify the causes of **sexual dysfunction** as either **organic** (physical or medical factors such as illness, injury, or drug effects) or **psychosocial** (including psychological, interpersonal, environmental, and cultural factors). The precise cause of a specific dysfunction in a given person cannot always be identified, and in some instances it may be a combination of several different factors.

Organic Factors

In the past, it was generally estimated that only 10 to 20 percent of sexual dysfunction cases are caused primarily by organic factors (Kolodny, Masters, and Johnson, 1979; Munjack and Oziel, 1980; Kaplan, 1983). Today, it is recognized that this category is much higher in cases of erectile dysfunction, where various estimates suggest that one-half to three-quarters of all cases have a primary organic cause (Goldstein and Rothstein, 1990; Wincze and Carey, 1991; Rosen and Leiblum, 1992; Masters, Johnson, and Kolodny, 1994). In the other sexual dysfunctions, "pure" organic causes are much less frequent, although medical problems interact with psychosocial factors to create sexual dysfunction in a significant number of cases. Given the frequency of these organic contributions, it is important for a person seeking treatment for a sexual dysfunction to have a thorough physical examination as well as appropriate laboratory testing to identify pertinent problems. We now review each sexual dysfunction to examine organic factors that may be important. Many of these factors are discussed more fully in the next chapter.

Male Sexual Dysfunction

Erectile dysfunction can result from many medical conditions. Diabetes (a condition in which the body improperly handles blood sugar regulation) and alcoholism are the two most prominent organic causes of erectile dysfunction. Together, they probably account for several million cases in the United States alone. Other organic causes of erectile dysfunction include spinal cord injury, multiple sclerosis, or other neurological disorders; infections or injuries of the penis, testes, urethra, or prostate gland; hormone deficiencies; and circulatory problems. Both prescription medications (such as drugs for high blood pressure) and street drugs like uppers (amphetamines), downers (barbiturates), and narcotics sometimes cause difficulty with erection.

Premature ejaculation rarely results from organic causes. In over 500 cases of premature ejaculation seen at the Masters & Johnson Institute, we have found only one instance where an organic condition proved to be of importance.

With *ejaculatory incompetence,* organic causes can be eliminated as a possibility if ejaculation occurs in noncoital situations. In cases of complete inability to ejaculate, drug use and neurological disorders are sometimes found, accounting for about 1 out of 20 cases. Drug use and alcoholism account for about 10 percent of cases of retarded ejaculation. Some prescription medicines, such as guanethidine (trade name Ismelin, used to treat high blood pressure) and monoamine oxidase inhibitors (used to treat depression) can also cause retarded ejaculation.

Painful intercourse in males can be due to several different organic problems, although psychosocial factors appear to cause at least half of such cases. Inflammation or infection of the penis, the foreskin, the testes, the urethra, or the prostate are the most likely organic causes of male dyspareunia. A few men experience pain if the tip of the penis is scratched or irritated by the tail of an IUD (the stringlike portion that protrudes through the cervix into the vagina). Other men develop painful penile

irritation when exposed to a vaginal contraceptive foam or cream.

Female Sexual Dysfunction

Vaginismus is most frequently a psychosocial problem rather than an organic one. However, any of the organic causes of female dyspareunia can condition a woman into vaginismus as a natural protective reflex (Kolodny, Masters, and Johnson, 1979). Even when the underlying organic problem is detected and successfully treated, the vaginismus may remain, particularly if it has been present for a long time.

Anorgasmia is linked to organic causes in less than 5 percent of cases. Severe chronic illness of almost any variety can impair female orgasmic response. Specific disorders that sometimes block orgasm include diabetes, alcoholism, neurological disturbances, hormone deficiencies, and pelvic disorders such as infections, trauma, or scarring from surgery. Drugs such as narcotics, tranquilizers, and blood pressure medications can also impair female orgasm. *Rapid orgasm* in women has no known physical causes.

Female dyspareunia can be caused by dozens of physical conditions, although psychosocial factors may be as frequent as organic ones (Lazarus, 1980). Any condition that results in poor vaginal lubrication can produce discomfort during intercourse. The chief culprits here seem to be drugs that have a drying effect (e.g.; antihistamines, used to treat allergies, colds, or sinus conditions; certain tranquilizers and marijuana) and disorders such as diabetes, vaginal infections, and estrogen deficiencies. Other causes of female dyspareunia include the following:

1. Skin problems (blisters, rashes, inflammation) around the vaginal opening or affecting the vulva.

rapid orgasm   the female counterpart of premature ejaculation, marked by characteristically having orgasm so quickly in a sexual encounter that it is distressful. This is a very rare complaint.

sexual dysfunction   conditions in which the ordinary physical resposes of sexual excitement or orgasm are impaired. Can be classified as **psychosocial** (caused by psychological, interpersonal, environmental, and cultural factors) or **organic** (caused by physical or medical factors such as illness, injury, or drugs).

2. Irritation or infection of the clitoris.

3. Disorders of the vaginal opening, such as scaring from an episiotomy, intact hymen or chronically infected remnants of the hymen that stretched during intercourse, or infection of the Bartholin glands.

4. Disorders of the urethra or anus.

5. Disorders of the vagina, such as infections, surgical scarring, thinning of the walls of the vagina (whether due to aging or estrogen deficiency), and irritation due to chemicals that are found in contraceptive materials or douches.

6. Pelvic disorders such as infection, tumors, abnormalities of the cervix or uterus, and torn ligaments that support the uterus.

Psychosocial Factors

It has been much more difficult to develop a clear understanding of how psychosocial factors "cause" sexual dysfunction. Much of the research to date has found *associations* between factors such as developmental traumas, psychological traits, behavior patterns, and relationship difficulties and the existence of a sexual dysfunction, but research of this sort cannot prove what *causes* sexual dysfunctions. Furthermore, many people whose histories are loaded with potentially devasting psychosexual events have completely normal sexual function, while others who have unremarkable histories turn up with sexual dysfunctions.

Despite these problems, we can identify some psychosocial factors that are currently thought to contribute to the origins of sexual dysfunction. Since many of these are nonspecific—that is, they may lead to a number of dysfunctions in either men or women—we consider them in terms of several broad categories.

Developmental Factors

Many authorities have suggested that troubled parent–child relationships, negative family attitudes toward sex, traumatic childhood or adolescent sexual experiences, and gender identity conflicts may all predispose one toward developing later sexual dysfunctions, either singly or in combination (Masters and Johnson, 1970; Kaplan, 1974; Wyatt, 1991; Becker and Kaplan, 1991; Mezey and King, 1992).

For example, a child who is brought up believing that sex is sinful and shameful may be handicapped in later sexual enjoyment. Children who have been repeatedly and severely punished for touching their genitals or for innocent sex play with other boys or girls are also liable to become fearful about sex in any form and may have difficulty developing a positive view of sex as an intimate, pleasurable, desirable activity.

A traumatic first coital experience—either physically or psychologically painful—is another common problem found in the backgrounds of many with sexual dysfunctions (Wernik, 1993). Such an experience can raise fear about sexual encounters, lead to avoidance, or cause considerable guilt. Another variation is shown in this comment from one of our patients:

> *A 48-year-old coitally anogasmic woman:* When I was 21 and still a virgin I had been looking forward to my wedding night in a romantic, idealized way. But the wedding day was exhausting, my husband and I both had too much to drink, and when we tried to make love for the first time, instead of being blissful and tender, it was hurried and disastrous. It seems as though we were never able to catch the spark of loving sex after that—it's always been disappointing and unpleasant for me. *(Authors' files)*

One other developmental factor will be mentioned briefly. In *Human Sexual Inadequacy* (Masters and Johnson, 1970), it was noted that a rigid religious background during childhood seemed to be associated with many sexual dysfunctions. What was striking about these cases was not the specific set of religious teachings (since these did not always condemn sexuality) but that sex was strongly regarded as evil and dirty in these rigidly religious families. Since 1970, when these findings were published, we have gathered more information in this area. We can now say that a rigid religious upbringing seems to be a common factor only in certain dysfunctions: vaginismus and primary anorgasmia in women and ejaculatory incompetence and primary impotence in men. Furthermore, by interviewing many individuals from similar backgrounds who did *not* have sexual dysfunctions, we have become even more confident that it is generally *not* the religious beliefs that are troublesome but the severely antisexual attitudes that are forced on the child.

Personal Factors

People's feelings obviously have a lot to do with how they function sexually. We have already noted that fears of performance often suppress sexual function. Other types of anxiety, including fears of pregnancy, venereal disease, rejection, loss of control, pain, intimacy, and even success, can also block the pathways of sexual response.

Other feelings can also affect sexual responsiveness. Guilt, depression, and poor self-esteem are encountered frequently in association with sexual dysfunction. Sometimes, though, it is difficult to know which came first, the feeling or the dysfunction. It is natural for people who have sexual problems to become depressed about them or to feel less good about themselves. Thus, identifying such a feeling does not always mean it caused the dysfunction.

Other personal factors that can play a part in sexual dysfunction are lack of sexual information and blind acceptance of cultural myths. Uncertainty about the location of the clitoris or lack of awareness of its importance in female sexual response are prime examples of lack of sexual information. Believing that the capacity for sexual function disappears with aging or that the pace of sexual activity must be set by the male are examples of how cultural myths can translate into personal attitudes and behavior.

Body image problems are another common causative element in primary orgasmic dysfunction, although these appear to be less of an issue in women who are orgasmic in some forms of sexual activity with a partner. On the other hand, it is not unusual to find that women who have orgasms during solitary masturbation but not with a partner are troubled about issues of personal attractiveness and sexual self-worth, just as they are often conflicted about the relationship itself.

Although a number of different studies have attempted to correlate sexual dysfunctions with particular types of personalities, no solid evidence exists documenting such a relationship.

Interpersonal Factors

Interpersonal factors are of tremendous importance in most sexual dysfunctions. The most common problem is poor communication, in both sexual and nonsexual areas of the relationship. Communication problems either can lead directly to a sexual dysfunction (through misunderstandings or defensiveness) or can play a key role in perpetuating a dysfunction. As we have stressed throughout this book, sex is a form of communication, and effective communication is extremely important in sexual relationships. Other interpersonal factors frequently involved in sexual dysfunctions include power struggles within a relationship, hostility toward a partner or spouse, preference for another partner, distrust or deceit, lack of physical attraction to a partner, and gender-role conflicts (which often become power struggles). Conflicts in the sex value systems of partners or widely different sexual preferences in terms of timing, frequency, or type of sexual activity may also contribute to dysfunctions.

It must be recognized, however, that such problems do not *always* lead to sexual difficulties. Some couples find that sex is most enjoyable when they are angry at each other. Other couples with terrible communication have fantastic sexual relationships. As always, we must be careful not to oversimplify.

Additional Considerations

Until the detailed studies of Masters and Johnson were released, it was generally thought that sexual dysfunctions were invariably due to deep-seated personality problems the originated in childhood (Kaplan, 1974; LoPiccolo and Heiman, 1978; Apfelbaum, 1980a). Today, most sexologists recognize that many people with sexual dysfunctions have completely normal personalities, no signs of emotional illness, and simple, straightforward explanations for their problems.

Yet there are still some major differences between how psychoanalysts and behaviorists explain sexual dysfunction. The traditional psychoanalytic viewpoint has been that the dysfunction is not the primary problem but is instead a symptom of a deeper psychological disturbance. Analysts have suggested that ejaculatory incompetence, erectile dysfunction, and premature ejaculation result from castration anxiety and unresolved Oedipal wishes that are usually present at the unconscious level. Similarly, the analytic viewpoint generally suggests that vaginismus and anorgasmia also reflect unresolved Electra conflicts as well as unconscious hostility toward men because of penis envy. In essence, old fears of being punished for sexual play that were supposedly learned in early childhood are reawakened (in the unconscious) by adult sexual encounters and cause psychological conflict, anxiety, and dysfunction.

Sexual Fakery

A 28-year-old married woman tells her husband that for six years of marriage she's been "faking" orgasms. He gets so angry at her that he kicks off the end of their bed. Later, with professional counseling, he admits that his anger was self-directed—he couldn't believe he didn't see through her act.

A 24-year-old man who's been having problems with erections finds himself with an intimate invitation from a girl he's just begun dating. "Look," he tells her, "I'm not feeling so good tonight, so don't expect too much." *(Authors' files)*

No one knows how many people lie to their partners by faking sexual responsivity or personal satisfaction. When one partner tenderly asks another, "How was that for you?" the usual answer ("terrific!") may be more a matter of tact than truth. Although there are certainly times when sexual deception may seem the better part of valor by allowing a person to save face or by protecting a partner's feelings, many problems may arise if it becomes habitual. This can be illustrated by considering what seems to be the most common form of sexual fakery: a woman who fakes orgasms. The woman who "fakes" is sabotaging communication rather than doing her partner a favor. Although she may succeed in temporarily massaging his ego by making him feel like a great lover, her pretense convinces him that he's doing everything "just right." As a result, he will probably continue doing what he thinks she enjoys, having no reason to change his style and being unaware of her need for anything different.

While men have an impossible time trying to fake erections and while male orgasm usually produces unmistakable external evidence, "faking" can still occur. This usually takes the form of trying to hide an inability to achieve erection, using fatigue or illness as an excuse. In other instances, a man may try to hide his own difficulties by convincing his partner that he wants only to please her—that *he* is satisfied when *she* is satisfied—although this pretense works only with noncoital acts. In a few cases of ejaculatory incompetence, men have faked intravaginal ejaculation successfully for years without their partner's detection. Whatever the particular deception, the result is very similar to the female version of sexual fakery. By undermining effective communication, the man cuts off an opportunity to gain his partner's understanding and thus lessens his chances of being able to change the situation.

Sexual fakery has no long-lasting advantages. It may save a partner's feelings temporarily, but this is usually at the cost of the other person's pleasure. The sexual lie is all too likely to become a barrier between partners. If the barrier becomes thick enough, it can dissolve the relationship.

In sharp distinction, the learning theory viewpoint sees sexual dysfunction as a conditioned, or learned, response. A man may develop erectile dysfunction if his partner constantly criticizes his performance or if he feels guilty after every sexual encounter. A woman may be anorgasmic because she was conditioned to believe that sex was "wrong" or shameful or because she was taught that "nice" girls don't enjoy sex. Premature ejaculation may originate from early sexual experiences in which ejaculating quickly was desirable. Such experiences might include situations with a risk of being discovered by someone else, as in sex in a parked car; sex with a prostitute who typically encourages speed so she can see more customers; or group masturbation, where ejaculatory speed was seen as a sign of virility. If the conditioning is powerful enough, it cannot be easily "unlearned" even when circumstances change.

The learning theory model also points out that some dysfunctions are maintained by positive reinforcement. That is, the dysfunction may result in increased tenderness or attention from a partner, or it may give a person the upper hand in a power struggle. Furthermore, behaviorists generally believe that a precise understanding of causation is less important in treating a sexual dysfunction than recognizing the conditions that *maintain* the difficulty, since these are the ones that need to be changed.

Perhaps as sex research becomes more sophisticated it will be possible to approach the question of causation with more certainty. At present, the understanding of this area remains limited.

DISORDERS OF SEXUAL DESIRE

Since the mid-1970s, sex therapists have become increasingly aware of a new category of sexual problems that are not, strictly speaking, sexual dysfunctions. In these conditions, which are collectively referred to as disorders of sexual desire, the capacity for physical sexual response is usually preserved, and the problem is one of lack of willingness to participate in sexual relations due to either disinterest or fear. If lack of interest in sex is the predominant problem, it is classified as **inhibited sexual desire (ISD).** If lack of participation in sex is mainly due to overwhelming fear, it is classified as **sexual aversion.**

In deciding when a disorder of sexual desire is present, it is necessary to remember that while some people seem to be interested in sex at almost any time, others have low or seemingly nonexistent levels of sexual interest. Only when lack of sexual interest is a source of personal or relationship distress, instead of voluntary choice, is it classified as ISD. Schover and co-workers (1982) suggest that ISD is present if there is both a low rate of sexual activity and "a subjective lack of desire for sexual activity; desire here includes sexual dreams and fantasies, attention to erotic materials, awareness of wishes for sexual activity, noticing attractive potent-ial partners, and feelings of frustration if deprived of sex."

People with ISD characteristically have low interest in initiating sexual behavior and are generally unreceptive to a partner's sexual advances, although they may reluctantly "give in" to their partner's wishes from time to time to preserve peace in the relationship. Generally, people with ISD are sexually functional (in physiological terms), but this disorder can also coexist with one or more sexual dysfunctions. ISD can be primary (lifelong) or secondary, and it can be either general-

ized (occurring all the time) or situational. Although the exact incidence of this problem is unknown, it has been appearing frequently in sex therapy clinics around the country in the recent past, accounting for as many as three out of ten cases in some clinics (Lief, 1977; Schover and LoPiccolo, 1982; Leiblum and Rosen, 1988).

The causes of inhibited sexual desire include both organic and psychosocial conditions. Hormone deficiencies, alcoholism, kidney failure, drug abuse, and severe chronic illness may each play a role. Ten to 20 percent of men with this disorder have pituitary tumors that produce excessive amounts of prolactin; the prolactin suppresses testosterone production and sometimes causes impotence as well as ISD (Schwartz and Bauman, 1981). A majority of cases of ISD appear to be psychosocial in origin, reflecting problems such as depression, prior sexual trauma, poor body image or self-esteem, interpersonal hostility, and relationship power struggles. In some cases, ISD seems to develop as a means of coping with a preexisting sexual dysfunction. For instance, a man with erectile dysfunction who develops a low interest in sex finds that this allows him to avoid the unpleasant consequences of sexual failure such as embarrassment, anxiety, loss of self-esteem, and frustration.

Women or men with ISD may be sexually functional or may have difficulties with sexual arousal and orgasm. In many cases, they seem not to be able to recognize early signs of sexual arousal in themselves and use a limited set of cues to define a situation as sexual (LoPiccolo, 1980). For example, such persons may ignore warmth and tenderness as possible signs of sexual feelings while waiting to be swept off their feet by a tidal wave of sexual passion. In addition, many people with ISD believe their initial desire is a good predictor of their ultimate response to a sexual situation, so if they are not feeling "turned on" at the first touch or kiss, they give up all hope of enjoying themselves.

ISD is not a source of difficulty in all marriages or relationships where it occurs. Sometimes a couple reaches an acceptable accommodation to the

inhibited sexual desire (ISD) a condition marked by very low interest in sexual behavior.
sexual aversion a severe phobia (irrational fear) of sexual activity or the thought of sexual activity, which generally leads to avoidance of sexual situations.

situation: for example, a person with ISD may agree to participate in sex when his or her partner requests it, regardless of personal interest. Alternatively, some couples reach a workable solution by allowing—or even encouraging—the partner with an intact sex drive to seek sexual activity outside the relationship. Most frequently, however, when only one person in the relationship has low sexual desire, it poses a major strain.

Sexual aversion is a severe phobia (irrational fear) to sexual activity or the thought of sexual activity which leads to avoidance of sexual situations. It too affects both males and females. The intense fear or dread found in sexual aversion is sometimes expressed in physiological symptoms such as profound sweating, nausea, diarrhea, or a racing, pounding heartbeat (Masters, Johnson and Kolodny, 1994). But in many cases, the phobia expresses itself in purely psychological terms: simply put, the person is terrified of sexual contact.

Perhaps surprisingly, people with sexual aversion are likely to be able to respond fairly naturally to sexual encounters—if they can get past the initial dread. Some patients with this disorder have told us they have more difficulty with undressing and touching in a sexual context than they do with participation in intercourse.

Between 1972 and 1992, we saw over 200 cases of sexual aversion at the Masters & Johnson Institute. The primary causes seem to be (1) severely negative parental sex attitudes, (2) a history of sexual trauma (e.g., rape, incest), (3) a pattern of constant sexual pressuring by a partner in a long-term relationship, and (4) gender identity confusion in men. In the typical case of sexual aversion, the frequency of sexual activity drops to only once or twice a year—if that often. This can obviously become a major source of relationship stress, and the partner of the person with sexual aversion often becomes angry and considers leaving the relationship. Fortunately, the success rate for treating sexual aversion is over 90 percent even in cases of long duration (Masters, and Johnson, and Kolodny, 1994). Schover and LoPiccolo (1982) have also reported that cases of ISD and sexual aversion usually have successful treatment outcomes.

SEX THERAPY

Prior to 1970 the treatment of sexual dysfunctions and problems was generally the province of psy-

chiatry (Levine, 1976). Treatment usually took a long time, and successful reversal of the sexual distress was very uncertain. The traditional psychiatric model of individual treatment (one therapist working with one patient) was almost always used.

Today, sex therapy is a field that includes practitioners of many different backgrounds—psychology, medicine (both psychiatry and other specialties), social work, nursing, counseling, and theology to name just a few. There are also many approaches to sex therapy, some of which are described below.

The Masters and Johnson Model

Beginning in 1959, Masters and Johnson began their innovative program for treating sexual dysfunctions. It is considerably different from prior approaches in a number of ways. For example, they primarily work only with couples (instead of individuals) because they feel that there is no such thing as an uninvolved partner in a committed relationship in which there is any form of sexual distress. This does not mean that the partner always *causes* the problem but points out that he or she is *affected* by it, as the relationship is affected. This strategy shifts the therapeutic focus to the relationship instead of the individual. Furthermore, it provides a more effective means of identifying the full dimensions of a problem. Masters and Johnson found that the input of both partners usually proved more useful than the one-sided view that an individual provided. Finally, this strategy provides an opportunity to gain the cooperation and understanding of both partners in overcoming the distress.

A logical extension of this approach is the use of *two* therapists—a man and woman working together as a *cotherapy team*. This team increases therapeutic objectivity and balance by adequately representing male and female viewpoints and gives each partner a same-sex therapist to whom he or she can (theoretically) relate more easily. The cotherapy team also provides a model for the patient couple in important ways: for example, they can easily demonstrate effective communication skills.

Another important element of the Masters and Johnson approach is the integration of physiologic and psychosocial data in assessment and treatment. In the past, many psychiatrists never examined their patients because they feared that this might trigger unwanted sexual feelings that could complicate the treatment relationship. Masters and Johnson recognized that it was important to identify organic conditions that might require medical or surgical treatment instead of sex therapy. They also found that explaining the anatomy and physiology of sexual response to patients often had important therapeutic benefits of its own.

Finally, the Masters and Johnson model involves a rapid, intensive approach to treating sexual problems. Couples are seen daily for a two-week period (the average duration of therapy is actually just under 12 days). This format permits a day-to-day continuity that appears to be beneficial in certain aspects of sex therapy, such as reducing anxiety or helping patients overcome mistakes. Couples are also urged to free themselves whenever possible from their ordinary work, family, and social activities during the two weeks of therapy to be able to devote their attention to their own relationship without outside distractions.

It became apparent during the pilot phase of this clinical model that the therapy process was much more effective when couples were seen on a daily basis than in cases where couples were seen in the prevailing format of the 50-minute hour once or twice a week.

Against this general background, some additional treatment concepts of the Masters and Johnson approach are important:

1. *Therapy is individualized to meet the specific needs of each couple.* The couple's values and objectives are the primary determinants of exactly what is done. Therapists must avoid imposing their own values on their patients.

2. *Sex is assumed to be a natural function, controlled largely by reflex responses of the body.* Although many different factors can interfere with sexual function by disrupting these natural reflexes, sex therapy does not generally involve "teaching" the desired sexual response. Masters and Johnson focus instead on identifying obstacles that block effective sexual function and on helping people remove or overcome these obstacles. When this happens, natural function usually takes over promptly.[1]

[1]Sometimes removing the obstacles to natural function is not enough, particularly for people who have a life-long pattern of sexual dysfunction. They may also need specific therapeutic attention to facilitate arousal or to improve sexual techniques. In this situation, there is some "teaching" going on.

3. *Because fears of performance and "spectatoring" are often central to cases of sexual dysfunction, therapy is approached at several levels.* Pressures to perform are removed initially by banning direct sexual contact. Couples are then helped to rediscover the sensual pleasures of touching and being touched without the goal of a particular sexual response (the "sensate focus" exercises). The therapists also help couples relabel their expectations so they do not judge everything they do as "success" or "failure." They also give people "permission" to be anxious, which helps them to talk about their anxiety more openly. This open communication often reduces the severity of the anxiety.

4. *Determining who's "to blame" for a sexual problem is discouraged as counterproductive.* Instead, couples are assisted in finding out what makes them feel comfortable and relaxed as opposed to tense or nervous. In this approach, each person is urged to take responsibility for himself or herself rather than waiting for his or her partner to provide the "right" mood, the "right" touch, or the "right" style of making love.

5. *Helping couples see that sex is just one component of their relationship is stressed.* Often, when a sexual problem occurs in people's lives, it causes them to worry about sex so much that they devote a disproportionate amount of time to thinking and talking about this topic. One typical objective of therapy is to help couples achieve a balanced perspective toward sex in which it is neither the totality of their relationship nor the most neglected part of their relationship. In fact, a general truism of sex therapy is that when a couple's relationship improves outside the bedroom, it is apt to have positive results inside the bedroom too.

The Masters and Johnson Therapy Format

On the first day of therapy, the couple begins by briefly meeting with their cotherapists, who introduce themselves and explain the events of the next few days. Following this overview, the patients are separated and a detailed history is taken from each partner by the same-sex therapist. After a break for lunch, when the cotherapists get together to discuss what they have learned, a second history is taken, but this time on a cross-sex basis: that is, the male therapist interviews the female patient and the female therapist interviews the male patient. Rounding out a busy day, each patient has a complete physical examination. Blood samples are obtained the following morning for laboratory evaluation of general health.

The second day of therapy is the time of the "roundtable session" in which the couple and both cotherapists meet together. Here, the therapists present their assessment of the sexual *and* nonsexual problems that the couple is facing and give an honest opinion of the chances of successful treatment. The patients are encouraged to comment on the therapists' impressions and to correct any factual errors that have been made. The therapists try to explain the most plausible causes of the sexual dysfunction(s) or problem(s) and begin to outline the approach for treatment. Generally, there is some discussion of sex as a natural function, how fears of performance originate, the effect of spectatoring, and the importance of communication skills. The roundtable usually concludes with suggestions to try the "sensate focus" exercises (described in the next section) in the privacy of their own home or hotel room.

Each initial history-taking session usually lasts one and one-half to two hours, and the cross-sex histories average about 45 minutes apiece. The roundtable generally lasts about 90 minutes, although any of these times are quite variable, depending in part on how talkative the couple is. Daily sessions after the roundtable average about an hour in length.

From the third day, the patient couple and the cotherapists continue to meet in a four-way interaction, although occasionally the therapists may see each patient separately to discover if there are any individual concerns that one partner is hesitant to discuss in the presence of the other. Each partner is asked to describe the events of the previous 24 hours, with particular attention to communication patterns and interaction during the sensate focus assignments.

Interestingly, a majority of time in the therapy sessions is usually spent on nonsexual issues (such as dealing with anger, self-esteem, and power struggles), although there is a direct attempt to provide information about sexual anatomy and physiology while attending to the couple's other needs. Couples who have negative sexual attitudes are encouraged to adopt new viewpoints.

Sensate Focus

At the beginning of therapy, each couple is asked to refrain from direct sexual interaction involving genital contact. This approach helps to remove performance pressures and provides a framework for breaking the fear–spectatoring–failure–fear cycle that is often deeply ingrained. To learn more effective ways of sexual interaction, the idea of sensate focus is introduced.

In the first stage of sensate focus exercises, the couple is told to have two sessions in which they will each have a turn touching their partner's body—with the breasts and genitals "off limits." The purpose of the touching is *not* to be sexual but to establish an awareness of touch sensations by noticing textures, contours, temperatures, and contrasts (while doing the touching) or to simply be aware of the sensations of being touched by their partner. The person doing the touching is told to do so on the basis of what interests him or her, *not* on any guesses about what his or her partner likes or doesn't like. It is emphasized that the touching should not be a massage or an attempt to arouse the partner sexually.

The initial sensate focus periods should be as silent as possible, since words can detract from the awareness of physical sensations. However, the person being touched must let his or her partner know—either nonverbally (by body language) or in words—if any touch is uncomfortable.

Although many people say, "Oh, we've touched lots of times before—can't we just skip this and go on to a more advanced level?" this first stage of sensate focus is critical in several ways. It allows the therapists to find out additional information about how a couple interacts that supplements their histories in important ways. This stage also has a specific treatment value of its own, as shown by the fact that many men who have not had erections for years in attempts at sex suddenly discover a king-size erection probably because the performance demand was removed. After all, they were told that sexual arousal was not expected but even if it occurred, it was not to be put into action. Finally, it provides an excellent means for reducing anxiety and teaching nonverbal communication skills.

In the next stage of sensate focus, touching is expanded to include the breasts and genitals. A more detailed discussion of the overall process is presented in Chapter 14.

Some Specific Treatment Strategies

The general features of the Masters and Johnson treatment model just described are supplemented by some additional methods used in the treatment of various dysfunctions.

In *erectile dysfunction,* it is important to help the man understand that he cannot "will" an erection to occur on demand any more than he can "will" his blood pressure to drop or his heart rate to increase. He *can* set the stage for his own natural reflexes to take over by not trying to have erections and by moving out of his performance fears. Not surprisingly, the man with erectile dysfunction often finds himself having firm erections during the early stages of sensate focus experience. While this can be reassuring to him, it is also important for the man (and his partner) to realize that losing an erection is *not* a sign of failure; it simply shows that erections come and go naturally. For this reason, the woman may be instructed to stop stroking or fondling the penis when an erection occurs, so the man has an opportunity to see that it will return with further touching. A related problem is that many men with erectile dysfunction try to rush their sexual performance once they get an erection out of fear that they will promptly lose it. The "rushing" adds one more performance pressure, and the usual result is a rapid loss of erection.

When intercourse is attempted (only after the man has gained considerable confidence in his erectile capacity *and* has been able to reduce his spectatoring behavior), the woman is advised to insert the penis. This reduces pressures on the man to decide when it is time to insert and removes the potential distraction of his fumbling to "find" the vagina.

In treating *premature ejaculation,* the couple approach is particularly important since the condition may actually be more distressing to the woman than the man. In addition to discussing the physiology of ejaculation, the therapists introduce a specific method called the "squeeze technique" that helps recondition the ejaculatory reflex. When genital touching is begun, the woman uses the "squeeze" periodically. As shown in Figure 21.2, the woman puts her thumb on the frenulum of the penis and places her first and second finger just above and below the coronal ridge on the opposite side of the penis. A firm, grasping pressure is applied for about four seconds and then abruptly released. The pressure is always applied front to back, never from side to side. It is important that the woman use the pads of her fingers and thumb and avoids pinching the penis or scratching it with her fingernails. For unknown reasons, the squeeze technique reduces the urgency to ejaculate (it also may cause a temporary, partial loss of erection). It should not be used, however, at the moment of ejaculatory inevitability: instead, it must begin at the early stages of genital play and continue periodically, every few minutes. The "squeeze" can be used whether the penis is erect or flaccid, but the firmness of the pressure should be proportionate to the degree of erection.

When the couple begins to have intercourse, the woman is asked to use the squeeze three to six times before attempting insertion. Once the penis is fully inside her, she should hold still for 15 to 30 seconds, with neither partner thrusting, and then move off the penis, apply the squeeze again, and reinsert. This time a slow thrusting pattern can begin. Once the man improves his ejaculatory control, both partners are taught the "basilar squeeze," another version of the squeeze technique (Figure 21.3), so that intercourse need not be interrupted by repeated dismounting to apply a squeeze.

The basilar squeeze should only be employed during coitus. The male partner should initiate the basilar squeeze because, once fully mounted, he has the easier anatomical access to the base of the penis, and he obviously is far more subjectively aware of his level of sexual excitation than is his female partner. For the first six months after introduction of the squeeze technique, the male partner is encouraged to avoid any attempts at "brinksmanship," that is, seeing how close he can come to the state of ejaculatory inevitability before initiating the appropriate squeeze technique. The squeeze techniques are far more effective if initiated before the plateau phase of the sexual response cycle has been attained.

Ejaculatory incompetence is treated by in-depth attention to the underlying psychological components combined with sensate focus experiences that seek to lead the man through a sequence of (1) ejaculating by masturbation while alone, (2) ejaculating by masturbation in the presence of his partner, (3) ejaculating by manual stimulation received from his partner, and (4) having the partner stimulate the penis vigorously to the point of ejaculatory inevitability and then quickly inserting it in the vagina. In most cases, when the man has ejaculated

Figure 21.2   The Squeeze Technique Used in Treating Premature Ejaculation

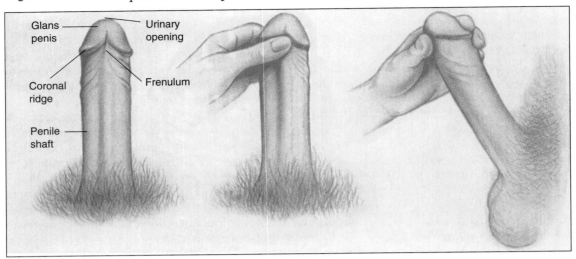

in the vagina once or twice, the fears or inhibitions about this act disappear completely. In some cases where the treatment sequence has not worked, it may be helpful to have the man ejaculate (via manual stimulation) externally onto the woman's genitals. After he becomes used to seeing his semen in genital contact with his partner, intravaginal ejaculation may occur more easily.

Vaginismus is treated by explaining the nature of the involuntary reflex spasm to the couple and demonstrating the reflex in a carefully conducted pelvic examination with the male partner present and the woman urged to watch by use of a mirror. After this is done, the physician teaches the woman some techniques for relaxing the muscles around the vagina. The most effective method seems to be

Figure 21.3   The Basilar Squeeze Technique Used in
Treating Premature Ejaculation

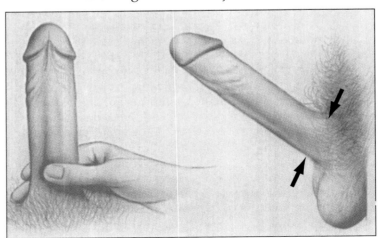

Unlike the squeeze at the coronal ridge, the basilar squeeze can be applied by the man during vaginal containment of the penis. Firm pressure is applied for about four seconds and then released; the pressure should always be from front to back (as shown by the arrows), never from side to side.

having her first deliberately tighten these muscles and then simply let go. It is much more difficult to relax on command. Next, the woman is given a set of various-sized plastic dilators. The smallest of these, slightly thinner than a finger, is gently inserted in the vagina by the physician—often to the amazement of the woman, who may have never been able to insert *anything* in her vagina. She is then shown how to insert the dilator herself, using plenty of sterile lubricating jelly, and is asked to practice this at home several times a day, keeping the dilators in place for 10 to 15 minutes at a time. Most women with vaginismus find that within five or six days they are able to use the largest dilator in the set, which is similar in thickness to an erect penis. If relationship issues have been dealt with adequately (often a key part of the therapy), the transition to successful intercourse is usually easy at this point. At this time, it is particularly important for the woman to insert the penis so she feels in control.

The strategies used in treating *anorgasmia* depend greatly on the nature of the dysfunction. Different approaches are needed for a woman who has never had an orgasm than for a woman who is easily orgasmic with masturbation, manual stimulation, or oral–genital sex. Similarly, depending on the cause(s) of the anorgasmia, treatment strategies will vary widely from case to case. For example, a woman with a poor body image may be helped to find various ways of regarding her body more positively. A woman who is distracted from high levels of arousal by disturbing fantasies might be taught thought-blocking techniques, while another woman who cannot get beyond plateau may be encouraged to experiment with fantasies as an aid to boosting her into orgasm.

Common techniques used in treating anorgasmia include (1) encouraging a woman to explore her own body, especially focusing on genital exploration and stimulation in a relaxed, undemanding fashion; (2) dealing with performance anxieties and spectatoring, with particular attention to reducing performance pressures from her partner; (3) fostering sexual communications so that the woman is able to let her partner know what type of touch or stimulation she prefers at a given moment; and (4) reducing inhibitions that limit the woman's capacity for arousal or that block orgasm. A woman helped by this last technique is often given "permission" to have sexual feelings and learns to overcome fears that orgasm involves losing consciousness or losing control of her bladder. In most cases, these strategies make it fairly simple for the woman to reach orgasm via masturbation or stimulation by her partner. To make the transition to having orgasms during intercourse, a "bridging" technique is used in which either partner stimulates the clitoris manually during coitus with active thrusting.

Plastic dilators used to treat vaginismus to allow the woman to learn how to recondition the reflex response of the muscles surrounding her vagina. Treatment begins with the smallest dilator and progresses gradually to the larger sizes.

These methods have now been used for more than 30 years in the treatment of sexual dysfunctions, with approximately four out of five patients successfully treated. Between 1959 and 1973, patients were followed for five years after therapy to evaluate the permanence of treatment results. More recently, a two-year follow-up has been used. About 1 couple in 20 returns to the Masters & Johnson Institute for additional therapy sometime after their two-week course of treatment. Statistics describing the Masters & Johnson Institute's experience for the various categories of dysfunction are shown in Table 21.1.

Other Approaches to Sex Therapy

Important contributions to sex therapy have been made by a number of other workers using treatment methods that differ from the Masters and Johnson model. Most therapists, for example, see patients once a week rather than daily (Schmidt and Lucas, 1976; Caird and Wincze, 1977; Schiller, 1981). Many therapists believe that a single therapist can work as effectively as a cotherapy team (H. Kaplan, 1974, 1979; Annon, 1976; Ellis, 1980; Schiller, 1981; Arentewicz and Schmidt, 1983; LoPiccolo et al., 1985), which reduces the expense of sex therapy. Others have experimented successfully with group therapy formats or individual therapy (Kaplan, 1974; Barbach, 1980; Zilbergeld, 1980; Cotten-Huston and Wheeler, 1983). Hypnosis has also been reported to be useful in treating sexual difficulties (Alexander, 1974; Fuchs et al., 1975; Fabbri, 1976; Brown and Chaves, 1980). Here, we consider some of the most common approaches used by other therapists.

Helen Kaplan: The New Sex Therapy

Psychiatrist Helen Kaplan (1974, 1979, 1989) has written extensively on the treatment of sexual dysfunctions, integrating many methods of Masters and Johnson with principles of psychoanalytic therapy. In her view, human sexual response is best seen as *triphasic,* or consisting of three separate but interlocking phases: desire, arousal, and orgasm. She believes that desire-phase disorders are most difficult to treat because they tend to be associated with deep-seated psychological difficulties (1979). She also states that "the standard sex therapy methods seem to be effective primarily for those sexual problems which have their roots in mild and easily diminished anxieties and conflicts" (1979, p.

xviii). To deal with more complex cases, she uses a lengthened form of sex therapy that seeks a deeper level of insight and addresses unconscious conflicts. One of her underlying theories is that a sexual disorder usually results from multiple levels of causes—some more immediate and accessible, some more remote and hidden.

The details of Kaplan's treatment methods differ considerably in some ways from the Masters and Johnson methods. In the treatment of premature ejaculation, for example, she advocates use of the "stop–start" technique instead of the squeeze. In the "stop–start" method, introduced by James Semans in 1956, the female partner stimulates the penis manually until the man feels that he is rapidly approaching ejaculation, at which time she stops all stimulation until the sense of ejaculatory urgency disappears. Stimulation then begins again, and the stop–start cycle is repeated several times before the man is allowed to ejaculate (Kaplan, 1974, 1989).

Behavioral Therapy

Modern behavioral methods for treating sexual difficulties are generally traced back to Joseph Wolpe (1958) and enjoy widespread acceptance today (Heiman and LoPiccolo, 1988; Leiblum and Rosen, 1989). While many methods used by Masters and Johnson are very similar to behavioral techniques, there are some theoretical and practical differences in approach.

The operant approach to behavioral therapy is to carefully analyze the problematic behavior (e.g., the sexual dysfunction) and to use positive and negative reinforcers best suited to the individual case. Gradual exposure to imaginary scenes of sexual activity may be used before exposure to real-life sexual situations in sensate focus exercises. These techniques are both forms of *desensitization,* in which the controlled exposure to limited amounts of anxiety helps to eliminate the anxiety. *Relaxation training* (learning specific breathing and muscle exercises to reduce tension) and *assertiveness training* (learning how to say what you feel and what you need) are other methods used to reduce anxiety. *Directed masturbation* (LoPiccolo and Lobitz, 1972; Wincze and Carey, 1991) which is used in the treatment of anorgasmia, is a nine-step program for helping a woman learn to masturbate to orgasm and then include her partner in her orgasmic response, first in manual stimulation and then during intercourse.

Table 21.1   Results of Sex Therapy at the Masters & Johnson Institute

	N[a]	Failures	Successes[b]	Success Rate
Primary impotence	65	21	44	67.7%
Secondary impotence	674	134	540	80.1
Premature ejaculation	543	35	508	93.6
Ejaculatory incompetence	113	27	86	76.1
Male totals	1395	217	1178	84.4
Anorgasmia	811	207	604	74.5
Vaginismus	130	2	128	98.5
Female totals	941	209	732	77.8
Combined totals	2336	426	1910	81.8

[a]*Cases seen between 1959 and 1985.*

[b]*A case was categorized as successful only if the change in sexual function was unequivocal and lasting. For all patients seen before 1973, follow-up lasted five years. From 1973, the follow-up period was reduced to two years. If a patient was successful during the two-week sex therapy program but then slipped back into dysfunction, the case was listed as a failure.*

An interesting and logical way of approaching sexual problems has been suggested by behavioral psychologist Jack Annon (1976). He uses a four-level model, represented by the acronym PLISSIT, to go from the simplest to more advanced levels of treatment. The four levels are P = permission, LI = limited information, SS = specific suggestions, and IT = intensive therapy. This model makes use of the fact that in simple cases of sexual difficulties, reassurance and education are sometimes enough to solve the problem. Specific suggestions might include instruction in the squeeze technique or in sensate focus, without dealing with major psychosocial issues. Intensive therapy goes beyond these steps to deal with relationship conflicts, psychological problems, and other complex issues that may be present.

Additional Psychotherapy Methods

There are now so many different approaches to sex therapy that it is practically impossible to describe them all. Only brief mention of a few other notable methods can be made here due to space limitations. Lonnie Barbach (1975, 1980) has pioneered in the use of women's groups for treating anorgasmia. These groups have the particular advantages of being relatively inexpensive and quite successful. Psychologist Albert Ellis has developed Rational-Emotive Therapy (RET) as a useful approach to sexual and nonsexual problems. RET helps people overcome irrational beliefs and unrealistic expectations that feed into their sexual dysfunction. Blending behavioral methods with unique strategies for dealing with emotional discomfort (such as shame-attacking exercises, risk-taking exercises), RET principles can be applied in individual, couple, or group therapy.

Wincze and Carey (1991) suggest that therapists should include a broad range of treatment approaches. For example, in addition to providing education to debunk common myths and misunderstandings people have about their sexuality, therapists can provide education about sexual health issues, from dealing with the menopause to sexual problems related to infertility or STDs. They also suggest cognitive restructuring techniques to help clients change their negative sex attitudes and reduce interfering thoughts. Wincze and Carey also describe several common areas of communication problems that usually require attention in couples with sexual difficulties.

1. *Off beam:* Partners start talking about one thing but lose their focus, drifting off into other (often trivial) matters.

2. *Mind reading:* Just what it says, as in: "I know what you're thinking because I can read you like a book."

3. *Kitchen sink:* A couple starts discussing one problem but quickly brings in so many other issues that there is an obvious data and problem overload.

4. *"Yes, but":* One person listens to the other but continually thinks up reasons that the other person is wrong. Sometimes these are verbal-

ized, sometimes not, but the end result is the same: defensive listening and blocked understanding.

5. *Cross-complaining:* Each response includes a new gripe or criticism.

6. *Standoff:* Both partners repeat the same complaints and arguments so often that they (a) become stale, and (b) become next-to-impossible to resolve.

As most sex therapists agree, until such communication impasses are solved, it is difficult to make much progress with sex therapy.

Another approach that has proven valuable is the use of systems theory applied to sexual dysfunction. In this context, systems theory asks how a sexual dysfunction maintains the equilibrium of the emotional interaction between two partners (LoPiccolo, 1992). For example, a problem such as erectile dysfunction may actually have certain benefits within a relationship, such as reducing intimacy or changing the balance of power from the man to the woman (or from one man to his male partner). Sometimes these "side benefits" are so powerful that they may help maintain the dysfunction. As LoPiccolo (1992) notes, such positive gains are usually denied by a couple at first, but emerge as therapy progresses.

Biomedical Methods

In the last decade, a number of significant advances have been made in treating organic forms of male sexual dysfunction by techniques other than "talking" therapies. The most dramatic example of this approach is the use of surgery to implant a device in the penis that makes intercourse possible when the physical capacity to have an erection has been lost due to illness or injury. This form of treatment, called a penile prosthesis, is discussed in more detail in Chapter 22.

Other types of surgery can also be useful for treating specific types of erectile dysfunction. For example, several different types of vascular surgery can be done to correct conditions of either too little blood flowing into the penis (a condition called "arterial blockage") or leaky veins causing blood to drain from the penis during sexual arousal (a condition technically called "venous insufficiency") (Melman and Tiefer, 1992). While the results of such surgery are unpredictable, for some men they offer a major improvement in sexual functioning.

A less invasive, "do-it-yourself" method has recently become widely used, as well: the external vacuum device. In this approach, a plastic cylinder is put over the penis and then a lever is pumped to pull the air out. (Safety note: this is NOT an electric vacuum, which could be dangerous). The suction draws blood into the penis, causing it to swell. When this occurs, a rubber ring or band is put tightly around the base of the penis and kept in place for up to 30 minutes to allow intercourse to occur. In general, these vacuum pumps have been well-received by men with erectile dysfunction, with about 80 percent of men in some studies reporting that they are able to have intercourse after using this method (Witherington, 1988; Althof and Turner, 1992). However, the erections that are produced as not as firm as most men would like, and since there is no erection at all at the base of the penis (between the body and the rubber ring or band), the penis tends to flop around more than normal. We have found that 32 percent of the men who have tried this device discarded this method after a month or two of use because of these problem (Masters, Johnson, and Kolodny, 1994). In addition, the vacuum pump device is painful for some men, especially when they are first getting used to it.

An even newer method that is currently being used in many centers involves drugs such as papaverine hydrochloride, phentolamine, and prostaglandin E1, which cause temporary erections after they are injected into the penis. Men are generally taught to administer these injections at home; after a successful injection, the drug-induced erection will usually last one to two hours. In general, the results of self-injection therapy have been encouraging (Zorgniotti et al., 1985; Sidi et al., 1986; Goldstein and Rothstein, 1990; Wagner and Kaplan, 1993). For example, Goldstein and Rothstein (1990, p. 116) claim, "Penile injections are a predictable, rational, successful and safe treatment; usually there are minimal side effects." However, they also note that like all treatments for erectile dysfunction, self-injection works best when a man has a supportive partner. On the other hand, one prominent UCLA urologist notes that 25 percent of the patients receiving such injections had no change at all in their erections and another 14 percent had such a slight improvement they were not able to have intercourse (Lue, 1988). Althof and Turner (1992) observed that patient acceptance of the self-injection method is only 40 to 50 percent. Priapism (persistent, painful erection) is one common side effect that can require emergency medical care; another problem is that local scarring can occur at the injection sites (Lue, 1988; Wagner and Kaplan, 1993).

Inhibited male sexual desire that is caused by excessive levels of prolactin in the blood can often be treated successfully with the use of a drug called bromocriptine. In addition, men with erectile dysfunction and/or low sex drive due to a deficiency of testosterone can usually be treated successfully with injections of testosterone on a monthly or bimonthly basis.

Unfortunately, there have not been corresponding treatment advances in dealing with female sexual dysfunction by using biomedical approaches.

THE EFFECTIVENESS OF SEX THERAPY

Because there are many different models of sex therapy and the specialty is still fairly young, evaluating the effectiveness of these approaches is difficult. Most studies to date have not had control groups, and many reports are based on a small number of cases. Other problems are (1) lack of uniform definitions of the dysfunctions, (2) differences in selection of patients, (3) differences in defining success or failure, and (4) lack of adequate follow-up (checking the results periodically after therapy is over). Additional methodological issues have been raised elsewhere (Leiblum and Rosen, 1989; Wincze and Carey, 1991; McCabe and Delaney, 1992; Hawton, 1992).

Psychologists Bernie Zilbergeld and Michael Evans (1980) have criticized the Masters and Johnson data on the effectiveness of sex therapy on a variety of methodological grounds. Specifically, they have questioned the criteria Masters and Johnson used to rate treatment outcomes, suggesting that the results obtained may have reflected undue leniency in deciding how to classify cases. In addition, they suggested that the Masters and Johnson results may have been artificially inflated by selecting only the best candidates for treatment (and rejecting fairly large numbers of cases that appeared "difficult"). In actuality, however, fewer than 1 out of 50 couples who apply to the Masters & Johnson Institute are turned down for therapy, and the criteria used to evaluate the outcome of sex therapy at the Masters & Johnson Institute are relatively strin-

gent (Kolodny, 1981a; Masters et al., 1983). These criticisms also seem to lose sight of the fact that other sex therapy programs are reporting rates of success that are similar to those of the Masters and Johnson program (Arentewitz and Schmidt, 1983; Kaplan, 1989; Leiblum and Rosen, 1989; Wincze and Carey, 1991). One specific example is the recent report of Hawton, Catalan, and Fagg (1992) showing a positive treatment outcome for 69.4 percent in couples treated for erectile dysfunction.

Some critics of sex therapy have suggested that it is a dehumanizing, mechanistic process. Psychiatrist Natalie Shainess (1973), for example, argues that sex therapy "debases" sex and that Masters and Johnson "have tended to detach the sex act from the moods, feelings, and emotions of desire and love." In her view, sex therapy is a kind of "coaching that reduces one partner to a push-button operator" (Cadden, 1978, p. 487). Psychiatrist Thomas Szasz (1980, p. xvi) sees sex therapists as "determined to conceal moral values and social policies as medical diagnoses and treatment."

As most sex therapists agree, success or failure is a subjective commodity. Some sex therapy patients who are classified as "failures" may see their treatment as very beneficial. Others, who attained enough change in their sexual function to be called a "success" by their therapists, may continue to feel unhappy or anxious. Sometimes two partners disagree about whether therapy was helpful. In all these situations, it is impossible to say that one viewpoint is right or wrong.

Although sex therapy offers no instant, magical cures, a variety of studies show that it can be of significant help to many people. Furthermore, the gains made in sex therapy tend to be long-lasting rather than short-lived (Leiblum and Pervin, 1980). Thus, while sex therapy is no cure-all and some people admittedly require a different type of professional help, sex therapy has managed to improve the lives of thousands of people with sexual distress.

CHOOSING A SEX THERAPIST

Unfortunately, sex therapy is an unregulated profession today. People can call themselves sex therapists even if their "training" consists only of attending a few workshops or reading a book. Judging from letters received at the Masters & Johnson Institute and from situations we have encountered with our patients, there are fraudulent sex therapists who are deliberately bilking the public, and there are hundreds of well-meaning persons who try to do sex therapy but simply are not qualified. Worse yet, emotional problems may be created by improper therapy, sexual problems may worsen, and the lack of success may discourage a person from seeking further care.

To minimize the risk of falling prey to unqualified sex therapists, the following guidelines may be of assistance:

1. Turn first to sex therapy centers that are affiliated with universities, medical schools, or hospitals. Alternately, your local medical society, psychological association, or your family physician may be able to provide a list of qualified therapists. Two professional organizations, the Society for Sex Therapy and Research (New York, NY) and the American Association of Sex Educators, Counselors, and Therapists (Washington, DC), publish national directories. AASECT has a sex therapist certification program; SSTAR has tougher membership requirements that it believes are equivalent to certification.

2. Ask about the education and training of the sex therapist. Unless he or she is willing to discuss this with you, do not continue any further. In addition to a genuine graduate degree from a recognized university, be sure to verify that the therapist has received postgraduate training in sex therapy that included personal supervision. Attendance at a weekend seminar isn't the same as in-depth training.

3. Avoid therapists who make unrealistic promises or guarantees of cure and therapists who tell you that part of your "treatment" includes having sexual relations with them.

4. Be sure the therapist is willing to discuss treatment costs, schedules, and plans in an open, straightforward fashion. (Many sex therapy clinics have a sliding scale fee arrangement where charges are adjusted to the client's ability to pay.)

PREVENTING SEXUAL DYSFUNCTION

The prevention of sexual dysfunctions probably begins in the parenting role by providing children with sex information appropriate for their age and by permitting them to discuss sexuality in an open, honest fashion. Severely negative family attitudes about sex may predispose a child to later sexual difficulties. After childhood, the following pointers apply:

1. Approach sex as an opportunity for exploration and intimacy instead of as a job to be done. Goal-oriented sex creates performance demands, which can lead to spectatoring and impaired responsivity. Remember that there's no "right" way of having sex; it's a matter of personal interest and comfort.

2. Try to develop open, effective lines of communication with your partner. Guessing about what your partner wants is difficult at best; making your partner guess about your needs is equally problematic. Effective communication includes being able to say no just as well as yes: if you never say no, your partner can't be sure if your yes is genuine or not.

3. Don't believe everything you read or hear about sex. Many books and articles about how people "should" respond are oversimplified at best and may be inaccurate and misleading. It's easy to talk yourself into a problem by comparing yourself to what "others" say.

4. If you're having a sexual problem of any sort, discuss it with your partner instead of pretending it doesn't exist. Often, by using some of the sensate focus methods or the self-help readings listed at the end of this chapter, a solution can be found. *However, if the problem doesn't go away fairly quickly, seek professional help.* It's usually much easier to treat recent problems than problems that have solidified over a long time.

SUMMARY

1. Sexual dysfunctions are conditions in which the physical responses of sexual function are impaired. In males, the principle sexual dysfunctions are erectile dysfunction, premature ejaculation, ejaculatory incompetence, and retarded ejaculation; in women, they are anorgasmia, vaginismus, and dyspareunia.

2. Overall, about 10 to 20 percent of cases of sexual dysfunction have organic causes such as diabetes, alcoholism, infection, neurologic disease, and drugs. Psychosocial causes can be

classified as developmental (e.g., negative sex attitudes, sexual trauma), personal (e.g., anxiety, depresssion, guilt), or interpersonal (e.g., poor communication, relationship conflicts, hostility).

3. Inhibited sexual desire and sexual aversion are examples of sexual problems that do not necessarily cause dysfunction but can lead to considerable emotional distress.

4. Sex therapy as a distinct specialty originated with the work of Masters and Johnson. Their approach involves a cotherapy team working with couples on a daily basis over a two-week period emphasizing integration of physiologic and psychosocial information. Sex is seen as a natural function; sensate focus exercises are used to reduce anxiety and improve spontaneity; and methods such as the "squeeze" technique (for premature ejaculation) and use of vaginal dilators (for vaginismus) are sometimes employed along with careful attention to relationship dynamics.

5. Other approaches to therapy include Helen Kaplan's work (integrating sex therapy and psychoanalytic methods), behavioral models, Rational-Emotive therapy, and group therapy.

6. Although sex therapy is not foolproof, it has been shown to be highly effective in most studies. Many so-called sex therapists, however, have little or no formal training in the field, so it is important to choose a sex therapist carefully.

Thought Questions

1. Researchers have concluded that about 10 percent of women have never experienced coital orgasm. Do you think this finding is correct? Why or why not?

2. The text states that ejaculatory incompetence may be a potential source of sexual pleasure due to the man's ability to prolong coitus. Do you agree or disagree with this idea? Explain.

3. Psychological, familial, cultural, and biological factors can all contribute to the development of sexual dysfunction. How should these factors be changed to reduce the number of people who are sexually dysfunctional in our population?

4. Why do women fake orgasms? What are their motives? Is it always wrong for a woman to fake an orgasm? Can men accurately discrimi-

nate fake from real orgasms? *Should* men wonder whether their partners are faking? How should a man deal with these suspicions? How should a woman who has not had an orgasm but whose partner thinks she has respond to the situation? How should a woman who has been habitually faking orgasms and wants to change handle the situation?

5. Should a sex therapist *ever* engage in sexual activities with a client? How often do you think this happens? What if the client is attracted to the therapist and wants to engage in sex with him or her?

6. What should a couple who are committed to their relationship do if they find that they have very different levels of sexual needs? What if one member experiences sexual aversion or inhibited sexual desire? How should the partner best respond?

7. For most men who develop erectile dysfunctions, do you think they would prefer to learn that the cause was physiological or psychological in nature? Assuming the cause was psychological, how should the partner act so that she demonstrates sexual desire but at the same time avoids making what could be interpreted as a demand for performance?

Suggested Readings

Belliveau, Fred, and Richter, Lin. *Understanding Human Sexual Inadequacy.* New York: Bantam, 1970. A translation into nontechnical language of *Human Sexual Inadequacy,* accurately summarizing the content in easily readable form.

Castleman, M. *Sexual Solutions.* New York: Touchstone, 1989. An updated revision of a comprehensive guide to dealing with sexual problems, this book covers a lot of territory concerning sexual dysfunctions and sex therapy.

Heiman, Julia R., and LoPicolo, Joseph. *Becoming Orgasmic: A Sexual and Personal Growth Program for Women,* revised ed. New York: Simon & Schuster, 1988. A sensitively written book designed to help women overcome sexual differences.

Kaplan, Helen S. *How to Overcome Premature Ejaculation.* New York: Brunner/Mazel, 1989. This slim book (only 118 pages with large type) describes the causes and treatment of premature ejaculation in easy-to-understand terms.

Leiblum, S. R., and Rosen, R. C. (eds.). *Sexual Desire Disorders*. New York: Guilford Press, 1988. An outstanding collection of thoughtful and carefully documented papers summarizing the various treatment approaches to disorders of sexual desire.

Rosen, Raymond C., and Leiblum, Sandra R. *Erectile Disorders: Assessment and Treatment*. New York: Guilford Press, 1992. An authoritative, in-depth discussion of virtually all aspects of this topic presented along with extensive lists of references of the research and clinical literature.

Snarch, David. *Constructing the Sexual Crucible*. New York: Norton, 1991. An integration of sex therapy, marital therapy and family systems therapy that is difficult reading but filled with original insights. Best suited to graduate students or students with an extensive background in psychology or family therapy.

Wagner, Gorm, and Kaplan, Helen S. *The New Injection Treatment for Impotence: Medical and Psychological Aspects*. New York: Brunner/Mazel, 1993. An informative, clear description of one of the newest medical methods used in the treatment of severe erectile problems.

Wincze, John P., and Carey, Michael P. *Sexual Dysnfunction: A Guide for Assessment and Treatment*. New York: Guilford Press, 1991. A concise overview of current thinking about the causes, prevalence, and treatments of the sexual difficulties, loaded with practical pointers and thoughtful commentary.

Sexual Disorders and Sexual Health

Sexual health is tightly interwoven with total health: both depend on freedom from physical and emotional limitations. The preceding chapter emphasized emotional causes of sexual distress and ways of dealing with these problems. In this chapter, we consider the physical conditions that affect sexuality. Our discussion covers four major topics: sex and disability, the impact of illness on sexuality, drugs and sex, and infections involving the sex organs. Learning about these problems is important because it increases our understanding of the physiology of sex and helps us better grasp the emotional dimension of such situations.

SEX AND DISABILITY

A number of common myths and stereotypes about sexuality of disabled people have been identified by the Sex & Disability Project of George Washington University. These myths, which "can drastically and unnecessarily curtail the sexual expression of disabled people" (Chipouras et al., 1979), are as follows:

1. Disabled people are asexual.
2. Disabled people are dependent and childlike, so they need to be protected.
3. Disability breeds disability.
4. Disabled people should stay with and marry their own kind.

The joy of loving and being loved is shared by disabled people. Despite popular misconceptions, the disabled also have sexual feelings and needs which can be expressed in many ways.

5. Parents of handicapped children don't want sex education for their children.

6. Sexual intercourse culminating in orgasm is essential for sexual satisfaction.

7. If a disabled person has a sexual problem, it's almost always the result of the disability.

8. If a nondisabled person has a sexual relationship with a disabled individual, it's because he or she can't attract anyone else.

These myths collectively show how uncomfortable our society is with the idea of disabled persons as sexual beings. Somehow, many people seem to think, the disabled should worry about more important things in their lives and not concern themselves with an area that is obviously intended for healthy, "normal" people to enjoy. Fortunately, many of those who are disabled have refused to be intimidated by this line of reasoning and have joined forces with a number of workers in the health-care professions as activists in seeking more attention to the sexual needs and feelings of people who have one form of disability or another. In fact, this movement has led to the development of a sexual bill of rights for the disabled (Chipouras et al., 1979) that covers the following items:

1. The right to sexual expression.

2. The right to privacy.

3. The right to be informed.

4. The right to have access to needed services such as contraceptive counseling, medical care, genetic counseling, and sex counseling.

5. The right to choose one's marital status.

6. The right to have or not to have children.

7. The right to make decisions that affect one's life.

8. The right to develop to one's fullest potential.

Although we are not yet in an era when the disabled are totally free to exercise these rights, we have made considerable progress in this direction in the last decade. As attitudes toward the disabled continue to change and as our society accepts sexuality as a positive, enhancing aspect of all of our lives, we may finally see the disappearance of myths and stereotypes and a more tolerant, open, and informed attitude taking their place.

Spinal Cord Injuries

A dramatic example of the impact of a disability on sexuality can be seen in people who have had injuries of the spinal cord. These injuries occur in a variety of circumstances, such as auto or motorcycle accidents, stab or bullet wounds, crushing industrial accidents, diving accidents, and serious falls. The injury usually results in **para-**

PERSONAL PERSPECTIVES

Sex and Disability

Understanding the impact of a major disability on a person's sexuality is not simply a matter of understanding sexual physiology or even the medical side of the disability. The following candid observations explain, in their own ways, other aspects of the disability that may be eye-opening.

First, Don Smith talks about his reactions after a spinal cord injury at age 19:

> I felt asexual for a long time because a man's sex was supposed to be in his penis, and I couldn't feel my penis. So that contributed to my feeling of being asexual; it didn't occur to me that it felt good to have the back of my neck licked, or that it felt good to have my arms stroked lightly. Stroking the wrists, then to the arms, then up the arms is a sequence that I've since learned can be very exciting.

> A lot of my first sexual contacts were just to gain experience. I wanted to find out what was going on and what I liked. With the help of two really excellent lovers, I learned about my body. I learned to take goals out of my lovemaking; I don't have to have intercourse or any kind of penetration if I'm going to have sex. I don't even have to do anything with the genitals if I'm going to have sex. I can take my time; I feel less pressure and less performance anxiety. That's not to say it's all gone, because it's there; I want to be there for my partner. *(Bullard and Knight, 1981, p. 16)*

A spinal-cord-injured woman discusses some aspects of her relationships with men:

> I find that I am often suspicious of the motives of men who are attracted to me sexually. That is, some men want to be caretakers; some men can't find able-bodied partners (and assume that disabled women are also unable to find partners). Other men are sexually intrigued with disabled women, believing they will have a "kinky" experience; some men want a "strong mother confessor" figure they can depend on or want a woman who will be totally dependent on them. I don't intend to do a general indictment of the whole male race, but I do believe disabled women must be very selective in choosing partners.

> Many of my relationships have matured into strong relationships with sexual dimensions, some of my partners have been "affairs," flings, one-night stands, etc. During my sexually active years, I have had several different partners; among them three long-term relationships. 1 with a gay woman. *(Becker, 1978)*

A 25-year-old woman with cerebral palsy talks about her sexual feelings:

plegia (paralysis of the legs) or quadriplegia (paralysis of all four limbs) and loss of all sensations in the body below the level of the injury. Normal bowel and bladder control is usually lost, and persons with spinal cord injuries are apt to have a significant loss of sexual function as well.

When I was a teenager, I was intensely jealous of the beautiful, able-bodied women I saw on television and in the movies. I thought that sex was for them, not me, and I was angry because I knew I'd never have a baby. In fact, I was pretty much resigned to never finding a husband and being celibate all my life.

Fortunately, I learned how to masturbate at age 12 or 13. I figured out a way of getting a rubber hose attachment from the faucet near my genitals while I was bathing, and I quickly found myself looking forward to baths for reasons quite apart from cleanliness. The almost electric, tingly feelings of sexual excitement began to build up for me slowly for hours before bath time, and the sudden surge of a climax was sheer joy. Even now, years later, I still get excited thinking about this wonderful way of stimulating myself or having a partner do it for me. But what was most important was that my discovery of the joys of masturbating let me know that I was a sexual being, that it was legitimate to have these feelings. *(Authors' files)*

Finally, consider the comments of a man remembering his reactions after a spinal cord injury resulting in quadriplegia at age 16:

At home I felt like the town eunuch for a few years. I saw a lot of the women I had been dating before I broke my neck, but now there was nothing sexual going on between us. I kept secretly blaming them for not giving me a chance, not treating me as needing or wanting or even being capable of having a sexual relationship. Now I realize that I wasn't acting like I needed or wanted or was capable of having a sexual relationship. The simple truth was that I was just plain scared. I didn't know what I could do, how I could plea-sure or be pleasured, and I sure didn't want to look like a jerk while trying to find out, or worse yet, find out I was a failure and face the eventual rejection.

My eunuch years also included a lot of martyrdom. I remember deciding that if I ever really fell in love with someone, I would end the relationship because I thought, being in a wheelchair, I could never really make anyone happy. *(Bullard and Knight, 1981, pp. 65–66)*

As these heartfelt recollections show, the disabled are very much interested in and able to have sexual feelings and relationships. It is the mistaken assumptions of an able-bodied society that impose an asexual image on these individuals, which is equivalent to denying the very core of their humanity.

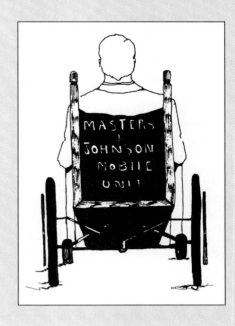

Most spinal-cord-injured (SCI) men lose the ability to have normal erections in response to psychological arousal, although they may be able to have

paraplegia paralysis of both lower extremities.
quadriplegia (kwahd ruh pleej' ee ah) paralysis of all limbs.

brief reflex erections (which they cannot feel) in response to mechanical stimulation such as pinching or rubbing close to the genitals. In some cases, SCI males have partial erections in response to psychological stimuli such as watching erotic movies or listening to erotic tapes but don't realize that they're responding in this manner (Kennedy and Over, 1990). Most (but not all) SCI males also become infertile and lose the ability to ejaculate. [Szasz and Carpenter (1989) state that under 10 percent of men with complete spinal cord injuries experience ejaculation with intercourse.] Those who are still able to ejaculate do so with no pelvic sensations of orgasm, and in many of the cases retrograde ejaculation (a backflow of semen into the bladder) occurs. On the other hand, intercourse may be possible for about four out of five men with incomplete spinal cord injuries. Even when erections do not occur, a technique called "stuffing" can be used. This involves tucking the soft or semifirm penis into the vagina, with the woman thrusting her hips, taking care not to move so the penis falls out.

Women with spinal cord injuries generally have normal fertility and can have children. While they usually retain their interest in sex, they typically lose their genital sensations and orgasmic responsiveness, and their vaginal lubrication is greatly reduced. Some SCI women—as well as SCI men—report experiencing "phantom" (nongenital) orgasms which include both psychological feelings of orgasm (e.g., intense pleasure) and physical sensations in some unaffected areas of the body that resemble prior patterns of orgasmic response.

Many people cannot understand why a spinal-cord-injured person who has no genital sensations would want to have intercourse. While the motivations of all cord-injured people are not the same, the following reasons are commonly given by people in this situation:

1. Having intercourse is a special act of sharing and intimacy quite apart from genital feelings.

2. Having intercourse can be intensely *psychologically* arousing.

3. Being able to engage in intercourse can provide a boost to a person's self-concept.

In addition, many cord-injured males mention that being able to have intercourse makes them feel more like a man, while some cord-injured females note that having intercourse enhances their sense of femininity. There are also some cord-injured persons who have intercourse primarily to please their partner (just as some people *without* cord injuries do, too).

While a number of people have pointed out that the SCI woman is less handicapped sexually than the SCI man because she is still able to have intercourse, this is an oversimplification of a complex issue and perpetuates a view of females as sexually passive. Many cord-injured women are distressed by their sexual limitations and require counseling to help them reaffirm their sexuality (Thornton, 1979). Unfortunately, as Zwerner (1982) points out, sexuality counseling is not included in many rehabilitation programs for SCI women, forcing many to seek out such services on their own or to do without their potential benefits.

The sexual abilities of the spinal-cord-injured and their ways of coping with their situation vary greatly. While some adopt a completely defeatist attitude and avoid all sexual opportunities, others have a continuing interest in sex which they express through active involvement with a partner. What must be stressed is that there are many methods of sexual interaction besides intercourse (Mooney, Cole, and Chilgren, 1975). Oral–genital sex, kissing, use of a vibrator (which a quadriplegic can sometimes apply by holding the base with his or her teeth), massage, and cuddling are only a few of the available options for having intimacy and sexual pleasure. In fact, recent research has shown that applying a vibrator directly to the penis of a cord-injured man produces a predictable series of body reactions that are quite similar to the nongenital physical changes found in the sexual response cycle of non-SCI men (Szasz and Carpenter, 1989). (Note: This type of stimulation should only be used in SCI males with medical consultation because there is a high risk of a dangerous reaction of soaring blood pressure and severe headache unless the proper medication is used in advance.) In addition, many SCI people find that unaffected regions of their body become extraordinarily sensitive and erotic, so that stimulation above the region of sensory loss can produce arousal and sometimes orgasm.

It is also possible for the SCI man with permanently impaired erections to have a device implanted surgically that will permit him to have erections and to participate in intercourse. (This topic is discussed in more detail on pages 625–626 later in this chapter.)

An experimental procedure called electroejaculation now offers some hope for fathering children to the nation's 145,000 spinal-cord-injured men who had previously been considered infertile (Raymond, 1987). The procedure, which is based on a method widely used in animal husbandry, involves inserting a probe into the rectum and then passing an electric current into the instrument until ejaculation is electrically induced. While this method is far from foolproof, and has a small but definite risk of injury to the rectum, success rates of about 45 percent have been attained so far (Bennett et al., 1988).

Blindness and Deafness

If a person is blind or deaf from birth (or from a very young age), the sexual learning that occurs during childhood and adolescence can be seriously hindered. The person who has been blind since birth, for instance, is deprived of the ability to see the various shapes of human bodies both clothed and undressed that most of us silently notice and learn from. As a result, the person with life-long blindness may be quite uncertain about the anatomic relation of one part of the body to another. (One 15-year-old boy was quite surprised to learn that the female breasts weren't located just above the waist, where he imagined them to be.) The person who has been deaf since birth often has difficulty understanding abstract concepts like maleness, parenting, and intimacy (FitzGerald and FitzGerald, 1977). Since very few parents of deaf children can communicate with them effectively with sign language, sex education in the home is often difficult.

Neither blindness nor deafness produces any physical limitations on the body's sexual responsivity in and of itself. However, the sexual ignorance of many deaf or blind persons may create a predisposition toward sexual and relationship problems. In addition, the distorted body image and poor self-esteem that many deaf or blind persons experience can also contribute to later sexual difficulties. Since blind persons do not have the visual cues surrounding sexual behavior that most of us depend on, and deaf people are apt to have significant problems in communicating with others, it's not surprising that such difficulties might occur.

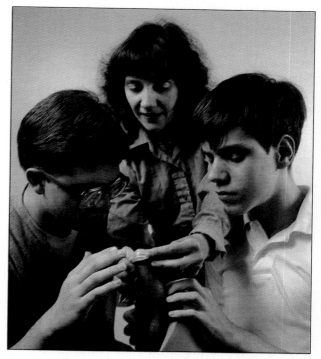

Two blind students are being educated about using condoms by an instructor using lifelike plastic models. This type of sex education is invaluable to persons with sensory disabilities.

Fortunately, sex education curricula have been devised for the deaf and blind. Most of these programs emphasize both social and biological aspects of sexuality and make good use of innovative methods of teaching as well. For instance, blind students may be given sex-related articles like condoms, tampons, birth control pill packages, and vibrators to handle, so they develop familiarity with these products by touch. In fact, in Europe the touch method is sometimes used for anatomy lessons with live nude models (Helsinga, 1974). Many deaf students are now being taught by sex educators trained in sign language, and special visual materials have been prepared to make sex education easier despite the existence of hearing impairment.

Mental Retardation

Until very recently, people who are mentally retarded have been viewed as either asexual (in a state of childlike innocence) or as totally impulse-ridden and unable to control their primitive sexual urges. These myths, along with the general public's distaste for seeing the retarded as persons in their own right, have combined to make the topic of sexuality and the retarded a threatening one that arouses indignation and sometimes anger. One reflection of this attitude that has recently been changed was the involuntary sterilization that was often performed on young retarded adults or even adolescents to ensure that they couldn't reproduce (even though there is no evidence that most forms of retardation are genetically transmitted).

It is important to recognize that not all mentally retarded people are alike in their learning capacity, emotional stability, social skills, or capacity for independent living. The mildly retarded, for example, are educable and often lead productive lives, holding jobs, marrying, and raising families. Their lives are often indistinguishable from the lives of "normal" people, and they are usually capable of learning responsible sexual behavior without difficulty (Monat, 1982). The moderately retarded do not fit into our society so easily and are more apt to behave in a childlike manner both sexually and in other areas of living. They may alarm people by masturbating or disrobing in public or acting in a fashion that appears to be reckless or aggressive when showing affection for others, and they often require a protected or restricted environment to live their lives as comfortably and safely as possible. Yet they too are capable of learning much about sexuality and reproduction; for example, they can be taught how babies are conceived, what menstruation is (and how to deal with it), and how to channel their sexual impulses into appropriate (i.e., nonpublic) masturbation. They also can learn how to avoid taking advantage of others and how to avoid sexual abuse. The severely or profoundly retarded, who must generally be institutionalized for their own safety, present a different range of problems since they are much more difficult to teach and are often capable of only the most rudimentary forms of communication.

The primary way of helping retarded people learn to handle their sexual feelings and express their sexual desires is through appropriate sex education. Kempton (1978) notes: "The retarded need sex education more than anyone else because they cannot readily learn about sexuality from friends, books, or from observing the behavior of others, and they have more than usual difficulty with sorting out reality from unreality" (p. 138). In addition, cause-and-effect relationships are not always clear

to the retarded; for instance, they may not realize that having intercourse can cause pregnancy. While some parents of retarded children have worried that sex education simply puts ideas into their children's heads, the available evidence suggests that withholding sex information does not deter sexual behavior and providing sex education does not lead to irresponsible sexual acts: in fact, just the opposite is likely to happen (Kempton, 1978; Monat, 1982).

A number of specific issues regarding sex and the mentally retarded are too complex to discuss meaningfully here. These issues include the following:

1. Providing privacy for the institutionalized retarded.

2. Providing appropriate contraceptive protection for the retarded. (In general, the IUD seems to be the best option for retarded women who are sexually active. Birth control pills are appropriate for use by the mildly retarded, but condoms, diaphragms, and foams are usually not practical since they are too easily forgotten and too difficult for many to use.)

3. Providing opportunities for long-term relationships and marriage, if desired.

Further information about these and related topics can be found in several books listed at the end of this chapter.

SEX AND MEDICAL ILLNESS

A wide variety of medical illnesses cause sexual problems. Until fairly recently, these situations were generally overlooked by health-care professionals, who were often uncomfortable discussing sexuality, uninformed about sexual aspects of illness, and untrained in providing useful ways of dealing with these problems. Fortunately, this situation is rapidly changing today because fundamental research in this area is increasing and most health-care schools include specific education about sexuality in their curricula.

Illnesses affect sexuality in direct and indirect ways. Physically, an illness can disrupt the normal reflexes of sexual response, as seen in persons with multiple sclerosis. Sometimes the treatment of an illness creates a sexual problem: medications that cause sexual side effects or surgery that results in sexual impairment are common examples. In other instances, sexual problems arise from the general effects of illness such as weakness, fatigue, or pain. There is an emotional side too: people with an illness may assume that it is "wrong" for them to have sexual feelings or may believe erroneously that their illness will prevent them from enjoying sex or from functioning sexually.

Now we describe the sexual problems encountered in some specific types of medical disorders.

Neurologic Conditions

Sexual behavior and sexual function are both controlled in important ways by the nervous system. The brain itself is the ultimate synthesizer of sensory input (touch, sight, sound, taste, smell) and transforms electric impulses sent to it by nerve fibers into perceptions of pleasure, pain, and human emotion. Similarly, impulses sent from the brain to other organs, including the genitals, translate sexual desire into sexual response. For these reasons, it is easy to see why many diseases or injuries of the nervous system can lead to sexual difficulties.

Multiple sclerosis (MS) is a disease that typically affects young adults and involves patchy damage to the protective covering of nerves throughout the body. Loss of erections and ejaculation eventually affects more than half of men with MS (Schover et al., 1988), while difficulty reaching orgasm (or complete anorgasmia) affects a similar fraction of women (Lilius, Valtonen, and Wikström, 1976). Early in the disease there may be a partial numbness in the genitals, and sometimes any type of touch to the affected body region produces irritating, unpleasant sensations (Lundberg, 1977). For this reason, painful intercourse is another common problem. The sexual effects of MS tend to vary over time, so a person may have difficulties for several weeks or months and then go through a period of relatively normal sexual function.

People with **brain tumors** are somewhat less likely to encounter sexual difficulties. Although pituitary or hypothalamic tumors commonly cause erectile dysfunction and decreased sexual desire (Lundberg and Wide, 1978), tumors in other regions of the brain do not usually lead to sexual problems. **Epilepsy** is another neurologic disorder with little physical effect on sexual function (Jensen et al., 1990). Some people with epilepsy,

however, feel inferior because of their condition and may avoid sexual opportunities in the mistaken fear that arousal will cause a seizure. Although **polio** can cause spinal cord damage, it affects muscular function, not sensations. For this reason, most people with paralysis from polio are not impaired in their sexual function, although their inability to move may create problems in coital thrusting.

Another common neurologic condition is **Alzheimer's disease,** which affects an estimated 2 to 4 percent of people over age 65 (American Psychiatric Association, 1987). Alzheimer's disease is a progressive form of degenerative brain disease of unknown cause that produces dementia, usually resulting in death after five to seven years. People with Alzheimer's disease usually have a loss of brain functions, including difficulties with memory, judgment, and abstract thought. There is usually speech impairment and deterioration in mental alertness, along with personality changes, but these features may be minimal early in the disease. According to Shapira and Cummings (1989), the most typical pattern of sexual behavior shown by male Alzheimer victims is a loss of interest in sex. However, there was marked variability in their sample, with a small number of Alzheimer patients showing a heightened interest in sex. These researchers also noted that it was common for the wife of the Alzheimer's patient to stop having sex with her husband as he became increasingly dependent and childlike, and as caring for him became more and more of a drain on her time. This sometimes caused considerable guilt on the wife's part, however.

multiple sclerosis (MS) a chronic neurological disorder affecting both motor and sensory function in an episodic but progressive fashion.

brain tumors abnormal growths in the brain which can either be malignant (cancerous) or nonmalignant.

epilepsy a disease of unknown origin marked by the periodic occurrence of seizures (convulsions).

polio an infection caused by a virus that can, in severe forms, cause paralysis.

Alzheimer's disease a progressive form of degenerative brain disease that causes dementia (deterioration of mental abilities).

FOCUS IN BRIEF

Sexual Dysfunction in Diabetic Males

- Erectile dysfunction affects approximately 50 percent of men with diabetes.
- In more than 90 percent of the cases, the erectile difficulties have a gradual onset, typically progressing from occasional episodes of erectile failure to complete impotence over a period of 6 to 12 months.
- Characteristically, the male's sex drive remains normal and ejaculation is undisturbed.
- The primary causes of erectile dysfunction due to diabetes are diabetic nerve damage and abnormalities in the small blood vessels supplying the penis.
- Approximately 1 percent of diabetic men develop retrograde ejaculation, a condition in which semen spurts backward into the bladder at the time of ejaculation.
- The erectile dysfunction caused by diabetes does not usually lessen genital sensations.
- Penile implants can be used to permit the diabetic male to have intercourse successfully.

Endocrine Conditions

The most common type of endocrine disorder is **diabetes,** which affects approximately 4 percent of the U.S. population. About 50 percent of diabetic men have erectile dysfunction, which either can be an early symptom of this disorder or may not occur for many years after the diagnosis (Podolsky, 1983; Pfeifer, 1988). Retrograde ejaculation occurs in about 1 percent of diabetic men, but sex drive is usually unaffected. Although the sexual difficulties of diabetic men had been well known for at least two centuries, sexual problems in diabetic women were not identified until the 1970s. Although one study found that about one-third of diabetic women have secondary anorgasmia, which usually occurs four to six years after the disease is discovered (Kolodny, 1971), other studies have not completely confirmed this finding. A report by Jensen

(1986), for instance, found that 14 percent of diabetic females had orgasmic dysfunction and 20 percent had reduced sexual desire. In addition, some diabetic women have problems with vaginal lubrication. Prather (1988) provides a review of previous research in this area.

The primary cause of these sexual problems in both diabetic men and women is a form of nerve damage that is a complication of diabetes (Rowland et al., 1989; Tejada et al., 1989). In a smaller fraction of cases, these dysfunctions are due to circulatory problems. Unfortunately, both types of problems tend to be permanent and untreatable (except for the possibility of using penile implants to overcome erectile dysfunction). In cases where diabetics have sexual difficulties for other reasons, such as anxiety or poor communication, sex therapy can be beneficial (Kolodny, Masters, and Johnson, 1979; Clarke, 1988).

Disorders of the pituitary, thyroid, or adrenal glands are also commonly associated with sexual difficulties. In each of these conditions, sex drive is likely to be altered along with sexual function. About 40 percent of women with an underactive thyroid or adrenal glands have orgasmic difficulties, and a similar percentage of men have problems with erections (Kolodny, Masters, and Johnson, 1979). Sexual dysfunction is even higher in people with underactive pituitary glands. Fortunately, these conditions are easily treatable by giving the proper amount of the "missing" hormone in pill form.

Heart Disease

In severe forms of chronic heart disease, the capacity for sexual activity is likely to be greatly limited. In milder types of heart problems, however, there may be no physical limitation on sexual activity. Nevertheless, several studies of men who had heart attacks have shown that six months to a year after recovery, sexual difficulties are common (Singh et al., 1970; Green, 1975; Mehta and Krop, 1979). The primary factor here is not a physical one but a mental one: anxiety, misconception, and avoidance conspire to create sexual difficulties. The man may be worried that his heart attack will cause sexual problems or that sexual excitement will cause another heart attack. This worry is also expressed in stories about men dying from a massive heart attack in the midst of a passionate sexual episode. There is no solid evidence to support this as a meaningful risk for most heart patients, and the cardiac cost of sexual activity—including intercourse and orgasm—seems to be about the same as the cost incurred in walking up two flights of steps (Masur, 1979; McLane, Krop, and Mehta, 1980). Women who have had heart attacks seem to be less likely to develop subsequent sexual problems than men (Kolodny, Masters, and Johnson, 1979; Schover and Jensen, 1988).

Cancer

Until the last decade, most people have automatically assumed that a person with cancer could not possibly have sexual feelings or sexual needs. Now it is clear that this view is incorrect, and increasing attention is being paid to the sexuality of people with cancer (Derogatis and Kourlesis, 1981). Several types of cancer and their impact on sexuality will be briefly examined.

Breast Cancer

According to the most recent statistics, an American woman has a 1 in 8 lifetime chance of developing breast cancer. In fact, breast cancer is now the most frequent female cancer and the second leading cause of cancer death in women after lung cancer (Elixhauser, 1992). More than 150,000 new cases of breast cancer are discovered each year, and late detection seriously lowers the chances of survival.

Unfortunately, more than a third of women with breast cancer only discover this condition accidentally (Lund, 1988; Harris et al., 1992). Most don't routinely examine their own breasts or have mammography (x-rays of the breasts), even though the medical evidence is strong that such procedures can be life-saving. In fact, for the first time ever, 11 major medical organizations such as the American Cancer Society, the National Cancer Institute, and the American Medical Association have finally come to agree that all women age 40 or over should undergo mammography. Indeed, the evidence from several research studies shows that deaths from breast cancer can be reduced by 20 to 40 percent by the routine use of mammography (Tabar et al., 1985; Roberts et al., 1990; Frisell et al., 1991; Day, 1991; Centers for Disease Control, SS-2, 1992).

Mammography is an important screening procedure to identify breast cancer in its earliest stages, when it is most easily treated.

A mammogram, which costs about $100, can detect tumors as small as the point of a pencil—tumors that are far too small to be detected by a woman during a breast self-exam (or a physician during a physical examination). The actual procedure involves x-raying each breast separately while it is placed in a compression device that exerts gentle pressure on the breast, flattening it so that an accurate x-ray picture can be taken. A side view and a front-to-back view of each breast are usually taken, for a total of four x-rays. The great majority of women (88 percent) undergoing mammography report no discomfort with the procedure or only mild discomfort; only 2 percent report severe discomfort or actual pain (Stomper et al., 1988).

While experts agree that there is no need for women under age 35 to have a mammogram because breast cancer is unusual in this age range, many suggest that women between the ages of 35

diabetes a chronic disorder of how the body handles sugar because of an insulin deficiency. Complications of this disease include circulatory and neurological problems.

FOCUS IN BRIEF

A Woman's Risk of Breast Cancer

By age 25: 1 in 19,608
By age 30: 1 in 2,525
By age 35: 1 in 622
By age 40: 1 in 217
By age 45: 1 in 93
By age 50: 1 in 50
By age 55: 1 in 33
By age 60: 1 in 24
By age 65: 1 in 17
By age 70: 1 in 14
By age 75: 1 in 11
By age 80: 1 in 10
By age 85: 1 in 9
Lifetime Risk: 1 in 8

Source: *National Cancer Institute, 1993.*

and 39 should have one mammogram done to serve as a baseline to be compared to future screenings. Current recommendations are that women in their 40s should have a mammogram every two years unless they have a family history of breast cancer, in which case they should be screened annually. From age 50 on, women should ideally have a mammogram every year.

In addition, recent studies by the Breast Cancer Detection Demonstration Project provide a way of calculating a woman's risk for developing breast cancer. The calculation involves an equation that utilizes four factors: age when menstruation began, whether her mother or sisters have had breast cancer, her age at the birth of her first live-born child, and the number of negative breast biopsies a woman has had.

A number of variables that are important predictors of breast cancer risk have been identified. Clearly, a family history of breast cancer is the single most important risk factor: if a woman's mother had breast cancer before age 60, the woman's relative risk is doubled, while if a woman has two first-degree relatives (mother, sisters, grandmothers) who have had this disease, her relative risk is three

to five times higher than for women without such a history (Gail et al., 1989; Harris et al., 1992).

It is hoped that by identifying women at particularly high risk for breast cancer, they can be encouraged to take steps geared toward both prevention and early detection. Possible preventive actions include, for example, losing weight if the woman is overweight, lowering fat consumption, and stopping the use of alcohol, since each of these factors has been tied to an increased risk of breast cancer. Early detection can be improved by regular monthly breast self-exams and by regular mammograms from age 40 on. The value of early detection is quite clear from this statistic: when found at a localized stage, five-year cancer survival rates usually exceed 85 percent (King, 1989).

In the past, breast cancer was typically treated by **mastectomy,** either **radical mastectomy,** an operation to remove the affected breast and lymph nodes adjacent to the breast, or by **total mastectomy,** which removed the entire affected breast. Since 1985, following the publication of a landmark study showing that less extensive (and disfiguring) surgery was equivalent in effectiveness to these approaches (Fisher, et al. 1985) many physicians (and many women) favor less drastic procedures such as "lumpectomy," which involves removing the tumor while conserving as much breast tissue as possible.

While such breast-conserving surgery is only suitable for women with breast cancer in an early stage (and is usually combined with radiation therapy for best results), it is notable that this approach is used far less often than would seem to be warranted (NIH Consensus Development Conference, 1991; Hand et al., 1991; Lazovich et al., 1991; Fisher et al., 1993; Veronesi et al., 1993; Swain, 1993). This is probably a reflection of several different factors. First, surgeons' attitudes towards their patients undoubtedly play a role. For example, surgeons seem to offer breast-conserving surgery more frequently to younger women and less frequently to older women (Greenfield et al., 1987; Silliman et al., 1989; Liberati et al., 1991; Ganz, 1992). (This ageist bias is accompanied by a second inherent bias among mostly male surgeons when it comes to treating breast cancer patients: from what we have seen [and this point has yet to be substantiated by formalized research], surgeons are more likely to recommend breast-conserving surgery to single women than to married women. As one male chauvinist surgeon explained to us, "A single woman needs to have her figure in order to find a husband; a married woman doesn't need to worry so much about her figure.")

Second, many women who are presented with the option of breast-conserving surgery choose to have the more extensive procedures because of their inherent fears about the nature of breast cancer. Since it might *seem* to the uninformed patient that more extensive surgery is, if not always more effective, at least safer (especially in terms of eliminating the risk of recurrence of cancer in the same breast, if a good portion of that breast is left intact), it should not be surprising that so many women opt for what seems to them a "better" form of surgery. Sadly, most physicians have not made an effort to educate women enough to counter this prevailing attitude. Certainly, evidence that women who undergo breast-conserving surgery have a better postoperative body image than those who have more extensive procedures should not be taken lightly.

Whatever type of surgery is chosen for the woman with breast cancer, concerns about subsequent sexuality abound. Although surgery of the breast does not directly affect a woman's sexuality in a physiological sense, the breasts have been so thoroughly eroticized and made an ersatz symbol of female sexuality in our society that most women react to the prospect of breast surgery with dread. This reaction, which may express itself to different degrees in different women, encompasses several component parts. First, many women feel a primary threat to their physical attractiveness as a result of cancer surgery on the breast. (This is largely because the breasts have been so enthusiastically enshrined as a cultural icon of a woman's femininity and sexual desirability; if a different body part had played this role, mastectomy would presumably be less threatening to us all.) This self-perceived loss of attractiveness translates for some women into diminished self-worth, a sense of helplessness, and (not surprisingly) an increased risk of depression.

Second, many women faced with the prospect of a mastectomy worry about sexual rejection by their partners or prospective partners. These worries reflect fundamental anxieties about the nature of intimacy, the partner's reaction to the cancer as well as the surgery, and, in some cases, the woman's fear that she may become less sexual herself because of her illness. As one sex therapist has described it (Witkin, 1975):

It almost goes without saying that the difficulties the woman might have in accepting and accommodating to the loss of a breast arise in large measure from her fears of how others will respond. The pain of rejection increases with intimacy, and the woman's greatest fears revolve around the man with whom she is most intimate. What many women fear is rejection not only in the form of aversion or denial but also rejection in the form of pity; for whereas empathy and concern imply an awareness of the woman's feelings of loss and fear, pity implies a belief that the woman has *really* been diminished, and involves not a sharing of her feelings but a reinforcement of her fantasies of incompleteness and worthlessness.

Even in relationships where a woman has no reason to doubt her mate's love or dedication, it is common to find that she harbors secret doubts that her partner will still find her desirable after her surgery. And we have found that after a mastectomy, many women question their sexual partners to check on the authenticity of their sexual interest and enjoyment so often that the male may become exasperated with the repetitive nature of the interrogation. As one husband said, "I can understand why Mary was worried, but after the twelfth time I'd told her that I still thought she was sexy and I still loved making love with her, you'd think the matter could be put to rest." The fact is that simple rational answers do not always sink in immediately and are often not accepted at face value in the understandably emotional aftermath of a health problem of such consequence as breast cancer; furthermore, while the best reassurances are undoubtedly the behavioral ones (what you do, instead of what you say), verbal reassurances can be extraordinarily valuable in helping a person adjust to a situation that seems threatening and unpredictable at its very core.

It is notable that the frequency of breast stimulation during sexual activity declines substantially after a mastectomy for many women (Frank et al., 1978). This reflects two separate facts: many men tend to avoid touching the uninvolved breast (fear-

mastectomy (mas tek′ tuh mē) surgical removal of the breast. In **radical mastectomy** the affected breast and lymph nodes are removed, while in **total mastectomy** the entire affected breast is removed.

ing that this will remind the woman of her illness and her loss), while many women who have had mastectomies clearly prefer to put any form of breast play off limits for reasons of psychological security. In addition, it is fairly common to find that women who have had mastectomies are especially self-conscious about complete nudity during sex. For some women, avoiding direct reminders of the existence of their surgical scar extends to a change in preferred coital positions. The number of women who never use the female-on-top position, which is the sexual position that involves the most direct visualization of the missing breast for the male, triples after a mastectomy.

Although there is clearly no uniform response pattern among women, and past responses to stressful situations may not reliably predict how any particular woman will react to the news of breast cancer and the psychological traumas of a mastectomy (or partial mastectomy), there does appear to be some evidence that single, younger women are more apt to see their prognosis as a devastating one in social terms. (Fortunately, breast cancer is far less common among younger women than those over 60.) On the other hand, there are also single younger women who survive breast cancer with aplomb, allowing it to have as little impact on their psyches and sex lives as possible. "It was a question of giving in to a sense of being invaded and impaired or insisting on leading the active sex life I always had," one single women told us. "Yes, there are some jerks out there who were put off by my mastectomy, but I would have realized these men were jerks even before my surgery."

As of this writing, the U.S. Food and Drug Administration's partial ban on silicone-gel breast implants because of safety concerns has made many breast cancer patients leery of reconstructive breast surgery even though the FDA permits such devices (and similar implants filled with saline rather than silicone gel) if the woman receiving it agrees to participate in an FDA-approved clinical trial.

Cancer of the Cervix and Uterus

Cancer of the cervix accounts for slightly more than 60,000 new cases of cancer annually, and cancer of the lining of the uterus is found in another 38,000 women (Silverberg, 1981). Risk factors include infection with herpes simplex virus type 2 or human papilloma virus (Raymond, 1987; Layde, 1989) and may also include cigarette smoking (Slattery et al.,

1989). There are two forms of cervical cancer: carcinoma in situ (CIS) and invasive cancer of the cervix (ICC). Although neither form is likely to cause symptoms, both can be detected by Pap smears during routine pelvic exams. CIS is really a precancerous condition involving cells on the surface of the cervix that do not invade other tissues. On average, it takes eight years or more for CIS to progress to true cancer, or ICC (Eddy, 1980; Richart and Barron, 1980). Treatment of CIS while it is still precancerous results in virtually 100 percent long-term survival. Treatment of ICC depends on whether the cancer cells have spread beyond the cervix: either surgical techniques or radiation therapy can be used. Sexual difficulties are common but depend on the amount of pelvic scarring that occurs (Abitbol and Davenport, 1974; Lamberti, 1979). One report suggests that surgery is less disruptive to sexual function than radiation therapy (Seibel, Freeman, and Graves, 1980).

Cancer of the lining of the uterus is rare before age 40 and is usually marked by abnormal bleeding early in its course. Later symptoms include cramping, pelvic discomfort, bleeding after intercourse, or lumps in the groin. Pap smears are *not* a foolproof way of detecting this form of cancer; usually a D&C (dilation and curettage, scraping the inside of the uterus) is done to establish the diagnosis. Depending on the findings, treatment ranges from surgery (removal of the uterus and ovaries) to radiation therapy, drug therapy, or hormone therapy. If the cancer has not spread beyond the uterus, the patient has an 83 percent chance of being cured—that is, of not having the cancer recur within the next five years (Silverberg, 1981). Surgical removal of the uterus, called **hysterectomy,** does not usually have any negative effects on female sexual function. It may actually be beneficial since physical problems such as bleeding or cramping are corrected. However, some women have impaired sexual responsiveness and/or decreased sexual interest after a hysterectomy because they see the operation as a lessening of their femininity (Utian, 1975; Dennerstein, Wood, and Burrows, 1977; Roeske, 1978).

Cancer of the Prostate

Cancer of the prostate is the second most common cancer and the second most common cause of death from cancer among men; in 1992, an estimated 132,000 men were diagnosed with this disease and 34,000 were estimated to have died (Office of Surveillance and Analysis, 1992). The condition is relatively rare under age 40 and often produces no physical symptoms; it is generally diagnosed by a rectal examination, although a newly developed blood test, the PSA test (for "prostate specific antigen") shows promise as a screening method (Catalona et al., 1991; Carter et al., 1992; Oesterling, 1992). However, prostate cancer is unusual because in at least three-quarters of cases, it will not spread and will not result in death (Moon, 1992; Johansson et al., 1992). Nevertheless, vigorous forms of treatment for prostate cancer, including surgery—called **prostatectomy** (the surgical removal of the prostate gland)—the use of estrogen therapy, and radiation therapy, have often been recommended in the past. Unfortunately, these treatments carry substantial risks of subsequent sexual dysfunction.

Prostate surgery done for cancer causes subsequent erectile insufficiency in a large number of cases, but the risk depends on the type of operation performed. In so-called radical surgery, where a wide operative dissection is performed (and the seminal vesicles are removed as well as the prostate), postoperative impotence is almost inevitable because of damage to the nerve pathways that control erection. In simpler surgical procedures also using the perineal approach (making an incision in the perineum, the area between the base of the penis and the rectum), there is still a 40 to 50 percent rate of postoperative erectile failure (Kolodny, Masters, and Johnson, 1979). Men who have penile implants inserted after such surgery to permit them to function sexually are generally unable to ejaculate, because all semen-producing glands have been surgically removed. In some cases, so-called "dry" orgasms—no ejaculation, but normal rhythmic orgasmic contractions in the rectal and pelvic area—occur in these men postoperatively, but most men complain that these give them a very minimal sort of orgasmic sensation (Schover and Jensen, 1988). Radiation treatment of prostatic cancer, which is often combined with estrogen therapy, also produces high rates of sexual dysfunction. Estrogen of course reduces the man's sex drive considerably and may also be the key component in this treatment regime that causes impotence, as well.

Cancer of the Testis
Cancer of the testis is a relatively rare condition that is most common in the twenties and thirties. Since only about half of these cancers are accompanied by pain, it is important for males to learn a method of testicular self-examination (see the boxed item on page 65) and to seek prompt medical attention if a testicular lump or swelling is noticed.

Treatment of testicular cancer (surgery, drugs, radiation) is sometimes a cause of sexual dysfunction and generally results in infertility. It is common to find that men with this form of cancer develop considerable guilt over their previous sexual practices, often blaming the problem incorrectly on masturbation, sexually transmitted disease, or an "overactive" sex life. Other men with this problem feel that the surgical removal of one testis makes them "less than a man." They may also develop fears of sexual performance and spectatoring, leading to difficulty with erection for strictly psychological reasons.

DES Daughters and Sons
Approximately 6 million people—pregnant women and their daughters and sons—were exposed to the synthetic estrogen DES (diethylstilbestrol) and other DES-like drugs from 1940 to 1971, when it was widely used to treat so-called high-risk pregnancies—those with a threatened miscarriage or those complicated by a medical problem such as diabetes. In 1971, physicians found evidence of a rare form of cancer of the vagina or cervix (technically called clear cell adenocarcinoma) in daughters whose mothers had taken DES and related drugs during pregnancy (Herbst, Ulfelder, and Poskanzer, 1971). Subsequently, a number of reproductive abnormalities were found in some of the sons of women given DES during pregnancy, including incomplete development of the testes, undescended testes (cryptorchidism), anatomical abnormalities of the penis, and preliminary evidence of infertility (Gill, Schumacher, and Bibbo, 1977). Still more recently, there is some preliminary concern about cancer of the testis in DES-exposed sons, although this finding requires further substantiation.

While the cancer found in DES daughters is relatively infrequent (it is estimated to occur in about one of every 800 exposed women), noncancerous abnormalities are found in the vagina in one-third of these individuals and abnormalities of the cervix are

hysterectomy (his' tur ek' tuh mē) partial or total removal of the uterus.

prostatectomy (pros' tuh tek' tuh mē) surgical removal of the prostate gland.

Pelvic Exams and Pap Smears

One aspect of sexual and reproductive health care that often seems shrouded in mystery is the pelvic exam, sometimes called a vaginal or internal exam. Many women are embarrassed or anxious about having a "female check-up" done, yet the information gained from such an exam is important in many ways. For instance, the pelvic exam can be used to diagnose such diverse conditions as pregnancy, vaginal infections, cancer of the cervix, certain causes of infertility, and tumors of the uterus. It is also needed to fit a diaphragm or to insert an IUD.

The pelvic exam is done with the woman lying flat on her back on an examination table with her knees bent, legs apart, and heels in special footrests called stirrups. The physician or nurse conducting the exam begins by inspecting the outer genital structures, checking the labia, clitoris, and vaginal opening for signs of infection, irritation, rashes, swellings, sores, or other problems. Next, wearing thin rubber gloves, the examiner gently inserts a finger just inside the vagina to check for vaginismus or other abnormalities. Following this, an instrument called a speculum is slipped into the vagina to spread the vaginal walls apart. (If the speculum is metal, it should be warmed first so it won't be shockingly cold.) Although some women find that insertion of the speculum may be a bit uncomfortable, it is generally not painful if properly positioned. Since this instrument comes in different sizes, a woman who has a lot of discomfort should ask the examiner to try a narrower or shorter instrument.

With the speculum in place, the cervix is visually inspected and a Pap smear is taken. The Pap smear (or, officially, the Papanicolaou smear, named for its inventor) is done by gently

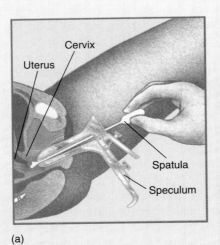
(a)

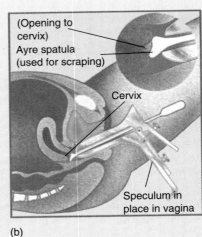
(b)

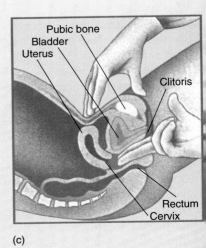
(c)

The pelvic exam. (a) The speculum in place for a pelvic exam. (b) The Ayre spatula is used to get a sample of cells for the Pap smear. (c) The bimanual pelvic exam.

present in almost every case (Robboy et al., 1981). It is not certain if a higher rate of vaginal/cervical cancer (or other forms of cancer, such as cancer of the breast or uterus) will emerge as this population of women ages, so that long-term medical follow-up is important. In fact, evidence suggests that there is an

scraping the area around the mouth of the cervix with a thin wooden spatula. Contrary to what many people believe, this is a painless procedure—most women don't even realize when it's been done (it takes only about two seconds). The scraping is then smeared on a glass microscope slide for later evaluation. The Pap smear shows early changes in cervical cancer or other abnormalities of the cervix. Generally, a second smear is also taken to examine vaginal secretions for microscopic signs of infection.

The speculum is then withdrawn slowly and gently from the vagina while the examiner carefully looks at the lining of the vagina for any unusual signs. Next, a bimanual exam is done. This involves inserting two gloved fingers into the vagina and pressing downward on the lower abdomen with the other hand. By this maneuver, the examiner can feel the size, shape, and position of the ovaries, uterus, and Fallopian tubes. Although there is often a sense of dull pressure during this part of the exam, it is not usually painful.

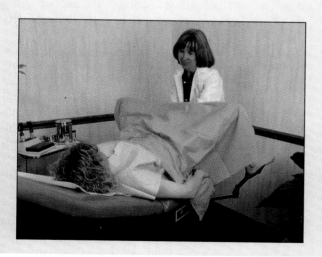

Not all health-care professionals are equally adept or sensitive to women's feelings when it comes to pelvic exams. It's important for a woman to find a doctor or nurse with whom she feels comfortable and is able to communicate. If a woman is tense and anxious before her pelvic exam, it can cause tenseness in her pelvic muscles so that it is more likely that the examination will be uncomfortable. A good health-care professional can help in this situation by teaching the woman several relaxation techniques and by using an unhurried approach. In addition, many women find that if each part of the exam is explained to them in advance and they are told at each step what is being done, they are less apprehensive. Finally, many women appreciate the opportunity to watch the exam in a hand-held mirror.

We strongly suggest that all women who are sexually active have a pelvic exam and Pap smear once a year. Women who are using birth control pills or who have a history of genital herpes should have a Pap smear twice a year. The most recent recommendations of the American Cancer Society are that (1) all women age 20 and over should have a Pap smear annually for two negative exams and then at least every three years until age 65; (2) pelvic exams should be done as part of a general physical exam every three years from age 20 to 40 and annually thereafter; (3) any of the following factors suggest the need for more frequent tests: early age at first intercourse, multiple sex partners, infertility, abnormal uterine bleeding, history of genital herpes or genital warts, obesity, or use of estrogens.

increased risk of cancer—including breast cancer—in the mothers who took the drug during pregnancy (Hoover, Gray, and Fraumeni, 1977; Meyers, 1983;

Greenberg et al., 1984). It also appears that there is a higher rate of ectopic pregnancies and miscarriages in DES daughters (Herbst, 1981).

If you were born after 1940, you should ask your mother whether she had any drugs prescribed for her during pregnancy—especially to prevent miscarriage or to treat a problem pregnancy associated with diabetes. If she did (or thinks she might have), go to your physician for evaluation. While it would be helpful to try to find out the dosage of the DES-type drug received, when in the pregnancy it was first administered, and for how long, such information is not always available. Nevertheless, a medical examination is in order if you (or your child) had such an exposure or think you may have.

DES daughters should undergo a pelvic examination including a Pap smear and should have a test using an iodine solution to stain the lining of the vagina temporarily. The physician may also use a special magnifying instrument called a colposcope for this examination, and if there are areas of the vagina that appear abnormal, a biopsy (removal and examination of tissue specimens) may be taken. Usually this type of biopsy causes relatively little discomfort, although a slight amount of bleeding (less than during menstrual flow) may occur for 12 to 24 hours after the procedure is done.

The situation for DES sons is not yet completely understood, but we suggest that until more information is available, they undergo a medical examination on an annual basis.

Generally, treatment is *not* required for DES-related abnormalities, and over 98 percent of exposed individuals will be found to be cancer-free. Nevertheless, follow-up examinations (advisable at least every six months if abnormalities are found, or once a year if not) are important because the success of treating the types of cancer that can develop is partly dependent on detecting it in its earliest stages.

Needless to say, knowledge of DES exposure can lead to anger, guilt, fear of cancer, and concerns about fertility and sex. One 24-year-old nurse summarizes her reactions:

> When I first learned that my mother had used DES while she was pregnant with me, I didn't fully comprehend what it meant. Now that I realize that the risk of cancer is remote, I'm less afraid, but I'd be dishonest if I didn't say that I consider myself abnormal and I constantly worry about what will happen. Statistics mean very little when you're on the line yourself. (*Authors' files*)

Other DES daughters voice dismay at being advised not to use birth control pills (it is possible that the pill might aggravate the DES-induced changes, although whether or not this actually happens is not currently clear) or worry about their future childbearing risks. Fortunately, there are several groups available to help them deal with such concerns, including DES Action (Long Island Jewish Hospital, New Hyde Park, NY 11040), National Women's Health Network (2025 I Street, N.W., Suite 105, Washington, DC 20006), and the National Cancer Institute (Department DES, Office of Cancer Communications, Bethesda, MD 20205).

Alcoholism

The alcoholic man or woman has a high chance of having sexual problems. Not all these problems result from the alcoholism, however: in more than a few cases preexisting sexual difficulties may have played an important role in starting a person on a path toward heavy drinking. Here, the use of alcohol may help people cope with feelings of sexual inadequacy by making them less interested in sex or less critical of their own performance. Given the popular notion that drinking is "manly" and that liquor can be used to seduce a woman by lowering her resistance, it is easy to see how drinking seems to be "beneficial" from a man's sexual viewpoint. Women who feel guilty or inhibited about sex may find that drinking loosens these restraints and lets them feel more comfortable.

We have found that about 40 percent of alcoholic men have problems with erections and 5 to 10 percent have retarded ejaculation. Thirty to 40 percent of alcoholic women have difficulties in sexual arousal, and 15 percent have problems being orgasmic (Kolodny, Masters, and Johnson, 1979; Murphy et al., 1980). Sexual desire is also apt to be low in alcoholics (Schiavi, 1990).

There are several reasons behind these problems. Alcoholism directly affects hormone production and lowers testosterone in men (Van Thiel, 1976; Lindholm et al., 1978) and estrogen in women (Ryback, 1977). Shrunken testes and breast enlargement are common in alcoholic men. Other medical complications of alcoholism include liver damage, nerve damage, lowered resistance to infection, and poor nutrition, all of which may provide a biological basis for sexual impairment. Relevant psychosocial factors include fears of performance and

Figure 22.1   The Inflatable Penile Implant

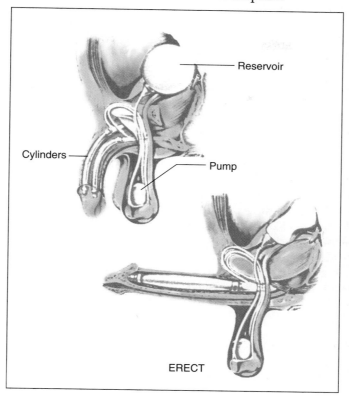

spectatoring, marital conflicts, low self-esteem, guilt, and depression.

Even when an alcoholic has stopped drinking completely, there is no guarantee that his or her sexual difficulties will disappear. About half of the time these problems continue, requiring professional counseling to be resolved.

Penile Implants

When injury or illness causes complete inability to have erections, sexual functioning can be restored to a significant degree by the use of various types of mechanical devices that can be implanted in the penis with surgery. Although these devices can provide firm enough erections for intercourse to take place, they cannot restore sensation to the penis or normal ejaculation if these have been lost due to organic causes.

There are two basic types of penile implants. The simplest is a pair of fixed, semirigid rods that are placed inside the shaft of the penis. The earliest version of these rods produced a permanent state

of partial erection that was embarrassing to some men. Now there are several additional types of rods that have either a bendable silver wire core or a hinge to allow the partly erect penis to be bent down against the inner thigh when the man is dressed, and embarrassment doesn't seem to be much of a problem.

More complicated and expensive, but more realistic in appearance and function, is an inflatable device (Figure 22.1) that also requires surgical placement. Two tapered inflatable cylinders are inserted into the penis and are connected by a tubing system to a fluid storage reservoir implanted in the lower abdomen. By pinching a simple pump and valve in the scrotum, fluid moves into the cylinders, causing a natural-looking erection. Releasing the valve moves the fluid out of the cylinders back to the reservoir (returning the penis to the flaccid state).

Either device may seem somewhat artificial to the man or his partner: in some cases this feeling is so problematic after surgery, the man only uses his implant a few times (Renshaw, 1979). For many men facing a "hopeless" situation, however, penile implants can restore a sense of manhood and improve self-esteem considerably. Thus, penile implants are currently used to treat men with erectile dysfunction resulting from spinal cord injuries, diabetes, multiple sclerosis and other neurological disease, and men with impotence resulting from severe vascular problems that are not correctable by surgery.

Unfortunately, penile implant surgery is not without its technical problems. In three reports, complications with the inflatable device—including infection and mechanical failure—were noted to occur in more than 40 percent of patients, often requiring removal of the device or at least one repeat operation to correct the problem (Apte, Gregory, and Purcell, 1984; Fallon, Rosenberg, and Culp, 1984; Joseph, Bruskewitz, and Benson, 1984). While the rate of complications with noninflatable rods is much lower, it is plain that this type of surgery is not the simple solution most men imagine it should be.

SEXUAL ASPECTS OF PSYCHIATRIC ILLNESSES

Mood Disorders

The mood disorders, also known as affective disorders, are marked by a prolonged disturbance of emotion that affects a person's whole life. These disturbances generally take the form of either depressed moods, elevated moods (euphoria or mania), or alterations of depressed and elevated moods (American Psychiatric Association, 1987). The latter condition has traditionally been called manic–depressive illness but is now also called bipolar disorder. Depression that occurs without accompanying bouts of mania is considered a unipolar disorder.

The features of depression are depressed mood (sometimes described as feelings of sadness, hopelessness, or despondency) and/or loss of interest in or pleasure from all or almost all of a person's ordinary activities (American Psychiatric Association, 1987). The most typical symptoms are loss of appetite, weight loss, difficulty sleeping, decreased energy, feelings of worthlessness or excessive or inappropriate guilt, difficulty thinking or concentrating, and recurrent thoughts of death or suicide (American Psychiatric Association, 1987; Goodwin and Guze, 1989).

The core features of mania are inappropriate, sustained euphoria; hyperactivity; and "flight of ideas"—the rapid, often chaotic, jumping from one idea to another. In unbridled mania, a person's speech generally changes from its natural style to a fast, rushing delivery; it may also be filled with puns, rhymes, and jokes, as well as highly dramatic pronouncements. There is usually a decreased need for sleep and a great sense of restlessness: manic people have a very tough time sitting still or listening, uninterruptingly, to anyone else. The person typically feels sublimely self-confident and advises others about matters in which he or she has no special knowledge—like how to attain world peace or how to run a world-class hotel. At the same time, the manic person often starts, and then abandons, ambitious projects for which he or she has little or no background, one minute announcing that they've started a novel, then calling friends to say that they've devised a new system for beating the stock market, then claiming that they've been hired to promote a U2 concert. The hallmark of such actions is their grandiosity, their impulsivity, and their disorganization; these features carry over into other behavior, as well, in which rash acts such as going on a major buying spree, driving recklessly, or resigning abruptly from a job occur.

Mood disorders are among the most common psychiatric conditions, with most studies reporting that more females are affected than males. The proportion of the adult population in the United States that currently has a mood disorder is thought to be approximately 5 percent (Myers, Weissman, and Tischler, 1984; Fishman, 1990). The lifetime risk of ever having a mood disorder has been estimated by Wing and Bebbington (1985) as 12 percent for men and 20 percent for women. Mania occurs far less often than depression, but both conditions tend to recur. About 70 percent of people with a major depressive episode will have at least one additional bout of depression in their lifetime, and about 12 percent will have subsequent bouts of mania (U.S. Public Health Service, 1986).

The sexual effects of the mood disorders are varied. The majority of depressed persons experience a marked reduction in their sex drives, but overt sexual dysfunction such as erectile dysfunction or anorgasmia occurs in less than one-third of these cases (Tamburello and Seppecher, 1977; Kolodny, Masters, and Johnson, 1979). In chronic depression, inhibited sexual desire is common (Kaplan, 1983), and the capacity for enjoying sexual fantasies is often lost (Woods, 1981). As we have noted elsewhere (Kolodny, Masters, and Johnson, 1979, p. 301):

> It is common to find that the depressed patient has few sexual fantasies or thoughts about sex; it is also common to find a significant decrease in initiatory sexual behavior, although the sexual receptivity of depressed persons is somewhat less affected. Mechanisms of sexual arousal (erectile function in the male and vaginal lubrication in the female) are more likely to be intact than to be impaired, but often the perception of sexual arousal is negatively affected.

When a true sexual dysfunction occurs as a result of depression, it is sometimes masked by other problems. In one case, a married 42-year-old man suffering from depression withdrew from virtually all social interaction with his wife, even insisting on eating his meals alone; months later, it turned out that this self-imposed social isolation was in part his response to guilt over erectile difficulties that first appeared as part of the depressive symptoms (*Authors' files*). Similarly, because depression in one partner obviously has some impact on many aspects of a couple's intimacy, it is no surprise that it may interfere with their sex relations.

Infrequently, depression may trigger unusual forms of sexual behavior, such as incest, pedophilia, or exhibitionism. And in some cases, depressed persons may start an affair to stimulate both their mood and their sexual performance.

Mania affects sexual behavior in a number of different ways, but its main effect is to make sexual behavior very impulsive. During a bout of mania (which typically lasts for weeks or months), hypersexuality is common (Tsuang, 1975). Ordinary social and sexual inhibitions may be loosened or shattered, with both male and female manics suddenly (and uncharacteristically) having sex with numerous partners, including partners who are total strangers, as the following case summaries show (*Authors' files*):

Case 1: A 28-year-old married female accountant who had a past history of psychiatric hospitalization for both manic and depressive episodes occurring sporadically since her early twenties called her husband from work one day to announce that she had taken all the money from their joint checking account and was off to the West Coast to see some friends. After flying from Boston to Los Angeles, she suddenly boarded another plane for Las Vegas. In four days there, she picked up seven different men at her hotel bar and had sex with them; the last two men agreed to a sexual threesome at her insistence.

Case 2: A 37-year-old sociology professor was taken to a psychiatrist after she suddenly disrobed at a faculty meeting and began masturbating. The psychiatrist discovered that she had cancelled all her office hours for the past several weeks and had squandered $25,000 from a research grant she had received earlier that semester. The diagnosis of mania was easily established.

Hospitalized manic patients often disrupt the psychiatric ward by similar displays of overt, inappropriate sexuality or by attempts to have sex with fellow patients or hospital staff members. In addition, some manic persons show their hypersexuality by a frantic search for sexual partners or constant seductive behavior (Woods, 1981), or by participation in forms of sexual activity that they never tried previously, including bisexuality, homosexuality, or group sex.

Mania is often treated with a drug called lithium carbonate. Although this is usually effective in controlling the manic episode and in preventing recurrences, lithium occasionally causes sexual difficulties in males, including erectile problems and decreased sexual desire (Blay, Ferraz, and Calil, 1982). One of the reasons for this effect may be that lithium decreases testosterone levels in the blood (Sanchez et al., 1976). There are no reports of lithium producing negative sexual effects in females.

A number of different medications are used to treat depression, often in combination with a program of cognitive psychotherapy (Goodwin and Guze, 1989). Virtually all the antidepressant drugs can affect sexual functioning adversely in both males and females, although this problem occurs in only a small minority of patients (Kolodny, Masters, and Johnson, 1979; Segraves et al., 1985; Jani and Wise, 1988; Segraves, 1988). (In males, the most common sexual difficulty is inhibited ejaculation, while in females inhibited orgasm is the most frequent problem.) As a practical matter, however, the sexual effects of antidepressant drugs are generally beneficial because they bring about an improvement in the mood disorder: they usually boost a person's sexual interest back to its pre-illness level.

In addition, if sexual dysfunction occurred as a result of the depression, as the depression lifts, the dysfunction often disappears.

Anorexia Nervosa and Bulimia

Anorexia nervosa, the self-starvation disorder, and **bulimia,** the binge–purge eating disorder, are related conditions marked by disturbances in body image and obsessive–compulsive concerns focusing on food and eating. Both disorders characteristically start in adolescence or young adulthood and affect females much more frequently than males (American Psychiatric Association, 1987). There is mounting evidence that anorexia and bulimia have increased in frequency in the general population in the past two decades; the problem of bulimia appears to be especially acute on college campuses throughout the nation, where some studies have estimated that more than 10 percent of college females engage in bulimic behavior, which they learn from other females in what has been termed a "copy cat" manner (Thompson and Schwartz, 1981; Pope et al., 1984; Johnson and Connors, 1987). The increased occurrence of both eating disorders may partly reflect the emphasis our culture puts on thinness as a way of providing attractiveness and personal self-worth (N. Kolodny, 1987).

The essential features of anorexia nervosa are: (1) progressive weight loss, to a point more than 15 percent below minimal normal weight for age and height (or failure to gain weight in a period of body growth); (2) disgust with food (often accompanied by a preoccupation with thoughts about food); (3) intense fear of gaining weight or becoming fat, even when the victim is so thin that she or he looks like a skeleton; (4) distorted body image so that the person "feels fat" even when emaciated; and (5) loss of menstrual periods in females (American Psychiatric Association, 1987; Goodwin and Guze, 1989). The disorder, while treatable, is sometimes fatal and often requires hospitalization.

Although the cause of anorexia is not known, one frequently expressed view is that it is a form of rejection of developing adult sexuality (Goodwin and Guze, 1989). Other theories have held that, through starvation, anorectic females reject a wish to be pregnant (Halmi, 1985) or that the anorexic's avoidance of food results from sexual and social tensions generated by the physical changes that occur with puberty (Crisp, 1967).

The anorectic female actually makes her body regress sexually by severely restricting her food intake. She can postpone the onset of menarche (if she hasn't yet started to have menstrual periods) or make her menstrual periods stop by losing a lot of weight; this effect occurs by suppression of luteinizing hormone and follicle stimulating hormone production (Copeland, 1985). By disrupting her ovarian functioning (estrogen production is kept at basically prepubertal levels in anorexia), the anorexic also can often postpone her breast development or cause her breasts to shrink back to a less threateningly sexual degree of flatness. Similarly, testosterone levels are low in male anorexics, and the development of secondary sex characteristics such as facial hair and lowering of the voice is delayed.

Anorectic females typically show little or no interest in sex; in fact, they often appear frightened of sex. Most anorectic females avoid dating, do not masturbate, and have no desire to give up their much-coveted virginity. Adolescents with anorexia nervosa are often shy and withdrawn and appear childlike in their social interactions. In some cases, a history of sexual abuse or assault precedes the development of anorexia (Goldfarb, 1987; Schecter, Schwartz, and Greenfeld, 1987). Even among married adult anorexics, avoidance of sex is common and sexual dysfunctions such as primary anorgasmia or vaginismus are frequently seen (Renshaw, 1990).

Bulimia is characterized by binge eating—the consumption of large amounts of food in a relatively short time period (generally less than two hours)—usually followed by self-induced vomiting or abuse of laxatives or diuretics. The binges, which are usually planned, typically involve rapidly eating food with a high calorie content and a lot of sugar—such as ice cream, donuts, cookies, or chocolates—and are usually carried out in private, gobbling down the food with little chewing (American Psychiatric Association, 1987). The bulimic feels out of control during a binge and worries that she won't be able to stop eating. Immediately after the binge, the bulimic is often depressed and guilty over her lack of control. Sometimes, but not always, there is an anorectic eating pattern between binges; more commonly, the bulimic is preoccupied with her weight and pursues various diet plans and stringent daily exercising as a way of staying thin.

In contrast to anorexics, bulimics tend to be socially outgoing and sexually active at an early age

(Hazard, 1985; Johnson and Connors, 1987; Haimes and Katz, 1988). However, as Renshaw (1990) points out, bulimics have a relatively high rate of sexual dysfunction as well as inhibited sexual desire. Renshaw also notes that many bulimics feel guilty about masturbation, which she observes is "strikingly similar to their binge–guilt–purge eating cycle." On the other hand, some bulimic females lead very satisfying sex lives, so it is incorrect to assume that anyone with bulimia is automatically sexually dysfunctional.

DRUGS AND SEX

For many centuries, there has been an avid search for **aphrodisiacs**—substances that could increase a person's sexual powers or desire. The long list of substances that have been claimed to have such an effect include oysters, ginseng root, powdered rhinoceros horn, animal testicles, and turtles' eggs, but there is no evidence that an actual aphrodisiac response occurs. "Spanish fly," the most famous supposed aphrodisiac, is made from beetles found in southern Europe. The beetles are ground into a powder and, when taken internally, the substance irritates the bladder and urethra and can also cause ulcers, diarrhea, and even death. The burning sensation in the penis due to irritation of the urethra has been interpreted by some men as a sign of lust.

Aphrodisiacs aside, both prescription drugs and drugs used recreationally (or illicitly, depending on your viewpoint) have some specific effects on sexuality.

Prescription Drugs

Many of the medications used to treat high blood pressure cause sexual difficulties for men and women. For example, Aldomet (alphamethyldopa), one of the drugs most commonly used to treat this condition, causes erectile dysfunction in 10 to 15 percent of men at low doses and in up to half of men in high doses (Kolodny, 1978a). Decreased libido and impaired sexual arousal is found in similar proportions of women using this drug. A different type of problem is found with Ismelin (guanethidine), which inhibits ejaculation in more than half of the men using it. Usually these difficulties disappear within a week or two after stopping the medication, but in some cases the sexual dysfunction may persist because of anxiety. Fortunately, there are many medications available to treat high blood pressure. Some have low rates of sexual side effects, and it is almost always possible to find a combination that will leave sexual function intact while simultaneously controlling high blood pressure (Croog et al., 1988).

Tranquilizers such as Librium (chlordiazepoxide) and Valium (diazepam) can sometimes cause erectile dysfunction, anorgasmia, or decreased sexual desire but in other instances may be beneficial by reducing sexual anxiety. Barbiturates and related drugs such as Quaalude (methaqualone) have also been reported to cause a variety of sexual problems (Gay et al., 1975; Bush, 1980), although Quaalude has developed a street reputation as an aphrodisiac.

In the last few years, fluoxetine (Prozac)—a drug used primarily as an antidepressant—has received considerable attention for its sexual effects. Some men have reported that Prozac improves premature ejaculation very dramatically, while others find that it causes an annoying form of retarded ejaculation. In women, the effects of Prozac are less dramatic, although orgasmic difficulties have also been reported (Jacobsen, 1992; Masters, Johnson, and Kolodny, 1994).

Antihistamines, used in allergy pills and sinus medications, can affect sexuality in two ways. Drowsiness is a prime side effect and one not likely to improve the quality of sex. In women, these drugs often cause a reduction in vaginal lubrication so they may sometimes cause painful intercourse.

The effects of hormones on sexual function were discussed in Chapter 4. A more detailed discussion of the sexual effects of prescription drugs is given in the several references listed at the end of this chapter.

anorexia nervosa an eating disorder marked by self-starvation. Anorexia nervosa usually occurs in females in their teens or early twenties.
bulimia an eating disorder marked by frequent episodes of binge eating (consuming large quantities of food) followed immediately by purging the food just eaten by self-induced vomiting or use of laxatives.
aphrodisiac (af' rō dēz' ē ak) a substance that increases or is believed to increase a person's sexual powers or desire.

Sex and Alcohol: Physiological Effects

1. Acute actions
   Male: Very low blood concentrations of alcohol seem to have a mildly enhancing effect on erections in men, but at blood concentrations corresponding to two to three shots of liquor, erections are mildly suppressed and ejaculation is delayed. At higher blood alcohol concentrations, many males are unable to ejaculate and have marked difficulty obtaining or maintaining erections.
   Female: Very low blood alcohol concentrations seem to have minimal effects on sexual responsivity, but moderate concentrations cause a reduction in vaginal blood flow, a delayed time to reach orgasm, and less orgasmic intensity. High blood alcohol concentrations can block orgasmic responsivity and can interfere with vaginal lubrication.
2. Chronic actions
   Male: Chronic alcohol abuse commonly causes low sex desire and erectile dysfunction possibly due to the depression of testosterone production.
   Female: Chronic alcohol abuse causes low sexual interest, difficulties becoming sexually aroused, and problems with orgasmic response. The cause of these problems is unclear.

Nonprescription Drugs

Alcohol

The effects of alcohol on sexuality have fascinated people throughout history. In *Macbeth,* Shakespeare reported that "it provokes the desire but it takes away the performance" (Act 2, scene 3, line 34), and modern research has shown that this view is fairly accurate. In one study, college men were given alcohol in three different doses while watching erotic movies (Farkas and Rosen, 1976). Amounts of alcohol well below the legal levels of intoxication suppressed erections. Similar studies in women showed that alcohol had a negative impact on physiologic signs of sexual arousal (Wilson and Lawson, 1976, 1978). Alcohol has also been shown to weaken male masturbatory effectiveness and to decrease the pleasure and intensity of male orgasm (Malatesta, 1979), and alcohol, even in moderate amounts, makes it more difficult for women to reach orgasm (Malatesta et al., 1982).

Despite the *physical* inhibition of even two or three drinks of an alcoholic beverage (due to a depressant effect on the nervous system), most people believe that alcohol *increases* their sexual responsiveness. This is partly because alcohol has a "disinhibiting" effect: it lowers the sexual inhibitions a person may ordinarily have, thus making it possible for sexual desire to emerge (Crowe and George, 1989). The belief that alcohol enhances sex also stems from advertising and cultural myths.

Narcotics

Addictive drugs such as heroin and morphine produce many sexual problems (Cushman, 1973; Mintz et al., 1974; Cicero et al., 1975). One large survey found that in 162 male addicts, erectile dysfunction occurred in 48 percent, retarded ejaculation in 59 percent, and low sexual interest in 66 percent; in 85 female addicts, 27 percent had orgasmic dysfunction and 57 percent had low sexual interest (Kolodny, 1983a). This is a complex area to evaluate, however, because drug addiction may be a means of trying to escape from preexisting sexual difficulties or may be a substitute for sex. Factors such as hormone problems (Azizi et al., 1973; Santen et al., 1975; Mirin et al., 1980), infections, and poor nutrition, which occur as a result of addiction, also play a role in causing sexual difficulties.

Narcotic addicts are also likely to have other problems that complicate their sex lives. Rosenbaum (1981) has noted that (1) female addicts usually have partners who are also addicted; (2) many addicts find that the "hit" of mainlining heroin is far more pleasurable, intense, and easy to get than an orgasm (in fact, many ex-addicts say the feeling is like dozens of orgasms rolled up into one); and (3) the sensuality and sharing that accompany narcotic use become a replacement for the sharing and sensuality of sex. Furthermore, since most female addicts must turn to prostitution to raise money for their habit, it is not surprising that sex becomes less appealing to them.

Amphetamines and Cocaine

Amphetamines ("speed," "uppers," "pep pills") reportedly increase sexual responsiveness when used in low doses but have the opposite effect in high doses or when used on a long-term basis.

Cocaine ("coke," "snow") has a street reputation as a strong sexual stimulant, but there are also reports of sexual dysfunction with its use (Gay et al., 1975; Bush, 1980; Cocores, Dackis, and Gold, 1986). Kolodny (1983) found that 17 percent of 168 male cocaine users had episodes of erectile failure when they used this drug, and 4 percent had experienced priapism (painful, persistent erections) at least once during or immediately after the use of cocaine. Similarly, Wesson (1982) found evidence of male erectile difficulties during the use of cocaine, and Siegel (1982) reported that the dangerous practice of "free-basing" cocaine consistently leads to sexual disinterest and situational impotence (20 of 23 men were affected in his study). In addition, the recent appearance of a highly potent form of cocaine called "crack" has led to addiction occurring very quickly. One study of 60 male crack users found that more than two-thirds of this group were sexually dysfunctional, while 23 of 30 female crack users reported decreased sexual interest and responsivity (Kolodny, 1987). A more recent report noted:

> At some point, nearly all chronic high-dose cocaine users become sexually dysfunctional (i.e., impotent and nonorgasmic). But despite their inability to perform physically, many chronic users find that their sexual feelings and fantasies are still heightened by cocaine, and their sexual acting-out behavior continues. At this point, however, sexual arousal and stimulation are often reduced to a purely mental (psychological) experience for the chronic user. *(Washton, 1989, p. 34)*

Because crack use is often combined with the practice of bartering sexual services in exchange for the drug, females who become addicted to crack commonly have sex with a number of partners each day in order to feed their habit (Macdonald et al., 1988; Fullilove and Fullilove, 1989). Partly because of this, crack use has been tied to soaring rates of STDs in the past few years (Goldsmith, 1988; Chaisson et al., 1989; Fullilove et al., 1990). In addition, Washton (1989) claims that many people who become addicted to crack are also driven to compulsive sexuality.

Cocaine use as a purported sexual stimulant is interesting for several other reasons. For one thing, many users believe that rubbing cocaine on the tip of the clitoris increases female sexual sensitivity and arousal, but how this could occur is difficult to understand since cocaine is used medically as a topical anesthetic, that is, to deaden nerve endings. The continued use of this practice may indicate how powerful expectations are in interpreting our experiences.

A second interesting point is that cocaine clearly acts as a sexual facilitator in a social sense. When a man offers cocaine to a woman (or vice versa) there is usually a sexual invitation implied. As Kolodny (1985) notes:

> Widely available at singles bars and in the economically advantaged "just-got-a-divorce" crowd, cocaine literally opens the doors of sexual access for many males and provides a convenient excuse for many females who otherwise might pass on having "instant sex" with a partner they hardly know.

Marijuana

Marijuana ("pot," "dope," "grass") is generally reported to enhance sexual feelings. In our own research with more than 1000 men and women aged 18 to 35 who had used this drug as an accompaniment to sex, 83 percent of the men and 81 percent of the women said that marijuana improved their sexual experience (Kolodny, Masters, and Johnson, 1979). Most users, however, denied that marijuana led to more sexual desire, quicker sexual arousal, or more intense orgasms. Instead, they indicated that marijuana gave them an increased awareness of touch all over their bodies, led to greater relaxation (both mentally and physically), and put them more in tune with their partners. These are highly subjective judgments which cannot be verified fully in experimental research. However, generally similar findings have been reported by others; for example, Halikas, Weller, and Morse (1982) described self-reports of enhanced touch awareness and physical closeness in a majority of both male and female users.

In nonsexual situations, it has been shown that instead of *increasing* touch sensitivity, marijuana actually produces no change or *lessens* touch perception (Reese, 1977). There is also considerable documentation that marijuana use slows reflex reactions (Klonoff, 1974; Manno et al., 1974; Jones,

1976; Jaffe, 1980). The fact that marijuana users say that if *they* are "high" but their partner is not, the sexual experience is unpleasant (disjointed?) also indicates that there is a strongly subjective element to the reported effects.

Some other research findings also bear examination. Erectile dysfunction has been found to affect about 20 percent of men using marijuana daily, although no association between marijuana use and sexual dysfunction in women has been noted (Kolodny, 1981). However, some women who use marijuana report that it causes temporary vaginal dryness, which can sometimes cause painful intercourse. Furthermore, heavy marijuana use has been reported to lower testosterone production in animals and men (Collu et al., 1975; Harmon et al., 1976; Smith et al., 1976; Kolodny et al., 1974, 1976, 1979) and to disturb sperm production as well (Kolodny et al., 1974; Hembree, Zeidenberg, and Nahas, 1976).[1] Although these effects are reversible once the drug is stopped, they may sometimes contribute to sexual problems. One study of chronic, frequent marijuana use in women showed menstrual cycle abnormalities and hormone changes but no negative sexual effects (Bauman et al., 1979).

Anabolic Steroids

Anabolic steroids are synthetic forms of testosterone that were developed in order to minimize the masculinizing effects of testosterone while amplifying its growth-promoting (anabolic) properties. While this class of hormones has authentic medical uses as a prescription drug (e.g., in the treatment of osteoporosis, endometriosis, breast cancer, and some anemias), they have become notorious because of their widespread illicit use by athletes. Because the anabolic properties of the drug increase the body's conversion of nitrogen from protein food sources into muscle, the drugs are commonly used by athletes in sports such as football, wrestling, weight lifting, bodybuilding, and track and field in which increased muscle size is beneficial. Whether anabolic steroids actually increase

strength or speed or otherwise improve athletic performance is unclear at present (Wilson, 1988).

Although use of anabolic steroids has long been "athletes' darkest and best-kept secret" (Hallagan, Hallagan, and Snyder, 1989), the world's attention was focused on this issue with the disqualification of Canadian sprinter Ben Johnson, winner of the 1988 Olympic 100-meter dash, after he acknowledged that he had used anabolic steroids during training (*Washington Post*, June 13, 1989, p. E1). But it is hardly just elite, world-class athletes who use anabolic steroids: one recent survey found that 6.6 percent of twelfth-grade male students ($N = 3403$) drawn from 46 public and private high schools across the country had used anabolic steroids, with two-thirds of this group starting at age 16 or younger (Buckley et al., 1988). Another survey documented that high school females, as well as males, sometimes use anabolic steroids; 1 percent of the female high school seniors in this study reported that they had used these drugs during their athletic careers (Newman, 1986). Among college athletes, usage is both far more common and far riskier because of higher doses and the frequent practice of "stacking"—using two or more anabolic drugs at the same time.

There are a number of undesirable or harmful side effects associated with the use of anabolic steroids. In most cases, the frequency and severity of these effects increase with the dose of the drug(s) used (Gilman, Goodman, and Gilman, 1988). Since it is not unusual for athletes who get anabolic steroids on the black market to use them in doses 10 to 50 times higher than the amounts used for medical purposes, the rates of harmful side effects are much higher than they are when used for strictly medical purposes. In both sexes, there is a significant risk of liver abnormalities (including chemically induced hepatitis, jaundice, and tumors), high blood pressure, and endocrine and reproductive effects. In women, the most visible effects are masculinizing ones: growth of facial and body hair, male pattern baldness, and enlargement of the clitoris. Women also are apt to have menstrual irregularities and blocked or inhibited ovulation as a result of using anabolic steroids. In males, these drugs typically cause a sharp drop in circulating testosterone (because their weak androgenic action is enough to keep the hypothalamus from triggering the hormonal signals for more testosterone production) and shrinkage of the testes. Sperm production is seri-

---

[1]One carefully designed research study found that three weeks of daily marijuana smoking under controlled conditions did *not* lower testosterone in men (Mendelson et al., 1974). However, a similar study, using the same carefully controlled conditions but administering marijuana daily over a three-*month* period found that the testosterone-lowering effect did not show up for five to six weeks (Kolodny, Masters, and Johnson, 1979, Figure 13.2).

ously impaired with prolonged use, and the resulting sterility is not always reversed after the anabolic steroids are discontinued (Lamb, 1984; Wilson, 1988). Gynecomastia (enlargement of the male breasts) is another common finding.

Many males using high doses of anabolic steroids develop low levels of sexual desire and erectile dysfunction—presumably as a result of their lowered testosterone production—but they are apt to attribute their lack of sexual interest to "being in training," rather than to hormonal changes of which they are unaware. Because they are not particularly interested in sex, they may not discover that they are having difficulties with erection until many months after the problem first begins.

There are also potential psychological effects from use of high doses of anabolic steroids. The most prominent is a form of increased aggressiveness known colloquially as "'roid rage." Rapid mood swings are also frequently noted, and one report found that 12 percent of users had psychotic symptoms (Pope and Katz, 1988). It has been theorized that the rapid mood swings and aggressiveness of steroid abuse may sometimes contribute to sexual assault committed by male athletes (Kolodny, 1990), although this is a complex issue in which blame should not be put entirely on the drugs.

Finally, when the anabolic steroids are injected (rather than taken in pill form), there is an increased risk of infections associated with sharing needles, including hepatitis and HIV (Sklarek et al., 1984).

INFECTIONS

Certain types of infections that affect the sex organs are not usually transmitted through sexual intercourse, unlike the sexually transmitted diseases that we have previously discussed. These infections, which *can* be sexually transmitted, can produce troublesome symptoms that interfere with sexual pleasure or cause considerable emotional turmoil. Fortunately, the most common of these infections are easily treatable and have no major health risks. We discuss them here to avoid the implication that they are always or usually of sexual origin.

Cystitis

Cystitis, or infection of the bladder, is closely related to sexual activity in women. Sexual inter-

course leads to an increase in bacteria in the urine (Buckley, McGuckin, and MacGregor, 1978) presumably because of inward pressure on the urethra during coital thrusting. Because the female urethra is short (about 2.5 cm, or 1 inch) compared to the male urethra (usually more than 15 cm, or 6 inches), cystitis is far more common in women than men (the bacteria have a shorter distance to travel).

The symptoms of cystitis include burning during urination, frequent urination, cloudy or bloody urine, and pain in the lower abdomen. The diagnosis can be made by examining a urine sample under the microscope and by taking a culture to identify the specific bacteria involved. Broad-spectrum antibiotics such as tetracycline or ampicillin are often prescribed.

One special variety of this infection is the so-called honeymoon cystitis that can occur either when a woman first becomes coitally active (not always on her honeymoon) or when coital activity is resumed after a prolonged period of inactivity.

Toxic Shock Syndrome

Toxic shock syndrome (TSS) first came to public attention in 1980 when it was widely reported as a serious, sometimes fatal illness suddenly striking healthy menstruating women who used tampons. Although TSS was named in 1978 by Todd and coworkers, who reported on a small number of cases appearing in children, it now is clear that it is actually a rare form of scarlet fever that was initially described in 1927 (Stevens, 1927; Reingold, 1983).

anabolic steroids synthetic hormones that promote the build-up of muscle mass. Commonly used by athletes in an attempt to increase their size and strength.

cystitis (sis tī' tis) infection or inflammation of the bladder.

toxic shock syndrome (TSS) an illness of rapid onset caused by infection with *Staphylococcus aureaus* bacteria; symptoms include fever, vomiting, muscle pain, and a sunburn-like skin rash. Most, but not all, cases have occurred in menstruating women, and the syndrome is thought to be related to the use of high-absorbency vaginal tampons.

TTS is marked by high fever, vomiting, diarrhea, muscle pain, and a skin rash that resembles a severe sunburn. Fainting spells, low blood pressure, and dizziness are other common symptoms. TTS is caused by a toxin, or poison, produced by a bacteria called *Staphylococcus aureus*, and it occurs primarily in menstruating women who use tampons. Most of the cases encountered in 1980 were associated with the use of Rely tampons, which were subsequently found to have a relative risk of developing TSS 11 times greater than Playtex tampons, 28 times higher than OB tampons, 38 times higher than Kotex tampons, and 77 times higher than Tampax (Schlech et al., 1982). However, both the absorbency and the chemical composition of tampons are thought to play a role, with low-absorbency tampons being much less risky (Berkley et al., 1987). After Rely tampons were withdrawn from the market, the number of cases of TSS linked with tampon use dropped (Reingold et al., 1982), and by 1983, approximately 15 percent of the cases being reported were unrelated to menstruation (Reingold, 1983). It is now clear that TSS can affect men as well as women and all age groups—including infants and the elderly—but the group at highest risk still seems to be tampon-using white females aged 15 to 25.

While women using tampons have the greatest risk of TSS and a few cases have been linked to use of the contraceptive sponge as well as to use of a diaphragm, the chances of developing this illness are very low. Preventive measures that can be taken to reduce this risk still further include (1) switching to sanitary napkins or minipads entirely; (2) alternating the use of tampons and minipads or sanitary napkins several times each day; or (3) changing tampons three or four times daily. If you develop symptoms suggestive of TSS while you are menstruating, you should immediately see a physician since TSS is a rapidly progressive illness that is fatal in about 4 percent of cases. Fortunately, with proper medical management—including hospitalization, treatment of shock, and aggressive antibiotic therapy—it is now clear that TSS is not as frightening as it first seemed to be.

Prostatitis

Prostatitis, or inflammation of the prostate, can be either acute (sudden) or chronic (long-lasting). The infecting organism is usually *E. coli,* a normal in-

habitant of the intestines. Acute prostatitis is marked by fever, chills, perineal or rectal pain, painful urination, and urinary frequency and is likely to interfere with sexual function (painful ejaculation is common). Chronic prostatitis may involve no symptoms at all, or low back pain or perineal discomfort may be present. Chronic prostatitis has sometimes been thought to cause premature or bloody ejaculation (Davis and Mininberg, 1976). Antibiotic treatment usually clears up acute prostatitis but may be ineffective in curing the chronic form of this disease.

SUMMARY

1. A number of myths exist about the sexuality of disabled people that present obstacles to their freedom of sexual expression. In recent years, these myths have been countered by a better understanding of the fact that being disabled does not prevent a person from having sexual feelings and needs and by recognition that a broad range of sexual expression is possible even if a disability partially interferes with sexual functioning.

2. Although spinal cord injury (SCI) commonly causes a variety of sexual problems (including erectile difficulties and disruption of ejaculation in men and impairment of vaginal lubrication and anorgasmia in women), as well as loss of sensations in the genitals, many SCI persons are able to be sexually active. In addition to noncoital options for intimacy and sexual sharing (such as oral–genital sex, massage, and cuddling), some SCI men can have intercourse using a "stuffing" technique and others choose to have a penile implant.

3. People who have been blind or deaf since birth are often hampered in learning about sex. While these conditions do not impair the physical reflexes of sexual response, they may at times create interpersonal problems that make sexual relationships difficult.

4. Many mildly or moderately mentally retarded persons are able to learn the basic facts necessary for responsible sexual behavior if this information is presented to them in a manner geared to their learning level.

5. A number of medical conditions can interfere physiologically with sexual function. For exam-

ple, neurologic problems such as multiple sclerosis commonly cause erectile dysfunction and female anorgasmia. Erectile dysfunction occurs in 50 percent of diabetic men and 40 percent of male alcoholics; anorgasmia is found in about one-third of diabetic women and 15 percent of female alcoholics. Other illnesses may be closely associated with anxiety about sex that limits sexual enjoyment. Heart attacks, breast cancer, and conditions that require hysterectomy are examples of such health problems.

6. Psychiatric illnesses frequently cause changes in sexual behavior. Loss of interest in sex is very common in depression, whereas hypersexual behavior is more typically seen with mania. Persons with anorexia nervosa are likely to be quite sexually withdrawn and childlike, whereas bulimia (the binge–purge eating disorder) has a far less noticeable impact on sexuality.

7. DES (diethylstilbestrol), which was widely used over three decades to treat problem pregnancies, is known to cause a variety of problems in the children of women who took this drug while pregnant. Although cancer of the vagina or cervix is infrequent in DES-exposed daughters, noncancerous abnormalities are common and should be followed closely by a physician. DES-exposed sons have an increased rate of reproductive abnormalities and may also have a heightened risk of cancer of the testis (although this has not been proved yet).

8. No true aphrodisiac has ever been found, although many people claim that alcohol, marijuana, cocaine, or amphetamines enhance their sexual experiences. Others report that these same substances lower their sexual desire or impair their sexual responses.

9. Prescription medications that can cause sexual problems include drugs used to treat high blood pressure, tranquilizers, barbiturates, and antihistamines.

10. Toxic shock syndrome (TSS) is a serious disorder caused by a toxin produced by the *Staphylococcus aureus* bacteria. Marked by an abrupt onset of fever, vomiting, muscle pain, skin rash, and low blood pressure, about 85 percent of TSS occurs in menstruating women. Although the TSS outbreak has slowed now compared to what it was in 1979–1980, it is advisable for women to change their tampons three or four times daily while they are menstruating or to switch to the use of sanitary napkins or minipads to minimize the risk of this illness.

11. Cystitis is inflammation of the bladder that can occur in either sex, while prostatitis is inflammation caused by infection of the prostate. Either condition may cause pain or burning with urination and can make sexual functioning uncomfortable.

Thought Questions

1. How have your friends and acquaintances responded to mastectomy or hysterectomy? Do you know of cases where orgasmic experience appeared to decline following hysterectomy? How do you think most men would respond to their wife or lover if she had to have a mastectomy? Is losing a breast different from losing an arm or leg from a sexual point of view?

2. Why is it that there are so many more operations done in this country to remove ovaries than to remove testes?

3. Imagine a friend of yours who is in a wheelchair who has lost a partner and is now ready to develop a new relationship. What should he or she do to get back into the mainstream again? What encouragement or advice would you give?

4. Researchers have shown that alcohol and marijuana have (if anything) deleterious effects on sexual functioning. But most users believe that they enhance sex. Why? What do you think?

5. Students and other young people often make fun of penile implants. Why? If you or your male partner lost the ability to get erect, would you want one of these implants? Why or why not?

Suggested Readings

Bullard, David, and Knight, Susan (eds.). *Sexuality and Physical Disability*. St. Louis: C. V. Mosby, 1981. The first half of this book provides an extraordinary collection of personal reflections on the sexual needs and experiences of the disabled. The second half of the book, which is less

prostatitis inflammation of the prostate, caused by infection.

engaging, consists of a number of papers of uneven quality discussing professional issues in this field.

Bush, Patricia. *Drugs, Alcohol and Sex.* New York: Richard Marek Publishers, 1980. Broad coverage of the physical and psychological effects of drugs and alcohol on sex, conveyed with a sense of humor.

Gregg, Charles. "Toxic Shock." In Gregg, C. (ed.), *A Virus of Love and Other Tales of Medical Detection,* pp. 93–112. New York: Charles Scribner 1983. A superb recounting of the whole toxic shock syndrome story including a scientific viewpoint and a revealing look at the commercial side of the issues involving Proctor & Gamble, the makers of Rely tampons.

Kolodny, Robert; Masters, William; and Johnson, Virginia. *Textbook of Sexual Medicine.* Boston: Little, Brown, 1979. A comprehensive but sometimes technical discussion of the impact of illness, drugs, and surgery on sexuality.

Love, Susan M. *Dr. Susan Love's Breast Book.* Boston: Addison-Wesley, 1990. This engaging, fact-filled book is full of expert advice rendered in a warm, caring manner. Outstanding discussion of breast cancer (as well as other breast diseases) and its diagnostic and treatment options.

Meadow, R. M., and Weiss, L. *Women's Conflicts About Eating and Sexuality.* Binghamton, NY: Harrington Press, 1993. A thoughtful discussion of how female sexuality is affected by pervasive cultural pressures to stay thin.

Meyers, Robert. *D.E.S.: The Bitter Pill.* New York: Putnam, 1983. The story of DES and its effects on millions is told with accuracy, insight, and compassion. Nontechnical but scientifically sound, this book is must reading for those who have been exposed to DES.

Monat, Rosalyn. *Sexuality and the Mentally Retarded.* San Diego: College-Hill Press, 1982. A thoughtful overview of a much-neglected topic.

Rabin, Barry. *The Sensuous Wheeler: Sexual Adjustment for the Spinal Cord Injured.* San Francisco: Multi-Focus Resource Center, 1980. A thoughtful, creative approach to a difficult subject, written in an informal tone. Deserves an award for its title!

Schover, L. R., and Jensen, S. B. *Sexuality and Chronic Illness: A Comprehensive Approach.* New York: Guilford Press, 1988. A concise yet comprehensive discussion of sexual aspects of many medical conditions.

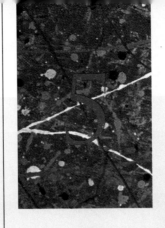

PART

Cultural Perspectives

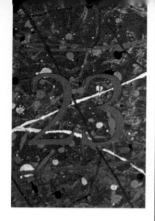

Sex and the Law

Throughout history, laws and other rules about behavior have existed for two very simple reasons: to give people guidelines about what is acceptable or "right" conduct and to keep people from doing "wrong" or unacceptable things (which may be harmful or offensive to others) by threatening them with punishment. Laws about sexual behavior have probably existed since the earliest days of civilization, but in the United States and in most of the Western world, most such laws can be traced back to sexual prohibitions found in the Judeo-Christian tradition. The original intent of such prohibitions was to preserve moral order as defined by particular sets of religious values. Today, even though the U.S. Constitution demands that our legal system function apart from any religious influence, the body of law that governs sexual behavior contains many remnants of the religious traditions from which it was derived.

Clearly, sexual behavior that victimizes another person—such as rape or incest—is difficult to defend on moral or philosophical grounds, so the fact that such acts are declared illegal is both logical and practical for most societies. But deciding what constitutes "proper" sex when both partners are consenting adults is more likely to be a matter of personal preference than to stem from the moral or philosophical principles necessary for the well-being of a given society.

In America and most of the Western world, we have restricted legally sanctioned sexual behavior to sex between the "right" people (e.g., married people but not blood relatives), in the "right" place (someplace private), and of the "right" type (generally, genital-to-genital sex is legal, while in most states oral–genital sex or anal sex is not). Of course, you may not always agree with the legal definitions of what kind of sex is "right" and what isn't, and that is partly what this chapter is about.

Most laws about sexual behavior in America are found at the state or local level. Since these laws vary quite a bit from one state to the next and change from year to year because of new legislation and new judicial decisions, it is not possible to provide a comprehensive, up-to-date listing of what is legal and what is not on a state-by-state basis. Instead, we discuss some general principles relating to legal issues about sexual behavior and some legal aspects of several related areas such as prostitution, obscenity, and pornography. If you need to get information about specific laws in your state, contact the local branch of the American Civil Liberties Union, an organization that can provide up-to-date answers.

RAPE AND SEXUAL ASSAULT

Although there are many definitions of rape, it is legally defined in most of the United States and Canada as sexual assault with penile penetration of the vagina without mutual consent (Estrich, 1987; Bourque, 1989; Muehlenhard et al., 1992; Fairstein, 1993). Thus, strictly speaking, penile penetration of the mouth or anus without mutual consent is usually not defined as rape but falls under other basic laws against sexual assault.

In recent years, some states have dropped the term rape entirely in favor of "sexual assault," hoping that this might increase the likelihood that survivors would report the crime and shifting more emphasis to the extent of physical and psychological injury the survivor has sustained rather than a focus on the sexual act itself (Wrightsman, 1991).

Other states now divide rape into several levels of criminal seriousness. For example, in the state of Washington, first-degree rape is defined as forcible compulsion under aggravated circumstances, such as use of a deadly weapon or during a kidnapping. The less serious charge of second-degree rape, which carries a lower prison sentence, requires

proving only the forcible compulsion. Third-degree rape is an even less serious charge that is defined as sexual intercourse without consent and without forcible compulsion. Such an arrangement has been thought to give jurors some leeway in decision making: when only one degree of rape covered all of the above circumstances, many juries found the possible sentence (such as the death penalty or life in prison) to be too extreme for certain cases and acquitted men accused of rape rather than expose them to these penalties (Wrightsman, 1991).

According to sex crimes prosecutor Alice Vachss (1993), virtually all of the accused's defenses to a charge of rape boil down to one of three basic categories: "It never happened," "She had sex with me willingly," or "Someone else did it, not me." Fortunately, as Fairstein (1993, p. 138) notes:

> There is no question that these trials present problems to survivors and prosecutors, but in large urban offices like ours,. . . [t]he experience of lawyers . . . enables them to anticipate the defense with a view to overcoming it, prepare the witness for the nature of her cross-examination, enhance the case by doing a more thorough investigation, and attempt to prove to the jury the absurdity of the defendant's claim.

Fairstein also observes that a fact of life in courtrooms today is that in acquaintance rape cases, jurors are greatly influenced by the appearance of the man who is being tried. Prospective jurors often observe, "I can't believe it—he doesn't *look* like a rapist," or "He doesn't look like he'd have to *force* someone to have sex with him," (Fairstein, 1993, p. 135). Other experts confirm this finding (Wrightsman, 1991; Vachss, 1992).

The Question of Consent

From a legal standpoint, one of the key elements in establishing that rape has occurred is the absence of meaningful consent. This is a somewhat tricky area legally for several reasons. First, the law has historically required that physical force or the threat of physical force be present in order to bring a charge of rape (some minor exceptions to this principle are discussed shortly). As a practical matter, this requirement has meant that to convict a man of rape, it has generally been necessary to show that the victim actively resisted. But exactly what constitutes a reasonable degree of resistance?

RESEARCH SPOTLIGHT

Beyond a Reasonable Doubt . . .

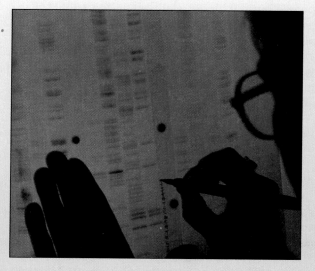

Just eight years ago, prosecutors and law enforcement personnel across the world became greatly excited by the development of a new technological breakthrough called "DNA fingerprinting" that could help them obtain convictions in cases of rape. DNA fingerprinting involves comparing samples of DNA (deoxyribonucleic acid, the basic genetic material in every cell in the human body) from sources such as semen, blood, or hair that may be found at the scene of a crime with samples obtained from a suspect. The samples are analyzed by a complicated series of tests that provide a biochemical "fingerprint" consisting of protein bands that experts believed initially were unique to each individual and would be as sure a means of identification as a more traditional fingerprint would. And because it is more likely that a speck of blood, a small piece of tissue, or semen will be left at the scene of a sex crime than it is that usable fingerprints will be found, this new technology was quickly pressed into use in courts across the country.

The first DNA fingerprints were accepted in American courtrooms in 1987. In several instances, the outcome of criminal trials hinged exclusively on the DNA evidence that was presented; jurors were enormously, and understandably, impressed by scientific expert testimony claiming that the odds of a match between two unrelated DNA fingerprints were 100 million to 1 or higher. In addition to obtaining convictions in many cases, DNA fingerprints were also used in some circumstances to establish innocence. Furthermore, DNA fingerprinting

---

If a woman kicks and screams and scratches at her assailant in an effort to fight him off, most juries would easily be convinced of her unwillingness to be a partner. But what if the rapist has a knife or a gun—or for that matter is 6'4" and 250 pounds: is it realistic or reasonable to expect that a woman must physically "fight back" in order to demonstrate that she was not consenting to sexual activity? It is certainly possible that a female might be so intimidated by the circumstances of such a rape that her wisest (and safest) course of action is to avoid any physical struggle. Yet the victim's lack of resistance in such a case would generally allow the rapist to claim in a court of law that the female was a willing participant who offered no opposition to his advances.

A second problem is that, in the past, it was often argued in rape trials that if the woman who claimed she had been raped was "unchaste,"

"promiscuous," or of "loose moral character," it was more likely that she had actually consented to having sex with the accused man, so no rape could have occurred. This led defense attorneys to focus great attention on examining the sex lives of the victims, although this practice has now generally been limited or banned entirely.

A third area relates to rapes that occur between people who have previously had voluntary, consenting sexual contact. Although clearly, as a matter of law, either partner has the absolute right to say no to any further sexual contact, as a practical matter this is one of the toughest areas to prosecute. In date rapes involving couples who have previously had sexual contact, for example, it may be very difficult for the female to convince a prosecutor to bring charges or to convince a jury that the sexual contact occurred without her consent. If the woman sustains bruises, scratches, torn clothing, or other

even seemed to have a deterrent potential: in Colorado and California, persons convicted of sex crimes must now give blood samples to the authorities for DNA fingerprinting before their release from prison in order to help solve any subsequent crimes they may commit.

Now, however, serious doubts have been raised about the validity of DNA fingerprinting—concerns both about its accuracy and about the ways of calculating the odds that the match of two samples is reliable. One researcher has noted that "two completely unrelated individuals will share a significant proportion of their [DNA] bands—some 20 to 40 percent—simply by chance" (Lewin, 1989, p. 1550). This can lead to mistaken "positive" identifications that turn out to be false—but if such a mistake went undiscovered, it could lead to a criminal conviction. Laboratories also can make mistakes—either by mistakenly identifying a match or saying that no match exists—and the available evidence suggests they do so at least 1 or 2 percent of the time (which is far from a reliability of 1 in 100 million). Laboratory mistakes occur both because of human error and because the technique for DNA fingerprinting is very complicated and subject to many sources or error. Another problem is that the actual DNA pattern in humans is not randomly determined; because of common ancestors, neighbors and friends may share more DNA bands than a South Sea Islander might be expected to share with a person whose family had lived in Alabama for generations.

Because of these concerns, the Minnesota Supreme Court has recently ruled that DNA fingerprints would be inadmissible until the scientific uncertainties are resolved. Other states are also reexamining their use of this form of evidence—and in some instances, appeals of earlier convictions have been mounted on the grounds that the jury was misled about the reliability of the scientific method being used. While this doesn't mean that a highly promising scientific technology must be discarded entirely, it does mean that—at least in the courtroom—this type of analysis must be viewed with caution until it is proved to be more accurate than it appears to be today.

Source: *Ford and Thompson, 1990.*

physical evidence of having resisted the sexual contact, however, there would be much less difficulty in bringing charges. The same principle applies even more strongly to cases of mate rape, where even states that permit such a charge also require ample evidence of coercion or force since marriage provides an implied consent to sexual intimacies.

Although various states (starting with Michigan in 1974) have passed legislation that shifts the focus from the conduct of the rape survivor to the actions of the rapist, as of the late 1980s, about four-fifths of the states still included a resistance standard in their definition of rape (Largen, 1988). Furthermore, in many states that implemented various degrees of rape law reform, the changes have had minimal impact both in and outside the courtroom (Goldberg-Ambrose, 1992). This poses a particular problem in jurisdictions that do not recognize how powerfully intimidated the victim feels by even an implied threat. For instance, when a grand jury in Texas refuses to indict because a woman who was terrified of AIDS begged the rapist to use a condom (Vachss, 1993), it reflects a fundamental misunderstanding of many in our society about just what rape is.

Rape charges can also be brought in cases where no force was involved. If at the time the sexual contact occurs the victim is either mentally incompetent, under the influence of drugs (including alcohol), unconscious, or defrauded into believing that she was married, rape charges can be brought because of the absence of a legally meaningful consent. Likewise, in cases of statutory rape (where the victim is under the age of consent), it does not matter legally if there was consent by both partners, since these laws are intended to protect minors who, by definition, cannot give a legally binding consent to a sexual act. (In a proven case of statutory rape, it is not the minor who is convicted and

Sexual Offenses: A Cross-Cultural Look

The legal boundaries established by our society about sexual behavior are hardly universal. In fact, concepts of what is acceptable, appropriate sexual behavior and what constitutes a form of sexual offense are largely culturally defined (Grubin, 1992). Behavior that is acceptable under some conditions in some societies is considered reprehensible and worthy of punishment in other societies.

Despite this, it is worth asking whether there are any universal areas of agreement about certain types of sexual offense. While it is clear that prohibitions of incest are as near to universal as any rules governing sexual behavior, most other forms of sexual behavior that the United States treats as deviant or offensive are subject to far less disapproval in other societies. For instance, although Americans consider rape to be an extreme example of unacceptable behavior, in many societies, including modern-day Bosnia, soldiers routinely rape women in villages they capture and see nothing wrong with such a practice. In primitive societies, too, rape is often regarded differently: for example, it may be part of ritualized behavior introducing the male or female to adulthood, or it might be part of ritualized punishment (as with the Cheyenne Indians of North America), or it is part of rivalries between separate clans (Grubin, 1992).

Sanday (1981) studied 156 different societies around the world and classified 18 percent as "rape-prone," 35 percent as exhibiting rape but not frequently enough to be considered rape-prone, and 47 percent as "free of rape." The last category consisted of societies in which rape was either nonexistent or very infrequent, including the Taureg of the Sahara Desert, the Pygmies of the Ituri rain forest in Africa, and the Arapesh of New Guinea. (Although it should be noted that it

is possible that the data about these societies are flawed, with the "rape free" societies actually being similar to others, but simply having very low rates of reporting rape.) Rape-free societies characteristically accord women considerable respect and attach prestige to a woman's reproductive role. Another nearly universal characteristic of rape-free societies is that they disapprove of interpersonal violence of any sort.

In contrast, in rape-prone societies there is almost invariably a lot of interpersonal violence, male dominance, and devaluing of the female role. Women are treated as property rather than as equals to men. Among industrialized nations, there is a partial parallel to Sanday's analysis. Japan has long had a much lower rate of rape than the United States, Great Britain, or France, for example. Japan fits Sanday's criterion of being a society that frowns on interpersonal violence, but at the same time it is a nation that has a long tradition of treating women as second-class citizens, so it doesn't really fit her second criterion. Another example of relatively rape-free industrialized societies can be found in modern Denmark and Sweden. In both countries, rape is far less frequent than in the United States, and both countries have a tradition of treating women in a relatively egalitarian manner. Furthermore, interpersonal violence is frowned on in these societies, so that they do, indeed, fit Sanday's predictions.

In the United States, of course, not only do we have an immense problem of uncontrolled violence—from seemingly irrational mass murders to frequent kidnappings, to domestic violence, to violence against the elderly (Kolodny, 1993)—we also treat women as less equal than men (see Chapter 11). Until these elements change, rape will remain a frequent crime in this country.

imprisoned, it is the adult.) Several states have laws that define a specific age—usually age 10—under which it is considered that no girl could possibly

have consented to sexual intercourse; anyone having sex with a girl below this age would be charged with actual rape rather than statutory rape (Mueller, 1980).

Sentencing the Rapist

Statutory rape is generally a felony—a serious crime—with some state statutes permitting prison terms of 20 years to life. Some states specify that the punishment depends on the age of the victim. For example, in Kentucky, if the victim is under age 12, the offender can be given either the death penalty or a life sentence, while if the victim is 12 to 15 years old, the sentence is 20 years, and if the victim is 16 or 17, the sentence is only 10 years.

In many states, forcible rape can be punished by death, although this penalty is not applied currently as often as it was in the past. [There has been some contention that black men convicted of raping white women were given death sentences in southern states far more often than white men were for raping either black or white women (MacNamara and Sagarin, 1977).] Lengthy prison terms for rape tend to be given for repeat offenders or in cases where the jury was convinced that extreme violence or cruelty was used (Estrich, 1987). However, it should be realized that many cases of rape eventually wind up being handled as misdemeanors since prosecutors frequently have to resort to plea bargaining (having both parties in a criminal case agree that the accused person will plead guilty to lesser charges). Plea bargaining avoids a trial that might be emotionally difficult for the victim (or difficult to prove to a jury's satisfaction), but it results in a greatly reduced sentence for the offender. This means that some rapists get out of prison within a year or two, given time off their sentences for "good behavior."

The Civil Suit Option

Although a criminal case can be filed and prosecuted only by the city, county, or state, rape victims may choose to file a civil action in which they sue their assailant for personal injury, pain and suffering, or punitive damages. (Some women also sue third parties—for instance, a motel chain or the corporate owner of a parking lot—if they believe that lack of safety on such premises materially contributed to their being raped.) In a civil suit, unlike criminal proceedings, people can hire their own attorney. In addition, since civil proceedings require that the suspect be proved guilty by "a preponderance of evidence," not by the more stringent "beyond a reasonable doubt" used in criminal proceedings, there may be greater likelihood of winning the case (Grossman and Sutherland, 1982/83). However, a civil suit will not succeed in putting even a convicted rapist in prison; it will only obtain a monetary judgment.

Attempted Rape

Before concluding this section, we should point out that *attempted* rape is also a serious crime. By definition, attempted rape occurs whenever the man assaults a woman but fails to achieve penile penetration of the vagina for any reason (losing his erection, being fought off by the woman, being interrupted by a third person who breaks up the attack, and so forth). If the man penetrates the vagina using a body part other than his penis (his tongue, a finger) or using an object (e.g., a dildo or beer bottle), then the crime is classified as a form of sexual assault, but it is not rape in the legal sense. In general, convictions for attempted rape or sexual assault carry somewhat less stringent sentences. If it can be established that a man is a repeat offender, however, it is much more likely that he will be given a far lengthier prison term than if it is his first conviction.

INCEST

Although incest is illegal throughout the United States, there is a great deal of variability from state to state in defining exactly what incest is. Most states limit the crime of incest to marriage or sexual contact between first- and second-degree blood relatives. As a practical matter, charges of incest are brought most often when the offense involves an adult–child interaction when the child is a minor, but this is not a legal necessity: in fact, charges of incest have been prosecuted successfully in cases involving a parent and an adult child or between adult siblings.

All states require that suspected cases of incest be reported under child abuse laws. Once state authorities have investigated a case and become convinced that the probability of incest having occurred is high enough to bring charges, the child–victim is usually removed from the home and placed in protective custody in a foster home arrangement. (This is not always an ideal solution, for a variety of reasons, so some states are now experimenting with keeping the child at home but requiring that the adult offender—usually the father—leave the home and enter treatment to avoid trial.) In the last decade, incest has increasingly come to be recognized as a matter best handled by family law and child welfare courts rather than by criminal courts. As a result, only a small number of incest cases are prosecuted, with most cases being handled by court workers who attempt to obtain psychological evaluation and counseling for the incest victim (even if he or she appears to be untroubled) as well as psychological therapy for the incest offender.

Cases that are prosecuted criminally tend to involve either repeat offenders, adults who have severely traumatized a child, a parent who has victimized several children over a period of time, or an adult who refuses to participate in treatment. In such cases, lengthy prison sentences can be handed out in most states. For example, in California and New Mexico the maximum sentence is 50 years; in Iowa it is 25 years; and in states such as Arizona, Arkansas, Connecticut, Maine, Maryland, Michigan, New York, Oklahoma, Texas, and Wisconsin it is 10 years.

SEXUAL ABUSE OF A CHILD

As with incest, sex between an adult and a child is strongly condemned in all jurisdictions in the United States, Canada, Europe, and most other countries. Sexual activity between an adult and a child is now widely regarded as a form of child abuse, so even if the child is a willing participant (and many authorities question whether a young child could possibly have the capacity to give consent) such acts are still illegal. The specific crime with which an adult may be charged may be rape, statutory rape, sexual assault, child molestation, impairing the morals of a minor, or incest, depending on the circumstances and the definitions used in a particular jurisdiction. Both men and women can be charged with these various forms of child sexual abuse.

Impairing the morals of a minor can be a crime that involves no physical sexual contact between the adult offender and the child. For example, recruiting a child to be photographed for "kiddie porn" would fall into this category, as would giving contraceptives or sexually explicit pictures to a child or bringing a minor to a brothel or gay bar. But the same statute can also apply to any non-

coital form of sexual contact between adult and child, whether it involves touching or fondling only or encompasses specific sex acts such as oral-genital contact. (If the adult–child act includes coitus, it is ordinarily prosecuted as rape.)

For adults who are convicted of child sexual abuse, the results are usually harsh. The severity of sentencing depends to some extent on the age of the child and the nature or length of the sexual acts in question. As a general rule, a sex act with an older teenage child is not judged as harshly as with a younger child unless force or injury was involved. The convicted sex offender is likely to receive a stiff prison term, particularly if it is a repeat conviction. In some jurisdictions, the offender may be given an indeterminate (open-ended) sentence. Depending on subsequent behavior and willingness to participate in treatment, the offender may be paroled in a shorter or longer time or may be imprisoned indefinitely.

Because the penalties for conviction of child sexual abuse are usually severe and because an accusation of such an act can play havoc with a person's life even if the charges are later dropped or the accused person is acquitted, there are several reasons to exercise caution in accepting as factual all claims made by children about sexual contacts with adults. First, there are many cases on record in which such accusations have been found to be fabrications, whether out of a child's wish to hurt someone or out of overimagination (Schetky, 1986). There is also the possibility that an adult may misunderstand a child, believing he or she meant that something sexual happened when the child's meaning was actually different.

This was a pivotal fact in the widely publicized McMartin preschool case in which an acquittal on most charges was handed down after a two and one-half year trial that cost the state of California over $15 million. The jurors were critical of videotaped interviews of the preschool children who had claimed to be molested under lurid circumstances involving satanic rites, mutilated rabbits and horses, and the drinking of blood, saying that "it appeared the children were coaxed into" making their charges (Reinhold, 1990).

This case illustrates the need to increase training in techniques of interviewing children for those professionals who gather testimony from the alleged victims of child sex abuse, so that those who conduct the interviews will resist asking the child leading questions and avoid pressuring the child's account in any direction (Eth, 1988; Mydans, 1990).

Establishing the credibility of a young child as a witness before a jury is not easy, and the rigors of the courtroom—including the requirement for cross-examination by a defense attorney—may be quite stressful and unsettling to the child. In fact, in some complex cases of child sexual abuse, pretrial hearings have gone on for years, so that by the time the case gets to trial the child–victim–witness may have difficulty recalling specific facts about the abuse. One other problem that law enforcement personnel and prosecutors encounter in cases of child sexual abuse is that repeatedly molested children, particularly those who are very young, have great difficulty distinguishing one act of abuse from another and pinpointing specific dates on which the abuse occurred. This makes it difficult to build the prosecution's case in a credible manner, especially because it is unlikely that there are witnesses available to provide corroborating testimony.

None of these reasons for caution means that suspected cases of child sexual abuse should not be vigorously investigated and prosecuted if warranted by the facts. Indeed, even when it might seem improbable at first that the child's story could be true—for instance, if the accused adult is an upstanding citizen, a prominent local figure, or a professionally distinguished person—careful investigation may finally show that the child has in fact been victimized and may even bring forward other child–victims of the same adult. But partly because of the strong sense of revulsion we have to child sexual abuse, it is important to realize that being accused is not the same as being found guilty. In fact, one recent study suggests that 58 percent of reported cases of child sexual abuse go unsubstantiated (Schetky, 1986).

When charges of sexual abuse of a child are made, there is almost invariably an attempt by the defense to claim that the child made up or imagined the whole matter. Recent research suggests that this is not apt to be the case. Saywitz and co-workers (1991) studied 72 5- and 7-year-old girls who were given standardized medical exams. For half, a vaginal and anal exam was included, while for the other half, there was no genital or anal contact at all. The girls who had not received vaginal exams never falsely reported having been touched on the genitals during the exam either in free recall discussions of the experience or while using anatomically detailed dolls to demonstrate the exam they had received, and even when they were asked misleading direct questions by the researchers, they did not make up inaccurate answers. While this research was certainly not an exact duplicate of sexual abuse situations (for one thing, the examining doctor was a woman; for another, the girl's mother was present in the examining room), it does suggest that in general children are not likely to lie about such "private" touching. However, this is a complicated issue, and there are certainly many instances in which false accusations are made for one reason or another, especially in families with a substantial number of problems (Hoorwitz, 1992).

SEXUAL HARASSMENT

The legal definition of sexual harassment is now quite specific:

> Unwelcome sexual advances, requests for sexual favors, and other verbal or physical conduct of a sexual nature constitute unlawful sexual harassment when (a) submission to such conduct is made either explicitly or implicitly a term or condition of an individual's employment, (b) submission to or rejection of such conduct by an individual is used as the basis for employment decisions affecting such individual, or (c) such conduct has the purpose or effect of unreasonably interfering with an individual's work performance or creating an intimidating, hostile, or offensive working environment. An employer is responsible for sexual harassment by its agents or supervisory employees regardless of whether the employer knew or should have known of their occurrence. An employer is responsible for acts of sexual harassment in the workplace committed by "non-supervisory employees" where the employer knows or should have known of the conduct and no immediate and appropriate corrective action was taken. (*EEOC Rules and Regulations, 1980*)

As more and more women have become aware of their legal rights in situations of sexual harassment, a large number of lawsuits have been filed with claims based primarily on sex discrimination under Title VII of the Civil Rights Act of 1964. Since few states have laws banning (or defining) sexual harassment at work, many of these cases have not been decided favorably for the women even when it was clear that sexual harassment did occur. Here, the situations were viewed as "personal" instances of harassment rather than sex discrimination (MacKinnon, 1979). Some landmark cases have been decided in the woman's favor, particularly in the past few years, and it may be anticipated that such judgments will become more realistically decided in the future. For example, in 1994 a jury awarded one woman more than five million dollars in a harassment case filed againt the law firm she had worked for, and one of the victims of the Tailhook scandal in Las Vegas was awarded millions of dollars in a case against the Hilton Hotel Corporation.

Coles (1986) reviewed 88 cases of sexual harassment (including 8 cases in which men were the complainants) that were filed with the San Bernadino County Office of the California Fair Employment and Housing Department between 1979 and 1983. She found that while the majority of people filing complaints were young, almost one-quarter were over 35. The instigators of sexual harassment were predominantly either a work supervisor (62 cases) or the owner of a business (19 cases). In 47 of these cases, a settlement—usually involving a payment for damages as well as lost wages, if a person had been wrongfully fired—was negotiated by the agency. Coles concluded that government agencies will act in cases of sexual harassment if witnesses to at least some of the charges are available (e.g., a co-worker who walks in on a supervisor pinching or grabbing at a victim), if there is some other type of corroborating evidence, or if several complaints have been filed against an individual or a firm.

In 1986, an important decision by the U.S. Supreme Court broadened the definition of sexual harassment to include behavior that creates a "hostile" or "intimidating" work environment whether it is linked with job advancement or not. The Supreme Court also ruled that, in certain circumstances, employers could be liable for damages even when they were unaware of sexual harassment occurring in their office or company.

The threat of economic penalties for businesses that allow sexual harassment to occur has led to a major effort on the part of large corporations like IBM, the Chase Manhattan Bank, Chrysler Corporation, and others to institute detailed company policies against sexual harassment and to educate

Teresa Harris talks to the media after attending agruments at the Supreme Court on her sexual harassment case.

their employees on this topic. Videotapes with titles such as "Power Pinch: Sexual Harassment in the Workplace" and "Shades of Gray" are being used to generate awareness and discussion among managers and workers about sexual harassment and how it can be prevented. As Foderaro (1986) notes: "Much of that discussion has centered . . . on what is sexual harassment. When does an arm around the shoulder cross the line between a show of affection and a come-on? When does an off-color joke go beyond harmless banter to being offensive and discriminatory?"

In 1993, the Supreme Court issued its first ruling since 1986 in a sexual harassment case and startled court observers by a unanimous 9 to 0 decision in which they broadened the definition of sexual harassment in the workplace considerably. The crux of the decision was that victims of harassment need not prove that the offensive behavior either damaged them psychologically or left them unable to perform their jobs. This was an important departure from previous legal precedent, since having to prove psychological damage from harassment was not always an easy task. Here is a portion of the

Figure 23.1 States Prohibiting Sodomy

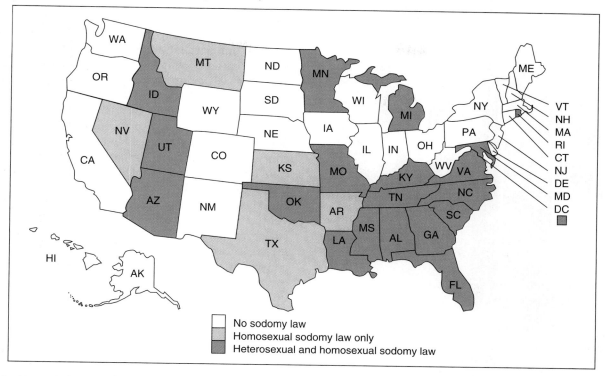

No sodomy law
Homosexual sodomy law only
Heterosexual and homosexual sodomy law

majority opinion in this case (officially known as *Harris v. Forklift Systems*), written by Associate Justice Sandra Day O'Connor:

Title VII comes into play before the harassing conduct leads to a nervous breakdown. A discriminatory abusive work environment, even one that does not seriously affect employees' psychological well-being, can and often will detract from employees' job performance, discourage employees from remaining on the job, or keep them from advancing in their careers. Moreover, even without regard to these tangible effects, the very fact that the discriminatory conduct was so severe or pervasive that it created a work environment abusive to employees because of their race, gender, religion, or national origin offends Title VII's broad rule of workplace equality. . . .

Certainly Title VII bars conduct that would seriously affect a reasonable person's psychological well-being, but the statute is not limited to such conduct. So long as the environment would reasonably be perceived, and is perceived, as hostile or abusive, there is no need for it to also be psychologically injurious.

The new standard described in the Supreme Court's decision will give juries more leeway in deciding when sexual harassment has occurred. More importantly, it sends a clear message to women that their complaints will receive a fair hearing and puts employers on notice that sexual harassment in the workplace will not be tolerated.

PRIVATE SEX BETWEEN CONSENTING ADULTS

It's safe to say that in any 24-hour period, millions of ordinary Americans unwittingly engage in sex acts that are defined as criminal and could lead to imprisonment. In many states, oral–genital sex is illegal (see Figure 23.1)—even between husband and wife—and extramarital sex, premarital sex, homosexual acts, and prostitution all fall within the long arm of the law.

Laws that regulate private sexual behavior between consenting adults are a source of dismay to many who argue that these are "victimless" crimes: no one is hurt by the activity, the public's sense of decency cannot be offended because the behavior is private, and the government should not be

"*I now pronounce you man and wife. Before you kiss the bride, Donald, I think I should remind you that the laws of this state specifically forbid the use of the tongue.*"

Source: *Reproduced by special permission of* Playboy *magazine. Copyright* © *1988 by* Playboy.

poking its nose into the bedrooms of the nation. Furthermore, such critics note, because it is practically impossible to detect such "crimes" and because it is clear that criminal sanctions do not "prevent" them, it is hypocritical to keep such laws on the books: it only encourages people to feel that breaking the law is a trivial matter. Supporters of laws governing sexual behavior note that they are no more arbitrary than laws pertaining to business, sports, taxes, or education and point out that many laws depend on first making a moral judgment that gets transformed into legislation.

While most people agree that these are indeed "victimless" crimes, not everyone agrees on just what "victimless" means. The prostitute is regarded as a victim by many; women may be victimized by an unintended pregnancy; anyone can be victimized by sexually transmitted disease. Defining "victim" in its broadest sense, some people believe that unrestricted sexual permissiveness may lead to the downfall of our civilization (the "victim").

Despite these philosophical and political disputes, if current laws regulating sexual behavior *were* enforced in a strict and uniform manner, our prisons would have to accommodate the great majority of our population. Recognizing this dilemma and recognizing that the common good could be better served if our criminal justice system turned its attention to crimes of violence and of a serious nature, the American Law Institute drafted a Model Penal Code, which recommends abolishing laws that regulate the private sexual behavior of consenting adults. The major provisions of this code have now been adopted by a number of states (including Illinois, Connecticut, Colorado, Oregon, and Hawaii), although political pressures have prevented it from becoming more widespread. The basic problem is that most politicians need to run for reelection and do not want to be accused by conservative groups or fundamentalist religious organizations of being "soft on crime" or "soft on sex."

Here are some of the ways in which sex laws categorize and criminalize private, consensual adult sexual acts.

Nonmarital Heterosexual Intercourse

The law usually differentiates between **fornication** (intercourse between unmarried heterosexual adults) and **adultery** (extramarital intercourse), with adultery being the more serious crime. In a few states, cohabitation is illegal. The statutes pertaining to fornication and adultery are infrequently enforced today; when they are, people on welfare or members of minority groups are usually involved. Not too long ago, in some states these laws applied only to biracial couples, but such laws have now been abolished as discriminatory and unconstitutional. In many states, adultery is judged to be unlawful only if it is committed "openly and notoriously," which sometimes meant that cases were prosecuted only if a couple registered falsely in a hotel or motel as husband and wife (Mueller, 1980). Punishment for those convicted of fornication or adultery is generally a fine, but in a few states a jail sentence may be given, depending on the discretion of the judge.

An interesting subcategory of fornication is called **seduction,** which is legally defined as a situation in which a woman is enticed into sexual intercourse by a promise of marriage. Only a male can be prosecuted under this statute (who said the law was always fair?) since the original intention of this law was to protect young, innocent females from exploitation by a more worldly man. Although laws against seduction are rarely enforced, because they are felonies they can carry prison sentences of five years or longer.

The laws applying to nonmarital heterosexual coitus have an interesting past. Adultery was originally frowned on because it violated the sanctity of the family and made it difficult to determine a child's paternity, complicating inheritance decisions (MacNamara and Sagarin, 1977). In addition, a married woman was considered the property of her husband, so if she engaged in extramarital sex, her husband's property rights were violated. A similar line of reasoning held in cases of seduction: the male who seduced a woman violated a verbal contract (his promise to marry her) just as surely as if he had pulled out of a business venture. The result of his broken promise was judged to be "damaged" or "used" property, which no longer had the value of the original, unsullied merchandise. His punishment? Take delivery of the "used" property (i.e., marry her, thus fulfilling the original "contract") or go to prison.

Noncoital Acts

In many states, most forms of noncoital sex are considered illegal even if they are done in private by consenting adult partners. As astonishing as it may seem in an age when oral sex is statistically the norm rather than the exception, a pleasant interlude of cunnilingus or fellatio can, theoretically, lead to arrest and imprisonment. Anal sex is similarly banned. In general, the statutes against such acts refer to them as sodomy or "crimes against nature," going back to the view that heterosexual intercourse (with its reproductive potential) is the only "natural," healthy, nonsinful way of having sexual relations.

While some states permit these sexual practices in legally recognized marriages, many states do not. Homosexual acts are banned by most states on the same grounds, and the likelihood of prosecution for gay men or women is substantially higher than it is for heterosexuals. Most arrests of homosexuals, however, are for public solicitation and not for specific sexual acts.

The Supreme Court and the Right to Privacy

Despite the large number of state laws making various types of sexual acts between consenting adults illegal, private sexual behavior has generally been thought to be protected by the reasoning implicit in a long line of judicial decisions. For instance, in 1965 the U.S. Supreme Court struck down a Connecticut law against selling or displaying contraceptive devices on the grounds that regulating reproductive behavior was outside the scope of state law (*Griswold v. Connecticut*). Later, in the 1973 landmark case *Roe v. Wade,* which established a woman's right to abortion, the Court further strengthened the notion of the right to privacy—without the interference of government—in matters of an intensely personal, intimate nature.

This long-standing tradition may have taken a sudden turn to the right in 1986, when a sharply divided Supreme Court decided that the U.S. Constitution does not protect homosexual activity between consenting adults even when it occurs in the privacy of their own homes. The background of the case is as follows. On August 3, 1982, a policeman went to the home of Michael Hardwick to serve him with a warrant because he had not paid a fine for public drunkenness. Another man answered the door and said he wasn't sure if Mr. Hardwick was at home but told the policeman he could check to see. As the policeman walked down the hallway, he looked through an open bedroom door and saw Michael Hardwick and another man engaged in oral sex. The policeman arrested both men, charging them with sodomy—a felony under Georgia law punishable by a prison term of up to 20 years.

Although Hardwick was not prosecuted, he decided to challenge the law on the grounds that it violated his right to privacy. In 1985, a three-judge panel of the U.S. Court of Appeals ruled in favor of Hardwick, finding that Georgia's sodomy law was unconstitutional because it interfered with per-

fornication (for' nuh kā' shun) coitus between unmarried heterosexual adults. A crime in some states.

adultery sexual intercourse between a married person and a partner other than his or her spouse.

seduction a situation in which a woman is enticed into sexual intercourse by a promise of marriage.

sonal freedom and privacy. Georgia officials appealed the ruling, arguing, among other points, that sodomy is an unnatural act and a crime against the laws of God and man alike and that antisodomy laws would help in the fight against AIDS.

In a highly controversial 5 to 4 decision announced on June 30, 1986, the U.S. Supreme Court ruled that Georgia's antisodomy law was constitutional and could be used to prosecute homosexuals who engage in oral or anal sex. At the same time, the Court sidestepped the broader question involved by declining to rule on whether such a law could be used to prosecute married couples or unmarried heterosexuals who engage in the same acts.

Later in 1986, the Supreme Court refused to hear a case in which it would have been confronted by the question of whether states have the right to make heterosexual sodomy between consenting adults a crime (*The New York Times*, October 15, 1986, p. B36). This suggests that, at least at present, the justices would rather not grapple with such an emotionally charged issue.

The homosexual community reacted to the Hardwick case with shock and dismay. Fearing that the Supreme Court action seriously eroded progress made by gays in the last decade on civil rights issues—at a time when homophobia and discrimination against gays were increasingly noticeable in reaction to the AIDS epidemic—many gay leaders were understandably alarmed. Jean O'Leary, executive director of the National Gay Rights Advocates, put it this way: "Homophobes want us to go back into the closet, [but] now the Supreme Court has even made the closet unsafe" (*Time*, July 14, 1986, p. 24).

A related aspect of the privacy issue involves the fairly common police practice of using surveillance cameras or officers stationed behind peepholes in public restrooms to detect male homosexual activity. In a case in Michigan, a judicial ruling said that such police practices are permissible and do not constitute an invasion of privacy (*The New York Times*, August 20, 1986, p. A8). Since public restrooms along highways or in parks, as well as in some gay bars or restaurants, are frequently used for quick, anonymous sexual encounters by homosexual or bisexual men, such police surveillance typically yields a substantial number of arrests. Readers whose first reaction to this practice is to view it as an unwarranted invasion of privacy should keep in mind that the amount of privacy expected in a "public" restroom is different from the privacy expected by a person in his or her own home and that an unsuspecting person entering such a public restroom may be offended by seeing strangers engaging in sex together.

PROSTITUTION

Although prostitution is legal in many countries throughout the world, where it is generally closely regulated by some form of government licensing and health check-ups, it is illegal in all U.S. jurisdictions except for several counties in Nevada. In spite of its illegality, prostitution flourishes in virtually all American cities, taking a variety of forms including low-status streetwalkers and male hustlers, massage parlor attendants, escorts for hire, call girls (and call boys), and the more traditional brothel-based prostitutes.

As pointed out in Chapter 17, there are male prostitutes as well as female prostitutes, although males make up only a small fraction of the overall population of persons working on a sex-for-hire basis. While some states and cities define the crime of prostitution in a way that applies to either gender, others have prostitution laws that pertain only to females. As with many other illegal acts, the crime of prostitution is defined in different ways in the penal codes of the various states and cities of the United States.

In general, prostitution is defined legally as the indiscriminate or promiscuous offer of a person's body for hire for the purpose of engaging in sexual activity. However, several fine points of distinction need to be kept in mind regarding this definition. First, it is not a single, specific act of sex for hire that legally defines a person as a prostitute; instead, prostitution is generally defined as a status crime (as in the crime of vagrancy) in which an ongoing pattern must be shown to obtain a conviction (Mueller, 1980). MacNamara and Sagarin (1977) point out that the requirement for sex with many partners—the "indiscriminate" or "promiscuous" criterion of the definition—is meant to exempt a "kept woman" or "paid mistress" from being legally considered a prostitute. A second point to keep in mind is that it is not necessary for a person to receive money as payment for sex to be legally

defined as a prostitute. The receipt of any item of value—for example, clothing, free rent, jewelry, or drugs—is enough to establish the commercial side of the sex-for-hire arrangement. Third, to charge and convict someone of prostitution in most jurisdictions, it is not necessary to have proof that a specific sex act was performed. Instead, it is usually necessary simply to prove that an offer to perform such an act was made for a specified price (making such an offer is legally called solicitation).

In most areas, laws against owning or operating brothels (houses of prostitution) specify that this crime is a misdemeanor, a crime of a less serious nature than a felony. As a result, people owning or operating brothels are usually treated leniently under the law—that is, with a fine but no prison term—except when they are repeat offenders or where the location of the brothel (e.g., near a public school or a church) is particularly offensive to the community. A place can be classified as a house of prostitution regardless of whether prostitutes live there, or whether it reveals its character publicly, and whether the activity is noisy or quiet (Mueller, 1980).

Customers of prostitutes can be arrested in some states but not in others. This discrepancy probably reflects the traditional view that it is the prostitute who is deviant and to be looked down on, while the man who patronizes her is seen as blameless (or, at worst, guilty of a minor indiscretion). In those locales where it is a crime to solicit or patronize a prostitute, including Dallas, New York, and St. Louis, the police regularly use policewomen "decoys" on street corners where prostitutes habitually try to attract customers. An unwary male approaches the decoy (usually by car), engages her in conversation (which is sometimes recorded by a hidden tape recorder or radio transmitter worn by the decoy), and—once he offers money in return for a sexual act—the decoy signals to her hidden police confederates, who move in to make the arrest.

Statistically, there are relatively few cases of men arrested for patronizing prostitutes in the United States, and the penalty for conviction is usually a small fine. Legislators apparently have taken the view that the deterrent effect of such laws is their major value—and that once having had the ignoble publicity of being arrested on such a charge, a man will likely think twice about dealing with a prostitute again.

Laws aimed against the prostitutes themselves take a variety of forms. As a practical matter, it is primarily streetwalkers and male hustlers who are vulnerable to arrest because their actions are the most visible. This is doubly true because many of the laws against prostitution are actually directed against loitering in a public place for purposes of prostitution or for solicitation; the call girl or call boy who works by appointment only and generally travels to the customer's home or hotel doesn't usually risk violating these statutes.

In some cities, police have mounted extensive campaigns against prostitution by posing as potential "johns" (in a variety of disguises) who arrest prostitutes once an offer for sex with a price tag has been made. Atkinson and Boles (1977) describe it this way:

> Many officers' costumes are highly idiosyncratic; one habitually wore a white fur hat, and another had an earring in one ear. Hair styles and length, beards and mustaches are part of the costume. . . . On special assignments officers may be dressed as conventioneers with badges, taxi-cab drivers, or street cleaners. *(p. 508)*

On the other hand, many prostitutes form a working alliance with vice squad officers by acting as informants, by keeping wayward hookers "in line," by paying "protection money," and by occasionally providing sexual favors to police officers, judges, journalists, and politicians (Atkinson and Boles, 1977; Barrows, 1986).

In most cases of women arrested for prostitution, conviction leads to a minimal fine, which is simply considered one of the expenses of doing business. Pimps often have a service contract with a lawyer who promptly arranges bail for any of their arrested "girls" so that their time off the streets and out of work is limited. If, on the other hand, a person is convicted not simply of prostitution but for another crime as well—for instance, robbery, assault, or blackmail—then a prison sentence is more likely.

Recruitment and the Mann Act

Pimps, madams, and others who recruit persons for prostitution are usually subject to prosecution under statutes against pandering or procurement. Whether or not someone consents to being a prostitute has no bearing on the illegal nature of recruiting them, although the original purpose of these statutes was to prevent females from being forced into prostitution—for example, holding a woman captive and demanding that she engage in prostitution to pay off her debts. Many antiprocurement statutes also extend to the activities of pimps who direct customers to prostitutes.

There are a number of special instances in which someone who recruits a female for prostitution is dealt with harshly by the legal system. A husband who entices or coerces his wife into becoming a prostitute is one such instance. This situation, sadly, is not as unusual as might be thought, especially in marriages where the husband gets hooked on drugs and uses his wife's earnings to pay for his daily habit. Far less common in the United States, fortunately, are families in which one or both parents introduce a daughter to prostitution.

A federal law passed in 1910 known as the Mann Act was aimed at preventing the abduction of females for purposes of prostitution. The Mann Act makes it illegal to transport a female across state lines (or into or out of this country) for "prostitution, debauchery, or any immoral purpose." Interestingly, the Mann Act is written in such a way that the female—even though she may already have been a prostitute and even though she may have willingly crossed state lines—has nothing to do with whether or not an accused offender is convicted.

Should Prostitution Be Legalized?

Not everyone in America agrees that prostitution should be illegal. Some argue that prostitution should be decriminalized since it will occur whether it is banned or not and since fighting it is not only relatively futile but also much less important than other uses of law enforcement personnel and funds. Others feel that decriminalization is not enough: they believe that legalizing prostitution is necessary to bring it under strict government supervision, which they believe can improve the overall safety of this activity for both the prostitute and her client.

One popular notion about prostitution that is often used to argue in favor of legalizing or decriminalizing it might be labeled the "social utility theory." According to this view, prostitutes provide a useful service to society. For instance, legalizing prostitution may reduce the chances that men would commit rape out of sexual frustration. In addition, prostitutes may also help build confidence among clients who are sexually insecure or who are unable to find their own sex partners because of physical deformities or disabilities. Furthermore, some suggest that regular visits to a prostitute may actually keep some marriages intact, when they would otherwise break up because of sexual problems.

Critics of the social utility theory point out the following difficulties with the above logic: (1) Most experts now believe that rape is not generally an act of sexual frustration (see Chapter 18). (2) The humanitarian benefits of prostitution are far overshadowed by prostitutes' roles in spreading sexually transmitted diseases (including HIV) and in committing crimes. (3) Even though large numbers of men use the services of prostitutes fairly regularly, it is quite unlikely that this saves many marriages from divorce. (No one has seriously suggested yet, to the best of our knowledge, that many women use the services of male prostitutes to save their marriages.)

Other issues relating to the need for reform in laws about prostitution continue to be murky. For instance, while it is thought that legalizing prostitution would result in all prostitutes registering to avoid arrest, the actual experiences in France, Germany, and the Netherlands have been that only about 10 to 20 percent of women engaged in prostitution register and become licensed to pursue their occupation (MacNamara and Sagarin, 1977; LaPoint, 1985). Some women do not register because they want to keep their earnings entirely to themselves, without having to pay taxes, licensing fees, or the costs of medical tests. Other women don't register because they don't want to work in government-approved brothels or because they want to keep their occupation a secret. Whatever the reason, in such a situation the general population gets the false impression that because prostitution has been legalized, it is completely safe. This is particularly the case with sexually transmitted diseases, where even weekly testing (which is expensive) is not 100 percent foolproof in preventing or detecting the existence of viral diseases such as genital herpes and AIDS.

Recently, Rio (1991) has argued that there are numerous advantages to legalizing prostitution, including: increasing government revenues by taxation, easing the enforcement burden on the criminal justice system, reducing the prostitute's vulnerability to her pimp, and eliminating the presence of streetwalkers. However, it is unlikely that such a social policy change will occur in the United States in the near future, for reasons that Green (1992, p. 203) explains:

> The major impediment to removing prostitution from the category of crime is, in the final analysis, a moral one, a vestige of the time (perhaps legendary) when sexual contact only occurred between married male and female partners and with a reproductive goal. . . . Sex-for-hire emphasizes too boldly the passing or undermining of this romantic ideal.

EROTICA

Pornography and Obscenity Laws

Webster's New Collegiate Dictionary (1980) defines **pornography** (from the Greek term meaning writings of or about prostitutes) as any form of communication intended to cause sexual excitement, while **obscenity** refers to anything that is "disgusting to the senses," "abhorrent to morality or virtue," and/or specifically designed to incite "lust or depravity." According to U.S. law, pornography is not illegal, but obscenity is.

U.S. obscenity laws date back to Massachusetts in the 1600s, where obscenity was first punishable by death and later by boring through the tongue with a hot iron. But obscenity meant something different then: it was an offense against religion—a blasphemy—and had nothing to do with sexual content of material. Obscenity did not encompass sexual materials until 1815 when a Pennsylvania court found several men who exhibited a painting of a nude couple in an "indecent posture" guilty of a common-law offense. In 1821 Massachusetts became the first state to convict booksellers of selling obscene literature. The book was John Cleland's *Fanny Hill,* and although the upper courts did not discuss the issue directly, the book seems to have been assumed to be obscene (Rembar, 1969, p. 15). By the mid-1800s several states had broadened their obscenity statutes to include sexual materials that "corrupted public morals."

In spite of the proliferation of obscenity laws and statutes during most of the nineteenth century, there was little enforcement at either a state or a federal level. A young grocery clerk named Anthony Comstock changed all that when he decided to personally check on the enforcement of an 1868 act that prohibited the distribution of obscene literature. Comstock, obsessed with the issue, joined forces with the YMCA, lobbied in Washington, and finally got Congress to broaden its federal mail act (later dubbed the Comstock Act) to prohibit the mailing of

pornography books or pictures that depict erotic behavior with the intent of causing sexual excitement. Technically, pornography is not illegal, obscenity is.

obscenity pictures or writing disgusting to the senses, abhorrent to morality or virtue, and/or specifically designed to incite lust or depravity. Obscenity is illegal, pornography is not.

obscene literature and to allow the post office to confiscate it (Talese, 1980). The mailing of birth control information particularly riled Comstock, and his crusade temporarily ended the practice.

In the first part of the twentieth century, obscenity laws in America were applied to a wide range of materials. Margaret Sanger's pioneering work advocating birth control for women ran afoul of these laws. Havelock Ellis's scholarly *Studies in the Psychology of Sex* was banned, and many books now recognized as literary classics were prohibited (Rembar, 1969; Bullough and Bullough, 1977).

The first breakthrough came in 1933 when Judge Woolsey of the New York District Court lifted the ban on importing *Ulysses,* a novel by the Irish writer James Joyce. Woolsey's famous decision noted that although *Ulysses* included many explicit sexual passages, its main purpose was not to incite lust. In addition, Woolsey's decision found that a work with serious artistic, literary, political, or scientific value could not be banned as obscene.

For the next two decades obscenity trials followed the guidelines of Woolsey's decision. However, in 1957 the U.S. Supreme Court established new standards for judging obscenity. The test now became whether the "average person, applying contemporary community standards" found the "dominant theme of the material taken as a whole appeals to prurient interest" (*Roth v. United States,* 1957). This decision was expanded in 1966 when the Supreme Court handed down a three-part definition of obscenity that is still used today: the material must appeal to a prurient interest in sex, offend contemporary community standards, *and* be "utterly without redeeming social value" (Rembar, 1969; Wilson, 1973).

These judicial opinions seemed to make obscenity judgment more objective and fair, but they led to a number of problems. For example, Supreme Court Justice Potter Stewart admitted that defining hardcore pornography was difficult, but said "I know it when I see it" (*Jacobelis v. Ohio,* 1965). Charles Rembar, who argued several important obscenity cases before the Supreme Court, also pointed out this subjective element when he noted that the difference between literature and pornography lies in the groin of the beholder (Rembar, 1969).

Other problems of these judicial decisions further complicate the issue. For instance, the Supreme Court has never defined what it means by "community." Does this refer to a geographic location or a group of people sharing similar cultural, political, or religious beliefs? On what basis is social value to be judged? Is the "average person" a man or a woman? Is it necessary for juries deciding obscenity cases to have equal numbers of males and females in order to strike an average?

In 1973 the Supreme Court ruled that *local* community standards could be used to obtain obscenity convictions (*Miller v. California,* 1973). Shortly after this decision, the Court made it clear that a rigid application of local standards could not be used to define obscenity. The case in point (*Jenkins v. Georgia,* 1974) was one in which a Georgia jury decided that the movie *Carnal Knowledge* was obscene. The Supreme Court overturned the conviction on grounds that local juries did not have "unbridled discretion" in judging what was obscene and what wasn't.

The combined impetus of *Miller v. California* (1973), with its emphasis on local community standards, and a slow but discernible national swing toward sexual conservatism has led to publishers of national newspapers and magazines and actors in pornographic movies being convicted in some communities for criminal violations of obscenity statutes although they had never been in those communities. In early 1990, many people were dismayed when an exhibit of photographs by the late Robert Mapplethorpe that included explicit depictions of sadomasochistic and homosexual acts was banned in Cincinnati by a notoriously antipornography district attorney. (The exhibit was reopened by court order; in a subsequent jury trial, the museum director was found to be innocent of obscenity charges.) Civil libertarians—concerned with protecting the constitutional rights of freedom of speech and freedom of the press—worried that the threat of such lawsuits would create a stifling climate of censorship. While this has not yet come to pass, further rulings from the Supreme Court are needed to clarify the ambiguities of current obscenity standards.

The movement toward more restrictiveness was fueled by a federal advisory commission convened by Attorney General Edwin Meese. The recommendations of the Meese Commission (1986) included a call for a national crackdown on pornography spearheaded by three different forms of action—action by citizens' groups, action by law enforcement agencies, and legislative action. Here is a representative summary of the commission's major recommendations:

- Religious and civic groups were encouraged to picket and protest or take other actions to disrupt the sale of material they find offensive even if such materials are not obscene.
- There should be more vigorous enforcement of current obscenity laws at federal, state, and local levels; there is no need, however, to broaden the current legal definition of obscenity.
- Second or subsequent violations of obscenity laws should become felonies punishable by at least one year in prison.
- Legislation should be passed at both the federal and state levels requiring convicted pornographers to forfeit their profits and permitting the confiscation of property they had used in the production or distribution of obscene material.
- Congress should ban obscene cable television programming.
- The Federal Communications Commission should ban dial-a-porn telephone services.
- Stringent regulations should be written to clamp down on the production and distribution of child pornography.

Earlier, a number of scientists on whose research findings the commission's report was supposedly based expressed dismay at how their work had been misinterpreted by the panel. Edward Donnerstein, a psychologist at the University of Wisconsin who is one of the leading researchers exploring the effects of violent pornography, said: "These conclusions seem bizarre to me. It is the violence more than the sex—and negative messages about human relationships—that are the problem. And these messages are everywhere" (*The New York Times*, May 17, 1986, p. A6). Another prominent researcher in the field, Neil Malamuth, had testified to the commission that no direct causal link has been scientifically established between viewing portrayals of sexual violence and committing sexually aggressive acts. Malamuth also disagreed with the commission's assessment of the current prevalence of violent pornography. "There has been an increase," he said, referring to the change since 1970, "but it's not like it went from zero to 50 percent. It's more likely the amount of sexually violent material went from a small amount to maybe 10 percent" (*Chicago Tribune*, July 13, 1986, Section 5, p. 9).

Other reactions to the report have been mixed. Barry Lynn, legislative counsel to the American Civil Liberties Union, called the report "a form of taxpayer financed consumer fraud" and "little more than prudishness and moralizing masquerading behind social science jargon." Jerry Falwell, president of the Liberty Foundation, praised the commission's findings and recommendations, calling it "a good and healthy report that places the United States government clearly in concert with grass roots America." The National Organization for Women (NOW) issued a statement agreeing with the commission's findings "that pornography harms women and children" but cautioned that there was danger that "the religious right" would "spread bigotry and hatred against lesbians and gay men" under the banner of fighting pornography. Showing the divisiveness of the issue even within feminist ranks, Betty Friedan and others joined in support of a Feminist Anti-Censorship Task Force that issued a critical pamphlet titled "The Meese Commission—A Menace to Women" (McNulty, 1986).

The Use of Erotica

Today, it is practically impossible to find a high school student in America who has not come across some form of sexually explicit material (erotica). Although there are bookstores, movie theaters, and videotape clubs catering to the "21 or older" crowd, there are ample supplies of so-called soft-core erotica in men's and women's magazines, best-selling novels, advertising campaigns, comic books, and general release movies to guarantee that anyone remotely interested in viewing such materials can have the opportunity.

There are many reasons why people show an interest in the use of erotica. Erotica provides a source of knowledge and comparative information about sexual behavior. These materials often produce sexual arousal which can be prolonged or abbreviated depending on a person's appetite at a particular moment. Like sexual fantasies, erotica triggers the imagination and so helps people deal with forbidden or frightening areas in a controlled way. Erotica gives people an opportunity to imaginatively rehearse acts that they hope to try or are curious about. Finally, just like westerns or spy thrillers, erotica can provide a kind of pleasurable recreation or entertainment separate and apart from its sexual turn-on effect.

There seem to be few differences in the sexual arousal induced by words, photographs, or movies (Byrne, 1977). Some people prefer the more vivid, real-life action of cinema, whereas others prefer to let their imaginations expand on a drawing or photograph or find that the printed word offers a greater ease in erotic interest. Such differences are matters of style and preference in just the same way that one person prefers a concert to a movie while someone else likes seeing a play, no matter what the subject matter. In contrast, the content of erotica, rather than its style of presentation, does have a specific effect. People are more likely to be sexually aroused by content to which they relate, rather than by portrayals of sexual acts which they find uncomfortable or offensive.

The sexual arousal that occurs with the use of erotic materials is not simply psychological. Many investigators have noted specific physiologic changes in people who watch erotic pictures or movies (Schmidt and Sigusch, 1970; McConaghy, 1974; Henson, Rubin, and Henson, 1979), read erotic passages (Englar and Walker, 1973), or listen to tape recordings of erotic stories (Heiman, 1977, 1980; Schreiner-Engel and Shiavi, 1980). Men often experience penile erection while women undergo changes in vaginal blood flow or lubrication.

In the past, it was generally assumed that men responded more frequently and powerfully to erotic readings, pictures, and films than women did. Research evidence, however, indicates that this is not the case: both sexes respond to erotica in similar ways (Englar and Walker, 1973; Byrne, 1977; Athanasiou, 1980). To be certain, some females—having been taught that it is not "ladylike" to allow oneself to be intrigued or excited by such materials—avidly avoid any exposure to erotica or do their best to block their own spontaneous responses by an act of will. The same reaction may occur among women who object to pornography on political grounds as exploitive of females. Other females may be more open to the opportunity but have difficulty noticing mild sexual arousal even when physiological changes such as increased vaginal blood flow can be detected. The male, in contrast, usually has more obvious external evidence of his arousal.

Another consideration is that while both males and females have a similar capacity to respond to erotica, the *type* of erotica (content, style, plot) may also be important in determining the response pattern. In the past, it was thought that males tend to be more object-oriented and respond to stark close-ups of sexual action, while females pay more attention to the style, setting, and mood. Other studies, however, show that males and females are actually quite similar in what they find erotically arousing (Fisher and Byrne, 1978).

The Effects of Erotica on Behavior

How the use of erotica affects behavior is a complicated question that provokes much controversy at present, with no single answer readily apparent. In the United States, President Lyndon Johnson established a special Commission on Obscenity and Pornography in 1968, which reviewed a large body of research over the next two years. The Commission's Report (1970) noted:

> When people are exposed to erotic materials, some persons increase masturbatory or coital behavior, a small proportion decrease it, but the majority of people report no change in their behaviors. Increases in either of these behaviors are short lived and generally disappear within 48 hours. . . .

> In general, established patterns of sexual behavior were found to be very stable and not altered substantially by exposure to erotica. *(pp. 28–29)*

In addition, in Denmark after hard-core pornography became widely available (and legal) in 1965, the rates of many sex crimes decreased substantially (Kutchinsky, 1970, 1973), while studies in America showed that rapists, child molesters, and other sex offenders actually had less exposure to sexually explicit materials during adolescence than other adults (Goldstein, 1973). Furthermore, repeated heavy exposure to erotica seems to lead to satiation and boredom rather than changes in sexual behavior (Lipton, 1983). Thus, a number of authorities have concluded that reading pornographic materials or viewing sexually explicit pictures of films doesn't turn people into sexual maniacs (Money, 1980) or incite men to rape or act in sexually impulsive ways (W.C. Wilson, 1978; Money, 1980; Athanasiou, 1980; Lipton, 1983; Green, 1992).[1] In addition, recent research has shown that re-

---

[1]The studies cited all have methodological flaws—as all research does—and their findings have not been universally accepted. For an alternative view of these and other studies on the effects of pornography, see Diamond (1980) and Bart and Jozsa (1980).

Violent Pornography and Aggression

Although most researchers agree that the use of erotica in and of itself doesn't lead to negative social consequences (Green, 1982; Linz, 1989), many feminists have suggested that there is a profound debasement of women found in most pornographic materials (Faust, 1980; Griffin, 1981; Steinem, 1983). Attention has focused on a particular form of pornography—violent pornography, defined as depictions of sex in which force or coercion is used against women. In the past decade, violent pornography has become more prominent in films such as *Maniac, Texas Chainsaw Massacre,* and *Tool Box Murders* and has been shown graphically in issues of *Hustler* and similar men's magazines. Now evidence linking the viewing of such violent pornography to aggression against women is beginning to emerge.

Neil Malamuth and Edward Donnerstein have been in the forefront of researchers studying this relationship. Their work has shown that it is the violence, rather than the sexual content, of such materials that produces negative effects. For instance, Donnerstein conducted a set of experiments that showed that exposure to X-rated depictions of sexual violence against women often increases the acceptance of myths about rape (such as the notions that women secretly want to be raped and enjoy the experience) and lead many men to say that they would commit rape if they were certain they wouldn't be caught (Donnerstein, 1983). In addition, viewing X-rated violent films increases men's aggressive behavior against women in laboratory settings and decreases male sympathy and sensitivity toward rape victims when the subjects are viewing videotapes of simulated rape trials (Donnerstein and Linz, 1984). Specifically, Donnerstein (1983) observed:

> Most startling, the men by the last day of viewing graphic violence against women were rating the material as significantly less debasing and degrading to women, more humorous, more enjoyable, and claimed a greater willingness to see this type of film again.

Malamuth's studies have previously shown that hostility toward women predicts rape-related attitudes, motivations, and behaviors (Malamuth and Donnerstein, 1984). In addition, he has found that men who score high on the likelihood-to-rape scale have more arousal fantasies after exposure to slides and tapes depicting rape than after exposure to mutually consenting coitus (Malamuth, 1981). However, some of the research findings are confusing, since "even men who score low on the likelihood-to-rape scale are sometimes highly sexually aroused by portrayals of rape" (Cunningham, 1983), and women themselves are also sometimes highly aroused by eroticized depictions of rape (Stock, 1983). On the contrary, women who listened to a description of rape that was realistic, emphasizing the victim's fright and pain without any attempt at eroticizing the scenario, generally registered lower genital responses and lower levels of subjective sexual arousal (Stock, 1983).

Although these studies are thought-provoking, they must be interpreted cautiously at present for several different reasons. Thus far, for example, they have involved relatively small samples and have been conducted primarily in college student populations. Furthermore, these studies have involved experimental methods that lead to somewhat artificial judgments of attitudes and (potential) behaviors; for ethical reasons, a true field study of the effects of violent pornography has not yet been conducted. Despite these limitations, however, the findings described above are particularly noteworthy because they have been based on the effects of viewing relatively brief amounts of violent pornography. Since loss of sensitivity to violence and even a proclivity toward violent behavior may well be a cumulative effect, studies are now under way examining aggressive behavior and attitudes toward violence after repeated, prolonged exposure (Donnerstein and Linz, 1984).

peated viewing of nonviolent pornography has no effects on attitudes toward women (Padgett, Brislin-Slütz, and Neal, 1989). However, there are conflicting findings in this general area. For example, Marshall (1988) reported that rapists and child molesters used hard-core pornography significantly more, both in adolescence and adulthood, than nonoffender controls.

There is another aspect to this question. A number of observers believe that in the past 20 years there has been a considerable increase in the appearance of violence in pornography (Eysenck and Nias, 1978; Lederer, 1980; Malamuth and Spinner, 1980; Stock, 1983; Donnerstein and Linz, 1984). Since both a 1960s presidential commission and a more recent task force of the National Institute of Mental Health have found clear evidence linking pictorial portrayals of violence in the media to increased aggressive behavior by observers, there is now much concern about whether this fusion of violence and pornography may have specific negative effects on behavior (see "Research Spotlight" on page 657). In addition to other uncertainties about violent pornography, many people are also concerned with the ways in which pornography debases and "objectifies" women, portrayals that they feel may contribute to sex discrimination by showing women as "mindless" sex objects. Thus, even if such materials do not directly affect behavior, by reinforcing existing stereotypes and prejudices about men and women they may strengthen or even create types of attitudes that are ultimately expressed in behavior (Linz, 1989).

There are several other sides to the question of the long-range effects of erotica. There is evidence that sexually explicit materials can sometimes help people to overcome sexual problems or can lessen their sexual inhibitions (W. C. Wilson, 1978; Money, 1988). Sometimes, however, these materials provoke anxiety—particularly when people compare their physical attributes or sexual response patterns to the stars of erotica. These heroes and heroines are not only highly attractive but engage in instantaneous, endless passion (the hallmark of erotica). Some people understandably respond to these images with guilt, embarrassment, or self-doubt.

Given the trend of the last 20 years toward a greater acceptability and accessibility of sexually explicit items—and the recent boom in uncensored cable TV and home video systems—it seems im-portant to gather more complete data on the effects of erotica. We should not overlook the possibility that use of erotica is sometimes accompanied by problems; neither should we be frightened by old negative attitudes reborn in the guise of modern morality.

Beyond the Meese Report: Where Are We Headed?

The essential elements of disagreement in the pornography debate continue much as they were even before the report of the Meese Commission. Those who want more restrictive legislation and further bans on the production and sale of pornography claim to represent the majority of citizens in the United States. Insisting that they are not vigilantes or censors, they argue that laws against pornography do not limit freedom of the press any more than laws against libel or plagiarism do. They also note that it is difficult, if not impossible, to prevent pornographic materials from being seen by children and teenagers, with no way of knowing whether such exposure may have long-term negative effects. In addition, they argue that even if pornography doesn't actually lead to sex crimes, it almost undoubtedly affects people's attitudes toward such crimes by fostering the myth that women enjoy being raped and by otherwise presenting females in a degrading manner.

Those on the other side of the fence argue that more restrictive laws would necessarily violate First Amendment rights, leading to legal bans on books that are widely acclaimed as having literary or artistic merit—as happened in the past with books such as James Joyce's *Ulysses* or D. H. Lawrence's *Lady Chatterley's Lover*.

Opponents of more restrictive legislation also point out that no one is forced to buy pornographic books, magazines, or videotapes, so the popularity of these materials shows that there is considerable demand for them among adults. The anticensorship camp also notes that the Meese Commission's finding of a link between violent pornography and sexual aggression is not supported by the scientific evidence and point out that there isn't an attorney general's commission trying to ban *Rambo* or *Dirty Harry* movies or other blatantly violent films. Thus, they argue, the latest move to crack down on pornography is just another round in the same ongoing battle—a battle they feel they must fight to keep the government from having the right to dictate what they can read or watch in the privacy of their own homes.

FUTURE DIRECTIONS IN SEX LAW REFORM

After reading about the many ways in which sexual behavior is regulated in the United States, it probably won't surprise you to realize that there are some major discrepancies in laws applying to sex. For instance, in most locations, the clients of a prostitute are not subject to arrest, but the prostitute is. In some states, oral or anal sex between two consenting heterosexual partners is legal if done in the privacy of *their* own home, but if the same act is done by two consenting men or two consenting women in the privacy of *their* own home, it is not only illegal but may be punishable by a lengthy prison term. In many states, laws pertaining to sex that were written more than a hundred years ago remain on the books. And there is little uniformity from state to state in penalties for many sexual offenses.

Not too long ago, many legal experts had hoped that the American Law Institute's Model Penal Code, which was written in the late 1950s, would eventually become the law of the land. Although Illinois adopted this set of laws in 1961 and was subsequently followed by 22 other states, there has recently been a virtual halt toward decriminalization of private sexual acts between adults in those states that haven't yet changed their laws. In fact, in several states where the Model Penal Code was approved, it did not last very long. In Idaho, the state legislature repealed the changes before they even took effect. In Arkansas, sexual reform lasted for one year, and then legislation was passed that restored criminal status to homosexual acts, although private heterosexual acts between consenting adults remained decriminalized.

The climate of religious and political conservatism in America in the mid-1990s does not seem likely to give rise to much liberalization in laws regarding sexual behavior. In fact, with increasing public concern over the AIDS epidemic and other sexually transmitted diseases, which in turn puts a negative spotlight on homosexual acts, prostitution, and all forms of nonmonogamous sex, it is quite possible that we may see an eventual shift toward a greater degree of sexual restrictiveness. If the Meese Commission report on pornography, and the 1986 Supreme Court decision upholding the constitutionality of Georgia's sodomy law, are any indications, this shift may actually have already begun.

SUMMARY

1. In the United States, many current laws about sexual behavior have their origins in the Judeo-Christian tradition. As a result of legislation and court decisions, however, these laws vary considerably from state to state.

2. Laws about rape and sexual assault generally depend on showing that the victim did not consent in a legally meaningful way to the sexual contact that occurred. While this is usually easiest to prove in cases of forcible rape where there was physical evidence of the victim's resistance, there are a number of circumstances in which lack of physical resistance does not preclude bringing rape charges or obtaining a conviction.

3. It is important to remember that rape is a criminal offense, which means that charges must be brought by the state or city rather than by the victim. A rape victim may, however, file a civil suit, in which she or he can sue for monetary damages.

4. Incest and other forms of child sexual abuse are generally dealt with harshly by the law when they are prosecuted, but in many instances offenders are permitted to enter treatment programs rather than face trial. Although it is important to give a fair hearing to all claims made by a child that such an act occurred, it is also important to realize that not all such accusations turn out to be factual.

5. The law deals with private sex between consenting adults in various ways from one state to another. There is much disagreement over whether these "victimless crimes" should ever be prosecuted. In the so-called Hardwick case, the U.S. Supreme Court upheld the constitutionality of Georgia's homosexual sodomy law, but it ducked the issue of whether heterosexual sodomy could be criminally prosecuted.

6. Although there are some advocates of decriminalizing or legalizing prostitution, prostitution

is currently illegal in all U.S. jurisdictions except some countries of Nevada. This hasn't seemed to stop the activity, however. Customers of prostitutes can be arrested or fined in some states, but most prostitution laws punish the prostitute or the person who recruited the prostitute rather than the customer.

7. Obscenity laws in the United States can be traced back to Anthony Comstock in the nineteenth century and continue to provoke much debate today. First Amendment advocates, who seek to preserve freedom of speech and freedom of the press, fear that anti-obscenity legislation will broadly be used as a type of unnecessary and inhibiting censorship, although most of them agree that laws against child pornography are necessary and proper. Those taking a more conservative view—including the majority of members of the Meese Commission, which issued its major report in 1986—advocate various measures to restrict pornography and obscenity since they contend they may lead to violent, abusive sexual behavior and since they tend to debase women.

8. If current trends are any indication, we may be about to witness a return to more restrictive laws governing sexual behavior as an outgrowth of public concerns about AIDS and other sexually transmitted diseases and as a result of a shift from a liberal to conservative political climate.

Thought Questions

1. What are the pros and cons of a civil suit versus a criminal trial in the case of a rape? Would it be wise for child sexual abuse victims to bring a civil suit against the alleged perpetrator? What if the case involved incest? Should an adult daughter sue her father for having been damaged by incest when she was a child?

2. The laws against incest usually involve a parent-figure and a minor. However, in 1979 a case occurred in which a young man and a woman met by accident, fell in love, and wanted to marry. They turned out to be brother and sister, separated as infants and adopted into different families. Should they be allowed to marry? Would such a union be incestuous? Would the State be justified in prosecuting this couple under laws prohibiting incest?

3. Should states be allowed to proscribe (i.e., make illegal) acts performed by homosexuals when the same acts are legal when performed by heterosexuals? Is this "equal protection under the law"? Is it the sexual act or the sexual orientation that is illegal?

4. In states that regulate sexual behavior according to the Model Penal Code, sexual acts that are mutual and performed in private by consenting adults are legal. Why then is prostitution illegal in these states? Should it be?

5. Regarding the myriad of usually unenforced laws that proscribe sexual acts, Kinsey was quoted as making the observation that "Most American men are sex offenders, and women are only a little less guilty." Since most Americans break these laws, why do state legislatures have difficulty in clearing up the situation by passing laws based on the Model Penal Code recommendations?

6. In terms of the complicated problems of the undesirable effects of censorship, our constitutional right to free speech, and the possible dangers to our society from widespread pornography: Is there a difference between the media in which pornographic materials are presented? Should society respond differently to pornographic books, paintings, films, photographs, videotapes, phone-answering services, etc.? Are some forms more potentially dangerous than others? Do the various forms represent equally important examples of speech that need to be protected?

Suggested Readings

Estrich, S. *Real Rape.* Cambridge, Massachusetts: Harvard University Press, 1987. A detailed look at rape laws and potential rape law reforms.

Fairstein, Linda A. *Sexual Violence: Our War Against Rape.* New York: William Morrow, 1993. A readable, detailed, thoughtful analysis of the legal treatment of rape written by one of the preeminent prosecutors in the field. This book is rich with insights into the criminal justice system vividly illuminated with numerous true stories of rape cases.

Final Report of the Attorney General's Commission on Pornography. Nashville, TN: Rutledge Hill Press, 1986. A one-volume, paperback edition of the controversial Meese Report.

Green, Richard. *Sexual Science and the Law.* Cambridge, MA: Harvard University Press, 1992. Thoughtful (but sometimes stuffy) discussions by a psychiatrist/attorney of a wide range of legal issues relating to sexuality, including child custody for homosexual parents, transsexuality, pornography, prostitution, and sexual privacy.

MacNamara, D. E., and Sagarin, E. *Sex, Crime, and the Law.* New York: Free Press, 1977. A comprehensive overview of the subject. Now somewhat dated, but still lively reading.

Rembar, Charles. *The End of Obscenity.* New York: Bantam Books, 1969. A fascinating journey through the trials of *Lady Chatterley's Lover, Tropic of Cancer,* and *Fanny Hill* written by the lawyer who defended these books before the U.S. Supreme Court.

Vachss, Alice. *Sex Crimes.* New York: Random House, 1993. This hard-hitting, fact-filled book about dealing with rapists, pedophiles, and other sex criminals is masterfully written. Here is what Vachss says on page 1 of her book: "The names of defendants and public figures are real. There is no reason to protect [their] identity. We're the ones who need protection from [them]."

Religious and Ethical Perspectives on Sexuality

The important role of personal and cultural values in sexual decision making has been mentioned in many places throughout this book.[1] We have also suggested that there is no single set of values and rules that fits all people in all societies all the time. This chapter addresses the two major ways in which individuals and societies approach questions of values: through religious beliefs and ethical analysis. The intent is not to present yes or no answers to difficult sexual choices but to examine ideas that have been important historical influences on sexual attitudes and practices and that continue to affect contemporary cultural patterns.

RELIGIOUS VIEWS OF SEXUALITY

Many books have been written about religion and sex, and it would be naive to think that thorough and detailed coverage is possible in these few pages. Instead, we highlight some of the similarities and differences in the ways that certain religions have dealt with sexual issues, remembering that these views have changed over the course of

[1]The first section of this chapter was written in collaboration with J. Robert Meyners, Ph.D., who was Associate Director of the Masters & Johnson Institute from 1983 to 1987 and Professor of Theology and Urban Culture at the Chicago Theological Seminary from 1966 until 1979.

time. While our discussion focuses on Jewish, Catholic, and Protestant thought, we also mention the sexual values found in several other religious traditions.

Judaism

Jewish views of sexuality stem from both the Hebrew Bible (called the Old Testament by Christians) and from the Talmud, a collection of writings interpreting the Bible and applying its teachings to everyday matters. Throughout these writings, the basic attitude of Judaism is that sexuality is a positive force, a gift of God the creator. This attitude is clearly expressed in the Song of Songs, supposedly written by King Solomon. This brief excerpt shows its decidedly erotic tone:

> Oh may your breasts be like clusters of the vine
> and the scent of your breath like apples
> And your kisses like the best wine.
> *(Song of Songs 7:8–9)*

Judaism teaches that it is irreverent to regard the sex organs or their functions as obscene (Gordis, 1978) since God created Adam and Eve in his own image and since he saw that all his creations were good (Genesis 1:27,31). Furthermore, although one purpose of sex is reproduction—as stated by the first positive command in the Bible, "Be fruitful and multiply" (Genesis 1:28)—sex is also meant to be enjoyed (Franzblau, 1975; Rosenheim, 1977; Fertel and Feuer, 1979). Judaism teaches that the joy of sexual activity is good in and of itself, apart from its procreative potential. However, sexual activity is seen as proper only within a marriage, a view reflecting that the Jewish family has "a supreme religious significance" (Rosenheim, 1977).

As indicated by many writings, the Jewish tradition has never believed that marriage exists only for the purpose of having children. Instead, companionship and mutuality between spouses are of major importance. For this reason, Jewish law urges that *all* people marry—including those who are infertile or elderly. Furthermore, Jewish law has always seen sexual activity between husband and wife as mandatory. The Talmud suggests how often sexual intercourse ought to take place according to the husband's occupation: for example, laborers should have intercourse at least twice a week and scholars should have intercourse at least once a

week, preferably on Friday evening (the eve of the Jewish Sabbath), since intercourse is sacred. The Talmud also declares, however, that a woman has the right to reject her husband's sexual advances, in which case he is forbidden to pressure her to try to change her mind (Gordis, 1978). Jewish wives have always been encouraged to take an active role in lovemaking and to initiate sex if they wish. Needless to say, this view of female sexuality was relatively unique 2000 years ago. Although the family structure of ancient Jews has often been regarded as male-dominated, this is certainly not the case today (in some branches of Judaism, women have been ordained as rabbis).

Sexual relations between husband and wife are relatively unrestricted. Oral and anal sex are permissible (although the male is expected to ejaculate only within the vagina), no limits are placed on the

In Orthodox Judaism, women are always segregated from men in the synagogue.

A gay pride march in New York City shows that not all Jewish congregations are opposed to homosexuality.

frequency of sexual activity, and both partners are expected to derive pleasure from their sexual interaction. Celibacy is not only valueless as a virtue, it is actually regarded as sinful. Since each spouse has an obligation to provide for the sexual fulfillment of his or her partner, a woman is permitted to divorce an impotent man or a man who is uninterested in sex, and a man may divorce a woman who refuses to have intercourse with him.

Although it supports the joy and pleasure of sexual activity within marriage, Judaism also condemns certain forms of sexual behavior. Adultery is forbidden (Leviticus 20:10). Premarital intercourse is strongly discouraged (Rosenheim, 1977). Incest is prohibited (Leviticus 18:6–18). Forcing daughters into prostitution is outlawed (Leviticus 19:20), although prostitution itself seems to be tolerated. Male homosexual acts are condemned (Leviticus 18:22 and 20:13), but female homosexual behavior is not mentioned in the Bible. Bestiality and pedophilia are also outlawed. However, Judaism generally takes the view that sex is good and has no concept to parallel the Christian notion of original sin.

In America today there are three basic categories of Judaism: Orthodox, Conservative, and Reform. Orthodox Jews, who follow the teachings of the Old Testament with a literal interpretation that has changed very little over the centuries, are strongly opposed to abortion (except in cases of grave danger to the mother's life) and observe the Laws of Niddah, which prohibit sexual contact between husband and wife during menstruation and for one week after menstrual flow has stopped (Fertel and Feuer, 1979). Orthodox Judaism also prohibits male masturbation if it leads to ejaculation, although female masturbation is not specifically banned. Reform Jews have discarded many of the rituals described in the Old Testament and Talmud—such as the dietary (kosher) laws and the Laws of Niddah—to adapt to changing times. Reform Judaism generally takes a liberal stance on matters such as abortion, masturbation, and premarital sex. Conservative Jews, on the other hand, fall midway between these positions, modifying the Orthodox tradition less drastically than the Reform movement.

Orthodox Judaism has been criticized by many people as a sexist religion. An Orthodox Jewish man must recite a prayer each morning that thanks God for not creating him as a woman; females are segregated from males in the synagogue during services (supposedly so as not to distract the men's attention from spiritual matters by the sight of tempting flesh); and women are not counted in calculating the minimum number of ten worshipers (called a *minyan*) needed for a service. Orthodox Jewish laws on marriage and divorce also treat women as second-class citizens, and the Laws of

Niddah strongly proclaim menstruation as unclean (Priesand, 1975).

Christianity

Christian teachings have often been silent or negative about sexuality. In fact, many people thought (and continue to think) that the principal Christian word about sex was "don't." As you may recall from Chapter 1, the earliest Christians were Jews and their views about sexuality came from Judaism. However, the early disciples of Jesus seem to have been strongly influenced by Greek ideas that separated physical from spiritual love. This outlook contrasted sharply with the Jewish view that body and soul are complementary parts of human nature and not antagonistic opposites. Since the disciples also believed that Jesus would return to earth in the near future to bring salvation (1 Thessalonians 5; 1 Corinthians 7:29ff), some of the early Christian teachings about sex that seem negative today were probably meant as temporary measures (Kosnik et al., 1977; Nelson, 1978). A few centuries later, St. Augustine's belief that sex was contaminated by original sin led him to view every sexual act—even marital intercourse—as sinful (see Chapter 1). With these historical points in mind, we now turn our attention to contemporary Christian viewpoints on sex.

Catholicism

The position of the Catholic church on sexuality is based not only on the Old and New Testaments but also on the teachings of the popes. While sexual activity in marriage is considered good as long as it has the potential for reproduction, all other forms of sexual behavior are condemned.

The "Declaration on Certain Questions Concerning Sexual Ethics," a position paper issued by the Sacred Congregation for the Doctrine of the Faith in 1976 and approved by the pope, spelled out the Catholic position on sexuality in more detail: "In the present period, the corruption of morals has increased, and one of the most serious indications of this corruption is the unbridled exaltation of sex." The declaration went on to make the following points: (1) It is incorrect to regard biblical writings about sex as "expressions of a form of a particular culture at a certain moment of history." Thus, the centuries-old teachings of the church still apply in full force today even though societies may have

changed. (2) Even in engaged couples where both persons have strong affection for each other, sexual activity is sinful, for "every genital act must be within the framework of marriage." (3) All homosexual orientation unaccompanied by homosexual acts is not in and of itself sinful. (4) Masturbation, even though not specifically condemned in the Bible, is a "grave moral disorder." (5) Chastity (either virginity or celibacy) is virtuous not only because it avoids sin but also because it attains a higher spiritual good.

In addition to these viewpoints on sexual matters, the Catholic church does not permit divorce except under special circumstances and prohibits the use of all artificial methods of contraception (i.e., any method other than abstinence or rhythm).

Within the modern-day church, many Catholic clergy believe that some of these teachings are outdated and have expressed serious misgivings about the church's positions. In 1977, for example, a study on human sexuality commissioned by the Catholic Theological Society of America recommended that all sexual behaviors be judged to see if they are self-liberating, other-enriching, honest, faithful, socially responsible, life-serving, and joyous. "Where such qualities prevail," the authors said, "one can be reasonably sure that the sexual behavior that has brought them forth is wholesome and moral" (Kosnik et al., 1977, p. 95).

United States and Canadian bishops attending a 1981 meeting on the subject of sexuality pointed out that although sexual union produces children, its primary role is "enabling the person to reach fulfillment." Furthermore, the Reverend Benedict M. Ashley criticized the church for having "failed to meet the actual problems of human beings in realistic compassionate ways" and suggested that the inseparable linkage between human sexuality and procreation "is by no means evident" (Schaeffer, 1981).[2] However, when Pope John Paul II held a bishops' synod in Rome in the fall of 1980, "the Vatican-dominated synod reaffirmed the prece-

---

[2]A few months before this meeting, Pope John Paul II created quite a stir when he said that a man is guilty of committing "adultery in the heart" if he looks at his wife in a lustful manner (*The New York Times*, Oct. 10, 1980). Although the pope later explained that he was trying to free women from the role of being sex objects, his remarks were widely taken to mean that even healthy sexual desire between spouses is sinful in the eyes of the church.

Source: © *Bill Mitchell—ROTHCO cartoons.*

dence of laws over compassion" (Murphy, 1981, p. 44) despite hopes that the church would reform its positions on some crucial sexual issues.

In 1983, the Vatican issued a set of guidelines on sex education that generally repeated the prohibitions voiced in the 1976 declaration, once again calling masturbation "a grave moral disorder" and speaking of extramarital sex as "a grave disorder" (*The New York Times,* December 2, 1983). Although the new guidelines specify that parents have the primary responsibility for providing sex education for their children, they do allow schools to assist and complete this education.

In 1987, the church issued guidelines that oppose virtually all modern technology used to foster reproduction, including artificial insemination, *in vitro* fertilization, and surrogate motherhood.

Protestantism

Protestantism as a separate branch of Christianity developed in the sixteenth century when Martin Luther led a split from the Catholic church. Luther rejected many elements of Catholic faith because he believed that salvation is freely available to the sinner and does not depend on human righteousness. He described this process as "salvation by faith through grace." Accordingly, the most conspicuous change in sexual attitudes was Luther's rejection of celibacy as a way to heaven. He encouraged priests

and nuns to marry because they did not possess special divine authority, because there was no religious meaning to trying to be especially holy, and because he saw sex as a natural part of human life.

In other respects, the Protestant Reformation followed traditional Christian ideals in sexual matters. Adultery, masturbation, and homosexuality were seen as sinful, and marriage was regarded as a life-long commitment. Although these rules were thought to be necessary to restrain the outbreak of sin and lawlessness, obedience was not thought of as contributing to individual salvation. John Calvin (1509–1564) originated another tradition in which the orderly development of social life, including sexual behavior, glorified God in grateful response to the gift of salvation.

The individualism that Luther and Calvin represent provided the basis for a number of divisions and wide differences of opinion within Protestantism. Today, therefore, there are many Protestant denominations with extremely diverse positions on sexual matters. In addition, the differences of opinion *within* the denominations are almost as great as those *between* denominations.

Protestant perspectives are usually classified into conservative, moderate, and liberal. In the conservative group are fundamentalists, who believe that a Christian must accept a specific set of beliefs (what they see as the fundamental teachings of the

Bible) in order to be saved. Also in this group are evangelicals, who, along with the fundamentalists, emphasize the necessity of a personal experience of Jesus Christ as Lord and savior but do not require the same degree of adherence to a specific set of beliefs. The sexual beliefs of such groups—including the opposition to abortion, rejection of premarital sex, skepticism about contraception, very negative judgments about divorce, and condemnation of homosexual behavior—are hardly distinguishable from those of the Catholic church. Moderate Protestantism places greater emphasis on Christian nurture in which children are educated to be Christians and to experience the power of faith in Christ. The sexual values of this group are somewhat diverse. Moderate Protestants generally accept abortion, are no longer willing to condemn premarital sex outright, regard contraception as a social and individual good, believe that divorce is often the lesser evil to a tormented marriage, and are more tolerant of homosexuality.

Liberal Protestants see Christian faith as a perspective on the world and on human life that is guided by human reason and the traditions of historic faith. They do not regard the Bible as an infallible source of truth but as the record of the human struggle to find meaning in life. Thus, liberal Protestants are likely to be open to completely new understandings of many aspects of human sexuality.

Some Protestant denominations are completely traditional in their sexual views. The Jehovah's Witnesses, for example, seek to follow the Bible literally and to find biblical rules for sexual behavior. At the other extreme is the Unitarian-Universalist Association, which affirms humanistic values and reveres religious tradition only to the extent to which it fosters human fulfillment. For them, sexual values must be continually reinterpreted in the light of modern knowledge and contemporary experience.

Very few denominations fit neatly into the conservative, moderate, or liberal categories. There are conservative and liberal Presbyterians, conservative and liberal Quakers. Some fundamentalist Baptists have joined with the Roman Catholic church in the right-to-life movement. Some liberal Baptists are in the forefront of the struggle for the rights of homosexuals. Both groups believe that sexual perspective is rooted in the history of their faith, yet they are poles apart.

The struggle to reevaluate and redefine a contemporary moral perspective has embroiled many Protestant denominations in controversy about sexual matters; other denominations are responding to the struggle by slowly evolving an openness to new sexual options. No one can now predict the conclusion of all these struggles and changes, but one thing is certain: the divisions of opinion will continue for decades to come.

Religion and Sex in Perspective

Many people who consider themselves religious find that in real life they make sexual decisions in ways that conflict with the teachings of their church or synagogue. While this dilemma has undoubtedly ocurred for many centuries, the problem seems to be more pressing today in light of changing cultural attitudes toward various types of sexual behavior.

This tug-of-war between traditional teachings and contemporary cultural attitudes affects people in many different ways. Some devout believers experience great guilt as a result of their sexual behavior. Others, who begin with a genuine desire to follow their religious orientation, decide that the teachings of their religion are so outdated in regard to sex that they either disregard them entirely or drop their participation in organized religion. There are also many people who feel completely comfortable with the sexual values of their religion and endorse its views in theory and practice.

The uneasiness with traditional religious viewpoints on sexuality is found not only among the laity (i.e., members of the churches) but among the clergy as well. For instance, there is a movement in today's Catholic clergy that advocates permitting priests and nuns to drop their vows of celibacy and marry. In each religion, there are members of the clergy who respond to the sexual problems of their congregants with flexible and inventive counseling, taking into account the relative merits of all the various issues (religious, social, psychological, etc.) in each individual situation. Overall, there seems to be much discussion among American clergy about the need to avoid cut-and-dried pronouncements on the morality or immorality of sexual behavior and to develop a dialogue about sex (Kosnik et al., 1977; Gordis, 1978; Nelson, 1978; Yates, 1988; Stackhouse, 1989/90).

Sexual Viewpoints in Other Religions

The perspectives found in the Judeo-Christian tradition are not the only ways in which religions view sexuality. Every known religion has teachings that relate to sexual ethics, although some of these religions express viewpoints that seem quite foreign to most Westerners. Here, we briefly mention three of these other religious perspectives.

Islam was the third major religion, along with Judaism and Christianity, to be born in the Middle East. Although its early followers (called Moslems) were Arabs, Islam has spread to many non-Arabic peoples across the world. Muhammad, who founded Islam in the seventh century A.D., influenced his followers on sexual matters through both his life and his teachings as recorded in the Koran (the Islamic holy scriptures). Muhammad had several wives and concubines, and Islam takes a very positive view of most forms of sexuality. Celibacy is discouraged, Moslem men may have up to four wives, and sexuality is regarded as a gift from God. While adultery is punishable by death (a penalty that is still sometimes enforced in countries such as Saudi Arabia and Iran), Islam takes a fairly tolerant position on other sexual issues. The institution of "admut'a," or temporary marriage, is one indication of this approach. Divorce is also permitted but is subject to many detailed regulations. Although generally tolerant on sexual issues, to Westerners Islam seems biased against women for several reasons: women must wear veils in public (except in Egypt and Turkey), harems still exist, and clitoridectomy (surgical removal of the clitoris) and other forms of female genital mutilation are still practiced in some sects.

In the oldest religion of India, *Hinduism,* sex is treated as a form of spiritual energy. Because Hinduism is a collection of many different approaches to life, it encompasses a number of different sexual philosophies. For example, those taking the path of Karma (the pursuit of pleasure) have very open and accepting attitudes toward sex, as shown by the *Kama Sutra,* a book written by a Hindu priest in the fourth century A.D. that provides a detailed discussion of sexual technique and coital positions. Others who choose the paths of Dharma (the moral life) or Moksha (liberation from the continuing cycle of rebirth by renunciation of physical pleasures and passions) may strive for celibacy at certain times in their lives in order to devote their attention to finding inner knowledge or peace. However, celibacy does not play a central role in Hinduism, and most Hindu priests marry.

Buddhism was founded in India in the fifth century B.C. and stresses a philosophy that sees suffering as a basic part of earthly life. Liberation from wordly suffering comes from mental and moral self-purification; thus, celibacy is highly desired. In actual practice, while celibacy is demanded of priests and encouraged for monks and nuns, other followers of this faith are usually married and are not restricted from sexual enjoyment. Interestingly, although Buddhism regards prostitution as lowly, it is not condemned because of the conviction that prostitutes are working out their "karma," the force that determines their destiny in their next existence.

While these three religions differ in many ways from Jewish or Christian teachings about sexuality, they provide a source of guidance for millions of people across the world.

SEXUAL ETHICS AND SEXUAL DECISIONS

Clearly, people base their sexual decisions on a variety of considerations in addition to their religious perspective. For example, some sexual decisions are based mainly on personal taste and preference. In reaching such decisions people may ask themselves questions like "Is this person (or act) attractive and pleasing?" "Am I in the mood?" "Is this the right time and place?" Questions of this sort are ethically value-free; that is, they are not a matter of right or wrong in a moral sense, any more than the question of whether to order a vanilla milkshake or to see a particular movie is morally "right" or "wrong."

Other sexual decisions are based on personal and social values or the priorities that we assign to these values. Here, people may ask questions like "Am I doing the right thing?" "Am I being honest?" "Is there a chance I'll hurt my partner?" These value-loaded questions *are* ethical questions, since they have to do with the moral quality (rightness or wrongness) of a particular course of action. Unlike making moral decisions based solely on religion, a process that requires faith, ethical decision making requires a process of rational thought. This is particularly important because the most difficult ethical problems are those that do not present black-and-white choices but involve choosing between several conflicting values. Of course, some people deal with ethical dilemmas on the basis of a mixture of faith and reason.

There is considerable variety in the way people resolve ethical conflicts. For example, Kinsey and his colleagues found that in the 1940s and 1950s, people generally judged what was "proper" sexual behavior in different ways depending on their educational background. People with only an elementary school education generally believed that permissible sexual acts were those that were "natural." Thus, intercourse was approved but masturbation, oral–genital sex, and homosexual acts were questioned or rejected. In contrast, people with a junior high school or high school education generally used respectability as the standard of right and wrong sexual behavior. College-educated people tended to regard sexual behavior in still another way: the primary standard was whether two people really loved each other. Kinsey concluded that educational level influenced people's views of sexual morality more than their formal religious affiliations did (Kinsey, Pomeroy, and Martin, 1948; Kinsey et al., 1953).

More recently, as more people are completing high school and college than in the 1950s, three other ways of judging the moral appropriateness of a sexual act have become widespread. First, some argue that any private sexual activity between consenting adults is moral. Second, others believe that good sexuality is anything that enhances interpersonal relationships and personal growth and development. Third, still others suggest that there are no absolute rules to follow and that decisions should be made on the basis of all the facts of a given situation (an approach called "situation ethics").

Whatever the attitudes toward sexuality, choices are always made in terms of values. Even if the terms *right* and *wrong* and *good* and *bad* are not used, similar distinctions are often made between healthy and unhealthy, neurotic and normal, inhibited and free. To what extent these attitudes are ethical must be decided by each person on the basis of the standards and values to which he or she is committed.

The concluding portion of this chapter discusses several sexual issues that are a continuing source of ethical and religious controversy. Because these are particularly complicated matters, this brief discussion should be seen as an outline of perspectives on each issue rather than the final word. No matter how strong your own feelings may be, it is helpful to recognize that many intelligent, thoughtful, honest people hold opposing views.

Abortion

Historical references to abortion go as far back as China 4600 years ago, with attitudes ranging from harsh penalties in Assyria to encouragement in Greece. However, throughout most of recorded history, abortion was generally disapproved of because it was a health risk. Abortion did not become a major moral issue until modern medicine made safe abortions possible.

In the last two decades, the discussion over abortion has exploded into a strident public controversy.

Many public opinion polls have been conducted over the years on the abortion issue, with results that have remained remarkably consistent, as shown in Figure 24.1. Fewer than one-quarter of American adults are opposed to abortion under any circumstances and about the same percentage take the opposite position that a woman is entitled to an abortion just because she wants one. The majority of Americans take a position in-between, supporting abortion rights under certain circumstances. Four nationally representative polls, conducted in 1988 and 1989 by the Gallup Organization and by *The Los Angeles Times* and *The New York Times,* asked participants about specific circumstances under

Figure 24.1   Public Support for Legal Abortion: 1975 to 1990

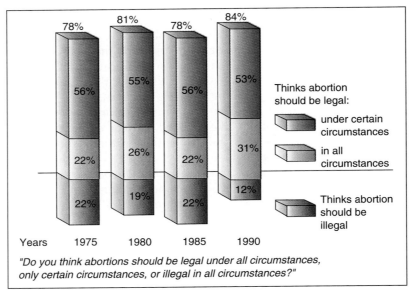

"Do you think abortions should be legal under all circumstances, only certain circumstances, or illegal in all circumstances?"

Source: *Gallup Organization*

which they thought abortion should be permitted or banned (*Family Planning Perspectives* 21:138–139, 1989). The findings showed that a great majority of Americans are in favor of legalized abortion if the woman's life is threatened by the pregnancy (86 to 94 percent), when the woman's health would be seriously damaged by the pregnancy (81 to 88 percent), when the pregnancy was due to rape or incest (84 to 86 percent), or when there is a high chance that the baby would be seriously deformed (60 to 74 percent).

There are three primary positions that people seem to take on abortion. At one extreme is the pro-life group, which wants to ban abortion under all circumstances and feels that the state has no right to endorse the destruction of the embryo or fetus by legalizing abortion. At the other end of the spectrum are those who believe that the state has no right to limit the freedom of the mother's choice and that abortion should be available to all pregnant women at their request (the "pro-choice" group). The middle ground is occupied by people who believe in restricting abortions to certain situations such as pregnancies that threaten the life of the mother or that result from rape or incest or who believe that abortion should not be used as a primary method of birth control.

The "pro-life" movement, which is highly organized and politically active, is largely supported by the Catholic church. However, Orthodox Jews, Eastern Orthodox followers, some nonreligious persons, and many conservative Protestants have also taken this position. The four central propositions of this viewpoint have been stated by Daniel Callahan (1970):

1. Every human being, even the child in its mother's womb, receives its right to life directly from God.

2. Human beings do not have the right to take the lives of other innocent human beings.

3. Human life begins at the moment of conception.

4. Abortion at whatever stage of development is the taking of innocent human life.

Many pro-lifers who do not accept all the above arguments agree with the position voiced by former President Ronald Reagan, who said, "If we don't know [when life begins], then shouldn't we morally opt on the side that is life? If you came upon an immobile body and could not determine whether it was dead or alive, you would consider it alive until somebody could prove it was dead. We should do the same thing with regard to abortion" (Emmens, 1987, p. 33).

However, the question of when human life begins is a deceptive one in the context of abortion. While both the sperm and egg are living cells, conception does not automatically lead to viable life. Most people would also agree that the zygote or the very tiny embryo is not a person in the ordinary sense of that term. The real question concerns when personhood begins. And this is a much more complicated issue—one that is probably more a matter of philosophy than science.

Nevertheless, even those who do not necessarily believe that an embryo or fetus is a person may hold to the anti-abortion position. These individuals are apt to argue that since a human embryo or fetus has the *potential* to become a person, killing it is immoral: in effect, you would be taking away its right to life.

Another point made by those who oppose abortion is that the embryo or fetus is innocent life: it never asked to be conceived, or to be born, but since it was brought into existence, and since it is alive, it has a compelling right not to be destroyed. In the Catholic view, for instance, human life can be taken only when it is not innocent, as in capital punishment, or when it is the unintended effect of some other action, as in the "just war." This is the principle of double effect. If, for example, a malignancy is removed from the uterus of a pregnant woman, the death of the fetus is not morally wrong because it is the unintended and indirect result of an action taken to save the woman's life. However, if the fetus itself is the cause of the danger to the mother's life, its destruction is not permissible because it would be a directly intended action.

Opponents of abortion also frequently point out that "every child is wanted—by someone" (Emmens, 1987). They believe that adoption is both a logical alternative and a better moral choice than abortion. Although they acknowledge that carrying a pregnancy to term may be inconvenient, expensive, and even physically harmful to the pregnant woman, they claim that the relative safety of pregnancy today and the opportunity to have the cost of prenatal care and childbirth paid by the adoptive parents are countering factors. And they believe that the moral scales tip firmly in their favor, as this statement shows:

> Abortion is forbidden morally because it is an abuse of human power. It is a destruction of a human being by another human being, and as such it strikes at the heart of human dignity. . . .

To give moral justification to abortion is to condemn all men to the level of expendable things. *(Granfield, 1969, pp. 15–41)*

Given these positions, it should not be difficult to see why people who think abortion is a form of murder are morally obligated to oppose it. As Anna Quindlen (1990) notes: "To say that that is imposing religious beliefs on others is absurd."

The "pro-choice" movement has also become well organized and politically active in recent years, with groups such as NARAL (National Association for the Repeal of Abortion Laws), Planned Parenthood, and NOW (National Organization for Women) lobbying on its behalf. What many people do not realize, however, is that the pro-choice stance is also supported by dozens of mainstream religious groups, including the American Baptist church, American Friends Service Committee, Episcopalian church, Lutheran Baptist Convention, Presbyterian church in the United States, Union of American Hebrew Colleges, Unitarian Universalist Association, and the United Methodist church. In fact, the majority of churches and religious organizations in the United States support legalized abortion (Emmons, 1987).

The central ethical points that pro-choice advocates make are as follows (Callahan, 1970; Terkel, 1988):

1. No one should have the right to make a woman remain pregnant against her will.

2. Unwanted children should not be brought into the world.

3. Abortion would not be banned if men were not the lawmakers (or, as one aphorism has it, "If men could get pregnant, abortion would be a sacrament").

4. Unless a woman has a right to control her own body, which includes the right to control her own reproduction, she has no real freedom at all.

Advocates of abortion generally believe that the government should not intrude into the private lives of women by regulating what happens to their pregnancies. They feel that each woman should have the choice of having an abortion or not—and they emphatically point out that having this choice available does not force anyone to do something they don't want to do. In addition, abortion rights advocates note that everyone should be free from government-mandated health risks, but when the government bans abortions, it exposes many pregnant women to the medical risks associated with pregnancy and childbirth as well as the risks of illegal abortions. Furthermore, those favoring abortions worry that if government regulation of abortion is permitted to safeguard the right to life of each zygote or embryo, politicians might next wish to regulate a woman's lifestyle during pregnancy—for instance, by forbidding women to smoke, or to consume alcohol, or to engage in strenuous physical exercise—on the grounds that such actions might jeopardize the health of the developing fetus and thus may threaten a "potential" life.

Many people who have taken a pro-choice position see a degree of hypocrisy in their opponents' philosophy. For example, the pro-choice people ask, if every baby is wanted by someone, why are there tens of thousands of minority children and children with birth defects or chronic illnesses who have not been adopted by those who insist that women should never be allowed to terminate a pregnancy? And why does it seem that the pro-life group is more worried about protecting unborn lives than improving the social or economic quality of the masses of impoverished people already born into our world? Another point raised to support the pro-choice position is that aborted or miscarried fetuses cannot be baptized or given Christian funerals as if they were persons (Maguire, 1990).

To be sure, the pro-choice contingent is divided on some issues. Some are uncomfortable with the idea of permitting abortions for birth defects or genetic disorders, wondering exactly where to draw the line. While it may seem completely defensible morally to abort a fetus that is developing without a brain, what about a fetus who will be mentally retarded, for example, even if its physical health won't be vastly impaired? And what about those who might live long, but sickly, lives: Is it right to prevent them from being born?

Another point on which pro-choice supporters disagree is how late in pregnancy abortions should be permitted. Most people who favor liberal abortion rights draw the line at or near the end of the second trimester, except in the most extenuating circumstances (e.g., a third-trimester pregnancy that threatens the woman's life). But some who favor freedom of choice are uncomfortable with the idea of abortions after the first trimester, while

others believe there should be no time limitations at all.

Many people are reluctant to support so-called abortions of convenience, but these are tricky to define. As one writer put it: "Semantics alone make it sound like a pregnancy ended because a woman wanted a child who was a Leo, not a Capricorn" (Quindlen, 1990). If a 13-year-old is impregnated by her seventh-grade boyfriend and has an abortion, is it fair to call this an abortion of convenience? If an unmarried, unemployed 24-year-old woman who is struggling to feed her four children with her meager welfare check becomes pregnant again and wants an abortion, is this also an abortion of convenience? Convenience, it might seem, lies in the eyes of the beholder in these situations.

In debating the ethical aspects of abortion, a great many arguments have been used to justify one position or another. Whatever one's personal viewpoints on this topic might be, it is important to be able to recognize lines of ethical logic that in fact are not so logical—even though they may be appealing because they sound like they *should* be logical. [Some of the examples we discuss here are drawn from Terkel (1988).]

One example of this is the *slippery slope argument*. This line of reasoning states that when a first step is taken down a "slippery slope"—even though the first step seems innocuous by itself—sliding further down the slope to more and more extreme actions will inevitably follow. An example of the "slippery slope" argument that many pro-lifers use is that if you permit abortion, even under limited circumstances, you are paving the way to euthanasia (mercy killing of the terminally ill) and eventually to killing off genetically defective people. Another version of this argument says that permitting legal abortions will destroy our society by undermining the family and making human lives simply "expendable commodities." In fact, many critics of abortion have likened it to the mass murders that occurred in Nazi Germany.[3]

The problem with this line of reasoning is that there is no inevitability of consequences. If you kill

[3]As a point of historical accuracy, it should be noted that one of the first things the Nazis did when they assumed power in Germany in 1933 was to outlaw abortion rights. Invoking the abortions = Nazi atrocities equation is particularly unconvincing since the Nazis could hardly be thought of as "pro-life," even though they prohibited abortions.

a fly, does it mean that you will "slip down the slope" and eventually kill your pet cat?

Another type of "logic" often used in the abortion debate is the example of Beethoven's mother. This was a sickly woman, badly affected by tuberculosis, married to a man with syphilis, who had already had four children, one of whom was blind, one of whom was deaf and mute, and one of whom was infected with tuberculosis. Although she was living in conditions of extreme poverty, and two of her children had already died, if she had had an abortion, the world would have been denied one of its greatest musical geniuses—Ludwig van Beethoven. Terkel (1988, p. 136) points out the fault of this reasoning:

> Perhaps if Mrs. Beethoven had access to a safe, legal abortion, she might still have elected to give birth. This argument, and the equally deplorable argument given by the pro-choice who counter that perhaps Adolf Hitler's mother should have had an abortion, totally ignores the slim chance that any woman's fetus will grow up to be either a genius or a lunatic. . . . There are enough compelling arguments for either side to use without resorting to blatantly outrageous ones.

One of the newer developments in the abortion debate involves a particularly thorny ethical issue: is it right to use deceptive practices to further what is thought to be a moral goal? The question of whether the end justifies the means has come into the picture because of a network of "problem-pregnancy" clinics that have sprung up around the country. These clinics advertise in newspapers and in the yellow pages and seem to offer abortions to women who desire them. The real goal of these clinics is, however, to prevent women from terminating their pregnancies: they do not perform abortions at all, even if the woman is a victim of rape or incest or is medically threatened by her pregnancy. To accomplish their goal, these clinics typically show women frightening pictures of bloody fetuses thrown into trash cans, lie about the safety statistics of current abortion methods, and try to keep women from seeking the services of clinics that actually perform abortions.

Proponents of such clinics argue that saving an unborn baby's life is worth treading in the moral gray zone of deceit. They claim that they are not actually lying (they are trained to never actually say that they perform abortions) and argue that deception has been hailed historically as the morally proper choice in certain situations (e.g., helping slaves to escape from the South prior to the Civil War or helping Jews to flee from the Nazis). Furthermore, proponents claim that what they are doing is just the opposite side of the coin to what abortion clinics are doing, since few abortion clinics try to provide balanced counseling about all the options available to a pregnant woman. Those opposed to the tactics employed by the "problem-pregnancy" clinics point out that by deceiving a pregnant woman in this situation and by delaying the time it takes for her to find a clinic to perform an abortion, the clinics may actually be endangering her health, since the safest abortions are the ones that are done earliest in pregnancy. In addition, many people see the use of fear and deceit to persuade a woman to keep a pregnancy as a form of coercion, limiting the woman's rights to freedom of choice.

The New Reproductive Technologies

In a time where IVF (*in vitro* fertilization) and GIFT (gamete intrafallopian transfer) have become commonplace, and where egg donation is no longer a theoretical possibility but a practical fact (see Chapter 5) many thorny ethical issues have arisen. In some instances, controversy over these issues has produced rifts within the Catholic church. Several Catholic medical institutions in Europe, for example, announced that they would defy the Vatican's ban on all forms of artificial fertilization and embryo transfer in order to continue providing help for infertile couples (Lewis, 1987). In other cases, advances in medical science have led to previously unanticipated dilemmas, as the following example shows.

A small number of medical centers now perform an unusual type of abortion that is not aimed at ending fetal life, but preserving it. This seemingly paradoxical situation arises when women are pregnant with more fetuses than they can safely carry to term—a situation that occurs with some frequency when women have been given drugs to help them ovulate. For example, in one case a woman was carrying octuplets, which led her doctors to tell her that all would die unless something was done. With her consent, the doctors performed what is called a selective abortion, eliminating six of the fetuses, thus reducing the number of fetuses to two. The woman was able to continue her pregnancy and gave birth to healthy twins.

The selective abortion is performed using ultrasound to allow a miniature needle to be inserted into the chest cavity of a fetus when it is still smaller than a thumb. A chemical is injected through the needle that causes the fetal heart to stop beating. The dead fetus is eventually absorbed into the woman's body.

This octuplet case seems to offer few problems to most observers: after all, it is clear that all the fetuses would have died if the octuplets were left undisturbed. But there have also been cases involving selective abortions as a matter of convenience for a couple—for example, reducing quadruplets to twins. (Ironically, these cases have sometimes arisen because of the practice of placing multiple embryos in the Fallopian tubes as part of a GIFT procedure, which is often done because most of the implanted embryos are not expected to survive.) If this is an ethically permissible practice, some wonder, where do you draw the line? What if a woman attending an IVF program conceives twins and then decides she only wants one baby: Is it morally correct to abort one of the developing fetuses? What if a woman carrying twins or triplets wants to abort the female fetuses and give birth only to a male?

A somewhat related matter is that of what to do with frozen pre-embryos preserved during a couple's participation in an IVF program. Once the couple has given birth to a child, and assuming they plan on no future pregnancies, should these frozen pre-embryos be destroyed? Opponents of this practice argue that this is a form of murder, while advocates feel that it's the only sensible solution. Still others feel that the frozen pre-embryos should be offered to other infertile couples who are unable to conceive on their own even with the assistance of modern techniques. To make the issue even more complicated, who "owns" the frozen embryos in the event that the couple divorces? This is not just a theoretical question. Tens of thousands of frozen human pre-embryos left over from IVF treatment cycles lie frozen in tanks of liquid nitrogen around the country (Kolata, 1992). In one case decided in 1992 by the Tennessee Supreme Court, a couple who divorced after IVF treatments could not agree on what to do with their frozen, stored pre-embryos. The woman wanted to become pregnant with them, but her ex-husband didn't want to permit this, and wanted to have them destroyed. The court ruled in his favor, saying the pre-embryos were "neither people nor property" (*The New York Times* June 6, 1992, Section 1, p. 22).

Few people have objected in the past to men donating their sperm for use in artificial insemination because of ethical concerns—although the Catholic church and Orthodox Judaism object to this practice on religious grounds. The parallel instance of women donating eggs for use by other women in IVF or GIFT programs has, however, raised more of an ethical outcry. Are these situations really very different? Critics contend that they are, in part because the egg donor must undergo surgery to retrieve the eggs, whereas sperm donors simply masturbate. In addition, egg donors are usually treated with hormones for a week or longer to increase the production of eggs in the donation cycle from one to six or more. While the risks are generally modest, there is a danger of overstimulating the ovaries so that they swell and even rupture. There is no counterpart to this sort of danger for sperm donors.

Others criticize egg donor programs that do not pay the donors, pointing out that this is a form of sex discrimination, since sperm donors are virtually always paid. Those programs that do not pay donors claim that this keeps the act of donation from being a commercial transaction, but there is a great deal of disagreement on this point. (As of mid-1990, most American egg donor programs do provide payment for the donors, usually on the order of $500 to $1000.) Since no one seems to criticize men who donate sperm for money, is this an ethical double standard of sorts?

One other troublesome issue about egg donation that is also unresolved at present is what would happen if an egg donor decided later on that she wanted to file a lawsuit claiming that the baby was really hers, since she was the biological mother—the one who contributed her genetic material to the child? Neither the ethical nor the legal answers to this situation are yet available, but it is not far-fetched to envision such a lawsuit arising. Most egg donor programs attempt to avoid this problem by having the donor sign a legal release of all claims to children who are conceived using her eggs. The validity of these releases has not yet been tested.

On the other side of the coin are those who see egg donation as an important advance in the treatment of infertility that gives hope and help to despairing couples. Advocates of egg donation argue that although medical progress is commonly accompanied by ethical complexity, this is no reason to ban the use of the latest medical knowledge. These people advocate the responsible use of new treatment technologies and point out that in many cases, egg donation would eliminate the need for surrogate mothers. In addition, they say, any treatment that produces new, wanted life cannot be regarded as ethically questionable.

Another ethical challenge posed by advancing technology is connected to the current scientific ability to detect hundreds of genetic defects. At one end of the spectrum, this allows IVF centers to undertake *preimplantation genetic diagnosis* in which a pre-embryo is screened for genetic abnormalities, such as chromosome defects, prior to being implanted in the uterus. [This involves sampling the nuclear material of a single cell at the cleavage or blastocyst stage, which does not appear to affect preimplantation development (Winston and Handyside, 1993).] Preimplantation diagnosis provides a means of preventing genetic abnormalities by not completing the IVF procedure in that particular cycle. At the other end of the spectrum, prenatal genetic diagnosis, such as testing done with either chorionic villus sampling or amniocentesis, identifies abnormalities once a pregnancy is well underway, but at a time when an abortion can still be performed if desired. There are numerous ethical questions surrounding these procedures. For example, is it right to perform an amniocentesis simply because the mother is anxious, but no solid medical reason exists? Is it ethical to use any of these methods as a form of sex selection—for example, if a couple has two daughters and wants a son? Is it proper to permit the woman to undertake the risks of either of these procedures "just" to find out the sex of her baby-to-be or for other nonmedical reasons?

These questions have taken on a new urgency in light of continuing technological advances in the field. The news in late 1993 that scientists had cloned human embryos for the first time startled the world and led many observers to moral outrage at the casual way in which it had been done. Although embryo-cloning is not some form of *Jurassic Park*–like genetic tampering, but is simply the duplication of existing immature cells, response to this news was sharp around the world. The Vati-

can issued an editorial saying that such procedures could lead humanity "down a tunnel of madness," French president Francois Miterrand called the experiment "horrible," and a spokesman for the Japan Medical Association said such a procedure was "unthinkable" (*Time,* October 31, 1993). Although the possibility of embryo-cloning certainly might have justifiable uses—for example, women who are infertile and only produce one egg per month could have a better chance of conceiving by IVF if a single embryo were cloned into four or five—many scientists, and the general public, remain largely skeptical about the process being too much "playing God." While it is too early to tell what government regulations or legal restrictions will be placed on such experiments in the future, it seems mandatory that scientists not barge ahead in such work without careful ethical analysis.

These are only a few examples of the difficult ethical issues that are posed by the applications of modern medical science. As further advances occur—for example, if sex preselection becomes a practical possibility—the intensity of ethical debates will undoubtedly escalate to new levels.

Surrogate Motherhood

The ethical and legal dilemmas posed by surrogate motherhood are particularly thorny. Today, a number of states (including New York) have banned this practice whenever it is done for pay. Japan and France have banned surrogate motherhood entirely, with the French Supreme Court saying that it violates a woman's body and improperly undermines adoptions (*The New York Times* June 23, 1991, p. A17). At the same time, the American Academy of Pediatrics supports the practice and published a policy statement in 1992 in which it said that the surrogate should be the one in control of any decisions up until the time of birth (*American Medical News* August 3, 1992, p. 27).

Opponents of this practice argue that surrogacy treats babies as commodities, leading to a situation in which affluent people can afford to hire women to bear their children. Opponents also contend that surrogacy makes motherhood a contractual business decision that, by its very nature, may be driven more by the profit motive than by what is good for the parties involved. In addition, many feminists believe that surrogate motherhood promotes the exploitation of women, and some church groups argue that surrogacy is a dehumanizing, immoral practice that undermines the sanctity of marriage and the family. There is also concern that some surrogate mothers may be harmed psychologically by giving up a child that is genetically theirs after the bonding that occurs during a nine-month pregnancy and delivery, even if they originally feel they will be able to part with the baby unemotionally.

Those in favor of the use of surrogate motherhood see it quite differently, of course. They point out that for couples where the woman is infertile or unable to bear a child because of medical problems, the use of a surrogate is the only practical way in which the husband can conceive and rear a child who is genetically "his." Advocates also note that surrogacy is a way of bringing a wanted child into the world and point out that it is not conceptually very different from adoption. They argue that rather than commercializing human reproduction or making babies commodities, the use of a surrogate motherhood arrangement is a profound act of love and creativity. In addition, they insist that although there are potential risks to the surrogate mother, these risks can be understood and consented to by the prospective participants, so that contracting to be paid for one's services as a surrogate is no riskier than many other occupational choices a woman might make. Advocates of surrogacy also deny that the practice exploits women, claiming instead that women who voluntarily choose to become surrogate mothers are offered reasonable compensation for their services and inconvenience as well as the opportunity to provide a socially desirable service.

Relatively little has been said about the child in such situations. The child can be affected by genetic defects the surrogate mother passes on (except for those infrequent instances in which the woman who hires the surrogate contributes an egg, which is fertilized *in vitro*, and implanted in the surrogate's uterus). Some of these conditions, unfortunately, cannot be detected by current screening techniques. The developing fetus can also be harmed if the surrogate mother is not sufficiently careful during her pregnancy—for instance, if she uses drugs or if she doesn't eat properly. Of equal importance, but unanswerable at present, are concerns about the psychological development of the child. If the child is told (or discovers accidentally) that he or she was born to a surrogate mother, will it create problems or psychological anguish? If the surrogate mother has continuing contact with the child after birth—as sometimes happens if the surrogate is a friend or relative—what impact will this have on the child later?

With so many unresolved questions surrounding the issue of surrogate motherhood at present, it should not be surprising that the Ethics Committee of the American Fertility Society (1986) voiced "serious ethical reservations about surrogacy that cannot be resolved until appropriate data are available for assessment of the risks and possible benefits of this alternative." In light of these reservations, the society recommended that if surrogate motherhood is used, it should be done as a clinical experiment with the following conditions attached:

1. Careful data should be gathered on the psychological effects of the procedure on surrogates, the couples employing them, and the children that result.

2. Special attention should be given to ensuring that the surrogate and couple have given a voluntary, informed consent.

3. The surrogate and the father should be carefully screened for infectious diseases and genetic defects.

4. Professionals involved in the process, such as doctors or lawyers, should be paid only their usual fees for their services and should *not* get a finder's fee for arranging a surrogate motherhood procedure.

Despite such recommendations, it is certain that some instances of surrogate motherhood will be arranged under less rigorous (and less professional) circumstances. It is already apparent that some women applying to be surrogate mothers are motivated primarily by the money involved, which may lead them to falsify certain information about their backgrounds or health status. In other cases, infertile couples looking for a likely candidate for a surrogate mother have tried to pressure a relative into accepting such an assignment. Unscrupulous or inattentive attorneys or physicians may be so attracted by the large fees they can earn for arranging surrogate mothers for a couple in need that they fail to act in the best interests of the parties involved. Nevertheless, as hundreds of parents of children born to surrogate mothers can attest, the rewards from this solution to childlessness can be immense.

The various moral issues discussed in this chapter represent problems that involve individual and social judgments about the nature of responsible sexual behavior. In earlier eras, these issues were regarded as questions that had *one* right answer. Today, we understand these judgments to be relative because of our exposure to world religions, to different cultures, and to vastly differing points of view and sexual practices. No one can any longer be sure what he or she prefers is right for everyone.

SUMMARY

1. Judaism accepts sexuality as a God-given gift and heartily endorses most forms of marital sex. Although Orthodox Jewish tradition is sexually restrictive in certain ways—such as by opposing abortion and male contraception and by banning sexual activity for at least 12 days after menstruation begins—Conservative and Reform Jews generally hold more liberal beliefs.

2. The official Catholic view of sexuality teaches that only marital sex with the potential for reproduction is permissible. All forms of premarital, extramarital, and solitary sexual activity are considered sinful by the church, which also bans "artificial" contraception, abortion, and divorce. However, many Catholic leaders in the United States, Canada, and other Western nations have been urging the Vatican to reassess these positions in favor of a more permissive approach.

3. Protestant views on sexuality stretch across the entire spectrum from very conservative positions that are almost identical to those of Catholicism to very liberal philosophies that endorse women's rights for abortion, permit homosexuals to be ordained ministers, and tolerate any sexual behavior that enhances personal relationships.

4. Many people find that the teachings of their church or synagogue about sexuality do not fit their own needs very well and move away from these "official" teachings. For example, more than 70 percent of American Catholic women of childbearing age use artificial methods of birth control.

5. Ethical analysis can be applied to situations in which one set of values conflicts with another. Abortion and certain aspects of the new reproductive technologies, including egg donation, the handling of frozen embryos, and surrogate motherhood, are examples of issues that currently provoke considerable controversy.

Thought Questions

1. The French "abortion pill" (RU-486) has been found to be a safe and inexpensive way to terminate a pregnancy during the first trimester. Although some small American companies want to market this pill in the United States, the federal government has failed to list RU-486 in the *Pharmacopia*, the list of legal drugs. Since abortion is at present legal in the United States, is the federal government's failure to act in favor of making RU-486 available to U.S. physicians and patients an ethical or an unethical act?

2. Why has Christianity been historically repressive and negative toward sexuality, compared to other religions? Has this relative negativity primarily been due to religious beliefs or to the needs of a developing society?

3. Right now in the United States, the right to reproduce is regarded as an absolute: no governmental agency can tell a woman that she may not get pregnant. Is this a moral position in an overpopulated world? What if the woman has already had ten children? Twenty children? Would it ever be right for a society to forcibly prevent a person from having as many children as he or she wants?

4. In the future, genetic engineering techniques could, without abortion, offer couples the ability to choose the characteristics of their offspring. Would it be ethical to use these techniques to ensure that your baby would be healthy and free from genetic disease? To ensure that your baby had certain physical features, like blond hair and blue eyes? Or should we continue to reproduce by "tossing the dice"?

5. Is there any moral or ethical difference between artificial insemination by a donor and egg donation? Or are these morally equivalent acts?

6. In the Baby M case, the New Jersey State Supreme Court ruled that contracts for "surro-

gate motherhood" were illegal and could not be enforced. Should a woman be allowed to deliver a baby to a genetic father and his infertile wife and be paid for her services? What if she likes being pregnant, wants no more children to raise herself, and wants to make a living by providing this service to infertile couples?

Suggested Readings

Callahan, Daniel. *Abortion: Law, Choice and Morality.* New York: Macmillan, 1970. A comprehensive, objective analysis of the abortion issue. Although now somewhat dated in its legal coverage, Callahan's discussion of the ethics of abortion is masterful.

Gordis, Robert. *Love and Sex: A Modern Jewish Perspective.* New York: Farrar, Straus & Giroux, 1978. A well-written and informative book that skillfully synthesizes historical and contemporary Jewish attitudes toward sexuality.

Gregory, Hamilton, ed. *The Religious Case for Abortion: Protestant, Catholic, and Jewish Perspectives.* Asheville, North Carolina: Madison & Polk, 1983. A slim, quick-reading, but provocative book that outlines the beliefs of representatives of three major faiths who feel that abortion need not be incompatible with religious commitment.

Kosnik, Anthony, et al. *Human Sexuality: New Directions in American Catholic Thought.* New York: Paulist Press, 1977. Catholic teachings on sexuality are reexamined and reinterpreted in a modern perspective in this insightful discussion.

Matthews, Robert J. *The Human Adventure: A Study Course for Christians on Sexuality.* Lima, OH: C.S.S. Publishing, 1980. An overview of Christian teachings on sexual ethics and issues.

McNeill, John J. *The Church and the Homosexual.* Kansas City: Sheed Andrews and McMeel, 1976. A provocative discussion of homosexuality from a religious viewpoint.

Nugent, Robert, ed. *A Challenge to Love: Gay and Lesbian Catholics in the Church.* New York: Crossroad Publishing Company, 1983. A book by liberal Catholic theologians and academics that argues that case for greater acceptance of homosexuals by the Catholic church. At times written in cumbersome language, the book is nevertheless an important indicator of an evolutionary direction within a segment of the Catholic community.

Parrinder, Geoffrey. *Sex in the World's Religions.* New York: Oxford University Press, 1980. A scholarly, comprehensive view of sexual attitudes and rules in religions around the world.

APPENDIX: RESOURCE GUIDE

MAJOR ORGANIZATIONS IN THE FIELD OF SEXUALITY

AASECT (American Association of Sex Educators, Counselors, and Therapists)
435 North Michigan Avenue, Suite 1717
Chicago, IL 60611
312-644-0828

  AASECT publishes the quarterly *Journal of Sex Education & Therapy* as well as a monthly newsletter, *Contemporary Sexuality*. It will provide a list of certified sex therapists in your locale if you need it.

SIECUS (Sex Information and Education Council of the U.S.)
130 West 42nd Street, Suite 2500
New York, NY 10036
212-819-9770

  SIECUS publishes the bimonthly *SIECUS Report* and maintains an extensive sexuality library at New York University. It provides pre-printed comprehensive bibliographies on many sexual topics and will arrange to do computer searches of its database on a very reasonable fee-for-service basis.

SOCIETY FOR THE SCIENTIFIC STUDY OF SEX
Box 208
Mount Vernon, IA 52314

  SSSS publishes the bimonthly *Journal of Sex Research*.

INSTITUTIONS IN THE FIELD OF SEXOLOGY

KINSEY INSTITUTE FOR RESEARCH IN SEX, GENDER, AND REPRODUCTION
Morrison Hall
Indiana University
Bloomington, IN 47405
812-855-7686

  The Kinsey Institute has the most extensive library collection of materials related to sexuality in the United States.

ORGANIZATIONS PROVIDING AIDS INFORMATION

AIDS ACTION COUNCIL
729 8th Street SE, Suite 200
Washington, DC 20003
202-547-3101

AIDS INFORMATION
U.S. Public Health Service
Office of Public Affairs, Room 721-H
200 Independence Avenue SW
Washington, DC 20201
202-245-6867

AIDS-RELATED DISCRIMINATION UNIT
American Civil Liberties Union
132 West 43rd Street

New York, NY 10036
212-944-9800, Ext. 545

AMERICANS FOR A SOUND AIDS POLICY
(ASAP)
P. O. Box 17433
Washington, DC 20041
703-471-7350

AMERICAN FOUNDATION FOR AIDS
RESEARCH (AMFAR)
1515 Broadway, Suite 3601
New York, NY 10036
212-719-0033

GAY MEN'S HEALTH CRISIS
P. O. Box 274
129 West 20th Street
New York, NY 10011
212-807-6655

NATIONAL AIDS NETWORK
2033 M Street, Suite 800
Washington, DC 20036
202-293-2437

NATIONAL ASSOCIATION OF PEOPLE WITH
AIDS
P. O. Box 65472
Washington, DC 20335
202-483-7979

HIV/AIDS HOTLINES

NATIONAL AIDS HOTLINE: 800-342-AIDS

NATIONAL AIDS INFORMATION
CLEARINGHOUSE: 800-458-5231
This service, provided by the Centers for Disease
Control, distributes up-to-date information
related to HIV/AIDS statistics and services. Its
data base contains descriptions of more than
12,000 organizations working in the field and
more than 6,000 AIDS-related educational
materials, as well as information about funding
opportunities for community-based HIV/AIDS
service organizations. All of the Clearinghouse's
services (including its publications) are free.

NATIONAL GAY TASK FORCE: 800-221-7044

Note: Additional listings of national and
community-based AIDS organizations can be
found in *AIDS Information Sourcebook: Second
Edition, 1989–90* (H. R. Malinowsky and G.

Perry, eds.), published by Oryx Press, Phoenix,
Arizona (800-457-6799)

ORGANIZATIONS PROVIDING RESEARCH ON CONTRACEPTION

ALAN GUTTMACHER INSTITUTE
111 Fifth Avenue
New York, NY 10003
212-254-5656
One of the most prolific sources of new research
in contraception, the AGI publishes two
outstanding journals, *Family Planning
Perspectives* and *International Family Planning
Perspectives,* as well as several useful newsletters
such as the biweekly "Washington Memo,"
which summarizes political actions and legal
decisions that affect family planning issues,
including the fast-changing area of abortion law.

PLANNED PARENTHOOD FEDERATION OF
AMERICA
810 Seventh Avenue
New York, NY 10019
212-541-7800
Planned Parenthood has local clinics in cities
throughout the country. (You can usually locate
them through your local telephone directory; if
not, you can contact the national office.) This
organization offers a broad range of information
on virtually every aspect of family planning and
sex education through a series of pamphlets and
classes, as well as providing clinical services
such as contraceptive counseling, pregnancy
testing, voluntary sterilization, preventive
health-care exams (including Pap smears and
breast exams), and early abortion services. (In
some locations, Planned Parenthood also offers
confidential testing for HIV.)

POPULATION INFORMATION PROGRAM
Johns Hopkins University
527 St. Paul Place
Baltimore, MD 21202
This program publishes the highly readable but
thoroughly documented *Population Reports*
about various family planning issues on a five-
times-a-year basis; back issues are available for
many issues. They also run POPLINE, a
computerized collection of more than 200,000

citations with abstracts, and will perform searches of this database for a nominal fee.

ORGANIZATIONS PROVIDING INFORMATION AND SERVICES RELATED TO HOMOSEXUALITY

INSTITUTE FOR THE PROTECTION OF GAY AND LESBIAN YOUTH
110 East 23rd Street
New York, NY 10010
212-473-1113

LAMBDA LEGAL DEFENSE AND EDUCATION FUND
132 West 43rd Street
New York, NY 10036
212-944-9488

NATIONAL GAY AND LESBIAN TASK FORCE
1517 U Street NW
Washington, DC 20009
202-332-6483

NATIONAL LESBIAN AND GAY HEALTH FOUNDATION
P. O. Box 65472
Washington, DC 20035
202-797-3708

ORGANIZATIONS HELPING INCEST VICTIMS OR SURVIVORS

ADULTS MOLESTED AS CHILDREN UNITED
P. O. Box 592
San Jose, CA 95108
408-280-5055

INCEST SURVIVORS ANONYMOUS
P. O. Box 5613
Long Beach, CA 90805
213-428-5599

INCEST RECOVERY ASSOCIATION
6200 North Central Expressway, Suite 209
Dallas, TX 75206
214-373-6607

LOOKING UP (for adult incest survivors)
P. O. Box K
Augusta, ME 04330
207-626-3402

NATIONAL CENTER ON CHILD ABUSE AND NEGLECT
P. O. Box 1182
Washington, DC 20013
202-245-2858

NATIONAL RESOURCE CENTER ON CHILD SEXUAL ABUSE
106 Lincoln Street
Huntsville, AL 35801
800-543-7006

VOICES IN ACTION, INC. (VOICES is an acronym for Victims of Incest Can Emerge Survivors.)
P. O. Box 148309
Chicago, IL 60614
312-327-1500

CHILD ABUSE/INCEST HOTLINES

NATIONAL CHILD ABUSE HOTLINE (Referral Service): 800-422-4453

ORGANIZATIONS PROVIDING INFERTILITY SERVICES

AMERICAN FERTILITY SOCIETY
2140 Eleventh Avenue, Suite 200
Birmingham, AL 35205
  Provides a large number of informational brochures on topics such as endometriosis, the medical evaluation of infertility, and IVF. Also makes referrals to medical specialists in your locale.

NATIONAL SOCIETY OF GENETIC COUNSELORS
233 Canterbury Drive
Wallingford, PA 19086
215-872-7608
  Provides information and referrals on genetic counseling services.

RESOLVE, INC.
5 Water Street
Arlington, MA 02174
617-643-2424
  A valuable, national self-help group for infertile couples that provides physician and IVF referrals, many informational brochures, a monthly newsletter, and telephone counseling. It has support groups throughout the nation. If

your are having problems with infertility and are thinking about obtaining treatment, we strongly recommend that you join this group, both for the information it will provide and the numerous ways in which it can help you deal with the emotional ups and downs of this odyssey.

ORGANIZATIONS PROVIDING PREGNANCY-RELATED SERVICES

AMERICAN COLLEGE OF NURSE MIDWIVES
1522 K Street NW
Washington, DC 20005
Provides information on midwife-assisted childbirth.

AMERICAN COLLEGE OF OBSTETRICIANS AND GYNECOLOGISTS
409 12th Street SW
Washington, DC 20024
202-638-5577
This national organization has a resource center that provides a number of educational pamphlets as well as lists of ob-gyns in various locations.

AMERICAN SOCIETY FOR PSYCHOPROPHYLAXIS IN OBSTETRICS/LAMAZE
1840 Wilson Boulevard, Suite 204
Arlington, VA 22201
Despite its intimidating name, this organization provides useful brochures about the Lamaze method and offers a referral service to certified Lamaze instructors in your area. It also publishes a magazine on pregnancy, childbirth, and early childhood.

INTERNATIONAL CHILDBIRTH EDUCATION ASSOCIATION
P. O. Box 20048
Minneapolis, MN 55420
Dedicated to family-centered maternity care and freedom of choice in childbirth, this organization publishes a number of informative brochures and periodicals and will refer you to the Childbirth Education Association in your area.

LaLECHE LEAGUE INTERNATIONAL
9616 Minneapolis Avenue
Franklin Park, IL 60131
A nationwide organization that offers practical advice about breast-feeding. Organizes local monthly meetings in many cities and provides a variety of useful publications.

STD INFORMATION

HEPATITIS HOTLINE: 404-332-4555
This service provided by the C.D.C. gives information on modes of transmission, prevention, and statistics related to all forms of viral hepatitis.

HERPES RESOURCE CENTER: 415-328-7710

STD NATIONAL HOTLINE: 800-227-8922
A service provided by the American Social Health Association, this hotline deals with questions on any STDs.

MAJOR JOURNALS

Archives of Sexual Behavior
Plenum Publishing Company
233 Spring Street
New York, NY 10013

Family Planning Perspectives
Alan Guttmacher Institute
111 Fifth Avenue
New York, NY 10003

Journal of Homosexuality
The Haworth Press
10 Alice Street
Binghamton, NY 13904

Journal of Psychology & Human Sexuality
Haworth Press
10 Alice Street
Binghamton, NY 13904

Journal of Sex Education & Therapy
435 North Michigan Avenue, Suite 1717
Chicago, IL 60611

Journal of Sex & Marital Therapy
Brunner/Mazel, Inc.
19 Union Square West
New York, NY 10003

Journal of Sex Research

P. O. Box 208
Mount Vernon, IA 52314

Medical Aspects of Human Sexuality
Cahners Publishing
249 West 17th Street
New York, NY 10011

Sex Roles
Plenum Publishing Company
233 Spring Street
New York, NY 10013

Sexuality and Disability
Human Sciences Press
233 Spring Street
New York, NY 10013

Siecus Report
130 West 42nd Street, Suite 2500
New York, NY 10036

MISCELLANEOUS

AMERICAN CANCER SOCIETY (National Office)
90 Park Avenue
New York, NY 10016

With more than 3,000 local units, which you can find by consulting your local telephone directory, this organization provides many informational and educational services related to cancer. The "Reach to Recovery" program for women who have had mastectomies is particularly noteworthy.

NATIONAL ABORTION RIGHTS ACTION
LEAGUE
1101 14th Street NW
Washington, DC 20005
202-371-0779

This is the leading pro-choice abortion group in America; it maintains a high political profile and is frequently in the news. NARAL produces a

number of educational materials, such as videotapes and brochures, advocating women's right to abortion.

NATIONAL CANCER INSTITUTE CANCER
INFORMATION SERVICE: 800-4-CANCER
Provides a wide range of brochures, reprints, and bibliographies at no charge, as well as answering all cancer-related questions.

NATIONAL CENTER FOR THE PREVENTION
AND CONTROL OF RAPE
National Institutes of Mental Health
5600 Fisher's Lane
Rockville, MD 20857
301-433-1910

NATIONAL COALITION AGAINST SEXUAL
ASSAULT
8787 State Street
East St. Louis, IL 62203
618-398-7764

NATIONAL RIGHT TO LIFE COMMITTEE
419 7th Street NW
Washington, DC 20004
202-626-8800

This is one of the leading anti-abortion groups. Like others in this field, it is primarily a political organization.

NATIONAL SELF-HELP CLEARINGHOUSE
33 West 42nd Street
New York, NY 10036
212-840-1259

If you need help in finding a self-help organization that we haven't listed here, this national clearinghouse will help you find it.

SEX ADDICTS ANONYMOUS
P. O. Box 3038
Minneapolis, MN 55403
612-871-1520

GLOSSARY

abortion Termination of a pregnancy before the fetus can survive outside the uterus. *Spontaneous* abortions occur naturally due to medical problems; *induced* abortions are done intentionally.

abstention (abstinence) The act of voluntarily not engaging in some act, such as sexual intercourse. A highly effective method of birth control if practiced consistently.

acquired immune deficiency syndrome See *AIDS*.

acrosome (ak' rosōm) Chemical reservoir in the head of the spermatozoon.

actual effectiveness The observed effectiveness of a contraceptive method in real life, including user failures and method failures.

adolescent growth spurt A period of fast bone growth usually occurring in the early or middle teens caused by the rising sex hormone levels of puberty.

adrenogenital syndrome (a drē' nō jen' i tul) An inherited disorder involving an enzyme block in the adrenal glands. Females born with this condition frequently have masculinized genitals because of excess androgen exposure prenatally. In males, genital appearance is usually unaffected.

adultery Sexual intercourse between a married person and a partner other than his or her spouse.

ageism An attitude of prejudice against the elderly.

AIDS (acquired immune deficiency syndrome) A condition of increased susceptibility to unusual forms of cancer and infection due to disturbances of the body's immune defenses; a majority of cases have occurred in male homosexuals.

AIDS-related complex (ARC) A constellation of signs and symptoms of infection with HIV, including such features as swollen lymph nodes and fevers or nightsweats, that falls short of a full-blown case of

AIDS. A substantial number of cases of ARC eventually progress to AIDS.

Alzheimer's disease A progressive form of degenerative brain disease that causes dementia (deterioration of mental abilities).

ambisexual (am' bē sek shoo ul) Term used by Masters and Johnson to refer to men or women who have no preference about the gender of their sex partners and who accept or reject sexual opportunities based on their own physical need.

amniocentesis (am' nē ō sen tē' sis) Procedure used to obtain a sample of amniotic fluid from the uterus of a pregnant woman to be analyzed for a variety of genetic disorders and biochemical abnormalities in the fetus.

amnion (am' nē on) The inner of the thin sacs of tissue (fetal membranes) that enclose the developing fetus.

amniotic fluid (am' nē ot' ik) The liquid in which the developing fetus is suspended. It keeps the temperature constant and cushions shock.

anabolic steroids Synthetic hormones that promote the build-up of muscle mass. Commonly used by athletes in an attempt to increase their size and strength.

anal stage According to Freud's theory of psychosexual development, the stage that occurs from about ages 1 to 3 when a child's sexual energies are focused on the anal zone and eliminative functions.

androcentrism Making the male perspective and male experience the cultural norm.

androgens (an' dro jinz) Hormones such as testosterone that develop and maintain secondary sex characteristics in males and, if in large quantities, promote masculinization in females.

androgynous Behavior that expresses aspects of stereotypically masculine and feminine characteristics by the same person either simultaneously or sequentially.

Long vowels are marked. Short vowels are left alone or changed to show the sound they make. Major (') and minor (') accents are marked.

androgyny (an droj' i nē) The combined presence of stereotyped feminine and masculine characteristics in one person.

anorexia nervosa An eating disorder marked by self-starvation. Anorexia nervosa usually occurs in females in their teens or early twenties.

anorgasmia (an' or gaz' mē uh) The inability of a woman to reach orgasm. Can be classified as primary (always existing), secondary (having been orgasmic in the past), situational (existing only in certain situations), coital (existing only during coitus), or random (existing on a frequent basis during different types of sexual activity).

anthropology The study of mankind, particularly involving comparative studies of nonliterate cultures.

aphrodisiac (af' rō dēz' ē ak) A substance that increases or is believed to increase a person's sexual powers or desire.

apotemnophilia Sexual excitement preferentially or exclusively from visualizing or touching an amputation, either in the person with the paraphilia or in his or her partner.

areola (a rē' o luh) The circular area of dark skin around the nipple.

assertiveness training (assertion training) A semi-structured teaching approach that emphasizes acquiring assertive skills through practice. It generally includes four basic procedures: (1) teaching people the difference between assertion and aggression and between nonassertion and politeness; (2) helping people identify and accept both their own personal rights and the rights of others; (3) reducing existing obstacles to acting assertively, e.g., irrational thinking, excessive anxiety, guilt, and anger; and (4) developing assertive skills through active practice methods.

asymptomatic carrier state The phase of HIV infection in which a person is symptom-free (although able to infect others); this period may last for years.

atrophy (a' truh fē) Reduction or wasting away of a cell, tissue, organ, or part.

autoerotic asphyxiation Strangulation during masturbation done in the belief it will heighten sexual arousal.

azidothymidine (or zidovudine) (AZT) A medication that has been shown to prolong life in HIV-infected persons and to slow the progression to symptomatic AIDS.

bacterial vaginosis A bacterial infection of the vagina marked by a malodorous grayish-white discharge and symptoms of burning or itching; this condition is caused by an overgrowth of various bacteria, including *Gardnerella vaginalis.*

Bartholin's glands (bahr' tō linz) Small glands adjacent to the vaginal opening. Although they produce minimal amounts of lubrication, their function is unknown.

basal body temperature (BBT) Temperature taken immediately after awakening and used to predict ovulation for the rhythm method of birth control. See *temperature method of birth control.*

bestiality (bes' tē al' i tē) Engaging in sexual activity with an animal.

biological essentialism The view that androcentrism and gender polarization are the inevitable expression of the innate biological nature of men and women.

bisexual (bī sek' shoo ul) A person sexually attracted to both males and females.

blastocyst (blas' tō sist) A spherical mass of cells with a hollow inner portion containing fluid produced by the cleavage of the fertilized egg.

bonding (parent–child) The emotional link partly created by cuddling, cooing, and physical and eye contact by the parent early in an infant's life.

brain tumors Abnormal growths in the brain, which can either be malignant (cancerous) or nonmalignant.

Braxton-Hicks contractions Painless short episodes of muscle tightening sometimes mistaken for the onset of labor.

breech presentation The childbirth presentation in which the buttocks or feet are the first part of the baby to pass through the opening of the vagina.

bulbocavernosus (bul' bō kav ur nō' sus) A muscle encircling and supporting the entrance to the vagina.

bulimia An eating disorder marked by frequent episodes of binge eating (consuming large quantities of food) followed immediately by purging the food just eaten by self-induced vomiting or use of laxatives.

calendar method of birth control A technique of determining the days in the menstrual cycle when the risk of pregnancy is low; a form of the rhythm method.

capacitation (kuh pas' i tā' shun) The process by which sperm become capable of penetrating an egg.

castration anxiety (kas trā' shun) According to Freud, the unconscious fear in boys about the possible loss of their penis as a terrible form of punishment.

celibacy (sel' uh buh sē) Abstention from sexual intercourse. The state of remaining unmarried, as some members of the clergy do.

cephalic presentation (se fal' ik) The childbirth presentation in which the head is the first part of the baby's body to pass through the birth canal.

cervical cap (ser' vi kul kap) A small plastic or rubber contraceptive device worn on the cervix to provide a barrier to sperm.

cervical os (ser' vi kul oss') The mouth or opening of the cervix.

cervix (ser' viks) The cylindrical part of the uterus that protrudes into the vagina. The point where sperm cells enter the uterus and menstrual flow exits is called the *cervical os.*

cesarean section (seez air' ee uhn) A surgical method of childbirth in which delivery occurs through an incision in the abdomen and uterus.

chancre (shan' ker) A painless sore that appears in the primary stage of syphilis.

chloasma (klō as' muh) Brown pigmented spots, usually on the face, caused either by birth control pills or hormones produced naturally during pregnancy.

chorion (kor ee on') The outer sac of tissue that encloses the developing fetus inside the uterus.

chorionic villi sampling (CVS) A method for diagnosing defects in the developing fetus; done by inserting a catheter through the vagina and cervix to take a small piece of tissue from the edge of the chorion, the membrane surrounding the fetus.

chromosomes (krō' muh sōmz) The genetic material in the nucleus of every cell in the body. Sperm and eggs each have 23 chromosomes; all other cells normally have 46.

cilia (sil' ē uh) The hairlike filaments in the inside of the Fallopian tubes that propel the egg along to the uterus.

circumcision (sur' kum sizh' un) Surgical removal of the foreskin of the penis.

climacteric (klī mak' tur ik) Syndrome experienced by about 5 percent of men over 60, marked by weakness, fatigue, poor appetite, decreased sexual drive, reduction or loss of potency, irritability, and impaired ability to concentrate. Also see *menopause*, which is sometimes called the female climacteric.

clitoral glans (klit' o rul) The tip or head and the only visible part of the clitoris, resembling a small button.

clitoral hood The fold of skin covering the clitoral shaft. Sometimes referred to as the female foreskin.

clitoral shaft Part of the external female genitals; two small erectile bodies enclosed in a fibrous membrane and ending in a glans. Corresponds to the *corpus cavernosa* in the penis.

clitoris (klit' o ris) Part of the external genitals of the female, situated at the anterior meeting of the labia minora and made up of two small erectile bodies, a glans and a hood. Its only known function is to focus and accumulate sexual sensations and erotic pleasure.

cohabitation A situation in which an unmarried heterosexual couple live together.

coitus interruptus (kō' i tus in tur rup' tus) The removal of the penis from the vagina before ejaculation occurs.

colostrum (kohl ah' strum) A thin, watery fluid secreted by the breasts late in pregnancy as a precursor to breast milk.

combination pill A birth control pill containing both estrogen and progesterone.

communal living Group cohabitation. The group shares economic resources and personal energies and gives emotional sharing and support. The lifestyle can include sexual sharing, but not necessarily.

complementation The process of learning the gender-appropriate responses of one's own assigned sex by interacting with a member of the opposite sex.

congenital syphilis Syphilis contracted by the fetus from an infected mother, causing various abnormalities in the unborn child.

control group Individuals in an experiment who are monitored but do not receive the experimental variable; in a treatment study, this group either receives no treatment or a placebo.

coprophilia Sexual excitement deriving from contact with feces.

coronal ridge (kor' ō nul) The rim of tissue that separates the glans from the shaft of the penis.

corpora cavernosa (kor' por ruh kav ur nō' suh) The two parallel cylindrical bodies of erectile tissue that make up the larger part of the shaft of the penis and the clitoris. Also called cavernous bodies.

corpus luteum (kor' pus lew' tē um) The part of the capsule of the ovarian follicle left in the ovary after an egg is expelled. It secretes hormones and, if pregnancy does not occur, degenerates.

corpus spongiosum (kor' pus spon' jē ō' sum) The cylinder of erectile tissue along the underside of the penis containing the urethra. The distal portion expands to form the *glans*. Also called spongy body.

cortisol (kor' ti sol) A hormone secreted by the adrenal glands that influences a wide range of body functions.

couvade syndrome (koo vahd') A condition in which a male experiences symptoms mimicking pregnancy and/or childbirth.

Cowper's glands (kow' perz) Two pea-sized structures connected to the urethra just below the prostate gland. They produce fluid before ejaculation but otherwise have no known function.

crowning In childbirth, the appearance of the baby's head at the opening of the vagina.

crura (kroo' ruh) The internal branches of the clitoral shaft and the corpus cavernosa attached to the bony pelvis.

cryptorchid (krip tor' kid) Undescended testes.

cunnilingus (kun' i ling' gus) Stimulation of the external genitals of the female by oral contact.

cystitis (sis tī' tis) Inflammation of the bladder.

diabetes A chronic disorder of how the body handles sugar because of an insulin deficiency. Complications of this disease include circulatory and neurological problems.

diaphragm (dī' uh fram) A dome-shaped rubber contraceptive device that is positioned inside the vagina so that it blocks the cervix; it must be used with a spermicide to be effective.

differential socialization The ways in which parents and others react differently to boys and girls and reinforce different behaviors for the two sexes.

dihydrotestosterone (dī hī′ drō tes tos′ ter ōn) A hormone similar to testosterone that stimulates development of the penis, scrotum, and prostrate gland in the embryo.

dilatation (dil′ uh tā′ shun) Opening of the mouth of the cervix in preparation for birth.

dilatation and curettage (D&C) (kyur e tazh′) Process involving dilating the cervix and then gently scraping the lining of the uterus with a metal instrument. Sometimes used as a form of abortion.

dilatation and evacuation (D&E) A method for abortion involving widening the mouth of the cervix, followed by removing the products of conception by a combination of suction and scraping.

douching (dūsh′ ing) Using a liquid to flush the vagina.

Down's syndrome A chromosome disorder that causes mental retardation and defects of the heart, kidneys, and intestines. Also known as trisomy 21 or mongolism.

dysfunctional (dis funk′ shun ul) Abnormally impaired.

dysmenorrhea (dis men′ or ē′ uh) Painful menstruation, usually including backache, headache, cramps, and a bloated feeling.

dyspareunia (dis′ puh roo′ nē uh) Painful intercourse.

eclampsia (e klamp′ sē uh) A condition occurring during the latter half of pregnancy marked by high blood pressure, edema, protein in the urine, and convulsions, sometimes resulting in coma or death. Also known as toxemia of pregnancy.

ectopic pregnancy (ek top′ ik) A misplaced pregnancy. The implantation of the blastocyst occurs outside the uterus, for example in the tubes or abdomen.

edema (e dē′ muh) Swelling due to fluid retention.

effacement (e fāce′ munt) The thinning of flattening of the cervix during labor.

effleurage (ef′ lu razh′) The circular stroking movement used in massage of the abdomen during labor in the Lamaze method.

egg donors Women who volunteer to provide their eggs for the purposes of treating anovulatory infertility or avoiding the transmittal of a genetic disorder in another woman.

ejaculatory ducts (ē jak′ you luh tō′ rē) Paired tubelike structures that carry sperm from the vas deferens and fluid from the seminal vesicles into the prostatic urethra.

ejaculatory incompetence The inability to ejaculate within the vagina. Can be classified as primary (always existing) or secondary (having been able to ejaculate in the past).

ejaculatory inevitability The first stage of orgasm in men, a feeling of having passed the point where ejaculation can be controlled as the vas deferens, seminal vesicles, and prostate start contracting.

Electra complex In Freudian theory, the sexual attraction of a young girl toward her father, usually accompanied by hostility toward her mother.

embryo (em′ brē o) The unborn child during the first eight weeks after fertilization.

embryo freezing A technique of freezing pre-embryo (usually zygotes or blastocysts) for use in subsequent menstrual cycles so as to reduce the risk of multiple gestations and reduce the cost of treating infertility.

embryo transplant A method of treating female infertility that involves artificially inseminating a donor female, then removing the pre-implantation pre-embryo and transplanting it to the infertile woman's uterus.

encephalitis A viral infection of the brain that is among the most serious opportunistic infections persons with AIDS face.

endocervical canal (en′ dō ser′ vi kul) The tubelike connection between the mouth of the cervix and the uterine cavity containing numerous secretory glands that produce mucus.

endogamy The custom of requiring that people marry partners from within their band or village.

endometriosis The occurrence of endometrial tissue in locations other than the uterus; a frequent cause of female infertility.

endometrium (en′ dō mē′ trē um) The inner lining of the uterus in which the egg implants and which is partially shed during menstruation.

engagement The settling of the fetal head into position against the pelvic bones for birth. It usually occurs during the last few weeks of pregnancy in women having their first child and during labor with subsequent pregnancies. Also called dropping or lightening.

enzyme-linked immunoabsorbent assay (ELISA) The screening test used to detect HIV antibodies in blood samples; positive ELISA results must always be confirmed with a second, more specific, test, such as the Western blot.

epideminological studies Research focusing on patterns of the prevalence and spread of a condition or disease, especially infectious diseases and epidemics.

epididymis (ep′ i did′ i mis) The tightly coiled tubing network folded against the back surface of each testis in which sperm cells spend several weeks maturing.

epilepsy A disease of unknown origin marked by the periodic occurrence of seizures (convulsions).

episiotomy (e piz′ ē ot′ uh mē) During a vaginal delivery, the incision in the mother's perineum that gives the baby's head more room to emerge.

erectile dysfunction The inability to have or maintain an erection firm enough for coitus. Can be classified as primary (always existing) or secondary (having functioned in the past). See *impotence.*

estrogens (es′ tro jinz) Hormones present in both sexes, but primarily considered female. Produced in the ovaries and adrenal glands in the female, they maintain the lining of the vagina and produce breast growth. Also important in controlling the menstrual cycle.

excitement phase First phase of the human sexual response cycle caused by physical and/or psychological stimulation. It is characterized by increasing levels of myotonia and by vasocongestion.

exhibitionism A condition in which a person repeatedly and preferentially exposes the sex organs to unsuspecting strangers to obtain sexual arousal.

exhibitionist A person who obtains sexual gratification by exposing the genitals to strangers. "Flasher" is a slang term.

exogamy The custom of requiring that people marry partners from outside their band or village.

extramarital sex Sexual activity involving a married person and a partner who isn't his or her spouse.

extra nipples More than two paired nipples; about one person in 1000 has this condition.

Fallopian tubes (fuh lō′ pē un) The tubes that transport eggs from the ovaries to the uterus. Also called oviducts.

false labor Irregular contractions that do not become regular. They are felt mainly in the lower abdomen and groin in contrast to true labor, which is felt in the back and abdomen.

fellatio (fe lā′ shē ō) Stimulation of the male genitals by oral contact.

fetal alcohol syndrome The effects on the unborn child of heavy use of alcohol by the pregnant woman, including growth deficiencies, nervous system damage, and facial abnormalities.

fetal membranes Two thin sacs of tissue, the inner amnion and the outer chorion, that enclose the developing baby.

fetal monitor Electronic equipment used during labor to check the progress of the baby, especially its heartbeat, and the duration, frequency, and intensity of uterine contractions.

fetishism (fet′ ish iz um) A condition in which sexual arousal occurs principally in response to an inanimate object or body part rather than a partner.

fetus (fē′ tus) The unborn child from the ninth week after fertilization until birth.

field study Research conducted in the natural environment of study subjects instead of in a laboratory.

fimbria (fim′ brē uh) Long, fingerlike extensions at the entrance to the Fallopian tubes.

first stage of labor The early portion of labor in which cervical effacement and dilatation occurs.

follicle (fol′ i kul) A thin capsule of tissue surrounding immature eggs.

follicle stimulating hormone (FSH) A substance produced in the pituitary gland that prepares the ovary for ovulation and stimulates the production of sperm cells in the testes.

follicular phase (fol ik′ ūlar) The first phase of the menstrual cycle, in which ovarian follicles begin to mature as a result of stimulation by FSH. See also *follice stimulating hormone.*

foreskin (for′ skin) The freely movable skin that covers the penis. Also the hood of the clitoris.

fornication (for′ nuh kā′ shun) Coitus between unmarried heterosexual adults. A crime in some states.

frenulum (fren′ ūlum) A small, triangular fold of skin on the underside of the penis connecting the glans with the foreskin.

frigidity (fri jid′ i tē) An outdated term formerly used to describe female sexual difficulties.

frotteurism Sexual arousal that results from rubbing the genitals against the body of a fully clothed person in crowded situation such as subways, buses, or elevators.

FSH See *follicle stimulating hormone.*

gamete intrafallopian transfer (GIFT) The direct placement of a mixture of sperm and eggs into the Fallopian tube as a treatment for infertility.

gender identity The inner sense a person has of being male or female.

gender polarization Mutually exclusive scripts and expectations for how males and females should act, with a person not following these scripts viewed as problematic or abnormal.

gender role Behavior that conveys to others that an individual is either male or female.

gender-role transcendence Behavior that is functional in a particular situation without regard to whether it fits stereotypical views of masculinity and femininity.

gender schema How we use gender-based classifications to view our beliefs about masculinity and femininity and to translate them into our own behavior.

generalizing Applying the findings of research from a sample to the population from which the sample was taken, or other, similar populations.

genital herpes (jen′ i tul her pēz) Painful blisters of the genitals caused by infection with the herpes virus; outbreaks typically are recurrent and are highly contagious.

genital stage In Freudian theory, the last stage of sexual development, which begins at puberty owing to internal biological forces. Characterized by growing independence and a final transition into adult genital sexuality.

genital warts Dry, painless warts on or near the genitals or anus that are caused by a sexually transmitted virus. Sometimes referred to as venereal warts.

genitals (jen′ i tulz) Sex organs in the pelvic region. Customarily refers to the penis, the testes, and scrotum in the male and the vulva and vagina in the female.

glans (glanz) The tip or head of the penis or clitoris.

gonad Ovary or testicle.

gonadotropin releasing hormone (GnRH) (gō nad′ ō trō′ pin) A substance produced by the hypothalamus that controls the production and release of LH and FSH by the pituitary.

gonorrhea A sexually transmitted disease caused by the bacterium *Neisseria gonorrheae*. First symptoms in men include a puslike discharge from the tip of the penis and frequent urination, but many affected women are symptomless. Untreated, gonorrhea can cause serious complications, especially infertility in women.

granulosa cells (gran′ ū lō′ suh) The cells lining the ovarian follicle that enlarge and form the corpus luteum.

G Spot (Gräfenberg spot) A proposed region of the front wall of the vagina claimed by some researchers to have a high degree of erotic sensitivity.

gynecomastia (jīn′ e kō mas′ tē uh) Enlargement of one or both male breasts.

Hawthorne effect The change in people's behavior that often occurs when they know they are being studied as part of a research project.

hepatitis (hep ah tie′ tis) An infection or inflammation of the liver.

hermaphrodite (hur maf′ rō dīt) A person with both testicular and ovarian tissue.

heterosexual (het′ ur ō sek′ shoo ul) A person with sexual preference for partners of the opposite sex.

homogeneity The degree to which individuals in a population are alike.

homophobia Obsessive hostility and fear toward homosexuals.

homosexual (hō′ mō sek′ shoo ul) A person with sexual preference for partners of his or her own sex.

hormone Chemical substance secreted by the endocrine system into the bloodstream to be carried directly to the tissue on which it acts.

hot flash Sudden sensations of warmth, blushing, and sweating, sometimes with dizziness, that occur commonly in menopausal women.

human immunodeficiency virus (HIV) The retrovirus that causes AIDS; prior to 1986, this virus was generally called HTLV-III.

H-Y antigen The substance that controls the transformation of the primitive gonads into testes in the embryo. If it is not present, the primitive gonads develop into ovaries.

hymen (hī′ mun) A thin tissue membrane covering the opening of the vagina.

hypersexual Having an extraordinarily high sex drive; "oversexed." Sometimes called *nymphomania* in women and *satyriasis* or Don Juanism in men.

hypothalamus (hī′ pō thal′ uh mus) The portion of the brain that has primary control over most endocrine pathways. It reacts to the level of hormones in the blood supply which regulate many sexual responses and directs their production.

hysterectomy (his′ tur ek′ tuh mē) Partial or total removal of the uterus.

hysterotomy (his tur ot′ uh mē) Incision of the uterus. Infrequently used for abortion during the second trimester.

implantation The attachment of the blastocyst to the lining of the uterus.

impotence (im′ puh tence) The inability to have or maintain an erection firm enough for coitus. See *erectile dysfunction.*

incest Sexual activity between close relatives.

induced labor Labor started artificially, usually by infusing oxytocin into a vein.

infertility The inability of a couple to achieve pregnancy, usually defined after a year or more of sexual intercourse without pregnancy.

inguinal canal (in′ gwuh nal) A passage about 4 cm long through which a nerve and the spermatic cord pass in the male and the round ligament of the uterus passes in the female.

inhibited sexual desire (ISD) A condition marked by very low interest in sexual behavior.

inner lips See *labia minora.*

intrauterine device (IUD) (in truh ū′ ter in) A small object, either plastic or metal, placed inside the uterus for birth control.

introitus The opening of the vagina.

inverted nipples Congenital condition in which the nipples are not protuberant.

in vitro **fertilization** A procedure involving removing eggs from a woman's body and fertilizing them with sperm in a laboratory. After successful fertilization, the pre-embryo is surgically implanted in the woman's uterus.

Kaposi's sarcoma A previously rare form of cancer of the small blood vessels, causing purplish spots on the skin or in the mouth; a common sign of AIDS in homosexual men.

Klinefelter's syndrome A sex chromosome abnormality marked by an extra X chromosome in a genetic male, giving a 47, XXY pattern. Most of these men tend to be tall with poor muscular development and small testes. Sexual desire is often low and impotence common.

klismaphilia Sexual excitement preferentially or exclusively resulting from the use of enemas.

labia majora (la′ bē uh muh jor′ uh) The two outer folds of skin on either side of the inner lips, the clitoris, and the urethral and vaginal openings.

labia minora (la′ bē uh mi nor′ uh) The two inner folds of skin enclosing the urethral and vaginal openings.

labor The processes involved in giving birth, especially uterine contractions.

lactation (lak tā′ shun) The production of milk by the breasts, usually beginning a few days after birth.

laparoscopy An exploratory visualization of the pelvic and abdominal organs using a tubelike instrument.

laparotomy (lap uh rot′ uh mē) Any operation involving an incision through the abdominal wall. Now used for sterilization only if other surgery is required in the abdomen.

larynx The voice box.

latency stage In Freudian theory, the period from about six years to puberty when sexual impulses are quiescent and are sublimated into nonsexual behaviors and interests.

latent stage (syphilis) Period in the course of syphilis when symptoms disappear and the disease is no longer contagious. During this stage infecting organisms burrow into most organs of the body.

lenses of gender According to Sandra Bem, assumptions about the nature of masculinity and femininity that people commonly employ.

Leydig cells (lī′ dig) The cells in the testes where hormone production occurs.

libido (li bē′ dō) In Freudian theory, psychic energy or drive, fundamentally sexual. Also refers to level of sexual desire.

limerence Word coined by Dorothy Tennov to describe a blind, intense kind of love outside a person's rational control.

longitudinal study Observations of one sample conducted over a period of time.

luteal phase (lū′ tē ul) The third phase of the menstrual cycle, after ovulation. The corpus luteum produces large amounts of progesterone and estrogen, which prepare the uterus to receive the fertilized egg.

luteinizing hormone (LH) (lū′ tē in īz′ ing) Produced by the pituitary gland, LH triggers ovulation and stimulates the Leydig cells to manufacture testosterone.

lymphokines Messenger proteins secreted by macrophages that activate the immune response.

macho Aggresively male. The adjective form of *machismo,* which describes a set of masculine attitudes and behaviors originally from South American and Mediterranean cultures.

macromastia (mak′ rō mas′ tē uh) Abnormally large breasts.

mammary hyperplasia or macromastia Abnormally large breasts.

masochism (mas′ ō kiz um) The need for experiencing pain and humiliation to achieve sexual gratification.

mastectomy (mas tek′ tuh mē) Surgical removal of the breast.

meiosis (mī ō′ sis) The process by which each immature egg divides into four cells, only one of which is a mature egg.

menarche (me nar′ kē) The onset of menses.

menopause (men′ ō paws) The period during which menstruation gradually stops, usually occurring in the late forties. Sometimes called female climacteric.

menstruation (men stroo′ ā′ shun) A flow of blood from the lining of the uterus occurring about once a month in females from puberty until the late forties or early fifties.

micropenis (mī krō pē′ nis) A penis that is correctly formed, but is less than 2 cm long.

minipill A contraceptive pill containing only progesterone in low dosage.

molluscum contagiosum A skin disease caused by a pox virus; the skin breaks out in small, bumpy lesions with a pearly top.

mongolism See *Down's syndrome.*

monilial vaginitis (mon il′ ee all vaj in eye′ tis) Infection of the vagina caused by a fungus; usually accompanied by a thick, cheesy discharge with intense itching.

monogamy A form of marriage in which a person can marry only one spouse at a time. In a broader sense, monogamy is sometimes used to describe sexual fidelity between partners in a marriage or other form of long-term, nonmarital relationship.

mons veneris (mōnz ven′ e ris) The area over the pubic bone of the female, which consists of a cushion of fatty tissue covered by skin and pubic hair. Also called mons pubis or mound of Venus.

morula (more′ u lah) A spherical mass of cells resulting from cleavage of the fertilized egg.

mucosa (mew kō′ suh) Mucous membrane. The membrane lining of the body openings, especially of the vagina, kept moist by the secretions of various types of glands.

Müllerian duct (mew ler′ ē un) One of two pairs of embryonic genital ducts. In females, this duct system develops into the Fallopian tubes, uterus, and inner part of the vagina. In males, a substance secreted by the embryonic testes causes the Müllerian duct system to shrink and practically disappear.

multiorgasmic (mul′ te or gaz′ mik) The potential ability of women to have a series of identifiable orgasmic responses without dropping below the plateau level of arousal. Men do not share this capacity.

multiple sclerosis (MS) A chronic neurological disorder affecting both motor and sensory function in an episodic but progressive fashion.

myometrium (mī′ ō mē′ trē um) The muscular component of the uterus, important in labor and delivery.

myotonia (mī′ ō tō nē uh) Involuntary contraction of muscle.

necrophilia Sexual arousal from viewing or having sexual contact with a corpse.

neuromuscular tension (new' rō mus' kew lur) Buildup of energy in the nerves and muscles sometimes caused by sexual arousal.

neurosis A psychological disorder usually characterized by anxiety and/or tension. In contrast to more severe forms of psychological problems, called psychoses, with a neurosis a person's sense of reality is not greatly altered.

nipple Protuberance located at the tip of the breast principally consisting of smooth muscle fibers and a network of nerve endings and containing in the female the outlets of the milk ducts.

nocturnal emissions Involuntary male orgasm and ejaculation during sleep (sometimes called wet dreams).

nonspecific urethritis (NSU) Inflammation of the male's urethra not caused by gonorrhea.

nymphomania (nim' fō mā' nē uh) In females, compulsive sexual activity that gives only fleeting satisfaction. The male form is *satyriasis*.

obscenity Pictures or writing disgusting to the senses, abhorrent to morality or virtue, and/or specifically designed to incite lust or depravity. Obscenity is illegal, pornography is not.

occiput presentation The childbirth presentation in which the back part of the baby's head is the first part to pass through the birth canal.

Oedipus complex (ed' i pus) In Freudian theory, the sexual attraction of a young boy toward his mother, accompanied by a mixture of fear and rivalry toward his father. See also *Electra complex.*

oral stage In Freudian theory, the first year of life, in which the sexual energies are focused in the region of the mouth.

orgasm (or' gas um) The third and shortest phase of the human sexual response cycle. A total body response involving the sudden discharge of accumulated sexual tension.

orgasmic dysfunction (or gaz' mik) The inability of a female to reach orgasm. See also *anorgasmia.*

orgasmic platform The narrowing of the vagina during sexual excitement due to vasocongestion.

orgasmic reconditioning An approach used to condition a person away from an unsuitable sexual fantasy by instructing the person to begin masturbating using the unsuitable fantasy and to switch to a more appropriate fantasy at the moment of orgasm.

osteoporosis (ah stee oh porh oh' sis) A condition in which the bones become thin and brittle due to mineral loss; a common occurrence in postmenopausal women.

outcome study A form of clinical research that evaluates the effect of one or more treatments on a particular condition, such as a disease.

outer lips See *labia majora.*

ovariectomy (ō vuh' rē ek' tuh mē) Surgical removal of the ovaries.

ovaries (ō' vur ēz) Paired structures located on each side of the uterus that contain and release eggs and secrete hormones such as estrogen and progesterone. The female gonads.

ovulation (ōv you lā' shun) The second phase of the menstrual cycle; the release of the egg from the ovary.

ovulation method of birth control A method that depends on changes in the cervical mucus thought to indicate the time of ovulation. The mucus changes from cloudy, white, and tacky to clear and stretchy at the time of ovulation. Intercourse is thought to be safe four days after the ovulatory mucus begins and when the mucus has returned to a cloudy, tacky consistency. Failure rate is high.

ovum (ō' vum) A mature egg cell that is capable, after maturation and fertilization, of becoming another member of the same species.

oxytocin (ahk' sē to' sin) A hormone made in the posterior pituitary thought to play a role in uterine contractions and lactation stimulation.

paraphilia (pair' uh fil' ē uh) A condition in which a person's sexual gratification is dependent on an unusual sexual experience (or fantasy). A neutral term for sexual alternatives that have been called deviant.

paraplegia Paralysis of both lower extremities.

parent–child bonding The process of attachment and identification that usually occurs during early infancy.

participant–observer method A form of research in which the researcher takes an active part in the situation being studied.

pedophilia (ped ō fil' ē uh) A sexual variation in which the preferred or exclusive method of achieving sexual excitement is by fantasizing about or engaging in sexual activity with children.

penis (pē' nis) The male organ of copulation. It consists primarily of three cylinders of spongy tissue, interspersed with many small, thin-walled blood vessels and bound in a thick membrane sheath.

penis envy In Freudian theory, the girl's unconscious sense of inadequacy and jealousy at not having a penis.

pentamidine A medication used to prevent *pneumocystis carinii* pneumonia.

perimenopausal years (perry men oh paws' uhl) The years immediately before and after menopause.

perineum (per i nē' um) The hairless area of skin between the vagina and anus in the female and between the scrotum and anus in the male.

peristalsis (per' i stal' sis) Waves of contractions in the muscle fibers in the walls of tubes such as the Fallopian tubes. These contractions, along with the beating of the cilia, move the fertilized egg along the

Fallopian tubes to the uterus. In the male, peristalic contractions of the urethra advance the ejaculate through the penis.

permissive society One in which there are few restraints on children and adolescents engaging in sexual activity.

phagocytes White blood cells that engulf invading microorganisms.

phallic stage In Freudian theory, the period from about 3 to 5 years of age when the child's sexual energies are focused on the genitals.

pituitary (pi tew' i ter' ē) An acorn-sized gland at the base of the brain which, at the direction of the hypothalamus, secretes several hormones important to sexual development and function. Once believed to control most of the endocrine system, it is now known to act only as a relay station.

placebo (pluh sē' bō) An inert substance or treatment that may cause improvements in a person's condition.

placebo effect The results observed in an experiment when people report various changes (e.g., sleeping better) from use of a placebo, or chemically inert drug; the effect is due to expectations of improvement.

placenta (pluh sen' tuh) The organ attached to the wall of the uterus that performs the functions of nutrition, respiration, and excretion for the unborn child. It is also an endocrine organ secreting large amounts of several hormones.

plateau phase The phase of human sexual response following excitement, in which a leveling off of sexual tensions occurs. The phase can be short or long prior to reaching levels required to trigger orgasm.

pneumocystis carinii A microorganism that causes life-threatening pneumonia in persons with AIDS; one of the leading causes of death in AIDS patients.

polar bodies Cells that arise in the development of the ovum during meiosis.

polio An infection caused by a virus that can, in severe forms, cause paralysis.

polyandry The practice of a woman's being married to more than one husband at a time.

polygamy Being married to more than one spouse at a time.

polygyny The practice of a man's being married to more than one woman at a time.

population In research, the overall group being studied from which a smaller sample is drawn.

pornography Books or pictures that depict erotic behavior with the intent of causing sexual excitement. Technically, pornography is not illegal, obscenity is.

postmenopausal years The period of a woman's life after menstruation ceases.

postpartum depression The letdown many women experience after giving birth. They are tearful and depressed and may have frightening dreams. Also called baby blues.

precocious puberty (pree koh' shus pew' burr tee) Physical changes of puberty occurring before age 8 in girls or age 10 in boys.

preeclampsia (prē' e klamp' sē uh) A condition occurring during the latter half of pregnancy characterized by high blood pressure, edema, and protein in the urine. May progress to *eclampsia*.

pre-embryo stage The interval from the completion of fertilization until the appearance of a single primitive streak.

premature ejaculation Unintentional ejaculation during noncoital play, while the male is trying to enter his partner, or soon after intercourse begins.

premenstrual syndrome Fatigue, irritability, depression, and bloated feeling some women experience a few days before menstruation. Physical, psychological, and social causes are debated.

prenatal care The combined efforts of doctor, nurse, and mother to see that the pregnant women stays healthy and the unborn child has everything needed to grow and develop.

prenatal period The time from conception to birth.

primary spermatocytes (spur mat' ō sīts) The matured spermatogonia that have divided by meiosis.

primitive streak An embryonic structure that appears on about the fourteenth day of development, eventually degenerating and disappearing.

procreational sex (prō' krē ā' shun ul) Sexual intercourse solely for reproduction. Sometimes advocated by some churches and groups as the only acceptable reason for sex.

progesterone (prō jes' tur ōn) A hormone present in both sexes, but primarily known as a female hormone. Present in high levels during pregnancy.

prolapsed cord Condition whereby the umbilical cord is compressed to the point where the blood supply to the baby is cut off.

prostaglandin-induced abortion Evacuation of the contents of the pregnant uterus produced by infusion of prostaglandins.

prostatectomy (pros' tuh tek' tuh mē) Surgical removal of the prostate gland.

prostate gland (pros' tāt) Gland located directly below the bladder, surrounding the urethra as it exits the bladder. It secretes part of the seminal fluid and is a major site of the synthesis of prostaglandins.

prostatitis (pros tuh tī' tis) Inflammation of the prostate, cause by infection.

pseudohermaphrodite (sue' dō hur maf' rō dīt) An individual born with gonads matching the sex chromosomes but a genital appearance that resembles the opposite sex.

pubic lice Parasites that invade the pubic region, often transmitted during sexual intercourse.

pubococcygeus (pew bō kock sij′ ē us) A muscle encircling and supporting the vagina.

quadriplegia (kwahd ruh pleej′ ee ah) Paralysis of all limbs.

quickening The time during pregnancy when a woman can first feel the fetus moving.

random sample A sample in which each member of the population has an identical chance of being selected.

rapid orgasm The female counterpart of premature ejaculation, marked by characteristically having orgasm so quickly in a sexual encounter that it is distressful. This is a very rare complaint.

recreational sex Sexual activity primarily for pleasure. Emotional involvement and intimacy are purposefully limited.

rectum (rek′ tum) The lower part of the large intestine.

refractory period In the male, the period immediately following ejaculation during which further orgasm is physiologically impossible. This period is not present in the female response cycle.

relational sex Sexual activity in the context of emotional involvement and intimacy in a relationship.

reliability In research, the consistency of repeated measurements with the same procedure.

resolution phase Last phase of human sexual response following orgasm or maximum excitement in which the body returns to an unaroused state.

restrictive society One in which adults attempt to prevent children and adolescents from engaging in sexual activity until marriage.

retarded ejaculation Condition in which ejaculation in the vagina occurs only after a lengthy time period and strenuous efforts.

retrograde ejaculation Condition in which the semen spurts backward into the bladder during orgasm because the bladder neck does not close off properly. It occurs in men with multiple sclerosis and diabetes and following some types of prostate surgery.

Rh incompatibility Condition in which antibodies from the mother's bloodstream destroy red blood cells in the fetus, causing anemia, mental retardation, or fetal death.

rhythm method Any form of birth control based on periodic abstinence. Although most rhythm methods seek to identify the most fertile portion of the menstrual cycle, they are generally of poor reliability. Rhythm methods are acceptable to the the Catholic church, which views them as "natural" forms of birth control.

rubella (roo bel′ uh) German measles. If the virus crosses the placental barrier to the fetus, it can cause serious malformations including deafness, eye problems, and mental retardation.

Rubin's test A procedure to check for obstructed Fallopian tubes. Carbon dioxide is inserted into the uterus to see if it passes into the abdomen.

sadism (sā′ diz um) The intentional infliction of pain on another person to achieve sexual excitement.

saline-induced abortion Evacuation of the contents of the pregnant uterus produced by infusion of a salt solution into the amniotic fluid.

sample In research, the portion of a larger population chosen to study.

sample selection The process of choosing a sample.

satyriasis (sat′ i rī′ uh sis) In males, compulsive sexual activity that gives only fleeting satisfaction. Also called Don Juanism. Female form is *nymphomania*.

scrotum (skrō′ tum) The thin, loose sac of skin that contains the testes and has a layer of muscle fibers that contract involuntarily.

second stage of labor The portion of labor from full cervical dilation to delivery of the baby.

secondary spermatocytes (spur mat′ ō sī tz) The product of the second division of the mature spermatogonia, which divide into spermatids.

seduction In legal terminology, situation in which a woman is enticed into sexual intercourse by a promise of marriage.

seminal fluid (sem′ uh nul) The thick white, yellow, or gray liquid portion of the male ejaculate.

seminal vesicles (sem′ uh nul ves′ e kulz) In the male, paired pouchlike bodies that empty into the ejaculatory ducts and provide the major part of the fluid in the ejaculate.

seminiferous tubules (sem′ i nif′ ur us tū′ bewls) Microscopic tube-shaped structures in the testes where sperm is produced.

sensate focus Graduated touching experiences (not necessarily sexual) assigned to couples in therapy to reduce anxiety and teach nonverbal communication skills.

serial monogamy The practice of remarrying after divorce or death of a spouse.

sex flush A temporary reddish, spotty rashlike color change sometimes developing during sexual excitement. Usually on the abdomen and breasts, it can spread to any areas of the body.

sexual aversion A severe phobia (irrational fear) of sexual activity or the thought of sexual activity, which generally leads to avoidance of sexual situations.

sexual differentiation The process that begins at the moment of conception to create a normal male or female.

sexual dysfunction Conditions in which the ordinary physical responses of sexual excitement or orgasm are impaired. Can be classified as psychosocial (caused by psychological, interpersonal, environmental, and cultural factors) or organic (caused by physical or medical factors such as illness, injury, or drugs).

sexual orientation Preference for sexual partners of the same sex (homosexual), of the opposite sex (heterosexual), or of either sex (bisexual).

sexual psychopath Variously defined in law; most generally, a person exhibiting compulsive, repetitive, and/or bizarre sexual behavior. This legal label, not a psychiatric diagnosis, permits courts to impose jail sentences and implies that people so labeled are a menace to society.

sexuality A broadly encompassing term used to refer to all aspects of being and feeling sexual.

sexually transmitted disease (STD) Infection spread mainly by sexual contact.

shingles A painful, blistering skin rash caused by the herpes zoster virus.

significance Statistically, the determination that the observed result was not a matter of chance alone.

smegma (smeg' muh) Glandular secretions, dead cells, dirt particles, and bacteria that accumulate under the foreskin of the penis or the hood of clitoris.

spermatids (spur' muh tids) The products of the third and last division of the male germ cell, which mature into spermatozoa.

spermatogonia (spur' muh to gō' nē uh) Primitive male germ cells that mature into primary spermatocytes.

spermatozoa (spur' muh to zō' uh) The mature male germ cell.

spongy body See *corpus spongiosum.*

squeeze technique Method for reducing the tendency for rapid ejaculation.

statutory rape Intercourse with a female below the legal age of consent.

stereotypes Fixed, conventional beliefs based on oversimplified evidence or uncritical judgments.

sterilization Surgical procedure performed on men (vasectomy) or women (tubal ligation; hysterectomy) to prevent union of sperm and egg.

swinging A form of consensual extramarital sex in which married couples switch partners with one or more other couples.

syphilis (sif' uh lis) A sexually transmitted disease caused by *Treponema pallidum.* Its stages consist of primary (characterized by chancres), secondary (characterized by rash, fever, aches and pains, weight loss, and hair loss), and tertiary (characterized by serious heart problems and brain or spinal cord damage.)

temperature method of birth control A technique of determining the part of the menstrual cycle when pregnancy is likely to occur so that intercourse can be avoided then. Involves daily recording of basal body temperature to pinpoint ovulation. Intercourse is not allowed from the day menstrual flow stops until two to four days after a temperature rise. Failure rate is high.

teratogen (teh rat' ō jin) A substance, such as a drug or chemical, that causes birth defects.

testes (tes' tēz) The paired male reproductive glands contained in the scrotum. The male gonads.

testicular feminization syndrome An inherited condition in which tissues are insensitive to the effects of testosterone. The individual is born with a 46, XY chromosome pattern (male) but with female genitals.

testosterone (tes tos' tur ōn) The most important hormone in sexual function, present in both sexes. Often called the male hormone, it is secreted by the testes and adrenals in the male and the ovaries and adrenals in the female.

theoretical effectiveness The ideal effectiveness of a contraceptive method when used correctly and consistently.

third stage of labor The period immediately following delivery of the baby, concluding with separation and expulsion of the placenta.

thrush An infection of the mouth and throat caused by monilia; this type of infection is more bothersome than life-threatening.

toxemia A complication of pregnancy marked by sudden increase in blood pressure, edema, and protein in the urine.

toxic shock syndrome (TSS) An illness of rapid onset caused by infection with *Staphylococcus aureas* bacteria; symptoms include fever, vomiting, muscle pain, and a sunburn-like skin rash. Most, but not all, cases have occurred in menstruating women, and the syndrome is thought to be related to the use of high-absorbency vaginal tampons.

transsexualism A rare condition in which there is a persistent sense of discomfort and inappropriateness about one's anatomical sex accompanied by the desire to change one's sexual anatomy and live as a member of the opposite biological sex.

transudation (trans' ū dā' shun) The passing of a fluid through a membrane, especially the lubrication in the vagina during sexual arousal.

transverse position The childbirth presentation in which the baby lies across the uterus and a shoulder or arm is first to be seen at the opening of the vagina. A cesarean section in often necessary if the baby cannot be turned.

transvestite (trans ves' tīt) An individual who receives sexual gratification and release from anxiety by dressing in the clothing of the opposite sex. Unlike transsexuals, transvestites are not interested in becoming a member of the opposite sex.

triad Three-partner marriage.

trichomonas vaginitis (trick ō mon' ess) An infection of the vagina caused by bacteria called trichomonas vaginalis. Accompanied by a frothy, thin, greenish or yellowish gray, foul-smelling discharge and burning and itching.

trimester A three-month period; generally used to describe the progression of pregnancy in three such periods.

trisomy 21 (trī′ sō mē) See *Down's syndrome*.

tubal ligation (tū′ bull lī gā′ shun) Literally, tying the tubes—cutting, cauterizing, and blocking the Fallopian tubes to prevent conception.

Turner's syndrome A sex chromosome abnormality caused by a missing chromosome. The individual has a 45, X chromosome pattern and may appear fairly normal until puberty, when nonfunctioning gonads prevent development of the secondary sex characteristics and the adolescent growth spurt. May also be accompanied by webbing of the neck, increased carrying angle of the elbow, heart defects, and other abnormalities.

umbilical cord The cylindrical structure connecting the fetus to the placenta. It contains two arteries and a vein.

urethra (u rē′ thruh) A tube beginning at the bladder and ending at the urethral meatus, carrying urine in the female and urine or semen in the male.

urethral meatus (u rē′ thral mē a′ tus) The urinary opening.

urinary stress incontinence A condition in which urine leaks from the urethra during coughing, laughing, and/or sexual arousal.

urophilia Sexual excitement deriving from contact with urine.

uterus (ū′ tur us) A hollow, pear-shaped muscular organ, part of the female internal genitals, in which the fertilized egg becomes embedded and the embryo and the fetus are nourished. Sometimes called the womb.

vacuum aspiration The method usually chosen for abortion during the first trimester. The cervix is dilated and the contents of the uterus are removed through a plastic tube connected to a pump.

vagina (va jī′ nuh) The canal in the female that receives the penis in copulation, existing as a potential space capable of contraction and expansion. The opening is called the vaginal introitus.

vaginismus (vaj in iz′ mus) Involuntary spasms of the muscles around the vagina in response to attempts at penetration.

vaginitis (vaj in ī′ tis) Vaginal inflammation from infection or chemical irritation.

validity The soundness of the the theoretically defined meaning of a measure or set of data.

vas deferens (vas def′ ur enz) One of two long, tubelike structures that convey spermatozoa from the testes.

vasectomy (vas ek′ tuh mē) Surgical procedure for sterilization of the male consisting of cutting and tying each vas deferens. The operation does not stop sperm production but blocks its passage from the testes.

vasocongestion (vas′ o kun jes′ chun) An increased amount of blood concentrated in body tissues, especially in the genitals and female breasts during sexual arousal. In the male it causes erection and in the female an increase in the size of the clitoris and transudation of fluid in the vagina.

venereal warts Dry, usually painless, sexually transmitted nodules that grow on or near the genitals and are caused by a virus.

vernix (ver′ niks) The cheeselike paste that appears on the surface of the fetus beginning about the sixth month.

vertex presentation (vur′ teks) The childbirth presentation in which the crown of the baby's head is first to be seen at the opening of the vagina.

viral hepatitis Infection of the liver by a virus causing a debilitating acute illness and sometimes a chronic condition.

volunteer bias A type of sampling bias in research in which the sample does not reflect the characteristics of the population because individuals with a certain characteristic or pattern of characteristics are more (or less) likely to volunteer to be studied.

voyeurism (voi yur′ iz um) A sexual variation in which a person obtains sexual gratification by witnessing the sexual acts of others or by spying on other people who are undressing or are nude.

vulva (vul′ vuh) The external sex organs of the female: the mons, labia, clitoris, and vaginal orifice.

Western blot test A confirmatory test used to supplement ELISA testing. Western blot tests are more accurate than ELISA tests, but their complexity and expense precludes their use as the primary screening method in testing for HIV.

wet dreams See *nocturnal emissions*.

withdrawal The removal of the penis from the vagina before ejaculation occurs. When used as a birth control method, failure rate is high. See *coitus interruptus*.

Wolffian duct (wool′ fē un) One of two primitive duct systems in the embryo. Develops in the male to form the epididymis, vas deferens, seminal vesicles, and prostate; it shrinks in the female to nonfunctioning remnants.

zona pellucida (zō′ nuh pe lew′ sē duh) The jellylike material surrounding the mature egg.

zoophilia (zō′ uh fil′ ē uh) A sexual variation in which a person prefers sexual activity with animals.

zygote (zī′ gōt) The single cell created by the penetration of an egg by the sperm. An organism produced by the union of two gametes.

zygote intrafallopian transfer (ZIFT) A technique of assisted reproductive technology in which the woman's eggs are fertilized *in vitro*, after which the zygote is placed in the Fallopian tube.

REFERENCES

Aarskog, D. "Maternal Progestins as a Possible Cause of Hypospadias." *New England Journal of Medicine* 300:75–78, 1979.

AAUW. *The AAUW Report: How Schools Shortchange Girls.* Annapolis Junction, MD: AAUW Educational Foundation and the National Education Association, 1992.

Abbey, A., and Melby, C. "The Effects of Nonverbal Cues on Gender Differences in Perception of Sexual Intent." *Sex Roles* 15:283–298, 1986.

Abel, G., et al. "Current Treatment of Paraphiliacs." *Annual Review of Sex Research* III:255–290, 1992.

Abel, G. G., and Blanchard, E. B. "The Role of Fantasy in the Treatment of Sexual Deviation." *Archives of General Psychiatry* 30:467–475, 1974.

Abel, G. G., et al. "The Components of Rapists' Sexual Arousal." *Archives of General Psychiatry* 34:895–903, 1977.

———. "Women's Vaginal Responses During REM Sleep." *Journal of Sex and Marital Therapy* 5:5–14, 1979.

Abitbol, M. M., and Davenport, J. H. "Sexual Dysfunction After Therapy for Cervical Carcinoma." *American Journal of Obstetrics and Gynecology* 119:181–189, 1974.

Aboulker, J. P., and Swart, A. M. "Preliminary Analysis of the Concorde Trial." *Lancet* 341:889–890, 1993.

Abramson, P. R. "Sexual Science: Emerging Discipline or Oxymoron?" *Journal of Sex Research* 27:147–166, 1990.

Abramson, P. R., and Mosher, D. L. "An Empirical Investigation of Experimentally Induced Masturbatory Fantasies." *Archives of Sexual Behavior* 8:27–39, 1979.

Adams, D. B., Gold, A. R., and Burt, A. D. "Rise in Female-Initiated Sexual Activity at Ovulation and Its Suppression by Oral Contraceptives." *New England Journal of Medicine* 299:1145–1150, 1978.

Adams, G. R., and Huston, T. L. "Social Perception of Middle-Aged Persons Varying in Physical Attractiveness." *Developmental Psychology* 11:657–658, 1975.

Adams, J. W., Kottke, J. L., and Padgitt, J. S. "Sexual Harassment of University Students." *Journal of College Student Personnel* 24:484–490, 1983.

Addiego, F., et al. "Female Ejaculation: A Case Study." *Journal of Sex Research* 17(1):13–21, 1981.

Ades, A. E., et al. "Prevalence of Maternal HIV-1 Infection in Thames Regions: Results from Anonymous Unlinked Neonatal Testing." *Lancet* 337:1562–1565, 1991.

Adler, N. E., et al. "Psychological Responses After Abortion." *Science* 248:41–44, 1990.

Agnew, J. "Hazards Associated with Anal Erotic Activity." *Archives of Sexual Behavior* 15:307–314, 1986.

Ahn, N. "Teenage Childbearing and High School Completion: Accounting for Individual Heterogeneity." *Family Planning Perspectives* 26:17–21, 1994.

Ainsworth, M. "The Effects of Maternal Deprivation: A Review of Findings and Controversy in the Context of Research Strategy." In *Deprivation of Maternal Care: A Reassessment of Its Effects.* Public Health Papers, No. 14. Geneva: World Health Organization, 1962.

Ainsworth, M., et al. *Patterns of Attachment: A Psychological Study of the Strange Situation.* Hillsdale, NJ: Laurence Erlbaum Associates, 1978.

Alderman, P. M. "The Lurking Sperm." *Journal of the American Medical Association* 259:3142–3144, 1988.

Alexander, C. S., et al. "Early Sexual Activity Among Adolescents in Small Towns and Rural Areas: Race and Gender Patterns." *Family Planning Perspectives* 21:261–266, 1989.

Alexander, L. "Treatment of Impotency and Anorgasmia by Psychotherapy Aided by Hypnosis." *American Journal of Clinical Hypnosis* 17:33–43, 1974.

Alington-MacKinnon, D., and Troll, L. E. "The Adaptive Function of the Menopause: A Devil's Advocate Position." *Journal of the American Geriatrics Society* 29:349–353, 1981.

Allen, D. M. "Young Male Prostitutes: A Psychosocial Study." *Archives of Sexual Behavior* 9:399–426, 1980.

Allen, J. A. "Premenstrual Frenzy." *New York Magazine,* pp. 37–42, November 1, 1982.

Allen, J. R. "Heterosexual Transmission of HIV: A View of the Future." *Journal of the American Medical Association* 266:1695–1696, 1991.

Allen, J. R., and Setlow, V. P. "Heterosexual Transmission of HIV." *Journal of the American Medical Association* 266:1695–1696, 1991.

Allen, L. S., and Gorski, R. A. "Sexual Orientation and the Size of the Anterior Commissure in the Human Brain." *Proceedings of the National Academy of Science of the United States* 89:7199–2020, 1992.

Alter, M., et al. "Hepatitis B Virus Transmission Between Heterosexuals." *Journal of the American Medical Association* 256:1307–1310, 1986.

———. "Risk Factors for Acute Non-A, Non-B Hepatitis in the United States and Association with Hepatitis C Virus Infection." *Journal of the American Medical Association* 264:2231–2235, 1990.

Alter, M. J., and Sampliner, R. E. "Hepatitis C: And Miles to Go Before We Sleep." *New England Journal of Medicine* 321:1538–1540, 1989.

Alter, M. J., et al. "The Importance of Heterosexual Activity and Intravenous Drug Use in the Transmission of Hepatitis B and Non-A, Non-B Hepatitis." *Journal of the American Medical Association* 262:1201–1205, 1989.

———. "The Changing Epidemiology of Hepatitis B in the United States." *Journal of the American Medical Association* 263:1218–1222, 1990.

Althof, S. E., and Turner, L. A. "Self-Injection Therapy and External Vacuum Devices in the Treatment of Erectile Dysfunction: Methods and Outcome." In Rosen, R. C., and Leiblum, S. R. (eds.), *Erectile Disorders: Assessment and Treatment*, pp. 283–309. New York: Guilford Press, 1992.

Altman, Dennis. *Homosexualization of America*. Boston: Beacon Press, 1982.

———. *AIDS in the Mind of America*. New York: Anchor Books, 1987.

Altman, I., Vinsel, A., and Brown, B. B. "Dialectic Conceptions in Social Psychology: An Application to Social Penetration and Privacy Regulation." *Advances in Experimental Social Psychology* 14:107–160, 1981.

Altman, L. K., "Who's Stricken and How: AIDS Pattern Is Shifting." *The New York Times*, Section 1, pp. 1 & 28, February 5, 1989.

———. "Some Optimism Amid Grim Predictions as 87-Nation AIDS Meeting Opens." *The New York Times*, p. B4, June 5, 1989a.

———. "Hopes Are Dashed on AIDS Therapy." *The New York Times*, p. A16, June 10, 1993.

———. "AIDS Cases Increase Among Heterosexuals." *The New York Times*, p. A14, March 11, 1994.

———. et al. "AIDS Link to V.D. Becomes Clearer." *The New York Times*, p. A6, June 11, 1993.

Alvarez, F., et al. "New Insights on the Mode of Action of Intrauterine Contraceptive Devices in Women." *Fertility and Sterility* 49:768–773, 1988.

Alzate, H., and Hoch, Z. "The 'G Spot' and 'Female Ejaculation': A Current Appraisal." *Journal of Sex & Marital Therapy* 12:211–220, 1986.

Alzate, H., and Londono, M. L. "Vaginal Erotic Sensitivity." *Journal of Sex & Marital Therapy* 10:49–56, 1984.

American Cancer Society. "Guidelines for the Cancer-Related Checkup." *Ca-A Cancer Journal for Clinicians* 30:194–240, 1980.

American Fertility Society. *Recurrent Miscarriage: A Guide for Patients*. Birmingham, AL: The American Fertility Society, 1991.

American Health Consultants. "Common Sense about AIDS." *AIDS Alert* 8(4):insert following p. 56, 1993.

American Journal of Psychiatry. "Historical Notes: A Letter from Freud." 107:786–787, 1951.

American Psychiatric Association. *Diagnostic and Statistical Manual of Mental Disorders*, 3rd ed. rev. Washington, DC: American Psychiatric Association, 1987.

American Psychiatric Association. *Diagnostic and Statistical Manual of Mental Disorders*, 3rd ed. (DSM-III). Washington, DC: American Psychiatric Association, 1980.

Amir, M. *Patterns in Forcible Rape*. Chicago: University of Chicago, 1971.

Analyse des Comportements Sexuels en France Investogators. "AIDS and Sexual Behavior in France." *Nature* 360:407–409, 1992.

Anderson, J. E., and Dahlberg, H. "High-risk Sexual Behavior in the General Population: Results from a National Survey, 1988–1990." *Sexually Transmitted Diseases* 19:320–325, 1992.

Anderson, T. P., and Cole, T. M. "Sexual Counseling of the Physically Disabled." *Postgraduate Medicine* 58:117–123, 1975.

Andrews, M. C., et al. "An Analysis of the Obstetric Outcome of 125 Consecutive Pregnancies Conceived *in vitro* and Resulting in 100 Deliveries." *American Journal of Obstetrics and Gynecology* 154:848–854, 1986.

Angell, M. "A Dual Approach to the AIDS Epidemic." *New England Journal of Medicine* 324:1498–1500, 1991.

Annas, G. J. "The Supreme Court, Liberty, and Abortion." *New England Journal of Medicine* 327:651–654, 1992.

Annon, J. S. *The Behavioral Treatment of Sexual Problems: Brief Therapy*. New York: Harper & Row, 1976.

[anonymous]. "The Concorde Study." *AIDS Clinical Care* 5(5):38, 42, 1993.

Antonarakis, S. E., and the Down Syndrome Collaborative Group. "Parental Origin of the Extra Chromosome in Trisomy 21 as Indicated by Analysis of DNA Polymorphisms." *New England Journal of Medicine* 324:872–876, 1991.

Antunes, C. M., et al. "Endometrial Cancer and Estrogen Use: Report of a Large Case–Control Study." *New England Journal of Medicine* 300:9–13, 1979.

Apfelbaum, B. (ed.). *Expanding the Boundaries of Sex Therapy*, rev. ed. Berkeley, CA: Berkeley Sex Therapy Group, 1980.

———. "Why We Should Not Accept Sexual Fantasies." In Apfelbaum, B. (ed.), *Expanding the Boundaries of Sex Therapy*, rev. ed., pp. 101–108. Berkeley, CA: Berkeley Sex Therapy Group, 1980a.

———. "Review of *The Hite Report on Male Sexuality*." *Journal of Sex Research* 18:85–88, 1982.

———. *Expanding the Boundaries of Sex Therapy*, 2nd ed. Berkeley, CA: Berkeley Sex Therapy Group, 1983.

Apte, S. M., Gregory J., and Purcell, M. "The Inflatable Penile Prosthesis: Reoperation and Patient Satisfaction." *Journal of Urology* 131:894–895, 1984.

Aptheker, B. *Tapestries of Life: Women's Work, Women's Consciousness, and the Meaning of Daily Experience*. Amherst: University of MA Press, 1989.

Arafat, I., and Cotton, W. L. "Masturbation Practices of Males and Females." *Journal of Sex Research* 10:293–307, 1974.

Arentewicz, G., and Schmidt, G. (eds.). *The Treatment of Sexual Disorders*. New York: Basic Books, 1983.

Arkkelin, D., and O'Connor, R., Jr. "The 'Good' Professional: Effects of Trait-profile Gender Type, Androgyny, and Likableness on Impressions of Incumbents of Sex-typed Occupations." *Sex Roles* 27:517–532, 1992.

Arms, S. *Immaculate Deception*. Boston: Houghton Mifflin, 1975.

Arthes, F. G., and Masi, A. T. "Myocardial Infarction in Younger Women: Associated Clinical Features and Relationship to Use of Oral Contraceptive Drugs." *Chest* 70:574–583, 1976.

Arvin, A. M., et al. "Failure of Antepartum Maternal Cultures to Predict the Infant's Risk of Exposure to Herpes Simplex Virus at Delivery." *New England Journal of Medicine* 315:796–800, 1986.

Ashford, J. *The Whole Birth Catalog*. Trumansburg, NY: The Crossing Press, 1983.

Athanasiou, R. "A Review of Public Attitudes on Sexual Issues." In Zubin, J., and Money, J. (eds.), *Contemporary Sexual Behavior: Critical Issues in the 1970s*, pp. 361–390. Baltimore: Johns Hopkins University Press, 1973.

———. "Pornography: A Review of Research." In Wolman, B. B., and Money, J. (eds.), *Handbook of Human Sexuality*, pp. 251–265. Englewood Cliffs, NJ: Prentice-Hall, 1980.

Athanasiou, R., and Sarkin, R. "Premarital Sexual Behavior and Postmarital Adjustment." *Archives of Sexual Behavior* 3:207–225, 1974.

Athanasiou, R., et al. "A Report to *Psychology Today* Readers on the Research Questionnaire on Sex." *Psychology Today* 4:37–52, 1970.

Atkinson, M., and Boles, J. "Prostitution as an Ecology of Confidence Games: The Scripted Behavior of Prostitutes and Vice Officers." In Gemme, R., and Wheeler,

C. C. (eds.), *Progress in Sexology*, pp. 505–512. New York: Plenum Press, 1977.

Atwater, L. *The Extramarital Connection: Sex, Intimacy, and Identity*. New York: Irvington Publishers, 1982.

Atwood, J. D., and Gagnon, J. "Masturbatory Behavior in College Youth." *Journal of Sex Education and Therapy* 13(2):35–42, 1987.

Avalah, D., and Weinstock, I. J. *Breasts*. New York: Summit Books, 1979.

Averill, J. R. *Anger and Aggression*. New York: Springer-Verlag, 1982.

Avery-Clark, C. "Sexual Dysfunction and Disorder Patterns of Husbands of Working and Nonworking Women." *Journal of Sex & Marital Therapy* 12:282–296, 1986.

Azizi, F., et al. "Decreased Serum Testosterone Concentration in Male Heroin and Methadone Addicts." *Steroids* 22:467–472, 1973.

Bach, G. R., and Wyden, P. *The Intimate Enemy*. New York: Aron Books, 1968.

Bachetti, P., and Moss, A. R. "Incubation Period of AIDS in San Francisco." *Nature* 338:251–253, 1989.

Backhouse, C., and Cohen, L. *Sexual Harassment on the Job*. Englewood Cliffs, NJ: Prentice-Hall, 1981.

Bahm, R. M. "The Influence of Nonsexual Cues, Sexual Explicitness, and Sex Guilt on Female's Erotic Response to Literature." Unpublished Ph.D. dissertation, University of Massachusetts, 1972.

Bailey, J. M., and Pillard, R. C. "A Genetic Study of Male Sexual Orientation." *Archives of General Psychiatry* 48:1089–1096, 1991.

Bailey, J. M., Willerman, L., and Parks, C. "A Test of the Maternal Stress Theory of Human Male Homosexuality." *Archives of Sexual Behavior* 20:277–293, 1991.

Bailey, J. M., et al. "Heritable Factors Influence Sexual Orientation in Women." *Archives of General Psychiatry* 50:217–223, 1993.

Baird, D. T., and Glasier, A. F., "Hormonal Contraception." *New England Journal of Medicine* 328:1543–1549, 1993.

Baker, C. D. "Preying on Playgrounds: The Sexploitation of Children in Pornography and Prostitution." In Schultz, L. (ed.), *The Sexual Victimology of Youth*. Springfield, IL: Charles C. Thomas, 1980.

Bakwin, H. "Erotic Feelings in Infants and Young Children." *Medical Aspects of Human Sexuality* 8(10):200–215, 1974.

Baldwin, J. D., and Baldwin, J. I. "Factors Affecting AIDS-Related Risk-Taking Behavior Among College Students." *Journal of Sex Research* 25:181–196, 1988.

Baldwin, Wendy. "Testimony on AIDS and Adolescents for the Presidential Commission on the HIV Epidemic," Washington, DC, May 18, 1988.

Ballinger, C. B. "The Menopause and Its Syndromes." In Howells, J. G. (ed.), *Modern Perspectives in the Psychiatry of Middle Age*, pp. 279–303. New York: Brunner/Mazel, 1981.

Banatvala, J. E., et al. "HIV Screening in Pregnancy." *Lancet* 337:1218, 1991.

Bancroft, J. "The Relationship Between Hormones and Sexual Behavior in Humans." In Hutchison, J. B. (ed.), *Biological Determinants of Sexual Behavior*, pp. 493–519. New York: Wiley, 1978.

———. "Hormones and Human Sexual Behavior." *Journal of Sex & Marital Therapy* 10:3–21, 1984.

Bancroft, J., et al. "Mood, Sexuality, Hormones and the Menstrual Cycle: III. Sexuality and the Role of Androgens." *Psychosomatic Medicine* 45:509–524, 1983.

Barbach, L. *The Pause: Positive Approaches to the Menopause*. New York: Dutton, 1993.

Barbach, L. G. *For Yourself: The Fulfillment of Female Sexuality*. New York: Doubleday, 1975.

———. *Women Discover Orgasm*. New York: Free Press, 1980.

———. *For Each Other: Sharing Sexual Intimacy*. Garden City, NY: Anchor Press, 1982.

Barbach, L. G., and Levine, L. *Shared Intimacies*. Garden City, NY: Anchor Press/Doubleday, 1980.

Barbaree, H. E., and Marshall, W. L. "The Role of Male Sexual Arousal in Rape: Six Models." *Journal of Consulting and Clinical Psychology* 59:621–630, 1991.

Barbaree, H. E., Marshall, W. L., and Lanthier, R. D. "Deviant Sexual Arousal in Rapists." *Behavior Research & Therapy* 17:215–222, 1979.

Barber, T. Y. *Pitfalls in Human Research*. New York: Pergamon Press, 1976.

Barlow, D. "Increasing Heterosexual Responsiveness in the Treatment of Sexual Deviation: A Review of the Clinical and Experimental Evidence." *Behavior Therapy* 4:655–671, 1973.

———. *Sexually Transmitted Diseases: The Facts*. New York: Oxford University Press, 1979.

Barocas, R., and Karoly, P. "Effects of Physical Appearance on Social Responsiveness." *Psychology Review* 31:495–500, 1972.

Barrett, F. M. "Sexual Experience, Birth Control Usage, and Sex Education of Unmarried Canadian University Students: Changes Between 1968 and 1978." *Archives of Sexual Behavior* 9:367–390, 1980.

Barrett-Connor, E. "Post-Menopausal Estrogen Replacement and Breast Cancer." *New England Journal of Medicine* 321:319–320, 1989.

Barrows, Sidney B. *Mayflower Madam*. New York: Arbor House, 1986.

Barry, H., III, and Schlegel, A. "Measurements of Adolescent Sexual Behavior in the Standard Sample of Societies." *Ethnology* 23:315–329, 1984.

———. "Cultural Customs that Influence Sexual Freedom in Adolescence." *Ethnology* 24:151–162, 1985.

Bart, P. B., and Grossman, M. "Menopause." In Notman, M. T., and Nadelson, C. C. (eds.), *The Woman Patient*, pp. 337–354. New York: Plenum Press, 1978.

Bart, P. B., and Jozsa, J. "Dirty Books, Dirty Films, Dirty Data." In Lederer, L. (ed.), *Take Back the Night*, pp. 204–217. New York: William Morrow, 1980.

Bartell, G. D. *Group Sex: A Scientist's Eyewitness Report on the American Way of Swinging*. New York: Wyden Books, 1971.

Bartlett, J. G., and Finkbeiner, A. K. *The Guide to Living with HIV Infection*. Baltimore: Johns Hopkins University Press, 1991.

Bass, E., and Davis, L. *The Courage to Heal: A Guide for Women Survivors of Child Sexual Abuse*. New York: Harper & Row, 1988.

———. *Beginning to Heal: A First Book for Survivors of Child Sexual Abuse*. New York: HarperCollins, 1993.

Bates, G. "On the Nature of the Hot Flash." *Clinical Obstetrics and Gynecology* 24(1):231–241, 1981.

Battaglia, F. C. "Reducing the Cesarean-Section Rate Safely." *New England Journal of Medicine* 319:1540–1541, 1988.

Baulieu, E. "Contragestion and Other Clinical Applications of RU 486, an Antiprogesterone at the Receptor." *Science* 245:1351–1357, 1989.

———. "RU 486 as an Antiprogesterone Steroid." *Journal of the American Medical Association* 262:1808–1814, 1989a.

Bauman, J. E. "Basal Body Temperature: Unreliable Method of Ovulation Detection." *Fertility and Sterility* 36:729, 1981.

Bauman, J. E., et al. "Effectos Endocrinos Del Uso Cronico De La Marijuana en Mujeres." *Cuadernos Cientificos Cemesam* 10:85–97, July 1979.

Baumeister, R. F. "Masochism as Escape from Self." *Journal of Sex Research* 25:28–59, 1988.

Bayer, R. *Homosexuality and American Psychiatry: The Politics of Diagnosis*. New York: Basic Books, 1981.

Beach, F. (ed.). *Sex and Behavior*. New York: Wiley, 1965.

———. *Human Sexuality in Four Perspectives*. Baltimore: Johns Hopkins University Press, 1977.

Becker, E. F. *Female Sexuality Following Spinal Cord Injury*. Bloomington, IN: Accent Special Publication, Cheever Publishing, 1978.

Becker, J. V., and Kaplan, M. S. "Rape Victims: Issues, Theories, and Treatment." *Annual Review of Sex Research* II:267–292, 1991.

Becker, J. V., et al. "Incidence and Types of Sexual Dysfunctions in Rape and Incest Victims." *Journal of Sex & Marital Therapy* 8:65–74, 1983.

———. "Level of Postassault Sexual Functioning in Rape and Incest Victims." *Archives of Sexual Behavior* 15:37–50, 1986.

Becker, M. H., and Joseph, J. G. "AIDS and Behavioral Change to Reduce Risk: A Review." *American Journal of Public Health* 78:394–410, 1988.

Beer, A. E. "Immunology, Contraception, and Preeclampsia." *Journal of the American Medical Association* 262:3184, 1989.

Beer, W. R. *Househusbands: Men and Housework in American Families.* New York: Praeger, 1983.

Beerthuizen, R. J., et al. "IUD and Salpingitis." *European Journal of Obstetrics, Gynecology, and Reproductive Biology* 13(1):31–41, 1982.

Bell, A. P., and Weinberg, M. S. *Homosexualities.* New York: Simon & Schuster, 1978.

Bell, A. P., Weinberg, M. S., and Hammersmith, S. K. *Sexual Preference: Its Development in Men and Women.* Bloomington: Indiana University Press, 1981.

Bell, R., and Bell, P. "Sexual Satisfaction Among Married Women." *Medical Aspects of Human Sexuality* 6(12):136–144, 1972.

Bell, R. T. "Friendships of Women and Men." *Psychology of Women Quarterly* 5:402–417, 1981.

Belliveau, F., and Richter, L. *Understanding Human Sexual Inadequacy.* New York: Bantam, 1970.

Belsky, J. "The Research Findings on Gender Issues in Aging Men and Women." In Wainrib, B. R. (ed.), *Gender Issues Across the Life Cycle,* pp. 163–171, NY: Springer, 1992.

Belsky, J. E., Wan, L. S., and Douglas, G. W. "Abortion." In Kaplan, H. I., and Sadock, B. J. (eds.), *Comprehensive Textbook of Psychiatry,* 4th ed., p. 1054. Baltimore: Williams & Wilkins, 1985.

Belzer, E. "Orgasmic Expulsions of Women: A Review and Heuristic Inquiry." *Journal of Sex Research* 17:1–12, 1981.

Bem, S. L. "Psychology Looks at Sex Roles: Where Have All the Androgynous People Gone?" Paper presented at the UCLA Symposium on Women, Los Angeles, May 1972.

———. "The Measurement of Psychological Androgyny." *Journal of Consulting and Clinical Psychology* 42(2):155–162, 1974.

———. "Sex Role Adaptability: One Consequence of Psychological Androgyny." *Journal of Personality and Social Psychology* 31(4):634–643, 1975.

———. "Gender Schema Theory: A Cognitive Account of Sex Typing." *Psychological Reviews,* 88:354–364, 1981.

———. "Genital Knowledge and Gender Constancy in Preschool Children." *Child Development,* 60:649–662, 1989.

———. *The Lenses of Gender: Transforming the Debate on Sexual Inequality.* New Haven, CT: Yale University Press, 1993.

Bem, S. L., Martyna, W., and Watson, C. "Sex Typing and Androgyny: Further Explorations of the Expressive Domain." *Journal of Personality and Social Psychology* 34:1016–1023, 1976.

Bender, L., and Blau, A. "The Reaction of Children to Sexual Relations with Adults." *American Journal of Orthopsychiatry* 7:500–518, 1937.

Bene, E. "On the Genesis of Male Homosexuality: An Attempt at Clarifying the Role of the Parents." *British Journal of Psychiatry* 111:803–813, 1965.

Benigni, A., et al. "Effect of Low-Dose Aspirin on Fetal and Maternal Generation of Thromboxane by Platelets in Women at Risk for Pregnancy-Induced Hypertension." *New England Journal of Medicine* 321:357–362, 1989.

Benjamin, M. *The Transsexual Phenomenon.* New York: Julian Press, 1966.

Bennett, C. J., et al. "Sexual Dysfunction and Electroejaculation in Men with Spinal Cord Injury." *Journal of Urology* 139:453–457, 1988.

Bennett, N. G., Bloom, D. E., and Craig, P. H. "Black and White Marriage Patterns: Why So Different?" Center Discussion Paper #500, Economic Growth Center, Yale University, March 1986.

Benson, M. D., Perlman, C., and Sciarra, J. J. "Sex Education in the Inner City." *Journal of the American Medical Association* 255:43–47, 1986.

Benson, P. L., Karabenick, S. A., and Lerner, R. M. "Pretty Pleases: The Effects of Physical Attractiveness, Race, and Sex on Receiving Help." *Journal of Experimental Social Psychology* 12:409–415, 1976.

Benson, R. C. *Current Obstetric & Gynecologic Diagnosis & Treatment.* Los Altos, CA: Lange Medical Publications, 1978.

Beral, V., et al. "Epidemiology of Kaposi's Sarcoma in AIDS Patients: United States." (Abstract #M.A.O.30, p. 50.) Fifth International Conference on AIDS, Montreal, June 4–9, 1989.

Berger, G., Goldstein, M., and Fuerst, M. *The Couple's Guide to Fertility.* New York: Doubleday, 1989.

Berger, R. M. *Gay and Gray: The Older Homosexual Male.* Urbana: University of Illinois Press, 1982.

Bergkvist, L., et al. "The Risk of Breast Cancer After Estrogen and Estrogen-Progestin Replacement." *New England Journal of Medicine* 321:293–297, 1989.

Bergman, L. "Dating Violence Among High School Students." *Social Work,* 37(1):21–27, 1992.

Berkeley, S. "AIDS in the Global Village." *Journal of the American Medical Association* 268:3368–3369, 1992.

Berkeley, S. F. "HIV in Africa: What Is the Future?" *Annals of Internal Medicine* 116:339–341, 1992.

Berkeley, S. F., et al. "The Relationship of Tampon Characteristics to Menstrual Toxic Shock Syndrome." *Journal of the American Medical Association* 258:917–920, 1987.

Berlin, F. S., and Meinecke, C. F. "Treatment of Sex Offenders with Antiandrogenic Medication." *American Journal of Psychiatry* 138:601–607, 1981.

Berndt, T. J., and Heller, K. A. "Gender Stereotypes and Social Influences: A Developmental Study." *Journal of Personality and Social Psychology,* 50:889–898, 1986.

Berne, E. *Sex in Human Loving.* New York: Pocket Books, 1971.

Bernstein, G., et al. "Results of a Comparative Study of the Diaphragm and Cervical Cap." Paper presented at the annual meeting of the American Public Health Association, Las Vegas, September 29–October 2, 1986.

Berscheid, E. "Some Comments on Love's Anatomy." In Sternberg, R. J., and Barnes, M. L. (eds.), *The Psychology of Love*, pp. 359–374. New Haven, CT: Yale University Press, 1988.

Berscheid, E., et al. "Physical Attractiveness and Dating Choice: A Test of the Matching Hypothesis." *Journal of Experimental Social Psychology* 7:173–189, 1971.

Bieber, I., et al. *Homosexuality: A Psychoanalytic Study.* New York: Basic Books, 1962.

Bigler, M. O. "Adolescent Sexual Behavior in the Eighties." *SIECUS Report* 18:6–9, October/November 1989.

Billy, J. O. G., et al. "Effects of Sexual Activity on Adolescent Social and Psychological Development." *Social Psychology Quarterly* 51:190–212, 1988.

———. "The Sexual Behavior of Men in the United States." *Family Planning Perspectives* 25:52–60, 1993.

Binkin, N. J., and Alexander, E. R. "Neonatal Herpes: How Can It Be Prevented?" *Journal of the American Medical Association* 250:3094–3095, 1983.

Blackwood, E. "Sexuality and Gender in Certain Native American Tribes: The Case of Cross–Gender Females." *Signs: Journal of Women in Culture and Society* 10:27–42, 1984.

———. (ed.). *Anthropology and Homosexual Behavior.* New York: Haworth Press, 1986.

Blay, S. L., Ferraz, M. P. T., and Calil, H. M. "Lithium-Induced Male Sexual Impairment." *Journal of Clinical Psychiatry* 43:497–498, 1982.

Blood, R. O., and Wolfe, D. J. *Husbands and Wives.* Glencoe, IL: Free Press, 1960.

Bloom, Alan. *The Closing of the American Mind.* New York: Simon & Schuster, 1987.

Blume, E. "Methodological Difficulties Plague PMS Research." *Journal of the American Medical Association* 249:2866, 1983.

Blumenfeld, W. J. (ed.). *Homophobia: How We All Pay the Price.* Boston: Beacon Press, 1992.

Blumstein, P. W., and Schwartz, P. "Bisexuality in Women." *Archives of Sexual Behavior* 5:171–181, 1976.

———. "Bisexuality: Some Social Psychological Issues." *Journal of Social Issues* 33(2):30–45, 1977.

———. *American Couples.* New York: William Morrow, 1983.

Boehm, D. "The Cervical Cap: Effectiveness as a Contraceptive." *Journal of Nurse-Midwifery* 28(1):3–6, 1983.

Bohlen, J. G. "Female Ejaculation" and Urinary Stress Incontinence." *Journal of Sex Research* 18:360–363, 1982.

Bohlen, J. G., et al. "Development of a Woman's Multiple Orgasm Pattern: A Research Case Report." *Journal of Sex Research* 18:130–145, 1982.

Bolton, F. G. *The Pregnant Adolescent: Problems of Premature Parenthood.* Beverly Hills, CA: Sage Publications, 1980.

Booth, A. "Sex and Social Participation." *American Sociological Review* 37:183–192, 1972.

Booth, A. W. "AIDS and Insects." *Science* 237:355–356, 1987.

Borneman, Ernest. "Progress in Empirical Research on Childhood Sexuality." Presented at the 6th World Congress of Sexology, Washington, DC, May 24, 1983.

Bors, E., and Comarr, A. E. "Neurological Disturbances of Sexual Function with Special Reference to 529 Patients with Spinal Cord Injury." *Urological Survey* 10:191–222, 1960.

Boston Women's Health Book Collective, *Our Bodies, Ourselves,* 2nd ed. New York: Simon & Schuster, 1976.

———. *The New Our Bodies, Ourselves.* New York: Simon & Schuster, 1984.

Boswell, J. *Christianity, Social Tolerance, and Homosexuality.* Chicago: University of Chicago Press, 1980.

———. *Same-Sex Unions in Premodern Europe.* New York: Villard, 1994.

———. "Searle, Last Major IUD Maker, Quits Market." *American Medical News,* pp. 3 & 49, February 14, 1986b.

Botwin, C. *Is There Sex After Marriage?* Boston: Little, Brown, 1985.

———. *Tempted Women: The Passions, Perils, and Agonies of Female Infidelity.* New York: William Morrow, 1994.

Bounds, W., Guillebaud, J., and Newman, G. B. "Female Condom (Femidom ™): A Clinical Study of Its Use-Effectiveness and Patient Acceptability." *British Journal of Family Planning* 18:36, 1992.

Bourque, L. *Defining Rape.* Durham, NC: Duke University Press, 1989.

Bower, D. W. "A Description and Analysis of a Cohabiting Sample in America." Unpublished master's thesis, University of Arizona, 1975.

Bower, D. W., and Christopherson, V. A. "University Student Cohabitation: A Regional Comparison of Selected Attitudes and Behaviors." *Journal of Marriage and the Family* 39:447–453, 1977.

Bozett, F. W. "Gay Fatherhood." In Bronstein, P., and Cowan, C. P. (eds.), *Fatherhood Today,* pp. 214–235. New York: Wiley, 1988.

———. "Gay Fathers: A Review of the Literature." *Journal of Homosexuality* 18(Nos. 1/2):137–162, 1989.

Bracken, M. B. "Spermicidal Contraceptives and Poor Reproductive Outcomes: The Epidemiologic Evidence Against an Association." *American Journal of Obstetrics and Gynecology* 151:552–556, 1985.

Bradford, J., and Pawlak, A. "Double-Blind Placebo Crossover Study of Cyproterone Acetate in the Treatment of the Paraphilias." *Archives of Sexual Behavior* 22:383–402, 1993.

———. "Effects of Cyproterone Acetate on Sexual Arousal Patterns of Pedophiles." *Archives of Sexual Behavior* 22:629–641, 1993a.

Braen, G. R. "Examination of the Accused: The Heterosexual and Homosexual Rapist." In Warner, C. G.

(ed.), *Rape and Sexual Assault*, pp. 85–91. Germantown, MD: Aspen Systems Corp., 1980.

Bragonier, J. R. "Influence of Oral Contraception on Sexual Response." *Medical Aspects of Human Sexuality* 10(10):130–143, October 1976.

Brandeau, M. L. "Screening Women of Childbearing Age for Human Immunodeficiency Virus: A Cost-benefit Analysis." *Archives of Internal Medicine* 152:2229–2237, 1992.

Branden, N. *The Psychology of Romantic Love*. Los Angeles: J. P. Tarcher, 1980.

———. *If You Could Hear What I Cannot Say*. New York: Bantam Books, 1983.

Brandt, E. N., Jr. "Physicians and Sexually Transmitted Disease: A Call to Action." *Journal of the American Medical Association* 248:2032, 1982.

Bravo, E., and Cassedy, E. *The 9 to 5 Guide to Combating Sexual Harassment*. New York: Wiley, 1992.

Brecher, E. *The Sex Researchers*. Boston: Little, Brown, 1969.

Brecher, E. M. "History of Human Sexual Research and Study." In Freedman, A. M., Kaplan, H. I., and Sadock, B. J. (eds.), *Comprehensive Textbook of Psychiatry/II*, pp. 1327–1357. Baltimore: Williams & Wilkins, 1975.

Brecher, E. M., and the Editors of *Consumers Union Report. Love, Sex, and Aging*. Boston: Little, Brown, 1983.

Breslow, N., Evans, L., and Langley, J. "On the Prevalence and Roles of Females in the Sadomasochistic Subculture." *Archives of Sexual Behavior* 14:303–317, 1985.

Bresters, D., et al. "Sexual Transmission of Hepatitis C Virus." *Lancet* 342:210–211, 1993.

Bretschneider, J. G., and McCoy, N. L. "Sexual Interest and Behavior in Healthy 80- to 102-Year-Olds." *Archives of Sexual Behavior* 17:109–129, 1988.

Brewer, M. B. "Further Beyond Nine to Five: An Integration and Future Directions." *Journal of Social Issues* 38(4):149–158, 1982.

Brick, P. "Toward a Positive Approach to Adolescent Sexuality." *SIECUS Report* 17(5):1–3, May/July 1989.

Briddell, D., and Wilson, G. T. "Effects of Alcohol and Expectancy Set on Male Sexual Arousal." *Journal of Abnormal Psychology* 85:225–234, 1976.

Bridges, J. S., and McGrail, C. A. "Attributions of Responsibility for Date and Stranger Rape." *Sex Roles* 21:273–286, 1989.

Brindley, G. S., and Gillan, P. "Men and Women Who Do Not Have Orgasms." *British Journal of Psychiatry* 45:351–356, 1982.

Brock, B. V., et al. "Frequency of Asymptomatic Shedding of Herpes Simplex Virus in Women with Genital Herpes." *Journal of the American Medical Association* 263:418–420, 1990.

Broderick, C. B. "Preadolescent Sexual Behavior." *Medical Aspects of Human Sexuality* 2(1):20–29, 1968.

Brody, Jane E. "Study Finds Women in 40's Benefit from Mammograms." *The New York Times*, p. B5, September 21, 1988.

Brody, J. E. "Scientists Trace Aberrant Sexuality." *The New York Times*, pp. C1 & C12, January 23, 1990.

Brok, A. J. "Some thoughts on gender role issues for men later in life." In Wainrib, B. R. (ed.), *Gender Issues Across the Life Cycle*, pp. 172–183, New York: Springer, 1992.

Brooke, J. "In Deception and Denial, an Epidemic Looms." *The New York Times*, pp. A1 & A6, January 25, 1993.

Brooks-Gunn, J., and Ruble, D. N. "The Menstrual Attitude Questionnaire." *Psychosomatic Medicine* 42(5):503–511, 1980.

Broude, G. J., and Greene, S. J. "Cross-Cultural Codes on Twenty Sexual Attitudes and Practices." *Ethnology* 15:409–429, 1976.

Broverman, I. K., et al. "Sex-Role Stereotypes: A Current Appraisal." *Journal of Social Issues* 28(2):59–78, 1972.

Brown, G. *The New Celibacy*. New York: McGraw-Hill, 1980.

Brown, G. R., and Collier, L. "Transvestites' Women Revisited: A Nonpatient Sample." *Archives of Sexual Behavior* 18:73–83, 1989.

Brown, J. *Nutrition for Your Pregnancy*. Minneapolis: University of Minnesota Press, 1983.

Brown, J. M., and Chaves, J. F. "Hypnosis in the Treatment of Sexual Dysfunction." *Journal of Sex & Marital Therapy* 6(1):63–74, 1980.

Brown, L. K., DiClemente, R. J., and Beausoleil, N. I. "Comparison of Human Immunodeficiency Virus Related Knowledge, Attitudes, Intentions, and Behaviors Among Sexually Active and Abstinent Young Adolescents." *Journal of Adolescent Health* 13:140, 1992.

Brown, L. M., and Gilligan, C. *Meeting at the Crossroads: Women's Psychology and Girls' Development*. Cambridge, MA: Harvard University Press, 1992.

Browning, D., and Boatman, B. "Incest: Children at Risk." *American Journal of Psychiatry* 134:69–72, 1977.

Brownmiller, S. *Against Our Will*. New York: Simon & Schuster, 1975.

Bry, A. *How to Get Angry Without Feeling Guilty*. New York: New American Library, 1977.

Bryne, D., and Fisher, W. (eds.). *Adolescents, Sex, and Contraception*. Hillsdale, NJ: Laurence Erlbaum Associates, 1983.

Bryson, Y. J., et al. "Treatment of First Episodes of Genital Herpes Simplex Virus Infection with Oral Acycolvir." *New England Journal of Medicine* 308:916–921, 1983.

Buchanan, R. "Breast-feeding: Aid to Infant Health and Fertility Control." *Population Reports*, Series J(4): July 1975.

Buchwald, E. "Raising Girls for the 21st Century." In Buchwald, E., Fletcher, P., and Roth, M. (eds.), *Transforming a Rape Culture*, pp. 179–200. Minneapolis, MN: Milkweed Editions, 1993.

Buchwald, E., Fletcher, P., and Roth, M. (eds.). *Transforming a Rape Culture*. Minneapolis: Milkweed Editions, 1993.

Buckley, R. M., Jr., McGuckin, M., and MacGregor, R. R. "Urine Bacterial Counts After Sexual Intercourse." *New England Journal of Medicine* 298:321–324, 1978.

Buckley, W. E., et al. "Estimated Prevalence of Anabolic Steroid Use Among Male High School Seniors." *Journal of the American Medical Association* 260:3441–3445, 1988.

Bullard, D. G., and Knight, S. E. (eds.). *Sexuality and Physical Disability*. St. Louis: Mosby, 1981.

Bullough, V. L. *Sexual Variance in Society and History*. New York: Wiley, 1976.

———. "Variant Life Styles: Homosexuality." In Murstein, B. I. (ed.), *Exploring Intimate Life Styles*, pp. 245–257. New York: Springer, 1978.

Bullough, V., and Bullough, B. *Sin, Sickness, and Sanity*. New York: New American Library, 1977.

Bumpass, L. L., and Sweet, J. A. "National Estimates of Cohabitation." *Demography* 26:615, 1989.

Bumpass, L. L., Sweet, J. A., and Cherlin, A. "The Role of Cohabitation in Declining Rates of Marriage." *Journal of Marriage and the Family* 53:913–927, 1991.

Burgess, A. W., and Holmstrom, L. L. *Rape: Victims of Crisis*. Bowie, MD: Robert J. Brady, 1974.

———. "Coping Behavior of the Rape Victim." *American Journal of Psychiatry* 133:413–418, 1976.

Burgess, A. W., et al. *Sexual Assault of Children and Adolescents*. Lexington, MA: D. C. Heath, 1978.

Burgess, A., et al. "Response Patterns in Children and Adolescents Exploited Through Sex Rings and Pornography." *American Journal of Psychiatry* 141:656–662, 1984.

Burke, D. S., et al. "Measurement of the False Positive Rate in a Screening Program for Human Immunodeficiency Virus Infections." *New England Journal of Medicine* 319:961–964, 1988.

———. "Human Immunodeficiency Virus Infections in Teenagers." *Journal of the American Medical Association* 263:2074–2077, 1990.

Burke, P. J., Stets, J. E., and Pirog-Good, M. A. "Gender Identity, Self-Esteem, and Physical and Sexual Abuse in Dating Relationships." *Social Psychology Quarterly* 51:272–285, 1988.

Burkhart, K. *Growing into Love*. New York: Putnam, 1981.

Burnell, G. M., and Norfleet, M. A. "Women's Self-reported Responses to Abortion." *The Journal of Psychology* 121:71–76, 1987.

Busch, M. P., et al. "Evaluation of Screened Blood Donations for Human Immunodeficiency Virus Type 1 Infection by Culture and DNA Amplification of Pooled Cells." *New England Journal of Medicine* 325:1–5, 1991.

Bush, P. *Drugs, Alcohol and Sex*. New York: Richard Marek Publishers, 1980.

Buss, D. M. "Love Acts: The Evolutionary Biology of Love." In Sternberg, R. J., and Barnes, M. L. (eds.), *The Psychology of Love*, pp. 100–118. New Haven, CT: Yale University Press, 1988.

Buss, David M. "Conflict Between the Sexes: Strategic Inference and the Evocation of Anger and Upset." *Journal of Personality and Social Psychology* 56:735–747, 1989.

Butler, R. M., and Lewis, M. I. *Sex After Sixty*. New York: Harper & Row, 1976.

Byne, W., and Parsons, B. "Human Sexual Orientation: The Biologic Theories Reappraised." *Archives of General Psychiatry* 50:228–239, 1993.

Byrne, D. "The Imagery of Sex." In Money, J., and Musaph, H. (eds.), *Handbook of Sexology*, pp. 327–350. New York: Elsevier/North-Holland, 1977.

Cadden, V. "The Psychiatrists Versus Masters and Johnson." In LoPiccolo, J., and LoPiccolo, L. (eds.), *Handbook of Sex Therapy*, pp. 485–490. New York: Plenum Press, 1978.

Cado, S., and Leitenberg, H. "Guilt Reactions to Sexual Fantasies During Intercourse." *Archives of Sexual Behavior* 19:49–64, 1990.

Cagen, R. "The Cervical Cap as a Barrier Contraceptive." *Contraception* 33:496, 1986.

Caird, W., and Wincze, J. P. *Sex Therapy: A Behavioral Approach*. New York: Harper & Row, 1977.

Calderone, M. "Fetal Erection and Its Message to Us." *SIECUS Report* XI(5/6):9–10, 1983.

Calderone, M. S. "Is Sex Education Preventative?" In Qualls, C. B., Wincze, J. P., and Barlow, D. H. (eds.), *The Prevention of Sexual Disorders*, pp. 139–155. New York: Plenum Press, 1978.

Calderone, M. S., and Johnson, E. *The Family Book About Sexuality*, 2nd ed. New York: Harper & Row, 1989.

Cale, A. R. J., et al. "Does Vasectomy Accelerate Testicular Tumor? Importance of Testicular Examinations Before and After Vasectomy." *British Medical Journal* 300:370, 1990.

Califia, P. "Lesbian Sexuality." *Journal of Homosexuality* 4(3):255–266, 1979.

Callahan, D. *Abortion: Law, Choice and Morality*. New York: Macmillan, 1970.

Callender, C., and Kochems, L. M. "Men and Not-Men: Male Gender-Mixing Statuses and Homosexuality." In Blackwood, E. (ed.), *Anthropology and Homosexual Behavior*, pp. 165–178. New York: Haworth Press, 1986.

Cancer and Steroid Hormone Study of the Centers for Disease Control and the National Institute of Child Health and Human Development. "Oral Contraceptive Use and the Risk of Breast Cancer." *New England Journal of Medicine* 315:405–411, 1986.

Cannon, R. O., et al. "Association of Herpes Simplex Virus Type 2 with HIV Infection in Heterosexual Patients Attending Sexual Transmitted Disease Clinics." (Abstract Book 2, p. 201.) Presented at the Fourth International Conference on AIDS, Stockholm, June 12–16, 1988.

Cantania, J. A., et al. "Predictors of Condom Use and Multiple Partnered Sex Among Sexually-Active Adolescent Women: Implications for AIDS-Related Health Interventions." *Journal of Sex Research* 25:514–524, 1989.

Cantor, M. H. "Family and Community: Changing Roles in an Aging Society." *Gerontologist* 31:3, 1991.

Cardell, M., Finn, S., and Marecek, J. "Sex-Role Identity, Sex-Role Behavior, and Satisfaction in Heterosexual, Lesbian, and Gay Male Couples." *Psychology of Women Quarterly* 5:488–494, 1981.

Carey, R. F., et al. "Effectiveness of Latex Condoms as a Barrier to Human Immunodeficiency Virus-sized Particles Under Conditions of Simulated Use." *Sexually Transmitted Diseases* 19:230, 1992.

Carmody, D. "Increasing Rapes on Campus Spur Colleges to Fight Back." *The New York Times*, Section 1, pp. 1 & 12, January 1, 1989.

Carnes, P. *Out of the Shadows: Understanding Sexual Addiction*. Minneapolis: CompCare Publications, 1983.

Caron, S. L., and McMullen, T. "AIDS and the College Student: The Need for Sex Education." *SIECUS Report* 15(6):6–7, July/August 1987.

Carrera, M. A., and Dempsey, P. "Restructuring Public Policy Priorities on Teen Pregnancy." *SIECUS Report* 16:6–9, January/February 1988.

Carrier, J. "Cultural Factors Affecting Urban Mexican Male Homosexual Behavior." *Archives of Sexual Behavior* 5(2):103–124, 1976.

———. "Homosexual Behavior in Cross-Cultural Perspective." In Marmor, J. (ed.), *Homosexual Behavior*, pp. 100–122. New York: Basic Books, 1980.

Carrier, J. M. "Childhood Cross-gender Behavior and Adult Homosexuality." *Archives of Sexual Behavior* 15:89–93, 1986.

Carroll, J. L., Volk, K., and Hyde, J. S. "Differences in Males and Females in Motives for Engaging in Sexual Intercourse." *Archives of Sexual Behavior* 14:131–140, 1985.

Carroll, James. "Change Starts with Our Own Attitudes." In Alyson, S. (ed.), *You Can Do Something About AIDS*, 2nd ed., pp. 19–21. Boston: The Stop AIDS Project, 1990.

Carson, S. A. "Sex Selection: The Ultimate in Family Planning." *Fertility & Sterility* 50:16–18, 1988.

Carson, S. A., and Buster, J. E. "Ectopic Pregnancy." *New England Journal of Medicine* 329:1174–1181, 1993.

Carter, C. S., and Greenough, W. T. "Sending the Right Sex Messages." *Psychology Today*, p. 112, September 1979.

Carter, D. B., and McCloskey, L. A. "Peers and the Maintenance of Sex-Typed Behavior: The Development of

Children's Conceptions of Cross-Gender Behavior in Their Peers." *Social Cognition*, 2:294–314, 1983–1984.

Carter, H. B., et al. "Longitudinal Evaluation of Prostate-Specific Antigen Levels in Men With and Without Prostate Disease." *Journal of the American Medical Association* 267:2215–2220, 1992.

Casper, R. F., Yen, S. S. C., and Wilkes, M. M. "Menopausal Flushes; A Neuroendocrine Link with Pulsatile Luteinizing Hormone Secretion." *Science* 205:823–825, 1979.

Cass, V. C. "Homosexual Identity Formation: A Theoretical Model." *Journal of Homosexuality* 4(3):219–235, 1979.

Catalona, W. J., et al. "Measurement of Prostate-Specific Antigen in Serum as a Screening Test for Prostate Cancer." *New England Journal of Medicine* 324:1156–1161, 1991.

Catania, J. A. "Prevalence of AIDS-related Risk Factors and Condom Use in the United States." *Science* 258:1101–1106, 1992.

Catania, J. A., and White, C. B. "Sexuality in an Aged Sample: Cognitive Determinants of Masturbation." *Archives of Sexual Behavior* 11:237–245, 1982.

Catania, J. A., et al. "Changes in Condom Use Among Heterosexual Men in San Francisco." *Health Psychology* 10:190–199, 1991.

Cates, W., Jr., and Stone, K. M. "Family Planning, Sexually Transmitted Diseases and Contraceptive Choice: A Literature Update—Part I." *Family Planning Perspectives* 24:75–84, 1992.

———. "Family Planning, Sexually Transmitted Diseases and Contraceptive Choice: A Literature Update—Part II." *Family Planning Perspectives* 24:122–128, 1992a.

Cates, W., Jr., Weisner, P. J., and Curran, J. W. "Sex and Spermicides: Preventing Unintended Pregnancy and Infection." *Journal of the American Medical Association* 248:1636–1637, 1982.

Catterall, R. D. *A Short Textbook of Venereology*. Philadelphia: Lippincott, 1974.

Cavero, C. "Modern Midwifery: Complicated Rebirth of an Ancient Art." *Family and Community Health* 2(3):29–39, November 1979.

Cefalu, E., et al. "Successful Gamete Intrafallopian Transfer Following Failed Artificial Insemination by Donor: Evidence for a Defect in Gamete Transfer?" *Fertility & Sterility* 50:279–282, 1988.

Centers for Disease Control. "Oral Contraceptive Use and the Risk of Ovarian Cancer." *Journal of the American Medical Association* 249:1596–1599, 1983.

———. "Oral Contraceptive Use and the Risk of Endometrial Cancer." *Journal of the American Medical Association* 249:1600–1604, 1983a.

———. "*Chalamydia Trachomatis* Infections: Policy Guidelines for Prevention and Control." *MMWR* 34(Suppl.):53S–74S, 1985.

————. "Classification System for Human T-Lymphotropic Virus Type III/Lymphadenopathy-Associated Virus Infections." *MMWR* 35(29):19, 1986.

————. "1989 Sexually Transmitted Diseases Treatment Guidelines." *Morbidity and Mortality Weekly Report* 38(S-8), 1989.

————. "Ectopic Pregnancy—United States, 1986." *Morbidity and Mortality Weekly Report* 38:481–484, 1989a.

————. "Increase in Rubella and Congenital Rubella Syndrome—United States, 1998–1990." *Morbidity and Mortality Weekly Report* 40:93–99, 1991.

————. "Summary of Notifiable Diseases, United States, 1990." *Morbidity and Mortality Weekly Report* 39(53) (published October 4, 1991) 1991a.

————. "Summary of Notifiable Diseases, United States, 1991." *Morbidity and Mortality Weekly Report* 40(53) (published October 2, 1992, for 1991) 1991b.

————. "1993 Revised Classification System for HIV Infection and Expanded Surveillance Case Definition for AIDS Among Adolescents and Adults." *Morbidity and Mortality Weekly Report* 41:RR-17, 1992.

————. "Breast and Cervical Cancer Surveillance, United States, 1973–1987." *Morbidity and Mortality Weekly Report* 41(SS-2):1–15, 1992a.

————. "Cancer Screening Behaviors Among U. S. Women: Breast Cancer, 1987–1989, and Cervical Cancer, 1988–1989." *Morbidity and Mortality Weekly Report* 41(SS-2):17–34, 1992b.

————. "Ectopic Pregnancy—United States, 1988–1989." *Morbidity and Mortality Weekly Report* 41:591–594, 1992c.

————. "Hepatitis A Among Homosexual Men—United States, Canada, and Australia." *Morbidity and Mortality Weekly Report* 41:155, 161–164, 1992d.

————. *HIV/AIDS Surveillance*, Technical Notes, p. 17, October 1992e.

————. "Sexual Behavior Among High School Students—United States, 1990." *Morbidity and Mortality Weekly Report* 40:885–888, 1992f.

————. "1993 Sexually Transmitted Diseases Treatment Guidelines." *Morbidity and Mortality Weekly Report* 42:RR-14, September 24, 1993.

————. *HIV/AIDS Surveillance*, January 1993a.

————. *HIV/AIDS Surveillance*, April 1993b.

————. "Impact of the Expanded AIDS Surveillance Case Definition on AIDS Case Reporting." *Morbidity and Mortality Weekly Report* 42:308–310, 1993c.

————. "Rates for Cesarean Delivery—United States, 1991." *Morbidity and Mortality Weekly Report* 42:285–289, 1993d.

————. "Recommendations for the Prevention and Management of *Chlamydia trachomatis* Infections, 1993." *Morbidity and Mortality Weekly Report* 42:(RR-12), August 6, 1993e.

————. "Sexual Behavior of STD Clinic Patients Before and After Earvin 'Magic' Johnson's HIV-Infection An-

nouncement—Maryland, 1991–1992." *Morbidity and Mortality Weekly Report* 42(3):45–48, 1993f.

————. "Surveillance for Gonorrhea and Primary and Secondary Syphilis Among Adolescents, United States—1981–1991." *Morbidity and Mortality Weekly Report* 42 (SS-3):1–11, 1993g.

————. "Teenage Pregnancy and Birth Rates—United States, 1990." *Morbidity and Mortality Weekly Report* 42(38):733–737, 1993h.

————. "Heterosexually-Acquired AIDS—United States, 1993." *Morbidity and Mortality Weekly Report* 43:155–160, 1994.

————. "Summary—Cases of Specified Notifiable Diseases, United States, Cumulative, Week Ending July 2, 1994." *Morbidity and Mortality Weekly Report* 43 (27): Table 1, 1994a.

Centers for Disease Control and World Health Organization. "AIDS Case Watch." *AIDS Clinical Care* 5(1):1, January 1993.

————. "Case Watch." *AIDS Clinical Care* 6(6):1, 1994.

Chaisson, R. E., et al. "Cocaine Use and HIV Infection in Intravenous Drug Users in San Francisco." *Journal of the American Medical Association* 261:561–565, 1989.

Chamberlain, G., et al. "HIV Screening in Pregnancy." *Lancet* 337:1219, 1991.

Chasnoff, I. J., et al. "Temporal Patterns of Cocaine Use in Pregnancy." *Journal of the American Medical Association* 261:1741–1744, 1989.

Chasnoff, I. J., Landress, H. J., and Barrett, M. E. "The Prevalence of Illicit-Drug or Alcohol Use During Pregnancy and Discrepancies in Mandatory Reporting in Pinellas County, Florida." *New England Journal of Medicine* 322:1202–1206, 1990.

Chavez, G. F., Mulinare, J., and Cordero, J. F. "Maternal Cocaine Use During Pregnancy as a Risk Factor for Congenital Urogenital Abnormalities." *Journal of the American Medical Association* 262:795–798, 1989.

Chelune, G. A. "A Multidimensional Look at Sex and Target Differences in Disclosure." *Psychological Reports* 39:259–263, 1976.

Chen, J. T., et al. "Menopausal Flushes and Calcitonin-Gene-Related Peptide." *Lancet* 342:49, 1993.

Cherfas, J. "The Pill of Choice?" *Science* 245:1319–1324, 1989.

Cherfas, J., and Palca, J. "Hormone Antagonist with Broad Potential." *Science* 245:1322, 1989.

Cherlin, A. J. *Marriage, Divorce, Remarriage*. Cambridge, MA: Harvard University Press, 1981.

————. *Marriage, Divorce, Remarriage*. (Revised ed.) Cambridge, MA: Harvard University Press, 1992.

Chernin, K. *The Hungry Self*. New York: Times Books, 1985.

Chiasson, M. A., Stoneburner, R. L., and Joseph, S. C. "Human Immunodeficiency Virus Transmission Through Artificial Insemination." *Journal of AIDS* 3:69–72, 1990.

Children's Defense Fund. *What About the Boys: Teenage Pregnancy Prevention Strategies*. Quoted in *SIECUS Report* 17:20, September/October 1988.

Chilman, C. *Adolescent Sexuality in a Changing American Society* (No. NIH 79-1426). Bethesda, MD: U.S. Department of Health, Education, and Welfare, 1979.

Chipouras, S., et al. *Who Cares? A Handbook on Sex Education and Counseling Services for Disabled People*. Washington, DC: George Washington University, 1979.

Chiriboga, D. A. "The Developmental Psychology of Middle Age." In Howells, J. G. (ed.), *Modern Perspectives in the Psychiatry of Middle Age*, pp. 3–25. New York: Brunner/Mazel, 1981.

Chodorow, N. *The Reproduction of Mothering: Psychoanalysis and the Sociology of Gender*. Berkeley: University of California Press, 1978.

Christensen, A., and Heavey, C. L. "Gender and Social Structure in the Demand/Withdraw Pattern of Marital Conflict." *Journal of Personality and Social Psychology* 59:73–81, 1990.

Christenson, C. V. *Kinsey: A Biography*. Bloomington: Indiana University Press, 1971.

Cicero, T. J., et al. "Function of the Male Sex Organs in Heroin and Methadone Users." *New England Journal of Medicine* 292:882–887, 1975.

Clark, D. *The New Loving Someone Gay*. Berkeley, CA: Celestial Arts, 1987.

Clark, L. "Is There a Difference Between a Clitoral and a Vaginal Orgasm?" *Journal of Sex Research* 6:25–28, 1970.

Clarke, D. H. "Erectile Dysfunction in Diabetes." *Clinical Diabetes* 6:103–105, 1988.

Clarkson, T. B., and Alexander, N. J. "Long-Term Vasectomy: Effects on the Occurrence and Extent of Atherosclerosis in Rhesus Monkeys." *Journal of Clinical Investigation* 65(1):15–25, 1980.

Clarren, S. K., and Smith, D. W. "The Fetal Alcohol Syndrome." *New England Journal of Medicine* 298:1063–1067, 1978.

Clifford, R., and Kolodny, R. "Sex Therapy for Couples." In Wolman, B. B., and Stricker, G. (eds.), *Handbook of Family and Marital Therapy*, pp. 421–449. New York: Plenum Press, 1983.

Cochran, S. D., and Mays, V. M. "Sex, Lies, and HIV." *New England Journal of Medicine* 322:774–775, 1990.

Cochran, W. G., Mosteller, F., and Tukey, J. W. "Statistical Problems of the Kinsey Report." *Journal of the American Statistical Association* 48:674–716, 1953.

Cocores, J., Dackis, C., and Gold, M. "Sexual Dysfunction Secondary to Cocaine Abuse." *Journal of Clinical Psychiatry* 47:384–385, 1986.

Cohen, H., Rosen, R. C., and Goldstein, L. "Electroencephalographic Laterality Changes During Human Sexual Orgasm." *Archives of Sexual Behavior* 5:189–199, 1976.

Cohen, J. "Can Combination Therapy Overcome Drug Resistance?" *Science* 260:1258, 1993.

———. "The HIV Vaccine Paradox." *Science* 264:1072–1074, 1994.

Cohen, M. L., Seghorn, T., and Calmas, W. "Sociometric Study of the Sex Offender." *Journal of Abnormal Psychology* 74:249–255, 1969.

Cohen, N. D., et al. "Transmission of Retroviruses by Transfusion of Screened Blood in Patients Undergoing Cardiac Surgery." *New England Journal of Medicine* 320:1172–1176, 1989.

Cohen, P. T., Sande, M. A., and Volberding, P. A. (eds.). *The AIDS Knowledge Base*. Waltham, MA: The Medical Publishing Group, 1990.

Colditz, G. A., et al. "Menopause and the Risk of Coronary Heart Disease in Women." *New England Journal of Medicine* 316:1105–1110, 1987.

Colditz, G. A., et al. "Prospective Study of Estrogen Replacement Therapy and Risk of Breast Cancer in Postmenopausal Women." *Journal of the American Medical Association* 264:2648–2653, 1990.

Cole, H. M. "Intrauterine Devices." *Journal of the American Medical Association* 261:1227–1230, 1989.

Cole, P. M., and Putnam, F. W. "Effect of Incest on Self and Social Functioning: A Developmental Psychopathology Perspective." *Journal of Consulting and Clinical Psychology* 60:174–184, 1992.

Coleman, E. "Developmental Stages of the Coming Out Process." *Journal of Homosexuality* 7(2/3):31–43, 1981/1982.

———. "Bisexual Women and Lesbians in Heterosexual Marriage." *Journal of Homosexuality* 11:87–113, 1985.

———. "Bisexuality: Challenging Our Understanding of Human Sexuality and Sexual Orientation." In Shelp, E. E. (ed.), *Sexuality and Medicine*, Vol. 1, pp. 225–242. New York: Reidel Publishing, 1987.

Coleman, E., Colgan, P., and Gooren, L. "Male Cross-Gender Behavior in Myanmar (Burma): A Description of the Acault." *Archives of Sexual Behavior* 21:313–321, 1992.

Coleman, E. M., Hoon, P. W., and Hoon, E. F. "Arousability and Sexual Satisfaction in Lesbian and Heterosexual Women." *Journal of Sex Research* 19:58–73, 1983.

Coleman, S. "A Developmental Stage Hypothesis for Nonmarital Dyadic Relationships." *Journal of Marriage and Family Counseling* 3:71–76, 1977.

Coleman, S., Piotrow, P. T., and Rinehart, W. "Tobacco: Hazards to Health and Human Reproduction." *Population Reports*, Series L(1): March 1979.

Coles, F. "Forced to Quit: Sexual Harassment Complaints and Agency Response." *Sex Roles* 14:81–95, 1986.

Collier, A. C., et al. "A Pilot Study of Low-Dose Zidovudine in Human Immunodeficiency Virus Infection." *New England Journal of Medicine* 323:1015–1021, 1990.

Collins, E., and Turner, C. "Maternal Effects of Regular Salicylate Ingestion in Pregnancy." *Lancet* 2:335–339, 1975.

Collins, G. "New Studies of 'Girl Toys' and 'Boy Toys.'" *The New York Times*, February 13, 1984.

Collins, J. A., et al. "Treatment-Independent Pregnancy Among Infertile Couples." *New England Journal of Medicine* 309:1201–1206, 1983.

Collu, R., et al. "Endocrine Effects of Chronic Administration of Psychoactive Drugs to Prepubertal Male Rats. I: Δ^9 - Tetrahydrocannabinol." *Life Sciences* 16:533–542, 1975.

Comfort, A. *The Joy of Sex.* (rev. ed.) New York: Crown, 1972.

———. *The Joy of Sex.* New York: Pocket Books, 1991.

Committee on Contraceptive Development, *Developing New Contraceptives: Obstacles and Opportunities*, Washington, DC: National Academy Press, 1990.

Committee on the Relationship Between Oral Contraceptives and Breast Cancer (ed.) *Contraceptives and Breast Cancer*. Washington, DC: National Academy Press, 1991.

Comstock, G. D. *Violence Against Lesbians and Gay Men*. New York: Columbia University Press, 1991.

Concorde Coordinating Committee. "Concorde: MRC/ANRS Randomized Double-blind Controlled Trial of Immediate and Deferred Zidovudine in Symptom-Free HIV Infection." *Lancet* 343:871–881, 1994.

Cone, R. W., et al. "Frequent Detection of Genital Herpes Simplex Virus DNA by Polymerase Chain Reaction Among Pregnant Women," *Journal of the American Medical Association* 272:792–796, 1994.

Conley, L. J., and Holmberg, S. D. "Transmission of AIDS from Blood Screened Negative for Antibody to the Human Immunodeficiency Virus." *New England Journal of Medicine* 326:1499–1500, 1992.

Connell, R. W., and Kippax, S. "Sexuality in the AIDS Crisis: Patterns of Sexual Practice and Pleasure in a Sample of Australian Gay and Bisexual Men." *Journal of Sex Research* 27:167–198, 1990.

Consensus Conference. "The Impact of Routine HTLV-III Antibody Testing of Blood and Plasma Donors on Public Health." *Journal of the American Medical Association* 256:1778–1783, 1986.

Consensus Development Conference. "Prophylaxis and Treatment of Osteoporosis." *The American Journal of Medicine* 90:107–110, 1991.

Constantine, L. L. "Multilateral Relations Revisited: Group Marriage in Extended Perspective." In Murstein, B. I. (ed.), *Exploring Intimate Life Styles*, pp. 131–147. New York: Springer, 1978.

Constantine, L. L., and Constantine, J. M. *Group Marriage: A Study of Contemporary Multilateral Marriage*. New York: Macmillan, 1973.

Constantine, L. L., and Martinson, F. M. (eds.). *Children and Sex*. Boston: Little, Brown, 1981.

Conway, G. A., et al. "Underreporting of AIDS Cases in South Carolina, 1986 and 1987." *Journal of the American Medical Association* 262:2859–2863, 1989.

Cook, E. P. *Psychological Androgyny*. New York: Pergamon Press, 1985.

Coombs, L. C. "Preferences for Sex of Children Among U.S. Couples." *Family Planning Perspectives* 9:259–265, 1977.

Cooper, D. A., et al. "Acute AIDS Retrovirus Infection: Definition of a Clinical Illness Associated with Seroconversion." *Lancet* I:537–546, 1985.

Copeland, P. M. "Neuroendocrine Aspects of Eating Disorders." In Emmett, S. W. (ed.), *Theory and Treatment of Anorexia Nervosa and Bulimia*, pp. 51–72. New York: Brunner/Mazel, 1985.

Corbitt, G.; Bailey, A. S.; and Williams, G. "HIV Infection in Manchester, 1959." *Lancet* 336:51, 1990.

Cordero, J. F., and Layde, P. M. "Vaginal Spermicides, Chromosomal Abnormalities, and Limb Reduction Defects." *Family Planning Perspectives* 15(1):16–18, 1983.

Corey, L., and Holmes, K. K. "Sexual Transmission of Hepatitis A in Homosexual Men: Incidence and Mechanism." *New England Journal of Medicine* 302:435–438, 1980.

———. "Genital Herpes Simplex Virus Infections: Current Concepts in Diagnosis, Therapy, and Prevention." *Annals of Internal Medicine* 98:973–983, 1983.

———. "Genital Herpes Simplex Virus Infections: Clinical Manifestations, Course, and Complications." *Annals of Internal Medicine* 98:958–972, 1983.

Corsan, G. H.; Ghazi, D.; and Kemmann, E. "Home Urinary Luteinizing Hormone Imunoassays: Clinical Applications," *Fertility & Sterility* 53:591–601, 1990.

Costello, John. *Virtue Under Fire*. Boston: Little, Brown, 1985.

Cotten-Huston, A. L., and Wheeler, K. A. "Preorgasmic Group Treatment: Assertiveness, Marital Adjustment and Sexual Function in Women." *Journal of Sex & Marital Therapy* 9:296–302, 1983.

———. "Mammographic Screening in Asymptomatic Women Aged 40 Years and Older." *Journal of the American Medical Association* 261:2535–2542, 1989.

Couzinet, B., et al. "Termination of Early Pregnancy by the Progesterone Antagonist RU 486." *New England Journal of Medicine* 315:1565–1569, 1986.

Covington, T. R., and McClendon, J. R. *Sex Care: The Complete Guide to Safe and Healthy Sex*. New York: Pocket Books, 1987.

Cowan, C., and Kinder, M. *Smart Women/Foolish Choices*. New York: Clarkson N. Potter, 1985.

Cramer, D. W., and Roach, A. J. "Coming Out to Mom and Dad: A Study of Gay Males and Their Relationships with Their Parents." *Journal of Homosexuality* 15(3/4):79–91, 1988.

Cramer, D. W., et al. "The Relationship of Tubal Infertility to Barrier Method and Oral Contraceptive Use."

Journal of the American Medical Association 257:2446–2450, 1987.

Crane, L. R. "Sentinel Surveillance for HIV Infection in Detroit: Heterosexual Transmission in a Medium Prevalence City." (Abstract PoC 4013.) Eighth International Conference on AIDS, Amsterdam, July 19–24, 1992.

Crenshaw, T. L. "Counseling the Family and Friends." In Halpern, S. (ed.), *Rape: Helping the Victim*, pp. 51–65. Oradell, NJ: Medical Economics Books, 1978.

———. "The Sexual Aversion Syndrome." *Journal of Sex & Marital Therapy* 11:285–292, 1985.

Crewdson, J. *By Silence Betrayed: Sexual Abuse of Children in America*. Boston: Little, Brown, 1988.

Crisp, A. H. "The Possible Significance of Some Behavioral Correlates of Weight and Carbohydrate Intake." *Journal of Psychosomatic Research* 11:117–131, 1967.

Croog, S. H., et al. "Sexual Symptoms in Hypertensive Patients." *Archives of Internal Medicine* 148:788–794, 1988.

Crowe, L. C., and George, W. H. "Alcohol and Human Sexuality: Review and Integration." *Psychological Bulletin* 105:374–386, 1989.

Crum, C., et al. "Human Papillomavirus Type 16 and Early Cervical Neoplasia." *New England Journal of Medicine* 310:880–883, 1984.

Culp, R. E., Cook, A. S., and Housley, P. C. "A Comparison of Observed and Reported Adult–Infant Interactions: Effect of Perceived Sex." *Sex Roles* 9:475–479, 1983.

Cunningham, F. G., and Gant, N. F. "Prevention of Preeclampsia—A Reality?" *New England Journal of Medicine* 321:606–607, 1989.

Cunningham, F. G., MacDonald, P. C., and Gant, N. F. (eds.). *Williams Obstetrics*, 18th ed. East Norwalk, CT: Appleton and Lange, 1989.

Cunningham, S. "Violent Pornography Said to Spur Aggression." *APA Monitor*, p. 30, March 1983.

Curran, J. W. "AIDS: Two Years Later." *New England Journal of Medicine* 309:609–611, 1983.

Currier, R. L. "Juvenile Sexuality in Global Perspective." In Constantine, L. L., and Martinson, F. M. (eds.), *Children and Sex: New Findings, New Perspectives*, pp. 9–19. Boston: Little, Brown, 1981.

Cushman, P., Jr. "Plasma Testosterone in Narcotic Addiction." *American Journal of Medicine* 55:452–458, 1973.

Cvetkovitch, G., et al. "On the Psychology of Adolescents' Use of Contraception." *Journal of Sex Research* 11:256–270, 1975.

Daling, J., et al. "Tubal Infertility in Relation to Prior Induced Abortion." *Fertility & Sterility* 43:389, 1985.

Dalton, K. "Menstruation and Acute Psychiatric Illness." *British Medical Journal*, pp. 148–149, January 17, 1959.

———. "Menstruation and Accidents." *British Medical Journal* 2:1425–1426, 1960.

———. *The Premenstrual Syndrome*. Springfield, IL: Charles C. Thomas, 1964.

———. "The Influence of Mother's Menstruation on Her Child." *Proceedings of the Royal Society of Medicine* 59:1014–1016, 1966.

———. "Menstruation and Examinations." *Lancet* 2:1386–1388, 1968.

———. "Children's Hospital Admissions and Mother's Menstruation." *British Medical Journal* 2:27–28, 1970.

———. "Cyclical Criminal Acts in Premenstrual Syndrome." *Lancet* 2:1070–1071, 1980.

Dan, A. J. "Behavioral Variability and the Menstrual Cycle." Presented at the American Psychological Association Annual Convention, Washington, DC, 1976.

Dan, B. D. "Sex and the Singles' Whirl: The Quantum Dynamics of Hepatitis B." *Journal of the American Medical Association* 256:1344, 1986.

Danforth, D. N. "Cesarean Section." *Journal of the American Medical Association* 253:811–818, 1985.

Daniel, W. A., Jr. "Obesity in Adolescence." In Wolman, B. B. (ed.), *Psychological Aspects of Obesity*, pp. 104–117. New York: Van Nostrand Reinhold, 1982.

Dank, B. M. "Coming Out in the Gay World." *Psychiatry* 34:180–197, 1971.

Darling, C. A.; Davidson, J. K.; and Conway-Welch, C. "Female Ejaculation: Perceived Origins, The Grafenburg Spot/Area, and Sexual Responsiveness." *Archives of Sexual Behavior* 19:29–47, 1990.

Darling, J., et al. "Primary Tubal Infertility in Relation to the Use of an Intrauterine Device." *New England Journal of Medicine* 312:937–941, 1985.

Darney, P. D., et al. "Acceptance and Perceptions of Norplant Among Users in San Francisco, USA." *Studies in Family Planning* 21:152–155, 1990.

Davenport, W. "Sexual Patterns and Their Regulation in a Society of the Southwest Pacific." In Beach, F. (ed.), *Sex and Behavior*. New York: Wiley, 1965.

———. "Sex in Cross-Cultural Perspective." In Beach, F. (ed.), *Human Sexuality in Four Perspectives*, pp. 115–163. Baltimore: Johns Hopkins University Press, 1977.

David. "The Commune Movement in the Middle 1970s." In Murstein, B. I. (ed.), *Exploring Intimate Life Styles*, pp. 69–82. New York: Springer, 1978.

Davidson, J. K., and Hoffman, L. E. "Sexual Fantasies and Sexual Satisfaction: An Empirical Analysis of Erotic Thought." *Journal of Sex Research* 22:184–205, 1986.

Davis, G. L., et al. "Treatment of Chronic Hepatitis C with Recombinant Interferon Alfa." *New England Journal of Medicine* 321:1501–1506, 1989.

Davis, J. E., and Mininberg, D. T. "Prostatitis and Sexual Function." *Medical Aspects of Human Sexuality* 10(8):32–40, 1976.

Davis, K. B. *Factors in the Sex Life of Twenty-Two Hundred Women*. New York: Harper, 1929.

Davis, L. J., and Brody, E. M. *Rape and Older Women*. Rockville, MD: U.S. Department of Health, Education, and Welfare, 1979.

Dawson, D. A. "The Effects of Sex Education on Adolescent Behavior." *Family Planning Perspectives* 18:163–165, 1986.

Day, N. E. "Screening for Breast Cancer." *British Medical Bulletin* 47:400–415, 1991.

DeBuono, B. A., et al. "Sexual Behavior of College Women in 1975, 1986, and 1989." *New England Journal of Medicine* 322:821–825, 1990.

DeCasper, A. J., and Fifer, W. P. "Of Human Bonding: Newborns Prefer Their Mothers' Voices." *Science* 208:1174–1176, 1980.

DeGowin, E. L., and DeGowin, R. L. *Bedside Diagnostic Examination*, 3rd ed. New York: Macmillan, 1976.

DeLamater, J. "Gender Differences in Sexual Scenarios," In Kelley, K. (ed.), *Females, Males, and Sexuality*. Albany, NY: SUNY Press, 1987.

DeLamater, J., and MacCorquodale, P. *Premarital Sexuality: Attitudes, Relationships, Behavior*. Madison: University of Wisconsin Press, 1979.

Delaney, J., Lupton, M. J., and Toth, E. *The Curse: A Cultural History of Menstruation*. New York: New American Library, 1977.

de la Vega, E. "Considerations for Reaching the Latino Population with Sexuality and HIV/AIDS Information and Education." *SIECUS Report* 18(3):1–8, February/March 1990.

del Rosario, N. C., Blair, E., and Rickman, L. "A Herpetic Hickey." *New England Journal of Medicine* 317:54–55, 1987.

DeMartino, M. F. (ed.). *Human Autoerotic Practices*. New York: Human Sciences Press, 1979.

de Mauro, D. "Sexuality Education 1990: A Review of State Sexuality and AIDS Education Curricula." *SIECUS Report* 18(2):1–9, December 1989/January 1990.

Dennerstein, L., and Burrows, G. D. "Hormone Replacement Therapy and Sexuality in Women." *Clinics in Endocrinology and Metabolism* 11(3):661–679, November 1982.

Dennerstein, L., Wood, C., and Burrows, G. D. "Sexual Response Following Hysterectomy and Oophorectomy." *Obstetrics and Gynecology* 49:92–96, 1977.

Deodhar, L. P., and Tendolkar, U. M. "Genital Ulcers and HIV Antibody." *Lancet* 336:112, 1989.

Derenski, A., and Landsburg, S. B. *The Age Taboo: Older Women/Younger Men*. Boston: Little, Brown, 1981.

Dermer, M., and Thiel, D. L. "When Beauty May Fail." *Journal of Personality and Social Psychology* 31:1168–1176, 1975.

Derogatis, L. R., and Kourlesis, S. M. "An Approach to Evaluation of Sexual Problems in the Cancer Patient." *Ca-A Cancer Journal for Clinicians* 31:46–50, 1981.

Devereux, G. "Institutionalized Homosexuality of the Mohave Indians." *Human Biology* 9:498–527, 1937.

Diagnostic and Statistical Manual and Mental Disorders (DSM-III). Washington, DC: American Psychiatric Association, 1980.

Diamond, I. "Pornography and Repression: A Reconsideration of 'Who' and 'What.'" In Lederer, L. (ed.), *Take Back the Night*, pp. 187–203. New York: William Morrow, 1980.

Diamond M. "Human Sexual Development." In Beach, F. (ed.), *Human Sexuality in Four Perspectives*, pp. 22–61. Baltimore: Johns Hopkins University Press, 1977.

———. "Sexual Identity, Monozygotic Twins Reared in Discordant Sex Roles and a BBC Follow-up." *Archives of Sexual Behavior* 11:118–186, 1982.

———. "Homosexuality and Bisexuality in Different Populations." *Archives of Sexual Behavior* 22:291–310, 1993.

Di Bisceglie, A. M., et al. "Recombinant Interferon Alfa Therapy for Chronic Hepatitis C." *New England Journal of Medicine* 321:1506–1510, 1989.

Dick-Read, G. *Childbirth Without Fear*. New York: Harper & Row, 1932.

DiClemente, R., Boyer, C., and Morales, E. "Minorities and AIDS: Knowledge, Attitudes, and Misconceptions Among Black and Latino Adolescents." *American Journal of Public Health* 78:55–57, 1988.

Dietz, P. E., Burgess, A. W., and Hazelwood, R. R. "Autoerotic Asphyxia, the Paraphilias, and Mental Disorder." In Hazelwood, R. R., Dietz, P. E., and Burgess, A. W., *Autoerotic Fatalities*, pp. 83–85. Lexington, MA: Lexington Books, 1983.

DiLapi, E. M. "Lesbian Mothers and the Motherhood Hierarchy." *Journal of Homosexuality* 18(Nos.1/2):101–121, 1989.

Dina, T. S. "Primary Central Nervous System Lymphoma Versus Toxoplasmosis in AIDS." *Radiology* 179:823–828, 1991.

Diokno, A. C., Brown, M. B., and Herzog, A. R. "Sexual Function in the Elderly." *Archives of Internal Medicine* 150:197–200, 1990.

Dion, K. K., and Berscheid, E. "Physical Attractiveness and Peer Perception Among Children." *Sociometry* 37:1–12, 1974.

Dion, K. K., Berscheid, E., and Walster, E. "What Is Beautiful Is Good." *Journal of Personality and Social Psychology* 24:285–290, 1972.

Dion, K. K., and Dion, K. L. "Self-Esteem and Romantic Love." *Journal of Personality* 43:39–57, 1975.

Dion, K. L., and Dion, K. K. "Correlates of Romantic Love." *Journal of Consulting and Clinical Psychology* 41:51–56, 1973.

———. "Love, Liking and Trust in Heterosexual Relationships." *Personality and Social Psychology Bulletin* 2:191–206, 1976.

Dionne, E. J., Jr. "On Both Sides, Advocates Predict a 50-State Battle." *The New York Times*, pp. 1 & 11, July 4, 1989.

Djerassi, C. *The Politics of Contraception*. New York: Norton, 1979.

Dodson, B. *Liberating Masturbation*. New York: Bodysex Designs, 1974.

Doel, et al. "Persistence of High Risk Sexual Behavior in Homosexual/Bisexual Men: A Multicenter Study." (Abstract # M.D.P. 23, p. 714.) Presented at the Fifth International Conference on AIDS, Montreal, June 1989.

Doerr, P., et al. "Plasma Testosterone, Estradiol, and Semen Analysis in Male Homosexuals." *Archives of General Psychiatry* 29:829–833, 1973.

Doe v. Kelley, reprinted in 6 FLR 3011(1980).

Dolcini, M. M. "Demographic Characteristics of Heterosexuals with Multiple Partners: The National AIDS Behavioral Surveys." *Family Planning Perspectives* 25:208–214, 1993.

Donahue, J. G., et al. "Transmission of HIV by Transfusion of Screened Blood." *New England Journal of Medicine* 323:1709, 1990.

Donnelly, D. A. "Sexually Inactive Marriages." *Journal of Sex Research* 30:171–179, 1993.

Donnerstein, E. "Massive Exposure to Sexual Violence and Desensitization to Violence and Rape." Presented at the 26th annual meeting of the Society for the Scientific Study of Sex, Chicago, November 20, 1983.

Donnerstein, E., and Linz, D. "Sexual Violence in the Media: A Warning." *Psychology Today* 18(1):14–15, 1984.

———. "Mass Media Sexual Violence and Male Viewers." *American Behavioral Scientist* 29(5):601–618, 1986.

Donnerstein, E., Linz, D., and Penrod, S. *The Question of Pornography*. New York: The Free Press, 1987.

Dorgan, M., Goebel, B. L., and House, A. E. "Generalizing About Sex Role and Self-Esteem: Results or Effects?" *Sex Roles* 9:719-724, 1983.

Dörner, G. "Hormonal Induction and Prevention of Female Homosexuality." *Journal of Endocrinology* 42:163–164, 1968.

———. *Hormones and Brain Differentiation*. Amsterdam: Elsevier Scientific Publishing, 1976.

Dörner, G., et al. "Prenatal Stress as Possible Aetiogenetic Factor of Homosexuality in Human Males." *Endokrinologie* 75:365–386, 1980.

———. "Stressful Events in Prenatal Life of Bi- and Homosexual Men." *Experimental and Clinical Endocrinology* 81:83–87, 1983.

Dorris, Michael. *The Broken Cord*. New York: Harper & Row, 1989.

Douglas, J., et al. "A Double-blind Study of Oral Acyclovir for Suppression of Recurrences of Genital Herpes Simplex Virus Infection." *New England Journal of Medicine* 310:1551–1556, 1984.

Douthitt, R. A. "The Division of Labor Within the Home: Have Gender Roles Changed?" *Sex Roles* 20:693–704, 1989.

Drill, V. A. "Oral Contraceptives: Relation to Mammary Cancer, Benign Breast Lesions, and Cervical Cancer." *Annual Review of Pharmacology* 15:367–385, 1975.

Duldt, B. W. "Sexual Harassment in Nursing." *Nursing Outlook*, pp. 336–343, June 1982.

Dunn, D. T., et al. "Risk of Human Immunodeficiency Virus Type 1 Transmission Through Breastfeeding." *Lancet* 340:585–588, 1992.

Dunn, H. G., et al. "Maternal Cigarette Smoking During Pregnancy and the Child's Subsequent Development, II: Neurological and Intellectual Maturation to the Age of $6\,^1/_2$ Years." *Canadian Journal of Public Health* 68:43–50, 1977.

Dunn, M. E., and Trost, J. E. "Male Multiple Orgasms: A Descriptive Study." *Archives of Sexual Behavior* 18:377–388, 1989.

Dutton, D., and Aron, A. "Some Evidence for Heightened Sexual Attraction Under Conditions of High Anxiety." *Journal of Personality and Social Psychology* 30:510–517, 1974.

Earle, R., and Crow, G. *Lonely All the Time*. New York: Pocket Books, 1989.

Eckert, P. *Jocks and Burnouts*. New York: Teachers College Press, 1989.

Eckholm, E. "AIDS, Fatally Steady in the U. S. Accelerates Worldwide," *The New York Times*, Section 4, p. 5, June 28, 1992.

Eckholm, E., and Tierney, J. "AIDS in Africa: A Killer Rages On." *The New York Times*, pp. 1, 15–16, September 16, 1990.

Eddy, D. M. *Screening for Cancer: Theory, Analysis and Design*. Englewood Cliffs, NJ: Prentice-Hall, 1980.

Eddy, D. M., et al. "The Value of Mammography Screening in Women under Age 50." *Journal of the American Medical Association* 259:1512–1519, 1988.

Edmiston, S. "Hers." *The New York Times*, p. Y20, July 22, 1982.

Ehrenberg, M., and Ehrenberg, O. *The Intimate Circle: The Sexual Dynamics of Family Life*. New York: Simon & Schuster, 1988.

Ehrhardt, A., and Meyer-Bahlburg, H. "Effects of Prenatal Sex Hormones on Gender-Related Behavior." *Science* 211(4488):1312–1318, 1981.

Ehrhardt, A. A., Evers, K., and Money, J. "Influence of Androgen and Some Aspects of Sexual Dimorphic Behavior in Women with the Late-Treated Adrenogenital Syndrome." *Johns Hopkins Medical Journal* 123:115–122, 1968.

Ehrhardt, A. A., Grisanti, G. C., and Meyer-Bahlburg, H. F. "Prenatal Exposure to Medroxyprogesterone Acetate (MPA) in Girls." *Psychoneuroendocrinology* 2:391–398, 1977.

Ehrhardt, A. A., Yingling, S., and Warne, P. A. "Sexual Behavior in the Era of AIDS: What Has Changed in the

United States?" *Annual Review of Sex Research* II:25–47, 1991.

Eidelberg, L. "A Contribution to the Study of Masturbation Fantasy." *International Journal of Psychoanalysis* 26:127–137, 1945.

Ekman, P., Levenson, R. W., and Friesen, W. V. "Autonomic Nervous System Activity Distinguishes Among Emotions." *Science* 221:1208–1210, 1983.

Ekstrand, M. L., et al. "Risky Sex Relapse, The Next Challenge for AIDS Prevention Programs." (Abstract # T.D.O.8, p. 699.) Fifth International Conference on AIDS, Montreal, June 4–9, 1989.

El-Sadr, W., et al. "Clinical and Laboratory Correlates of Human Immunodeficiency Virus Infection in a Cohort of Intravenous Drug Users from New York, NY." *Archives of Internal Medicine* 152:1653–1659, 1992.

Eliasson, R., and Lindholmer, C. "Functions of Male Accessory Genital Organs." In Hafez, E. S. (ed.), *Human Semen and Fertility Regulation in Men*. St. Louis, MO: Mosby, 1976.

Ellerbock, T. V., et al. "Epidemiology of Women with AIDS in the United States, 1981 through 1990." *Journal of the American Medical Association* 265:2971–2975, 1991.

Ellis, A. *The American Sexual Tragedy*. New York: Twayne Publishers, 1959.

———. *Sex Without Guilt*. New York: Grove Press, 1965.

———. "Treatment of Erectile Dysfunction." In Leiblum, S. R., and Pervin, L. A. (eds.), *Principles and Practice of Sex Therapy*, pp. 235–262. New York: Guilford Press, 1980.

Ellis, L. "A Synthesized (Biosocial) Theory of Rape." *Journal of Consulting and Clinical Psychology* 59:631–642, 1991.

Ellis, L., et al. "Sexual Orientation of Human Offspring May Be Altered by Severe Maternal Stress During Pregnancy." *Journal of Sex Research* 25:152–157, 1988.

Elixhauser, A. "Public Health Focus: Mammography." *Morbidity and Mortality Weekly Report* 41:454–459, 1992.

Emmens, C. *The Abortion Controversy*. New York: Julian Messner (Simon & Schuster), 1987.

Endlemen, R. "Homosexuality in Tribal Societies." *Transcultural Psychiatric Research Review* 23:187–218, 1986.

Englar, R. C., and Walker, C. E. "Male and Female Reactions to Erotic Literature." *Psychological Reports* 32:481–482, 1973.

Englund, J. A., et al. "Herpes Simplex Virus Resistant to Acyclovir." *Annals of Internal Medicine* 112:416–422, 1990.

Enoch, J., Herrman, C., and Walsh, S. "Sexual Abuse and Eating Disorders." Workshop presented at the 4th International Conference on Eating Disorders, New York, NY, April 27–29, 1990.

Ensminger, M. E. "Adolescent Sexual Behavior as It Relates to Other Transition Behaviors in Youth." In Hofferth, S. L., and Hayes, C. D. (eds.), *Risking the Future:*

Adolescent Sexuality, Pregnancy, and Childbearing, Vol. 11. Washington, DC: National Academy Press, 1987.

Erickson, W. D., Walbek, N. H., and Seely, R. K. "The Behavior Patterns of Child Molesters." *Archives of Sexual Behavior* 17:77–86, 1988.

Erikson, E. *Childhood and Society*, 2nd ed. New York: Norton, 1963.

———. *Identity: Youth and Crisis*. New York: Norton, 1968.

Erlich, K. S., et al. "Acyclovir-Resistant Herpes Simplex Virus Infections in Patients with the Acquired Immunodeficiency Syndrome." *New England Journal of Medicine* 320:293–296, 1989.

Erlik, Y., et al. "Association of Waking Episodes with Menopausal Hot Flushes." *Journal of the American Medical Association* 245:1741–1744, 1981.

Essex, M., and Kanki, P. "The Origins of the AIDS Virus." *Scientific American*, pp. 64–71, October 1988.

Estrich, S. *Real Rape*. Cambridge, MA: Harvard University Press, 1987.

Eth, S. "The Child Victim as Witness in Sexual Abuse Proceedings." *Psychiatry* 51:221–231, 1988.

Ethics Committee of the American Fertility Society. *Ethical Consideration of the New Reproductive Technologies: Fertility & Sterility* 46(3):Suppl. 1, September 1986.

Ettinger, B., et al. "Long-Term Estrogen Replacement Prevents Bone Loss and Fractures." *Annals of Internal Medicine* 102:319–329, 1985.

European Collaborative Study. "Mother-to-Child Transmission of HIV Infection." *Lancet* Ii:1039–1043, 1988.

European Study Group. "Risk Factors for Male to Female Transmission of HIV." *British Medical Journal* 298:411–415, 1989.

Evans, D. R. "Exhibitionism." In Costello, C. G. (ed.), *Symptoms of Psychopathology*. New York: Wiley, 1970.

Evans-Pritchard, E. E. "Sexual Inversion Among the Azande." *American Anthropologist* 72:1428–1434, 1970.

———. *The Azande*. Oxford: Oxford University Press, 1971.

Everstine, D. S., and Everstine, L. *Sexual Trauma in Children and Adolescents*. New York: Brunner/Mazel, 1989.

Ewigman, B. G., et al. "Effect of Ultrasound Screening on Perinatal Outcome." *New England Journal of Medicine* 329:821–827, 1993.

Eysenck, N., and Nias, D. K. B. *Sex, Violence, and the Media*. New York: St. Martin's Press, 1978.

Eyster, M. E., et al. "Predictive Markers for the Acquired Immunodeficiency Syndrome (AIDS) in Haemophiliacs: Persistence of P24 Antigen and Low T4 Cell Count." *Annals of Internal Medicine* 110:963–969, 1989.

Fabbri, R., Jr. "Hypnosis and Behavioral Therapy: A Coordinated Approach to the Treatment of Sexual Disorders." *American Journal of Clinical Hypnosis* 19:4–8, 1976.

Fabes, R. A., and Martin, C. L. "Gender and Age Stereotypes of Emotionality." *Personality and Social Psychology Bulletin* 17:532–540, 1991.

Faderman, L. *Odd Girls and Twilight Lovers: A History of Lesbian Life in Twentieth-Century America.* New York: Penguin Books, 1991.

Fagot, B. I. "Consequences of Moderate Cross-Gender Behavior in Pre-school Children." *Child Development* 48:902–907, 1977.

Fagot, B. I., and Leinbach, M. D. "The Young Child's Gender Schema: Environmental Input, Internal Organization." *Child Development* 60:663–672, 1989.

Fagot, B. I., Leinbach, M. D., and O'Boyle, C. "Gender Labeling, Gender Stereotyping, and Parenting Behaviors." *Developmental Psychology* 28:225–230, 1992.

Fahey, B. J., and Henderson, D. K. "Minimizing Risks for Occupational Blood-borne Infections." *Journal of the American Medical Association* 264:1189–1190, 1990.

Faich, G., et al. "Toxic Shock Syndrome and the Vaginal Contraceptive Sponge." *Journal of the American Medical Association* 255:216–218, 1986.

Fairchild, B., and Hayward, N. *Now That You Know: What Every Parent Should Know About Homosexuality.* New York: Harcourt Brace Jovanovich, 1979.

Fairstein, L. *Sexual Violence: Our War Against Rape.* New York: William Morrow, 1993.

Falicov, C. J. "Sexual Adjustment During First Pregnancy and Post-Partum." *American Journal of Obstetrics and Gynecology* 117:991–1000, 1973.

Fallon, B., Rosenberg, S., and Culp, D. "Long-Term Follow-up in Patients with an Inflatable Penile Prosthesis." *Journal of Urology* 132:270–271, 1984.

Farkas, G. M., and Rosen, R. C. "Effect of Alcohol on Elicited Male Sexual Response." *Journal of Studies on Alcohol* 37:265–272, 1976.

Farkas, G. M., Sine, L. F., and Evans, I. M. "Personality, Sexuality, and Demographic Differences Between Volunteers and Nonvolunteers for a Laboratory Study of Male Sexual Behavior." *Archives of Sexual Behavior* 7:513–520, 1978.

Farizo, K. M. "Spectrum of Disease in Persons with Human Immunodeficiency Virus Infection in the United States." *Journal of the American Medical Association* 267:1798–1805, 1992.

Farzadegan, H. "Loss of Human Immunodeficiency Virus Type 1 (HIV-1) Antibodies with Evidence of Viral Infection in Asymptomatic Homosexual Men." *Annals of Internal Medicine* 108:785–790, 1988.

Fast, J. *Body Language.* New York: M. Evans, 1972.

Faundes, A., et al. "Ovulatory Dysfunction During Continuous Administration of Low-dose Levonorgestrel by Subdermal Implants." *Fertility & Sterility* 56:27–31, 1991.

Fausto-Sterling, A. *Myths of Gender: Biological Theories about Women and Men.* New York: Basic Books, 1985.

Faux, M. *Roe v. Wade.* New York: Mentor Books, 1989.

Fay, R. E., et al. "Prevalence and Patterns of Same-Gender Sexual Contact Among Men." *Science* 243:338–348, 1989.

Feather, N. T. "Values in Adolescence." In Adelson, J. (ed.), *Handbook of Adolescent Psychology*, pp. 247–294. New York: Wiley, 1980.

Feitel, L. F. "My Body, My Self." *Sesame Street Magazine Parents Guide*, pp. 20–25, April 1990.

Feldblum, P. J., Bernardik, E., and Rosenberg, M. J. "Spermicide Use and Sexually Transmitted Disease." *Journal of the American Medical Association* 259:2851, 1988.

Feldblum, P. J., and Fortney, J. A. "Condoms, Spermicides, and the Transmission of Human Immunodeficiency Virus: A Review of the Literature." *American Journal of Public Health* 78:52–54, 1988.

Feldman, M. P., and MacCulloch, M. J. *Homosexual Behavior: Therapy and Assessment.* Oxford: Pergamon Press, 1971.

Feldman-Summers, S., Gordon, P., and Meagher, J. R. "The Impact of Rape on Sexual Satisfaction." *Journal of Abnormal Psychology* 88:101–105, 1979.

Felson, D. T., et al. "The Effect of Postmenopausal Estrogen Therapy on Bone Density in Elderly Women." *New England Journal of Medicine* 329:1141–1146, 1993.

Fertel, N. S., and Feuer, E. G. "Marital and Sexual Counseling in the Orthodox Jewish Community." *Journal of Sex Education and Therapy* 1(6):62–65, Winter 1979.

Fielding, J. E. "Adolescent Pregnancy Revisited." *New England Journal of Medicine* 299:893–896, 1978.

Finkelhor, D. "Psychological, Cultural and Family Factors in Incest and Family Sexual Abuse." *Journal of Marriage and Family Counseling*, pp. 41–49, October 1978.

———. "Sex Among Siblings: A Survey on Prevalence, Variety, and Effects." *Archives of Sexual Behavior* 9:171–194, 1980.

———. "Sex Between Siblings." In Constantine, L. L., and Martinson, F. M. (eds.), *Children and Sex: New Findings, New Perspectives*, pp. 129–149. Boston: Little, Brown, 1981.

———. *Child Sexual Abuse.* New York: Free Press, 1984.

Finkelhor, D., and Araji, S. "Explanations of Pedophilia: A Four Factor Model." *Journal of Sex Research* 22:145–161, 1986.

Fiscella, K. "Relationships of Weight Change to Required Size of Vaginal Diaphragm." *Nurse Practitioner* 7(7):21, 25, July–August 1982.

Fischer, J. L., and Narus, L. R., Jr. "Sex Roles and Intimacy in Same Sex and Other Sex Relationships." *Psychology of Women Quarterly* 5:444–455, 1981.

Fischl, M., et al. "Evaluation of Heterosexual Partners, Children, and Household Contacts of Adults with AIDS." *Journal of the American Medical Association* 257:640–644, 1987.

Fischl, M. A., et al. "The Efficacy of Azidothymidine (AZT) in the Treatment of Patients with AIDS and AIDS Related Complex." *New England Journal of Medicine* 317:192–197, 1987.

Fischl, M. A., et al. "Seroprevalence of HIV Antibody in a Sexually Active Heterosexual Population." (Abstract #4067, 1988a.) Presented at the Fourth International AIDS Conference, Stockholm, June 1988.

Fischl, M. A., et al. "A Randomized Controlled Trial of a Reduced Daily Dose of Zidovudine in Patients with Acquired Immunodeficiency Syndrome." *New England Journal of Medicine* 323:1009–1014, 1990.

Fisher, B., et al. "Five Year Results of a Randomized Clinical Trial Comparing Total Mastectomy and Segmental Mastectomy with or without Radiation in the Treatment of Breast Cancer." *New England Journal of Medicine* 312:665–673, 1985.

Fisher, B., et al. "Lumpectomy Compared with Lumpectomy and Radiation Therapy for the Treatment of Intraductal Breast Cancer." *New England Journal of Medicine* 328:1581–1586, 1993.

Fisher, Bernard, et al. "Eight-Year Results of a Randomized Clinical Trial Comparing Total Mastectomy and Lumpectomy With or Without Irradiation in the Treatment of Breast Cancer." *New England Journal of Medicine* 320:822–828, 1989.

Fisher, S. *The Female Orgasm.* New York: Basic Books, 1973.

Fisher, W. A., and Byrne, D. "Sex Differences in Response to Erotica? Love vs. Lust." *Journal of Personality and Social Psychology* 36:117–125, 1978.

Fisher, W. A., Branscombe, N. R., and Lemery, C. R. "The Bigger the Better? Arousal and Attributional Responses to Erotic Stimuli That Depict Different Size Penises." *Journal of Sex Research* 19:337–396, 1983.

Fishman, H. "Clinical Issues in Treatment-Resistant Depression." *The Psychiatric Times* Supplement, October 1990.

Fitzgerald, L. F., and Ormerod, A. J. "Perceptions of Sexual Harassment." *Psychology of Women Quarterly* 15:281–294, 1991.

FitzGerald, M., and FitzGerald, D. "Deaf People Are Sexual Too!" *SIECUS Report* 6(2):1, 13–15, 1977.

Fitzpatrick, M. A. *Between Husbands and Wives: Communication in Marriage.* Newbury Park, CA: Sage, 1988.

Fleming, M., MacGowan, B., and Costos, D. "The Dyadic Adjustment of Female-to-Male Transsexuals." *Archives of Sexual Behavior* 14:47–55, 1985.

Foderaro, L. "New Focus on Sexual Harassment." *The New York Times*, pp. C1 & C4, July 23, 1986.

Food and Drug Administration. "Panel Recommendations on Silicone Gel-Filled Breast Implants Follow Moratorium." *FDA Medical Bulletin* 22:3–4, 1992.

Ford, C. S., and Beach, F. A. *Patterns of Sexual Behavior.* New York: Harper & Brothers, 1951.

Ford, S., and Thompson, W. C. "A Question of Identity: Some Reasonable Doubts About DNA Fingerprints." *The Sciences*, pp. 37–43, January/February 1990.

Forrest, B. "Women, HIV, and Mucosal Immunity." *Lancet* 337:835–836, 1991.

Forrest, J. D., and Fordyce, R. R. "Women's Contraceptive Attitudes and Use in 1992." *Family Planning Perspectives* 25:175–179, 1993.

Forrest, J. D., and Silverman, J. "What Public School Teachers Teach About Preventing Pregnancy, AIDS and Sexually Transmitted Diseases. *Family Planning Perspectives* 21:65–72, 1989.

Forrest, J. D., and Singh, S. "Public-Sector Savings Resulting from Expenditures for Contraceptive Services." *Family Planning Perspectives* 22:6–15, 1990.

Forrest, K. A., et al. "Vaginal Douching as a Risk Factor for Pelvic Inflammatory Disease." *Journal of the National Medical Association* 81:159–165, 1989.

Foster, R. S., Jr., et al. "Breast Self-Exam Practices and Breast-Cancer Stage." *New England Journal of Medicine* 299:265–270, 1978.

Fox, C. A., and Fox, B. "Blood Pressure and Respiratory Patterns During Human Coitus." *Journal of Reproduction and Fertility* 19:405–415, 1969.

Fraiberg, S. H. *The Magic Years.* New York: Scribner's, 1959.

Francis, D., and Chin, J. "The Prevention of Acquired Immunodeficiency Syndrome in the United States." *Journal of the American Medical Association* 257:1357–1366, 1987.

Francis, D. P. "Toward a Comprehensive HIV Prevention Program for the CDC and the Nation." *Journal of the American Medical Association* 268:1444–1447, 1992.

Francis, D. P., et al. "Targeting AIDS Prevention and Treatment Toward HIV-1-Infected Persons: The Concept of Early Intervention." *Journal of the American Medical Association* 262:2572–2576, 1989.

Francke, L. B. *The Ambivalence of Abortion.* New York: Random House, 1978.

Frank, D., et al. "Mastectomy and Sexual Behavior: A Pilot Study." *Sexuality and Disability* 1:16–26, 1978.

Frank, E., Anderson, C., and Rubinstein, D. "Frequency of Sexual Dysfunction in 'Normal' Couples." *New England Journal of Medicine* 299:111–115, 1978.

Frank, R. "The Hormonal Causes of Premenstrual Tension." *Archives of Neurology and Psychiatry* 26:1053–1057, 1931.

Franzblau, A. N. "Religion and Sexuality." In Freedman, A. M., Kaplan, H. I., and Sadock, B. J. (eds.), *Comprehensive Textbook of Psychiatry/II*, pp. 1599–1608. Baltimore: Williams & Wilkins, 1975.

Frazier, P., and Cohen, B. "Research on the Sexual Victimization of Women." *The Counseling Psychologist* 20:141–158, 1992.

Freed, G. L. "Breast-Feeding." *Journal of the American Medical Association* 269:243–245, 1993.

Freeman, E., et al. "Ineffectiveness of Progesterone Suppository Treatment for Premenstrual Syndrome." *Journal of the American Medical Association* 264:349–353, 1990.

Freud, S. *A General Introduction to Psychoanalysis*. Garden City, NY: Garden City Publishing, 1943.

———. "Formulations Regarding Two Principles in Mental Functioning." In *Selected Papers* 4:13–21. London: Hogarth Press, 1946.

Friday, N. *My Secret Garden*. New York: Trident, 1973.

———. *Forbidden Flowers*. New York: Pocket Books, 1975.

———. *Men in Love*. New York: Delacorte, 1980.

———. *Women on Top*. New York: Pocket Books, 1991.

Fried, P. A. "Postnatal Consequences of Maternal Marijuana Use in Humans." *Annals of the New York Academy of Sciences* 562:123–132, 1989.

Friedland, G., et al. "Lack of Transmission of HTLV-III/LAV Infection to Household Contacts of Patients with AIDS or AIDS-Related Complex with Oral Candidiasis." *New England Journal of Medicine* 314:344–349, 1986.

Friedland, G. H. "Early Treatment for HIV." *New England Journal of Medicine* 322:1000–1002, 1990.

Friedman, H. J. "The Divorced in Middle Age." In Howells, J. G. (ed.), *Modern Perspectives in the Psychiatry of Middle Age*, pp. 103–115. New York: Brunner/Mazel, 1981.

Frieze, I. "Investigating the Causes and Consequences of Marital Rape." *Signs* 8:532–553, 1983.

Frieze, I. H., et al. *Women and Sex Roles: A Social Psychological Perspective*. New York: Norton, 1978.

Frisch, R. E., and McArthur, J. W. "Menstrual Cycles: Fatness as a Determinant of Minimum Weight for Height Necessary for Their Maintenance or Onset." *Science* 185:949–951, 1974.

Frisch, R. E., Wyshak, G., and Vincent, L. "Delayed Menarche and Amenorrhea in Ballet Dancers." *New England Journal of Medicine* 303:17–19, 1980.

Frisell, J., et al. "Randomized Study of Mammography Screening—Preliminary Report on Mortality in the Stockholm Trial." *Breast Cancer Research and Therapy* 18:49–56, 1991.

Froland, S. S., et al. "HIV-1 Infection in a Norwegian Family Before 1970." *Lancet* 1:1344–1345, 1988.

Fromm, E. *The Art of Loving*. New York: Harper & Row, 1956.

Fuchs, E. *The Second Season: Life, Love and Sex for Women in the Middle Years*. Garden City, NY: Anchor Books, 1978.

Fuchs, K., et al. "Vaginismus: The Hypno-Therapeutic Approach." *Journal of Sex Research* 11:39–45, 1975.

Fugger, E. F. "Clinical Status of Human Embryo Cryopreservation in the United States of America," *Fertility & Sterility* 52:986–990, 1989.

Fullilove, M. T., and Fullilove, R. E. "Intersecting Epidemics: Black Teen Crack Use and Sexually Transmitted Disease." *Journal of the American Medical Women's Association* 44:146–153, 1989.

Fullilove, R. E., et al. "Risk of Sexually Transmitted Disease Among Black Adolescent Crack Users in Oakland and San Francisco, Calif." *Journal of the American Medical Association* 263:851–855, 1990.

Furstenberg, F., Jr., Menken, J., and Lincoln, R. *Teenage Sexuality, Pregnancy, and Childbearing*. Philadelphia: University of Pennsylvania Press, 1981.

Furstenberg, F. F., et al. "Race Differences in the Timing of Adolescent Intercourse." *American Sociological Review* 52:511–518, 1987.

Furstenberg, F. F., Jr. "The Social Consequences of Teenage Parenthood." *Family Planning Perspectives* 8:148–164, 1976.

Furstenberg, F. F., Moore, K. A., and Peterson, J. L. "Sex Education and Sexual Experience Among Adolescents." *American Journal of Public Health* 75:1331–1332, 1985.

Gabuzda, D. H., and Hirsch, M. H. "Neurologic Manifestations of Infection with Human Immunodeficiency Virus," *Annals of Internal Medicine* 107:383–391, 1987.

Gadpaille, W. J. *The Cycles of Sex*. New York: Scribner, 1975.

Gager, N., and Schurr, C. *Sexual Assault: Confronting Rape in America*. New York: Grosset & Dunlap, 1976.

Gagnon, J. H. *Human Sexualities*. Glenview, IL: Scott, Foresman, 1977.

———. "Sexuality Across the Life Course in the United States." In Turner, C. F., Miller, H. G., and Moses, L. E. (eds.), *AIDS: Sexual Behavior and Intravenous Drug Use*, pp. 500–536. Washington, DC: National Academy Press, 1989.

Gagnon, J. H., and Simon, W. *Sexual Conduct: The Social Origins of Human Sexuality*. Chicago: Aldine, 1973.

———. "The Sexual Scripting of Oral Genital Contacts." *Archives of Sexual Behavior* 16:1–25, 1987.

Gail, M. H., et al. "Projecting Individualized Probabilities of Developing Breast Cancer for White Females Who Are Being Examined Annually." *Journal of the National Cancer Institute* 81:1879–1886, 1989.

Gambrell, R. D., Jr., et al. "Reduced Incidence of Endometrial Cancer Among Postmenopausal Women Treated with Progestogens." *Journal of the American Geriatrics Society* 27:389–398, 1979.

Ganz, P. A. "Treatment Options for Breast Cancer—Beyond Survival." *New England Journal of Medicine* 326:1147–1149, 1992.

Garrett-Gooding, J., and Senter, R. "Attitudes and Acts of Sexual Aggression on a University Campus." *Sociological Inquiry* 57:348–371, 1987.

Garry, R. F., et al. "Documentation of an AIDS Virus Infection in the United States in 1968." *Journal of the American Medical Association* 260:2085–2087, 1988.

Gartrell, N. K., Loriaux, D. L., and Chase, T. N. "Plasma Testosterone in Homosexual and Heterosexual Women." *American Journal of Psychiatry* 134:117–119, 1977.

Gay, G. R., et al. "Drug–Sex Practice in the Haight-Ashbury or 'The Senses Hippie.'" In Sandler, M., and Gessa, G. L. (eds.), *Sexual Behavior: Pharmacology and Biochemistry*, pp. 63–79. New York: Raven Press, 1975.

Gay, J. "Mummies and Babies and Friends and Lovers in Lesotho." In Blackwood, E. (ed.), *Anthropology and Homosexual Behavior*, pp. 97–116. New York: Haworth Press, 1986.

Gay, P. *The Bourgeois Experience: Victoria to Freud*, Vol. 1: *Education of the Senses*. New York: Oxford University Press, 1983.

Gay Liberation v. *University of Missouri*. [416F.Suppl.1350 (W. D. Mo. 1976)] 1977.

Gebhard, P. H. "Factors in Marital Orgasm." *Journal of Social Issues* 22(4):88–95, 1966.

———. "Postmarital Coitus Among Widows and Divorcees." In Bohannan, P. (ed.), *Divorce and After*. Garden City, NY: Doubleday, 1968.

———. "The Acquisition of Basic Sex Information." *Journal of Sex Research* 13:148–169, 1977.

Gebhard, P., and Johnson, A. B. *The Kinsey Data: Marginal Tabulations of the 1938–1963 Interviews Conducted by the Institute for Sex Research*. Philadelphia: Saunders, 1979.

Gebhard, P., et al. *Sex Offenders: An Analysis of Types*. New York: Harper & Row, 1965.

General Accounting Office. *Sexual Exploitation of Children: A Problem of Unknown Magnitude* (HRD-82-64). Washington, DC: U.S. General Accounting Office, 1982.

George, L. K., and Weiler, S. J. "Sexuality in Middle and Later Life." *Archives of General Psychiatry* 38:919–923, 1981.

Giallombardo, R. *The Social World of Imprisoned Girls*. New York: Wiley, 1974.

Gianelli, D. "Ruling Fuels Abortion Debate." *American Medical News*, pp. 1, 40, June 10, 1991.

Gibbs, C. J., et al. "HIV Immunization and Challenge of HIV Seropositive and Seronegative Chimpanzees." (Abstract #C.Th.C.O. 46, p. 541.) Fifth International Conference on AIDS, Montreal, June 4–9, 1989.

Giesecke, J., et al. "Efficacy of Partner Notification for HIV Infection." *Lancet* 338:1096–1100, 1991.

Gilbaugh, J. H., Jr., and Fuchs, P. C. "The Gonococcus and the Toilet Seat." *New England Journal of Medicine* 301:91–93, 1979.

Gilgun, J. F. "Toward an Explanation of Child Sexual Abuse." Presented at the 26th annual meeting of the Society for the Scientific Study of Sex, Chicago, November 20, 1983.

Gill, W. B., Schumacher, G. F. B., and Bibbo, M. "Pathological Semen and Anatomical Abnormalities of the Genital Tract in Human Male Subjects Exposed to Diethylstilbestrol in Utero." *Journal of Urology* 117:477–480, 1977.

Gillespie, O. *Herpes: What to Do When You Have It*. New York: Grosset & Dunlap, 1982.

Gilman, A. G., Goodman, L. S., and Gilman, A. (eds.) *The Pharmacological Basis of Therapeutics*. New York: Macmillan, 1988.

Gilmartin, B. G. "Sexual Deviance and Social Networks: A Study of Social, Family, and Marital Interaction Patterns Among Co-Marital Sex Participants." In Smith, J. R., and Smith, L. R. (eds.), *Beyond Monogamy*, pp. 291–322. Baltimore: Johns Hopkins University Press, 1974.

Giovannucci, E., et al. "A Long-Term Study of Mortality in Men Who Have Undergone Vasectomy." *New England Journal of Medicine* 326:1392–1398, 1992.

Gissmann, L., and Schwarz, E. "Persistence and Expression of Human Papillomavirus DNA in Genital Cancer." In Everd, D., and Clark, S. (eds.), *Papillomaviruses*, pp. 190–197. Chicester, England: Wiley, 1986.

Gladue, B. A., Green, R., and Hellman, R. E. "Neuroendocrine Response to Estrogen and Sexual Orientation." *Science* 225:1496–1499, 1984.

Glaser, J. B., Strange, T. J., and Rosati, D. "Heterosexual Human Immunodeficiency Virus Transmission Among the Middle Class." *Archives of Internal Medicine* 149:645–649, 1989.

Glaser, R., et al. "Stress, Loneliness, and Herpesvirus Latency." *Journal of Behavioral Medicine* 8:249–260, 1985.

Glass, S. P., and Wright, T. L. "Justification for Extramarital Relationships: The Association between Attitudes, Behaviors, and Gender." *Journal of Sex Research* 29:361–387, 1992.

Glasier, A., et al. "Mifepristone (RU 486) Compared with High-Dose Estrogen and Progestogen for Emergency Postcoital Contraception." *New England Journal of Medicine* 327:1041–1044, 1992.

Gleason, J. B. "Sex Differences in Parent-Child Interaction." In Philips, S. U., Steele, S., and Tanz, C. (eds.) *Language, Gender, and Sex in Comparative Perspective*, pp. 189–199. Cambridge: Cambridge University Press, 1987.

Gochros, J. S. *When Husbands Come Out of the Closet*. New York: Harrington Park Press, 1989.

Goedert, J. J. "A Prospective Study of Human Immunodeficiency Virus Type 1 Infection and the Development of AIDS in Subjects with Hemophilia." *New England Journal of Medicine* 321:1141–1148, 1989.

Goedert, J., et al. "Three Year Incidence of AIDS in Five Cohorts of HTLV-III Infected Risk Groups." *Science* 231:992–995, 1986.

Goldberg, D. C., et al. "The Grafenberg Spot and Female Ejaculation: A Review of Initial Hypotheses." *Journal of Sex and Marital Therapy* 9:27–37, 1983.

Goldberg-Ambrose, C. "Unfinished Business in Rape Law Reform." *Journal of Social Issues* 48:173–185, 1992.

Goldenring, J. M. "Neonatal Circumcision." *New England Journal of Medicine* 323:1205–1206, 1990.

Goldfarb, L. A. "Sexual Abuse Antecedent to Anorexia Nervosa, Bulimia, and Compulsive Overeating: Three Case Reports." *International Journal of Eating Disorders,* 6:675–680, 1987.

Goldman, B. D. "Developmental Influences of Hormones on Neuroendocrine Mechanisms of Sexual Behavior: Comparisons with Other Sexually Dimorphic Behaviors." In Hutchison, J. B. (ed.), *Biological Determinants of Sexual Behavior,* pp. 127–152. New York: Wiley, 1978.

Goldman, L., and Tosteson, A. N. A. "Uncertainty about Postmenopausal Estrogen." *New England Journal of Medicine* 325: 800–802, 1991.

Goldman, R., and Goldman, J. *Children's Sexual Thinking.* Boston: Routledge and Kegal Paul, 1982.

———. "Children's Sexual Thinking: Report of a Cross-national Study." *SIECUS Report* 10(3):3–7, January 1982a.

Goldscheider, F. K., and DaVanzo, J. "Pathways to Independent Living in Early Adulthood: Marriage, Semi-autonomy, and Premarital Residential Independence." *Demography* 26:597–612, 1989.

Goldsmith, M. "Sexually Transmitted Diseases May Reverse the 'Revolution.'" *Journal of the American Medical Association* 255:1665–1672, 1986.

Goldsmith, M. F. "Sex in the Age of AIDS Calls for Common Sense and Condom Sense." *Journal of the American Medical Association* 257:2261–2266, 1987.

———. "Sex Tied to Drugs = STD Spread." *Journal of the American Medical Association* 260:2009, 1988.

———. "'Silent Epidemic' of 'Social Disease' Makes STD Experts Raise Their Voices." *Journal of the American Medical Association* 261:3509–3510, 1989.

———. "As Data on Antiprogesterone Compounds Grows, Societal and Scientific Aspects Are Scrutinized." *Journal of the American Medical Association* 265:1628–1629, 1991.

———. "Specific HIV-related Problems of Women Gain More Attention at a Price—Affecting More Women." *Journal of the American Medical Association* 268:1814–1816, 1992.

Goldstein, I., and Rothstein, L. *The Potent Male: Facts, Fiction, Future.* New York: The Body Press/Perigee Books, 1990.

Goldstein, M. J. "Exposure to Erotic Stimuli and Sexual Deviance." *Journal of Social Issues* 29:197–220, 1973.

Golub, S. "The Effect of Premenstrual Anxiety and Depression on Cognitive Function." *Journal of Personality and Social Psychology* 34:99–104, 1976.

———. (ed.) *Menarche: The Transition from Girl to Woman.* Lexington, MA: Lexington Books, D. C. Heath, 1983.

Goodwin, D. W., and Guze, S. B. *Psychiatric Diagnosis.* New York: Oxford University Press, 1989.

Goodwin, F. K. "Which Kids Use Condoms—Or Don't." *Journal of the American Medical Association* 264:1389, 1990.

Goodwin, J. M., Cheeves, K., and Connell, V. "Borderline and Other Severe Symptoms in Adult Survivors of Incestuous Abuse." *Psychiatric Annals* 20:22–32, 1990.

Goodwin, M. H. *He-Said-She-Said: Talk as Social Organization Among Black Children.* Bloomington: Indiana University Press, 1990.

Gooren, L., Fliers, E., and Courtney, K. "Biological Determinants of Sexual Orientation." *Annual Review of Sex Research* I:175–196, 1990.

Gordis, R. "Designated Discussion." In Masters, W. H., Johnson, V. E., and Kolodny, R. C. (eds.), *Ethical Issues in Sex Therapy and Research,* pp. 32–38. Boston: Little, Brown, 1977.

———. *Love and Sex: A Modern Jewish Perspective.* New York: Farrar, Straus & Giroux, 1978.

Gordon, M. T., and Riger, S. *The Female Fear.* New York: Free Press, 1989.

Gordon, S., and Gordon, J. *Raising a Child Conservatively in a Sexually Permissive World.* New York: Simon & Schuster, 1983.

Gostin, L. O. "Public Health Strategies for Confronting AIDS." *Journal of the American Medical Association* 261:1621–1630, 1989.

Gotlib, I. H., and McCabe, S. B. "Marriage and Psychopathology." In Fincham, F. D., and Bradbury, T. N. (eds.), *The Psychology of Marriage.* New York: Guilford Press, 1990, pp. 226–227.

Gottlieb, B. "Incest: Therapeutic Intervention in a Unique Form of Sexual Abuse." In Warner, C. (ed.), *Rape and Sexual Assault,* pp. 121–140. Germantown, MD: Aspen Systems Corp., 1980.

Gottman, J. M. *Marital Interaction: Experimental Investigations.* New York: Academic Press, 1979.

———. "The Roles of Conflict Engagement, Escalation, and Avoidance in Marital Interaction: A Longitudinal View of Five Types of Couples." *Journal of Consulting and Clinical Psychology* 61:6–15, 1993.

Gottman, J. M., and Krokoff, L. J. "The Relationship Between Marital Interaction and Marital Satisfaction: A Longitudinal View." *Journal of Consulting and Clinical Psychology* 57:47–52, 1989.

Gould, J. B., et al. "Socioeconomic Differences in Rates of Cesarean Sections." *New England Journal of Medicine* 321:233–239, 1989.

Gould, R. L. "Men's Desires: *The Hite Report on Male Sexuality.*" *The New York Times Book Review,* pp. 8–9 & 19, July 12, 1981.

Gould, S. J. "The Terrifying Normalcy of AIDS." *The New York Times Magazine,* pp. 32–33, April 19, 1987.

Goyert, G. L., et al. "The Physician Factor in Cesarean Birth Rates." *New England Journal of Medicine* 320:706–709, 1989.

Graber, B. (ed.). *Circumvaginal Musculature and Sexual Function.* New York: Karger, 1982.

Graber, B., and Kline-Graber, G. "Clitoral Foreskin Adhesions and Female Sexual Function." *Journal of Sex Research* 15:205–212, 1979.

Grad, R., et al. *The Father Book: Pregnancy and Beyond.* Washington, DC: Acropolis Books, 1981.

Grafenberg, E. "The Role of the Urethra in Female Orgasm." *International Journal of Sexology* 3:145–148, 1950.

Graham, S. "Alcohol and Breast Cancer." *New England Journal of Medicine* 316:1211–1213, 1987.

Graham, S., et al. "Sex Patterns and Herpes Simplex Virus Type 2 in the Epidemiology of Cancer of the Cervix." *American Journal of Epidemiology* 115:729–735, 1982.

Granfield, D. *The Abortion Decision.* New York: Doubleday, 1969.

Gray, J. *Men Are From Mars, Women Are From Venus.* New York: HarperCollins, 1993.

Gray, J. P. "Growing Yams and Men: An Interpretation of Kimam Male Ritualized Homosexual Behavior." In Blackwood, E. (ed.), *Anthropology and Homosexual Behavior*, pp. 55–68. New York: Haworth Press, 1986.

Green, A. W. "Sexual Activity and the Postmyocardial Infarction Patient." *American Heart Journal* 89:246–252, 1975.

Green, C. P., and Potteiger, K. "Teenage Pregnancy: A Major Problem for Minors." Washington, DC: Zero Population Growth, 1977.

Green, R. "Homosexuality as a Mental Illness." *International Journal of Psychiatry* 10(1):77–98, 1972.

———. *Sexual Identity Conflict in Children and Adults.* New York: Basic Books, 1974.

———. "Should Homosexuals Adopt Children?" In Brady, J. P., and Brodie, H. K. (eds.), *Controversy in Psychiatry*, pp. 813–828. Philadelphia: Saunders, 1978.

———. "Pornography, Sexual Violence, and Censorship." *Sexual Medicine Today*, p. 32, April 1982.

———. "Gender Identity in Childhood and Later Sexual Orientation." *American Journal of Psychiatry* 142:339–341, 1985.

———. *The "Sissy Boy Syndrome" and the Development of Homosexuality.* New Haven, CT: Yale University Press, 1987.

———. *Sexual Science and the Law.* Cambridge, MA: Harvard University Press, 1992.

Green, R., and Fleming, D. T. "Transsexual Surgery Follow-Up: Status in the 1990s." *Annual Review of Sex Research* I:163–174, 1990.

Green, R., and Money, J. (eds.). *Transsexualism and Sex Reassignment.* Baltimore: Johns Hopkins University Press, 1969.

Greenblatt, C. S. "The Salience of Sexuality in the Early Years of Marriage." *Journal of Marriage and the Family* 45:289–299, 1983.

Greenblatt, R., et al. "Update on the Male and Female Climacteric." *American Geriatrics Society* 27(11):481–490, 1979.

Greendale, G. A., and Judd, H. L. "The Menopause: Health Implications and Clinical Management." *Journal of the American Geriatrics Society* 41:426–436, 1993.

Greendlinger, V., and Byrne, D. "Coercive Sexual Fantasies of College Men as Predictors of Self-Reported Likelihood to Rape and Overt Sexual Aggression." *Journal of Sex Research* 23:1–11, 1987.

Greenfield, S., et al. "Patterns of Care Related Age of Breast Cancer Patients." *Journal of the American Medical Association* 257:2766–2770, 1987.

Greenhouse, S. "A Fierce Battle." *The New York Times Magazine*, pp. 23–26, February 12, 1989.

Greenwald, E., and Leitenberg, H. "Long-Term Effects of Sexual Experiences with Siblings and Nonsiblings During Childhood." *Archives of Sexual Behavior* 18:389–400, 1989.

Greer, D. M., et al. "A Technique for Foreskin Reconstruction and Some Preliminary Results." *Journal of Sex Research* 18:324–330, 1982.

Greer, G. *The Female Eunuch.* New York: Bantam Books, 1972.

Greer, W. R. "Violence Against Homosexuals Rising, Groups Seeking Wider Protection Say." *The New York Times*, p. 36, November 23, 1986.

Greico, A. "Cutting the Risks for STDs." *Medical Aspects of Human Sexuality*, pp. 70–84, March 1987.

Griffin, S. *Pornography and Silence.* New York: Harper & Row, 1981.

Grimes, D. A., and Cook, R. J. "Mifepristone (RU 486)—An Abortifacient to Prevent Abortion?" *New England Journal of Medicine* 327:1088–1089, 1992.

Grob, C. S. "Female Exhibitionism." *Journal of Nervous and Mental Disease* 173:253, 1985.

Grosskopf, D. *Sex and the Married Woman.* New York: Simon & Schuster, 1983.

Grossman, F., Eichler, L., and Winickoff, S. *Pregnancy, Birth and Parenthood.* San Francisco: Jossey-Bass, 1980.

Grossman, R., and Sutherland, J. (eds.). *Surviving Sexual Assault.* New York: Congdon & Weed, 1982/83.

Groth, A. N. *Men Who Rape.* New York: Plenum Press, 1979.

Groth, A. N., and Burgess, A. W. "Sexual Dysfunction During Rape." *New England Journal of Medicine* 297:764–766, 1977.

———. "Male Rape: Offenders and Victims." *American Journal of Psychiatry* 137:806–810, 1980.

Groth, A. N., Burgess, A. W., and Holmstrom, L. "Rape: Power, Anger, and Sexuality." *American Journal of Psychiatry* 134:1239–1243, 1977.

Gruber, J. E. "How Women Handle Sexual Harassment: A Literature Review." *Sociology and Social Research* 74:3–7, 1989.

———. "A Typology of Personal and Environmental Sexual Harassment: Research and Policy Implications for the 1990s." *Sex Roles* 26:447–464, 1992.

Grubin, D. "Sexual Offending Across Cultures." *Annual Review of Sex Research* III:201–217, 1992.

Grumbach, M. "The Neuroendocrinology of Puberty." *Hospital Practice*, pp. 51–60, March 1980.

Gurman, A. S., and Klein, M. "Marital and Family Conflicts." In Brodsky, A. M., and Hare-Mustin, R. (eds.), *Women and Psychotherapy*, pp. 159–188. New York: Guilford Press, 1980.

Gutis, P. S. "Attacks on U.S. Homosexuals Held Alarmingly Widespread." *The New York Times*, p. A24, June 8, 1989.

Guttmacher, Alan, Institute. *Teenage Pregnancy: The Problem That Hasn't Gone Away*. New York: Alan Guttmacher Institute, 1981.

Gutman, D. L. *Reclaimed Powers: Towards a New Psychology of Men and Women in Later Life*. New York: Basic Books, 1987.

Gwinn, M., et al. "Prevalence of HIV Infection in Childbearing Women in the United States." *Journal of the American Medical Association* 265:1704–1708, 1991.

Hacker, H. M. "Blabbermouths and Clams: Sex Differences in Self-disclosure in Same-sex and Cross-sex Friendship Dyads." *Psychology of Women Quarterly* 5:385–401, 1981.

Hadler, S., et al. "Long-Term Immunogenicity and Efficacy of Hepatitis B Vaccine in Homosexual Men." *New England Journal of Medicine* 315:209–214, 1986.

Haggstrom, G. W., et al. *Teenage Parents: Their Ambitions and Attainments*. Santa Monica, CA: Rand Corporation, 1981.

Hahn, R. A., et al. "Prevalence of HIV Infection Among Intravenous Drug Users in the United States." *Journal of the American Medical Association* 261:2677–2684, 1989.

Hahn, S. R., and Paige, K. E. "American Birth Practices: A Critical Review." In Parsons, J. E. (ed.), *The Psychobiology of Sex Differences and Sex Roles*, pp. 145–175. New York: McGraw-Hill/Hemisphere, 1980.

Haimes, A. L., and Katz, J. L. "Sexual and Social Maturity Versus Social Conformity in Restricting Anorectic, Bulimic, and Borderline Women." *International Journal of Eating Disorders* 7:331–341, 1988.

Halbreich, U., Endicott, J., and Nee, J. "Premenstrual Depressive Changes." *Archives of General Psychiatry* 40:535–542, 1983.

Halikas, J., Weller, R., and Morse, C. "Effects of Regular Marihuana Use on Sexual Performance." *Journal of Psychoactive Drugs* 14:59–70, 1982.

Hallagan, J. B., Hallagan, L. F., and Snyder, M. B. "Anabolic–Androgenic Steroid Use by Athletes." *New England Journal of Medicine* 321:1042–1045, 1989.

Haller, J. S., and Haller, R. M. *The Physician and Sexuality in Victorian America*. New York: Norton, 1977.

Hallstrom, T. "Sexuality of Women in Middle Age: The Goteborg Study." *Journal of Biosocial Sciences* (Suppl.) 6:165–175, 1979.

Halmi, K. A. "Anorexia Nervosa." In Kaplan, H. I., and Sadock, B. J. (eds.), *Comprehensive Textbook of Psychiatry*, 4th ed., pp. 1143–1148, Baltimore: Williams & Wilkins, 1985.

Halstead, M. M., and Halstead, L. S. "A Sexual Intimacy Survey of Former Nuns and Priests." *Journal of Sex and Marital Therapy* 4:83–90, 1978.

Hamer, D. H., et al. "A Linkage Between DNA Markers on the X Chromosome and Male Sexual Orientation." *Science* 261:321–327, 1993.

Hand, R., et al. "Hospital Variables Associated with Quality of Care for Breast Cancer Patients." *Journal of the American Medical Association* 266:3429–3432, 1991.

Handsfield, H. "Gonorrhea and Uncomplicated Gonococcal Infection." In Holmes, K. K., et al. (eds.), *Sexually Transmitted Diseases*, pp. 205–220. New York: McGraw-Hill, 1984.

Handsfield, H., et al. "Criteria for Selective Screening for *Chlamydia trachomatis* Infection in Women Attending Family Planning Clinics." *Journal of the American Medical Association* 255:1730–1734, 1986.

Handsfield, H. H., et al. "Localized Outbreak of Penicillinase-Producing *Neisseria gonorrhoeae*." *Journal of the American Medical Association* 261:2357–2361, 1989.

Hanson, S., Morrison, D. R., and Ginsburg, A. L. "The Antecedents of Teenage Fatherhood." *Demography* 26:579–596, 1989.

Harbison, R. D., and Mantilla-Plata, B. "Prenatal Toxicity, Maternal Distribution and Placental Transfer of Tetrahydrocannabinol." *Journal of Pharmacology and Experimental Therapy* 180:446–453, 1972.

Hardy, Janet B., et al. "Fathers of Children Born to Young Urban Mothers." *Family Planning Perspectives* 21:159–163, 187, 1989.

Hariton, E. B., and Singer, J. L. "Women's Fantasies During Marital Intercourse: Normative and Theoretical Implications." *Journal of Consulting and Clinical Psychology* 42(3):313–322, 1974.

Harlap, S. "Gender of Infants Conceived on Different Days of the Menstrual Cycle." *New England Journal of Medicine* 300:1445–1448, 1979.

Harlow, H., and Harlow, M. "The Effect of Rearing Conditions on Behavior." *Bulletin of the Menninger Clinic* 26:213–224, 1962.

Harlow, H. F. "The Nature of Love." *American Psychologist* 13:673–685, 1958.

Harmon, J. W., et al. "Interference with Testicular Development with Δ^9 tetrahydrocannabinol." *Surgical Forum* 27:350–352, 1976.

Harris, J., et al. "Breast Cancer" (first of three parts). *New England Journal of Medicine* 327:319–328, 1992.

Harris, M. B., and Turner, P. H. "Gay and Lesbian Parents." *Journal of Homosexuality* 12(2):101–113, 1986.

Harrison, F. *The Dark Angel: Aspects of Victorian Sexuality*. New York: University Books, 1977.

Harry, Joseph. *Gay Children Grown Up*. New York: Praeger, 1982.

Haskett, R. F., et al. "Severe Premenstrual Tension: Delineation of the Syndrome." *Biological Psychiatry* 15:121–139, 1980.

Hass, A. *Teenage Sexuality*. New York: Macmillan, 1979.

Hatfield, E. "Passionate Love, Companionate Love, and Intimacy." In Fisher, M., and Stricker, G. (eds.), *Intimacy*, pp. 267–292. New York: Plenum Press, 1982.

———. "Passionate and Companionate Love." In Sternberg, R. J., and Barnes, M. L. (eds.), *The Psychology of Love*, pp. 191–217. New Haven, CT: Yale University Press, 1988.

Hatfield, E., and Rapson, R. L. *Love, Sex, and Intimacy*. New York: HarperCollins, 1993.

Hatfield, E., and Sprecher, S. "Measuring Passionate Love in Intimate Relations." *Journal of Adolescence* 9:383–410, 1986.

Hatterer, L. J. *Changing Homosexuality in the Male*. New York: McGraw-Hill, 1970.

Haverkos, H. W., and Edelman, R. "The Epidemiology of Acquired Immunodeficiency Syndrome Among Heterosexuals." *Journal of the American Medical Association* 260:1922–1929, 1988.

Hawton, K. "Sex Therapy Research: Has It Withered on the Vine?" *Annual Review of Sex Research* III:49–72, 1992.

Hawton, K., Catalan, J., and Fagg, J. "Sex Therapy for Erectile Dysfunction: Characteristics of Couples, Treatment Outcome, and Prognostic Factors." *Archives of Sexual Behavior* 21:161–175, 1992.

Haynes, B. F. "Scientific and Social Issues of Human Immunodeficiency Virus Vaccine Development." *Science* 260:1279–1286, 1993.

Hays, D., and Samuels, A. "Heterosexual Women's Perceptions of Their Marriages to Bisexual or Homosexual Men." *Journal of Homosexuality* 18(1/2):81–100, 1989.

Hazard, C. *Feminine Self-Concept in Bulimic Women*. Unpublished manuscript, Texas A&M University, 1985; cited in Johnson and Connors, 1985.

Hazelwood, R. R., Dietz, P. E., and Burgess, A. W. "The Investigation of Autoerotic Fatalities." *Journal of Police Science and Administration* 9:404–411, 1981.

Heaton, D. "Out of the Closet." *Women's Sports and Fitness*, pp. 60–66, September 1992.

Hegger, S. "Falling in Love Again . . . and Again . . . and Again." *The Riverfront Times* (St. Louis), pp. 17–19, January 26, 1983.

Heilman, M. E. "Sex Discrimination." In Wolman, B. E., and Money, J. (eds.), *Handbook of Human Sexuality*, pp. 227–249, Englewood Cliffs, NJ: Prentice-Hall, 1980.

Heiman, J. "A Psychophysiological Exploration of Sexual Arousal Patterns in Females and Males." *Psychophysiology* 14:266–274, 1977.

———. "Female Sexual Response Patterns." *Archives of General Psychiatry* 37:1311–1316, 1980.

Heiman, J. R., and LoPiccolo, J. *Becoming Orgasmic: A Sexual and Personal Growth Program for Women*, rev. ed. New York: Simon & Schuster, 1988.

Heinlein, R. *Stranger in a Strange Land*. New York: Putnam, 1961.

Heinonen, O. P., et al. "Cardiovascular Birth Defects and Antenatal Exposure to Female Sex Hormones." *New England Journal of Medicine* 296:67–70, 1977.

Helsinga, K. *Not Made of Stone: The Sexual Problems of Handicapped People*. Springfield, IL: Charles C. Thomas, 1974.

Hembree, W. C., Zeidenberg, P., and Nahas, G. G. "Marihuana Effects upon Human Gonadal Function." In Nahas, G. G. (ed.), *Marihuana: Chemistry, Biochemistry and Cellular Effects*. New York: Springer-Verlag, 1976.

Henderson, B. E., Paganini-Hill, A., and Ross, R. K. "Decreased Mortality in Use of Estrogen Replacement Therapy." *Archives of Internal Medicine* 151:75–78, 1991.

Henderson, D. K., et al. "Risk for Occupational Transmission of Human Immunodeficiency Virus Type 1 (HIV-1) Associated with Clinical Exposures." *Annals of Internal Medicine* 113:740–746, 1990.

Hendricks, S. E., Graber, B., and Rodrigues-Sierra, J. F. "Neuroendocrine Responses to Exogenous Estrogen: No Differences Between Heterosexual and Homosexual Men." *Psychoneuroendocrinology* 14:177–185, 1989.

Henshaw, S. K. "Abortion Trends in 1987 and 1988: Age and Race." *Family Planning Perspectives* 24:85–86, 1992.

Henshaw, S. K., and O'Reilly, K. "Characteristics of Abortion Patients in the United States, 1979 and 1980." *Family Planning Perspectives* 15(1):5–15, 1983.

Henshaw, S. K., and Silverman, J. "The Characteristics and Prior Contraceptive Use of U.S. Abortion Patients." *Family Planning Perspectives* 20:158–168, 1988.

Henshaw, S. K., and Van Vort, J. "Teenage Abortion, Birth, and Pregnancy Statistics: An Update. *Family Planning Perspectives* 21:85–88, 1989.

———. (eds.). *Abortion Factbook, 1992 Edition: Readings, Trends, and State and Local Data to 1988*. New York: Alan Guttmacher Institute, 1992.

Henson, C., Rubin, H. B., and Henson, D. E. "Women's Sexual Arousal Concurrently Assessed by Three Genital Measures." *Archives of Sexual Behavior* 8:459–479, 1979.

Herbst, A. L., Ulfelder, H., and Poskanzer, D. C. "Adenocarcinoma of the Vagina: Association of Maternal Stilbestrol Therapy with Tumor Appearance in Young Women." *New England Journal of Medicine* 284:878–881, 1971.

Herdt, G. *Guardians of the Flutes: Idioms of Masculinity*. New York: McGraw-Hill, 1981.

———. (ed.). *Ritualized Homosexuality in Melanesia*. Berkeley: University of California Press, 1984.

———. *The Sambia: Ritual and Gender in New Guinea*. New York: Holt, Rinehart and Winston, 1986.

Herman, J., and Hirschman, L. "Father–Daughter Incest." *Journal of Women in Culture and Society* 2:735–756, 1977.

Herman, W. A., et al. "A Simulated Physiologic Test of Latex Condoms." (Abstract # W.A.P. 101, p. 136.) Presented at the Fifth International Conference on AIDS, Montreal, Canada, June 4–9, 1989.

Herzberg, B. N., et al. "Oral Contraceptives, Depression, and Libido." *British Medical Journal* 3:495–500, 1971.

Herzog, L. W. "Urinary Tract Infections and Circumcision: A Case–Control Study." *American Journal of Diseases of Children* 143:348–350, 1989.

Heston, L., and Shields, J. "Homosexuality in Twins." *Archives of General Psychiatry* 18:149–160, 1968.

Heyn, D. *The Erotic Silence of the American Housewife.* New York: Random House, 1992.

Heywood, W. L., and Curran, J. W. "The Epidemiology of AIDS in the U.S." *Scientific American* 259(4):72–81, 1988.

Hicks, D. R., et al. "Inactivation of HTLV-III-Infected Cultures of Normal Human Lymphocytes by Nonoxynol-9 in Vitro." *Lancet* ii:1422–1423, 1985.

Hicks, J. M., and Iosefsohn, M. "Reliability of Home Pregnancy-Test Kits in the Hands of Laypersons." *New England Journal of Medicine* 320:320–321, 1989.

Hiebert, W. J. "Intimacy, Limits, and Lake Wobegon." *Family Therapy News*, 18:7, January/February 1987.

Hier, D. B., and Crowley, W. F., Jr. "Spatial Ability in Androgen-Deficient Men." *New England Journal of Medicine* 306:1202–1205, 1982.

Higham, E. "Sexuality in the Infant and Neonate: Birth to Two Years." In Wolman, B. B., and Money, J. (eds.), *Handbook of Human Sexuality*, pp. 16–27. Englewood Cliffs, NJ: Prentice-Hall, 1980.

Hilberman, E. "Rape: The Ultimate Violation of the Self." *American Journal of Psychiatry* 133:436, 1976.

———. "The Impact of Rape." In Notman, M., and Nadelson, C. (eds.), *The Woman Patient*, Vol. 1, pp. 303–322. New York: Plenum Press, 1978.

Hill, C. T., Rubin, Z., and Peplau, L. A. "Breakups Before Marriage: The End of 103 Affairs." *Journal of Social Issues* 32:147–168, 1976.

Hill, I. (ed.). *The Bisexual Spouse.* New York: Harper & Row, 1989.

Hillier, S., and Holmes, K. K. "Bacterial Vaginosis." In Holmes, K. K., et al. (eds.), *Sexually Transmitted Diseases*, 2nd ed. New York: McGraw-Hill, 1990.

Hilton, E., et al. "Ingestion of Yogurt Containing *Lactobacillus acidophilus* as Prophylaxis for Vaginal Candidal Vaginitis." *Annals of Internal Medicine* 116:353–357, 1992.

Hilts, P. J. "World AIDS Epidemic Draws New Warnings." *The New York Times*, p. D19, December 1, 1989.

Hirsch, M. S., and Schooley, R. T. "Resistance to Antiviral Drugs: The End of Innocence." *New England Journal of Medicine* 320:313–314, 1989.

Hite, S. *The Hite Report.* New York: Dell, 1976.

———. *The Hite Report on Male Sexuality.* New York: Alfred A. Knopf, 1981.

———. *Women and Love.* New York: Knopf, 1987.

Ho, D. D., et al. "The Acquired Immunodeficiency Syndrome (AIDS) Dementia Complex." *Annals of Internal Medicine* 111:400–410, 1989.

Hockenberry, S. L., and Billingham, R. E. "Sexual Orientation and Boyhood Gender Conformity." *Archives of Sexual Behavior* 16:475–482, 1987.

Hoffman, M. "Homosexuality." In Beach, F. (ed.), *Human Sexuality in Four Perspectives*, pp. 164–189. Baltimore: Johns Hopkins University Press, 1977.

Hoffman, R. J. "Some Cultural Aspects of Greek Male Homosexuality." *Journal of Homosexuality* 5(3):217–226, 1980.

Hogge, W., Schonberg, S., and Golbus, M. "Chorionic Villus Sampling: Experience of the First 1,000 Cases." *American Journal of Obstetrics and Gynecology* 154:1249–1252, 1986.

Hogue, C. J. "Impact of Abortion on Subsequent Fecundity." *Clinical Obstetrics and Gynecology* 13:951, 1986.

Holden, C. "House Chops Sex-Pot Probe." *Science* 192:450, 1976.

Holden, C. "Koop Finds Abortion Evidence 'Inconclusive'." *Science* 243:730–731, 1989.

Hollender, M. H. "Women's Sexual Fantasies During Intercourse." *Archives of General Psychiatry* 8:86–90, 1963.

———. "Women's Wish to Be Held: Sexual and Nonsexual Aspects." *Medical Aspects of Human Sexuality* 5(10):12–26, 1971.

Hollender, M. H., Brown, C. W., and Roback, H. B. "Genital Exhibitionism in Women." *American Journal of Psychiatry* 134:436–438, 1977.

Holmberg, S. D., et al. "Prior Herpes Simplex Virus Type 2 Infection as a Risk Factor for HIV Infection." *Journal of the American Medical Association* 259:1048–1050, 1988.

Holmes et al. (eds.). *Sexually Transmitted Diseases*, 2nd ed. New York: McGraw-Hill, 1990.

Holmes, K. K. "Syphilis." In Isselbacher, K. J., et al. (eds.), *Harrison's Principles of Internal Medicine*, 9th ed., pp. 716–726. New York: McGraw-Hill, 1980.

Holmes, K. K., et al. (eds.). *Sexually Transmitted Diseases*, 2nd ed. New York: McGraw-Hill, 1989.

Holmes, L. "Vaginal Spermicides and Congenital Disorders: The Validity of a Study." *Journal of the American Medical Association* 256:3096, 1986.

Hoofnagle, J. H. "Type D (Delta) Hepatitis." *Journal of the American Medical Association* 261:1321–1325, 1989.

———. "Toward Universal Vaccination Against Hepatitis B Virus." *New England Journal of Medicine* 321:1333–1334, 1989a.

Hooker, E. "The Adjustment of the Male Overt Homosexual." *Journal of Projective Techniques* 21:18–31, 1957.

Hooper, R. R., et al. "Cohort Study of Veneral Disease, I: The Risks of Gonorrhea Transmission from Infected

Women to Men." *American Journal of Epidemiology* 108:136–144, 1978.

Hoorwitz, A. N. *The Clinical Detective: Techniques in the Evaluation of Sexual Abuse.* New York: Norton, 1992.

Hoover, R. N., Gray, L. A., and Fraumeni, J. D., Jr. "Stilbestrol (Diethylstilbestrol) and the Risk of Ovarian Cancer." *Lancet* 2:533–534, 1977.

Hopkins, J. R. "Sexual Behavior in Adolescence." *Journal of Social Issues* 33(2):67–85, 1977.

Hopkins, K. R., and Johnston, W. B. *The Incidence of HIV Infection in the United States,* Indianapolis: Hudson Institute, 1988.

Hosken, F. P. *The Hosken Report: Genital and Sexual Mutilation of Females,* 2nd ed. Lexington, MA: Women's International Network News, 1979.

Howard, L., et al. "Evaluation of Chlamydiazyme for the Detection of Genital Infection Caused by *Chlamydia trachomatis.*" *Journal of Clinical Microbiology* 23:329–332, 1986.

Howard, M., and McCabe, J. B. "Helping Teenagers Postpone Sexual Involvement." *Family Planning Perspectives* 22:21–26, 1990.

Howells, J. G. (ed.). *Modern Perspectives in the Psychiatry of Middle Age.* New York: Brunner/Mazel, 1981.

Hubbard, R. "The Search for Sexual Identity." *The New York Times,* p. A15, August 2, 1993.

Hudak, M. A. "Gender Schema Theory Revisited: Men's Stereotypes of American Women." *Sex Roles* 28:279–293, 1993.

Hudson, W. W., and Ricketts, W. A. "A Strategy for the Measurement of Homophobia." *Journal of Homosexuality* 5:357–372, 1980.

Huggins, S. L. "A Comparative Study of Self-Esteem of Adolescent Children of Divorced Lesbian Mothers and Divorced Heterosexual Mothers." *Journal of Homosexuality* 18(1/2):123–135, 1989.

Humphreys, L. *Tearoom Trade: Impersonal Sex in Public Restrooms.* Chicago: Aldine, 1970.

Hunt, D. D., Carr, J. E., and Hampson, J. L. "Cognitive Correlates of Biologic Sex and Gender Identity in Transsexualism." *Archives of Sexual Behavior* 10:65–78, 1981.

Hunt, M. *Sexual Behavior in the 1970s.* New York: Dell, 1975.

———. "The Future of Marriage." In DeBurger, J. E. (ed.), *Marriage Today,* pp. 683–698. New York: Wiley, 1977.

Hutchison, J. B. (ed.). *Biological Determinants of Sexual Behavior.* New York: Wiley, 1978.

Hunter, N. D., and Rubenstein, W. B. (eds.). *AIDS Agenda: Emerging Issues in Civil Rights.* New York: The New Press, 1992.

Hurlbert, D. F., and Whittaker, K. E. "The Role of Masturbation in Marital and Sexual Satisfaction: A Comparative Study of Female Masturbators and Nonmasturbators." *Journal of Sex Education & Therapy* 17:272–282, 1991.

Hyde, J. S., Krajnik, M., and Skuldt-Niederberger, K. "Androgyny Across the Life-span: A Replication and Longitudinal Follow-up." *Developmental Psychology* 27:516–519, 1991.

Hyde, J. S., and Phillis, D. E. "Androgyny Across the Life Span." *Developmental Psychology* 15:334–336, 1979.

Illa, R. V. "Possible Salivary Transmission of AIDS: Case Report." Abstract #3.6. First International Symposium on Oral AIDS, Montreal, June 1–3, 1989.

Imagawa, D. T., et al. "Human Immunodeficiency Virus Type 1 Infection in Homosexual Men Who Remain Seropositive for Prolonged Periods." *New England Journal of Medicine* 320:1458–1462, 1989.

Imperato-McGinley, J., and Peterson, R. "Male Pseudohermaphroditism: The Complexities of Male Phenotypic Development." *American Journal of Medicine* 61:251–272, 1976.

Imperato-McGinley, J., et al. "Androgens and the Evolution of Male-Gender Identity Among Male Pseudohermaphrodites with 5a-Reductase Deficiency." *New England Journal of Medicine* 300(22):1233–1237, 1979.

Innala, S. M., and Ernulf, K. E. "Asphyxiophilia in Scandinavia." *Archives of Sexual Behavior* 18:181–189, 1989.

Inoue, M., et al. "Human Papillomavirus (HPV) Type 16 in Semen of Partners of Women with HPV Infection." *Lancet* 339:1114–1115, 1992.

Institute of Medicine/National Academy of Sciences. *Confronting AIDS: Directions for Public Health, Health Care, and Research.* Washington, DC: National Academy Press, 1986.

———. *Confronting AIDS: Update 1988.* Washington, DC: National Academy Press, 1988.

———. *Confronting AIDS: Update.* Washington, DC: National Academy Press, 1989.

Jacobelis v. *Ohio.* 378 U.S. 184 (1965).

Jacobs, L. S., et al. "Primary Microsurgery for Postinflammatory Tubal Infertility." *Fertility & Sterility* 50:855–859, 1988.

Jacobson, N. S. "The Politics of Intimacy." *Behavior Therapist* 12(2):29–32, 1989.

Jaffe, J. H. "Drug Addiction and Drug Abuse." In Gilman, A. S., Goodman, L. S., and Gilman, A. (eds.), *The Pharmacological Basis of Therapeutics,* pp. 535–583. New York: Macmillan, 1980.

Jaffe, L., et al. "Anal Intercourse and Knowledge of AIDS Among Minority-Group Adolescents." *Journal of Pediatrics* 112:1005–1007, 1988.

James, Robin. "HIV Testing and Counseling: Crisis and Coping for Adolescents and Adults." In Anderson, G. (ed.), *Courage to Care,* pp. 271–283. Washington, DC: Child Welfare League of America, 1990.

James, W. *The Principles of Psychology.* New York: Dover, 1950. (Originally published in 1890.)

James, W. H. "Coital Rates and the Pill." *Nature* 234:555–556, 1971.

Jamison, P. L., and Gebhard, P. G. "Penis Size Increase Between Flaccid and Erect States: An Analysis of the Kinsey Data." *Journal of Sex Research* 24:177–183, 1988.

Janerich, D. T., Piper, J. M., and Glebatis, D. M. "Oral Contraceptives and Congenital Limb-Reduction Defects." *New England Journal of Medicine* 291:697–700, 1974.

Jani, N. N., and Wise, T. N. "Antidepressants and Inhibited Female Orgasm: A Literature Review." *Journal of Sex & Marital Therapy* 14:279–284, 1988.

Janssen, R. S. "HIV Infection Among Patients in U.S. Acute Care Hospitals." *New England Journal of Medicine* 327:445–452, 1992.

Jelliffe, D. B. "Community and Sociopolitical Considerations of Breast-Feeding." In Ciba Foundation Symposium 45 (new series), *Breast-Feeding and the Mother*, pp. 231–245. New York: Elsevier/North-Holland, 1976.

Jenkins v. *Georgia.* 418 U.S. 153 (1974).

Jensen, G. D. "Childhood Sexuality." In Green, R. (ed.), *Human Sexuality: A Health Practitioner's Text*, 2nd ed., pp. 46–57. Baltimore: Williams & Wilkins, 1979.

———. "Cross-cultural Studies and Animal Studies of Sex." In Kaplan, H. I., Freedman, A. M., and Sadock, B. J. (eds.), *Comprehensive Textbook of Psychiatry/III*, pp. 1723–1734. Baltimore: Williams & Wilkins, 1980.

Jensen, P., et al. "Sexual Dysfunction in Male and Female Patients with Epilepsy: A Study of 86 Outpatients." *Archives of Sexual Behavior* 19:1–14, 1990.

Jensen, S. "Sexual Dysfunction in Insulin-Treated Diabetics." *Archives of Sexual Behavior* 15:271–283, 1986.

Jessor, S. L., and Jessor, R. "Transition from Virginity to Nonvirginity Among Youth: A Social–Psychological Study Over Time." *Developmental Psychology* 11:473–484, 1975.

———. *Problem Behavior and Psychosocial Development: A Longitudinal Study of Youth.* New York: Academic Press, 1977.

Jick, H., et al. "Myocardial Infarction and Other Vascular Diseases in Young Women: Role of Estrogens and Other Factors." *Journal of the American Medical Association* 240:2548–2552, 1978.

———. "Replacement Estrogens and Breast Cancer." *American Journal of Epidemiology* 112:586, 1980.

———. "Vaginal Spermicides and Congenital Disorders." *Journal of the American Medical Association* 245(13):1329–1332, 1981.

———. "Vaginal Spermicides and Gonorrhea." *Journal of the American Medical Association* 248:1619–1621, 1982.

Johansson, J., et al. "High 10-Year Survival Rate in Patients with Early, Untreated Prostatic Cancer." *Journal of the American Medical Association* 267:2191–2196, 1992.

Johnson, A. M., et al. "Sexual Lifestyles and HIV Risk." *Nature* 360:410–412, 1992.

Johnson, C., and Connors, M. E. *The Etiology and Treatment of Bulimia Nervosa.* New York: Basic Books, 1987.

Johnson, D. "Privacy vs. the Pursuit of Gay Rights." *The New York Times*, p. A21, March 27, 1990.

Johnson, J. H. "Weighing the Evidence on the Pill and Breast Cancer." *Family Planning Perspectives* 21:89–92, 1989.

Johnson, M. I., and Hoth, D. F. "Present Status and Future Prospects for HIV Therapies." *Science* 260:1279–1286, 1993.

Johnson, R. E., et al. "A Seroepidemiologic Survey of the Prevalence of Herpes Simplex Virus Type 2 Infection in the United States." *New England Journal of Medicine* 321:7–12, 1989.

Johnson, V. E., and Masters, W. H. "Intravaginal Contraceptive Study, Phase I: Anatomy." *Western Journal of Surgery, Obstetrics, and Gynecology* 70:202–207, 1962.

Jonas, H. S., and Dooley, S. L. "The Search for a Lower Cesarean Rate Goes On." *Journal of the American Medical Association* 262:1512–1513, 1989.

Jones, E. F., and Forrest, J. D. "Contraceptive Failure in the United States: Revised Estimates from the 1982 National Survey of Family Growth." *Family Planning Perspectives* 21:103–109, 1989.

Jones, H. W., Jr., and Schrader, C. "And Just What Is A Pre-Embryo?" *Fertility & Sterility* 52:189–191, 1989.

Jones, J. L., et al. "Partner Acceptance of Health Department Notification of HIV Exposure, South Carolina." *Journal of the American Medical Association* 264:1284–1286, 1990.

Jones, K. L., et al. "Pattern of Malformations in the Children of Women Treated with Carbamazepine During Pregnancy." *New England Journal of Medicine* 320:1661–1666, 1989.

Jones, R. B., et al. "Recovery of *Chlamydia trachomatis* from the Endometrium of Women at Risk for Chlamydial Infection." *American Journal of Obstetrics and Gynecology* 155:35–39, 1986.

Jones, R. T. "Human Effects." In Petersen, R. C. (ed.), *Marihuana Research Findings: 1976*, pp. 128–178. NIDA Dept. of HEW (ADM) 78–501. Washington, DC: U.S. Government Printing Office, 1976.

Jones, T. S., and Remland, M. S. "Sources of Variability in Perceptions of and Responses to Sexual Harassment." *Sex Roles* 27:121–141, 1992.

Jong, E. *Fear of Flying.* New York: Signet, 1974.

Joseph, D., Bruskewitz, R., and Benson, R. "Long-Term Evaluation of the Inflatable Penile Prosthesis." *Journal of Urology* 131:670–673, 1984.

Joseph, R. A., Markus, H. R., and Tafarodi, R. W. "Gender and Self-esteem." *Journal of Personality & Social Psychology* 63:391–402, 1992.

Jost, A. "Problems of Fetal Endocrinology: The Gonadal and Hypophyseal Hormones." *Recent Progress in Hormone Research* 8:379–418, 1953.

————. "A New Look at Mechanisms Controlling Sex Differentiation in Mammals." *Johns Hopkins Medical Journal* 130:38–53, 1972.

Joyce, J. *Ulysses*. New York: Random House, 1961.

Judson, F. "Fear of AIDS and Gonorrhea Rates in Homosexual Men." *Lancet* ii:159–160, 1983.

Kaeser, L. "Reconsidering Age Limits on Pill Use." *Family Planning Perspectives* 21:273–274, 1989.

Kagan, J. "Psychology of Sex Differences." In Beach, F. (ed.), *Human Sexuality in Four Perspectives*, pp. 87–114. Baltimore: Johns Hopkins University Press, 1976.

Kaiser, F. E., et al. "Impotence and Aging: Clinical and Hormonal Factors." *Journal of the American Geriatric Society* 36:511–519, 1988.

Kallen, D. J., Stephenson, J. J., and Doughty, A. "The Need to Know: Recalled Adolescent Sources of Sexual and Contraceptive Information and Sexual Behavior." *Journal of Sex Research* 19:137–159, 1983.

Kallman, F. J. "Comparative Twin Study on the Genetic Aspects of Male Homosexuality." *Journal of Nervous and Mental Disease* 115:283–298, 1952.

Kalter, H., and Warkany, J. "Congenital Malformations." *New England Journal of Medicine* 308:491–497, 1983.

Kanin, E. "Selected Dyadic Aspects of Male Sex Aggression." *Journal of Sex Research* 5:12–28, 1969.

————. "Date Rapists: Differential Sexual Socialization and Relative Deprivation." *Archives of Sexual Behavior* 14:219–231, 1985.

Kanki, P., et al. "New Human T-Lymphotropic Retrovirus Related to Simian T-Lymphotropic Virus Type III (STLV III)." *Science* 232:238–243, 1986.

Kanter, R. M. *Men and Women of the Corporation*. New York: Basic Books, 1977.

Kantner, J. F., and Zelnik, M. "Sexual Experiences of Young Unmarried Women in the U.S." *Family Planning Perspectives* 4(4):9–17, 1972.

————. "Contraception and Pregnancy: Experience of Young Unmarried Women in the United States." *Family Planning Perspectives* 5:21–35, 1973.

Kaplan, A. "Clarifying the Concept of Androgyny: Implications for Therapy." *Psychology of Women Quarterly* 3:223–230, 1979.

Kaplan, A., and Sedney, M. A. *Psychology and Sex Roles: An Androgynous Perspective*. Boston: Little, Brown, 1980.

————. Kaplan, H. *The Evaluation of Sexual Disorders*. New York: Brunner/Mazel, 1983.

Kaplan, H. S. *The New Sex Therapy*. New York: Brunner/Mazel, 1974.

————. *The Illustrated Manual of Sex Therapy*. New York: Quadrangle/New York Times, 1975.

————. *Disorders of Sexual Desire*. New York: Brunner/Mazel, 1979.

————. *How to Overcome Premature Ejaculation*. New York: Brunner/Mazel, 1989.

Kaplan, J. E., et al. "Lymphadenopathy Syndrome in Homosexual Men." *Journal of the American Medical Association* 257:335–337, 1987.

Kaplowitz, L. G., et al. "Prolonged Continuous Acyclovir Treatment of Normal Adults with Frequently Recurring Genital Herpes Simplex Virus Infection." *Journal of the American Medical Association* 265:747–751, 1991.

Karbon, M., et al. "Preschoolers' Beliefs About Sex and Age Differences in Emotionality." *Sex Roles* 27:377–390, 1992.

Karlen, A. *Sexuality and Homosexuality: A New View*. New York: Norton, 1971.

————. "Homosexuality in History." In Marmor, J. (ed.), *Homosexual Behavior*, pp. 75–99. New York: Basic Books, 1980.

————. *Threesomes*. New York: Beech Tree Books, 1988.

Karmel, M. *Thank You, Dr. Lamaze*. Philadelphia: Lippincott, 1959.

Kasan, P. N., and Andrews, J. "Oral Contraception and Congenital Anomalies." *British Journal of Obstetrics and Gynaecology* 87:548–551, 1980.

Kasl, C. D. *Women, Sex, and Addiction*. New York: Ticknor & Fields, 1989.

Kassel, V. "Sex in Nursing Homes." *Medical Aspects of Human Sexuality* 10(3):129–131, March 1976.

Katchadourian, H. *The Biology of Adolescence*. San Francisco: W. H. Freeman, 1977.

Kaufman, D. W., et al. "Decreased Risk of Endometrial Cancer Among Oral Contraceptive Users." *New England Journal of Medicine* 303:1045–1047, 1980.

Kay, C. R., and Hannaford, P. C. "Breast Cancer and the Pill." *British Journal of Cancer* 58:675–680, 1988.

Keating, J. N., et al. "Evidence of Brain Methyltransferase Inhibition and Early Brain Involvement in HIV-positive Patients." *Lancet* 337:935–939, 1991.

Kegel, A. "Sexual Functions of the Pubococcygeus Muscle." *Western Journal of Surgery, Obstetrics, and Gynecology* 60:521–524, 1952.

Kegeles, S., Adler, N., and Irwin, C., Jr. "Sexually Active Adolescents and Condoms: Changes Over One Year in Knowledge, Attitudes, and Use." *American Journal of Public Health* 78:460–461, 1988.

Kelley, D. B., and Pfaff, D. W. "Generalizations from Comparative Studies on Neuroanatomical and Endocrine Mechanisms of Sexual Behavior." In Hutchison, J. B. (ed.), *Biological Determinants of Sexual Behavior*, pp. 225–254. New York: Wiley, 1978.

Kelly, J. A., et al. "Situational Factors Associated with AIDS Risk Behavior Lapses and Coping Strategies Used by Gay Men to Successfully Avoid Lapses." *American Journal of Public Health* 81:1335–1338, 1991.

————. "Acquired Immunodeficiency Syndrome/Human Immunodeficiency Virus Risk Behavior Among Gay Men in Small Cities." *Archives of Internal Medicine* 152:2293–2297, 1992.

Kemeny, M. E., et al. "Psychological and Immunological Predictors of Genital Herpes Recurrence." *Psychosomatic Medicine* 51:195–208, 1989.

Kempton, W. "Sex Education for the Mentally Handicapped." *Sex and Disability* 1(2):137–146, 1978.

Kenig, S., and Ryan, J. "Sex Differences in Levels of Tolerance and Attribution of Blame for Sexual Harassment on a University Campus." *Sex Roles* 15:422–438, 1986.

Kennard, E. A. D., et al. "A Program for Matched, Anonymous Oocyte Donation." *Fertility & Sterility* 51:655–660, 1989.

Kennedy, J. G. "Circumcision and Excision in Egyptian Nubia." *Man* 5:175–191, 1970.

Kennedy, L. "Human Papillomavirus: A Study of Male Sexual Partners." *Medical Journal of Australia* 149:309–311, 1988.

Kennedy, S., and Over, R. "Psychophysiological Assessment of Male Sexual Arousal Following Spinal Cord Injury." *Archives of Sexual Behavior* 19:15–28, 1990.

Kenney, A. M., Guardad, S., and Brown, L. "Sex Education and AIDS Education in the Schools." *Family Planning Perspectives* 21:56–64, 1989.

Kern, S. "Freud and the Discovery of Child Sexuality." *History of Childhood Quarterly* 1:117–141, 1973.

Kessler, I. I. "On the Etiology and Prevention of Cervical Cancer: A Status Report." *Obstetrics and Gynecological Survey* 34:790–794, 1979.

Keye, W. R. "Update: Premenstrual Syndrome." *Endocrine & Fertility Forum* 6(4):1–3, Fall 1983.

Kilmann, P. R., et al. "The Treatment of Sexual Paraphilias: A Review of the Outcome Research." *Journal of Sex Research* 18:193–252, 1982.

Kilpatrick, A. C. *Long-Range Effects of Child and Adolescent Sexual Experiences: Myths, Mores, and Menaces.* Hillsdale, NJ: Lawrence Erlbaum, 1992.

Kimball, M. M. "A New Perspective on Women's Math Achievement." *Psychological Bulletin* 105:198–214, 1989.

Kimmel, D. "Adult Development and Aging: A Gay Perspective." *Journal of Social Issues* 34(3):113–130, 1978.

King, M., and McDonald, E. "Homosexuals Who Are Twins: A Study of 46 Probands." *British Journal of Psychiatry* 160:407–409, 1992.

King, S. "Not Everyone Agrees with New Mammographic Screening Guidelines Designed to End Confusion." *Journal of the American Medical Association* 262:1154–1155, 1989.

Kingsley, L. A., et al. "Sexual Transmission Efficiency of Hepatitis B Virus and Human Immunodeficiency Virus Among Homosexual Men." *Journal of the American Medical Association* 264:230–234, 1990.

Kinsey, A. C., et al. *Sexual Behavior in the Human Female.* Philadelphia: Saunders, 1953.

Kinsey, A. C., Pomeroy, W. B., and Martin, C. E. *Sexual Behavior in the Human Male.* Philadelphia: Saunders, 1948.

Kirby, D., Alter, J., and Scales, P. *An Analysis of U.S. Sex Education Programs and Evaluation Methods.* Atlanta, GA: U.S. Department of Health, Education, and Welfare, Public Health Service, Centers for Disease Control, Bureau of Health Education, Report CDC-2021-79-DK-FR, 1979.

Kirby, D., et al. "A Direct Mailing to Teenage Males About Condom Use." *Family Planning Perspectives* 21:12–18, 1989.

Kirkham, G. L. "Homosexuality in Prison." In Henslin, J. M. (ed.), *Studies in the Sociology of Sex.* New York: Appleton-Century-Crofts, 1971.

Kish, L. S., et al. "An Ancient Method and a Modern Scourge: The Condom as a Barrier Against Herpes." *Journal of the American Academy of Dermatology* 9:769–770, 1983.

Klaus, M. H., et al. "Maternal Attachment: Importance of the First Post-Partum Days." *New England Journal of Medicine* 286:460–463, 1972.

Kleck, R. E., Richardson, S. A., and Ronald L. "Physical Appearance Cues and Interpersonal Attraction in Children," *Child Development* 45:305–310, 1974.

Klein, F. *The Bisexual Option.* New York: Arbor House, 1978.

Kline-Graber, G., and Graber, B. "Diagnosis and Treatment Procedures of Pubococcygeal Deficiencies in Women." In LoPiccolo, J., and LoPiccolo, L. (eds.), *Handbook of Sex Therapy*, pp. 227–239. New York: Plenum Press, 1978.

Klitsch, M. "FDA Approval Ends Cervical Cap's Marathon." *Family Planning Perspectives* 20:137–138, 1988.

———. *RU 486: The Science and the Politics.* New York: Alan Guttmacher Institute, 1989.

Klonoff, H. "Marijuana and Driving in Real-Life Situations." *Science* 186:317–324, 1974.

Klonoff-Cohen, H. S., et al. "An Epidemiologic Study of Contraception and Preeclampsia." *Journal of the American Medical Association* 262:3143–3147, 1989.

Knapp, J. J., and Whitehurst, R. N. "Sexuality, Open Marriage and Relationships: Issues and Prospects." In Murstein, B. I. (ed.), *Exploring Intimate Life Styles*, pp. 35–51. New York: Springer, 1978.

Koch, P. B. "College Students: The Concerns They Experience in Their Sexual Lives." Presented at the 15th Annual National Meeting of the American Association for Sex Educators, Counselors, and Therapists, New York, March 13, 1982.

Koeske, R. "Lifting the Curse of Menstruation: Toward a Feminist Perspective on the Menstrual Cycle." *Women and Health* 8:1–16, 1983.

Koeske, R. K. "Premenstrual Emotionality: Is Biology Destiny?" *Women and Health* 1:11–14, 1976.

Koeske, R. K., and Koeske, G. F. "An Attributional Approach to Moods and the Menstrual Cycle." *Journal of Personality and Social Psychology* 31:474–478, 1975.

Kohlberg, L. "A Cognitive-Developmental Analysis of Children's Sex-Role Concepts and Attitudes." In Maccoby, E. E. (ed.), *The Development of Sex Differences*, pp. 82–172. Stanford, CA: Stanford University Press, 1966.

Kolata, G. "AIDS Is Spreading in Teen-Agers, A New Trend Alarming to Experts." *The New York Times*, Section 1, pp. 1 & 30, October 8, 1989.

———. "Frozen Embryos: Few Rules in a Rapidly Growing Field." *The New York Times*, p. A10, June 5, 1992.

Kolata, G. B. "In Vitro Fertilization Goes Commercial." *Science* 221:1160–1161, 1983.

———. "Math Genius May Have Hormonal Basis." *Science* 222:1312, 1983a.

———. "Math and Sex: Are Girls Born with Less Ability?" *Science* 210:1234–1235, 1980.

———. "NIH Panel Urges Fewer Cesarean Births." *Science* 210:176–177, 1980a.

Kolodny, N. *When Food's a Foe*. Boston: Little, Brown, 1987.

Kolodny, R. "The Roots of Violence in Contemporary Society." Keynote speech presented at the Chicago Social Services Agencies Annual Conference, "The Many Faces of Violence," March 1993.

———. "Current Trends in Heterosexual Behavior." Paper presented at the Symposium of Sexuality in the 1990s, New York, May 4, 1994.

Kolodny, R., and Kolodny, N. "Current Trends in Sexual Behavior and the Impact of AIDS Anxiety." Presented at the Third Annual Symposium of the Behavioral Medicine Institute, New York, April 25, 1987.

Kolodny, R. C. "Sexual Dysfunction in Diabetic Females." *Diabetes* 20(8):557–559, 1971.

———. "Effects of Alpha-Methyldopa on Male Sexual Function." *Sexuality and Disability* 1:223–228, 1978.

———. "Ethical Issues in the Prevention of Sexual Problems." In Qualls, C. B., Wincze, J. P., and Barlow, D. H. (eds.), *The Prevention of Sexual Disorders*, pp. 183–196. New York: Plenum Press, 1978a.

———. "Effects of Marihuana on Sexual Behavior and Function." Paper presented at the Midwestern Conference on Drug Use, St. Louis, February 16, 1981.

———. "Evaluating Sex Therapy: Process and Outcome at the Masters & Johnson Institute." *Journal of Sex Research* 17:301–318, 1981a.

———. "Sexual Issues in Mid-Adulthood." Presented at the Las Vegas Psychiatric Symposium, Las Vegas, NV, January 23, 1983.

———. Unpublished research, 1983a.

———. "The Clinical Management of Sexual Problems in Substance Abusers." In Bratter, T. E., and Forrest, G. (eds.), *Current Management of Alcoholism and Substance Abuse*. New York: Free Press, 1985.

———. "Anabolic Steroids and Sexual Assault." Presented at the First Annual Florida Sex Therapy Association Training Program, Miami, March 16, 1990.

Kolodny, R. C., and Bauman, J. E. "Female Sexual Activity at Ovulation" (letter). *New England Journal of Medicine* 300:626, 1979.

Kolodny, R. C., et al. "Plasma Testosterone and Semen Analysis in Male Homosexuals." *New England Journal of Medicine* 285:1170–1174, 1971.

———. "Depression of Plasma Testosterone Levels After Chronic Intensive Marijuana Use." *New England Journal of Medicine* 290:872–874, 1974.

———. "Sexual Dysfunction in Diabetic Men." *Diabetes* 23:306–309, 1974a.

———. "Depression of Plasma Testosterone with Acute Marihuana Administration." In Braude, M. C., and Szara, S. (eds.), *The Pharmacology of Marihuana*, pp. 217–225. New York: Raven Press, 1976.

———. "Endocrine Status of Men During Chronic Marihuana Use." Paper presented at Washington University Medical Center Research Seminar. St. Louis, April 1979.

———. "Endocrine Effects of Chronic Marihuana Use by Women." Paper presented at the University of Rochester Medical School Endocrine Grand Rounds, Rochester, NY, February 1980.

Kolodny, R. C., Masters, W. H., and Johnson, V. E. *Textbook of Sexual Medicine*. Boston: Little, Brown, 1979.

Kols, A., et al. "Oral Contraceptives in the 1980s." *Population Reports*, Series A, No. 6, May–June, 1982.

Komaroff, A. L., et al. "Chlamydial Pharyngitis." *Annals of Internal Medicine* 111:537–538, 1989.

Komaromy, M., et al. "Sexual Harassment in Medical Training." *New England Journal of Medicine* 328:322–326, 1993.

Komarovsky, M. *Dilemmas of Masculinity*. New York: Norton, 1976.

Konner, Melvin. "The Gender Option." *The Sciences* 27(6):2–4, November–December 1987.

Koonin, L. M., et al. "Maternal Mortality Surveillance, United States, 1979–1986." In *CDC Surveillance Summaries* July 1991; *Morbidity and Mortality Weekly Reports* 40 (No. SS-2), Table 1, p. 8, 1991.

Koop, C. E. "The U.S. Surgeon General on the Health Effects of Abortion." *Population and Development Review* 15:172–175, 1989.

Koralnik, I. J., et al. "A Controlled Study of Early Neurologic Abnormalities in Men with Asymptomatic Human Immunodeficiency Virus Infection." *New England Journal of Medicine* 323:864–870, 1990.

Kosnik, A., et al. *Human Sexuality: New Directions in American Catholic Thought*. New York: Paulist Press, 1977.

Koss, M. P. "The Underdetection of Rape: Methodological Choices Influence Incidence Estimates." *Journal of Social Issues* 48:61–75, 1992.

Koss, M. P., et al. "Stranger and Acquaintance Rape: Are There Differences in the Victim's Experience?" *Psychology of Women Quarterly* 12:1–23, 1988.

Kost, K., and Forrest, J. D. "American Women's Sexual Behavior and Exposure to Risk of Sexually Transmitted Diseases." *Family Planning Perspectives* 24:244–254, 1992.

Koutsky, L. A., et al. "A Cohort Study of the Risk of Cervical Intraepithelial Neoplasia Grade 2 or 3 in Relation to Papillomavirus Infection." *New England Journal of Medicine* 327:1272–1278, 1992.

Kramer, Larry. "A 'Manhattan Project' for AIDS." *The New York Times*, p. A15, July 16, 1990.

Krane, R. J., and Siroky, M. B. "Neurophysiology of Erection." *Urologic Clinics of North America* 8:91–102, 1981.

Krebs, D., and Adinolfi, A. A. "Physical Attractiveness, Social Relations, and Personality Style." *Journal of Personality and Social Psychology* 31:245–253, 1975.

Kreiss, J., et al. "Efficacy of Nonoxynol 9 Contraceptive Sponge Use in Preventing Heterosexual Acquisition of HIV in Nairobi Prostitutes." *Journal of the American Medical Association* 268:477–482, 1992.

Kriess, J. K., et al. "AIDS Virus Infection in Nairobi Prostitutes." *New England Journal of Medicine* 314:414–418, 1986.

Kruttschnitt, C. "A Sociological, Offender-Based, [sic] Study of Rape." *The Sociological Quarterly* 30(2):305–329, 1989.

Ku, L. C., Sonenstein, F. L., and Pleck, J. H. "The Association of AIDS Education and Sex Education with Sexual Behavior and Condom Use Among Teenage Men." *Family Planning Perspectives* 24:100–106, 1992.

Kuo, G., et al. "An Assay for Circulating Antibodies to a Major Etiologic Virus of Non-A, Non-B Hepatitis." *Science* 244:362–364, 1989.

Kurinij, N., Shiono, P., and Rhodes, G. "Breast-Feeding Incidence and Duration in Black and White Women." *Pediatrics* 81:365–371, 1988.

Kutchinsky, B. "Sex Crimes and Pornography in Copenhagen: A Study of Attitudes." *Technical Reports of the Commission on Obscenity and Pornography*, Vol. 7. Washington, DC: U.S. Government Printing Office, 1970.

———. "The Effect of Easy Availability of Pornography on the Incidence of Sex Crimes." *Journal of Social Issues* 29:163–182, 1973.

Labovitz, S., and Hagedorn, R. *Introduction to Social Research*. New York: McGraw-Hill, 1976.

Lacoste-Utamsing, C., and Holloway, R. L. "Sexual Dimorphism in the Human Corpus Callosum." *Science* 216:1431–1432, 1982.

Ladas, A. K., Whipple, B., and Perry, J. D. *The G Spot and Other Recent Discoveries About Human Sexuality*. New York: Holt, Rinehart & Winston, 1982.

Lader, L. *RU 486: The Pill That Could End the Abortion Wars and Why American Women Don't Have It*. Boston: Addison-Wesley, 1991.

Lafferty, W. E., et al. "Recurrences After Oral and Genital Herpes Simplex Virus Infection." *New England Journal of Medicine* 316:1444–1449, 1987.

Lake, A. "Childbirth in America." *McCall's*, p. 128, January 1976.

Lakoff, R. T. *Taking Power: The Politics of Language*. New York: Basic Books, 1990.

Lamaze, F. *Painless Childbirth*. Chicago: Regnery, 1970.

Lamb, D. R. "Anabolic Steroids in Athletes: How Well Do They Work and How Dangerous Are They?" *American Journal of Sports Medicine* 12:31–38, 1984.

Lamb, E. J., and Leurgans, S. "Does Adoption Affect Subsequent Fertility?" *American Journal of Obstetrics and Gynecology* 134:138–144, 1979.

Lambert, B. "10 Years Later, Hepatitis Study Still Yields Critical Data on AIDS." *The New York Times*, p. C3, July 17, 1990.

Lamberti, J. "Sexual Adjustment After Radiation Therapy for Cervical Carcinoma." *Medical Aspects of Human Sexuality* 13(3):87–88, 1979.

Lammer, E., et al. "Retinoic Acid Embryopathy." *New England Journal of Medicine* 313:837–841, 1985.

Lande, R. "Controlling Sexually Transmitted Diseases." *Population Reports* Series L, Number 9, June 1993.

Landis, S. E., et al. "Results of a Randomized Trial of Partner Notification in Cases of HIV Infection in North Carolina." *New England Journal of Medicine* 326:101–106, 1992.

Langenberg, A., et al. "Development of Clinically Recognizable Genital Lesions Among Women Previously Identified as Having 'Asymptomatic' Herpes Simplex Virus Type 2 Infection." *Annals of Internal Medicine* 110:882–887, 1989.

Langfeldt, T. "Sexual Development in Children." In Cook, M., and Howells, K. (eds.), *Adult Sexual Interest in Children*. London: Academic Press, 1981.

Langston, D. *Living with Herpes*. Garden City, NY: Doubleday, 1983.

Larder, B. A., Draby, G., and Richman, D. D. "HIV with Reduced Sensitivity to Zidovudine (AZT) Isolated During Prolonged Therapy." *Science* 243:1731–1734, 1989.

Largen, M. A. "Rape-law Reform: An Analysis." In Burgess, A. W. (ed.), *Rape and Sexual Assault*, Vol. 2. New York: Garland, 1988.

LaRossa, R. "Fatherhood and Social Change." *Men's Studies Review* 6(2):1–9, 1989.

Larsen, B., and Galask, R. P. "Vaginal Microbial Flora: Composition and Influence of Host Physiology." *Annals of Internal Medicine* 96 (Part 2):926–930, 1982.

Larson, T., and Bryson, Y. "Fomites and Herpes Simplex Virus: The Toilet Seat Revisited (abstract)." *Pediatric Research* 16:244, 1982.

Lasater, M. "Sexual Assault: The Legal Framework." In Warner, C. (ed.), *Rape and Sexual Assault*, pp. 231–264. Germantown, MD: Aspen Systems Corp., 1980.

LaTorre, R., and Wendenberg, K. "Psychological Characteristics of Bisexual, Heterosexual, and Homosexual Women." *Journal of Homosexuality* 9(1):87–97, 1983.

Lattimer, J. K., et al. "The Optimum Time to Operate for Cryptorchidism." *Pediatrics* 53:96–99, 1974.

Laumann, E. O., et al. "Monitoring the AIDS Epidemic in the United States: A Network Approach." *Science* 244:1186–1189, 1989.

Laumann, E. O., et al. *The Social Organization of Sexuality: Sexual Practices in the United States*. Chicago: University of Chicago Press, 1994.

Laurence, L. T. *Couple Constancy: Conversations with Today's Happily Married People*. Ann Arbor, MI: UMI Research Press, 1982.

Lawrence, D. H. *Lady Chatterley's Lover*. New York: Grove Press Black Cat Edition, 1962.

Laws, D., and Marshall, W. "Masturbatory Reconditioning with Sexual Deviates: An Evaluative Review." *Advances in Behavior Research and Therapy* 13:13–25, 1991.

Laws, D. R. (ed.). *Relapse Prevention with Sex Offenders*. New York: Guilford Press, 1989.

Lawson, C. "Surrogate Mothers Grow in Numbers Despite Questions." *The New York Times*, pp. C1 & C18, October 1, 1986.

Layde, P. M. "Smoking and Cervical Cancer: Cause or Coincidence?" *Journal of the American Medical Association* 261:1631–1633, 1989.

Lazarus, A. A. "Psychological Treatment of Dyspareunia." In Leiblum, S. R., and Pervin, L. A. (eds.), *Principles and Practice of Sex Therapy*, pp. 147–166. New York: Guilford Press, 1980.

Lazovich, D., et al. "Underutilization of Breast-Conserving Surgery and Radiation Therapy Among Women with Stage I or Stage II Breast Cancer." *Journal of the American Medical Association* 266:3433–3438, 1991.

Leary, W. E. "Sharp Rise in Rare Sex-Related Diseases." *The New York Times*, p. B6, July 14, 1988.

———. "Why Fewer Blacks Choose to Breast-Feed Than Do Whites." *The New York Times*, p. B7, April 7, 1988a.

LeBolt, S. A., Grimes, D. A., and Cates, W., Jr. "Mortality from Abortion and Childbirth." *Journal of the American Medical Association* 248:188–191, 1982.

Lebovitz, P. S. "Feminine Behavior in Boys: Aspects of Its Outcome." *American Journal of Psychiatry* 128:1283–1289, 1972.

Leboyer, F. *Birth Without Violence*. New York: Knopf, 1975.

Lederer, L. (ed.) *Take Back the Night*. New York: William Morrow, 1980.

Lee, J. *At My Father's Wedding: Reclaiming Our True Masculinity*. New York: Bantam, 1991.

Lee, J. A. *The Colours of Love*. Toronto: New Press, 1973.

———. *The Colors of Love*. Englewood Cliffs, NJ: Prentice-Hall, 1976.

———. "Love-Styles." In Sternberg, R. J., and Barnes, M. L. (eds.), *The Psychology of Love*, pp. 38–67. New Haven, CT: Yale University Press, 1988.

Lee, N. C., Rubin, G. L., and Borucki, R. "The Intrauterine Device and Pelvic Inflammatory Disease Revisited: New Results from the Women's Health Study." *Obstetrics and Gynecology* 72:1–6, 1988.

Lee, P. A. "The Relationship of Concentrations of Serum Hormones to Pubertal Gynecomastia." *Journal of Pediatrics* 86:212–215, 1975.

Lee, S. H., et al. "Resurgence of Congenital Rubella Syndrome in the 1990s." *Journal of the American Medical Association* 267:2616–2620, 1992.

Leiblum, S., and Rosen, R. (eds.). *Sexual Desire Disorders*. New York: Guilford Press, 1988.

———. *Principles and Practice of Sex Therapy: Update for the 1990s*, 2nd ed. New York: Guilford Press, 1989.

Leiblum, S., et al. "Vaginal Atrophy in the Postmenopausal Woman: The Importance of Sexual Activity and Hormones." *Journal of the American Medical Association* 249:2195–2198, 1983.

Leiblum, S. R., and Pervin, L. A. *Principles and Practice of Sex Therapy*. New York: Guilford Press, 1980.

Leinbach, M. D., and Hort, B. "Bears Are for Boys: Metaphorical Associations in the Young Child's Gender Schema." Paper Presented at Biennial Meeting of the Society for Research in Child Development, Kansas City, MO, April 1989.

Leitenberg, H., Detzer, M. J., and Srebnik, D. "Gender Differences in Masturbation and the Relation of Masturbation Experience in Preadolescence and/or Early Adolescence to Sexual Behavior and Sexual Adjustment in Young Adulthood." *Archives of Sexual Behavior* 22:87–98, 1993.

Lenton, E. A., Weston, G. A., and Cooke, I. D. "Problems in Using Basal Body Temperature Recordings in an Infertility Clinic." *British Medical Journal* 1:803–805, 1977.

Leo, J. "Stomping and Whomping Galore." *Time*, pp. 73–74, May 4, 1981.

Lessing, D. *The Four-Gated City*. New York: Bantam Books, 1970.

LeVay, S. "A Difference in Hypothalamic Structure Between Heterosexual and Homosexual Men." *Science* 253:1034–1037, 1991.

———. *The Sexual Brain*. Cambridge, MA: MIT Press, 1993.

Levin, R. J. "The Redbook Report on Premarital and Extramarital Sex: The End of the Double Standard?" *Redbook*, pp. 38–44, 190–192, October 1975.

Levin, R. J., and Levin, A. "Sexual Pleasure: The Surprising Preferences of 100,000 Women." *Redbook*, pp. 51–58, September 1975.

Levine, A., et al. "Immunization with Inactivated, Envelope-Depleted HIV Immunogen in HIV Infected Men with ARC." (Abstract #Th.B.O.44, p. 219.) Fifth International Conference on AIDS, Montreal, June 4–9, 1989.

Levine, M. P., and Troiden, R. R. "The Myth of Sexual Compulsivity." *Journal of Sex Research* 25:347–363, 1988.

Levine, R. "Gusii Sex Offenses: A Study in Social Control." *American Anthropologist* 61(6):965–990, 1959.

Levine, S. B. "Marital Sexual Dysfunction: Introduction Concepts." *Annals of Internal Medicine* 84:448–453, 1976.

Levinger, G. "Can We Picture Love?" In Sternberg, R. J., and Barnes, M. L. (eds.), *The Psychology of Love*, pp. 139–158. New Haven, CT: Yale University Press, 1988.

Levinger, G., and Rausch, H. L. (eds.). *Close Relationships: Perspectives on the Meaning of Intimacy*. Amherst, MA: University of Massachusetts Press, 1977.

Levinson, D. J., et al. *The Seasons of a Man's Life*. New York: Ballantine, 1978.

Levy, N. L. "The Middle-aged Male and Female Homosexual." In Howells, J. G. (ed.), *Modern Perspectives in the Psychiatry of Middle Age*, pp. 116–131. New York: Brunner/Mazel, 1981.

Levy, J. A. "Human Immunodeficiency Viruses and the Pathogenesis of AIDS." *Journal of the American Medical Association* 261:2997–3006, 1989.

Lewin, R. "Limits to DNA Fingerprinting." *Science* 243:1549–1551, 1989.

Lewin, T. "Fewer Teen Mothers, But More Are Unmarried." *The New York Times*, Section 4, p. 6, March 20, 1988.

Lewis, M. "State as an Infant-Environment Interaction: An Analysis of Mother-Infant Interaction as a Function of Sex." *Merrill-Palmer Quarterly* 18:95–121, 1972.

Lewis, P. "Catholic Hospitals in Europe Defy Vatican on In-Vitro Fertilization," *The New York Times*, pp. A1 & A12, March 18, 1987.

Lewis, R. A. "Parents and Peers: Socialization Agents in the Coital Behavior of Young Adults." *Journal of Sex Research* 9:156–170, 1973.

Lewis, R. J., and Janda, L. H. "The Relationship Between Adult Sexual Adjustment and Childhood Experiences Regarding Exposure to Nudity, Sleeping in the Parental Bed, and Parental Attitudes Toward Sexuality." *Archives of Sexual Behavior* 17:349–362, 1988.

Liang, A. P., et al. "Risk of Breast, Uterine Corpus and Ovarian Cancer in Women Receiving Medroxyprogesterone Injections." *Journal of the American Medical Association* 249:2909–2912, 1983.

Liberati, A., et al. "The Role of Attitudes, Beliefs, and Personal Characteristics of Italian Physicians in the Surgical Treatment of Early Breast Cancer." *American Journal of Public Health* 81:38–42, 1991.

Liebowitz, M. R. *The Chemistry of Love*. Boston: Little, Brown, 1983.

Lief, H. I. "Inhibited Sexual Desire." *Medical Aspects of Human Sexuality* 11(7):94–95, 1977.

Lief, H. I., and Hubschman, L. "Orgasm in the Postoperative Transsexual." *Archives of Sexual Behavior* 22:145–155, 1993.

Lilius, H. G., Valtonen, E. J., and Wikström, J. "Sexual Problems in Patients Suffering from Multiple Sclerosis." *Journal of Chronic Diseases* 29:643–647, 1976.

Lindemalm, G., Korlin, D., and Uddenberg, N. "Long-Term Follow-up of 'Sex Change' in 13 Male-to-Female Transsexuals." *Archives of Sexual Behavior* 15:187–210, 1986.

Lindholm, F. B., et al. "Pituitary-Testicular Function in Patients with Chronic Alcoholism." *European Journal of Clinical Investigation* 8:269–272, 1978.

Linn, L. S., et al. "Recent Sexual Behaviors Among Homosexual Men Seeking Primary Care." *Archives of Internal Medicine* 149:2685–2690, 1989.

Linz, D. "Exposure to Sexually Explicit Materials and Attitudes Toward Rape: A Comparison of Study Results." *Journal of Sex Research* 26:50–84, 1989.

Lipkin, M., Jr., and Lamb, G. S. "The Couvade Syndrome: An Epidemiologic Study." *Annals of Internal Medicine* 96:509–511, 1982.

Lipsett, M. B. "Estrogen Use and Cancer Risk." *Journal of the American Medical Association* 237:1112–1115, 1977.

Lipton, M. A. "The Problem of Pornography." In Fann, W. E., et al. (eds.), *Phenomenology and Treatment of Psychosexual Disorders*, pp. 113–134. New York: Spectrum, 1983.

Liskin, L., Benoit, E., and Blackburn, R. "Vasectomy: New Opportunities." *Population Reports*, Series D, Number 5, March 1992.

Liskin, L., and Blackburn, R. "AIDS: A Public Health Crisis." *Population Reports*, Series L. Number. 6, July–August 1986.

Lo, B., et al. "Voluntary Screening for Human Immunodeficiency Virus (HIV) Infection." *Annals of Internal Medicine* 110:727–733, 1989.

Loche, M., and Mach, B. "Identification of HIV-infected Seronegative Individuals by a Direct Diagnosis Test Based on Hybridization to Amplified Viral DNA." *Lancet* ii:418–421, 1988.

Long Laws, J. *The Second X*. New York: Elsevier, 1979.

LoPiccolo, J. "Direct Treatment of Sexual Dysfunction in the Couple." In Money, J., and Musaph, H. (eds.), *Handbook of Sexology*, pp. 1227–1244. Amsterdam: Elsevier/North Holland, 1977.

LoPiccolo, J., and Heiman, J. "The Role of Cultural Values in the Prevention and Treatment of Sexual Problems." In Qualls, C. B., Wincze, J. P; and Barlow, D. H. (eds.), *The Prevention of Sexual Disorders*, pp. 43–71. New York: Plenum Press, 1978.

LoPiccolo, J., and Lobitz, W. C. "The Role of Masturbation in the Treatment of Orgasmic Dysfunction." *Archives of Sexual Behavior* 2:163–171, 1972.

LoPiccolo, J., and LoPiccolo, L. (eds.). *Handbook of Sex Therapy*. New York: Plenum Press, 1978.

LoPiccolo, J., et al. "Effectiveness of Single Therapists Versus Cotherapy Teams in Sex Therapy." *Journal of Consulting & Clinical Psychology* 53:287–294, 1985.

LoPiccolo, L. "Low Sexual Desire." In Lieblum, S. R., and Pervin, L. A. (eds.), *Principles and Practice of Sex Therapy*, pp. 29–64. New York: Guilford Press, 1980.

Loraine, J. A., et al. "Endocrine Function in Male and Female Homosexuals." *British Medical Journal* 4:406–408, 1970.

Loren, R. E. A., and Weeks, G. R. "Sexual Fantasies of Undergraduates and Their Perceptions of the Sexual Fantasies of the Opposite Sex." *Journal of Sex Therapy and Education* 12(2):31–36, 1986.

Louik, C., et al. "Maternal Exposure to Spermicides in Relation to Certain Birth Defects." *New England Journal of Medicine* 317:474–476, 1987.

Lowry, T. P. "The Volatile Nitrites as Sexual Drugs: A User Survey." *Journal of Sex Education and Therapy* 1:8–10, 1979.

Lowry, T. P., and Williams, G. R. "Brachioproctic Eroticism." *Journal of Sex Education and Therapy* 9(1):50–52, 1983.

Lue, T. "Office Treatment: Papaverine Injections for Impotence." In Tanagho, E., Lue, T., and McClure, R. (eds.), *Contemporary Management of Impotence and Infertility*, pp. 162–163. Baltimore: Williams & Wilkins, 1988.

Lui, K.-J., Darrow, W. W., and Rutherford, G. W., III. "A Model-Based Estimate of the Mean Incubation Period for AIDS in Homosexual Men." *Science* 240:1333–1335, 1988.

Lund, D. S. "Survey: Many Women Found Breast Cancer 'Accidentally'." *American Medical News*, p. 35, June 17, 1988.

Lundberg, P. O. "Sexual Dysfunction in Patients with Neurological Disorders." In Gemme, R., and Wheeler, C. C. (eds.), *Progress in Sexology*, pp. 129–139. New York: Plenum Press, 1977.

Lundberg, P. O., and Wide, L. "Sexual Function in Males with Pituitary Tumors." *Fertility & Sterility* 29:175–179, 1978.

Lunde, I., et al. "Sexual Desire, Orgasm, and Sexual Fantasies: A Study of 625 Danish Women Born in 1910, 1936, and 1958." *Journal of Sex Education & Therapy* 17:111–115, 1991.

Lundstrom, B. *Gender Dysphoria*. Akademiforlaget, Gothenberg, Sweden: Scandinavian University Books, 1981.

Lycke, E., et al. "The Risk of Transmission of Genital *Chlamydia trachomatis* Infection Is Less Than That of Genital *Neisseria gonorrhea* Infection." *Sexually Transmitted Diseases* 7:6, 1980.

McCabe, M. P., and Delaney, S. M. "An Evaluation of Therapeutic Programs for the Treatment of Secondary Inorgasmia in Women." *Archives of Sexual Behavior* 21:69–89, 1992.

McCandlish, B. M. "Therapeutic Issues with Lesbian Couples." *Journal of Homosexuality* 7(2–3):71–78, 1981/82.

McCarthy, B. W. "Sexual Dysfunctions and Dissatisfactions among Middle-years Couples." *Journal of Sex Education and Therapy* 8(2):9–12, 1982.

———. "Sexual Trauma: The Pendulum Has Swung Too Far." *Journal of Sex Education and Therapy* 18:1–10, 1992.

McCarthy, J., and Radish, E. S. "Education and Child-bearing Among Teenagers." *Family Planning Perspectives* 14:154–155, 1982.

McClintock, M. "Menstrual Synchrony and Suppression." *Nature (London)* 229:244–245, 1971.

Maccoby, E., and Jacklin, C. *The Psychology of Sex Differences*. Stanford, CA: Stanford University Press, 1974.

McConaghy, N. "Penile Volume Responses to Moving and Still Pictures of Male and Female Nudes." *Archives of Sexual Behavior* 3:566–570, 1974.

McCormick, M. C., Shapiro, S., and Starfield, B. "High Risk Young Mothers: Changes in Infant Mortality and Morbidity in Four Areas in the United States, 1973–1978." Presented at the Annual Meeting of the American Pediatric Association. San Francisco, April 30, 1981.

McDonald, A. P. "Bisexuality: Some Comments on Research and Theory." *Journal of Homosexuality* 6(3):21–35, 1981.

MacDonald, K. L., et al. "Performance Characteristics of Serologic Tests for Human Immunodeficiency Virus Type 1 (HIV-1) Among Minnesota Blood Donors." *Annals of Internal Medicine* 110:617–621, 1989.

MacDonald, N. E., et al. "High-Risk STD/HIV Behavior Among College Students." *Journal of the American Medical Association* 263:3155–3159, 1990.

Macdonald, P. T., et al. "Heavy Cocaine Use and Sexual Behavior." *Journal of Drug Issues* 18:437–455, 1988.

McDougall, J. K., et al. "Cervical Carcinoma: Detection of Herpes Simplex Virus RNA in Cells Undergoing Neoplastic Change." *International Journal of Cancer* 25:1–8, 1980.

McEwen, B. "Neural Gonadal Steroid Actions." *Science* 211(4488):1303–1311, 1981.

McGee, E. A. *Too Little, Too Late: Services for Teenage Parents*. New York: Ford Foundation, 1982.

McGuinness, D., and Pribram, K. "The Origins of Sensory Bias in the Development of Gender Differences in Perception and Cognition." In Bortner, M. (ed.), *Cognitive Growth and Development: Essays in Honor of Herbert G. Birch*, pp. 3–56. New York: Brunner/Mazel, 1978.

McGuire, R. J., Carlisle, J. M., and Young, B. G. "Sexual Deviations as Conditioned Behavior: A Hypothesis." *Behavioral Research and Therapy* 2:185–190, 1965.

Maciak, B. J., et al. "Pregnancy and Birth Rates Among Sexually Experienced US [sic] Teenagers—1974, 1980, and 1983." *Journal of the American Medical Association* 258:2069–2071, 1987.

Macionis, J. J. "Intimacy, Structure and Process in Interpersonal Relationships." *Alternative Lifestyles* 1:113–130, 1978.

McKinley, H., and Drew, B. "The Nursing Home: Death of Sexual Expression." *Health and Social Work* 2(3):180–187, August 1977.

MacKinnon, C. A. *Sexual Harassment of Working Women.* New Haven, CT: Yale University Press, 1979.

Macklin, E. "Nontraditional Family Forms." In Sussman, M. B., and Steinmetz, S. K. (eds.), *Handbook of Marriage and the Family*, pp. 320–354. New York: Plenum Press, 1987.

Macklin, E. D. "Unmarried Heterosexual Cohabitation on the University Campus." In Wiseman, J. P. (ed.), *The Social Psychology of Sex*, pp. 108–142. New York: Harper & Row, 1976.

———. "Review of Research on Nonmarital Cohabitation in the United States." In Murstein, B. I. (ed.), *Exploring Intimate Life Styles*, pp. 197–243. New York: Springer, 1978.

———. "Nontraditional Family Forms: A Decade of Research." *Journal of Marriage and the Family* 42:905–922, 1980.

McKusick, L., and Hoff, C. C. "Relationship Between HIV Awareness, Partner Selection Criteria, and Early Relationship Formation in Two Groups of San Francisco Bar Patrons." (Abstract #W.D.O. 2, p. 704.) Presented at the Fifth International Conference on AIDS, Montreal, June 1989.

McLane, M., Krop, H., and Mehta, J. "Psychosexual Adjustment and Counseling After Myocardial Infarction." *Annals of Internal Medicine* 92:514–519, 1980.

MacLusky, N., and Naftolin, F. "Sexual Differentiation of the Central Nervous System." *Science* 211(4488):1294–1303, 1981.

MacNamara, D. E., and Sagarin, E. *Sex, Crime, and the Law.* New York: Free Press, 1977.

McNeill, J. J. *The Church and the Homosexual.* Kansas City, KS: Sheed Andrews and McMeel, 1976.

McNulty, T. J. "Pornography Blind Spot." *Chicago Tribune*, Section 6, pp. 5 & 9, July 13, 1986.

McWhirter, D. P., and Mattison, A. M. *The Male Couple: How Relationships Develop.* Englewood Cliffs, NJ: Prentice-Hall, 1984.

Maguire, D. C. "The Governor and the Bishop." *The New York Times*, p. A23, January 30, 1990.

Major, B., McFarlin, D. B., and Gagnon, D. "Overworked and Underpaid: On the Nature of Gender Differences in Personal Entitlement." *Journal of Personality and Social Psychology* 47:1399–1412, 1984.

Malamuth, N. "Rape Proclivity Among Males." *Journal of Social Issues* 37:138–157, 1981.

Malamuth, N., and Donnerstein, E. (eds.). *Pornography and Sexual Aggression.* New York: Academic Press, 1984.

Malamuth, N., and Spinner, B. "A Longitudinal Content Analysis of Sexual Violence in the Best-Selling Erotic Magazines." *Journal of Sex Research* 16(3):226–237, 1980.

Malatesta, V. J. "Alcohol Effects on the Orgasmic-Ejaculatory Response in Human Males." *Journal of Sex Research* 15:101–107, 1979.

Malatesta, V. J., et al. "Acute Alcohol Intoxication and Female Orgasmic Response." *Journal of Sex Research* 18:1–17, 1982.

Malinowski, B. *The Sexual Life of Savages.* New York: Harcourt, Brace & World, 1929.

Maltz, W., and Holman, B. *Incest and Sexuality: A Guide to Understanding and Healing.* Lexington, MA: Lexington Books, 1987.

Mandelson, M. T., Maden, C. B., and Daling, J. R. "Low Birth Weight in Relation to Multiple Induced Abortions." *American Journal of Public Health* 82:391–394, 1992.

Mann, J., Tarantola, D. J. M., and Netter, T. W. (eds.). *AIDS in the World.* Cambridge, MA: Harvard University Press, 1992.

Mann, J. I., and Inman, W. H. "Oral Contraceptives and Death from Myocardial Infarction." *British Medical Journal* 2:245–248, 1975.

Mannion, R. "Penile Laceration" (letter). *Journal of the American Medical Association* 224:1763, 1973.

Manno, J. E., et al. "Motor and Mental Performance with Marijuana: Relationship to Administered Dose of Δ^9-tetrahydrocannabinol and Its Interaction with Alcohol." In Miller, L. L. (ed.), *Marihuana: Effects on Human Behavior*, pp. 45–72. New York: Academic Press, 1974.

Mant, D., et al. "Myocardial Infarction and Angina Pectoris in Young Women." *Journal of Epidemiology and Community Health* 41:215–219, 1987.

March, C. "Update: Home Tests for Ovulation and Pregnancy." *Endocrine & Fertility Forum* 8(4):2–6, 1985.

Marchbanks, P. A., et al. "Risk Factors for Ectopic Pregnancy." *Journal of the American Medical Association* 259:1823–1827, 1988.

Marcus, I. M., and Francis, J. J. (eds.). *Masturbation: From Infancy to Senescence.* New York: International Universities Press, 1975.

Marcus, R., et al. "Surveillance of Healthcare Workers Exposed to Blood from Patients Infected with the Human Immunodeficiency Virus." *New England Journal of Medicine* 319:1118–1123, 1988.

Marcus, S. *The Other Victorians.* New York: Bantam Books, 1967.

Margolin, L., Miller, M., and Moran, P. B. "When a Kiss Is Not Just a Kiss: Relating Violations on Consent in Kissing to Rape Myth Acceptance." *Sex Roles* 20:231–243, 1989.

Margolin, G. "A Social Learning Approach to Intimacy." In Fisher, M., and Stricker, G. (eds.), *Intimacy*, pp.

175–201. New York: Plenum Press, 1982.

Margolis, A. J., and Greenwood, S. "Gynecology and Obstetrics." In Schroeder, S. A., et al. (eds.), *Current Medical Diagnosis & Treatment*, pp. 554–607. Norwalk, CT: Appleton & Lange, 1992.

Marin, Peter. "A Revolution's Broken Promises." *Psychology Today*, pp. 50–57, July 1983.

Markel, N., Long, J., and Saine, T. "Sex Effects on Conversational Interaction." *Human Communication Research* 2:356–364, 1976.

Markle, G. E. "Sex Ratio at Birth: Values, Variance and Some Determinants." *Demography* 11:131–142, 1974.

Marks, J. S., and Cates, W. "Sex Education: How Should It Be Offered?" *Journal of the American Medical Association* 255:85–86, 1986.

Marks, M. A., and Nelson, E. S. "Sexual Harassment on Campus: Effects of Professor Gender on Perception of Sexually Harassing Behavior." *Sex Roles* 28:207–217, 1993.

Markus, H., and Cross, S. "The Interpersonal Self." In Pervin, L. A. (ed.), *Handbook of Personality: Theory and Research*, pp. 576–608. New York: Guilford Press, 1990.

Markus, H., and Kitayama, S. "Culture and the Self: Implications for Cognition, Emotion, and Motivation." *Psychological Review* 98:224–253, 1991.

Marmor, J. "'Normal' and 'Deviant' Sexual Behavior." *Journal of the American Medical Association* 217:165–170, 1971.

———. (ed.). *Homosexual Behavior*. New York: Basic Books, 1980.

———. "Clinical Aspects of Male Homosexuality." In Marmor, J. (ed.), *Homosexual Behavior*, pp. 267–279. New York: Basic Books, 1980a.

———. "Comments on Sexuality Survey and Discussion." In Hill, I. (ed.), *The Bisexual Spouse*, pp. 211–221. New York: Harper & Row, 1989.

Marshall, D. "Sexual Behavior on Mangaia." In Marshall, D., and Suggs, R. (eds.). *Human Sexual Behavior*, pp. 103–162. New York: Basic Books, 1971.

Marshall, D., and Suggs, R. (eds.), *Human Sexual Behavior*. New York: Basic Books, 1971.

Marshall, E. "Sullivan Overrules NIH on Sex Survey." *Science* 253:502, 1991.

Marshall, W. A. "Growth and Sexual Maturation in Normal Puberty." *Clinics in Endocrinology and Metabolism* 4:3–25, 1975.

———. *Human Growth and Its Disorders*. New York: Academic Press, 1977.

Marshall, W. A., and Tanner, J. M. "Variation in the Pattern of Pubertal Changes in Girls." *Archives of Disease in Childhood* 44:291–303, 1969.

———. "Variation in the Pattern of Pubertal Changes in Boys." *Archives of Disease in Childhood* 45:13–23, 1970.

Marshall, W. L. "The Use of Sexually Explicit Stimuli by Rapists, Child Molesters, and Nonoffenders." *Journal of Sex Research* 25:267–288, 1988.

Marsiglio, William. "Adolescent Fathers in the United States: Their Initial Living Arrangements, Marital Experience and Educational Outcomes." *Family Planning Perspectives* 19:240–251, 1987.

Martin, A. D., and Hetrick, E. S. "The Stigmatization of Gay and Lesbian Youth." *Journal of Homosexuality* 15:163–183, 1988.

Martin, C. E. "Sexual Activity in the Aging Male." In Money, J., and Musaph, H. (eds.), *Handbook of Sexology*, pp. 813–824. New York: Elsevier/North Holland Biomedical Press, 1977.

Martin, J. L. "Psychological, Social and Serological Correlates of Sexual Behavior Changes Among Gay Men." Paper presented at the International Academy of Sex Research 12th Annual Meeting, Amsterdam, the Netherlands, September 19, 1986.

Martin, K. A., and Freeman, M. W. "Postmenopausal Hormone-Replacement Therapy." *New England Journal of Medicine* 328:1115–1116, 1993.

Martinson, F. M. "Eroticism in Infancy and Childhood." *Journal of Sex Research* 12:251–262, 1976.

———. "Childhood Sexuality." In Wolman, B. B., and Money, J. (eds.), *Handbook of Human Sexuality*, pp. 29–59. Englewood Cliffs, NJ: Prentice-Hall, 1980.

———. "Eroticism in Infancy and Childhood." In Constantine, L. L., and Martinson, F. M. (eds.), *Children and Sex: New Findings, New Perspectives*, pp. 23–35. Boston: Little, Brown, 1981.

Marx, J. L. "Circumcision May Protect Against the AIDS Virus." *Science* 245:470–471, 1989.

———. "How DNA Viruses May Cause Cancer." *Science* 243:1012–1013, 1989a.

Massey, F. J., et al. "Vasectomy and Health." *Journal of the American Medical Association* 252:1023–1029, 1984.

Masters, W. H. "Update on Sexual Physiology." Paper presented at the Masters & Johnson Institute's Postgraduate Workshop on Human Sexual Function and Dysfunction, St. Louis, October 20, 1980.

———. "Update on Sexual Physiology." Presented at the Masters & Johnson Institute's Advanced Workshop on Human Sexuality, St. Louis, June 12, 1982.

Masters, W. H., et al. *Ethical Issues in Sex Therapy and Research*, Vol. 2. Boston: Little, Brown, 1980.

———. "Outcome Studies at the Masters & Johnson Institute." Presented at the Sixth World Congress of Sexology, Washington, DC, May 26, 1983.

Masters, W. H., and Johnson, V. E. *Human Sexual Response*. Boston: Little, Brown, 1966.

———. *Human Sexual Inadequacy*. Boston: Little, Brown, 1970.

———. *The Pleasure Bond*. New York: Bantam Books, 1976.

———. *Homosexuality in Perspective*. Boston: Little, Brown, 1979.

———. "Facts and Fallacies in Sexual Physiology." Paper presented at the Fifth National Meeting of the American Association of Sex Educators, Counselors, and Therapists, San Francisco, April 4, 1981.

Masters, W. H., Johnson, V. E., and Kolodny, R. C. *Crisis: Heterosexual Behavior in the Age of AIDS.* New York: Grove Press, 1988.

———. *Heterosexuality.* New York: HarperCollins, 1994.

Masterson, A., et al. "Marked Underreporting of CDC Defined AIDS Due to Poor Utilization of the HIV Antibody Test." (Abstract T.A.O. 5, p. 55.) Fifth International Conference on AIDS, Montreal, June 4–9, 1989.

Mastroianni, L., Jr., Donaldson, P. J., and Kane, T. T. "Development of Contraceptives—Obstacles and Opportunities." *New England Journal of Medicine* 322:482–484, 1990.

Masur, F. T. "Resumption of Sexual Activity Following Myocardial Infarction." *Sexuality and Disability* 2:98–114, 1979.

Matthews, R. J. *The Human Adventure: A Study Course for Christians on Sexuality.* Lima, OH: C.S.S. Publishing, 1980.

May, R. "Mood Shifts and the Menstrual Cycle." *Journal of Psychosomatic Research* 20:125–130, 1976.

Mazer, D. G., and Percival, E. F. "Ideology or Experience? The Relationships Among Perceptions, Attitudes, and Experiences of Sexual Harassment in University Students." *Sex Roles* 20:135–147, 1989.

Medical Research International and Society for Assisted Reproductive Technology. "In Vitro Fertilization–Embryo Transfer in the United States: 1988 Results from the IVF–ET Registry." *Fertility & Sterility* 53:13–20, 1990.

Mehrabian, A. *Nonverbal Communication.* Chicago: Aldine Atherton, 1972.

Mehta, J., and Krop, H. "The Effect of Myocardial Infarction on Sexual Functioning." *Sexuality and Disability* 2:115–121, 1979.

Meiselman, K. C. *Incest.* San Francisco: Jossey-Bass, 1978.

Meisler, A. W., et al. "Success and Failure in Penile Prosthesis Surgery: Two Cases Highlighting the Importance of Psychosocial Factors." *Journal of Sex & Marital Therapy* 14:108–119, 1988.

Melman, A., and Tiefer, L. "Surgery for Erectile Disorders: Operative Procedures and Psychological Issues." In Rosen, R. C., and Leiblum, S. R. (eds.), *Erectile Disorders: Assessment and Treatment*, pp. 255–282. New York: Guilford Press, 1992.

Mendelson, J. H., et al. "Plasma Testosterone Levels Before, During, and After Chronic Marihuana Smoking." *New England Journal of Medicine* 291:1051–1055, 1974.

Merson, M. H. "Slowing the Spread of AIDS: Agenda for the 1990s." *Science* 260:1266–1268, 1993.

Mertz, G. J., et al. "Double-Blind Placebo-Controlled Trial of Oral Acyclovir in First-Episode Genital Herpes Simplex Virus Infection." *Journal of the American Medical Association* 254:1147–1151, 1984.

———. "Long-Term Acyclovir Suppression of Frequently Recurring Genital Herpes Simplex Virus Infection." *Journal of the American Medical Association* 260:201–206, 1988.

———. "Transmission of Genital Herpes in Couples with One Symptomatic and One Asymptomatic Partner: A Prospective Study." *Journal of Infectious Disease* 157:1169–1177, 1988a.

———. "Risk Factors for the Sexual Transmission of Genital Herpes." *Annals of Internal Medicine* 116:197–202, 1992.

Merz, B. "Greater IUD Perforation Risk, Lactation Linked." *Journal of the American Medical Association* 249:3152, 1983.

Messenger, J. "Sex and Repression in an Irish Folk Community." In Marshall, D., and Suggs, R. (eds.), *Human Sexual Behavior*, pp. 3–37. New York: Basic Books, 1971.

Messenger, M. *The Breastfeeding Book.* New York: Van Nostrand Reinhold, 1982.

Mettlin, C., Natarajan, N., and Huben, R. "Vasectomy and Prostate Cancer Risk." *American Journal of Epidemiology* 132:1056–1061, 1990.

Metzger, D. "It Is Always the Woman Who Is Raped." *American Journal of Psychiatry* 133:405–408, 1976.

Meyer, H. "Prostitutes, Politics Heighten Thailand's AIDS Dilemma." *American Medical News*, pp. 3 & 26–28, July 27, 1990.

Meyer, J. K., and Hoopes, J. E. "The Gender Dysphoria Syndromes: A Position Statement on So-Called 'Transsexualism.'" *Plastic and Reconstructive Surgery* 54:444–451, 1974.

Meyer, J. K., and Reter, D. J. "Sex Reassignment." *Archives of General Psychiatry* 36:1010–1015, 1979.

Meyer-Bahlburg, H. F. "Sex Hormones and Male Homosexuality in Comparative Perspective." *Archives of Sexual Behavior* 6:297–325, 1977.

———. "Behavioral Effects of Estrogen Treatment in Human Males." *Pediatrics* 62(Suppl.):1171–1177, 1978.

———. "Sex Hormones and Female Homosexuality: A Critical Examination." *Archives of Sexual Behavior* 8:101–120, 1979.

Meyer-Bahlburg, H., et al. "HIV-Positive Gay Men: Sexual Dysfunction." (Abstract # T.D.O. 22, p. 701.) Fifth International Conference on AIDS, Montreal, 1989.

Meyers, Robert. *D.E.S.: The Bitter Pill.* New York: Putnam, 1983.

Meyners, R., and Wooster, C. *Sexual Style.* New York: Harcourt Brace Jovanovich, 1979.

Mezey, G. C., and King, M. B. (eds.). *Male Victims of Sexual Assault.* New York: Oxford University Press, 1992.

Michael, R. T., and Tuma, N. B. "Entry into Marriage and Parenthood by Young Men and Women: The Influence of Family Background." *Demography* 22:515–544, 1985.

Michael, R. T., et al. *Sex in America.* Boston: Little, Brown, 1994.

Miedzian, M. "How Rape Is Encouraged in American Boys and What We Can Do to Stop It." In Buchwald, E., Fletcher, P., and Roth, M. (eds.), *Transforming a Rape Culture*, pp. 155–163. Minneapolis, MN: Milkweed Editions, 1993.

Miller v. California. 413 U.S. 15(1973).

Miller, D. B. "Sexual Practices and Administrative Policies in Long Term Care Institutions." In Solnick, R. L. (ed.), *Sexuality and Aging*, rev. ed., pp. 163–175. Los Angeles: University of Southern California Press, 1978.

Miller, D. R., et al. "Breast Cancer Before Age 45 and Oral Contraceptive Use: New Findings." *American Journal of Epidemiology* 129:269–277, 1989.

Miller, H. *Tropic of Cancer*. New York: Grove Press, 1961.

———. *Tropic of Capricorn*. New York: Grove Press, 1961a.

Miller, H. G., Turner, C. F., and Moses, L. E. (eds.). *AIDS—The Second Decade*. Washington, DC: National Academy Press, 1990.

Miller, L., Downer, A., and Krueger, L. "Reported Sexual Behavior Differences Between Heterosexual and Gay/Bisexual Populations." Presented at the IV International Conference on AIDS, Stockholm, June 12–16, 1988.

Miller, J. B. *Toward a New Psychology of Women*, 2nd ed. Boston: Beacon, 1986.

Miller, P., and Biele, N. "Twenty Years Later: The Unfinished Revolution." In Buchwald, E., Fletcher, P. R., and Roth, M. (eds.), *Transforming a Rape Culture*, pp. 49–53. Minneapolis, MN: Milkweed Editions, 1993.

Miller, P. Y., and Simon, W. "The Development of Sexuality in Adolescence." In Adelson, J. (ed.), *Handbook of Adolescent Psychology*, pp. 383–407. New York: Wiley, 1980.

Millett, K. *Sexual Politics*. New York: Doubleday, 1970.

Mills, J. L., et al. "Maternal Alcohol Consumption and Birth Weight." *Journal of the American Medical Association* 252:1875–1879, 1984.

Mindel, A., et al. "Prophylactic Oral Acyclovir in Recurrent Genital Herpes." *Lancet* ii:57–59, 1984.

Minkoff, H. L., et al. "Routinely Offered Prenatal HIV Testing." *New England Journal of Medicine* 319:1018, 1988.

Mintz, J., et al. "Sexual Problems of Heroin Addicts." *Archives of General Psychiatry* 31:700–703, 1974.

Minuk, G. Y., Bohme, C. E., and Bower, T. J. "Condoms and Hepatitis B Virus Infection." *Annals of Internal Medicine* 104:584, 1986.

Mirin, S., et al. "Opiate Use and Sexual Function." *American Journal of Psychiatry* 173:909–915, 1980.

Mishell, D. R., Jr. "Contraception." *New England Journal of Medicine* 320:777–787, 1989.

———. "Current Status of Intrauterine Devices." *New England Journal of Medicine* 312:984–985, 1985.

———. "Intrauterine Devices." *Journal of the American Medical Association* 263:235–236,1990.

Moffat, A. S. "Another Sex Survey Bites the Dust." *Science* 253:1483, 1991.

Moghissi, K. S. "Accuracy of Basal Body Temperature for Ovulation Detection." *Fertility and Sterility* 27:1415–1421, 1976.

Mohr, J. C. *Abortion in America: The Origins and Evolution of National Policy, 1800–1900*. New York: Oxford University Press, 1978.

Mohr, J. W., Turner, R. E., and Jerry, M. B. *Pedophilia and Exhibitionism*. Toronto: University of Toronto Press, 1964.

Moller, L. C., Hymet, S., and Rubin, K. H. "Sex Typing in Play and Popularity in Middle Childhood." *Sex Roles* 26:331–353, 1992.

Monat, R. K. *Sexuality and the Mentally Retarded*. San Diego: College-Hill Press, 1982.

Money, J. "Ablatio Penis: Normal Male Infant Sex-Reassigned as a Girl." *Archives of Sexual Behavior* 4:65–72, 1975.

———. "Childhood: The Last Frontier in Sex Research." *The Sciences* 16(6):12–15, 1976.

———. *Love and Love Sickness*. Baltimore: Johns Hopkins University Press, 1980.

———. *Lovemaps*. New York: Irvington Press, 1986.

———. *Gay, Straight, and In-Between*. New York: Oxford University Press, 1988.

———. "The Ethics of Pornography in the Era of AIDS." *Journal of Sex & Marital Therapy* 14:177–183, 1988a.

———. "Treatment Guidelines: Antiandrogen and Counseling of Paraphilic Sex Offenders." *Journal of Sex and Marital Therapy* 13:219–223, 1987.

Money, J., and Bohmer, C. "Prison Sexology: Two Personal Accounts of Masturbation, Homosexuality, and Rape." *Journal of Sex Research* 16:258–266, 1980.

Money, J., and Ehrhardt, A. E. *Man & Woman, Boy & Girl*. Baltimore: Johns Hopkins University Press, 1972.

Money, J., and Lamacz, M. *Vandalized Lovemaps*. Buffalo, NY: Prometheus Books, 1989.

Money, J., and Ogunro, C. "Behavioral Sexology: Ten Cases of Genetic Male Intersexuality with Impaired Prenatal and Pubertal Androgenization." *Archives of Sexual Behavior* 3:181–205, 1974.

Money, J., and Russo, A. J. "Homosexual Outcome of Discordant Gender Identity/Role in Childhood: Longitudinal Follow-up." *Journal of Pediatric Psychology* 4(1):29–41, 1979.

Money, J., and Schwartz, M. "Dating, Romantic and Nonromantic Friendships, and Sexuality in 17 Early-Treated Adrenogenital Females, Aged 16–25." In Lee, P. A., et al. (eds.), *Congenital Adrenal Hyperplasia*. Baltimore: University Park Press, 1977.

Money, J., and Wiedeking, C. "Gender Identity/Role: Normal Differentiation and Its Transpositions." In Wolman, B. B., and Money, J. (eds.), *Handbook of Human Sexuality*, pp. 269–284. Englewood Cliffs, NJ: Prentice-Hall, 1980.

Money, J., Jobaris, R., and Furth, G. "Apotemnophilia: Two Cases of Self-Demand Amputation as a Paraphilia." *Journal of Sex Research* 13:115–125, 1977.

Montagu, Ashley. *Touching: The Human Significance of the Skin.* New York: Harper & Row, 1978.

Monzon, O. T., and Capellan, J. M. "Female-to-Female Transmission of HIV." *Lancet* 2:40–41, 1987.

Moody, Lt. J., and Hayes, V. "Responsible Reporting: The Initial Step." In Warner, C. (ed.), *Rape and Sexual Assault.* Germantown, MD: Aspen Systems Corp., 1980.

Moon, T. D. "Prostate Cancer." *Journal of the American Geriatric Society* 40:622–627, 1992.

Mooney, T. O., Cole, T. M., and Chilgren, R. A. *Sexual Options for Paraplegics and Quadraplegics.* Boston: Little, Brown, 1975.

Moore, D. E., et al. "Transmission of Genital Herpes by Donor Insemination." *Journal of the American Medical Association* 261:3441–3443, 1989.

———. "Congenital Syphilis—New York City, 1986–1988." *Morbidity and Mortality Weekly Report* 38:825–829, 1989.

Moore, K. A., et al. *Teenage Motherhood: Social and Economic Consequences.* Washington, DC: The Urban Institute, 1979.

Moore, K. A., Nord, C. W., and Peterson, J. L. "Nonvoluntary Sexual Activity Among Adolescents." *Family Planning Perspectives* 21:110–114, 1989.

Moos, R. H. "Typology of Menstrual Cycle Symptoms." *American Journal of Obstetrics and Gynecology* 103:390–402, 1969.

Morbidity and Mortality Weekly Report 38:561–563, 1989.

Morin, Jack. *Anal Pleasure and Health.* Burlingame, CA: Down There Press, 1981.

Morin, N. C., et al. "Congenital Malformations and Psychosocial Development in Children Conceived by In Vitro Fertilization." *Journal of Pediatrics* 115:222–227, 1989.

Morris, J. *Conundrum.* New York: New American Library, 1974.

Morris, L. "Young Adults in Latin America and the Caribbean: Their Sexual Experience and Contraceptive Use." *International Family Planning Perspectives* 14:153–158, 1988.

Morrison, T. (ed.). *Race-ing Justice, En-gendering Power: Essays on Anita Hill, Clarence Thomas, and the Construction of Social Reality.* New York: Pantheon Books, 1992.

Moser, C. "Sadomasochism." *Journal of Social Work and Human Sexuality* 7:43–56, 1988.

Mosher, D. L., and Tomkins, S. S. "Scripting the Macho Man: Hypermasculine Socialization and Enculturation." *Journal of Sex Research* 25:60–84, 1988.

Mosher, W. D., and Pratt, W. F. "AIDS-Related Behavior Among Women 15–44 Years of Age: United States, 1988 and 1990." Advance Data from *Vital Health Statistics* No. 239, 1993.

Moss, A. R., et al. "Seropositivity for HIV and the Development of AIDS or AIDS Related Condition." *British Medical Journal* 296:745–750, 1988.

Moultroup, D. J. *Husbands, Wives, and Lovers: The Emotional System of the Extramarital Affair.* New York: Guilford Press, 1990.

Muehlenhard, C. L., and Linton, M. A. "Date Rape and Sexual Aggression in Dating Situations: Incidence and Risk Factors." *Journal of Counseling Psychology* 34:186–196, 1987.

Muehlenhard, C. L., Harney, P. A., and Jones, J. M. "From 'Victim-Precipitated Rape' to 'Date Rape': How Far Have We Come?" *Annual Review of Sex Research* III:219–253, 1992.

Muehlenhard, C. L., et al. "Definitions of Rape: Scientific and Political Issues." *Journal of Social Issues* 48:23–44, 1992.

Mueller, G. O. *Sexual Conduct and the Law.* Dobbs Ferry, NY: Oceana Publications, 1980.

Mulligan, T., and Katz, P. G. "Erectile Failure in the Aged: Evaluation and Treatment." *Journal of the American Geriatrics Society* 36:54–62, 1988.

Mulligan, T., et al. "The Role of Aging and Chronic Disease in Sexual Dysfunction." *Journal of the American Geriatrics Society* 36:520–524, 1988.

Munjack, D. J., and Kanno, P. H. "Retarded Ejaculation: A Review." *Archives of Sexual Behavior* 8:139–150, 1979.

Munjack, D. J., and Oziel, L. J. *Sexual Medicine and Counseling in Office Practice.* Boston: Little, Brown, 1980.

Munroe, R. L. "Male Transvestism and the Couvade: A Psycho-Cultural Analysis." *Ethos* 8:49–59, 1980.

Murphy, F. X. "Of Sex and the Catholic Church." *Atlantic Monthly* 247(2):44–57, February 1981.

Murphy, W. D., et al. "Sexual Dysfunction and Treatment in Alcoholic Women." *Sexuality and Disability* 3:240–255, 1980.

Murphy-Corb, M., et al. "A Formalin-Inactivated Whole SIV Vaccine Confers Protection in Macaques." *Science* 246:1293–1297, 1989.

Murray, A. B., et al. "Coincident Acquisition of *Neisseria Gonorrhoeae* and HIV From Fellation." *Lancet* 338:830, 1991.

Murray, P. P., et al. "Oral Contraceptive Use in Women with a Family History of Breast Cancer." *Obstetrics and Gynecology* 73:977–983, 1989.

———. "Oral Contraceptive Use in Women with a Family History of Breast Cancer." *Obstetrics and Gynecology* 73:977–983, 1989a.

Murstein, B. I. *Love, Sex and Marriage Through the Ages.* New York: Springer, 1974.

———. *Who Will Marry Whom? Theories and Research on Marital Choice.* New York: Springer, 1976.

———. (ed.). *Exploring Intimate Life Styles.* New York: Springer, 1978.

———. "Swinging, or Comarital Sex." In Murstein, B. I. (ed.), *Exploring Intimate Life Styles,* pp. 109–130. New York: Springer, 1978a.

————. "Mate Selection in the 1970s." *Journal of Marriage and the Family* 42:777–792, 1980.

Mydans, S. "For Jurors, Facts Could Not Be Sifted from Fantasies." *The New York Times*, p. A18, January 19, 1990.

Myers, J. K., Weissman, M. M., and Tischler, G. C. "Six-month Prevalence of Psychiatric Disorders in Three Communities." *Archives of General Psychiatry* 41:959–967, 1984.

Myers, S. A., and Gleicher, N. "A Successful Program to Lower Cesarean-Section Rates." *New England Journal of Medicine* 319:1511–1516, 1988.

Nabulsi, A. A., et al. "Association of Hormone-Replacement Therapy with Various Cardiovascular Risk Factors in Postmenopausal Women." *New England Journal of Medicine* 328:1069–1075, 1993.

Nadelson, C. C. "The Emotional Impact of Abortion." In Notman, M. T., and Nadelson, C. C. (eds.), *The Woman Patient*, Vol. 1, pp. 173–179. New York: Plenum Press, 1978.

Nadelson, C. C., et al. "A Follow-up Study of Rape Victims." *American Journal of Psychiatry* 139:1266–1270, 1982.

Nahmias, A. J., et al. "Evidence for Human Infection with an HTLV-III/LAV-like Virus in Central Africa, 1959. *Lancet* 1:1279–1280, 1986.

Nanda, S. *Neither Man nor Woman: The Hijras of India*. Belmont, CA: Wadsworth, 1990.

Nankin, H. R., and Calkins, J. H. "Decreased Bioavailable Testosterone in Aging Normal and Impotent Men." *Journal of Clinical Endocrinology & Metabolism* 63:1418–1426, 1986.

National Center for Health Statistics. U.S. Department of Health and Human Services, vol. 30, no. 12, March 18, 1982.

————. *Health, United States, 1990*. (DHHS Pub. No. PHS 91–1232.) Washington, DC: U.S. Public Health Service, 1991.

Navarro, M. "In the Age of AIDS, Sex Clubs Proliferate Again." *The New York Times*, pp. B1 & B5, March 5, 1993.

Navot, D., et al. "Poor Oocyte Quality Rather Than Implantation Failure as a Cause of Age-Related Decline in Female Fertility." *Lancet* 337:1375–1377, 1991.

Nelson, J. B. *Embodiment*. Minneapolis: Augsburg Publishing House, 1978.

Nerurkar, L. S., et al. "Survival of Herpes Simplex Virus in Water Specimens Collected from Hot Tubs in Spa Facilities and on Plastic Surfaces." *Journal of the American Medical Association* 250:3081–3083, 1983.

Newcomb, M. "Sexual Behavior of Cohabitors: A Comparison of Three Independent Samples." *Journal of Sex Research* 22:492–513, 1986.

Newcomer, S. F., and Udry, J. R. "Oral Sex in an Adolescent Population." *Archives of Sexual Behavior* 14:41–46, 1985.

Newhouse, M. L., et al. "A Case–Control Study of Carcinoma of the Ovary." *British Journal of Preventive and Social Medicine* 31(3):148–153, September 1977.

Newman, G., and Nichols, C. R. "Sexual Activities and Attitudes in Older Persons." *Journal of the American Medical Association* 173:117–119, 1960.

Newman, L. E. "Treatment for the Parents of Feminine Boys." *American Journal of Psychiatry* 133:683–687, 1976.

Newman, M. *Michigan Consortium of Schools Student Survey*. Minneapolis: Hazelden Research Services, 1986.

Nichols, M. "Low Sexual Desire in Lesbian Couples." In Leiblum, S. R., and Rosen, R. C. (eds.), *Sexual Desire Disorders*, pp. 387–412. New York: Guilford Press, 1988.

Nielsen, L. *Adolescence: A Contemporary View*, 2nd ed. New York: Harcourt Brace Jovanovich, 1991.

Nightingale, S. L. "Didanosine (DDI) Approved for Advanced HIV Infection." *Journal of the American Medical Association* 266:2528, 1991.

NIH Consensus Development Conference. "Treatment of Early-stage Breast Cancer." *Journal of the American Medical Association* 265:391–395, 1991.

Nillson, L. et al. *A Child is Born*. New York: Delacorte/Seymour Lawrence, 1977.

Niruthisard, S., Roddy, R. E., and Chutivongse, S. "Use of Nonoxynol-9 and Reduction in Rate of Gonococcal and Chlamydial Cervical Infections." *Lancet* 339:1371–1375, 1992.

Nora, A. H., and Nora, J. J. "Maternal Exposure to Exogenous Progestogen/Estrogen as a Potential Cause of Birth Defects." *Advances in Planned Parenthood* 12(3):156–169, 1978.

Nora, J. J., and Nora, A. H. "Birth Defects and Oral Contraceptives." *Lancet* i:941–942, 1973.

Norman, C. "Politics and Science Clash on African AIDS." *Science* 230:1140–1141, 1986.

Norris, R. V., and Sullivan, C. *PMS: Premenstrual Syndrome*. New York: Rawson Wade, 1983.

North, B. B., and Vorhauer, B. W. "Use of the Today Contraceptive Sponge in the United States." *International Journal of Fertility* 30:81–84, 1985.

Norwood, R. *Women Who Love Too Much*. Los Angeles: Tarcher/St. Martin's, 1985.

Notarius, C. I., et al. "Exploring the Interface Between Perception and Behavior: An Analysis of Marital Interaction in Distressed and Nondistressed Couples." *Behavioral Assessment* 11:39–64, 1989.

Notman, M. T. "A Psychological Consideration of Mastectomy." In Notman, M. T., and Nadelson, C. C. (eds.), *The Woman Patient*, Vol. 1, pp. 247–255. New York: Plenum Press, 1978.

Notman, M. T., and Nadelson, C. C. "The Rape Victim: Psychodynamic Considerations." *American Journal of Psychiatry* 113:408–413, 1976.

———. (ed.). *The Woman Patient*, Vol. 1. New York: Plenum Press, 1978.

Notzon, F. C., Placek, P. J., and Taffel, S. M. "Comparisons of National Cesarean-Section Rates." *New England Journal of Medicine* 316:386–389, 1987.

Nurcombe, Barry. "The Child as Witness: Competency and Credibility." *Journal of the American Academy of Child Psychiatry* 25:473–480, 1986.

Nutter, D. E., and Condron, M. K. "Sexual Fantasy and Activity Patterns of Females with Inhibited Sexual Desire Versus Normal Controls." *Journal of Sex & Marital Therapy* 9:276–282, 1983.

———. "Sexual Fantasy and Activity Patterns of Males with Inhibited Sexual Desire and Males with Erectile Dysfunction Versus Normal Controls." *Journal of Sex & Marital Therapy* 11:91–98, 1985.

O'Connell, L., Betz, M., and Kurth, S. "Plans for Balancing Work and Family Life: Do Women Pursuing Nontraditional and Traditional Occupations Differ?" *Sex Roles* 20:35–45, 1989.

O'Donohue, W., and Geer, J. H. (eds.). *The Sexual Abuse of Children*, Vol. I (*Theory and Research*) and Vol. II (*Clinical Issues*). Hillsdale, NJ: Lawrence Erlbaum, 1992.

Oesterling, J. E. "Prostate-Specific Antigen—Improving Its Ability to Diagnose Early Prostate Cancer." *Journal of the American Medical Association* 267:2236–2238, 1992.

Offer, D., and Offer, J. *From Teenage to Young Motherhood.* New York: Basic Books, 1975.

Office of Surveillance and Analysis. "Trends in Prostate Cancer—United States, 1980–1988." *Morbidity and Morality Weekly Report* 41:401–404, 1992.

Offit, A. *The Sexual Self*. New York: Ballantine, 1977.

O'Hara, M. W., et al. "Prospective Study of Postpartum Blues." *Archives of General Psychiatry* 48:801–806, 1991.

O'Neil, N. *The Marriage Premise.* New York: Bantam Books, 1978.

O'Neill, N., and O'Neill, G. *Open Marriage: A New Life Style for Couples.* New York: M. Evans and Company, 1972.

———. "Open Marriage: A Synergic Model." In De-Burger, J. E. (ed.), *Marriage Today: Problems, Issues and Alternatives*, pp. 287–296. New York: Wiley, 1977.

O'Neill, T. M., Abbot, A. V., and Radecki, S. E. "Risk of Needlesticks and Occupational Exposures Among Residents and Medical Students." *Archives of Internal Medicine* 152:1451–1456, 1992.

Orr, M. T. "Sex Education and Contraceptive Education in U.S. Public High Schools." *Family Planning Perspectives* 14:304–313, 1982.

Ory, H. W., Rosenfeld, A., and Landman, L. C. "The Pill at 20: An Assessment." *Family Planning Perspectives* 12:278–283, 1980.

Ory, S. J. "Ectopic Pregnancy: Current Evaluation and Treatment." *Mayo Clinic Proceedings* 64:874–877, 1989.

Orzek, A. M. "Sexual Assault: The Female Victim, Her Male Partner, and Their Relationship." *Personnel and Guidance Journal* 62(3):143–146, November 1983.

Osborne, N. G., Grubin, L., and Pratson, L. "Vaginitis in Sexually Active Women: Relationship to Nine Sexually Transmitted Organisms." *Obstetrics and Gynecology* 142:962–967, 1982.

Osmond, D. H., et al. "Risk Factors for Hepatitis C Virus Seropositivity in Heterosexual Couples." *Journal of the American Medical Association* 269:361–365, 1993.

Osofsky, H. J. "Efficacious Treatments of PMS: A Need for Further Research." *Journal of the American Medical Association* 264:387, 1990.

Ouellette, E. M., et al. "Adverse Effects on Offspring of Maternal Alcohol Abuse During Pregnancy." *New England Journal of Medicine* 297:528–530, 1977.

Overby, C., Lo, B., and Litt, T. "Knowledge and Concerns About Acquired Immunodeficiency Syndrome and Their Relationship to Behavior Among Adolescents with Hemophilia." *Pediatrics* 83:204–210, 1989.

Padgett, V. R., Brislin-Slutz, J. A., and Neal, J. A. "Pornography, Erotica, and Attitudes Toward Women: The Effects of Repeated Exposure." *Journal of Sex Research* 26:479–491, 1989.

Paige, K. E. "Women Learn to Sing the Menstrual Blues." *Psychology Today*, pp. 41–46, April 1973.

Paige, K. "The Declining Taboo Against Menstrual Sex." *Psychology Today* 12(7):50–51, 1978.

Palca, J. "Dallas AIDS Survey Raises Expectations." *Science* 247:1023, 1990.

———. "The Sobering Geography of AIDS." *Science* 252:372–373, 1991.

Paludi, Michelle (ed.). *Ivory Power: Sexual Harassment on Campus.* Albany, NY: State University of New York Press, 1990.

Palmore, E. "Published Reactions to the Kinsey Report." *Social Forces* 31:165–170, December 1952.

Pam, A., Plutchik, R., and Conte, H. R. "Love: A Psychometric Approach." *Psychological Reports* 37:83–88, 1975.

Pantaleo, G., Graziosi, C., and Fauci, A. "The Immunopathogenesis of Human Immunodeficiency Virus Infection." *New England Journal of Medicine* 328:327–335, 1993.

Parlee, M. B. "The Premenstrual Syndrome." *Psychological Bulletin* 80:454–465, 1973.

Parrinder, G. *Sex in the World's Religions.* New York: Oxford University Press, 1980.

Parrot, A. *Coping with Date Rape & Acquaintance Rape*. New York: The Rosen Publishing Group, 1988.

Parrot, A., and Bechhofer, L. (eds.). *Acquaintance Rape: The Hidden Crime*. New York: Wiley, 1991.

Parsons, J. E. "Psychosexual Neutrality: Is Anatomy Destiny?" In Parsons, J. E. (ed.), *The Psychobiology of Sex Differences and Sex Roles*, pp. 3–29. New York: Hemisphere Publishing, 1980.

Pauly, B., and Edgerton, M. "The Gender-Identity Movement." *Archives of Sexual Behavior* 15:315–329, 1986.

Pauly, I. B. "Female Transsexualism: Part I." *Archives of Sexual Behavior* 3:487–507, 1974.

Payne, S. F., et al. "Effect of Multiple Disease Manifestations on Length of Survival for AIDS Patients in San Francisco." (Abstract # W.A.P. 80, p. 133.) Fifth International Conference on AIDS, Montreal, June 4–9, 1989.

Peele, S. "Fools for Love." In Sternberg, R. J., and Barnes, M. L. (eds.), *The Psychology of Love*, pp. 159–188. New Haven, CT: Yale University Press, 1988.

Peele, S., with Brodsky, A. *Love and Addiction*. New York: New American Library, 1976.

Pelligrini, A. "S(h)ifting the Terms of Hetero/Sexism: Gender, Power, and Homophobias." In Blumenfeld, W. J. (ed.), *Homophobia: How We All Pay the Price*. Boston: Beacon Press, 1992.

Peplau, L. A., and Gordon, S. L. "The Intimate Relationships of Lesbians and Gay Men." In Allgeier, E. R., and McCormick, N. B. (eds.), *Gender Roles and Sexual Behavior*. Palo Alto, CA: Mayfield, 1982.

Perelman, M. A. "Treatment of Premature Ejaculation." In Leiblum, S. R., and Pervin, L. A. (eds.), *Principles and Practice of Sex Therapy*, pp. 199–233. New York: Guilford Press, 1980.

Perkins, R. P. "Sexual Behavior and Response in Relation to Complications of Pregnancy." *American Journal of Obstetrics and Gynecology* 134:498–505, 1979.

Pernoll, M. L., and Benson, R. C. *Current Obstetric and Gynecologic Diagnosis & Treatment*. Norwalk, CT: Appleton & Lange, 1987.

Perrin, E. B., et al. "Long-Term Effect of Vasectomy on Coronary Heart Disease." *American Journal of Public Health* 74:128–132, 1984.

Perrone, J. "Controversial Abortion Approach." *American Medical News*, pp. 9 & 18–22, January 12, 1990.

Perry, J. D., and Whipple, B. "Pelvic Muscle Strength of Female Ejaculators: Evidence in Support of a New Theory of Orgasm." *Journal of Sex Research* 17(1):22–39, 1981.

Perry, S., Jacobsberg, L., and Fogel, K. "Orogenital Transmission of Human Immunodeficiency Virus (HIV)." *Annals of Internal Medicine* 11:951–952, 1989.

Persky, H. "Reproductive Hormones, Moods and the Menstrual Cycle." In Friedman, R. C., Richard, R. M., and Vande Wiele, R. L. (eds.), *Sex Differences in Behavior*, pp. 455–466. New York: Wiley, 1974.

Persky, H., et al. "Plasma Testosterone Level and Sexual Behavior of Couples." *Archives of Sexual Behavior* 7:157–173, 1978.

Person, E. S., et al. "Gender Differences in Sexual Behaviors and Fantasies in a College Population." *Journal of Sex & Marital Therapy* 15:187–198, 1989.

Peter, J. B., Bryson, Y., and Lovett, M. A. "Genital Herpes: Urgent Questions, Elusive Answers." *Diagnostic Medicine*, pp. 71–74, 76–88, March/April 1982.

Peterman, D. J., Ridley, C. A., and Anderson, S. M. "A Comparison of Cohabitating and Non-Cohabitating College Students." *Journal of Marriage and the Family* 36:344–354, 1974.

Peterman, T. A., and Curran, J. W. "Sexual Transmission of Human Immunodeficiency Virus." *Journal of the American Medical Association* 256:2222–2226, 1986.

Peterman, T. A., et al. "Risk of HIV Transmission from Heterosexual Adults with Transfusion-Associated Infections." *Journal of the American Medical Association* 259:55–58, 1988.

Peters, B. *Terrific Sex in Fearful Times*. New York: St. Martin's Press, 1988.

Peters, D. K., and Cantrell, P. J. "Gender Roles and Role Conflict in Feminist Lesbian and Heterosexual Women." *Sex Roles* 28:379–391, 1993.

Peters, J. "Children Who Are Victims of Sexual Assault and the Psychology of Offenders." *American Journal of Psychotherapy* 30:398–421, 1976.

Petersen, A. C. "Biopsychosocial Processes in the Development of Sex-Related Differences." In Parsons, J. E. (ed.), *The Psychobiology of Sex Differences and Sex Roles*, pp. 31–55. New York: Hemisphere Publishing, 1980.

Peterson, L. "The Issue—and Controversy—Surrounding Adolescent Sexuality and Abstinence." *SIECUS Report* 17:1–8, September/October 1988.

Petravage, J. B. "Outcomes of Three Birthing Rooms." *Journal of Family Practice* 16:929, 1983.

Petty, J. A. "An Investigation of Factors Which Differentiate Between Types of Cohabitation." Unpublished masters thesis, Indiana University, 1975.

Peyron, R., et al. "Early Termination of Pregnancy with Mifepristone (RU 486) and the Orall Active Prostaglandin Misoprostol." *New England Journal of Medicine* 328:1509–1513, 1993.

Pfeiffer, E., and Davis, G. C. "Determinants of Sexual Behavior in Middle and Old Age." *Journal of the American Geriatrics Society* 20:151–158, 1972.

Pfeiffer, E., Verwoerdt, A., and Davis, G. C. "Sexual Behavior in Middle Life." *American Journal of Psychiatry* 128:1262–1267, 1972.

Pfeffer, M. A. "Diabetic Sexual Dysfunction," *Clinical Diabetes* 6:97–100, 118, 1988.

Phillips, D. I. W. "Twin Studies in Medical Research: Can They Tell Us Whether Diseases Are Genetically Determined?" *Lancet* 341:1008–1009, 1993.

Piazza, M., et al. "Passionate Kissing and Microlesions of the Oral Mucosa: Possible Role in AIDS Transmission." *Journal of the American Medical Association* 261:244–245, 1989.

Piotrow, P. T., Rinehart, W., and Schmidt, J. C. "IUDs: An Update on Safety, Effectiveness, and Research." *Population Reports*, Series B(3), May 1979.

Pivar, D. J. *Purity Crusade, Sexual Morality, and Social Control, 1868–1900.* Westport, CT: Greenwood Press, 1973.

Placek, P., Taffel, S., and Liss, T. "The Cesarean Future." *American Demography* 9:46–47, 1987.

Plapinger, L., and McEwen, B. S. "Gonadal Steroid–Brain Interactions in Sexual Differentiation." In Hutchison, J. B. (ed.), *Biological Determinants of Sexual Behavior*, pp. 153–218. New York: Wiley, 1978.

Platt, R., Rice, P. A., and McCormack, W. M. "Risk of Acquiring Gonorrhea and Prevalence of Abnormal Adnexal Findings Among Women Recently Exposed to Gonorrhea." *Journal of the American Medical Association* 250:3205–3209, 1983.

Pleck, J. H. "Masculinity–Femininity: Current and Alternative Paradigms." *Sex Roles* 1:161–178, 1975.

———. *Working Wives/Working Husbands.* Beverly Hills, CA: Sage Publications, 1985.

Pleck, J. H., Sonenstein, F. L., and Ku, L. "Changes in Adolescent Males' Use of and Attitudes Toward Condoms, 1988–1991." *Family Planning Perspectives* 25:106–109 and 117, 1993.

Pleck, J. H. *The Myth of Masculinity.* Cambridge: MIT Press, 1981.

Plummer, F. A., et al. "Co-factors in Male-Female Sexual Transmission of Human Immunodeficiency Virus Type 1." *Journal of Infectious Diseases* 163:233, 1991.

Podolsky, S. "Erectile Impotence in the Diabetes Patient." *Practical Gastroenterology* 7(1):40–43, January/February 1983.

Pogrebin, L. C. *Growing Up Free: Raising Your Child in the 80's.* New York: McGraw-Hill, 1980.

Pokrovsky, V. V., and Eramova, E. U. "Nosocomial Outbreak of HIV Infection in Elista, USSR. (Abstract # W.A.O.5, p. 63.) Fifth International Conference on AIDS, Montreal, June 4–9, 1989.

Poland, R. L. "The Question of Routine Neonatal Circumcision." *New England Journal of Medicine* 322:1312–1315, 1990.

Pomerantz, R. J., et al. "Human Immunodeficiency Virus (HIV) Infection of the Uterine Cervix." *Annals of Internal Medicine* 108:321–327, 1988.

Pomeroy, W. B. "The Masters–Johnson Report and the Kinsey Tradition." In Brecher, R., and Brecher, E. (eds.), *An Analysis of Human Sexual Response*, pp. 111–123. New York: Signet Books, 1966.

Pomeroy, W. B., Flax, C. C.; and Wheeler, C. C. *Taking a Sex History.* New York: Free Press, 1982.

Pool, R. "Evidence for Homosexuality Gene." *Science* 261:291–292, 1993.

Pope, H. G., and Katz, D. L. "Affective and Psychotic Symptoms Associated with Anabolic Steroid Use." *American Journal of Psychiatry* 145:487–490, 1988.

Pope, H. G., et al. "Prevalence of Anorexia Nervosa and Bulima in Three Student Populations." *International Journal of Eating Disorders* 3:45–51, 1984.

Pope, K. S. "Defining and Studying Romantic Love." In Pope, K. S. (ed.), *On Love and Loving*, pp. 1–26. San Francisco: Jossey-Bass, 1980.

Population Reports. Published five times per year by Population Information Program of the Johns Hopkins University, 624 N. Broadway, Baltimore, MD 21205.

Porter, S. B., and Sande, M. A. "Toxoplasmosis of the Central Nervous System in the Acquired Immunodeficiency Syndrome." *New England Journal of Medicine* 327:1643–1648, 1992.

Potter, L. B., and Anderson, J. E. "Patterns of Condom Use and Sexual Behavior Among Never-Married Women." *Sexually Transmitted Diseases* 20:201–208, 1993.

Powell, M. G., et al. "Contraception with the Cervical Cap: Effectiveness, Safety, Continuity of Use, and User Satisfaction." *Contraception* 33:215–232, 1986.

Powledge, T. M. "Unnatural Selection." In Holmes, H. B., Hoskins, B. B., and Gross, M. (eds.), *The Custom-Made Child? Women Centered Perspectives.* Clifton, NJ: Humana Press, 1981.

Prather, R. C. "Sexual Dysfunction in the Diabetic Female: A Review." *Archives of Sexual Behavior* 17:277–284, 1988.

Presidential Commission on the Human Immunodeficiency Virus Epidemic. *Report of the Presidential Commission on the Human Immunodeficiency Virus Epidemic.* Washington, DC: U.S. Government Printing Office, 1988.

Priesand, S. *Judaism and the New Woman.* New York: Behrman House, 1975.

Prober, C. G., et al. "Low Risk of Herpes Simplex Virus Infections in Neonates Exposed to the Virus at the Time of Vaginal Delivery to Mothers with Recurrent Genital Herpes Simplex Infections." *New England Journal of Medicine* 316:240–244, 1987.

———. "Use of Routine Viral Cultures at Delivery to Identify Neonates Exposed to Herpes Simplex Virus." *New England Journal of Medicine* 318:887–891, 1988.

Proctor, F., Wagner, N., and Butler, J. "The Differentiation of Male and Female Orgasm: An Experimental Study." In Wagner, N. (ed.), *Perspectives on Human Sexuality.* New York: Behavioral Publications, 1974.

Pugh, B. "An Evaluation of the Effects of Various Lubricants on Latex Condoms." (Abstract # W.A.P.95, p. 135.) Presented at the Fifth International Conference on AIDS, Montreal, June 4–9, 1989.

Quadagno, D. M., et al. "Postpartum Moods in Men and Women." *American Journal of Obstetrics and Gynecology* 154:1018–1023, 1986.

Queenan, J. T. "The C-Section Crisis: Why We Must Solve It Ourselves." *Contemporary Obstetrics and Gynecology* 31(2):9–10, 1988.

Quindlen, Anna. "A Time to Choose." *The New York Times*, p. E21, January 28, 1990.

Quinn, T. C. "Screening for HIV Infection—Benefits and Costs." *New England Journal of Medicine* 327:445–452, 1992.

Quinn, T. C., et al. "Human Immunodeficiency Virus Infection Among Patients Attending Clinics for Sexually Transmitted Diseases. *New England Journal of Medicine* 318:197–203, 1988.

Rabin, B. *The Sensuous Wheeler: Sexual Adjustment for the Spinal Cord Injured*. San Francisco: Multi-Focus Resource Center, 1980.

Rada, R. T. (ed.). *Clinical Aspects of the Rapist*. New York: Grune & Stratton, 1978.

Rainwater, L. "Marital Sexuality in Four 'Cultures of Poverty.'" In Marshall, D., and Suggs, R. (eds.), *Human Sexual Behavior*, pp. 187–205. New York: Basic Books, 1971.

Raisz, L. G. "Local and Systemic Factors in the Pathogenesis of Osteoporosis." *New England Journal of Medicine* 318:818–828, 1988.

Ramalingaswami, V. "India: National Plan for AIDS." *Lancet* 339:1162–1163, 1992.

Ramcharan, S. *The Walnut Creek Contraceptive Drug Study: A Prospective Study of the Side Effects of Oral Contraceptives*. Bethesda, MD: U.S. Department of Health and Human Services, National Institutes of Health (publication NIH 81–564), 1981.

Ramstedt, K., et al. "Contact Tracing for Human Immunodeficiency Virus Infection." *Sexually Transmitted Diseases* 17:37–41, 1990.

Rando, R. F. "Human Papillomavirus: Implications for Clinical Medicine." *Annals of Internal Medicine* 108:628–630, 1988.

Ranki, A., et al. "Long Latency Precedes Overt Seroconversion in Sexually Transmitted Human Immunodeficiency Virus Infections." *Lancet* ii:589–593, 1987.

Raymond, C. A. "New Use for Old Method of Inducing Ejaculation May Give Hope of Fatherhood to Some Spinal Cord-Injured Men." *Journal of the American Medical Association* 258:743–744, 1987.

———. "Cervical Dysplasia Upturn Worries Gynecologists, Health Officials." *Journal of the American Medical Association* 257:2397–2398, 1987a.

———. "In Vitro Fertilization Enters Stormy Adolescence as Experts Debate the Odds." *Journal of the American Medical Association* 259:464–469, 1988.

Raz, R., and Stamm, W. E. "A Controlled Trial of Intravaginal Estriol in Postmenopausal Women with Recurrent Urinary Tract Infections." *New England Journal of Medicine* 329:753–756, 1993.

Rebecca, M., Hefner, R., and Oleshansky, B. "A Model of Sex-Role Transcendence." *Journal of Science Issues* 32:197–206, 1976.

Redfield, R., and Birx, D. "HIV-specific Vaccine Therapy: Concepts, Status, and Future Directions." *AIDS Research and Human Retroviruses* 8(6):1051–1058, 1992.

Redfield, R. R., and Burke, D. S. "HIV Infection: The Clinical Picture." *Scientific American* 259(4):90–98, October 1988.

Reese, C. R. "Neurophysiological Studies of Cannabis in Human Subjects." *Journal of Substance Use and Abuse* 4:118–127, 1977.

Reeves, W. C., et al. "Human Papillomavirus Infection and Cervical Cancer in Latin America." *New England Journal of Medicine* 320:1437–1441, 1989.

Regelson, W., Loria, R., and Kalimi, M. "Beyond Abortion: RU-486 and the Need of the Crisis Constituency." *Journal of the American Medical Association* 264:1026–1027, 1990.

Reichman, R. C., et al. "Treatment of Recurrent Genital Herpes Simplex Infections with Oral Acyclovir." *Journal of the American Medical Association* 251:2103–2107, 1984.

Reid, I. R., et al. "Effect of Calcium Supplementation on Bone Loss in Postmenopausal Women." *New England Journal of Medicine* 328:460–464, 1993.

Reid, R. L. "Premenstrual Syndrome." *New England Journal of Medicine* 324:1208–1210, 1991.

Reiner, N. E., et al. "Asymptomatic Rectal Mucosal Lesions and Hepatitis B Surface Antigen at Sites of Sexual Contact in Homosexual Men with Persistent Hepatitis B Virus Infection." *Annals of Internal Medicine* 96:170–173, 1982.

Reingold, A. L. "Nonmenstrual Toxic Shock Syndrome: The Growing Picture." *Journal of the American Medical Association* 249:932, 1983.

———. "Toxic Shock Syndrome and the Contraceptive Sponge." *Journal of the American Medical Association* 255:242–243, 1986.

Reingold, A. L., et al. "Toxic Shock Syndrome Surveillance in the United States, 1980 to 1981." *Annals of Internal Medicine* 96(Part 2):875–880, 1982.

Reinhold, R. "2 Acquitted of Child Molestation in Nation's Longest Criminal Trial." *The New York Times*, pp. A1 & A18, January 20, 1990.

Reinisch, J., and Beasley, R. *The Kinsey Institute New Report on Sex*. New York: St. Martin's Press, 1990.

Reinisch, J. M. "Fetal Hormones, the Brain, and Human Sex Differences: A Heuristic, Integrative Review of the Recent Literature." *Archives of Sexual Behavior* 3:51–90, 1974.

———. "Prenatal Exposure to Synthetic Progestins Increases Potential for Aggression in Humans." *Science* 211:1171–1173, 1981.

Reinisch, J. M., et al. "High-Risk Sexual Behavior Among Heterosexual Undergraduates at a Midwestern University." *Family Planning Perspectives* 24:116–121 & 145, 1992.

Reinisch, J. *The Kinsey Institute New Report on Sex*. New York: St. Martin's Press, 1990.

Reiss, A. J. "The Social Integration of Queers and Peers." In Becker, H. S. (ed.), *The Other Side: Perspectives on Deviance*, pp. 181–210. New York: Free Press, 1967.

Reiss, B. F. "Psychological Tests in Homosexuality." In Marmor, J. (ed.), *Homosexual Behavior*, pp. 296–311. New York: Basic Books, 1980.

———. "The Sexual Renaissance: A Summary and Analysis." *Journal of Social Issues* 22:123–137, 1966.

Reiss, I. L. *Journal Into Sexuality: An Exploratory Voyage*. Englewood Cliffs, NJ: Prentice-Hall, 1986.

———. *The Social Context of Premarital Sexual Permissiveness*. New York: Holt, Rinehart and Winston, 1967.

———. *Family Systems in America*, 3rd ed. New York: Holt, Rinehart and Winston, 1980.

Reiss, I. L., et al. *A Guide for Researching Heterosexual Relationships*. University of Minnesota, Minnesota Family Study Center, 1980.

Rekers, G. A., et al. "Sex-Role Stereotype and Professional Intervention for Childhood Gender Disturbance." *Professional Psychology* 9:127–136, 1978.

Remafedi, G. "The Healthy Sexual Development of Gay and Lesbian Adolescents." *SIECUS Report* 17(5):7–8, May–July 1989.

Rembar, C. *The End of Obscenity*. New York: Bantam Books, 1969.

Renshaw, D. "Inflatable Penile Prosthesis." *Journal of the American Medical Association* 241:2637–2638, 1979.

———. *Incest: Understanding and Treatment*. Boston: Little, Brown, 1983.

Renshaw, D. C. "Young Children's Sex Play: Counseling the Parents." *Medical Aspects of Human Sexuality* 22(12):68–72, December 1988.

———. "Sex and Eating Disorders." *Medical Aspects of Human Sexuality* 24(4):68–77, 1990.

Report of the Commission on Obscenity and Pornography. New York: Bantam Books, 1970.

Rheingold, H. L., and Cook, K. V. "The Contents of Boys' and Girls' Rooms as an Index of Parents' Behavior." *Child Development* 46:459–463, 1975.

Rhoads, G. G., et al. "The Safety and Efficacy of Chorionic Villus Sampling for Early Prenatal Diagnosis of Cytogenetic Abnormalities." *New England Journal of Medicine* 320:609–617, 1989.

Richart, R. M., and Barron, B. A. "Screening Strategies for Cervical Cancer and Cervical Intraepitheleal Neoplasia." Presented at the American Cancer Society National Conference on Cancer Prevention and Detection, Chicago, April 17–19, 1980.

Richwald, G. A., et al. "Are Condom Instructions Readable? Results of a Readability Study." *Public Health Reports* 103:355–358, 1988.

Rietmeijer, C. A. M., et al. "Condoms as Physical and Chemical Barriers Against Human Immunodeficiency Virus." *Journal of the American Medical Association* 259:1851–1853, 1988.

Rinehart, W., and Piotrow, P. T. "OCs: Update on Usage, Safety, and Side Effects." *Population Reports*, Series A(5):January 1979.

Rio, L. M. "Psychological and Sociological Research and the Decriminalization or Legalization of Prostitution." *Archives of Sexual Behavior* 20:205–218, 1991.

Rivenbark, W. H., III. "Self-disclosure Among Adolescents." *Psychological Reports* 28:35–42, 1971.

Rizley, R. "Psychobiological Basis of Romantic Love." In Pope, K. S., et al., *On Love and Loving*, pp. 104–113. San Francisco: Jossey-Bass, 1980.

Robbins, M., and Jensen, G. D. "Multiple Orgasm in Males." *Journal of Sex Research* 14:21–26, 1978.

Robboy, S. J., et al. *Prenatal Diethylstilbestrol (DES) Exposure: Recommendations of the Diethylstilbestrol Adenosis (DESAD) Project for the Identification and Management of Exposed Individuals*. Washington, DC: U.S. Department of Health and Human Services, NIH Publication No. 81–2049, 1981.

Roberts, C. L., and Lewis, R. A. "The Empty Nest Syndrome." In Howells, J. G. (ed.), *Modern Perspectives in the Psychiatry of Middle Age*, pp. 328–336. New York: Brunner/Mazel, 1981, 1990.

Roberts, M. M., et al. "Edinburgh Trial of Screening for Breast Cancer: Mortality at Seven Years." *Lancet* 335:241–246, 1990.

Robertson, D. H., McMillan, A., and Young, H. *Clinical Practice in Sexually Transmissible Diseases*. Kent, England: Pitman Medical, 1980.

Robinson, B. E. *Teenage Fathers*. Lexington, MA: D.C. Heath, 1988.

Robinson, I., and Jedlicka, D. "Change in Sexual Attitude and Behavior of College Students from 1965 to 1980: A Research Note." *Journal of Marriage and the Family* 44:237–240, 1982.

Robinson, J. E., and Short, R. V. "Changes in Breast Sensitivity at Puberty, During the Menstrual Cycle, and at Parturition." *British Medical Journal* 1:1188–1191, 1977.

Robinson, P. A. "What Liberated Males Do." *Psychology Today* 15:18–84, 1981.

Roeske, N. C. "Hysterectomy and Other Gynecological Surgeries: A Psychological View." In Notman, M. T., and Nadelson, C. C. (eds.), *The Woman Patient*, Vol. 1, pp. 217–232. New York: Plenum Press, 1978.

Rogers, C. R. *Becoming Partners*. New York: Delacorte Press, 1972.

Roiphe, K. *The Morning After: Sex, Fear and Feminism on Campus*. Boston: Little, Brown, 1993.

Romieu, I., et al. "Prospective Study of Oral Contraceptive Use and Risk of Breast Cancer in Women." *Journal of the National Cancer Institute* 81:1313–1321, 1989.

Ronald, A. R., and Albritton, W. L. "Chancroid and *Haemophilus ducreyi*." In Holmes, K. K., et al. (eds.),

Sexually Transmitted Diseases, pp. 385–393. New York: McGraw-Hill, 1984.

Rooks, J. P., et al. "Outcomes of Care in Birth Centers." *New England Journal of Medicine* 321:1804–1811, 1989.

Rooney, J. F., et al. "Acquisition of Genital Herpes from an Asymptomatic Sexual Partner." *New England Journal of Medicine* 314:1561–1564, 1986.

Rosen, M. G., and Thomas, L. *The Cesarean Myth*. New York: Viking Penguin, 1989.

Rosen, R. C., and Leiblum, S. R. *Erectile Disorders: Assessment and Treatment*. New York: Guilford Press, 1992.

Rosenbaum, M. "When Drugs Come into the Picture, Love Flies Out the Window: Women Addicts' Love Relationships." *International Journal of the Addictions* 16:1197–1206, 1981.

Rosenberg, L., et al. "Oral Contraceptive Use in Relation to Nonfatal Myocardial Infarction." *American Journal of Epidemiology* 111:59–66, 1980.

———. "Vasectomy and the Risk of Prostate Cancer." *American Journal of Epidemiology* 132:1051–1055, 1990.

Rosenberg, M. J., et al. "Effect of the Contraceptive Sponge on Chlamydia Infection, Gonorrhea, and Candidiasis." *Journal of the American Medical Association* 257:2308–2312, 1987.

Rosenblatt, R. "The Baby in the Factory." *Time*, p. 90, February 14, 1983.

Rosenblum, L., et al. "Sexual Practices in the Transmission of Hepatitis B Virus and Prevalence of Hepatitis Delta Virus in Female Prostitutes in the United States." *Journal of the American Medical Association* 267:2477–2481, 1992.

Rosenblum, S., and Faber, M. M. "The Adolescent Sexual Asphyxia Syndrome." *Journal of the American Academy of Child Psychiatry* 18:546–558, 1979.

Rosenfield, A. "Mifepristone (RU 486) in the United States: What Does the Future Hold?" *New England Journal of Medicine* 328:1560–1561, 1993.

Rosenheim, E. "Sexual Attitudes and Regulations in Judaism." In Money, J., and Musaph, H. (eds.), *Handbook of Sexology*, pp. 1315–1323. New York: Elsevier/North-Holland, 1977.

Rosenheim, M. K., and Testa, M. F. (eds.). *Early Parenthood and Coming of Age in the 1990s*. New Brunswick, NJ: Rutgers University Press, 1993.

Rosenthal, E. "As More Tiny Infants Live, Choices and Burdens Grow." *The New York Times*, pp. 1 & 26, September 29, 1991.

Rosoff, J. L. "Sex Education in the Schools: Policies and Practice." *Family Planning Perspectives* 21:52, 64, 1989.

Ross, C., and Piotrow, P. T. "Birth Control Without Contraceptives." *Population Reports*, Series I(1):June 1974.

Ross, J. A. "Contraception: Short-Term vs. Long-Term Failure Rates." *Family Planning Perspectives* 21:275–277, 1989.

Ross, M. W. "Retrospective Distortion in Homosexual Research." *Archives of Sexual Behavior* 9:523–532, 1980.

Rossi, A. S., and Rossi, P. E. "Body Time and Social Time: Mood Patterns by Menstrual Cycle and Day of Week." *Social Science Research* 6:273–308, 1977.

Rousseau, S., et al. "The Expectancy of Pregnancy for 'Normal' Infertile Couples." *Fertility & Sterility* 40:768–772, 1983.

Rowland, D. L., et al. "Penile and Finger Sensory Thresholds in Young, Aging, and Diabetic Males." *Archives of Sexual Behavior* 18:1–12, 1989.

Rozenbaum, W., et al. "HIV Transmission by Oral Sex." *Lancet* ii:1395, 1988.

Rubenstein, C. "The Modern Art of Courtly Love." *Psychology Today*, pp. 43, 49, July 1983.

Rubenstein, C., and Shaver, P. *In Search of Intimacy*. New York: Random House, 1982.

Rubin, A. M., and Adams, J. R. "Outcomes of Sexually Open Marriages." *Journal of Sex Research* 22:311–319, 1986.

Rubin, J., Provenzano, F., and Luria, Z. "The Eye of the Beholder: Parents' Views on Sex of Newborns." *American Journal of Orthopsychiatry* 44:512–519, 1974.

Rubin, L. "Sex and Sexuality: Women at Midlife." In Kirkpatrick, M. (ed.), *Women's Sexual Experiences: Explorations of the Dark Continent*, pp. 61–82. New York: Plenum Press, 1982.

———. *Intimate Strangers: Men and Women Together*. New York: Harper & Row, 1983.

Rubin, R., Reinisch, J., and Haskett, R. "Postnatal Gonadal Steroid Effects on Human Behavior." *Science* 211(4488):1318–1324, 1981.

Rubin, T. I. *The Angry Book*, New York: Collier, 1970.

Rubin, Z. "Measurement of Romantic Love." *Journal of Personality and Social Psychology* 16(2):265–273, 1970.

———. *Liking and Loving: An Introduction to Social Psychology*. New York: Holt, Rinehart and Winston, 1973.

Rubin, Z., and Shenker, S. "Friendship, Proximity, and Self-disclosure." *Journal of Personality* 46:1–22, 1978.

Rubin, Z., et al. "Self-disclosure in Dating Couples: Sex-Roles and the Ethic of Openness." *Journal of Marriage and the Family* 42:305–317, 1980.

Ruble, D. N., Brooks-Gunn, J., and Clarke, A. "Research on Menstrual-Related Psychological Changes: Alternative Perspectives." In Parsons, J. E. (ed.), *The Psychobiology of Sex Differences and Sex Roles*, pp. 227–243. New York: McGraw-Hill/Hemisphere, 1980.

Rush, D., and Callahan, K. R. "Exposure to Passive Cigarette Smoking and Child Development: A Critical Review." *Annals of the New York Academy of Sciences* 562:74–100, 1989.

Rush, F. "The Sexual Abuse of Children: A Feminist Point of View." In Connell, N., and Wilson, C. (eds.), *Rape: The First Sourcebook for Women*, pp. 65–75. New York: New American Library, 1974.

Russell, D. E. H. *Rape in Marriage*. New York: Macmillan, 1982.

Russell-Brown, P., et al. "Comparison of Condom Breakage During Human Use with Performance in Laboratory Testing." *Contraception* 45:429, 1992.

Rwandan HIV Seroprevalence Study Group. "Nationwide Community-based Serological Survey of HIV-1 and Other Human Retrovirus Infection in a Central African Country." *Lancet* i:941–943, 1989.

Ryan, A. S., Lewandowski, G., and Krieger, F. W. "The Recent Decline in Breast-Feeding, 1984–1989." *Pediatrics* 8:873–874, 1991.

Ryback, R. S. "Chronic Alcohol Consumption and Menstruation" (letter). *Journal of the American Medical Association* 238:2143, 1977.

Ryder, N. B. "Contraceptive Failure in the United States." *Family Planning Perspectives* 5(3):133–142, 1973.

Sachs, J. "Young Children's Language Use in Pretend Play." In Philips, S. U., Steele, S., and Tanz, C. (eds.), *Language, Gender, and Sex in Comparative Perspective.* Cambridge: Cambridge University Press, 1987.

Sachs, M. K. "Antiretroviral Chemotherapy of Human Immunodeficiency Virus Infections Other Than with Azidothymidine." *Archives of Internal Medicine* 152:485–501, 1992.

Sacred Congregation for the Doctrine of the Faith. "Declaration on Certain Questions Concerning Sexual Ethics." Translated by the National Catholic News Service. *Origins* 5(31):485–494, 1976.

Sadoff, R. L. "Other Sexual Deviations." In Freedman, A. M., Kaplan, H. I., and Saddock, B. J. (eds.), *Comprehensive Textbook of Psychiatry/II,* pp. 1539–1544, Baltimore: Williams & Wilkins, 1975.

Safran, C. "What Men Do to Women on the Job: A Shocking Look at Sexual Harassment." *Redbook,* pp. 148–150, 156, November 1976.

———. "Sexual Harassment: The View from the Top." *Redbook,* pp. 47–51, March 1981.

Sagarin, E. "Prison Homosexuality and Its Effect on Postprison Sexual Behavior." *Psychiatry* 39:245–257, 1976.

Sager, C. "A Typology of Intimate Relationships." *Journal of Sex and Marital Therapy* 3:83–112, 1977.

Sager, C., et al. *Treating the Remarried Family.* New York: Brunner/Mazel, 1983.

Saghir, M. T., and Robins, E. *Male and Female Homosexuality.* Baltimore: Williams & Wilkins, 1973.

Salholz, E., et al. "The Future of Gay America." *Newsweek,* pp. 20–25, March 12, 1990.

Salvesen, K. A., et al. "Routine Ultrasonography In Utero and School Performance at Age 8–9 Years." *Lancet* 339:85–89, 1992.

Sanchez, R. S., et al. "Pituitary–Testicular Axis in Patients on Lithium Therapy." *Fertility & Sterility* 27:667–669, 1976.

Sanday, P. R. "The Sociocultural Context of Rape: A Cross-Cultural Study." *Journal of Social Issues* 37(4):5–27, 1981.

Sanders, L. L., Jr., et al. "Treatment of Sexually Transmitted Chlamydial Infections." *Journal of the American Medical Association* 255:1750–1756, 1986.

Sandfort, T. "Pedophile Relationships in the Netherlands: Alternative Lifestyle for Children?" *Alternative Lifestyles* 5(3):164–183, 1983.

Sandoval, J. A. "IMPACT 88: Dallas' Countywide Plan for Reducing Teen Pregnancy." *SIECUS Report* 16:1–5, January/February 1988.

Sanford, L. T. *Come Tell Me Right Away.* Fayetteville, NY: Ed-U Press, 1982.

Santen, R. J., et al. "Mechanism of Action of Narcotics in the Production of Menstrual Dysfunction in Women." *Fertility & Sterility* 26:538–548, 1975.

Sarafino, E. "An Estimate of Nationwide Incidence of Sexual Offenses against Children." *Child Welfare* 58:127–134, 1979.

Sarrel, L. J., and Sarrel, P. M. *Sexual Unfolding: Sexual Development and Sex Therapies in Late Adolescence.* Boston: Little, Brown, 1979.

Sarrel, P. "Male Rape." Paper presented at the Annual Meeting of the International Academy of Sex Research, Phoenix, AZ, November 1980.

Sarrel, P. M., and Masters, W. H. "Sexual Molestation of Men by Women." *Archives of Sexual Behavior* 11:117–131, 1982.

Sauer, M. V., et al. "Establishment of a Nonananonymous Donor Oocyte Program: Preliminary Experience at the University of Southern California." *Fertility & Sterility* 52:433–436, 1989.

Saunders, E. J. "Life-Threatening Autoerotic Behavior: A Challenge for Sex Educators and Therapists." *Journal of Sex Education and Therapy* 15:82–91, 1989.

Sayers, S. L., and Baucom, D. H. "Role of Femininity and Masculinity in Distressed Couples' Communication." *Journal of Personality and Social Psychology* 61:641–647, 1991.

Saywitz, K. J., et al. "Children's Memories of a Physical Examination Involving Genital Touch: Implications for Reports of Child Sexual Abuse." *Journal of Consulting and Clinical Psychology* 59:682–691, 1991.

Scacco, A. M., Jr. *Male Rape.* New York: AMS Press, 1982.

Scanzoni, J., and Fox, G. L. "Sex Roles, Family and Society: The Seventies and Beyond." *Journal of Marriage and the Family* 42:743–758, 1980.

Schachter, S. "The Interaction of Cognitive and Physiological Determinants of Emotional State." In Berkowitz, L. (ed.), *Advances in Experimental Social Psychology,* Vol. 1, pp. 49–80. New York: Academic Press, 1964.

Schacter, J., Stone, E., and Moncada, J. "Screening for Chlamydial Infections in Women Attending Family Planning Clinics." *Western Journal of Medicine* 138:375–379, 1983.

Schaeffer, P. "Bishops' Study Data on Sexuality Published." *St. Louis Post-Dispatch,* p. 9D, February 27, 1981.

Schatten, G., and Schatten, H. "The Energetic Egg." *The Sciences* 23(5):28–34, 1983.

Schatzkin, A., et al. "Alcohol Consumption and Breast Cancer in the Epidemiologic Follow-up Study of the First National Health and Nutrition Examination Survey." *New England Journal of Medicine* 316:1169–1173, 1987.

Schecter, J. O., Schwartz, H. P., and Greenfield, D. G. "Sexual Assault and Anorexia Nervosa." *International Journal of Eating Disorders* 6:313–316, 1987.

Schesselman, J. J. "Cancer of the Breast and Reproductive Tract in Relation to Use of Oral Contraceptives." *Contraception* 40:1–38, 1989.

Schetky, D. H. "Emerging Issues in Child Sexual Abuse." *Journal of the American Academy of Child Psychiatry* 25:490–492, 1986.

Schiavi, R. C. "Sexuality and Aging in Men." *Annual Review of Sex Research* I:227–249, 1990.

Schiavi, R. "Chronic Alcoholism and Male Sexual Dysfunction." *Journal of Sex & Marital Therapy* 16:23–33, 1990.

Schiff, E., et al. "The Use of Aspirin to Prevent Pregnancy-Induced Hypertension and Lower the Ratio of Thromboxane A2 to Prostacyclin in Relatively High Risk Pregnancies." *New England Journal of Medicine* 321:351–356, 1989.

Schiller, P. *The Sex Profession.* Washington, DC: Shilmark House, 1981.

Schlech, W. F., III, et al. "Risk Factors for Development of Toxic Shock Syndrome." *Journal of the American Medical Association* 248:835–839, 1982.

Schlegel, A., and Barry, H., III. "Adolescent Initiation Ceremonies: Cross-Cultural Codes." *Ethnology* 18:199–210, 1979.

———. "The Evolutionary Significance of Adolescent Initiation Ceremonies." *American Ethnologist* 7:696–715, 1980.

Schmid, G. P., et al. "Chancroid in the United States." *Journal of the American Medical Association* 258:3265–3268, 1987.

Schmidt, C. W., and Lucas, J. "The Short-Term, Intermittent, Conjoint Treatment of Sexual Disorders." In Meyer, J. K. (ed.), *Clinical Management of Sexual Disorders.* Baltimore: Williams & Wilkins, 1976.

Schmidt, G., and Clement, V. "Does Peace Prevent Homosexuality?" *Archives of Sexual Behavior* 19:183–187, 1990.

Schmidt, G., and Sigusch, V. "Sex Differences in Responses to Psychosexual Stimulation by Films and Slides." *Journal of Sex Research* 6:268–283, 1970.

Schmidt, P. J., Grover, G. N., and Rubinow, D. R. "Alprazolam in the Treatment of Premenstrual Syndrome." *Archives of General Psychiatry* 50:467–473, 1993.

Schoen, E. J. "The Status of Circumcision of Newborns." *New England Journal of Medicine* 322:1308–1312, 1990.

Schoenbaum, S., et al. "Outcome of Delivery Following an Induced or Spontaneous Abortion." *American Journal of Obstetrics and Gynecology* 136:19, 1980.

Schofield, C. B. *Sexually Transmitted Diseases.* New York: Churchill Livingstone, 1979.

Scholl, T. O., et al. "Effects of Vaginal Spermicides on Pregnancy Outcome." *Family Planning Perspectives* 15:244–250, 1983.

Schover, L. R., and LoPiccolo, J. "Treatment Effectiveness for Dysfunctions of Sexual Desire." *Journal of Sex & Marital Therapy* 8:179–197, 1982.

Schover, L. R., et al. "The Multi-axial Problem-Oriented Diagnostic System for the Sexual Dysfunctions: An Alternative to DSM-III." *Archives of General Psychiatry* 39:614–619, 1982.

Schover, L. R., et al. "Orgasm Phase Dysfunction in Multiple Sclerosis." *Journal of Sex Research* 25:548–554, 1988.

Schover, L. R., and Jensen, S. B. *Sexuality and Chronic Illness: A Comprehensive Approach.* New York: Guilford Press, 1988.

Schreeded, M. T., et al. "Hepatitis B in Homosexual Men: Prevalence of Infection and Factors Related to Transmission." *Journal of Infectious Diseases* 146:7–15, 1982.

Schreiner-Engel, P., and Schiavi, R. "Sexual Arousability in Women." Paper presented at the Sixth Annual Meeting of the Society for Sex Therapy and Research, Cambridge, MA, May 31, 1980.

Schreiner-Engel, P., et al. "Sexual Arousability and the Menstrual Cycle." *Psychosomatic Medicine* 43:199–214, 1981.

Schulman, A. "Organs and Orgasms." In Gornick, V., and Moran, B. K. (eds.), *Women in Sexist Society.* New York: Basic Books, 1971.

Schultz, L. G. (ed.). *The Sexual Victimology of Youth.* Springfield, IL: Charles C. Thomas, 1980.

Schultz, W. C. M., et al. "Vaginal Sensitivity to Electric Stimuli: Theoretical and Practical Implications." *Archives of Sexual Behavior* 18:87–95, 1989.

Schwartz, D. "Female Fecundity as a Function of Age." *New England Journal of Medicine* 306:404–406, 1982.

Schwartz, M., Jewelewicz, R., and Vande Wiele, R. L. "Application of Orthodox Jewish Law to Reproductive Medicine." *Fertility & Sterility* 33:471–474, 1980.

Schwartz, M. F. "Incest: Its Many Facets." Presentation at the Special Symposium on Incest of the Masters & Johnson Institute, St. Louis, MO, June 4, 1983.

Schwartz, M. F., and Bauman, J. E. "Hyperprolactinemia and Sexual Dysfunction in Men." Presented at the Seventh Annual Meeting of the Society for Sex Therapy and Research, New York, March 1981.

Schwartz, M. F., and Brasted, W. S. "Sexual Addiction." *Medical Aspects of Human Sexuality* 19:103–107, 1985.

Schwartz, M. F., and Masters, W. H. "Conceptual Factors in the Treatment of Paraphilias: A Preliminary Report." *Journal of Sex & Marital Therapy* 9:3–18, 1983.

Schwartz, P., et al. "Type II Herpes Simplex Virus and Vulvar Carcinoma in Situ." *New England Journal of Medicine* 305:517–518, 1981.

Science. "News and Comments." *Science* 221:436, 1983.

Scott, J. F. *The Sexual Instinct: Its Use and Dangers as Affecting Heredity and Morals,* 3rd ed. Chicago: Login Brothers, 1930.

Segal, S. J., et al. "Norplant Implants: The Mechanism of Contraceptive Action." *Fertility & Sterility* 56:273–275, 1991.

Segraves, R. T. "Psychiatric Drugs and Inhibited Female Orgasm." *Journal of Sex and Marital Therapy* 14:202–207, 1988.

Segraves, R. T., et al. "Erectile Dysfunction Association with Pharmacologic Agents." In Segraves, R. T., and Schoenberg, H. W. (eds.), *Diagnosis and Treatment of Erectile Disturbances.* New York: Plenum Press, 1985.

———. "Spontaneous Remission in Erectile Dysfunction: A Partial Replication." *Behavioral Research and Therapy* 23(2):203–204, 1985.

Seibel, M. "A New Era in Reproductive Technology." *New England Journal of Medicine* 318:828–834, 1988.

Seibel, M., Ranoux, C., and Kearnan, M. "In Vitro Fertilization: How Much Is Enough?" *New England Journal of Medicine* 321:1052–1053, 1989.

Seibel, M. M., Freeman, M., and Graves, W. "Carcinoma of the Cervix and Sexual Function." *Obstetrics and Gynecology* 55:484–487, 1980.

Semmens, J. P., and Wagner, G. "Estrogen Deprivation and Vaginal Function in Postmenopausal Women." *Journal of the American Medical Association* 248:445–448, 1982.

Serpenti, L. *Cultivators in the Swamps.* Assen: Van Gorcum, 1965.

Sevely, J., and Bennett, J. "Concerning Female Ejaculation and the Female Prostate." *Journal of Sex Research* 14:1–20, 1978.

Shafer, M. A., et al. "Urinary Leukocyte Esterase Screening Test for Asymptomatic Chlamydial and Gonococcal Infections in Males." *Journal of the American Medical Association* 262:2562–2566, 1989.

Shainess, N. "How 'Sex Experts' Debase Sex." *World* 2(1):21–25, 1973.

Shane, J. M., Schiff, I., and Wilson, E. A. The Infertile Couple: Evaluation and Treatment. *Clinical Symposia* 28(5), 1976.

Shanor, K. *The Fantasy Files.* New York: Dial Press, 1977.

Shapira, J., and Cummings, J. L. "Alzheimer's Disease: Changes in Sexual Behavior." *Medical Aspects of Human Sexuality* 23(No.6):32–36, June 1989.

Shapiro, S., et al. "Birth Defects and Vaginal Spermicides." *Journal of the American Medical Association* 247:2381–2384, 1982.

Shaver, P., Hazan, C., and Bradshaw, D. "Infant-Caretaker Attachment and Adult Romantic Love: Similarities and Differences." Paper presented at the 2nd International Conference on Personal Relationships, Madison, WI, 1984.

———. "Love As Attachment." In Sternberg, R. J., and Barnes, M. L. (eds.), *The Psychology of Love,* pp. 68–99. New Haven, CT: Yale University Press, 1988.

Sheehy, G. *Prostitution: Hustling in Our Wide-Open Society.* New York: Delacorte, 1973.

———. *Passages: Predictable Crises of Adult Life.* New York: E. P. Dutton, 1976.

———. *Pathfinders.* New York: William Morrow, 1981.

———. *The Silent Passage.* New York: Simon & Schuster, 1992.

Sherfey, M. J. *The Nature and Evolution of Female Sexuality.* New York: Random House, 1972.

Sherif, C. W. "A Social Psychological Perspective on the Menstrual Cycle." In Parsons, J. E. (ed.), *The Psychobiology of Sex Differences and Sex Roles,* pp. 245–268. New York: McGraw-Hill/Hemisphere, 1980.

Sherman, B. "A New Recognition of the Realities of Date Rape." *The New York Times,* pp. C1 & C14, October 23, 1985.

Sherris, J. D., Moore, S. H., and Fox, G. "New Developments in Vaginal Contraception." *Population Reports,* Series H, No. 7, January/February 1984.

Sherwin, B. B. "The Psychoendocrinology of Aging and Female Sexuality." *Annual Review of Sex Research* 2:181–198, 1991.

Shettles, L., and Rorvik, D. *Your Baby's Sex: Now You Can Choose.* New York: Dodd, Mead, 1970.

Shilts, R. *And the Band Played On: Politics, People, and the AIDS Epidemic.* New York: St. Martin's Press, 1987.

———. "Is 'Outing' Gays Ethical?" *The New York Times,* p. A26, April 12, 1990.

Shiono, P. H., Klebanoff, M. A., and Rhoads, G. G. "Smoking and Drinking During Pregnancy." *Journal of the American Medical Association* 255:82–84, 1986.

Shostak, A., McLouth, G., and Seng, L. *Men and Abortions: Lessons, Losses, and Love.* New York: Praeger, 1984.

Shuckit, M. A., et al. "Premenstrual Symptoms and Depression in a University Population." *Diseases of the Nervous System* 36:516–517, 1975.

Shuster, R. "Sexuality as a Continuum: The Bisexual Identity." In *Lesbian Psychologies: Explorations and Challenges,* pp. 56–71. Edited by the Boston Lesbian Psychologies Collective. Urbana: University of Illinois Press, 1987.

Shusterman, L. R. "Predicting the Psychological Consequences of Abortion." *Social Science and Medicine* 13:683–689, 1979.

Sibai, B. M., et al. "Prevention of Preeclampsia with Low-Dose Aspirin in Healthy, Nulliparous Pregnant Women." *New England Journal of Medicine* 329:1213–1218, 1993.

Sidi, A. A., et al. "Recent Advances in the Diagnosis and Management of Impotence." *Urology Clinics of North America* 13(3):489–500, August 1986.

Siegel, K., et al. "Patterns of Change in Sexual Behavior Among Gay Men in New York City." *Archives of Sexual Behavior* 17:481–497, 1988.

Siegel, O. "Personality Development in Adolescence." In Wolman, B. B., et al. (eds.), *Handbook of Development Psychology*, pp. 537–548. Englewood Cliffs, NJ: Prentice-Hall, 1982.

Siegel, R. K. "Cocaine and Sexual Dysfunction." *Journal of Psychoactive Drugs* 14:71–74, 1982.

Siegelman, M. "Parental Background of Male Homosexuals and Heterosexuals." *Archives of Sexual Behavior* 3:3–18, 1974.

Silliman, R. A., et al. "Age as a Predictor of Diagnostic and Initial Treatment Intensity in Newly Diagnosed Breast Cancer Patients." *Journal of Gerontology* 44:M46–M50, 1989.

Silver, H. "Autologous Blood Donation." *Transfusion Medicine Topic Update* 2(1):1–4, January 1989.

Silverberg, E. "Cancer Statistics, 1981." *Ca-A Cancer Journal for Clinicians* 31(1):13–28, 1981.

Silverman, S. "Scope, Specifics of Maternal Drug Use, Effects on Fetus Are Beginning to Emerge from Studies." *Journal of the American Medical Association* 261:1688–1689, 1989.

Silvestre, L., Bouali, Y., and Ulmann, A. "Postcoital Contraception: Myth or Reality?" *Lancet* 338:39–41, 1991.

Simenauer, J., and Carroll, D. *Singles: The New Americans.* New York: Simon & Schuster, 1982.

Simmons, R. G., and Rosenberg, F. "Sex, Sex-Roles, and Self-Image." *Journal of Youth and Adolescence* 4:225–258, 1975.

Simon, W., and Gagnon, J. "1967 Research Data." Cited in Gagnon, J. H., *Human Sexualities*, p. 157. Glenview, IL: Scott, Foresman, 1967.

Simonds, R. J., et al. "Transmission of Human Immunodeficiency Virus Type 1 from a Seronegative Organ and Tissue Donor." *New England Journal of Medicine* 326:726–732, 1992.

Singer, J., and Singer, I. "Types of Female Orgasm." *Journal of Sex Research* 8:255–267, 1972.

Singh, J., et al. "Sex Life and Psychiatric Problems After Myocardial Infarction." *Journal of the Association of Physicians of India* 18:503–507, 1970.

Sklarek, H. M., et al. "AIDS in a Bodybuilder Using Anabolic Steroids." *New England Journal of Medicine* 311:1701, 1984.

Slattery, M. L. "Cigarette Smoking and Exposure to Passive Smoke Are Risk Factors for Cervical Cancer." *Journal of the American Medical Association* 261:1593–1598, 1989.

Sloan, L. A. "Abortion Attitude Scale." *Health Education* 14(3):41–42, 1983.

Slovenko, R. *Psychiatry and Law*, pp. 59–60. Boston: Little, Brown, 1973.

———. "Homosexuality and the Law: From Condemnation to Celebration." In Marmor, J. (ed.), *Homosexual Behavior*, pp. 194–218. New York: Basic Books, 1980.

Smith, C. G., et al. "Effect of Delta-9-tetrahydrocannabinol (THC) on Secretion of Male Sex-Hormone in Rhesus Monkey." *Pharmacologist* 18:248, 1976.

Smith, D. G. "Thailand: AIDS Crisis Looms." *Lancet* 335:781–782, 1990.

Smith, D. W. "The Fetal Alcohol Syndrome." *Hospital Practice*, pp. 121–128, October 1979.

Smith, J., and Smith, L. "Co-marital Sex and the Sexual Freedom Movement." *Journal of Sex Research* 6:131–142, 1970.

Smith, P. B., and Mumford, D. M. (eds.). *Adolescent Pregnancy: New Perspectives for the Health Professional.* Boston: G. K. Hall, 1980.

Smith, P. C. "Saving Lives with a Testicular Self-Examination." *Sexual Medicine Today* 4(6):11–12, 1980.

Smith, T. F., et al. "The Phylogenetic History of Immunodeficiency Viruses." *Nature* 333:573–575, 1988.

Smith, T. M. "Specific Approaches and Techniques in the Treatment of Gay Male Alcohol Abusers." *Journal of Homosexuality* 7(4):53–69, 1982.

Smith, T. W. "Sex Counts: A Methodological Critique of Hite's Women and Love." In Turner, C. F., Miller, H. G., and Moses, L. E. (eds.), *AIDS: Sexual Behavior and Intravenous Drug Use*, pp. 537–547. Washington, DC: National Academy Press, 1989.

———. "Adult Sexual Behavior in 1989: Number of Partners, Frequency of Intercourse and Risk of AIDS." *Family Planning Perspectives* 23:102–107, 1991.

Smukler, A. J., and Schiebel, D. "Personality Characteristics of Exhibitionists." *Diseases of the Nervous System* 36:600–603, 1975.

Snarch, D. *Constructing the Sexual Crucible.* New York: Norton, 1991.

Sobel, J. D. "Bacterial Vaginosis—An Ecologic Mystery." *Annals of Internal Medicine* 111:551–561, 1989.

Sokolov, J. J., Harris, R. T., and Hecker, M. R. "Isolation of Substances from Human Vaginal Secretions Previously Shown to Be Sex Attractant Pheromones in Higher Primates." *Archives of Sexual Behavior* 5:269–274, 1976.

Solberg, D. A., Butler, J., and Wagner, N. N. "Sexual Behavior in Pregnancy." *New England Journal of Medicine* 288:1098–1103, 1973.

Solomon, R., et al. "Human Immunodeficiency Virus and Hepatitis Delta Virus in Homosexual Men: A Study of Four Cohorts." *Annals of Internal Medicine* 108:51–54, 1988.

Solomon, R. C. *Love: Emotion, Myth and Metaphor.* Garden City, NY: Anchor Press, 1981.

———. *About Love: Reinventing Romance for Our Times.* New York: Touchstone, 1989.

Somers, A. "Sexual Harassment in Academia: Legal Issues and Definitions." *Journal of Social Issues* 38(4):23–32, 1982.

Sonenstein, F. L., Pleck, J. H., and Ku, L. C. "Sexual Activity, Condom Use, and AIDS Awareness Among

Adolescent Males." *Family Planning Perspectives* 21:152–158, 1989.

Sorenson, R. C. *Adolescent Sexuality in Contemporary America.* New York: World Publishing, 1973.

Sorenson, T. "A Follow-up Study of Operated Transsexual Males." *Acta Psychiatrica Scandinavia* 63:486–503, 1981.

Sorokin, P. A. *The American Sex Revolution.* Boston: Porter Sargent, 1956.

Spach, D. H., Stapleton, A. E., and Stamm, W. E. "Lack of Circumcision Increases the Risk of Urinary Tract Infection in Young Men." *Journal of the American Medical Association* 267:679–681, 1992.

Spanier, G. B., and Cole, C. L. "Mate Swapping: Participation, Knowledge, and Values in a Midwestern Community." Presented at the Annual Meeting of the Midwest Sociological Society, Kansas City, MO, April 21, 1972.

Spanier, G. B., and Furstenberg, F. F., Jr. "Remarriage After Divorce: A Longitudinal Analysis of Well-being." *Journal of Marriage and the Family* 44:709–720, 1982.

Spear, L. P., Kirstein, C. L., and Frambes, N. A. "Cocaine Effects on the Developing Central Nervous System: Behavioral, Psychopharmacological, and Neurochemical Studies." *Annals of The New York Academy of Sciences* 562:290–307, 1989.

Spence, J. T., and Helmreich, R. L. *Masculinity & Femininity: Their Psychological Dimensions, Correlates, and Antecedents.* Austin: University of Texas Press, 1978.

Sperling, F. "Gonococcal Infections." In Wyngaarden, J. B., Smith, L. H., Jr., and Bennett, J. C. (eds.), *Cecil Textbook of Medicine,* 19th ed., pp. 1755–1759. Philadelphia: Saunders, 1992.

Speroff, L., and Darney, P. *A Clinical Guide for Contraception.* Baltimore: Williams & Wilkins, 1992.

Speroff, L., Glass, R. H., and Kase, N. G. *Clinical Gynecologic Endocrinology and Infertility,* 3rd ed. Baltimore: Williams & Wilkins, 1983.

Spitz, R. A. "Autoeroticism: Some Empirical Findings and Hypotheses on Three of Its Manifestations in the First Year of Life." In *The Psychoanalytic Study of the Child* 3(4):85–120. New York: International Universities Press, 1949.

Spitzer, P. G., and Weiner, N. J. "Transmission of HIV Infection from a Woman to a Man by Oral Sex." *New England Journal of Medicine* 320:251, 1989.

Spitzer, R. L., et al. *DSM-III-R Case Book.* Washington, DC: American Psychiatric Press, 1989.

Spohn, H. L., Willms, J., and Steinhausen, H. C. "Prenatal Alcohol Exposure and Long-Term Developmental Consequences." *Lancet* 341:907–910, 1993.

Spring-Mills, E., and Hafez, E. S. "Male Accessory Sexual Organs." In Hafez, E. S. (ed.), *Human Reproduction,* pp. 60–90. New York: Harper & Row, 1980.

St. Louis, M. E. "Human Immunodeficiency Virus Infection in Disadvantaged Adolescents: Findings from the U.S. Job Corps." *Journal of the American Medical Association* 266:2387–2391, 1991.

Stack, S., and Gundlach, J. H. "Divorce and Sex." *Archives of Sexual Behavior* 21:359–367, 1992.

Stackhouse, B. "The Impact of Religion on Sexuality Education." *SIECUS Report* 18:21–24 & 27, December 1989/January 1990.

Stall, R., et al. "Alcohol and Drug Use During Sexual Activity and Compliance with Safe Sex Guidelines for AIDS." *Health Education Quarterly* 13:359–371, 1986.

Stamm, W. E. "Diagnosis of *Chlamydia trachomatis* Genitourinary Infections." *Annals of Internal Medicine* 108:710–717, 1988.

———. "Effect of Treatment Regimens for *Neisseria gonorrhoeae* on Simultaneous Infection with *Chlamydia trachomatis.*" *New England Journal of Medicine* 310:545–549, 1984.

———. "CDC Update: *Chlamydia trachomatis* Infections." *Urban Health* 14:10–29, July/August 1985.

Stamm, W. E., et al. "The Association Between Genital Ulcer Disease and Acquisition of HIV Infection in Homosexual Men." *Journal of the American Medical Association* 260:1429–1433, 1988.

Stampfer, M. J., et al. "Postmenopausal Estrogen Therapy and Cardiovascular Disease: Ten-Year Follow-Up from the Nurses' Health Study." *New England Journal of Medicine* 325:756–762, 1991.

Stanley, J. P., and Wolfe, S. J. *The Coming Out Stories.* Watertown, MA: Persephone Press, 1980.

Starr, B. D., and Weiner, M. B. *The Starr–Weiner Report on Sex and Sexuality in the Mature Years.* New York: Stein & Day, 1981.

Staver, S. "Women Found Contracting HIV via Unprotected Sex." *American Medical News,* p. 4, June 1, 1990.

Stearns, P. "Interpreting the Medical Literature on Aging." Presented at the Family and Community History Colloquia: The Physician and Social History, Chicago, October 30, 1975 (cited in Bart and Grossman, 1978).

Steece, R., and Fleming, D. W. "False-Positive HIV Antibody Tests in RPR-Reactive Patients." *Journal of the American Medical Association* 260:923–924, 1988.

Steinberg, K. K., et al. "A Meta-analysis of the Effect of Estrogen Replacement Therapy on the Risk of Breast Cancer." *Journal of the American Medical Association* 265:1985–1990, 1991.

Steinem, G. "Erotica vs. Pornography." In Steinem, G. (ed.), *Outrageous Acts and Everyday Rebellions.* New York: Holt, Rinehart and Winston, 1983.

Stempel, R. R., and Moss, A. R. "Changes in Sexual Behavior by Gay Men in Response to AIDS." (Abstract # 6538.) Fourth International Conference on AIDS, Stockholm, June 12–16, 1988.

Stermac, L., Hall, K., and Henskens, M. "Violence Among Child Molesters." *Journal of Sex Research* 26:450–459, 1989.

Sternberg, R. J. *The Triangle of Love*. New York: Basic Books, 1988a.

———. "Triangulating Love." In Sternberg, R. J., and Barnes, M. L. (eds.), *The Psychology of Love*, pp. 119–138. New Haven, CT: Yale University Press, 1988.

Sternberg, R. J., and Barnes, M. L. (eds.). *The Psychology of Love*. New Haven, CT: Yale University Press, 1988.

Stevens, C. E., et al. "Epidemiology of Hepatitis C. Virus." *Journal of the American Medical Association* 263:49–53, 1990.

Stevens, F. A. "The Occurrence of *Staphyloccocus aureus* Infection with a Scarlatiniform Rash." *Journal of the American Medical Association* 88:1957–1958, 1927.

Stevens, W. K. "Fear of AIDS Brings Explicit Advice to Campus, Caution to Singles Bars." *The New York Times*, p. 9, February 17, 1987.

Stewart, A. J., and Lykes, M. B. (eds.). "Conceptualizing Gender in Personality Theory and Research." In *Gender and Personality: Current Perspectives on Theory and Research*. Durham, NC: Duke University Press, 1985.

Stewart, F., et al. *My Body, My Health: The Concerned Woman's Guide to Gynecology*. New York: Wiley, 1979.

Stock, W. E. "Effects of Exposure to Violent Pornography." Presented at the 26th Annual Meeting of the Society for the Scientific Study of Sex, Chicago, November 20, 1983.

Stockard, J., and Johnson, M. M. *Sex and Gender in Society*, 2nd ed. Englewood Cliffs, NJ: Prentice Hall, 1992.

Stoddart, T., and Turiel, E. "Children's Concepts of Cross-Gender Activities." *Child Development* 56:1241–1252, 1985.

Stoenner, H. "Child Sexual Abuse Growing in the United States." In *Plain Talk About Child Abuse*, pp. 11–13. Denver: Denver Humane Society, 1972.

Stoller, R. J. "Etiological Factors in Female Transsexualism: A First Approximation." *Archives of Sexual Behavior* 2:47–64, 1972.

———. "Gender Identity." In Freedman, A. M., Kaplan, H. I., and Sadock, B. J. (eds.), *Comprehensive Textbook of Psychiatry/III*, pp. 1400–1408. Baltimore: Williams & Wilkins, 1975.

———. *Perversion: The Erotic Form of Hatred*. New York: Pantheon Books, 1975a.

———. "Sexual Deviations." In Beach, F. (ed.), *Human Sexuality in Four Perspectives*, pp. 190–214. Baltimore: Johns Hopkins University Press, 1977.

———. *Sexual Excitement*. New York: Pantheon Books, 1979.

Stomper, P. C., et al. "Is Mammography Painful?" *Archives of Internal Medicine* 148:521–524, 1988.

Stone, R. "Living Dangerously After an AIDS Test." *Science* 257:615, 1992.

Stout, A. L., et al. "Premenstrual Symptoms in Black and White Community Samples." *American Journal of Psychiatry* 143:1436–1439, 1986.

Stovall, T. G., Ling, F. W., and Buster, J. E. "Outpatient Chemotherapy of Unruptured Ectopic Pregnancy." *Fertility & Sterility* 51:435–438, 1989.

Straus, S. E., et al. "Suppression of Frequently Recurring Genital Herpes: A Placebo-Controlled Double-Blind Trial of Oral Acyclovir." *New England Journal of Medicine* 310:1545–1550, 1984.

———. "Herpes Simplex Virus Infections: Biology, Treatment, and Prevention." *Annals of Internal Medicine* 103:404–419, 1985.

———. "Acyclovir Suppression of Frequently Recurring Genital Herpes." *Journal of the American Medical Association* 260:2227–2230, 1988.

Streissguth, A. P., Sampson, P., and Barr, H. M. "Neurobehavioral Dose–Response Effects of Prenatal Alcohol Exposure in Humans from Infancy to Adulthood." *Annals of the New York Academy of Sciences* 562:145–158, 1989.

Struckman-Johnson, C., and Struckman-Johnson, D. "Men Pressured and Forced into Sexual Experience." *Archives of Sexual Behavior* 23:93–114, 1994.

Stryker, J. "IV Drug Use and AIDS: Public Policy and Dirty Needles." *Journal of Health Politics, Policy and Law* 14:719–740, 1989.

Stuart, R. B. *Helping Couples Change*. New York: Guilford Press, 1980.

Stubblefield, P., et al. "Fertility After Induced Abortion: A Prospective Follow-up Study." *Obstetrics & Gynecology* 62:186, 1984.

Stumbo, B. "The State of Hate." *Esquire*, pp. 73–78, September 1993.

Sue, D. "Erotic Fantasies of College Students During Coitus." *Journal of Sex Research* 15:299–305, 1979.

Suggs, R., and Marshall, D. "Anthropological Perspectives on Human Sexual Behavior." In Marshall, D., and Suggs, R. (eds.), *Human Sexual Behavior*, pp. 218–243. New York: Basic Books, 1971.

Sullivan, J. M., et al. "Postmenopausal Estrogen Use and Coronary Atherosclerosis." *Annals of Internal Medicine* 108:358–363, 1988.

———. "Estrogen Replacement and Coronary Artery Disease: Effect On Survival in Postmenopausal Women." *Archives of Internal Medicine* 150:2557–2562, 1990.

Sullivan, R. "Revolution Number 9: Postcard from Oregon." *The New Yorker*, pp. 67–73, November 9, 1992.

Sullivan-Bolyai, J., et al. "Neonatal Herpes Simplex Virus Infection in King County, Washington." *Journal of the American Medical Association* 250:3059–3062, 1983.

Sulloway, F. J. *Freud: Biologist of the Mind*. New York: Basic Books, 1979.

Sultan, F. E., and Chambles, D. L. "Pubococcygeal Function and Orgasm in a Normal Population." In Graber, B. (ed.), *Circumvaginal Musculature and Sexual Function*, pp. 74–87. New York: Karger, 1982.

Summers, G. F., and Hammonds, A. D. "Toward a Paradigm of Respondent Bias in Survey Research." University of Wisconsin, 1965. Cited in Rosenthal, R., *Experimental Effects in Behavioral Research*. New York: Appleton-Century-Crofts, 1966.

Summers, R. J., and Myklebust, K. "The Influence of a History of Romance on Judgments and Responses to a Complaint of Sexual Harassment." *Sex Roles* 27:345–357, 1992.

Summit, R., and Kryso, J. "Sexual Abuse of Children: A Clinical Spectrum." *American Journal of Orthopsychiatry* 48:237–251, 1978.

Surgeon General, U.S. Public Health Service. *Surgeon General's Report on Acquired Immune Deficiency Syndrome*. Washington, DC: U.S. Government Printing Office, 1986.

Sussman, N. "Sex and Sexuality in History." In Sadock, B. J., Kaplan, H. I., and Freedman, A. M. (eds.), *The Sexual Experience*, pp. 7–70. Baltimore: Williams & Wilkins, 1976.

Sutherland, S., and Scherl, D. "Patterns of Response Among Victims of Rape." *American Journal of Orthopsychiatry* 40:503–511, 1970.

Swaab, D. F., and Hoffman, M. A. "An Enlarged Suprachiasmic Nucleus in Homosexual Men." *Brain Research* 537:141–148, 1990.

Swain, S. M. "In Situ or Localized Breast Cancer—How Much Treatment Is Needed?" *New England Journal of Medicine* 328:1633–1634, 1993.

Sweet, E. "Date Rape." *Ms.*, pp. 54–59 & 84–85, October 1985.

Sweet, J. A., and Bumpass, L. L. *American Families and Households*. New York: Russell Sage Foundation, 1987.

Szasz, G., and Carpenter, C. "Clinical Observations in Vibratory Stimulation of the Penis of Men with Spinal Cord Injury." *Archives of Sexual Behavior* 18:461–474, 1989.

Szasz, T. *Sex by Prescription*. New York: Anchor Press/Doubleday, 1980.

Tabar, L., et al. "Reduction in Mortality from Breast Cancer After Mass Screening with Mammography." *Lancet* i:829–832, 1985.

Talese, G. *Thy Neighbor's Wife*. New York: Doubleday, 1980.

Tallent, N. "Sexual Deviation as a Diagnostic Entity: A Confused and Sinister Concept." *Bulletin of the Menninger Clinic* 41:40–60, 1977.

Tamburello, A., and Seppecher, M. F. "The Effects of Depression on Sexual Behavior: Preliminary Results of Research." In Gemme, R., and Wheeler, C. C. (eds.), *Progress in Sexology*, pp. 107–128. New York: Plenum Press, 1977.

Tan, S. L., et al. "Cumulative Conception and Livebirth Rates After In Vitro Fertilization [sic]." *Lancet* 339:1390–1394, 1992.

Tanfer, K. "National Survey of Men: Design and Execution." *Family Planning Perspectives* 25:83–86, 1993.

Tanfer, K., and Schoorl, J. J. "Premarital Sexual Careers and Partner Change." *Archives of Sexual Behavior* 21:45–68, 1992.

Tanfer, K., et al. "Condom Use Among U.S. Men, 1991." *Family Planning Perspectives* 25:61–66, 1993.

Tangri, S. S., Burt, M. R., and Johnson, L. B. "Sexual Harassment at Work: Three Explanatory Models." *Journal of Social Issues* 38(4):33–54, 1982.

Tannahill, R. *Sex in History*. New York: Stein & Day, 1980.

Tannen, D. *You Just Don't Understand: Women and Men in Conversation*. New York: William Morrow, 1990.

Tanner, J. M. "Sequence and Tempo in the Somatic Changes in Puberty." In Grumbach, M. M., Grave, G. D., and Mayer, F. E. (eds.), *Control of the Onset of Puberty*. New York: Wiley, 1974.

Tatum, H. L., "Contraception and Family Planning." In Pernoll, M. L., and Benson, R. C. (eds.), *Current Obstetric & Gynecologic Diagnosis and Treatment*. Norwalk, CT: Appleton & Lange, 1987.

Tavris, C. *Anger: The Misunderstood Emotion*. New York: Simon & Schuster, 1982.

———. *The Mismeasure of Woman*. New York: Simon & Schuster, 1992.

———. "Beware the Incest-Survivor Machine." *The New York Times Book Review*, pp. 1 & 16–17, January 3, 1993.

Tavris, C., and Offir, C. *The Longest War: Sex Differences in Perspective*. New York: Harcourt Brace Jovanovich, 1977.

Tavris, C., and Sadd, S. *The Redbook Report on Female Sexuality*. New York: Delacorte Press, 1977.

Taylor, G. R. *Sex in History*. New York: Vanguard, 1954.

Tejada, I. S. D., et al. "Impaired Neurogenic and Endothelium-Mediated Relaxation of Penile Smooth Muscle from Diabetic Men with Impotence." *New England Journal of Medicine* 320:1025–1030, 1989.

Tennov, D. *Psychotherapy: The Hazardous Cure*. New York: Abelard-Schuman, 1975.

———. *Love and Limerance*. New York: Stein & Day, 1979.

Terkel, S. N. *Abortion: Facing the Issues*. New York: Franklin Watts, 1988.

Terman, L. M., and Miles, C. C. *Sex and Personality: Studies in Masculinity and Femininity*. New York: McGraw-Hill, 1936.

Teti, D. M., Lamb, L. E., and Elster, A. B. "Long-Range Socioeconomic and Marital Consequences of Adolescent Marriage in Three Cohorts of Adult Males." *Journal of Marriage and the Family* 49:499–513, 1987.

Thomas, J. L. "The Catholic Tradition for Responsibility in Sexual Ethics." In Wynn, J. C. (ed.), *Sexual Ethics and Christian Responsibility*. New York: Association Press, 1970.

Thompson, A. P. "Extramarital Sex: A Review of the Research Literature." *Journal of Sex Research* 19:1–22, 1983.

Thompson, M., and Schwartz, D. "Life Adjustment of Women with Anorexia Nervosa and Anorexia-like Behavior." *International Journal of Eating Disorders* 2:47–60, 1981.

Thompson, S. E., and Washington, A. E. "Epidemiology of Sexually Transmitted *Chlamydia trachomatis* Infections." *Epidemiology Review* 5:96–123, 1983.

Thompson, S. K. "Gender Labels and Early Sex Role Development." *Child Development* 46:339–347, 1975.

Thomson, J. J. "A Defense of Abortion." *Philosophy and Public Affairs* 1(1):47–66, 1971.

Thorne, B. *Gender Play: Girls and Boys in School.* New Brunswick, NJ: Rutgers University Press, 1993.

Thornton, C. E. "Sexuality Counseling of Women with Spinal Cord Injuries." *Sexuality and Disability* 2:267–277, 1979.

Todd, J., et al. "Toxic-Shock Syndrome Associated with Phage-Group-I Staphylococci." *Lancet* ii:1116–1118, 1978.

Todd, W. D., and Tapley, D. F. *The Columbia University College of Physicians and Surgeons Complete Guide to Pregnancy.* New York: Crown Publishers, 1988.

Tollison, C. D., and Adams, H. E. *Sexual Disorders: Treatment, Theory, Research.* New York: Gardner Press, 1979.

Tolor, A., and DiGrazia, P. V. "Sexual Attitudes and Behavior Patterns During and Following Pregnancy." *Archives of Sexual Behavior* 5:539–551, 1976.

Toubia, N. "Female Circumcision as a Public Health Issue." *New England Journal of Medicine* 331:712–716, 1994.

Tourney, G. "Hormones and Homosexuality." In Marmor, J. (ed.), *Homosexual Behavior*, pp. 41–58. New York: Basic Books, 1980.

Trause, M. A., Kennell, J., and Klaus, M. "Parental Attachment Behavior." In Money, J., and Musaph, H. (eds.), *Handbook of Sexology*, pp. 789–799. New York: Elsevier/North-Holland, 1977.

Treiman, K., and Liskin, L. "IUDs—A New Look." *Population Reports*, Series B, No. 5, March 1988.

Tripp, C. A. *The Homosexual Matrix.* New York: McGraw-Hill, 1975.

Troiden, R. R., and Goode, E. "Variables Related to the Acquisition of a Gay Identity." *Journal of Homosexuality* 5(4):383–392, 1980.

Trudel, G., and Saint Laurent, S. "A Comparison Between the Effects of Kegel's Exercises and a Combination of Sexual Awareness Relaxation and Breathing on Situational Orgasmic Dysfunction in Women." *Journal of Sex & Marital Therapy* 9:204–209, 1983.

Trussell, J. "Teenage Pregnancy in the United States." *Family Planning Perspectives* 20:262–272, 1988.

Trussell, J., and Grummer-Strawn, L. "Contraceptive Failure of the Ovulation Method of Periodic Abstinence." *Family Planning Perspectives* 22:65–75, 1990.

Trussell, J., Warner, D. L., and Hatcher, R. "Condom Slippage and Breakage Rates." *Family Planning Perspectives* 24: 20, 1992.

Trussell, J., and Westoff, C. F. "Contraceptive Practice and Trends in Coital Frequency." *Family Planning Perspectives* 12:246–249, 1980.

Trussell, J. Strickler, J. and Vaughan, B. "Contraceptive Efficacy of the Diaphragm, the Sponge, and the Cervi-

cal Cap." *Family Planning Perspectives* 25:100–105 and 135, 1993.

Trussell, James, et al. "Emergency Contraceptive Pills: A Simple Proposal to Reduce Unintended Pregnancies." *Family Planning Perspectives* 24:269–273, 1992.

Tsuang, M. T. "Hypersexuality in Man Patients." *Medical Aspects of Human Sexuality* 9(11):83–89, 1975.

Tucker, J., et al. "HTLV-III Infection Associated with Glandular-Fever-like Illness in a Hemophiliac." *Lancet* i:585, 1985.

Turner, B. F., and Adams, C. G. "Reported Change in Preferred Adult Sexual Activity Over the Adult Years." *Journal of Sex Research* 25:289–303, 1988.

Turner, C. F., Miller, H. G., and Moses, L. E. (eds.). *AIDS: Sexual Behavior and Intravenous Drug Use.* Washington, DC: National Academy Press, 1989.

Turnock, B. J., and Kelly, C. J. "Mandatory Premarital Testing for Human Immunodeficiency Virus—The Illinois Experience." *Journal of the American Medical Association* 261:3415–3418, 1989.

Udry, J. R., and Cliquet, R. L. "A Cross-Cultural Examination of the Relationship Between Ages at Menarche, Marriage, and First Birth." *Demography* 19:53–63, 1982.

Udry, J. R., and Morris, N. "Distribution of Coitus in the Menstrual Cycle." *Nature* 220:593–596, 1968.

Unger, R. K. "Toward a Redefinition of Sex and Gender." *American Psychologist* 34(11):1085–1094, 1979.

[unsigned editorial]. "Anonymous HIV Testing: Latest Results." *Lancet* 337:1572–1573, 1991.

———. "Partner Notification for Preventing HIV Infection." *Lancet* 338:1112–1113, 1991a.

———. "PML: More Neurological Bad News for AIDS Patients." *Lancet* 340:943–944, 1992.

———. "Hetereosexual AIDS: Pessimism, Pandemics, and Plain Hard Facts." *Lancet* 341:863–864, 1993.

U.S. Bureau of the Census. "Perspectives on American Husbands and Wives." *Current Population Reports*, Series P-23(77):December 1978.

U.S. Department of Health, Education, and Welfare. *Age at Menarche in the United States.* DHEW Publication No. (HRA)74:1615, p. 3, 1973.

U.S. Preventive Services Task Force. "Estrogen Prophylaxis." *American Family Physician* 42:1293–1296, 1990.

U.S. Public Health Service. *Mood Disorders: Pharmacologic Prevention of Recurrence.* Washington, DC: Department of Health and Human Services, Public Health Service Monograph Vol. 5, No. 4, 1986.

Upchurch, D. W., and McCarthy, J. "Adolescent Childbearing and High School Completion in the 1980s: Have Things Changed?" *Family Planning Perspectives* 21:199–202, 1989.

Upton, G. V. "Lipids, Cardiovascular Disease, and Oral Contraceptives: A Practice Perspective." *Fertility & Sterility* 53:1–12, 1990.

Utian, W. H. "Effect of Hysterectomy, Oophorectomy and Estrogen Therapy on Libido." *International Journal of Obstetrics and Gynaecology* 13:97–100, 1975.

Utian, W. H., et al. "Successful Pregnancy After In Vitro Fertilization and Embryo Transfer from an Infertile Woman to a Surrogate." *New England Journal of Medicine* 313:1351–1352, 1985.

Vachss, A. *Sex Crimes.* New York: Random House, 1993.

Valentine-French, S., and Radtke, H. L. "Attributions of Responsibility for an Incident of Sexual Harassment in a University Setting." *Sex Roles* 21:545–555, 1989.

Van De Perre, P., et al. "Postnatal Transmission of Human Immunodeficiency Virus Type 1 from Mother to Infant." *New England Journal of Medicine* 325:593–598, 1991.

———. "Postnatal Transmission of HIV-1 Associated with Breast Abscess." *Lancet* 339:1490–1491, 1992.

Van Griesven, G. J. P., et al. "Effect of Human Immunodeficiency Virus (HIV) Antibody Knowledge on High-Risk Sexual Behavior with Steady and Non-steady Sexual Partners Among Homosexual Men." *American Journal of Epidemiology* 129:596–603, 1989.

Van Thiel, D. H. "Testicular Atrophy and Other Endocrine Changes in Alcoholic Men." *Medical Aspects of Human Sexuality* 10(6):153–154, 1976.

Veldhuis, J. D., Urban, R. J., and Dufua, M. L. "Evidence That Androgen Negative Feedback Regulates the Hypothalamic Gonadotropin-Releasing Hormone Impulse Strength and the Burst-Like Secretion of Biologically Active Luteinizing Hormone in Men." *Journal of Clinical Endocrinology and Metabolism* 74:1227–1235, 1992.

Vella, S., et al. "Survival of Zidovudine-Treated Patients with AIDS Compared with that of Contemporary Untreated Patients." *Journal of the American Medical Association* 267:1232–1236, 1992.

Vermeulen, A. "Decline in Sexual Activity in Aging Men: Correlation with Sex Hormone Levels and Testicular Changes." *Journal of Biosocial Science* 6(Suppl.):5–18, 1979.

———. "Clinical Review 24: Androgens in the Aging Male." *Journal of Clinical Endocrinology and Metabolism* 73:221–224, 1991.

Vermeulen, A., and Kaufman, J. M. "Role of the Hypothalamo-Pituitary Function in the Hypoandrogenism of Healthy Aging." *Journal of Clinical Endocrinology and Metabolism* 74:1226A–1226C, 1992.

Vermund, S. H., et al. "Acquired Immunodeficiency Syndrome Among Adolescents." *American Journal of Diseases of Children* 143:1220–1225, 1989.

Veronesi, U., et al. "Radiotherapy after Breast-Preserving Therapy in Women with Localized Cancer of the Breast." *New England Journal of Medicine* 328:1587–1591, 1993.

Vessey, M. P. "Oral Contraceptives and Breast Cancer." *International Planned Parenthood Federation Medical Bulletin* 21(6):1–2, 1987.

Vessey, M., et al. "Fertility After Stopping Different Methods of Contraception." *British Medical Journal* 1:265–267, 1978.

———. "Pelvic Inflammatory Disease and the Intrauterine Device." *British Medical Journal* 282(6267):855–857, 1981.

Vittecoq, D., et al. "Acute HIV Infection After Acupuncture Treatment." *New England Journal of Medicine* 320:250–251, 1989.

Voelker, R. "How, Why, and When Do We Do It? Researchers Say It's Time to Find Out." *American Medical News*, p. 6, April 20, 1990.

Voeller, B. "Persistent Condom Breakage." (Abstract W.A.P. 99, p. 136.) Presented at the Fifth International Conference on AIDS, Montreal, June 4–9, 1989.

———. "Society and the Gay Movement." In Marmor, J. (ed.), *Homosexual Behavior*, pp. 232–254. New York: Basic Books, 1980.

———. "AIDS and Heterosexual Anal Intercourse." *Archives of Sexual Behavior* 20:233–276, 1991.

Voeller, B. Personal communication, November 1986.

Voger, F. T. "Sex Life of American Indians." In Ellis, A., and Abarbanel, A. (eds.), *The Encyclopedia of Sexual Behavior*, pp. 90–109. New York: Hawthorn Books, 1961.

Voigt, L. F., et al. "Progestagen Supplementation of Exogenous Oestrogens and Risk of Endometrial Cancer." *Lancet* 338:274–277, 1991.

Volberding, P. A., et al. "Zidovudine in Asymptomatic Human Immunodeficiency Virus Infection." *New England Journal of Medicine* 322:941–949, 1990.

Vollman, R. F. *The Menstrual Cycle.* Philadelphia: Saunders, 1977.

Vontver, L. A., et al. "Recurrent Genital Herpes Simplex Virus Infection in Pregnancy: Infant Outcome and Frequency of Asymptomatic Recurrences." *American Journal of Obstetrics and Gynecology* 143:75–81, 1982.

Wagner, G., and Kaplan, H. S. *The New Injection Treatment for Impotence: Medical and Psychological Aspects.* New York: Brunner/Mazel, 1993.

Wainrib, B. R. (ed.). *Gender Issues Across the Life Cycle.* New York: Springer, 1992.

Walker, E., et al. "Relationship of Gender and Marital Status with Symptomatology in Psychotic Patients." *Journal of Abnormal Psychology* 94:42–50, 1985.

Wallace, J. I., Mann, J., and Beatrice, S. "HIV-1 Exposure Among Clients of Prostitutes." Fifth International Conference on AIDS, Stockholm, June 12–16, 1988.

Walsh, F. M., et al. "Autoerotic Asphyxial Deaths: A Medicolegal Analysis of Forty-Three Cases." In Wecht, C. H. (ed.), *Legal Medicine Annual 1977*, pp. 157–182. New York: Appleton-Century-Crofts, 1977.

Walsh, R. N., et al. "The Menstrual Cycle, Sex and Academic Performance." *Archives of General Psychiatry* 38:219–221, 1981.

Walshok, M. L. "The Emergence of Middle Class Deviant Subcultures: The Case of Swingers." *Social Problems* 18:488–496, 1971.

Walster, E., and Walster, G. W. *A New Look at Love.* Reading, MA: Addison-Wesley, 1978.

Walster, E., Walster, G. W., and Berscheid, E. *Equity: Theory and Research.* Boston: Allyn & Bacon, 1978.

Walster, E., et al. "'Playing Hard to Get': Understanding an Elusive Phenomenon." *Journal of Personality and Social Psychology* 26:113–121, 1973.

Walum, L. R. *The Dynamics of Sex and Gender: A Sociological Perspective.* Chicago: Rand McNally College Publishing, 1977.

Ward, J. W., et al. "Transmission of Human Immunodeficiency Virus (HIV) by Blood Transfusions Screened as Negative for HIV Antibody." *New England Journal of Medicine* 318:473–478, 1988.

Warner, C. G. (ed.). *Rape and Sexual Assault.* Germantown, MD: Aspen Systems Corp., 1980.

Warner, P. K. "Aural Assault: Obscene Telephone Calls." *Qualitative Sociology* 11(4):302–318, 1988.

Warshaw, R. *I Never Called it **Rape**: The Ms. Report on Recognizing, Fighting, and Surviving Date and Acquaintance Rape.* New York: *Ms.* Foundation/Sara Lazin Books, Harper & Row, 1988.

Warshaw, Robin. *I Never Called It Rape.* New York: Harper & Row, 1988.

Washburn, S. *Partners: How to Have a Loving Relationship After Women's Liberation.* New York: Atheneum, 1981.

Washington, A. E., and Katz, P. "Cost of and Payment Source for Pelvic Inflammatory Disease." *Journal of the American Medical Association* 266:2565–2569, 1991.

Washton, A. M. "Cocaine Abuse and Compulsive Sexuality." *Medical Aspects of Human Sexuality* 23(12):32–39, December 1989.

Wasow, M., and Loeb, M. "Sexuality in Nursing Homes." *Journal of the American Geriatrics Society* 27:73–79, 1979.

Wasserheit, J. N. "Epidemiological Synergy: Inter-relationships Between HIV Infection and Other STDs." In Chen, L., et al. (eds.), *AIDS and Women's Reproductive Health.* New York: Plenum Press, 1992.

Waterman, C. K., and Chiauzzi, E. J. "The Role of Orgasm in Male and Female Sexual Enjoyment." *Journal of Sex Research* 18:146–159, 1982.

Watkins, R. N. "Vaginal Spermicides and Congenital Disorders: The Validity of a Study." *Journal of the American Medical Association* 256:3095, 1986.

Webb, A. M. C., Russell, J., and Elstein, M. "Comparison of Yuzpe Regimen, Danazol, and Mifepristone (RU 486) in Oral Postcoital Contraception." *British Medical Journal* 305:927, 1992.

Webb, S. L. *Step Forward: Sexual Harassment in the Workplace.* New York: MasterMedia, 1991.

Webster, S. K., Bauman, J. E., and Kolodny, R. C. "The Biochemistry of Dysmenorrhea: Failure to Validate the Distinction Between Spasmodic and Congestive Dysmenorrhea." Presented at the First Dysmenorrhea Symposium, St. Louis University, St. Louis, MO, 1978.

Weinberg, S. K. *Incest Behavior.* New York: Citadel, 1955.

Weinberg, T. S. "On 'Doing' and 'Being' Gay: Sexual Behavior and Homosexual Male Self-Identity." *Journal of Homosexuality* 4:143–156, 1978.

Weinstein, M., and Thornton, A. "Mother–Child Relations and Adolescent Sexual Attitudes and Behavior." *Demography* 26:563–578, 1989.

Weinstock, H. S., et al. "Factors Associated with Condom Use in a High-Risk Heterosexual Population." *Sexually Transmitted Diseases* 20:14–20, 1993.

———. "Hepatitis C Virus Infection Among Patients Attending a Clinic for Sexually Transmitted Diseases." *Journal of the American Medical Association* 269:392–394, 1993a.

Weisfuse, I. "Delta Hepatitis in Homosexual Men in the United States." *Hepatology* 9:872–874, 1989.

Weisman, C. S., et al. "AIDS Knowledge, Perceived Risk and Prevention Among Adolescent Clients of a Family Planning Clinic." *Family Planning Perspectives* 21:213–217, 1989.

Weiss, H. D. "The Physiology of Human Penile Erection." *Annals of Internal Medicine* 76:793–799, 1972.

Weiss, N. S., and Sayvetz, T. A. "Incidence of Endometrial Cancer in Relation to the Use of Oral Contraceptives." *New England Journal of Medicine* 302:551–554, 1980.

Weiss, S. H. "Links Between Cocaine and Retroviral Infection." *Journal of the American Medical Association* 261:607–609, 1989.

Weissman, M. "Depression." In Brodsky, A. M., and Hare-Mustin, R. (eds.), *Women and Psychotherapy*, pp. 97–112. New York: Guilford Press, 1980.

Weitz, C. M. "Vaginal Birth After Cesarean Section." *Postgraduate Obstetrics and Gynecology* 5(11):1–4, 1985.

Weitzman, L. J. "Sex-Role Socialization." In Freeman, J. (ed.), *Women: A Feminist Perspective.* Palo Alto, CA: Mayfield, 1975.

Weitzman, L. J., et al. "Sex Role Socialization in Picture Books for Pre-School Children." *American Journal of Sociology* 77:1125–1150, 1972.

Wellesley College Center for Research on Women. *The AAUW Report: How Schools Shortchange Girls.* Wellesley, MA: Cheever House, 1992.

Wellisch, D. K., Jamison, K. R., and Pasnau, R. O. "Psychosocial Aspects of Mastectomy, II: The Man's Perspective." *American Journal of Psychiatry* 135:543–546, 1978.

Wells, B. L. "Predictors of Female Nocturnal Orgasms." *Journal of Sex Research* 22:421–437, 1986.

Weniger, B. G., et al. "The Epidemiology of HIV Infection and AIDS in Thailand." *AIDS* 5(suppl 2):S71–S85, 1991.

Werner, D. "A Cross-Cultural Perspective on Theory and Research on Male Homosexuality." *Journal of Homosexuality* 4:345–362, 1979.

Wernik, U. "The Role of the Traumatic Component in the Etiology of Sexual Dysfunctions and Its Treatment with Eye Movement Desensitization Procedures." *Journal of Sex Education and Therapy* 19:212–222, 1993.

Wertz, R. W., and Wertz, D. C. *Lying-in: A History of Childbirth in America*. New York: Free Press, 1977.

Wesson, D. R. "Cocaine Use by Masseuses." *Journal of Psychoactive Drugs* 14:75–76, 1982.

Westoff, C. F., and McCarthy, J. "Sterilization in the United States." *Family Planning Perspectives* 11:147–152, 1979.

Westoff, C. F., and Rindfuss, R. R. "Sex Preselection in the U.S.: Some Implications." *Science* 184:633–636, 1974.

Wharton, C., and Blackburn, R. "Lower-Dose Pills." *Population Reports*, Series A, No. 7, November, 1988.

Whiffen, V. E., and Gotlib, I. H. "Comparison of Postpartum and Nonpostpartum Depression." *Journal of Consulting and Clinical Psychology* 61:485–494, 1993.

White, G. L., Fishbein, S., and Rustein, J. "Passionate Love and the Misattribution of Arousal." *Journal of Personality and Social Psychology* 41:56–62, 1981.

Whitehead, H. "The Bow and the Burden Strap: A New Look at Institutionalized Homosexuality in Native North America." In Ortner, B., and Whitehead, H. (eds.), *Sexual Meaning: The Cultural Construction of Gender and Sexuality*, pp. 80–115. New York: Cambridge University Press, 1981.

Whitham, F. L. "Culturally Invariable Properties of Male Homosexuality: Tentative Conclusions from Cross-Cultural Research." *Archives of Sexual Behavior* 12:207–226, 1983.

Whitham, F. L., and Mathy, R. M. *Male Homosexuality in Four Societies*. New York: Praeger, 1986.

Whitley, M. P., and Berke, P. A. "Sexual Response in Diabetic Women." *Journal of Sex Education and Therapy* 9(2):51–56, 1983.

Wickware, F. S. "Report on the Kinsey Report." *Life* 25:86–90, August 2, 1948.

Wilcox, A. J., et al. "Incidence of Early Loss of Pregnancy." *New England Journal of Medicine* 319:189–194, 1988.

Wilcox, D., and Hager, R. "Toward Realistic Expectation for Orgasmic Response in Women." *Journal of Sex Research* 16:162–179, 1980.

Williams, K. B., and Cyr, R. R. "Escalating Commitment to a Relationship: The Sexual Harassment Trap." *Sex Roles* 27:47–72, 1992.

Williams, W. M., and Barnes, M. L. "Love Within Life." In Sternberg, R. J., and Barnes, M. L. (eds.), *The Psychology of Love*, pp. 311–329. New Haven, CT: Yale University Press, 1988.

Williams-Deane, M., and Potter, L. S. "Current Oral Contraceptive Use Instructions: An Analysis of Patient Package Inserts." *Family Planning Perspectives* 24:111–115, 1992.

Wills, T. A., Weiss, R. L., and Patterson, G. R. "A Behavioral Analysis of the Determinants of Marital Satisfaction." *Journal of Consulting and Clinical Psychology* 42:802–811, 1974.

Wilson, C. "Pornography: The Emergence of a Social Issue and the Beginning of a Psychological Study." *Journal of Social Issues* 29(3):7–17, 1973.

Wilson, E. O. *On Human Nature*. Cambridge, MA: Harvard University Press, 1978.

Wilson, G. T., and Lawson, D. M. "Effects of Alcohol on Sexual Arousal in Women." *Journal of Abnormal Psychology* 85:489–497, 1976.

———. "Effects of Alcohol on Sexual Arousal in Male Alcoholics." *Journal of Abnormal Psychology* 87:609–616, 1978.

Wilson, J., George, F., and Griffin, J. "The Hormonal Control of Sexual Development." *Science* 211(4488):1278–1284, 1981.

Wilson, J. D. "Androgen Abuse by Athletes." *Endocrine Reviews* 9:181–199, 1988.

Wilson, J. G. "Embryotoxicity of Drugs in Man." In Wilson, J. G., and Fraser, F. C. (eds.), *Handbook Teratology*, Vol. 1: *General Principles and Etiology*, pp. 209–255. New York: Plenum Press, 1977.

Wilson, S. N., and Sanderson, C. A. "The Sex Report Curriculum: Is 'Just Say No' Effective?" *SIECUS Report* 17(1):10–11, 1988.

Wilson, W. C. "Can Pornography Contribute to the Prevention of Sexual Problems?" In Qualls, C. B., Wincze, J. P., and Barlow, D. H. (eds.), *The Prevention of Sexual Disorders*, pp. 159–179. New York: Plenum Press, 1978.

Wincze, J. P., Hoon, E. F., and Hoon, P. W. "Physiological Responsivity of Normal and Sexually Dysfunctional Women During Erotic Stimulus Exposure." *Journal of Psychosomatic Research* 20:445–451, 1976.

Wincze, J. P., and Carey, M. P. *Sexual Dysfunction: A Guide for Assessment and Treatment*. New York: Guilford Press, 1991.

Winder, A., and Winder, B. "Patient Counseling: Clarifying a Woman's Choice for Breast Reconstruction." *Patient Education and Counseling* 7:65–75, 1985.

Wing, J. K., and Bebbington, P. "Epidemiology of Depression." In Beckham, E. E., and Leber, W. R. (eds.), *Handbook of Depression*, pp. 765–794. Homewood, IL: Dorsey Press, 1985.

Winkelstein, W., Jr., et al. "Selected Sexual Practices of San Francisco Heterosexual Men and Risk of Infection by the Human Immunodeficiency Virus." *Journal of the American Medical Association* 257:1470–1471, 1987.

Winkenwerder, W., Kessler, A. R., and Stolec, R. M. "Federal Spending for Illness Caused by the Human Immunodeficiency Virus." *New England Journal of Medicine* 320:1598–1603, 1989.

Winston, R. M. L., and Handyside, A. H. "New Challenges in Human In Vitro Fertilization." *Science* 260:932–936, 1993.

Wise, T. N., and Meyer, J. K. "The Border Area Between Transvestism and Gender Dysphoria: Transvestitic Applicants for Sex Reassignment." *Archives of Sexual Behavior* 9(4):327–342, 1980.

Wiswell, T. E., et al. "Declining Frequency of Circumcision: Implications for Changes in the Absolute Incidence and Male to Female Sex Ratio of Urinary Tract Infections in Early Infancy." *Pediatrics* 79:338–342, 1987.

Witherington, R. "Suction Device Therapy in the Management of Erectile Impotence." *Urologic Clinics of North America* 15:123–128, 1988.

Witkin, M. H. "Sex Therapy and Mastectomy." *Journal of Sex & Marital Therapy* 1:290–304, 1975.

Wofsy, C. B., et al. "Isolation of AIDS-Associated Retrovirus from Genital Secretions of Women with Antibodies to the Virus." *Lancet* i:527–529, 1986.

Wolchik, S. A., Spencer, S. L., and Lisi, I. S. "Volunteer Bias in Research Employing Vaginal Measures of Sexual Arousal." *Archives of Sexual Behavior* 12:399–408, 1983.

Wolf, E. S. "Self-theory and Intimacy." In Fisher, M., and Stricker, G. (eds.), *Intimacy*, pp. 65–77. New York: Plenum Press, 1982.

Wolfe, J., and Baker, V. "Characteristics of Imprisoned Rapists and Circumstances of the Rape." In Warner, C. (ed.), *Rape and Sexual Assault*, pp. 265–278. Germantown, MD: Aspen Systems Corp., 1980.

Wolfe, L. "The Sexual Profile of that Cosmopolitan Girl." *Cosmopolitan*, pp. 254–265, September 1980.

Wolff, C. *Love Between Women*. New York: Harper & Row, 1971.

Wolman, B., and Stricker, G. (eds.), *Handbook of Family and Marital Therapy*. New York: Plenum Press, 1983.

Wolner-Hanssen, P., et al. "Association Between Vaginal Douching and Acute Pelvic Inflammatory Disease." *Journal of the American Medical Association* 263:1936–1941, 1990.

Wolpe, J. *Psychotherapy by Reciprocal Inhibition*. Stanford, CA: Stanford University Press, 1958.

———. *The Practice of Behavior Therapy*. Oxford: Pergamon, 1969.

Wong, H. "Typologies of Intimacy." *Psychology of Women Quarterly* 5:435–443, 1981.

Woods, S. M. "Sexuality and Mental Disorders." In Lief, H. L. (ed.), *Sexual Problems in Medical Practice*, pp. 199–209. Chicago: American Medical Association, 1981.

Working Group on the Very Low Birth Weight Infant. "European Community Collaborative Study of Pregnancy Between 22 and 28 Weeks' Gestation." *Lancet* 336:782–784, 1990.

World Health Organization. *Special Programme of Research, Development and Research Training: Seventh Annual Report*. Geneva: WHO, November 1978.

———. "A Prospective Multicentre Trial of the Ovulation Method of Natural Family Planning II: The Effectiveness Phase." *Fertility & Sterility* 36:591–598, 1981.

World Health Organization Collaborative Study of Neoplasia and Steroid Contraceptives. "Breast Cancer and Depot-Medroxyprogesterone Acetate: A Multinational Study." *Lancet* 338:833–836, 1991.

World Health Organization Global Programme on AIDS. *Current and Future Dimensions of the HIV/AIDS Pandemic: A Capsule Summary, January, 1992*. Publication WHO/GPA/RES/SFI/92.1. World Health Organization, 1992.

Wortman, J. "Vasectomy: What Are the Problems?" *Population Reports*, Series D(2), January 1975.

———. "The Diaphragm and Other Intravaginal Barriers: A Review." *Population Reports*, Series H(4), January 1976.

Wortman, J., and Piotrow, P. T. "Laparoscopic Sterilization, II: What Are the Problems?" *Population Reports*, Series C(2), March 1973.

Wright, N. H., et al. "Neoplasia and Dysplasia of the Cervix Uteri and Contraception: A Possible Protective Effect of the Diaphragm." *British Journal of Cancer* 38(2):273–279, August 1978.

Wrightsman, L. S. *Psychology and the Legal System*. Pacific Grove, CA: Brooks/Cole, 1991.

Wyatt, G. E. "Ethnic and Cultural Differences in Women's Sexual Behaviors." In Blumenthal, S. J., and Eichler, A., chairpersons, NIMH/NIDA *Workshop on Women and AIDS: Promoting Healthy Behaviors*. [Background papers] Rockville, MD: National Institute of Mental Health, 1988.

———. "Child Sexual Abuse and Its Effects on Sexual Functioning." *Annual Review of Sex Research* II:249–266, 1991.

Wyatt, G. E., Peters, S. D., and Guthrie, D. "Kinsey Revisited, Part I: Comparisons of the Sexual Socialization and Sexual Behavior of White Women Over 33 Years." *Archives of Sexual Behavior* 17:201–239, 1988.

———. "Kinsey Revisited, Part II: Comparisons of the Sexual Socialization and Sexual Behavior of Black Women Over 33 Years." *Archives of Sexual Behavior* 17:289–332, 1988a.

Wyatt, G., et al. *The Effects of Child Sexual Abuse on Women's Sexual and Psychological Functioning*. Newbury Park, CA: Sage, 1992.

Wycoff, R. F., et al. "Notification of the Sex and Needle-sharing Partners of Individuals with Human Immunodeficiency Virus in Rural South Carolina: 30 Month Experience." *Sexually Transmitted Diseases* 18:217–222, 1991.

Wyngaarden, J. B. "Identifying Factors That Reactivate Herpes Simplex Virus." *Journal of the American Medical Association* 259:1922, 1988.

Wynne, L. C., and Wynne, A. R. "The Question for Intimacy." *Journal of Marital and Family Therapy* 12:383–394, 1986.

Yalom, I. D. "Aggression and Forbiddenness in Voyeurism." *Archives of General Psychiatry* 3:305–319, 1960.

Yalom, I. D., Green, R., and Fisk, N. "Prenatal Exposure to Female Hormones." *Archives of General Psychiatry* 28:554–561, 1973.

Yates, W. "The Church and Its Holistic Paradigm of Sexuality." *SIECUS Report* 16:1–5, May/June 1988.

Yorukoglu, A., and Kemph, J. P. "Children Not Severely Damaged by Incest with a Parent." *Journal of the American Academy of Child Psychiatry* 5:111–124, 1966.

Young, M. "Attitudes and Behavior of College Students Related to Oral–Genital Sexuality." *Archives of Sexual Behavior* 9:61–67, 1980.

Zabin, L. S., Hirsch, M. B., and Emerson, M. R. "When Urban Adolescents Choose Abortion: Effects on Education, Psychological Status and Subsequent Pregnancy." *Family Planning Perspectives* 21:248–255, 1989.

Zabin, L. S., et al. "The Baltimore Pregnancy Prevention Program for Urban Teenagers: I. How Did it Work?" *Family Planning Perspectives* 20:182–187, 1988.

———. "The Baltimore Pregnancy Prevention Program for Urban Teenagers: II. What Did It Cost?" *Family Planning Perspectives* 20:188–192, 1988a.

Zacharias, L., and Wurtman, R. J. "Age at Menarche: Genetic and Environmental Influences." *New England Journal of Medicine* 280:868–875, 1969.

Zarutskie, P. W., et al. "The Clinical Relevance of Sex Selection Techniques." *Fertility & Sterility* 52:891–905, 1989.

Zeiss, A. M. "Expectation for the Effects of Aging on Sexuality in Parents and Average Married Couples." *Journal of Sex Research* 18:47–57, 1982.

Zelnick, M., and Kantner, J. F. "Sexual Activity, Contraceptive Use, and Pregnancy Among Metropolitan-Area Teenagers: 1971–1979." *Family Planning Perspectives* 12:230–237, 1980.

Zelnik, M., and Kim, Y. J. "Sex Education and Its Association with Teenage Sexual Activity, Pregnancy and Contraceptive Use." *Family Planning Perspectives* 14:117–126, 1982.

Zelnik, M., and Shah, F. K. "First Intercourse Among Young Americans." *Family Planning Perspectives* 15:64–70, 1983.

Zelnik, M., Kantner, J. F., and Ford, K. *Sex and Pregnancy in Adolescence*. Beverly Hills, CA: Sage Publications, 1981.

Zeman, N., and Meyer, M. "No 'Special Rights' for Gays." *Newsweek*, November 23, 1992, p. 32.

Ziegler, J. B., et al. "Postnatal Transmission of AIDS-associated Retrovirus from Mother to Infant." *Lancet* i:896–898, 1985.

Zilbergeld, B. *Male Sexuality: A Guide to Sexual Fulfillment*. Boston: Little, Brown, 1978.

———. "Alternatives to Couples Counseling for Sex Problems: Group and Individual Therapy." *Journal of Sex & Marital Therapy* 6(1):3–18, 1980.

———. *The New Male Sexuality*. New York: Bantam Books, 1992.

Zilbergeld, B., and Evans, M. "The Inadequacy of Masters and Johnson." *Psychology Today* 14:29–43, 1980.

Zillman, D. *Connections Between Sex and Aggression*. Hillsdale, NJ: Lawrence Erlbaum, 1984.

Zitter, S. "Coming Out to Mom: Theoretical Aspects of the Mother–Daughter Process." In *Lesbian Psychologies: Explorations and Challenges*, pp. 177–194. Edited by the Boston Lesbian Psychologies Collective. Urbana: University of Illinois Press, 1987.

Zorgniotti, A. W., et al. "Auto-injection of the Corpus Cavernosum with a Vasoactive Drug Combination for Vasculogenic Impotence." *Journal of Urology* 133:39–41, 1985.

Zuckerman, A. J. "Viral Hepatitis." *Practical Gastroenterology* 6(6):16, 21–27, November/December 1982.

Zuckerman, B., et al. "Effects of Maternal Marijuana and Cocaine Use on Fetal Growth." *New England Journal of Medicine* 320:762–768, 1989.

Zuger, B. "Monozygotic Twins Discordant for Homosexuality: Report of a Pair and Significance of the Phenomenon." *Comprehensive Psychiatry* 17:661–669, 1976.

———. "Early Effeminate Behavior in Boys: Outcome and Significance for Homosexuality." *Journal of Nervous and Mental Diseases* 172:90–97, 1984.

———. "Homosexuality in Families of Boys with Early Effeminate Behavior: An Epidemiological Study." *Archives of Sexual Behavior* 18:155–166, 1989.

Zussman, J. U., Zussman, P. P., and Dalton, K. K. "Postpubertal Effect of Prenatal Administration of Progesterone." Paper presented at the Society for Research in Child Development, Denver, April 1975.

———. Abstract, Third Annual Meeting of the International Academy of Sex Research, Bloomington, IN, 1977.

Zussman, L., et al. "Sexual Response After Hysterectomyoophorectomy: Recent Studies and Reconsideration of Psychogenesis. *American Journal of Obstetrics and Gynecology* 140:725–729, 1981.

Zwerner, J. "Sexual Issues of Women with Spinal Cord Injury." *Sexuality and Disability* 5:158–171, 1982.

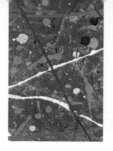

INDEX

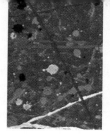

PHOTO CREDITS